W9-CSV-825

2002

POET'S
MARKET

**1,800 PLACES TO
PUBLISH YOUR POETRY**

EDITED BY **NANCY BREEN**

WRITER'S DIGEST BOOKS
CINCINNATI, OH

Important market listing information

- Listings are based on questionnaires and verified copy. They are not advertisements *nor* are markets necessarily endorsed by the editors of this book.
- Information in the listings comes directly from the publishers and is as accurate as possible. However, publications and editors come and go, and poetry needs fluctuate between the publication date of this directory and the customer's purchase date.
- *Poet's Market* reserves the right to exclude any listing that does not meet its requirements.

Complaint procedure

If you feel you have not been treated fairly by a listing in *Poet's Market*, we advise you to take the following steps:

- First try to contact the listing. Sometimes one phone call or a letter can quickly clear up the matter.
- Document all your correspondence with the listing. When you write to us with a complaint, provide the details of your submission, the date of your first contact with the listing and the nature of your subsequent correspondence.
- We will enter your letter into our files and attempt to contact the listing.
- The number and severity of complaints will be considered in our decision whether or not to delete the listing from the next edition.

If you are a poetry publisher and would like to be considered for a listing in the next edition of *Poet's Market*, send a SASE (or SAE and IRC) with your request for a questionnaire to *Poet's Market*—QR, 1507 Dana Ave., Cincinnati OH 45207. Questionnaires received after February 15, 2002, will be held for the 2004 edition.

Editorial Director, Annuals Department: Barbara Kuroff
Managing Editor, Annuals Department: Doug Hubbuch
Production Editor: Vanessa Lyman

Writer's Market website: www.writersmarket.com
Writer's Digest Books website: www.writersdigest.com

International Standard Serial Number 0883-5470
International Standard Book Number 1-58297-048-3

Attention Booksellers: This is an annual directory of F&W Publications. Return deadline for this edition is December 31, 2002.

Contents

INDEXES

From the Editor

"Too much information!" We hear that catchphrase a lot these days, from sitcoms to radio commercials. I shout it at the TV when the media rushes me with the gory details of the latest sex scandal. My sister shouts it at me if I try to discuss my problems with . . . well, never mind. "Too much information!" you'd say. "More than we wanted to know!"

Yet we live in the Information Age, cruise the Information Superhighway, prowl cable channels looking for every possible outlet of information. Okay, then, which is it? Too much information or not enough?

We ponder that question at *Poet's Market* as well. Are we giving you enough of the right kind of information you need to market your poetry successfully? We try to provide the hard data as well as helpful hints, poetry samples, and editorial suggestions—a balance of information without approaching "overload." And we aspire to make it as clear and easy to understand as possible. This year we've reformatted the contact information and streamlined the content to make each listing a smoother read. We haven't scrimped on the important stuff, though—you'll notice a significant increase in e-mail and website addresses throughout the book, plus there are 300 publishing opportunities new to this edition.

And while lots of you already know the ins and outs of poetry submission, we're aware that many of our readers are taking their first peek into the world of publishing. For you, we've provided **Publishing Your Poetry: Eight Quick Tips** and **Who Wants to Be a Published Poet?**, basic but thorough information about most aspects of the submission process. We also offer **The Art of Self-Promotion** with valuable insights from poet Leah Maines about putting yourself and your work in the public eye.

Too much information? If you need a break from the numbers, needs, and requirements, kick back with our **Insider Reports**. Explore a variety of perspectives on poetry with Joseph Enzweiler, Jane Hirshfield, David Wojahn, Cynthia Huntington, and Beth Gylys. Learn from Toi Derricotte and Cornelius Eady how the workshop Cave Canem was founded. Let all these talented poets remind you of the soulful origins of poetry, far removed from the mechanics of manuscript preparation and the nitty-gritty of editorial preferences. (However, when you're ready to get back to "business," check out Robin Travis-Murphree's advice on poetry and the Internet.)

The modern world may overwhelm us with information at times. However, the upside is it's easier today to locate what we want and need to know. I hope you'll feel the same way about the 2002 edition of *Poet's Market* and find the information we've provided an indispensable resource as you create and market your poetry.

Nancy Breen
poetsmarket@fwpubs.com

Publishing Your Poetry: Eight Quick Tips

Delving into the pages of *Poet's Market* indicates a commitment—you've decided to take that big step and begin submitting your poems for publication. Three cheers for you! How do you *really* begin, though? To smooth the way, here are eight quick tips to help make sense of the marketing/submission process. Follow these suggestions, study the markets in this book carefully, and give proper attention to the preparation of your manuscript. Before you know it you'll be well under way in pursuit of your dream—seeing your poems in print.

1. **Read. And read. Then read some more.** There's a tendency among poets, young and old, not to read poetry. Kind of a puzzle, isn't it? It's also a big mistake. You'll never develop your skills if you don't immerse yourself in poetry of all kinds. It's essential to study the masters; but from a marketing standpoint, it's equally vital to read what your contemporaries are writing and publishing. Read journals and magazines, chapbooks and collections, anthologies for a variety of voices; scope out the many poetry sites on the Internet. Develop an eye for quality, then use that eye to assess your own work. Don't rush to publish until you know you're writing the best poetry you're capable of producing.

2. **Know what you like to write—and what you write best.** Ideally you should be experimenting with all kinds of poetic forms, from free verse to villanelles. However, there's sure to be a certain style with which you feel most comfortable, that conveys your true "voice." Whether you're into more formal, traditional verse or avant-garde poetry that breaks all the rules, you should identify which markets publish work similar to yours. Those are the magazines and presses you should target to give your submissions the best chance of being read favorably—and accepted! (See the Subject Index beginning on page 518 to get an idea of how some magazines and presses specify their needs.)

3. **Learn the "biz."** Poetry may not be a high-paying writing market, but there's still a right way to go about the "business" of submitting and publishing poems. Learn all you can by reading writing-related magazines like *Writer's Digest*, *Poets & Writers*, and *The Writer*, as well as others. Read the articles and interviews in this book for plenty of helpful advice. Surf the Net for a wealth of sites filled with writing advice, market news, and informative links. (See Websites of Interest on page 468 for some leads.)

4. **Research those markets.** Start by studying the listings in *Poet's Market*. Each gathers the names, addresses, figures, editorial preferences, and other pertinent information all in one place. (The Publishers of Poetry section begins on page 17, with the Contests & Awards section following on page 391. Also, the indexes at the back of this book provide insights to what a publication or publisher might be looking for.)

   You're already reading a variety of published poetry (or at least you should be). That's the best way to gauge the kinds of poetry a market publishes. However, you need to go a step further. It's best to study several issues of a magazine/journal or several of a press's books to get a feel for the style and content of each. If the market has a Web address (when available, websites are included in the contact information for each listing in this book), log on and take a look. Check out the site for poetry samples, reviews and other content, and especially guidelines! If a market isn't online, send for guidelines and sample copies. Guidelines give you the lowdown on what an editor expects of submissions, the kind of "insider information" that's too valuable to ignore.

5. **Start slowly.** As tempting as it may be to send your work straight to *The New Yorker*, try to adopt a more modest approach if you're just starting out. Most listings in this book show symbols that reflect the level of writing a magazine or publisher would prefer to receive. The (☐) symbol indicates those markets where the work of beginning or unpublished poets is most welcome. As you gain confidence and experience (and increased skill in your writing), move on to markets coded with the (◑) symbol. Later, when you've built a publication history, submit to the more prestigious magazines and presses (the ● markets). Although it may tax your patience, slow and steady progress is a proven route to success.

6. **Be professional.** Professionalism, on the other hand, is not something you should "work up to." Make it show in your very first submission, from the way you prepare your manuscript to the attitude you project in your communications with editors.

    Follow guidelines. Submit a polished manuscript. (See Who Wants to Be a Published Poet? on page 8 for details on manuscript formatting and preparation.) Choose poems carefully with the editor's needs in mind. *Always* include a SASE (self-addressed stamped envelope) with any submission or inquiry. Not only do such practices show respect for the editor, the publication, and the process; they reflect *your* self-respect and the fact that you take your work seriously. Editors love that; and even if your work is rejected, you've made a good first impression that could help your chances with your next submission.

7. **Keep track of your submissions.** First, do *not* send out your only copies of your work. There are no guarantees that your submission won't get lost in the mail, misplaced in a busy editorial office, or vanish into a black hole if the market winds up closing shop. Create a special file folder for poems you are submitting. Even if you use a word processing program and store your manuscripts on disk, keep a hard copy file as well.

    Second, establish a tracking system so you always know which poems are where. This can be extremely simple: index cards, a chart made up on the computer, or even a simple notebook used as a log. Note the titles of the poems submitted (or the title of the manuscript, if submitting a collection); the name of the publication, press, or contest; date sent; and date returned *or* date accepted. Additional information you may want to log includes the name of the editor/contact, date the accepted piece is published, the pay received, rights acquired by the publication or press, and any pertinent comments.

    Without a tracking system you risk forgetting where and when pieces were submitted. This is even more problematic if you simultaneously send the same poems to different magazines. And if you learn of an acceptance at one magazine, you must notify the others that the poem you sent them is no longer available. You have a bigger chance of overlooking someone without an organized approach. This causes hard feelings among editors you may have inconvenienced, hurting your chances with these markets in the future.

    Besides, a tracking system gives you a sense of accomplishment, even if your acceptances are infrequent at first. After all, look at all those poems you've sent out! You're really working at it, and that's something to be proud of.

8. **Learn from rejection.** Oh, the dreaded "r" word. No one enjoys rejection, but every writer faces it. The best way to turn a negative into a positive is to learn as much as you can from your rejections. Don't let them get you down. A rejection slip isn't a permission slip to doubt yourself, condemn your poetry, or give up. Look over the rejection. Did the editor provide any comments about your work or reasons why your poems were rejected? Probably he or she didn't. Editors are extremely busy and don't necessarily have time to comment on rejections. If that's the case, move on to the next magazine or publisher you've targeted and send your work out again.

    If, however, the editor *has* commented on your work, pay attention. It counts for something that the editor took the time and trouble to say anything, however brief, good, or bad. And consider any remark or suggestion with an open mind. You don't have to agree, but you shouldn't automatically disregard it, either. Tell your ego to sit down and be quiet, then use the editor's comments to review your work from a new perspective. You might be surprised how much you'll learn from a single scribbled word in the margin; or how encouraged you'll feel from a simple "Try again!" written on the rejection slip.

Keep these eight tips in mind as you prepare your poetry manuscript, and keep *Poet's Market* close at hand to help you along. Believe in yourself and don't give up! As the 1,800+ listings in this book show, there are many opportunities for beginning poets to become published poets. Why shouldn't you be one of them?

GUIDE TO LISTING FEATURES

Below is an example of the market listings you'll find in the Publishers of Poetry section. Note the callouts that identify various format features of the listing. The front and back covers of this book contain a key to the symbols used at the beginning of all listings.

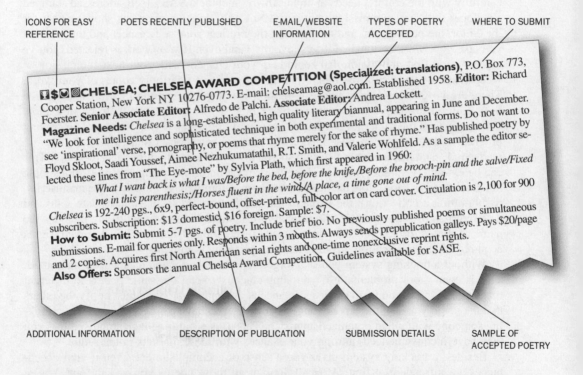

ICONS FOR EASY REFERENCE   POETS RECENTLY PUBLISHED   E-MAIL/WEBSITE INFORMATION   TYPES OF POETRY ACCEPTED   WHERE TO SUBMIT

CHELSEA; CHELSEA AWARD COMPETITION (Specialized: translations), P.O. Box 773, Cooper Station, New York NY 10276-0773. E-mail: chelseamag@aol.com. Established 1958. **Editor:** Richard Foerster. **Senior Associate Editor:** Alfredo de Palchi. **Associate Editor:** Andrea Lockett.
Magazine Needs: *Chelsea* is a long-established, high quality literary biannual, appearing in June and December. "We look for intelligence and sophisticated technique in both experimental and traditional forms. Do not want to see 'inspirational' verse, pornography, or poems that rhyme merely for the sake of rhyme." Has published poetry by Floyd Skloot, Saadi Youssef, Aimee Nezhukumatathil, R.T. Smith, and Valerie Wohlfeld. As a sample the editor selected these lines from "The Eye-mote" by Sylvia Plath, which first appeared in 1960:
What I want back is what I was/Before the bed, before the knife,/Before the brooch-pin and the salve/Fixed me in this parenthesis;/Horses fluent in the wind,/A place, a time gone out of mind.
Chelsea is 192-240 pgs., 6x9, perfect-bound, offset-printed, full-color art on card cover. Circulation is 2,100 for 900 subscribers. Subscription: $13 domestic, $16 foreign. Sample: $7.
How to Submit: Submit 5-7 pgs. of poetry. Include brief bio. No previously published poems or simultaneous submissions. E-mail for queries only. Responds within 3 months. Always sends prepublication galleys. Pays $20/page and 2 copies. Acquires first North American serial rights and one-time nonexclusive reprint rights.
Also Offers: Sponsors the annual Chelsea Award Competition. Guidelines available for SASE.

ADDITIONAL INFORMATION   DESCRIPTION OF PUBLICATION   SUBMISSION DETAILS   SAMPLE OF ACCEPTED POETRY

For More Information
If you're interested in writing for greeting card companies, *Writer's Market* (Writer's Digest Books, www.writersmarket.com) includes a section devoted to the greeting card/giftware industry. If you write song lyrics as well as poetry, *Songwriter's Market* (Writer's Digest Books) is an ideal resource for this field. Both books are available through your local library or bookstore, or can be ordered directly through the publisher at (800) 289-0963 or www.writersdigest.com.

The Art of Self-Promotion

BY LEAH MAINES

"Don't wait for your publisher to promote you!" This is the best advice I could offer a fellow poet, whether seasoned or starting out. Even if you already have a book under your belt, it's unlikely your publisher will do much to promote your latest collection (unless you're being picked up by a big-name press). If you're new to the trade with no book or chapbook in print, you need to work even harder to get your name out to the public.

This isn't to say having work published by a small press is a bad thing. In fact, it's wonderful! I never would have seen my poems in journals and anthologies if it weren't for small presses, or my book in print (at least, I don't think so). The truth is, though, most small presses just don't have the time, staff, or resources to promote their writers beyond the initial book ad or new book announcement mailers. The poet who wants to be successful must step up and take charge of the promotion effort.

There are numerous ways you can promote your work. The following suggestions are presented to help you make a splash in your local literary community. They worked for me, and I'm sure they'll work for you.

Make business cards

When I first started writing poetry for publication, I made business cards using the title of "writer/researcher," my name, telephone number, e-mail address, and regular mail address. (Although I'm mainly a poet, using "writer/researcher" kept my options open for other writing opportunities.)

I didn't spend a lot of money on the cards. In fact, I did a nice job using my computer and printer. (Later I made cards showing a picture of my book cover, and I still use them.) I distributed cards at poetry readings, social events, pretty much everywhere. Once I got an e-mail from a radio host with a talk show about writers and artists. He'd been given my card by a woman I'd met at a college alumni reception. I'd given her my card casually and told her about my poetry. (She'd never read one of my poems, but she liked me and was impressed by my business cards.) The talk show host asked if I was interested in being on his show. Not only did I do a 50-minute interview, I returned several times to promote events and talk about new writing projects.

Another time I gave my card to an old friend who was working for a local cable television show. She passed my card along to the producer and in less than a month I was on the air. All that from a tiny business card and a little bit of friendly conversation. Which leads me to my next point—networking.

Make connections

Networking is vital to a poet's career. You may be saying, "It's talent that will get me published." True to a certain extent. However, persistence and networking can make the difference. The talented poet who throws himself into the spotlight will get the coffeehouse gigs,

LEAH MAINES *is the author of* Looking to the East with Western Eyes *(Finishing Line Press), which was nominated for a Pushcart Prize. She serves as Poet-in-Residence at Northern Kentucky University and her work has appeared in* Flyway, Kaleidoscope, *and other literary publications. She has many media appearances to her credit.*

radio and TV appearances, newspaper write-ups, and so forth. The exposure you get from these various media outlets can lead to more demand for your work in print. I've been approached by several editors and publishers who heard me on the radio, saw me on TV, or read about me in the newspaper and asked me to submit poems to their journals. Publicity sparked interest in my work, and I've had some nice publishing opportunities (and successes) because of it.

Not sure how to start networking? Why not . . .

Join a local writer's group. This is the best way to make contacts in your literary community. Getting together with others who share your passion for the written word is always helpful and motivating, and it's a good way to keep informed about what's going on locally. Such groups may offer workshops and public speaking opportunities. My writer's group often arranges poetry readings at local bookstores and occasionally publishes anthologies. If you have few or no publishing credits, appearing in your group's anthology can be a good start to building publication credits. (And it feels great to see your name and work in print.)

Join your state poetry society. You'll stay better informed about what's happening around your state. These groups often put out a monthly newsletter with publication and grant opportunities as well as information about which members are publishing and where. If you get a poem accepted, win an award, or schedule an appearance or reading, inform your newsletter editor—it's a great way to keep your name in the public eye. In addition to the free publicity, it encourages your fellow poets to share their accomplishments as well.

Do a public reading

I know this sounds a little scary. It is at first, but it can really boost your reputation. If you suffer from stage fright, try reading at an open mic (i.e., microphone) event. These have become very popular at bookstores and coffeehouses. Open mic readings are easy, and there's no pressure to read unless you want to. Usually there's a sign-up sheet at the door, so go, sign up, read a poem or two. It's fun, and there's always the possibility that an editor is in the audience. (I know of a noted poet who met his future publisher at an open mic. The publisher heard him read some of his poems and the next thing he knew, he had a book deal.) Check your newspaper for listings, and keep an eye out for flyers and bulletin board notices at coffeehouses and bookstores. And when you go, don't forget to take along your business cards.

Once you've braved an open mic reading, consider going solo. Let the manager of a local coffeehouse know you're a poet and available to do special readings. Suggest that you could be their featured reader with an open mic to follow. If you've published a book or chapbook, show the manager a copy. If you don't have a book but your work has appeared in journals and magazines, inform the manager (you could even make copies of the printed poems to show him). Volunteer to prepare flyers and write a news release. This is no time to be shy. Remember to be polite, though, not pushy.

You could also offer to do a reading at your local bookstore. (This can be a little tricky to maneuver, but it's worth a shot.) Contact the bookstore manager or events coordinator, if they have one. Show her your book or copies of your published poems and explain that you've given successful readings in other venues. Maybe the bookstore would be open to hosting a local poets night; you could gather fellow poets, perhaps from your writing group, to stage a reading. I've participated in such events and they've always been a great success.

Again, be bold but polite. The bookstore will probably handle the news release, but when in doubt you can send one out yourself.

Contact your local newspapers

Whether the newspaper is a big urban daily or a community weekly, send them a news release. Most papers have a calendar or similar section where they announce various events of public interest. Contact the paper for the name of the section editor to whom you should submit information. Follow the paper's guidelines and respect deadlines! Your release should be brief and to the point. No fluff—just the "who, what, when, where, and why" of the event. And remember, if the deadline is Tuesday, make sure the editor has your release on or before Tuesday (the earlier the better).

While you're at it, why not contact the appropriate editor and let her know you're available to be interviewed? Tell her about your publication successes and any other information she might find unusual and interesting about you.

It worked for me. While living in Japan, I decided to keep a daily journal in which I wrote poems that eventually grew into a book. I thought my story was unique and hoped the editors of my local newspaper would think the same. As the cliché says, one thing led to another. Much to my pleasure, *The Kentucky Post* ran a half-page article about my life in Japan and my poetry book.

Do *you* have any unique hobbies or life experiences related to your poetry that your newspaper editor should know about?

Contact your local radio and cable stations

This sounds like a big step, but if I can do it successfully (and I have), so can you. When you schedule a poetry reading, let your radio and cable stations know. Find out if the station has a program that might be interested in having you come on and talk about your event, maybe even read some of your poems (public radio and television stations are more likely to have such shows). Don't be afraid to ask! The worst they can say is no.

A side note about public stations: Local PBS stations often have annual televised auctions where merchants donate goods to be sold on air. This is a fantastic way to get some free publicity. Does your writing group publish an anthology? Suggest they donate some copies for the auction. Do you have a book or chapbook of poems? Donate some to the station; or better yet, ask your publisher to contribute some. My publisher donated copies of my book to our local PBS Action Auction, and they did a great-looking on air display. If you don't have a book but still want to tap into this free publicity source, why not donate something else and attach a note "donated by local poet *insert your name here*"? Every year I donate items I've purchased from my travels abroad, and I always meet someone who heard my name announced on TV or radio as a result of my donation.

Self-promotion is an art that can really open doors. There's nothing sweeter to a poet than to see his or her poems in print. The promotional work you do to further your writing career is meant to spark people's interest in your poetry. So keep writing and submitting your work to keep up with your public's demand. And remember that exciting possibilities will open up for you when you promote yourself!

Editor's Note: *Although this article focuses on self-promotion for poets, there's no reason these same techniques wouldn't work for journals and magazines, book and chapbook publishers, and others.*

Who Wants to Be a Published Poet?

What if you were going to appear on a game show called *Who Wants to Be a Published Poet?* Could you answer such questions as "What is a chapbook?" or "How many poems per page in a manuscript?"

These are the kinds of questions we hear regularly at *Poet's Market*, so it made sense to provide our readers with a handy FAQ section ("frequently asked questions"). Study the answers and prepare to win! Okay, there aren't any million dollar jackpots up for grabs, but there *is* a valuable prize to claim—the expert knowledge it takes to submit your poetry like a pro.

Important Note: Most basic questions such as "How many poems should I send?", "How long should I wait for a reply?", and "Are simultaneous submissions okay?" can be answered by simply reading the listings in the Publishers of Poetry section. See the introduction to that section for an explanation of the information contained in the listings. Also, see the Glossary of Listing Terms on page 471.

Is it okay to submit handwritten poems?

Usually no. Now and then a publisher or editor makes an exception and accepts handwritten manuscripts. However, check the preferences stated in each listing. If no mention is made of handwritten submissions, assume your poetry should be typed or computer-printed.

How should I format my poems for submission to magazines and journals?

If you're submitting poems by regular mail (often referred to as *snail mail*), follow this format:

Poems should be typed or computer-printed on white 8½ × 11 paper of at least 20 lb. weight. Left, right, and bottom margins should be at least one inch. Starting ½ inch from the top of the page, type your name, address, telephone number, and e-mail address (if you have one), and number of lines in the poem in the *upper right* corner, individual lines, single spaced. Space down about six lines and type the poem title, either centered or flush left. The title may appear in all caps or in upper and lower case. Space down another two lines (at least) and begin to type your poem. Poems are usually single spaced, although some magazines may request double-spaced submissions. (Be alert to each market's preferences.) Double space between stanzas. Type one poem to a page. For poems longer than one page, type your name in the *upper left* corner; on the next line type a key word from the title of your poem, the page number, and indicate whether the stanza begins or is continued on the new page (i.e., HAYWIRE, Page 2, continue stanza *or* begin new stanza).

If you're submitting poems by e-mail:

First, make sure the publication accepts e-mail submissions. This information, when available, is included in all *Poet's Market* listings (also see Publications Accepting E-Mail Submissions on page 469 for an easy cross reference). In most cases include poems within the body of your e-mail, *not* as attachments. This is the preference of many editors accepting e-mail submissions because of the danger of viruses, the possibility of software incompatibility, and other concerns. Editors who consider e-mail attachments taboo may even delete the message without ever opening the attachment.

Of course, other editors do accept, and even prefer e-mail submissions as attachments. This information should be clearly stated in the market listing. If it's not, you're probably safer submitting your poems in the body of the e-mail. (All the more reason to pay close attention to details given in the listings.)

Note, too, the number of poems the editor recommends including in the e-mail submission. If no quantity is given specifically for e-mails, go with the number of poems an editor recommends submitting in general. Identify your submission with a notation in the subject line. Some editors simply want the words "Poetry Submission" while others want poem titles. Check the market listing for preferences. If you're uncertain about any aspect of e-mail submission formats, double-check the website (if available) for information or contact the publication for directions. (For more advice about submitting poetry electronically, see An Online Editor Looks at Poetry on the Web, by Robin Travis-Murphree, page 266.)

If you're submitting poems by disk:

Submit poems by disk *only* when the publication indicates this is acceptable. Even then, if no formatting preferences are given, contact the publisher for specifics before sending the disk. Always include a hardcopy (i.e., printed copy) of your submission with the disk.

What is a chapbook? How is it different from a regular poetry book?

A chapbook is a booklet averaging 24-50 pages in length (some may be shorter), usually digest sized (5½ × 8½, although chapbooks can come in all sizes, even published within the pages of a magazine). Typically a chapbook is saddle-stapled with a soft cover (card or special paper); however, chapbooks can also be produced with a plain paper cover the same weight as the pages, especially if the booklet is photocopied.

A chapbook is a much smaller collection of poetry than a full-length book (which runs anywhere from 50 pages to well over 100 pages, longer for "best of" collections and retrospectives). However, there are probably more poetry chapbooks being published than full-length books, and that's an important point to consider. Don't think of the chapbook as a poor relation to the full-length collection. While it's true a chapbook won't attract big reviews, qualify for major prizes, or find national distribution through large bookstores, it's a terrific way for a poet to build an audience (and reputation) in increments, while developing the kind of publishing history that may eventually attract the attention of a book publisher.

Although some presses consider chapbook-length submissions, many choose manuscripts through competitions. Check each publisher's listing for requirements, send for guidelines or visit the website (absolutely vital if a competition is involved), and check out some sample chapbooks the press has already produced (these are usually available from the publisher). Keep in mind that chapbook publishers are usually just as choosy as book publishers about the quality of work they accept. Submit your best work in a professional manner. (See the Chapbook Publishers Index on page 474 for markets that consider chapbook manuscripts.)

How do I format a collection of poems to submit to a book/chapbook publisher?

Before you send a manuscript to a book/chapbook publisher, request guidelines (or consult the publisher's website, if one is available). Requirements vary regarding formatting, query letters and samples, length, and other considerations. Usually you will be using 8½ × 11 20 lb. paper; left, right, and bottom margins of at least one inch; your name and title of your collection in the top left corner of every page; one poem to a page (although poems certainly may run longer than one page); and pages numbered consecutively. Individual publisher requirements may include a title page, table of contents, credits page (indicating where previously published poems originally appeared), and biographical note.

If you're submitting your poetry book or chapbook manuscript to a competition, you *must* read and follow the guidelines. Failure to do so could disqualify your manuscript. Often guidelines for a competition call for a special title page, a minimum and maximum number of pages, the absence of the poet's name anywhere in the manuscript, and even a special entry form to accompany the submission.

What is a cover letter? Do I have to send one? What should it say?

A cover letter is your introduction to the editor, telling him a little about yourself and your work. Most editors have indicated their preferences regarding cover letters in their listings in the Publishers of Poetry section. If an editor states that a cover letter is "required," absolutely send one! It's also better to send one if a cover letter is "preferred." Experts disagree on the necessity and appropriateness of cover letters, so use your own judgment when preferences aren't clear in the listing.

A cover letter should be professional but also allow you to present your work in a personal manner. (See the fictional cover letter on page 11 as an example.) Keep your letter brief, no more than one page. Address your letter to the correct contact person. (Use "Poetry Editor" if no contact name appears in the listing.) Include your name, address, phone number, and e-mail address (if available). If a biographical note is requested, include 2-3 lines about your job, interests, why you write poetry, etc. Avoid praising yourself or your poems in your letter (your submission should speak for itself). Include titles (or first lines) of the poems you're submitting. List a few of your most recent publishing credits, but no more than five. (If you haven't published any poems yet, you may skip this. However, be aware that some editors are interested in and make an effort to publish new writers.) Show your familiarity with the magazine to which you're submitting—comment on a poem you saw printed there, tell the editor why you chose to submit to her magazine, mention poets the magazine has published. Use a business-style format for a professional appearance, and proofread carefully; typos, misspellings, and other errors make a poor first impression. Remember that editors are people, too. Respect, professionalism, and kindness go a long way in poet/editor relationships.

What is a SASE? An IRC (with SAE)?

A SASE is a self-addressed stamped envelope. Don't let your submission leave home without it! You should also include a SASE if you send an inquiry to an editor. If your submission is too large for an envelope (for instance a bulky book-length collection of poems), use a box and include a self-addressed mailing label with adequate postage paper clipped to it.

An IRC is an International Reply Coupon, enclosed in place of a SASE with manuscripts submitted to foreign markets. Each coupon is equivalent in value to the minimum postage rate for an unregistered airmail letter. IRCs may be exchanged for postage stamps at post offices in all foreign countries that are members of the Universal Postal Union (UPU). When you provide the adequate number of IRCs and a self-addressed envelope (SAE), you give a foreign editor financial means to return your submission (U.S. postage stamps cannot be used to send mail *to* the United States from outside the country). Purchase price is $1.75 per coupon. Call your local post office to check for availability (sometimes only larger post offices sell them).

To save trouble and money, poets sometimes send disposable manuscripts to foreign markets and inform the editor to discard the manuscript after it's been read. Some enclose an IRC and SAE for reply only; others establish a deadline after which they will withdraw the manuscript from consideration and market it elsewhere.

How much postage does my submission need?

As much as it takes; you do *not* want your manuscript to arrive postage due! Purchase a postage scale or take your manuscript to the post office for weighing. Remember you'll need postage on two envelopes: the one containing your submission and SASE, and the return envelope itself. Submissions without SASEs usually will not be returned (and possibly may not even be read).

At press time U.S. first class postage rates were 34 cents for the first ounce, 23 cents for each additional ounce up to 13 ounces. So, if your submission weighs in at five ounces, you'll need to apply $1.26 in postage. Note that three pages of poetry, a cover letter, and a SASE can be mailed for one first-class stamp using a #10 (business-size) envelope; the SASE should be

Perry Lineskanner
1954 Eastern Blvd.
Pentameter, OH 45007
(852)555-5555
soneteer@trochee.vv.cy

April 24, 2002

Spack Saddlestaple, Editor
The Squiggler's Digest
Double-Toe Press
P.O. Box 54X
Submission Junction, AZ 85009

Dear Mr. Saddlestaple:

Enclosed are three poems for your consideration for *The Squiggler's Digest*: "His Tired Feet," "Boogie Lunches," and "Circling Piccadilly."

Although I'm a long-time reader of *The Squiggler's Digest*, this is my first submission to your publication. However, my poetry has appeared in other magazines, including *The Bone-Whittle Review*, *Bumper Car Reverie*, and *Stock Still*. I've won several awards through the annual *Buckeye Versefest!* contests and my chapbook manuscript was a finalist in the competition sponsored by Hollow Banana Press. While I devote a great deal of time to poetry (both reading and writing), I'm employed as a grocery store manager—which inspires more poetry than you might imagine!

Thank you for the opportunity to submit my work. Your time and attention are much appreciated, and I look forward to hearing from you.

Sincerely,

Perry Lineskanner

Enc: 3 poems

What to include in a cover letter. Note: The names used in this letter are intended to be fictional; any resemblance to real people, publications, or presses is purely coincidental.

either a #10 envelope folded in thirds or a #9 envelope. Larger envelopes may require different rates, so check with your post office.

First Class mail over 13 ounces is classified Priority; for $3.95 you can mail a package of up to two pounds with two-day service offered to most domestic destinations. You can simply mark your envelope "Priority Mail" or use labels, envelopes, or boxes provided free by the Postal Service. Matter sent in a flat-rate envelope provided by the Postal Service can also be mailed for $3.95, regardless of weight or destination.

For complete U.S. Postal Service information, including rates, a postage calculator, and the option to buy stamps online with a credit card, see their website at www.usps.gov. Canadian Postal Service information is available at www.canadapost.ca.

What does it mean when an editor says "no previously published" poems? Does this include poems that have appeared in anthologies?

If your poem appears *anywhere* in print for a public audience, it's considered "previously" published. That includes magazines, anthologies, websites and online magazines, and even programs (say for a church service, wedding, etc.). See the following explanation of rights, especially *second serial (reprint) rights* and *all rights* for additional concerns about previously published material.

What rights should I offer for my poems? What do these different rights mean?

Usually editors indicate in their listings what rights they acquire. Most journals and magazines license *first rights* (a.k.a. *first serial rights*), which means the poet offers the right to publish the poem for the first time in any periodical. All other rights to the material remain with the poet. (Note that some editors state that rights to poems "revert to authors upon publication" when first rights are acquired.) When poems are excerpted from a book prior to publication and printed in a magazine/journal, this is also called *first serial rights*. The addition of *North American* indicates the editor is the first to publish a poem in a U.S. or Canadian periodical. The poem can still be submitted to editors outside of North America or to those who acquire reprint rights.

When a magazine/journal licenses *one-time rights* to a poem (also known as *simultaneous rights*), the editor has *nonexclusive* rights to publish the poem once. The poet can submit that same poem to other publications at the same time (usually markets that don't have overlapping audiences).

Editors/Publishers who are open to submissions of work that already has been published elsewhere seek *second serial (reprint) rights*. The poet is obliged to inform them where and when the poem previously appeared so they can give proper credit to the original publication. In essence, chapbook or book collections license reprint rights, listing the magazines in which poems previously appeared somewhere in the book (usually on the copyright page or separate credits page).

If a publisher or editor requires you to relinquish *all rights*, be aware that you are giving up ownership of that poem or group of poems. You cannot resubmit the work elsewhere, nor can you include it in a poetry collection without permission or negotiating for reprint rights to be returned to you. Before you agree to this type of arrangement, ask the editor first if she is willing to acquire first rights instead of all rights. If she refuses, simply write a letter withdrawing your work from consideration. Some editors will reassign rights to a writer after a given amount of time, such as one year.

With the growth in Internet publishing opportunities, *electronic rights* have become very important. These cover a broad range of electronic media, including online magazines, CD recordings of poetry readings, and CD-ROM editions of magazines. When submitting to an electronic market of any kind, find out what rights the market acquires upfront (many online magazines also stipulate the right to archive poetry they've published so it's continually available on their websites).

What is a copyright? Should I have my poems copyrighted before I submit them for publication?

Copyright is a proprietary right that gives you the power to control your work's reproduction, distribution, and public display or performance, as well as its adaptation to other forms. In other words, you have legal right to the exclusive publication, sale, or distribution of your poetry. What's more, your "original works of authorship" are protected as soon as they are "fixed in a tangible form of expression," or written down. Since March 1989, copyright notices are no longer required to secure protection, so it's not necessary to include them on your poetry manuscript. Also, in many editors' minds copyright notices signal the work of amateurs who are distrustful and paranoid about having work stolen.

If you still want to indicate copyright, use the (c) symbol or the word *copyright*, your name, and the year. Furthermore, if you wish you can register your copyright with the Copyright Office for a $30 fee. (Since paying $30 per poem is costly and impractical, you may prefer to copyright a group of poems for that single fee.) Further information is available from the U.S. Copyright Office, Library of Congress, Washington DC 20559. You can also call the Copyright Public Information Office at (202)707-3000 between 8:30 a.m. and 5:00 p.m. weekdays (EST). Copyright forms can be ordered from (202)707-9100 or downloaded from http://lcweb.loc.gov/copyright (this Library of Congress website includes advice on filling out forms, general copyright information, and links to copyright-related websites).

Are You Being Taken?

There are many publishing opportunities for poets, from traditional magazines and journals to contests, websites, and anthologies. Along with that good news comes this warning: There are also many opportunities for poets to be taken. How do you know whether an opportunity is legitimate? Listed below are some of the most common situations that cost poets disappointment, frustration—and cash. Watch out for them when you're submitting your work, and *don't* let your vanity be your guide.

Anthologies

You know the drill. There's an ad in a perfectly respectable publication announcing a poetry contest with big cash prizes. You enter and receive a glowing letter congratulating you on your exceptional poem, which the contest sponsor wants to include in his deluxe hardbound anthology of the best poetry submitted to the contest. The anthology costs only $25 (or whatever, could be more). You don't have to buy it to have your poem published, of course, but wouldn't you be proud to own one? And wouldn't it be nice to buy additional copies to give to family and friends? And for an extra charge you can include a biographical note. And so on . . .

Of course, when the anthology arrives you may be disappointed. The quality of the poetry isn't what you were expecting, with several poems crammed unattractively onto a page. It turns out everyone who entered the contest was invited to be published, and you basically paid cash to see your poem appear in a phone book-like volume with no literary merit at all.

Are you being taken? Depends on how you look at it. If you bought into the flattery heaped on you and believed you were being published in an exclusive, high quality publication, no doubt you feel duped. On the other hand, if all you were after was seeing your poem in print, even knowing you'd have to pay for the privilege, then you got what you wanted. (Unless you've deceived yourself into believing you've truly won an honor and now have a worthy publishing credit; you don't).

You'll really feel taken if you fall for any other spiels, like having your poem printed on coffee mugs and t-shirts (you can do this much cheaper yourself through quick-print centers) or spending large sums on awards banquets and conferences. Also, find out what rights the contest sponsor acquires before you submit a single line of poetry. You may be relinquishing all rights to your poem simply by mailing it in or submitting it through a website. From then on the poem no longer belongs to you and the publisher can do whatever he wishes with it. Don't let your vanity propel you into a situation you'll always regret.

Reading and contest fees

You notice a promising market for your poetry, but the editor requires a set fee simply to consider your work. You see a contest that interests you, but the sponsors want money from you just to enter. Are you being taken?

In the case of reading fees, keep these points in mind: Is the market so exceptional that you feel it's worth risking the cost of the reading fee to have your work considered? What makes it so much better than markets that do *not* charge fees? Has the market been around awhile, with an established publishing schedule? What are you paid if your work is accepted? Are reasonably priced samples available so you can judge the production values and quality of the writing?

Reading fees don't necessarily signal a suspicious market. In fact, they're becoming increasingly popular as editors struggle with the costs of publishing books and magazines, including the man-hours required to read loads of (often bad) submissions. However, fees represent an additional financial burden on poets, who often don't receive any monetary reward for their poems to begin with. It's really up to individual poets to decide whether paying a fee is beneficial to their publishing efforts. Think long and hard about fee-charging markets that are new and untried, don't pay poets for their work (at the very least a print publication should offer a contributor's copy), charge high prices for sample copies, or set fees that seem unreasonable ($1/poem is an average fee).

Entry fees for contests are less worrisome. Usually these funds are used to establish prizes, pay judges, cover the expenses of running and promoting the contest (including publishing a "prize" issue of a magazine). Other kinds of contests charge entry fees, from Irish dancing competitions to bake-offs at a county fair. Why not poetry contests?

That's not to say you shouldn't be cautious. Watch out for contests that charge fees that are higher than average, especially if the fees are out of proportion to the amount of prize money being given. (Look through the Contests & Awards section beginning on page 391 to get a sense of what most competitions charge; you'll also find contests in listings throughout the Publishers of Poetry section, page 17.) Try to find out how long the contest has been around and whether prizes have been awarded each year. In the case of book and chapbook contests, send for a sample copy to confirm that the publisher puts out a quality product. Beware any contest that tells you you've won something, then demands payment for an anthology, trophy, or other item. (It's okay if a group offers an anthology for a modest price without providing winners with free copies. Most state poetry societies have to do this, but they also present cash awards in each category of the contest and charge low entry fees.)

Subsidy Publishers

Poetry books are a hard sell. Few of the big publishers handle them, and those that do feature the "name" poets, major prize winners and contemporary masters with breathtaking reputations. Even the small presses publish only so many books per year—far less than the number of poets writing.

No wonder poets feel desperate enough to turn to subsidy publishers (also called "vanity publishers"). These operations charge a sum to print a given number of copies of a poetry book. They promise promotion and distribution, and the poet receives a certain percentage of the print run along with a promise of royalties after the printing costs are met.

Are you being taken? Sounds okay, except the whole picture is painted rosier than it really is. Often the sum the publisher charges is inflated and the finished books may be of dubious quality. Bookstores won't stock subsidy-published books (especially poetry), and promotion efforts often consist of sending review copies far and wide, even though such volumes are rarely reviewed. In some particularly tricky situations the poet may not even own rights to his or her own work any more. Regardless, the poet is left with a stack of unsold books, perhaps with an offer from the publisher to sell the balance of the print run to the poet for a certain price. What seemed to be a dream realized turns out to be a dead end.

Before shelling out huge sums of money to a subsidy publisher for more books than you'll ever need, consider self-publishing. Literary history is starred with great poets who published their own works (Walt Whitman is one of the most well known). Talk to some local printers about the kind of book you have in mind, see what's involved, and get some price quotes. If the cost is too high for your budget, consider doing a more modest publication through a quick-print center. Chapbooks (about 24 pages) are an ideal length and can be produced attractively, softbound and saddle-stapled, for a reasonable cost. (You can even lay out and typeset the whole chapbook on your computer.) You'll have something beautiful to share with family and friends, to sign and sell at readings, and you might be able to persuade a supportive local bookstore to put a few copies on its shelves. Best of all, you'll still own and control your work; and if you turn a profit, every cent goes to you.

Obviously, poets who don't stay on their toes may find themselves preyed upon. And a questionable publishing opportunity doesn't have to be an out-and-out rip-off for you to feel cheated. In every situation, you have a choice *not* to participate. Exercise that choice, or at least develop a healthy sense of skepticism before you fling yourself and your poetry at the first smooth talker who compliments your work. Poets get burned because they're much too impatient to see their work in print. Calm your ego, slow down, and devote that time, energy, and money toward reading other poets and improving your own writing. You'll find that getting published will eventually take care of itself.

The Markets

Publishers of Poetry

In these early years of the 21st century, poetry is being published in a variety of venues: in magazines; in literary and academic journals; in books and chapbooks produced by both large and small presses; in anthologies assembled by poetry societies and other groups; on CDs and tapes that feature poets reading their own work; and on the Internet in sites ranging from individual web pages to sophisticated digital publications. There are probably others as well, not to mention new cutting-edge opportunities not yet widely known.

In this edition of *Poet's Market* we've striven to gather as much information about these markets as possible. Each listing in the Publishers of Poetry section gives an overview of the various activities for a single operation as indicated by the responses of the editors/publishers we queried. These include magazines/journals, books/chapbooks, contests, workshops, readings, organizations, and whatever else the editor/publisher thinks will be of interest to you. For those few publishers with projects at different addresses, or who requested their activities to be broken out into the appropriate sections of the book, we've cross-referenced the listings so the overview will be complete.

HOW LISTINGS ARE FORMATTED

To organize all this information within each listing, we follow a basic format:

Symbols. Each listing begins with symbols that reflect various aspects of that operation: (🅽) a market new to this edition; (🍁) a Canadian or (🌐) international market; (💻) an online or electronic market; (🏆) an award-winning market (including publications with work appearing in *The Best American Poetry*); (✅) a market with contact information that has changed since the last edition; ($) a cash-paying market (as opposed to one that pays in copies); (🔲) a market that accepts poetry written by children; (🔳) a market open to beginners; (◑) a market open to both beginners and experienced poets; (🌑) a market open to mostly experienced poets with few beginners; (◎) a specialized market; and (⊘) a market that does not consider unsolicited manuscripts. (These symbols and their explanations are listed on the inside front and back covers of this book; they also appear in blurbs at the bottom of pages scattered throughout each section.)

Contact Information. Next you'll find all the information you need to contact the market, as provided by each editor/publisher: names (in bold) of all operations associated with the market (with areas of specialization noted in parenthesis where appropriate); regular mail address; telephone number; fax number; e-mail address; website address; year the market was established; the name of the person to contact (with that person's title in bold); and membership in small press/publishing organizations (when provided).

Magazine Needs. This is an important section to study as you research potential markets. Here you'll find the editor's or publisher's overview of the operation and stated preferences (often in his or her own words), plus a list of recently published poets; poetry sample; production information about the market (size of publication, printing/binding methods, art/graphics); statistics regarding the number of submissions the market receives vs. the number accepted; and distribution and price information.

How to Submit: Another important section! This one gets down to specifics—how many poems to send; minimum/maximum number of lines; preferences regarding previously published poems and simultaneous submissions, as well as electronic submissions; payment, rights, and response times; and a lot more.

Book/Chapbook Needs and How to Submit. Same as the information for magazines with added information tailored to book/chapbook publishers.

Also Offers: The section to check for contests, conferences/workshops, readings, or organizations sponsored by or affiliated with the market.

Advice: Want to hear what an editor or publisher has to say? In this section you'll find direct quotes about everything from pet peeves to tips on writing to views on the state of poetry today.

WHERE TO START?

If you don't have a specific publisher in mind, dive right in and start reading through the listings, possibly making notes as you go (don't be afraid to write in the margins, underline, use highlighters; it also helps to flag markets that interest you with Post-it Notes). Browsing the listings is an effective way of familiarizing yourself with the information presented and the publishing opportunities available.

If you do want information about a particular market, however, begin with the General Index. This is where *all* listings are alphabetized (i.e., all the markets included within a single listing). For instance, you may want to check out the *Native American Poetry Anthology*. If you turn to the "N" listings in Publishers of Poetry section, you won't find this publication. The information appears as part of the Indian Heritage Publishing listing (along with *Indian Heritage Council Quarterly*). In the General Index, though, *Native American Poetry Anthology* is listed individually with the page number for Indian Heritage Publishing so you can go straight to the source for the information you need. (Sound confusing? Try it, it works.)

The General Index also lists those markets in the 2001 edition which do not appear in this book, along with a two-letter code explaining the absence (see the introduction to the General Index on page 529 for an explanation of these codes). You can also find markets that have changed names in the General Index, cross-referenced to the new titles.

REFINE YOUR SEARCH

In addition to the General Index, we provide several more specific indexes to help you refine your marketing plan for your poems. Note that the editors/publishers themselves indicate how and where they want their listings indexed, and not every listing appears in an index. Therefore, use indexes only to supplement your other research efforts:

Chapbook Publishers Index provides a breakdown of markets that publish chapbooks, along with corresponding page numbers.

Book Publishers Index indicates which markets are looking for book-length collections of poetry.

Openness to Submissions Index provides lists of markets according to the Openness to Submissions symbols that appear at the beginning of each listing: (□) for beginning poets, (◨) for beginning and experienced poets, (●) for mostly experienced poets, few beginners, and (◎) for specialized markets.

Geographical Index shows markets listed state by state. Some markets are more open to poets submitting from their geographical area, so use this index when you're pinpointing local activities.

Subject Index takes specialized markets (◎) a step farther by grouping them into subsections by areas of interest. Look for subheadings ranging from animals, bilingual/foreign language, and ethnic/nationality to gay/lesbian/bisexual, regional, and sports/recreation, among many others.

THE NEXT STEP

Once you know how to interpret the listings in this section, using the information they contain to identify markets for your work, the next step is to start submitting your poems. See Publishing Your Poetry: Eight Quick Tips on page 2 and Who Wants to Be a Published Poet? on page 8 for advice and guidelines about preparing your manuscript and following proper submission procedures.

ADDITIONAL INFORMATION

The Publishers of Poetry section includes six Insider Reports—five interviews with poets **Joe Enzweiler**, **Jane Hirshfield**, **David Wojahn**, **Cynthia Huntington**, and **Beth Gylys**, and an overview of poetry on the Internet by editor **Robin Travis-Murphree**. These pieces provide insights, commentary, and valuable advice from some of the top names in contemporary poetry.

This section also features the covers of nine literary magazines reflecting the range of print publications being produced today. Such images tell a lot about a publication's style and content, as do the accompanying comments by editors regarding why the cover images were selected. (When evaluating a potential market for your work, consider everything that makes up the product—poets published, style and quality of content, guidelines, editorial comments, cover art, and even ads.)

And remember that the opportunities in the Publishers of Poetry section are only part of the picture. Be sure to look at the sections that follow (Contests & Awards, Conferences & Workshops, Organizations, and Publications of Interest) for additional market leads, competitions, and educational and informational sources of special interest to poets.

🌐 🖥️ 💟 **AABYE; AABYE'S BABY**, 20 Werneth Ave., Gee Cross, Hyde, Cheshire SK14 5NL United Kingdom. E-mail: newhope@iname.com. Website: www.nhi.clara.net/nhihome.htm (includes guidelines, information on books and magazines available for sale, samples of poetry published by *New Hope International,* and links to other sites. A separate website, www.nhi.clara.net/online.htm, publishes reviews of books, magazines, audio material, PC software, videos of interest to all lovers of words, arts, and music). Established 1969 as *Headland*, 1980 as *New Hope International*, 1998 as *Aabye*. **Editor:** Gerald England.
Magazine Needs: *Aabye* publishes all types of poetry from traditional to avant-garde, from haiku to long poems, including collaborative poetry, translations (usually with the original), long poems, short poems, prose poems, haiku, englynion. Has published poetry by David Cobb, Graham High, Kona McPhee, Rochelle Hope Mehr, Frances Nagle, and Lucien Stryk. As a sample the editor selected these lines from "On Perennial Gardens: Rocks and Holes" by Kenneth D. Smith:

> A potted rose can survive/At least a season or two/Without a garden./But a rock without its hole,/Or
> a hole without its rock,/Or a perennial garden without both/Does not exist.

Aabye is 52 pgs., digest-sized, printed offset-litho from computer typesetting, saddle-stapled, glossy cover using color artwork. Press run is 500 for 200 subscribers of which 20 are libraries. Subscription: £10 (£13 non-UK)/3 issues. Sample: £3.75 (£5 non-UK). Make checks payable to Gerald England. "Non-sterling cheques not accepted. Payment by International Giro (available from Post Offices worldwide), or currency notes to the sterling equivalent preferred."
How to Submit: Submit up to 6 poems at a time on separate sheets; put name and address on each sheet. Include SASE (or SAE with IRCs) or submissions will not be considered. No simultaneous submissions. No e-mail submissions, "except by prior arrangement." Cover letter required. Translations should include copy of original. "If you do not require the ms returned (and disposable mss are preferred, especially from overseas) please advise, but do note that an SAE or IRC is still required for reply." Guidelines available for SASE (or SAE with IRC) or by e-mail. Responds usually within 1 month. Always sends prepublication galleys. Pays 1 contributor's copy. Acquires first British serial rights. Poets may send books for review consideration.
Book/Chapbook Needs & How to Submit: "Only writers with a body of work already published in periodicals should consider approaching us. Always query before submitting."
Also Offers: The associated website *Aabye's Baby* (www.aabyesbaby.ukpoets.net) publishes poetry only electronically. Its content differs entirely from that published in the printed magazine *Aabye*. Poems not selected for *Aabye* may be considered for *Aabye's Baby*. Contributors should indicate when submitting whether or not they wish their work to be considered for the website.
Advice: "Long lists of previous publications do not impress; perceptive, interesting, fresh writing indicative of a live, thinking person makes this job worthwhile."

⬛ ◯ ◪ ◎ **THE AARDVARK ADVENTURER; THE ARMCHAIR AESTHETE; PICKLE GAS PRESS (Specialized: humor)**, 31 Rolling Meadows Way, Penfield NY 14526. (716)388-6968. E-mail: bypaul @netacc.net. Established 1996. **Editor:** Paul Agosto.

Magazine Needs: *The Aardvark Adventurer* is "a quarterly family-fun newsletter-style zine of humor, thought, and verse. Very short stories (less than 500 words) are sometimes included." Prefers "light, humorous verse; any style; any 'family acceptable' subject matter; length limit 32 lines. Nothing obscene, overly forboding, no graphic gore or violence." Accepts poetry written by children. Has published poetry by Paul Humphrey, Ray Gallucci, Harry Roman, and Najwa Brax. As a sample the editor selected his poem "Squiggles and Doodles":

> wandering, pointless, meandering line/serving one purpose: to occupy time./without you i'm certain
> i'd probably find/i'd have to resort back to using my mind.

The Aardvark Adventurer is 6-12 pgs., 8½×14, photocopied, corner-stapled, with many playful b&w graphics. Receives about 500 poems/year, accepts about 40%. Press run is 150 for 100 subscribers. Single copy: $2; subscription: $5. Sample: $2. Make checks payable to Paul Agosto. "Subscription not required but subscribers given preference."

Magazine Needs: Also publishes *The Armchair Aesthete*, a quarterly digest-sized zine of "fiction and poetry of thoughtful, well-crafted concise works. Interested in more fiction submissions than poetry though." Line length for poetry is 30 maximum. *The Armchair Aesthete* is 40-60 pgs., 5½×8½, quality desktop-published, photocopied, card cover, includes ads for other publications and writers' available chapbooks. Each issue usually contains 10-15 poems and 9-14 stories. Receives about 300 poems/year, accepts about 25-30%. Subscription: $10/year. Sample postpaid: $3. Make checks payable to Paul Agosto.

How to Submit: For both publications, accepts previously published poems and simultaneous submissions, if indicated. Accepts disk and e-mail submissions, include in body of message. Cover letter preferred. Time between acceptance and publication is 1 year. Seldom comments on rejected poems. *The Aardvark Adventurer* occasionally publishes theme issues, but *The Armchair Aesthete* does not. Guidelines available by SASE for both publications. Responds in 2 months. Pay 1 contributor's copy. Acquire one-time rights. The staff of *The Aardvark Adventurer* reviews books and chapbooks of poetry in 100 words. The staff of *The Armchair Aesthete* occasionally reviews chapbooks. Send books for review consideration.

Advice: "*The Aardvark Adventurer* is a perfect opportunity for the aspiring poet, a newsletter-style publication with a very playful format."

◪ **ABBEY; ABBEY CHEAPOCHAPBOOKS**, 5360 Fallriver Row Court, Columbia MD 21044. E-mail: greisman@aol.com. Established 1970. **Editor:** David Greisman.

Magazine Needs & How to Submit: *Abbey*, a quarterly, aims "to be a journal but to do it so informally that one wonders about my intent." Wants "poetry that does for the mind what that first sip of Molson Ale does for the palate. No pornography or politics." Has published poetry and artwork by Richard Peabody, Vera Bergstrom, D.E. Steward, Carol Hamilton, Harry Calhoun, Wayne Hogan, and Cheryl Townsend. *Abbey* is 20-26 pgs., magazine-sized, photocopied. Publishes about 150 of 1,000 poems received/year. Press run is 200. Subscription: $2. Sample: 50¢. Guidelines are available for SASE. Responds in 1 month. Pays 1-2 copies.

Book/Chapbook Needs & How to Submit: *Abbey Cheapochapbooks* come out 1-2 times/year averaging 10-15 pgs. For chapbook consideration query with 4-6 samples, bio, and list of publications. Responds in 2 months. Pays 25-50 copies.

Advice: The editor says he is "definitely seeing poetry from two schools—the nit'n'grit school and the textured/reflective school. I much prefer the latter."

🌐 ✓ ◪ ◎ **ABIKO ANNUAL WITH JAMES JOYCE FW STUDIES (Specialized: translations)**, 8-1-7 Namiki, Abiko-shi, Chiba-ken 270-1165 Japan. Phone/fax: 011-81-471-84-5873. E-mail: hce@mil.allnet.ne .jp. Website: www.user3.allnet.ne.jp/hce/. Established 1988. Founding Editor: Laurel Willis. **Contact:** Dr. Tatsuo Hamada.

Magazine Needs: *Abiko* is a literary-style annual journal "heavily influenced by James Joyce's *Finnegan's Wake*. We publish all kinds, with an emphasis like Yeats's quote: 'Truth seen in passion is the substance of poetry!' We prefer poetry like Eliot's or Donne's. We include originals and translations from Japanese and other languages." Has published poetry by Eileen Malone, James Fairhall, and Danetta Loretta Saft. *Abiko Annual* is about 350 pgs., 14.8cm×21cm, perfect-bound, coated paper cover. Press run is 300 for 50 subscribers of which 10 are libraries. Sample: $25.

How to Submit: "See *Writer's Digest*, *Poets & Writers*, and *AWP Chronicle* for details." Writers may send books for review consideration.

Advice: "Please remember U.S. postage does not work in Japan with SAEs! Send 2 International Reply Coupons."

✓ ▣ ◪ ◎ **ABLE MUSE (Specialized: form/style); ERATOSPHERE**, 467 Saratoga Ave., #602, San Jose CA 95129-1326. Phone/fax: (801)729-3509. E-mail: submission@ablemuse.com. Website: www.ablemuse.c om. Established 1999. **Editor:** Alex Pepple.

Magazine Needs: *Able Muse: a review of metrical poetry* "spotlights formal poetry via a quarterly online presentation, in the supportive environment of art and photography, essays, interviews, book reviews, fiction, and a literary forum. Also includes electronic books of poetry. *Able Muse* exclusively publishes formal poetry.

We are looking for well-crafted poems of any length or subject that employ skillful and imaginative use of meter, or meter and rhyme, executed in contemporary idiom, that reads as naturally as your free-verse poems. Do not send us free-verse, greeting card verse, or poetry campaigning for the revival of archaic language." Has published poetry by Mark Jarman, Andrea Hollander Budy, Rhina P. Espaillat, Len Krisak, John William Watkins, and Patrick Daly. As a sample the editor selected these lines from "Heart Attack" by Beth Houston:

> Even now, her last day blessed with a flood/Of roses, only one closed flower will do,/One last bud clinging to color like blood/Flowing from its thorn, her old heart's issue,/Love held so deep, so cold, that stillborn bud/In ice, that wound's child clutching one fist, two.

Receives about 800 poems/year, accepts about 10%. Publish 20 poems/issue.
How to Submit: Submit 1-5 poems at a time. No previously published poems or simultaneous submissions. Accepts e-mail and disk submissions. "E-mail is the preferred medium of submission, but we also welcome snail mail, or submit directly from the website with the automated online submission form." Cover letter preferred. Time between acceptance and publication is 4-10 weeks. Often comments on rejected poems. Occasionally publishes theme issues. Guidelines and a list of upcoming themes available by e-mail or on website. Responds in 1 month. Sometimes sends prepublication galleys. Acquires first rights. Reviews books of poetry. Poets may send books for review consideration.
Also Offers: *Eratosphere* is provided online for the posting and critique of poetry and other literary work. It is a 'virtual' workshop! Literary online chats also provided featuring the scheduled appearance of guest celebrity poets."
Advice: "Despite the rush to publish everything online, most of web-published poetry has been free verse. This is surprising given formal poetry's recent rise in popularity and number of print journals that exclusively publish formal poetry. *Able Muse* attempts to fill this void bringing the best contemporary formalists online. Remember, content is just as important as form."

ABRAXAS MAGAZINE; GHOST PONY PRESS, P.O. Box 260113, Madison WI 53726-0113. E-mail: irmarkha@students.wisc.edu. Website: www.geocities.com/Paris/4614 or www.litline.org/html/ABRAXAS.html (include guidelines and submission dates; book prices; and links to the editor). *Abraxas* established in 1968 by James Bertolino and Warren Woessner; Ghost Pony Press in 1980 by editor/publisher Ingrid Swanberg.
Contact: Ingrid Swanberg (for both presses).
Magazine Needs & How to Submit: *Abraxas* no longer considers unsolicited material, except as announced as projects arise. Interested in poetry that is "contemporary lyric, experimental, and poetry in translation." Does not want to see "political posing; academic regurgitations. Please include original with submissions of translation." Has published poetry by William Stafford, Ivan Argüelles, Denise Levertov, César Vallejo, and Andrea Moorhead. As a sample the editor selected these lines from "the silence of lascaux" by próspero saíz:

> in the silence of lascaux a wavering light is fading/outside the cave the bones of slaughter linger still/ traces of mass killings beneath the cliffs of stone/yet far from the equine ossuary stubby ponies tumble/ in the vanishing lines of the sacred terror of the horse . . .

Abraxas is up to 80 pgs. (160 pgs., double issues), 6 × 9, flat-spined (saddle stapled with smaller issues), litho-offset, original art on matte card cover, with "unusual graphics in text, original art and collages, concrete poetry, exchange ads only, letters from contributors, essays." Appears "irregularly, 4- to 9-month intervals or longer." Press run is 600 for 500 subscribers of which 150 are libraries. Subscription: $16/4 issues, $20/4 issues Canada, Mexico, and overseas. Sample: $4 ($8 double issues). *Abraxas* will announce submission guidelines as projects arise. Pays 1 copy plus 40% discount on additional copies.
Book/Chapbook Needs & How to Submit: To submit to Ghost Pony Press, inquire with SASE plus 5-10 poems and cover letter. Accepts previously published material for book publication by Ghost Pony Press. Editor sometimes comments briefly on rejected poems. Responds to queries in 1-3 months, to mss in 3 months or longer. "We currently have a considerable backlog of mss." Payment varies per project. Send SASE for catalog to buy samples. Has published three books of poetry by próspero saíz including *the bird of nothing & other poems*; 168 pgs., 7 × 10, sewn and wrapped binding, paperback available for $20 (signed and numbered edition is $35), as well as *Zen Concrete Ex Etc.*, by d.a. levy; 268 pgs., 8½ × 11, perfect-bound, illustrated, paperback for $27.50.
Advice: "Ghost Pony Press is a small press publisher of poetry books; *Abraxas* is a literary journal publishing contemporary poetry, criticism, and translations. Do not confuse these separate presses!"

ACM (ANOTHER CHICAGO MAGAZINE); LEFT FIELD PRESS; CHICAGO LITERARY PRIZE, 3709 N. Kenmore, Chicago IL 60613. Website: www.anotherchicagomag.com (includes guidelines, contest guidelines, subscription info, and current issues info). Established 1977. **Poetry Editor:** Barry Silesky.
• Work published in *ACM* has been included in *The Best American Poetry* (1995, 1996, and 1997) and *Pushcart Prize* anthologies.
Magazine Needs: *ACM* is a literary biannual, with emphasis on quality, experimental, politically aware prose, fiction, poetry, reviews, cross-genre work, and essays. No religious verse. Has published prose and poetry by Albert Goldbarth, Michael McClure, Jerome Sala, Nadja Tesich, Wanda Coleman, Charles Simic, and Diane Wakoski. *ACM* is 220 pgs., digest-sized, offset printed, with b&w art and ads. Appreciates traditional to experimental verse with an emphasis on message, especially poems with strong voices articulating social or political concerns. Press run is 2,000 for 500 subscribers of which 100 are libraries.

How to Submit: Submit 3-4 typed poems at a time. Accepts simultaneous submissions; no previously published poems. Responds in 3 months, has 3- to 6-month backlog. Sends prepublication galleys. Pays "if funds permit," and/or 1 contributor's copy and 1 year subscription. Acquires first serial rights. Reviews books of poetry in 250-800 words. Poets may send books for review consideration.

Also Offers: Sponsors Chicago Literary Prize. Deadline: December.

Advice: "Buy a copy—subscribe and support your own work."

N ☐ ☑ ◎ ACORN: A JOURNAL OF CONTEMPORARY HAIKU (Specialized: forms, haiku); REDFOX PRESS, P. O. Box 186, Philadelphia PA 19105. E-mail: missias@earthlink.net. Website: http://home.e arthlink.net/~missias/Acorn.html (includes examples, guidelines, info on special issues, price and ordering info). Established 1998. **Editor:** A. C. Missias.

Magazine Needs: *Acorn: a journal of contemporary haiku* appears biannually and is dedicated to publishing "the best of contemporary English language haiku, and in particular to showcasing individual poems that reveal the extraordinary moments found in everyday life." No restrictions on form or absolute subject matter, "but the approach should generally be that of 'traditional' haiku: images taken from reality, juxtaposed in a way that elicits (indirectly) an emotional response, insight, or deeper resonance." Does not want "epigrams, musings, and overt emotion poured into 17 syllables; surreal, sci-fi, or political commentary 'ku'; strong puns or raunchy humor. Syllable counting generally discouraged." Accepts poetry written by children. Recently published poetry by Bruce Ross, Michael Ketchek, Francine Porad, Pamela Miller Ness, Michael Dylan Welch, and Cindy Zacko-witz. As a sample the editor selected this haiku by john crook:

> heatwave/the cat rests her head/on today's paper

Acorn is 60 pgs. plus flyleaf, 4¼ × 7, offset-printed/photocopied, saddle-stapled, cardstock cover with set graphic. Receives about 2,000 poems/year, accepts about 12%. Publishes about 115 poems/issue. Press run is 350 for 180 subscribers of which 6 are libraries, 30 shelf sales; 20 are distributed free to potential subscribers. Single copy: $5; subscription: $9.50. Sample: $5. Make checks payable to redfox press.

How to Submit: Submit 5-25 poems at a time. Line length for poetry is 1 minimum, 5 maximum. No previously published poems or simultaneous submissions. Accepts e-mail submissions; no fax or disk submissions. "Snail mail should include SASE; e-mail submissions in e-mail text only (no attachments); several poems/page preferred." Reads submissions year round. Deadlines: February 28(9) and August 31 for spring and fall issues. Time between acceptance and publication is 1-6 months. "Decisions made by editor on a rolling basis. Poems judged purely on their own merits, not dependent on other work taken. Sometimes acceptance conditional on minor edits. Attempt to respond to submissions within 2 weeks." Often comments on rejected poems. Occasionally publishes theme issues, supplemental volumes only (released with every 3rd issue; solicited content only). Guidelines are available in magazine and on website. Responds in 3 weeks. Pays $2/accepted snail mail submission with SASE, $1/accepted e-mail submission. Acquires first rights and one-time rights. Poets may send books for review consideration to A. C. Missias, c/o redfox press (reviews posted online, not in journal).

Book/Chapbook Needs & How to Submit: redfox press publishes "occasional book projects, mostly solicited. Focus on haiku, with some interest in poets whose work spans haiku and other poetry."

Also Offers: Periodic supplement issues released with *Acorn* on particular topics chosen by the editor. Descriptions and ordering information available on website.

Advice: "This is primarily a journal for those with a focused interest in haiku, rather than an outlet for the occasional short jottings of longer-form poets. It is a much richer genre than one might surmise from many of the recreational websites that claim to promote 'haiku' and bound to appeal to many readers and writers, especially those attuned to the world around them."

☐ ◎ THE ACORN; EL DORADO WRITERS' GUILD (Specialized: regional), P.O. Box 1266, El Dorado CA 95623-1266. (530)621-1833. Fax: (530)621-3939. E-mail: theacorn@visto.com. Established 1993. **Editors:** Kirk Colvin, Harlon Stafford, Frank Seveson, Joy Burris.

Magazine Needs: *the ACORN* is a quarterly journal of the Western Sierra, published by the El Dorado Writers' Guild, a nonprofit literary organization. It includes "fiction and nonfiction, history and reminiscence, story and legend, and poetry." Wants poetry "up to 30 lines long, though we prefer shorter. Focus should be on western slope Sierra Nevada. No erotica, pornography, or religious poetry." Has published poetry by Nancy Cherry, Jeanne Wagner, Joyce Odam, and Edward C. Lynskey. As a sample the poetry consultant selected these lines from "Talking Water" by Blaine Hammond:

It has been the hawk/after it was a rat/eaten by the hawk. Listen!/It was your lover/after she breathed moist oxygen/once exhaled by the pine,/which gave its limbs a perch/to the hawk, breathed/carbon dioxide expiration.//It has passed through so many cells,/been alive so many times/without dying, by now/it has become aware./You should taste/its memory.

the ACORN is 44 pgs., 5½ × 8½, offset-printed, saddle-stapled, light card cover. Receives about 400 poems/year, accepts about 15%. Press run is 200 for 110 subscribers. Subscription: $12. Sample: $3.

How to Submit: Submit 3-5 poems, neatly typed or printed, at a time. Accepts previously published poems—indicate where published; no simultaneous submissions. E-mail submissions encouraged; "prefer attachment in MSWord format. However, in body of message is acceptable." Cover letter with short (75-word) bio and publication credits preferred. "Our issues favor topical items suitable for the season." Deadlines are February 1, May 1, August 1. "December is our contest issue." Time between acceptance and publication is 1 month. "Five editors score the poems for content, form, and suitability. Graphics editor selects to fit space available." Often comments on rejected poems. Responds within 1 month after deadline. Pays 2 copies.

Also Offers: Sponsors annual contest. 1st Prize: $100, 2nd Prize: $50, 3rd Prize: $20, 2 $10 honorable mentions. Entry fee: $8/3 poems, 40 lines maximum/poem. Deadline: Novermber 1. All winning entries are published in the contest edition of *the ACORN* in December. Send SASE for complete rules.

Advice: "If your poetry is about nature, be accurate with the species' names, colors, etc. If you describe a landscape, be sure it fits our region. Metered rhyming verse had better be precise. (We have an editor with an internal metronome!) Slant rhyme and free verse are welcome. Avoid trite phrases."

🌐 ◯ ◪ **ACUMEN MAGAZINE; EMBER PRESS; THE LONG POEM GROUP NEWSLETTER**, 6 The Mount, Higher Furzeham, Brixham, South Devon TQ5 8QY England. Phone: (01803)851098. Press established 1971. *Acumen* established 1984. **Poetry Editor:** Patricia Oxley.

Magazine Needs: *Acumen* appears 3 times/year (in January, May, and September) and is a "small press publisher of a general literary magazine with emphasis on good poetry." Wants "well-crafted, high quality, imaginative poems showing a sense of form. No experimental verse of an obscene type." Has published poetry by Elizabeth Jennings, William Oxley, Gavin Ewart, D.J. Enright, Peter Porter, Kathleen Raine, and R.S. Thomas. As a sample the editor selected these lines from "Learning A Language" by Danielle Hope:

> . . . *And I walk to the sea/to look for messages in dunes/and sea-grass/but I find a tangle of red flowers I cannot identify./The sea shuffles/illegible scatters of sand.*

Acumen is 100 pgs., A5, perfect-bound. "We aim to publish 120 poems out of 12,000 received." Press run is 650 for 400 subscribers of which 20 are libraries. Subscription: $45 surface/$50 air. Sample copy: $15.

How to Submit: Submit 5-6 poems at a time. Accepts simultaneous submissions, if not submitted to UK magazines; no previously published poems. Responds in 1 month. Pays "by negotiation" and 1 copy. Staff reviews books of poetry up to 300 words, single format or 600 words, multi-book. Send books for review consideration to Glyn Pursglove, 25 St. Albans Rd., Brynmill, Swansea, West Glamorgan SA2 0BP Wales.

Also Offers: Publishes *The Long Poem Group Newsletter*, established in 1995, which features short articles about long poems and reviews long poems. Free for large SASE (or SAE with IRC).

Advice: "Read *Acumen* carefully to see what kind of poetry we publish. Also read widely in many poetry magazines, and don't forget the poets of the past—they can still teach us a great deal."

◪ **ADASTRA PRESS**, 16 Reservation Rd., Easthampton MA 01027-2536. Established 1980. **Publisher:** Gary Metras.

Book/Chapbook Needs: "Adastra is primarily a chapbook publisher using antique equipment and methods, i.e., hand-set type, letterpress printed, hand-sewn bindings. Any titles longer than chapbook length are by special arrangement and are from poets who have previously published a successful chapbook or two with Adastra. Editions are generally released with a flat-spine paper wrapper, and some titles have been bound in cloth. Editions are limited, ranging from 200-400 copy print runs. Some of the longer titles have gone into reprint and these are photo-offset and perfect-bound. Letterpress chapbooks by themselves are not reprinted as single titles. Once they go out of print, they are gone. Instead, I have released *The Adastra Reader, Collected Chapbooks, 1979-1986* (1987), and am assembling *The Adastra Reader II, Collected Chapbooks, 1987-1992*. These anthologies collect the first twelve chapbooks and the second twelve, respectively, and I am now planning the third series. I am biased against poems that rhyme and/or are religious in theme. Sequences and longish poems are always nice to present in a chapbook format. There are no guidelines other than these. Competition is keen. Less than .5% of submissions are accepted." Poets published include W.D. Ehrhart (*Beautiful Wreckage, New & Selected Poems*), Linda Lee Harper (*Blue Flute*), Martha Carlson-Bradley (*A Nest Full of Cries*), Ed Ochester (*Cooking in Key West*). As a sample the editor selected these lines from "Two Years After a Death" by Richard Jones from *The Stone It Lives On:*

> *Taking shelter in the cleft of a rock/on a cliff face lashed by rain,/I waited for lightning to pass/and thought of him, how suffering/is like rock, hard and bare.*

Publishes 2-4 chapbooks/year. Sample hand-crafted chapbook: $6

How to Submit: Send a complete chapbook ms of 12-18 pgs., double-spaced preferred, during the month of February. Notification of acceptance/rejection by April. "I choose 1 or 2 mss to publish the following year."

Query with a sample of 5 poems from a chapbook ms in the Fall. "If I like what I see, I'll ask you to submit the chapbook ms in February. Always include an SASE." Time between acceptance and publication is up to 2 years. Payment is 10% of the print run in copies with a discount on additional copies.

ADEPT PRESS; SMALL BRUSHES, P.O. Box 391, Long Valley NJ 07853-0391. Established 1999. **Editor:** Jan Epps Turner.
Magazine Needs: Published quarterly, *Small Brushes* wants "to be another showcase for good poetry from many voices. Although we prefer poems of 36 lines or fewer, we will occasionally run an excellent two-page poem (up to 72 lines). We want poetry of all forms springing from important human emotions, ethics, and realizations. We value unity, coherence, emphasis, and accessibility. We will not use material containing vulgarity, explicit sexual references, or words or descriptions that might reasonably offend anyone. We avoid issues of a narrow religious, social, or political nature." Has published poetry by Claudia Showers Drezga, Jane M. Long, R. Paul Muni, Ann DeFalco, M.Z. Reed, and Anne Abrams Nadel. As a sample the editor selected these lines from "Captured Heat: Leaves Wide Between Filaments" by Bruce E. Litton:
> The sky, dense; water,/trapped in a lifted vase,/flushed from the gills/of a leaping bass./Life expanse: entity, romance.

Small Brushes is 32 pgs., digest-sized, desktop-published with some photocopying, saddle-stapled, parchment cover, with b&w cartoons, or occasionally color graphics. Receives about 140 poems/year, accepts about 40%. Publish 25-28 poems/issue. Press run is 80 for 15 subscribers, 26 shelf sales; 33 distributed free to contributors and libraries. Single copy: $3; subscription: $10/year (4 issues). Sample: $2. Make checks payable to Adept Press. "There are no requirements for contributors. The poetry stands on its own merit. Ours is a labor of love and not for profit. We do urge our regular contributors to subscribe, so that our magazine can continue."
How to Submit: Submit 3-4 poems at a time. No previously published poems or simultaneous submissions. Cover letter required. "Please include a brief bio in your cover letter, place your name and address at the top of each manuscript page and type or print clearly. Please send SASE for our comments or contact." Reads submissions all year. Submit seasonal poems 2 months in advance. Time between acceptance and publication is up to 15 months. Seldom comments on rejected poems. Guidelines are available for SASE. Responds in 2 months. Sometimes sends prepublication galleys. Pays 1 copy/published poem. Rights remain with authors and artists.
Advice: "Read poetry, including the masters. Ignore the trends. Write from your own experiences and deep feelings."

$ ADRIFT (Specialized: nationality), 46 E. First St., #3D, New York NY 10003. Established 1980. **Editor:** Thomas McGonigle.
Magazine Needs: *Adrift* appears twice/year. "The orientation of the magazine is Irish, Irish-American. I expect the reader-writer knows and goes beyond Yeats, Kavanagh, Joyce, O'Brien." Open to all kinds of submissions, but does not want to see "junk." Has published poetry by James Liddy, Thomas McCarthy, Francis Stuart, and Gilbert Sorrentino. *Adrift* is 32 pgs., magazine-sized, offset-printed on heavy stock, saddle-stapled, matte card cover. Circulation is 1,000 with 200 subscriptions, 50 of which are libraries. Single copy: $4; subscription: $8. Sample: $5. Make checks payable to T. McGonigle.
How to Submit: Accepts simultaneous submissions. Magazine pays, rate varies; contributors receive 1 copy. Reviews books of poetry. Poets may send books for review consideration.

ADVOCATE, PKA's PUBLICATION, 301A Rolling Hills Park, Prattsville NY 12468. (518)299-3103. Established 1987.
Magazine Needs: *Advocate* is a bimonthly advertiser-supported tabloid, 12,000 copies distributed free, using "original, previously unpublished works, such as feature stories, essays, 'think' pieces, letters to the editor, profiles, humor, fiction, poetry, puzzles, cartoons, or line drawings." Wants "nearly any kind of poetry, any length, but not religious or pornographic. Poetry ought to speak to people and not be so oblique as to have meaning only to the poet. If I had to be there to understand the poem, don't send it. Now looking for horse-related poems, stories, drawings, and photos." Accepts about 25% of poems received. Sample: $4.
How to Submit: No previously published poems or simultaneous submissions. Time between acceptance and publication is an average of 6 months. "Occasionally" comments on rejected poems. Responds in 2 months. Pays 2 copies. Acquires first rights only.
Advice: "All submissions and correspondence must be accompanied by a self-addressed, stamped envelope with sufficient postage."

AETHLON: THE JOURNAL OF SPORT LITERATURE (Specialized: sports/recreation), Dept. PM, English Dept., East Tennessee State University, Box 70270, Johnson City TN 37614-0270. Established 1983. **General Editor:** Don Johnson, Dean, Arts & Sciences, ETSU. **Poetry Editor:** Robert W. Hamblin, Professor of English, Southeast Missouri State University, Cape Girardeau MO 63701.
Magazine Needs: *Aethlon* publishes a variety of sport-related literature, including scholarly articles, fiction, poetry, and reviews; two issues annually in fall and spring. Subject matter must be sports-related; no restrictions regarding form, length, style, or purpose. Does not want "doggerel, cliché-ridden, or oversentimental" poems. Poets published include Neal Bowers, Joseph Duemer, Robert Fink, Jan Mordenski, H.R. Stoneback, and Don

Welch. *Aethlon* is 200 pgs., digest-sized, offset-printed, flat-spined, with illustrations and some ads. Publishes 12-15 poems/issue. Circulation is 1,000 for 750 subscribers of which 250 are libraries. Subscription included with membership ($40) in the Sport Literature Association. Sample: $15.
How to Submit: "Only typed mss with SASE considered." No simultaneous submissions. Responds in up to 2 months. Backlog is up to 1 year. Pays 5 offprints and a copy of the issue in which their poem appears.

⊔ **AFFABLE NEIGHBOR**, P.O. Box 3635, Ann Arbor MI 48106-3635. Established 1994. **Editor-in-Chief:** Joel Henry-Fisher. **Poetry Editor:** Leigh Chalmers.
Magazine Needs: Published various times throughout the year, *Affable Neighbor* "pushes the boundaries of what a magazine is supposed to be/can be and provides a good laugh too." Wants "shocking, groundbreaking work that 'pushes the envelope' whatever that means, and sometimes short." No religious, flowery, uninspired poetry. Has published poetry by Robin Clenard, Geoff O'Daley, Lexi Menter, and Tom T. *Affable Neighbor* is photocopied and stapled with cardstock cover, includes "photos, drawings, etc., very visual." Receives about 500-1,000 poems/year, accepts about 1%. Single copy: $2; subscription: $20. Make checks payable to Joel Fisher.
How to Submit: Accepts previously published poems and simultaneous submissions. Cover letter preferred. "If a response is desired, please say so and include a SASE." Time between acceptance and publication is "several months or years." Poems are circulated to an editorial board. "A poem must be unanimously accepted by the editors and staff of *Affable Neighbor*." Often comments on rejected poems. Occasionally publishes theme issues. Responds in 2 weeks. Pays copies. Staff reviews other magazines.
Book/Chapbook Needs & How to Submit: Affable Neighbor Press publishes 0-5 poetry titles/year. "We publish exciting and groundbreaking work that can find no other outlet." Query first, with a few sample poems and cover letter with brief bio and publication credits. Pays royalties of 50% maximum. "We work out terms with individual authors."
Advice: "*Affable Neighbor* appreciates writing that includes or is mixed with visuals. For beginners: keep working. Photographs are also appreciated."

▣ ◯ ▨ ◎ **AFRICAN VOICES (Specialized: ethnic)**, 270 W. 96th St., New York NY 10025. (212)865-2982. Fax: (212)316-3335. E-mail: annebutts@aol.com. Website: www.africanvoices.com (includes history of magazine, submission guidelines, subscription information, spotlighted artists, a calendar of events, flash animation, etc.). Established 1992. **Poetry Editor:** Layding Kalida.
Magazine Needs: *African Voices* is a quarterly "art and literary magazine that highlights the work of people of color. We publish ethnic literature and poetry on any subject. We also consider all themes and styles: avant-garde, free verse, haiku, light verse, and traditional. We do not wish to limit the reader or author." Accepts poetry written by children. Has published poetry by Reg E. Gaines, Maya Angelou, Jessica Care Moore, Asha Bandele, Tony Medina, and Louis Reyes Rivera. *African Voices* is about 48 pgs., 8½ × 11, professionally printed, saddle-stapled, paper cover, with b&w photos and illustrations. Receives about 100 submissions/year, accepts approximately 30%. Press run is 20,000 for 5,000 subscribers of which 30 are libraries, 40% shelf sales. Single copy: $3; subscription: $12. Sample: $5.
How to Submit: Submit no more than 5 poems at any one time. Accepts previously published poems and simultaneous submissions. Accepts e-mail and fax submissions; include in body of e-mail message. Cover letter and SASE required. Seldom comments on rejected poems. Guidelines and a list of upcoming themes available for SASE or on website. Responds in 3 months. Pays 5 copies. Acquires first or one-time rights. Reviews books of poetry in 500-1,000 words. Poets may send books for review consideration, attn. Layding Kaliba.
Also Offers: Sponsors periodic poetry contests and readings. Send SASE for details.
Advice: "We strongly encourage new writers/poets to send in their work and not give up if their work is not accepted the first time. Accepted contributors are encouraged to subscribe."

◩ $ ◨ **AGNI**, Boston University, 236 Bay State Rd., Boston MA 02215. (617)353-7135. Fax: (617)353-7134. E-mail: agni@bu.edu. Website: www.bu.edu.agni/ (includes writer's guidelines, names of editors, poetry, and interviews, plus information on back issues). Established 1972. **Editors:** Askold Melnyczuk and Eric Grunwald.
  ● Work published in *AGNI* has been included in *The Best American Poetry* (1995, 1997, 1998, and 1999) and *Pushcart Prize* anthologies.
Magazine Needs: *AGNI* is a biannual journal of poetry, fiction, and essays "by both emerging and established writers. We publish quite a bit of poetry in forms as well as 'language' poetry, but we don't begin to try and place parameters on the 'kind of work' that *AGNI* selects." Wants readable, intelligent poetry—mostly lyric free verse (with some narrative and dramatic)—that somehow communicates tension or risk. Has published poetry by Adrienne Rich, Seamus Heaney, Maxine Scates, Rosanna Warren, Chinua Achebe, and Ha Jin. *AGNI* is typeset, offset-printed and perfect-bound. Publishes about 40 poems/issue. Circulation is 1,500 for subscription, mail order and bookstore sales. Subscription: $15. Sample: $9.
How to Submit: "Our next reading period will run October 1st, 2001 until February 15, 2002. Please submit no more than five poems at a time. No fancy fonts, gimmicks, or preformatted reply cards. No work accepted via e-mail. Brief, sincere cover letters." Accepts simultaneous submissions; no previously published poems. Pays $10/page, $150 maximum, plus 2 copies and one-year subscription. Acquires first serial rights.

Also Offers: *AGNI* also publishes Take Three, an annual series of work by three young poets in conjunction with Graywolf Press. Poets are chosen by *AGNI*'s editorial board.

✔️ ◻️ $ ◻️ ◐ ◎ **AG-PILOT INTERNATIONAL MAGAZINE (Specialized: agricultural aviation); VOLANDO**, P.O. Box 1607, Mt. Vernon WA 98273. (360)734-3881 Fax: (888)490-8206. E-mail: agpilot 78@aol.com. Website: www.agpilot.com. **Publisher:** Tom Wood. **Contact:** Krista Salinas.
Magazine Needs: *AG-Pilot* appears monthly, "is intended to be a fun-to-read, technical, as well as humorous and serious publication for the ag pilot and operator. Interested in agricultural aviation (crop dusting) and aerial fire suppression (air tanker pilots) related poetry ONLY—something that rhymes and has a cadence." Accepts poetry written by children. As a sample we selected these lines from "Freedom" by Jack B. Harvey:

> So now I dress in faded jeans/And beat up cowboy boots./My flying's done on veg'tables,/The row
> crops, and the fruits.//My wife now drives the flaggin' truck/And marks off all my fields./She tells me
> all about the crops/And talks about the yields.

Ag-Pilot is 64-96 pgs., 8½×10⅞, saddle-stapled. Circulation is 7,109.
How to Submit: Buys 1 poem/issue. Accepts e-mail submissions. Pays about $50.
Also Offers: Publishes a Spanish-language version of *Ag-Pilot* titled *Volando*. For more information, contact managing editor Iris Carias at the above address.

◻️ ◐ ◎ **THE AGUILAR EXPRESSION (Specialized: social issues); EROS ERRANT (Specialized: love/romance/erotica)**, 1329 Gilmore Ave., Donora PA 15033. (724)379-8019. Established 1986. **Editor/Publisher:** Xavier F. Aguilar.
Magazine Needs: *Aguilar Expression* appears 2 times/year. "In publishing poetry, I try to exhibit the unique reality that we too often take for granted and acquaint as mediocre. We encourage poetics that deal with *now*, which our readers can relate to. We are particularly interested in poetry dealing with social issues." Has published poetry by Martin Kich and Gail Ghai. As a sample the editor selected these lines from "The Water Truck" by Donna Taylor Burgess:

> But pockets are as empty/As the taps/In a government day/And water has never been free.

Aguilar Expression is 4-20 pgs., photocopied on 8½×11 sheets, corner-stapled. Receives about 20-30 poems/month, accepts about 5-10. Circulation is 300. Sample: $6. Make checks payable to *Aguilar Expression*.
How to Submit: "We insist that all writers send a SASE for writer's guidelines before submitting." Submit up to 3 poems at a time. 24-line limit, any topic/style. Cover letter, including writing background, and SASE for contact purposes, required with submissions. "Send copies; mss will not be returned." Responds in 2 months. Pays 1 copy. Open to unsolicited reviews.
Magazine Needs: *Eros Errant* appears 2 times/year (June and December) and publishes poetry, fiction, and b&w line art. Wants poems that "exhibit the sexual travels of various characters and situations—diversity is our call. All situations with adults considered. The more graphic the better. No fetish." As a sample the editor selected these lines from "Obsessed" by Corrine DeWinter:

> I whispered to you,/told you secrets./I asked you to come,/to bring me stars,/to say my name.

Eros Errant is 4-12 pgs., photocopied on 4¼×5½ sheets. Circulation is 100. Sample: $5. Make checks payable to *Aguilar Expression*.
How to Submit: "We ask that writers send a SASE for guidelines before submitting work." Submit up to 5 poems at a time, 20-line limit/poem. Accepts previously published poems; no simultaneous submissions. Pays 1 copy. Acquires one-time rights.

$ ◻️ ◐ ◎ **AIM MAGAZINE (Specialized: social issues, ethnic, political)**, P.O. Box 1174, Maywood IL 60153. (773)874-6184. Fax: (206)543-2746. E-mail: mapilado@aol.com. Website: www.aimmagazine.org (includes advertising, subscription information). Established 1974. **Poetry Editor:** Ruth Apilado.
Magazine Needs: *Aim* appears quarterly, "dedicated to racial harmony and peace." Uses 3-4 poems ("poetry with social significance mainly"—average 32 lines) in each issue. Accepts poetry written by high school students. Has published poetry by J. Douglas Studer, Wayne Dowdy, Ned Pendergast, and Maria DeGuzman. *Aim* is magazine-sized with glossy cover. Receives about 30 submissions/year, accepts about half. Circulation is 10,000 for 3,000 subscribers of which 15 are libraries. Single copy: $3; subscription: $12. Sample: $4.
How to Submit: Accepts simultaneous submissions. A list of upcoming themes is available for SASE. Responds in 6 weeks. Pays $3/poem and 1 copy. Does not send an acceptance notice: "We simply send payment and magazine copy."
Advice: "Read the work of published poets."

✔️ ◐ **ALASKA QUARTERLY REVIEW**, University of Alaska Anchorage, 3211 Providence Dr., Anchorage AK 99508. Phone/fax: (907)786-6916. E-mail: ayaqr@uaa.alaska.edu. Website: www.uaa.alaska.edu/aqr. Established 1981. **Executive Editor:** Ronald Spatz.

> • Poetry published in *Alaska Quarterly Review* has been selected for inclusion in *The Best American Poetry*, *Pushcart Prize,* and *Beacon's Best* anthologies.

Magazine Needs: *Alaska Quarterly Review* "is a journal devoted to contemporary literary art. We publish both traditional and experimental fiction, poetry, literary nonfiction, and short plays." Has published poetry by Kim Addonizio, Tom Lux, Pattiann Rogers, John Balaban, Albert Goldbarth, Jane Hirshfeld, Billy Collins, and Dorianne Laux. Wants all styles and forms of poetry with the most emphasis perhaps on voice and content that displays "risk," or intriguing ideas or situations. Publishes two double-issues/year, each using between 25-50 pgs. of poetry. *Alaska Quarterly Review* is 262 pgs., 6×9, professionally printed, perfect-bound, card cover with b&w photo. Receives up to 3,000 submissions/year, accepts about 40-60. Circulation is 2,200 for 500 subscribers of which 32 are libraries. Subscription: $10. Sample: $6.

How to Submit: Does not accept fax or e-mail submissions. Manuscripts are *not* read from May 15 through August 15. Responds in up to 4 months, sometimes longer during peak periods in late winter. Pay depends on funding. Acquires first North American serial rights. Guest poetry editors have included Stuart Dybek, Jane Hirshfield, Stuart Dischell, Maxine Kumin, Pattiann Rogers, Dorianne Laux, and Billy Collins.

◖ ◎ **ALBATROSS; THE ANABIOSIS PRESS (Specialized: nature)**, 2 South New St., Haverhill MA 01835. (978)469-7085. E-mail: rsmyth@massed.net. Website: www.massed.nef/~rsmyth/anabiosis. **Editor:** Richard Smyth.

Magazine Needs: *Albatross* appears "as soon as we have accepted enough quality poems to publish an issue. We consider the albatross to be a metaphor for an environment that must survive. This is not to say that we publish only environmental or nature poetry, but that we are biased toward such subject matters. We publish mostly free verse, 200 lines/poem maximum, and we prefer a narrative style, but again, this is not necessary. We do not want trite rhyming poetry which doesn't convey a deeply felt experience in a mature expression with words." Also publish interviews with established writers. Has published poetry by William Miller, Simon Perchik, Virgil Suarez, and James Doyle. As a sample the editors selected these lines by Lorraine Tolliver:

> It still feels safe/to hear the young being trained,/even if all this busy rearranging the planet/may have
> us—trees, animals, people—way down the road to dead and gone.

Albatross is 28-36 pgs., 5½×8½, laser-typeset, linen cover, with some b&w drawings. Circulation is 300 for 75 subscribers of which 10 are libraries. Many complimentary copies are sent out to bookstores, poets, and libraries. Subscription: $5/2 issues. Sample: $3.

How to Submit: Submit 3-5 poems at a time. "Poems should be typed single-spaced, with name, address, and phone number in upper left corner." No simultaneous submissions. Accepts e-mail submissions if included in body of message. Cover letter not required; "We do, however, need bio notes and SASE for return or response." Guidelines available for SASE. Responds in 6 months, has 6- to 12-month backlog. Pays 1 copy. Acquires all rights. Returns rights provided that "previous publication in *Albatross* is mentioned in all subsequent reprintings."

Also Offers: Holds a chapbook contest. Submit 20 pgs. of poetry, any theme, any style. Deadline is June 30 of each year. Include name, address, and phone number on the title page. Charges $7 reading fee (check payable to Anabiosis Press). Winner receives $100 and 25 copies of his/her published chapbook. All entering receive a free copy of the winning chapbook. "The Anabiosis Press is a nonprofit, tax-exempt organization. Membership fee is $20/year."

Advice: "We expect a poet to read as much contemporary poetry as possible. We seek deeply felt experiences expressed maturely within a unique style of writing. We want to be moved. When you read our poetry, we hope that it moves you in the same way that it moves us. We try to publish the kind of poetry that you would want to read again and again."

☑ ▣ $▢ ◯ ◖ **ALDEN ENTERPRISES; GRACIE PUBLICATIONS; POETIC VOICES MAGAZINE; WRITERS CLUB.COM**, 2206 Bailey St. NW, Hartselle AL 35640-4219. E-mail: editor@poeticvoices.com (for Robin Travis-Murphree) or poetryeditor@poeticvoices.com (for Ursula T. Gibson). Website: www.poeticvoices.com (includes poetry, poetry events, workshops, conferences, book reviews, and more). Established 1997. **Executive Editor (Alden Ent.):** Robin Travis-Murphree. **Submissions Editor (*Poetic Voices*):** Ursula T. Gibson.

Magazine Needs: E-mailed to subscribers monthly, *Poetic Voices* is "informational and educational in content. Articles include feature interviews, columns on the mechanics of writing, questions on writing and publishing, information on organizations useful to poets, contest and award opportunities, publishing opportunities, workshops and conferences, book reviews and more. We are open to most forms, styles, and subjects. No pornography, scatology, racial slurs, or dehumanizing poems." Accepts poetry written by children. Has published poetry by Lyn Lifshin, David Lehman, Michael McClure, Kevin Stein, Molly Peacock, Afaa Weaver, and others. As a sample the editors selected these lines from "The Created" by Sue Scalf:

> . . . from this body made of dirt, spinning/like a wind lifted in that turning,/he is making a porcelain,/
> fired in the kiln and glowing,/a vessel of intricate filligree/planned and wrought/before the world was
> made . . .

Poetic Voices is an electronic magazine containing 30-60 pgs. It can be accessed at members.aol.com/gracieami/arch.htm. Receives about 1,200 poems/year, accepts about 10%. Circulation is "over 10,000 poets in 20 countries each month."

How to Submit: Submit up to 4 poems/month by e-mail, text in body of message, to Ursula T. Gibson. Accepts previously published poems and simultaneous submissions. Cover letter preferred. Often comments on rejected poems. Guidelines available for SASE or on website. Responds in 2 months. Sometimes sends prepublication galleys. Acquires one-time rights. Reviews books and chapbooks of poetry and other magazines in 200-500 words. Poets may send books for review consideration to Robin Travis-Murphree or e-mail.

Creating the writing life

In 1975, Joseph Enzweiler attended graduate school in Alaska and fell in love with the state. He has remained there for the past twenty-six years, currently living in a primitive cabin he built himself and writing his poetry. Enzweiler has published four books of poems: *Home Country* (Fireweed Press, 1986); *Stonework of the Sky* (Graywolf Press, 1995); *A Curb in Eden* (Salmon Press, Ireland, 1999, with a second, revised edition due in 2002); and the recently completed *The Man Who Ordered Perch*. His poem "Karla Faye" won the Green River Grand Poetry Prize in 2000.

At one time Enzweiler's great passions were astronomy, math, and physics. Now it's the poetry of these scientific disciplines he loves.

Joseph Enzweiler

As a man drawn to the sciences, why did you choose to devote your life to poetry?
I see poetry in most things. Separating poetry from the sciences is an artificial division, and it's something fairly recent, in the last few centuries. I don't know that I consciously chose to be a poet. I found that I'm best able to comprehend life that way, in terms of language and how I organize and see the world.

I really don't want to write anything else. Poetry for me is a sacred thing. I've created a life around that concept.

What experiences affect you as a poet?
Unusual experiences affect me all the time. The course of life as it's lived, little and big events, that's the stuff of poetry. For example, once I saw a strange woman walking with her dog in eastern Colorado right at sunset, casting this huge shadow. The sunset was deep red, she was walking in front of her farm, and there was something very powerful about the image. I was driving and I kept working on this: Who was she? What does it all mean?

Seeing a flower blooming out of the side of a locust trunk—what is that a symbol of? Should we ask the "meaning" of this? So, it's the ordinary things. If you look closely and let them work inside you, they can become extraordinary.

My father's death created an entire book for me, *A Curb in Eden*. It was about the interweaving of the experiences in memories and thoughts about my dad, this girl I was in love with when I was a kid, and how that all blends together and meets somewhere in the middle with this guy in his 40s who's thinking about life. Big issues—love, death, and so on—but they begin with the smallest moments: a glance through a window, my first cup of coffee with my father in the cold.

You've described your cabin as being "at the edge of the wilderness." Do you have plumbing, electricity?
I don't have plumbing. I didn't have electricity for three years, but I wanted to get it because

I really like having a steady light to read by, real simple things. I don't own a computer. For me it's just not something I have room or time for in my life. Word processors are a great tool. I've used them. But as a poet with a book about every seven years, my old Smith-Corona works just fine. One's tools should match one's life. I don't watch TV either. I like silence.

Living as you do, alone and with few distractions, you must devote a great deal of time to writing poetry. How much time do you actually spend on your craft?
Usually two or three hours a day, give or take. But actually, within myself, I'm writing all the time. I'm always working on things. If something gets in me, for example the Karla Faye poem, it starts to cook, and then sitting down and putting it on paper becomes critical. The act of becoming physical with it can change your perception, your understanding of the subject. It's a very mysterious thing. And that ties in with inspiration. Often I end up in a completely different place at the end of a poem than where I thought I was going. But it's only by going that I discover that.

"Karla Faye"

The day is nearly gone, an orange bead
in the gun sight of evening.
When a key turns, you hear the kingdom open.
"Just a little food to tide me over."
Bread is a comfort. The butter tastes sweet.
Death is a white cotton shirt, drawstring,
slippers. That corridor ahead is tiled
with footsteps of the vanished,
each thought a twelve inch square.
Forgiveness. Love. Justice.
Death is a stainless table, a clean sheet
folded down sharp as a military bunk.
But your eyes are in the treetops now.
The Lord blinks in the Texas sun,
a smoke on the tailgate, his pickup
by the side door idling.
Climb in and he'll forgive you.

The law strikes six o'clock, 6:01.
Night is a man in black leather shoes.
He is kind to you, you'll be human
for some minutes yet. His smile's
a passport on the night train, a cold water.
He tightens the straps where the needles go,
one in each arm, a fearsome symmetry
close to beauty. Straps on your ankles,
across your chest, as if the soul might drag
the body with it. The body stays.
It's a matter for the record.

The woman you killed those years ago
in blind stupid rage, you'll see her
in a minute. Her husband is happy
watching the gauge in your face wind down.
The poison kisses you and he calls out
"Here she comes baby doll, she's all yours now,"
as if she was a lioness pacing the cage
of paradise. The two of you go at it
stripped and mean, while Jude
and all the betting saints
lean on the bars of heaven.

The sky's a neutral place for hate
and earth's at peace, the husband sleeps,
the journalists are fed. You lie there,
a dazzling blackness, blood pooling
in the underworld. Repentance is meant
for the soil above. This is justice.
This is the world. Turn the lights off.
Secure the iron hasp.

A pickup glides now across the prairie,
glides west and disappears. In deep twilight
a love song comes on the radio.
The road is flat and straight forever,
no one ahead of you, none behind.
Maybe you watch the cotton fields pass,
the farms of heaven. Maybe he tells you
of Abraham, his friend, who obeyed
the voice of God though his heart
was breaking to lift the knife, how the boy
was spared at last, his hands unbound,
how good things die sometimes
and what is owed the sky and what the ground.

(© Joseph Enzweiler; used by permission)

How would you advise those seriously contemplating the writing life?

I'd say live a moral life with values and principles. Find out what you're meant to do on earth and live it fully and passionately. There are always compromises, of course. I had a really great job with benefits, retirement, security. But I didn't like it, I needed to get out. By now I'd have a hell of a retirement, but I wouldn't have four books of poems.

I'm not suggesting everyone should quit their jobs, especially if they love what they do. I don't have a family to support, so it was easier for me to create a life where I could write. I live on very little money and work seasonally. But it's different for everyone. My friend Dick Hague in Cincinnati is a high school teacher and family man. He's terribly busy in his life, but writes these fine poems and essays regularly, year after year. I don't know how he does it! Yet many people never write that novel or book of poems and it bothers them, especially as they get older and feel something slipping away. That's the paradox. Life sweeps us along, we're caught up in other things. But to really write, you must create, in some fashion, the time and silence to do it. It requires choices. It means giving up something, and we'd rather not do that.

What is the best a poem can set out to do? When you write a poem, what are you trying to accomplish?

The best a poem can do is honor the subject, be true to it, change people's perceptions. Poems should be transforming experiences. I want those poems to reach out. If I'm going to publish and it's not going to be just for myself but for a public, then I want a reader to say, "You made me think about things."

"Karla Faye" is about Karla Faye Tucker, who was executed in Texas. It's a poem that takes no stand on capital punishment. It does make a statement that maybe she was good, but that good things die and what do you owe the state, what do you owe the sky? Are there different forms of redemption? Do you have to let the state kill you because that's the rules? If you are truly saved, does it matter? The only way I could write the poem was to believe that she'd reached her peace with these questions. There are people who have taken great offense at that poem because they're pro-capital punishment. They failed to really see what the poem was saying, the fact that the response was emotional if, according to me, misunderstood. Still I took it as a positive response that someone felt something about this issue, that it triggered something. At least that's effective. You don't have to preach or take a definitive stand on something in order to transform life.

—*Pamala Shields*

Book/Chapbook Needs & How to Submit. Gracie Publications, a division of Alden Enterprises, seeks "to promote new and talented poets, and their work, via the publication of chapbooks of poetry. All styles of poetry are welcome. . . . We are open to new writers, look for variety and excellence, are open to concrete forms, traditional, and free verse as well as other varieties. We do accept religious theme poems." Publishes 6-10 chapbooks/year. Chapbooks are usually 20-40 pgs., 8½×5½, laser-printed, saddle-stapled, cardstock cover with art. Submit ms containing 20-30 poems ("no epic poetry please"), typed and double spaced on 8½×11 paper. ("We ask that you also include a disk copy of your poetry saved in text format.") No e-mail submissions. Include cover letter with address and phone number. Poems must be original. Accepts simultaneous submissions and previously published poetry if noted. **Reading fee:** $10, must be included with submission. Make checks payable to Alden Enterprises. Reads submissions March 15 through September 15. Responds to queries in 2 months; to mss in 4 months. Pays royalties of 8-15% and 10 author's copies (out of a press run of 200). Order sample books or chapbooks by sending $5 to above address.

Also Offers: Sponsors WritersClub.com, the online community for writers (www.writersclub.com). Includes chats, genre newsletters, searchable agents and publishers database, courses, message boards, reviews, author interviews, and horoscopes for writers. The Alden website, www.poeticvoices.com, uses original content. Needs poetry, book reviews, essays, criticism, features, and interviews. Please submit poetry submissions to poetryeditor @poeticvoices.com and all other submissions to editor@poeticvoices.com.

Advice: "Make sure you read and follow guidelines. Make sure your work is neatly presented. There is nothing worse than receiving messy work or work that does not conform to the guidelines."

ALICE JAMES BOOKS; NEW ENGLAND/NEW YORK AWARD, BEATRICE HAWLEY AWARD, JANE KENYON CHAPBOOK AWARD (Specialized: regional, women), University of Maine at Farmington, 238 Main St., Farmington ME 04938. (207)778-7071. Fax: (207)778-7573. E-mail: ajb@umf.main e.edu. Website: www.umf.maine.edu/~ajb (includes information on press, guidelines, sample poems, and individual pages on published poets). Established 1973. **Contest Coordinator:** Alice James Books.

Book/Chapbook Needs: *Alice James Books* is "a nonprofit author's collective which only publishes poetry. Authors are primarily from the New England area. We emphasize poetry by women, though we now seek poetry by any contemporary voice." Has published poetry by Jane Kenyon, Jean Valentine, and B.H. Fairchild. Publishes flat-spined paperbacks of high quality, both in production and contents, no children's poetry or light verse. Publishes 4-5 books, 80 pgs., each year in editions of 1,500, paperbacks—no hardbacks.

How to Submit: Query first (with SASE), but no need for samples: simply ask for dates of reading period, which is in early fall and winter. No phone queries. Send 2 copies of the ms. Accepts simultaneous submissions, but "we would like to know when a manuscript is accepted elsewhere." Responds in 4 months.

Also Offers: Beatrice Hawley Award for poets living anywhere in the US. Also, winners of the New England/ New York Competition become members of the collective with a three-year commitment to editorial board. Each winner in both competitions receives a cash award of $1,000. Also offers the Jane Kenyon Chapbook Award every 2 years. Next chapbook competition is in 2003. Send SASE for guidelines.

$ ☐ ◎ ALIVE NOW (Specialized: spirituality, themes); POCKETS (Specialized: religious, children, themes); DEVO'ZINE (Specialized: religious, youth, themes); WEAVINGS; THE UPPER ROOM, 1908 Grand Ave., P.O. Box 340004, Nashville TN 37203-0004. Website www.upperroom.org (include guidelines, subscription information, daily devotionals, news, bookstore, etc.). This publishing company brings out about 30 books/year and 5 magazines: *The Upper Room, Alive Now, Pockets, Devo'Zine,* and *Weavings*. Of these, three use unsolicited poetry.

Magazine Needs & How to Submit: *Pockets, Devotional Magazine for Children,* which comes out 11 times/ year, circulation 90,000, is for children 6-12. "Offers stories, activities, prayers, poems—all geared to giving children a better understanding of themselves as children of God. Some of the material is not overtly religious but deals with situations, special seasons and holidays, and ecological concerns from a Christian perspective." Uses 3-4 pgs. of poetry/issue. Sample free with 7½×10½ SAE and 4 first-class stamps. Ordinarily 24-line limit on poetry. Upcoming themes and guidelines available for SASE and on website. Pays $25-50.

Magazine Needs & How to Submit: *Alive Now* is a bimonthly, circulation 65,000, for a general Christian audience interested in reflection and meditation. Buys 20 poems/year, avant-garde and free verse. Submit 5 poems, 10-45 lines. Guidelines and a list of upcoming themes available for SASE and on website. Pays $25-50.

Magazine Needs & How to Submit: *Devo'Zine: Just for Teens* is a bimonthly devotional magazine for youth ages 13-18. Offers meditations, scripture, prayers, poems, stories, songs, and feature articles to "aid youth in their prayer life, introduce them to spiritual disciplines, help them shape their concept of God, and encourage them in the life of discipleship." Ordinarily 20-line limit on poetry. Guidelines and a list of upcoming themes available for SASE and on website. Pays $25.

Also Offers: *The Upper Room* magazine does not accept poetry.

✓ ◯ ◎ THE ALLEGHENY REVIEW (Specialized: undergraduate students); THE ALLEGHENY REVIEW AWARD IN POETRY, Box 32, Allegheny College, Meadville PA 16335. (814)332-6553. E-mail: review@allegheny.edu. Website: http://review.allegheny.edu. Established 1983. **Faculty Advisor:** Christopher Bakken.

Magazine Needs: "Each year *The Allegheny Review* compiles and publishes a review of the nation's best undergraduate literature. It is entirely composed of and by college undergraduates." *The Allegheny Review* is 6×9, flat-spined, professionally printed, b&w photo on glossy card cover. Single copy: $4. Sample: $4 and 11×18 SASE.

How to Submit: Submit 3 poems. No fax or e-mail submissions. "Each poem should have author's name and address clearly indicated. Only submissions accompanied by a SASE should expect a response from the editors." Submissions should be accompanied by cover letter "stating which college the poet is attending, year of graduation, and a very brief bio." Call or e-mail for current deadlines. Responds 2 months following deadline.

Also Offers: "Submissions for *The Allegheny Review* Award in Poetry are read in the Fall semester of each year. All submissions accompanied by an entry fee receive an one-year subscription to the journal and are considered for publication. In January a nationally-recognized poet awards $150 to the contest winner." Guidelines available by e-mail or on website. *The Allegheny Review* also welcomes b&w art submissions. Send copies (not originals) and SASE.

Advice: "Familiarize yourself with any journal to which you submit your work for publication and send only your very best work. While *The Allegheny Review* has no particular stylistic preferences, you will have a better sense of the kind of writing we tend to publish if you do. And when you submit, please take enough pride in your work to do so professionally. Handwritten or poorly typed and proofed submissions definitely convey an impression—a negative one."

✓ ◯ ◎ ALLISONE PRESS; STAR RISING MAGAZINE; STAR RISING PUBLISHING, INC., (Specialized: wicca, psychic/occult, religious, science fiction/fantasy, social issues, spirituality/inspirational), P.O. Box 3790, Sedona AZ 86340. (877)249-6894. Fax: (526)634-8102. E-mail: webmaster@allisonepress.com. Website: www.allisonepress.com (includes guidelines, submissions, poetry, monthly updates for writers, referrals to other contests, help typing submissions, advertising, books, address, and subscriptions). Established 1996. **Editor:** Robin Vance.

● **NOTE: Readers are advised that we received complaints at press time that the P.O. Box for Allisone Press has been closed. Their website is no longer accessible and we have been unable to reach them by phone.**

The Allegheny Review's editorial board unanimously selected the b&w photograph entitled "Coffee" for the cover of this volume. Impressed by the exemplary quality of Ann Stichler's work, the board believed that the Valencia Community College student had created "a visual reflection of what we try to achieve with the literature between the cover pages."

Magazine Needs: *Star Rising Magazine* is published annually and contains "all types of writing—poetry, short stories, and articles." Wants "poetry that speaks from experience and the heart. Be creative. No pornographic material." Has published poetry by Anna Laxague and Anmol Bhagchand. As a sample the editor selected these lines from "Melancholy" by May:

> *A parable of phrases enter my mind/with it a gentle stroke to be so kind/a wish, a prayer, the dagger's edge/gazing ever intently through the hedge.*

Star Rising Magazine is about 60 pgs., magazine-sized, photocopied, glued into a folder-like card cover, with art/graphics and ads. Receives about 200 poems/year, accepts about 60%. Press run is 500 for 200 subscribers of which 50 are libraries, 100 shelf sales; 50 distributed free to "hospitals, rest homes, etc." Subscription: $17.95/year, $35/2 years. Sample: $8.95. Make checks payable to Star Rising Publishing, Inc.
How to Submit: Submit 5 poems at a time. Accepts previously published poems and simultaneous submissions. No fax, e-mail, or disk submissions. Cover letter preferred. Time between acceptance and publication is 4 months. Poems are circulated to an editorial board. Often comments on rejected poems. Guidelines available for SASE, by e-mail, or on website; "please read our guidelines before submitting." Responds in 1 month. Pays 1 copy, more copies available at wholesale cost. Acquires one-time rights. Reviews books of poetry in single book format. Poets may send books for review consideration to Robin B. May, publisher.
Book/Chapbook Needs & How to Submit: Star Rising Publishers considers all types and forms of poetry. Publishes 2 paperbacks/year. Books are usually 60-200 pgs., 5½×8½, digitally-printed, perfect-bound, cover stock, with art/graphics. Send complete ms (both in hard copy and saved on disk as text or rtf) with cover letter, list of credits, and brief bio. Responds to queries in 1 month; to mss in 4 months. Pays royalties of 10-20% and 10 author's copies (out of a press run of 100). Order sample books by sending $10.

ALONG THE PATH (Specialized: nature, spirituality), P.O. Box 9204, Chico CA 95927-9204. E-mail: gpiper@thegrid.net or pitsaki@netzero.net. Established 1995. **Editors:** Gloria Piper and Andrea Workman.
Magazine Needs: *Along the Path* appears quarterly to "uplift and refresh readers with essays, stories, poems, and drawings on nature and the spiritual. Nature may include the scientific. Spiritual may include the religious. We interpret broadly. We like the personal touch." Wants "whatever fits our speciality on nature and/or spirituality. Should be uplifting. Can be personal experience, philosophical, inspirational, humorous, thought-provoking. No vulgarity, unredeemed pessimism, preachiness, or poetry longer than page-length." As a sample the editors selected these lines from "Leaving This Valley" by Megan Duffy:

> *I want a tattoo of/the way Wyoming smells,/with colors that sink and mix./I want it in me, on me,/ burning through the tunnels of me/like it is part of the system*

Along the Path is 16 pgs., 8½×11, photocopied, stapled, with b&w line drawings. Receives about 500 poems/year, accepts about 75%. Press run is 60. Single copy: $3.25 plus 55¢ postage; subscription: $12/year.
How to Submit: *Along the Path* **is currently not accepting unsolicited poetry but is rather focusing on its backlog of poetry.** Submit up to 4 poems at a time. Shorter is better. Accepts previously published poems and

simultaneous submissions. Accepts e-mail submissions if included in body of text. Cover letter is "nice but not required. Send disposable copies." Time between acceptance and publication varies. Often comments on rejected poems. Responds in 2 weeks. Pays 1 copy. Acquires one-time and reprint rights.

☑ ◔ THE ALSOP REVIEW. 7381 Swan Point Way, Columbia MD 21045. E-mail: alsop@alsopreview.c om. Website: www.alsopreview.com/ (includes poetry and fiction showcases, a variety of reviews, a chatroom, a workshop, poem of the day, etc.). Established 1998. **Editor:** Jamie Wasserman. **Founder:** Jaimes Alsop.
Magazine Needs: *The Alsop Review* "aims to merge the print and Web world, to bring established print writers to the Web and highlight those writers whose reputations are still word-of-mouth." Wants "well-crafted verse with a strong voice. No pornography; overtly religious work, greeting card verse, or sloppy writing." Has published poetry by Lola Haskins, Gwendolyn MacEwen, A.E. Stallings, and Kim Addonizio. As a sample the editors selected these lines from "To Play Pianissimo" by Lola Haskins:

> To play pianissimo/is to carry sweet words/to the old woman in the last dark row/who cannot hear anything else,/and to lay them across her lap like a shawl.

Receives about 1,000 poems/year, accepts about 2%.
How to Submit: Submit 3-5 poems at a time. Accepts simultaneous submissions; no previously published poems. Cover letter preferred. "Submissions may only be sent via e-mail in body of message." Time between acceptance and publication is 1 month. Seldom comments on rejected poems. Guidelines are available by e-mail or on website. Responds in 1 month. Acquires first rights.
Also Offers: *The Alsop Review* "sponsors annual poetry and fiction contests, and runs the most popular workshop on the Web (The Gazebo)."

$ ▨ ◎ AMELIA; CICADA; SPSM&H; THE AMELIA AWARDS (Specialized: form), 329 "E" St., Bakersfield CA 93304 or P.O. Box 2385, Bakersfield CA 93303, (805)323-4064. Established 1983. **Poetry Editor:** Frederick A. Raborg, Jr.
Magazine Needs & How to Submit: *Amelia* is a quarterly magazine that publishes chapbooks as well. Central to its operations is a series of contests, most with entry fees, spaced evenly throughout the year, awarding more than $3,500 annually, but they publish many poets who have not entered the contests as well. Among poets published are Pattiann Rogers, Larry Rubin, Charles Bukowski, Maxine Kumin, Charles Edward Eaton, and Shuntaro Tanikawa. "Receptive to all forms to 100 lines. We do not want to see the patently-religious or overtly-political. Erotica is fine; pornography, no." *Amelia* is digest-sized, flat-spined, offset-printed on high-quality paper, sometimes features original four-color cover. Circulation is about 1,642 for 702 subscribers of which 28 are libraries. Subscription: $30/year. Sample: $10.95. Submit 3-5 poems at a time. No simultaneous submissions except for entries to the annual Amelia Chapbook Award. Responds in up to 3 months. Pays $2-25/poem plus 2 copies. "Almost always" tries to comment. "*Amelia* is not afraid of strong themes, but we do look for professional, polished work even in handwritten submissions. Poets should have something to say about matters other than the moon. We like to see strong traditional pieces as well as the contemporary and experimental. And neatness *does* count." Typically swamped with submissions, so response times can exceed stated parameters. *Amelia* continues to place in outside surveys as a top market, because of editorial openness. Brief reviews are also featured.
Magazine Needs & How to Submit: *Cicada* is a quarterly magazine that publishes haiku, senryu, and other Japanese forms, plus essays on the form—techniques and history—as well as fiction which in some way incorporates haiku or Japanese poetry in its plot. Also reviews books pertaining to Japan and its poetry or collections of haiku. Has published Roger Ishii, H.F. Noyes, Knute Skinner, Katherine Machan Aal, Ryah Tumarkin Goodman, and Ryokufu Ishizaki. Receptive to experimental forms as well as the traditional. "Try to avoid still-life as haiku; strive for the *whole* of an emotion, whether minuscule or panoramic. Erotica is fine; the Japanese are great lovers of the erotic." *Cicada* is offset-printed on high-quality paper. Circulation is 800, with 562 subscribers of which 36 are libraries. Subscription: $18/year. Sample: $6. Submit 3-10 haiku or poems. No simultaneous submissions. Responds in 2 weeks. No payment, except three "best of issue" poets each receive $10 on publication plus copy. "I try to make some comment on returned poems always."
Magazine Needs & How to Submit: *SPSM&H* is a quarterly magazine that publishes only sonnets, sonnet sequences, essays on the form—both technique and history—as well as romantic or Gothic fiction which, in some way, incorporates the form. Also reviews sonnet collections or collections containing a substantial number of sonnets. "Receptive to experimental forms as well as the traditional, and appreciate wit when very good." Has published Margaret Ryan, Harold Witt, Sharon E. Martin, Rhina P. Espaillat, and Robert Wolfkill. Editor's

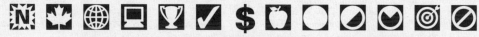

**FOR EXPLANATIONS OF THESE SYMBOLS,
SEE THE INSIDE FRONT AND BACK COVERS OF THIS BOOK.**

favorite Shakespearean sonnet is #29; he feels John Updike clarified the limits of experimentation with the form in his "Love Sonnet" from *Midpoint*. *SPSM&H* is offset-printed on high-quality paper. Circulation is 602 for 409 subscribers of which 26 are libraries. Subscription: $18/year. Sample: $6. Submit 3-5 poems at a time. No simultaneous submissions. Responds in 2 weeks. No payment, except two "best of issue" poets each receive $14 on publication plus copy. "I always try to comment on returns."

Also Offers: The following annual contests have various entry fees: The Amelia Awards (six prizes of $200, $100, $50, plus three honorable mentions of $10 each); The Anna B. Janzen Prize for Romantic Poetry ($100, annual deadline January 2); The Bernice Jennings Traditional Poetry Award ($100, annual deadline January 2); The Georgie Starbuck Galbraith Light/Humorous Verse Prizes (six awards of $100, $50, $25, plus three honorable mentions of $5 each, annual deadline March 1); The Charles William Duke Longpoem Award ($100, annual deadline April 1); The Lucille Sandberg Haiku Awards (six awards of $100, $50, $25, plus three honorable mentions of $5 each, annual deadline April 1); The Grace Hines Narrative Poetry Award ($100, annual deadline May 1); The Amelia Chapbook Award ($250, book publication and 50 copies, annual deadline July 1); The Johanna B. Bourgoyne Poetry Prizes (six awards of $100, $50, $25, plus three honorable mentions of $5 each); The Douglas Manning Smith Epic/Heroic Poetry Prize ($100, annual deadline August 1); The Hildegarde Janzen Prize for Oriental Forms of Poetry (six awards of $50, $30, $20, and three honorable mentions of $5 each, annual deadline September 1); The Eugene Smith Prize for Sonnets (six awards of $100, $50, $25, and three honorable mentions of $5 each); The A&C Limerick Prizes (six awards of $50, $30, $20, and three honorable mentions of $5 each); The Montegue Wade Lyric Poetry Prize ($100, annual deadline November 1).

✓ $ ◒ **AMERICA; FOLEY POETRY CONTEST**, 106 W. 56th St., New York NY 10019. (212)581-4640. Fax: (212)399-3596. Website: www.americapress.org. Established 1909. **Poetry Editor:** Paul Mariani

Magazine Needs: *America* is a weekly journal of opinion published by the Jesuits of North America. Primarily publishes articles on religious, social, political, and cultural themes. "Looking for imaginative poetry of all kinds. We have no restrictions on form or subject matter, though we prefer to receive poems of 35 lines or less." Has published poetry by Philip Levine, Kelly Cherry, and Dabney Stuart. *America* is 36 pgs., magazine-sized, professionally printed on thin stock, thin paper cover. Circulation is 39,000. Subscription: $42. Sample: $2.25.

How to Submit: Send SASE for "excellent" guidelines. Responds in 2 weeks. Pays $2.50/line plus 2 copies.

Also Offers: The annual Foley Poetry Contest offers a prize of $1,000, usually in June. Send SASE for rules. "Poems for the Foley Contest should be submitted between January and April. Poems submitted for the Foley Contest between July and December will be returned unread."

Advice: "*America* is committed to publishing quality poetry as it has done for the past 89 years. We encourage more established poets to submit their poems to us."

✓ ◯ ◎ **THE AMERICAN DISSIDENT(Specialized: political, social issues)**, 1837 Main St., Concord MA 01742. E-mail: enmarge@aol.com. Website: www.geocities.com/enmarge (includes guidelines, sample poems and essays, names of editors, and contact information). Established 1998. **Editor:** G. Tod Slone

Magazine Needs: *The American Dissident* appears 2-3 times/year to "provide an outlet for critics of America." Wants "well-written dissident work (non-rhyming poetry and short 250-950 word essays) in English, French, or Spanish. Submissions should be iconoclastic and anti-obfuscatory in nature and should criticize some aspect of the American scene." *The American Dissident* is 56 pgs., digest-sized, offset-printed, perfect-bound, card cover, with political cartoons. Press run is 200. Single copy: $7. Subscription: $14.

How to Submit: Submit 3 poems at a time. Accepts simultaneous submissions; no previously published poems. No e-mail submissions. "Include SASE and cover letter containing short bio (Manifest humility! Don't list credits and prizes), including de-programing and personal dissident information and specific events that may have pushed you to shed the various national skins of indoctrination and stand apart from your friends and/or colleagues to howl against corruption." Time between acceptance and publication up to 6 months. Almost always comments on rejected poems. Guidelines available for SASE. Responds in 1 month. Pays 1 copy. Acquires first North American serial rights. Reviews books and chapbooks of poetry and other magazines in 250 words, single book format. Poets may send books for review consideration.

Advice: "Do not submit work apt to be accepted by the multitudinous valentine and academic journals and presses that clog up the piping of the nation's bowels. *The American Dissident* is concerned about the overly successful indoctrination of the citizenry and resultant pervasive happy-face fascism. It is concerned that too many citizens have become clonified team players, networkers, and blind institutional patriots for whom loyalty (*semper fi*) has overwhelming priority over the truth. *The American Dissident* is interested in unique insights and ways of looking at the national infrastructure of hypocrisy, fraud, and corruption, the glue that seems to be holding America together."

◯ **AMERICAN LITERARY REVIEW**, University of North Texas, P.O. Box 311307, Denton TX 76203-1307. (940)565-2755. Website: www.engl.unt.edu/alr. **Editor:** Lee Martin. **Poetry Editors:** Bruce Bond and Corey Marks.

Magazine Needs: *American Literary Review* is a biannual publishing all forms and modes of poetry and fiction. "We are especially interested in originality, substance, imaginative power, and lyric intensity." Has published poetry by Christopher Howell, David Citino, Laura Kasischke, Pattiann Rogers, Eric Pankey, and David St. John. *American Literary Review* is about 120 pgs., 6×9, attractively printed, perfect-bound, color card cover with photo. Subscription: $10/year, $18/2 years. Sample: $6 (US), $7 (elsewhere).

How to Submit: Submit up to 5 typewritten poems at a time. No fax or e-mail submissions. Cover letter with author's name, address, phone number, and poem titles required. Responds in 2 months. Pays 2 contributor's copies.

Also Offers: Sponsors poetry and fiction contest in alternating years. Next poetry contest will be in 2002. Send SASE for details.

AMERICAN RESEARCH PRESS (Specialized: paradoxism); "FLORENTIN SMARANDACHE" AWARD FOR PARADOXIST POETRY, P.O. Box 141, Rehoboth NM 87322. E-mail: M_L_Perez@yahoo.com. Website: www.gallup.unm.edu/~smarandache (includes features of paradoxism). Established 1990. **Publisher:** Minh Perez.

Book/Chapbook Needs: American Research Press publishes 2-3 poetry paperbacks per year. Wants experimental poetry dealing with paradoxism. No classical poetry. See website for poetry samples. Has published poetry by Al. Florin Tene, Anatol Ciocanu, Nina Josu, and Al Bantos.

How to Submit: Submit 3-4 poems at a time. No previously published poems or simultaneous submissions. Cover letter preferred. Submit seasonal poems 1 month in advance. Time between acceptance and publication is 1 year. Seldom comments on rejected poems. Responds to queries in 1 month. Pays 100 author's copies. Order sample books by sending SASE.

Also Offers: Sponsors the "Florentin Smarandache" Award for Paradoxist Poetry.

AMERICAN TANKA (Specialized: form/style), P.O. Box 120-024, Staten Island NY 10312. E-mail: editor@americantanka.com. Website: www.americantanka.com (includes guidelines, sample poems from issues, information about the tanka form, a tanka bibliography, and an on-line submission form). Established 1996. **Contact:** Editor.

Magazine Needs: *American Tanka* appears twice/year (Spring and Fall) and is devoted to single English-language tanka. Wants "concise and vivid language, good crafting, and echo of the original Japanese form." Does not want anything that is not tanka. Has published poetry by Sanford Goldstein, ai li, Jane Reichhold, and George Swede. As a sample the editor selected this tanka by Marianne Bluger:

> Headed back/from good-byes at the airport/I keep checking/in rear-view the sky/where your contrail lingers.

American Tanka is 120-140 pgs., 8½×5½, perfect-bound, glossy cover, with b&w original drawings. Single copy: $8; subscription: $16. Sample: $8.

How to Submit: Submit up to 5 poems at a time; "submit only once per reading period." No previously published poems or simultaneous submissions. Accepts submissions on website and by e-mail, "send submissions in the text of the e-mail." Reads manuscripts from November 1 to February 15; May 1 to August 15. Guidelines available for SASE or on website. Responds up to 2 months. Pays 1 copy. Acquires first North American serial rights.

Advice: "The tanka form is rapidly growing in popularity in the West because of its emotional accessibility and because it is an exquisite way to capture a moment in one's life."

AMERICAN TOLKIEN SOCIETY; MINAS TIRITH EVENING-STAR; W.W. PUBLICATIONS (Specialized: science fiction/fantasy), P.O. Box 7871, Flint MI 48507-0871. Phone/fax: (727)585-0985. Established 1967. **Editor:** Philip W. Helms.

Magazine Needs & How to Submit: Journals and chapbooks use poetry of fantasy about Middle-Earth and Tolkien. Accepts poetry written by children. Has published poetry by Thomas M. Egan, Anne Etkin, Nancy Pope, and Martha Benedict. *Minas Tirith Evening-Star* is digest-sized, offset from typescript, with cartoon-like b&w graphics. Press run is 400 for 350 subscribers of which 10% are libraries. Single copy: $3.50; subscription: $10. Sample: $1.50. Make checks payable to American Tolkien Society. No simultaneous submissions; previously published poems "maybe." Cover letter preferred. "We do not return phone calls unless collect." Editor sometimes comments on rejected poems. Occasionally publishes theme issues. Guidelines available for SASE. Responds in 2 weeks. Sometimes sends prepublication galleys. Pays contributor's copies. Reviews related books of poetry; length depends on the volume, "a sentence to several pages." Poets may send books to Paul Ritz, Reviews, P.O. Box 901, Clearwater FL 33757 for review consideration.

Book/Chapbook Needs & How to Submit: Under the imprint of W.W. Publications, publishes collections of poetry 50-100 pgs. For book or chapbook consideration, submit sample poems. Publishes 2 chapbooks/year.

Also Offers: Membership in the American Tokien Society is open to all, regardless of country of residence, and entitles one to receive the quarterly journal. Dues are $10 per annum to addresses in US, $12.50 in Canada, and $15 elsewhere. Sometimes sponsors contests.

AMERICAN WRITING: A MAGAZINE; NIERIKA EDITIONS (Specialized: form/style), 4343 Manayunk Ave., Philadelphia PA 19128. Established 1990. **Editor:** Alexandra Grilikhes.
  • Since *American Writing* began, 50 of their authors have won national awards after appearing in the magazine.

Magazine Needs: *American Writing* appears twice/year using poetry that is "experimental and the voice of the loner, writing that takes risks with form, point of view, language, and ways of perceiving. Interested in the powers of intuition and states of being, the artist as shaman. No cerebral, academic poetry. Poets often try to make an experience 'literary' through language, instead of going back to the original experience and finding the original images. What we are interested in: the voice that speaks those images." Has published poetry by Ivan Argüelles, Antler, Eleanor Wilner, Diane Glancy, and Margaret Holley. *American Writing* is 96 pgs., digest-sized, professionally printed, flat-spined, matte card cover. Press run is 1,800 for 1,000 subscribers. Subscription: $10. Sample: $6.

How to Submit: Submit 8 poems at a time. Accepts simultaneous submissions; no previously published poems. Guidelines available for SASE. Responds anywhere from 6 weeks to 6 months. Pays 2 copies/accepted submission group.

Advice: "Many magazines print the work of the same authors (the big names) who often publish 'lesser' works that way. *American Writing* is interested in the work itself, its particular strength, energy, and voice, not necessarily in the 'status' of the authors. We like to know *something* about the authors, however. We recommend reading a sample issue before just blindly submitting work."

AMETHYST & EMERALD PUBLISHING, 1556 Halford Ave., Suite #124, Santa Clara CA 95051. Fax: (408)249-7646. E-mail: amem@earthlink.net. Website: www.amethystandemerald.com. Established 1997. **Publisher:** Cathyann Ortiz.

Book/Chapbook Needs: "Amethyst & Emerald Publishing seeks to publish written works to inspire a collective change toward universal fellowship." Publishes 3 poetry titles, 1 paperback, and 2 chapbooks per year. Wants strong images, emotions, and messages. "Poetry must move the reader in content and form." No greeting card verse or pornographic material. Books are usually 70-90 pgs. (chapbooks 40 pgs.), offset-printed, (chapbook photocopied), perfect-bound (chapbook saddle-stapled), paper cover, with some art/graphics.

How to Submit: Submit 5 sample poems with $10 reading fee. Accepts simultaneous submissions. Accepts e-mail and disk submissions. Cover letter preferred. "Poems are selected monthly." Reads submissions January 1 through June 30 only. Time between acceptance and publication is 6 months. Often comments on rejected poems. Responds to queries in 2 weeks; to mss in 1 month. Pays 20 author's copies (out of a press run of 100).

Also Offers: Publishes individual poems through a contest on their website at the Poetry Café.

THE AMETHYST REVIEW, 23 Riverside Ave., Truro, Nova Scotia B2N 4G2 Canada. (902)895-1345. E-mail: amethyst@col.auracom.com. Website: www.col.auracom.com/~amethyst (includes guidelines, links, and samples of published work). Established 1992. **Editors:** Penny Ferguson and Lenora Steele.

• *The Amethyst Review* nominates short stories for the Journey Prize.

Magazine Needs: *The Amethyst Review* is a biannual publication (May and November) of poetry, prose, and black ink art. Wants "quality, contemporary poetry to 200 lines. No bad rhyme and meter." Has published poetry by Joe Blades and Liliane Welch. As a sample the editors selected these lines from "Shade Garden of Your Bones" by Shawna Lemay:

> For me, it was not the rape itself/which leaves its trace on the body/the way espresso stains white
> linen/and on the heart which is soft and spongy and forgets/for me, it was not even the seven months
> trial,/but the sibille

The Amethyst Review is 84 pgs., about $7 \times 8\frac{1}{2}$, perfect-bound, colored recycled paper cover, with b&w art on the cover and inside. Receives 1,000 poems/year, accepts about 4%. Press run is 180 for 200 subscribers of which 5 are libraries. Single copy: $6 Canadian; subscription: $12 Canadian, $14 US, $24 international. Sample (including guidelines): $4 Canadian, $6 US. Make checks payable to *The Amethyst Review* or Marcasite Press.

How to Submit: Submit 3-5 poems at a time. No previously published poems or simultaneous submissions. Accepts inquiries by e-mail; no e-mail submissions. Cover letter preferred. Guidelines available for SASE (or SAE and IRC) or on website. "No American stamps please!" Submission deadlines: January 31 and August 31. Responds in 6 months maximum, "usually in 1-2 months." Pays 1 copy. Acquires first North American serial rights.

Also Offers: Sponsors an annual contest. The contest fee is the cost of (and includes) a subscription. First prize is $100 Canadian. Send SASE (or SAE and IRC) for details after May. Deadline: January 31.

Advice: "Therapy is not always good poetry. The craft must be the important focus."

THE AMHERST REVIEW, Box 2172, Amherst College, P.O. Box 5000, Amherst MA 01002-5000. E-mail: review@amherst.edu. **Editor-in-Chief:** Josh Friedman.

Magazine Needs: *The Amherst Review*, appearing in April, is an annual (inter)national literary magazine seeking quality submissions in fiction, poetry, nonfiction, and photography/artwork. "All kinds of poetry welcome." *The Amherst Review* is 80 pgs., 5×8, soft cover with photography, art, and graphics. Receives 800-900 mss/year, accepts approximately 30. Sample: $6. Make checks payable to *The Amherst Review*.

How to Submit: Accepts simultaneous submissions; no previously published poems. No e-mail submissions. Reads submissions from September through March only. Magazine staff makes democratic decision. Seldom comments on rejected poems. Guidelines available for SASE. Responds in April. Pays 1 copy.

$ 🔄 ⓞ THE AMICUS JOURNAL; E-AMICUS, (Specialized: nature/rural/ecology), 40 W. 20th St., New York NY 10011. (212)727-4412. Fax: (212)727-1773. E-mail: amicus@nrdc.org. Website: www.nrdc.org/eamicus/home.html. **Poetry Editor:** Brian Swann.

Magazine Needs: The quarterly journal of the Natural Resources Defense Council, *The Amicus Journal* publishes about 15 poems/year and asks that submitted poetry be "rooted in nature" and no more than one ms page in length. Has published poetry by some of the best-known poets in the country, including Mary Oliver, Gary Snyder, Denise Levertov, Reg Saner, John Haines, and Wendell Berry. As a sample the editor selected these lines from "Into the Light" by Pattiann Rogers:

> There may be some places the sun/never reaches—into the stamen/of a prairie primrose bud burned/
> and withered before blooming,/or into the eyes of a fetal/lamb killed before born. I suppose . . .

The Amicus Journal is 48 pgs., about 7½×10½, finely printed, saddle-stapled, on high quality paper, with glossy cover, with art, photography, and cartoons. Circulation is 150,000. Sample: $4.

How to Submit: "All submissions must be accompanied by a cover note (with notable prior publications) and self-addressed, stamped envelope. We prefer to receive submissions by mail, no fax or e-mail. However, poets can request information by e-mail." Pays $50/poem plus 1 contributor's copy and a year's subscription.

Also Offers: Publishes *e Amicus*, an online magazine.

✓ ⓞ ANAMNESIS PRESS; ANAMNESIS PRESS POETRY CHAPBOOK AWARD CONTEST, P.O. Box 95, Ridgecrest CA 93556. (760)375-8555. Fax: (760)375-8559. E-mail: anamnesis@cs.com. Website: www.anamnesispress.com (includes history of Anamnesis Press, online book catalog, and chapbook contest guidelines). Established 1990. **Publisher:** Keith Allen Daniels.

Book/Chapbook Needs: Primarily publishes chapbooks selected through its annual contest, though occasionally publishes a larger volume "to preserve poetry that might otherwise be forgotten. We wish to see poems of intellectual and emotional depth that give full rein to the imagination, whether free verse or formalist. Please don't send us trite, sappy, maudlin, or 'inspirational' poetry." Has published poetry by Robert Frazier, David Lunde, Marjorie Maddox, Joe Haldeman, David R. Bunch, and Steven Utley. Chapbooks are 25-40 pgs., photo offset-printed, saddle-stapled, 2-color covers.

How to Submit: For the Anamnesis Press Poetry Chapbook Award Contest, submit 20-30 pgs. of poetry with a cover letter, SASE, and $15 entry fee postmarked by March 15. Accepts previously published poems (if author provides acknowledgments) and simultaneous submissions. "Poets can request guidelines via fax and e-mail and obtain guidelines via our website, but we do not accept poetry submissions via e-mail or fax." Winners are selected in June. Prize: $1,000, an award certificate, publication, and 20 copies of winning chapbook.

Advice: "We encourage poets to purchase a sample chapbook for $6 before submitting, to get a feel for what we're looking for. We use free verse and well done formal poetry."

✓ 🖳 $ 🔄 ⓞ ANCIENT PATHS (Specialized: religious), PMB #223 2000 Benson Rd. S. #115, Renton WA 98055. E-mail: skylar.burris@gte.net. Website: http://ancientpaths.LiteratureClassics.com (includes submission guidelines, online seasonal issues, sample literature, advice and resources for writers, and bible trivia). Established 1998. **Editor:** Skylar H. Burris.

- The online journal contains original content not found in the print edition. "Easter and Christmas poems needed for online seasonal issues. Authors published online will receive one free copy of the printed publication (no cash payment for online publication)." Contact Skylar H. Burris.

Magazine Needs: *Ancient Paths* is published semiannually in February and August "to provide a forum for quality Christian literature. It contains poetry, short stories, and art." Wants "traditional forms or free verse; Christian images, issues, events or themes. I seek poetry that makes the reader both think and feel. No 'preachy' poetry or obtrusive rhyme; no stream of conscious or avant-garde work; no esoteric academic poetry ." Has published poetry by Giovanni Malito, Diane Glancy, and Donna Farley. As a sample the editor selected these lines from "A Sudden Death in the House" by Jene Erick Beardsley:

> How thoughtless of you to get up on that morning—unsteady/In bathrobe and slippers, with toothbrush
> and washcloth ready,/Breakfast frying in the kitchen, son leaving for work—merely/To die, the day in
> your absence resuming so queerly.

Ancient Paths is 40 pgs., digest-sized, photocopied, side-stapled, cardstock cover, with b&w art. Receives about 350 poems/year, accepts about 15%. Press run is 150 for about 40 paid subscribers, 30 individual copy sales; 80 distributed free to churches, libraries, and authors. Subscriptions: $12/2 years. Sample: $3. Make checks payable to Skylar Burris.

How to Submit: Submit up to 5 poems at a time, single-spaced. Line length for poetry is 60 maximum; 20-50 lines preferred. Accepts previously published poems and simultaneous submissions. Accepts e-mail submissions, but regular mail submissions preferred. "E-mail submissions should be pasted directly into the message, single spaced, one poem per message, using a small or normal font size, with name and address at the top of each submission. Specify that it is a submission to the *Ancient Paths* printed journal." Cover letter not required. "Name, address, and line count on first page. Note if the poem is previously published and what rights (if any) were purchased." Do not submit mss in January and July. Time between acceptance and publication is up to a year. Often comments on rejected poems. Guidelines available for SASE. Responds in "2-3 weeks if rejected, longer if being seriously considered." Pays $1/poem and 1 copy. Acquires one-time or reprint rights. Reviews other magazines and chapbooks in 100 words.

⊘ ANGELFLESH; ANGELFLESH PRESS, P.O. Box 141123, Grand Rapids MI 49514. Established 1994. **Editor:** Jim Buchanan.
Magazine Needs: *Angelflesh* appears up to 2 times/year and publishes "today's best cutting-edge fiction, poetry, and art." Wants poetry that is "strong, real and gutsy, with vivid images, emotional and spiritual train wrecks. No taboos, no 'Hallmark' verse." Has published poetry by Elizabeth Florio, Todd Balazic, Juliet Cook, Gerald Locklin, and Joseph Shields. As a sample the editor selected these lines from "Voyeur" by Karla Hutson:

> I stand at my window/offer bare breasts, press them/like lillies into the cold glass./They flatten like
> new moons./I wonder who watches,/who might enter the space between.

Angelflesh is 40-50 pgs., 5½ × 8½, photocopied, saddle-stitched, or paperback. Receives about 1,000 poems/year, accepts about 2-5%. Press run is up to 500. Subscription: $10. Sample: $4.
How to Submit: Submit 3-5 poems at a time. Accepts simultaneous submissions. No fax or e-mail submissions. Cover letter preferred. Time between acceptance and publication is up to 12 months. Seldom comments on rejected poems. Responds in up to 2 months. "I will respond to submissions via e-mail if the poets do not need their material returned." Pays 1 copy.
Book/Chapbook Needs & How to Submit: Under Angelflesh Press the editor also publishes 1-2 perfect-bound paperbacks/year. Responds in 1 month. Pay negotiable.

⊘ ANHINGA PRESS; ANHINGA PRIZE, P.O. Box 10595, Tallahassee FL 32302-0595. (850)521-9920. Fax: (850)442-6323. E-mail: info@anhinga.org. Website: www.anhinga.org. Established 1972. **Poetry Editors:** Rick Campbell and Van Brock.
Book/Chapbook Needs: The press publishes "books and anthologies of poetry. We want to see contemporary poetry which respects language. We're inclined toward poetry that is not obscure, that can be understood by any literate audience." Has published *The Secret History of Water* by Silvia Curbelo; and *Conversations During Sleep* by Michele Wolf (the 1997 Anhinga Prize winner).
How to Submit: Considers simultaneous submissions. Include SASE with all submissions.
Also Offers: The annual Anhinga Prize awards $2,000 and publication to a book-length poetry manuscript. Send SASE for rules. Submissions accepted January 1 to March 31 only. Entry fee: $20. The contest has been judged by such distinguished poets as William Stafford, Louis Simpson, Henry Taylor, Hayden Carruth, Marvin Bell, Donald Hall, and Joy Harjo. "Everything we do is on our website."

☑ ◯ ◎ ANNA'S JOURNAL (Specialized: childlessness issues), P.O. Box 341, Ellijay GA 30540. Phone/fax: (706)276-2309. E-mail: annas@ellijay.com. Website: www.annasjournal.com. Established 1995. **Editor:** Catherine Ward-Long.
Magazine Needs: *Anna's Journal* appears quarterly to offer "spiritual support for childless couples who for the most part have decided to stay that way." Wants any type of poetry as long as it relates to childless issues. Receives about 10 poems/year, accepts approximately 50%.
How to Submit: Submit 3 poems at a time. Accepts previously published poems; no simultaneous submissions. Accepts e-mail submissions; include text in body of message. Cover letter preferred. Publishes theme issues occasionally. Acquires first rights and reprint rights. Reviews books of poetry, single book format. Poets may send books for review consideration.
Advice: "Poetry must relate to childlessness issues. It helps if writer is childless."

⊘ ◎ THE ANTHOLOGY OF NEW ENGLAND WRITERS; ROBERT PENN WARREN POETRY AWARDS (Specialized: form); NEW ENGLAND WRITERS CONFERENCE; VERMONT POETS ASSOCIATION; NEWSCRIPT, P.O. Box 483, Windsor VT 05089. (802)674-2315. Fax: (802)674-5503. E-mail: newvtpoet@aol.com. Website: www.hometown.aol.com/newvtpoet/myhomepage/profile.html (includes names of the panelists, workshop leaders, judges of fiction and poetry contests, and conference date and location). Established 1986. **Editor:** Frank Anthony. **Associate Editor:** Susan Anthony.
Magazine Needs: *The Anthology of New England Writers* appears annually in November. All poems published in this annual are winners of their contest. Wants "unpublished, original, free verse poetry only; 10-30 line limit." Open to *all* poets, not just New England. Has published poetry by Richard Eberhart, Rosanna Warren, David Kirby, and Vivian Shipley. *Anthology* is 44 pgs., 5½ × 8½, professionally printed, perfect-bound, colored card cover, with b&w illustrations. Press run is 400. Single copy: $3.95. Sample: $3. Make checks payable to New England Writers.
How to Submit: Submit 3-9 poems at a time with contest reading fee (3 poems: $6; 6 poems: $10; 9 poems: $15). Include 3 × 5 card with name, address, and titles of poems. No previously published poems or simultaneous submissions. Reads submissions September through June 15 (post mark) only. Guidelines available for SASE or by e-mail. Responds 6 weeks after June 15 deadline. Sometimes sends prepublication galleys. Pays 1 copy. All rights revert to author upon publication.
Also Offers: Sponsors an annual free verse contest with The Robert Penn Warren Poetry Awards. Awards $300 for first, $200 for second, and $100 for third. Also awards 10 Honorable Mentions ($20 each), 10 Commendables, and 10 Editor's Choice. Entry fee: $6/3 poems. Winners announced at the New England Writers Conference in July. All submissions are automatically entered in contest. The Vermont Poets Association was established in 1986 "to encourage precision and ingenuity in the practice of writing and speaking, whatever the form and style." Currently has 500 members. Writing information is included in the biannual newsletter, *NewScript*.

Meetings are held several times/year. Membership dues: $9, $6 senior citizens and students. Send SASE for additional information. Also sponsors the annual New England Writers Conference with nationally known writers and editors involved with workshops, open mike readings, and a writer's panel. 2001 date: July 21. Conference lasts one day and is "affordable," and open to the public.

☑ $⊚ ANTIETAM REVIEW (Specialized: regional), Washington County Arts Council, 41 S. Potomac St., Hagerstown MD 21740-5512. Phone/fax: (301)791-3132. Established 1982. **Managing Editor:** Chreryl Winger. **Poetry Editor:** Paul Grant.

• Public Radio's series *The Poet and the Poem* recognized *The Antietam Review* as an "outstanding contributor to American Letters."

Magazine Needs: *The Antietam Review* appears annually in June and looks for "well-crafted literary quality poems. We discourage inspirational verse, haiku, doggerel." Uses poets (natives or residents) from the states of Maryland, Pennsylvania, Virginia, West Virginia, Delaware, and District of Columbia. Needs 25 poems/issue, up to 30 lines each. Has published poetry by Paul Grant, Rick Cannon, and Kathy Anderson. As a sample the editor selected these lines from "The Black Fish" by Lois Marie Harrod:

> Later that evening he took the black fish that was swimming through the air/and gave it to her to swallow so that it could grow as a pumpkin seed/in her belly, and for days she could feel it flipping inside her . . .

Antietam Review is 76 pgs., 8½×11, saddle-stapled, glossy paper with glossy card cover and b&w photos throughout. Press run is 1,000. Sample: $3.25 back issue, $6.30 current.

How to Submit: Submit 5 typed poems at a time. "We prefer a cover letter stating other publications, although we encourage new and emerging writers. We do not accept previously published poems and reluctantly take simultaneous submissions." No fax or e-mail submissions; "we share offices with the Washington County Arts Council, and this creates a problem for other staff." Do not submit mss from February through August. "We read from September 1 through February 1 annually." Guidelines available for SASE. Sends prepublication galleys, if requested. Pays between $15-25/poem, depending on funding, plus 2 copies. Acquires first North American serial rights.

Also Offers: Sponsors a contest for natives or residents of DC, DE, MD, PA, VA, and WV. Send SASE for details.

☑ ❧ ⊘ THE ANTIGONISH REVIEW, St. Francis Xavier University, P.O. Box 5000, Antigonish, Nova Scotia B2G 2W5 Canada. (902)867-3962. Fax: (902)867-5563. E-mail: TAR@stfx.ca. Website: www.stfx.ca/people/TAR. Established 1970. **Editor:** George Sanderson. **Poetry Editor:** Peter Sanger.

Magazine Needs: *The Antigonish Review* appears quarterly and "tries to produce the kind of literary and visual mosaic that the modern sensibility requires or would respond to." Wants poetry not over "80 lines, i.e., 2 pgs.; subject matter can be anything, the style is traditional, modern, or post-modern limited by typographic resources. Purpose is not an issue." No "erotica, scatalogical verse, excessive propaganda toward a certain subject." Has published poetry by Andy Wainwright, W.J. Keith, Michael Hulse, Jean McNeil, M. Travis Lane, and Douglas Lochhead. *The Antigonish Review* is 150 pgs., 6×9, flat-spined with glossy card cover, offset printing, using "in-house graphics and cover art, no ads." Receives 2,500 submissions/year; about approximately 10%. Press run is 850 for 700 subscribers. Subscription: $24. Sample: $4.

How to Submit: Submit 5-10 poems at a time. No simultaneous submissions or previously published poems. Include SASE (or SAE and IRCs if outside Canada). Accepts e-mail and fax submissions. Time between acceptance and publication is up to 8 months. Editor sometimes comments on rejected poems. Guidelines available for SASE or by e-mail. Responds in 2 months. Pays 2 copies. Acquires first North American serial rights.

☑ ☑ $⊙ THE ANTIOCH REVIEW, P.O. Box 148, Yellow Springs OH 45387. (937)754-6808. Established 1941. **Poetry Editor:** Judith Hall.

• Work published in this review has also been included in *The Best American Poetry* (1998, 1999, and 2000) and *Pushcart Prize* anthologies.

Magazine Needs: *The Antioch Review* "is an independent quarterly of critical and creative thought . . . For well over 50 years, creative authors, poets and thinkers have found a friendly reception . . . regardless of formal reputation. We get far more poetry than we can possibly accept, and the competition is keen. Here, where form and content are so inseparable and reaction is so personal, it is difficult to state requirements or limitations. Studying recent issues of *The Review* should be helpful. No 'light' or inspirational verse." Has published poetry by Ralph Angel, Jorie Graham, Jacqueline Osherow, and Mark Strand. Receives about 3,000 submissions/year, publishes 16 pages of poetry in each issue, and has about a 6-month backlog. Circulation is 5,000, with 70% distributed through bookstores and newsstands. Large percentage of subscribers are libraries. Subscription: $35. Sample: $6.

How to Submit: Submit 3-6 poems at a time. No previously published poems. Reads submissions September 1 through May 1 only. Guidelines available for SASE. Responds in 2 months. Pays $10/published page plus 2 copies. Reviews books of poetry in 300 words, single format.

$⊚ ANTIPODES (Specialized: regional, Australia), 8 Big Island, Warwick NY 10990. E-mail: kane@vassar.edu. Established 1987. **Poetry Editor:** Paul Kane.

Magazine Needs: *Antipodes* is a biannual of Australian poetry, fiction, criticism, and reviews of Australian writing. Wants work from Australian poets only. No restrictions as to form, length, subject matter, or style. Has published poetry by A.D. Hope, Judith Wright, and Les Murray. The editor says *Antipodes* is 180 pgs., 8½×11, perfect-bound, with graphics, ads, and photos. Receives about 500 submissions/year, accepts about 10%. Press run is 500 for 200 subscribers. Subscription: $20. Sample: $17.
How to Submit: Submit 3-5 poems at a time. No previously published poems or simultaneous submissions. Cover letter with bio note required. Prefers submission of photocopies which do not have to be returned. Seldom comments on rejected poems. Responds in 2 months. Pays $20/poem plus 1 copy. Acquires first North American serial rights. Staff reviews books of poetry in 500-1,500 words. Send books for review consideration.

✅ ◐ ◎ **APALACHEE REVIEW; APALACHEE PRESS (Specialized: themes)**, (formerly *Apalachee Quarterly*), P.O. Box 10469, Tallahassee FL 32302. Established 1971. **Editors:** Laura Newton, Mary Jane Ryals, and Michael Trammell.
Magazine Needs: Has published poetry by David Kirby, Peter Meinke, Alfred Corn, and Virgil Suarez. *Apalachee Review* is 160 pgs., 6×9, professionally printed, perfect-bound, card cover. There are 55-95 pgs. of poetry in each issue. "Every year we do an issue on a special topic. Past issues include Dental, Revenge, Cocktail Party, and Noir issues." Press run is 700 for 350 subscribers of which 75 are libraries. Subscription: $15. Sample: $5.
How to Submit: Submit clear copies of 3-5 poems, name and address on each. Accepts simultaneous submissions. "We don't read during the summer (June 1 through August 31)." Sometimes comments on rejected poems. Publishes theme issues. Guidelines and a list of upcoming themes available for SASE. Pays 2 copies. Staff reviews books of poetry. Send books for review consideration.

◐ **APHASIA PRESS**, P.O. Box 1626, Orange CA 92856. (714)663-9701. E-mail: aphasiapress@hotmail.com. Website: www.csulb.edu/~rroden (includes chapbook information with sample poems, bios and photos of authors, ordering information). Established 1998. **Editor:** Robert Roden.
Book/Chapbook Needs & How to Submit: Aphasia Press publishes 2 chapbooks per year, minimum. Has published *Armageddon's Garden/Between Genesis and 666* by Jerry Gordon/Robert Roden. Chapbooks are usually 24-48 pgs., digest-sized, photocopied, saddle-stapled with card cover. Submit 10 sample poems with SASE for inquiry. "Check website for some indication of appropriate material." Reads submissions June through August only. Responds in 3 months. Pays 25-50 author's copies (out of an initial press run of 50-100). Order sample chapbooks by sending $5. "I encourage poets to order a sample chapbook before sending in their completed manuscript to see the quality of the work I do."

◐ ◎ **APPALACHIA; THE APPALACHIA POETRY PRIZE (Specialized: nature)**, 5 Joy St., Boston MA 02108. Established 1949. **Poetry Editor:** Parkman Howe.
Magazine Needs: *Appalachia* is a "semiannual journal of mountaineering and conservation which describes activities outdoors and asks questions of an ecological nature." Open to all forms of poetry relating to the outdoors and nature—specifically weather, mountains, rivers, lakes, woods, and animals. "No conquerors' odes." Recently published poetry by Mary Oliver, Jean Hollander, Francis Blessington, and Thomas Reiter. As a sample the editor selected these lines from "Early October" by Carolyn Miller:

> So many bronze torches to lead us down/into darkness, dark lamb's blood/of dogwood, low flames of
> sumac/and sassafras, and here and there, a few bright coins/for the hooded boatman on the shore

Appalachia is 160 pgs., digest-sized, professionally printed, perfect-bound, color cover using photos, with art/graphics and a few ads. Receives about 200 poems/year, accepts about 5%. Press run is 15,000. Subscription: $10/year. Sample: $5. Make checks payable to *Appalachia*.
How to Submit: Submit 5 poems at a time. "We favor shorter poems—maximum of 36 lines usually." No previously published poems or simultaneous submissions. Cover letter preferred. SASE required. Time between acceptance and publication is 6 months. Seldom comments on rejected poems. Occasionally publishes theme issues. Guidelines are available for SASE. Responds in 3 months. Pays 1 contributor's copy. Acquires first rights. Staff reviews books of poetry in 500 words, multi-book format. Poets may send book for review consideration to Parkman Howe, poetry editor.
Also Offers: An annual award, The Appalachia Poetry Prize, given since 1975 to poets published in the journal. Write for details.
Advice: "Our readership is very well versed in the outdoors—mountains, rivers, lakes, animals. We look for poetry that helps readers see the natural world in fresh ways. No generalized accounts of the great outdoors."

⑂ ▣ ◐ **APPLES & ORANGES INTERNATIONAL POETRY MAGAZINE; RED FOX AWARD FOR MAINE POETRY; LA GRANDE POMME AWARD**, E-mail: aopoetry@yahoo.com. Website: www.aopoetry.com. Established 1997. **Editor:** Tom Fallon.
Magazine Needs: *Apples & Oranges International Poetry Magazine* appears online. "All poetry forms accepted from international, U.S., Maine, and student poets. Three sections: aopoetry.com for international and U.S. poets; Fox in the Snow for Maine poets; Blue Zebra for students. See Submission Guide at http://aopoetry.com/pmsubmit.html." Wants "any poetry form: free verse, prose poems, traditional poetry, experimental forms. Satire,

the erotic, humorous, serious religious poetry okay." Does not want greeting card, pornographic, or discriminatory poetry. Recently published poetry by Brendan O'Neill, Kucinta Setia, Ruth Daigon, Yala Korwin, Miguel de Asen, and Jill Chan. As a sample the editor selected these lines from "Absence" by Robert Phelps:

> Absence doesn't do a thing for me/Doesn't make my heart grow anything but/weeds, and those weeds grow down into my soul soil/where the worms follow. Like some terrible dow jones/the life in my heart rides bulls and bears,/and the falls and surges blow ulcer holes in who I am.

Apples & Oranges is published online. Receives about 2,000 poems/year, accepts about 10%. Publishes about 50 poems/issue.

How to Submit: Poets should submit 3-5 poems at a time. Accepts simultaneous submissions; no previously published poems. Accepts e-mail submissions; no fax or disk submissions. Cover letter is preferred. "E-mail submission only: poems in the body of the message. No attachments. See Submission Guide." Reads submissions September 1 through May 1. Submit seasonal poems 3 months in advance. Time between acceptance and publication is 3 months. "The three-month selection period allows multiple readings of each submission." Never comments on rejected poems. Guidelines are available on website. Responds in 3 months. Acquires one-time rights.

Also Offers: Red Fox Award for Maine Poetry in 2001; La Grande Pomme Award for international and US poetry in 2002; alternate years thereafter. No submission fee. $300 cash award for each.

Advice: "I strongly encourage beginning poets to visit the *AOIPM* Submission Guide before submitting to the website. I encourage them also to use *Poet's Market* to learn manuscript formatting. Most new poets have not done their homework and thereby court rejection."

APROPOS (Specialized: subscribers), Ashley Manor, 450 Buttermilk Rd., Easton PA 18042. Established 1989. **Editor:** Ashley C. Anders.

Magazine Needs: *Apropos* publishes all poetry submitted by subscribers except that judged by the editor to be pornographic or in poor taste. As a sample the editor selected her own poem "With Pen in Hand":

> With pen in hand I can confess/my innermost unhappiness,/or wonder in the things I see—/a newborn bird; a lovely tree.//This gift that God has given me/Allows my feelings to be free./With pen in hand I always say/whatever's on my mind each day.

Apropos is 90 pgs., desktop-published, digest-sized, plastic ring bound, with heavy stock cover. $25 for 6 issues. Sample: $3.

How to Submit: Submit 1 poem at a time. Line length for poetry is 40 maximum—50 characters/line. Editor prefers to receive sample of poetry prior to acceptance of subscription. Samples will not be returned. Accepts previously published poems; no simultaneous submissions. Does not accept fax or e-mail submissions. Guidelines available for SASE. All poems are judged by subscribers. Prizes for regular issues are $50, $25, $10, and $5.

ARCTOS PRESS; HOBEAR PUBLICATIONS, P.O. Box 401, Sausalito CA 94966-0401. (415)331-2503. E-mail: runes@aol.com. Established 1997. **Editor:** C.B. Follett.

Book/Chapbook Needs: Arctos Press, under the imprint HoBear Publications, publishes 1-2 paperbacks each year. "We publish quality books and anthologies of poetry, usually theme-oriented, in runs of 1,000, paper cover, perfect-bound." Has published poetry by Robert Hass, Kay Ryan, Brenda Hillman, and Jane Hirshfield. As a sample the editor selected these lines from "Every Day" by Ellery Akers:

> It is not impersonal, the world./Or strict. If she is awake to every stalk./If she can watch the hyacinths hammer their green beaks/through the ground.

How to Submit: "We do not accept unsolicited mss unless a current call has been posted in *Poets & Writers* and/or elsewhere, at which time up to 5 poems related to the theme should be sent." Accepts previously published poems (if author holds the rights) and simultaneous submissions ("if we are kept informed.").

Also Offers: *Runes, A Review of Poetry* (see separate listing in this section).

ARJUNA LIBRARY PRESS; JOURNAL OF REGIONAL CRITICISM, 1025 Garner St. D, Space 18, Colorado Springs CO 80905-1774. Library established 1963; press established 1979. **Editor-in-Chief:** Count Prof. Joseph A. Uphoff, Jr.

Magazine Needs: "The Arjuna Library Press is avant-garde, designed to endure the transient quarters and marginal funding of the literary phenomenon (as a tradition) while presenting a context for the development of current mathematical ideas in regard to theories of art, literature, and performance; photocopy printing allows for very limited editions and irregular format. Quality is maintained as an artistic materialist practice." Publishes "surrealist prose poetry, visual poetry, dreamlike, short and long works; no obscene, profane (will criticize but not publish), unpolished work." Has published work by David P. Cain, Kenneth Kahn, Richard C. Lulay, Bill Jackson, Don Phelps, and Joshua Miller. As a sample the editor selected these lines from "Norwegian Blue" by Sheila Campbell:

> Sunken ship/Thought it was over/Sailors swam quietly off to their graves/Rest in peace/Stay asleep/For ever and ever.

Journal of Regional Criticism is published on loose photocopied pages of collage, writing, and criticism, appearing frequently in a varied format. Press run is 1 copy each. Reviews books of poetry "occasionally." Poets may send books for review consideration. "Upon request will treat material as submitted for reprint, one-time rights."

Book/Chapbook Needs & How to Submit: Arjuna Library Press publishes 6-12 chapbooks/year, averaging 50 pgs. Sample: $2.50. Currently accepting one or two short poems, with a cover letter and SASE, to be considered for publication.

Advice: "Poets and visual poets have a vast publishing advantage through the personal computer, however identity is detached. Secrecy is an insufficient compromise or transient irony. To retain individual presence and control of interpersonal assumptions, it remains necessary to make contact with the audience and manifest live appearances."

ARKANSAS REVIEW: A JOURNAL OF DELTA STUDIES (Specialized: regional), P.O. Box 1890, State University AR 72467-1890. (870)972-3043. Fax: (870)972-2795. E-mail: delta@toltec.astate.edu. Website: www.clt.astate/arkreview (includes past table of contents, guidelines for contributors, list of editors). Established 1968 (as *Kansas Quarterly*). **General Editor:** William M. Clements. **Creative Materials Editor:** Norman E. Stafford.

Magazine Needs: Appearing 3 times/year, the *Arkansas Review* is "a regional studies journal devoted to the seven-state Mississippi River Delta. Interdisciplinary in scope, we publish academic articles, relevant creative material, interviews, and reviews. Material must respond to or evoke the experiences and landscapes of the seven-state Mississippi River Delta (St. Louis to New Orleans)." Has published poetry by Errol Miller, Mary Kennan Herbert, Lora Dunetz, and Mark DeFoe. As a sample the editors selected this untitled poem:

> On her good old stove, her hardy skillet/waits, iron sentinel guarding those grim days/when her food
> stuck to the field hand's ribs./Her stove is as yellow now as an old/wedding gown. It stands, perfuming
> the air/with the just aroma of Mr. Clean.

Arkansas Review is 92 pgs., magazine-sized, photo offset-printed, saddle-stapled, 4-color cover, with photos, drawings, and paintings. Receives about 500 poems/year, accepts about 5%. Press run is 600 for 400 subscribers of which 300 are libraries, 20 shelf sales; 50 distributed free to contributors. Subscription: $20. Sample: $7.50. Make checks payable to ASU Foundation.

How to Submit: No limit on number of poems submitted at a time. No previously published poems or simultaneous submissions. Accepts e-mail and disk submissions. Cover letter with SASE preferred. Time between acceptance and publication is about 6 months. Poems are circulated to an editorial board. "The Creative Materials Editor makes the final decision based—in part—on recommendations from other readers." Often comments on rejections. Occasionally publishes theme issues. Guidelines available by e-mail or for SASE. Responds in 4 months. Pays 5 copies. Acquires first rights. Staff reviews books and chapbooks of poetry in 500 words, single and multi-book format. Send books for review consideration to William M. Clements. ("Inquire in advance.")

ARNAZELLA, Bellevue Community College, 3000 Landerholm Circle SE, Bellevue WA 98007-6484. (206)603-4032. E-mail: arnazella@prostar.com. Established 1979. **Advisor:** Woody West.

Magazine Needs: *Arnazella* is a literary annual, published in spring, using well-crafted poetry, no "jingles or greeting card" poetry. Has published poetry by Judith Skillman and Colleen McElroy. Student publication (which uses work from off campus). *Arnazella* is 75 pgs., 6×8, offset-printed, using photos and drawings. Of 150-200 poems received/year they use about 20. Press run is 500 for 3 subscriptions, one of which is a library. Sample: $10.

How to Submit: Submit up to 3 poems. Deadline is usually at the end of December or early January. Guidelines available for SASE. Responds in 4 months. Pays 1 copy.

$ ARSENAL PULP PRESS, 103-1014 Homer St., Vancouver, British Columbia V6B 2W9 Canada. Website: http://arsenalpu/p.com. Established 1980. Publishes 1 paperback book of poetry/year. Only publishes the work of Canadian poets; *currently not accepting any unsolicited mss.*

ARSENIC LOBSTER, P.O. Box 484, Pocatello ID 83204. Established 2000. **Editors:** Martin Vest and Jen Hawkins.

Magazine Needs: *Arsenic Lobster* appears biannually, "prints succulent poems for toxic people. Honed lyricisms or stripped narratives." Wants "surgical steel punk, disasters that die laughing, riddles that end with a gunshot—poetry written down on its knees. BE NOT AFRAID to send us your words, be they formal profanities or faiths scraped from the bottom of your shoe." Does not want "marmalade, hyacinths, or the art of gardening. No cicadas, wheelbarrows, or fond reflections on the old county fair. Nothing about Tai Chi. Nothing written with a cat on your lap." *Arsenic Lobster* is 30 pgs., digest-sized, saddle-stapled, illustrated card stock cover. Publishes about 20-30 poems/issue. Press run is 200. Single copy $4; subscription: $8/year. Make checks payable to Jen Hawkins.

How to Submit: Submit 4-7 poems at a time. Accepts previously published poems and simultaneous submissions. ("Please inform us.") No fax, e-mail, or disk submissions. Cover letter preferred. "We prefer free verse; biographical cover letters, not credit lists; SASE." Reads submissions all year. Time between acceptance and publication is 9 months. "If both editors like a piece, it's accepted." Occasionally publishes theme issues. A list of upcoming themes is not currently available. Guidelines are available in magazine. Responds in 6 weeks. Pays 1 contributor's copy. Acquires first rights, one-time rights. Reviews chapbooks of poetry and other magazine/journals in 100 words, single book format. Poets may send books for review consideration Attn: Jen Hawkins.

☑ ◎ **ART TIMES: COMMENTARY AND RESOURCE FOR THE FINE & PERFORMING ARTS**, P.O. Box 730, Mount Marion NY 12456-0730. Phone/fax: (845)246-6944. E-mail: poetry@arttimesjournal.com. Website: www.arttimesjournal.com. **Poetry Editor:** Raymond J. Steiner.

Magazine Needs: *Art Times* is a monthly tabloid newspaper devoted to the arts. Focuses on cultural and creative articles and essays, but also publishes some poetry and fiction. Wants "poetry that strives to express genuine observation in unique language; poems no longer than 20 lines each." As a sample the editor selected these lines from "Satin" by Paul Camacho:

> *an encounter with a noticed article,/the satin of a bias smile,/which causes the novice to speak/of no experience save his own:/what is beauty, but articulate bone?*

Art Times is 20-26 pgs., newsprint, with reproductions of artwork, some photos, advertisement-supported. Receives 300-500 poems/month, accepts about 40-50/year. Circulation is 23,000, of which 5,000 are subscriptions; most distribution is free through galleries, theatres, etc. Subscription: $15/year. Sample: $1 with 9 × 12 SAE and 3 first-class stamps.

How to Submit: Submit 4-5 typed poems at a time, up to 20 lines each. "All topics; all forms." Include SASE with all submissions. No e-mail submissions. Has an 18-month backlog. Guidelines available for SASE. Responds in 6 months. Pays 6 copies plus 1-year subscription.

Ⓝ $ ☑ ◎ **ARTFUL DODGE (Specialized: translations)**, Dept. of English, College of Wooster, Wooster OH 44691. Established 1979. **Poetry Editor:** Daniel Bourne.

Magazine Needs: *Artful Dodge* is an annual literary magazine that "takes a strong interest in poets who are continually testing what they can get away with successfully in regard to subject, perspective, language, etc., but who also show mastery of current American poetic techniques—its varied textures and its achievement in the illumination of the particular. What all this boils down to is that we require high craftsmanship as well as a vision that goes beyond one's own storm windows, grandmothers, or sexual fantasies—to paraphrase Hayden Carruth. Poems can be on any subject, of any length, from any perspective, in any voice, but we don't want anything that does not connect with both the human and the aesthetic. Thus, we don't want cute, rococo surrealism, someone's warmed-up, left-over notion of an avant-garde that existed 10-100 years ago, or any last bastions of rhymed verse in the civilized world. On the other hand, we are interested in poems that utilize stylistic persuasions both old and new to good effect. We are not afraid of poems which try to deal with large social, political, historical, and even philosophical questions—especially if the poem emerges from one's own life experience and is not the result of armchair pontificating. We often offer encouragement to writers whose work we find promising, but *Artful Dodge* is more a journal for the already emerging writer than for the beginner looking for an easy place to publish. We also have a sustained commitment to translation, especially from Polish and other East European literatures, and we feel the interchange between the American and foreign works on our pages is of great interest to our readers. We also feature interviews with outstanding literary figures." Has published poetry by Gregory Orr, Julia Kasdorf, Denise Duhamel, Gary Gildner, and John Haines. As a sample the editor selected these lines from "How It Was" by Jeff Gundy:

> *. . . It was the last year of the old world, the last spring/of the old time, you don't believe me but watch it/or next thing you know you'll be carving sticks/by the scant fire and waiting for somebody to ask you,/hey grandpa, about all that, and nobody will.*

Artful Dodge is digest-sized, perfect-bound, professionally printed, glossy cover, with art, ads. There are about 60-80 pgs. of poetry in each issue. Receives at least 2,000 poems/year, accepts about 60. Press run is 1,000 for 100 subscribers of which 30 are libraries. Sample: $7 for current issue, $3 for others.

How to Submit: "No simultaneous submissions. Please limit submissions to 6 poems. Long poems may be of any length, but send only one at a time. We encourage translations, but we ask as well for original text and statement from translator that he/she has copyright clearance and permission of author." Responds in up to 1 year. Pays 2 copies, plus, currently, $5/page honorarium because of grants from Ohio Arts Council. Poets may send books for review consideration; however, "there is no guarantee we can review them!"

Ⓞ ◎ **ARTISAN, A JOURNAL OF CRAFT**, P.O. Box 157, Wilmette IL 60091. E-mail: artisanjnl@aol.com. Website: http://members.aol.com/artisanjnl (includes writer's guidelines, excerpts from current issue, and contest announcements). Established 1995. **Editor:** Joan Daugherty.

Magazine Needs: *artisan* is a tri-quarterly publication based on the idea that "anyone who strives to express themselves with skill is an artist and artists of all kinds can learn from each other. We want poetry that is vital, fresh, and true to life; evocative. Nothing trite, vague, or pornographic." Has published poetry by Gary Myers, Giovanni Malito, and Gayle Elen Harvey. Accepts poetry written by children. As a sample the editor selected these lines by Bhikshuni Weisbrot (poem untitled):

> *Perhaps poetry is this truth telling, the eye of the poet/waiting like a camera to say, yes, this is exactly as it was:/the prison chain of dogs being dragged down the ragged top of a driveway,/Buddha, placid and porcelain, gesturing to you at 4 a.m.*

artisan is 36 pgs. (including cover), 8½ × 11, saddle-stapled with card stock cover, with minimal graphics and ads. Receives about 450 poems/year, accepts about 10%. Press run is 300 for 100 subscribers; 100 distributed free to coffeehouses and local libraries. Subscription: $18. Sample: $6. Make checks payable to artisan, ink.

How to Submit: Submit 2-3 poems at a time. No previously published poems or simultaneous submissions. Accepts e-mail submissions and queries in attached file, ASCII text format. Cover letter not necessary, however "if you send a cover letter, make it personal. We don't need to see any writing credentials; poems should stand on their own merit." Guidelines available for SASE or on website. Responds in 8 months. Pays 2 copies. Acquires first rights.

Also Offers: *artisan* sponsors an annual poetry contest. 1st prize: $150, 2nd prize: $75. Prize winners and works meriting honorable mention are published in an upcoming issue. Entry fee is $5/poem. Postmark deadline: December 31. Send SASE for guidelines.

ARTWORD QUARTERLY; MERISTEM PRESS, P.O. Box 14760, Minneapolis MN 55414-0760. (612)378-3261. E-mail: editors@meristempress.com. Website: www.meristempress.com. Established 1995. **Editors:** Karen Kraco and Sherry Kempf.

Magazine Needs: *ArtWord Quarterly* welcomes well-crafted poetry of any style. "Please send your finest work: editors are attentive readers of other journals and recognize less-than-best efforts." Has published poetry by Joyce Sutphen, William Reichard, and Virgil Suarez. As a sample the editor selected these lines from "A Russian Sailor Recalls Dying on the Kursk" by Richard Broderick:

> *"Near the end, in the dark and utter cold, the hearts/of some of us grew buoyant, rising like bubbles/ to bump against the frozen bulkhead. Outside/the groans of deep sea pressure became the song/of wood spirits flitting in and out of birch groves/back home and the icy grate beneath our feet/sprang up as sun-warmed rye grass between bare toes."*

ArtWord Quarterly is 40 pgs., 5½ × 8½, offset-printed, saddle-stapled, 2-color glossy card cover. Receives about 2,000 poems/year, accepts about 10%. Press run is 250 for 150 subscribers, 25 shelf sales and 5 libraries. Subscription: $18 (International: $22). Sample: $5. Back issues: $3 each.

How to Submit: Submit 3-5 poems at a time. "Poems of 33 lines or fewer work best but longer poems that merit two pages are considered." No previously published poems or simultaneous submissions. No e-mail submissions. Cover letter preferred. "Name, address, phone, and e-mail address should appear on each page. No more than one poem per page, single-spaced. Include brief bio, plus publication credits, and SASE." Current submission deadlines are March 1, June 1, September 1, and December 1; "a transition to a triquarterly schedule might occur during 2002." Editors often offer feedback on "near misses" and work with contributors on final edits on poems. Responds in up to 3 months. Pays 1 copy. All rights revert to author upon publication.

Also Offers: ArtWord Quarterly/Meristem Press features a few pages of quality work by young poets (ages 14-20) in each issue. Submit 3-5 poems, with name, age, address, and phone on each page, SASE, and brief bio. Meristem Press also plans on offering a contest and a theme publication in 2002. Details available for SASE or on website.

ASHEVILLE POETRY REVIEW, P.O. Box 7086, Asheville NC 28802. (828)649-0217. Established 1994. **Founder/Managing Editor:** Keith Flynn.

Magazine Needs: *Asheville Poetry Review* appears biannually. "We publish the best regional, national, and international poems we can find. We publish translations, interviews, essays, historical perspectives, and book reviews as well." Wants "quality work with well-crafted ideas married to a dynamic style. Any subject matter is fit to be considered so long as the language is vivid with a clear sense of rhythm." Has published poetry by Robert Bly, Yevgeny Yevtushenko, Eavan Doland, and Fred Chappell. *Asheville Poetry Review* is 160-180 pgs., 6×9, perfect-bound, laminated, full-color cover, b&w art inside. Receives about 1,200 poems/year, accepts about 10-15%. Press run is 600-750. Subscription: $22.50/1 year, $43.50/2 years. Sample: $13. "We prefer poets purchase a sample copy prior to submitting."

How to Submit: Submit 3-5 poems at a time. Accepts simultaneous submissions; no previously published poems. Cover letter required. Include comprehensive bio, recent publishing credits, and SASE. Submission deadlines: January 15 and July 15. Time between acceptance and publication is up to 5 months. Poems are circulated to an editorial board. Seldom comments on rejected poems. Publishes theme issues occasionally. Guidelines and upcoming themes available for SASE. Responds in up to 5 months. Pays 1 copy. Rights revert back to author upon publication. Reviews books and chapbooks of poetry. Poets may send books for review consideration.

ASIAN PACIFIC AMERICAN JOURNAL; ASIAN AMERICAN WRITERS' WORKSHOP (Specialized: ethnic/nationality, anthology), 16 W. 32nd St., Suite 10A, New York NY 10001. (212)494-0061. Fax: (212)494-0062. E-mail: desk@aaww.org. Website: www.aaww.org (includes information about AAWW publications, creative writing workshops, programs and events, guidelines, and a comprehensive seasonal calendar). Established 1992. **Contact:** poetry editor.

Magazine Needs: The *APA Journal* is a biannual published by the AAWW, a not-for-profit organization. It is "dedicated to the best of contemporary Asian-American writing." Has published poetry by Arthur Sze, Meera Alexander, Luis Cabalquinto, and Sesshu Foster. *APA Journal* is 200 pgs., digest-sized, typeset, perfect-bound, 2-color cover, with ads. Receives about 150 poems/year, accepts about 30%. Press run is 1,500 for 400 subscribers of which 50 are libraries, 800 shelf sales. Single copy: $10; subscription/membership: $45; institutional membership: $55. Sample: $12.

How to Submit: Submit 4 copies of up to 10 pages of poetry, maximum of one poem/page. No previously published poems. No fax or e-mail submission. Cover letter with phone and fax numbers and 1- to 4-sentence biographical statement required. Deadlines are usually August 15 for the issue appearing December 1 and March

15 for the issue appearing June 1. "We will work with authors who are promising." Guidelines available for SASE or on website. Responds in up to 4 months. Pays 2 copies. Acquires one-time rights. In 1999, *The Nuyorasian Anthology: Asian American Writings about NYC* was published followed by *Take Out: Queer Writing from Asian America* in 2001.

Also Offers: The AAWW offers creative writing workshops, a newsletter, a bookselling service, readings, and fellowships to young Asian-American writers. Write for details.

ATLANTA REVIEW; POETRY 2002, P.O. Box 8248, Atlanta GA 31106. E-mail: dan@atlantarevie w.com. Website: www.atlantareview.com (includes submission and contest guidelines, names of editors, poetry samples from several issues, and a free issue offer). Established 1994. **Editor:** Dan Veach.

● Work published in this review has been included in the *Pushcart Prize* anthologies.

Magazine Needs: *Atlanta Review* is a semiannual primarily devoted to poetry, but also featuring fiction, interviews, essays, and fine art. Wants "quality poetry of genuine human appeal." Has published poetry by Seamus Heaney, Derek Walcott, Maxine Kumin, Rachel Hadas, Charles Simic, Louis Simpson, and Naomi Shihab Nye. As a sample the editor selected these lines from "Signature" by R.T. Smith:

> It's plain. When the world is torn/we all transform/to spiders. We bring//our private language to the
> wound/like cobwebs. We mend it with our name.

Atlanta Review is 128 pgs., 6×9, professionally printed on acid-free paper, flat-spined, glossy color cover, with b&w artwork. Receives about 10,000 poems/year, accepts about 1%. Press run is 3,500 for 1,000 subscribers of which 50 are libraries, 2,000 shelf sales. Single copy: $6; subscription: $10. Sample: $5.

How to Submit: No previously published poems. No e-mail submissions. Issue deadlines are June 1 and December 1. Time between acceptance and publication is 3 months. Seldom comments on rejected poems. Each spring issue has an International Feature Section. Guidelines available for SASE. Responds in 2 weeks. Pays 2 copies plus author's discounts. Acquires first North American serial rights.

Also Offers: *Atlanta Review* also sponsors POETRY 2002, an annual international poetry competition. Prizes are $2,000, $500, and $250, plus 50 International Merit Awards. Winners are announced in leading literary publications. All entries are considered for publication in *Atlanta Review*. Entry fee is $5 for the first poem, $2 for each additional. No entry form or guidelines necessary. Send to POETRY 2002 at the above address. Postmark deadline: May 1, 2002.

Advice: "We are giving today's poets the international audience they truly deserve."

THE ATLANTIC MONTHLY, Dept. PM, 77 North Washington St., Boston MA 02114. (617)854-7700. Website: www.theatlantic.com. Established 1857. **Poetry Editor:** Peter Davison. **Assistant Poetry Editor:** David Barber.

● Poetry published here has been included in every volume of *The Best American Poetry.*

Magazine Needs: *The Atlantic Monthly* publishes some of the most distinguished poetry in American literature, including work by William Matthews, Andrew Hudgins, Stanley Kunitz, Rodney Jones, May Swenson, Galway Kinnell, Philip Levine, Richard Wilbur, Jane Kenyon, Donald Hall, and W.S. Merwin. Has a circulation of 500,000, of which 5,800 are libraries. Receives some 50,000 poems/year, accepts about 30-35, has an "accepted" backlog of 6-12 months. Sample: $3.

How to Submit: Submit 3-5 poems with SASE. No simultaneous submissions. No fax or e-mail submissions. Publishes theme issues. Responds in 3 weeks. Always sends prepublication galleys. Pays about $4/line. Acquires first North American serial rights only.

Advice: Wants "to see poetry of the highest order; we do *not* want to see workshop rejects. Watch out for workshop uniformity. Beware of the present tense. Be yourself."

ATTIC MAGAZINE, 8501 Candlewood Dr. #105, Oklahoma City OK 73132. E-mail: editor@attic-magazine.com. Website: www.attic-magazine.com (includes submission guidelines, online magazines). Established 1999. **Editor/Owner:** Lindsey Duncan.

Magazine Needs: *Attic Magazine* appears quarterly and strives to publish cutting edge, thoughtful writing and art. Wants polished poetry, open form; no sexually explicit material or overly confessional poetry. Accepts poetry written by children. Recently published poetry by Carol Hamilton and Ryan G. Van Cleave. As a sample the editor selected these lines from "Ice Boat" by River Montijo:

> My chest shelters a frozen craft in its rib cove,/mute vessel glued with frost to silvery moorings.

Attic Magazine is 46 pgs., digest-sized, saddle-stapled, card stock cover, with b&w art/graphics. Receives about 1,000 poems/year, accepts about 20%. Publishes about 15 poems/issue. Press run is 200. Single copy $7.95; subscription: $24.95. Sample: $6. Make checks payable to Lindsey Duncan.

How to Submit: Submit 3-6 poems at a time. Accepts previously published poems and simultaneous submissions. Accepts e-mail submissions; no fax or disk submissions. "Prefer e-mailed submissions." Reads submis-

---

FOR AN EXPLANATION of symbols used in this book, see the Key to Symbols on the front and back inside covers.

sions year round. Submit seasonal poems 6 months in advance. Time between acceptance and publication is up to 4 months. Single editor decides on submissions. Seldom comments on rejected poems. Guidelines are available for SASE, by e-mail, or on website. Responds in up to 3 months. Pays 1 contributor's copy. Acquires one-time rights.

Also Offers: "Entire magazine is also published on website."

THE AURROREAN: A POETIC QUARTERLY; THE UNROREAN; ENCIRCLE PUBLICATIONS, P.O. Box 219, Sagamore Beach MA 02562. Phone/fax: (508)833-0805 (call before faxing; sometimes used at deadline for last-minute bios or changes in proofs). E-mail: cafpoet37@aol.com. Press established 1992. Magazine established 1995. **Editor:** Cynthia Brackett-Vincent.

Magazine Needs: *The Aurorean*, which appears in March, June, September, and December, seeks to publish "poetry that is inspirational (but not religious), meditational, or reflective of the Northeast. Strongly encouraged (but not limited to) topics: positiveness, recovery, and nature. Maximum length: 38 lines. Typographical oddities are OK as long as it can be reproduced on our page. No hateful, overly religious or poetry that uses four-letter words for four-letter words' sake. Use mostly free-verse; occasional rhyme; I am biased toward haiku and well-written humor. I'm *always* in need of short (2-6 lines), seasonal poems. For seasonal poems, please note specific deadlines in our guidelines." Has published poetry by Lisa Alexander Baron, Michael Keshigian, Linda Porter, and Virgil Suarez. As a sample the editor selected these lines from "Cages" by Gene Fehler:

> *Week mornings/climb coolly into my own cage,/sense a Pat cat drooling on me./I know what it's like to have no place to hide/and to eat something like a gift of spiders.*

The Aurorean is 35 pgs. of poetry, 5 pgs. of contributor's bios, $5\frac{1}{2} \times 8\frac{1}{2}$, professionally printed, perfect-bound with papers and colors varying from season to season. Open to exchange ads. Press run is 500. Single copy: $5 US, $6 international. Subscription: $17 US, $21 international. Make checks payable to Encircle Publications or *The Aurorean*.

How to Submit: Submit 3-5 poems at a time. No previously published poems or simultaneous submissions. No e-mail or fax submissions. "Make it clear what you're submitting. Type if possible; if not, write as clearly as possible." Cover letter strongly preferred (especially with first submission). Sometimes comments on rejected poems. Guidelines available for SASE. "I notify authors of receipt of manuscripts immediately (if you did not receive an acknowledgement card, we did not receive your submission or you did not include a SASE) and report on decisions in one week to three-and-a-half months maximum." Always sends prepublication galleys. Pays 3 copies/poem with an up-to 50-word bio in the "Who's Who" section. Also features a "Poet-of-the-Quarter" each issue with publication of up to 3 poems and an extended bio (100 words). The "Poet-of-the-Quarter" receives 10 copies and a 1-year subscription.

Also Offers: "New contests for *The Aurorean*: each issue an independent judge picks Best-Poems-of-Last-Issue; winner receives $20. Send entries for Poetic-Quote-of-the-Season (cannot be acknowledged or returned); 4 lines maximum, quote by not-too-obscure poet. Winner receives 2 free issues." "New broadsheet, *The Unrorean*, will appear 2/year . . . experimental, risque, and for poems that might not fit *The Aurorean*. Still, nothing hateful. SASE for return/reply. No proofs, acknowledgements, deadlines, or bio listings. 11×17; laser-printed. $2 ed. postpaid." Pays one copy/poem published. Unless otherwise requested, work sent to *The Aurorean* will also be considered for the broadsheet.

Advice: "Study *Poet's Market*. Be familiar with our journal before submitting. Always have a ms out there. Stop saying you want to be a writer. You are a writer if you write. Remember, editors are people too. What one editor rejects one day, another may jump at the next. Invest in small presses with samples. Invest in yourself with postage. Always include enough postage for the return/reply process!!! When in doubt, an extra first-class stamp or SASE is appreciated. Read more poetry than you write, and read your poetry out loud. Editors: I'm open to subscription and ad-swapping with other markets."

AUSTRALIAN GOTHICA, P.O. Box 6492, Destin FL 32550. Established 1993. **Editor:** Rebecca Lu Kiernan.

Magazine Needs: Currently accepting mss by invitation only. *Australian Gothica* appears biannually. "We publish tightly crafted, impressive works of art, poetry, short stories, the exotic and erotic, and science fiction of the highest literary value." As a sample, the editor selected these lines from "Pre-emptive" by Rebecca Lu Kiernan:

> *I will have a rib removed/and mail it to you/in a sanitary jar/saving you the/trouble/of robbing me/in my sleep.//Incision is easier sewn/than the slow jagged/tearing/of stealing back/a bone.*

Australian Gothica is 38-50 pgs., 6×9, professionally printed, flat spined. Press run is 1,000 for 600 subscribers.

Advice: "We have a sense of horror and humor. Tell us something we will never forget!"

AVALANCHE; ROCK PILE PRESS, 512 Rahm, Salina KS 67401 or 1422 Derby Ave., Salina KS 67401. (785)823-7557. E-mail: AvalanchePoetry@hotmail.com. Website: http://communities.msn.com/AVAL ANCHEPoetry/website/home.htm (includes guidelines, names of editors). Established 1995. **Co-Editors:** Bob Sears and Ross Bolejack.

Magazine Needs: *Avalanche* appears biannually. Its goal is "to present a wide range of poems by new and well-known poets." Wants modern, contemporary poetry. Recently published poetry by Michael Hathaway, Ruth Moon Kempher, Lyn Lifshin, Tony Moffett, Kyle Laws, and Debra Drake. As a sample the editors selected these lines from "Hilo" by Lyn Lifshin which appear in *Mad Girl*:

> wild orchid/in the field of fern/Mangoes blue/leis in the ohi/blue morning glories/growing out/of rippled lava

Avalanche is 20-30 pgs., magazine-sized, copier printed, stapled, card stock cover. Receives about 200 poems/year, accepts about 45%. Publishes about 30-45 poems/issue. Press run is 1,000. Single copy: $3; subscription: $6. Sample: $3. Make check payable to *Avalanche*.

How to Submit: No previously published poems or simultaneous submissions. "Must have cover letter, SASE, and b&w photo (if possible)." Reads submissions January 1-May 30. Time between acceptance and publication is 6 months. Always comment on rejected poems. Occasionally publishes theme issues. A list of upcoming themes and guidelines are available for SASE. Responds in 3 months. Pays 1 contributor's copy. Acquires first rights. Reviews chapbooks of poetry in 300 words in single book format. Poets may send books for review consideration to *Avalanche*.

Book/Chapbook Needs & How to Submit: Rock Pile Press publishes 1-3 chapbooks/year. Chapbooks are usually 18-20 pgs. copy-printed, stapled, card stock cover. Query first, with a few sample poems and a cover letter with brief bio and publication credits. Responds to queries in 6 months. Pays 1 author's copy (out of a press run of 100-200). Order sample chapbooks by sending $3 to *Avalanche*.

AVOCET; AVOCET PRESS (Specialized: nature, spirituality), P.O. Box 8041, Calabasas CA 91372-8041. E-mail: patricia.j.swenson@csun.edu. Website: www.csun.edu/~pjs44945/avocet.html (includes writer's guidelines, editor's e-mail address, deadlines, and sample poems). First issue published fall 1997. **Editor:** Patricia Swenson.

Magazine Needs: *Avocet* is a quarterly poetry journal "devoted to poets seeking to understand the beauty of nature and its interconnectedness with humanity." Wants "poetry that shows man's interconnectedness with nature; discovering the Divine in nature." Does not want "poems that have rhyme or metrical schemes, cliché, abstraction ,and sexual overtones." Has recently published poetry by Donna J. Waidtlow, Fred Boltz, Joan Goodwin, and John Greg. *Avocet* is 30 pgs., $4\frac{1}{4} \times 5\frac{1}{2}$, professionally printed, saddle-stapled, card cover, with some illustrations. Single copy: $3.50; subscription: $14. Make checks payable to Pat Swenson.

How to Submit: Submit up to 5 poems at a time. Accepts previously published poems if acknowledged; no simultaneous submissions. Accepts e-mail submissions with name, city, state, and e-mail address; include submission in body of message, no attachments. Cover letter required including SASE. Time between acceptance and publication is up to 6 months. Responds in 8 weeks. Pays 1 contributor's copy.

THE AWAKENINGS REVIEW (Specialized: people living with mental illness), University of Chicago, Center for Psychiatric Rehabilitation, 7230 Arbor Dr., Tinley Park IL 60477. (708)614-4770. Fax: (708)614-4780. E-mail: rklundin@uchicago.edu. Website: www.ucpsychrehab.org (includes excerpts, guidelines, names of editors). Established 1999. **Editor:** Robert Lundin.

Magazine Needs: *The Awakenings Review* appears biannually to publish works by people living with mental illness: consumers, survivors, family members, ex-patients. Wants "meaningful work, good use of the language. Need not be about mental illness." Recently published poetry Joan Rizzo, Wanda Washko, Ben Beyerlein, and Trish Evers. As a sample the editor selected these lines from "Electro-Convulsive 'Therapy' " by Joan Rizzo:

> At your bedside/I forge dread into denial/trying to convince myself/that nothing about you will change./ I wrap a finger round one of yours.

The Awakenings Review is 150 pgs., digest-sized, perfect-bound, b&w, glossy cover, with some art/graphics. Receives about 400 poems/year, accepts about 40%. Publishes about 90 poems/issue. Press run is 1,000 for 100 subscribers of which 2 are libraries, 800 shelf sales; 300 are distributed free to contributors, friends. Single copy $12; subscription: $22. Sample: $6.50. Make checks payable to *Awakenings Review*.

How to Submit: Submit 5 poems at a time. No previously published poems or simultaneous submissions. Accepts e-mail, fax, and disk submissions. Cover letter is preferred. Include SASE and short bio. Submit seasonal poems 6 months in advance. Time between acceptance and publication is 4 months. Poems are read by 3 editors. Often comments on rejected poems. Poet "must live with mental illness: consumer, survivor, family member, ex-patient." Occasionally publishes theme issues. Guidelines are available in magazine, for SASE, by e-mail. Responds in 1 month. Always sends prepublication galleys. Pays 4 contributor's copies. Acquires first rights. Poets may send books for review consideration.

Advice: "Include a cover letter with your publishing experience."

AXE FACTORY REVIEW; CYNIC PRESS, P.O. Box 40691, Philadelphia PA 19107. *Axe Factory* established 1986. Cynic Press established 1996. **Editor/Publisher:** Joseph Farley.

● We highly recommend obtaining a sample before submitting as the editor has displayed, in his answers to our questionnaire, a quirky sense of humor.

Magazine Needs: *Axe Factory* is published 1-4 times/year and its purpose is to "spread the disease known as literature. The content is mostly poetry and essays. We now use short stories too." Wants "eclectic work. Will look at anything but suggest potential contributors purchase a copy of magazine first to see what we're like. No greeting card verse." Accepts poetry written by children. "Parents should read magazine to see if they want their children in it as much material is adult in nature." Has published *River Architecture: poems from here & there* by Louis McKee and poetry by Taylor Graham, A.D. Winans, Normal, and Kimberly Brittingham. As a sample the editor selected these lines from "Starting Over" by Louis McKee:

> *I kept the doll I found/in the yard, a Barbie with matted/blond hair and not a stitch/of clothing. A new wife,/I thought, and I proposed to her*

Axe Factory is 20-40 pgs., 8½×11, saddle-stapled, neatly printed with light card cover. Press run is 100. Single copy: $8; subscription: $20 for 3 issues. Sample: $3 for old issue, $8 for recent. Make checks payable to Joseph Farley.

How to Submit: Submit up to 10 poems. Accepts previously published poems "sometimes, but let me know up front" and simultaneous submissions. Cover letter preferred "but not a form letter, tell me about yourself." Often comments on rejected poems. Pays 1-2 copies. " 'Featured poet' receives more." Reserves right to anthologize poems under Cynic Press; all other rights returned. Reviews books of poetry in 10-1,000 words. Poets may send books for review consideration.

Book/Chapbook Needs & How to Submit: Cynic Press occasionally publishes chapbooks. Published *Yellow Flower Girl* by Xu Juan, *Under The Dogwood* by Joseph Barford, and *13 Ways of Looking at Godzilla* by Michael Harper. Send $10 reading fee with ms. No guarantee of publication. All checks to Joseph Farley.

Advice: "Writing is a form of mental illness, spread by books, teachers, and the desire to communicate."

◑ BABYSUE, P.O. Box 8989, Atlanta GA 31106-8989. Established 1985. Website: www.babysue.com. **Editor/Publisher:** Don W. Seven.

Magazine Needs: *babysue* appears twice/year publishing obtuse humor for the extremely open-minded. "We are open to all styles, but prefer short poems." No restrictions. Has published poetry by Edward Mycue, Susan Andrews, and Barry Bishop. *babysue* is 32 pgs., offset printed. "We print prose, poems, and cartoons. We usually accept about 5% of what we receive." Subscription: $12 for 4 issues. Sample: $3.

How to Submit: Accepts previously published poems and simultaneous submissions. Deadlines are March 30 and September 30 of each year. Seldom comments on rejected poems. Responds "immediately, if we are interested." Pays 1 copy. "We do occasionally review other magazines."

Advice: "We have received no awards, but we are very popular on the underground press circuit and sell our magazine all over the world."

N ◑ ◎ "BACK TO BASICS" POETRY PROGRAM (Specialized: family values), WASN (1330 AM), 401 N. Blaine Ave., Youngstown OH 44505. (330)746-1330. Fax: (330)746-6711. E mail: talkradio@wasn.com. Website: www.wasn.com. Established 1998. **Host:** Tom Gilmartin, Sr.

Magazine Needs: "Back To Basics" is a radio program hosted by Tom Gilmartin. The on-the-air poetry reading includes poets reading their own work. Wants poetry that reflects "family values—no sex or porno." Recently published poetry by Tom Williams, Lulu Bernardich, Corry Dama, Oliver Crumb, Cora Armstrong, and William Phipps. Special purpose of the program is "to help shut-ins, uplifting people who live alone."

How to Submit: Prefers short poems, "even one-liners." Accepts previously published poems and simultaneous submissions. No e-mail or disk submissions. Reads submissions all year. Regularly broadcasts theme programs. Guidelines available for SASE. Responds "now." No pay for poetry read on the air.

Also Offers: "We had a Mother's Day contest—well received. We provide a $100 bond to the winner."

Advice: "Keep writing, keep trying—self-publish."

☑ ◑ THE BALTIMORE REVIEW; BALTIMORE WRITER'S ALLIANCE, P.O. Box 410, Riderwood MD 21139. (410)377-5265. Fax: (410)377-4325. E-mail: hdiehl@bcpl.net. Website: ww.baltimorewriters.org (includes writer's guidelines and distributor information). *Baltimore Review* established 1996, Baltimore Writers' Alliance established 1980. **Editor:** Barbara Diehl.

Magazine Needs: *The Baltimore Review* appears 2 times/year (winter and summer) and showcases the "best short stories and poems of writers from the Baltimore area and beyond." No restrictions on poetry except they do not want to see "sentimental-mushy, loud, or very abstract work; corny humor; poorly crafted or preachy poetry." Has published poetry by Fredrick Zydek, Allison Joseph, Barbara F. Lefcowitz, and Simon Perchik. *Baltimore Review* is 128 pgs., 6×9, offset lithography, perfect-bound with 10 pt. CS1 cover, back cover photo only. Publish 20-30 poems/issue. Press run is 1,000. Single copy: $7.95; subscription: $14/year (2 issues). Sample: $8. Make checks payable to Baltimore Writers' Alliance.

How to Submit: Submit up to 5 poems at a time. Accepts simultaneous submissions; no previously published poems. No e-mail or fax submissions. Cover letter preferred. Time between acceptance and publication is up to 6 months. "Poems and short stories are circulated to at least 2 reviewers." Sometimes comments on rejected poems. Guidelines available for SASE. Responds in up to 4 months. Pays 2 copies, reduced rate for additional copies.

Also Offers: The Baltimore Writers' Alliance is "a vital organization created to foster the professional growth of writers in the metro Baltimore area." The Alliance meets monthly and sponsors workshops, an annual conference, and an annual contest. It also publishes *WordHouse*, a monthly newsletter for members. Write for details.

◻ ◕ **BARBARIC YAWP; BONEWORLD PUBLISHING**, 3700 County Route 24, Russell NY 13684. (315)347-2609. Established 1996. **Editors:** John and Nancy Berbich.

Magazine Needs: *Barbaric Yawp* appears quarterly, "publishing the best fiction, poetry, and essays available"; encourages beginning writers. "We are not preachers of any particular poetic or literary school. We publish any type of quality material appropriate for our intelligent and wide-awake audience; all types considered, blank, free, found, concrete, traditional rhymed and metered forms. We do not want any pornography, gratuitous violence, or any whining, pissing, or moaning." Has published poetry by Errol Miller, Mark Spitzer, and Gary Jurechka. As a sample the editors selected these lines from "A Good Day" by Virginia Burnett:

> He will step outside/with certainty in his boots./He will listen to his buckets,/and judge the breeze with
> his face./He will turn to us/with a smile/and he will tell me why/this is a good day for sugarin'.

Barbaric Yawp is a 60-page booklet, stapled with 67 lb. cover, line drawings. Receives 1,000 poems/year, accepts about 5%. Press run is 120 for 40 subscribers of which 3 are libraries. Single copy: $4; subscription: $15/year for 4 issues. Sample: $3. Make checks payable to John Berbich.

How to Submit: Submit up to 5 poems at a time, no more than 50 lines each, and include SASE. All types considered. Accepts previously published poems and simultaneous submissions. No fax or e-mail submissions. One-page cover letter preferred, include a short publication history (if available) and a brief bio. No deadlines; reads year round. Time between acceptance and publication is up to 6 months. Often comments on rejected poems. Guidelines available for SASE. Responds in up to 2 months. Pays 1 copy. Acquires one-time rights.

Advice: "We are primarily concerned with work that means something to the author but which is able to transcend the personal into the larger more universal realm. Send whatever is important to you. We will use yin and yang. We really like humor."

✓ $◕ **BARNWOOD PRESS; BARNWOOD**, P.O. Box 146, Selma IN 47383. (765)285-8409. Fax: (765)285-3765. E-mail: tkoontz@gw.bsu.edu. Website: www.barnwoodpress.org. Established 1975. **Editor:** Tom Koontz.

Magazine Needs: *Barnwood* appears 3 times/year "to serve poets and readers by publishing excellent poems." Does not want "expressions of prejudice such as racism, sexism." Has published poetry by Bly, Goedicke, and Stafford. As a sample the editor selected these lines from "Prophecy" by Alice Friman:

> I've already told you what I want:/that sloshing sea of you turned in this direction,/my arms reaching
> into you like jetties./The tides taking care of the rest.

Barnwood is 12 pgs., magazine-sized, photocopied and saddle-stitched with paper cover. Receives about 500 poems/year, accepts about 4%. Press run is 200 for 150 subscribers of which 30 are libraries. Single copy: $5; subscription: $15/3 issues. Sample: $5.

How to Submit: Submit 1-3 poems at a time. Accepts simultaneous submissions; no previously published poems. Does not accept fax or e-mail submissions. "SASE or no response." Reads submissions September 1 through May 31 only. Time between acceptance and publication is 6 months. Poems are circulated to an editorial board. "Submissions screened by assistant editors. Editor makes final decisions." Seldom comments on rejected poems. Responds in 1 month. Pays $25/poem and 2 copies. Acquires one-time rights.

Book/Chapbook Needs & How to Submit: Barnwood Press publishes 1 paperback and 1 chapbook of poetry/year. Chapbooks are usually 12-32 pgs., size varies, offset printed and saddle-stitched with paper cover and cover art. Query first with a few sample poems and cover letter with brief bio and publication credits. Responds to queries and mss in 1 month. Payment varies. Order sample books or chapbooks by sending price of book plus $2.50.

✓ ⚐ ◕ **BARROW STREET**, P.O. Box 2017, Old Chelsea Station, New York NY 10113-2017. E-mail: info@barrowstreet.org. Website: www.barrowstreet.org. Established 1998. **Editors:** Patricia Carlin, Peter Covino, Lois Hirshkowitz, Melissa Hotchkiss.

● Poetry published in *Barrow Street* has been selected for inclusion in *The Best American Poetry 2000* and *2001*.

Magazine Needs: "*Barrow Street*, a poetry journal appearing twice yearly, is dedicated to publishing new and established poets." Wants "poetry of the highest quality; open to all styles and forms." Has published poetry by Kim Addonizio, Brian Henry, Jane Hirshfield, Phillis Levin, Jeffrey Levine, and Molly Peacock. *Barrow Street* is 96-120 pgs., 6×9, professionally printed and perfect-bound with glossy cardstock cover with color and photography. Receives about 3,000 poems/year, accepts about 3%. Press run is 1,000. Subscription: $15/1 year, $28/2 years, $42/3 years. Sample: $8.

How to Submit: Submit up to 5 poems at a time. Accepts simultaneous submissions (when notified); no previously published poems. Cover letter with brief bio preferred. Reads submissions year round. Poems are circulated to an editorial board. Seldom comments on rejected poems. Publishes theme issues occasionally. Guidelines available for SASE or on website. Responds in approximately 6 months. Always sends prepublication galleys. Pays 2 copies. Acquires first rights.

✓ ◻ ◕ **BATHTUB GIN; PATHWISE PRESS; THE BENT**, P.O. Box 2392, Bloomington IN 47402. E-mail: charter@bluemarble.net. Website: www.bluemarble.net/~charter/btgin.htm (includes guidelines, subscription and patronage info, outlets, links to small presses, and resources). Established 1997. **Editor:** Christopher Harter.

Magazine Needs: *Bathtub Gin*, a biannual, is "an eclectic aesthetic . . . we want to keep you guessing what is on the next page." Wants poetry that "takes a chance with language or paints a vivid picture with its imagery . . . has the kick of bathtub gin, which can be experimental or a sonnet. No trite rhymes . . . Bukowski wannabes (let the man rest) . . . confessional (nobody cares about your family but you)." Has published poetry by A.D. Winans, Laurel Speer, John Grey, and Patrick McKinnon. As a sample the editor selected these lines from "The Water Horses" by John Gohmann:

> *Whiskey had slit poetry's throat in a barfight/So painting was the only exorcism I could muster/And as I set out my oils and brushes,/Cubism seemed the logical tool/To pulverise two separate nightmares/ Into a communal pile of rubble*

Bathtub Gin is approximately 60 pgs., digest-sized, laser-printed, saddle stapled, 54 lb. cover stock cover, includes "eclectic" art. "We feature a 'News' section where people can list their books, presses, events, etc." Receives about 800 poems/year, accepts about 10%. Press run is 160 for 30 subscribers, 60 shelf sales; 7 distributed free to reviewers, other editors, and libraries. Subscription: $10. Sample: $5; foreign orders add $2; back issues: $3. Make checks payable to Christopher Harter.

How to Submit: Submit 4-6 poems at a time. Include SASE. Accepts previously published poems and simultaneous submissions. Accepts e-mail submissions (include in text of message); no fax submissions. "Three to five line bio required if you are accepted for publication . . . if none [given], we make one up." Cover letter preferred. Reads submissions July 1 through September 15 and January 1 through March 15 only. Time between acceptance and publication is up to 4 months. Often comments on rejected poems. Guidelines available for SASE. Responds in 2 months. Pays 1 contributor's copy. "We also sell extra copies to contributors at a discount, which they can give away or sell at full price." Reviews books and chapbooks of poetry and spoken word recordings. Poets may send books for review consideration.

Book/Chapbook Needs & How to Submit: Pathwise Press's goal is to publish chapbooks, broadsides, and "whatever else tickles us." For co-operative publishing guidelines, send SASE.

Also Offers: "We also publish a newsletter, *The Bent*, with reviews, ads, and news items. Price is $1."

Advice: "The small presses/magazines are where it's at. They are willing to take chances on unknown and experimental writers and because of that they are publishing the most interesting work out there—have been for years."

BAY AREA POETS COALITION (BAPC); POETALK, P.O. Box 11435, Berkeley CA 94712-2435. E-mail: poetalk@aol.com. Established 1974. Direct submissions to Editorial Committee. Coalition sends quarterly poetry journal, *Poetalk*, to over 300 people. Also publishes an annual anthology (23rd—100 pgs., out in Spring 2002), giving one page to each member of BAPC (minimum 6 months) who has had work published in *Poetalk* during the previous year.

Magazine Needs: *Poetalk* publishes approximately 70 poets each issue. BAPC has 150 members, 70 subscribers, but *Poetalk* is open to all. No particular genre. Short poems (under 40 lines) are preferred. "Rhyme must be well done." Membership: $15/year of *Poetalk*, copy of anthology and other privileges; extra outside US. Also offers a $50 patronage, which includes a subscription and anthology for another individual of your choice, and a $25 beneficiary/memorial, which includes membership plus subscription for friend. Subscriptions: $6/year. As a sample the editors selected these lines from "At the Beach On My 50th" by Blaine Hammond:

> *frantic shorebirds lift/off together, turn one way a black swarm/of bees, the other a flash of moving sculpture, white/as laundry. They are like a mind.*

Poetalk is 36 pgs., 5½×8½, photocopied, saddle-stapled with heavy card cover. Send SASE with 78¢ postage for a free complimentary copy.

How to Submit: Submit up to 4 poems, typed and single-spaced, 40 lines maximum preferred, with SASE, no more than twice a year. "A poem will be rejected outright if there are spelling errors." Accepts simultaneous and previously published work, but must be noted. "All subject matter should be in good taste." Response time is up to 4 months. Pays 1 copy. All rights revert to authors upon publication.

Also Offers: BAPC holds monthly readings, yearly contest, etc. BAPC's annual contest, established in 1980, awards a $40 1st Prize, $25 2nd Prize, $10 3rd Prize, certificates for 1st, and 2nd honorable mentions, plus publication in and 1 copy of BAPC's annual anthology. Submissions must be unpublished. Submit 2 copies of up to 8 poems on any subject of 15-35 lines (blank lines count), with SASE for winners list. Include name, address, and whether member or nonmember on 1 copy only. Entry fee: $1/poem for members and $1.50/poem for nonmembers. Submission period: October 1 through November 15, 2002. Winners will be announced by mail in January 2003. People from many states and countries have contributed to *Poetalk* or entered their annual contests. Send SASE in early September for contest guidelines.

Advice: "If you don't want suggested revisions you need to say so clearly in your cover letter or indicate on each poem submitted."

BAY WINDOWS (Specialized: gay/lesbian), 631 Tremont St., Boston MA 02118. Fax: (617)266-5973. E-mail: rKikel@baywindows.com. Established 1983. **Poetry Editor:** Rudy Kikel.

Magazine Needs: *Bay Windows* is a weekly gay and lesbian newspaper published for the New England community, regularly using "short poems of interest to lesbians and gay men. Poetry that is 'experiential' seems to have a good chance with us, but we don't want poetry that just 'tells it like it is.' Our readership doesn't read poetry all the time. A primary consideration is giving pleasure. We'll overlook the poem's (and the poet's) tendency not to be informed by the latest poetic theory, if it does this: pleases. Pleases, in particular, by articulating common gay or lesbian experience, and by doing that with some attention to form. I've found that a lot of our choices were made because of a strong image strand. Humor is always welcome—and hard to provide with craft. Obliquity, obscurity? Probably not for us. We won't presume on our audience." Has published poetry by Carol Guess, Walter Holland, Christina Hutchins, Christopher Thomas, and Dennis Rhodes. As a sample the editor selected these lines from "Words" by Barbara Brooks:

> *I have to treat the word* friend/*carefully; often it becomes/*end.///*I need to practice* together,/*knowing how often one becomes/alone.*

"We try to run four poems each month." Receives about 300 submissions/year, accepts about 1 in 10, has a 3-month backlog. Press run is 13,000 for 700 subscribers of which 15 are libraries. Single copy: 50¢; subscription: $40. Sample: $3.

How to Submit: Submit 3-5 poems at a time, "up to 30 lines are ideal; include short biographical blurb and SASE. No submissions via e-mail, but poets may request info via e-mail." Responds in 3 months. Pays 1 copy "unless you ask for more." Acquires first rights. Editor "often" comments on rejected poems. Reviews books of poetry in about 750 words—"Both single and omnibus reviews (the latter are longer)."

BAYBURY REVIEW, 40 High St., Highwood IL 60040. Website: www.bayburyreview.com (includes "samples from current and back issues, subscription form, information on staff, and editorial approach"). E-mail: baybury@flash.net (queries only). Established 1997. **Editor:** Janet St. John.

Magazine Needs: *Baybury Review* appears annually and publishes "any style or form of poetry as long as it demonstrates attention to craft and fresh insight." Has published poetry by Susan Aizenberg, Mary Crow, Jim Elledge, Mark Halperin, David Jauss, Lyn Lifshin, William Orem, and Virgil Suarez. As a sample the editor selected these lines from "To an Absent Husband, After the Nightly News" by Jan Worth:

> *. . . a sound/of the desert, a survivor's keen/from somewhere parched and dangerous—/not of this overgrown yard, its green life/incessant, surging up wall and windows,/takeover green, and you not here.*

Baybury Review is 70-115 pgs., 5½ × 8½, professionally printed and flat-spined with card cover, occasional b&w graphics, accepts exchange ads. Receives about 600 poems/year, accepts about 5%. Press run is 500. Subscription: $8 (current issues, includes postage). Sample: $6 (back issue).

How to Submit: Submit 3-6 poems at a time. Simultaneous submissions OK; no previously published poems. Cover letter preferred. "Manuscripts should be clearly typewritten and include author's name and address on each page. Please indicate simultaneous submissions in cover letter. An adequate SASE must accompany the submission to receive a response or have work returned." Reads submissions August 1 through December 31 only. Time between acceptance and publication is up to 9 months. May comment on rejected poems. Responds in 3 months. Pays 2 copies. Acquires first North American serial rights. Accepts reviews of very recent poetry books (350 word maximum) as well as critical (literary) essays.

Advice: "We encourage submissions from emerging, as well as established writers, but suggest that, before submitting, writers spend some time reading literary magazines to get a feel for where their work might belong."

BEACON STREET REVIEW (Specialized: graduate-level writers), 100 Beacon St., Emerson College, Boston MA 02116. E-mail: beaconstreetreview@hotmail.com. Website: www.beaconstreetreview. emerson.edu (publishes chosen works simultaneously with bound edition; also includes submission guidelines). Established 1986. **Editor:** Joy Williams. **Poetry Editor:** Krista Miranda.

Magazine Needs: *Beacon Street Review* appears biannually "to publish the best prose (fiction and nonfiction) and poetry we receive; to publish specifically the poetry that evidences the highest degree of creative talent and seriousness of effort and craft. Facile poetry that is not polished and crafted and poems that lack a strange sense of the 'idea' will not be ranked highly. Submissions from Emerson students as well as writers across the country are welcomed and encouraged." Has published poetry by Charlotte Pence, John McKernan, and Paul Berg. As a sample the editors selected these lines from "Umbrella," by Ted O'Callahan:

> *A wheel/with a dubious hub, sliding on a stalk,/expected to stop/with apoplectic tension in the nick of a racket.//Click. Skin taut in a manic grin--/all jointy spider legs and bones full of wires—/so close to lashing out.//Spill the wind.//Or snap of ribs/shattered rag—broken spokes—it beetles away.*

Beacon Street Review is 96-104 pgs., 5½ × 8½, offset-printed and perfect-bound with 4-color, matte finish cover with art/photo. Receives about 700 poems/year, accepts about 4%. Press run is 1,000; 200 distributed free to Emerson College students. Subscription: $7/year (2 issues), $15/2 years (4 issues). Sample: $4.

How to Submit: Submit 3-5 poems at a time. Accepts simultaneous submissions; no previously published poems. No fax, e-mail, or disk submissions. Cover letter required. "Poets should include four copies of each poem. The poet's name and address should not appear on those copies but should appear on the cover letter with all titles clearly listed." Reads submissions year round but responds only during early December and early April. Time between acceptance and publication is 2 months. Poems are circulated to an editorial board. "We have reading boards who read and rate all poems, submitting ranks and comments to a poetry editor. The poetry editor and the editor-in-chief confer with those ranks and comments in mind and then make final decisions." Send SASE for guidelines. Responds in 2 months. Pays 3 copies. Acquires first rights. Staff reviews of poetry in 250 words, single book format. Send books for review consideration to editor-in-chief.

Also Offers: Sponsors the Editor's Choice Awards. Selected by local established poets, the award gives a cash prize for the best poem published in *Beacon Street Review* during the year.

$ ◎ THE BEAR DELUXE (Specialized: nature/ecology), P.O. Box 10342, Portland OR 97296-0342. (503)242-1047. Fax: (503)243-2645. E-mail: bear@teleport.com. Website: www.orlo.org. Established 1993. **Editor:** Tom Webb. **Contact:** poetry editor.

• Note: *The Bear Deluxe* is published by Orlo, a nonprofit organization exploring environmental issues through the creative arts.

Magazine Needs: *The Bear Deluxe*, formerly *Bear Essential*, is a quarterly that "provides a fresh voice amid often strident and polarized environmental discourse. Street-level, non-dogmatic, and solution-oriented, *The Bear Deluxe* presents lively creative discussion to a diverse readership." Wants poetry with "innovative environmental perspectives, not much longer than 50 lines. No rants." Has published poetry by Judith Barrington, Robert Michael Pyle, Mary Winters, Stephen Babcock, Carl Hanni, and Derek Sheffield. As a sample the editor selected these lines from "Smoking" by Leanne Grabel:

> I wonder what I/think's going to/happen if I/breathe only/air.

Bear Deluxe is 60 pgs., 11 × 14, newsprint with brown Kraft paper cover, saddle-stapled, with lots of original graphics and b&w photos. Receives about 1200 poems/year, accepts about 20-30. Press run is 17,000 for 750 subscribers of which 20 are libraries, 16,000 distributed free on the streets of the Western US and beyond. Subscription: $16. Sample: $3. Make checks payable to Orlo.

How to Submit: Submit 3-5 poems at a time up to 50 lines each. Accepts previously published poems and simultaneous submissions, "so long as noted." Accepts e-mail submissions, "in body of message. We can't respond to e-mail submissions but do look at them." Poems are reviewed by a committee of 7-9 people. Publishes 1 theme issue/year. Guidelines and a list of upcoming themes available for SASE. Responds in 6 months. Pays $10/poem, 5 copies (more if willing to distribute), and subscription. Acquires first or one-time rights.

$ ◐ ◎ BEAR STAR PRESS; DOROTHY BRUNSMAN POETRY PRIZE (Specialized: regional), 185 Hollow Oak Dr., Cohasset CA 95973. (530)891-0360. Website: www.bearstarpress.com (includes sample poems from books published, guidelines for the annual contest, information about the press, and a link to a secure-server for credit card trancations). Established 1996. **Publisher/Editor:** Beth Spencer.

Book/Chapbook Needs: Bear Star Press accepts work by poets from Western and Pacific states ("Those in Mountain or Pacific time zones"). "Bear Star is committed to publishing the best poetry it can attract. Each year it sponsors a contest open to poets from Western and Pacific states, although other eligibility requirements change depending on the composition of our list up to that point. From time to time we add to our list other poets from our target area whose work we admire." Wants "well-crafted poems. No restrictions as to form, subject matter, style or purpose." Has published *Poems in Which* by Joseph Di Prisco, *The Archival Birds* by Melissa Kwaswy, and *The Orphan Conducts the Dovehouse Orchestra* by Deborah Woodard. As a sample the publisher selected these lines from "Beeman" by Deborah Woodard:

> Bitten near the mouth, he keeps/completely still under his burred coat./The bees have flung a leopard skin/over the shoulders of a strong man./And then intractable as ivy,/they dedicate themselves to hanging on,

Publishes 1-2 paperbacks and occasionally chapbooks. Books are usually 35-75 pgs., size varies, professionally printed, and perfect-bound.

How to Submit: "Poets should enter our annual book competition. Other books are occasionally solicited by publisher, sometimes from among contestants who didn't win." Accepts previously published poems and simultaneous submissions. "Prefer single-spaced manuscripts in plain font such as Times New Roman. SASE required for results. Manuscripts not returned but are recycled." Generally reads submissions September through November. Guidelines available for SASE or on website. Contest entry fee: $16. Time between acceptance and publication is up to 9 months. Poems are circulated to an editorial board. "I occasionally hire a judge. More recently I have taken on the judging with help from poets whose taste I trust." Seldom comments on rejected poems. Responds to queries regarding competitions in 1-2 weeks. Contest winner notified February 1 or before. Contest pays $1,000 and 25 author's copies (out of a press run of up to 750).

Advice: "Send your best work, consider its arrangement. A 'Wow' poem early on keeps me reading."

◖ THE BEATNIK PACHYDERM, P.O. Box 161, Deadwood SD 57732. Established 1998. **Editor:** Tim Brennan. **Editor:** Randall K. Rogers.

Magazine Needs: *The Beatnik Pachyderm* appears 3 times/year and publishes poems, prose, artwork, letters, and short stories. Wants "shorter poems; poems from social philosopher poets of the everyday life; humor, experimental, slice of life poems; Beat-influenced." As a sample they selected these lines from "Bank Job" by editor Tim Brennan:

> I had this strange dream early this morning/it was about me four or five people I work with and Bing Crosby/we were successful bank robbers/celebrating a major bank job/my dreams aren't always like this/in this one Bing kept his clothes on

The Beatnik Pachyderm is 25-30 pgs., magazine-sized, photocopied, artwork contributions desired. Receives about 400 poems/year, accepts about 20%. Press run is 250. Single copy: $5; subscription: $13. Make checks payable to Tim Brennan.

How to Submit: Submit up to 6 poems at a time. Line length for poetry is 60 maximum. Accepts previously published poems and simultaneous submissions. No fax or e-mail submissions. Cover letter preferred. "Name and address on each page; include SASE." Time between acceptance and publication is 6 months. Poems are circulated to an editorial board of 3 editors. Often comments on rejected poems. Responds in 6 months. Pays 1 copy. Acquires one-time rights.

Advice: "Enjoy writing, reflect, tell a unique or twisted observation."

$◯◐ BEGGAR'S PRESS; THE LAMPLIGHT; RASKOLNIKOV'S CELLAR; BEGGAR'S RE-VIEW, 8110 N. 38th St., Omaha NE 68112-2018. (402)455-2615. Website: http://angelfire.com/journal/begpress. Established 1977. **Editor:** Richard R. Carey. **Contact:** Danielle Staton.

Magazine Needs: *The Lamplight* is a semiannual (more frequent at times) publication of short stories, poetry, humor, and unusual literary writings. "We are eclectic, but we like serious poetry, historically orientated. Positively no religious or sentimental poetry. No incomprehensible poetry." Has published poetry by Fredrick Zydek and Heidi von Palleske. As a sample the editor selected these lines (poet unidentified):

> Lord, why did you curse me with doubt!/I'm a shot discharged in a wood without trees,/like a scream
> that began as a shout./Never too far from famine or mire;/hunger and cold, and all creatures turn
> bold—/But, Lord, why did you give me desire!

The Lamplight is 40-60 pgs., 8½×11, offset-printed and perfect-bound with 65 lb. cover stock. Receives about 600 poems/year, accepts about 10-15%. Press run is 500 for 300 subscribers of which 25 are libraries. Single copy: $9.50. Sample: $7 plus 9×12 SASE.

How to Submit: Accepts simultaneous submissions; no previously published poems. No fax or e-mail submissions. Cover letter required—"must provide insight into the poet's characteristics. What makes this poet different from the mass of humanity?" Time between acceptance and publication is up to 12 months. Always comments on rejected poems. Also offers "complete appraisals and evaluations" for $4/standard sheet, double-spaced. Responds in 1 month or less. Pays 1 copy. Acquires first North American serial rights. *Raskolnikov's Cellar* is an irregular magazine of the same format, dimensions, and terms as *The Lamplight*. However, it deals in "deeper psychologically-orientated stories and poetry. It is more selective and discriminating in what it publishes. Guidelines and brochure are an essential to consider this market." Guidelines and brochures available for SASE. *Beggar's Review* is 20-40 pgs., 8½×11, offset-printed and saddle-stapled. It lists and reviews books, chapbooks, and other magazines. "It also lists and reviews unpublished manuscripts: poetry, short stories, book-length, etc. Our purpose is to offer a vehicle for unpublished work of merit, as well as published material. We like to work with poets and authors who have potential but have not yet been recognized." Lengths of reviews range from a listing or mere caption to 1,000 words, "according to merit." Single copy: $6.

Advice: "We look for poets with unique qualities of expression and who meet our uncustomary requirements. Beggar's Press is different from most publishers. We are impressed with concrete poetry, which is without outlandish metaphors. Keep it simple but don't be afraid to use our language to the fullest. Read Poe, Burns, and Byron. Then submit to us. There is still a place for lyrical poetry."

☑◐ BELLINGHAM REVIEW; 49TH PARALLEL POETRY AWARD, M.S. 9053, Western Washington University, Bellingham WA 98225. E-mail: bhreview@cc.wwu.edu. Website: www.wwu.edu/~bhreview/ (includes submissions and contest guidelines, names of editors and staff, and selections from recent issue). Established 1975. **Editor:** Brenda Miller.

Magazine Needs: *Bellingham Review* appears twice/year. "We want well-crafted poetry but are open to all styles," no specifications as to form. Has published poetry by David Shields, Tess Gallagher, Gary Soto, Jane Hirshfield, Albert Goldbarth, R.T. Smith, and Rebecca McClanahan. As a sample the editor selected these lines from "Sitting at Dusk in the Back Yard After the Mondrian Retrospective" by Charles Wright:

> Form imposes, structure allows—/the slow destruction of form/So as to bring it back resheveled,
> reorganized,/Is the hard heart of the enterprise./Under its camouflage,/The light, relentless shill and
> cross-dresser, pools and deals./Inside its short skin, the darkness burns.

Bellingham Review is 6×9, perfect-bound, with art and glossy cover. Each issue has about 60 pgs. of poetry. Circulation is 1,500 with 500 subscriptions. Subscription: $10/year, $19/2 years. Sample: $5. Make checks payable to The Western Foundation/*Bellingham Review*.

How to Submit: Submit 3-5 poems at a time with SASE. Accepts simultaneous submissions with notification. No fax or e-mail submissions. Reads submissions October 1 through February 1 only. Guidelines available for SASE or on website. Responds in 2 months. Pays 1 copy, a year's subscription plus monetary payment (if funding allows). Acquires first North American serial rights.

Also Offers: The 49th Parallel Poetry Award, established in 1983, awards a $1,000 first prize, $300 second prize and $200 third prize, plus a year's subscription to the *Bellingham Review*. Submissions must be unpublished and may be entered in other contests. Guidelines available for SASE or website. Most recent award winner was Ellen Andolsek (2000). Judge was Reginald Shepard. Winners will be announced in summer.

◐ BELLOWING ARK; BELLOWING ARK PRESS, P.O. Box 55564, Shoreline WA 98155. (206)440-0791. Established 1984. **Editor:** Robert R. Ward.

Magazine Needs: *Bellowing Ark* is a bimonthly literary tabloid that "publishes only poetry which demonstrates in some way the proposition that existence has meaning or, to put it another way, that life is worth living. We have no strictures as to length, form or style; only that the work we publish is to our judgment life-affirming." Does not want "academic poetry, in any of its manifold forms." Has published poetry by Irene Culver, Mary-Marcia Casolt, Esther Cameron, Ute Carbone, Jacqueline Hill, and Elizabeth Biller Chapman. *Bellowing Ark* is 32 pgs., tabloid-sized, printed on electrobright stock with b&w photos and line drawings. Circulation is 1,000, of which 275 are subscriptions and 500 are sold on newsstands. Subscription: $15/year. Sample: $3.

How to Submit: Submit 3-6 poems at a time. "Absolutely *no* simultaneous submissions." No fax or e-mail submissions. Responds to submissions in up to 12 weeks and publishes within the next 1 or 2 issues. Occasionally will criticize a ms if it seems to "display potential to become the kind of work we want." Sometimes sends prepublication galleys. Pays 2 copies. Reviews books of poetry. Send books for review consideration.

Book/Chapbook Needs & How to Submit: Bellowing Ark Press publishes collections of poetry by *invitation only.*

BELL'S LETTERS POET (Specialized: subscribers), P.O. Box 2187, Gulfport MS 39505-2187. E-mail: jimbelpoet@aol.com. Established 1956. **Publisher/Editor:** Jim Bell.

Magazine Needs: *Bell's Letters Poet* is a quarterly which you must buy ($5.50/issue, $22 subscription) to be included. "Many say they stop everything the day it arrives," and judging by the many letters from readers, that seems to be the case. Though there is no payment for poetry accepted, many patrons send cash awards to the poets whose work they especially like. Poems are "four to 20 lines in good taste." Accepts poetry written by children, ages 8-12. Has published poetry by Nancy Dodrils, C. David Hay, Gary Edwards, William Middleton, and Helen Webb. As a sample we selected these lines from "Awakening" by William J. Middleton:

> I doubt I heard a call to live or die./I only knew, somehow, that I must cry.

Bell's Letters Poet is about 52 pgs., digest-sized, photocopied on plain bond paper (including cover) and saddle-stapled. Sample (including guidelines): $5. "Send a poem (20 lines or under, in good taste) with your sample order and we will publish in our next issue."

How to Submit: Submit 4 poems/year. No simultaneous submissions. Accepts previously published poems "if cleared by author with prior publisher." Accepts e-mail submissions. Accepted poems by subscribers go immediately into the next issue. Deadline for poetry submissions is 3 months prior to publication. Reviews books of poetry by subscribers in "one abbreviated paragraph." "The Ratings" is a competition in each issue. Readers are asked to vote on their favorite poems, and the "Top 40" are announced in the next issue, along with awards sent to the poets by patrons. *Bell's Letters Poet* also features a telephone and e-mail exchange among poets and a birth-date listing.

Advice: "Tired of seeing no bylines this year? Subscription guarantees a byline in each issue."

THE BELOIT POETRY JOURNAL; CHAD WALSH POETRY PRIZE, 24 Berry Cove Rd., Lamoine ME 04605-4617. (207)667-5598. E-mail: sharkey@maine.edu (for information only). Website: www.bpj .org (includes writer's guidelines, magazine history, names of editors, sample poems, a 50-year index, and table of contents of recent issues). Established 1950. **Editor:** Marion K. Stocking.

● Poetry published in *The Beloit Poetry Journal* has also been included in *The Best American Poetry* (1994, 1996, and 2000) and *Pushcart Prize* anthologies.

Magazine Needs: *The Beloit Poetry Journal* is a well-known, long-standing quarterly of quality poetry and reviews. "We publish the best poems we receive, without bias as to length, school, subject, or form. It is our hope to discover the growing tip of poetry and to introduce new poets alongside established writers. We publish occasional chapbooks to diversify our offerings. These are almost never the work of one poet." Wants "fresh, imaginative poetry, with a distinctive voice. We tend to prefer poems that make the reader share an experience rather than just read about it, and these we keep for up to four months, circulating them among our readers, and continuing to winnow for the best. At the quarterly meetings of the Editorial Board we read aloud all the surviving poems and put together an issue of the best we have." Has published poetry by Bei Dao, A.E. Stallings, Albert Goldbarth, and Janet Holmes. As a sample the editor selected the poem "The Menstrual Hut" by Annie Finch:

> How can I listen to the moon?/Your blood will listen, like a charm.//I had a way to feel the sun/as if
> a statue felt warm eyes./Your blood can listen, every time.//Now I am the one with eyes./Even with
> ruins on the moon,/your blood will listen, every time.

The Beloit Poetry Journal averages 48 pgs., 6×9, saddle-stapled, and attractively printed with tasteful art on the card cover. Circulation is 1,200 for 724 subscribers of which 227 are libraries. Subscription: individuals $18/year, institutions $23/year. Sample (including guidelines): $5. Guidelines without sample available for SASE.

How to Submit: Submit any time, without query, any legible form. "No previously published poems or simultaneous submissions. Any length of ms, but most poets send what will go in a business envelope for one stamp. Don't send your life's work." No e-mail submissions. Pays 3 copies. Acquires first serial rights. Editor reviews books by and about poets in an average of 500 words, usually single format. Send books for review consideration.

Also Offers: The journal awards the Chad Walsh Poetry Prize ($4,000 in 2000) to a poem or group of poems published in the calendar year. "Every poem published in 2002 will be considered for the 2002 prize."

Advice: "We'd like to see more strong, imaginative, experimental poetry; more poetry with a global vision; and more poetry with fresh, vigorous language."

BENEATH THE SURFACE, % The Dept. of English, Chester New Hall, McMaster University, Hamilton, Ontario L8S 4L9 Canada. Established 1911. Editor changes yearly.

Magazine Needs: *Beneath the Surface* is an annual using "top quality poetry/prose that achieves universality through individual expression." Wants "quality poetry; any form; no restrictions." Also interested in short stories. Has published poetry by Janice Knapp and Jeffrey Donaldson. *Beneath the Surface* is 30-50 pgs., professionally printed, saddle-stapled, with cover art, drawings and b&w photographs. Receives about 250 submissions/year, accepts approximately 10%. Press run is 75 for 8 subscribers of which 3 are libraries, 92 shelf sales. Subscription: $3/2 years. Sample: $1.50.

How to Submit: No previously published poems or simultaneous submissions. No fax or e-mail submissions. Submit poems with cover letter, including short bio and summary of previous publications, if any. Reads submissions September through April only. Pays 1 copy. Acquires first North American serial rights. Rarely reviews books of poetry, "though we do include literary essays when submitted." Responds in up to 10 months.

BENNETT & KITCHEL (Specialized: form), P.O. Box 4422, East Lansing MI 48826. (517)355-1707. Established 1989. **Editor:** William Whallon.

Book/Chapbook Needs: Publishes 1-2 hardbacks/year of "poetry of form and meaning. No free verse or blank verse." As an example of what he admires, the editor selected these lines by Anthony Lombardy:

> *From recent fires surrounding groves are ashen,/Are like the Trojan women mad with thirst,/Who begged for water while the one accursed/Allowed the guards to fill her pool to splash in.*

Sample: $4.

How to Submit: Submit 6 poems at a time. Accepts simultaneous submissions and previously published poems if copyright is clear. Minimum volume for a book "might be 750 lines." Time between acceptance and publication is 9 months. Seldom comments on submissions. Responds in 2 weeks. Terms are "variable, negotiable."

Advice: "To make a bad rhyme not from incompetence but willfully is like stubbing your toe on purpose."

BETWEEN WHISPER AND SHOUT POETRY. E-mail: KXZX@hotmail.com. Website: http://homestead.juno.com/zark-3/index.html. Established 1999. **Editor:** Kate Zielinski.

Magazine Needs: *Between Whisper and Shout Poetry* is a website that publishes only poetry. Wants "poetry from new or experienced poets. Any form or style is welcome as well as any purpose. No pornography, epic, or extremely violent poems are even considered." Submit 2-3 poems at a time. Line length for poetry is 40 maximum. Accepts previously published poems and simultaneous submissions. Accepts e-mail submissions; no disk submissions. "Include all poems in the body of the e-mail; no attachments! Include e-mail address. Poet may include a brief bio to be posted with submission(s)." Reads submissions constantly, but "cutoff for an update is the last day of the previous month." Submit seasonal poems 2 months in advance. Editor reads all submissions and chooses according to available space on the website and the quality of the poems. Seldom comments on rejections.

Also Offers: "*Between Whisper and Shout* offers a poet's showcase that will post 5 original works by one poet, absolutely free. Also has a help page with links to literary help having to do with homework and writing."

Advice: "Send in poetry that you are proud of and never, ever be afraid of rejection; it fuels better work in the future."

BIBLE ADVOCATE (Specialized: religious), P.O. Box 33677, Denver CO 80233. E-mail: bibleadvocate@cog7.org (includes writer's guidelines). Website: www.cog7.org/BA. Established 1863. **Associate Editor:** Sherri Langton.

Magazine Needs: *Bible Advocate*, published monthly, features "Christian content—to advocate the Bible and represent the church." Wants "free verse, some traditional; 5-20 lines, with Christian/Bible themes." Does not want "avant garde poetry." *Bible Advocate* is 24 pgs., $8\frac{3}{4} \times 11\frac{7}{8}$ with most poetry set up with 4-color art. Receives about 30-50 poems/year, accepts about 10-20. Press run varies for 13,500 subscribers with all distributed free.

How to Submit: Submit no more than 5 poems at a time, 5-20 lines each. Accepts previously published poems (with notification) and simultaneous submissions. Accepts e-mail submissions with text included in body of message; no attachments. "No fax or handwritten submissions, please." Cover letter preferred. Time between acceptance and publication is up to 12 months. "I read them first and reject those that won't work for us. I send good ones to editor for approval." Seldom comments on rejected poems. Publishes theme issues. Guidelines available for SASE and on website. Responds in 2 months. Pays $20. Acquires first, reprint, electronic, and one-time rights.

Advice: "Avoid trite, or forced rhyming. Be aware of the magazine's doctrinal views (send for doctrinal beliefs booklet)."

BIBLIOPHILOS (Specialized: animals, bilingual/foreign language, ethnic/nationality, structured form, humor, nature/rural/ecology, political, social issues, writing, anti-technology/ "Ludditism"), 200 Security Building, Fairmont WV 26554. (304)366-8107. Established 1981. **Editor:** Gerald J. Bobango.

Magazine Needs: "*Bibliophilos* is a quarterly academic journal, for the literati, illuminati, amantes artium, and those who love animals; scholastically oriented, for the liberal arts. Topics include fiction and nonfiction; literature and criticism, history, art, music, theology, philosophy, natural history, educational theory, contemporary issues and politics, sociology, and economics. Published in English, French, German, Romanian." Wants "traditional forms, formalism, structure, rhyme; also blank verse. Aim for concrete visual imagery, either in words or on the page. No inspirational verse, or anything that Ann Landers or Erma Bombeck would publish." Accepts poetry written by children, ages 12-17. Has published poetry by Belle Randall, Lois Greene Stone, and Jack Lloyd Packard. As a sample the editor selected these lines from "Trademark" (poet unidentified):

> *superimposed on a picture too faint to see,/printed in red in English and Chinese,/concludes: ". . . should not be poured out/until five minutes have passed/when the taste will come out/in its full glory."*

Bibliophilos is 64 pgs., 5½×8, laser photography printed and saddle-stapled with light card, includes clip art, ads. Receives about 100 poems/year, accepts about 33%. Press run is 200 for 150 subscribers. Subscription: $18/year. Sample: $5. Make checks payable to *The Bibliophile*. West Virginia residents please add 6% sales tax.

How to Submit: Query first with SASE and $5 for sample and guidelines. Then, if invited, submit 3-5 poems at a time. Accepts previously published poems and simultaneous submissions. Cover letter with brief bio preferred. Does not read submissions September 1 through December 31. Time between acceptance and publication is 3 months. Often comments on rejected poems. Guidelines available for SASE. Responds in 2 weeks. Pays 2 copies plus offprints. Acquires first North American serial rights. Staff reviews books and chapbooks of poetry in 750-1,000 words, single book format. Send books for review consideration.

Also Offers: Sponsors poetry contest. Send SASE for rules. 1st Prize $25 plus publication and offprints.

Advice: "There is too much maudlin over-emotionalism and instant pop psychology in this touchy-feely world. We need some good traditional, hearty, Kiplingesque poetry that stirs, inspires, and hits you between the eyes. Also, we need more peristaltic belchings of crabbed organisms arguing that malls, 'feeling everyone's pain,' and building self-esteem as opposed to educating people, should all be extinguished as blights."

$© BILINGUAL REVIEW PRESS; BILINGUAL REVIEW/REVISTA BILINGÜE (Specialized: ethnic/Hispanic, bilingual/Spanish), Hispanic Research Center, Arizona State University, Box 872702, Tempe AZ 85287-2702. (480)965-3867. Journal established 1974, press in 1976. **Managing Editor:** Karen Van Hooft.

Magazine Needs: "We are a small press publisher of U.S. Hispanic creative literature and of a journal containing poetry and short fiction in addition to scholarship." *Bilingual Review/Revista Billingüe,* published 3 times/year, contains some poetry in most issues. "We publish poetry by and/or about U.S. Hispanics and U.S. Hispanic themes. We do not publish translations in our journal or literature about the experiences of Anglo-Americans in Latin America. We have published a couple of poetry volumes in bilingual format (Spanish/English) of important Mexican poets." Has published poetry by Alberto Ríos, Martín Espada, Judith Ortiz Cofer, and Marjorie Agosín. The journal is 96 pgs., 7×10, offset-printed and flat-spined, with 2 color cover. Accepts less than 10% of hundreds of submissions received each year. Press run is 1,000 for 700 subscribers. Subscriptions: $23 for individuals, $38 for institutions. Sample: $7 individuals/$12 institutions.

How to Submit: Submit "two copies, including ribbon original if possible, with loose stamps for return postage." Cover letter required. Pays 2 copies. Acquires all rights. Reviews books of US Hispanic literature only. Send books, Attn: Editor, for review consideration.

Book/Chapbook Needs & How to Submit: Bilingual Review Press publishes flat-spined paperback collections of poetry. For book submissions, inquire first with 4-5 sample poems, bio, and publication credits. Pays $250 advance, 10% royalties, and 10 copies. Over the years, books by this press have won 6 American Book Awards and 2 Western States Book Awards.

$◑© BIRCH BROOK PRESS (Specialized: anthology, nature, social issues, themes), P.O. Box 81, Delhi NY 13753. (212)353-3326. Website: www.birchbrookpress.com ("tells how we produce our books, lists media coverage, and our latest titles"). Established 1982. **Contact:** Tom Tolnay.

● Birch Brook Press acquired the poetry publishing activities of Persephone Press in 1998 and is a member of the American Academy of Poets.

Book/Chapbook Needs: Birch Brook "is a letterpress book printer/typesetter/designer that uses monies from these activities to publish several titles of its own each year with cultural and literary interest." Has published *The Melancholy of Yorick* by Joel Chace; *Waiting On Pentecost* by Tom Smith; *The Derelict Genius of Martin M* by Frank Fagan, *Repercussions* by Marcus Rome; and *Risking the Wind* by Warren Carrier. Publishes 4-6 paperbacks and/or hardbacks per year. The press specializes "mostly in anthologies with specific subject matter. Birch Brook Press publishes one or two books annually by individuals with high-quality literary work on a co-op basis." Books are "handset letterpress editions printed in our own shop."

How to Submit: Query first with sample poems or send entire ms. "Must include SASE with submissions." Occasionally comments on rejected poems. Authors may obtain sample books by sending SASE for catalog. Pays from $5-20 for publication in anthology.

Advice: "Send your best work, and see other Birch Brook Press books."

◑© BIRMINGHAM POETRY REVIEW (Specialized: translations), English Dept., HB205, 1530 Third Ave. S, University of Alabama at Birmingham, Birmingham AL 35294. (205)934-4250. Website: www.uab.edu/english/bpr (includes guidelines, contents of current issue, subscription information, list of editors, and sample poems). Established 1988. **Co-Editors:** Robert Collins and Adam Vines.

Magazine Needs: The review appears twice/year using poetry of "any style, form, length or subject. We are biased toward exploring the cutting edge of contemporary poetry. Style is secondary to the energy, the fire the poem possesses. We don't want poetry with cliché-bound, worn-out language." Has published poetry by Hague, Harrod, McDonald, Murawski, and Steinman. *Birmingham Poetry Review* is 50 pgs., 6×9, offset-printed, with b&w cover. Press run is 700 for 300 subscribers. Subscription: $4/year; $7/2 years. Sample: $2.

How to Submit: Submit 3-5 poems, "no more. No cover letters. We are impressed by good writing; we are unimpressed by publication credits." SASE required. No simultaneous or multiple submissions, and previously published poems only if they are translations. Editor sometimes comments on rejected poems. Guidelines available for SASE. Responds in 6 months. Pays 2 copies and one-year subscription.

Advice: "Advice to beginners: Read as much good contemporary poetry, national and international, as you can get your hands on. Then be persistent in finding your own voice."

THE BITTER OLEANDER; FRANCES LOCKE MEMORIAL AWARD, 4983 Tall Oaks Dr., Fayetteville NY 13066-9776. (315)637-3047. Fax: (315)637-5056. E-mail: bones44@ix.netcom.com. Website: www.bitteroleander.com. Established 1974. **Editor/Publisher:** Paul B. Roth.

● Poetry published in *The Bitter Oleander* has been included in *The Best American Poetry 1999*.

Magazine Needs: *The Bitter Oleander* appears biannually, publishing "imaginative poetry; poetry in translation; serious language." Wants "highly imaginative poetry whose language is serious. We prefer short poems of no more than 25 lines. We are not interested in very long poems and prefer not to receive poems about the common values and protests of society." Has published poetry by Robert Bly, Alan Britt, Duane Locke, and Ray Gonzalez. *The Bitter Oleander* is 128 pgs., digest-sized, offset-printed, perfect-bound with glossy 2-color cover, cover art, ads. Receives about 5,000 poems/year, accepts about 2%. Press run is 1,500; 1,000 shelf sales. Single copy: $8; subscription: $15. Make checks payable to Bitter Oleander Press.

How to Submit: Submit up to 8 poems at a time with name and address on each page. No previously published poems or simultaneous submissions. No e-mail submissions. Cover letter preferred. Does not read mss during July. Time between acceptance and publication is 6 months. "All poems are read by the editor only and all decisions are made by this editor." Often comments on rejected poems. Responds within a month. Pays 1 copy.

Also Offers: Sponsors the Frances Locke Memorial Award, awarding $500 and publication. Submit any number of poems. Entry fee: $10/5 poems, $2 each additional poem. Open to submissions March 15 through June 15 only.

Advice: "We simply want poetry that is imaginative and serious in its performance of language. So much flat-line poetry is written today that anyone reading one magazine or another cannot tell the difference."

BLACK BEAR PUBLICATIONS; BLACK BEAR REVIEW (Specialized: social issues), 1916 Lincoln St., Croydon PA 19021-8026. E-mail: BBReview@earthlink.net. Website: http://home.earthlink.net/~BB Review (includes recent issues, a list of upcoming themes, complete guidelines, links, and current needs). Established 1984. **Poetry and Art Editor:** Ave Jeanne. **Business Manager:** Ron Zettlemoyer.

Magazine Needs: *Black Bear Review* is a semiannual international literary and fine arts magazine in print and online. "We like well-crafted poetry that mirrors real life—void of camouflage. We seek energetic poetry, avant-garde, free verse and haiku which relate to the world today. We seldom publish the beginner. No traditional poetry is used. The underlying theme of *Black Bear Publications* is social and political, but the review is interested also in environmental, war/peace, ecological, and minorities themes. We would like to receive more ideas on AIDS awareness, life styles, and current political topics." Has recently published poetry by Juan Sequeira, A.D. Winans, Gerald Wheeler, Juan Sequeira, and Adam Perry. As a sample the editor selected these lines from "Poets W/Alarm Clocks in their Foreheads" by Peter Conners:

> *I despise your dream/am of the nightmares of your dream: a/legion of hungry poets w/minds for souls./*
> *These heartfelt visions of your awakening.*

Black Bear Review is 64 pgs., digest-sized, perfect-bound, offset from typed copy on white stock, with line drawings, collages, and woodcuts. Circulation is 500 for 300 subscribers of which 15 are libraries. Subscription: $12, $18 overseas. Sample: $6; back copies when available are $5 (overseas add $3/copy). Make checks payable to Ron Zettlemoyer.

How to Submit: Submit 5 poems at a time by e-mail only. "E-mail submissions are answered within a week, use Arial font. Include snail mail address. No attached files please." Simultaneous submissions are not considered. Time between acceptance and publication is 6 months. Guidelines available for SASE or on website. Pays 1 copy. Acquires first North American serial rights and electronic rights, "as work may appear on our website."

Book/Chapbook Needs & How to Submit: Publishes 2 chapbooks/year. "Publication is now on a subsidy basis." Chapbook series requires a **reading fee of $5**, complete ms, and cover letter sent via snail mail. Guidelines available for SASE. For book publication, they require that "*Black Bear Publications* has published the poet and is familiar with his/her work." Author receives one-half print run. Recently published *Tracers* by Gerald Wheeler.

ALWAYS include a self-addressed, stamped envelope (SASE) when sending a ms or query to a publisher within your own country. When sending material to other countries, include a self-addressed envelope and International Reply Coupons (IRCs), available at many post offices.

Also Offers: "Our yearly poetry competition offers cash awards to poets." Deadline: November 30. Guidelines available for SASE. "Our website is designed and maintained by Ave Jeanne and is updated regularly to meet the diverse needs of our readers. *Bear Facts* is our online newsletter, which readers can subscribe to for free. Details can be found on website. Mark Zettlemoyer, *Bear Facts* Editor Zettlemoyer@mail.com."

Advice: "We appreciate a friendly, brief cover letter. All submissions are handled with objectivity and quite often rejected material is directed to another market. We are always interested in aiding those who support small press. We frequently suggest poets keep up with the current edition of *Poet's Market*. We make an effort to keep our readers informed and on top of the small press scene. Camera-ready ads are printed free of charge as a support to small press publishers. We also run an ad page on the Internet, 'InterActions,' for all interested poets and writers to advertise. We do suggest poets and artists read issues before submitting to absorb the flavor and spirit of our publication. Send your best!" "Visit our applauded website. *Black Bear* will continue to print in our paperback format as well as art and poems online. We are financially supported by our poets, artists, readers, and editors."

BLACK BUZZARD PRESS; BLACK BUZZARD REVIEW; VISIONS—INTERNATIONAL, THE WORLD JOURNAL OF ILLUSTRATED POETRY; THE BLACK BUZZARD ILLUSTRATED POETRY CHAPBOOK SERIES; INTERNATIONAL—VISIONS POETRY SERIES, 1007 Ficklen Rd., Fredericksburg VA 22405. Established 1979. **Poetry Editor:** Bradley R. Strahan. **Associate Editor:** Shirley G. Sullivan.

Magazine Needs: "*Visions* is international in both scope and content, publishing poets from all over the world and having readers in 48 U.S. states, Canada, and 24 other countries." *Visions*, a digest-sized, saddle-stapled magazine finely printed on high-quality paper, appears 3 times/year, uses 56 pages of poetry in each issue. Press run is 800 with 400 subscribers of which 50 are libraries. Receives *well* over 1,000 submissions/year, accepts about 150, has a 3- to 18-month backlog. Sample: $5.50. Current issue: $5.50. *Black Buzzard Review* is a "more or less annual informal journal, dedicated mostly to North American poets and entirely to original English-language poems. In *Black Buzzard Review*, we are taking a more wide-open stance on what we accept (including the slightly outrageous)." *Black Buzzard Review* is 48 pgs., magazine-sized, side-stapled, with matte card cover. Sample: $4.50. Current issue: $5.50.

How to Submit: Submit 3-6 poems at a time. "Poems must be readable (not faded or smudged) and not handwritten. We resent having to pay postage due, so use adequate postage! No more than six pages, please." No previously published poems or simultaneous submissions. Does not accept fax or e-mail submissions. Publishes theme issues. Upcoming themes available for SASE. Responds in 3 weeks. Pays 1 copy or $5-10 "if we get a grant." Acquires first North American serial rights. Staff reviews books of poetry in "up to two paragraphs." Send books for review consideration.

Book/Chapbook Needs & How to Submit: "We are an independent nonsubsidized press dedicated to publishing fine accessible poetry and translation (particularly from lesser-known languages such as Armenian, Gaelic, Urdu, Vietnamese, etc.) accompanied by original illustrations of high quality in an attractive format. We want to see work that is carefully crafted and exciting, that transfigures everyday experience or gives us a taste of something totally new; all styles except concrete and typographical 'poems.' Nothing purely sentimental. No self-indulgent breast beating. No sadism, sexism, or bigotry. No unemotional pap. No copies of Robert Service or the like. Usually under 80 lines but will consider longer." Has published poetry by Michael Mott, Sharon Olds, Eamon Grennan, Miller Williams, Phillip Appleman, Naomi Shihab Nye, and Lawrence Ferlinghetti. To submit for the chapbook series, send samples (5-10 poems) and a brief cover letter "pertinent to artistic accomplishments." Responds in up to 3 weeks. Pays in copies. Usually provides criticism. Send $4.50 for sample chapbook. Also publishes the International-Visions Poetry Series. Send SASE for flyer describing titles and order information.

Advice: In *Visions*, "We sometimes publish helpful advice about 'getting published' and the craft of poetry, and often discuss poets and the world of poetry on our editorial page."

$ BLACK DIASPORA MAGAZINE; BLACK DIASPORA COMMUNICATIONS, LTD. (Specialized: ethnic/nationality), 298 Fifth Ave., 7th Floor, New York NY 10001. (212)268-8348. Fax: (212)268-8370. E-mail: blakdias@earthlink.net. Established 1979. **Executive Editor:** Michelle Phipps. **Publisher:** Rene John-Sandy.

Magazine Needs: Published 7 times/year, *Black Diaspora Magazine* is a "general interest publication for African-Americans, Caribbeans, Africans, Hispanics. Covers general topics in all facets of their lives." Wants "long and short poems—creatively done. Sonnets are good. They should all follow editorial guidelines. Be imaginative. No five-page poems." Has published poetry by Sabrina Smith and Annan Boodram. As a sample they selected these lines from "Altered Mind" by Barbara Grant-Richardson:

> We are the family of Black/America standing at the turning/point of life/Silently absorbed in a world/
> misunderstood by many./Where the human spirit and level/of admiration are steadily stripped of their
> luster.

Black Diaspora Magazine is 68-84 pgs., magazine-sized, flat-spined with glossy cover, includes photos and ads. Receives about 60 poems/year, accepts about 100%. Single copy: $2.95; subscription: $15/year. Sample: $5.

How to Submit: Submit up to 2 poems at a time. Accepts previously published poems; no simultaneous submissions. Accepts disk submissions; "Format should be in Word Perfect 5.1." Cover letter preferred. Time between acceptance and publication is 3 months. Seldom comments on rejected poems. Publishes theme issues. Guidelines and a list of upcoming themes available for SASE. Responds in 3 weeks. Pays $15. Acquires first North American serial rights or one-time rights. Reviews books of poetry in 200-300 words, single book format. Open to unsolicited reviews. Poets may send books for review consideration to Michelle Phipps.

Advice: "Please do not call editors. They're very busy and don't have time for all calls. Be patient. Make friends with editorial assistants and assistant editors."

BLACK SPRING PRESS; BLACK SPRING REVIEW, 63-89 Saunders, 6G, Rego Park NY 11374. E-mail: stjulian66@juno.com. Established 1997. **Editor/Publisher:** John Gallo.

Magazine Needs: *Black Spring Review* is published 2-4 times/year. "We are seeing poetry from two different camps: Those who use poetry as a form of expression and those who use poetry as a craft. We prefer poetry as expression. Don't be afraid to let it all hang out. We don't care if you have a Ph.D. in Literature or if you began writing on a napkin yesterday. Make the reader feel what you feel. No 'Sword & Sorcery'/Hallmark/Gothic Vampire Romance type poems." Has published poetry by Linda La Porte, Ana Christy, Ed Galing, A.D. Winans, Frank Lima, Raymond Mason, and Kate Greene. As a sample the editor selected these lines from "Nonsense" by Laura Joy Lustig:

> Sense is known/only/but its/non./& only 1/is/usable

Black Spring Review is about 20 pgs., 8½ × 5½ chapbook, cardstock cover, and saddle-stapled. Receives approximately 500-600 poems/year, accepts approximately 30%. Press run is 200 for 50 subscribers. Single copy: $5; subscription: $20/4 issues. Make checks/money orders payable to John Gallo, not Black Spring Press.

How to Submit: Submit 6 poems maximum. Accepts previously published poems and simultaneous submissions. "Please ensure that name and address appears on each page. I can't tell you how many times poems accepted for submission have gone by the wayside due to the fact that I couldn't tell who wrote it or where it came from. Writing name and address on envelope is not good enough, since there are hundreds and they tend to get torn and tossed. Also be sure to send SASE. Any submission without an SASE will be discarded." Accepts e-mail submissions (must be an attached file for MSWord); no fax submissions. Time between acceptance and publication varies. "Please refrain from sending letter upon letter about when you will see your poem in print. If it's accepted it will be published." Sometimes comments on rejected poems. Guidelines available for SASE. Responds in up to 2 months. "There are a ton of submissions and only one man going through them. Please be patient." Pays 1 copy.

Book/Chapbook Needs & How to Submit: Black Spring Press wants "strong, emotional writing that isn't afraid to be bold, hard, and risky" and publishes 4-6 chapbooks/year. "We also publish a small series called 'Mezzotints' for individual poets." Has published *Bloody and Living* by Ed Galing, *Naked Brunch* by Laura Joy Lustig, *Poems Not For Your Aunt Nora* by Raymond Mason, *Egotesticle* by Laura Joy Lustig, and *Suck Out the Marrow of Life* by Linda La Porte. Chapbooks are usually 20-40 pgs., 5½ × 8½, photocopied, and saddle-stapled with card stock cover. Query first. "Please do not send the entire manuscript, especially if it's over 200 pages long. However, books and chapbooks are usually solicited, but we are open to unsolicited mss provided that the poet queries first. We do offer co-op publishing of chapbooks. Write for details." Responds to queries and mss in 2 weeks. Pays 40 author's copies (out of a press run of 100). Write to obtain sample books or chapbooks.

Advice: "Write from deep within you. Find your own voice. Bukowski already did Bukowski and Ginsberg already did Ginsberg. Black Spring Press respects the Beat tradition but is not interested in resurrecting a by-gone era. It's the 21st century now. Time to move forward. Also, take whatever you may have learned in college literature courses or writing workshops and ignore it. Good writing does not necessarily come out of the universities. Keep your ego in check. There are an awful lot of people writing out there, and a small press will not make you rich and famous beyond your wildest dreams. However small presses have been a nice stepping stone to bigger and better things. Just don't think I am going to get you the Pulitzer prize. Remember what small in 'small press' means. We feel it should be a network of independent writers and artists to share ideas and their work since none of the large houses would ever look our way unless there's a million dollars to be made."

BLACK THISTLE PRESS, 491 Broadway 6th Floor, New York NY 10012. (212)219-1898. Fax: (212)431-6044. E-mail: bthistle@netcom.com. Website: www.blackthistlepress.com. Established 1990. **Publisher:** Ms. Hollis Melton. "We are no longer accepting submissions because we are not publishing new projects at this time."

BLACK TIE PRESS, P.O. Box 440004, Houston TX 77244-0004. Fax: (713)789-5119. Established 1986. **Publisher and Editor:** Peter Gravis.

Book/Chapbook Needs: "Black Tie Press is committed to publishing innovative, distinctive, and engaging writing. We publish books; we are not a magazine or literary journal. We are not like the major Eastern presses, university presses, or other small presses in poetic disposition. To get a feel for our publishing attitude, we urge you to buy one or more of our publications before submitting. Prefer the exotic, the surreal, the sensual—work that provokes, shocks . . . work that continues to resonate long after being read. Surprise us." Does not want "rhyme or fixed forms, unless remarkably well done. No nature, animal, religious, or pet themes." Has published poetry by Steve Wilson, Guy Beining, Laura Ryder, Donald Rawley, Harry Burrus, and Jenny Kelly. As a sample the editor selected these lines from "Late November, Los Angeles" in *Steaming* by Donald Rawley:

In this rubbed dusk,/the false fall sky/silvers itself/into a pale, nude witch,/a sun of mother's cologne,/ and a neck of distanced chill

Sample: $8.

How to Submit: "We have work we want to publish, hence, unsolicited material is not encouraged. However, we will read and consider material from committed, serious writers as time permits. Query with four sample poems. Write, do not call about material. No reply without SASE." Cover letter with bio preferred. Responds in 6 weeks. Always sends prepublication galleys. Author receives percent of press run.

Advice: "Too many writers are only interested in getting published and not interested in reading or supporting good writing. Black Tie hesitates to endorse a writer who does not, in turn, promote and patronize (by actual purchases) small press publications. Once Black Tie publishes a writer, we intend to remain with that artist."

⚑ $⬯ BLACK WARRIOR REVIEW, P.O. Box 862936, Tuscaloosa AL 35486-0027. (205)348-4518. Website: www.sa.ua.edu/osm/bwr (includes guidelines, names of editors, poetry, and subscription information). Established 1974. **Poetry Editor:** Mark Neely. **Editor:** T. J. Beitelman.

• Poetry published in *Black Warrior Review* has been included in the 1997, 1999, and 2000 volumes of *The Best American Poetry* and *Pushcart Prize* anthologies.

Magazine Needs: *Black Warrior Review* is a semiannual review. Has published poetry by W.S. Merwin, Tomaz Salamun, Nancy Eimers, Alice Notley, Thomas Rabbitt, and C.D. Wright. As a sample the editor selected these lines from "The Birth of a Saint" by Bob Hicok:

If there's a gun in her theory of Heaven it's unloaded,/pearl-handled, graced with the feel of flesh/ extending from hand to steel, the confidence/of her palm radiating to the man . . .

Black Warrior Review is 200 pgs., 6×9. Press run is 2,000. Subscription: $14. Sample: $8.

How to Submit: Submit 3-6 poems at a time. Accepts simultaneous submissions if noted. No electronic submissions. Responds in 4 months. Pays $30-45/poem plus 2 copies. Acquires first rights. Reviews books of poetry in single or multi-book format. Poets may send books for review consideration.

Also Offers: Awards one $500 prize annually to a poet whose work appeared in either the fall or spring issue.

Advice: "We solicit a nationally-known poet for a chapbook section. The remainder of the issue is chosen from unsolicited submissions. Many of our poets have substantial publication credits, but our decision is based simply on the quality of the work submitted."

⊕ ⬯ ◎ BLACKWATER PRESS (Specialized: regional), P.O. Box 5115, Leicester LE2 8ZD Great Britain. Established 1996. **Contact:** Hilary Solanki.

Book/Chapbook Needs: Blackwater Press "aims to publish poets based in the United Kingdom who have established a reputation in journals, pamphlets, etc., but who have not yet had a full collection published." The press publishes 3-4 paperbacks/year. Has published *A Year Without Apricots* by Kate Foley, *The Getting of Vellum* by Catherine Byron, and *Einstein's Bumblebee* by Colin Sutherill. Books are usually about 50 pgs., 21 × 15cm, professionally printed and perfect bound with soft cover. Blackwater Press is currently not accepting unsolicited mss.

N: ◎ BLIND BEGGAR PRESS; LAMPLIGHT EDITIONS; NEW RAIN (Specialized: ethnic, anthology, children), P.O. Box 437, Williamsbridge Station, Bronx NY 10467. Phone/fax: (914)683-6792. Established 1976. **Literary Editor:** Gary Johnston. **Business Manager:** C.D. Grant.

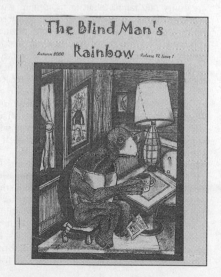

Because cover art submissions proved to be unpredictable, Melody Sherosky, editor of *Blind Man's Rainbow,* now works "closely with one of three artists to produce a cover." This pen and ink drawing originated as a "seed" concept of a turtle drinking coffee; Mark Gardner, a graphic artist from Pittsburgh, decided to set the image in a local coffee shop.

Book/Chapbook Needs: Publishes work "relevant to Black and Third World people, especially women." *New Rain* is an annual anthology of such work. Wants to see "quality work that shows a concern for the human condition and the condition of the world—art for people's sake." Has published work by Judy D. Simmons, A.H. Reynolds, Mariah Britton, Kurt Lampkin, Rashidah Ismaili, Jose L. Garza, and Carletta Wilson. *New Rain* is a 60- to 200-page book, digest-sized, finely printed, saddle-stapled or perfect-bound, with simple art, card covers. Sample: $5. Also publishes about 3 collections of poetry by individuals each year, 60-100 pgs., flat-spined paperback, glossy, color cover, good printing on good paper. Sample: $5.95.

How to Submit: For either the anthology or book publication, first send sample of 5-10 poems with cover letter including biographical background, philosophy, and poetic principles. Considers simultaneous submissions. Reads submissions January 15 through September 1 only. Responds to queries in 4 weeks, to submissions in 3 months. Pays copies (the number depending on the print run). Acquires all rights. Returns them "unconditionally." Willing to work out individual terms for subsidy publication. Catalog available for SASE.

Also Offers: Lamplight Editions is a subsidiary that publishes "educational materials such as children's books, manuals, greeting cards with educational material in them, etc."

THE BLIND MAN'S RAINBOW, P.O. Box 1557, Erie PA 16507-0557. E-mail: bmrainbow@excite.com. Website: www.angelfire.com/on2/blindmansrainbow (includes writer's guidelines, subscription information, poets, and covers from latest issues). Established 1993. **Editor:** Melody Sherosky.

Magazine Needs: *Blind Man's Rainbow* is a quarterly publication "whose focus is to create a diverse collection of quality poetry and art." Wants "all forms of poetry (Beat, rhyme, free verse, haiku, etc.), though excessively long poems are less likely to be accepted. All subject matter accepted." Does not want "anything graphically sexual or violent." Accepts poetry written by children. As a sample the editor selected these lines from "Fiddlehead Harvest" by Maija Barnett:

> Hunched over mud/and last summer's leaves/my fingers dig/into/thick clumps of ferns/curled like a
> fetus/inside their coppery sheaths.

The Blind Man's Rainbow is 20-24 pgs., 8½×11, photocopied and side-stapled, paper cover with art, line drawings inside. Receives about 500 submissions a month. Subscription: $10 US, $14 foreign. Sample: $3 US, $4 foreign. Make checks payable to Melody Sherosky.

How to Submit: Submit 2-10 poems at a time with name and address on each poem. Include SASE. Accepts previously published poems and simultaneous submissions, "but it is nice to let us know." No e-mail submissions. Cover letter preferred. "Submissions only returned if requested and with adequate postage." Time between acceptance and publication is up to 6 months. Often comments on rejected poems. Guidelines available for SASE, by e-mail or on website. Responds in 3 months. Pays 1 copy. Acquires one-time rights.

BLUE COLLAR REVIEW; PARTISAN PRESS; WORKING PEOPLE'S POETRY COMPETITION (Specialized: political, social issues, women/feminism, working class), P.O. Box 11417, Norfolk VA 23517. E-mail: redart@infi.net. Website: www.angelfire.com/va/bcr (includes mission statement, sample poetry, rate of publication, subscription information, and a list of available chapbook collections). *Blue Collar Review* established 1997. Partisan Press established 1993. **Editor:** A. Markowitz. **Co-Editor:** Mary Franke.

Magazine Needs: *Blue Collar Review* (*Journal of Progressive Working Class Literature*) is published quarterly and contains poetry, short stories, and illustrations "reflecting the working class experience, a broad range from the personal to the societal. Our purpose is to promote and expand working class literature and an awareness of the connections between workers of all occupations and the social context in which we live. Also to inspire the creativity and latent talent in 'common' working people." Wants "writing of high quality which reflects the working class experience from delicate internal awareness to the militant. We accept a broad range of style and focus—but are generally progressive, political/social. Nothing racist, sexist-misogynist, right wing, or overly religious. No 'bubba' poetry, nothing overly introspective or confessional, no acedemic/abstract or 'Vogon' poetry. No simple beginners rhyme or verse." Has published poetry by Martín Espada, Robert Edwards, Anne Wilson, Jeff Vande Zande, Charles Pott, Theresinka Pereira, and Rob Whitbeck. As a sample the editor selected these lines from "Note to Wall Street" by Rob Whitbeck:

> And you, parasites, with your paper stakes/claimed in that ancient place/where you add our
> substraction,/look once at me./I am a worker./Your dead weight/aches in our limbs.

Blue Collar Review is 56 pgs., 8½×5½, offset-printed and saddle-stapled with colored card cover, includes b&w illustrations and literary ads. Receives hundreds of poems/year, accepts about 30%. Press run is 350 for 200 subscribers of which 8 are libraries, 50 shelf sales. Subscription: $15/year. Sample: $5. Make checks payable to Partisan Press.

How to Submit: Submit up to 4 poems at a time; "no complete manuscripts please." Accepts previously published poems and simultaneous submissions. No e-mail submissions. Cover letter preferred. "Poems should be typed as they are to appear upon publication. Author's name and address should appear on every page. Overly long lines reduce chances of acceptance as line may have to be broken to fit the page size and format of the journal." Time between acceptance and publication is 3 months to 1 year. Poems are reviewed by editor and co-editor. Seldom comments on rejected poems. SASE for response. Responds in 3 months. Sends prepublication galleys only upon request. Pays 1-3 copies. Reviews of chapbooks and journals accepted.

Book/Chapbook Needs & How to Submit: Partisan Press looks for "poetry of power that reflects a working class consciousness and which moves us forward as a society. Must be good writing reflecting social/political issues, militancy desired but not didactic screed." Publishes about 3 chapbooks/year and are not presently open to unsolicited submissions. "Submissions are requested from among the poets published in the *Blue Collar Review*." Chapbooks are usually 20-60 pgs., 5½ × 8½, offset-printed and saddle-stapled with card or glossy cover. Sample chapbooks are $5 and listed on website.

Also Offers: Sponsors the Working People's Poetry Competition. Entry fee: $15 per entry. Prize: $100 and 1-year subscription to *Blue Collar Review*. Deadline: May 1. Winner of the 2000 Working People's Poetry Competition is Anne Babson. "Include cover letter with entry and make check payable to Partisan Press."

Advice: "Don't be afraid to try. Read a variety of poetry and find your own voice. Write about reality, your own experience, and what moves you."

BLUE LIGHT PRESS; THE BLUE LIGHT POETRY PRIZE AND CHAPBOOK CONTEST, P.O. Box 642, Fairfield IA 52556. (641)472-7882. E-mail: bluelightpress@aol.com. Established 1988. **Chief Editor:** Diane Frank.

Book/Chapbook Needs: Publishes 2 paperbacks, 3 chapbooks/year. "We like poems that are imagistic, emotionally honest, and uplifting, where the writer pushes through the imagery to a deeper level of insight and understanding. No rhymed poetry." Has published poetry by Kate Gray, Viktor Tichy, Tom Centolella, and Diane Averill. As a sample the editor selected these lines from *Where She Goes* by Kate Gray:

> On the river rowing blind, all I really know/is her voice, its tone and thickness consistent as/blood
> flowing through veins. In the double, she tells me/when to risk, how to jump at "Attention,/Go," to
> push through pain of breathing without/air. Each a Ruth for the other, we back away/from some
> women's warnings . . .

Where She Goes is 32 pgs., digest-sized, professionally printed and flat-spined with elegant matte card cover, includes woodcuts by Molly Bellman: $8 plus $1 p&h. Also published 3 anthologies of visionary poets.

How to Submit: Does not accept e-mail submissions. Send SASE for submission deadlines. Has an editorial board and "work in person with local poets, have an ongoing poetry workshop, give classes, and will edit/critique poems by mail—$30 for 4-5 poems."

Also Offers: Sponsors the Blue Light Poetry Prize and Chapbook Contest. "The winner will be published by Blue Light Press, receive a $100 honorarium and 50 copies of his or her book, which can be sold for $8 each, for a total of $500." Submit ms of 10-24 pages, typed or printed with a laser or inkjet printer, between March 1, 2002 and May 1, 2002. Entry fee: $10. Make checks payable to Blue Light Press. Include SASE. No ms will be returned without a SASE. Winner will be announced on or before September 1, 2002, and the book will be published in December, 2002. Send SASE for more information.

BLUE MESA REVIEW, Dept. of English, Humanities Bldg. #217, University of New Mexico, Albuquerque NM 87131-1106. (505)277-6155. Fax: (505)277-5573. E-mail: bluemesa@unm.edu. Website: www.unm. edu/~bluemesa (includes current news about recent issues, sample cover art and writing, and guidelines). Established 1989 by Rudolfo Anaya. **Managing Editor:** Elise McHugh.

Magazine Needs: *Blue Mesa Review* is an annual review of poetry, short fiction, creative essays, and book reviews. Wants "all kinds of free, organic verse; poems of place encouraged. Limits: four poems or six pages of poetry; one story; one essay. We accept theoretical essays as well as fiction, poetry, nonfiction, and book reviews." Has published poetry by Virgil Suarez, David Axelrod, and Brian Swann. As a sample they selected these lines from "Que Milagro" by Melissa Flores:

> a poco piensas que you can hold/back the swelling tide with one hand/leading the pledge of allegiance
> with the other/then you believe/in the power la fuerza/of miracles

Blue Mesa Review is about 250 pgs., 6 × 9, professionally printed and flat-spined with glossy cover, photos, and graphics. This hefty publication includes a number of long poems—several spanning 3 pages. Receives about 1,000 poems/year, accepts about 10% or less. Press run is 1,000 for 600 shelf sales. Sample: $12.

How to Submit: "Please submit two copies of everything with your name, address and telephone number on each page. Fax numbers and e-mail addresses are also appreciated." No previously published poems or simultaneous submissions. No electronic submissions. Cover letter required. Accepts mss from July 1 through October 1 only. Poems are then passed among readers and voted on. Guidelines available on website. Reports on mss by mid-December to mid-January. Pays 2 copies. Reviews books of poetry and fiction. Poets may send books for review consideration.

BLUE UNICORN, A TRIQUARTERLY OF POETRY; BLUE UNICORN POETRY CONTEST, 22 Avon Rd., Kensington CA 94707. (510)526-8439. Established 1977. **Poetry Editors:** Ruth G. Iodice, Martha E. Bosworth, and Fred Ostrander.

Magazine Needs: *Blue Unicorn* wants "well-crafted poetry of all kinds, in form or free verse, as well as expert translations on any subject matter. We shun the trite or inane, the soft-centered, the contrived poem. Shorter poems have more chance with us because of limited space." Accepts poetry written by children. Has published poetry by James Applewhite, Kim Cushman, Patrick Worth Gray, Joan LaBombard, James Schevill, and Gail White. As a sample the editors selected these lines from "Laura, At Thirteen" by Deborah Warren:

> . . . When nouns and declensions/pale, will you, so serious, receive/everything the way you do this
> sentence?/Will the petals of your cheeks be scored/by persons, places, actions, older words,/and harder,
> than the Latin that you leave?

Blue Unicorn is "distinguished by its fastidious editing, both with regard to contents and format." It is 56 pgs., narrow digest-sized, finely printed, saddle-stapled, with some art. It features 40-50 poems in each issue, all styles, with the focus on excellence and accessibility. Receives over 35,000 submissions/year, accepts about 200, has a year's backlog. Single copy: $6, foreign add $2; subscription: $14/3 issues, foreign add $6.

How to Submit: Submit 3-5 typed poems on 8½×11 paper. No simultaneous submissions or previously published poems. "Cover letter OK, but will not affect our selection." Guidelines available for SASE. Responds in 3 months (generally within 6 weeks), sometimes with personal comment. Pays 1 copy.

Also Offers: Sponsors an annual contest with small entry fee, with prizes of $150, $75, $50, and sometimes special awards, distinguished poets as judges, publication of 3 top poems and 6 honorable mentions in the magazine. Entry fee: $6 for first poem, $3 for others to a maximum of 5. Write for current guidelines. Criticism occasionally offered.

Advice: "We would advise beginning poets to read and study poetry—both poets of the past and of the present; concentrate on technique; and discipline yourself by learning forms before trying to do without them. When your poem is crafted and ready for publication, study your markets and then send whatever of your work seems to be compatible with the magazine you are submitting to."

BLUELINE (Specialized: regional), Dept. PM, English Dept., Potsdam College, Potsdam NY 13676. Fax: (315)267-2043. E-mail: blueline@potsdam.edu. Established 1979. **Editor-in-Chief:** Rick Henry and an editorial board.

Magazine Needs: *Blueline* "is an annual literary magazine dedicated to prose and poetry about the Adirondacks and other regions similar in geography and spirit." Wants "clear, concrete poetry pertinent to the countryside and its people. It must go beyond mere description, however. We prefer a realistic to a romantic view. We do not want to see sentimental or extremely experimental poetry." Usually uses poems of 75 lines or fewer, though "occasionally we publish longer poems" on "nature in general, Adirondack Mountains in particular. Form may vary, can be traditional or contemporary." Has published poetry by L.M. Rosenberg, John Unterecker, Lloyd Van Brunt, Laurence Josephs, Maurice Kenny, and Nancy L. Nielsen. *Blueline* is 200 pgs., 6×9, with 90 pgs. of poetry in each issue. Press run is 600. Sample copies: $4 for back issues.

How to Submit: Submit 3 poems at a time. Include short bio. No simultaneous submissions. Submit September 1 through November 30 only. Occasionally comments on rejected poems. Guidelines available for SASE or by e-mail. Responds in 10 weeks. Pays 1 copy. Acquires first North American serial rights. Reviews books of poetry in 500-750 words, single or multi-book format.

Advice: "We are interested in both beginning and established poets whose poems evoke universal themes in nature and show human interaction with the natural world. We look for thoughtful craftsmanship rather than stylistic trickery."

BOA EDITIONS, LTD., 260 East Ave., Rochester NY 14604. (716)546-3410. E-mail: boaedit@frontiernet .net. Website: www.info-boaeditions.org. Established 1976. **Poetry Editor:** Thom Ward. Has published some of the major American poets, such as W.D. Snodgrass, John Logan, Isabella Gardner, Richard Wilbur, and Lucille Clifton. Also publishes introductions by major poets of those less well-known. For example, Gerald Stern wrote the foreword for Li-Young Lee's *Rose*. Guidelines available for SASE. Pays 10 copies.

BOGG PUBLICATIONS; BOGG, (Specialized: experimental), 422 N. Cleveland St., Arlington VA 22201-1424. Established 1968. **Poetry Editors:** John Elsberg (USA), George Cairncross (UK: 31 Belle Vue St., Filey, N. Yorkshire YO 14 9HU England), Wilga Rose (Australia: 13 Urara Rd., Avalon Beach, NSW 2107 Australia), and Sheila Martindale (Canada: P.O. Box 23148, 380 Wellington St., London, Ontario NGA 5N9 Canada).

Magazine Needs: Appearing at least twice/year, *Bogg* is "a journal of contemporary writing with an Anglo-American slant. Its contents combines innovative American work with a range of writing from England and the Commonwealth. It includes poetry (to include haiku, prose poems, and experimental/visual poems), very short experimental or satirical fiction, interviews, essays on the small press scenes both in America and in England / the Commonwealth, reviews, review essays, and line art. We also publish occasional free-for-postage pamphlets." The magazine uses a great deal of poetry in each issue (with several featured poets)—"poetry in all styles, with a healthy leavening of shorts (under ten lines). Prefer original voices." Accepts all styles, all subject matter. "Some have even found the magazine's sense of play offensive. Overt religious and political poems have to have strong poetical merits—statement alone is not sufficient." *Bogg* started in England and in 1975 began including a supplement of American work; it now is published in the US and mixes US, Canadian, Australian, and UK work with reviews of small press publications from all of those areas. Has published work by Martin Galvin, John M. Bennett, Marcia Arrieta, Harriet Zinnes, and Steve Sneyd. As a sample the editors selected these lines from "The Word" by American poet Harriet Zinnes:

> It is time to be open. To be free of metaphor. To let desire walk/naked. In the word. The word, stripped,
> bare, not even in swaddling/clothes. The word that is not an object. Not a frame of meaning. Like/a
> stone, the word.

Bogg is about 72 pgs., typeset, saddle-stapled, in a 6×9 format that leaves enough white space to let each poem stand and breathe alone. There are about 50 pgs. of poetry/issue. Receives over 10,000 American poems/year, accepts about 100-150. Press run is 850 for 400 subscribers of which 20 are libraries. Single copy: $4.50; subscription: $12 for 3 issues. Sample: $3.50.

How to Submit: Submit 6 poems at a time. No simultaneous submissions. Cover letters preferred. "They can help us get a 'feel' for the writer's intentions/slant." SASE required or material discarded ("no exceptions.") Prefer typewritten manuscripts, with author's name and address on each sheet. "We will reprint previously published material, but with a credit line to a previous publisher." Guidelines available for SASE. Responds in 1 week. Pays 2 copies. Acquires one-time rights. Reviews books and chapbooks of poetry in 250 words, single book format. Poets may send books to relevant editor (by region) for review consideration.

Book/Chapbook Needs & How to Submit: Their occasional pamphlets and chapbooks are by *invitation only*, the author receiving 25% of the print run, and you can get chapbook samples free for 6×9 SASE. "Better make it at least 2 ounces worth of postage."

Advice: "Become familiar with a magazine before submitting to it. Long lists of previous credits irritate me. Short notes about how the writer has heard about *Bogg* or what he or she finds interesting or annoying in the magazine I read with some interest."

✓ ◑ **BOMBAY GIN**, Naropa University, 2130 Arapahoe Ave., Boulder CO 80302. (303)546-3540. Fax: (303)546-5297. E-mail: bgin@naropa.edu or jhuntera@naropa.edu. Website: www.naropa.edu/gin.html (includes writer's guidelines, sample poems from most recent issue, and current cover art). Established 1974. **Contact:** Judith Huntera.

Magazine Needs: "*Bombay Gin*, appearing in June, is the annual literary magazine of the Jack Kerouac School of Disembodied Poetics at Naropa University. Produced and edited by MFA students, *Bombay Gin* publishes established poets and fiction writers alongside new writers. It has a special interest in works that push conventional literary boundaries." Recent issues have included works by Lisa Jarnot, Anne Waldman, Wang Ping, Keith Abbott, and Ted Berrigan. As a sample the editor selected these lines from "Evidence" by Max Regan:

> both of us today/with an aversion to dreams/both of us stacking tasks/like cordwood/both asleep inside/
> the iris of an eye.

Bombay Gin is 124 pgs., 6×9, professionally printed, perfect-bound with color card cover, includes art and photos. Receives about 300 poems/year, accepts about 5%. Press run is 500, 400 shelf sales; 100 distributed free to contributors. Single copy: $10. Sample: $5.

How to Submit: "Submit up to 3 pages of poetry or up to 8 pages of prose/fiction (12 pt. Times New Roman). Art may be submitted as slides, negatives, or prints." No previously published poems or simultaneous submissions. Accepts disk submissions (PC format). Cover letter preferred. Reply with SASE only. Deadline: December 1. Submissions read December 15 through March 15. Guidelines available for SASE or on website. Notification of acceptance/rejection: April 15. Pays 2 copies. Acquires one-time rights.

◑ **THE BOOKPRESS: THE NEWSPAPER OF THE LITERARY ARTS**, The DeWitt Bldg., 215 N. Cayuga St., Ithaca NY 14850. (607)277-2254. Fax: (607)275-9221. E-mail: bookpress@clarityconnect.com. Website: www.thebookery.com/Bookpress. Established 1990. **Editor/Publisher:** Jack Goldman.

Magazine Needs: *Bookpress* appears 8 times/year, each month except January, June, July, and August. As for poetry, the editor says, "The only criterion is a commitment to the aesthetic power of language. Avoid the hackneyed and formulaic." Has published poetry by Phyllis Janowitz, Kathleen Gemmell, and A.R. Ammons. *The Bookpress* is a 12-page tabloid. Receives about 50 poems/year, accepts about 10%. Press run is 6,500 for 300 subscribers of which 15 are libraries. Subscription: $12/year. Sample copies free.

How to Submit: No previously published poems or simultaneous submissions. Accepts e-mail submissions, include in body of message. Cover letter preferred. Reads submissions August 1 through April 1 only. SASE required. Time between acceptance and publication is 1 month. Often comments on rejected poems. Guidelines available for SASE. Responds in 3 months. Pays 2 copies. Acquires first North American serial rights. Reviews books of poetry. Length of reviews varies, typically between 1,500-2,000 words, sometimes longer. Poets may send books for review consideration.

◑ ◎ **BORDERLANDS: TEXAS POETRY REVIEW (Specialized: regional, translations, bilingual/foreign language)**, P.O. Box 33096, Austin TX 78764. E-mail: cgilbert@austin.rr.com. Website: www.borderlands.org (includes submission guidelines, sample poems, calendar of events, etc.). Established 1992. **Contact:** editor.

Magazine Needs: *Borderlands* appears twice/year publishing "high-quality, outward-looking poetry by new and established poets, as well as brief reviews of poetry books and critical essays. Cosmopolitan in content, but particularly welcomes Texas and Southwest writers." Wants "outward-looking poems that exhibit social, political, geographical, historical, feminist, or spiritual awareness coupled with concise artistry. We also seek poems in two languages (one of which must be English), where the poet has written both versions. Please, no introspective work about the speaker's psyche, childhood, or intimate relationships." Has published poetry by Walter McDonald, Naomi Shihab Nye, Mario Susko, Wendy Barker, Larry D. Thomas, and Reza Shirazi. As a sample the editors selected these lines from "Good Sense, Fine Food" by Robert Parhem:

> . . .Reason is an easy thing/to render up in the land of madness.

Borderlands is 80-120 pgs., 5½ × 8½, offset, perfect-bound, with 4-color cover, art by local artists. Receives about 2,000 poems/year, accepts about 120. Press run is 1,000. Subscription: $17/year; $33/2 years. Sample: $10. **How to Submit:** Submit 5 typed poems at a time. No previously published poems or simultaneous submissions. No e-mail submissions. Include SASE (or SAE and IRCs) with sufficient postage to return poems. Seldom comments on rejected poems. Guidelines are available on website. Responds in 6 months. Pays 1 copy. Acquires first rights. Reviews books of poetry in one page. Also uses 3- to 6-page essays on single poets and longer essays (3,500-word maximum) on contemporary poetry in some larger context (query first). Address poetry submissions to "Editors, *Borderlands*."
Also Offers: The Writers' League of Texas is a state-wide group open to the general public. Established in 1981, the purpose of the Writers' League of Texas is "to provide a forum for information, support, and sharing among writers; to help members improve and market their skills; and to promote the interests of writers and the writing community." Currently has 1,600 members. Annual membership dues are $45. Send SASE for more information to: The Writers' League of Texas, 1501 W. 5th St., Suite E-2, Austin TX 78703.

BORDERLINES; ANGLO-WELSH POETRY SOCIETY, Nant Y Brithyll, Llangynyw, Powys SY21 OJS United Kingdom. Established 1977. **Editor:** Kevin Bamford. **Editor:** Dave Bingham.
Magazine Needs: *Borderlines* is published biannually to encourage reading and writing of poetry. "We try to be open-minded and look at anything. We do not normally publish very long poems. Most poems fit on one page. No poems about poems; unshaped recitals of thoughts and/or feelings." Has published poetry by Peter Abbs, Mike Jenkins, and Vuyelwa Carlin. As a sample we selected this poem, "fane" by Gigliola Millard:

> supine in the cathedral wood/summer light faint/through green-dark eaves/for the briefest of moments/
> out hands are still-/carved sinners reminded of repentant days

Borderlines is 40-48 pgs., 7 × 10, neatly printed and saddle-stapled with light card cover, art on cover only. Receives about 600 poems/year, accepts about 16%. Press run is 200 for 100 subscribers of which 8 are libraries. Single copy: £1.50; subscription: £3, other EU countries £4, non-EU countries £5. Make checks payable to Anglo-Welsh Poetry Society.
How to Submit: Cover letter preferred. "Please write name and address on each poem sheet." Time between acceptance and publication is up to 6 months. Seldom comments on rejected poems. Guidelines available for SASE (or SAE and IRC). Responds in 6 weeks. Sometimes sends prepublication galleys. Pays 1 copy.
Also Offers: "The Anglo-Welsh Poetry Society is a group of people interested in the reading, writing, and promotion of poetry, particularly in the Marches—the Anglo-Welsh border country. It is based in the border counties of Shropshire and Montgomeryshire, though there are members all over the country. A core group of members meets on the first Tuesday of the month at the Loggerheads pub in Shrewsbury. Other meetings such as readings, workshops, poetry parties are arranged at intervals over the course of the year. A monthly newsletter gives information of interest to members on events, publications, competitions, and other news of the poetry world." Membership fee for AWPS is £7.50/year.

BORDIGHERA, INC.; VOICES IN ITALIAN AMERICANA; VIA FOLIOS; THE BORDIGHERA POETRY PRIZE; ANIELLO LAURI AWARD (Specialized: ethnic/nationality), P.O. Box 1374, Lafayette IN 47902-1374. Phone/fax: (765)474-6330. E-mail: atamburri@fau.edu. Established 1990. **Editors:** Anthony Julian Tamburri, Paolo Giordano, and Fred Gardaphé.
Magazine Needs: *Voices in Italian Americana* (*VIA*) is "a semiannual literary and cultural review devoted to the dissemination of information concerning the contributions of and about Italian Americans to the cultural and art worlds of North America." Open to all kinds of poetry. Has published poetry by Daniela Gioseffi, David Citino, Felix Stefanile, and Dana Gioia. As a sample the editor selected these lines from "Coming To Know Empedokles" by Diane diPrima:

> A couple of millennia seems like a moment:/This song cd be planting rite of black Sicilians/in autumn
> fields behind a small house/the sounds / the colors as if/intervening greys & anglo stillness/had never
> entered.

VIA is about 250 pgs., 8½ × 5½, docutech printed, perfect-bound with glossy paper cover, includes art and ads. Receives about 150 poems/year, accepts about 25%. Press run is 500 for 300 subscribers of which 50 are libraries, 50 shelf sales; 50 distributed free to contributors. Subscription: $20 individual; $15 student/senior citizen; $25 institutional; $30 foreign. Sample: $10. Make checks payable to Bordighera, Inc.
How to Submit: No previously published poems or simultaneous submissions. Accepts e-mail and disk submissions. Cover letter required. Reads submissions October 1 through May 31 only. Time between acceptance and publication is 3 months. Poems are circulated to an editorial board. Often comments on rejected poems. Publishes theme issues occasionally. Guidelines and upcoming themes available for SASE. Responds in 6 weeks. Always sends prepublication galleys. Acquires all rights. Rights returned upon publication. "But in subsequent publications, poet must acknowledge first printing in *VIA*." Reviews books and chapbooks of poetry in 500-1,000 words, single book format. Poets may send books for review consideration to Fred Gardaphé, Center for Italian Studies, State University of New York, Stony Brook NY 11794-3358.
Book/Chapbook Needs & How to Submit: Bordighera, under the imprint *VIA* Folios, has published *The Silver Lake of Love Poems* by Emmanuel di Pasquale, *Going On* by Daniela Gioseffi, *Sardinia/Sardegna* by Robert Lima, and *The Book of Madness and Love* by Arthur L. Clements. Publishes 5 titles/year with the print run for each paperback being 550. Books are usually 50-75 pgs., 8½ × 5½, docutech printed and perfect-bound

with glossy paper cover and art. Query first, with a variety of sample poems and a cover letter with brief bio and publication credits. Responds to queries in 2 weeks; to mss in 6 weeks. Pays 10% royalties. Offers subsidy arrangements. Poets are required to subsidize 50% of publishing costs. "Author regains subsidy through sales with 50% royalties up to subvention paid, 10% thereafter."

Also Offers: Sponsors the Bordighera Poetry Prize, which awards book publication and $2,000, and the Aniello Lauri Award, which awards $150 plus publication in *Voices in Italian Americana*. Contest rules available for SASE.

BOREALIS PRESS; TECUMSEH PRESS LTD.; JOURNAL OF CANADIAN POETRY (Specialized: regional), 110 Bloomingdale St., Ottawa, Ontario K2C 4A4 Canada. (613)798-9299. Fax: (613)798-7974. E-mail: borealis@istar.ca. Website: www.borealispress.com. Established 1972. Presently not considering unsolicited submissions.

Also Offers: The *Journal of Candian Poetry* is an annual that publishes articles, reviews, and criticism, not poetry. Sample: $15.95.

$ BOSTON REVIEW, E53-407, MIT, 30 Wadsworth St., Cambridge MA 02139-4307. (617)253-3642. Fax: (617)252-1549. Website: www.polisci.mit.edu/BostonReview/. Established 1975. **Poetry Editors:** Mary Jo Bang and Timothy Donnelly.

• Poetry published by this review has been included in *The Best American Poetry* (1998 and 2000 volumes).

Magazine Needs: *Boston Review* is a bimonthly tabloid format magazine of arts, culture, and politics which uses about 30 poems/year, for which they receive about 3,000 submissions. "We are open to both traditional and experimental forms. What we value most is originality and a strong sense of voice." Has published poetry by Gilbert Sorrentino, Heather McHugh, Richard Howard, Allen Grossman, Cole Swenson, Tan Lin, and Claudia Rankine. Circulation is 20,000 nationally including subscriptions and newsstand sales. Single copy: $3.50; subscription: $17. Sample: $4.50.

How to Submit: Submit 3-5 poems at a time. Submissions and inquiries are accepted via regular mail only. Cover letter with brief bio encouraged. Has a 6-12 month backlog. Responds in 3 months. Pays $40/poem plus 5 copies. Acquires first serial rights. Reviews books of poetry. Only using *solicited* reviews. Publishers may send books for review consideration.

Also Offers: Sponsors an annual poetry contest. Awards publication and $1,000. Submit up to 5 unpublished poems, no more than 10 pgs. total, with postcard to acknowledge receipt. Deadline: June 1. Entry fee: $15. Guidelines available for SASE.

$ BOULEVARD, 4579 Laclede Ave. #332, St. Louis MO 63108-2103. (314)361-2986. Website: www.boulevardmagazine.com. Established 1985. **Editor:** Richard Burgin.

• Poetry published in *Boulevard* has been inclined in *The Best American Poetry* and *Pushcart Prize* anthologies.

Magazine Needs: *Boulevard* appears 3 times/year. "*Boulevard* strives to publish only the finest in fiction, poetry, and nonfiction (essays and interviews; we do not accept book reviews). While we frequently publish writers with previous credits, we are very interested in publishing less experienced or unpublished writers with exceptional promise. We've published everything from John Ashbery to Donald Hall to a wide variety of styles from new or lesser known poets. We're eclectic. Do not want to see poetry that is uninspired, formulaic, self-conscious, unoriginal, insipid." Has published poetry by Amy Clampitt, Molly Peacock, Jorie Graham, and Mark Strand. *Boulevard* is 200 pgs., digest-sized, professionally printed, flat-spined, with glossy card cover. Their press run is 3,500 with 1,200 subscribers of which 200 are libraries. Subscription: $15. Sample: $8 plus 5 first-class stamps and SASE.

How to Submit: Submit up to 5 poems at a time. Line length for poetry is 200 maximum. Does not accept fax or e-mail submissions. "Prefer name and number on each page. All submissions must include an SASE. Encourage cover letters but don't require them. Will consider simultaneous submissions but not previously published poems." Reads submissions October 1 through April 1 only. Editor sometimes comments on rejected poems. Responds in about 3 months. Pays $25-250/poem, depending on length, plus 1 copy. Acquires first-time publication and anthology rights.

Advice: "Write from your heart as well as your head."

BRANDO'S HAT; TARANTULA PUBLICATIONS, 14 Vine St., Kersal, Salford, Manchester M7 3PG United Kingdom. Phone/fax: (0161)792 4593. E-mail: tarantula_pubs@lineone.net. Established 1998. **Contact:** Sean Body.

Magazine Needs: *Brando's Hat* appears 3 times/year. Wants "extremely high-quality poetry only. No restrictions on subject matter, form or style." Does not want "careless, unrhythmical, boring, unoriginal work—i.e., 90 percent of what we get." Has published poetry by Tony Curtis, Peter Sansom, Kevin Crossley-Holland, and John Latham. As a sample they selected these lines from "Searching" by Gaia Holmes:

*Night falls/like you slip into my head/I smell the scent of something late./You're curled into yourself/
like paper when it burns/and a hundred black moths*

Brando's Hat is 42 pgs., A5, laser-printed, and saddle-stapled with color card cover. Receives about 1,300 poems/year, accepts about 10%. Press run is 250 for 200 subscribers. Subscription: £13 Sterling. Sample: £5 Sterling. Make checks (Sterling only) payable to Tarantula Publications.

How to Submit: Submit 6 or more poems at a time. No previously published poems or simultaneous submissions. Cover letter required. "Cover letters should give brief (just a few lines) biographical details, publications, etc. Must include SAE with appropriate postage [or IRCs], otherwise discarded." Time between acceptance and publication is 3 months. Poems are circulated to an editorial board. "There are four editors (all poets). Decisions for publishing have to be unanimous." Seldom comments on rejected poems. Responds in 3 months or less. Pays 1 copy. Acquires first rights.

N 🖊 ◎ **BREAKAWAY BOOKS (Specialized: sports)**, P.O. Box 24, Halcottsville NY 12438-0024. (212)898-0408. E-mail: Garth@breakawaybooks.com. Website: www.breakawaybooks.com. Established 1994. **Publisher:** Garth Battista.

Book/Chapbook Needs & How to Submit: Breakaway Books publishes "sports literature—fiction, essays, and poetry on the athletic experience." Wants "Poetry on sports only—for intelligent, literate athletes; book-length collections or book-length poems only." Accepts previously published poems and simultaneous submissions. Accepts e-mail submissions; no disk submissions. Query first, with a few sample poems and a cover letter with brief bio and publication credits. Responds to queries in 2 weeks; to mss in 2 months. Seldom comments on rejections. Pays royalties of 7-12%.

🏆 🖊 ◎ **THE BRIAR CLIFF REVIEW (Specialized: regional)**, Briar Cliff College, 3303 Rebecca St., Sioux City IA 51104-2340. E-mail: emmons@briar-cliff.edu. Website: www.briar-cliff.edu/administrative/publications/bccrevie/bcreview.htm (includes writer's guidelines, annual contest guidelines, and sample contest winners). Established 1989. **Managing Editor:** Tricia Currans-Sheehan. **Poetry Editor:** Jeanne Emmons.

• *The Briar Cliff Review* received the 1998 Columbia Scholastic Association Gold Crown.

Magazine Needs: *The Briar Cliff Review*, appearing in April, is an attractive annual "eclectic literary and cultural magazine focusing on (but not limited to) Siouxland writers and subjects." Wants "quality poetry with strong imagery; especially interested in regional, Midwestern content with tight, direct, well-wrought language. No allegorical emotional landscapes." Has published poetry by Sandra Adelmund, Vivian Shipley, and Michael Carey. As a sample the editor selected these lines from "Eden of the New Moon" by Jonathan Stull:

> *and the apple drops, shaking the limb/that draws light from the back of the moon,/as the unpressed
> winesaps rise/and fall like some red,/unholy thunder*

The Briar Cliff Review is 64 pgs., 8½×11, professionally printed on 70 lb. matte paper, saddle-stapled, four-color cover on 10 pt. coated stock, b&w photos inside. Receives about 100 poems/year, accepts about 12. Press run is 500, all shelf sales. Sample: $9.

How to Submit: Submissions should be typewriten or letter quality, with author's name and address on the first page, with name on following pages. Accepts simultaneous submissions; no previously published poems. No fax or e-mail submissions. "We will assume that submissions are not simultaneous unless notified." Cover letter with short bio required. "No manuscripts returned without SASE." Reads submissions August 1 through November 1 only. Time between acceptance and publication is up to 6 months. Seldom comments on rejected poems. Responds in 6 months. Pays 2 copies. Acquires first serial rights.

🖊 ◎ **BRICKHOUSE BOOKS, INC.; NEW POETS SERIES, INC./CHESTNUT HILLS PRESS; STONEWALL SERIES (Specialized, Stonewall only: gay/lesbian/bisexual)**, 541 Piccadilly Rd., Baltimore MD 21204. (410)830-2869 or 828-0724. Fax: (410)830-3999. E-mail: charriss@towson.edu. Website: www.towson.edu/harriss/ (includes writer's guidelines, names of editors, list of in-print publications, plus sample poetry from individual books). Established 1970. **Editor/Director:** Clarinda Harriss, NPS. Along with Chestnut Hills Press, Stonewall is now a division of BrickHouse Books.

Book/Chapbook Needs: BrickHouse and The New Poets Series, Inc. brings out first books by promising new poets. Poets who have previously had book-length mss published are not eligible. Prior publication in journals and anthologies is strongly encouraged. Wants "excellent, fresh, nontrendy, literate, intelligent poems. Any form (including traditional), any style." BrickHouse Books and New Poets Series pay 20 author's copies (out of a press run of 1,000), the sales proceeds going back into the corporation to finance the next volume. "BrickHouse has been successful in its effort to provide writers with a national distribution; in fact, The New Poets Series was named an Outstanding Small Press by the prestigious Pushcart Awards Committee, which judges some 5,000 small press publications annually." Chestnut Hills Press publishes author-subsidized books—"High quality work only, however. Chestnut Hills Press has achieved a reputation for prestigious books, printing only the top 10% of mss Chestnut Hills Press and New Poets Series receive." Chestnut Hills Press authors receive proceeds from sale of their books. The Stonewall series publishes work with a gay, lesbian, or bisexual perspective. New Poets Series/Chestnut Hills Press has published books by Chester Wickwire, Ted McCrorie, Sharon White, Mariquita McManus, and Jeff Mann. As a sample the editor selected these lines from *To Move Into the House* from "Just After Dawn" by Richard Fein:

> *I woke to the murmur of my words./Leaning against the headboard/I yielded to the words that took
> me back/to my mother's slow death, how I finally stopped wishing/I had a sister to take her off my
> hands,/how we worked through that long illness to embrace/and she called me* Ruvn. Ruvn.

Brickhouse publishes 64-112 page works. Chapbooks: $8. Full-length books: $10.
How to Submit: Send a 50- to 55-page ms, $10 reading fee and cover letter giving publication credits and bio. Indicate if ms is to be considered for BrickHouse, New Poets Series, Chestnut Hills Press or Stonewall. Accepts simultaneous submissions. No e-mail submissions. Cover letters should be very brief, businesslike and include an accurate list of published work. Editor sometimes comments briefly on rejected poems. Responds in up to 1 year. Mss "are circulated to an editorial board of professional, publishing poets. BrickHouse is backlogged, but the best 10% of the mss it receives are automatically eligible for Chestnut Hills Press consideration," a subsidy arrangement. Send $5 and a 7×10 SASE for a sample volume.
Also Offers: Stonewall Series offers a chapbook contest whose winner is published by New Poets Series. Send 20-30 poems with $20 entry fee, postmarked no later than August 15. Rane Arroyo's *The Naked Thief* is a recent Stonewall winner.

$ ☺ BRIDGES: A JOURNAL FOR JEWISH FEMINISTS AND OUR FRIENDS (Specialized: Ethnic, women/feminism, social issues), P.O. Box 24839, Eugene OR 97402. Phone/fax: (541)343-7617. E-mail: ckinberg@pond.net. Website: www.pond.net/~ckinberg/bridges. Established 1990. **Managing Editor:** Clare Kinberg.
Magazine Needs: The biannual *Bridges* is "a showcase for Jewish women's creativity and involvement in social justice activism." Wants "anything original by Jewish women, not purely religious." Has published poetry by Emily Warn, Willa Schneberg, and Ellen Bass. As a sample the managing editor selected these lines from "I'll Tell You What My People Know of the Land" by Judith Arcana:
> Later, much later, who can say how it came to be, there were market stalls in Kiev, Bobroisk, the Ukraine, changing names and shifting borders with the decades. Every war made new rules to learn, new names, but still they came in the night to burn and tear at us. So we climbed on the wagon, hid our boxes under the straw, and rode out across the meadows by moonlight. The leather straps creaked all night, they made me think of something, something before.

Bridges is 128 pgs., 7×10, professionally printed on 50% recycled paper, perfect-bound, with 2-color cover, b&w photos inside. Receives about 200 poems/year, accepts about 20. Press run is 3,000 for 1,500 subscribers of which 70 are libraries, 300 shelf sales; 200 distributed free to exchanges, board members, funders. Subscription: $15/year. Sample: $7.50.
How to Submit: Submit 6-10 poems at a time. No previously published poems or simultaneous submissions. Cover letter preferred with 40 word bio. Time between acceptance and publication is 6 months. Poems are circulated to an editorial board. "Two poetry readers and sometimes others decide on poems." Often comments on rejected poems. Publishes theme issues. Guidelines available for SASE. Responds in 9 months. Sometimes sends prepublication galleys. Pays $50 per selection plus 3 copies. Sometimes reviews books of poetry. Poets may send books for review consideration.

✔ ◗ ☺ BRILLIANT CORNERS: A JOURNAL OF JAZZ & LITERATURE (Specialized: jazz-related literature), Lycoming College, Williamsport PA 17701. (570)321-4279. Fax: (570)321-4090. E-mail: bc@lycoming.edu. Website: www.lycoming.edu/BrilliantCorners. Established 1996. **Editor:** Sascha Feinstein.
Magazine Needs: *Brilliant Corners*, a biannual, publishes jazz-related poetry, fiction, and nonfiction. "We are open to length and form, but want work that is both passionate and well crafted—work worthy of our recent contributors. No sloppy hipster jargon or improvisatory nonsense." Has published poetry by Amiri Baraka, Jayne Cortez, Philip Levine, Colleen McElroy, and Al Young. As a sample the editor selected these lines from "Rhythm Method" by Yusef Komunyakaa:
> If you can see blues/in the ocean, light & dark,/can feel worms ease through/a subterranean path/
> beneath each footstep,/Baby, you got rhythm.

Brilliant Corners is 100 pgs., 6×9, commercially printed and perfect-bound with color card cover with original artwork, ads. Accepts about 5% of work received. Press run is 1,800 for 200 subscribers. Subscription: $12. Sample: $7.
How to Submit: Submit 3-5 poems at a time. Previously published poems "very rarely, and only by well established poets"; no simultaneous submissions. No e-mail or fax submissions. Cover letter preferred. Reads submissions September 1 through May 15 only. Seldom comments on rejected poems. Responds in 2 months. Pays 2 copies. Acquires first North American serial rights. Staff reviews books of poetry. Poets may send books for review consideration.

🌐 ☺ BRITISH HAIKU SOCIETY; BLITHE SPIRIT; THE MUSEUM OF HAIKU LITERATURE; JAMES W. HACKETT HAIKU AWARD (Specialized: membership, form/style, translations), Lena-cre Ford, Woolhope, Hereford HR1 4RF England. Website: www.britishhaikusociety.org. Established 1990. **Secretary:** David Walker.
Magazine Needs & How to Submit: *Blithe Spirit*, a quarterly journal, publishes mainly haiku, senryu, haibun, and tanka sent in by society members. Staff reviews books of poetry. Send books for review consideration. The British Haiku Society also publishes a newsletter and other occasional publications (pamphlets, folios).
Also Offers: The Museum of Haiku Literature, Tokyo, gives a quarterly best-of-issue award (£50). In addition, the British Haiku Society administers the annual James W. Hackett Haiku Award (currently £70). Rules of entry

are available annually in the spring. Send SASE (or SAE and IRC from outside England) to J.W. Hackett Award, % D. Cobb, Sinodun, Shalford, Essex CM7 5HN England. Also, the Sasakawa Prize for original contribution to haikai literatue is awarded biennially. Next deadline is December 31, 2001.

THE BROBDINGNAGIAN TIMES, 96 Albert Rd., Cork, Ireland. Phone: 353-21-311 227. Established 1996. **Editor:** Giovanni Malito.

Magazine Needs: *The Brobdingnagian Times* appears quarterly. "Its purpose and contents are international and eclectic. We wish to present a small sample of what is happening out there in the 'world' of poetry." Open to all kinds of poetry of 40 lines or less. "Translations are very welcome. Not very partial to rhyming forms." Accepts poetry written by children. Has published poetry by Miroslav Holub, Leonard Cirino, Ion Codescru, John Martone, and John Millet. *The Brobdingnagian Times* is 8 pgs., A3 sheet folded twice, photocopied from laser original. Receives about 300 poems/year, accepts about 10%. Press run is 250 for 65 subscribers, variable shelf sales; 12 distributed free to writers' groups. Subscription: $4. Sample: $1 or postage. Make checks payable to Giovanni Malito.

How to Submit: Submit 4-8 poems at a time. Line length for poetry is 1 minimum, 40 maximum. Accepts previously published poems and simultaneous submissions. Cover letter preferred. "SASE is required. If IRCs are not convenient then loose stamps for trade with Irish stamps are fine." Time between acceptance and publication is up to 6 months. Often comments on rejected poems. Publishes theme issues occasionally. Note: the theme issues appear as supplements. Guidelines and a list of upcoming themes are available for SASE. Responds in 1 month. Pays 2 copies. Acquires one-time rights. Staff reviews books and chapbooks of poetry in 300-500 words, single book format. Send books for review consideration.

Book/Chapbook Needs & How to Submit: The Brobdingnagian Times Press is open to any type of prose and/or poetry and publishes 2-8 chapbooks/year. Chapbooks are usually "palmtop" in size, photocopied from laser original and side-stapled with slightly heavier stock colored paper, cover art only. "The palmtops are quite small. They may be one long poem (8 pages) or several (8-16) short poems (less than 6 lines) or something in between. Collections (unless haiku/senryu) must be more or less themed." Responds to queries in 1 week; to mss in up to 3 weeks. Pays 50 author's copies (out of a press run of 100). "Poets outside of Ireland are asked to cover the postage." Order sample chapbooks by sending 2 IRCs.

Advice: "Nerve and verve and the willingness to edit: these are three qualities a poet must possess."

BROKEN BOULDER PRESS; GESTALTEN; NEOTROPE (Specialized: form/style), P.O. Box 6305, Santa Barbara CA 93160. E-mail: apowell10@hotmail.com or paulsilvia@hotmail.com. Website: www.brokenboulder.com (includes editor's information, submission guidelines, catalog, samples of previous offerings). Established 1996. **Co-Editor:** Adam Powell. **Co-Editor:** Paul Silvia.

Magazine Needs & How to Submit: *gestalten* appears 2 times/year and publishes experimental poetry from new and established writers. "We want experimental, abstract, collage, visual, language, asemic, found, system, proto, non, and simply strange forms of poetry. Coherence and words are optional. No vampire poetry; religious/inspirational poetry; Bukowski rip offs; no poems containing the word 'poetry'." Has published poetry by John Lowther, Spencer Selby, Peter Ganick, John M. Bennett, Michael Lenhart, and the Atlanta Poet's Group. As a sample the editors selected this poem, "24/7" by Sheila E. Murphy:

> Allow forth format, gem/The interimshot letterfest/Play to altercations/Summative in form of plenty/
> folded latitude

gestalten is a 100 page perfect-bound journal with full-color cover, includes "tons" of art/graphics and a few small-press ads. Receives about 750 poems/year, accepts about 10%. Publish 70 poems/issue. Press run is 1,000 for 250 subscribers of which 50 are libraries, 250 shelf sales; 200 distributed free to friends, editors and educational/community organizations. Subscription: $8/2 issues, $15/4 issues. Sample: $5. Make checks payable to Broken Boulder Press. Submit 5-20 poems at a time. No previously published poems or simultaneous submissions. No fax or e-mail submissions. Cover letter preferred. "SASE required. No e-mail submissions, please. We like casual and quirky cover letters." Time between acceptance and publication is up to 8 months. Always comments on rejected poems. Guidelines available for SASE. Responds in 3 weeks. Sometimes sends prepublication galleys. Pays 2 copies. Acquires one-time rights.

Magazine Needs & How to Submit: Published annually, *neotrope* "focuses primarily on experimental fiction and drama, with some visual poetry and abstract art. We publish primarily fiction and want to see visual poetry, collages, and abstract art only (Visual/text hybrids OK.) No traditional or text poetry. If you send text poems we will send them back unread." Has published poetry by Jim Leftwich, John M. Bennett, Michael Basinski, and Dave Chirot. *neotrope* is 160 pgs., digest-sized, professionally printed and perfect-bound with full-color glossy cover, includes 10-20 pgs. of art per issue, some ads included on an exchange basis. Receives about 30 poems/year, accepts about 20%. Publish 5-8 poems/issue. Press run is 1,500 for 250 subscribers of which 50 are libraries, 1,000 shelf sales; 30 distributed free to review publications. Subscription: $8/2 issues, $15/4 issues. Sample: $5. Make checks payable to Broken Boulder Press. Submit up to 10 poems at a time. Accepts simultaneous submissions; no previously published poems. Accepts e-mail submissions. Cover letter with brief bio preferred. "Electronic submissions should be sent in Quark or Pagemaker format, if possible. E-mail us to make other arrangements." Time between acceptance and publication is about 6 months. Always comments on rejected poems. Guidelines available for SASE. Responds in 1 month. Sometimes sends prepublication galleys. Pays 2 copies. Acquires one-time rights.

Book/Chapbook Needs & How to Submit: Broken Boulder Press publishes 6 chapbooks per year. "We want to promote experimental writing; we're biased toward work by underappreciated and beginning poets." Chapbooks are usually 24-32 pgs., 5½×8½, photocopied, and saddle-stapled with cardstock cover, includes lots of art. "Normally we like to see the whole manuscript, but if it's a long one you can send 5-10 sample poems. Publishing in our journals is certainly not required but nearly all of our chapbook authors have done so." Responds to queries and mss in 1 month. Pays 12 author's copies (out of a press run of 50). Order sample chapbooks by sending $1.50 per title.

Advice: "You can't do anything new until you know what's already been done. For every hour you spend writing, spend five hours reading other writers."

 **BROTHER JONATHAN REVIEW; TWOCATS PRESS**, 2145 Heather Lane #3, Arcata CA 95521. (707)825-8667. E-mail: brotherjonathan@lycos.com. Established 1999. **Editor:** Patrick K. Schulze.

Magazine Needs: *Brother Jonathan Review* appears biannually. Publishes "poetry that 'shows rather than tells' from poets who enjoy reading as much as writing." Also considers essays and flash fiction. Recently published poetry by James Bertolino, Barbara Brinson Curiel, Ken Letko, Jerry Martien, C. Rose, and Ann Wehrman. As a sample the editor selected these lines from "New Year. New Fool" by Jerry Martien:

> We meet under a certain oak on a ridge between our worlds./In spite of the season it's always a fine
> day for a picnic./I eat my food. She eats hers. We say nothing./We look into each others' eyes as fools
> always do.

Brother Jonathan Review is 40-60 pgs., digest-sized, photocopied, saddle-stapled with card cover. Receives about 100 poems/year, accepts about 20%. Publishes about 10 poems/issue. Press run is 100 for 25 subscribers of which 2 are libraries, 20 shelf sales; 40 distributed free to contributors and writing centers. Single copy: $4.50; subscription: $9. Sample: $4.50. Make checks payable to Patrick K. Schulze.

How to Submit: Submit 5 poems at a time. Accepts simultaneous submissions; no previously published poems. Accepts disk and e-mail submissions; attach file, Word/Wordperfect. Cover letter is preferred. Reads submissions January 15 through November 15 only. Time between acceptance and publication is 6 months. Poems are circulated to an editorial board. Seldom comments on rejected poems. Guidelines available for SASE. Responds in 3 months. Pays 1-2 contributors copies. Acquires first North American serial rights.

 **THE BROWN BOTTLE**, 21A Grove St., Concord NH 03301. E-mail: ngrazio@aol.com. Established 1999. **Editor:** Nate Graziano.

Magazine Needs: Appearing biannually, *The Brown Bottle* publishes poetry, short fiction, and essays. Each issue includes some b&w art. Wants "work that cuts the vein. Open to any style/form, although rhymed verse stands less of a chance. No sappy love poetry; poems about rabbits munching lillies in the garden; anything timid. No 'Hallmark' verse." Has published poetry by A.D. Winans, Mark Senkus, Ana Christy, Taylor Graham, and Joseph Shields. As a sample the editor selected these lines from "Soapbox" by Joseph Verrilli:

> I laugh and sneer at all of you/on silly little pads of paper/just like this one./Maybe it's not much of a
> life to you,/but to me/it's everything . . ./it's all I've got left.

The Brown Bottle is 36 pgs., digest-sized, saddle-stapled with cardstock cover, includes b&w art. Receives about 10%. Publish 10-15 poems/issue. Press run is 100. Single copy: $3; subscription: $6. Sample: $2. Make checks payable to Nate Graziano.

How to Submit: Submit 3-5 poems at a time. Accepts simultaneous submissions; no previously published poems. No e-mail submissions. Cover letter preferred. "Include name and address on every page. Send an SASE with all submissions or they'll be returned unread." Time between acceptance and publication is 5 months. Often comments on rejected poems. Guidelines available for SASE. Responds in 1 month. Pays 1 copy. Acquires one-time rights. Reviews books and chapbooks of poetry in 100 words. Poets may send books for review consideration.

Also Offers: Also publishes a broadside series titled *Happy Hour*. It includes poetry, articles, and reviews.

Advice: "Editors are not gods. We make mistakes. A rejection letter doesn't mean your work is poorly written. It just means it doesn't fit in that particular magazine. There are thousands of others. Look at this book! Also, great poets are great *writers*. Too many poets see the genre as exclusive—it is *NOT*! Good poets write fiction, essays, reviews, etc. Good writing is good writing. Don't think being a poet gives license to exclude grammar, syntax, and basic composition."

 **BUGLE: JOURNAL OF ELK COUNTRY AND THE HUNT (Specialized: animals, nature/rural/ecology, conservation)**, Rocky Mountain Elk Foundation, P.O. Box 8249, Missoula MT 59807-8249. (406)523-4570. Fax: (406)523-4550. E-mail: bugle@rmef.org. Website: www.rmef.org. Established 1984. **Assistant Editor:** Lee Cromrich.

Magazine Needs: *Bugle* is the bimonthly publication of the nonprofit Rocky Mountain Elk Foundation, whose mission is to ensure the future of elk, other wildlife, and their habitat. "The goal of *Bugle* is to advance this

---

OPENNESS TO SUBMISSIONS: ⬭ beginners; ⬯ beginners and experienced; ⬮ mostly experienced, few beginners; ◉ specialized; ⬰ closed to unsolicited mss.

mission by presenting original, critical thinking about wildlife conservation, elk ecology, and hunting." Wants "high quality poems that explore the realm of elk, the 'why' of hunting, or celebrate the hunting experience as a whole. Prefer one page. Free verse preferred. No 'Hallmark' poetry." *Bugle* is 130 pgs., 8½ × 11, professionally printed on coated stock and saddle-stapled with full-color glossy cover containing photos, illustrations, ads. Receives about 50 poems/year, accepts about 10%. Press run is 195,000 for 120,000 subscribers, 85,000 shelf sales. Subscription: $30 membership fee. Sample: $5.95. Make checks payable to Rocky Mountain Elk Foundation.

How to Submit: "Poets may submit as many poems as they'd like at a time." Accepts simultaneous submissions. Accepts e-mail (prefer attached file in Word), fax, and disk submissions. Cover letter preferred. Time between acceptance and publication varies. "Poems are screened by assistant editor first, those accepted then passed to editorial staff for review and comment, final decision based on their comments. We will evaluate your poem based on content, quality, and our needs for the coming year." Rarely comments on rejected poems. Publishes special sections. Guidelines and a list of upcoming themes available for SASE. Responds in 3 months. Pays $100/poem plus 3 copies. Acquires first North American serial rights. Staff reviews other magazines.

Advice: "Although poetry has appeared periodically in *Bugle* over the years, it has never been a high priority for us, nor have we solicited it. A lack of high-quality work and poetry appropriate for the focus of the magazine has kept us from making it a regular feature. However, we've decided to attempt to give verse a permanent home in the magazine. . . . Reading a few issues of *Bugle* prior to submitting will give you a better sense of the style and content of the magazine. The Rocky Mountain Elk Foundation is a nonprofit conservation organization committed to putting membership dollars into protecting elk habitat. So we appreciate, and still receive, donated work. However, if you would like to be paid for your work, our rate is $100 a poem, paid on acceptance. Should your poem appear in *Bugle*, you will receive three complimentary copies of the issue."

N ■ ◐ BULK HEAD; BRIDGE BURNER'S PUBLISHING, P.O. Box 5255, Mankato MN 56002-5255. E-mail: editor@bulkhead.org. Website: www.bulkhead.org. Established 2000. **Editor:** Curtis Meyer.

Magazine Needs: *Bulk Head* appears online quarterly, publishing quality poetry, fiction, and nonfiction. "We like angst. We like anything experimental. Shorter poems. No religious stuff (unless angry). Nothing rhyming. No song lyrics." Recently published poetry by Paul Dilsaver, Janet Buck, Greg Kosmicki, Leslie Bentley, Matt Mason, and Duane Locke. As a sample the editor selected these lines from "Date with Pete" by Cassandra Labairon:

> We stop at McDonalds/for soda. His brother/is there, giggling/with a group/of high school/girls, Pete winks/and whispers,/"Ladies man./It's in the genes."

Bulk Head is published online only with b&w photos. Receives about 120 poems/year, accepts about 30%. Publishes about 10-20 poems/issue. Single copy: free online; subscription: free online.

How to Submit: Submit 3 poems at a time. Line length for poetry is 2-4 minimum, 50 maximum. No previously published or simultaneous submissions. Accepts e-mail and disk submissions; no fax submissions. Cover letter is required. "Include a short bio." Reads submissions up to the date of publication. Time between acceptance and publication is up to 3 months. "For now, this is a one-man operation." Seldom comments on rejected poems. Guidelines are available in magazine and on website. Responds in up to 3 months. Acquires first rights, one-time rights. Reviews books and chapbooks of poetry and other magazines/journals. Poets may send books for review consideration.

Book/Chapbook Needs & How to Submit: Bridge Burner's Publishing presents work of "genius, anger, unpublished greatness." Publishes 1-2 paperback, 1-2 chapbooks/year. Books/chapbooks are usually 16-80 pgs. Query first, with a few sample poems and a cover letter with brief bio and publication credits. "We will consider polished collections for chapbooks." Responds to queries in 2 weeks; to mss in 2 months. Order sample books/chapbooks by sending $15 to Bridge Burner's.

Also Offers: Annual Bulk Head Poetry Contest. Entry fee: $1. Check website for details. "We've decided to publish a print edition of *Bulk Head* starting later this year. Details will be on the website."

Advice: "We are open to anything, but we prefer writing stripped of all romance and glamour. We especially like constructive angst. Don't shoot up your office or school! Write a poem instead."

◐ ◑ ◉ BURNING BUSH PUBLICATIONS; PEOPLE BEFORE PROFITS POETRY PRIZE, P.O. Box 9636, Oakland CA 94613. (510)482-9996. E-mail: editor@bbbooks.com. Website: www.bbbooks.com (includes "the inspiration behind Burning Bush Publications, lists our mail order titles, writer's guidelines, contest guidelines, and features a literary e-zine). Established 1996. **Contact:** acquisitions editor.

Book/Chapbook Needs: Burning Bush serves "voices that are underserved by mainstream presses." Wants "uplifting writing that believes in a more harmonious and equitable world with an emphasis on social justice and conscience." Does not want "any work that is degrading to humans or other lifeforms." Has published poetry by Morton Marcus, Lyn Lifshin, Patti Sirens, Opal Palmer Adisa, and Grace Paley. As a sample the editor selected these lines from "like a red tail" by Abby Bogomolny:

> i scope out your canyon/clearing the ridge and view your landscape,/a shifting of your desire/steaming, brown, dusty/and ride the hot wind high

Publishes 1 paperback/year. Books are usually 144 pgs., 5½ × 8½, offset, perfect-bound with medium card cover and photographs.

How to Submit: "Send ten sample poems with a description of the audience you wish to reach. Explain the scope of work in a cover letter and include any previous publications including references." Accepts previously published poems; no simultaneous submissions. Accepts e-mail submissions if included in body of message; no fax submissions. Time between acceptance and publication is 1 year. Poems are circulated to an editorial board. "Board meets once per month and reviews all submissions that have passed our acquisitions editors approval." Seldom comments on rejected poems. Responds to queries and mss in 2 months. Authors are paid by individual contract.

Also Offers: People Before Profits Poetry Prize awards a $100 first prize and two Honorable Mentions. Submit up to 3 poems in any style or form. Attach index card with name, title of poems, address, entry fee, phone and e-mail address. Entry fee: $10. Poems accepted through February 17. Send SASE for guidelines or obtain via website. Winners published in their e-zine. Our books are distributed to the trade by Bookpeople, Baker & Taylor, and Small Press Distribution.

BUTTON MAGAZINE; BUTTON 2002 POETRY CONTEST, 3 Oak Ave., Lunenburg MA 01462. E-mail: buttonx26@aol.com. Established 1993. **Poetry Editor:** D.E. Bell.

Magazine Needs: *Button* "is New England's tiniest magazine of fiction, poetry, and gracious living." Wants "poetry about the quiet surprises in life, not sentimental, and true moments carefully preserved. Brevity counts." Has published poetry by William Corbett, Amanda Powell, Diana Der-Hovanessian, Kevin McGrath, and Sappho ("Hey, we have a fabulous translator in Julia Dubnoff!"). As a sample the editor selected these lines from "Flying Back" by Diana Der-Hovanessian:

> We are escaping the thin gruel oatmeal/made with salt Armenian style/my grandmother/and mother
> prefer/to get the lumpy kind, thick with/cream which I can cover with sugar./my grandfather has the
> same . . .

Button appears twice/year and is 30 pgs., 4¼×5½, saddle-stapled, card stock 4-color cover with illustrations that incorporate one or more buttons. Press run is 1,200 for more than 500 subscribers; 750 shelf sales. Subscription: $5/2 years, $25/lifetime. Sample: $2 and a 34 cent stamp.

How to Submit: Submit up to 3 poems at a time. No previously published poems. Cover letter required. Time between acceptance and publication is up to 6 months. Poems are circulated to an editorial board. Often comments on rejected poems. Guidelines available for SASE or by e-mail. Responds in 4 months. Pays honorarium, 2-year subscription, and author's copies. Acquires first North American serial rights.

Also Offers: Sponsors the Button 2000 Poetry Contest. Submit poems on any topic, 25 lines or fewer, with SASE. Entry fee: $10/2 poems ($5 for each additional poem). Deadline: July 1, 2000. Awards $100 and publication. Guidelines available for SASE.

Advice: "*Button* was started so that a century from now when people read it they'll say, 'Gee, what a wonderful time to have lived. I wish I lived back then.' Our likes include wit and humanity, intelligence and eccentricity. Button tries to reflect a world one would *want* to live in. Please don't submit more than twice in a twelve-month period. If we send your poems home for further work, they really won't have matured that much in mere months."

BYLINE MAGAZINE; BYLINE LITERARY AWARDS (Specialized: writing), P.O. Box 130596, Edmond OK 73013-0001. (405)348-5591. E-mail: mPreston@bylinemag.com. Website: www.bylinemag.com (features guidelines, contest listings, subscription info, and sample column or article from magazine). Established 1981. **Poetry Editor:** Sandra Soli. **Editor:** Marcia Preston.

Magazine Needs: *ByLine* is a magazine for the encouragement of writers and poets, using 8-10 poems/issue about writers or writing. Has published poetry by Judith Tate O'Brien, Katheryn Howd Machan, and Henry B. Stubbs. *ByLine* is magazine-sized, professionally printed, with illustrations, cartoons, and ads. Has more than 3,000 subscriptions and receives about 2,500 poetry submissions/year, of which about 100 are used. Subscription: $22. Sample: $4.

How to Submit: Submit up to 3 poems at a time, no reprints. No e-mail or fax submissions, please. Guidelines available for SASE or on website. Responds within 6 weeks. Pays $10/poem. Acquires first North American serial rights.

Also Offers: Sponsors up to 20 poetry contests, including a chapbook competition open to anyone. Send #10 SASE for details. Also sponsors the *ByLine* Short Fiction and Poetry Awards. Prize: $250. Send SASE for guidelines.

Advice: "We are happy to work with new writers, but please read a few samples to get an idea of our style. We would like to see more serious poetry about the creative experience (as it concerns writing)."

THE CAFÉ REVIEW, c/o Yes Books, 20 Danforth St., Portland ME 04101. E-mail: all@seegerlab.com. Website: www.thecafereview.com. Established 1989. **Editor-in-Chief:** Steve Luttrell.

Magazine Needs: *The Café Review* is a quarterly which has grown out of open poetry readings held at a Portland cafe. The editors say they aim "to print the best work we can!" Wants "free verse, 'beat' inspired, and fresh. Nothing clichéd." Has published poetry by Charles Bukowski, Robert Creeley, Janet Hamill, and Diane Wakoski. *The Café Review* is 70-80 pgs., 5½×8½, professionally printed and perfect-bound with card cover, b&w art, no ads. Receives over 1,000 submissions/year, accepts approximately 15%. Press run is 500 for 100 subscribers of which 10 are libraries, 75-100 shelf sales. Subscription: $25. Sample: $6.

How to Submit: Submit 3 poems at a time. No previously published poems or simultaneous submissions. No e-mail submissions. Cover letter with brief bio required. Charges a $1 reading fee "which we put directly back into the production of our publication." "We usually respond with a form letter indicating acceptance or rejection of work, seldom with additional comments." Responds in 4 months. Pays 1 copy.

Book/Chapbook Needs: Publishes 1-2 chapbooks/year.

☑ ◐ ◑ **CALIFORNIA QUARTERLY; CALIFORNIA STATE POETRY SOCIETY**, P.O. Box 7126, Orange CA 92863-7126. (949)854-8024. E-mail: Jipalley@aol.com. Established 1972. **Editorial Board Chair:** Julian Palley.

Magazine Needs: *California Quarterly* is the official publication of the California State Poetry Society (an affiliate of the National Federation of State Poetry Societies) and is designed "to encourage the writing and dissemination of poetry." Wants poetry on any subject, 60 lines maximum. "No geographical limitations. Quality is all that matters." Has published poetry by Michael L. Johnson, Lyn Lifshin, and Robert Cooperman. *California Quarterly* is 64 pgs., 5½×8½, offset-printed, perfect-bound, heavy paper cover with art. Receives 3,000-4,000 poems/year, accepts about 5%. Press run is 500 for 300 subscribers of which 24 are libraries, 20-30 shelf sales. Membership in CSPS is $20/year and includes a subscription to *California Quarterly*. Sample (including guidelines): $5. Guidelines available for SASE.

How to Submit: Submit up to 6 "relatively brief" poems at a time; name and address on each sheet. Include SASE. Prefer no previously published poems or simultaneous submissions. Seldom comments on rejected poems. Responds in up to 4 months. Pays 1 contributor's copy. Acquires first rights. Rights revert to poet after publication.

Also Offers: CSPS also sponsors an annual poetry contest. Awards vary. All entries considered for *California Quarterly*.

Advice: "Since our editor changes with each issue, we encourage poets to resubmit."

Ⓝ ⓨ ◯ ◑ ◎ **CALLALOO (Specialized: ethnic)**, Dept. of English, P.O. Box 400121, University of Virginia, Charlottesville VA 22904-4121. (804)924-6637. Fax: (804)924-6472. E-mail: callaloo@virginia.edu. Website: www.people.virginia.edu/~callaloo. Established 1976. **Editor:** Charles H. Rowell.

● Poetry published in *Callaloo* has been included in the 1992, 1994, 1995, and 1996 volumes of *The Best American Poetry*.

Magazine Needs: Devoted to poetry dealing with the African Diaspora, including North America, Europe, Africa, Latin and Central America, South America, and the Caribbean. Has published poetry by Nathaniel Mackey, Lucille Clifton, Harryette Mullen, Audre Lorde, Will Alexander, and Cave Canem poets. This thick quarterly journal features about 15-20 poems (all forms and styles) in each issue along with short fiction, interviews, literary criticism, and concise and scholarly book reviews. Circulation is 1,600 subscribers of which half are libraries. Subscription: $36, $92 for institutions.

How to Submit: Submit complete ms in triplicate. Include cover letter with name, mailing address, e-mail address if available, and SASE. No fax or e-mail submissions. Responds in 6 months. Pays copies.

◐ **CALYPSO PUBLICATIONS**, 5810 Osage, #205, Cheyenne WY 82009. Established 1989.

Book/Chapbook Needs: Calypso Publications seeks to print "excellent and accessible contemporary poetry." Publishes occasional chapbooks and anthologies. Wants "contemporary poetry, no limitations on form, etc. No traditional rhyming or inspirational poetry." Has published poetry by William Kloefkorn, Jean Nordhaus, Lyn Lifshin, William Dickey, Barbara Crooker, and Dennis Saleh. Books are usually 60-100 pgs., 6×9, perfect-bound, some with multi-color covers, includes line drawing on covers.

How to Submit: "We don't accept queries. We accept full manuscripts and only when we request them through writing magazines. Poems for book publication can be previously published." Accepts simultaneous submissions. SASE required. Time between acceptance and publication is up to 1 year. Often comments on rejected poems. Responds to mss in 2 months. Payment varies. Order sample books by sending $5.

Advice: "For our first three years, we published an annual magazine called *Calypso*. We now publish occasional anthologies and chapbooks. Writers should check writing magazines periodically to learn of our future projects."

◯ ◎ **CALYX, A JOURNAL OF ART & LITERATURE BY WOMEN (Specialized: women, lesbian, multicultural); CALYX BOOKS**, P.O. Box B, Corvallis OR 97339-0539. (541)753-9384. Fax: (541)753-0515. E-mail: calyx@proaxis.com. Established 1976. **Senior Editor:** Beverly McFarland. **Managing Editor:** Micki Reaman.

Magazine Needs: *Calyx* is a journal edited by a collective editorial board. Publishes poetry, prose, art, book reviews, and interviews by and about women. Wants "excellently crafted poetry that also has excellent content." Has published poetry by Maurya Simon, Robin Morgan, Carole Boston Weatherford, and Eleanor Wilner. As a sample the editor selected these lines from "Transparent Woman" by Donna Henderson:

> in the basement of the science museum,/half-lit, naked, and marvelous with her perfect/posture, lucite arms straight and slightly apart,/palms turned toward us like the Blessed Virgin's,/helplessly welcoming.

Calyx appears 3 times every 18 months and is 6×8, handsomely printed on heavy paper, flat-spined, glossy color cover, 128-144 pgs., of which 50-60 are poetry. Poems tend to be lyric free verse that makes strong use of image and symbol melding unobtrusively with voice and theme. Single copy: $9.50. Sample: $11.50.

How to Submit: Send up to 6 poems with SASE and short bio. "We accept copies in good condition and clearly readable. We focus on new writing, but occasionally publish a previously published piece." Accepts simultaneous submissions, "if kept up-to-date on publication." No fax or e-mail submissions. *Calyx* is open to submissions October 1 through December 15 only. Mss received when not open to reading will be returned unread. Guidelines available for SASE or e-mail. Responds in 9 months. Pays 1 copy/poem and subscription. Poets may send books for review consideration.

Book/Chapbook Needs & How to Submit: Calyx Books publishes 1 book of poetry/year. All work published is by women. Recently published: *Details of Flesh* by Cortney Davis. However, Calyx Books is closed for ms submissions until further notice.

Advice: "Read the publication and be familiar with what we have published."

CANADIAN DIMENSION: THE MAGAZINE FOR PEOPLE WHO WANT TO CHANGE THE WORLD (Specialized: political), 2B-91 Albert St., Winnipeg, Manitoba R3B 1G5 Canada. (204)957-1519. Fax: (204)943-4617. E-mail: info@canadiandimension.mb.ca. Website: www.canadiandimension .mb.ca. Established 1964. **Editorial Contact:** Ed Janzen.

Magazine Needs: *Canadian Dimension* appears 6 times/year, using "short poems on labour, women, native, gay/lesbian, and other issues. Nothing more than one page." Has published poetry by Tom Wayman and Milton Acorn. *Canadian Dimension* is 48-56 pgs., magazine-sized, slick, professionally printed, with glossy paper cover. Press run is 3,500 for 2,500 subscribers of which 800 are libraries, 1,000 shelf sales. Subscription: $34.50 US ($24.50 Canadian). Sample: $2.

How to Submit: Submit up to 5 poems at a time. Previously published poems are unlikely to be accepted. Accepts simultaneous submissions, if notified. Editor comments on submissions "rarely." Publishes theme issues. A list of upcoming themes is available for SASE (or SAE with IRC). Reviews books of poetry in 750-1,200 words, single or multi-book format.

Advice: "We are broadly political—that is, not narrowly sloganeering, but profoundly sensitive to the connections between words and the state of the world. Topics can be personal as well as political. Also, American writers are reminded to include Canadian return postage or its equivalent in reply coupons, etc."

CANADIAN LITERATURE (Specialized: regional), Buchanan E158-1866 Main Mall, University of British Columbia, Vancouver, British Columbia V6T 1Z2 Canada. (604)822-2780. Fax: (604)822-5504. Website: www.cdn-lit.ubc.ca. Established 1959. **Editor:** E.M. Kröller.

Magazine Needs: *Canadian Literature* is a quarterly review which publishes poetry by Canadian poets. "No limits on form. Less room for long poems." Has published poetry by Atwood, Ondaatje, Layton, and Bringhurst. "See recent issue for poetry sample." Each issue is professionally printed, digest-sized, flat-spined, with 175-200 pgs., of which about 10 are poetry. Receives 500 poetry submissions/year, accepts 10-40. Circulation is 1,200, two-thirds of which are libraries. Sample for the cover price: $15 Canadian plus postage and GST.

How to Submit: No simultaneous submissions or reprints. Cover letter and SASE (or SAE and IRC) required. Responds within the month. "Accepted poems must be available on diskette." *Canadian Literature* retains full copyright for articles and reviews published. Reviews books of poetry in 500-1,000 words.

CANADIAN WOMAN STUDIES (Specialized: women), 212 Founders College, York University, 4700 Keele St., North York, Ontario M3J 1P3 Canada. (416)736-5356. Fax: (416)736-5765. E-mail: cwscf@yorku .ca. Website: www.yorku.ca/org/cwscf/home.html (includes tables of contents, policies, order information, guidelines for submissions, and calls for papers). Established 1978. **Literary Editor:** Marlene Kadar.

Magazine Needs: *Canadian Woman Studies* appears quarterly and focuses on "women's studies; experiential and academic articles, poetry, book reviews, and artwork." Wants poetry "exploring women's lives/perspectives. No long poems (i.e., more than 50 lines)." Has published poetry by Libby Scheier, Patience Wheatley, and Lyn Lifshin. *Canadian Woman Studies* is about 152 pgs., magazine-sized, offset-printed and perfect-bound with full color cover, includes art and ads. Receives 400 poems/year, accepts about 15%. Press run is 4,000 for 1,500 subscribers of which 500 are libraries, 1,000 shelf sales; 250 distributed free to women's groups. Single copy: $10; subscription: $36 plus $2.10 gst/year. Sample: $13.

How to Submit: Submit 5 poems at a time. No previously published poems or simultaneous submissions. Accepts e-mail submissions. Cover letter required. "SASE (or SAE and IRC) appreciated, bio note must accompany submission." Time between acceptance and publication is 5 months. Publishes theme issues. Responds in 5 months. Pays 1 copy. "Poets maintain copyright of their work at all times." Reviews books and chapbooks of poetry in 750 words, single and multi-book format. Poets may send books for review consideration to Fran Beer, book review editor.

CANADIAN WRITER'S JOURNAL (Specialized: writing), White Mountain Publications, Box 5180, New Liskeard, Ontario P0J 1P0 Canada. (705)647-5424. Fax: (705)647-8366. E-mail: cwj@ntl.sympat ico.ca. Website: www.nt.net/~cwj/index.htm (includes writer's guidelines, names of editors, and table of contents). **Owner:** Deborah Ranchuk. **Managing Editor:** Carole Roy.

Magazine Needs: *Canadian Writer's Journal* is a digest-sized bimonthly, publishing mainly short "how-to" articles of interest to writers at all levels. Use a few "short poems or portions thereof as part of 'how-to' articles

relating to the writing of poetry and occasional short poems with tie-in to the writing theme. We try for 90% Canadian content but prefer good material over country of origin, or how well you're known." Subscription: $22.50/year, $42/2 years. Sample: $5.
How to Submit: Submit up to 5 poems (identify each form). Include SASE ("U.S. postage accepted; do not affix to envelope"). No previously published poems. Accepts e-mail and fax submissions. "Include in body of message, not as attachment. Write 'Submission' in the subject line." Hard copy and SASE (or SAE and IRC) required if accepted." Responds in 3 months. Token payment. Pays $2-5 and 1 copy/poem.

N ◯ ◑ THE CANDLE, W2314 Second Ave., Apt. B, Spokane WA 99204. (509)838-2994. E-mail: silentdr agonjkr@37.com. Established 2000. **Editor:** J. K. Reid.
Magazine Needs: *The Candle* appears annually in February. "The purpose has an Emersonian flair: To speak to, for, and about the parts and particles of the whole." Wants "free verse mainly, but not opposed to rhymed lines as long as they don't have a Hallmark feel to them. *The Candle* aims to publish contemporary verse lighting man's relationship to himself and his universe." Does not want touchy-feely love poems of the rhymed variety. Recently published poetry by A. W. Milam, Lyn Lifshin, Scott Poole, Jason Olsen, and G. R. Esox. As a sample the editor selected these lines from "I Walk the Sixty" by G. R. Esox:
> I have moved to the desert, towed a mobile home to the middle of it/I have yet to take off my headphones since my satellite was installed on the mountain/away from me./My lips are always dry, and my eyes hurt in the day./They deliver my supplies sixty miles away/I walk . . .
The Candle is 32 pgs., digest-sized, Xeroxed, saddle-stapled, cardstock cover, with photography and sketches. Receives about 75 poems/year, accepts about 33%. Publishes about 26 poems/issue. Press run is 100 for 15 subscribers, 25 are shelf sales; balance is distributed free to coffee shops and cafes. Single copy: $3; subscription: $3.50. Sample: $3.50. Make checks payable to Jennifer Reid.
How to Submit: Submit 3-7 poems at a time. Line length for poetry is open. No previously published poems or simultaneous submissions. Accepts e-mail and disk submissions; no fax submissions. Cover letter is preferred. "Send a SASE or submit via e-mail (subject heading should state 'Submission for *The Candle*.')" Reads submissions May through November. Time between acceptance and publication is 2-6 months. "Anything that is fresh, captivating, and alive grabs my interest. I can usually tell right away if a poem will find its place in the next issue, and I stop reading submissions when I have enough acceptances to fill the magazine's needs." Often comments on rejected poems. "I recommend purchasing a sample copy." Occasionally publishes theme issues. Guidelines are available in magazine, for SASE, or by e-mail. Responds in 2 months. Pays 1 contributor's copy. Acquires one-time rights.
Advice: "While many in the literary community would agree that the writing of today has a cynicism to it, thus communicating a sense of disconnectedness with place and language, I am beginning to see a turn in this trend. Much of contemporary poetry is returning to a sense of optimism (or at the very least acceptance of the world as is) and finding beauty and connection among people and places that writers hold dear. Balance is becoming restored."

N ◑ THE CAPE ROCK, Dept. of English, Southeast Missouri State University, Cape Girardeau MO 63701. (314)651-2500. Established 1964. **Editor:** Dr. Harvey Hecht.
Magazine Needs: *Cape Rock* appears twice yearly and consists of poetry and photography. "No restrictions on subjects or forms. Our criterion for selection is the quality of the work. We prefer poems under 70 lines; no long poems or books; no sentimental, didactic, or cute poems." Has published poetry by Stephen Dunning, Joyce Odam, Judith Phillips Neeld, Lyn Lifshin, Virginia Brady Young, Gary Pacernick, and Laurel Speer. *Cape Rock* is a 64-page, handsomely printed, flat-spined, digest-sized magazine. Press run 500 for 200 subscribers of which half are libraries. Single copy: $5; subscription: $7/year. Sample: $4.
How to Submit: Submit 3-7 poems at a time. Do not submit mss in May, June, or July. Guidelines available for SASE. Has a 2- to 8-month backlog and responds in up to 3 months. Pays 2 copies.
Also Offers: Also offers a $200 prize for the best poem in each issue and $100 for featured photography.

✹ ✓ $◑ THE CAPILANO REVIEW, 2055 Purcell Way, North Vancouver, British Columbia V7J 3H5 Canada. (604)984-1712. Fax: (604)990-7837. E-mail: tcr@capcollege.bc.ca. Website: www.capcollege.bc.ca/dept/TCR/ (includes guidelines, excerpts, subscription info, contest info, etc.). Established 1972. **Editor:** Carol Hanshaw.
Magazine Needs: *The Capilano Review* is a literary and visual arts review appearing 3 times/year. Wants "avant-garde, experimental, previously unpublished work, poetry of sustained intelligence and imagination. We are interested in poetry that is new in concept and in execution." Has published poetry by bill bissett, Phyllis Webb, and Michael Ondaatje. *The Capilano Review* comes in a handsome digest-sized format, 115 pgs., flat-spined, finely printed, semi-glossy stock with a glossy full-color card cover. Circulation is 900. Sample: $9 prepaid.
How to Submit: Submit 5-6 poems, minimum, with cover letter and SAE and IRC. No simultaneous submissions. No e-mail or disk submissions. Responds in up to 5 months. Pays $50-200, subscription, plus 2 copies. Acquires first North American serial rights.
Advice: "*The Capilano Review* receives several manuscripts each week; unfortunately the majority of them are simply inappropriate for the magazine. The best advice we can offer is to read the magazine before you submit."

$ ☐ ◯ CAPPER'S, 1503 SW 42nd St., Topeka KS 66609-1265. (785)274-4300. Fax: (785)274-4305. Website: www.cappers.com (includes guidelines and summary of current issue). Established 1879. **Editor:** Ann Crahan.

Magazine Needs: *Capper's* is a biweekly tabloid (newsprint) going to 240,000 mail subscribers, mostly small-town and rural families. Wants short poems (4-16 lines preferred, lines of one-column width) "relating to everyday situations, nature, inspirational, humorous. Most poems used in *Capper's* are upbeat in tone and offer the reader a bit of humor, joy, enthusiasm, or encouragement." Accepts poetry written by children, ages 12 and under and 13-19. Has published poetry by Elizabeth Searle Lamb, Robert Brimm, Margaret Wiedyke, Helena K. Stefanski, Sheryl L. Nelms, and Claire Puneky. Send $1.95 for sample. Uses 6-8 poems in each issue. Not available on newsstand.

How to Submit: Submit 5-6 poems at a time, 14-16 lines. No simultaneous submissions. No e-mail or fax submissions. Returns mss with SASE. Publishes seasonal theme issues. A list of upcoming themes available for SASE. Responds in 3 months. Pays $10-15/poem. Additional payment of $5 if poem is used on website. Acquires one-time rights.

Advice: "Poems chosen are upbeat, sometimes humorous, always easily understood. Short poems of this type fit our format best."

✔ ◯ ◎ THE CARIBBEAN WRITER (Specialized: regional, Caribbean); THE DAILY NEWS PRIZE; THE CANUTE A. BRODHURT PRIZE; THE CHARLOTTE AND ISIDOR PAIEWONSKY PRIZE; DAVID HOUGH LITERARY PRIZE; THE MARGUERITE COBB MCKAY PRIZE, University of the Virgin Islands, RR 02, P.O. Box 10,000, Kingshill, St. Croix, USVI 00850. (340)692-4152. Fax: (340)692-4026. E-mail: qmars@uvi.edu. Website: http://rps.uvi.edu/CaribbeanWriter (includes work from previous issues and current issue, along with biographies and photos of contributors). Established 1987. **Editor:** Dr. Erika Waters. **Contact:** Ms. Quilin Mars.

Magazine Needs: *The Caribbean Writer* is a literary anthology, appearing in July, with a Caribbean focus. The Caribbean must be central to the literary work or the work must reflect a Caribbean heritage, experience or perspective. Has published poetry by Virgil Suarez, Thomas Reiter, Kamau Brathwaite, and Opal Palmer Odisa. *The Caribbean Writer* magazine is over 300 pgs., 6×9, handsomely printed on heavy stock, perfect-bound, with glossy card cover, using advertising and b&w art by Caribbean artists. Press run is 1,000. Single copy: $12 plus $2 postage; subscription: $20. Sample: $7 plus $2 postage. Guidelines are available for SASE. (Note: Postage to and from the Virgin Islands is the same as within the US.)

How to Submit: Submit up to 5 poems. Accepts simultaneous submissions; no previously published poems. Accepts submissions by e-mail (attached file); no fax submissions. Blind submissions only: name, address, phone number, and title of ms should appear in cover letter along with brief bio. Title only on ms. Deadline is September 30 of each year. Publishes theme issues. Pays 2 copies. Acquires first North American serial rights. Reviews books of poetry and fiction in 1,000 words. Poets may send books for review consideration.

Also Offers: The magazine annually awards the Daily News Prize ($300) for the best poem or poems, The Marguerite Cobb McKay Prize to a Virgin Island author ($100), the David Hough Literary Prize to a Caribbean author ($500), the Canute A. Brodhurst Prize for Fiction, and the Charlotte and Isidor Paiewonsky Prize ($200) for first-time publication.

Ⓝ ▨ ◯ CARLETON ARTS REVIEW, Box 78, 18th Floor, Davidson Dunton Tower, Carleton University, Ottawa, Ontario K1S 5B6 Canada. (613)237-9381. Established 1985. **Editor-in-Chief:** Jason MacDonald.

Magazine Needs: *Carleton Arts Review* is a 90-page semiannual publishing poetry, prose, drama, visual art (b&w) and reviews. "All kinds of poetry accepted and encouraged." Has published poetry by Stan Rogal, Brian Burke, Calvin White, and Alan Packwood. Receives 200-300 poems/year, accepts about 10%. Press run is 300 for 50 subscribers most of which are libraries, 150 shelf sales. Subscription: $15. Sample: $6.

How to Submit: No previously published poems or simultaneous submissions. Accepts e-mail submissions; no fax submissions. "Please include a short biography and list of publications plus a SASE or SAE and IRC." Always comments on rejected poems. Responds in 4 months. Pays 2 copies.

⊕ ◎ CARN; THE CELTIC LEAGUE (Specialized: foreign language, ethnic), 11 Hilltop View, Braddan, Isle of Man. Phone/fax: (UK)(0)1624-627128. Website: www.manxman.co.im/cleague. Established 1973. **General Secretary:** Bernard Moffatt.

Magazine Needs: *Carn* is a magazine-sized quarterly, press run 2,000. "The aim of our quarterly is to contribute to a fostering of cooperation between the Celtic peoples, developing the consciousness of the special relationship which exists between them, and making their achievements and their struggle for cultural and political freedom better known abroad."

How to Submit: "Contributions to *Carn* come through invitation to people whom we know as qualified to write more or less in accordance with that aim. We would welcome poems in the Celtic languages if they are relating to that aim. If I had to put it briefly, we have a political commitment, or, in other words, *Carn* is not a literary magazine." Reviews books of poetry only if in the Celtic languages.

✓ ◎ ⊘ **CAROLINA WREN PRESS (Specialized: women, ethnic, gay/lesbian, social issues)**, 120 Morris St., Durham NC 27701. (919)560-2738. E-mail: carolina@carolinawrenpress.org. Website: www.carolina. wrenpress.org. Established 1976.

Book/Chapbook Needs: Publishes 1 book/year, "primarily women and minorities, though men and majorities also welcome." Has published poetry by Jaki Shelton Green, Mary Kratt, and Steven Blaski.

How to Submit: Currently are not accepting any unsolicited mss. Send 9½×12 SASE for catalog (include postage for 3 ounces).

Also Offers: "We are launching our new North American Poetry Chapbook Series with George Elliott Clarke's *Gold Indigoes.*"

⊘ ◎ **CATAMOUNT PRESS; COTYLEDON (Specialized: anthology, short poems, haiku, tanka, nature/rural/ecology)**, 2519 Roland Rd. SW, Huntsville AL 35805-4147. Established 1992. **Editor:** Georgette Perry.

Magazine Needs: *Cotyledon*, established in 1997 and published 4 times/year, is a miniature magazine. Wants poems up to 8 lines. Nature and the environment are favorite subjects, but a variety of subject matter is needed. Poets recently published include Gerrye Payne, John Cantey Knight, and Ross Figgins. As a sample the editor has selected these lines by Dorothy McLaughlin:

> Wind's sound follows/bare trees' flickering shadows/into the house.

Cotyledon is 16 pgs., 3½×4¼, photocopied, saddle-stapled, with bond cover and b&w art.

How to Submit: Submit 3-6 poems at a time with cover letter and SASE. Accepts previously published poems if identified as such. Send three unattached first-class stamps for a sample *Cotyledon*, guidelines, and news of press offerings and plans. Responds in 2 months. Pays at least 2 copies.

Book/Chapbook Needs & How to Submit: "Catamount Press publishes very few chapbooks, so please do not submit a ms. Get acquainted with us first by submitting to *Cotyledon*, or querying."

⊘ **CAVEAT LECTOR**, 400 Hyde St., Apt. 606, San Francisco CA 94109-7445. Phone/fax: (415)928-7431. Established 1989. **Editors:** Christopher Bernard, James Bybee, and Andrew Towne.

Magazine Needs: Appearing 2 times/year, "*Caveat Lector* is devoted to the arts and to cultural and philosophical commentary. We publish visual art and music as well as literary and theoretical texts. We are looking for accomplished poems, something that resonates in the mind long after the reader has laid the poem aside. We want work that has authenticity of emotion and high craft; whether raw or polished, that rings true—if humorous, actually funny, or at least witty. Classical to experimental. 500-line limit." Not accepting submissions in 2002. Has published poetry by Deanne Bayer, Simon Perchik, Alfred Robinson, and E.S. Kilbert. As a sample the editor selected these lines from "To A Friend Who Has Not Written," by Christopher Hewitt:

> You must have some news./I do. The asters bloomed. There's/still no rain./Oh and I go often to/A place
> I found/Where leaves are letters falling/All of which I've written.//How I exhaust myself/Catching
> them!

Caveat Lector is 36-64 pgs., 11×4¼, photocopied and saddle-stitched with b&w card cover. Receives 600-800 poems/year, accepts about 2%. Press run is 300 for 30 subscribers, 200 shelf sales. Single copy: $3.50; subscription: $15/4 issues. Sample: $3.

How to Submit: Submit up to 6 short poems (up to 50 lines each), 3 medium length poems (51-100 lines), or 1 long poem (up to 500 lines) at a time "on any subject, in any style, as long as the work is authentic in feeling and appropriately crafted." Place name, address, and (optional) telephone number on each page. Include SASE, cover letter, and brief bio (30 words or less). Accepts simultaneous submissions, "but please inform us." Time between acceptance and publication is 1 year. Sometimes comments on rejected poems. Responds in 1 month. Pays 5 copies. Acquires first publication rights.

Advice: "The two rules of writing are: 1. Rewrite it again. 2. Rewrite it again. The writing level of most of our submissions is pleasingly high. A rejection by us is not always a criticism of the work, and we try to provide comments to our more promising submitters."

$ ☐ ⊘ **CC. MARIMBO COMMUNICATIONS**, P.O. Box 933, Berkeley CA 94701-0933. Established 1996. **Editor:** Peggy Golden.

Book/Chapbook Needs: CC. Marimbo Communications "promotes the work of underpublished poets/artists by providing a well-crafted, cheap (people's prices) and therefore affordable/accessible, collection." Publishes 2-3 poetry titles per year. "Books are issued as 'minichaps' to introduce underpublished poets/artists to the public. Runs done by alphabet, lettered A-Z, AA-ZZ, etc. Short poems for the small format, styles, and content welcome in whatever variation. We do not want to see already published work, unless poems previously in print in magazines (attributed), i.e., poems OK, reprintable books not OK." Has published poetry by Errol Miller, Don A. Hoyt, and Bert Glick. As a sample the editor selected this poem, "These Kids," from *My Back Yardstick* by Tom Plante:

> Singing, these kids/kicking that eternal ball

Chapbooks are usually 40 pgs., 4¼×5¼ or 5½×4¼, offset-printed and photocopied, mainly handsewn binding with matt cover, includes art/graphics according to project.

How to Submit: Query first, with a few sample poems and cover letter with brief bio and publication credits, include SASE. Line length for poetry is 25 maximum. Responds in 2 months to queries; 3 months to mss. Pays

5 author's copies (out of a press run of 26), additional copies paid for larger press runs. "Author gets 10% of cover price on all copies sold, except for copies sold to author." Order sample chapbooks by sending $5 (5¢ for p&h).

Advice: "We must keep seeking."

✔ ◐ **CENTER PRESS; MASTERS AWARDS**, Box 17897, Encino CA 91416. E-mail: news7@letterbox.com. Website: http://members.nbci.com/CenterPress. Established 1980. **Publisher:** Gabriella Stone.

Book/Chapbook Needs & How to Submit: Center Press is "a small press presently publishing 6-7 works per year including poetry, photojournals, calendars, novels, etc. We look for quality, freshness, and that touch of genius." In poetry, "we want to see verve, natural rhythms, discipline, impact, etc. We are flexible but verbosity, triteness, and saccharine make us cringe. *We now read and publish only mss accepted from the Masters Award.*" Has published books by Bebe Oberon, Walter Calder, Exene Vida, Carlos Castenada, and Sandra Gilbert. As a sample the editor selected these lines from "The Patriot" by Scott A. Sonders:

> Underwire bras/and other implements/of torture, are remnants of the Inquisition./It would be best to
> set/the breast free to hang, as a proud silk flag/on a windless day.

Their tastes are for poets such as Adrienne Rich, Li-Young Lee, Charles Bukowski, and Czeslaw Milosz. "We have strong liaisons with the entertainment industry and like to see material that is media-oriented and au courant."

Also Offers: "We sponsor the Masters Awards, established in 1981, including a $1,000 grand prize annually plus each winner (and the five runners-up in poetry) will be published in a clothbound edition and distributed to selected university and public libraries, news mediums, etc. There is a one-time only $15 administration and reading fee per entrant. Submit a maximum of five poems or song lyric pages (no tapes) totaling no more than 150 lines. Any poetic style or genre is acceptable, but a clear and fresh voice, discipline, natural rhythm, and a certain individuality should be evident. Further application and details available with a #10 SASE."

Advice: "Please study what we publish before you consider submitting."

◑ **CHACHALACA POETRY REVIEW**, English Dept., UT-Brownsville, Brownsville TX 78521. Fax: (956)544-8988. Established 1997. **Contact:** Marty Lewis.

Magazine Needs: *Chachalaca Poetry Review* is "published once or twice/year, depending on number of submissions. We are looking for thematic substance and crafted lines in the poetry we publish. That doesn't often mean standard stanza pattern or any particular style, but there should be some connection between form and content. We don't accept poems with skinny, three syllable lines, intrusive rhymes, arbitrary line breaks, random indentation, or center justification just because the PC can do it. No haikus or prose poems. Because of space limitations, we usually can't use poems of more than 60 lines." Has published poetry by Lola Rodriquez, Vivian Shipley, Virgil Suarez, and Nathan Whiting. As a sample the editor selected these lines from "What to Do with Hands" by Anne Giles Rimbey:

> My pain lets down like milk and whitens our tea./I am trying to tell you what my father/said:
> Understanding is not black or white but/surface with typography Equal heights reached/here or there
> I shape hands in a hill over/teapots like I am conjuring. Or praying.

Chachalaca is 50-100 pgs., professionally printed and perfect-bound with no ads. Press run is 500 with 200 distributed free to libraries, 100 shelf sales. Single copy: $8. Sample: $4.

How to Submit: Submit 5-10 poems at a time. Include SASE. Accepts simultaneous submissions "if you alert us"; no previously published poems. Cover letter with short bio preferred. Time between acceptance and publication varies. Poems are circulated to an editorial board of 3 readers. Seldom comments on rejected poems. Responds in 2 months or more. Pays 2 copies. Acquires all rights. Returns rights.

Advice: "*Chachalaca*'s editors are experienced and the journal is well supported."

◑ ◯ **CHAFF**, 4400 Shamrock, Unit 1A, McHenry IL 60050. E-mail: jordan5450@aol.com. Established 1996. First issue 1997. **Editor:** Jordan Taylor Young.

Magazine Needs: *Chaff* is a semiannual publication "dedicated to the Lord, for the express purpose of reaching out to a lost and hurting world, as well as uniting Christian poets through the publication of their work." Wants "free verse poetry—rhyme and meter only if exceptional quality—romance, nature, aging, friendship, family life, animals, mystery, senior citizens, social issues, children, and humor. Nothing satanic, obscene, violent, sensual, erotic, or homosexual." Accepts poetry written by children, ages 8 and older. As a sample the editor selected this poem, "This Miracle Mile" by Jordan Taylor Young:

> Who gives music to the songbird, feathered limbs for flight, what determines when the stars should
> shine, and bid the morning night. I often ask on bended knee by what possessed this smile, for I am
> but a feeble guest upon this miracle mile.

Chaff is 20-30 pgs., 5½×8, laser-printed and stapled. Press run is 50-100. Single copy: $6. Poetry may be complemented by appropriate photographs, illustrations, or scripture. In addition, *Chaff* includes a "Featured Poet" segment, consisting of a short bio and photograph.

How to Submit: Submit no more than 5 poems at a time with **$2/poem reading fee**. Make checks payable to Jordan Taylor Young, editor. Accepts previously published poems and simultaneous submissions. Accepts e-mail submissions; no fax submissions. Cover letter and SASE required. Responds in 1 month. Pays 2 copies, 3 copies to Featured Poet.

Advice: "Often poets are not recognized for their artistry, separated like chaff from wheat. The name *Chaff* stems from my deep conviction that we are like chaff, and separated from God we can do nothing. We intend to provide a stronger link to self, helping new and aspiring poets to find their own voices through the publication of their work. 'For where your treasure is, there will your heart be also.' (Matthew 6:21)."

N ⦿ **CHAFFIN JOURNAL**, Dept. of English, Case Annex 467, Eastern Kentucky University, Richmond KY 40475-3102. (859)622-3080. Established 1998. **Editor:** Robert W. Witt.
Magazine Needs: *The Chaffin Journal* appears annually. Publishes quality short fiction and poetry by new and established writers/poets. Wants any form, subject matter, or style. Does not want "poor quality." Recently published poetry by Pat Boran, James Doyle, Corey Mesler, Simon Perchik, Philip St. Clair, and Virgil Suarez. As a sample the editor selected these lines from "The Home Place" by Philip St. Clair:

> It's Saturday morning, and a fiftyish woman sits in a booth/in a family-style restaurant, staring/out of the window as she smokes mentholated cigarettes/one after another. The walls/are hung with sepia photos and antique tools, conjuring/bygone days, country virtues . . .

The Chaffin Journal is 120 pgs., digest-sized, offset-printed, perfect-bound, plain cover with title only. Receives about 200 poems/year, accepts about 25%. Publishes about 40-50 poems/issue. Press run is 300 for 65 subscribers of which 3 are libraries, 180 shelf sales; 40-50 are distributed free to contributors. Single copy: $5; subscription: $5 annually. Make checks payable to *The Chaffin Journal*.
How to Submit: Submit 5 poems at a time. Accepts simultaneous submission; no previousy published poems. No fax, e-mail, or disk submissions. Cover letter is preferred. "Submit typed, double-spaced pages with only one poem per page. Enclose SASE." Reads submissions June 1 through November 1. Time between acceptance and publication is 6 months. Poems are reviewed by the general editor and 2 poetry editors. Never comments on rejected poems. Guidelines are available in magazine. Responds in 3 months. Pays 1 contributor's copy. Acquires one-time rights.

⬥ ◯ ◗ ◎ **CHALLENGER INTERNATIONAL; MCNAUGHTON EDITIONS (Specialized: teen/young adult)**, 440 McNaughton Ave., McNaughton Center, Quesnel, British Columbia V2J 3K8 Canada. (250)991-5567. E-mail: lukivdan@hotmail.com. Established 1978. **Editor:** Dan Lukiv.
Magazine Needs: *Challenger international*, a literary quarterly, contains poetry, short fiction, novel excerpts, and black pen drawings. Open to "any type of work, especially by teenagers (*Ci*'s mandate: to encourage young writers, and to publish their work alongside established writers), providing it is not pornographic, profane, or overly abstract." He has published poetry from Canada, the US, Switzerland, Russia, and Columbia. As a sample the editor selected "United They Stood" by Dan Lukiv:

> A good-as-naked man,/A bloodless alloy,/Beats his sword/Into a plowshare.//Concrete, glass, and steel/ Tower like Babel.//And mothers will drink their children.

Ci is about 20 pgs., 8½ × 11, photocopied and side-stapled. Press run is 100. *Ci* is distributed free to McNaughton Center-secondary alternate-students.
How to Submit: Accepts previously published poems and simultaneous submissions. Cover letter required with list of credits, if any. Accepts e-mail submissions. Sometimes comments on rejected poems. "No SASE (or SAE and IRC) means submission goes into the garbage. Sometimes we edit to save the poet rejection." Responds in 4 months. Pays 1 copy.
Book/Chapbook Needs & How to Submit: McNaughton Editions publishes chapbooks of work by authors featured in *Ci*. Pays 3 copies. Copyright remains with authors. Has published *Forgive Us Our Sins*, by Julia Shtromberg (Russia). Distribution of free copies through the Quesnel Library.
Advice: "Don't send U.S. stamps as return postage."

✓ ⊕ ◎ **CHAPMAN (Specialized: ethnic); CHAPMAN PUBLISHING**, 4 Broughton Place, Edinburgh EH1 3RX Scotland. Phone: (0131)557-2207. Fax: (0131)556-9565. E-mail: editor@chapman-pub.co.uk. Website: www.chapman-pub.co.uk (includes sample of current issue, guidelines, back list of issues, and publications). Established 1970. **Editor:** Joy Hendry.
Magazine Needs: "*Chapman* magazine is controversial, influential, outspoken, and intelligent. Established in 1970, it has become a dynamic force in Scottish culture covering theatre, politics, language, and the arts. Our highly-respected forum for poetry, fiction, criticism, review, and debate makes it essential reading for anyone interested in contemporary Scotland. *Chapman* publishes the best in Scottish writing—new work by well-known Scottish writers in the context of lucid critical discussion. It also, increasingly, publishes international writing. With our strong commitment to the future, we energetically promote new writers, new ideas and new approaches." Has published poetry and fiction by Alasdair Gray, Liz Lochhead, Sorley MacLean, T.S. Law, Edwin Morgan, Willa Muir, Tom Scott, and Una Flett. As a sample the editor selected these lines from Judy Steel's poem "For Nicole Boulanger" who, Steel says, "was born in the same year as my daughter and died in the Lockerbie air disaster of 1988":

> You died amongst these rolling Border hills:/The same our daughters played and rode and walked in -/ They make a nursery fit to shape and mould/A spirit swift as water, free as air.//But you, west-winging through the Christmas dark/Found them no playground but a mortuary -/Your young life poised for flight to woman's years/Destroyed as wantonly as moorland game.

Chapman appears 3 times/year in a 6×9, perfect-bound format, 144 pgs., professionally printed in small type on matte stock with glossy card cover, art in 2 colors. Press run is 2,000 for 900 subscribers of which 200 are libraries. Receives "thousands" of poetry submissions/year, accepts about 200, has a 4- to 6-month backlog. Sample: £4 (overseas).

How to Submit: "We welcome submissions which must be accompanied by a SASE/IRC. Please send sufficient postage to cover the return of your manuscript. Do not send foreign stamps." Submit 4-10 poems at a time, one poem/page. "We do not usually publish single poems." No simultaneous submissions. Cover letter required. Responds "as soon as possible." Always sends prepublication galleys. Pays copies. Staff reviews books of poetry. Send books for review consideration.

Book/Chapbook Needs: Chapman Publishing is currently not accepting submissions.

Advice: "Poets should not try to court approval by writing poems especially to suit what they perceive as the nature of the magazine. They usually get it wrong and write badly." Also, they are interested in receiving poetry dealing with women's issues and feminism.

$Ⓩ THE CHARITON REVIEW, Truman State University, Kirksville MO 63501. (816)785-4499. Established 1975. **Editor:** Jim Barnes.

Magazine Needs: *The Chariton Review* began in 1975 as a twice yearly literary magazine and in 1978 added the activities of the press (now defunct). The poetry published in the magazine is, according to the editor, "open and closed forms—traditional, experimental, mainstream. We do not consider verse, only poetry in its highest sense, whatever that may be. The sentimental and the inspirational are not poetry for us. Also, no more 'relativism': short stories and poetry centered around relatives." Has published poetry by Michael Spence, Kim Bridgford, Sam Maio, Andrea Budy, Charles Edward Eaton, Wayne Dodd, and J'laine Robnolt. There are 40-50 pages of poetry in each issue of the *The Chariton Review*, a 6×9, flat-spined magazine of over 100 pages, professionally printed, glossy cover with photographs. Receives 8,000-10,000 submissions/year, accepts about 35-50, with never more than a 6-month backlog. Press run is about 600 for 400 subscribers of which 100 are libraries. Subscription: $9/1 year, $15/2 years. Sample: $5.

How to Submit: Submit 5-7 poems at a time, typescript single-spaced. No simultaneous submissions. Do *not* write for guidelines. Responds quickly; accepted poems often appear within a few issues of notification. Always sends prepublication galleys. Pays $5/printed page. Acquires first North American serial rights. Contributors are expected to subscribe or buy copies. Poets may send books for review consideration.

N Ⓩ CHASE PARK, P.O. Box 9136, Oakland CA 94613-0136. E-mail: twentymule@yahoo.com. Established 2000. **Editor:** David Horton.

Magazine Needs: *Chase Park*, published biannually, is a journal of poetry and poetics. "We attempt to publish a wide range of voices in the contemporary national and international schools and scenes as well as new and independent voices. Open to style and form. Open to experimental, language, concrete, visual, and more traditional approaches." Recently published poetry by Richard Kostelanetz and Rosmarie Waldrop. *Chase Park* is 60-80 pgs., digest-sized, perfect-bound, card stock cover with art/graphics on cover only. Receives about 1,000 poems/year, accepts about 5-10%. Publishes about 40-60 poems, 50-70 pages/issue. Press run is 500 for 10 subscribers of which 10 are libraries, 300 shelf sales. Single copy: $7; subscription: $12. Sample: $5. Make checks payable to *Chase Park*.

How to Submit: Submit 3-7 poems at a time. Accepts simultaneous submissions if notified of acceptance elsewhere immediately. No previously published poems. SASE required. No e-mail or disk submissions. "If submitting visual poetry, you may be asked for disk upon acceptance." Reads submissions year-round, "but responses may be slower in summer." Submit seasonal poems 4 months in advance. Time between acceptance and publication is up to 6 months. "Poems are read by editorial assistants who make recommendations to editor. Editor makes final decisions." Seldom comments on rejected poems. Guidelines available for SASE or by e-mail. Responds in 4 months. Sometimes sends prepublication galleys. Pays 5 contributor's copies. Acquires first North American serial rights. Reviews chapbooks and books of poetry and other magazines/journals in 250-500 words, single and multi-book format. Send books for review consideration to the review editor.

✓ $Ⓩ THE CHATTAHOOCHEE REVIEW, Georgia Perimeter College, 2101 Womack Rd., Dunwoody GA 30338. (770)551-3019. Website: www.gpc.peachnet.edu/~twadley/cr/index.htm. Established 1980. **Editor-in-Chief:** Lawrence Hetrick. **Poetry Editors:** (Mr.) Collie Owens and Steven Beauchamp.

Magazine Needs: *The Chattahoochee Review* is a quarterly of poetry, short fiction, essays, reviews, and interviews, published by Georgia Perimeter College. "We publish a number of Southern writers, but *Chattahoochee Review* is not by design a regional magazine. All themes, forms, and styles are considered as long as they impact the whole person: heart, mind, intuition, and imagination." Has published poetry by A.E. Stalling, Carolyne Wright, Coleman Barks, Ron Rash, and Fred Chapp. *Chattahoochee Review* is 140 pgs., 6×9, professionally printed on cream stock with reproductions of artwork, flat-spined, with one-color card cover. Recent issues feature a wide range of forms and styles augmenting prose selections. Press run is 1,250, of which 300 are complimentary copies sent to editors and "miscellaneous VIPs." Subscription: $16/year. Sample: $6.

How to Submit: Writers should send 1 copy of each poem and a cover letter with bio material. No simultaneous submissions. Time between acceptance and publication is up to 4 months. Publishes theme issues. Guidelines and a list of upcoming themes available for SASE. Queries will be answered in 1-2 weeks. Responds in 3 months. Pays $50/poem and 2 copies. Acquires first rights. Staff reviews books of poetry and short fiction in 1,500 words, single or multi-book format. Send books for review consideration.

■ $ ◗ ◎ CHELSEA; CHELSEA AWARD COMPETITION (Specialized: translations), P.O. Box 773, Cooper Station, New York NY 10276-0773. E-mail: chelseareview@yahoo.com. Established 1958. **Editor:** Richard Foerster. **Senior Associate Editor:** Alfredo de Palchi. **Associate Editor:** Andrea Lockett.
  ● Work published in *Chelsea* has been included in the 1995, 1997, and 1998 volumes of *The Best American Poetry* and the 1999 and 2000 *Beacon's Best* anthologies.
Magazine Needs: *Chelsea* is a long-established, high quality literary biannual, appearing in June and December, that aims to promote intercultural communication. "We look for intelligence and sophisticated technique in both experimental and traditional forms. We are also interested in translations of contemporary poets. Although our tastes are eclectic, we lean toward the cosmopolitan avant-garde. We would like to see more poetry by writers of color. Do not want to see 'inspirational' verse, pornography or poems that rhyme merely for the sake of rhyme." Has published poetry by Floyd Skloot, C. Dale Young, Saadi Youssef, Aimee Nezhukumatathil, R.T. Smith, and Valerie Wohlfeld. As an example of "the kind of attention to language and imagery" wanted for *Chelsea*, the editor selected these lines from "The Eye-mote" by Sylvia Plath, which first appeared in *Chelsea* in 1960:

> What I want back is what I was/Before the bed, before the knife,/Before the brooch-pin and the salve/
> Fixed me in this parenthesis;/Horses fluent in the wind,/A place, a time gone out of mind.

Chelsea is 192-240 pgs., 6×9, perfect-bound, offset-printed, full-color cover art on card cover, occasional photos, ads. Press run is 2,100 for 900 subscribers of which 200 are libraries. Subscription: $13 domestic, $16 foreign. Sample: $7.
How to Submit: *Chelsea* will again be accepting submissions after October 1, 2001. Submissions of 5-7 pgs. of poetry are ideal; long poems should not exceed 10 pgs.; must be typed; include brief bio. No previously published poems or simultaneous submissions. E-mail for queries only, not for submissions. "We try to comment favorably on above-average mss; otherwise, we do not have time to provide critiques." Responds within 3 months. Always sends prepublication galleys. Pays $20/page and 2 copies. Acquires first North American serial rights and one-time nonexclusive reprint rights.
Also Offers: Sponsors the annual Chelsea Award Competition (deadline December 15), $1,000 for poetry. Guidelines available for SASE.
Advice: "Beginners should realize editors of little magazines are always overworked and that it is necessary haste and not a lack of concern or compassion that makes rejections seem coldly impersonal."

☑ ▢ ◯ CHILDREN, CHURCHES AND DADDIES; SCARS PUBLICATIONS, 824 Brian Court, Gurnee IL 60031. E-mail: ccandd96@aol.com. Website: www.yotko.com/scars (includes writer's guidelines, past issues, archives, past books archives, writers' work, art, awards, interactive poetry, names of editors, poetry, interviews). Established 1993. **Editor/Publisher:** Janet Kuypers.
Magazine Needs: *Children, Churches and Daddies (the unreligious, non-family oriented literary magazine)* is published "monthly or bimonthly depending on year and contains news, humor, poetry, prose, and essays. We specialize in electronic issues and collection books. We accept poetry of almost any genre, but we're not keen on rhyme for rhyme's sake, and we're not keen on religious poems (look at our current issue for a better idea of what we're like). We like gay/lesbian/bisexual, nature/rural/ecology, political, social issues, women/feminism. We do accept longer works, but within two pages for an individual poem is appreciated. We don't go for racist, sexist (therefore we're not into pornography either), or homophobic stuff." Has published poetry by Rochelle Holt, Virginia Love Long, Pete McKinley, and Janine Canan. As a sample we selected these lines from the publisher's own poem "Scars 1997":

> I wear my scars like badges./These deep marks show through from under my skin/like war paint on
> an Apache chief./Decorated with feathers, the skins of his prey.

The print version of *Children, Churches and Daddies* is about 100 pgs., 8×11, photocopied and saddle-stapled, cover, with art and ads. Receives hundreds of poems/year, accepts about 40%. Press run "depends." Sample: $5.50. Make checks payable to Janet Kuypers.
How to Submit: Prefers electronic submissions. Submit via e-mail in body of message, explaining in preceding paragraph that it is a submission. Or mail floppy disk with ASCII text or Macintosh disk. Accepts previously published poems and simultaneous submissions. Seldom comments on rejected poems. Guidelines available for SASE, e-mail, or on website. Responds in 2 weeks.
Also Offers: Scars Publications sometimes sponsors a book contest. Write or e-mail for information. "The website is a more comprehensive view of what *Children, Churches and Daddies* does. All the information is there."

◐ ◯ ◑ CHIRON REVIEW; CHIRON BOOKS; KINDRED SPIRIT PRESS, 702 N. Prairie, St. John KS 67576-1516. (316)549-6156 or (316)786-4955. E-mail: chironreview@hotmail.com. Website: www.geocities. com/SoHo/Nook/1748/ (includes guidelines, sample poems, news and notes, and Personal Publishing Program information). Established 1982 as *The Kindred Spirit*. **Editor:** Michael Hathaway. **Contributing Editor (poetry):** Gerald Locklin.

Magazine Needs: *Chiron Review* is a quarterly tabloid using photographs of featured writers. No taboos. Accepts poetry written by children. Has published poetry by John Gilgun, Douglas Airmet, Paul Snoek, Alison Pelegrin, Paul Agostino, and Hafiz. As a sample the editor selected this poem, "Blue Cellophane" by Melissa Huseman:

> How about that neat piece of blue/cellophane floating into your yard on the wind?//See, Lorna, God
> still loves you./God dropped his eye into your sky.//Go grab that piece of blue. To love it you gotta/
> look at the world as if you're not in it.

Each issue "contains dozens of poems." Press run is about 1,000. Sample: $5 ($10 overseas or institutions).
How to Submit: Submit 3-6 poems at a time, "typed or printed legibly." No simultaneous submissions or previously published poems. No e-mail submissions. Very seldom publishes theme issues. Guidelines and list of upcoming themes available for SASE or on website. Responds in 2 months. Pays 1 copy. Acquires first-time rights. Reviews books of poetry in 500-700 words. Poets may send books for review consideration.
Book/Chapbook Needs & How to Submit: For book publication, query. Publishes 1-3 chapbooks/year, flat-spined, professionally printed, paying 25% of press run of 100-200 copies.
Also Offers: Personal Publishing Program is offered under the Kindred Spirit Press imprint. "Through special arrangements with a highly specialized printer, we can offer extremely short run publishing at unbelievably low prices." Information available for SASE.

$ ☐ ☑ THE CHRISTIAN SCIENCE MONITOR, The Home Forum Page, One Norway St., Boston MA 02115. Website: www.csmonitor.com (includes all of the daily paper, submission guidelines, and original content). Established 1908. **Poetry Editor:** Elizabeth Lund.
Magazine Needs: *Christian Science Monitor* is an international daily newspaper. Poetry used regularly in The Home Forum. Wants "finely crafted poems that explore and celebrate daily life. Seasonal material always needed. Especially interested in poems with an urban flavor. No violence or sensuality. Poems about illness, death, or suffering are not a good fit. Short work preferred." Has published work by Diana Der-Hovanessian, Marilyn Krysl, and Michael Glaser. As a sample the editor included these lines from "Carpe Diem" by Marilyn Krysl:

> Three bees seize/this opportunity to/buzz me, but see://now, instead of three,/there are many: lazy,/
> buzzing me and the blue//felicias, three convened/to please the powers that/be, bees and me and this

How to Submit: Submit up to 5 poems at a time, single-spaced. No previously published poems or simultaneous submissions. SASE must be included. "No faxed submissions please." Usually responds within 2 months. Pays varying rates, upon publication.
Also Offers: A "small (but growing) poetry section includes interviews, reviews, a teacher's guide, Poem of the Month, and more." Also sponsors an annual poetry contest for children (preschool through high school). Entries are accepted from October 1 to November 30.

[N] ◎ ☑ CHRONICLES OF DISORDER (Specialized: themes), 20 Edie Rd., Saratoga Springs NY 12866. Established 1996. **Editor:** Thomas Christian
Magazine Needs: Published biannually, each issue of *Chronicles of Disorder* is based on a theme poetry, prose, art influenced by that theme. "Understand this quote from Antonin Artaud: 'If there is one hellish, accursed thing in our time, it is our artistic dallying with form, instead of being like victims burnt at the stake, signaling through the flames.' " Has published poetry by Thurston Moore, Ron Whitehead, Arthur Winfield Knight, and G.J. Bassett. As a sample the editor selected these lines from his poem "Daimonswey":

> The poet sings. She is Sikelianos./Our spears are twisted. Mangled./A churchbell bangs/A string of
> gongs/the Laconian bitches howl

Chronicles of Disorder is 48 pgs., digest-sized, photocopied and stapled with cardstock cover, includes photography and art sketches. Receives about 150 poems/year, accepts approximately 20%. Press run is 500 for 50 subscribers of which 10 are libraries, 300 shelf sales; 100 distributed free to review publications. Single copy: $2.95. Sample: $4. Make checks payable to Thomas Christian.
How to Submit: Not accepting unsolicited submissions at present. "*Chronicles of Disorder* is currently being reformatted to an online publication with an annual print version featuring the 'best of the year'. Please enclose a SASE for most current information and inquiries."
Advice: "Be in love with your life. Realize that existence is a gift; a temporary window of opportunity in time; a lusting. Find the language as your expression."

☑ CIDER PRESS REVIEW, P.O. Box 881914, San Diego CA 92168. Established 1997. **Co-Editors:** Caron Andregg and Robert Wynne.

USE THE GENERAL INDEX, located at the back of this book, to find the page number of a specific publisher. Also, publishers that were listed in last year's edition but not included in this edition are listed in the General Index with a notation explaining why they were omitted.

Magazine Needs: *Cider Press Review* appears twice/year and features "the best new work from contemporary poets." Wants "thoughtful, well-crafted poems with vivid language and strong images. We prefer poems that have something to say. We would like to see more well-written humor. No didactic, inspirational, greeting-card verse; therapy or religious doggerel." Has published poetry by Jackson Wheeler, Janet Holmes, W.D. Snodgrass, Thomas Lux, Linda Pastan, and Gary Young. As a sample the editors selected these lines from "The Lesser Days" by Cecilia Woloch:

> And I mean to make the most of what has/fallen in my path. The brown-haired man; the smiling clerk; the/branch I've broken from the branch. I mean you can. Give in or not./Take something like the juice of too few stars, anoint yourself.

Cider Press Review is 120 pgs., digest-sized, offset printed and perfect-bound with 2-color coated card cover. Receives about 1,500 poems/year, accepts about 5%. Press run is 750. Subscription: $22/2 issues. Sample: $10.

How to Submit: Submit up to 5 poems at a time. Accepts simultaneous submissions; no previously published poems. Cover letter with short bio preferred. "Please include a SASE. Poets whose work is accepted will be expected to provide a copy of the poem on disk. Do not send unsolicited disk submissions." Time between acceptance and publication is up to 10 months. Poems are circulated to an editorial board. Seldom comments on rejected poems. Responds in up to 6 months. Pays 1 copy. Acquires first North American serial rights.

$⬚ CIMARRON REVIEW, 205 Morrill Hall, Oklahoma State University, Stillwater OK 74078-0135. Established 1967. **Poetry Editor:** Lisa Lewis.

Magazine Needs: *Cimarron* is a quarterly literary journal. "We take pride in our eclecticism. We like evocative poetry (lyric or narrative) controlled by a strong voice. No sing-song verse. No quaint prairie verse. No restrictions as to subject matter. We look for poems whose surfaces and structures risk uncertainty and which display energy, texture, intelligence, and intense investment." Among poets they have published are Dorothy Barresi, Cesare Pauese, Mark Doty, Tess Gallagher, David Rivard, and Albert Goldbarth. *Cimarron Review*, 100-150 pgs., 6×9, perfect-bound, boasts a handsome design, including a color cover and attractive printing. Poems lean toward free verse, lyric, and narrative, although all forms and styles seem welcome. There are 15-25 pages of poetry in each issue. Circulation is 500 of which most are libraries. Single copy: $5; subscription: $16/year ($20 Canada), $45/3 years ($55 Canada), plus $2.50 for all international subscriptions.

How to Submit: Submit 3-5 poems, name and address on each, typed single- or double-spaced. No simultaneous submissions. No response without SASE. No fax or e-mail submissions. Responds in 3 months. Pays $15 for each poem published, 1 copy, and a subscription. Acquires first North American serial rights only. Reviews books of poetry in 500-900 words, single book format, occasionally multi-book. All reviews are assigned.

🍁 ✔ 🍎 ⬚ ⬚ ◎ THE CLAREMONT REVIEW (Specialized: teens/young adults), 4980 Wesley Rd., Victoria, British Columbia V8Y 1Y9 Canada. (250)658-5221. Fax: (250)658-5387. E-mail: review@claremont.victoria.bc.ca. Website: www.members.home.net/review (includes guidelines, samples, and monthly contest information). Established 1991. **Contact:** Susan Stenson.

THE CLAREMONT REVIEW   NUMBER 18
FALL   2000

"Our covers must capture our interest," say the editors of *The Claremont Review*. "Some covers are chosen over others because they offer variety from a previous cover." Richard Greenwood, an artist enrolled in the University of Victoria's Visual Arts program, designed the computer-generated image "Tryest" featured on this volume's cover.

Magazine Needs: *The Claremont Review* is a biannual review which publishes poetry and fiction written by those ages 13 to 19. Each fall issue also includes an interview with a prominent Canadian writer. Wants "vital, modern poetry with a strong voice and living language. We prefer works that reveal something of the human condition. No clichéd language nor copies of 18th and 19th century work." Has published poetry by Jen Wright, Erin Egan, and Max Rosenblum. As a sample the editors selected these lines from "The Last Room" by Jen Wright:

> These men study death./They say it is congestive heart failure,/brain hemorrhage, invasive tumor./But
> that's not what you showed me/one child's day/after we found a robin, frozen, on the porch.

The Claremont Review is 110 pgs., 6×9, professionally printed and perfect-bound with an attractive color cover. Receives 600-800 poems/year, accepts about 120. Press run is 700 for 200 subscribers of which 50 are libraries, 250 shelf sales. Subscription: $12/year, $20/2 years. Sample: $6.
How to Submit: Submit poems typed one to a page with author's name at the top of each. Accepts simultaneous submissions; no previously published poems. Cover letter with brief bio required. Reads submissions September through June only. Always comments on rejected poems. Guidelines available for SASE (or SAE and IRC). Responds in up to 6 weeks (excluding July and August). Pays 1 copy and funds when grants allow it. Acquires first North American serial rights.
Advice: "We strongly urge potential contributors to read back issues of *The Claremont Review*. That is the best way for you to learn what we are looking for."

☑ ◐ ◉ **CLARK STREET REVIEW (Specialized: form/style, narrative poetry)**, P.O. Box 1377, Berthoud CO 80513. (970)669-5175. E-mail: clarkreview@earthlink.net. Website: http://home.earthlink.net/~clarkreview/ (includes submission guidelines). Established 1998. **Editor:** Ray Foreman.
Magazine Needs: Appearing 8 times/year, *Clark Street Review* publishes narrative poetry and short shorts—"to give writers and poets cause to keep writing by publishing their best work." Wants "narrative poetry under 100 lines that reach readers who are mostly published poets and writers. Subjects are open. No obscure and formalist work." Has published poetry by Sean Carney, Sam Vargo, Alan Catlin, Gary Blanenburg, Albert Huffstickler, Anselm Brocki, and Lamar Thomas. As a sample the editor selected these lines from "those days" by Lamar Thomas:

> Through fog and smoke a long ash crooks/at my cigarette's end./It feels like a Hopper diner,/stark, sad
> eyes, a conversation stalls,/she sits steady, pieta-like in blue light./I stare through the steam of my
> coffee.

Clark Street Review is 20 pgs., digest-sized, photocopied, and saddle-stapled with paper cover. Receives about 500 poems/year, accepts about 25%. Press run is 200 for 90 subscribers. Subscription: $10 for 10 issues postpaid. Sample: $2. Make checks payable to R. Foreman. "prefer cash or stamps."
How to Submit: Submit 1-10 poems at a time. Line length for poetry is 30 minimum, 100 maximum. Accepts previously published poems and simultaneous submissions. "Disposable copies only—sharp copies. Maximum width—65 characters. SASE or e-mail address for reply. No cover letter." Time between acceptance and publication is 3 months. "Editor reads everything with a critical eye of 30 years of experience in writing and publishing small press work." Often comments on rejected poems. Publishes theme issues occasionally. Guidelines available for SASE, by e-mail, or on website. "If one writes narrative poetry, they don't need guidelines. They feel it." Responds in 3 weeks. Pays 1 copy. Acquires one-time rights.
Advice: "*Clark Street Review* is geared to the more experienced poet and writer. There are tips throughout each issue writers appreciate. As always, the work we print speaks for the writer and the magazine. We encourage communication between our poets by listing their e-mail and home addresses. Publishing excellence and giving writers a cause to write is our only aim."

☑ ◉ **THE CLASSICAL OUTLOOK (Specialized: themes, translations, classics, Latin)**, Classics Dept., Park Hall, University of Georgia, Athens GA 30602-6203. (706)542-9257. Fax: (706)542-8503. E-mail: mricks@arches.uga.edu. Website: www.classics.uga.edu/classout.html. Established 1924. **Editor:** Prof. Richard LaFleur. **Poetry Editors:** Prof. David Middleton (original English verse) and David Slavitt (translations and original Latin verse).
Magazine Needs: *The Classical Outlook* "is an internationally circulated quarterly journal (4,200 subscriptions, of which 250 are libraries) for high school and college Latin and Classics teachers, published by the American Classical League." They invite submissions of "original poems in English on classical themes, verse translations from Greek and Roman authors, and original Latin poems. Submissions should, as a rule, be written in traditional poetic forms and should demonstrate skill in the use of meter, diction, and rhyme if rhyme is employed. Original poems should be more than mere exercise pieces or the poetry of nostalgia. Translations should be accompanied by a photocopy of the original Greek or Latin text. Latin originals should be accompanied by a literal English rendering of the text. Submissions should not exceed 50 lines." Has published work by Jack Flavin and Robert Cooperman. As a sample the editors selected these lines from "Penelope in Progress" by Lisa Barnett:

> Her subject matter is the warp and weft/of pure design—it's not the body's landscape,/it's not the text
> of deep-felt,wifely grief,/Her weaving is the work of artist's hands.

There are 2-3 magazine-sized pgs. of poetry in each issue. Receives about 350 submissions/year, uses 15%. Has a 12- to 18-month backlog, 4-month lead time. Single copy: $10.

How to Submit: Submit 2 anonymous copies, double-spaced, no more than 5 poems at a time. No previously published or simultaneous submissions. No fax or e-mail submissions. "Please include a floppy disk containing work, if possible. Also, please identify the name and version number of word-processing package used." Poetry is refereed by poetry editors. Guidelines available for SASE, by e-mail, or by fax. Responds in up to 3-6 months. Pays 2 copies. Sample copies are available from the American Classical League, Miami University, Oxford OH 45056 for $10. Reviews books of poetry "if the poetry is sufficiently classical in nature."

Advice: "Since our policy is to have poetry evaluated anonymously, names and addresses on poems, etc., just make work at this end. Cover letters are not forwarded to the poetry editors. Also, we never knowingly publish any works which have been or will be published elsewhere."

CLAY PALM REVIEW: ART AND LITERARY MAGAZINE, 8 Huntington St., Suite 307, Shelton CT 06484-5228. E-mail: claypalm@cs.com. Website: www.claypalmreview.com (includes guidelines, statement of purpose, sample poetry, sample artwork, contact information, list of contributors, purchasing information, advice to writers, retail outlets, advertising information, and quotes). Established 1999 (premier issue, spring/summer 2000). **Founder/Editor:** Lisa Cisero.

Magazine Needs: Published biannually, *Clay Palm Review* "aims to introduce new and already established poets. We would like to create a place for the imagination to flourish. The public needs to become culturally aware, and I feel that poets and artists understand their connection to life and one another. We accept well-crafted poetry with specific attention to detail and imagery. The poem must appeal to the senses and be full of texture, void of cliché language. Translations are always welcomed. We encourage the writer to experiment with their language, to be unique and different. There will also be a 'special to this issue' section including featured essays or interviews." *Clay Palm Review* does not accept rhyme, vulgarity, social or political content, science fiction, or depressive material. Has published poetry by Naomi Shihab Nye, Marge Piercy, Duane Locke, Virgil Suarez, and John Smelcer. As a sample the editor selected these lines from "Seven Reasons" by Heather MacLeod:

> She takes me to a woman, covered/in Egyptian cotton, pale, irises like tattoos/inside the palms of her
> hands. Maps instead/of veins, journeys instead of blood./. . . Muslims praying, holy water on my
> forehead,/geography all over the soles of my feet.

Clay Palm Review is about 120 pgs., "a bit larger than digest-sized," offset-printed and perfect-bound with glossy cover, includes colored artwork, b&w photography, short fiction, essays, interviews, collage, sculpture, and ads. Single copy: $9.95; subscription: $17.95.

How to Submit: Submit 5-6 poems at a time. Accepts previously published poems "only with written consent from publisher"; no simultaneous submissions. Accepts e-mail submissions from foreign writers; include in body of text. Accepts disk submissions. Cover letter required. "Each poem must include the name and address of the poet in the upper right hand corner, along with copyright date. A SASE must always be included. No handwritten submissions." Reads submissions July through September for fall/winter issue and December through March for spring/summer issue. Submit seasonal poems 3-4 months in advance. Time between acceptance and publication is up to 6 months. "Submissions are given an extensive review, in order to decide whether they meet the satisfaction of the editor. They are then accepted, rejected, or held for future use. Comments upon the drafts, creating a working relationship with the poet." Publishes theme issues occasionally. Guidelines available on website. "Also welcome to e-mail any questions." Responds in up to 6 months. Pays 1 copy. Acquires first North American serial rights. "The rights revert back to the poet after publication. We do need to be recognized as the first-time publisher."

Advice: "Poets should always review guidelines before submitting. Purchasing a copy is best to determine whether your writing style meets our needs. Revise, revise, revise! The more you write the more 'polished' you become. As long as you are passionate about what you write, you will succeed."

$ ◎ CLEANING BUSINESS MAGAZINE; CLEANING CONSULTANT SERVICES, INC. (Specialized: cleaning, self-employment), P.O. Box 1273, Seattle WA 98111. (206)622-4241. Fax: (206)622-6876. E-mail: wgriffin@cleaningconsultant.com. Website: www.cleaningconsultants.com. Established 1976. **Poetry Editor:** William R. Griffin.

Magazine Needs: *Cleaning Business Magazine* is "a monthly magazine for cleaning and maintenance professionals" and uses some poetry relating to their interests. "To be considered for publication in *Cleaning Business*, submit poetry that relates to our specific audience—cleaning and self-employment." Has published poetry by Don Wilson, Phoebe Bosche, Trudie Mercer, and Joe Keppler. *Cleaning Business Magazine* is 100 pgs., 8½×11, offset litho printed, using ads, art, and graphics. Receives about 50 poems/year, accepts about 10. Press run is 5,000 for 3,000 subscribers of which 100 are libraries, 500 shelf sales. Single copy: $5; subscription: $20. Sample: $3.

How to Submit: Accepts simultaneous submissions; no previously published poems. Send SASE and $3 for guidelines. Pays $5-10 plus 1 copy.

Advice: "Poets identify a specific market and work to build a readership that can be tapped again and again over a period of years with new books. Also write to a specific audience that has a mutual interest. We buy poetry about cleaning, but seldom receive anything our subscribers would want to read."

◢ ◎ CLEVELAND STATE UNIVERSITY POETRY CENTER; CSU POETRY SERIES; CLEVELAND POETS SERIES; CSU POETRY CENTER PRIZE (Specialized: regional), 1983 E. 24 St., Cleveland OH 44115-2440. (216)687-3986 or toll-free: (888)278-6473. Fax: (216)687-6943. E-mail: poetrycenter@csu ohio.edu. Website: www.csuohio.edu/poetrycenter (including contest guidelines and catalog of publications). The Poetry Center was established in 1962, first publications in 1971. **Coordinator:** Rita Grabowski. **Director:** Ted Lardner.

Book/Chapbook Needs: The Poetry Center publishes the CSU Poetry Series for poets in general and the Cleveland Poets Series for Ohio poets. "Open to many kinds of form, length, subject matter, style, and purpose. Should be well-crafted, clearly of professional quality, ultimately serious (even when humorous). No light verse, devotional verse or verse in which rhyme and meter seem to be of major importance." Has published *Hammerlock* and *Hurdy-Gurdy* by Tim Seibles; *The Book of Orgasms* by Nin Andrews; *Attendant Ghosts* by George Looney; *A Short History of Pets* by Carol Potter; and *The Obsidian Ranfla* by Anthony R. Vigil. As a sample the editors selected this excerpt from "Bad Date" from *The Largest Possible Life* by Alison Luterman:

> *Now he has taken a deep breath and looked moistly into my eyes./I think that means I am responsible*
> *for his emotional well-being./He is getting ready to recite/one of his poems. Maybe there will be an*
> *earthquake/and the chandelier will fall on our heads and I'll be spared*

Books are chosen for publication from the entries to the CSU Poetry Center Prize contest. (Write and send $2 for catalog of Poetry Center books.) Postmark deadline: February 1. Entry fee: $20. The winner receives $1,000 and publication. Publishes some other entrants in the Poetry Series, providing 50 copies (out of a press run of 1,000) and $300 lump sum. The Cleveland Poets Series (for Ohio poets) offers 100 copies of a press run of 600.

How to Submit: To submit for all series, send ms between November 1 and February 1 only. Responds to all submissions for the year by the end of July. No e-mail submissions. Mss should be for books of 50-100 pgs. ("should contain a minimum of 40 pages of poems, table of contents"); pages numbered; poet's name, address and phone number on cover sheet, clearly typed. Poems may have been previously published (listed on an acknowledgement page). Accepts simultaneous submissions, if notified and "poet keeps us informed of change in status." Guidelines available for SASE or on website.

🍎 🌙 ◑ ◎ **THE CLIMBING ART (Specialized: nature/rural/ecology, sports/recreation)**, 6390 E. Floyd Dr., Denver CO 80222. Phone/fax: (303)757-0541. E-mail: rmorrow@dnur.uswest.net. Established 1986. **Editor:** Ron Morrow.

Magazine Needs: *The Climbing Art* is a biannual journal "read mainly by mountain enthusiasts who appreciate good writing about mountains and mountaineering. We are open to all forms and lengths. The only requirement is that the work be fresh, well-written, and in some way of interest to those who love the mountains." Accepts poetry written by children. Has published poetry by Terry Gifford, Allison Hunter, Paul Willis, Denise K. Simon, and Barry Govenor. *The Climbing Art* is 160 pgs., digest-sized, professionally printed on heavy stock with glossy card cover. Accepts 12-20 poems/issue, receives 50 submissions/month. Press run is 1,500 for 700 subscribers of which 10 are libraries, 500 shelf sales. Subscription: $18. Sample: $4.

How to Submit: Accepts simultaneous submissions and previously published poems. Accepts fax and e-mail submissions. Responds in 6 months. Sometimes sends prepublication galleys. Pays 2 copies and subscription. Acquires one-time rights. Reviews books of poetry only if they concern mountains.

🌐 ◎ **CLÓ IAR-CHONNACHTA (Specialized: bilingual/foreign language)**, Indreabhán, Co. Galway, Ireland. Phone: +353-91-593307. Fax: +353-91-593362. E-mail: cic@iol.ie. Website: www.cic.ie. Established 1985. **Contact:** Deirdre O'Toole.

Book/Chapbook Needs: Publishes paperback books of Irish language poetry, one of which is selected through a competition. Has published collections of poetry by Cathal Ó Searcaigh, Nuala Ni Dhomhnaill, Gabriel Rosenstock, Michael Davitt, and Liam Ó Muirthile.

How to Submit: Query with 20 sample poems and a cover letter with brief bio and publication credits. Mss are read by an editorial panel. Often comments on rejected poems. No payment information provided.

$ ◙ **CLOUD RIDGE PRESS**, 815 13th St., Boulder CO 80302. Established 1985. **Editor:** Elaine Kohler.

Book/Chapbook Needs: Cloud Ridge Press is a "literary small press for unique works in poetry and prose." Publishes letterpress and offset books in both paperback and hardcover editions. In poetry, publishes "strong images of the numinous qualities in authentic experience grounded in a landscape and its people." The first book, published in 1985, was *Ondina: A Narrative Poem* by John Roberts. The book is 6×9¼, handsomely printed on buff stock, cloth bound in black with silver decoration and spine lettering, 131 pgs. 800 copies were bound in Curtis Flannel and 200 copies bound in cloth over boards, numbered, and signed by the poet and artist. This letterpress edition, priced at $18/cloth and $12/paper, is not available in bookstores but only by mail from the press. The trade edition was photo-offset from the original, in both cloth and paper bindings, and is sold in bookstores. The press plans to publish 1-2 books/year.

How to Submit: Since the press is not accepting unsolicited mss, writers should query first. Queries will be answered in 2 weeks and mss reported on in 1 month. Simultaneous submissions are acceptable. Royalties are 10% plus a negotiable number of author's copies. A brochure is free on request; send #10 SASE.

✓ ♟ 🍎 $ ◑ ◎ **CLUBHOUSE JR. (Specialized: children, religious)**, 8605 Explorer Dr., Colorado Springs CO 80920. Fax: (719)531-3499. Established 1988. **Assistant Editor:** Suzanne Hadley. **Editor:** Annette Bourland.

● *Clubhouse Jr.* won the Evangelical Press Association Award for Youth Publication.

Magazine Needs: *Clubhouse Jr.* is a monthly magazine published by Focus on the Family for 4-8 year olds. Wants short poems—less than 100 words. "Poetry should have a strong message that supports traditional values. No cute, but pointless work." As a sample the editors selected this poem, "My Friend," by Mary Ryer:

> If I'm feeling very sad/And don't know what to do./If I'm feeling all alone/Or angry through and
> through./I really shouldn't worry/Or sit alone and cry./I always have a friend to help./Jesus is nearby.

Clubhouse Jr. is 16-20 pgs., magazine-sized, web-printed on glossy paper and saddle-stapled with 4-color paper cover, includes 4-color art. The magazine has 96,000 subscribers. Single copy: $1.50; subscription: $15/year. Sample: $1.25 with 8 × 10 SASE. Make checks payable to Focus on the Family.

How to Submit: Submit up to 5 poems at a time. Accepts simultaneous submissions; no previously published poems. Cover letter preferred. Accepts fax submissions; no e-mail submissions. Time between acceptance and publication is in up to 1 year. Seldom comments on rejected poems. Occasionally publishes theme issues. Guidelines available for SASE. Responds in up to 2 months. Pays $50-100. Acquires first rights.

COAL CITY REVIEW, English Dept., University of Kansas, Lawrence KS 66045. Established 1989. **Editor:** Brian Daldorph.

Magazine Needs: Published in the fall, *Coal City Review* is an annual publication of poetry, short stories, reviews, and interviews—"the best material I can find." As for poetry, the editor quotes Pound: " 'Make it new.' " Does not want to see "experimental poetry, doggerel, five-finger exercises, or beginner's verse." Has published poetry by Taylor Graham, David Ray, Gary Lechliter, and Elliot Richman. As a sample the editor selected these lines from "How to Be a Gay Literary Icon" by Michael Gregg Michaud:

> Say you knew Tennessee Williams./Say you slept with him./He's dead, who'll know?/Enter your latest
> book/in the annual Lambda Literary Awards/and vote for yourself./Be sullen./Be fat with a receding
> hairline/a 44 inch waist/and a mother complex./Frequent hustler bars./Be photographed with Sandra
> Bernhard, Madonna,/or Jeff Stryker.

Coal City Review is 100 pgs., 5½ × 8½, professionally printed on recycled paper and perfect-bound with light, colored card cover. Accepts about 5% of the material received. Press run is 200 for 50 subscribers of which 5 are libraries. Subscription: $10. Sample: $6.

How to Submit: Submit 6 poems at a time. Accepts previously published poems occasionally; prefers not to receive simultaneous submissions. "Please do not send list of prior publications." Seldom comments on rejected poems. Guidelines available for SASE. Responds in up to 3 months. Pays 1 copy. Reviews books of poetry in 300-1,000 words, mostly single format. Poets may send books for review consideration.

Book/Chapbook Needs & How to Submit: *Coal City Review* also publishes occasional chapbooks as issues of the magazine but does not accept unsolicited chapbook submissions. Their most recent chapbook is *Slowly Along the Riverbeds* by Phil Wedge.

Advice: "Care more (much more) about writing than publication. If you're good enough, you'll publish."

COCHRAN'S CORNER (Specialized: subscribers), 1003 Tyler Court, Waldorf MD 20602-2964. Established 1985. **Executive Editor:** Jeanie Saunders. **Poetry Editor:** Billye Keene.

Magazine Needs: *Cochran's Corner* is a "family type" quarterly open to beginners, preferring poems of 20 lines or less. Must be a subscriber to submit. "Any subject or style (except porn)." Accepts poetry written by children. Has published poetry by Jean B. York, Brian Duthins, C.J. Villiano, and Annette Shaw. As a sample the editor selected this poem, "Journey," (poet unidentified):

> You take me to places/Within myself/Where I have never been—/foreign places/Timidly I follow you
> through/Subterranian chambers/And/Undiscovered essences/to the/mainstream/that/is/I

Cochran's Corner is 58 pgs., desktop-published, saddle-stapled, with matte card cover. Press run is 500. Subscription: $20. Sample: $5 plus SASE.

How to Submit: Submit 5 poems at a time. Accepts simultaneous submissions and previously published poems. Guidelines available for SASE. Responds in 3 months. Pays 2 copies. Acquires first or one-time rights. Reviews books of poetry. Send books for review consideration.

Also Offers: Sponsors contests in March and July; $5 entry fee for unlimited poems "if sent in the same envelope. We provide criticism if requested at the rate of $1 per page."

Advice: "Write from the heart, but don't forget your readers. You must work to find the exact words that mirror your feelings, so the reader can share your feelings."

COFFEE HOUSE PRESS, 27 N. Fourth St., Suite 400, Minneapolis MN 55401. (612)338-0125. Established 1984. **Managing Editor:** Chris Fischbach.

● Coffee House Press books have won numerous honors and awards. As an example, *The Book of Medicines* by Linda Hogan won the Colorado Book Award for Poetry and the Lannan Foundation Literary Fellowship.

Book Needs: Publishes 12 books/year, 4-5 of which are poetry. Wants poetry that is "challenging and lively; influenced by the Beats, the NY School, or Black Mountain." Has published poetry collections by Victor Hernandez Cruz, Anne Waldman, and Paul Metcalf.

How to Submit: Submit 8-12 poems at a time. Accepts previously published poems. Cover letter and vita required. "Please include a SASE for our reply and/or the return of your ms." Seldom comments on rejected poems. Responds to queries in 1 month; to mss in up to 8 months. Always sends prepublication galleys. Send SASE for catalog. No phone, fax, or e-mail queries.

☑ ☒ $ ◲ **COLORADO REVIEW; COLORADO PRIZE FOR POETRY**, Dept. of English, Colorado State University, Ft. Collins CO 80523. (970)491-5449. E-mail: creview@colostate.edu. Website: www.colorador eview.com (includes writer's guidelines, list of editorial staff, subscription guidelines, and Colorado Prize for Poetry guidelines). Established 1955 as *Colorado State Review*, resurrected 1967 under "New Series" rubric, renamed *Colorado Review* 1985. **Editor:** David Milofsky. **Poetry Editors:** Jorie Graham and Donald Revell.
  ● Poetry published in *Colorado Review* has been included in the 1995, 1996, and 1997 volumes of *The Best American Poetry*.
Magazine Needs: *Colorado Review* is a journal of contemporary literature which appears 3 times/year combining short fiction, poetry, and personal essays. Has published poetry by Karen Volkman, Cal Bedient, Susan Wheeler, and Tracy Philpot. *Colorado Review* is about 180 pgs., 6×9, professionally printed and perfect-bound with glossy card cover. Press run is 1,500 for 1,000 subscribers of which 100 are libraries. Receives about 10,000 submissions/year, accepts about 2%. Subscription: $24/year. Sample: $10.
How to Submit: Submit about 5 poems at a time. No previously published poems or simultaneous submissions. Submissions must include SASE for response. Reads submissions September 1 through May 1 only. Responds in 2 months. Pays $5/printed page for poetry. Acquires first North American serial rights. Reviews books of poetry and fiction, both single and multi-book format. Poets may send books for review consideration.
Also Offers: Also sponsors the annual Colorado Prize for Poetry, established in 1995, offering an honorarium of $2,000. Complete book must be unpublished. Submit a book-length ms on any subject in any form. Guidelines available for SASE. Entry fee: $25. Deadline: January 8. Most recent award winner was Sally Keith (2000). Judge was Allen Grossman. Winner announced in May.

⅗ ▣ ◐ **COMFUSION REVIEW**, 304 S. Third St., San Jose CA 95112. E-mail: wright@comfusionreview .com. Website: www.comfusionreview.com (includes poetry, interviews, reviews, fiction, academic essays, rant/ friction, photography, and artwork in varied mediums). Established 1995. **Editors:** Jaime Wright and Stephen Wiley.
Magazine Needs: *Comfusion* appears annually; www.comfusion.com is updated monthly. "Our purpose is to showcase new and established talent skillfully manifested within the medium of poetry. We want well-crafted material that is original and edgy. We encourage innovative formal and free verse poetry." Also accepts essays, fiction, and photography. "We do not want to see sappy-sentimental love or devotional poetry. And please, absolutely no inspirational." Recently published poetry by Richard Linker, Vadim Litvak, Samuel Maio, James Brown, Ginger Pielage, and Marc David Pinate. As a sample the editors selected these lines from "Photographer" by Ginger Pielage:
> *he penetrates the silver solution/grasps the skin of film/casts me/a dripping rag/drying out in his hands*
Comfusion is 60-80 pgs., magazine-sized, saddle-stapled, glossy cover, with art/graphics and ads. "Many poems that go unprinted in our yearly publication are featured on our website." Receives about 120 poems/year, accepts about 10%. Publishes 12-20 poems/issue. Press run is 1,000 for 200 subscribers; 800 distributed free to independent book stores and cafes. Single copy: free; subscription: $10 for 2 years. Sample: $5. Make checks payable to *comfusion*/Lotus Foundation.
How to Submit: Submit 3 poems at a time. Accepts previously published poems; no simultaneous submissions. Accepts e-mail submissions and disk submissions. Cover letter is preferred. "Cover letter should include bio information. Please include SASE with submission. E-mail poems to wright@comfusionreview.com. Each submission needs name, address, phone, and e-mail." Reads submission year round. Submit seasonal poems 2 months in advance. Time between acceptance and publication is 6 months. Poems are circulated to an editorial board. Seldom comments on rejections. "We encourage poets and other artists to check out our website, comfusion review.com, or purchase one of our back issues before submission." Guidelines available for SASE, by e-mail, or on website. Responds in 3 months. Always sends prepublication galleys. Pays 2 contributor's copies. Acquires one-time rights. Reviews books and chapbooks of poetry and other magazines in 1,000 words, single book format. Poets may send books for review consideration to *comfusion*.
Advice: "Poets should take into account a broad spectrum of poetic tradition as refracted through the spectrum of their own personal irreverence and respect. Please don't insult your collective readers' intelligence by attempting to speak in the voice of the 'common man.' But feel free to make sure we know what you're talking about (James Brown)."

☑ ▢ ◎ **COMMON THREADS; OHIO HIGH SCHOOL POETRY CONTESTS; OHIO POETRY ASSOCIATION (Specialized: membership, students)**, 3520 State Route 56, Mechanicsburg OH 43044. (937)834-2666. Website: www.crosswinds.net/~opa (includes the history of the OPA, most recent newsletter, membership applications, poets' library, and links). Established 1928. **Editor:** Amy Jo Zook. Ohio Poetry Association (Michael Lepp, treasurer, 1798 Sawgrass Dr., Reynoldsburg OH 43068), is a state poetry society open to members from outside the state, an affiliate of the National Federation of State Poetry Societies.

Magazine Needs: *Common Threads* is their poetry magazine, appearing twice/year. Only members of OPA may submit poems. Does not want to see poetry which is highly sentimental, overly morbid, or pornograpic—and nothing over 40 lines. "We use beginners' poetry, but would like it to be good, tight, revised. In short, not first drafts. Too much is sentimental or prosy when it could be passionate or lyric. We'd like poems to make us think as well as feel something." Accepts poetry written by children "if members or high school contest winners." Has published poetry by Yvonne Hardenbrook, Betsy Kennedy, Rose Ann Spaith, and Dalene Workman Stull. As a sample the editor selected these lines from "Talking to Flowers," by Cathryn Essinger:

> And then we spoke about silence/and the fragile gestures made by flowers/and the single word spoken/
> by each blossom, mouth to mouth.

Common Threads is 52 pgs., digest-sized, computer-typeset, with matte card cover. "Ours is a forum for our members, and we do use reprints, so new members can get a look at what is going well in more general magazines." Annual dues including *Common Threads*: $15. Senior (over 65): $12. Single copies: $2.

How to Submit: Accepts previously published poems, if "author is upfront about them. All rights revert to poet after publication."

Also Offers: Ohio Poetry Association sponsors an annual contest for unpublished poems written by high school students in Ohio with categories of traditional, modern, and several other categories. March deadline, with 3 money awards in each category. For contest information write Ohio Poetry Association, % Elouise Postle, 4761 Willow Lane, Lebanon OH 45036. "Also, we have a quarterly contest open to all poets, entry fee, two money awards and publication. Write to Janeen Lepp, president, 1798 Sawgrass Dr., Reynoldsburg OH 43068 (#10 SASE) or e-mail janeenlepp@juno.com for dates and themes." (Also see separate listing for Ohio Poetry Association in the Organizations section.)

$ ✉ ◎ COMMONWEAL (Specialized: religious), 475 Riverside Dr., New York NY 10115. Fax: (212)662-4183. Website: www.commonwealmagazine.org (includes writer's guidelines, names of editors, poetry, interviews, samples from current issue, and back issues with table of contents). **Poetry Editor:** Rosemary Deen.

Magazine Needs: *Commonweal* appears every 2 weeks, circulation 20,000, is a general-interest magazine for college-educated readers by Catholics. Prefers serious, witty, well-written poems of up to 75 lines. Does not publish inspirational poems. As a sample the editor selected these lines from "One is One," a sonnet by Marie Ponsot:

> Heart, you bully, you punk, I'm wrecked, I'm shocked/stiff. You? you still try to rule the world—though/
> I've got you: identified, starving, locked/in a cage you will not leave alive . . .

Subscription: $44. Sample: $3.

How to Submit: Considers simultaneous submissions. Does not accept fax or e-mail submissions. Reads submissions September 1 through June 30 only. Pays 50¢ a line plus 2 copies. Acquires all rights. Returns rights when requested by the author. Reviews books of poetry in 750-1,000 words, single or multi-book format.

✎ THE COMSTOCK REVIEW; COMSTOCK WRITERS' GROUP INC.; MURIEL CRAFT BAILEY MEMORIAL PRIZE, 4958 St. John Dr., Syracuse NY 13215. (315)488-8077. E-mail: kniles1@twcny.rr.com. Website: www.comstockreview.org. Established 1987 as *Poetpourri*, published by the Comstock Writers' Group, Inc. **Coordinator:** Kathleen Bryce Niles.

Magazine Needs: *The Comstock Review* appears biannually. Uses "well-written free and traditional verse. No obscene, obscure, patently religious, or greeting card verse." Has published poetry by Ellen Bass, Ryan G. Van Cleave, Virgil Suarez, Susan Terris, Robert Cooperman, and Katharyn Howd Machan. As a sample they selected these lines from "Numberology" by Ute Carbone:

> Nine is not an easy number/it always leaves something hanging./It's not perfect like eight,/with its two
> worlds one atop/the other, flowing in a single/fluid line, a mobius strip,/divisible by fours and twos.

The Comstock Review is about 100 pgs., digest-sized, professionally printed, perfect-bound. Press run is 600. Subscription: $15/year; $8/issue. Sample from past years: $6.

How to Submit: Submit 3-6 poems at a time, name and address on each page, unpublished poems only. No fax or e-mail submissions. Cover letter with short bio preferred. Poems are read January 1 through February 28 and July 1 through August 31 only. Poems are held until next reading period for consideration. Editors sometimes comment on returned submissions. Pays 1 copy. Acquires first North American serial rights.

Also Offers: Offers the Muriel Craft Bailey Memorial Prize yearly with $1,000 1st Prize, $200 2nd Prize, $100 3rd Prize, honorable mentions, publication of all finalists. Entry fee: $3/poem. 40-line limit. Deadline: July 1. Judge for 2001: Mary Oliver; judge for 2002: Kelly Cherry.

✎ CONCHO RIVER REVIEW; FORT CONCHO MUSEUM PRESS, P.O. Box 10894, Angelo State University, San Angelo TX 76909. (915)942-2273. Fax: (915)942-2155. E-mail: jbradley@mail.wtamu.edu. Website: www.angelo.edu (includes writer's guidelines and names of editors). Established 1984. **Editor:** James A. Moore. **Poetry Editor:** Jerry Bradley.

Magazine Needs: *Concho River Review* is a literary journal published twice/year. "Prefer shorter poems, few long poems accepted; particularly looking for poems with distinctive imagery and imaginative forms and rhythms. The first test of a poem will be its imagery." Short reviews of new volumes of poetry are also published. *Concho*

River Review is 120-138 pgs., digest-sized, professionally printed and flat-spined, with matte card cover. Accepts 35-40 of 600-800 poems received/year. Press run is 300 for about 200 subscribers of which 10 are libraries. Subscription: $14. Sample: $5.

How to Submit: "Please submit 3-5 poems at a time. Use regular legal-sized envelopes—no big brown envelopes; no replies without SASE. Type must be letter-perfect, sharp enough to be computer scanned." Accepts e-mail submissions. Responds in 2 months. Pays 1 copy. Acquires first rights.

Advice: "We're always looking for good, strong work—from both well-known poets and those who have never been published before."

CONCRETE WOLF, P. O. Box 10250, Bedford NH 03110-0250. E-mail: concretewolf@yahoo.com. Website: www.concretewolf.homestead.com (includes submission guidelines, excerpts, audio poems). Established 2001. **Editors:** Brent Allard and Lana Ayers.

Magazine Needs: *Concrete Wolf* appears quarterly. "We like to see fresh perspectives on common human experiences, with careful attention to words. No specifications as to form, subject matter, or style. Poems that give the impression the poet is in the room." Does not want "poetry that is all head or preaches rather than speaks." Recently published poetry by Martha Miller, Paul Szlosek, Brian Moreau, Sharon Desmarais, Ed Nelson, and Ute Carbone. As a sample the editors selected these lines from "September 30, 1992" by Sean Patrick Murphy:

> *He awoke in the middle of the night/and lied/"It is October first and my love/has died"/In the darkness*
> *he fumbled for matches/said a prayer for every suffocated child*

Concrete Wolf is 75 pgs., magazine-sized, duplex-printed, perfect-bound, matte card stock cover, with b&w art. Receives about 800 poems/year, accepts about 30%. Publishes about 60 poems/issue. Press run is 1,000 for 50 subscribers of which 3 are libraries, 50% shelf sales; 20% are distributed free to writing organizations. Single copy: $6; subscription: $20. Sample: $5. Make checks payable to *Concrete Wolf*.

How to Submit: Submit up to 5 poems at a time. Line length for poetry is 300 maximum. Accepts previously published poems and simultaneous submissions. Accepts e-mail and disk submissions; no fax submissions. "For e-mail submissions, type into body or attach Word file." Reads submissions year round. Time between acceptance and publication is 3-6 months. "Poetry is individually reviewed by two editors and then discussed. Poems agreed upon by both editors are accepted." Often comments on rejected poems. Guidelines are available for SASE, by e-mail, and on website. Responds in 6 weeks. Pays 2 contributor's copies. Acquires one-time rights.

Also Offers: Website will occasionally post writing exercises. Future plans include a supplementary CD of poets reading their work.

Advice: "Poetry exists for everyone, not just the academic. Remember that poetry is work that requires crafting."

CONFLUENCE PRESS (Specialized: regional), 500 Eighth Ave., Lewis-Clark State College, Lewiston ID 83501. (208)799-2336. Fax: (208)799-2850. E-mail: conpress@lcsc.edu. Website: www.confluencepress.com (includes guidelines and recent titles). Established 1975. **Poetry Editor:** James R. Hepworth.

• "We have received four Western States Book Awards and two awards from The Pacific Northwest Booksellers within the last decade."

Book/Chapbook Needs: Confluence is an "independent publisher of fiction, poetry, creative nonfiction, and literary scholarship. We are open to formal poetry as well as free verse. No rhymed doggerel, 'light verse,' 'performance poetry,' 'street poetry,' etc. We prefer to publish work by poets who live and work in the northwestern United States." Has published poetry by John Daniel, Greg Keeler, Nancy Mairs, and Sherry Rind. Prints about 2 books/year.

How to Submit: "Please query before submitting manuscript." Query with 6 sample poems, bio, and list of publications. No fax or e-mail submissions. Responds to queries in 6 weeks. Pays 10% royalties plus copies. Acquires all rights. Returns rights if book goes out of print. Send SASE for catalog to order samples.

CONFRONTATION MAGAZINE, English Dept., C.W. Post Campus of Long Island University, Brookville NY 11548-1300. (516)299-2720. Fax: (516)299-2735. E-mail: mtucker@liu.edu. Established 1968. **Editor-in-Chief:** Martin Tucker. **Poetry Editor:** Michael Hartnett.

Magazine Needs: *Confrontation Magazine* is "a semiannual literary journal with interest in all forms. Our only criterion is high literary merit. We think of our audience as an educated, lay group of intelligent readers. We prefer lyric poems. Length generally should be kept to two pages. No sentimental verse." Has published poetry by Karl Shapiro, T. Alan Broughton, David Ignatow, Philip Appleman, Jane Mayhall, and Joseph Brodsky. *Confrontation* is about 300 pgs., digest-sized, professionally printed, flat-spined, with a press run of 2,000. Receives about 1,200 submissions/year, accepts about 150, has a 6- to 12-month backlog. Subscription: $10/year. Sample: $3.

How to Submit: Submit no more than 10 pgs., clear copy. No previously published poems. Accepts fax submissions. Do not submit mss June through August. "Prefer single submissions." Publishes theme issues. A list of upcoming themes available for SASE. Responds in 2 months. Sometimes sends prepublication galleys. Pays $5-50 and copy of magazine. Staff reviews books of poetry. Send books for review consideration.

Also Offers: Basically a magazine, they do on occasion publish "book" issues or "anthologies." Their most recent "occasional book" is *Clown at Wall*, stories and drawings by Ken Bernard.

$ ◨ **THE CONNECTICUT POETRY REVIEW**, P.O. Box 818, Stonington CT 06378. Established 1981.
Poetry Editors: J. Claire White and Harley More.
Magazine Needs: *The Connecticut Poetry Review* is a "small press annual magazine. We look for poetry of quality which is both genuine and original in content. No specifications except length: 10-40 lines." Has published such poets as John Updike, Robert Peters, Diane Wakoski, and Marge Piercy. Each issue seems to feature a poet. As a sample the editors selected these lines from "Sea" by Miguel Torga (translated by Alexis Levitin):

> *"Sea!/And when will all the suffering reach an end!/And when will we at last no longer bow/To your*
> *enchantments, oh, false friend!"*

The flat-spined, large digest-sized journal is "printed letterpress by hand on a Hacker Hand Press from Monotype Bembo." Most of the 45-60 pgs. are poetry, but they also have reviews. Receives over 2,500 submissions/year, accepts about 20, has a 3-month backlog. Press run is 400 for 80 subscribers of which 35 are libraries. Sample: $3.50.
How to Submit: Reads submissions April through June and September through December only. Responds in 3 months. Pays $5/poem plus 1 copy.
Advice: "Study traditional and modern styles. Study poets of the past. Attend poetry readings and write. Practice on your own."

▓ ◨ **CONNECTICUT REVIEW**, Southern Community State University, 501 Crescent St., New Haven CT 06473. (203)392-6737. Established 1968. **Editor:** Dr. Vivian Shipley.
  ● Poetry published in this review has been included in *The Best American Poetry* and *The Pushcart Prize XXIII*, has received special recognition for Literary Excellence from Public Radio's series *The Poet and the Poetry*, and has won the Phoenix Award for Significant Editorial Achievement from the Council of Editors of Learned Journals (CELJ).
Magazine Needs: *Connecticut Review*, published biannually, contains essays, poetry, articles, fiction, b&w photographs, and color artwork. Has published poetry by Robert Phillips, Sherod Santos, Colette Inez, Maxine Kumin, Pattiann Rogers, Alberto Riós, Dana Gioia, and Walt McDonald. *Connecticut Review* is 176 pgs., digest-sized, offset-printed, perfect-bound, with glossy 4-color cover and 8-color interior art. Receives about 2,500 poems/year, accepts about 5%. Press run is 3,000 of which 400 are libraries, with 1,000 distributed free to Connecticut State libraries and high schools. Sample: $6. Make checks payable to Connecticut State University.
How to Submit: Submit 3-5 typed poems at a time with name, address, and phone in the upper left corner on 8½×11 paper with SASE for return only. Publishes theme issues. Guidelines and a list of upcoming themes available for SASE. Pays 2 copies. Acquires first or one-time rights.

◨ **CONNECTICUT RIVER REVIEW; BRODINE CONTEST; WINCHELL CONTEST; LYNN DE-CARO HIGH SCHOOL COMPETITION; CONNECTICUT POETRY SOCIETY**, P.O. Box 4053, Waterbury CT 06704-0053. Website: http://pages.prodigy.net/mmwalker/cpsindex.html. Established 1978. **Editor:** Kevin Carey.
Magazine Needs: *Connecticut River Review* appears biannually. Looking for "original, honest, diverse, vital, well-crafted poetry; any form, any subject. Translations and long poems accepted." Has published poetry by Jana Harris, Lewis K. Parker, Alyce Miller, Walt McDonald, and Miguel Torga. As a sample the editor selected these lines from "Bicycler's Sonnet" by Fileman Waitts:

> *On pedals I have climbed as steep as spires,/have sweated fiercely in the glaring noon;/and coasted*
> *straight down into sunset fires/to hang my handlebars upon the moon.*

Connecticut River Review is attractively printed, digest-sized and contains about 40 pgs. of poetry, has a press run of about 500 with 175 subscriptions of which 5% are libraries. Receives about 2,000 submissions/year, accepts about 80. Subscription: $20. Sample: $6.
How to Submit: Submit up to 3 poems at a time. Include SASE for return of mss. No previously published poems or simultaneous submissions. Cover letter with current bio appreciated. "SASE must be sufficient for additional communication. SASE with insufficient postage will not be returned." Guidelines available with SASE and online. Responds in up to 6 weeks. Pays 1 copy. International submissions must be accompanied by a minimum of 2 IRCs.
Also Offers: The Brodine Contest has a $2 entry fee/poem and 3 cash awards plus publication in the *Connecticut River Review*. Entries must be postmarked between May 1 and July 31. The Winchell Contest has a $2 entry fee/poem and 3 cash awards plus publication in the *Connecticut River Review*. Entries must be postmarked between October 1 and December 31. The Lynn DeCaro Competition for Connecticut high school students only has no entry fee and 3 cash prizes plus publication in the *Connecticut River Review*. Entries must be postmarked between September 1 and February 27. Connecticut Poetry Society was established in 1974 to encourage the art of poetry. State-wide organization open to all who are interested in poetry. Affiliated with the National Federation of State Poetry Societies. Currently has 150 members. Sponsors conferences, workshops. Publishes *Poets at Work*, for members only, appearing irregularly; and *Newsletter*, a bimonthly publication, also available to nonmembers for SASE. Members or nationally known writers give readings that are open to the public. Sponsors open-mike readings. Membership dues are $25/year. Members meet monthly. Send SASE for additional information.

[N] [symbols] **COPIOUS MAGAZINE**, Box 276, 2416 Main St., Vancouver, British Columbia V5T 3A6 Canada. E-mail: copious_zine@hotmail.com. Website: www.copiousmagazine.com (includes excerpts, guidelines). Established 2000. **Editor:** Andrea Grant.

Magazine Needs: *Copious Magazine* appears bimonthly, featuring poetry, artwork, b&w photographs, pulp fiction novel covers, interviews, music, and a new comic series called *Minx*. "I want poems that have that aching knife twist in them. Darker themes of nocturne, superheroes, mythology and fairy tales. Poems about people. *Copious* features 'the doyenne,' the vixen of *film noir* and hardboiled pulp novels. She defies social expectations as seduction melds with her tragic side - a strong female force! Love poems are always nice, Native Indian themes also." Does not want rhyming, overly sentimental poetry. Accepts poetry written by children. As a sample the editor selected these lines from her own "When Captured, Snakes Shed a Layer of Skin":

> The snakes under my pillow are unfortunate,/but they remind me of boundaries. I tied their bodies in
> my hair/and entered a circus sideshow, but nobody believed/I was Medusa's descendant. They said my
> eyes were not devious,/so I heightened my mystery.

Copious Magazine is 46 pgs., digest-sized, professionally-printed, glossy cover, with contributed artwork and photos, pulp fiction pictures, and ads for related industries or of reader interest. Publishes about 20 poems/issue. Press run is 1,000 and growing. Single copy: $5; subscription: $35 US/$30 Canada. Sample: $4. Make checks payable to Andrea Grant.

How to Submit: Submit 3-5 poems at a time. Accepts previously published poems and simultaneous submissions. Accepts e-mail submissions; no fax or disk submissions. Cover letter is required. "Please provide a short bio, send SASE." Reads submissions year round. Submit seasonal poems 4 months in advance. Time between acceptance and publication is up to 4 months. "Whatever I like, I will publish." Often comments on rejected poems. Occasionally publishes theme issues. A list of upcoming themes is available for SASE, by e-mail, or on website. Guidelines are available in magazine, for SASE, by e-mail, or on website. Responds in 1 month. Pays 1 contributor's copy. Acquires one-time rights; reserves right to republish in future anthologies. Poets may send books for review consideration to Andrea Grant.

Advice: "Take risks—the dream is in your head. Create your own reality, and shamelessly self-promote."

[symbol] **COPPER CANYON PRESS; HAYDEN CARRUTH AWARD**, P.O. Box 271, Port Townsend WA 98368. (360)385-4925. Fax: (360)385-4985. E-mail: poetry@coppercanyonpress.org. Website: www.coppercany onpress.org. Established 1972. **Editor:** Sam Hamill.

Book/Chapbook Needs: Copper Canyon publishes books of poetry. Has published books of poetry by Lucille Clifton, Hayden Carruth, Carolyn Kizer, Olga Broumas, and Jim Harrison. As a sample, the editor selected these lines from "Comice" in *Below Cold Mountain* by Joseph Stroud:

> I think of Issa often these days, his poems about the loneliness/of fleas, watermelons becoming frogs
> to escape from thieves./Moon in solstice, snowfall under the earth, I dream of a pure life./Issa said of
> his child, She smooths the wrinkles from my heart./Yes, it's a dewdrop world. Inside the pear there's
> a paradise/we will never know, our only hint the sweetness of its taste

How to Submit: Currently accepts no unsolicited poetry. E-mail queries and submissions will go unanswered.

Also Offers: Copper Canyon Press publishes 1 volume of poetry each year by a new or emerging poet through its Hayden Carruth Award. "For the purpose of this award an emerging poet is defined as a poet who has published not more than two books." Winning poet receives a book contract with Copper Canyon Press and $1,000. Send SASE for contest guidelines.

[N] [symbols] **CORRECTION(S): A LITERARY JOURNAL (Specialized: poetry from prisoners only); CORRECTION(S) CHAPBOOK CONTEST**, P.O. Box 1234, New York NY 10276. Established 2002. **Editor:** K. Adams.

Magazine Needs: "*Correction(s)* is a biannual journal dedicated to the poetics and vision of incarcerated, American writers." Wants "good writing with a sense of one's own poetics." Does not want blatant pornography. Recently published poetry by David Bowman, Torrance Mimms, and Dwight Jordan. *Correction(s)* is 60 pgs., digest-sized, printed through www.chapbooks.com, perfect-bound, glossy and card stock cover, sometimes with art/graphics. Publishes 25-30 poems/issue. Single copy price: $3 (inmates), $8 (everyone else). Make checks payable to *Correction(s)*.

How to Submit: Submit 3-8 poems at a time. Accepts simultaneous submissions, no previously published poems. Accepts disk submissions; no fax or e-mail submissions. Cover letter is preferred. "Include SASE and brief bio. Handwritten submissions are accepted. Please print as neatly as possible." Reads submissions "all year/all the time." Time between acceptance and publication is about 6 months. Seldom comments on rejected poems. Will occasionally publish theme issues. A list of upcoming themes and guidelines are available for SASE. Responds in 6 weeks. Pays 2 contributor's copies. Acquires first rights. Reviews books and chapbooks of poetry and other magazines/journals. Poets may send books for review consideration to *Correction(s)*.

Book/Chapbook Needs & How to Submit: Correction(s) Press "seeks to publish quality literature written by incarcerated individuals." Publishes one paperback, one chapbook/year. Selects chapbook through competition (see **Also Offers** below). Chapbooks are usually 30-45 pgs., printed through www.chapbooks.com, perfect-bound, varied covers, sometimes with art/graphics. Responds to queries in 6 weeks; to mss in up to 1 year. Pays 30 author's copies. Guidelines available for SASE.

Also Offers: The *Correction(s)* Chapbook Contest accepts submissions in poetry and short fiction. Handwritten mss accepted. Manuscript must not exceed 60 handwritten (45 typed) pgs. for poetry; 50 handwritten (35 typed) pgs. for short fiction. **Contest open to incarcerated individuals only.** Prize is 30 copies and publication in *Correction(s)*. Entry fee: $1. Deadline: December 1, 2001. Winners will be notified by January 30, 2002.

N ▣ ◔ THE CORTLAND REVIEW, 2061 NE 73rd St., Seattle WA 98115. Website: www.cortlandrevie w.com. Established 1997. **Editor-in-Chief:** Guy Shahar. **Contact:** Poetry Submission Reader.
Magazine Needs: *The Cortland Review* is an online literary magazine only (no print version) "publishing in text and audio, and its free. We publish poetry, essays, interviews, fiction, book reviews, etc." Has published poetry by W.S. Merwin, Charles Simic, Yehuda Amichai, Dick Allen, Linda Pastan, Billy Collins, David Lehman, Marge Piercy, and R.T. Smith. As a sample the editor selected these lines from "The Kindnesses of Bad Neighbors" by Neal Bowers:

> *Whenever they absolutely must discharge a gun/in celebration or anger or simple idleness,/they try to*
> *aim low so the bullet won't carry;/and none of the fires they've set/by accident with cigarettes or*
> *overloaded outlets/has ever spread beyond their walls*

How to Submit: Submit 3-5 poems at a time. No previously published poems or simultaneous submissions. *The Cortland Review* "prefers online submissions through either our Online Submission Form or through e-mail. No attachments will be accepted. Please visit website for full submission guidelines. Snail mail is also acceptable." Cover letter required. Time between acceptance and publication is up to 12 months. Seldom comments on rejected poems. Guidelines available at www.cortlandreview.com/subs.htm. Always sends prepublication galleys. Acquires first rights. Staff reviews books and chapbooks of poetry and other magazines in 100 words, multibook format. Send books for review consideration.

◔ ◎ COTTONWOOD; COTTONWOOD PRESS (Specialized: regional), 400 Kansas Union-Box J, University of Kansas, Lawrence KS 66045. (913)864-3777. E-mail: cottonwd@falcon.cc.ukans.edu. Website: www.falcon.cc.ukans.edu/~cottonwd (includes guidelines, names of editors and staff, information on publications, and subscription order form). Established 1965. **Poetry Editor:** Philip Wedge.
Magazine Needs: *Cottonwood* is published biannually. Wants "strong narrative or sensory impact, non-derivative, not 'literary,' not 'academic.' Emphasis on Midwest, but publishes the best poetry received regardless of region. Poems should be 60 lines or fewer, on daily experience, *perception.*" Has published poetry by Rita Dove, Virgil Suarez, Walt McDonad, and Luci Tapahonso. As a sample the editors selected these lines from "The World Remade" by Lyn Plath:

> *Sunlight becomes a room in the city,/an angle of windows, a bar of gold on the floor./In a white vase*
> *on a table in the corner/flowers open, pulling the day into themselves,/into the rush and flutter of*
> *yellow petals/the way one body draws another body into itself.*

Cottonwood is 112 pgs., 6×9, flat-spined, printed from computer offset, with photos, using 10-15 pages of poetry in each issue. Receives about 4,000 submissions/year, accepts about 30, have a maximum of 1-year backlog. Press run of 500-600, with 150 subscribers of which 75 are libraries. Single copy: $8.50. Sample: $5.
How to Submit: Submit up to 5 pgs. of poetry at a time. No simultaneous submissions. Sometimes provides criticism on rejected mss. Responds in up to 5 months. Pays 1 copy.
Book/Chapbook Needs & How to Submit: The press "is auxiliary to *Cottonwood Magazine* and publishes material by authors in the region. Material is usually solicited." The press published *Violence and Grace* by Michael L. Johnson and *Midwestern Buildings* by Victor Contoski.
Advice: "Read the little magazines and send to ones you like."

✓ ◎ COUNTRY FOLK, HC 77, Box 608, Pittsburg MO 65724. Phone/fax: (417)993-5944. E-mail: salaki@ countryfolkmag.com. Website: www.countryfolkmag.com. Established 1994. **Editor:** Susan Salaki.
Magazine Needs: "*Country Folk* is a quarterly magazine written for, by, and about people living in country and rural areas. We publish poetry that reflects the serenity and peace of mind one feels when living close to nature. We also like humorous poetry. We do not want to see poetry with images of violence or meanness." Has published poetry by Goldena Trolinger of Hermitage MO and Reed Shook of Zion IL. *Country Folk* is 40 pgs., 2-color cover, includes rare old photos and ads. Receives about 100 poems/year, accepts about 10%. Press run is 2,000 for 500 subscribers. Single copy: $2.75; subscription: $15/6 issues. Sample: $4.25.
How to Submit: Submit up to 3 poems at a time. Line length for poetry is 8 minimum, 30 maximum. Accepts previously published poems and simultaneous submissions. Accepts e-mail submissions. No fax submissions. Cover letter preferred. "Include SASE if you want your poetry returned." Time between acceptance and publication is 2 months. Seldom comments on rejected poems. Occasionally publishes theme issues. Guidelines available for SASE. Pays 1 contributor's copy. Acquires one-time rights. Staff reviews other magazines in 500 words, single book format.
Advice: "We strongly suggest poets read a copy of *Country Folk* to get a flavor of what we like. Your poetry may be outstanding work but if you mail it to the wrong magazine for review it will get rejected. Know your market. It's the least you can do for your poetry. Without exception, most of the poems we read could be improved with additional revisions. Yet we find that poets usually decline to revise when asked to do so because they feel

it was an inspirational work and should not be tampered with. At that point, we must either reject the work, which we often do, or publish it 'as is' because it's the best we have been able to find, a sad conclusion but true."

$ ◎ COUNTRY WOMAN; REIMAN PUBLICATIONS (Specialized: women, humor), P.O. Box 643, Milwaukee WI 53201. Established 1970. **Executive Editor:** Kathy Pohl.

Magazine Needs: *Country Woman* "is a bimonthly magazine dedicated to the lives and interests of country women. Those who are both involved in farming and ranching and those who love country life. In some ways, it is very similar to many women's general interest magazines, and yet its subject matter is closely tied in with rural living and the very unique lives of country women. We like short (4-5 stanzas, 16-20 lines) traditional rhyming poems that reflect on a season. No experimental poetry or free verse. Poetry will not be considered unless it rhymes. Always looking for poems that focus on the seasons. We don't want rural putdowns, poems that stereotype country women, etc. All poetry must be positive and upbeat. Our poems are fairly simple, yet elegant. They often accompany a high-quality photograph." Has published poetry by Hilda Sanderson, Edith E. Cutting, and Ericka Northrop. *Country Woman* is 68 pgs., magazine-sized, printed on glossy paper with much color photography. Receives about 1,200 submissions of poetry/year, accepts about 40-50 (unless they publish an anthology). One of their anthologies, *Cattails and Meadowlarks: Poems from the Country*, is 90 pgs., saddle-stapled with high-quality color photography on the glossy card cover, poems in large, professional type with many b&w photo illustrations. Backlog is 1-3 months. Subscription: $16.98/year. Sample: $2.

How to Submit: Submit up to 6 poems at a time. Photocopy OK if stated not a simultaneous submission. Responds in 3 months. Pays $10-25/poem plus 1 copy. Acquires first rights (generally) or reprint rights (sometimes).

Also Offers: Holds various contests for subscribers only.

Advice: "We're always welcoming submissions, but any poem that does not have traditional rhythm and rhyme is automatically passed over."

Ⓝ ◐ ◎ CRAB CREEK REVIEW (Specialized: themes), P.O. Box 840, Vashon Island WA 98070. E-mail: editor@crabcreekreview.org. Website: www.crabcreekreview.org (includes back issue samples, subscriber information, guidelines, and information on readings and appearances). Established 1983. **Editorial Collective:** Harris Levinson, Laura Sinai, and Terri Stone.

Magazine Needs: Published biannually, *Crab Creek Review* publishes "an eclectic mix of energetic poems, free or formal, and more interested in powerful imagery than obscure literary allusion. Wit? Yes. Punch? Sure. Toast dry? No thank you. Translations are welcome—please submit with a copy of the poem in its original language, if possible." Has published poetry by Pauls Toutonghi, Molly Tenenbaum, Judith Skillman, Derek Sheffield, David Lee, and Kevin Miller. *Crab Creek Review* is an 80 to 100-page, perfect-bound paperback. Subscription: $10 (2 issues). Sample: $5.

How to Submit: Submit up to 5 poems at a time. No fax or e-mail submissions. Include SASE ("without one we will not consider the work"). Responds in up to 4 months. Pays 2 copies. Publishes themes issues. Guidelines available for SASE or on website.

▼ $ ◐ CRAB ORCHARD REVIEW; CRAB ORCHARD AWARD SERIES IN POETRY, English Dept., Faner Hall, Southern Illinois University at Carbondale, Carbondale IL 62901-4503. Website: www.siu.edu/~crborchd (includes guidelines, details of past issues, book reviews, list of contributors, contest requirements and results, editors' biographies, and calls for submissions). Established 1995. **Poetry Editor:** Allison Joseph. **Managing Editor:** Jon C. Tribble. **Editor-in-Chief:** Richard Peterson.

• *Crab Orchard Review* received a 2000 Literary Award from the Illinois Arts Council. Poetry from *Crab Orchard Review* has also appeared in *The Best American Poetry 1999* and *2000* and *Beacon Best of 1999* and 2000.

Magazine Needs: *Crab Orchard Review* appears biannually in May and December. "We are a general interest literary journal publishing poetry, fiction, creative nonfiction, interviews, book reviews, and novel excerpts." Wants all styles and forms from traditional to experimental. No greeting card verse; literary poetry only. Has published poetry by Kyoko Mori, Maria Terrone, Jim Daniels, and Cathy Song. In response to our request for sample lines of poetry the editors say, "We'd prefer not to, since no one excerpt can convey the breadth of poetry we'd like to receive." *Crab Orchard Review* is 250 pgs., 5½ × 8½, professionally printed and perfect-bound with photos, usually glossy card cover containing b&w photo. Receives about 7,000 poems/year, accepts about 1%. Each issue usually includes 35-40 poems. Press run is 1,600 for 1,100 subscribers of which 60 are libraries, 390 shelf sales; 50 distributed free to exchange with other journals. Subscription: $10. Sample: $6.

How to Submit: Submit up to 5 poems at a time. Accepts simultaneous submissions with notification; no previously published poems. No fax or e-mail submissions. Cover letter preferred. "Indicate stanza breaks on

THE SUBJECT INDEX, located at the back of this book, can help you select markets for your work. It lists those publishers whose poetry interests are specialized ◎ .

poems of more than one page." Reads submissions April to October for our Spring/Summer special issue, November to April for regular, non-thematic Fall/Winter issue. Time between acceptance and publication is 6-12 months. Poems are circulated to an editorial board. "Poems that are under serious consideration are discussed and decided on by the editor-in-chief, managing editor, and poetry editor." Seldom comments on rejected poems. Publishes theme issues. Theme for Spring/Summer 2002 issue is "Stage and Screen: Writers Take on Entertainment." Deadline: October 15, 2001. Guidelines and a list of upcoming themes available for SASE or on website. Responds in up to 8 months. Pays $10/page, $50 minimum plus 2 copies and 1 year's subscription. Acquires first North American serial rights. Staff reviews books of poetry in 500-700 words, single book format. Send books for review consideration to managing editor Jon C. Tribble.

Also Offers: Sponsors the Crab Orchard Award Series in Poetry. The publisher of the books will be Southern Illinois University Press. The competition is open from October 1 to November 16 for US citizens and permanent residents. "The Crab Orchard Award Series in Poetry, launched in 1997, is committed to publishing two book-length manuscripts each year. We also run an annual fiction/nonfiction contest." Books are usually 50-70 pgs., 9×6, perfect-bound with color paper covers. Entry fee: $20/submission. 1st and 2nd Prize winners each receive a publication contract with Southern Illinois University Press. In addition, the 1st Prize winner will be awarded a $2,000 prize and $1,000 as an honorarium for a reading at Southern Illinois University at Carbondale; also, the 2nd Prize winner will receive $1,000 as an honorarium for a reading at Southern Illinois University at Carbondale. Both readings will follow the publication of the poets' collections by Southern Illinois University Press. Recent winners are J. Allyn Rosser's *Misery Prefigured* (2000 winner), Julianna Baggott *(This Country of Mothers)* and Oliver de la Paz *(Names Above Horses)* were co-winners of the 2000 second prize. Also, first book competition for the publication of a poet's first book. Deadline: June 15, 2001. 2000 winner: Vandana Khanna for *Train to Agra*. Details available for SASE.

CRANIAL TEMPEST; CANNEDPHLEGM PRESS, 410 El Dorado St., Vallejo CA 94590. E-mail: cranialtempest@hotmail.com. Established 1991 (press); 2000 (publication). **Editor:** Jeff Fleming.

Magazine Needs: *Cranial Tempest* appears bimonthly "to publish the best in poetry and short fiction." Wants poetry of all kinds, "we are wide open." Recently published poetry by John Grey, Michael Brownstein, Ed Galing, Tim Scannell, normal, and John Sweet. As a sample the editor selected these lines from "In Traffic" by John Grey:

> you're on the streets,/on a bed of rubber/and rusty springs,/steering life out/of the faraway,/the misty-eyed

Cranial Tempest is 26 pgs., digest-sized, photocopied, saddle-stapled, card stock cover. Receives about 600 poems/year, accepts about 40%. Publishes about 25 poems/issue. Press run is 150 for 75 subscribers.

Book/Chapbook Needs & How to Submit: CannedPhlegm Press publishes 3-5 chpbooks/year. Chapbooks are usually 15-30 pgs., photocopied, saddle-stapled, card stock cover. Query first, with 3-5 sample poems and a cover letter with brief bio and publication credits. Responds to queries in 2 weeks; to mss in 1 month. Pays 2 author's copies. Order sample chapbooks by sending $3 to Jeff Fleming.

CREATIVE JUICES; FORESTLAND PUBLICATIONS (Specialized: animals, humor, love/romance/erotica, mystery, social issues, writing), 423 N. Burnham Highway, Canterbury CT 06331. E-mail: forestland1@juno.com. Website: www.geocities.com/geraldinepowell (includes guidelines, submission info, and subscription forms). Established 1989 (Forestland Publications). **Editor:** Geraldine Hempstead Powell.

Magazine Needs: *Creative Juices*, published bimonthly, features poetry, arts, photos, "something to inspire everyone's creative juices." Wants "any style or subject, 50 lines or less." Does not want pornography. Accepts poetry written by children. Has published poetry by Geraldine Powell, Ernest Stableford, and Peter Betrano. Press run is 100 for 65 subscribers, 30 shelf sales. Receives about 1,000 poems/year, accepts about 350. Single copy: $3; subscription: $20/year; $35/2 years. Sample: $2. Make checks payable to Geraldine Powell.

How to Submit: Submit 3-5 poems at a time. Accepts previously published poems (with credits) and simultaneous submissions. Accepts e-mail submissions; prefers attached file. Cover letter preferred. Time between acceptance and publication is up to 3 months. Submissions reviewed by editor. Often comments on rejected poems. Publishes theme issues. Guidelines and a list of upcoming themes available for SASE, on website, or by e-mail. Responds in 1 month. Sometimes sends prepublication galleys. Pays 1 or more copies. Acquires first North American serial or one-time rights. Always returns rights. Reviews books of poetry. Poets may send books for review consideration.

Book/Chapbook Needs & How to Submit: Forestland Publications publishes 4-6 chapbooks/year. Chapbooks are usually 5×7, 20 pgs. Query first with sample poems and cover letter with brief bio and publication credits. Responds to queries in 1 week, to mss in 1 month. Obtain sample chapbooks by sending SASE and $3. "Beginning in 1999, non-subscribers [to *Creative Juices*] should remit a $10 reading fee for chapbook submissions."

CREATIVE WITH WORDS PUBLICATIONS (C.W.W.); SPOOFING (Specialized: themes); WE ARE WRITERS, TOO (Specialized: children); THE ECLECTICS (Specialized: adults),

P.O. Box 223226, Carmel CA 93922. Fax: (831)655-8627. E-mail: geltrich@usa.net or cwwpub@usa.net. Website: http://members.tripod.com/CreativeWithWords (includes guidelines, themes, editing information, contest for children and winners). Established 1975. **Poetry Editor:** Brigitta Geltrich.

Magazine Needs: Creative with Words Publications focuses "on furthering folkloristic tall tales and such; creative writing abilities in children (poetry, prose, language art); creative writing in adults (poetry and prose)." Publishes on a wide range of themes relating to human studies and the environment that influence human behaviors. **Reading fee:** $5/poem (includes critique). The publications are anthologies of children's poetry, prose, and language art; anthologies of 'special-interest groups' poetry and prose; *Spoofing: An Anthology of Folkloristic Yarns and Such*; and anthologies with announced themes (nature, animals, love, travel, etc.). "Do not want to see: too mushy; too religious; too didactic; expressing dislike for fellow men; political; pornographic; death and murder poetry and prose." Guidelines and upcoming themes available for SASE or on website. Has published poetry by Daniel Mohler, Hannah Shefsky, Elizabeth Kapp, Nick Emanuele, and Alex Beck. As a sample the editor selected these lines by Ruth Margarete Boehnke:

> *Love does not guarantee everthing,/Love is fighting a battle in deepest understanding*

Spoofing! and *We are Writers, Too!* are low-budget publications, photocopied from typescript, saddle-stapled, card covers with cartoon-like computer art. Samples: $6 plus p&h. Single copy: $9-12, depending on length; subscription: 12 issues for $60; 6 issues for $36; 3 issues for $21. Libraries and schools receive 10% discount. Make checks payable to Brigitta Ludgate.

How to Submit: Submit poems of 20 lines or less, 46 character maximum line length, poems geared to specific audience and subject matter. No simultaneous submissions or previously published poems. No fax submissions. "Query with sample poems (one poem/page, name and address on each), short personal biography, other publications, poetic goals, where you read about us, for what publication and/or event you are submitting. SASE is a must." Accepts queries by fax. Has "no conditions for publication, but **C.W.W. is dependent on author/poet support by purchase of a copy or copies of publication.**" Offers a 20% reduction on any copy purchased.

Also Offers: Sponsors "Best of the Month" contest, awards publication certificate and 1 copy.

Advice: "Trend is proficiency. Poets should research topic; know audience for whom they write; check topic for appeal to specific audience; should not write for the sake of rhyme, rather for the sake of imagery and being creative with the language. Feeling should be expressed (but no mushiness). Topic and words should be chosen carefully; brevity should be employed; and author should proofread for spelling and grammar. We would like to receive more positive and clean, family-type poetry."

CREATIVITY UNLIMITED PRESS®; ANNUAL CREATIVITY UNLIMITED PRESS® POETRY COMPETITION, 30819 Casilina, Rancho Palos Verdes CA 90275. E-mail: sstockwell@earthlink.net. Established 1978. **Editor:** Shelley Stockwell.

Book/Chapbook Needs: Creativity Unlimited® uses poetry submitted to their contest in published text. $5 fee for 1-5 poems; prizes of $50, $35, and $25 and possible publication. Deadline: December 31. "Clever, quippy, humor, and delightful language encouraged. No inaccessible, verbose, esoteric, obscure poetry. Limit three pgs. per poem, double-spaced, one side of page."

How to Submit: "Poems previously published will be accepted provided writer has maintained copyright and notifies us." Accepts e-mail submissions. Often uses poems as chapter introductions in self-help books. Always comments on rejected poems. Publishes theme issues. A list of upcoming themes is available for SASE. Sometimes sends prepublication galleys. Pays 2 copies.

Advice: "We are interested in receiving more humorous poetry."

CREOSOTE, Department of English, Mohave Community College, 1977 W. Acoma Blvd., Lake Havasu City AZ 86403. Established 2000. **Editor:** Ken Raines.

Magazine Needs: *Creosote* is an annual publication of poetry, fiction, and literary nonfiction. Has "a bias favoring more traditional forms, but interested in any and all quality poems." Has "a bias against confessional and beat-influenced poetry, but will consider everything." Recently published poetry by William Wilborn, Ruth Moose, and Star Coolbrooke. As a sample the editor selected these lines from "Chinook" by William Wilborn:

> *Then wind like starlight or, maybe, the Grace Of God, drops silent, freshening the face/Of mountain ranges, sweeps the valleys, swirls/Around you sleeping, turning all the world/To tender sucking sweetly breathing mood/Of spring, of our brief aching dream of earth.*

Creosote is 48 pgs., digest-sized, saddle stapled, card cover. Receives about 150-200 poems/year, accepts about 10%. Publishes about 15 poems/issue. Press run is 500 for 30 subscribers of which 5 are libraries, 200 shelf sales; 100+ are distributed free to contributors and others. Single copy: $3. Sample: $1.50. Make checks payable to Mohave Community College.

How to Submit: Submit up to 5 poems at a time. Line length for poetry is open. Accepts simultaneous submissions "but please notify us ASAP if accepted elsewhere"; no previously published poems. Accepts disk submissions; no fax or e-mail submissions. Cover letter is preferred. "Disk submissions must be accompanied by a hard copy." Reads submissions September 1-February 28. Time between acceptance and publication is 2-3 months. Poems are circulated to an editorial board. "All work which passes initial screening is considered by at least 2 (usually more) readers." Seldom comments on rejected poems. Guidelines are available for SASE.

Responds in 6 months "at most, usually sooner." Pays 2 contributor's copies. Acquires one-time rights. Occasionally reviews books of poetry in 250-500 words. Poets may send books for review consideration to Ken Raines, editor.

Advice: "Love words more than the feelings and ideas you think you mean to express. Resist the urge to pontificate. Beware a self-congratulatory tone. Shun sloppy expression."

$ ⊚ CRICKET; SPIDER, THE MAGAZINE FOR CHILDREN; LADYBUG, THE MAGAZINE FOR YOUNG CHILDREN; BABYBUG, THE LISTENING AND LOOKING MAGAZINE FOR INFANTS AND TODDLERS (Specialized: children); CICADA (Specialized: teens), P.O. Box 300, Peru IL 61354-0300. Website: www.cricketmag.com. *Cricket* estab. 1973. *Ladybug* estab. 1990. *Spider* estab. 1994. *Babybug* estab. 1995. *Cicada* estab. 1998. **Editor-in-Chief:** Marianne Carus.

Magazine Needs: *Cricket* (for ages 9-14) is a monthly, circulation 67,000, using "serious, humorous, nonsense rhymes" for children and young adults. Does not want "forced or trite rhyming or imagery that doesn't hang together to create a unified whole." Sometimes uses previously published work. *Cricket* is 64 pgs., 8 × 10, saddle-stapled, with color cover and full-color illustrations inside. *Ladybug*, also monthly, circulation 123,000, is similar in format and requirements but is aimed at younger children (ages 2-6). *Spider*, also monthly, circulation 74,000, is for children ages 6-9. Format and requirements similar to *Cricket* and *Ladybug*. *Cicada*, appearing bimonthly, is a magazine for ages 14 and up publishing "short stories, poems, and first-person essays written for teens and young adults." Wants "serious or humorous poetry; rhymed or free verse." *Cicada* is 128 pgs., 5½ × 8½, perfect-bound with full-color cover and b&w illustrations. *Babybug*, published at 6-week intervals, circulation 40,000, is a read-aloud magazine for ages 6 months to 2 years; premier issue published January 1995. *Babybug* is 24 pgs., 6¼ × 7, printed on cardstock with nontoxic glued spine and full-color illustrations. The magazines receive over 1,200 submissions/month, use 25-30, and have up to a 2-year backlog. Sample of *Cricket*, *Ladybug*, *Spider*, or *Babybug*: $5; sample of *Cicada*: $8.50.

How to Submit: Do not query. Submit no more than 5 poems—up to 50 lines (2 pgs. max.) for *Cricket*; up to 20 lines for *Spider* and *Ladybug*, up to 25 lines for *Cicada*, up to 8 lines for *Babybug*, no restrictions on form. Guidelines available for SASE and on website. Responds in 4 months. Payment for all is up to $3/line and 2 copies. "All submissions are automatically considered for all five magazines."

Also Offers: *Cricket* and *Spider* hold poetry contests every third month. *Cricket* accepts entries from readers of all ages; *Spider* from readers ages 10 and under. Current contest themes and rules appear in each issue.

N ◯ ⊘ CROOKED RIVER PRESS, 41 Washington Ave., Waltham MA 02453. E-mail: editor@crookedriverpress.com. Website: www.crookedriverpress.com (includes deadlines, guidelines, recently published poets, samples of poetry from back issue). Established 2000. **Editor:** Elizabeth Borges.

Magazine Needs: *Crooked River Press* appears quarterly. Recently published poetry by Richard Wilhelm, Doug Holder, Lyn Lifshin, H. Lamar Thomas, Robert K. Johnson, and Elizabeth Borges. As a sample the editor selected these lines from "The End" by Richard Wilhelm:

> Dawn in the city—/The dirty rain that could never cleanse us/Cools at least our feverish heads/And
> forces a quick departure./At least even this is impossible—/A decade aches in my throat.

Crooked River Press is 65-85 pgs., 6 × 9, perfect-bound, paper cover with illustrations. Publishes about 60-70 poems/issue. Press run is 100 with 25 shelf sales. Single copy: $7; subscription: $6.50. Sample: $6.25 plus $1.50 s&h. Make checks payable to Elizabeth Borges.

How to Submit: Submit at least 3 but no more than 6 poems at time. Accepts previously published poems and simultaneous submissions. Prefers e-mail submissions (poems in the body of the message only); no disk submissions. Cover letter is preferred; include titles of poems, bio, and contact information for author. "Hard copies must include either a SASE or a note that specifically mentions that the poems do not need to be returned." Reads submissions all year. Submit seasonal poems 3 months in advance. Time between acceptance and publication is 3 months. Seldom comments on rejected poems. Occasionally publishes theme issues. Guidelines available on website. Responds in 6 weeks. Pays 1 contributor's copy. Acquires one-time rights. Reviews books and chapbooks of poetry. Poets may send books for review consideration to editor, *Crooked River Press*.

⊘ ⊚ CROSS-CULTURAL COMMUNICATIONS; CROSS-CULTURAL REVIEW OF WORLD LITERATURE AND ART IN SOUND, PRINT, AND MOTION; CROSS-CULTURAL MONTHLY; CROSS-CULTURAL REVIEW CHAPBOOK ANTHOLOGY; INTERNATIONAL WRITERS SERIES (Specialized: translations, bilingual), 239 Wynsum Ave., Merrick NY 11566-4725. (516)868-5635. Fax: (516)379-1901. E-mail: cccmia@juno.com or cccpoetry@aol.com. Established 1971. **Contact:** Stanley H. and Bebe Barkan.

Magazine Needs & How to Submit: *Cross-Cultural Monthly* focuses on bilingual poetry and prose. Subscription (12 issues/editions): $50. Sample postpaid: $7.50. Pays 1 copy.

Book/Chapbook Needs & How to Submit: *Cross-Cultural Review* began as a series of chapbooks (6-12/year) of collections of poetry translated from various languages and continues as the Holocaust, Women Writers, Latin American Writers, African Heritage, Asian Heritage, Italian Heritage, International Artists, Art & Poetry, Jewish, Israeli, Yiddish, Hebrew, Arabic, American, Bengali, Cajun, Chicano, Czech, Dutch, Finnish, Gypsy (Roma), Indian, Polish, Russian, Serbian, Sicilian, Swedish, Scandinavian, Turkish, and Long Island and Brooklyn Writers Chapbook Series (with a number of other permutations in the offing)—issued simultaneously in palm-sized and regular paperback and cloth-binding editions and boxed and canned editions, as well as audiocassette and videocassette. Cross-Cultural International Writers Series, focusing on leading poets from various countries, includes titles by Leo Vroman (Holland) and Pablo Neruda (Chile). The Holocaust series is for survivors. In addition to publications in these series, Cross-Cultural Communications has published anthologies, translations, and collections by dozens of poets from many countries. As a sample the editor selected the beginning of a poem by Rainer Maria Rilke, as translated by Stephen Mitchell:

> *She was no longer that woman with blue eyes/who once had echoed through the poet's songs,/no longer the wide couch's scent and island,/and that man's property no longer.//She was already loosened like long hair,/poured out like fallen rain,/shared like a limitless supply.*

That's from the bilingual limited poetry and art edition, *Orpheus. Eurydice. Hermes: Notations on a Landscape* (1996) which is 35 pgs., 10½ × 13½, smythe-sewn cloth. Sample chapbook: $10 postpaid. All submissions should be preceded by a query letter with SASE. Guidelines available for SASE. Pays 10% of print run.

Also Offers: Cross-Cultural Communications continues to produce the International Festival of Poetry, Writing and Translation with the International Poets and Writers Literary Arts Week in New York. Cross-Cultural Communications won the Poor Richards Award "for a quarter century of high-quality publishing," presented by The Small Press Center in New York.

CRUCIBLE; SAM RAGAN PRIZE, Barton College, College Station, Wilson NC 27893. (252)399-6456. E-mail: tgrimes@barton.edu. Established 1964. **Editor:** Terrence L. Grimes.

Magazine Needs: *Crucible* is an annual published in November using "poetry that demonstrates originality and integrity of craftsmanship as well as thought. Traditional metrical and rhyming poems are difficult to bring off in modern poetry. The best poetry is written out of deeply felt experience which has been crafted into pleasing form. No very long narratives." Has published poetry by Robert Grey, R.T. Smith, and Anthony S. Abbott. *Crucible* is 100 pgs., 6×9, professionally printed on high-quality paper with matte card cover. Press run is 500 for 300 subscribers of which 100 are libraries, 200 shelf sales. Sample: $7.

How to Submit: Submit 5 poems at a time between Christmas and mid-April only. No previously published poems or simultaneous submissions. Responds in up to 4 months. "We require three unsigned copies of the manuscript and a short biography including a list of publications, in case we decide to publish the work." Pays contributor's copies.

Also Offers: Send SASE for guidelines for contests (prizes of $150 and $100), and the Sam Ragan Prize ($150) in honor of the former Poet Laureate of North Carolina.

Advice: Editor leans toward free verse with attention paid particularly to image, line, stanza, and voice. However, he does not want to see poetry that is "forced."

CUTBANK; THE RICHARD HUGO MEMORIAL POETRY AWARD, English Dept., University of Montana, Missoula MT 59812. (406)243-6156. E-mail: cutbank@selway.umt.edu. Website: www.umt.edu/cutbank (includes "pretty much the whole magazine"). Established 1973. **Contact:** poetry editor.

Magazine Needs: *Cutbank* is a biannual literary magazine which publishes regional, national and international poetry, fiction, reviews, interviews, and artwork. Has published poetry by Jane Miller, Sheryl Noethe, Nance Van Winckel, and Jane Hirshfield. There are about 100 pgs. in each issue, 25 pgs. of poetry. Circulation is 400 for 250 subscribers of which 30% are libraries. Single copy: $6.95; subscription: $12/2 issues. Sample: $4.

How to Submit: Submit 3-5 poems at a time, single-spaced with SASE. Simultaneous submissions discouraged but accepted with notification. "We accept submissions from August 15 through March 15 only. Deadlines: Fall issue, November 15; Spring issue, March 15." Guidelines are available for SASE or by e-mail. Responds in 2 months. Pays 2 copies. All rights return to author upon publication.

Also Offers: It also offers 2 annual awards for best poem and piece of fiction published in the magazine, The Richard Hugo Memorial Poetry Award, and The A.B. Guthrie, Jr. Short Fiction Award. Winners are announced in the spring issue.

CYBER LITERATURE, c/o Dr. Chhote Lal Khatri, Khetan Ln., Jehanabad, Bihar 804408 India. Phone: 0621-363326. Fax: 0612-669188. Established 1997. **Contact:** Dr. Chhote Lal Khatri or Dr. Shaileshwar Sati Prasad.

Magazine Needs: *Cyber Literature* appears biannually to "nurture creativity and serve humanity by spreading the voice of muse and foster world peace and fellow-feeling." "Open to all sorts of poems within 25 lines that have authenticity of experience and vitality of expression, well knit, compact and crisp, preference to structural verse. No sermons, prosaic, experimental work without any purpose." Has published poetry by Ruth Wildes Schuler, R.K. Singh, and I.H. Rizvi. *Cyber Literature* is 70-80 pgs., offset-printed and saddle-stapled with paper back cover, includes ads. Receives about 200 poems/year, accepts about 30-40%. Press run is 500 for 300 subscribers of which 20 are libraries, 100 shelf sales; 40-60 distributed free to editors, celebrities. Single copy: $5; subscription: $10. Sample: $5. Make checks payable to Dr. Chhote Lal Khatri.

How to Submit: Submit 3-6 poems at a time. Line length for poetry is 25 maximum. Accepts previously published poems and simultaneous submissions. Cover letter preferred. Include SASE or IRC and a bio. Reads submissions March 1-April 30 and September 1-October 30 only. Time between acceptance and publication is 6 months. "Poems are circulated among associate editors. They are returned to the editor for final decision."

Seldom comments on rejections. Membership or purchase of copy required for consideration. Responds in 1 month. Pays 1 contributor's copy. Acquires one-time rights. Reviews books and chapbooks of poetry and other magazines in 500 words, single book format. Poets may send books for review consideration.
Also Offers: Publishes an anthology of poets from both India and abroad.

$ CYBER OASIS. Fax: (603)971-5013. E-mail: eide491@earthlink.net. Website: www.sunoasis.com/oasis.html. Established 1996. **Contact:** David Eide.
Magazine Needs: *Cyber Oasis* is a monthly online journal containing poems, stories, personal essays, articles for writers, and commentary. "The purpose is two-fold. Number one is to publish excellent writing and number two is to explore the web for all the best writing and literary venues. Not only does *Cyber Oasis* publish original material but it investigates the web each month to deliver the very best material it can find." Wants "poetry that has an active consciousness and has artistic intention. Open on form, length, subject matter, style, purpose, etc. It must deliver the active consciousness and artistic intention. No sing song stuff, fluff stuff, those who write poems without real artistic intent because they haven't given the idea a thought." Has published poetry by Yvonne Linck-Osborne, Tom Daley, Deborah Byrne, and Leonore Wilson. "I'm trying to find the right style for the Web. I was inspired by the literary magazine phenomena but find the Web to be a new medium. One that is terrific for poetry." Receives "hundreds" of poems/year, accepts about 15%.
How to Submit: Submit 5 poems at a time. Accepts previously published poems; no simultaneous submissions. Accepts fax and e-mail submissions; "try to include submission in ASCII plain-text in body of e-mail message." Time between acceptance and publication is about 3 months. "If I know I don't want it I'll turn it back that day. If there is something there that warrants further reading I'll put it into a review folder. As the day of publication approaches I'll get the review folder out and start to eliminate stuff. If I eliminate something that I like, I'll put it into next month's folder. Then I come down to a chosen few. One or two I pick for publication, the others I schedule for another month. I then notify the writer of acceptance, I notify the others that I want to publish their poems later and give them updates on that." Often, but not always, comments on rejected poems. Guidelines available for e-mail or website. Responds in 1 month. Pays $10/poem. Acquires first, first North American serial, one time, and reprint rights.
Advice: "Seek to improve the writing; take poetry seriously, treat it as an art and it will treat you well."

DALHOUSIE REVIEW, Dalhousie University, Halifax, Nova Scotia B3H 3J5 Canada. (902)494-2541. Fax: (902)494-3561. E-mail: dalhousie.review@dal.ca. Website: www.dal.ca/~dalrev. Established 1921. **Editor:** Dr. Ronald Huebert.
Magazine Needs: *Dalhousie Review* appears 3 times/year. Recently published poetry by Joy Hewitt Mann, Elizabeth Brewster, Elana Wolff, A. Mary Murphy, Leonard Ferry, and David Winwood. *Dalhousie Review* is 144 pgs., 6×9. Accepts about 10% of poems received. Press run is 800 for 650 subscribers. Single copy: $10 (Canadian); subscription: $22 (Canadian); 28 (US). Sample: $10 (Canadian). Make checks payable to *Dalhousie Review*.
How to Submit: Accepts simultaneous submissions; no previously published poems. Accepts e-mail and disk submissions. "Contributions should be typed on plain white paper, double-spaced throughout. Spelling preferences are those of *The Canadian Oxford Dictionary*: catalogue, colour, program, travelling, theatre, and so on. Beyond this, writers of fiction and poetry are encouraged to follow whatever canons of usage might govern the particular story or poem in question, and to be inventive with language, ideas and form. Poems should in general not exceed 40 lines, but there will of course be valid exceptions to these rules. Initial submissions are by means of hard copy only." Reads submissions year-round. Seldom comments on rejected poems. Occasionally publishes theme issues. A list of upcoming themes and guidelines available for SAE and IRC. Pays 2 contributor's copies.

$ DANA LITERARY SOCIETY ONLINE JOURNAL, P.O. Box 3362, Dana Point CA 92629-8362. Website: www.danaliterary.org (includes poetry, fiction, and nonfiction, also editorial commentary, writer's guidelines, and recommended resources; edited by Ronald D. Hardcastle). Established 2000. **Director:** Robert L. Ward.
Magazine Needs: *Dana Literary Society Online Journal* appears monthly. Contains poetry, fiction, and nonfiction. "All styles are welcome—rhyming/metrical, free verse, and classic—but they must be well-crafted and throught-provoking. We want no pornography. Neither do we want works that consist of pointless flows of words with no apparent significance." Recently published poetry by Christina Rolf, Ronald V. Laskow, William R. Siltes, and Sarah R. Roark. As a sample the editor selected these lines from "Nimby" by A.B. Jacobs:

> Whether lots to be filled,/Or huge structures to build,/I will back any scheme, to be sure./This is
> progress, you see . . . /For support, count on me./I'm a genuine entrepreneur.

Dana Literary Society Online Journal is equivalent to approximately 40 printed pages. Receives about 600 poems/year, accepts about 10%. Publishes about 5 poems/issue.
How to Submit: Submit up to 3 poems at a time. Line length for poetry is 120 maximum. Accepts previously published poems and simultaneous submissions. No fax, e-mail, or disk submissions. Time between acceptnce and publication is 3 months. Poems are selected by Society director and *Online Journal* editor. Often comments on rejected poems. Guidelines are available on website. Responds in 2 weeks. Pays $25 for each poem accepted. Acquires right to display in *Online Journal* for one month.
Advice: "View our website."

🌐 🔲 📖 **DANDELION ARTS MAGAZINE; FERN PUBLICATIONS (Specialized: membership/subscription)**, 24 Frosty Hollow, East Hunsbury, Northants NN4 OSY England. Fax: 01604-701730. Established 1978. **Editor/Publisher:** Mrs. Jacqueline Gonzalez-Marina M.A.

• Fern Publications subsidizes costs for their books, paying no royalties.

Magazine Needs: *Dandelion Arts Magazine*, published biannually, is "a platform for new and established poets and prose writers to be read throughout the world." Wants poetry "not longer than 35-40 lines. Modern but not wild." Does not want "bad language poetry, religious or political, nor offensive to any group of people in the world." Has published poetry by Andrew Duncan, Donald Ward, Andrew Pye, John Brander, and Gerald Denley. As a sample the editor selected these lines from her own poem:

> . . . *The human spirit without a planned path/to follow, is a sad landscape,/only grass and weeds, and nothing more/to expect.*

Dandelion is about 25 pgs., A4, thermal binding with b&w and color illustrations, original cover design, some ads. Receives about 200-300 poems/year, accepts about 40%. Press run is up to 1,000 for 100 subscribers of which 10% are universities and libraries, some distributed free to chosen organizations. Subscription: £10 (Europe), £25 (other). Sample: half price of subscription. Make checks payable to J. Gonzalez-Marina.

How to Submit: Poets must become member-subscribers of *Dandelion Arts Magazine* and poetry club in order to be published. Submit 4-6 poems at a time. Accepts simultaneous submissions; no previously published poems. Cover letter required. "Poems must be typed out clearly and ready for publication, if possible, accompanied by a SAE or postal order to cover the cost of postage for the reply. Reads submissions any time of the year. Time between acceptance and publication is 2-6 months. "The poems are read by the editor when they arrive and a decision is taken straight away." Some constructive comments on rejected poems. Guidelines available for SASE (or SAE and IRC). Responds within 3 weeks. Reviews books of poetry. Poets may send books for review consideration.

Also Offers: *Dandelion* includes information on poetry competitions and art events.

Book/Chapbook Needs & How to Submit: Fern Publications is a subsidy press of artistic, poetic, and historical books and publishes 2 paperbacks/year. Books are usually 50-80 pgs., A5 or A4, "thermal bound" or hand finished. Query first with 6-10 poems. Requires authors to subscribe to *Dandelion Arts Magazine*. Responds to queries and mss in 3 weeks. "All publications are published at a minimum cost agreed beforehand and paid in advance."

Advice: "Consider a theme from all angles and to explore all the possibilities, never forgetting grammar! Stay away from religious or political or offensive issues."

💲 📖 **JOHN DANIEL AND COMPANY, PUBLISHER; FITHIAN PRESS**, a division of Daniel & Daniel, Publishers, Inc., P.O. Box 21922, Santa Barbara CA 93121-1922. (805)962-1780. Fax. (805)962-8835. E-mail: dandd@danielpublishing.com. Website: www.danielpublishing.com (includes writer's guidelines, author profiles, description of books, and "opinionated advice for writers"). Established 1980. Reestablished 1985.

Book/Chapbook Needs: John Daniel, a general small press publisher, specializes in literature, both prose, and poetry. "Book-length mss of any form or subject matter will be considered, but we do not want to see pornographic, libelous, illegal, or sloppily written poetry." Has published *Flying Horses* by Jeanne Lohmann, *Mending The Skies* by Celia Brown, and *What Counts* by Jay Liveson. As a sample John Daniel selected "After Love" from the book *Sustenance*, by Julia Cunningham:

> Sometimes when Oyster shells lie open/on the abandoned rowboat bleached from sun/and barnacles are heavy with mud in the salt marsh./a loon yodels across the breeding waters/as I make my way through long, brown grass.

Publishes about 4 flat-spined poetry paperbacks, averaging 80 pgs., each year. Press runs average between 500-1,000. For free catalog of either imprint, send #10 SASE.

How to Submit: Send 12 sample poems and bio. Responds to queries in 2 weeks, to mss in 2 months. Accepts simultaneous submissions. No fax or e-mail submissions. Always sends prepublication galleys. Pays 10% royalties of net receipts. Acquires English-language book rights. Returns rights upon termination of contract.

Also Offers: Fithian Press (50% of his publishing) are subsidized, the author paying production costs and receiving royalties of 60% of net receipts. Books and rights are the property of the author, but publisher agrees to warehouse and distribute for one year if desired.

Advice: "We receive over five thousand unsolicited manuscripts and query letters a year. We publish only a few books a year, of which fewer than half were received unsolicited. Obviously the odds are not with you. For this reason we encourage you to send out multiple submissions and we do not expect you to tie up your chances while waiting for our response. Also, poetry does not make money, alas. It is a labor of love for both publisher and writer. But if the love is there, the rewards are great."

🌐 💟 📖 **DARENGO; SESHAT: CROSS-CULTURAL PERSPECTIVES IN POETRY AND PHILOSOPHY (Specialized: translation)**, P.O. Box 9313, London E17 8XL United Kingdom. Phone/fax: (44)181-679-4150. Darengo established 1989. *Seshat* established 1997. **Editor/Proprietor:** Terence DuQuesne. **Editor:** Mark Angelo de Brito.

Magazine Needs: *Seshat*, published biannually, "provides a focus for poetry enthusiasts by publishing high-quality poems in English and in translation. It also prints prose articles which highlight connections between the poetic, the philosophical, and the spiritual. *Seshat* is committed to the view that poetry and other art-forms are vitalizing and raise consciousness and thus should not be regarded as minority interests. Poetry is not merely an aesthetic matter: it can and should help to break down the barriers of class, race, gender, age, and sexual preference. *Seshat* is named for the Egyptian goddess of sacred writing and measurement." Has published poetry by Sappho, Anthony James, Martina Evans, Ellen Zaks, and Dwina Murphy-Gibb. *Seshat* is 80 pgs., offset-printed with stitched binding, laminated paper cover, includes graphics. Press run is 200. Single copy: £10 (payable in sterling only plus £5 postage outside UK); subscription: £20.

How to Submit: Submit up to 5 poems at a time. Accepts previously published poems; no simultaneous submissions. Accepts disk submissions. Cover letter required. Time between acceptance and publication is 3 months. Often comments on rejected poems. Guidelines available for SASE (or SAE and IRC). Responds in 2 weeks. Always sends prepublication galleys. Pays 1 contributor's copy, more on request. Poets retain copyright. Reviews books and chapbooks of poetry and other magazines in 1,000 words. Poets may send books for review consideration.

Book/Chapbook Needs & How to Submit: Darengo currently does not accept unsolicited mss.

$ ⊘ ◎ DARK REGIONS (Specialized: horror, science fiction/fantasy), P.O. Box 6301, Concord CA 94524. Established 1985. **Poetry Editor:** Bobbi Sinha-Morey.

Magazine Needs: *Dark Regions* is a quarterly magazine "dedicated to putting out an on-time quality product that will entertain as well as make the reader think. We publish weird fantasy and horror and occasionally weird science fiction. Our magazine is intended for mature readers. We want inventive tales that push the boundaries of originality and invention. We dislike overused themes like Friday the 13th, Conan, and invaders from Mars." Wants "dark fantasy, disturbing horror, vampires, gothicism, psychological verse, magic, and wonder. For horror poetry, make it eerie and tantalizing. Use plenty of imagery and be passionate about your writing. Use your imagination and make your work fly. More fantasy!" Free verse and traditional verse. Has published poetry by Bruce Boston, Ann K. Schwader, and Kendall Evans. As a sample the editor selected these lines from "Pyramid of the Moon" by Ann K. Schwader:

> The wind off Cerro Blanco is crying/tonight with the tongues of dead warriors.

Dark Regions is 64-80 pgs., 5½×8½, offset-printed, and saddle-stapled with full color cover. Receives about 100 poems/year, accepts about 25%. Press run is 1,000 for 300 subscribers of which 50 are libraries, 500 shelf sales; 150 distributed free to reviewers, writers, poets, advertising. Single copy: $3.95; subscription: $13. Make checks payable to Dark Regions Press.

How to Submit: Submit 4 poems at a time, either single-spaced or double-spaced, 1 poem/page. Line length for poetry is 35 maximum. Accepts previously published poems; no simultaneous submissions. Cover letter preferred. "I take care of all poetry submissions and respond personally to each one." Often comments on rejected poems. Occasionally publishes theme issues. Guidelines and a list of upcoming themes available for SASE. Responds in 3 weeks. Always sends prepublication galleys. Pays $5-10/poem plus 1 copy. Acquires first North American serial rights.

✓ ▣ $ ⬚ ♥ DEAD END STREET, LLC, 813 Third St., Hoquiam WA 98550. (415)378-7401. E-mail: submissions@deadendstreet.com. Website: http://deadendstreet.com. Established 1997. **Director of Submissions:** John Rutledge. **Director of Publications:** Ivan Black.

Book/Chapbook Needs: Dead End Street Publications publishes electronic collections of poetry and seeks "cutting edge authors who represent the world's dead end streets." Accepts poetry written by children. Has published poetry by Circe, CD Reed, T. Rening, Larry Jaffe, and Von Enemy. As a sample they offer their mission statement:

> It must be known/that where I have been,/has both things to despise/and knowledge to lend.

How to Submit: "We request complete collections so the depth and experience of the poet can be adequately judged." Accepts simultaneous submissions; no previously published poems. "We require electronic submissions via e-mail in MS Word or Word Perfect." Cover letter required. Time between acceptance and publication is 6 months. Poems are circulated to an editorial board. Seldom comments on rejected poems. "Complete submission guidelines provided on company website." Responds to queries in 1 month. Pays royalties of 10% minimum, 40% maximum and 10 author's copies. Sample books available on website.

✓ ⊘ ◎ DEAD FUN (Specialized: gothic/horror), P.O. Box 752, Royal Oak MI 48068-0752. E-mail: terror@deadfun.com. Website: www.deadfun.com (includes submission guidelines, previews of issues, and other information). **Editoress:** Kelli.

Magazine Needs: *Dead Fun* appears sporadically. "I have to refrain from accepting poetry submissions this time around. I've gotten absolutely swamped with submissions and my 'hold' file is overflowing. I'll still read and respond to those who send submissions but all I can offer at this time is for their work to be placed in our files for possible future use." Prefers "gothic and horror-related, religious/sacrilegious material." Does not want poetry that is "political, flowery." Has published poetry by Jessica Ocasio, Ben Wilensky, and Rod Walker. As a sample the editor selected these lines from "After the Feast" by John Grey:

> What a meal,/no . . . a banquet:/eyes like grapes,/spaghetti veins,/flesh tender/on the bone./I lick her lips,/knowing she would/if she could.

Dead Fun is about 50 pgs., digest-sized, photocopied and stapled with cardstock cover, includes pen and ink drawings, charcoal art, photography, as well as ads for zines, bands, and "anything relative." Accept approximately 30% of poetry submitted. Sample: $3 plus 77¢ postage (inside US) or IRC. Make money orders payable to Kelli or send well-concealed cash.
How to Submit: Submit up to 3 poems at a time. Accepts previously published poems and simultaneous submissions. Accepts e-mail submissions; no fax submissions. Cover letter strongly preferred. Time between acceptance and publication up to 6 months "unless otherwise agreed." Guidelines available for SASE, on website, or by e-mail. Responds in 6 weeks or a few days for e-mail requests. Pays 1 contributor's copy. Staff reviews books of poetry in approximately 40 words. Send books for review consideration.

DEAD METAPHOR PRESS, P.O. Box 2076, Boulder CO 80306-2076. Established 1992. **Contact:** Richard Wilmarth.
Book/Chapbook Needs: Publishes 3-5 chapbooks of poetry and prose/year through an annual chapbook contest. "No restrictions in regard to subject matter and style." Has published poetry by John McKernan, Patrick Pritchett, Mark DuCharme, Thomas R. Peters, Jr., and Randy Roark. As a sample we selected these lines from "currently" by Richard Wilmarth:
> the refrigerator motor is my companion/we have coffee together/talk sports/interface with the phone
> system/we keep everything cold

Chapbooks are usually 20-80 pgs., sizes differ, printed, photocopied, saddle-stapled or perfect-bound, some with illustrations.
How to Submit: Submit 24 pgs. of poetry or prose with a bio, acknowledgments. Manuscripts are not returned. "Entries must be typed or clearly reproduced and bound only by a clip. Do not send only copy of manuscript." Accepts previously published poems and simultaneous submissions. Does not accept fax or e-mail submissions. SASE for notification. Guidelines and booklist available for SASE. Reading fee: $10. Deadline: October 31. Winner receives 10% of press run plus discounted copies. For sample chapbooks, send $6.

DEBUT REVIEW, P.O. Box 412184, Kansas City MO 64141-2184. Established 1999. **Editor:** M.L. Acksonj.
Magazine Needs: *Debut Review* appears annually to "showcase the work of a select few talented poets. Although we favor form, we are looking for poetry of the highest order in traditional form or free verse. We prize the voice that demonstrates both objectivity and control. We look for the use of poetic devices such as: alliteration, simile, metaphor, etc. Wit is fine, but nothing overly humorous, trite, or unpolished." *Debut Review* is "somewhere between 25-30 pages, printed in a somewhat informal manner, but highly professsional. After a few issues, the review will be perfect-bound by a printer, and presented to contributors and libraries."
How to Submit: *Debut Review* is currently not accepting unsolicited submissions.

DEFINED PROVIDENCE PRESS, 34-A Wayawanda Rd., Warwick NY 10990. E-mail: definedprovidence@mail.com. Website: www.definedprovidence.com. Established 1992. **Editor:** Gary J Whitehead.
Book/Chapbook Needs & How to Submit: "Defined Providence Press, which published a journal from 1992 to 1999, is now dedicated to publishing high quality volumes of poetry. For 2002, the press will hold two full-length book competitions, to be judged by well known poets. For both contests, the author of the winning 48-120 page ms will receive a prize of $1,000 and 100 copies of a perfect-bound, professionally printed book, selling in paperback for $12. The deadlines are February 1 and June 1. For additional details, or to sample previous books, visit the website or send a SASE."

DENVER QUARTERLY; LYNDA HULL POETRY AWARD, Dept. of English, University of Denver, Denver CO 80208. (303)871-2892. Fax: (303)871-2853. Established 1965. **Editor:** Bin Ramke.
● Poetry published here has also been included in the 1997, 1998, and 1999 volumes of *The Best American Poetry*.
Magazine Needs: *Denver Quarterly* is a quarterly literary journal that publishes fiction, poems, book reviews and essays. There are no restrictions on the type of poetry wanted. Poems here focus on language and lean toward the avant-garde. Length is open, with some long poems and sequences also featured. Translations are also published. Has published poetry by John Ashbery, Jorie Graham, Arthur Sze, and Paul Hoover. *Denver Quarterly* is about 130 pgs., 6×9, handsomely printed on buff stock and perfect-bound with 2-color matte card cover. Press run is 1,900 for 900 subscribers of which 300 are libraries, about 700 shelf sales. Subscription: $20/year to individuals and $24 to institutions. Sample: $6.
How to Submit: Submit 3-5 poems at a time. Include SASE. Accepts simultaneous submissions. Do not submit between May 15 and September 15 each year. Publishes theme issues. Responds in 3 months. "Will request diskette upon acceptance." Pays 2 copies and $5/page. Reviews books of poetry.
Also Offers: The Lynda Hull Poetry Award of $500 is awarded annually for the best poem published in a volume year. All poems published in the *Denver Quarterly* are automatically entered.

DESCANT (Specialized: themes), Box 314, Station P, Toronto, Ontario M5S 2S8 Canada. (416)593-2557. E-mail: descant@web.net. Website: www.descant.on.ca (includes writer's guidelines, editors, themes, subscription info, and excerpts). Established 1970. **Editor-in-Chief:** Karen Mulhallen.

Magazine Needs: *Descant* is "a quarterly journal of the arts committed to being the finest in Canada. While our focus is primarily on Canadian writing we have published writers from around the world." Has published are Lorna Crozier, Eric Ormsby, and Jan Zwicky. *Descant* is 140 pgs., over-sized digest format, elegantly printed and illustrated on heavy paper, flat-spined with colored, glossy cover. Receives 1,200 unsolicited submissions/ year, accepts less than 100, has a 2-year backlog. Press run is 1,200. Sample: $8.50 plus postage.
How to Submit: Submit typed ms of no more than 6 poems, name and address on first page and last name on each subsequent page. Include SASE with Canadian stamps or SAE and IRCs. "Please include an extra stamp, or an e-mail address, or fax number, so that we may acknowledge receipt of your submission." No previously published poems or simultaneous submissions. Guidelines and a list of upcoming themes available for SASE (or SAE and IRC). Responds within 4 months. Pays "approximately $100." Acquires first rights.
Advice: "The best advice is to know the magazine you are submitting to. Please read the magazine before submitting."

☑ ◯ DESCANT: FORT WORTH'S JOURNAL OF POETRY AND FICTION, English Dept., Box 297270, Texas Christian University, Fort Worth TX 76129. Fax: (817)257-6239. E-mail: descant@tcu.edu. Web-site: www.eng.tcu.edu./usefulsites/descant.htm. Established 1956. **Editor:** Dave Kuhne.
Magazine Needs: *descant* appears annually during the summer months. Wants "well-crafted poems of interest. No restrictions as to subject matter or forms. We usually accept poems 60 lines or fewer but sometimes longer poems." *descant* is more than 100 pgs., 6×9, professionally printed and bound with matte card cover. "We publish 30-40 pgs. of poetry per year. We receive probably 3,000 poems annually." Press run is 500 for 350 subscribers. Double issue: $12, $18 outside US. Sample: $6.
How to Submit: No simultaneous submissions. No fax or e-mail submissions. Reads submissions September through April only. Responds in 6 weeks. Pays 2 copies.
Also Offers: The Betsy Colquitt Award for poetry, $500 prize awarded annually to the best poem or series of poems by a single author in an issue. Complete contest rules and guidelines available for SASE or by e-mail.

◐ DEVIL BLOSSOMS, P.O. Box 5122, Seabrook NJ 08302-3511. Established 1997. E-mail: theeditor@asteri uspress.com. Website: www.asteriuspress.com (includes guidelines, publication information, contest updates, etc). **Editor:** John C. Erianne.
Magazine Needs: *Devil Blossoms* appears irregularly, 1-2 times/year, "to publish poetry in which the words show the scars of real life. Sensual poetry that's occasionally ugly. I'd rather read a poem that makes me sick than a poem without meaning." Wants poetry that is "darkly comical, ironic, visceral, horrific; or any tidbit of human experience that moves me." Does not want religious greetings, 'I'm-so-happy-to-be-alive' tree poetry. Has published poetry by John Sweet, T. Kilgore Splake, Dennis Saleh, and Alan Catlin. As a sample the editor selected these lines from "The Big News" by Karl Wachter:

> A serpent is waiting/beneath the sewer drain/winged angels are asked/for change and the darkness/in
> a god's eyes is mistaken/for dirt.

Devil Blossoms is 24 pgs., 8½×11, saddle-stapled, with a matte-card cover and ink drawings (cover only). Receives about 1,500 poems/year, accepts about 2-3%. Press run is 500, 200 shelf sales. Single copy: $5; subscription: $14. Make checks payable to John C. Erianne.
How to Submit: Submit 2-5 poems at a time. Accepts simultaneous submissions. Accepts e-mail submissions; include in body of message. Cover letter preferred. Time between acceptance and publication is up to 6 months. "I promptly read submissions, divide them into a 'no' and a 'maybe' pile. Then I read the 'maybes' again." Seldom comments on rejected poems. Guidelines available for SASE. Responds in up to 5 weeks. Pays 1 contributor's copy. Acquires first rights.
Advice: "Write from love; don't expect love in return, don't take rejection personally and don't let anyone stop you."

🌐 ◐ DIALOGOS: HELLENIC STUDIES REVIEW, Dept. of Byzantine and Modern Greek Studies, King's College, Strand Campus, London WC2R 2LS England. Fax: 0044-020-7848-2830. E-mail: david.ricks@k cl.ac.uk. Website: www.frankcass.com (includes current table of contents). Established 1994. **Co-Editors:** David Ricks and Michael Trapp.
Magazine Needs: *Dialogos* is an annual of "Greek language and literature, history and archaeology, culture and thought, present and past." Wants "poems with reference to Greek or the Greek world, any period (ancient, medieval, modern), translations of Greek poetry." Does not want "watery mythological musings." Has published poetry by Homer (translated by Oliver Taplin) and Nikos Engonopoulos (translated by Martin McKinsey). As a sample the editor selected these lines by C. Haim Gouri, translated by Avi Sharon:

> "Error always returns" said Odysseus to his weary heart/and came to the crossroads of the next town/
> to find that the way home was not water.

Dialogos is 150 pgs., professionally printed and bound. Receives about 50 poems/year, accepts about 2%. Press run is 500 for 150 subscribers of which 100 are libraries. Sample: $45. Make checks payable to Frank Cass & Co. Ltd.
How to Submit: Submit 6 poems at a time. No previously published poems or simultaneous submissions. No e-mail or fax submissions. Time between acceptance and publication is 1 year. Poems are circulated to an editorial

board of 2 editors. Seldom comments on rejected poems. Responds within 6 weeks. Always sends prepublication galleys. Pays 1 copy and 25 offprints. Acquires all rights. Returns rights. Reviews books of direct Greek interest, in multi-book review. Poets may send books for review consideration.

THE DIDACTIC, 11702 Webercrest, Houston TX 77048. Established 1993. **Editor:** Charlie Mainze.
Magazine Needs: *The Didactic* is a monthly publishing "only, only didactic poetry. That is the only specification. Some satire might be acceptable as long as it is didactic."
How to Submit: Accepts previously published poems and simultaneous submissions. Time between acceptance and publication is about a year. "Once it is determined that the piece is of self-evident quality and is also didactic, it is grouped with similar or contrasting pieces. This may cause a lag time for publication." Responds "as quickly as possible." Pay is "nominal." Acquires one-time rights. Considering a general review section, only using staff-written reviews. Poets may send books for review consideration.

DINER; POETRY OASIS, P.O. Box 60676, Greendale Station Worcester MA 01606-2378. Website: www.spokenword.to/diner (includes guidelines, editors, feature information). Established 2000. **Editors:** Eve Rifkah and Abby Millager.
Magazine Needs: *Diner* appears biannually. Its goal is to continue the Worcester poetry tradition—Bishop, Knight, Kunitz, O'Hara. Features 1-2 native poets per issue. Encourages general submissions from all regions and will also include short reviews. "Open to all types of poetry. Like to see imaginative work, with attention to diction sound, imagery. Surprise us." Recently published poetry by Fran Quinn. *Diner* is 100 pgs., digest-sized, perfect-bound, glossy card cover with photo. Publishes about 50 poems/issue. Press run is 500. Single copy: $8; subscription: $15. Sample: $6. Make checks payable to Poetry Oasis.
How to Submit: Submit no more than 5 poems. Line length for poetry is open. Accepts simultaneous submissions "if polite about it"; no previously published poems. No fax, e-mail, or disk submissions. Cover letter is required. "SASE a must. Cover letter should include your name and poems submitted." Reads submissions year round. Time between acceptance and publication up to 6 months. Often comments on rejected poems. Guidelines are available for SASE or on website. Responds in up to 6 months. Pays 1 contributor's copy. Acquires first rights. Reviews books and chapbooks of poetry in single book format. Poets may send books for review consideration if poet "is from central New England."
Advice: "Find a group, share your work, get feedback. Read not only classics but also work currently being published. Don't worry about rejections—buy lots of stamps."

DIRIGIBLE (Specialized: form/style, avant-garde), 101 Cottage St., New Haven CT 06511. E-mail: dirigibl@javanet.com. Established 1994. **Co-Editors:** David Todd and Cynthia Conrad.
Magazine Needs: "*Dirigible* is a quarterly avant-garde journal of language art which publishes prose, poetry, selective reviews, translations, and hybrid genres. We seek language-centered poetry, controlled experiments, fiction that is postmodern, paraliterary, nonlinear, or subjective, and work that breaks with genre, convention, or form. Hybrid forms of writing and essays on aesthetics, poetics, reader experience, and writing processes are also of interest to us. No social issues, no inspirational, scatological, or emotional exhibitionism. *Dirigible* publishing was suspended for most of 2000, but will resume this year." Has published poetry by Sheila E. Murphy, W.B. Keckler, Simon Perchik, Ron Padgett, Richard Kostelanetz, Scott Keeney, and Dennis Holt. As a sample the editor selected these lines from "Weights and Measures" by Morgan Avery Sispoidis:

> I hold your steadfastness/like a spirit level/to keep a balance that/does not fall/to guide me past the
> worn down chairs/away from spoon-faces and kitchen knives/and things that linger in thin curtains/
> sharp and white like razor blades.

Dirigible is 40-48 pgs., 4¼×7, photocopied, saddle-stapled with buff card cover, in-house graphics; "will swap ads with similar publications." Accepts about 10% of poems received each year. Press run is 500-800, 60% shelf sales. Subscription: $10/year. Sample: $3. Make checks payable to Dirigible.
How to Submit: Submit up to 8 poems at a time. No previously published poems or simultaneous submissions. No e-mail submissions. Cover letter preferred. Time between acceptance and publication is up to 3 months. Responds in up to 3 months. Pays 2 copies. Acquires first rights. Staff reviews books of poetry—"selective reviews; length and type vary."
Advice: "We are interested in a phenomenological lyricism which recreates the texture and logic of interior experience. We are grinding an aesthetic ax and acceptance is dependent upon our editorial vision."

DISQUIETING MUSES; THE MUSES AWARD, P.O. Box 640746, San Jose CA 95164-0746. E-mail: editors@disquietingmuses.com. Website: www.disquietingmuses.com (includes full text of magazine). **Editor-in-Chief:** Dancing Bear. **Managing Editor:** C.J. Sage.
Magazine Needs: *Disquieting Muses* appears quarterly as "a quality online magazine of poetry, presented with visual art, interviews, reviews, and public service surveys/articles." Wants "intriguing themes, unique, strong imagery, metaphor and fresh, concise language over a base of smarts and discovery. The best poems enter the reader like songs and make the body rock. We'd like to see more deep-image (mature) work, but we are interested in high quality poetry of any style." Does not want "Hallmarkish writing, form without compelling content,

narratives without interesting imagery or underlying musicality." Recently published poetry by Gary Short, Dorianne Laux, Rainer Marie Rilke, Federico Garcia Lorca, Julia Alter, Jane Hirshfield, Joy Harjo, and Grace Butcher. As a sample the editor selected these lines from "Psalm" by Gary Short:

> Then the boy breathes harder into the goose,/cradles it and listens,//until there is music, a swell of air/ returned over the bird's vocal chords, a purr,/a dirge, a lost-soul quaver./A blue cone of sound, human-made,/or made human.

Disquieting Muses is published online; art/photography appears with the poetry. Receives about 3,000-5,000 poems/year, accepts about 3%. Publishes about 20-25 poems/issue.

How to Submit: Submit 3-5 poems at a time. Accepts simultaneous submissions (with notifications only); no previously published poems. E-mail submissions preferred; no fax or disk submissions. "Paste poems in the body of an e-mail only; no attachments will be read. Please refer to complete submissions guidelines on our website and submit accordingly." Reads submissions year round. Time between acceptance and publication is 1-3 months. Poems circulated to an editorial board. "The editor-in-chief, managing editor, and a third editor read and vote on all submissions. Seldom comments on rejected poems. Responds in up to 6 weeks. Acquires first rights. Reviews books and chapbooks of poetry and other magazines/journals. Poets may send books for review consideration to *Disquieting Muses* editors.

Also Offers: The Muses Award, an annual prize of $100 for the best poem to first appear in *Disquieting Muses* during the year. No entry fee or special entry process. "Our editors will select a winner from all poems first published in the magazine. To be eligible, contributors must simply adhere to all regular submission guidelines as outlined in our Submission Guidelines page; and, if using a pen name, include their legal name with the submission. Previously published poems are ineligible for the award." Also nominates 6 poems/year for the Pushcart Prize. "We also consider submissions of visual art, which we publish with the poems in the magazine with links to artists' sites."

Advice: "Read the magazine carefully before submitting, then send your very best work."

DOC(K)S; AKENATON, 4 Cours Grandval, F 20 000 AJACCIO France. **Contact:** Philippe Castellin. **Magazine Needs:** *Doc(k)s* uses "concrete, visual, sound poetry; performance; mail-art; metaphysical poetry." Has published work by Nani Balestrini, Bernard Heidsieck, James Koller, Julien Blaine, Philippe Castellin, and Franco Beltrametti. The magazine *Doc(k)s* is published 4 times/year and has a circulation of 1,100, of which 150 are subscriptions. It is an elegantly produced volume of over 300 pgs., 7×10, flat-spined, using heavy paper and glossy full-color card covers. Since 1996, each volume has included either a CD-rom or audio CD. Most of it is in French. "We cannot quote a sample, because concrete poetry, a cross between poetry and graphic art, requires the visual image to be reproduced."

How to Submit: There are no specifications for submissions. Pays 5 copies.

Book/Chapbook Needs: Akenaton publishes collections of poetry, mostly in French.

DOLPHIN-MOON PRESS; SIGNATURES (Specialized: regional), P.O. Box 22262, Baltimore MD 21203. Established 1973. **President:** James Taylor.

Book/Chapbook Needs: Dolphin-Moon is "a limited-edition (500-1,000 copies) press which emphasizes quality work (regardless of style), often published in unusual/'radical' format." The writer is usually allowed a strong voice in the look/feel of the final piece. "We've published magazines, anthologies, chapbooks, pamphlets, perfect-bound paperbacks, records, audio cassettes, and comic books. All styles are read and considered, but the work should show a strong spirit and voice. Although we like the feel of 'well-crafted' work, craft for its own sake won't meet our standards either." Has published work by Teller, Michael Weaver, John Strausbaugh, Josephine Jacobsen, and William Burroughs. Send SASE for catalog and purchase samples or send $15 for their 'sampler' (which they guarantee to be up to $25 worth of their publications).

How to Submit: To submit, first send sample of 6-10 pgs. of poetry and a brief cover letter. No fax or e-mail submissions. Responds to query or to submission of whole work (if invited) in up to 4 weeks. Always sends prepublication galleys. Pays in author's copies, negotiable, though usually 10% of the run. Acquires first edition rights.

Advice: "Our future plans are to continue as we have since 1973, publishing the best work we can by local, up-and-coming, and nationally recognized writers—in a quality package."

$ DOVETAIL: A JOURNAL BY AND FOR JEWISH/CHRISTIAN FAMILIES (Specialized: interfaith marriage), 775 Simon Greenwell Lane, Boston KY 40107. (502)549-5499. Fax: (502)549-3543. E-mail: DI-IFR@Bardstown.com. Website: www.dovetailpublishing.com. Established 1991. **Editor:** Mary Rosenbaum.

Magazine Needs: *Dovetail*, published bimonthly, provides "strategies and resources for interfaith couples, their families and friends." Wants poetry related to Jewish/Christian marriage issues, no general religious themes.

THE GEOGRAPHICAL INDEX, located at the back of this book, can help you discover the publishers in your region.

Dovetail is 12-16 pgs., magazine-sized, stapled, includes 1-5 ads. Receives about 10 poems/year, accepts about 1%. Press run is 1,000 for 700 subscribers. Single copy: $4.50; subscription: $25. Sample: $5.28. Make checks payable to DI-IFR.

How to Submit: Submit 1 poem at a time. Accepts previously published poems and simultaneous submissions. Accepts e-mail and disk submissions. Time between acceptance and publication is up to 1 year. Poems are circulated to an editorial board. "Clergy and other interfaith professionals review draft issues." Seldom comments on rejected poems. Publishes theme issues. Guidelines and a list of upcoming themes available for SASE. Responds in 1 month. Pays $10-20 plus copies. Acquires first North American serial rights. Reviews other magazines in 500 words, single and multi-book format.

⬜ ◎ **DREAM INTERNATIONAL QUARTERLY (Specialized: dreams)**, 809 W. Maple St., Champaign IL 61820-2810. Established 1981. **Editor-in-Chief/Publisher:** Charles I. (Chuck) Jones. **Senior Poetry Editor:** Carmen M. Pursifull.

Magazine Needs: "Poetry must be dream-inspired and/or dream-related. This can be interpreted loosely, even to the extent of dealing with the transitory as a theme. Nothing written expressly or primarily to advance a political or religious ideology. We have published everything from neo-Romantic sonnets to stream-of-consciousness, a la 'Beat Generation.' " Has published poetry by Carmen M. Pursifull, Ursula Le Guin, Errol Miller, and Dr. Dimitri Mihalas. As a sample the senior poetry editor selected these lines from Heather Winters' poem "Ripening":

> *she opens purple eyes/yawning shaking wiping/away Past's sleep sand/to a young man with/a sunrise*
> *beard &/a red wine twinkle/in his eyebound eye/*

Dream International Quarterly is 120-150 pgs., 8½×11, with vellum cover and drawings. Receives 300 poems/year, accepts about 30. Press run is 300 for 20 subscribers. Subscription: $56/year, $112/2 years. Sample: $14. All orders should be addressed to Chuck Jones, Editor-in-Chief/Publisher, *DIQ*, 411 14th St., #H-, Ramona CA 92605-2769. All checks/money orders should be in US Funds and made payable to Charles I. Jones.

How to Submit: Submit up to 3 typed poems at a time. Accepts previously published poems and simultaneous submissions. No fax or e-mail submissions. Cover letter including publication history, if any. "As poetry submissions go through the hands of two readers, poets should enclose 2 loose stamps, along with the standard SASE." Do not submit mss in September or October. Time between acceptance and publication is up to 2 years. Comments on rejected poems if requested. Send large SASE with 2 first-class stamps plus $2 for guidelines. Responds in 2 weeks. Sometimes sends prepublication galleys. Pays 1 copy, "less postage. Postage/handling for contributor's copy costs $4." Also, from time to time, "exceptionally fine work has been deemed to merit a complimentary subscription." Acquires first North American serial or nonexclusive reprint rights.

Advice: "We consider all types of poetry from blank verse to sonnets, from shape poems to haiku. However, nothing will turn me off more quickly on a submission than 'sing-song' greeting card style verse. Be very careful with rhyming poetry."

N $ ⬜ ◎ DREAMS OF DECADENCE: VAMPIRE POETRY AND FICTION (Specialized); ABSOLUTE MAGNITUDE (Specialized: science fiction); DNA PUBLICATIONS, INC., P.O. Box 2988, Radford VA 24143-2988. Phone/fax: (413)772-0725. Established 1995 (*Dreams of Decadence*), 1993 (*Absolute Magnitude* and DNA Publications). **Editor:** Angela Kessler. **Editor-in-Chief:** Warren Lapine.

Magazine Needs: *Dreams of Decadence* and *Absolute Magnitude* are published quarterly. *Dreams of Decadence* features vampire poetry and fiction. Wants "all forms; however, the less horrific and more explicitly vampiric a poem is, the more likely it is to be accepted." Has published poetry by Denise Dumars and Nancy Ellis Taylor. *Absolute Magnitude* is one of the largest science fiction fiction magazines in America and is looking to use poetry as a filler; wants only science fiction-related poetry. *Dreams of Decadence* is 64 pgs., digest-sized, web-offset, saddle-stapled, desktop-published, with full-color slick cover, illustrations, and clip art. *Absolute Magnitude* is 96 pgs., 8½×11, newsprint paper, offset-printed on web press, saddle-stapled, with glossy 4-color cover, cover art, b&w illustrations, and ads. *Dreams of Decadence* receives about 1,000 poems/year, accepts about 100; *Absolute Magnitude* accepts about 20 poems. *Dreams of Decadence*'s press run is 2,000 for 200 subscribers, 1,000 shelf sales. *Absolute Magnitude*'s press run is 9,000 for 1,000 subscribers of which 5% are libraries, the remaining are shelf sales. Subscriptions: $16. Samples: $5. Make checks payable to DNA Publications.

How to Submit: Submit 5 poems at a time. Accepts simultaneous submissions with notification; no previously published poems. Cover letter preferred. Time between acceptance and publication is 6 months. Often comments on rejected poems. Send SASE for *Dreams of Decadence*'s guidelines. Responds in 1 month. Sometimes sends prepublication galleys. *Dreams of Decadence* pays 1 copy; *Absolute Magnitude* pays 10¢ per line and 1 copy. Acquires first North American serial rights. *Dreams of Decadence*'s staff reviews books or chapbooks of poetry. Poets may send book for review consideration to Angela Kessler at the above address.

Advice: "Write as often as you can. Send your work out and keep it out. A helpful hint: as we pay by the line many poets are tempted to truncate their lines to maximize their payment. This is not a good idea. Each line of a poem has a natural length and if it is truncated this will affect your poems' chances."

◎ **THE DRIFTWOOD REVIEW (Specialized: regional)**, P.O. Box 2042, Bay City MI 48707. E-mail: driftwdmi@aol.com. Established 1996. **Poetry Editor:** Jeff Vande Zande.

Magazine Needs: "An annual publication, *The Driftwood Review* strives to publish the best poetry and fiction being written by Michigan writers—known and unknown. We consider any style, but are particularly fond of poetry that conveys meaning through image. Rhyming poetry stands a poor chance. Give up the ghost; rhyme is dead—good riddance." Has published poetry by Daniel James Sundahl, Anca Vlasopolos, Terry Blackhawk, and Joe Sheltraw. As a sample the editor selected these lines from "Tattooed" by Matthew Echelberger:

> I remember when he bought me a speed bag/for Christmas and made the red leather sing,/his sinew
> and muscle straining/against the anchor tattooed on his forearm

The Driftwood Review is 100-125 pgs., digest-sized, professionally-printed, perfect-bound with glossy card cover containing b&w artwork. Receives about 500 poems/year, accepts about 5-7%. Press run is 200 for 75 subscribers. Subscription: $6.

How to Submit: Submit 3-5 poems at a time. No previously published poems or simultaneous submissions. Cover letter preferred. "Cover letter should include a brief bio suitable for contributors notes. No SASE? No reply." Reads submissions January 1 through October 1 only. Time between acceptance and publication is 9 months. Seldom comments on rejected poems. "Will comment on work that's almost there." Responds in 3 months. Pays 1 copy and includes the opportunity to advertize a book. Acquires first North American serial rights. Staff reviews chapbooks of poetry by Michigan writers only in 500 words, single book format. Send chapbooks for review consideration.

Also Offers: Sponsors a Reader's Choice Award. "Our readers vote by e-mail and the winner receives a cash award.'

Advice: "There are too many writers and not enough readers."

◑ ◎ DWAN (Specialized: gay/lesbian/bisexual, translations, bilingual/foreign language), Box 411, Swarthmore PA 19081-0411. E-mail: dsmith3@swarthmore.edu. Established 1993. **Editor:** Donny Smith.

Magazine Needs: Published every 2 to 3 months, *Dwan* is a "queer poetry zine; some prose; some issues devoted to a single poet or a single theme ('Jesus' or 'Mom and Dad,' for instance)." Wants "poetry exploring gender, sexuality, sex roles, identity, queer politics, etc. Heterosexuals usually welcome." Has published poetry by Melanie Hemphill, Susana Cattaneo, and Fabián Iriarte. As a sample the editor selected these lines from "The Russian Twins" by Lola Arias:

> To kill the father./The twin kisser her sister on the mouth./Shameless, snow falls on the impossible
> kiss./That country, that father.

Dwan is 20 pgs., 5½×8½, photocopied on plain white paper, and stapled. Receives 400-500 pgs. of poetry/year, accepts less than 10%. Press run is 100. Sample available for $2 (free to prisoners). Make checks payable to Donny Smith.

How to Submit: Submit 5-15 poems typed. Accepts previously published poems and simultaneous submissions. Accepts e-mail submissions, "include in body of message, no attachments." Cover letter required. Time between acceptance and publication is 6-18 months. Often comments on rejected poems. Upcoming themes available for SASE. Responds in 3 months. Pays copies. The editor reviews books, chapbooks, and magazines usually in 25-150 words. Send books for review consideration.

Advice: "Our guidelines: Queer. Legible. You decide what that means."

○ ◑ ◎ EAGLE'S FLIGHT; EAGLE'S FLIGHT BOOKS (Specialized: translations), 1505 N. Fifth St., Sayre OK 73662. (580)928-2298. Established 1989. **Editor/Publisher:** Shyamkant Kulkarni.

Magazine Needs: *Eagle's Flight* is a quarterly "platform for poets and short story writers—new and struggling to come forward." Wants "well-crafted literary quality poetry, any subject, any form, including translations. Translations should have permission of original poets." Has published poetry by Robert O. Schulz, Amrita Kulkarni, and Kim Klemm. As a sample the editor selected these lines from "Midnight" by Camille E. Torok:

> Midnight calls, I respond./The force of nature beckons/me from constraint. Dawn is a lifetime away/
> and the darkness lasts forever.

Eagle's Flight is 8-12 pgs., 7×8½, printed on colored paper and saddle-stapled, including simple art, few ads. Receives about 200 poems/year, accepts about 10%. Press run is 200 for 100 subscribers. Subscription: $5. Sample: $1.25.

How to Submit: Submit up to 5 poems at a time, no more than 21 lines each. No previously published poems or simultaneous submissions. Cover letter required; include short bio, up to 4 lines. Reads submissions January 1 through June 30 only. Time between acceptance and publication is up to 3 years. Seldom comments on rejected poems. "All material accepted for publication is subject to editing according to our editorial needs." Guidelines available for SASE. Responds in 3 months. Pays 1 copy. Acquires first publication rights. Reviews books of poetry in 250-750 words, single format.

Advice: "We expect poets to be familiar with our publication and our expectations and our limitations. To be a subscriber is one way of doing this. Everybody wants to write poems and, in his heart, is a poet. Success lies in getting ahead of commonplace poetry. To do this one has to read, to be honest, unashamed and cherish decent values of life in his heart. Then success is just on the corner of the next block."

⚑ $ ☻ ◎ ÉCRITS DES FORGES; ESTUAIRE; ARCADE; EXIT (Specialized: foreign language, women), 1497 Laviolette, Trois-Rivières, Québec G9A 5G4 Canada. (819)379-9813. Fax: (819)376-0774. E-mail: ecrits.desforges@aiqnet.com. Established 1971. **Président:** Gaston Bellemare. **Directrice Générale:** Maryse Baribeau.

Magazine Needs: Écrits des Forges publishes 3 poetry journals each year: *Estuaire* appears 5 times/year and wants poetry from well-known poets; *Exit* appears 4 times/year and wants poetry from beginning poets; and *Arcade* appears 3 times/year and wants poetry from women only. All three publications only accept work in French. Wants poetry that is "authentic and original as a signature." "We have published poetry from more than a thousand poets coming from most of the francophone's countries: André Romus (Belgium), Amadou Lamine Sall (Sénégal), Nicole Brossard, Claudine Bertrand, Denise Brassard, Tony Tremblay, and Jean-Paul Daoust (Québec)." As a sample the editor selected these lines from "La peau fragile du ciel" by Bernard Pozier:

> *l'infini défait ses gris hérités de la pluie/dans la brume laiteuse du soir/et l'on tente de distinguer la plage le ciel et l'océan/en flottant dans ce néant/et c'est comme essayer enfin de savoir/s'il est plus facile de faire parler le poème/ou bien faire taire la mer*

The 3 journals are 88-108 pgs., 5½×8, perfect-bound with art on cover, includes ads from poetry publishers. Receives more than 1,000 poems/year, accepts less than 5%. Press run for *Estuaire* is 750 for 450 subscribers of which 250 are libraries. Press run for *Arcade* is 650 for 375 subscribers of which 260 are libraries. Press run for *Exit* is 500 for 110 subscribers of which 235 are libraries. Subscription for *Estuaire* is $45 plus p&h; for *Arcade* is $27 plus p&h; for *Exit* is $36 plus p&h. Samples: $10 each. For *Exit* make checks payable to Éditions Gaz Moutarde. For *Estuaire* and *Arcade*, make checks payable to the respective publication.

How to Submit: Submit 10 poems at a time. No previously published poems or simultaneous submissions. "We make decisions on submissions in February, May, September, and December." Time between acceptance and publication is 3-12 months. Poems are circulated to an editorial board. "Nine persons read the submissions and send their recommendations to the editorial board." *Arcade* publishes theme issues. Upcoming themes are listed in the journal. Guidelines available by e-mail. Responds in 5 months. Pays "10% of the market price based on number of copies sold." Acquires all rights for 1 year. Retains rights to reprint in anthology for 10 years. Staff reviews books and chapbooks of poetry and other magazines on 1 page, double-spaced, single book format. Send books for review consideration.

Book/Chapbook Needs & How to Submit: Écrits des Forges inc. publishes poetry only—40-50 paperbacks/year. Books are usually 80-88 pgs., 5½×8, perfect-bound with 2-color cover with art. Query first with a few sample poems and cover letter with brief bio and publication credits. Responds to queries in 3-6 months. Pays royalties of 10-20%, advance of 50% maximum, and 25 author's copies. Order sample books by writing or faxing.

Also Offers: Sponsors the International Poetry Festival. "250 poets from 30 countries based on the 5 continents read their poems over 10-day period in 70 different cafés, bars, restaurants, etc. 30,000 persons attend. All in French." For more information, see website: www.aiqnet.com/fiptr.

⚑ ⊘ ECW PRESS, 2120 Queen St. E., Suite 200, Toronto, Ontario M4E 1E2 Canada. (416)694-3348. Fax: (416)698-9906. E-mail: ecw@sympatico.ca. Website: www.ecwpress.com Established 1979. **Literary Editor:** Michael Holmes.

Book/Chapbook Needs: ECW Press typically publishes 4 Canadian-authored paperback titles/year. Wants interesting—structurally challenging poetry. No greeting card doggerel. Has published poetry by Robert Priest, Sky Gilbert, David McGimpsey, Mark Sinnett, and Libby Scheier. Books are usually 96-150 pgs., 5×8, perfect-bound with full color covers.

How to Submit: Not accepting unsolicited manuscripts.

▯ ⊘ ◎ EDGAR: DIGESTED VERSE (Specialized: macabre), 486 Essex Ave., Bloomfield NJ 07003. (973)748-5794. E-mail: dragoons5@aol.com. Established 1999. **Editor:** John Picinich. **Associate Editor:** Victoria Picinich.

Magazine Needs: *EDGAR* is a "quarterly eclectic collection of the darkly bizarre, erotic, and offbeat." Wants "horror, gothic, surreal, science fiction. Go for the jugular, but give the reader something to chew over." Does not want "prose poems; werewolf and vampire verse; sappy sweet stuff." Accepts poetry written by teenagers. Has published poetry by Kurt Newton, Marge Simon, c.s. anderson, Jennifer Crow, and Marie Kazalia. As a sample the editors selected these lines from "Awake" by Lorelei K. Hickman:

> *If I were to tell you the truth/about the sorts of things/that plague my dreams—/the visions of your blood/spattering the walls/dripping from my hands and chin—/would you still/smooth back my sweaty hair in the dark/and whisper gentle words/to ease my transition/back into reality?*

EDGAR is 28 pgs., digest-sized, offset-printed and saddle-stapled with b&w card cover with illustrations. Receives about 300 poems/year, accepts about 30%. Press run is 150 for 75 subscribers, 30 shelf sales; 6 distributed free to reviewers. Subscription: $10. Sample: $2.50. Make checks payable to John Picinich.

How to Submit: Submit up to 3 poems at a time; "prefer disposable copies." No previously published poems or simultaneous submissions. Cover letter required. Accepts e-mail submissions. "For e-mail submissions, do not send poem as an attached file; keep within the body of the e-mail message along with street and e-mail addresses. Snail mail submissions must have a SASE. Also, include publishing credits, if any, and tell us a little bit about yourself in the cover letter." Time between acceptance and publication is 6-9 months. Always comments on rejected poems. Guidelines available for SASE. Responds in 5 weeks. Pays 1 copy. Acquires first North American serial rights.

Advice: "We recommend poets send SASE for guidelines and buy a sample copy. Each issue runs one or two Poe-ish poems and one or two food poems. We run mostly free verse. Poems of 40 lines or less have a good chance of getting accepted but have run poems of up to 75 lines. We have debuted several new poets."

EDGEWISE PRESS, INC., 24 Fifth Ave., #224, New York NY 10011. Website: www.edgewise.com. Has published Alan Jones, Cid Corman, and Nanni Cagnone. Order sample books by sending $10, plus $2 p&h. Currently accepts no unsolicited poetry.

EDGZ, Edge Publications, P.O. Box 799, Ocean Park WA 98640. Established 2000. **Publisher/Editor:** Blaine R. Hammond.

Magazine Needs: *Edgz* appears semiannually and publishes "poetry of all sorts of styles and schools. Our purpose is to present poetry with transpersonal intentions or applications and to put poets on a page next to other poets they are not used to appearing next to." Wants "a broad variety of styles with a transpersonal intent. *Edgz* has two main reasons for existence: My weariness with the attitude that whatever kind of poetry someone likes is the only legitimate poetry; and my desire to present poetry addressing large issues of life: meaning; oppression; exaltation; and whatever else you can think of. Must be engaged; intensity helps." Does not want "anything with a solely personal purpose; dense language poetry, which I'm not good at; poetry that does not take care with the basics of language, or displays an ignorance of modern poetry. No clichés, gushing, sentimentalism, or lists of emotions. Nothing vague or abstract. No light verse, but humor is fine" *Edgz* is digest-sized, laser-printed, saddle-stapled or perfect-bound (depends on number of pages), 94 lb. card stock cover with art/graphics (not comix). Printed on tree-free paper (hemp, flax, cotton) when available. 2002 prices are single copy: $6; subscription: $11 (2 issues). Sample: $3.50 when available. Make checks payable to Edge Publications.

How to Submit: Submit 3-5 poems at a time; "a longer poem may be submitted by itself." No limits on line length. Accepts simultaneous submissions; no previously published poems. No e-mail submissions. "I don't mind more than one poem to a page or well-traveled submissions; these are ecologically sound practices. I like recycled paper. Submissions without SASE will be gratefully used as note paper. Handwritten OK if poor or incarcerated." Reads submissions all year. Deadlines: February 1 and August 1 for winter and summer issues. Time between acceptance and publication is 1-6 months. Often comments on rejections "as I feel like it. I don't provide criticism services." Guidelines available for SASE. Responds in up to 6 months. Pays 1 contributor's copy/poem. Acquires first rights plus anthology rights ("just in case").

Advice: "It is one thing to require subscriptions in order to be published. It is something else to charge reading fees. In a world that considers poetry valueless, reading fees say it is less than valueless—editors should be compensated for being exposed to it. I beg such editors to cease the practice. I advise everyone else not to submit to them, or the practice will spread."

1812; NEW WRITING AWARDS, P.O. Box 1812, Amherst NY 14226. E-mail: info@newwriting.com. Website www.newwriting.com/contest.html or members.aol.com/newwriting (includes complete magazine content—poetry, stories, artwork, music). Established 1993. **Editors:** Richard Lynch, Rick Lupert, and Sam Meade.

Magazine Needs: *1812* is an annual electronic, literary arts publication appearing in February. Wants "material with a bang." Receives about 1,000 poems/year, accepts about 1-3%.

How to Submit: Accepts previously published poems; no simultaneous submissions. Accepts e-mail submissions; "do not use attached files. Submit poems in the body of the e-mail only." Cover letter required. Time between acceptance and publication is up to 1 year. Sometimes comments on rejected poems. Guidelines available for SASE. Payment is "arranged." Acquires one-time rights.

Also Offers: Sponsors New Writing Awards with $3,000 in prizes plus publication. "See www.newwriting.com/contest.html for more information." Entry fee: $10. Forms and guidelines available for SASE or on website.

THE EIGHTH MOUNTAIN PRESS, 624 SE 29th Ave., Portland OR 97214. Established 1985. **Editor:** Ruth Gundle.

Book/Chapbook Needs: Eighth Mountain is a "small press publisher of literary works by women." Has published poetry by Lucinda Roy, Maureen Seaton, Irena Klepfisz, Almitra David, Judith Barrington, and Elizabeth Woody. Publishes 1 book of poetry averaging 128 pgs., every other year. "Our books are handsomely designed and printed on acid-free paper in both quality trade paperbacks and library editions." Initial press run for poetry is 2,500.

How to Submit: "We expect to receive a query letter along with a few poems. A résumé of published work, if any, should be included. Work should be typed, double-spaced, and with your name on each page. If you want to know if your work has been received, enclose a separate, stamped postcard." No e-mail or fax submissions. Responds within 6 weeks. SASE (#10 envelope) must be included for response. "Full postage must be included if return of the work submitted is desired." Pays 7-8% royalties. Acquires all rights. Returns rights if book goes out of print.

[N] [symbol] 88: A JOURNAL OF CONTEMPORARY AMERICAN POETRY, P. O. Box 2872, Venice CA 90294. (310)712-1238. Fax: (310)828-4860. E-mail: T88AJournal@aol.com. Established 1999. **Managing Editor:** Denise Stevens. Member: PMA.

Magazine Needs: 88: A Journal of Contemporary American Poetry appears annually, includes essays on poetry and poetics, also reviews. Wants mainstream, lyric, lyric narrative, prose poems. "Will consider work that incorporates elements of humor, elements of surrealism. No light verse, limericks, children's poetry, concrete poetry." 88 is 150 pgs., 6×9, printed on-demand, perfect-bound, 4-color soft cover, with very limited art/graphics, ads. Publishes about 80 poems/issue. Single copy: $13.95.

How to Submit: Submit 5 poems at a time. No previously published poems or simultaneous submissions. No fax, e-mail, or disk submissions. Cover letter is required. Poems should be typed, single spaced on one side, indicate stanza breaks if poem is longer than one page. Name and address should appear on every page. "Unsolicited submissions accompanied by a proof-of-purchase coupon clipped from the back of the journal are read year round. Without proof-of-purchase, unsolicited submissions are considered March 1 through May 31 only. Unsolicited submissions received outside these guidelines will be returned unread. Submissions sent without SASE will be discarded." Time between acceptance and publication is 5-9 months. "Managing editor has the final decision of inclusion, but every poem is considered by an editorial board consisting of contributing editors whose suggestions weigh heavily in the process." Guidelines are available in magazine and for SASE. Responds in 3 months. Sometimes sends prepublication galleys. Pays 1 contributor's copy. Acquires one-time rights. Reviews books of poetry in 500-1,000 words, single book and multi-book format. Poets may send books for review consideration to Denise Stevens, managing editor.

Advice: "We believe it's important for poets to support the journals to which they submit. Because of print-on-demand, 88 is always available. We recommend becoming familiar with the journal before submitting."

[symbol] [symbol] EKPHRASIS (Specialized: ekphrastic verse); FRITH PRESS; OPEN POETRY CHAPBOOK COMPETITION, P.O. Box 161236, Sacramento CA 95816-1236. Website: www.hometown.aol.com/ekphrasis1 (includes journal and competition guidelines as well as a list of publications). Ekphrasis established Summer 1997, Frith Press 1995. **Editors:** Laverne Frith and Carol Frith.

• Patricia Terry's "South of Iquitos" was winner of the 2000 Open Poetry Chapbook Competition.

Magazine Needs: Ekphrasis is a biannual "outlet for the growing body of poetry focusing on individual works from any artistic genre." Wants "poetry whose main content is based on individual works from any artistic genre. Poetry should transcend mere description. Form open. No poetry without ekphrastic focus. No poorly crafted work. No archaic language." They nominate for Pushcart Prize. Has published poetry by Rhina Espaillat, Linda Nemec Foster, William Greenway, Simon Perchik, Joseph Stanton, and Virgil Suarez. Ekphrasis is 40-50 pgs., digest-sized, photocopied and saddle-stapled. Subscription: $12/year. Sample: $6. Make checks payable, in US funds, to Laverne Frith.

How to Submit: Submit 3-7 poems at a time with SASE. Accepts previously published poems "occasionally, must be credited"; no simultaneous submissions. Cover letter required including short bio with representative credits and phone number. Time between acceptance and publication is up to 1 year. Seldom comments on rejected poems. Guidelines available for SASE. Responds in 4 months. Pays 1 copy. Acquires first North American serial or one-time rights.

Book/Chapbook Needs & How to Submit: Frith Press publishes well-crafted poems—all subjects and forms considered—through their annual Open Poetry Chapbook Competition. Submit 16-24 pages of poetry with $10 reading fee. Include cover sheet with poet's name, address, phone number, and e-mail. Previously published poems must be credited. "No poems pending publication elsewhere." Deadline: October 31. Winner receives $100, publication, and 50 copies of their chapbook.

Advice: "With the focus on ekphrastic verse, we are bringing attention to the interconnections between various artistic genres and dramatizing the importance and universality of language. Study in the humanities is essential background preparation for the understanding of these interrelations."

[N] [symbol] [symbol] [symbol] ELEMENTS MAGAZINE, 2820 Houston St., Alexandria LA 71301. (318)445-5055. Established 1979. **Editor/Publisher:** Bernard Washington.

Magazine Needs: Elements appears bimonthly and is "designed to be a communications tool to be used to demonstrate positive contributions from all sorts of writers. All poetry is accepted. None is excluded." Accepts poetry written by children. Recently published poetry by Tim Scannell, Joanne Lowery, Christopher Mulrooney, Ralph E. Pray, Michael L. Smith, and B.Z. Niditch. As a sample the editor selected these lines from "Antal the Gypsy Violinist to His Audience" by Joanne Lowery:

> you come to watch and listen/I wear my best black hat/for a coin or two/let my violin become yours/
> my love tremble like yours though there is no resemblance/And it's/true I know your truth/Life is one
> bitter nettle stew

Element is 50 pgs., magazine-sized, commercial inkjet-printed, stapled, soft cover, with b&w, cut and paste art/graphics and business and personal ads. Receives about 15 poems/year, accepts about 100%. Publishes about 15 poems/issue. Press run is 500 subscribers of which 2 are libraries, 10 shelf sales; 3 are distributed free to individuals. Single copy: $6.50/US, $9/foreign. Subscription: $25/year, $45/2 years, $60/3 years. Make checks payable to Bernard Washington.

How to Submit: Line length for poetry is open. Accepts previously published poems and simultaneous submissions. No fax, e-mail, or disk submissions. Cover letter is required. "All submissions must be put on both sides of paper. Always include a SASE, biographical info in cover letter, very short stories." Reads submissions January 1-December 24. Submit seasonal poems 1 month in advance. Time between acceptance and publication is weeks. "Poems are read for clarity and content and accepted on the basis of their merit." Never comments on rejected poems. Occasionally publishes theme issues. A list of upcoming themes and guidelines are available for SASE. Responds in 3 weeks. Sometimes sends prepublication galleys. Pays 2 contributor's copies. Acquires one-time rights. Reviews books and chapbooks of poetry and other magazines/journals in 1,200 words, single book format. Poets may send books for review consideration to *Elements Magazine*.

Advice: "Young poets should remember a poem is about teaching. A poet explains himself or herself over and over and further and further. The poet must write to please self and ultimately please others. Always seek knowledge, not just pieces of information."

N $ ⊘ ELLIPSIS MAGAZINE, Westminster College of Salt Lake City, 1840 S. 1300 East, Salt Lake City UT 84105. (801)832-2321. E-mail: Ellipsis@wcslc.edu. Website: www.wcslc.edu. Established 1967.

Magazine Needs: *Ellipsis* is an annual appearing in April. Needs "good literary poetry, fiction essays, plays, and visual art." Has published work by Allison Joseph, Molly McQuade, Virgil Suarez, Maurice Kilwein-Guevara, Richard Cecil, and Ron Carlson. *Ellipsis* is 130 pgs., digest-sized, perfect-bound, with color cover an color art insert. Sample: $7.50.

How to Submit: Submit 3-5 poems. No previously published submissions. No fax or e-mail submissions. Include SASE and brief bio. Reads submissions August 1 to November 1. Pays $10/poem, plus 1 copy.

Also Offers: "All accepted poems are eligible for the *Ellipsis* Award which includes a $100 prize. Past judges have included Jorie Graham, Sandra Cisneros, and Stanley Plumly."

✓ ◐ ◯ ◑ ◎ EMERALD COAST REVIEW; THE LEGEND (Specialized: Membership); WEST FLORIDA LITERARY FEDERATION; FRANCIS P. CASSIDY LITERARY CENTER; W.I.S.E. (WRITERS IN SERVICE TO EDUCATION); W.I.S.T.S. (WRITERS IN SERVICE TO SENIORS) PROGRAMS (Specialized: regional), 400 S. Jefferson St., Suite 212, Pensacola FL 32501. (850)435-0942. E-mail: WFLitFed@aol.com. Website: www.WestFloridaLiteraryFed.com. The WFLF was established in 1987 and began the Francis P. Cassidy Literary Center, a regional writers' resource and special collections library. *Emerald Coast Review* **Contact:** Submissions Committee. *Legend* **Editor:** Robin Travis-Murphree.

Magazine Needs & How to Submit: The *Emerald Coast Review* is published every odd year and is usually limited to Coast regional writers and members of the West Florida Literary Federation. Sample: $11. Guidelines available for SASE or on website. Submit with required form (included in guidelines) January 1 through May 15 only. Pays copies.

Magazine Needs & How to Submit: "*The Legend*, the WFLF monthly newsletter, publishes literary art news, events and contests, members' poetry, essays, and articles. Members may submit poetry short essays and articles in the body of an e-mail at WFLitFed@aol.com (no more than three poems or one article/essay per month), or by snail mail to the WFLF office attn: Robin Travis-Murphree, *Legend* Editor. Deadline is the 15th of each month for the next month's newsletter."

Also Offers: The WFLF offers many programs for writers. One program, W.I.S.E. (Writers In Service to Education), allows area writers to volunteer their time and talents to local students. Sponsors a Student Writers Network for students in grades 9-12 and also sponsors a PenWISE poetry contest for grades 1-12. Back Door Poets, one of their subgroups, conducts open microphone poetry readings the third Saturday of each month. WFLF also hosts a writing workshop the first Saturday of every month. W.I.S.T.S. (Writers In Service to Seniors) provides volunteer area writers to nursing homes and assisted living facilities to read and entertain the residents. Membership dues range from $10/year for students and senior citizens to $100 for patrons and corporate memberships.

◕ EMOTIONS LITERARY MAGAZINE; WINGS OF DAWN PUBLISHING, 17216 Saticoy St. PMB 370, Van Nuys CA 91406. (818)345-9759. Toll Free fax: (877)WINGS-90. E-mail: wingsbooks@aol.com Website: www.wingsofdawn.com (includes poems, guidelines, and general information). Established 1997. **Editor-in-Chief:** Lupi Basil.

Magazine Needs: Appearing 6 times/year, *Emotions*, "*where the pen meets the heart*," welcomes "good quality work from talented writers as they share their thoughts and emotions in their own unique style and form." Wants "all styles and topics as long as they are in good taste, and not degrading to the human spirit. Each line in the poem should not exceed 65 characters in length, including spaces. We also consider fiction, short stories, essays and articles if they are between 1,000-2,500 words, b&w photos/artwork and 4×6 landscape color photos for front cover." Has published poetry by award-winning novelist Ben Bova, Dr. C. David Hay, Dave Taub, k.t. Frankovich, and J.E. Dorsey (Doug Claybourne). *Emotions* is 40 pgs., 8½×11, printed on 70 lb. good quality paper and saddle-stapled with glossy color cover, includes b&w photos, artwork and ads. Receives up to 2,000 submissions/year, accepts about 10%. Press run is 500 for 50% subscribers. Single copy: $4.99 US, $6 international; subscription: $25/year US, $40/year international. Make checks payable to Wings of Dawn Publishing Co. or fax credit card orders.

How to Submit: Submit 3 poems at a time. Accepts previously published poems (sometimes); no simultaneous submissions unless previously notified. Accepts e-mail submissions, if mailing address and bio included. "Submission must be in body of the e-mail, no attachments." Cover letter with 50-word bio required. Time between acceptance and publication is 2-4 months. Rarely comments on rejected poems. Publishes theme issues. Guidelines available for SASE, by e-mail or on website. Responds in up to 5 months. Pays 1 copy. Acquires first North American serial or one-time rights.

Chapbook Needs & How to Submit: Wings of Dawn publishes 1 paperback and 2 chapbooks of poetry/year, averaging 50-60 pages. "We do not accept unsolicited manuscripts unless a current call is posted on our website for a certain theme. We suggest you check our website periodically for information."

Advice: "We are a small press but internationally acclaimed. Our magazine is distributed in 15 countries. We strongly recommend you order a sample of our magazine to get a feel for what type of material we accept."

EMPLOI PLUS; DGR PUBLICATION, 1256 Principale N. St. #203, L'Annonciation, Quebec J0T 1T0 Canada. Phone/fax: (819)275-3293. Established 1988 (DGR Publication), 1990 (*Emploi Plus*). **Publisher:** Daniel G. Reid.

Magazine Needs: *Emploi Plus*, published irregularly, features poems and articles in French or English. Has published poetry by Robert Ott. Recently published *Alexville, Planet Earth* by D.G. Reid online. *Emploi Plus* is 12 pgs., $7 \times 8\frac{1}{2}$, photocopied, stapled, with b&w drawings, and pictures, no ads. Press run is 500 distributed free. Sample: free.

How to Submit: *Does not accept unsolicited submissions.*

EMRYS JOURNAL, P.O. Box 8813, Greenville SC 29604. Established 1982. **Editor:** Jeanine Halva-Neubauer. **Contact:** poetry editor.

Magazine Needs: *Emrys Journal* is an annual appearing in April. Wants "the accessible poem over the fashionably sophisticated, the touching dramatic or narrative poem over the elaborately meditative, the humorous poem over the ponderously significant, the modest poem over the showily learned." Has published poetry by Ken Autrey, Virgil Suarez, Michael S. Smith, and Rosanne Singer. As a sample the editor selected these lines from "Florida Straight" by Virgil Suarez:

> Out here on the high seas, the ocean ispossessed/of a thousand hues between lapis lazuli and emerald,/
> and on this makeshift raft headed north, another/family prays to Santa Barbara, Holy Mother

Emrys Journal is up to 120 pgs., 6×9, handsomely printed, flat-spined. Press run is 400 for 250 subscribers of which 10 are libraries. "About 10 poems are selected for inclusion." Single copy: $12.

How to Submit: Submit up to 5 poems. "No individual poem may exceed three pages. Include phone number, fax and/or e-mail, if desired." Reads submissions August 15 through December 1. Responds in about 2 months. Guidelines available for SASE. Pays 5 copies.

ENITHARMON PRESS, 36 St. George's Ave., London N7 0HD England. Phone: (020)7607-7194. Fax: (020)7607-8694. E-mail: books@enitharmon.demon.co.uk. Established 1967. **Poetry Editor:** Stephen Stuart-Smith.

Book/Chapbook Needs: Enitharmon is a publisher of fine editions of poetry and literary criticism in paperback and some hardback editions, about 15 volumes/year averaging 100 pages. Has published books of poetry by John Heath-Stubbs, Ted Hughes, David Gascoyne, Thom Gunn, Ruth Pitter, and Anthony Thwaite.

How to Submit: "Substantial backlog of titles to produce, so no submissions possible before 2004."

EPICENTER, P.O. Box 367, Riverside CA 92502. Website: www.geocities.com/Athens/Delphi/2884. Established 1994.

Magazine Needs: *Epicenter* is a biannual poetry and short story forum open to all styles. "*Epicenter* is looking for ground-breaking poetry and short stories from new and established writers. No angst-ridden, sentimental, or earthquake poetry. We are not adverse to graphic images if the work is well presented and contains literary merit." Has published poetry by Lon Risley, Max Berkovitz, Stan Nemeth, and Vicki Solheid. *Epicenter* is 24 pgs., digest-sized, and saddle-stapled with semi-glossy paper cover and b&w graphics. Receives about 1,000 submissions/year, accepts about 5%. Press run is 400 for 250 shelf sales. Single copy: $3. Sample: $3.50. Make checks payable to Rowena Silver.

How to Submit: Submit up to 5 poems. Include SASE with sufficient postage for return of materials. Accepts previously published poems and simultaneous submissions. Seldom comments on rejected poems. Guidelines available for SASE. Pays 1 copy. Acquires one-time and electronic rights.

$ EPOCH, 251 Goldwin Smith, Cornell University, Ithaca NY 14853. (607)255-3385. Established 1947. **Poetry Editor:** Nancy Vieira Couto.

Magazine Needs: *Epoch* has a distinguished and long record of publishing exceptionally fine poetry and fiction. Has published work by such poets as Ashbery, Ammons, Eshleman, Wanda Coleman, Molly Peacock, Robert Vander Molen, and Alvin Aubert. *Epoch* appears 3 times/year in a 6×9, professionally printed, flat-spined format with glossy color cover, 128 pgs., which goes to 1,000 subscribers. Accepts less than 1% of the many submissions received each year, have a 2- to 12-month backlog. Sample: $5.

How to Submit: "We don't read unsolicited mss between April 15 and September 15." Responds in 2 months. Occasionally provides criticism on mss. Pays $5-10/page. Acquires first serial rights.

Advice: "It's extremely important for poets to read other poets. It's also very important for poets to read the magazines that they want to publish in. Directories are not enough."

☑ ◯ ◪ **ETHEREAL GREEN**, 238 W. Saginaw St. #106, East Lansing MI 48823. E-mail: etherealgreen@h ome.com. Website: www.angelfire.com/yt/etherealgreenpoetry/index.html (includes guidelines, sample poems, poet polls, and prices). Established 1996. **Contact:** Sarah Hencsie.

Magazine Needs: *Ethereal Green*, published quarterly, strives "to feed readers unknown talent." Contains poetry, art, and articles. Wants "Shakespearian, love, nature, and romance poetry. Poems should be less than 30 lines." Does not want "religious, ethnic, or edited poems." As a sample the editor selected these lines by Jaime Morrison:

> *Because it's raining . . . you're/falling from the sky, from/your soul being drained . . .*

Ethereal Green is 30-70 pgs., approximately 6×8, with cover art. Receives hundreds of poems/year, accepts about 50%. Press run is 250 for about 70 subscribers, 60% shelf sales. Subscription: $27. Sample: $7. Make checks payable to Sarah C. Hencsic.

How to Submit: Submit 3-7 typed poems at a time. SASE absolutely required. Accepts previously published poems and simultaneous submissions. Accepts e-mail submissions (no attachments). Cover letter required; "if no cover letter is submitted, submission will be automatically rejected." Time between acceptance and publication is 3-7 months. Poems are circulated to an editorial board with "poems edited twice; once by publisher and again by select editors on board." Always comments on rejected poems. Guidelines and upcoming themes available for SASE. Responds in 4 months. Sometimes sends prepublication galleys. Pays 1 copy. Acquires first North American serial or one-time rights.

🌐 ♡ ◎ **EUROPEAN JUDAISM (Specialized: religious, ethnic)**, Kent House, Rutland Gardens, London SW7 1BX England. Established 1966. **Poetry Editor:** Ruth Fainlight.

Magazine Needs: *European Judaism* is a "twice-yearly magazine with emphasis on European Jewish theology/philosophy/literature/history, with some poetry in every issue. It should preferably be short and have some relevance to matters of Jewish interest." Has published poetry by Linda Pastan, Elaine Feinstein, Daniel Weissbort, and Dannie Abse. As a sample the editor selected these lines from a poem by Michael Heller:

> *I took silence into time, marking the absence/of our late vocabularies in their conspirings,/these new mythologies, as they fell from on high//through our skies and through our roofs/scouring the mind as cosmic rays leave/traceries in the cool white lime of tunnels.*

European Judaism is a glossy, elegant, 6×9, flat-spined magazine, rarely art or graphics, 110 pgs. Has a press run of 950, about 50% of which goes to subscribers (few libraries). Subscription: $27.

How to Submit: Submit 3-4 poems at a time. No material dealt with or returned if not accompanied by SASE (or SAE with IRCs). "We cannot use American stamps. Also, I prefer unpublished poems, but poems from published books are acceptable." Cover letter required. Pays 1 copy.

🐦 $ ◪ **EVENT**, Douglas College, P.O. Box 2503, New Westminster, British Columbia V3L 5B2 Canada. (604)527-5293. Fax: (604)527-5095. E-mail: event@douglas.bc.ca. Website: http://event.douglas.bc.ca (includes submission guidelines, contest information, past and current issues, as well as subscription and contact information). Established 1971. **Poetry Editor:** Gillian Harding-Russell.

Magazine Needs: *Event* appears 3 times/year and is "a literary magazine publishing high-quality contemporary poetry, short stories, creative nonfiction, and reviews. In poetry, we tend to appreciate the narrative and sometimes the confessional modes. In any case, we are eclectic and always open to content that invites involvement. We publish mostly Canadian writers." Has published poetry by Tom Wayman, Lorna Crozier, Russell Thornton, Don McKay, A.F. Moritz, Marlene Cookshaw, and Tim Bowling. *Event* is 136 pgs., 6×9, finely printed and flat-spined with glossy cover. Press run is 1,300 for 700 subscribers of which 50 are libraries. Subscription: $22/year, $35/2 years. Sample back issue: $5; current issue: $8. Prices include GST. US subscribers please pay in US funds. Overseas and institutions: $32/year, $48/2 years. Sample: $9.

How to Submit: Submit 5 poems at a time. No previously published poems. No fax or e-mail submissions. Brief cover letter with publication credits required. Include SASE (Canadian postage only) or SAE and IRCs. "Tell us if you'd prefer your manuscript to be recycled rather than returned." Time between acceptance and publication is within 1 year. Comments on some rejected poems. Responds in 4 months. Pays honorarium. Acquires first North American serial rights.

◎ **EXIT 13 (Specialized: geography/travel)**, % Tom Plante, P.O. Box 423, Fanwood NJ 07023-1162. (908)889-5298. E-mail: plante@bellatlantic.net. Established 1987. **Editor:** Tom Plante.

Magazine Needs: *Exit 13* is a "contemporary poetry annual" using poetry that is "short, to the point, with a sense of geography." Has published poetry by Charles Plymell, Errol Miller, Adele Kenny, Varese Layzer, and Randy Fingland. As a sample the editor selected these lines by M.E. Grow:

> *Under the trees in the wind's paw reds scream./Torn by the sun time folds into rock.*

Exit 13, #9, was 64 pgs. Press run is 300. Sample: $6.50.

How to Submit: Accepts simultaneous submissions and previously published poems. Accepts e-mail submissions, include in body of message. Guidelines available for SASE. Responds in 4 months. Pays 1 copy. Acquires one-time and possible anthology rights. Staff reviews books of poetry and magazines in a "Publications Received" column, using 25-30 words/listing. Send books for review consideration.

Advice: "Write about what you know. Study geography. *Exit 13* looks for adventure. Every state, region, and ecosystem is welcome. Send a snapshot of an 'Exit 13' road sign and receive a free copy of the issue in which it appears."

☑ ☺ **EXPEDITION PRESS**, 411 Stanwood St., Apt. E, Kalamazoo MI 49006-4543. (616)349-6413. Established 1978. **Publisher:** Bruce W. White.

Book/Chapbook Needs: Expedition Press publishes chapbooks that are "offbeat and bohemian with egalitarian appeal." Open to any style. This press is "not for snobs." He has published poetry by J. Kline Hobbs, Robin Reish, Todd Zimmerman, Margaret Tyler, Martin Cohen and C. VanAllsburg. As a sample the publisher selected his own couplet:

> *The moon is always full/The sun is always high.*

Sample chapbooks: $5. Make checks payable to Bruce White.

How to Submit: Submit typed ms of 20-30 pgs. and cover letter with brief bio. **Reading fee: $5.** Please send SASE. Responds in 1 month. Sometimes sends prepublication galleys. Pays 100 contributor's copies. Bruce White provides "much" criticism on rejected mss.

☑ ◯ ◎ **EXPERIMENTAL FOREST PRESS (Specialized: bilingual/foreign language, political, social issues)**, 223 A Bosler Ave., Lemoyne PA 17043. (717)730-2143. E-mail: xxforest@yahoo.com. Website: http://maxpages.com/xxforest. Established 1999. **Co-Editors:** Jeanette Trout and Kevyn Knox.

Magazine Needs: *Experimental Forest* is published bimonthly "to show the world that there is more out there than meets the eye. Please, no sappy love poetry!" Has published poetry by Richard Kostelanetz, John M. Bennett, Taylor Graham, T. Kilgore Splake, Marty Esworthy, and Snow. As a sample the editor selected these lines by Kerry Shawn Keys:

> *E-mail is humming in pythagorean space/Chopin composes the flesh of a nocturne/Pink white apple blossoms/inner-tubes bearing naiads drift down the Delaware.*

Experimental Forest is 60 pgs., 5½ × 8½, stapled, b&w artwork on cover stock, also inside art. Receives about 1,000 poems/year, accepts about 20%. Publishes 30 poems/issue. Press run is 250 for 25 subscribers of which 5 are libraries, 75 shelf sales; 25 distributed free to fellow editors. Single copy: $5; subscription: $21.50/year. Sample: $5. Make checks payable to Jeanette Trout and/or Kevyn Knox.

How to Submit: Submit up to 5 poems at a time. Accepts simultaneous submissions. Accepts e-mail submissions; no fax submissions. Cover letter preferred. "We prefer to have a short bio for our contributors page. We also require a SASE." Time between acceptance and publication is 6 months. Often comments on rejected poems. Publishes theme issues occasionally. A list of upcoming themes available for SASE. Responds in 2 months. Pays 1 copy. Acquires one-time rights.

Also Offers: Sponsors a poetry contest every fall with a $100 1st Prize and a short story contest each spring with a $100 1st Prize. Guidelines available for SASE or by e-mail.

Advice: "We accept poetry of any style or subject. We look for poetic voices that have something fresh and new to say. Remember, we are called '*Experimental*' *Forest*."

☑ ◐ **EXPLORATIONS; EXPLORATIONS AWARD FOR LITERATURE**, UAS, 11120 Glacier Highway, Juneau AK 99801-8761. E-mail: art.petersen@uas.alaska.edu. Established 1981. **Editor:** Professor Art Petersen.

Magazine Needs: *Explorations* is the literary magazine of the University of Alaska Southeast and appears annually in July. "The editors respond favorably to language really spoken by men and women. Standard form and innovation are encouraged as well as appropriate and fresh aspects of imagery (allusion, metaphor, simile, symbol . . .)." *Explorations* is digest-sized, nicely printed and saddle-stapled, with front and back cover illustration in one color. The editors tend to go for smaller-length poems (with small line breaks for tension) and often print two on a page—mostly lyric free verse with a focus on voice. Sample: $5.

How to Submit: An entry/reading fee is required: $6 for 1 or 2 poems (60 lines/poem maximum), $3/poem for more than 2 poems (no more than 60 lines each); those paying reader/contest entry fees receive a copy of the publication. Checks should be made payable to "UAS Explorations." Mss must be typed with name, address, and 3- to 4-line biography on the back of each first page. Accepts simultaneous submissions. Submit January through May 15 only. Mss are not returned. Guidelines available for SASE or by e-mail. Responds in July. Pays 2 copies. Acquires one-time rights.

Also Offers: Sponsors the Explorations Awards for Literature. First place (for a poem or short story): $1,000; second place (for best work in a genre different from first place winner): $500; and third places for poetry and prose: $100. Entry fee: $6 for 1-2 poems, $3/poem for 3-5 poems. Judge for 2000 contest was Editor Art Petersen. Guidelines available for SASE.

N ◨ ◷ **FAILBETTER.COM**, 63 Eighth Ave., #3A, Brooklyn NY 11217. E-mail: submissions@failbetter. com. Website: www.failbetter.com (portal to current issue and archive of past issues). Established 2000. **Editors:** Thom Didato and David McLendon.

Magazine Needs: *failbetter.com* is a quarterly e-zine "in the spirit of a traditional literary journal, dedicated to publishing quality fiction, poetry, and artwork. While the Web plays host to hundreds, if not thousands, of genre-related literary sites (i.e., science fiction and horror, many of which have merit), *failbetter.com* is not one of them. We place a high degree of importance on originality, believing that even in this age of trends it is still possible." Recently published poetry by Amy Holman, Jonah Winter, Lee Upton, Jack Shuler, Terrance Hayes, and Mary Whittemore. As a sample the editors selected these lines from "Texan" by Jonah Winter:

> When you come towards me/you come towards Texas./And Texas is not/just a way of tipping back a
> beer bottle./Texas is whatever happens/after the bottle is empty.

failbetter.com is published exclusively online with art/graphics. Receives about 200 poetry submissions/year, accepts about 9-12. Publishes 3-4 poets/issue.

How to Submit: Submit 4-6 poems at a time. Line length for poetry is open. "We are not concerned with length: One good sentence may find a home here; as the bulk of mediocrity will not." Accepts simultaneous submissions; no previously published poems. Encourages e-mail submissions. "All e-mail submissions should include title in header. All poetry submissions must be included in the body of your e-mail. Please do not send attached files. If for whatever reason you wish to submit a MS Word attachment, please query first." Submissions also accepted by regular mail. "Please note, however, any materials accepted for publication must ultimately be submitted in electronic format in order to appear on our site." Cover letter is preferred. Reads submissions year round. Time between acceptance and publication ranges from 1-4 months. Poems are circulated to an editorial board. Often comments on rejected poems. "In fact, there have been several incidences where poets have been asked to re-submit, and their subsequent submissions have been accepted." Guidelines are available on website. Responds in 3 weeks to e-mail submissions; up to 3 months for submissions by regular mail. "We will not respond to any e-mail inquiry regarding receipt confirmation or status of any work under consideration." No payment. Acquires exclusive first-time Internet rights; works will also be archived online. All other rights, including opportunity to publish in traditional print form, revert to the artist.

Also Offers: *failbetter presents*, a New York-based reading series featuring both established and emerging poets and fiction writers. Inquiries regarding reading series can be made at failbetterpresents@yahoo.com.

Advice: "We strongly recommend that you not only read the previous issue, but also sign up on our e-mail list (subscribe@failbetter.com) to be notified of future publications. Most importantly, know that what you are saying could only come from you. When you are sure of this, please feel free to submit."

N ◨ ◷ ◯ **THE FAIRFIELD REVIEW**, 544 Silver Spring Rd., Fairfield CT 06430-1947. (203)255-1119. E-mail: fairfieldreview@hpmd.com. Website: www.fairfieldreview.org (includes all publications and related info). Established 1997. **Editors:** Janet and Edward Granger-Happ.

Magazine Needs: *The Fairfield Review* appears 3 times/year as an e-zine featuring poetry and short stories from new and established authors. "We prefer free style poems, approachable on first reading, but with the promise of a rich vein of meaning coursing along under the consonants and vowels." Does not want "something better suited for a Hallmark card." Accepts poetry written by children. Recently published poetry by David Meuel, Halsted, Richard Fewell, E. Doyle-Gillespie, and Doug Tanoury. As a sample the editors selected these lines from "Bulb & Seed" by Taylor Graham:

> The old dogs are blooming where we planted/them with daffodils, the lemon-yellow heads/nodding
> this March afternoon, with ruffs/as bright as egg yolk. I name them/to remember: Lady-Bear and
> Pepper, Roxy,/Pattycake . . .

Fairfield Review is 20-30 pgs. published online (HTML). Receives about 350 poems/year, accepts about 8%. Publishes about 10 poems/issue.

How to Submit: Submit 3 poems at a time. Line length for poetry is 75 maximum. Accepts previously published poems with permission; no simultaneous submissions. Accepts fax, e-mail, and disk submissions. Cover letter is preferred. "We prefer submission via e-mail or e-mail attachment." Reads submissions continually. Time between acceptance and publication is up to 3 months. Poems are circulated to an editorial board. Often comments on rejected poems, if requested and submitted via e-mail. Guidelines are available on website. Responds in up to 4 months. Always sends prepublications galleys (online only). Acquires first rights and right to retain publication in online archive issues. Reviews books of poetry. "We consider reviews of books from authors we have published or who are referred to us."

Also Offers: "We select poems from each issue for 'reader's choice' awards based on readership frequency."

Advice: "Read our article on 'Writing Qualities to Keep in Mind.' "

◯ ◑ ◎ **FANTASTIC STORIES OF THE IMAGINATION (Specialized: science fiction/fantasy)**, (formerly Pirate Writings), P.O. Box 329, Brightwaters NY 11718. Established 1992. **Editor:** Edward J. McFadden. (Published by DNA Publications. Send all business-related inquiries and subscriptions to DNA Publications, P.O. Box 2988, Radford VA 24143.)

Magazine Needs: *Fantastic Stories* is a quarterly magazine "filled with fiction, poetry, art, and reviews by top name professionals and tomorrow's rising stars." Wants all forms and styles of poetry "within our genres—literary (humorous or straight), fantasy, science fiction, and adventure. Best chance is 20 lines or less. No crude language or excessive violence. No pornography, horror, western, or romance. Poems should be typed with exact capitalization and punctuation suited to your creative needs." Has published poetry by Nancy Springer, Jane Yolen, and John Grey. *Fantastic Stories* is 72 pgs., magazine-sized and saddle-stapled with a full-color cover, interior spot color and b&w art throughout. Receives about 150 poetry submissions/year, accepts about 15-25 poems. Subscription: $16/4 issues, $27/8 issues. Sample: $4.95.

How to Submit: Accepts simultaneous submissions. Cover letter required; include credits, if applicable. Often comments on rejected poems. Guidelines available for SASE. Responds in 4 months. Pays 1-2 copies and 50¢ a line. Acquires first North American serial rights. Also "reserves the right to print in future volumes of *Fantastic Stories* anthology."

$ ☑ ◎ **FARRAR, STRAUS & GIROUX/BOOKS FOR YOUNG READERS (Specialized: children)**, 19 Union Square W., New York NY 10003. (212)741-6900. Established 1946. **Contact:** Editorial Dept./Books for Young Readers.

Book/Chapbook Needs: Publishes one book of children's poetry "every once in a while," in both hardcover and paperback editions. Open to book-length submissions of children's poetry only. Has published collections of poetry by Valerie Worth and Deborah Chandra.

How to Submit: Query first with sample poems and cover letter with brief bio and publication credits. Accepts previously published in magazines and simultaneous submissions. Seldom comments on rejected poems. Send SASE for reply. Responds to queries in up to 2 months, to mss in up to 4 months. "We pay an advance against royalties; the amount depends on whether or not the poems are illustrated, etc." Also pays 10 copies.

☑ ◻ ◯ **FAT TUESDAY**, 560 Manada Gap Rd., Grantville PA 17028. (717)469-7159. E-mail: cotolo@excite.com. Website: www.egroups.com/group/FatTuesday. Established 1981. **Editor-in-Chief:** F.M. Cotolo. **Editors:** Kristen Cotolo and Lionel Stevroid.

Magazine Needs: *Fat Tuesday* publishes irregularly as "a Mardi Gras of literary, visual, and audio treats featuring voices, singing, shouting, sighing, and shining, expressing the relevant to irreverent." Wants "prose poems, poems of irreverence, gems from the gut. Particularly interested in hard-hitting 'autofiction.' " Accepts poetry written by children, ages 10 and up. Has published poetry by Mark Cramer, Mary Lee Gowland, Patrick Kelly, Gerald Locklin, and Julia Solis, as well as material by unknown authors. *Fat Tuesday* is up to 60 pgs., typeset (large type, heavy paper), saddle-stapled, card covers, usually chapbook style (sometimes magazine-sized, unbound) with cartoons, black line art, and ads. Press run is 1,000/year with poetry on 80% of the pages. Receives hundreds of submissions each year, accepts about 3-5%, have a 3- to 5-month backlog "but usually try to respond with personal, not form, letters." All editions are $5, postage paid.

How to Submit: Submit any number of poems at a time. No previously published poems or simultaneous submissions. Accepts e-mail submissions (text in body of message). "Cover letters are fine, the more amusing the better." Publishes theme issues. Guidelines available for SASE. Responds in 2 weeks. Pays 2 copies if audio. Rights revert to author after publication.

Also Offers: "In 1998 *Fat Tuesday* was presented in a different format with the production of a stereo audio cassette edition. *Fat Tuesday's Cool Noise* features readings, music, collage, and songs, all in the spirit of *Fat's* printed versions. Other *Cool Noise* editions will follow. *Fat Tuesday* solicits artists who wish to have their material produced professionally in audio form. Call the editors about terms and prices on how you can release a stereo audio cassette entirely of your own material. *Fat Tuesday* has released *Seven Squared*, by Frank Cotolo and is looking for other audio projects. In-print magazines will still be produced as planned. You can hear Cotolo music and purchase CDs at our website."

Advice: "Be yourself. Use your own voice. We don't care about trends, we listen for unique and individual voices. We rely on sales to subsidize all projects so writers should be sensitive to this hard truth and buy sample editions. Join the *Fat Tuesday* e-group!"

☑ ◙ **FAULTLINE**, Dept. of English & Comparative Literature, University of California—Irvine, Irvine CA 92697-2650. (949)824-1573. E-mail: faultline@uci.edu. Website: www.humanities.uci.edu/faultline. Established 1991. **Managing Editor:** Thomas Babayan. **Contact:** Jonathan Farmer.

● Poetry published by this journal has also been selected for inclusion in a *Pushcart Prize* anthology.

Magazine Needs: *Faultline* is an annual journal of art and literature occasionally edited by guest editors and published at the University of California, Irvine. Has published poetry by Thomas Lux, Heather McHugh, Amy Geistler, and Yusef Komunyakaa. As a sample the editor selected these lines from "Late for Work" by Ralph Angel:

> *Maybe I knelt there/for since they have vanished the lamps/in the shop windows//flicker within.*
> *Somebody/flinching. A red/umbrella and that part of the town swept from the hip*

Faultline is approximately 120 pgs., 6 × 9, professionally printed on 60 lb. paper, perfect-bound with 80 lb. cover stock and featuring color and b&w art and photos. Receives about 1,500 poems/year, accepts about 5%. Press run is 500 for 50 subscribers, 175 shelf sales. Single copy: $8. Sample: $5.

How to Submit: Submit up to 5 poems at a time. Accepts simultaneous submissions. No fax or e-mail submissions. Cover letter preferred. Do not include name and address on ms to assist anonymous judging. Reads submissions September 15 to March 1 only. Poems are selected by a board of up to 6 readers. Seldom comments on rejected poems. Guidelines available for SASE. Responds in 3 months. Pays 2 copies. Acquires first or one-time rights.

$ ☑ FAUQUIER POETRY JOURNAL, P.O. Box 68, Bealeton VA 22712-0068. Established 1994. **Managing Editor:** D. Clement.

Magazine Needs: *Fauquier Poetry Journal* is a quarterly that contains poetry, poetry commentary, editorials, contest announcements, and book reviews. Wants "fresh, creative, well-crafted poetry, any style. Due to format, longer poems over 40 lines are not often used. Do not want overly sentimental or religious themes, overdone subjects, or overly obscure work." Has published poetry by Sean Brendan-Brown, Robert Cooperman, Maura Ramer, Nancy Ryan, and Kenneth Wanamaker. *Fauquier Poetry Journal* is 40-50 pgs., digest-sized, laser-printed on plain white paper and saddle-stapled with bright colored paper cover. Press run is more than 300 for 100 subscribers, including libraries. Subscription: $20. Sample: $5.

How to Submit: The editor encourages subscriptions by requiring a **reading fee for nonsubscribers** ($5 for 1-5 poems only per month); no reading fee for subscribers. Submit up to 5 poems with name and address in the upper left corner of each page and include SASE. Accepts previously published poems and simultaneous submissions. Sometimes comments on rejected poems. Guidelines and upcoming themes available for SASE. Responds within 6 weeks. Offers Editor's Choice Awards of $5-25 for the best entries in each issue. Pays 1 copy to remainder of published poets. Acquires one-time rights.

Also Offers: Sponsors quarterly poetry contests, explained in the journal. Entry fee: $5. Prizes range from $15-75, and winners are published in the following issue. In addition to poetry, *Fauquier Poetry Journal* occasionally prints articles by guest columnists. Articles should deal with some aspect of poetry, the writing experience, reactions to particular poems or poets, the mechanics (how to), etc. No reading fee, no guidelines other than word limit (around 1,000 words). "Pretty much anything goes as long as it's interesting and well-written." Pays 2¢/word.

Advice: "Let us see a variety in your submission; what one editor likes, another won't. Send a range of work that illustrates the breadth and depth of your talent; this helps us decide if there's something we like. We encourage submissions from anyone who is writing mature, well-crafted poetry."

☑ ⊕ ◖ ◗ ◎ FEATHER BOOKS; THE POETRY CHURCH MAGAZINE; CHRISTIAN HYMNS & SONGS (Specialized: anthology, humor, religious), Fairview, Old Coppice, Lyth Bank, Shrewsbury, Shropshire SY3 0BW United Kingdom. Phone/fax: (01743)872177. E-mail: john@waddysweb.freeuk.com. Website: www.waddysweb.freeuk.com (includes directors and editors and their specialized areas, a list of publications, and the top twenty most popular selling books). Feather Books established 1982. *Poetry Church Magazine* established 1996. **Contact:** Rev. John Waddington-Feather.

Magazine Needs: *The Poetry Church Magazine* appears quarterly and contains Christian poetry and prayers. Wants "Christian or good religious poetry—usually around 20 lines, but will accept longer." Does not want "unreadable blasphemy." Accepts poetry written by children over ten. Has published poetry by M.A.B. Jones, Joan Smith, Idris Caffrey, Walter Nash, and the Glyn family. *The Poetry Church Magazine* is 40 pgs., digest-sized, photocopied, saddle-stapled with laminated cover and b&w cover art. Receives about 1,000 poems/year, accepts about 500. Press run is 1,000 for 400 subscribers of which 10 are libraries. Single copy free; subscription: £7 ($15 US). Sample: $5. Make checks payable in sterling to Feather Books. Payment can also be made through website.

How to Submit: Submit 2 typed poems at a time. Accepts previously published poems and simultaneous submissions. Accepts e-mail submissions in attached file. Cover letter preferred with information about the poet. All work must be submitted by mail with SASE (or SAE and IRC). Time between acceptance and publication is 4 months. "The editor does a preliminary reading; then seeks the advice of colleagues about uncertain poems." Always comments on rejected poems. Guidelines available for SASE (or SAE and IRC), by e-mail, or by fax. Responds within 1 week. Pays 1 copy. Poets retain copyright.

Book/Chapbook Needs & How to Submit: Feather Books publishes the Feather Books Poetry Series, books of Christian poetry, and prayers. Has recently published poetry collections by the Glyn family, Walter Nash, David Grieve, and Rossi Morgan Barry. "We have now published 124 poetry collections by individual Christian poets." Books are usually photocopied and saddle-stapled with laminated covers. "Poets' works are selected for publication in collections of around 20 poems in our Feather Books Poetry Series. We do not insist, but most poets pay for small run-offs of their work, e.g., around 50-100 copies for which we charge $200 per fifty. If they can't afford it, but are good poets, we stand the cost. We expect poets to read our *Poetry Church Magazine* to get some idea of our standards." Pays 5% royalty "where we sell copies of poetry" or 1 author's copy (out of a press run of 50) "if we pay cost."

Also Offers: Feather Books also publishes *Christian Hymns & Songs*, a quarterly supplement by Grundy and Feather. And, each fall, selected poems that have been published throughout the year in *Poetry Church Magazine* appear in *The Poetry Church Anthology*, the leading Christian poetry anthology used in churches and schools. Began a new chapbook collection, the "Christianity and Literature Series," which focuses on academic work. "The first, just published, is a paper by Dr. William Ruleman, of Wesley College, Tennessee, entitled *W.H. Auden's Search for Faith*. Future numbers will include *Six Contemporary Women Christian Poets*, by Dr. Patricia

Batstone and *'The Dream of the Road,' 'The Wanderer,' 'The Seafarer': Three Old English Early Christian Poems of the 8th Century,* newly translated by Reverend John Waddington-Feather, with an introduction by Professor Walter Nash."

Advice: "We find it better for poets to master rhyme and rhythm before trying free verse. Many poets seem to think that if they write 'down' a page they're writing poetry, when all they're doing is writing prose in a different format."

N: ○ ○ FEELINGS OF THE HEART, P.O. Box 1022, Gulfport MS 39502-1022. (228)864-0766. E-mail: AHARNISCH1@aol.com. Website: www.feelingsoftheheart.net (includes Meet the Staff, featured authors, guidelines, subscription information). Established 1999. **Editor/Publisher/Founder:** Alice M. Harnisch-Fitchie.

Magazine Needs: *Feelings of the Heart,* a journal of fiction and poetry, appears quarterly. "I look for all forms of poetry styles and purposes that touch a string inside the heart, a poem that will be relted to one's life." Does not want childish, clichés. Recently published poetry by Lawrence E. Harnisch, Barry Elisofon, Robert Spector, Scott D. Kelly, Aaron Hillman, Vernon A. Fitchie, and Kenya Blue. As a sample the editor selected these lines from "Ecstasy" by Dorothy Birdwell:

> *A lover's kiss/soft as the wings/of a butterfly touches the cheek/for only a moment/but the fire it ignites/ burns for eternity . . .*

Feelings of the Heart is 50 pgs., magazine-sized, computer-printed, spiral-bound, artist cover, with ads from other zines. Receives about 100 poems/year, accepts about 50%. Publishes 20+ poems/issue. Press run is 100 for 60 subscribers; 5 distributed free. Single copy: $4.50; subscription; $17/year. Sample: $4.50. Make checks payable to Alice M. Harnisch.

How to Submit: Submit 5 poems at a time. Line length for poetry is 20-40. Accepts previously published poems and simultaneous submissions. Accepts e-mail submissions and disk submissions. Cover letter is required. "Please enclose up to 5 e-mail submissions a day—but if you prefer snail mail, enclose a SASE or IRC!" Reads submissions throughout the year. Submit seasonal poems 2 months in advance. Time between acceptance and publication is 2 weeks. Poems "are read by me, the editor, and decided on merit of quality." Often comments on rejections. Occasionally publishes theme issues. List of upcoming themes and guidelines available for SASE or on website. Responds in 2 weeks with SASE. Sometimes sends prepublication galleys. Acquires first rights. Reviews books and chapbooks of poetry and other magazines in 200 words or less, single book format. Poets may send books for review consideration to Alice M. Harnisch-Fitchie.

Advice: "Please send SASE for guidelines."

○ ○ ◎ FEMINIST STUDIES (Specialized: women/feminism), ℅ Dept. of Women's Studies, P.O. Box 30507, University of Maryland, College Park MD 14603-0507. (301)405-7415. Fax: (301)314-9190. E-mail: femstud@umail.umd.edu. Website: www.inform.umd.edu/femstud. Established 1969. **Poetry Editor:** Shirley Geok-Lin Lim.

Magazine Needs: *Feminist Studies* "welcomes a variety of work that focuses on women's experience, on gender as a category of analysis, and that furthers feminist theory and consciousness." Has published poetry by Janice Mirikitani, Paula Gunn Allen, Cherrie Moraga, Audre Lorde, Valerie Fox, and Diane Glancy. The elegantly printed, flat-spined, 250-page paperback appears 3 times/year. Press run is 8,000 for 7,000 subscribers, of which 1,500 are libraries. There are 4-10 pgs. of poetry in each issue. Sample: $15.

How to Submit: No simultaneous submissions; will only consider previously published poems under special circumstances. No fax or e-mail submissions. Manuscripts are reviewed twice a year, in May and December. Deadlines are May 1 and December 1. Authors will receive notice of the board's decision by June 30 and January 30. Guidelines are available on website. Always sends prepublication galleys. Pays 2 copies. Commissions reviews of books of poetry. Poets may send books to Claire G. Moses for review consideration.

▼ $ ○ ◎ FIELD: CONTEMPORARY POETRY AND POETICS; FIELD TRANSLATION SERIES; FIELD POETRY PRIZE; FIELD POETRY SERIES; OBERLIN COLLEGE PRESS (Specialized: translations), Rice Hall, Oberlin College, Oberlin OH 44074. (440)775-8408. Fax: (440)775-8124. E-mail: oc.press@oberlin.edu. Website: www.oberlin.edu/~ocpress (includes information on all publications, including excerpts and ordering information). Established 1969. **Editors:** David Young, Alberta Turner, David Walker, Martha Collins, and Pamela Alexander.

  • Work published in *Field* has also been included in the 1992, 1993, 1994, 1995, and 1998 volumes of *The Best American Poetry.*

Magazine Needs: *Field* is a literary journal appearing twice/year with "emphasis on poetry, translations, and essays by poets." Wants the "best possible" poetry. Has published poetry by Marianne Boruch, Miroslav Holub,

---

THE CHAPBOOK INDEX, located at the back of this book, lists those publishers who consider chapbook mss. A chapbook, a small volume of work (usually under 50 pages), is often a good middle step between magazine and book publication.

Charles Wright, Billy Collins, Jon Loomis, Charles Simic, and Sandra McPherson. The handsomely printed, digest-sized journal is flat-spined, has 100 pgs., rag stock with glossy card color cover. Although most poems fall under the lyrical free verse category, you'll find narratives and formal work here on occasion, much of it sensual, visually appealing, and resonant. Press run is 1,500, with 400 library subscriptions. Subscription: $14/year, $24/2 years. Sample: $7.

How to Submit: Submit up to 5 poems at a time. Cover letters preferred. Reads submissions year-round. No previously published poems; no simultaneous submissions. Does not accept fax or e-mail submissions. Seldom comments on rejected poems. Responds in 2 months. Time between acceptance and publication is 1-6 months. Always sends prepublication galleys. Pays $15-20/page plus 2 copies. Staff reviews books of poetry. Poets and publishers may send books for review consideration.

Book/Chapbook Needs & How to Submit: Publishes books of translations in the Field Translation Series, averaging 150 pgs., flat-spined and hardcover editions. Query regarding translations. Pays 7½-10% royalties and author's copies. Also has a Field Poetry Series. Has published *Ill Lit* by Franz Wright; *A Saturday Night at the Flying Dog* by Marcia Southwick. This series is by invitation only. Write for catalog to buy samples.

Also Offers: Sponsors the *Field* Poetry Prize, the winning ms will be published in their poetry series and receive $1,000 award. Submit mss of 50-80 pgs. with a $22 reading fee in May only. Contest guidelines available for SASE.

☑ 🌐 ◲ ◯ ◑ **FIRE**, Field Cottage, Old Whitehill, Tackley, Kidlington, Oxfordshire OX5 3AB United Kingdom. Website: www.poetical.org (includes information about the magazine, a list of contributors, the immediate past and future issues, a few selected poems from the current issue). Established 1994. **Editor:** Jeremy Hilton.

Magazine Needs: *Fire* appears 3 times/year "to publish little-known, unfashionable or new writers alongside better known ones." Wants "experimental, unfashionable, demotic work; longer work encouraged." Accepts poetry written by children. No rhyming verse. Has published poetry by Marilyn Hacker, Adrian C. Louis, Tom Pickard, Allen Fisher, Gael Turnbull, and David Hart. *Fire* is 150 pgs., A5. Receives about 400 poems/year, accepts about 35%. Press run is 250 for 180 subscribers of which 20 are libraries. Single copy: £4, add £1 postage Europe, £2 postage overseas. Subscription (3 issues): £7, add £2 postage Europe, £4 postage overseas.

How to Submit: Accepts previously published poems; no simultaneous submissions. Cover letter preferred. Time between acceptance and publication "varies enormously." Often comments on rejected poems. Guidelines available for SASE. Responds in 2 months. Sometimes sends prepublication galleys, "but rarely to overseas contributors." Pays 2 copies.

🆕 ◲ ◑ **FIREFLY MAGAZINE**, Volunteer State College, 1480 Nashville Pike, Gallatin TN 37066. (615)452-8600, ext. 3398. E-mail: ahofer@vscc.cc.tn.us. Established 1972. **Managing Editor:** Anthony Hofer.

Magazine Needs: *Firefly Magazine* appears semiannually in April and November. "We seek to publish the best in poetry and short fiction. We are not restrictive as to what forms and styles we will publish. Quality is our main concern. Originality is highly encouraged. We do not wish to see anything that does not—in the end—say something positive about what it means to be in this world." Accepts poetry written by children. Recently published poetry by Matthew Brennan, Susan Luther, J. Cailin Oakes, Marge Piercy, Charles Wright, and Betty Palmer Nelson. As a sample the editor selected these lines from "Admission" by J. Cailin Oakes:

> I sought words/of the vein and the slow pull of sap, of hair/rising at the nape. Out here, the moon flashes/from the eyes of the hungry. Every outer thing/has a voice, and none of it is human.

Firefly Magazine is 104 pgs., digest-sized, professionally printed, perfect-bound, original 3-color cover art. Receives about 500 poems/year, accepts about 10%. Publishes about 45-60 poems/issue. Press run is 1,000 for 500 subscribers of which 300 are libraries; 2 each are distributed free to contributors. Single copy: free; subscription and sample: free (as of now) by request.

How to Submit: Submit 3-4 poems at a time. Accepts simultaneous submissions; no previously published poems. Accepts fax and disk submissions; no e-mail submissions. Cover letter preferred. "Poets should include four copies of each poem—one with name and address, three without, along with brief bio." Reads submissions January 1-February 28. Time between acceptance and publication is 6-8 weeks. Poems circulated to an editorial board. "Each judge provides a numerical ranking, and poems averaging the best scores are considered for publication." Seldom comments on rejected poems. Guidelines are available for SASE. Responds in up to 4 months. Sometimes sends prepublication galleys. Pays 2 contributor's copies. Acquires one-time rights. Poets may send books for review consideration to Anthony Hofer, managing editor.

Advice: "We would love to publish poets from all over. We encourage new poets, while welcoming more established poets. Above all, express your humanity in all you do."

☑ 🌐 ◑ **FIREWATER PRESS INC.; VARIOUS ARTISTS**, 31, Northleaze, Long Ashton, Bristol BS41 9HT United Kingdom. Established 1989. **Editor:** Tony Lewis-Jones for *Various Artists*.

Magazine Needs: *Various Artists* appears annually "to encourage good accessible poetry by new and established writers. Wants any format/style "so long as the work is not anti-minority. Prefer short poems (up to 40 lines)." Has published poetry by Sophie Hannah, Robert Etty, Michael Daugherty, and Martin Holroyd. As a sample editor Tony Lewis-Jones selected his own haiku:

> Mist on the river/Skies are as fickle/As love, as snow.

Various Aritsts is approximately 30 pgs., A5, saddle-stapled with graphics. Accepts 10% of poems received a year; receives approximately 2,000. Press run is 250 for 100 subscribers of which 10 are libraries. Single copy: $5; subscription: $10. Sample: $3. Make checks payable to A. Lewis-Jones (currency from the US is preferred).
How to Submit: Submit 6 poems at a time. No previously published poems or simultaneous submissions. Cover letter preferred. Time between acceptance and publication is up to 12 months. Always comments on rejected poems. Guidelines available for SASE (or SAE and IRC). *Various Artists* responds in 2 weeks. Pays 1 contributor's copy. Returns rights upon publication. Staff reviews books of poetry. Send books for review consideration.
Also Offers: Firewater Press also sponsors a number of awards for poets working in the United Kingdom.
Advice: "Write from the heart, don't compromise and keep trying. If you're good enough, you'll make it."

✔ ◉ **FIRST CLASS; FOUR-SEP PUBLICATIONS**, P.O. Box 12434, Milwaukee WI 53212. E-mail: chriftor@execpc.com. Website: www.execpc.com/~chriftor (includes guidelines, recent books and chapbooks, current issue information, etc.). Established 1994. **Editor:** Christopher M.
Magazine Needs: *First Class* appears 3 times/year and "publishes excellent/odd writing for intelligent/creative readers." Wants "short postmodern poems, also short fiction." No traditional work. Has published poetry by Bennett, Locklin, Roden, Splake, Catlin, and Huffstickler. *First Class* is 50-54 pgs., 8½×11, printed, saddle-stapled with colored cover. Receives about 1,500 poems/year, accepts about 30. Press run is 200-400. Sample (including guidelines): $5 or mini version $1. Make checks payable to Christopher M.
How to Submit: Submit 5 poems at a time. Accepts previously published poems and simultaneous submissions. Does not accept fax or e-mail submissions. Cover letter preferred. Time between acceptance and publication is 2-4 months. Often comments on rejected poems. Responds in 3 weeks. Pays in 1 copy. Acquires one-time rights. Reviews books of poetry. Poets may send books for review consideration.
Also Offers: Chapbook production available.
Advice: "Belt out a good, short, thought-provoking, graphic, uncommon piece."

N ⊕ ○ ◉ **FIRST TIME; INTERNATIONAL HASTINGS POETRY COMPETITION**, The Snoring Cat, 136 Harold Rd., Hastings, East Sussex TN35 5NN England. Phone/fax: 01424 428855. E-mail: firsttime @carefree.net. Established 1981. **Editor:** Josephine Austin.
Magazine Needs: *First Time*, published biannually, is open to "all kinds of poetry—our magazine goes right across the board—which is why it is one of the most popular in Great Britain." As a sample the editor selected these lines from "Why a Poet?" by R.M. Griffiths:

> *Of all types of people/and all their differences in depth,/the poet is the deepest,/Or is it just the most vacuous?*

First Time is digest-sized, 80-100 pgs., saddle-stapled, contains several poems on each page, in a variety of small type styles, on lightweight stock, glossy one-color card cover. Subscription: $13. Sample: $2 plus postage. "Please send dollars."
How to Submit: Submit 6 poems with name and address of poet on each. Poems submitted must not exceed 30 lines. No previously published poems. Does not accept e-mail submissions. Cover letter and SAE required. Time between acceptance and publication is up to 2 months. "Although we can no longer offer a free copy as payment, we can offer one at a discounted price of $3 and postage."
Also Offers: The annual International Hastings Poetry Competition for poets 18 and older offers awards of £150, £75, and £50; £2/poem entry fee.
Advice: "Keep on 'pushing your poctry.' If one editor rejects you then study the market and decide which is the correct one for you. Try to type your own manuscripts as longhand is difficult to read and doesn't give a professional impression. Always date your poetry — ©1997 and sign it. Follow your way of writing, don't be a pale imitation of someone else—sooner or later styles change and you will either catch up or be ahead."

◉ **FISH DRUM**, P.O. Box 966, Murray Hill Station, New York NY 10156. Website: www.fishdrum.com. Established in 1988 by Robert Winson (1959-1995). **Editor:** Suzi Winson.
Magazine Needs: *Fish Drum* is a literary magazine appearing 2/year. Wants "West Coast poetry, the exuberant, talky, often elliptical and abstract 'continuous nerve movie' that follows the working of the mind and has a relationship to the world and the reader. Philip Whalen's work, for example, and much of *Calafia, The California Poetry*, edited by Ishmael Reed. Also magical-tribal-incantatory poems, exemplified by the future/primitive *Technicians of the Sacred*, ed. Rothenberg. *Fish Drum* has a soft spot for schmoozy, emotional, imagistic stuff. Literate, personal material that sings and surprises, OK?" Has published poetry by Philip Whalen, Arthur Sze, Nathaniel Tarn, Alice Notley, Jessica Hagedorn, and Leo Romero. As a sample the editor selected these lines from "Glossolalia" by Kate Bremer:

> *Everywhere I look I see amino acids on the ground./When I close my eyes, I see molecules and pieces of Sanskrit:/I hear syllables and alphabets.*

Fish Drum is approximately 80 pgs., professionally printed, perfect-bound. Press run is 2,000 for subscribers, libraries, and shelf sales. Subscription: $24/4 issues. Sample: $6.
How to Submit: Publishes theme issues. Sends prepublication galleys. Pays 2 copies. Acquires first serial rights. Reviews books or chapbooks of poetry in long essays and/or capsule reviews. Open to unsolicited reviews. Poets may send books for review consideration.

Advice: "We're looking for prose, fiction, essays, what-have-you, and artwork, scores, cartoons, etc.—just send it along. We are also interested in poetry, prose, and translations concerning the practice of Zen. We publish chapbooks, but solicit these from our authors." She also adds, "It is my intention to complete Robert's work and to honor his memory by continuing to publish *FishDrum*."

5 AM, P.O. Box 205, Spring Church PA 15686. Established 1987. **Editors:** Ed Ochester and Judith Vollmer. **Magazine Needs:** *5 AM* is a poetry publication that appears twice/year. Open in regard to form, length, subject matter, and style. However, they do not want poetry that is "religious or naive rhymers." Has published poetry by Virgil Suarez, Nin Andrews, Ron Koertge, Charles Webb, and Denise Duhamel. *5 AM* is a 24-page, offset tabloid. Receives about 3,000 poems/year, accepts about 2%. Press run is 1,000 for 550 subscribers of which 25 are libraries, about 300 shelf sales. Subscription: $12/4 issues. Sample: $4.
How to Submit: No previously published poems or simultaneous submissions. Seldom comments on rejected poems. Responds within 1 month. Pays 2 copies. Acquires first rights.

580 SPLIT, P.O. Box 9982, Mills College, Oakland CA 94613-0982. (510)430-2217. Fax: (510)430-3398. E-mail: five80split@yahoo.com. Website: www.mills.edu/SHOWCASE/F99/580SPLIT/580.html (includes guidelines, current editors, table of contents to past issues). Established 1999. **Contact:** poetry editor. Member: CLMP.
Magazine Needs: *580 Split* appears annually. Publishes "high-quality, innovative poetry and fiction. Open to style and form. Rhyming poetry must be stellar. Open to experimental, visual, language, and concrete poetry." Recently published poetry by David Starkey, Tyehimba Jess, Wenceslao Maldonado, and Dan Godston. *580 Split* is 100 pgs., digest-sized, professionally printed, perfect-bound, cardstock cover with b&w photo, b&w art/graphics. Receives about 2,000 poems/year, accepts 1-5%. Publishes about 25 pages/issue. Press run is 625 for 20 subscribers of which 15 are libraries, 500 shelf sales. Single copy: $7.50; subscription: $7.50. Sample: $5. Make checks payable to *580 Split*.
How to Submit: Submit 5 poems at a time. No previously published poems or simultaneous submissions. No e-mail or disk submissions. Cover letter is preferred. "Poems not accompanied by SASE are recycled immediately." Reads submissions July 1 through November 1. Time between acceptance and publication is 4 months. Poems circulate to an editorial board and are voted on. Seldom comments on rejected poems. Guidelines available by e-mail or on website. Responds in up to 5 months. Sometimes sends prepublication galleys. Pays 2 contributor's copies. Acquires first North American serial rights.

FIVE POINTS; JAMES DICKEY PRIZE FOR POETRY, Georgia State University, University Plaza, Atlanta GA 30303-3083. (404)651-0071. Fax: (404)651-3167. Website: www.webdelsol.com/Five-Points. Established 1996. **Managing Editor:** Megan Sexton.
Magazine Needs: *Five Points* appears 3 times/year and "publishes quality poetry, fiction, nonfiction, interviews and art by established and emerging writers. Wants "poetry of high quality which shows evidence of an original voice and imagination." Has published poetry by Charles Wright, Kate Daniels, and Philip Levine. As a sample the editor selected these lines from "Talc" by Jane Hirschfield:

> When you phoned I was far, and sleeping,/but they brought me the message and I ran,/I ran to the
> phone where you were,/You were speaking, we two were speaking,/When I ran back to the room I no
> longer/knew we would speak again.

Five Points is about 200 pgs., 6½×9, professionally printed and perfect-bound with 4-color card cover, includes b&w photos and ads. Receives about 2,000 poems/year, accepts about 5%. Press run is 2,000 for about 1,000 subscribers of which 10% are libraries, 40% shelf sales. Single copy: $7. Sample: $7.
How to Submit: Submit no more than 3 poems at a time. No previously published poems. No simultaneous submissions. Accepts 2 sumisssions per reading period. Cover letter preferred. Reads submissions September 1 through May 30 only. Time between acceptance and publication is 3 months. Poems are circulated to an editorial board. "First reader culls poems then send them to the final reader." Seldom comments on rejected poems. Guidelines available for SASE. Responds in 3 months. Always sends prepublication galleys. Pays $50/poem plus 2 copies and 1-year subscription. Acquires first North American serial rights.
Also Offers: Sponsors the James Dickey Prize for Poetry which awards $1,000 and publication in the Spring issue. Reading fee: $12 for up to 3 poems, no more than 50 lines each. Entries must be typed. Fee includes 1-year subscription. Deadline: November 30. Complete contest guidelines available for SASE.

FLAMING ARROWS, County Sligo VEC, Riverside, Sligo, Ireland. Phone: (+353)7145844. Fax: (+353)7143093. E-mail: leoregan@eircom.net. Established 1989. **Editor:** Leo Regan, A.E.O.
Magazine Needs: *Flaming Arrows*, published annually in January, features poetry and prose. Wants "cogent, lucid, coherent, technically precise poetry. Poems of the spirit, mystical, metaphysical but sensuous, tactile, and immediate to the senses." Has published poetry by Sydney Bernard Smith, Medbh McGuckian, Ben Wilensky, James Liddy, and Ciaran O'Driscoll. As a sample the editor selected these lines from "Alickadoo's Great Debate About Nothing" by S.B. Smith:

> . . . Re-enter Plato, expectation buoyed/by proven fact. Fact is, we're mostly hole;/which-body apart-
> leaves lots of room for-soul!//"That is, if soul were willing to subsist/within the same continuum or
> space/as petty particles, however wist-/ful, winsome, energetic, full of grace

Flaming Arrows is 80-102 pgs., A5, offset-printed, perfect-bound or saddle-stapled, with 2-color cover stock. Receives about 500 poems/year, accepts about 6%. Press run is 600 for 150 subscribers of which 30 are libraries, 180 shelf sales; 100 distributed free to writer's groups, contributors, literary events. Issues 2 and 3 are $6; issues 4, 5, and 6 are $3; postage $1.25. Make checks payable to *Flaming Arrows*.

How to Submit: Submit 5 poems "typed, A4, in 10 or 12 pt. for scanning or discs for Word 7 in Windows 95." Accepts previously published poems and simultaneous submissions. Cover letter required. Time between acceptance and publication is 10 months. Responds in 3 months. Pays 1 copy, additional copies at cost. Include SASE with IRC.

Advice: "Inspection of previous issues, especially 2, 3, 5, or 6 will inform prospective contributors of style and standard required."

N: ⃝ ◑ FLAMING OMELET PRESS; THE FLAMING OMELET, P.O. Box 25407, Baltimore MD 21217. E-mail: flaming_omelet@yahoo.com. Established 2001. **Editor-in-Chief:** Dani Dennis.

Magazine Needs: *The Flaming Omelet* appears bimonthly as a "zine that follows the life of a city-dwelling single woman in her mid-20s. It explores poetry, art, music, the oddities, of people and other elements of daily life. We accept rants and take-offs on everyday life." Wants haiku, tanka, senryu, other poems under 7 lines with strong imagery. Does not want science fiction poetry. *The Flaming Omelet* is magazine-sized, photocopied, stapled, with art/graphics. Receives about 50 poems/year, accepts about 30%. Publishes about 2 poems/issue. Press run is 200 for 50 subscribers of which 20 are shelf sales; 100 are distributed free to libraries and book stores. Single copy: $2; subscription: $10/6 issues. Sample: $3. Make checks payable to *The Flaming Omelet*.

How to Submit: Submit 3-5 poems at a time. Line length for poetry is 7 maximum. Accepts previously published poems and simultaneous submissions. Accepts e-mail submissions, no fax or disk submissions. "Include SASE with all correspondence; cover letter unnecessary." Reads submissions year round. Submit seasonal poems 3 months in advance. Time between acceptance and publication is 4-6 months. Often comments on rejected poems. "We suggest that you subscribe to get the feel of our zine." Occasionally publishes theme issues. A list of upcoming themes is available by e-mail. Guidelines are available for SASE and by e-mail. Responds in 3 months. Pays 2 contributor's copies. Acquires first North American serial rights. Reviews books and chapbooks of poetry and other magazines/journals in 250 words, single book format. Poets may send books for review consideration to *The Flaming Omelet*.

Book/Chapbook Needs & How to Submit: The goal of the Flaming Omelet Press is "to publish a wide variety of short, powerful poetry from a diverse group of authors. We solicit work worldwide." Publishes 2-4 chapbooks/year. Chapbooks are usually 24 pgs., photocopied, various types of binding, 80 lb. cover, with block prints/illustrations. "Submit 3-5 poems; cover letter not necessary. Multiple submission okay. Include SASE with all correspondence. Previously published submissions okay with credits." Responds to queries in up to 6 months. Pays 1 author's copy (out of a press run of 100). Order sample chapbooks by sending $5 to Flaming Omelet Press.

Also Offers: "We also accept illustrations, photography, reviews, short memoir, rants, and 'a day in the life' articles for the zine."

Advice: "We are a completely independent press committed to creating unique books that shape the literary landscape. We consider our books works of art."

⊕ $ ⃝ ◑ FLARESTACK PUBLISHING; OBSESSED WITH PIPEWORK, 15 Market Place, Redditch, Worcestershire B98 8AR England. Phone: (01527)63291. Fax: (01527)68571. E-mail: flare.stack@virgin.net. Established 1995. **Editor:** Charles Johnson.

Magazine Needs: *Obsessed with Pipework* appears quarterly. "We are very keen to publish strong new voices— 'new poems to surprise and delight' with somewhat of a high-wire aspect. We are looking for original, exploratory poems—positive, authentic, oblique maybe—delighting in image and in the dance of words on the page." Does not want "the predictable, the unfresh, the rhyme-led; the clever, the sure-of-itself. No formless outpourings, please." Has published "Searching For Salsa" by Jennifer Ballerini and poetry by David Hart, Jennifer Compton, Susan Wicks, and Vuyelwa Carlin. As a sample the editor selected these lines from "Fixtures and Fittings" by Di Neoh:

> That summer/we folded up the contents of our lives/and placed them into boxes./Even I became of use/
> sanctioning the closure of the dolls house/and removal of toys.

Obsessed With Pipework is 49 pgs., A5, photocopied and stapled with card cover, ads "by arrangement." Receives about 1,500 poems/year, accepts about 10%. Press run is 70-100. Single copy: £3.50; subscription: £12. Sample: £2 if available. Make checks payable to Flarestack Publishing.

How to Submit: Submit maximum of 6 poems at a time. No previously published poems or simultaneous submissions. Cover letter preferred. Accepts e-mail and fax submissions. "If sending by e-mail, send a maximum 3 poems in the body of the message, as attached files may become lost or corrupted." Time between acceptance and publication is 4 months maximum. Often comments on rejected poems. Guidelines available for SASE, by fax, or by e-mail. Responds in 2 months. Pays 1 copy. Acquires first rights.

Book/Chapbook Needs: Flarestack Publishing ("talent to burn") aims to "find an audience for new poets, so beginners are welcome, but the work has to be strong and clear." Publishes 12 chapbooks/year. Chapbooks are usually 12-40 pgs., A5, photocopied and stapled with card cover.

How to Submit: Query first with a few sample poems and cover letter with brief bio and publication credits. "Normally we expect a few previous magazine acceptances, but no previous collection publication." Responds to queries in 6 weeks; to mss in 2 months. Pays royalties of 25% plus 6 author's copies (out of a press run of 50-100). Order sample chapbooks by sending £3.50.

Advice: "Most beginning poets show little evidence of reading poetry before writing it! Join a poetry workshop. For chapbook publishing, we are looking for coherent first collections that take risks, make leaps, and come clean."

$ 🖊 ◎ FLESH AND BLOOD: QUIET TALES OF DARK FANTASY & HORROR (Specialized: horror, dark fantasy, off-beat, supernatural), 121 Joseph St., Bayville NJ 08721. E-mail: HorrorJack@aol.com. Website: www.geocities.com/soho/lofts/3459/Fnb.html (includes guidelines, updates, news, editors, issue contents, etc.). Established 1997. **Senior Editor:** Jack Fisher. **Associate Editor:** Matt Doeden.

Magazine Needs: Appearing 3 times/year, *Flesh and Blood* publishes work of dark fantasy and the supernatural. Wants surreal, bizarre, and avant-garde poetry. No "rhyming or love poems, epics, killers, etc." Has published poetry by Charles Jacob, Mark McLaughlin, Kurt Newton, Wendy Rathbone, J.W. Donnelly and Donna Taylor Burgess. *Flesh and Blood* is 44-52 pgs., 5½×8½, saddle-stapled with glossy 2-color cover, includes art/graphics and ads. Receives about 200 poems/year, accepts about 10%. Publishes 4-6 poems/issue. Press run is 500 for 400 subscribers, 100 shelf sales; 50 distributed free to reviewers. Subscription: $11. Sample: $4. Make checks payable to John Fisher.

How to Submit: Submit up to 5 poems at a time. Line length for poetry is 3 minimum, 30 maximum. Accepts previously published poems; no simultaneous submissions. Accepts e-mail submissions (include text in body of e-mail). Cover letter preferred. "Poems should be on separate pages, each with the author's address. Cover letter should include background credits." Time between acceptance and publication is up to 10 months. Guidelines available for SASE or on website. Responds in 2 months. Pays $5/poem and 1 copy.

Advice: "Be patient, professional, tactful, and courteous."

○ 🖊 FLINT HILLS REVIEW, Department of English, Box 4019, Emporia State University, Emporia KS 66801. (316)341-5216. Fax: (316)341-5547. E-mail: heldricp@emporia.edu or webbamy@emporia.edu. Website: www.emporia.edu/fhr (includes guidelines, samples, "a comprehensive web presence"). Established 1995. **Editors:** Phil Heldrich and Amy Sage Webb.

Magazine Needs: Published annually in June, *Flint Hills Review* is "a regionally focused journal presenting writers of national distinction alongside burgeoning authors." Open to all forms except "rhyming, sentimental or gratuitous verse." Has published poetry by E. Ethelbert Miller, Elizabeth Dodd, Vivian Shipley, and Gwendolyn Brooks. *Flint Hills Review* is about 100 pgs., digest-sized, offset-printed and perfect-bound with glossy card cover with b&w photo, also includes b&w photos. Receives about 2,000 poems/year, accepts about 5%. Single copy: $5.50.

How to Submit: Submit 3-5 poems at a time. Accepts simultaneous submissions; no previously published poems. Accepts disk submissions. Cover letter with SASE required. Reads submissions January through March only. Time between acceptance and publication is about 1 year. Seldom comments on rejected poems. Occasionally publishes theme issues. Guidelines and a list of upcoming themes available for SASE or on website. Pays 1 copy. Acquires first rights.

Also Offers: Sponsors the annual Bluestem Press Award. See listing in the Contests & Awards section of this book.

Advice: "Subscribe for examples of what we publish, understand our guidelines, and see our website."

◎ FLOATING BRIDGE PRESS (Specialized: regional), P.O. Box 18814, Seattle WA 98118. E-mail: ppereira5@aol.com. Website: www.scn.org/arts/floatingbridge (includes guidelines, sample poems, poet bios, ordering information, and links to other sites of interest to poets). Established 1994. **Contact:** editor.

Book/Chapbook Needs: Floating Bridge press is "supported by Seattle Arts Commission, King County Arts Commission, Washington State Arts Commission, and the Allen Foundation for the Arts." The press publishes chapbooks and anthologies by Washington state poets, selected through an annual contest. Recently published *X: a poem* by Chris Forhan; *Sonnets from the Mare Imbrium* by Bart Baxter; and *Blue Willow* by Molly Tenenbaum. In 1997 the press began publishing *Pontoon*, an annual anthology featuring the work of Washington state poets. *Pontoon* is 96 pgs., digest-sized, offset-printed and perfect-bound with matte cardstock cover. For a sample chapbook or anthology, send $7 postpaid.

How to Submit: For consideration, Washington poets (only) should submit a chapbook ms of 20-24 pgs. of poetry with $10 entry fee and SASE (for results only). The usual reading period is November 1 to February 15. Accepts previously published individual poems and simultaneous submissions. Author's name must not appear on the ms; include a separate page with title, name, address, telephone number, and acknowledgments of any previous publication. Mss are judged anonymously and will not be returned. In addition to publication, the winner receives $500 (minimum), 50 copies, and a reading in the Seattle area. All entrants receive a copy of the winning chapbook. All entrants will be considered for inclusion in *Pontoon*, a poetry anthology.

"With this issue, we began including informal self-portraits by the authors," says *Flyway* editor Stephen Pett. This striking self-portrait by Shelley Buffalo complemented the design shift well; the painting was selected to usher in the new format.

**FLYWAY, A LITERARY REVIEW**, 206 Ross Hall, Iowa State University, Ames IA 50011-1201. Fax: (515)294-6814. E-mail: flyway@iastate.edu. Website: www.engl.iastate.edu/journals/flyway. Established 1961. **Editor:** Stephen Pett.
Magazine Needs: Appearing 3 times/year, *Flyway* "is one of the best literary magazines for the money; it is packed with some of the most readable poems being published today—all styles and forms, lengths and subjects." The editor shuns elite-sounding free verse with obscure meanings and pretty-sounding formal verse with obvious meanings. *Flyway* is 112 pgs., 6×9, professionally printed and perfect-bound with matte card cover with color. Press run is 600 for 400 subscribers of which 100 are libraries. Subscription: $20. Sample: $7.
How to Submit: Submit 4-6 poems at a time. Cover letter preferred. "We do not read mss between the end of May and mid-August." May be contacted by fax. Publishes theme issues (Chicano, Latino). Responds in 6 weeks (often sooner). Pays 1 copy. Acquires first rights.
Also Offers: Sponsors an annual award for poetry, fiction, and nonfiction. Details available for SASE.

FOR POETRY.COM, E-mail: editor@forpoetry.com. Website: www.forpoetry.com. Established March 1999. **Editor:** Jackie Marcus.
Magazine Needs: *For Poetry.Com* is a web magazine with daily updates. "We wish to promote new and emerging poets, with or without MFAs. We will be publishing established poets, but our primary interest is in publishing excellent poetry, prose, essays, reviews, paintings, and photography. We are interested in lyric poetry, vivid imagery, open form, natural landscape, philosophical themes but not at the expense of honesty and passion: model examples: Robert Hass, James Wright, Charles Wright's *The Other Side of the River*, Montale, Neruda, Levertov, and Karen Fish. No city punk, corny sentimental fluff, or academic workshop imitations." Has published poetry by Charles Simic, Marilyn Hacker, and Karen Fish. As a sample the editor selected these lines from "Elegy" by Joseph Duemer:
> Wind lifts the curtains/in an empty room./I'm somewhere else—/a line storm moving up from the Gulf/
> meaning a downpour in Tennessee./Like all the weather—a blessing & a curse.
"We receive lots of submissions and are very selective about acceptances, but we will always try to send a note back on rejections."
How to Submit: Submit no more than 2 poems at a time. Accepts simultaneous submissions; no previously published poems. E-mail submissions only; include text in body of message. Cover letter preferred. Reads submissions September through May only. Time between acceptance and publication is 2-6 weeks. Poems are circulated to an editorial board. "We'll read all submissions and then decide together on the poems we'll publish." Comments on rejected poems "as often as possible." Guidelines available on website. Responds in 2 weeks. Reviews books and chapbooks of poetry and other magazines in 800 words.
Advice: "As my friend Kevin Hull said, 'Get used to solitude and rejection.' Sit on your poems for several months or more. Time is your best critic."

THE FORMALIST; HOWARD NEMEROV SONNET AWARD (Specialized: form, translations), 320 Hunter Dr., Evansville IN 47711. Established 1990. **Editor:** William Baer.
Magazine Needs: *The Formalist*, appears twice/year, "dedicated to contemporary *metrical* poetry written in the great tradition of English-language verse. We're looking for well-crafted poetry in a contemporary idiom which uses meter and the full range of traditional poetic conventions in vigorous and interesting ways. We're

especially interested in sonnets, couplets, tercets, ballads, the French forms, etc. We're not, however, interested in haiku (or syllabic verse of any kind) or sestinas. Only rarely do we accept a poem over 2 pages, and we have no interest in any type of erotica, blasphemy, vulgarity, or racism. Finally, we suggest that those wishing to submit to *The Formalist* become familiar with the journal beforehand. We are also interested in metrical translations of the poetry of major, formalist, non-English poets—from the ancient Greeks to the present." Has published poetry by Derek Walcott, John Updike, Maxine Kumin, X.J. Kennedy, May Swenson, W.D. Snodgrass, and Louis Simpson. As a sample the editor selected the opening stanza from "The Amateurs of Heaven" by Howard Nemerov:

> *Two lovers to a midnight meadow came/High in the hills, to lie there hand in hand/Like effigies and look up at the stars,/The never-setting ones set in the North/To circle the Pole in idiot majesty,/And wonder what was given them to wonder.*

The Formalist is 128 pgs., digest-sized, offset-printed on bond paper and perfect-bound, with colored card cover. Subscription: $12/year; $22/2 years (add $4/year for foreign subscription). Sample: $6.50.

How to Submit: Submit 3-5 poems at a time. No simultaneous submissions, previously published work, or disk submissions. A brief cover letter is recommended and a SASE is necessary for a reply and return of ms. Responds within 2 months. Pays 2 copies. Acquires first North American serial rights.

Also Offers: The Howard Nemerov Sonnet Award offers $1,000 and publication in *The Formalist* for the best unpublished sonnet. The final judge for 2001 was X.J. Kennedy. Entry fee: $3/sonnet. Postmark deadline: June 15. Guidelines available for SASE. See also the contest listing for the World Order of Narrative and Formalist Poets. Contestants must subscribe to *The Formalist* to enter.

4*9*1 NEO-NAIVE IMAGINATION (Specialized: neo-naive), P.O. Box 91212, Lakeland FL 33804-1212. Phone/fax: (863)687-9850. E-mail: stompdncr@aol.com or juanbeaumontez@aol.com. Website: www.fournineone.com. Established 1997. **Editor:** Donald Ryburn. **Assistant Editor:** Juan Beauregard-Montez.

Magazine Needs: *4*9*1 Neo-Naive Imagination* appears continuously as an online publication and publishes poetry, art, photography, essays and interviews. Wants "poetry of neo-naive genre. No academic poetry, limited and fallacious language." Accepts poetry written by children. Has published poetry by Rhonda Roszell and Jesus Morales-Montez. As a sample the editor selected these lines from "the shadow of a raven" by Juan Beauregaard-Montez:

> *Inside my body great flocks of swallows/sang and dove deep within/coming and going/carried off the roots and insects/of my life in Chiapas/carried off the tiny bones/of the woman who had punctured my veins*

How to Submit: Submit 3-6 poems at a time. Accepts previously published poems and simultaneous submissions. E-mail, fax, disk, and CD-ROM submissions preferred; include e-mail submissions in body of message. "No attachments accepted or opened." Note "submission" in subject area. "Would like to hear the poets own words not some standard format." Cover letter with picture and SASE preferred. Time between acceptance and publication varies. Response time varies. Payment varies. Acquires first or one-time rights. Reviews books and chapbooks of poetry and other magazines. Poets may send books for review consideration.

Also Offers: Sponsors a series of creative projects. Write for details or visit the website.

FOX CRY REVIEW, University of Wisconsin-Fox Valley, 1478 Midway Rd., Menasha WI 54952-1297. (920)832-2600. Website: www.uwfoxvalley.uwc.edu. E-mail: lmills@uwc.edu. Established 1974. **Editor:** Laurel Mills.

Magazine Needs: *Fox Cry Review* is a literary annual, published in August, using poems of any length or style, include brief bio, deadline February 1. Has published poetry by Doug Flaherty, Paula Sergi, and Matt Welter. As a sample the editor selected these lines from "Let the Words of My Mouth" by Beverly Voldseth, which was nominated for a Pushcart Prize:

> *We take comfort in these lines/that wait on our tongues—/to be rolled out to bank tellers//neighbors we pass on the street/strangers in the post office./What little boredoms our lives//are made up of, how they stand/in the mouth like truth.*

Fox Cry Review is 115 pgs., digest-sized, professionally printed and perfect-bound with light card cover with b&w illustration, also contains b&w illustrations. Press run is 300. Single copy: $6 plus $1 postage.

How to Submit: Submit maximum of 3 poems from September 1 through February 1 only. Include SASE. "Include name, address and phone number on each poem." No previously published poems. No fax or e-mail submissions. Guidelines available by e-mail. Pays 1 copy.

FREE FOCUS (Specialized: women/feminist); OSTENTATIOUS MIND (Specialized: form/style), P.O. Box 7415, JAF Station, New York NY 10116. *Free Focus* established 1985. *Ostentatious Mind* established 1987. **Poetry Editor:** Patricia D. Coscia.

Magazine Needs: *Free Focus* "is a literary magazine only for creative women, who reflect their ideas of love, nature, beauty, and men and also express the pain, sorrow, joy, and enchantment that their lives generate. *Free Focus* needs poems of all types on the subject matters above. Nothing X-rated, please. The poems can be as short as two lines or as long as two pages. The objective of this magazine is to give women poets a chance to be fullfilled in the art of poetry, for freedom of expression for women is seldom described in society." Has published poetry by Jill Bornstein, Joan Mazza, Janet Stuart, Patricia A. Pierkowski, Crystal Beckner, and Carol L. Clark. *Ostentatious Mind* "is a co-ed literary magazine for material of stream of consciousness and experimental poems. The poets deal with the political, social, and psychological." Has published poetry by Edward Janz, J. Fyfe, Tom Baer, Matt Hutchinson, Rod Farmer, and Joe Lackey. Both magazines are printed on 8 × 14 paper, folded in the middle and stapled to make a 10-page (including cover) format, with simple b&w drawings on the cover and inside. The two magazines appear every 6-8 months. Sample of either is $4.

How to Submit: Submit only 3 poems at a time. Poems should be typed neatly and clearly on white typing paper. Accepts simultaneous submissions and previously published poems. Publishes theme issues. Guidelines and a list of upcoming themes available for SASE. Responds "as soon as possible." Sometimes sends prepublication galleys. Pays 1 copy.

Advice: "I think that anyone can write a poem who can freely express intense feelings about their experiences. A dominant thought should be ruled and expressed in writing, not by the spoken word, but the written word."

✔️ 🌀 **FREE LUNCH**, P.O. Box 7647, Laguna Niguel CA 92607-7647. Website: http://poetsfreelunch.org (includes information about *Free Lunch*, submission guidelines, a poem and the cover art from most recent issue, and order form for sample copies or subscriptions). Established 1988. **Editor:** Ron Offen.

Magazine Needs: *Free Lunch* is a "poetry journal interested in publishing the whole spectrum of what is currently being produced by American poets. Features a 'Mentor Series,' in which an established poet introduces a new, unestablished poet. Mentors have included Maxine Kumin, Billy Collins, Lucille Clifton, Donald Hall, Carolyn Forché, Wanda Coleman, Lyn Lifshin, and Stephen Dunn. Especially interested in experimental work and work by unestablished poets. Hope to provide all serious poets living in the US with a free subscription. For details on free subscription send SASE. Regarding the kind of poetry we find worthwhile, we like metaphors, similes, arresting images, and a sensitive and original use of language. We are interested in all genres—experimental poetry, protest poetry, formal poetry, etc. No restriction on form, length, subject matter, style, purpose. No aversion to form, rhyme." Poets published include Neal Bowers, Thomas Carper, Jared Carter, Billy Collins, Donald Hall, D. Nurkse, and Marge Piercy. As a sample the editor selected "Coastline" by Billy Collins:

> I draw a fingernail over your skin/like the pen-point/of a blind mapmaker/tracing the outline of an
> island.//Let us go slowly now/in the dark/as the moon rises/into the curtainless window./Let me print
> the name of every bay and cove.

Free Lunch, published 2 times/year, is 32-40 pgs., digest-sized, attractively printed and designed, saddle-stapled, featuring free verse that shows attention to craft with well-knowns and newcomers alongside each other. Press run is 1,200 for 1,000 free subscriptions and 200 paid of which 15 are libraries. Subscription: $12 ($15 foreign). Sample: $5 ($6 foreign).

How to Submit: "Submissions must be limited to three poems and are considered only between September 1 and May 31. Submissions sent at other times will be returned unread. Although a cover letter is not mandatory, I like them. I especially want to know if a poet is previously unpublished, as I like to work with new poets." Accepts simultaneous submissions; no previously published poems. Editor comments on rejected poems and tries to return submissions in 2 months. Guidelines available for SASE. Pays 1 copy plus subscription.

Also Offers: "A prize of $200 will be awarded to one poem in each issue of *Free Lunch*. The winning poem of the Rosine Offen Memorial Award will be selected solely by the Board of Directors of Free Lunch Arts Alliance." Winners announced in next issue.

Advice: "Archibald MacLeish said, 'A poem should not mean/ But be.' I have become increasingly leery of the ego-centered lyric that revels in some past wrong, good-old-boy nostalgia, or unfocused ecstatic experience. Poetry is concerned primarily with language, rhythm, and sound; fashions and trends are transitory and to be eschewed; perfecting one's work is often more important than publishing it."

🅽 🌀 **FREEFALL**, Undead Poets Press, 612 S. Center St. #302, Royal Oak MI 48067-3839. (248)543-6858. E-mail: mauruspoet@yahoo.com. Established 1999. **Editor/Publisher:** Marc Maurus.

Magazine Needs: *freefall* appears biannually, publishing the quality work of beginners as well as established poets. "Free verse or formal poetry is okay, and our acceptance policy is broad. No concrete, shape, or greeting card verse. No gratuitous language or sex. No fuzzy animals or syrupy nature poems." Recently published poetry by T. Anders Carson, Kristin Hatch, Mary Hedger, Ann Holdreith, and Cara Jane Houlberg. As a sample the editor selected these lines from "Winter Wolf" by Nathan Roberts:

> silent howls deafen/the lonely moonlit sky/and the raven carries/a fletched twig arrow/to build his nest
> of souls

freefall is 40 pgs., digest-sized, laser-printed, saddle-stapled, card stock cover. Receives about 200 poems/year, accepts about 50%. Publishes about 30-40 poems/issue. Press run is 250 for 50 subscribers fo which 10 are libraries, 25 shelf sales; 25 are distributed free to small press reviewers. Single copy: $5; subscription: $7.50. Sample: $5. Make checks payable to Marc Maurus.

How to Submit: Submit 5-10 poems at a time. Line length for poetry is 3 minimum, 80 maximum. Accepts previously published poems with notification; no simultaneous submissions. Accepts e-mail submissions; no fax or disk submissions. Cover letter is preferred. "Snail mail preferred, please send SASE. E-mail submissions in body, not attached." Reads submissions all year. Submit seasonal poems 6 months in advance. Time between acceptance and publication is 6 months. Poems are circulated to an editorial board. "If a poem is high quality, I accept it right away, poor work is rejected immediately, and those on the fence are circulated to as many as 3

other guest editors." Often comments on rejected poems. ***Poems may be sent for critique only for $2 each plus SASE.*** Guidelines are available for SASE. Responds in 2 weeks. Always sends prepublication galleys. Pays 2 contributor's copies. Acquires first rights; rights always revert to author on publication. Reviews chapbooks of poetry and other magazines/journals in 500 words, single book format. Poets may send books for review consideration to Marc Maurus.
Advice: "We prefer to see crafted work, not unedited one-offs. We welcome as much formal verse as we can because we feel there is a place for it."

☑ ⬇ $⊘ **FREEFALL MAGAZINE**, Alexandra Writers' Centre Society, 922 Ninth Ave. SE, Calgary, Alberta T2G 0S4 Canada. Phone/fax: (403)264-4730. E-mail: awcs@writtenword.org. Website: www.writtenword.org (includes guidelines, a subscription form, and a listing of Alexandra Writers' Centre activities). Established 1990. **Editor:** Barbara Howard. **Managing Editor:** Sherring Amsden.
Magazine Needs: "Published biannually, *FreeFall's* mandate is to encourage the voices of new, emerging, and experienced writers and provide an outlet for their work. Contains: fiction, nonfiction, poetry, interviews related to writers/writing; artwork and photographs suitable for b&w reproduction." Wants "poems in a variety of forms with a strong voice, effective language, and fresh images." Has published poetry by Anne Burke, David Groulx, Norma Linder, Julie Lockhart, T.M. McDade, and Renee Norman. *FreeFall* is 40-44 pgs., magazine-sized, "xerox digital" printing and saddle-stapled with 60 lb. paper cover, includes art/graphics. Receives about 50-60 poems/year, accepts about 20%. Publishes 12-18 poems/issue. Press run is 350 for 270 subscribers of which 20 are libraries, 80 shelf sales; 30 distributed free to contributors, promotion. Single copy: $8.50 US, $7.50 Canadian; subscription: $14 US, $12 Canadian. Sample: $6.50 US, $5.50 Canadian.
How to Submit: Submit 2-5 poems at a time. Line length for poetry is 60 maximum. No previously published poems or simultaneous submissions. Accepts disk submissions (ASCII, text format) with hard copy but no fax or e-mail submissions. Cover letter with 2-line bio and SASE required. Reads submissions March through April and October through November only. Time between acceptance and publication is 6 months. Poems are circulated to an editorial board. "All submissions read by four editors." Seldom comments on rejected poems. Occasionally publishes theme issues. Guidelines and upcoming themes available for SAE and IRC, by e-mail, or on website. Responds in 3 months. Pays $5 Canadian/page and 1 copy. Acquires first North American serial rights.
Also Offers: See website for information about the Alexandra Writers' Centre Society activities and services and for additional information about *FreeFall* magazine.
Advice: "Check guidelines carefully before submitting material."

🌐 ◯ ⊘ **FREEXPRESSION**, P.O. Box 4, West Hoxton NSW 2171 Australia. Phone: (02)9607 5559. Fax: (02)9826 6612. E-mail: frexprsn@bigpond.com.au. Established 1993. **Managing Editor:** Peter F. Pike.
Magazine Needs: *FreeXpresSion* is a monthly publication containing "creative writing, how-to articles, short stories, and poetry including cinquain, haiku, etc., and bush verse." Open to all forms. "Christian themes OK. Humorous material welcome. No gratuitous sex; bad language OK. We don't want to see anything degrading." Has published poetry by Ron Stevens, John Ryan, and Ken Dean. As a sample the editor selected these lines from "The Riding of Tearaway" by Ellis Campbell:

> *I wasn't scared of any horse—or of the ringer's jeers—/I'd rode the worst to come my way since early childhood years./While droving with my father—since the day my mother died—/I'd often bested older men and showed them how to ride./But years diminish glory and I'm weary of the fray;/I had no inclination for the scalp of Tearaway.*

FreeXpresSion is 24 pgs., magazine-sized, offset-printed and saddle-stapled with paper cover, includes b&w graphics. Receives about 1,500 poems/year, accepts about 50%. Press run is 500 for 300 subscribers of which 20 are libraries. Single copy: $2.50 AUS; subscription: $25 AUS ($40 overseas airmail). For sample, send large SAE with $1 stamp.
How to Submit: Submit 3-4 poems at a time. Accepts previously published poems and simultaneous submissions. Accepts fax and e-mail submissions (include in body of message). Cover letter preferred. "Very long poems are not desired but would be considered." Time between acceptance and publication is 2 months. Seldom comments on rejected poems. Publishes theme issues. Guidelines and upcoming themes available for fax or SAE and IRC. Responds in 2 months. Sometimes sends prepublication galleys. Pays 1 copy, additional copies available at half price. Acquires first Australian rights only. Reviews books of poetry in 500 words. Poets may send books for review consideration.
Also Offers: Sponsors annual contest with 2 categories for poetry: blank verse (up to 40 lines), traditional verse (up to 80 lines). 1st Prize (in both categories): $200, 2nd Prize: $100. *FreeXpresSion* also publishes books up to 200 pgs. through subsidy arrangements with authors.
Advice: "Enter some of the many competitions listed in *FreeXpresSion*; compare your work with competition winners."

☑ ◯ ◎ **FRISSON: DISCONCERTING VERSE; SKULL JOB PRODUCTIONS (Specialized: form/style)**, 1012 Pleasant Dale Dr., Wilmington NC 28412-7617. Website: http://members.tripod.com/erdoni/skulljob/index.htm (includes the cover images of all issues and a listing of contents and authors in each issue). Established 1995. **Editor:** Scott H. Urban.

Magazine Needs: *frisson: disconcerting verse*, published quarterly, "presents poetry that is disturbing, haunting, macabre, yet subtle—poetry that attempts to elicit 'frisson.' " Wants "poetry that takes readers past the edge of comfort and into disturbing realms of experience. Poems should attempt to elicit the delicate sensation of 'frisson.' Any form or length, although shorter poems stand better chance." Does not want "light verse, romantic verse, inspirational verse, humorous verse." Has published poetry by Tom Piccirilli, Wendy Rathbone, Lee Ballentine, and Steve Sneyd. As a sample, the editor selected the poem "green drowning" by Peter Roberts:

    i sit with a cup of tea/filled with drowning/green circles/& i wait for her/to come/down

frisson is 20-24 pgs., digest-sized, photocopied, saddle-stapled with cardstock cover, original artwork on cover and in interior with limited ads. Receives about 150-200 poems/year, accepts approximately 10-15%. Press run is 100 for 50 subscribers, with 15 distributed free to reviewers. Subscription: $10. Sample: $2.50. Make checks payable to Scott H. Urban.

How to Submit: Submit 4-10 poems at a time in standard poem ms format. "Shorter ones (50 lines or less) stand a better chance of acceptance." Accepts simultaneous submissions; no previously published poems. No fax or e-mail submissions. Cover letter preferred. Time between acceptance and publication is up to 5 months. Poems chosen "solely according to editor's personal taste—how well each individual poem is applicable to the concept of 'disconcerting verse.' " Often comments on rejected poems. Guidelines available for SASE. Responds within a week. Sometimes sends prepublication galleys. Pays 1 contributor's copy upon publication. Acquires first North American serial rights. There is no review column as such, although editor recommends material in the introductory 'Foreshadowings' article. Send books for review consideration.

Also Offers: In 2000, Skull Job Productions published *A Student in Hell*, a collection of poems by Tom Piccirilli.

Advice: "Open others' perceptions to that shadowy, half-glimpsed world that you as a poet are aware lurks just at the edge of each dream. . . ."

✔ ⊕ Ⓜ **FROGMORE PAPERS; FROGMORE POETRY PRIZE**, 18 Nevill Rd., Lewes, East Sussex BN7 1PF England. Website: www.frogmorepress.co.uk (includes list of titles in print, submission guidelines, details of the Frogmore Poetry Prize). Established 1983. **Poetry Editor:** Jeremy Page.

Magazine Needs: *Frogmore Papers* is a biannual literary magazine with emphasis on new poetry and short stories. "Quality is generally the only criterion, although pressure of space means very long work (over 100 lines) is unlikely to be published." Has published "Other Lilies" by Marita Over and "A Plutonian Monologue" by Brian Aldiss and poetry by Carole Satyamurti, John Mole, Linda France, Elizabeth Garrett, John Harvey, and John Latham. As a sample the editor selected these lines by Tobias Hill:

    if I stand just here, just right/and look up, I can see the rain/coming, and light on aeroplanes/high and
    certain, crossing time zones.

The magazine is 42 pgs., saddle-stapled with matte card cover, photocopied in photoreduced typescript. Accepts 3% of the poetry received. Their press run is 300 for 120 subscribers. Subscription: £7 ($20). Sample: £2 ($5). (US payments should be made in cash, not check.)

How to Submit: Submit 5-6 poems at a time. Considers simultaneous submissions. Editor rarely comments on rejected poems. Responds in 6 months. Pays 1 copy. Staff reviews books of poetry in 2-3 sentences, single book format. Send books for review consideration to Catherine Smith, 24 South Way, Lewes, East Sussex BN7 1LU England.

Also Offers: Sponsors the annual Frogmore Poetry Prize. Write for information.

Advice: "My advice to people starting to write poetry would be: Read as many recognized modern poets as you can and don't be afraid to experiment."

⧉ ◎ **FROGPOND: INTERNATIONAL HAIKU JOURNAL; HAIKU SOCIETY OF AMERICA; HAIKU SOCIETY OF AMERICA AWARDS/CONTESTS (Specialized: form/style, haiku and related forms; translation)**, P.O. Box 2461, Winchester VA 22604-1661. (540)722-2156. Fax: (708)810-8992. E-mail: redmoon@shentel.net. Website: www.octet.com/~hsa/ (includes general information on haiku and the Haiku Society of America, plus contests, guidelines, publications, and special features). Established 1978. **Editor:** Jim Kacian.

Magazine Needs: *Frogpond* is the international journal of the Haiku Society of America and is published triannually. Wants "contemporary English-language haiku, ranging from 1-4 lines or in a visual arrangement, focusing on a moment keenly perceived and crisply conveyed, using clear images and non-poetic language." Also accepts "related forms: senryu, sequences, linked poems, and haibun. It welcomes translations of any of these forms." Accepts poetry written by children. As a sample the editor selected these poems by Phillip Rowland, John Stevenson, and Marko Hudnik:

    spring height:/two strangers walking/perfectly in step/along the platform/—Philip Rowland (Japan)//
    snow/accumulating/traffic/—John Stevenson (U.S.)//a mountain crow/hiding himself/in the dazzling
    winter sky/—Marko Hudnik (Slovenia)

Frogpond is 96 pgs., 5½×8½, perfect-bound, and has 60 pgs. of poetry. Receives about 20,000 submissions/year, accepts about 500. *Frogpond* goes to 800 subscribers, of which 15 are libraries, as well as to over a dozen foreign countries. Sample back issues: $7. Make checks payable to Haiku Society of America.

How to Submit: Submit 5-10 poems, with 5 poems per 8½×11 sheet, with SASE (send submissions to Jim Kacian at address mentioned above). No simultaneous submissions. Accepts fax and e-mail submissions (include in body of message). Information on the HSA and submission guidelines available for SASE. Responds "usually" in 3 weeks or less. Pays $1/accepted item. Poetry reviews usually 1,000 words or less. "Authors are urged to send their books for review consideration."

Also Offers: *Supplement* publishes longer essays, articles, and reviews from quarterly meetings and other haiku gatherings. *Supplement* is 96 pgs., 5½×8½, perfect-bound. *HSA Newsletter*, edited by Charles Trumbull, appears 6 times/year and contains reports of the HSA Quarterly meetings, regional activities, news of upcoming events, results of contests, publications activities, and other information. A "best of issue" prize is awarded for each issue through a gift from the Museum of Haiku Literature, located in Tokyo. The Society also sponsors The Harold G. Henderson Haiku Award Contest, the Gerald Brady Senryu Award Contest, the Bernard Lionel Einbond Memorial Renku Contest, the Nicholas A. Virgilio Memorial Haiku Competition for High School Students and the Merit Book Awards for outstanding books in the haiku field.

Advice: "Submissions to *Frogpond* are accepted from both members and nonmembers, although familiarity with the magazine will aid writers in discovering what it publishes."

✓ $ ◑ **FUGUE**, Brink Hall, Room 200, University of Idaho, Moscow ID 83844-1102. (208)885-6937. E-mail: Fugue@uidaho.edu. Website: www.uidaho.edu/LS/Eng/Fugue (includes writer's guidelines, names of editors, poetry samples, and cover art). Established 1989. **Managing Editor:** Andrea Mason.

Magazine Needs: *Fugue* is a biannual literary magazine of the University of Idaho. "There are no limits on type of poetry; however, we are not interested in trite or quaint verse." Has published poetry by Robert Wrigley, Phillip Dacey, and Sonia Sanchez. As a sample the editor selected these lines from "The Burned Diary" by Sharon Olds:

> . . . And when the dawn came up/on the black water of the house, they found it/by the side of her bed,
> its pages scorched,/a layer of them arched, the corners curled up/like the tips of wings, a messenger/
> from the other world, the solitary heart.

Fugue is up to 150 pgs., and perfect-bound. Receives about 400 poems/semester, accepts only 5-12 poems/issue. Press run is 250 plus an online version. Sample: $5.

How to Submit: No previously published poems or simultaneous submissions. Submit with #10 SASE or submission will not be considered. No e-mail or fax submissions. Reads submissions September 1 through May 1 only. Time between acceptance and publication is up to 1 year. "Submissions are reviewed by staff members and chosen with consensus by the editorial board. No major changes are made to a manuscript without authorial approval." Guidelines and a list of upcoming themes available for SASE and on website. Responds in 3 months. Pays at least 1 contributor's copy and honorarium. Acquires first North American serial rights.

Advice: "Proper manuscript format and submission etiquette are expected; submissions without proper SASE will not be read or held on file."

Ⓝ ▣ ◯ **FULLOSIA PRESS; THE ROCKAWAY PARK PHILOSOPHICAL SOCIETY**, 299-9 Hawkins Ave., #865, Ronkonkoma NY 11779. Fax: (631)588-9428. E-mail: dean@rpps.freeservers.com. Website: www.angelfire.com/bc2/FULLOSIAPRESS (includes online magazine, submission guidelines). Established 1971. **Contact:** H.A. Andrews.

Magazine Needs: *11694: Fullosia Press* appears online monthly, presenting news, information, satire, and right-conservative perspective. Wants any style of poetry. "If you have something to say, say it. We consider many different points of view." Does not want "anti-American, anti-Christian." Recently published poetry by John Grey, Lisa Marie Smith, J.D. Collins, D.G. Deman, H.A. Andrews, Dr. Duane Locke, and B.Z. Niditch. As a sample the editor selected these lines from "New Hampshire October" by John Grey:

> Oaks shudder and limbs break away like shutters in/storms. Browns and reds set the trees afire.
> Churches,/cabins and cheap motels . . . what cannot change color,/rusts.//High as the pile of pine
> needles and the boy with his lips/around his older brother's cigarette is what we have/arrived at . . .

11694: Fullosia Press is published online only. Receives about 50 poems/year, accepts about 40%. Publishes a varied number of poems/issue. Single copy: $5 and SASE—free online. Sample: $5. Make checks payable to RPPS-Fullosia Press.

How to Submit: Accepts fax, e-mail, and disk submissions. Cover letter is required. "Electronic submission by disk to address; e-mail preferred. Final submission by disk or e-mail only." Reads submissions when received. Submit seasonal poems 1 month in advance. Time between acceptance and publication varies. "I review all poems: (1) do they say something; (2) is there some thought behind it; (3) is it more than words strung together?" Always comments on rejected poems. A list of upcoming themes and guidelines are available for SASE and on website. Acquires one-time rights. Reviews books and chapbooks of poetry and other magazines/journals. Poets may send books for review consideration to RPPS-Fullosia Press.

Advice: "Say what you have in mind without tripping over your own symbolism. We like poems which are clear, concise, to the point; American traditional heroes; Arthur is nice; American states. Everybody sings about Texas, has anyone written a poem to New Jersey?"

✓ ◖ $ ◯ ◪ ◎ **THE FUNNY PAPER; F/J WRITERS SERVICE (Specialized: children/teen/young adult, humor, senior citizen, students, writing)**, P.O. Box 22557, Kansas City MO 64113-0557. E-mail: felix22557@aol.com. Website: www.angelfire.com/biz/funnypaper (includes guidelines, jokes, descriptive page, and bulletin boards). Established 1985. **Editor:** F.H. Fellhauer.

Magazine Needs: *The Funny Paper* appears 4 times/year "to provide readership, help and the opportunity to write for money to budding authors/poets/humanists of all ages." Accepts poetry written by children, ages 8-15. Wants "light verse; space limited; humor always welcome. No tomes, heavy, dismal, trite work, or pornography." As a sample we selected this poem, "Farewell" by Betty R. Cevoli:

> *Roughly grasping at my fingers,/They pull at my tee-shirt/My arms scratched as I/clutch them//Bright, sunny orange with/dark hills and valleys/covering their skin.//Roadmaps—promising tender,/juicy, rich flavor—/The last canteloupes of summer.*

The Funny Paper is 10 pgs., 8½×11, photocopied on colored paper and unbound, includes clip art and cartoons. Receives about 300 poems/year, accepts about 10%. Single copy: $2. Make checks payable to F/J Writers Service.

How to Submit: Submit 1-2 poems at a time. Accepts e-mail submissions (include in body of message). "We encourage beginners; handwritten poems OK. Submissions not returned." Seldom comments on rejected poems. Publishes contest theme issues regularly. Guidelines and upcoming themes available for SASE or on website. Pays $5-25/published poem and 1 copy. Acquires one-time rights.

Also Offers: Sponsors contests with $100 prize. Guidelines available for SASE or on website.

Advice: "When trying for $100 prize, take us seriously. The competition is fierce."

✔ $ ◎ **FUTURES MAGAZINE**, 3039 38th Ave. S, Minneapolis MN 55406-2140. (612)724-4023. E-mail: poemfutures@hotmail.com. Website: http://futuresforstorylovers.com (includes writer's guidelines, names of editors, artwork and illustrations, greeting cards for writers, cover art, contests, etc.). Established 1997. **Poetry Editor:** Scott Robison.

Magazine Needs: *Futures* is a bimonthly magazine containing short stories, essays, poetry, artwork and "inspiration for artists of all kinds." Has "no specific poetry needs—everything considered." However, they do not want to receive gratuitous profanity or pornography. Has published poetry by R.C. Hildebrandt, Simon Perchik, Kristin Masterson, John Bennett, Karen Davenport, and Ally Reith. *Futures* is 90 pgs., 8½×11, with 4-color semigloss cover, includes art and ads. Receives about 250 poems/year, accepts about 10%. Publishes 5-10 poems/issue. Press run is 2,000. Single copy: $7.95; subscription: $42. Sample (including guidelines): $5.

How to Submit: Submit up to 5 poems at a time. Accepts previously published poems. Accepts only e-mail submissions. "We are asking for submissions via e-mail because our writers, artists, and staff are all over the world. If you need me to make an exception, write and tell me why you cannot follow our guidelines." Cover letter preferred. Reads submissions January 31 through October 31 only. Submit seasonal poems 6 months in advance. Time between acceptance and publication is up to 6 months. Often comments on rejected poems. "If you want to assure a critique of your work, you may enclose a SASE and $3 with your request." Occasionally publishes theme issues. Guidelines available on website. Pays up to $50 "for best of the year."

Also Offers: There are 2 Publisher's Choice Awards per issue (not necessarily for poetry). Winners receive $15 plus an award certificate and "their caricature done by our cartoonist James Oddie."

Advice: "If it is flat on the page, it is not a poem. You have to make an impact in few words. In poetry the line is really all—like a commercial—you have to make an emotional statement in a flash."

🌐 ◎ **GAIRM; GAIRM PUBLICATIONS (Specialized: ethnic, foreign language)**, 29 Waterloo St., Glasgow G2 6BZ Scotland. Phone/fax: (0141)221-1971. Established 1952. **Editor:** Derick Thomson.

Magazine Needs: *Gairm* is a quarterly that uses modern/cosmopolitan and traditional/folk verse in Scottish Gaelic only. Has published the work of all significant Scottish Gaelic poets, and much poetry translated from European languages. An anthology of such translations, *European Poetry in Gaelic*, is available for £7.50 or $15. A recent collection is Derick Thomson's *Meall Garbh/The Rugged Mountain*, £7.50 or $15. *Gairm* is 96 pgs., digest-sized, flat-spined with coated card cover. Circulation is 1,000. Sample: $3.50.

How to Submit: Submit 3-4 poems at a time, Gaelic only. Staff reviews books of poetry in 500-700 words, single format; 100 words, multi-book format. Occasionally invites reviews. Send books for review consideration. All of the publications of the press are in Scottish Gaelic. Catalog available.

◖ **GECKO**, P.O. Box 6492, Destin FL 32550. (606)271-4028. E-mail: geckogalpoet@hotmail.com. Established 1998. **Editor:** Rebecca Lu Kiernan.

Magazine Needs: Published annually, *Gecko* "is an ambitious literary journal desirous of showcasing exciting new talent as well as established writers. A featured writer is chosen for each issue. All writers submitting will be treated with respect! Give me vivid imagery; make me feel like I am in the work, not outside looking in. Make me laugh, cry, pound my fists. Say it in a fresh, new way that no one else could have expressed. Knock me out!" Does not wish to see "anything degrading to women. Also no haiku, no rhyme and please, God, no limerick! Please don't put a gecko in your work just for me." Has published poetry by Bright Majikay, Grant Logan Jambors, Chaney Keblusek, Neal Bowers, Aleksey Katkov, and Chelsea Rummaway. As a sample the editor selected these lines from her poem "Intrepid Vagina":

> *Does my desire unnerve you?/Unblinking, lips parted/my breath/condensating in your ear/down on my haunches/like a jaguar/muscled for the strike./Are you happier to hunt me/over a half scrubbed toilet/in yellow gloves,/pinned hair/woefully accommodating you/like wet, underfoot grass?*

Gecko is 32-40 pgs., 5½ × 8½, professionally printed and flat-spined, color card cover with art/graphics. Receives about 2,000 poems/year, accepts under 3%. Press run is 1,000 for 450 subscribers; 250 distributed free to writers, libraries, media, colleges.

How to Submit: Submit 3-5 poems at a time. Line length for poetry is 12 minimum, 42 maximum. Accepts simultaneous submissions; no previously published poems. Cover letter required. "Writers must enclose SASE." Reads submissions year-round, slow during summer months. Time between acceptance and publication is up to 10 months. Seldom comments on rejected poems. Responds in 4 months. Pays 1 copy. Acquires first North American serial rights.

Advice: "I choose the best of the best. If I must reject, don't give up until you have been rejected by every appropriate listing in *Poet's Market*. If you have any talent, I promise you someone will discover it. Poetry published here has gone on to appear in *Ms. Magazine*."

✅ ◎ ⊘ **GENERATOR; GENERATOR PRESS (Specialized: visual poetry)**, 3503 Virginia Ave., Cleveland OH 44109. (216)351-9406. E-mail: generator@dellmail.com. Established 1987. **Editor:** John Byrum.

Magazine Needs: *Generator* is an annual magazine "devoted to the presentation of all types of experimental poetry, focusing on language poetry and 'concrete' or visual poetic modes."

Book/Chapbook Needs: Generator Press also publishes the Generator Press chapbook series. Approximately 1 new title/year.

How to Submit: Currently not accepting unsolicited manuscripts for either the magazine or chapbook publication.

🌐 ◖ ⊘ **GENTLE READER**, 8 Heol Pen-y-Bryn, Penyrheol, Caerphilly, Mid Glam, South Wales CF83 2JX United Kingdom. Phone: (029)20 886369. E-mail: lynne_jones@hotmail.com. Established 1994. **Editor:** Lynne E. Jones.

Magazine Needs: Published quarterly, *Gentle Reader* is "a short story magazine to encourage mostly new and unpublished writers worldwide. Poems provide food for thought and sometimes light relief." Wants "general easy to read verse, not too long, that appeals to a wide audience. Nothing obscure, odd, or esoteric." As a sample the editor selected these lines from "A Coffee-Shop Conversation" by Yvonne Eve Walus:

> *You say I'm brooding/my clock is talking/the age old instinct/emerging/from the sea of documents/and references*

Gentle Reader is 48 pgs., A5, desktop-published and stapled with paper cover, includes clip art and scanned photos, reciprocal ads from other small presses. Receives about 50 poems/year, accepts up to 80%. Press run is 80 for 65 subscribers of which 5 are libraries; 10 distributed free to writers, other presses. Single copy: £2.50, overseas £3.50; subscription: £8.50, overseas £12.00. Sample: £2.00. Make checks payable (in sterling) to L.E. Jones.

How to Submit: Submit 2-3 poems at a time. Line length for poetry is 12 minimum, 30 maximum. Accepts previously published poems and simultaneous submissions. Accepts e-mail and disk submissions. "E-mail in body of document message with/for lines; disks, save file as text, use slashes for lines. IRCs please for reply and return of work." Cover letter preferred. Time between acceptance and publication is up to 1 year. Guidelines available for SAE and IRC. Responds in 2 months. Pays 1 copy. Acquires first British serial rights. Staff reviews other magazines in 50 words, single book format. Send books for review consideration.

Advice: "Keep it simple."

✅ ◖ ◗ ⊘ ◎ **THE GENTLE SURVIVALIST (Specialized: ethnic, nature, inspirational)**, P.O. Box 4004, St. George UT 84770. E-mail: gentle-survivalist@rocketmail.com. Website: www.infowest.com/gentle/. Established 1991. **Editor/Publisher:** Laura Martin-Bühler.

Magazine Needs: *The Gentle Survivalist* is a quarterly newsletter of "harmony—timeless truths and wisdom balanced with scientific developments for Native Americans and all those who believe in the Great Creator." Wants poetry that is "positive, inspirational, on survival of body and spirit, also man's interconnectedness with God and all His creations. Nothing sexually oriented, occult, negative, or depressing." Also accepts poetry written by children. Has published poetry by Keith Moore and C.S. Churchman. The issues we have received discuss environmental illness, Eastern medicine, and list common household toxins to avoid. They also offer money-saving tips and ideas on writing a personal history. "We print four poems average per issue." Press run is 200. Subscription: $20. Sample: $5.

How to Submit: Submit 4 poems at a time. Accepts previously published poems and simultaneous submissions. No e-mail submissions. Cover letter required; "just a note would be fine. I find noteless submissions too imper-

---

🍁 🌐 **SENDING TO A COUNTRY** other than your own? Be sure to send International Reply Coupons (IRCs) instead of stamps for replies or return of your manuscript.

sonal." Time between acceptance and publication is up to 4 months. For written evaluation and editing, send $5. "Written evaluation money is returned if writing is inappropriate or rejected. Evaluation and editing does not guarantee writing will be published." Guidelines are available for SASE and $5; no guidelines sent without sample request. "Folks need to see what they are getting into and I need to weed out frivolous submitters." Responds within 2 months. Does not return poetry. Pays 1 copy.

Also Offers: Sponsors annual contest. Awards a 1-year subscription to the winner. Winner announced in Spring issue.

Advice: "To succeed, one must not seek supporters, but seek to know whom to support. *The Gentle Survivalist* receives a great deal of poetry that is too general in nature. We seek poems of inspiration about God, Man, and our interconnectedness with all living."

$ ⬛ GEORGE & MERTIE'S PLACE: ROOMS WITH A VIEW, P.O. Box 10335, Spokane WA 99209-1335. (509)325-3738. E-mail: geomert@icehouse.net. Established 1995. **Editors:** George Thomas and Mertie Duncan.

Magazine Needs: Appearing monthly except for January, *George & Mertie's Place* is "a monthly journal of opinion and imagination or any realm between. We are open to any form but our limited format prohibits long poetry." Has published poetry by Simon Perchik, Dennis Saleh, and Eric Howard. As a sample the editors selected these lines from "Why I Don't Vote" by Geoff Peterson:

> Some columnist said it best./He said remember the shiny boys and girls/who courted your vote/to be
> president/when you were horny and failing math/and too crazy to drive a car? . . .

George & Mertie's Place is a 4- to 8-page, 8½×11, "micromagazine," printed (unbound) on colored paper with b&w graphics. In addition to poetry it may contain essays, short-short stories, letters, opinions, and "tidbits with a twist." Press run is 100 for 60 subscribers, 20 shelf sales. Subscription: $15/year. Sample: $2.

How to Submit: Submit 3-5 poems at a time. No previously published poems or simultaneous submissions. Accepts e-mail submissions; include text in body of message. Cover letter preferred, "but not a long list of credits; we're looking for historical comments to personalize your submission." Time between acceptance and publication is 3 months. Comments on rejected poems. Responds in 2 months. Pays 1¢/word ($2 minimum) and 1 copy. A $25 "Dick Diver" prize is awarded each month; poetry, fiction and essays compete.

Also Offers: An annual $100.00 prize to a work of prose or poetry which most pleases the taste of writer (yet to be selected) who is not a part of the regular editorial staff of *George & Mertie's Place*."

Advice: "As Baudelaire says, 'Be always drunken—with wine, with poetry or with virtue—as you will—but be always drunken.' "

🅽 ◐ GEORGIA POETRY REVIEW; GEORGIA POETRY REVIEW POETRY PRIZE, 3963 Wolcott Circle, Atlanta GA 30340. E-mail: georgiapoetryreview@altavista.com. Established 2001. **Editors:** Chad Prevost and Travis Denton.

Magazine Needs: *Georgia Poetry Review* is a biannual journal of poetry, fiction, creative nonfiction, and art. Strives "to achieve a balance between high creativity and quality. We seek the best writing nationwide from established and emerging writers." Wants poetry "which is quality and accessible. Innovative images. Narrative or lyric, any form welcome. Any subject, especially when handled with skill and taste." Does not want "jingly verses or pornographic material." *Georgia Poetry Review* is 88-112 pgs., digest-sized, perfect bound, full color. Single copy: $6; subscription: $12/year or $20/2 years. Sample: $6.

How to Submit: Submit 3-7 poems at a time. Accepts simultaneous submissions ("just please notify us as soon as you have news of publication elsewhere."); no previously published poems. No e-mail submissions "though queries and requests are welcome." Cover letter is preferred. "Manuscripts without a SASE cannot be returned." Reads submissions year round. Time between acceptance and publication is 3-12 months. Usually comments on returned poems "if we'd like to see more." Responds in up to 3 months. Pays 1 contributor's copy. Acquires first rights.

Also Offers: "Each year we award two prizes—one for the best poem we publish for the year, and one for the winner of the *Georgia Poetry Review* Poetry Prize. Contest Deadline: March 1, 2002. Entry fee: $10 for three poems, $14 for four, $17 for five. Any length, style. With unbiased, nonstaff finalist judges. $100 for best poem published and $250 for Poetry Prize Winner."

Advice: "Help support us! We are an independent journal, not supported by an academic institution. We depend on subscriptions and grants. Subscribe today."

$ ◐ THE GEORGIA REVIEW, The University of Georgia, Athens GA 30602-9009. (706)542-3481. Website: www.uga.edu/garev (includes writer's guidelines, names of staff, subscription and advertising information, and samples). Established 1947. **Acting Editor:** Stephen Corey.

Magazine Needs: *Georgia Review* appears quarterly. "We seek the very best work we can find, whether by Nobel laureates and Pulitzer Prize-winners or by little-known (or even previously unpublished) writers. All manuscripts receive serious, careful attention." Has published poetry by Peter Davison, Rita Dove, Stephen Dunn, Philip Levine, Linda Pastan, and Pattiann Rogers. "We have featured first-ever publications by many new voices over the years, but encourage all potential contributors to become familiar with past offerings before submitting." As a sample the editor selected these lines from "The Voice of the Light" by John Engels:

*thins and hurls itself away./I've begun to starve/for memories, and memory//is beginning to speak/
another language, difficult/to understand; but I think//it likely to be telling me/we've all flown from
one another,/and in every direction at once.*

The Georgia Review is 208 pgs., 7×10, professionally printed, flat-spined with glossy card cover. Uses 60-70
poems/year, less than one-half of one percent of those received. Press run is 5,500. Subscription: $24/year.
Sample: $8.

How to Submit: Submit 3-5 poems at a time. No simultaneous submissions. Rarely uses translations. No
submissions accepted during June, July, and August. Occasionally publishes theme issues. Responds in 3 months.
Always sends prepublication galleys. Pays $3/line, 1-year subscription, and a copy of issue in which work appears.
Acquires first North American serial rights. Reviews books of poetry. "Our poetry reviews range from 500-word
'Book Briefs' on single volumes to 5,000-word essay reviews on multiple volumes."

Advice: "Needless to say, competition is extremely tough. All styles and forms are welcome, but response times
can be slow during peak periods in the fall and late spring."

N ▢ ◑ **GERONIMO REVIEW; MAOMAO PRESS**, Box 88, San Geronimo CA 94963-0088. E-mail:
geronimoreview@yahoo.com. Website: http://home.att.net/~geronimoreview (includes poetry, reviews, essays).
Established 1998. **Editor:** bassetti. **Factotumus Maximus:** Mark C. Peery.

Magazine Needs: At this time *Geronimo Review* appears randomly as a zine. Wants "only the freshest, most
original of any form or subject. Must have sight, sound, sense; or imagery, music, and meaning." Does not want
"the boring, the earnest, the lifeless—poetry currently in style (i.e. the dead end non sequitur)." Recently published poetry by Mark C. Peery, dada rambass, Albert de Silver, E.E. Glazer, geronimo bassetti, and Élan B.
Yergmoul. As a sample the editor selected these lines from "Oily Mourning" by Élan Batieri Yergmoul:

> *OILY MOURNING/INSTILL EMBED//bear giddup/ice head/tomb eyes/elf*

How to Submit: Submit 3 poems at a time. Line length for poetry is 100 maximum (or the length demanded
by the poem). Accepts simultaneous submissions; no previously published poems. Accepts e-mail submissions
only. "Text within body of mail, not as an attachment." Reads submissions all year. Time between acceptance
and publication is 2 weeks. Poems are "read by Wired Writers Group (of San Rafael); final decision made by
Geronimo Bassetti and Mark C. Peery." Seldom comments on rejections. Charges fee for criticism by special
arrangement at request of author. Occasionally publishes theme issues. List of upcoming themes and guidelines
available on website. Responds in 3 weeks. Pays "eternal fame" and 2 contributor's copies "when printing
occurs." Acquires all rights; returns to poet "on request." Reviews books and chapbooks of poetry and other
magazines in 250-500 words, single book format. Poets may send books for review consideration to *Geronimo
Rreview.*

Book/Chapbook Needs & How to Submit: MaoMao Press will publish essays on and reviews of poetry in
the future. "Not presently accepting book submissions—watch our website."

Also Offers: "We are currently calling for submissions of essays by poets (only) on Shakespeare's sonnets,
1,000-1,500 words."

Advice: "Don't throw up. Act up. Burn the wagon train of poetic fashion."

N ◯ ◑ ◎ **GERTRUDE: A JOURNAL OF VOICE & VISION (Specialized: social issue, women/
feminism, gay/lesbian/bisexual/transgender)**, P.O. Box 270814, Fort Collins CO 80527-0814. E-mail: editor
@gertrudejournal.com. Website: www.gertrudejournal.com (includes excerpts from previous issues, writer/artist
guidelines, and subscription information). Established 1998. **Founding Editor:** Eric Delehoy. **Art Editor:** Ronda
Stone.

Magazine Needs: "Published two times/year, *Gertrude* is a literary journal showcasing the voices and visions of
the gay, lesbian, bisexual, transgendered and straight-supportive community. Provides a positive, nonpornographic
forum. Open to all forms and subjects, we'd like to see positive poetry." Does not want "bitter ex-love poetry,
five-minute poetry, or Hallmark verse; steer clear of work that portrays gays as victims." Has published poetry
by Deanna Kern Ludwin, Christopher Thomas, Demrie Alonzo, Stephen Kopel, and Francisco Aragón. As a
sample the editor selected these lines from "leap the gate" by Stephen Kopel:

> *the moon and I/tip-toe your slumber/and I wonder/can you tell me, mother,/tell me if I'm in your satin
> dream*

Gertrude is 36-48 pgs., digest-sized, professionally printed and saddle-stapled with glossy cardstock cover,
includes b&w art/photography. Receives about 200 poems/year, accepts up to 10%. Press run is 500 for about
100 subscribers, 250 shelf sales; 50 distributed free to gay/lesbian/bisexual/transgender organizations. Single
copy: $4.95; subscription: $9/year. Sample: $5.95.

How to Submit: Submit 3-5 poems at a time. Accepts previously published poems; no simultaneous submis-
sions. No fax or e-mail submissions. Cover letter preferred. Include previous publication credits, short bio, and
SASE. Time between acceptance and publication is up to 2 months. Poems are circulated to an editorial board.
"Three editors apply initial rating system to determine final selections. Final selections are re-read by all editors."
Seldom comments on rejected poems. Occasionally publishes theme issues. Guidelines available for SASE and
on website. Responds in 4 months. Pays 1 copy plus discount on additional copies. All rights revert to authors
upon publication.

Also Offers: Sponsors Editors' Choice Awards in poetry. Also invite contributors to an annual contributors'
reading.

Advice: "Write for yourself, not for publication. In this you find your voice and produce your best."

🏆 $🔲 **THE GETTYSBURG REVIEW**, Gettysburg College, Gettysburg PA 17325. (717)337-6770. Fax: (717)337-6775. Website: www.gettysburgreview.com (includes guidelines, current masthead and staff bios, ordering information and forms, and most importantly, reprints of works published in recent issues. Works—poems, stories, essays—appear in their entirety). Established 1988. **Editor:** Peter Stitt.
- Work appearing in *The Gettysburg Review* has been included in *The Best American Poetry* (1998, 1999, and 2000) and *Pushcart Prize* anthologies. As for the editor, Peter Stitt won the first PEN/Nora Magid Award for Editorial Excellence.

Magazine Needs: *The Gettysburg Review* is a multidisciplinary literary quarterly considering "well-written poems of all kinds." Has published poetry by Rita Dove, Donald Hall, Linda Pastan, Pattiann Rogers, Mark Doty, and Charles Simic. As a sample, we selected these lines from "Epistle to Gerard Manley Hopkins" by Margaret Gibson:

> . . . *But there on the glass/foreshortened, the whole bird, ghosted, is-/its shrugged head sideways, soft breast full on,/plush the arc of its extended wind, the front edge/of its flying there . . .*

Accepts 1-2% of submissions received. Press run is 4,500 for 2,700 subscriptions. Subscription: $24/year. Sample: $7.

How to Submit: Submit 3-5 poems at a time, with SASE. No previously published poems. Simultaneous submissions OK. Cover letter preferred. Reads submissions September through May only. Occasionally publishes theme issues. Response times can be slow during heavy submission periods, especially in the late fall. Pays 1 copy plus subscription plus $2/line. Essay-reviews are featured in each issue. Poets may send books for review consideration.

✅ 🌐 $🔲 **GINNINDERRA PRESS**, P.O. Box 53, Charnwood ACT 2615 Australia. E-mail: gp@dynamit e.com.au. Website: www.ginninderrapress.com.au (includes press history, a full listing of titles published, book extracts, and ordering information). Established 1996. **Publisher:** Stephen Matthews.

Book/Chapbook Needs: Ginninderra Press works "to give publishing opportunities to new writers." Has published poetry by Alan Gould and Geoff Page. Books are usually up to 56 pgs., A5, laser printed and saddle-stapled with board cover, sometimes includes art/graphics.

How to Submit: Query first, with a few sample poems and cover letter with brief bio and publication credits. Accepts previously published poems; no simultaneous submissions. No fax or e-mail submissions. Time between acceptance and publication is 2 months. Seldom comments on rejected poems. Responds to queries in 1 week; to mss in 2 months. Pays royalties of 12½%.

N 🔲 **THE GLASS CHERRY PRESS**, 901 Europe Bay Rd., Ellison Bay WI 54210-9643. Established 1994. **Editor:** Judith Hirschmiller.

Book/Chapbook Needs & How to Submit: The Glass Cherry Press also plans to publish 3 books of poetry/year. Poems included in book-length mss need not be previously published. The editor reads book-length submissions (20-60 pgs.) from January through April only. Guidelines available for SASE. Responds in 4 months. Samples are available from the press for $10 and a SASE.

N 🔲 **GLASS TESSERACT**, P. O. Box 702, Agoura Hills CA 91376. E-mail: editor@glasstesseract. com. Website: www.glasstesseract.com (includes excerpts guidelines, names of editors, price). Established 2001. **Editor:** Michael Chester.

Magazine Needs: *Glass Tesseract* appears biannually and publishes poems and short stories. "Our purpose is to help bring works of art into the world. Our interests are eclectic." Wants poetry that is "rich in imagery, emotion, ideas, or the sound of language. We are open to all forms from rhyming sonnets to unrhymed, open-ended anything—so long as we feel that the poem is a work of art. We don't want sentimental, moralizing, devotional, cute, coy, or happy face poems." Recently published poetry by Carl Bramblett, Thomas Neuburger, and Bill Sapsis. As a sample the editor selected these lines from "A Sighting of Several Ghosts" by Carl Bramblett:

> *the dead like to feel my hot breath on the glass,/and I peer through the blur, stars diffusing./The dead speak with great effort. Their voices/amplify the dull, electric prattle of streetlights,/blue tongues nostalgic, regretful . . .*

Glass Tesseract is 48-96 pgs., digest-sized, laser-printed, spiral comb-bound, card stock cover with art, some issues with b&w line art illustrations. Publishes about 12-20 poems/issue. Single copy: $5; subscription: $9. Sample: $5. Make checks payable to *Glass Tesseract*.

How to Submit: Submit 1-5 poems at a time. Accepts previously published poems and simultaneous submissions. Accepts e-mail submissions; no fax or disk submissions. Cover letter is optional. Include SASE for hard copy submissions. Reads submissions year round. Time between acceptance and publication is 3-9 months. "Poems are always read by the editor and are subsequently reviewed by one or more consulting editors. We are particularly alert to strong poems that differ from our own preferred styles." Always comments on rejected poems. Guidelines are available in magazine, for SASE, by e-mail, or on website. Responds in up to 6 weeks. Sometimes sends prepublication galleys. Pays 2 contributor's copies. Acquires one-time rights which revert to author upon publication.

Advice: "Steep yourself in the best enduring poetry found in anthologies or taught in literature classes—then go your own way. Experiment until you find your voice. Keep reading other poets in the magazines that interest you for your own poems."

⊘ **DAVID R. GODINE, PUBLISHER**, 9 Hamilton Place, Boston MA 02108. Website: www.godine.com (includes titles and ordering information). "Our poetry program is completely filled through 2002, and we do not accept any unsolicited materials."

❖ ⊘ ◎ **GOOSE LANE EDITIONS (Specialized: regional)**, 469 King St., Fredericton, New Brunswick E3B 1E5 Canada. (506)450-4251. Established 1956. **Editorial Director:** L. Boone.
Book/Chapbook Needs: Goose Lane is a small press publishing Canadian fiction, poetry and literary history. Writers should be advised that Goose Lane considers mss by Canadian poets only. Receives approximately 400 mss/year, publishes 10-15 books yearly, 2 of these being poetry collections. Has published *She* by Claire Harris and *Certifiable* by Pamela Mordecai.
How to Submit: Not currently reading submissions. "Call to inquire whether we are reading submissions." Always sends prepublication galleys. Authors may receive royalty of up to 10% of retail sale price on all copies sold. Copies available to author at 40% discount.

✔ ○ ◑ ◎ **GOTTA WRITE NETWORK LITMAG; MAREN PUBLICATIONS (Specialized: Writing)**, 515 E. Thacker, Hoffman Estates IL 60194. Phone/fax: (847)882-8054 (nights only). E-mail: netera@aol.com or gwnlitmag@aol.com. Website: http://members.aol.com/gwnlitmag/. Established 1988. **Editor/Publisher:** Denise Fleischer.
Magazine Needs: *Gotta Write Network Litmag* features "contemporary poetry, articles, short stories, and market listings for a multi-genre audience. A short checklist of what I look for in all poems and stories would be: drawing the reader into the protagonist's life from the beginning; presenting a poem's message through powerful imagery and sensory details; and language that is fresh and dynamic. I prefer free verse. Would also like to receive experimental, multicultural, feminist, humor, contemporary, and translations. The poetry I publish expresses today's society with a tell-it-like-it-is voice. Contributors dive into subjects where others turn away. They speak of rape, suicide, the lives of Native Americans, the Holocaust, and the sign of the times." *Gotta Write Network* has published poetry by Debbi McIntyre, Toni Diol, Robert Cooperman, and Dorothy Wake. As a sample the editor has selected the poem "I am the daughter of Crazy Horse and Black Buffalo Woman" by Raven:

> I came from that mad morning/dash across Yellowstone Country,/I came from the loins of that strange/
> man sprang from the belly of that/woman "warm and good as May/earth," I am the love that blood/
> could not kill the love that no/bullets could end . . .

The semiannual is 48-76 pgs., magazine-sized, desktop-published, saddle-stapled. "*Gotta Write Network* subscribers receive more than a magazine. When submitting, one becomes part of a support group of both beginners and established poets. Readers are from all walks of life. I'm striving to give beginners a positive starting point (as well as promote the work of established writers and editors) and to encourage them to venture beyond rejection slips and writer's block. Publication can be a reality if you have determination and talent. There are over a thousand U.S. litmags waiting for submissions. So take your manuscripts out of your desk and submit them today!" Sample: $6. Overseas add $3.
How to Submit: Submit up to 5 poems at a time. Name and address on each page. No previously published poems or simultaneous submissions. Accepts fax and e-mail submissions (no attachments). Include a cover letter and SASE. "No SASE, no response!" Responds in up to 4 months. Acquires electronic rights. Pays $10 for assigned by-mail interviews with established big press authors and small press editors.
Advice: "Write the way you feel the words. Don't let others mold you into another poet's style. Poetry is about personal imagery that needs to be shared with others."

❖ $⊘ **GRAIN; SHORT GRAIN CONTEST**, Box 1154, Regina, Saskatchewan S4P 3B4 Canada. (306)244-2828. Fax: (306)244-0255. E-mail: grain.mag@sk.sympatico.ca. Website: www.skwriter.com (includes contest winners, submission guidelines, sample work from current issue, back issues available, contest rules, subscription information/online ordering, and mandate). Established 1973. **Editor:** Elizabeth Philips. **Poetry Editor:** Séan Virgo.
Magazine Needs: "*Grain*, a literary quarterly, strives for artistic excellence and seeks poetry that is well-crafted, imaginatively stimulating, distinctly original." *Grain* is 128-144 pgs., digest-sized, professionally printed. Press run is 1,300 for 1,100 subscribers of which 100 are libraries. Receives about 1,200 submissions of poetry/year, accepts 80-140 poems. Subscription: $26.95/1 year, $39.95/2 years, for international subscriptions provide $4 postage for 1 year, $8 postage for 2 years in US dollars. Sample: $7.95 plus IRC.
How to Submit: Submit up to 8 poems, typed on 8½×11 paper, single-spaced, one side only. No previously published poems or simultaneous submissions. Cover letter required. Include "the number of poems submitted, address (with postal or zip code), and phone number. Submissions accepted by regular post only. No e-mail submissions." Reads submissions August through May only. Guidelines available for SASE (or SAE and IRC), by e-mail, or on website. Responds in 3 months. "Response by e-mail if address provided (ms recycled). Then IRCs or SASE not required." Pays over $30/poem plus 2 copies. Acquires first North American serial rights.

Also Offers: Holds an annual Short Grain Contest. Entries are either prose poems (a lyric poem written as a prose paragraph or paragraphs in 500 words or less), dramatic monologues, or postcard stories (also 500 words or less). Also sponsors the Long Grain of Truth contest for nonfiction and creative prose (5,000 words or less). Prizes for all categories are $500 first, $250 second, $125 third; also honorable mentions. All winners and honorable mentions receive regular payment for publication in *Grain*. Entry fee of $22 allows up to two entries in the same category, and includes a 1-year subscription. Additional entries are $5 each. "U.S. and international entrants send fees in U.S. funds ($22 for two entries in one category plus $4 to help cover postage)." Entries are normally accepted between September 1 and January 31.

Advice: "Only work of the highest literary quality is accepted. Read several back issues."

✔ ▣ ⬇ ◔ **GRAND STREET**, 214 Sullivan St., 6C, New York NY 10012. (212)533-2944. Fax: (212)533-2737. E-mail: info@grandstreet.com. Website: www.grandstreet.com. **Poetry Editor:** James Lasdun.
   ● Work published in *Grand Street* has been included in the 1995 and 1997 volumes of *The Best American Poetry*.

Magazine Needs: *Grand Street* is now an online magazine publishing poetry, fiction, nonfiction, and art (with one printed anthology printed each year). "We have no writer's guidelines, but publish the most original poetry we can find—encompassing quality writing from all schools." Has published poetry by John Ashbery, Nicholas Christopher, Fanny Howe, Robert Kelly, August Kleinzahler, and Charles Simic.

How to Submit: Submit 5 poems at a time. No fax or e-mail submissions. Publishes theme issues. Upcoming themes available for SASE. Responds in 2 months.

✔ ◯ ◑ **GRASSLANDS REVIEW**, P.O. Box 626, Berea OH 44017. E-mail: GLReview@aol.com. Website: http://hometown.aol.com/GLReview/prof/index.htm (includes guidelines, sample poems, and contest information). Established 1989. **Editor:** Laura B. Kennelly.

Magazine Needs: *Grasslands Review* is a biannual magazine "to encourage beginning writers and to give adult creative writing students experience in editing fiction and poetry; using any type of poetry; shorter poems stand best chance." Has published poetry by Lauren Bower Smith, Linda Roth, Lynne Martin Bowmans, Stfn Comack, and Michael Cuanach. As a sample the editor selected these lines from "A Brief Bio" by Barbara Wouters:

> My mother was an apron,/my father was a hat./From her, frown and work,/from him, jokes and sales./
> I refused to be an apron, couldn't be a hat;/became a book instead,/escaped in fairy tales,/sewed long
> sheets of words/to cover my nakediness/when I left.

Grasslands Review is 80 pgs., digest-sized, professionally printed, photocopied, saddle-stapled with card cover. Accepts 30-50 of 600 submissions received. Press run is 200. Subscription (2 issues): $10 for individuals, $20 institutions. Sample: $4 for older issues, $5 for more recent.

How to Submit: Submit only during October and March, no more than 5 poems at a time. No previously published poems or simultaneous submissions. No e-mail submissions. Short cover letter preferred. Send #10 SASE for response. Editor comments on submissions "sometimes." Responds in 4 months. Sometimes sends prepublication galleys. Pays 1 copy.

Also Offers: Sponsors annual Editors' Prize Contest. Prize: $100 and publication. Deadline: April 30. Entry fee: $12 for 5 poems, $1/poem extra for entries over 5 poems. Entry fee includes 1-year subscription. Send SASE for reply.

Ⓝ ◑ **THE GRASSY KNOLL**, PMB #230, 5730 N. First St., #105, Fresno CA 93710. Established 2000. **Co-Editors:** Doug Cox, Joseph Voth.

Magazine Needs: *The Grassy Knoll* appears biannually and publishes high-quality poems written by established and emerging writers. Wants quality poems with no limitation on form, subject matter, or style. No "beginning verse." Recently published poetry by Alan Shapiro, Dorianne Laux, Kevin Clark, and Virgil Suarez. *The Grassy Knoll* is 60-80 pgs., digest-sized, perfect-bound. Receives about 3,000 poems/year, accepts about 2%. Publishes about 15-20 poems/issue. Press run is 500. Single copy: $5; subscription: $10. Make checks payable to *The Grassy Knoll*.

How to Submit: Submit up to 4 poems at a time. Accepts previously published poems (rarely) and simultaneous submissions. No fax, e-mail, or disk submissions. Cover letter is preferred. Include SASE. Reads submissions year round. Time between acceptance and publication is 2 months. "Co-editors read every poem." Seldom comments on rejected poems. Guidelines are available in magazine and for SASE. Responds in 3 months. Pays 1 contributor's copy. Acquires first North American serial rights. Reviews books of poetry in 1,000 words, single book and multi-book format. Poets may send books for review consideration to *The Grassy Knoll*.

Advice: "Please only submit poems that are memorable."

✔ $◯ **GRAVITY PRESSES; NOW HERE NOWHERE**, 27030 Havelock, Dearborn Heights MI 48127-3639. (313)563-3663. E-mail: barney@gravitypresses.com. Website: www.gravitypresses.com (includes contact information, guidelines, and subscription information). Established 1998. **Publisher:** Michael J. Barney. **Editor-in-Chief:** Paul Kingston.

Magazine Needs: *Now Here Nowhere* is a quarterly magazine publishing "the best poetry and short prose (fiction and nonfiction) that we can find. We are primarily a poetry magazine but will publish one to two prose pieces per issue. We have no restrictions or requirements as to form, content, length, etc. We publish what we like and what we think is good. No greeting card verse or song lyrics (unless by Leonard Cohen and Tom Waits)." Has published poetry by Simon Perchik, Taylor Graham, Richard Kostelanetz, and Alan Catlin. As a sample the editor selected these lines from "Communication" by Patti Couture:

> Sometimes my words seemed carved/with the dull clumsy chisels barely scratching/the granite air/I
> long for sharp clean edges/to cut precisely/deep through the silent stone

Now Here Nowhere is 48-52 pgs., 6¾×8½, offset-printed or photocopied, saddle-stapled with glossy card cover, includes b&w illustrations. Receives about 500 poems/year, accepts up to 30%. Press run is 100 for 10 subscribers, 85 shelf sales. Single copy: $5.50; subscription: $20/4 issues. Sample: $6. Make checks payable to Gravity Presses.

How to Submit: Submit 5 poems at a time. Accepts simultaneous submissions; no previously published poems. Accepts disk submissions. "International submissions only will be accepted in ASCII format via e-mail." Cover letter preferred. "SASEs should accompany all submissions." Time between acceptance and publication is up to 12 months. Poems are circulated to an editorial board. "All work is seen by at least two editors (of four) and must be accepted by at least two editors. Controversies are settled by the editor-in-chief with no appeals." Seldom comments on rejected poems. Publishes theme issues occasionally. Guidelines and upcoming themes available for SASE. Responds in 6 months. Sometimes sends prepublication galleys. Pays $3-5/issue plus 1 copy. Acquires first North American serial rights.

Book/Chapbook Needs & How to Submit: Gravity Presses is currently not accepting unsolicited mss.

Advice: "The only advice we have for beginners is to write well and submit fearlessly and unrelentingly."

⊘ GREEN BEAN PRESS, P.O. Box 237, Canal Street Station, New York NY 10013. Phone/fax: (718)302-1955. E-mail: gbpress@earthlink.net. Website: http://home.earthlink.net/~gbpress. Established 1993. **Editor:** Ian Griffin.

● Their journal, *Brouhaha*, is no longer being published.

Book/Chapbook Needs: Green Bean Press publishes 1-2 chapbooks and 1-2 full-length books/year. Chapbooks are usually 20-30 pgs., priced $3-5 occasional graphics; cover art sometimes provided by author, other times by publisher." Average press run is 125. "Chapbook arrangements consist of payment in copies only." Full-length books can range from 78-300 pgs., usually 5½×8½, list prices $10-16, catalog available upon request. Average press run is 600. Has published *Long Live the 2 of Spades*, by Daniel Crocker and *North Beach Revisited*, by A.D. Winans.

How to Submit: No unsolicited mss are read for full-length books. For chapbooks query first, with 5-10 sample poems and cover letter with brief bio and publication credits by mail, fax, or e-mail. "Not the entire manuscript, please." E-mail submissions preferred in attached RTF file. Responds to queries and mss in 1 month. Pays 35% author's copies out of a press run of 100-125.

⊘ GREEN HILLS LITERARY LANTERN, P.O. Box 375, Trenton MO 64683. (660)359-3948, ext. 324. Fax: (660)359-3202. E-mail: jsmith@mail.ncmc.cc.mo.us. Website: www.ncmc.cc.mo.us (includes current issue, back issues, subscription info, submission info, contact e-mail, etc.). **Editors:** Jack Smith and Ken Reger. **Poetry Editor:** Joe Benevento.

Magazine Needs: *Green Hills Literary Lantern* is the annual journal of North Central Missouri College and the North Central Missouri Writer's Guild and is open to short fiction and poetry of "exceptional quality." Wants "the best poetry, in any style, preferably understandable. There are no restrictions on subject matter, though pornography and gratuitous violence will not be accepted. Obscurity for its own sake is also frowned upon. Both free and formal verse forms are fine, though we publish more free verse overall. No haiku, limericks, or anything over two pages." Has published poetry by R. Nikolas Macioci, Jim Thomas, Marilyn Shelton, and Yvette A. Schnoeker-Shorb. As a sample the editor selected these lines from "Snowstorm" by Francine Tolf:

> A man's black eyes/roll over me,/cool basalt across/shoulders, thighs,/slide/from my knees/back to a
> newspaper/of sickled alphabet/I do not understand.

Green Hills Literary Lantern is 200 pgs., 6×9, professionally printed and perfect-bound with glossy, 4-color cover. Receives work by more than 200 poets/year and publishes about 10% of the poets submitting—less than 10% of all poetry received. Press run is 500. Sample: $7.

How to Submit: Send submissions to Joe Benevento, Truman State University, Division of Language and Literature, McClain Hall 310, 100 E. Normal, Kirksville MO 63501-4221. Submit 3-7 poems at a time, typed, 1 poem/page. Accepts simultaneous submissions but not preferred; no previously published poems. No fax or e-mail submissions. Cover letter with list of publications preferred. Often comments on rejected poems. Guidelines available for SASE or by e-mail. Responds within 4 months. Always sends prepublication galleys. Pays 2 copies. Acquires one-time rights.

Advice: "Read the best poetry and be willing to learn from what you encounter. A genuine attempt is made to publish the best poems available, no matter who the writer. First time poets, well-established poets, and those in-between, all can and have found a place in the *Green Hills Literary Lantern*. We try to supply feedback, particularly to those we seek to encourage."

Ⓝ ♥ ⊘ ⊘ GREEN MOUNTAINS REVIEW, Johnson State College, Johnson VT 05656. (802)635-1350. Fax: (802)635-1294. E-mail: gmr@badger.jsc.vsc.edu. Established 1975. **Poetry Editor:** Neil Shepard.

● Poetry published in *Green Mountain Review* has been selected for inclusion in *The Best American Poetry* (1997 and 1999) and the 1998 *Pushcart Prize* anthology.

Magazine Needs: *Green Mountains Review* appears twice/year and includes poetry (and other writing) by well-known authors and promising newcomers. Has published poetry by Dean Young, Maureen Seaton, Jane Hirshfield, Linda Gregg, and Bob Hicok. *Green Mountains Review* is digest-sized, flat-spined, 150-200 pgs. Of 3,000 submissions they publish 30 authors. Press run is 1,800 for 200 subscribers of which 30 are libraries. Subscription: $14/year. Sample back issue: $5, current issue $8.50.

How to Submit: Submit no more than 5 poems at a time. Accepts simultaneous submissions. Reads submissions September 1 through March 1 only. Editor sometimes comments on rejection slip. Publishes theme issues. Guidelines and upcoming themes are available for SASE. Responds in up to 6 months. Pays 1 copy plus 1-year subscription. Acquires first North American serial rights. Send books for review consideration.

GREENHOUSE REVIEW PRESS, 3965 Bonny Doon Rd., Santa Cruz CA 95060. Established 1975. Publishes a series of poetry chapbooks and broadsides. "Unsolicited mss are not accepted."

GREEN'S MAGAZINE, P.O. Box 3236, Regina, Saskatchewan S4P 3H1 Canada. Established 1972. **Editor:** David Green.

Magazine Needs: *Green's Magazine* is a literary quarterly with a balanced diet of short fiction and poetry. Publishes "free/blank verse examining emotions or situations." Does not want greeting card jingles or pale imitations of the masters. Accepts poetry written by children. Has published poetry by Robert Cooperman, B.Z. Niditch, and Jill Williams. As a sample the editor selected these lines from "Grey-Spoked Dreams" by Josh Auerbach:

> & I too see the woods/blacken; the bare face/of winter comes strong/into our land, beneath/smoke, beneath fog/lifting off grey-spoked dreams.

Green's is 96 pgs., digest-sized, typeset on buff stock with line drawings, matte card cover, saddle-stapled. Press run is 300. Subscription: $15. Sample: $5.

How to Submit: Submit 4-6 poems at a time. Prefers typescript, complete originals. No simultaneous submissions. "If © used, poet must give permission to use and state clearly the work is unpublished." Time between acceptance and publication is usually 6 months. Comments are usually provided on rejected mss. Guidelines available for SASE (or SAE and IRC). Responds in 2 months. Pays 2 copies. Acquires first North American serial rights. Occasionally reviews books of poetry in "up to 150-200 words." Send books for review consideration.

Advice: "Would-be contributors are urged to study the magazine first."

THE GREENSBORO REVIEW; GREENSBORO REVIEW LITERARY AWARDS, English Dept., Room 134, McIver Bldg., University of North Carolina, P.O. Box 26170, Greensboro NC 27402. (336)334-5459. Fax: (336)334-3281. E-mail: jlclark@uncg.edu. Website: www.uncg.edu/eng/mfa (writer's guidelines, subscription information, and literary award information). Established 1966. **Editor:** Jim Clark. **Contact:** Poetry Editor.

● Work published in this review has been consistently anthologized or cited in the Pushcart Prize.

Magazine Needs: *The Greensboro Review* appears twice yearly and showcases well-made verse in all styles and forms, though shorter poems (under 50 lines) seem preferred. Has published poetry by Brendan Galvin, Stanley Plumly, Adrienne Su, and Michael Collier. As a sample the poetry editor selected these lines from "Double Life" by Daniel Tobin:

> To have driven along blue levitating roads/this far into land's end, golden, rumpled,/these humps that could be the goddess's bedclothes,/and the red broach of a bridge pinning the continent/together, it is all ample and errant

The Greensboro Review is 128 pgs., digest-sized, professionally printed and flat-spined with colored matte cover. Uses about 25 pgs. of poetry in each issue, about 1.5% of the 2,000 submissions received for each issue. Subscription: $10. Sample: $5.

How to Submit: "Submissions (no more than five poems) must arrive by September 15 to be considered for the Spring issue (acceptances in December) and February 15 to be considered for the Fall issue (acceptances in May). Manuscripts arriving after those dates will be held for consideration with the next issue." No previously published poems or simultaneous submissions. No fax or e-mail submissions. Cover letter not required but helpful. Include number of poems submitted. Responds in 4 months. Always sends prepublication galleys. Pays 3 copies. Acquires first North American serial rights.

Also Offers: Sponsors an open competition for *The Greensboro Review* Literary Awards, $250 for both poetry and fiction each year. Deadline: September 15. Guidelines available for SASE.

GSU REVIEW; GSU REVIEW ANNUAL WRITING CONTEST, Georgia State University, Campus Box 1894, Atlanta GA 30303. (404)651-4804. Fax: (404)651-1710. Website: www.gsu.edu (includes guidelines and samples). Established 1980. **Poetry Editor:** Josephine Pallos. **Editor:** Katie Chaple.

Magazine Needs: *GSU Review* is a biannual literary magazine publishing fiction, poetry, and photography. Wants "original voices searching to rise above the ordinary. No subject or form biases." Does not want pornography or Hallmark verse. Has published poetry by Bert Hedin, Gary Sange, Virgil Suarez, and Dana Littlepage Smith. *GSU Review* is 112 pgs. Press run is 2,500 for 500 subscribers, 600 shelf sales; 500 distributed free to students. Single copy: $5; subscription: $8. Sample: $3.

How to Submit: Submit 3 poems at a time. Accepts simultaneous submissions; no previously published poems. Cover letter with 3- to 4-line bio preferred. Time between acceptance and publication is 3 months. Seldom comments on rejected poems. Guidelines available for SASE. Responds in 1 month. Pays 1 copy.

Also Offers: Sponsors the *GSU Review* Annual Writing Contest, an annual award of $1,000 for the best poem; copy of issue to all who submit. Submissions must be previously unpublished. Submit up to 3 poems on any subject or in any form. "Specify 'poetry' on outside envelope." Guidelines available for SASE. Accepts inquiries via fax and e-mail. Postmark deadline: January 31. Competition receives 200 entries. Past judges include Sharon Olds, Jane Hirschfield, Anthony Hecht, and Phil Levine. Winner will be announced in the Spring issue.

Advice: "Avoid cliched and sentimental writing but as all advice is filled with paradox—write from the heart. We look for a smooth union of form and content."

GUERNICA EDITIONS INC.; ESSENTIAL POET SERIES, PROSE SERIES, DRAMA SERIES; INTERNATIONAL WRITERS (Specialized: regional, translations, ethnic/nationality), P.O. Box 117, Toronto, Ontario M5S 2S6 Canada. Fax: (416)657-8885. E-mail: guernicaeditions@cs.com. Website: www.guernicaeditions.com. Established 1978. **Poetry Editor:** Antonio D'Alfonso.

Book/Chapbook Needs: "We wish to bring together the different and often divergent voices that exist in Canada and the U.S. We are interested in translations. We are mostly interested in poetry and essays on pluriculturalism." Has published work by Eugénio de Andrade (Portugal), Eugenio Cirese (Italy), Antonio Porta (Italy), Pasquale Verdicchio (Canada), Robert Flanagan (Canada), and Brian Day (Canada).

How to Submit: Query with 1-2 pgs. of samples. Send SASE (Canadian stamps only) or SAE and IRCs for catalog.

Advice: "We are interested in promoting a pluricultural view of literature by bridging languages and cultures. Besides our specialization in international translation."

GUERRILLA POETRY, 21265 Stevens Creek Blvd., Suite 205-550, Cupertino CA 95014-5715. E-mail: GuerrillaPoetry@yahoo.com. Website: www.GuerrillaPoetry.20m.com (includes excerpts, guidelines, statement of purpose, contact info, etc.). Established 1999. **Editor:** Aaron Gardner.

Magazine Needs: *Guerrilla Poetry* appears quarterly online and in print and "seeks to move poetry into places it has never entered. Our poetry actively forces itself and its world onto the reader." Wants poetry "which is focused, polished, mature, and grounded; poetry which takes risks in style and content, which avoids or reinvents cliches; poetry which is active, vibrant, expressive. Particularly enthused by prose poem, and other experimental styles and orphic poetry." Does not want "poetry which is predictable, unpolished, cliche, passive." *Guerrilla Poetry* is 6-20 pgs., published online and in print, Cover art with art/graphics. Receives about 200 poems/year, accepts about 5%. Publishes about 10 poems/issue. Press run is 750 for 50 subscribers; 700 are distributed free to public postings. Single copy: $2; subscription: $5. Sample: $2.

How to Submit: Submit 3-5 poems at a time. Accepts previously published poems and simultaneous submissions. Accepts fax and e-mail submissions; no disk submissions. Cover letter is preferred. "SASE required for notification of acceptance/rejection. We do not return manuscripts. Due to format we can only publish short works limited to one page typed." Time between acceptance and publication is 4 months usually. "Our editor reviews all submissions and makes decisions based on the input of a small board of assistant editors." Seldom comments on rejected poems. Guidelines are available in magazine, for SASE, by e-mail, or on website. Responds in 1 month. Pays 1 contributor's copy. Acquires one-time rights; reserves right "to publish on our website, or in the occasion of an anthology."

Advice: "Keep cover letters to the point. We don't want to hear about your dog's name or who else likes your poetry. Rather a list of some prior pubs and statement on what your poetry is trying to *do*. The audience of most poetry magazines is highly limited and exclusive. *Guerrilla Poetry* seeks to avoid this problem. Poets shouldn't be singing only to each other, critics, and the select few that will buy a literary magazine, but to everyone."

GUIDE MAGAZINE (Specialized: regional, New York state); FOR THE NATURAL POET, The Catskill Mountain Foundation Inc., P. O. Box 924, 7967 Main St., Hunter NY 12442. (518)263-4908. Fax: (518)263-4459. E-mail: catskillmtn@yahoo.com. Website: www.theguidemagazine.com (includes events, Elderhostel program, guidelines). Established 1992, new owner since 1999. **Literary Editor:** Faith Lieberman.

Magazine Needs: *Guide Magazine* appears as a monthly journal of arts and culture, outdoor recreation, and country and farm life for the Catskill Mountains and valleys of the Hudson, Mohawk, Delaware, and Susquehana River regions. "All types of verse are acceptable as long as they are accessible. If you use a particular form, please give a brief description. Not interested in profanity or shock value." Accepts poetry by teens. Recently published poetry by Anne-Marie Macari, Gerald Stern, Jason Shinder, Diane Wakoski, Anna DiBello, and Tony Coiro. As a sample the editor selected these lines from "The World Loved by Moonlight" by Jane Hirshfield:

> You must try,/the voice said, to become colder./I understood at once./It is like the bodies of gods: cast
> in bronze,/braced in stone. Only something heartless could bear the full weight

Guide Magazine is 110 pgs., magazine-sized, web press- and sheet fed press-printed, saddle-stapled, 80 lb. coated stock cover with 4-color photography, and ads (commercial, arts, sports). Receives about 500 poems/year, accepts about 5%. Publishes about 2 poems/issue. Press run is 20,000 for 250 subscribers of which 20 are libraries; 20,000 (more or less) are distributed free to commercial establishments and tourist info centers for 8 counties.

How to Submit: Submit 3 poems at a time. Line length for poetry is 32 maximum. Accepts simultaneous submissions; no previously published poems unless solicited. Accepts fax, e-mail, and disk submissions. Cover letter is preferred. Include SASE. Reads submissions year round. Submit seasonal poems 3 months in advance. Time between acceptance and publication is 2-3 months. Seldom comments on rejected poems. Occasionally publishes theme issues. A list of upcoming themes is available for SASE or by fax. Responds in 2 months. Pays 1 contributor's copy and admission (2) to poetry series and readings. All rights revert to author on publication. Poets may send books for review consideration to Faith Lieberman at the Catskill Mountain Foundation.

Also Offers: " 'For the Natural Poet' series with four or more dates on Saturdays, including seminars, readings, open mics. Bookstore accepts consignment. Happy to hear new ideas and voices, especially teachers and students."

Advice: "To be heard is to be validated. Make punctuation or the lack of it work for you. The spoken word can improve the written word. Poetry should be ageless and timeless."

$ ☑ **GULF COAST: A JOURNAL OF LITERATURE AND FINE ART**, Dept. of English, University of Houston, Houston TX 77204-3012. (713)743-3223. Website: www.gulfcoast.uh.edu (includes current magazine, submission and subscription information, events and links, contact information, cover art, etc.). Established 1986.
Poetry Editors: Michael Theune, Julie Chisolm, and Matt Otremba.
Magazine Needs: *Gulf Coast* is published twice/year in May and December. While the journal features work by a number of established poets, editors are also interested in "providing a forum for new and emerging writers who are producing well-crafted work that takes risks." Each issue includes poetry, fiction, essays, interviews, and color reproductions of work by artists from across the nation. Has published poetry by Heather McHugh, Robert Pinsky, Marilyn Nelson, William Logan, Lisa Lewis, Gail Mazur, and Asha Shahid Ali. As a sample the editors selected these lines from "Answer to Crowd" by Ed Skoog:

> You have to ask, what was your war crime?/This is social work, walking around the crowd,/wanting
> to tell the woman who left hours ago/that her scarf still lies across the bench,/another coworker at a
> crossroad like yours./At the end of the world one feels worldlier.

Gulf Coast is 140 pgs., 6×9, offset-printed, perfect-bound. Single copy: $7; subscription: $12/year, $22/2 years.
How to Submit: Submit up to 4 poems at a time. Accepts simultaneous submissions with notification; no previously published poems. Cover letter with previous publications, "if any," and a brief bio required. Does not read submissions June through August. Guidelines available for SASE or on website. Responds in 6 months. Pays 2 copies and $15 per poem. Returns all rights (except electronic) upon publication.

☑ **GULF STREAM MAGAZINE**, English Dept. Florida International University, 3000 NE First St., North Miami Campus, North Miami FL 33181. (305)919-5599. Established 1989. **Editor:** Lynne Barrett. **Associate Editors:** Terri Carrion and George Tucker.
Magazine Needs: *Gulf Stream* is the biannual literary magazine associated with the creative writing program at FIU. Wants "poetry of any style and subject matter as long as it is of high literary quality." Has published poetry by Gerald Costanzo, Naomi Shihab Nye, Jill Bialosky, and Catherine Bowman. *Gulf Stream* is 96 pgs., digest-sized, flat-spined, printed on quality stock, glossy card cover. Accepts less than 10% of poetry received. Press run is 750. Subscription: $9. Sample: $5.
How to Submit: Submit no more than 5 poems and include cover letter. Accepts simultaneous submissions (with notification in cover letter). Reads submissions September 15 through April 30 only. Editor comments on submissions "if we feel we can be helpful." Publishes theme issues. Guidelines available for SASE. Responds in 3 months. Pays 2 copies and 2 subscriptions. Acquires first North American serial rights.

☑ **$** ☐ ☺ **HADROSAUR TALES(Specialized: science fiction/fantasy)**, P.O. Box 8468, Las Cruces NM 88006-8468. (505)527-4163. E-mail: hadrosaur.productions@verizon.net. Website: http://hadrosaur.com (includes writer's guidelines, a staff description and company history, links to authors' websites, and an online bookstore through Amazon.com). Established 1995. **Editor:** David L. Summers.
Magazine Needs: "*Hadrosaur Tales* is a literary journal that appears 2 times/year and publishes well written, thought-provoking science fiction and fantasy." Wants science fiction and fantasy themes. "We like to see strong visual imagery; strong emotion from a sense of fun to more melancholy is good. We do not want to see poetry that strays too far from the science fiction/fantasy genre." Has published poetry by Louise Webster, Jennifer Crow, K.S. Hardy, and C.A. Gardner. As a sample the editor selected these lines from 'Crescendo/Decrescendo" by Jennifer Crow:

> Begin in the first, faint glow/of a million distant stars,/and drift through the bubbles/of emptiness in
> search of matter/to fill your void. You breed annihilation,/and endings that never end,/suspended in
> the moment when time/stops.

Hadrosaur Tales is about 100 pgs., digest-sized, "high quality photocopy," perfect-bound with black drawing on card stock cover, uses cover art only, includes minimal ads. Receives about 100 poems/year, accepts up to 25%. Press run is 100 for 25 subscribers. Single copy: $5.95; subscription: $10/year. Sample: $6.95. Make checks payable to Hadrosaur Productions.
How to Submit: Submit 1-5 poems at a time. Accepts previously published poems and simultaneous submissions. Accepts e-mail submissions (include in body of message). Cover letter preferred. "For electronic mail submissions, please place the word, 'Hadrosaur' in the subject line. Poetry will not be returned unless sufficient

insider report

Poetry and the interconnectedness of being

In the preface of her book of essays, *Nine Gates: Entering the Mind of Poetry*, Jane Hirshfield writes, "Poetry's work is the clarification and magnification of being." Her poetry, heavily influenced by Japanese and Chinese verse, consistently delves into the question, "What is the human experience?"

W. S. Merwin compared Hirshfield's poetry in her newest collection, *Given Sugar, Given Salt* (HarperCollins Publishers, 2001) to light beams, "searching, discovering, pausing to make sure." *Kirkus Review* said her work "seeps into one's consciousness, like the aftertaste of some delectable meal."

Sensual and moving, Hirshfield's poems explore "the interconnectedness of being on which poetry rests." She considers the nature of things such as a button or a pillow, then quietly and bravely moves into the mysterious realm of the human soul.

Jane Hirshfield

Photo by Shawn Cady Spelman

In *Nine Gates* you say, "In poetry, landscape is never only outer, it is also a portrait of a state of soul." Are you saying that external landscape is always a vehicle for internal description?

Yes, that is exactly what I was saying—that whatever enters into a poem is part of its deepest meaning and can never, in a good poem, be merely window-dressing. Nothing in a good poem is surface only.

But I want also to clarify that I don't mean by that statement that the outer world exists only in service of our human thoughts, emotions, purposes. I feel more that there is a two-fold movement—that sometimes an outer landscape is the "objective correlative," to use Eliot's term, of our preexisting condition, and other times, in attempting an "objective" description of a rock, a mountain, a horse, our beings can become more infused with rock-nature, mountain-nature, horse-nature. All existence is inseparable, and the more attention we bring to either realm—inner, outer—the larger and more precise both become.

For some reason, a statement of Basho's comes to mind. He once said, "The problem with most poetry is that it is either subjective or objective." A student inquired, "Don't you mean, too subjective or too objective?" He answered, simply, "No."

Then are you saying that no matter the poet's intention the poem brings a relationship of its own?

For me, each poem and the offering it brings to my life does have its own energies and wisdom, far beyond anything within my own intentions. This is as true, of course, of poems I read as of poems I write. It is almost like being given an additional sense organ. Poetry offers a way of knowing, seeing, and feeling the world and our existence in it that is unlike any other. It is close in one way to painting, in another to dream, in another to music; but each of these modes of knowledge is a necessary part of our lives because each is in fact unique, offering a gate into a part of experience that could not be known in any other way.

Yet the relationship we feel between beings and things in a poem is not arbitrary or fanciful or superficial. It is an entrance into the real. The interconnectedness of being on which poetry rests, aesthetically and conceptually, is revealed in a particular way by assonance, rhyme, metaphor, the way images can speak. But it is also, surely, one of the deepest substances of a human life, along with grief, joy, loss, desire, fear, curiosity, love.

"The Envoy"

One day in that room, a small rat.
Two days later, a snake.

Who, seeing me enter,
whipped the long stripe of his
body under the bed,
then curled like a docile house-pet.

I don't know how either came or left.
Later, the flashlight found nothing.

For a year I watched
as something—terror? happiness? grief?—
entered and then left my body.

Not knowing how it came in,
Not knowing how it went out.

It hung where words could not reach it.
It slept where light could not go.
Its scent was neither snake nor rat,
neither sensualistic nor ascetic.

There are openings in our lives
of which we know nothing.

Through them
The belled herds travel at will,
long-legged and thirsty, covered with foreign dust.

(from *Given Sugar, Given Salt*, HarperCollins Publishers, Inc., © 2001 by Jane Hirshfield; used by permission)

The expression of this interconnectedness is one of your strengths. Are there certain poems you feel express this more fully than the others?
Each poem, large or small, has to be a full and sufficient expression, if it's a poem worth reading.

Some may be more explicitly about interconnectedness than others, but that isn't what we're talking about here. It's the underpinning of connection, like the below-surface joists that support a floor and the rafters that hold up a roof, which are always there whether you can see them or not.

Still, since you ask, one example of a poem that is seated in interconnection is the title poem of my 1997 book, *The Lives of the Heart*; a poem which catalogues the range the heart inhabits and must inhabit, reaching out into whales, plastics, fossils, shoes, 19th-century lace-making children going blind. If we want to lead a fully human life, we can leave nothing of this world outside of our working definition of the self.

Has there been any one area or subject that has been particularly difficult to write about?

Every poem, each subject I take on is in some way difficult. What is easy to say doesn't require a poem, does it? That can be left to everyday talk over coffee.

I write a poem because something in my life needs working out—an emotional circumstance, an intellectual or metaphysical puzzlement, a grief or frustration, a loss or a hunger. One poem that was terribly difficult to write was "History as the Painter Bonnard," a poem in *The October Palace* on the political transitions that took place in Eastern Europe in 1989. I knew that I wasn't thinking or feeling deeply enough about those events, I felt inadequate to the magnitude of their meaning, and so I turned to poem-making in order to force myself to greater depth of response. But because the subject was so complex, because the history of that part of the world is so complex and so pivotal, finding my way through that poem was like walking a high wire blindfolded: I kept falling off and having to start over. I think it took 87 drafts.

No one thinks of me as a poet who deals with the political realm, yet if you look, you'll see that in each of my books in some small way I do. But you know, even the poems that come quickly feel somehow hard-won, pulled out of the ground of my life like extracted ore, rather than plucked like a plum from a tree. I don't think we escape leaving our fingerprints, our whole story, on the pages.

Many young writers are often given two pieces of advice: "Focus on things outside of yourself" and "Write what you know." Is there any way to resolve the conflict these statements create?

Almost all the sayings we learn as young writers have some merit and are useful to consider, and at the same time each is only a single small facet of an infinite craft. Writing good poems is not a matter of "either/or," it is a matter of "and/and/and." When I offer such guidelines in a workshop, I always add that every rule of "good" writing can be broken, if it is broken superbly well.

But my thought, today, on these particular two sentences, is that there is no contradiction at all. No good writing could emerge from ignorance, so of course you must write what you know—only remember that knowledge can be had through the imagination, through the tongue's delicious discoveries and inventions, through library research, through the results, even, of chance operations. The seeming contradiction dissolves once you realize that "what you know" does not mean only what you have personally lived in the narrowest sense. It means anything you can wrest with assurance and courage and honed attention into language that is particular, beautiful, and honest to both your certainties and your uncertainties.

> And in any case, what a limitation it would be to think that "you" and "the things outside yourself" are actually separate. All existence travels together: the trees and we conspire in a single breathing, and even the simplest-seeming of our words are, as Emerson said, "fossil poetry"—rooted in the metaphors of physical being, of the earth and the body connected to the earth. How much more connected to the wide world, then, must be the words of good poems.
> —Amy Ratto

postage is provided." Time between acceptance and publication is 1 year. Often comments on rejected poems. Occasionally publishes theme issues. Guidelines and upcoming themes available for SASE. Responds in 1 month. Sends prepublication galleys on request. Pays $2/poem plus 2 copies. Acquires one-time rights.

Advice: "Unfortunately, science fiction/fantasy poetry doesn't appear to have a strong 'main stream' market. However, science fiction poetry often provides the most evocative images and intriguing ideas."

HAIGHT ASHBURY LITERARY JOURNAL (Specialized: social issues, themes), 558 Joost Ave., San Francisco CA 94127. Established 1979-1980. **Editors:** Indigo Hotchkiss, Alice Rogoff, and Conyus.

Magazine Needs: *Haight Ashbury* is a newsprint tabloid that appears 1-3 times/year. Use "all forms including haiku. Subject matter sometimes political, but open to all subjects. Poems of background—prison, minority experience—often published, as well as poems of protest and of Central America. Few rhymes." Has published poetry by Molly Fisk, Laura del Fuego, Dancing Bear, Lee Herrick, Janice King, and Laura Beausoleil. As a sample the editors selected these lines from "in the lines" by Tia Blassingame:

> color boys and girls/leaves the trees in flower/triggers the metal from which year olds drop/drug addict
> babes born on/crack open their skulls/on the ground/color boys and girls/does not become men and
> women

Haight Ashbury Literary Journal is 16 pgs. with graphics and ads. Press run 2,500. $35 for a lifetime subscription, which includes 3 back issues. Subscription: $12/4 issues. Sample: $3.

How to Submit: Submit up to 6 poems. "Please type one poem to a page, put name and address on every page and include SASE." No previously published poems. Each issue changes its theme and emphasis. Guidelines and a list of upcoming themes available for SASE. Responds in 4 months. Pays 3 copies, small amount to featured writers. Rights revert to author. An anthology of past issues, *This Far Together*, is available for $15.

Also Offers: Writing contest with cash award. Deadline: May 1, 2001.

HAIKU HEADLINES: A MONTHLY NEWSLETTER OF HAIKU AND SENRYU (Specialized: form), 1347 W. 71st St., Los Angeles CA 90044-2505. (323)778-5337. Established 1988. **Editor/Publisher:** Rengé/David Priebe.

Magazine Needs: *Haiku Headlines* is "America's only monthly publication dedicated to the genres of haiku and senryu only." Prefers the 5/7/5 syllabic discipline, but accepts irregular haiku and senryu which display pivotal imagery and contrast. Has published haiku by Dorothy McLaughlin, Jean Calkins, Günther Klinge, and Mark Arvid White. Here are examples of haiku and senryu by Rengé:

> HAIKU: By the very sound/of the splash in the water/—invisible frog!
> SENRYU: The silent facades/of the tall city buildings/teeming with people.

Haiku Headlines is 8 pgs., 8½ × 11, corner-stapled and punched for a three-ring binder. "Each issue has a different color graphic front page. The back page showcases a Featured Haiku Poet with a photo-portrait, biography, philosophy, and six of the poet's own favorite haiku." *Haiku Headlines* publishes 100 haiku/senryu a month, including, on the average, work from 6 newcomers. Has 225 subscribers of which 3 are libraries. Single copy: $2 US and Canada, $2.50 overseas; subscription: $24 US and Canada, $30 overseas.

How to Submit: Haiku/senryu may be submitted with 12 maximum/single page. Unpublished submissions from subscribers will be considered first. Nonsubscriber submissions will be accepted only if space permits and SASE is included. Responds in 2 months. Pays subscribers half price rebates for issues containing their work; credits applicable to subscription. Nonsubscribers are encouraged to prepay for issues containing their work.

Also Offers: Monthly Readers' Choice Awards of $25, $15, and $10 are shared by the "Top Three Favorites." The "First Timer" with the most votes receives an Award of Special Recognition ($5).

HANDSHAKE; THE EIGHT HAND GANG (Specialized: science fiction), 5 Cross Farm, Station Rd., Padgate, Warrington, Cheshire WA2 OQG United Kingdom. Established 1992. **Contact:** J.F. Haines.

Magazine Needs: *Handshake*, published irregularly, "is a newsletter for science fiction poets. It has evolved into being one side of news and information and one side of poetry." Wants "science fiction/fantasy poetry of all styles. Prefer short poems." Does not want "epics or foul language." Has published poetry by Margaret B. Simon, Fleming A. Calder, and Jacqueline Jones. As a sample the editor selected these lines from "A Home in Space" by Jacqueline Jones:

> *Blueish splinters and a lightning beauty/Saw us through the orbits throat on earth*

Handshake is 1 sheet of A4 paper, photocopied with ads. Receives about 50 poems/year, accepts up to 50%. Press run is 60 for 30 subscribers of which 5 are libraries. Subscription: SAE with IRC. Sample: SAE with IRC.

How to Submit: Submit 2-3 poems, typed and camera-ready. No previously published poems or simultaneous submissions. Cover letter preferred. Time between acceptance and publication varies. Editor selects "whatever takes my fancy and is of suitable length." Seldom comments on rejected poems. Publishes theme issues. Responds ASAP. Pays 1 copy. Acquires first rights. Staff reviews books or chapbooks of poetry or other magazines of very short length. Send books for review consideration.

Also Offers: *Handshake* is also the newsletter for The Eight Hand Gang, an organization for British science fiction poets, established in 1991. They currently have 60 members. Information about the organization is found in their newsletter.

HANDSHAKE EDITIONS; CASSETTE GAZETTE, Atelier A2, 83 rue de la Tombe Issoire 75014, Paris, France. Phone: 33.1.43.27.17.67. Fax: 33.1.43.20.41.95. E-mail: jim_haynes@wanadoo.fr. Established 1979. **Publisher:** Jim Haynes.

Magazine Needs & How to Submit: *Cassette Gazette* is an audiocassette issued "from time to time. We are interested in poetry dealing with political/social issues and women/feminism themes." Poets published include Yianna Katsoulos, Judith Maĩna, Elaine Cohen, Amanda Hoover, Roy Williamson, and Mary Guggenheim. Single copy: $10 plus postage. Pays in copies.

Book/Chapbook Needs & How to Submit: Handshake Editions does not accept unsolicited mss for book publication. New Book: "a bilingual English/Spanish edition by Cuban poet, Pablo Armando Fernandez to be co-published with Mosaic Press, Toronto" in early 2001.

Advice: Jim Haynes, publisher, says, "I prefer to deal face to face."

HANGING LOOSE PRESS; HANGING LOOSE, 231 Wyckoff St., Brooklyn NY 11217. Website: http://omega.cc.umb.edu/~hangloos/ (includes guidelines, index, new titles, etc.). Established 1966. **Poetry Editors:** Robert Hershon, Dick Lourie, Mark Pawlak, and Ron Schreiber.

• Poetry published in *Hanging Loose* has been included in the 1995, 1996, and 1997 volumes of *The Best American Poetry.*

Magazine Needs: *Hanging Loose* appears 3 times/year. The magazine has published poetry by Sherman Alexie, Paul Violi, Donna Brook, Kimiko Hahn, Ron Overton, Jack Anderson, and Ha Jin. *Hanging Loose* is 120 pgs., flat-spined, offset on heavy stock with a 4-color glossy card cover. One section contains poems by high-school-age poets. The editor says it "concentrates on the work of new writers." Sample: $9.

How to Submit: Submit 4-6 "excellent, energetic" poems. No simultaneous submissions. "Would-be contributors should read the magazine first." Responds in 3 months. Pays small fee and 2 copies.

Book/Chapbook Needs & How to Submit: *Hanging Loose* Press does not accept unsolicited book mss or artwork.

HANOVER PRESS, LTD.; THE UNDERWOOD REVIEW, P.O. Box 596, Newtown CT 06470-0596. (203)426-3388. Fax: (203)426-3398. E-mail: faith@hanover-press.com. Website: www.hanover-press.com (includes poetry calendar, mission statement, guidelines, online bookstore, and online poetry newsletter). Established 1994. **Editor:** Faith Vicinanza.

Magazine Needs: *The Underwood Review* appears annually each spring and publishes poetry, short stories, essays, and b&w artwork including photographs. Wants "cutting-edge fiction, poetry, and art. We are not afraid of hard issues, love humor, prefer personal experience over nature poetry. We want poetry that is strong, gutsy, vivid images, erotica accepted. No religious poems; no 'Hallmark' verse." Accepts poetry written by children. Has published poetry by award winning poets Patricia Smith ("Queen of Performance Poetry"), Marc Smith ("Father of Slam Poetry"), Michael Brown, and Vivian Shipley. As a sample the editor selected these lines from "Mommy's Hubby" by Leo Connellan (Poet Laureate of Connecticut):

> *Yes, it's Fisk tellin' you split./Imagine it, Fisk tellin' you leave!/Because now I'm Mommy's Hubby and*
> *we've got our coffins/picked out/plots and perpetual flowers.*

The Underwood Review is 120-144 pgs., 6×9, offset-printed and perfect-bound with card cover with computer graphics, photos, etc. Receives about 1,000 poems/year, accepts up to 5%. Press run is 1,000. Subscription: $13. Sample: $13. Make checks payable to Hanover Press, Ltd./Faith Vicinanza.

THE OPENNESS TO SUBMISSIONS INDEX at the back of this book lists all publishers in this section by how open they are to submissions.

How to Submit: Submit up to 4 poems at a time. Accepts simultaneous submissions; no previously published poems. Accepts disk submissions; no e-mail submissions. Cover letter with short bio (up to 60 words) preferred. Time between acceptance and publication is up to 8 months. Guidelines available for SASE. Responds in 5 months. Pays 2 copies. Acquires one-time rights.

Book/Chapbook Needs & How to Submit: Hanover Press, Ltd. seeks "to provide talented writers with the opportunity to get published and readers with the opportunity to experience extraordinary poetry." Has published *Crazy Quilt* by Vivian Shipley; *Short Poems/City Poems* by Leo Connellan; *We Are What We Love* by Jim Scrimgeour; *Full Circle* by Elizabeth Thomas; *Dangerous Men* by David Martin; and *The Space Between* by Sandra Bishop Ebner. Publishes 5 paperbacks/year. Books are usually 6×9, offset-printed and perfect-bound with various covers, include art/graphics. Query first with a few sample poems and cover letter with brief bio and publication credits. Responds to queries in 2 months; to mss in 6 months. Pays 100 author's copies (out of a press run of 1,000). Order sample books by sending $11.

✓ ◐ ◑ ◎ **HARD ROW TO HOE; POTATO EYES FOUNDATION (Specialized: nature/rural/ecology)**, P.O. Box 541-I, Healdsburg CA 95448. (707)433-9786. **Editor:** Joe E. Armstrong.

Magazine Needs: *Hard Row to Hoe,* taken over from Seven Buffaloes Press in 1987, is a "book review newsletter of literature from rural America with a section reserved for short stories (about 2,000 words) and poetry featuring unpublished authors. The subject matter must apply to rural America including nature and environmental subjects. Poems of 30 lines or less given preference, but no arbitrary limit. No style limits. Do not want any subject matter not related to rural subjects." As a sample the editor selected these lines from "The Big River" by Armando Garcia Davila:

> There, reflected in the baptismal water is a/man in fine clothes and hair/that is combed and trimmed
> regularly. This is/what The Big River/offers, and it is all his to seize if he simply/crosses to El otro
> lado/undetected by those who would keep him from his fate.

Hard Row to Hoe is 12 pgs., magazine-sized, side-stapled, appearing 3 times/year, 3 pgs. reserved for short stories and poetry. Press run is 300. Subscription: $7/year. Sample: $2.

How to Submit: Submit 3-4 poems at a time. No simultaneous submissions. Accepts previously published poems only if published in local or university papers. Guidelines available for SASE. Editor comments on rejected poems "if I think the quality warrants." Pays 2 copies. Acquires one-time rights. Reviews books of poetry in 600-700 words. Poets may send books for review consideration.

▒N▒ ◑ **HARPERCOLLINS PUBLISHERS**, 10 East 53rd St., New York NY 10022. Website: www.HarperCollins.com (includes poets, recorded poetry, books and events, workshop, free electronic newsletter subscription). Top publisher of some of America's premier poets. **"Unfortunately the volume of submissions we receive prevents us from reading unsolicited manuscripts or proposals."**

▒N▒ ◑ **HARP-STRINGS POETRY JOURNAL; EDNA ST. VINCENT MILLAY "BALLAD OF THE HARP WEAVER" AWARD; VERDURE PUBLICATIONS**, P.O. Box 640387, Beverly Hills FL 34464-0387. Fax: (352)746-7817. E-mail: verdure@digitalusa.net. Website: www.verdurepubs.com (includes sample poems, guideline for each publication, names, photos and bios of editorial staff, contest rules, and previous winning poems). Established 1989. **Editor:** Madelyn Eastlund.

Magazine Needs: *Harp-Strings* appears quarterly. Wants "narratives, lyrics, ballads, sestinas, rondeau, redouble, blank verse. Nothing 'dashed off,' trite, broken prose masquerading as poetry." Recently published poetry by Joyce Odum, Todd Palmer, Gail White, Viktor Tichy, Norman Kraeft, and Helen Mar Cook. As a sample we selected these lines from "Canadian Geese in Early December" by Norman Kraeft:

> Fluid formations form as these birds fly./I watch as drill-team squadrons come and go,/and light up
> celebrations in the sky.//The rustle in their wings electrify/the evening. Hosts of lyric measures grow:/
> fluid formations form as these birds fly.

Harp-Strings is 16-20 pgs., digest-sized, saddle-stapled, professionally printed on quality colored matte stock with matte card cover. Accepts about 1% of poems received. Publishes about 12-16 poems/issue. Press run is 200 for 105 subscribers. Subscription: $12. Sample: $3.50.

How to Submit: Submit 3-5 poems at a time. Line length for poetry is 14 minimum, 80 maximum ("but more often find 40-60 line poems have best chance"). Accepts previously published poems. Accepts fax and e-mail submissions; no disk submissions. Cover letter is preferred. "Always an SASE—lately poets seem to forget." Brief cover letter, information about poet or poem. *Harper Strings* does use brief contributor notes." Reads submissions in January and February; April and May; July and August; October and November. "We do not hold poems until the next issue unless a poem is so good and we have no room in which case we so inform the author." Uses accepted poems in the next issue being planned. "Editor chooses; however, editor and associate editor do always conference before each issue is firmed, and there are times one or two poems will be discussed." Seldom comments on rejected poems. "A poem might not be right for us, but right for another publication. Rejection does not imply poem needs revisions." Guidelines are available for SASE, by e-mail, or on website. Responds at the end of each reading period. Pays 1 contributor's copy. Acquires one-time rights.

Also Offers: Sponsors the Edna St. Vincent Millay "Ballad of the Harp Weaver" Awards (narrative from 40 to 100 lines, deadline August 15). Entry fee: 1-3 poems for $5. Make checks payable to Madelyn Eastlund. One cash award of $50 and publication.

Advice: "Stanley Kunitz once said, 'Poetry today has become easier to write but harder to remember.' We want poetry to remember, poetry that haunts, poetry the reader wants to read again and again."

▨ $◩ THE HARPWEAVER; CANADIAN AUTHORS ASSOCIATION PRIZE FOR POETRY,

Dept. of English, 500 Glenridge Ave., St. Catharines, Ontario L2S 3A1 Canada. (905)688-5550, ext. 3469. Fax: (905)688-5550, ext. 4492. E-mail: harpweav@spartan.ac.BrockU.ca. Established 1996. **Contact:** editor.

Magazine Needs: "*the Harpweaver* biannually publishes the creative work of emerging and established artists. We want poetry embodying the best words in the best order. This poetry is always consistent with innovation in form and content." Has published poetry by George Elliott Clarke and James Reaney. *the Harpweaver* is 100-128 pgs., 5½×8½, offset-printed and perfect-bound, card cover with artwork. Receives about 200 poems/year, accepts up to 8-10%. Press run is 1,000. Subscription: $10/year (2 issues). Sample: $7/issue.

How to Submit: Submit up to 12 poems at a time. No previously published poems or simultaneous submissions. Cover letter required. Accepts e-mail and disk submissions. Reads submissions in June and January. Time between acceptance and publication is 3 months. Poems are circulated to an editorial board—"student board to faculty editor to journal editors." Guidelines available for SASE, by fax, or by e-mail. Responds in 3 months. Pays $10. Reviews books and chapbooks of poetry in 5,000 words, single book format. Poets may send books for review consideration.

Also Offers: Sponsors the Canadian Authors Association Prize for Poetry, a cash award of $100 given "to the author of the poem that our judges consider to be the most noteworthy among the many fine poems *the Harpweaver* has the opportunity to publish in its two yearly issues."

☑ ◩ HAWAII PACIFIC REVIEW, 1060 Bishop St., Honolulu HI 96813. (808)544-1107. Fax: (808)544-

0862. E-mail: hpreview@hpu.edu. Website: www.hpu.edu (includes tables of content from back issues, selected sample poems, contributor bios, and guidelines). Established 1986. **Poetry Editor:** Patrice Wilson.

Magazine Needs: *Hawaii Pacific Review* is an annual literary journal appearing in September. Wants "quality poetry, short fiction, and personal essays from writers worldwide. Our journal seeks to promote a world view that celebrates a variety of cultural themes, beliefs, values, and viewpoints. We wish to further the growth of artistic vision and talent by encouraging sophisticated and innovative poetic and narrative techniques." Has published poetry by Wendy Bishop, B.Z. Niditch, Rick Bursky, and Linda Bierds. *Hawaii Pacific Review* is 80-120 pgs., 6×9, professionally printed on quality paper, perfect-bound, with coated card cover; each issue features original artwork. Receives 800-1,000 poems/year, accepts up to 30-40. Press run is approximately 1,000 for 200 shelf sales. Single copy: $8.95. Sample: $5.

How to Submit: Submit up to 5 poems, maximum 100 lines each. 1 submission/issue. "No handwritten manuscripts." Accepts simultaneous submissions with notification; no previously published poems. No fax or e-mail submissions. Cover letter with 5-line professional bio including prior publications required. "Our reading period is September 1 through December 31 each year." Seldom comments on rejected poems. Guidelines available for SASE or by e-mail. Responds within 3 months. Pays 2 copies. Acquires first North American serial rights.

Advice: "We'd like to receive more experimental verse. Good poetry is eye-opening; it investigates the unfamiliar or reveals the spectacular in the ordinary. Good poetry does more than simply express the poet's feelings; it provides both insight and unexpected beauty."

▧ $◩ HAYDEN'S FERRY REVIEW, Box 871502, Arizona State University, Tempe AZ 85287-1502.

(480)965-1243. Website: www.haydensferryreview.com (includes guidelines, submission information, back issues, and excerpts). Established 1986.

● Poetry published in *Hayden's Ferry Review* has been included in the *Pushcart Prize* anthology for 2001.

Magazine Needs: *Hayden's Ferry* is a handsome literary magazine appearing in December and May. Has published poetry by Dennis Schmitz, Raymond Carver, Maura Stanton, Ai, and David St. John. *Hayden's Ferry Review* is 6×9, 120 pgs., flat-spined with glossy card cover. Press run is 1,300 for 200 subscribers of which 30 are libraries, 800 shelf sales. Accepts about 3% of 5,000 submissions annually. Subscription: $10. Sample: $6.

How to Submit: "No specifications other than limit in number (six) and no simultaneous submissions." Submissions circulated to two poetry editors. Editor comments on submissions "often." Guidelines available for SASE. Responds in 3 months of deadlines. Deadlines: February 28 for Spring/Summer issue; September 30 for Fall/Winter. Sends contributor's page proofs. Pays $25/page (maximum $100) and 2 copies.

◩ HAZMAT REVIEW; CLEVIS HOOK PRESS, P.O. Box 30507, Rochester NY 14603-0507. Established

1996. **Editor:** Norm Davis. **Fiction Editor:** Nick DiChario.

Magazine Needs: *HazMat Review* is a biannual literary review, "about 70% poetry; 25% short story; 5% misc. (essays, review, etc.). *HazMat Review* stands for 'hazardous material,' which we believe poetry most definitely may be!" Wants "your best material; take chances; political pieces welcome; also experimental and/or alternative; especially welcome pieces that show things are not what they appear to be. We think poetry/fiction of the highest quality always has a chance. New Age, witches, ghosts, and goblins, vampires, probably not." Has published poetry by Eileen Myles, Marc Olmstead, Steve Hirsch, Jim Cohn, bobby johnson, Thom Ward, Lawrence Ferlinghetti, and Anne Waldman. As a sample the editor selected this untitled poem by Larry Hilf:

> full moon/hides/in cloud thicket/ambush.

HazMat Review is 96 pgs., digest-sized, professionally printed and perfect-bound with glossy color or b&w cover, sometimes includes photographs or original art. Receives about 700 poems/year, accepts up to 20%. Press run is 500 for 35 subscribers of which 5 are libraries, 100 shelf sales; 100 distributed free to coffeehouses for publicity. Single copy: $8; subscription: $15/year. Sample: $5.

How to Submit: Submit 3 poems at a time. Accepts previously published poems; no simultaneous submissions. Accepts disk submissions. Cover letter preferred. SASE requested. Time between acceptance and publication is up to 1 year. Poems are circulated to an editorial board. "Editors pass promising material to staff readers for second opinion and suggestions, then back to editors for final decision." Often comments on rejected poems. Guidelines available for SASE. Responds in 3 months. Pays 1-2 copies. Acquires one-time rights. Staff reviews chapbooks of poetry. "Best chance for fiction, 2,500 words or less."

Advice: "We are encouraged by the renewed interest in poetry in recent years. If at all possible, read the magazine first before submitting to get a feel for the publication."

HEART—HUMAN EQUITY THROUGH ART (Specialized: social issues); AN-NUAL HEART POETRY CONTEST, P.O. Box 81038, Pittsburgh PA 15217-0538. (412)244-0122. Fax: (412)244-0210. E-mail: lesanne@ix.netcom.com. Website: http://trfn.clpgh.org/heart/ (includes contest guidelines, journal excerpts, events, subscription/submission info, links). Established 1997. **Poetry Editor:** Leslie Anne Mcilroy. Member: CLMP.

- Named one of "Others to Watch" in literature by the 1998 *Pittsburgh Magazine* Harry Schwalb Excellence in Arts Awards; received Honorable Mention from 1998 Pushcart Prize for "Elizabeth Tines" by Jane McCafferty.

Magazine Needs: *HEArt* appears 3 times/year. "*HEArt* is the nation's only journal of contemporary art, literature, and review devoted to confronting discrimination and promoting social justice. We encourage the role of artists as human rights activists. All poems should address social justice issues including, but not limited to racial, sexual, gender, and class discrimination. Fresh language, vivid imagery, strong craft, concise word choice, economy of language, and poems that 'show,' not tell. Must be accessible, not 'academic,' though intellectual is fine." Does not want "ethereal, romantic, pastoral, or highly academic and inaccessible poetry. We steer away from preachy or rambling work. Personal poems with no social significance are inappropriate." Accepts poetry written by children. Recently published poetry by Tim Seibles, Sherod Santos, Sapphire, Amiri Baraka, Sonia Sanchez, and Linda McCarriston. As a sample the editor selected these lines from "Really Breathing" by Tim Seibles:

> Fresh prisons and bottom lines/everywhere: terrible jobs, terrible/choices, terrible. Look at the flies/ dead, so close to freedom—/the window smiling,/the glass sweet as a guillotine.

HEArt is 80 pgs., 5 × 7½, offset/full-bleed-printed, saddle-stapled, computer art graphic/100 lb. uncoated/cover, with art/graphics (encouraged) and 4-8 pgs. of retail/art/literary ads. Receives about 150 poems/year, accepts about 20%. Publishes about 12 poems/issue. Press run is 1,000 for 500 subscribers of which 5 are libraries, 100 shelf sales; 250 are distributed free to potential subscribers, writing conferences, shelters, social service agencies. Single copy: $7.50; subscription: $21. Sample: $8.50. Make checks payable to *HEArt*.

How to Submit Submit 3 poems at a time. Accepts simultaneous submissions; no previously published poems. Accepts fax, e-mail, and disk submissions. Cover letter is preferred. "Require final version hard copy to proof as well as electronic version to place, preferably in rich text format." Reads submissions all year. Time between acceptance and publication is 4 months. "Poems are reviewed by poetry editor and accepted or rejected. Poems that raise some question or are printable with minor revisions are given to fiction editor for review/suggestions." Seldom comments on rejected poems. Occasionally publishes theme issues. A list of upcoming themes and guidelines are available in magazine, for SASE, by fax, by e-mail, or on website. Responds in up to 6 months. Pays $25 and 2 contributor's copies. Acquires first North American serial rights. Reviews books of poetry in 1,000-1,500 words, single book format. Poets may send books for review consideration to Leslie Anne Mcilroy.

Also Offers: The annual HEArt (Human Equity Through Art) Poetry & Short Fiction Contest. First prize in both categories is publication in *HEArt* and $500. Entries must be previously unpublished and address social justice issues, including but not limited to racial, sexual, gender, and class discrimination. Submissions must be postmarked by December 31. A $15 entry fee includes a copy of the winning issue. For $21, entrants receive a year's subscription to the journal beginning with the winning issue. Make check payable to HEArt. Additional information and guidelines available for SASE, by fax, e-mail, or on website.

Advice: "*HEArt* believes in the power of poetry to affect readers, and thereby affect social change. We encourage poets to use their voices to recognize injustice in the tradition of Pablo Neruda. This is not easy. Many submissions are preachy and trite, though well-meaning. Show, don't tell and balance message with craft."

HEAVEN BONE MAGAZINE; HEAVEN BONE PRESS; HEAVEN BONE PRESS INTERNATIONAL CHAPBOOK COMPETITION (Specialized: spiritual, nature/rural/ecology), P.O. Box 486, Chester NY 10918. (914)469-9018. E-mail: heavenbone@aol.com. Established 1986. **Poetry Editor:** Steve Hirsch.

Magazine Needs: *Heaven Bone* publishes poetry, fiction, essays, and reviews with "an emphasis on spiritual, metaphysical, surrealist, experimental, esoteric, and ecological concerns." Has published poetry and fiction by Richard Kostelanetz, Charles Bukowski, Marge Piercy, Kirpal Gordon, Diane di Prima, and Michael McClure. As a sample the editor selected these lines from "Message of Hope" by G. Sutton Breiding:

> *The screech owl's call/Is vertical: a tower/Rippling in the mist,/A door of oracles/Hung between night/*
> *And dawn that opens/And shuts softly/In the white places/Of sleep.*

Heaven Bone is approximately 144 pgs., magazine-sized, perfect-bound, using b&w art, photos on recycled bond stock with glossy 4-color recycled card cover. Receives up to 1,000 poems/year, accepts up to 30. Press run is 2,000. Sample: $10.

How to Submit: Submit 3-10 poems at a time. "I will not read submissions without SASEs." Accepts simultaneous submissions and previously published poems, "if notified." Accepts e-mail submissions (PDF, Microsoft Word). Time between acceptance and publication is up to 1 year. Occasionally publishes theme issues. A list of upcoming themes available for SASE. Responds in up to 6 months. Sometimes sends prepublication galleys. Pays 2 copies. Acquires first North American serial rights. Reviews books of poetry. Poets may send books for review consideration.

Also Offers: The press sponsors the biannual Heaven Bone Press International Chapbook Competition which awards $100 plus publication to an original, unpublished poetry ms of 30 pgs. or less. Reading fee $10. Guidelines available for SASE.

Advice: Editor advises, "Please be familiar with the magazine before sending mss. We receive too much religious verse. Break free of common 'poetic' limitations and speak freely with no contrivances. No forced end-line rhyming please. Channel the muse and music without being an obstacle to the poem."

N. ◒ HEELTAP; PARIAH PRESS, 604 Hawthorne Ave. E., St. Paul MN 55101. Established 1985 (Pariah Press); 1997 (*Heeltap*). **Editor:** Richard Houff.

Magazine Needs: *Heeltap* appears 2 times/year. Contains "social issues: people connecting with people/surviving chaos and government brain washing/re-establishing a literate society and avoiding the corporate machine." Very open to all kinds of poetry. "We don't believe in censorship." Does not want "early to mid-19th century rhyme about mother's lilacs, etc." Recently published poetry by Tom Clark, Gerald Locklin, Albert Huffstickler, Theodore Enslin, Charles Plymell, and Marge Piercy. As a sample the editor selected these lines from "Micro Histories" by Lillian Oglethorpe:

> *Afterward//:skies bleeding global/landscapes hacked to ribbons/—enough already*

Heeltap is 48-64 pgs. ("varies depending on finances"), digest-sized, laser/high speed-printed, saddle-stapled, cardstock cover (covers done by Mama Rue Day), ads for books and chapbooks from individuals and publishers. Receives about 10,000 poems/year, accepts about 2-5%. Publishes varied number of poems/issue. Press run is 500 for 50 subscribers of which 20 are libraries, 300 shelf sales. Single copy: $5; subscription: 4 issues/$18. Sample: $5 postage paid. "We encourage poets to buy samples." Make checks payable to Richard Houff.

How to Submit: Submit 3-5 poems at a time. Line length for poetry is 1 line minimum, 1 page maximum. Accepts previously published poems and simultaneous submissions. No fax, e-mail, or disk submissions. Cover letter is preferred. Reads submissions all year. Time between acceptance and publication is 1 year. Often comments on rejected poems. Responds in 3 months. Pays 1 contributor's copy. Acquires one-time rights. Reviews books and chapbooks of poetry, a half page in single book format. "We will do reviews on occasion—generally, we list books received in the magazine with comments."

Book/Chapbook Needs & How to Submit: Pariah Press publishes *only* solicited material. Published 12 titles in 2000 ("varies depending on cash flow"). Chapbooks are 24 pgs., laser/high speed-printed, saddle-stapled, with cover that varies from 150 lb. glossy to card stock, art/graphics on cover only. No unsolicited mss. "We solicit established poets and writers to send a complete manuscript." Responds to queries in 2 months. Pays 50 author's copies (out of a press run of 100). Order sample books/chapbooks by sending $5 (postage paid) to Richard Houff.

Advice: "The beginning poet should study the classics, from the early Greek tradition to the present. On the current scene, try to be yourself. Draw inspiration from others and you'll eventually find your voice. Let Bukowski rest—there are thousands of clones. Buk wouldn't approve."

☑ ◒ HELICON NINE EDITIONS, 3607 Pennsylvania Ave., Kansas City MO 64111. (816)753-1095. Fax: (816)753-1016. E-mail: twpkcmo@aol.com. Website: www.heliconnine.com. Established 1977. **Editor:** Gloria Vando Hickok.

Book/Chapbook Needs & How to Submit: Helicon Nine publishes poetry. "We do not accept unsolicited mss for Helicon Nine Editions without prior inquiry." Has published *One Girl* by Sheila Kohler and *Flesh* by Susan Gubernat. As a sample the editor selected these lines from "Night Ritual" by Marjorie Stelmach from her book *Night Drawings*:

> *Finger things: a silver hook/lifted and lowered on the screen-porch door,/a lamp-key turned to lower*
> *the flame,/a gown's hem lifted for stairs, one/slippered foot suspended.*

No electronic submissions.

☑ ◒ HELIOTROPE, P.O. Box 20037, Spokane WA 99204. E-mail: gribneal@omnicast.net. Established 1996. **Editors:** Tom Gribble and Iris Gribble-Neal.

Magazine Needs: *Heliotrope*, published annually in January, is "an outlet for poetry, fiction, prose and criticism." Wants "poetry of any form, length, subject matter, style or purpose with no restrictions." Has published poetry by Bill Tremblay, Carlos Reyes, and Raue Arroyo. As a sample the editors selected these lines from "Therapist: 'Tell Me About Your Mother's Kitchen . . '" by Kris Christensen:

I never went there/except once when my aunt was spinning/vodka and orange juice in a green/glass
making a strange brown light.

Heliotrope is 100 pgs., 6×9, perfect-bound with glossy cover with art. Press run is 200-300 for 75 subscribers. Subscription: $8. Make checks payable to Tom Gribble/*Heliotrope*.

How to Submit: Submit 5 poems at a time. No previously published poems or simultaneous submissions. Accepts e-mail submissions; include text in body of message. Cover letter preferred. Reads submissions June 21 through September 21 only. Poems are circulated to an editorial board. Seldom comments on rejected poems. Guidelines available for SASE. Responds 2 months after end of reading period. Sometimes sends prepublication galleys. Pays 1 copy.

Advice: "We are open to all writers."

$ ◎ HERALD PRESS; PURPOSE; STORY FRIENDS; ON THE LINE; WITH; CHRISTIAN LIV-ING (Specialized: religious, children), 616 Walnut Ave., Scottdale PA 15683-1999. (724)887-8500. Send submissions or queries directly to the editor of the specific magazine at address indicated.

Magazine Needs & How to Submit: *Herald Press*, the official publisher for the Mennonite Church in North America, seeks also to serve a broad Christian audience. Each of the magazines listed has different specifications, and the editor of each should be queried for more exact information. *Purpose*, edited by James E. Horsch, a "religious young adult/adult monthly in weekly parts," press run 13,000, its focus: "action oriented, discipleship living." It is 5⅜×8⅜, with two color printing throughout. Buys appropriate poetry up to 12 lines. *Purpose* uses 3-4 poems/week, receives about 2,000/year of which they use 150, has a 10- to 12-week backlog. Guidelines and a free sample are available for SASE. Mss should be double-spaced, one side of sheet only. Accepts simultaneous submissions. Responds in 2 months. Pays $7.50-20/poem plus 2 copies. *On the Line*, edited by Mary C. Meyer, a monthly religious magazine, for children 9-14, "that reinforces Christian values," press run 6,000. Sample free with SASE. Wants poems 3-24 lines. Submit poems "each on a separate 8½×11 sheet." Accepts simultaneous submissions and previously published poems. Responds in 1 month. Pays $10-25/poem plus 2 copies. *Story Friends*, edited by Rose Mary Stutzman, is for children 4-9, a "monthly magazine that reinforces Christian values," press run 6,500, uses poems 3-12 lines. Send SASE for guidelines/sample copy. Pays $10. *With*, Editorial Team, Box 347, Newton KS 67114, (316)283-5100. This magazine is for "senior highs, ages 15-18," focusing on empowering youth to radically commit to a personal relationship with Jesus Christ, and to share God's good news through word and actions." Press run 4,000, uses a limited amount of poetry. Poems should be 4-50 lines. Pays $10-25. *Christian Living*, edited by Sarah Kehrberg, published 8 times/year, is "for family, community, and culture," uses poems up to 30 lines. Has published poetry by Julia Kasdorf. As a sample the editor selected these lines from "Sometimes Hope" by Jean Janzen:

But sometimes hope/is a black ghost/in a fantastic twist,/an old dream that flickers/in the wind.

Christian Living is 28-44 pgs., 8×10, 1-3 color with photos and artwork. Receives about 75 poems/year, accepts 15-20. Press run is 4,000 for 4,000 subscribers of which 8-10 are libraries, 10-20 shelf sales; 100-300 distributed free. Single copy: $3; subscription: $23.95. Sample free with 9×12 SASE ($1). Make checks payable to *Christian Living*. Submit 3-5 poems at a time. Accepts previously published poems and simultaneous submissions. Time between acceptance and publication is up to 14 months. Seldom comments on rejected poems. Guidelines available for SASE. Responds within 6 months. Pays $1/line plus 2 copies. Acquires first or one-time rights. Staff reviews books or chapbooks of poetry in 200-800 words. Poets may send books for review consideration.

✓ ◖ ◯ ◎ THE HERB NETWORK (Specialized: herbs), P.O. Box 152, Oshkosh NE 69154. (308)772-4320. E-mail: editor@herbnetwork.com. Website: www.herbnetwork.com (includes writer's guidelines, membership information, articles, and an interview with the editor). Established 1995. **Editor:** Kathleen O'Mara.

Magazine Needs: *The Herb Network* is a quarterly newsletter of information for herbal enthusiasts. Wants poetry related to herbs or plants—real or folklore. Short poems to 250 words. Also accepts poetry written by children. Has published poetry by Louise Webster, Nancy Dahl, and Jim DeWitt. As a sample the editor selected "Dandelions" by Elizabeth Willis DeHuff:

Slim little girls with green flounced dresses,/Dandelions stand with yellow shaggy hair./Soon they grow
to gray haired ladies,/Whose locks sail away through the air./Ashamed of their baldness, each of these
dears,/Fringes a cap which she always wears.

The newsletter is 24 pgs., 8½×11, neatly printed on plain white paper with a few b&w graphics. The issue we received included recipes, information about herbs used by midwives, an article focusing on lavender, book reviews, and classified ads. Press run is 7,500 for 7,000 subscribers. Subscription: $35/year; student rate; $27/year; international: $45/year.

How to Submit: Submit up to 3 poems at a time, typed double-spaced, one poem/page, name and address on each. Line length for poems is 25 maximum. Accepts previously published poems and simultaneous submissions. Accepts e-mail submissions; include text in body of message. Cover letter preferred. Publishes theme issues. Guidelines available by e-mail or for SASE; upcoming themes available for SASE. Responds in up to 3 months. Pays with 1 copy and 2 tearsheets or by barter, offering free advertisements, or copies or $1-5 as budget allows. Acquires first or one-time rights.

◖N◗ ◖ ◯ HERNANDO MEDIC, 7443 Oak Tree Lane, Spring Hill FL 34607-2324. (352)688-8116. Fax: (352)686-9477. E-mail: mariasingh@cs.com. Established 2001. **Editor-in-Chief:** Pariksith Singh, MD.

Magazine Needs: *Hernando Medic* appears quarterly, published by the Hernando County Medical Society. Deals with health, healing, and medical aspects of the human experience. Wants any form, style of poetry dealing with health and healing." Does not want slander, racism, or bigotry. Accepts poetry written by children. *Hernando Medic* is 24-36 pgs., magazine-sized, offset-printed, stapled, glossy cover, with $1,200/page. Publishes about 2-3 poems/issue. Press run is 500 for 70 subscribers of which 10 are libraries; rest are distributed free to physicians and medical personnel. Single copy: $5; subscription: $20. Sample: $6. Make checks payable to Hernando County Medical Society.

How to Submit: Submit up to 5 poems at a time. Line length for poetry is 100 lines maximum. Accepts previously published poems and simultaneous submissions. Accepts fax, e-mail, and disk submissions. Cover letter is preferred. Submissions should be double-spaced, one side of 8½ × 11 sheet. Include SASE. Time between acceptance and publication is 2-3 months. "Editorial board is composed of 5-6 members. We meet every quarter to review the material received." Always comments on rejected poems. Occasionally publishes theme issues. A list of upcoming themes is available by e-mail. Guidelines are available in magazine, for SASE, or by e-mail. Responds in up to 1 month. Pays up to $50/page and 1 contributor's copy. Acquires first North American serial rights. Staff reviews books of poetry in 1,000 words, multi-book format. Poets may send books for review consideration to Pariksith Singh, MD.

Also Offers: "I also publish *Midwest Poetry Review*, a journal of poetry." (See separate listing for *Midwest Poetry Review* in this section.)

○ **HEY, LISTEN!; SEAWEED SIDESHOW CIRCUS**, 3820 Miami Rd., Apt. 3, Cincinnati OH 45227. (513)271-2214. E-mail: sscircus@aol.com. Website: http://hometown.aol.com/SSCircus/sscweb.html. Established 1994. **Editor:** Andrew Wright Milam.

Magazine Needs: *Hey, listen!* is an annual "small press magazine created to bring personal response back into publishing." Open to all poetry, except rhyme. Has published poetry by Jim Daniels, Susan Firer, James Liddy, and Sarah Fox. As a sample the editor selected these lines from "he found being in love/more difficult than driving/52 hours home" by Erich Ebert:

> no one wants to be sad/from saying "in 52 hours I'll be home."/especially since we should be/asking
> someone "Do the leaves change/when I touch your skin?"

Hey, listen! is 30 pgs., magazine-sized, photocopied, and saddle-stapled with cardstock cover. Receives about 50-100 poems/year, accepts 20-30%. Press run is 100. Subscription: $5/2 years. Sample: $2. Make checks payable to Seaweed Sideshow Circus.

How to Submit: Submit 3-5 poems at a time. No previously published poems or simultaneous submissions. Accepts e-mail submissions (include in body); no fax submissions. Include SASE and name and address on each page. Cover letter preferred. Time between acceptance and publication is 1-2 months. Often comments on rejected poems. Guidelines available for SASE. Responds in 2 months. Pays 1 contributor's copy. Rights revert to author upon publication.

Book/Chapbook Needs & How to Submit: Seaweed Sideshow Circus is "a place for young or new poets to publish a chapbook." Publishes 1 chapbook/year. Chapbooks are usually 30 pgs., 8½ × 5½, photocopied and saddle-stapled with cardstock cover. Send 5-10 sample poems and cover letter with bio and credits. Responds to queries in 3 weeks; to mss in 3 months. Pays royalties of 50% plus 10 author's copies (out of a press run of 100). Order sample chapbooks by sending $6.

Ⓝ ○ **HIDDEN OAK**, P.O. Box 2275, Philadelphia PA 19103. E-mail: hidoak@att.net. Established 1999. **Editor:** Louise Larkins.

Magazine Needs: *Hidden Oak* appears 3 times/year. "Hidden Oak seeks well-crafted poems which make imaginative use of imagery to reach levels deeper than the immediate and personal. Both traditional forms and free verse are accepted. Especially welcome are poems which include time-honored poetic devices and reveal an ear for the music of language. Nothing erotic, narrowly religious, or sentimental." *Hidden Oak* is 60-68 pgs., 5½ × 8½, photocopied, stapled, original art/photograph on cover, with b&w margin sketches; occasionally full-page b&w drawing. Receives about 500 poems/year, accepts up to 40%. Publishes about 50-60 poems/issue, usually 1 on a page. Press run is 80-100. Single copy: $4; subscription: $11. Sample: $3. Make checks payable to Louise Larkins.

How to Submit: Submit 3-6 poems at a time. Line length for poetry is 30 maximum. Accepts previously published poems; no simultaneous submissions. Accepts e-mail submissions; no disk submissions. Cover letter is preferred. Include SASE. Also accepts small b&w drawings, whether or not they are poem-related. Submit seasonal poems 2-3 months in advance. Time between acceptance and publication is up to 3 months. Seldom comments on rejected poems. Might publish theme issues in the future. Guidelines available for SASE or by e-mail. Responds in 1 week. Pays 1 contributors copy. Does not review books or chapbooks, but will list any chapbook sent under "Publications Received."

○ **THE HIGGINSVILLE READER; THE HIGGINSVILLE WRITERS**, P.O. Box 141, Three Bridges NJ 08887. (908)788-0514. E-mail: hgvreader@yahoo.com. Established 1990. **Editors:** Amy Finkenaur, Frank Magalhaes, Kathe Palka.

Magazine Needs: *The Higginsville Reader* is a "quarterly litmag for a general adult audience. *Higginsville Reader* prints poetry, short fiction, and essays; also b&w artwork and photographs." Wants "work rich in imaginative language. We are open to all forms and styles, accept both very short poems and longer works and are always more concerned with quality than name. We do not want poems that wander without aim, overt sentimentality, assaultive negativism." Has published poetry by Taylor Graham, Ron Offen, Duane Locke, Michael Foster, Glen Grundle, and Eric Howard. As a sample the editor selected these lines from "Early in May" by Gayl Ellen Harvey:

> We had almost forgotten the tenderness/of such a month/yeserday's trees, wordless,/rain-soaked, launching into green whispers,/page after page filling up.with the blossoms.

The Higginsville Reader is 16 pgs., 7×8½, laser-printed, unbound, b&w artwork and photography inside only—no cover art. Receives about 750-1,000 poems/year, accepts 8-10%. Press run is 150-200 for 125 subscribers. Subscription: $5/year. Sample (including guidelines): $1.50. Make checks payable to The Higginsville Writers.
How to Submit: Submit 3-6 poems at a time. Accepts previously published poems ("but prefer new work") and simultaneous submissions (if advised and notified). Accepts e-mail submissions, as attached Microsoft Word file or plain text in body of message. Time between acceptance and publication is up to 12 months. Poems are circulated to an editorial board. "Two editors (out of three) must agree on a piece for it to be accepted." Seldom comments on rejected poems. Guidelines available for SASE or by e-mail. Responds in 2 months. Pays 1 copy. Acquires one-time rights.

N **$ HIGH PLAINS LITERARY REVIEW**, 180 Adams St., Suite 250, Denver CO 80206. (303)320-6828. Established 1986. **Editor:** Robert O. Greer. **Associate Poetry Editor:** Ray Gonzalez.
Magazine Needs & How to Submit: *High Plains Literary Review* appears 3 times/year using "high quality poetry, fiction, essays, book reviews, and interviews." The format is 135 pgs., 70 lb. paper, heavy cover stock. Subscription: $20. Sample: $4. Guidelines available for SASE. Pays $10/published page for poetry.

$ 🔲 HIGH PLAINS PRESS (Specialized: regional), P.O. Box 123, Glendo WY 82213. (307)735-4370. Fax: (307)735-4590. Website: www.highplainspress.com. Established 1985. **Poetry Editor:** Nancy Curtis.
Book/Chapbook Needs: High Plains Press considers books of poetry "specifically relating to Wyoming and the West, particularly poetry based on historical people/events or nature. We're mainly a publisher of historical nonfiction, but do publish one book of poetry every year." Has published *Close at Hand* by Mary Lou Sanelli and *Bitter Creek Junction* by Linda Hasselstrom. As a sample the editor selected these lines from "Gathering Mint" from the book *Glass-Eyed Paint in the Rain* by Laurie Wagner Buyer:

> He returned at dusk, drunk on solitude, singing/in time with the gelding's rocky trot,/moccasined feet wet with mud,/the burlap bag he tossed me/stuffed full of mint/from the beaver slough.

How to Submit: Query first with 3 sample poems (from a 50-poem ms). Accepts fax submissions. Responds in 2 months. Time between acceptance and publication is up to 24 months. Always sends prepublication galleys. Pays 10% of sales. Acquires first rights. Catalog available on request; sample books: $5.

$ 🔲 HIGH/COO PRESS; MAYFLY (Specialized: form, haiku), 4634 Hale Dr., Decatur IL 62526. (217)877-2966. E-mail: brooksbooks@q-com.com. Website: www.family-net.net/~brooksbooks (includes sample poetry, book reviews, featured haiku writers, and online collections). Established 1976. **Editors:** Randy and Shirley Brooks.
• Their books have received the Haiku Society of America Merit Awards.
Magazine Needs: High/Coo Press is a small press publishing nothing but haiku in English. "We publish haiku poemcards, minichapbooks, anthologies, and a bibliography of haiku publications in addition to paperbacks and cloth editions and the magazine *Mayfly*, evoking emotions from contemporary experience. We are not interested in orientalism nor Japanese imitations." Wants "well-crafted haiku, with sensual images honed like a carved jewel, to evoke an immediate emotional response as well as a long-lasting, often spiritual, resonance in the imagination of the reader." Publishes no poetry except haiku. Has published haiku by George Swede, Peggy Lyles, and Masajo Suzuki. *Mayfly* is 16 pgs., 3½×5, professionally printed on high-quality stock, saddle-stapled, one haiku/page. It appears in January and August. Publishes 32 of an estimated 1,800 submissions. Subscription: $8. Sample: $4; or send $17 (Illinois residents add 7½% tax) for the *Midwest Haiku Anthology* which includes the work of 54 haiku poets. A Macintosh computer disk of haiku-related stacks is available for $10.
How to Submit: Submit no more than 5 haiku/issue. No previously published poems or simultaneous submissions. Accepts e-mail submissions. Deadlines are March 15 and October 15. Guidelines available for SASE. Pays $10/poem; no copies.
Book/Chapbook Needs & How to Submit: High/Coo Press considers mss "by invitation only."
Advice: "Publishing poetry is a joyous work of love. We publish to share those moments of insight contained in evocative haiku. We aren't in it for fame, gain, or name. We publish to serve an enthusiastic readership."

✓ 🔲 🔲 🔲 HIGHLIGHTS FOR CHILDREN (Specialized: children), 803 Church St., Honesdale PA 18431. (570)253-1080. E-mail: editorial@highlights-corp.com. Established 1946. **Contact:** Beth Troop.
Magazine Needs: *Highlights* appears every month using poetry for children ages 2-12. Wants "meaningful and/or fun poems accessible to children of all ages. Welcome light, humorous verse. Rarely publish a poem longer than 16 lines, most are shorter. No poetry that is unintelligible to children, poems containing sex, violence,

or unmitigated pessimism." Accepts poetry written by children. "We print, but do not purchase, from individuals under age 16." Has published poetry by Ruskin Bond, Aileen Fisher, Eileen Spinelli, and Carl Sandburg. As a sample we selected these lines from "Lone Fox Dancing" by Ruskin Bond:

> As I walked home last night,/I saw a lone fox dancing/in the bright moonlight//I stood and watched,/ Then took the low road, knowing/The night was his by right.

Highlights is generally 42 pgs., magazine-sized, full-color throughout. Receives about 300 submissions/year, accepts up to 30. Press run is 3.3 million for approximately 2.8 million subscribers. Subscription: $29.64/year (reduced rates for multiple years).

How to Submit: Submit typed ms with very brief cover letter. Please indicate if simultaneous submission. No e-mail submissions. Editor comments on submissions "occasionally, if ms has merit or author seems to have potential for our market." Responds "generally within 1 month." Always sends prepublication galleys. Payment: "money varies" plus 2 copies. Acquires all rights.

Advice: "We are always open to submissions of poetry not previously published. However, we purchase a very limited amount of such material. We may use the verse as 'filler,' or illustrate the verse with a full-page piece of art. Please note that we do not buy material from anyone under 16 years old."

HILLTOP PRESS (Specialized: science fiction), 4 Nowell Place, Almondbury, Huddersfield, West Yorkshire HD5 8PB England. Website (online catalog): www.bbr-online.com/catalogue. Established 1966. **Editor:** Steve Sneyd.

Book/Chapbook Needs: Hilltop publishes "mainly science fiction poetry nowadays." Publications include a series of books on poetry in US and UK SFanzines as well as collections, new and reprint, by individual science fiction poets including, recently, Andrew Darlington, Peter Layton, Gavin Salisbury, J.P.V. Stewart, and Andrei Lubensky. As a sample the editor selected these lines from the book *Euroshima, Mon amour: Poems from the Inner Mind to the Outer Limits*, by Andrew Darlington:

> and this man, frozen involcanic glaze/carbon-dated 50 million years old//to show we've passed this way before//he points at Earth, and he smiles that particular smile

Hilltop titles are distributed in the USA by the New Science Fiction Alliance. For full list of UK publications NSFA distributes, send SAE/IRC to A. Marsden, 31192 Paseo Amapola, San Juan Capistrano CA 92675-2227 or see website.

How to Submit: Does not accept unsolicited mss. Query (with SAE/IRC) with proposals for relevant projects.

Advice: "My advice for beginning poets is (a) persist—don't let any one editor discourage you. 'In poetry's house are many mansions,' what one publication hates another may love; (b) be prepared for long delays between acceptance and appearance of work—the small press is mostly self-financed and part time, so don't expect it to be more efficient than commercial publishers; (c) *always* keep a copy of everything you send out, put your name and address on *everything* you send and *always* include adequately stamped SAE."

HIPPOPOTAMUS PRESS (Specialized: form); OUTPOSTS POETRY QUARTERLY; OUTPOSTS ANNUAL POETRY COMPETITION, 22 Whitewell Rd., Frome, Somerset BA11 4EL England. Phone/fax: 01373-466653. *Outposts* established 1943, Hippopotamus Press established 1974. **Poetry Editor:** Roland John.

Magazine Needs: "*Outposts* is a general poetry magazine that welcomes all work either from the recognized or the unknown poet." Wants "fairly mainstream poetry. No concrete poems or very free verse." Has published poetry by Jared Carter, John Heath-Stubbs, Lotte Kramer, and Peter Russell. As a sample we selected these lines from "The Lotus-Eaters" by Ashleigh John:

> Our lives are one long Sunday, when it rained./There were so many things we might have done—/We watched the television-set instead,/And the day ended as it had begun./We are the quick who may as well be dead:/The nothing-ventured, and the nothing gained.

Outposts is 60-120 pgs., A5, litho printed and perfect-bound with laminated card cover, includes occasional art and ads. Receives about 46,000 poems/year, accepts approximately 1%. Press run is 1,600 for 1,200 subscribers of which 400 are libraries, 400 shelf sales. Single copy: $8; subscription: $26. Sample (including guidelines): $6. Make checks payable to Hippopotamus Press. "We prefer credit cards because of bank charges."

How to Submit: Submit 5 poems at a time. "IRCs must accompany U.S. submissions." Accepts simultaneous submissions; no previously published poems. Accepts fax submissions. Cover letter required. Time between acceptance and publications is 9 months. Seldom comments on rejected poems, "only if asked." Occasionally publishes theme issues. Upcoming themes available for SASE (or SAE and IRC). Responds in 2 weeks plus post time. Sometimes sends prepublication galleys. Pays £8/poem plus 1 copy. Copyright remains with author. Staff reviews books of poetry in 200 words for "Books Received" page. Also uses full essays up to 4,000 words. Send books for review consideration, attn. M. Pargitter.

Book/Chapbook Needs & How to Submit: Hippopotamus Press publishes 6 books/year. "The Hippopotamus Press is specialized, with an affinity with Modernism. No Typewriter, Concrete, Surrealism." For book publication query with sample poems. Accepts simultaneous submissions and previously published poems. Responds in 6 weeks. Pays 7½-10% royalties plus author's copies. Send for book catalog to buy samples.

Also Offers: The magazine also holds an annual poetry competition.

$ ☐ ◯ ◑ ◉ HODGEPODGE SHORT STORIES & POETRY (Specialized: subscribers), P.O. Box 6003, Springfield MO 65801. E-mail: fictionpub@aol.com. Website: http://members.aol.com/fictionpub/hppub.html. Established 1994. **Editor:** Vera Jane Goodin. **Contact:** poetry editor.

Magazine Needs: *Hodgepodge* appears quarterly to "provide a showcase for new as well as established poets and authors; to promote writing and offer encouragement." Open to all kinds of poetry. Accepts poetry written by children (but makes no special allowance for them). Has published poetry by Estelle Jones-Langston and M.D. LeDoux. As a sample the editor selected these lines from "Death of a Beatnik Poet, 1959" by Wanda Sue Parrott:

> *Summertime poets haunted the Gas House/along the strand in Venice West/seeking . . . like what?*
Hodgepodge is a 24- to 32-page chapbook, photocopied and saddle-stapled with self cover, includes clip art. Receives about 100 poems/year, accepts up to 50%. Press run is about 100 for about 100 subscribers. Single copy: $3; subscription: $10 US/$15 foreign. Sample: $2. Make checks payable to Goodin Communications. "Potential contributors either need to purchase a copy or be annual subscribers."

How to Submit: Submit up to 4 poems at a time. Accepts previously published poems and simultaneous submissions. Accepts e-mail submissions; include text in body of message, no attachments. SASE required for return of poems. Time between acceptance and publication is 3 months. Seldom comments on rejected poems. Guidelines available for SASE. Responds in 2 months. Pays $1/poem. Acquires one-time rights. Staff reviews books and chapbooks of poetry and other magazines in 250 words, single and multi-book format. Send books for review consideration to Review Editor.

Also Offers: Sponsors a Best-of-the-Year Contest. Any poem published in *Hodgepodge* is eligible for the contest. 1st Place $30, 2nd Place $15, 3rd Place free subscription. Also awards honorable mentions and certificates. "Judging is done by staff, but readers are asked for input." Sponsors the Sunny Edition contest; deadline: June 30, 2001—poems and short stories that are uplifting, touching or funny. Reading fee of $5 covers up to 3 entries. Awards: work published and 1st Place: $25, 2nd Place: $15, 3rd Place: $10, 4th Place: $5. Published in fall. Details available for SASE.

◑ ◉ HOLIDAY HOUSE, INC. (Specialized: children), 425 Madison Ave., New York NY 10017. Established 1936. **Editor-in-Chief:** Regina Griffin. A trade children's book house. Has published hardcover books for children by Myra Cohn Livingston and John Updike. Publishes 1 poetry book/year averaging 32 pages. "The acceptance of complete book manuscripts of high-quality children's poetry is limited." Send a query with SASE before submitting.

$ ◑ THE HOLLINS CRITIC, P.O. Box 9538, Hollins University, Roanoke VA 24020-1538. (540)362-6275. Website: www.hollins.edu/academics/critic. Established 1964. **Editor:** R.H.W. Dillard. **Poetry Editor:** Cathryn Hankla.

Magazine Needs: *The Hollins Critic*, appears 5 times/year, publishing critical essays, poetry, and book reviews. Uses a few short poems in each issue, interesting in form, content or both. Has published poetry by John Engels, Lyn Lifshin, George Garrett, Dara Wier. As a sample the editor selected these lines from "Carving the Salmon" by John Engels:

> *And then it is recognizable, a fish,/and ready for finishing. It quivers//a little at the skew chisel, flinches/ at the spoonbit. With the straight gouge/I give it eyes, and with the veiner, gills,//and it leaps a little in my hand.*
The Hollins Critic is 24 pgs., magazine-sized. Press run is 500. Subscription: $6/year ($7.50 outside US). Sample: $1.50.

How to Submit: Submit up to 5 poems, must be typewritten with SASE, to Cathryn Hankla, poetry editor. Responds in 6 weeks (slower in the summer). Pays $25/poem plus 5 copies.

◑ HOME PLANET NEWS, Box 415, Stuyvesant Station, New York NY 10009. Established 1979. **Co-Editor:** Enid Dame. **Co-Editor:** Donald Lev.

Magazine Needs: *Home Planet News* appears 3 times/year. "Our purpose is to publish lively and eclectic poetry, from a wide range of sensibilities, and to provide news of the small press and poetry scenes, thereby fostering a sense of community among contributors and readers." Wants "honest, well-crafted poems, open or closed form, on any subject. Poems under 30 lines stand a better chance. We do not want any work which seems to us to be racist, sexist, agist, anti-Semitic, or imposes limitations on the human spirit." Has published poetry by Layle Silbert, Robert Peters, Lyn Lifshin, and Gerald Locklin. As a sample the editor selected these lines from "Milk" by Barry Wallenstein:

> *In my tired hand—milk/in my memory—it glows/a white shadow/smear around my younger mouth/ around what I used to know*
Home Planet News is a 24-page tabloid, web offset-printed, includes b&w drawings, photos, cartoons and ads. Receives about 1,000 poems/year, accepts up to 3%. Press run is 1,000 for 300 subscribers. Subscription: $10/4 issues, $18/8 issues. Sample: $3.

How to Submit: Submit 3-6 poems at a time. No previously published poems or simultaneous submissions. Cover letter preferred. "SASEs are a must." Reads submissions February 1 through May 31 only. Time between acceptance and publication is 1 year. Seldom comments on rejected poems. Occasionally publishes theme issues. "We announce these in issues." Guidelines available for SASE, "however, it is usually best to simply send work." Responds in 4 months. Pays 1-year gift subscription plus 3 copies. Acquires first rights. All rights revert to author on publication. Reviews books and chapbooks of poetry and other magazines in 1,200 words, single and multi-book format. Poets may send books for review consideration to Enid Dame. "Note: we do have guidelines for book reviewers; please write for them. Magazines are reviewed by a staff member."

Advice: "Read many publications, attend readings, feel yourself part of a writing community, learn from others."

$ ☐ ◯ HOME TIMES, 3676 Collins Dr. #12, West Palm Beach FL 33406. (561)439-3509. Website: www.hometimes.org. Established 1988. **Editor/Publisher:** Dennis Lombard.

Magazine Needs: *Home Times* is a monthly "independent, conservative, pro-Christian, pro-Jewish," 24-page newsprint tabloid of "local, national, and world news and views, including information in the areas of home and family, arts and entertainment, and religion. *Home Times* tries not to moralize but to just be positive and Biblical in perspective. Our goal is to publish godly viewpoints in the marketplace, and to counteract the culturally elite of media and politics who reject Judeo-Christian values, traditional American values, true history, and faith in God." Wants poetry that is "short or humorous or spiritual—not 'religious'; for a general audience. Prefer traditional or light verse up to 16 lines." Accepts poetry written by children. Receives about 200 poems/year, accepts up to 3%. Press run is 5,200. Single copy: $2. Samples: $3 for 2 current issues.

How to Submit: Submit 3 poems at a time. Accepts previously published poems and simultaneous submissions. Time between acceptance and publication is up to 6 months. Sometimes comments on rejected poems. Guidelines available for SASE. Responds in 1 month. Pays $5-10 "generally" or a subscription, if requested. Acquires one-time rights.

Advice: "*Home Times* is very different! Please read guidelines and sample issues." Also, the editor has written a 12-chapter report for new writers entitled "101 Reasons Why I Reject Your Mss"—which is "an effective training course for new freelancers, easy to understand and written with lots of humor."

Ⓝ ☐ ◙ HOMESTEAD REVIEW, Box A-5, 156 Homestead Ave., Hartnell College, Salinas CA 93901. (831)755-6943. Fax: (831)755-6751. E-mail: mtabor@jafar.hartnell.cc.ca.us. Established 1985. **Editor:** Maria Garcia Tabor.

Magazine Needs: *Homestead Review* appears biannually (fall/winter and spring/summer). Wants to see "avant-garde poetry as well as fixed form styles of remarkable quality and originality. We do not want to see Hallmark-style writing or first drafts." Accepts poetry written by children. Recently published poetry by Ray Gonzalez, Dana Garrett, Janet Fujimoto, Deanna Shelor, and Alejandro Murguia. As a sample the editor selected these lines from "Why There Can Be No More Chinese Departure Poems" by Dana Garrett:

> *Under the digital blue theater sign outside the mall,/White faces stream out behind us./Here we must*
> *offer our "Later" and "Yea, Later,"/And trek a thousand feet of parking lot in broken glass.*

Receives about 1,000 poems/year, accepts about 15%. Publishes about 65 poems/issue. Press run is 500 for 300 subscribers of which 300 are libraries; 200 are distributed free to poets, writers, bookstores. Single copy: $5, subscription: $10/year. Make checks payable to *Homestead Review*.

How to Submit: Submit 3 poems at a time. No previously published poems or simultaneous submissions. No fax, e-mail, or disk submissions. Cover letter is required. "A brief bio should be included in the cover letter." Reads submissions all year. Submit seasonal poems 3 months in advance. Time between acceptance and publication is 2 months. "Manuscripts are read by the staff and discussed. Poems/fiction accepted by majority consensus." Often comments on rejected poems. Guidelines available for SASE. Responds in 2 months. Pays 1 contributor's copy. Acquires one-time rights.

Also Offers: "We accept short fiction, book reviews, and b&w photography/art, and interviews."

Advice: "Poetry is language distilled; do not send unpolished work. Join a workshop group if at all possible."

◯ HORSE LATITUDES PRESS, P.O. Box 294, Rhododendron OR 97049. Established 1982. **Publisher:** Michael P. Jones.

Book/Chapbook Needs: The publisher of Horse Latitudes Press says, "Those which are unique—poetry, short stories, manuscripts, etc.—can find a home with us." Publishes 15 paperbacks, 5 hardbacks, and 25 chapbooks per year. Books are usually 50-125 pgs., 5½ × 8½ or 8½ × 11, offset-printed, perfect-bound, and Velobind, include b&w art/graphics.

How to Submit: Query first, with sample poems ("the more the better") and cover letter with brief bio and publication credits. Accepts previously published poems and simultaneous submissions. Cover letter preferred. Poems are circulated to an editorial board. "They are read by a panel of 3. If we like them, we'll try to find a slot for them in a project." Seldom comments on rejected poems. Responds to queries in 2 weeks. Pays 5 author's copies (out of a press run of 500). Order sample books by writing and requesting a list with prices.

Advice: "We need enough poems to conduct a review of your work, so please send us enough samples."

☑ $ ⊘ HOUGHTON MIFFLIN CO., 222 Berkeley St., Boston MA 02116. Website: www.houghtonmifflinbooks.com. Established 1850.

Book/Chapbook Needs: Houghton Mifflin is a high-prestige trade publisher that puts out both hardcover and paperback books. Has published poetry books by Donald Hall, May Swenson, Rodney Jones, Geoffrey Hill, Galway Kinnell, Thomas Lux, Erica Funkhouser, William Matthews, Margaret Atwood, Linda Gregerson, Mary Oliver, Glyn Maxwell, and Andrew Hudgins.

How to Submit: *Poetry submission is by invitation only.* Currently not seeking new poets. Always sends prepublication galleys. Authors are paid 10% royalties on hardcover books, 6% royalties on paperbacks (minimum), $1,000 advance, and 12 author's copies.

☑ ↯ $ ⊘ ◎ **HOUSE OF ANANSI PRESS (Specialized: regional)**, 895 Don Mills Road, 400-2 Park Centre, Toronto, Ontario M3C 1W3 Canada. (416)445-3333. Fax: (416)445-5967. E-mail: info@anansi.ca. Website: www.anansi.ca (includes submission guidelines, front list, back list, contact info). Established 1967. **Publisher:** Martha Sharpe. **Assistant Editor:** Adrienne Leahey.
Book/Chapbook Needs: House of Anansi publishes literary fiction and poetry by Canadian writers. "We seek to balance the list between well-known and emerging writers, with an interest in writing by Canadians of all backgrounds. We publish Canadian poetry only, and poets must have a substantial publication record—if not in books, then definitely in journals and magazines of repute. No children's poetry and no poetry by previously unpublished poets." Has published *Power Politics* by Margaret Atwood and *Ruin & Beauty* by Patricia Young. As a sample they selected these lines from "The Ecstasy of Skeptics" in the book *The Ecstasy of Skeptics* by Steven Heighton:

> *This tongue/is a moment of moistened dust, it must learn/to turn the grit of old books/into hydrogen, and burn/The dust of the muscles must burn/down the blood-fuse of the sinews, . . .*

Their books are generally 96-144 pgs., trade paperback with French sleeves, a matte finish cover and full-color cover art.
How to Submit: Canadian poets should query first with 10 sample poems (typed double-spaced) and a cover letter with brief bio and publication credits. Accepts previously published poems and simultaneous submissions. Poems are circulated to an editorial board. Often comments on rejected poems. Responds to queries within 3 months, to mss (if invited) within 4 months. Pays 8-10% royalties, a $750 advance and 10 author's copies (out of a press run of 1,000).
Advice: To learn more about their titles, check their website or write to the press directly for a catalog. "We strongly advise poets to build up a publishing résumé by submitting poems to reputable magazines and journals. This indicates three important things to us. One, that he or she is becoming a part of the Canadian poetry community; two, that he or she is building up a readership through magazine subscribers; and three, it establishes credibility in his or her work. There is a great deal of competition for only three or four spots on our list each year—which always includes works by poets we have previously published."

🌐 ◪ ◔ **HQ POETRY MAGAZINE (THE HAIKU QUARTERLY); THE DAY DREAM PRESS**, 39 Exmouth St., Kingshill, Swindon, Wiltshire SN1 3PU England. Phone: 01793-523927. Website: www.nogs.dial.pi pex.com/HQ.htm (includes poetry from past and present issues). Established 1990. **Editor:** Kevin Bailey.
Magazine Needs: *HQ Poetry Magazine* is "a platform from which new and established poets can speak and/ or experiment with new forms and ideas." Wants "any poetry of good quality." Accepts poetry written by children. Has published poetry by Peter Redgrove, Alan Brownjohn, James Kirkup, and Cid Corman. *HQ Poetry magazine* is 48-64 pgs., A5, perfect-bound with art, ads, and reviews. Accepts about 5% of poetry received. Press run is 500-600 for 500 subscribers of which 30 are libraries. Subscription: £10 UK, £13 foreign. Sample: £2.70.
How to Submit: No previously published poems or simultaneous submissions. Cover letter and SASE (or SAE and IRCs) required. Time between acceptance and publication is 3-6 months. Often comments on rejected poems. Responds "as time allows." Pays 1 copy. Reviews books of poetry in about 1,000 words, single book format. Poets may send books for review consideration.
Also Offers: Sponsors "Piccadilly Poets" in London, and "Live Poet's Society" based in Bath, Somerset England.

◖ **HUBBUB; VI GALE AWARD; ADRIENNE LEE AWARD**, 5344 SE 38th Ave., Portland OR 97202. Established 1983. **Editors:** L. Steinman and J. Shugrue.
Magazine Needs: Appearing once/year (in August/September), *Hubbub* is designed "to feature a multitude of voices from interesting contemporary American poets. We look for poems that are well-crafted, with something to say. We have no single style, subject, or length requirement and, in particular, will consider long poems. No light verse." Has published poetry by Madeline DeFrees, Cecil Giscombe, Carolyn Kizer, Primus St. John, Shara McCallum, and Alice Fulton. *Hubbub* is 60-70 pgs., 5½ × 8½, offset-printed and perfect-bound, cover art only, usually no ads. Receives about 1,200 submissions/year, accepts up to 2%. Press run is 350 for 100 subscribers of which 12 are libraries, about 150 shelf sales. Subscription: $5/year. Sample: $3.35 (back issues), $5 (current issue).
How to Submit: Submit 3-6 typed poems (no more than 6) with SASE. No previously published poems or simultaneous submissions. Guidelines available for SASE. Responds in 4 months. Pays 2 copies. Acquires first North American serial rights. "We review two to four poetry books/year in short (three-page) reviews; all reviews are solicited. We do, however, list books received/recommended." Send books for consideration.
Also Offers: Outside judges choose poems from each volume for two awards: Vi Gale Award ($100) and Adrienne Lee Award ($50). There are no special submission procedures or entry fees involved.

$ ⃝ **THE HUDSON REVIEW**, 684 Park Ave., New York NY 10021. **Contact:** Emily D. Montjoy.
 ● Work published in this review has been included in the 1997 and 1998 volumes of *The Best American Poetry.*
Magazine Needs: *The Hudson Review* is a high-quality, flat-spined quarterly of 176 pgs., considered one of the most prestigious and influential journals in the nation. Editors welcome all styles and forms. However, competition is extraordinarily keen, especially since poems compete with prose. Subscription: $28 ($32 foreign)/ 1 year, institutions $34 ($38 foreign)/1 year. Sample: $9.
How to Submit: Nonsubscribers may submit poems between April 1 and July 31 only. "Simultaneous submissions are returned unread." Responds in 2 months. Always sends prepublication galleys. Pays 2 copies and 50¢/ line.

✓ ⃝ ◎ **HUNGER MAGAZINE; HUNGER PRESS (Specialized: form, translations)**, P.O. Box 505, Rosendale NY 12472. (845)658-9273. E-mail: hungermag@aol.com. Website: www.Hungermagazine.com. Established 1997. **Publisher/Editor:** J.J. Blickstein.
Magazine Needs: *Hunger Magazine* is an international zine based in the Hudson Valley and appears 2 times/ year. "*Hunger* publishes mostly poetry but will accept some short fiction, essays, translations, cover art drawings, and book reviews. Although there are no school/stylistic limitations, our main focus is on language-image experimentation with an edge. We publish no names for prestige and most of our issues are dedicated to emerging talent. Well known poets do grace our pages to illuminate possibilities. No dead kitty elegies; Beat impersonators; Hallmark cards; 'I'm not sure if I can write poems'. All rhymers better be very, very good. We have published poetry by Amiri Baraka, Paul Celan, Robert Kelly, Ray Gonzalez, Anne Waldman, Janine Pommy Vega, Antonin Artaud, and Clayton Eshleman." *Hunger* is 85-100 pgs., magazine-sized, saddle-stapled with glossy full-color card cover, uses original artworks and drawings. Accepts about 10% of submissions. Press run is 250-500. Single issue: $7, $10 (foreign); subscription: $14, $20 foreign. Back issue: $7. Chapbooks: $5. Make checks payable to Hunger Magazine & Press.
How to Submit: Submit 3-10 poems at a time. Accepts simultaneous submissions, if notified; no previously published poems. Accepts e-mail submissions and queries; include text in body of message "unless otherwise requested." Brief cover letter with SASE preferred. "Manuscripts without SASEs will be recycled. Please proof your work and clearly indicate stanza breaks." Time between acceptance and publication is 1-6 months. Full critiques available for $1 per page/poem (10 pages maximum). Guidelines available for SASE. Responds in 3 months. Sends prepublication galleys upon request. Pays 1-5 copies depending on amount of work published. "If invited to be a featured poet we pay a small honorarium and copies." Acquires first North American serial rights.
Also Offers: Sponsors a chapbook contest. Entry: $10. Accepting original mss, 25 pgs. maximum between January and May only. Chapbooks are 5½×8½, photocopied, saddle-stapled with full color card stock cover. Pays $25-50 and at least 20% of press run. Guidelines available for SASE or by e-mail.
Advice: "Read, read, read."

⃞ ⃝ ⃝ **THE HUNTED NEWS; THE SUBOURBON PRESS**, P.O. Box 9101, Warwick RI 02889. (401)826-7307. Established 1990. **Editor:** Mike Wood.
Magazine Needs: *The Hunted News* is an annual "designed to find good writers and give them one more outlet to get their voices heard." As for poetry, the editor says, "The poems that need to be written are those that need to be read." Does not want to see "the poetry that does not need to be written or which is written only to get a reaction or congratulate the poet." Accepts poetry written by children. *The Hunted News* is 25-30 pgs., 8½×11, photocopied, unstapled. "I receive over 200 poems per month and accept perhaps 10%." Press run is 150-200. Sample free with SASE.
How to Submit: Accepts previously published poems; no simultaneous submissions. Always comments on rejected poems. Publishes theme issues. Guidelines and a list of upcoming themes available for SASE. Responds in 1 month. Pays 3-5 copies, more on request. "I review current chapbooks and other magazines and do other random reviews of books, music, etc. Word count varies."
Advice: "I receive mostly beginner's poetry that attempts to be too philosophical, without much experience to back up statements, or self-impressed 'radical' poems by poets who assume that I will publish them because they are beyond criticism. I would like poets to send work whose point lies in language and economy and in experience, not in trite final lines, or worse, in the arrogant cover letter."

⃞ ◎ **HURRICANE ALICE (Specialized: feminist)**, Dept. of English, Rhode Island College, Providence RI 02908. (401)456-8377. Fax: (401)456-8379. E-mail: mreddy@ric.edu. Established 1983. **Submissions Manager:** Joan Dagle.

THE BOOK PUBLISHERS INDEX, located at the back of this book, lists those publishers who consider full-length book collections.

Magazine Needs: *Hurricane Alice* is a quarterly feminist review. Poems should be "infused by a feminist sensibility (whether the poet is female or male)." Accepts poetry written by children. Has published poetry by Alice Walker, Ellen Bass, Patricia Hampl, Nellie Wong, Edith Kur, and Kristen Williams. As a sample the editor selected these lines from "The Gift" by Marjorie Roemer:

> *I would give you my right hand/My mother always said/Too many times/As if she really wanted to/As if she needed to.*

Hurricane Alice is a "12-page folio with plenty of graphics." Press run is 1,000, of which 450 are subscriptions, about 50 go to libraries, and about 100 shelf sales. Subscription: $12 (or $10 low-income). Sample: $2.50.

How to Submit: Submit no more than 3 poems at a time. Considers simultaneous submissions. Time between acceptance and publication is up to 6 months. Publishes theme issues. Upcoming themes available for SASE. Responds in 1 year. Pays 6 copies. Reviews books of poetry.

IBBETSON ST. PRESS, 33 Ibbetson St., Somerville MA 02143. (617)628-2313. E-mail: Dianner@iop ener.net. Website: http://homepage.mac.com/rconte (includes contact info and samples). Established 1999. **Editor:** Doug Holder. **Co-Editors:** Dianne Robitaille and Marc Widershien.

Magazine Needs: Appearing 4 times/year, *Ibbetson St. Press* is "a poetry magazine that wants 'down to earth' poetry that is well-written; has clean, crisp images; with a sense of irony and humor. We want mostly free verse, but open to rhyme. No maudlin, trite, overly political, vulgar for vulgar's sake, poetry that tells but doesn't show." Has published poetry by Dianne Robitaille, Robert K. Johnson, Joanne Holdridge, Don Divecchio, and Ed Chaberek. As a sample the editors selected these lines by Ed Chaberek:

> *It's down a curving brick/stair, where the cool beer-stale/air gets thick; it's past/the piss-stains and the cracks/left by some wise guy's skull.*

Ibbetson St. Press is 30 pgs., 8½×11, desktop-published with plastic binding and cream cover stock cover, includes b&w prints and classified ads. Receives about 300 poems/year, accepts up to 40%. Press run is 100 for 20 subscribers. Single copy: $4; subscription: $7. Sample: $2. Make checks payable to Ibbetson St. Press.

How to Submit: Submit 3-5 poems at a time. Accepts previously published poems and simultaneous submissions. Cover letter required. Time between acceptance and publication is up to 5 months. Poems are circulated to an editorial board. "Three editors comment on submissions." Guidelines available by SASE. Responds in 2 weeks. Pays 1 copy. Acquires one-time rights. Reviews books and chapbooks of poetry and other magazines in 250-500 words. Poets may send books for review consideration.

Book/Chapbook Needs & How to Submit: "We also publish chapbooks by newer, little exposed poets of promise. In some cases we pay for all expenses, in others the poet covers publishing expenses." Has published *ADD* by Marc Widershien and *Inaccessibility of the Creator* by Jack Powers. Chapbooks are usually 20-30 pgs., 8½×11, photocopied with plastic binding, white coverstock cover, includes b&w prints. "Send complete manuscript for consideration, at least 20-30 poems with or without artwork." Responds to queries in 1 month. Pays 50 author's copies (out of a press run of 100). Order sample books or chapbooks by sending $4.

Advice: "Please buy a copy of the magazine you submit to—support the small press."

$ THE ICONOCLAST, 1675 Amazon Rd., Mohegan Lake NY 10547-1804. Established 1992. **Editor/Publisher:** Phil Wagner.

Magazine Needs: *The Iconoclast* is a general interest literary publication appearing 7 times/year. Wants "poems that have something to say—the more levels the better. Nothing sentimental, obscure, or self-absorbed. Try for originality; if not in thought, then expression. No greeting card verse or noble religious sentiments. Look for the unusual in the usual, parallels in opposites, the capturing of what is unique or often unnoticed in an ordinary, or extraordinary moment. What makes us human—and the resultant glories and agonies. Our poetry is accessible to a thoughtful reading public." Has published poetry by Anselm Brocki, Nelson James Dunford, and George Held. As a sample, the editor selected these lines from "Letter to Ranek Living in Doubt, Nebraska" by Frederick Zydek:

> *The wind is waiting for the words you will/send into its seasons. Let them be as flocks/of geese. Let them waddle on the ground/when they must, soar like swans when they can.*

The Iconoclast is 40-64 pgs., journal-sized, photo offset on #45 white wove paper, with b&w art, graphics, photos and ads. Receives about 2,000 poems/year, accepts up to 3%. Press run is 500-2,000 for 335 subscribers. Subscription: $15 for 8 issues. Double issue: $3. Sample: $2.50.

How to Submit: Submit 3-4 poems at a time. Accepts previously published poems and simultaneous submissions, when noted, though they say "previously published submissions must be demonstrably better than others." Time between acceptance and publication is 4-12 months. Sometimes comments on rejected poems. Responds in 1 month. Pays 1 copy per published page or poem, 40% discount on extras, and $2-5 per poem for first North American rights on acceptance. Otherwise, acquires one-time rights. Reviews books of poetry in 250 words, single format.

IDIOM 23; BAUHINIA LITERARY AWARDS, Regional Centre of the Arts, Central Queensland University, Rockhampton 4702 Australia. Phone: (07)49309511. Website: www.ejournalism.au.com/idiom. Established 1988. **Editor:** Liz Huf.

Magazine Needs: "Named for the Tropic of Capricorn, *Idiom 23* is dedicated to developing the literary arts throughout the Central Queensland region. Submissions of original short stories, poems, and articles, b&w

drawings and photographs are welcomed by the editorial collective. *Idiom 23* is not limited to a particular viewpoint but on the contrary hopes to encourage and publish a broad spectrum of writing. The collective seeks out creative work from community groups with as varied backgrounds as possible. The magazine hopes to reflect and contest idiomatic fictional representations of marginalised or non-privileged positions and values." Accepts poetry written by children 10 years of age and older. *Idiom 23*, published annually, is about 140 pgs., 7¾×10, professionally printed and perfect-bound with 4-color cover, includes photos and line drawings, ads appear on last few pages. Single copy: $10.

How to Submit: Accepts previously published poems. Accepts e-mail submissions. Cover letter required. Poems are circulated to an editorial board. Reviews books of poetry in single book format. Poets may send books for review consideration to Liz Huf.

Also Offers: Sponsors the Bauhinia Literary Awards for short stories and poetry. For poetry, offers the Open Award $200 and Student Award $100. Submit up to 3 poems, 50 lines in length. Entry fee: $5. Postmark deadline: June 29. Winning entries will be announced at the MultiCultural Day on August 12. Outstanding entries will be published in the *Morning Bulletin*. Send SAE and IRC for complete details.

☑ ◎ **THE IDIOT (Specialized: humor)**, P.O. Box 69163, Los Angeles CA 90069. E-mail: slavinginsrilanka@hotmail.com. Established 1993. **President for Life:** Sam Hayes.

Magazine Needs: *The Idiot* is a biannual humor magazine. "We mostly use fiction, articles, and cartoons, but will use anything funny, including poetry. Nothing pretentious. We are a magazine of dark comedy. Death, dismemberment, and the Talmud are all subjects of comedy. Nothing is sacred. But it needs to be funny, which brings us to . . . Laughs! I don't want whimsical, I don't want amusing, I don't want some fanciful anecdote about childhood. I mean belly laughs, laughing out loud, fall on the floor funny. If it's cute, give it to your sweetheart or your puppy dog. Length doesn't matter, but most comedy is like soup. It's an appetizer, not a meal. Short is often better. Bizarre, obscure, and/or literary references are often appreciated but not necessary." Has published poetry by Brian Campbell, Joe Deasy, Jessica Kochis, and Dave Littman. As a sample the editor selected these lines from "Red Squared" by Dave 'Kaptain Kommunist' Littman:

> *Jump in the slammer/With a sickle and hammer,/start up a clamor—/Ra! Ra! Ra!*

The Idiot is 48 pgs., 5½×8½, professionally printed and staple-bound with glossy cover. Receives about 100 submissions/year, accepts up to 3-4. Press run is 300. Single copy: $4. Sample: $5.

How to Submit: Accepts previously published poems and simultaneous submissions. Accepts e-mail submissions if included in body of message. Seldom comments on rejected poems. Responds in 6 months. Pays 1 copy. Acquires one-time rights.

Advice: "If it ain't funny, don't send it! I mean it! We're talkin' belly laughs, damn it!"

◐ **ILLUMINATIONS, AN INTERNATIONAL MAGAZINE OF CONTEMPORARY WRITING**, % Dept. of English, College of Charleston, 66 George St., Charleston SC 29424-0001. (843)953-1993. Fax: (843)953-3180. E-mail: lewiss@cofc.edu. Website: www.cofc.edu/~lewis/illums.html. Established 1982. **Editor:** Simon Lewis.

Magazine Needs: *Illuminations* is published annually "to provide a forum for new writers alongside already established ones." Open as to form and style. Do not want to see anything "bland or formally clunky." Has published poetry by Peter Porter, Michael Hamburger, Geri Doran and Anne Born. As a sample the editor selected these lines from "For Stephen Spender" by Louis Bourne:

> *Old romantic, imprisoned in your speech,/Steeled in a world racing to its doom,/We've taken in the news from your compass-points./You've given us some signs that still can teach.*

Illuminations is 64-88 pgs., 8×5, offset-printed and perfect-bound with 2-color card cover, includes photos and engravings. Receives about 1,500 poems/year, accepts up to 5%. Press run is 400. Subscription: $20 for 3 issues. Sample: $10.

How to Submit: Submit up to 6 poems at a time. No previously published poems or simultaneous submissions. Accepts e-mail and fax submissions. Brief cover letter preferred. Time between acceptance and publication "depends on when received. Can be up to a year." Publishes theme issues occasionally; "issue 16 [2000] was a Vietnamese special; issue 17 [2001] focuses on Cuban and Latin American writing." Guidelines available by e-mail. Responds within 2 months. Pays 2 copies plus one subsequent issue. Acquires all rights. Returns rights on request.

◫ ◐ **ILLYA'S HONEY**, P.O. Box 225435, Dallas TX 75222-5435. Website: www.dallaspoets.org (includes current information on submissions, contests, and readings, biographies of members, link to *Illya's Honey* with sample poems). Established 1994 by Stephen W. Brodie, acquired by The Dallas Poets Community in January, 1998. **Managing Editor:** Ann Howells.

Magazine Needs: *Illya's Honey* is a quarterly journal of poetry and micro fiction. "All subjects and styles are welcome, but we admit a fondness for free verse. Poems may be of any length but should be accessible, thought-provoking, fresh, and should exhibit technical skill. Every poem is read by at least three members of our editorial staff, all of whom are poets. No didactic or overly religious verse, please." Recently published poetry by Lyn Lifshin, Joe Ahern, Seamus Murphy, Robert Eastwood, and Brandon Brown. *Illya's Honey* is 40 pgs., digest-sized, and saddle-stapled, glossy card cover with b&w photographs. Receives about 2,000 poems/year, accepts about 5-10%. Press run is 250 for 80 subscribers, 50 shelf sales. Subscription: $18. Sample: $5.

How to Submit: Submit 3-5 poems at a time. No previously published poems or simultaneous submissions. Cover letter preferred. Include short biography. Occasionally comments on rejected poems. Guidelines available for SASE or through website e-mail link. Responds in up to 5 months. Pays 1 contributor's copy.
Also Offers: See listing for The Dallas Poets Community under Organizations.

☑ $ ◐ ◎ **IMAGE: A JOURNAL OF ARTS & RELIGION (Specialized: religious)**, 3307 3rd Ave. W., Seattle WA 98119. E-mail: image@imagejournal.org. Website: www.imagejournal.org (includes sample material from all back issues; info on The Glen Workshop, an annual writers workshop sponsored by *Image*; guidelines; *Image* Artist of the Month; as well as information on advertising; back issue and subscription ordering). Established 1989. **Publisher:** Gregory Wolfe.
Magazine Needs: *Image*, published quarterly, "explores and illustrates the relationship between faith and art through world-class fiction, poetry, essays, visual art, and other arts." Wants "poems that grapple with religious faith, usually Judeo-Christian." Has published poetry by Philip Levine, Scott Cairns, Annie Dillard, Mary Oliver, Mark Jarman, and Kathleen Norris. As a sample we selected these lines from "Receptionism" by Marjorie Maddox:

> Does our kneeling/bring him down/again, from the wood,/unhinge his stone,/trumpet for ourselves/our
> catalytic salvation?

Image is 136 pgs., 10×7, perfect-bound, acid free paper with glossy 4-color cover, averages 10 pgs. of 4-color art/issue (including cover), ads. Receives about 800 poems/year, accepts up to 2%. Has 4,700 subscribers of which 100 are libraries. Subscription: $30. Sample. $10.
How to Submit: Submit up to 4 poems at a time. No previously published poems. Cover letter preferred. No e-mail submissions. Time between acceptance and publication is 1 year. Guidelines available on website. Responds in 3 months. Always sends prepublication galleys. Pays 4 copies plus $2/line ($150 maximum). Acquires first North American serial rights. Reviews books of poetry in 1,000-1,300 words, single or multi-book format. Poets may send books for review consideration.

▣ ◑ **IMAGES INSCRIPT**, P.O. Box 44894, Columbus OH 43204-4894. E-mail: submit@ImagesInscript. com or comments@ImagesInscript.com. Website: www.ImagesInscript.com (includes writer's guidelines, names of staff, best poem, best short story, subscription information, latest edition, and back issues). Established 1998. **Publisher:** Roger Baker II. **Editor:** Carla Radwanski.
Magazine Needs: *Images Inscript* is a bimonthly online publication "to provide a showcase of poetry and short stories. *Images Inscript* is a place for writers to submit and comment on poetry and interact with other writers. We want to see creative well-written poetry that showcases the writer's talent. We do not want to see excessive use of 'adult' language." Has published poetry by Julie Rogers, Maryann Hazen, David Hunter Sutherland, and Cindy O'Connor. As a sample they selected these lines from "Breasts" by Maryann Hazen:

> A man will glance at breasts before/he decides whether or not/to continue on up to the face./Will it be
> worth the effort? Or not?

Receives about 600 poems/year, accepts up to 10%.
How to Submit: Submit 1 poem at a time. Line length for poetry is 60 maximum. Accepts previously published poems and simultaneous submissions. Accepts e-mail submissions. Cover letter preferred. "Electronic submissions preferred, subject line should read 'Images Inscript submission' with name, address and age included in 75 word maximum biography—sent to submit@imagesinscript.com." Time between acceptance and publication is up to 6 weeks. Seldom comments on rejected poems. Guidelines available by e-mail or on website. Responds in 5 weeks. Sometimes sends prepublication galleys. Acquires "right to appear in *Images Inscript* and *Images Inscript: Reflections*."
Also Offers: Sponsors a yearly contest where the best poetry and short story writers are awarded $50.
Advice: "With the gradual acceptance of online publishings, more quality Internet publications will be established to compete with the traditional print industry."

☑ ⊕ ◑ ◎ **IMAGO: NEW WRITING (Specialized: regional)**, School of Media & Journalism, Q.U.T., GPO Box 2434, Brisbane 4001 Queensland, Australia. E-mail: imago@qut.edu.au. Website: www.imago. qut.edu.au (includes current and past issues, links, and sample articles). Established 1988. **Managing Editor:** Helen Horton.
Magazine Needs: *Imago*, appears three times/year, publishing "the best Australian writing, placing particular emphasis on Queensland writing and culture, but also welcoming submissions from overseas. Poems preferably short—up to about 50 lines, most from 12-25 lines. Our main criterion is good writing." Has published poetry by Tom Shapcott, Peter Rose, and Philip Hammial. *Imago* is 160 pgs., digest-sized, with glossy card cover. Accepts about 10% of 500 poems from about 150 writers. Press run is 750 for 300 subscribers of which 36 are libraries. Subscription: $39.40 in Australia; $A42.70, overseas (airmail). Sample: $A10.50.
How to Submit: Submit 6-8 poems at a time. Accepts e-mail submissions. "A brief biography (few lines) of the writer accompanying the submission saves time if the work is accepted. We have a Notes on Contributors column." Responds in 6 months. Never sends prepublication galleys "unless specifically asked for by contributor." Pays 1 contributor's copy. Acquires first Australian serial rights. Reviews books of poetry in 600 words— "usually commissioned. Unsolicited reviews would have to be of books relevant to *Imago* (Queensland or writing)." Send books for review consideration.

$ 🔘 **IN THE FAMILY (Specialized: gay/lesbian/bisexual)**, P.O. Box 5387, Takoma Park MD 20913. (301)270-4771. E-mail: lmarkowitz@aol.com. Website: www.inthefamily.com. Established 1995. **Fiction Editor:** Helena Lipstadt.

Magazine Needs: *In the Family* is a quarterly "therapy magazine exploring clinical issues for queer people and their families." We're open to anything but it must refer to a gay/lesbian/bisexual theme. No long autobiography. No limericks." Has published poetry by Benjamin Goldberg, Susan Spilecki, Alden Reimonenq, and Susan Landers. As a sample the editor selected these lines from "Haiku" by Shoshana T. Daniel:

> Smoke and whiskey sours,/whatever it takes to make/your mouth taste like hers./Idiot splashes/grown
> dumb with her absence. Blue/pool no orange koi./Thumbs shoved under rind/you split the orange.
> Your hands/sting me everywhere

In the Family is 32 pgs., 8½×11, offset-printed and saddle-stapled with 2-color cover, includes art and ads. Receives about 50 poems/year, accepts approximately 10%. Press run is 10,000 for 8,000 subscribers of which 10% are libraries, 5% shelf sales; 10% distributed free to direct mail promos. Subscription: $22. Sample: $5.50. Make checks payable to ITF.

How to Submit: Submit 5 poems at a time. Accepts simultaneous submissions; no previously published poems. No e-mail submissions. Cover letter required. Time between acceptance and publication is up to 2 months. Poems are circulated to an editorial board. "Fiction editor makes recommendations." Publishes theme issues. Responds in 2 months. Always sends prepublication galleys. Pays $35 and 5 copies. Acquires first rights. Reviews books of poetry in 1,000 words, multi-book format. Poets may send books for review consideration to attn. Reviews.

◣ 🔘 **IN THE GROVE (Specialized: regional)**, P.O. Box 16195, Fresno CA 93755. (559)442-4600, ext. 8105. Fax: (559)265-5756. E-mail: inthegrove@rocketmail.com. Website: www.freeyellow.com/members7/lherrick/inthegrove.html (includes writer's guidelines, submission deadlines, samples from recent issues). Established 1996. **Editor:** Lee Herrick. **Poetry Editor:** Optimism One.

Magazine Needs: *In the Grove* appears 2 times/year and publishes "short fiction, essays and poetry by new and established writers born or currently living in the Central Valley and throughout California." Wants "poetry of all forms and subject matter. We seek the originality, distinct voice and craftsmanship of a poem. No greeting card verse or forced rhyme. Be fresh. Take a risk." Has published poetry by Gillian Wegener, Andres Montoya, Loren Palsgaard, Michael Roberts, Amy Uyematsu, and Renny Christopher. *In The Grove* is 80-100 pgs., 5½×8½, photocopied and perfect-bound with heavy card stock cover, 4-5 pgs. of ads. Receives about 500 poems/year, accepts up to 10%. Press run is 150 for 50 subscribers, 75 shelf sales; 25 distributed free to contributors, colleagues. Subscription: $16. Sample: $6.

How to Submit: Submit 3-5 poems at a time. Accepts previously published poems and simultaneous submissions. Cover letter preferred. Time between acceptance and publication is up to 6 months. "Poetry editor reads all submissions and makes recommendations to editor, who makes final decisions." Seldom comments on rejected poems. Guidelines available for SASE or on website. Responds in 3 months. Pays 1 copy. Acquires first or one-time rights. Rights return to poets upon publication.

◪ $ ▢ ◯ 🔘 **IN 2 PRINT MAGAZINE (Specialized: children/teen/young adult, national)**, P.O. Box 102, Port Colborne, Ontario L3K 5V7 Canada. (905)834-1539. Fax: (905)834-1540. Established 1994. **Publisher:** Jean Baird.

Magazine Needs: *In 2 Print*, a national forum for emerging artists, is a quarterly, award-winning, glossy color magazine which promotes and showcases the creativity of young Canadians: the magazine publishes original works by young adults ages 12-21 including poetry, short stories, plays, painting, photography, computer art, and cartoons. *In 2 Print* also publishes an eclectic array of interviews and reviews of books, music and theatre." Open to all forms and styles. "No mush, no gush! No class assignments or work produced to please teachers." As a sample we selected these lines from "angelfish" by Amelinda Berube:

> i cast my nets every day,/trying so desperately to capture you,/stars in a winter sky//ever remote, you
> are also fire/in a hearth i left so long ago to stand/here where everything is gray as ice/sea sky ropes/
> whose bite leaves blood on my hands//every day my nets come back/empty—

In 2 Print is 48 pgs., magazine-sized, web offset-printed and saddle-stapled with color paper cover, includes b&w and color photos and artwork, ads. Receives about 5,000 poems/year, accepts 1%. Press run is 25,000 for 9,000 subscribers of which 300 are libraries, 2,000 shelf sales; balance distributed free to qualified lists. Sample: $4.

How to Submit: Submit 4 poems at a time with SASE (or SAE and IRC). No previously published poems or simultaneous submissions. Cover letter with brief bio required. "Submissions can only be made by the author, artist or photographer. While the magazine is delighted by all the teachers and educators who encourage their students to submit work for publication, the submission must be made by the creator(s) of the work. Bulk submissions from teachers or schools are not accepted." Time between acceptance and publication is 4 months. Poems are circulated to an editorial board. "Peer review to short-list. Short-list goes to six of Canada's finest poets—including Susan Musgrave, Christopher Dewdney, Lorna Crozier, Patrick Lane—for final recommendation." Guidelines available for SASE (or SAE and IRC). Responds in 4 months. Sometimes sends prepublication galleys. Pays $50. Acquires first rights. Reviews books and chapbooks of poetry and other magazines in 500-1,200 words. Poets may send books for review consideration.

Advice: "Great writers are great readers."

◧ $▯ ◯ ◎ **INDIAN HERITAGE PUBLISHING; INDIAN HERITAGE COUNCIL QUAR-TERLY; NATIVE AMERICAN POETRY ANTHOLOGY (Specialized: ethnic/nationality, spiritual-ity/inspirational)**; P.O. Box 2302, Morristown TN 37816. (423)581-4448. Established 1986. **CEO:** Louis Hoo-ban.

● Indian Heritage Publishing's Native American Poetry Anthology won first prize in literature from the Green Corn Festival 1999 and received the Best Native Literature Award at the National Pow-Wow.

Magazine Needs: *Indian Heritage Council Quarterly* devotes 1 issue to poetry with a Native American theme. Wants "any type of poetry relating to Native Americans, their beliefs, or Mother Earth." Does not want "dog-gerel." Has published poetry by Running Buffalo and Angela Evening Star Dempsey. As a sample the editor selected these lines from his poem "the Pow-wow":

> *And listen! You can/hear it/as the drum beats tune in/to the heartbeats of/Mother Earth/giving birth*
> *to life/in the center/of the Dance Circle.*

Indian Heritage Council Quarterly is 6 pgs., 5½×8½ (8½×11 folded sheet with 5½×8½ insert), photocopied. Receives about 300 poems/year, accepts up to 30%. Press run and number of subscribers vary, 50% shelf sales; 50 distributed free to Indian reservations. Subscription: $10. Sample: "negotiable." Make checks payable to Indian Heritage Council.

How to Submit: Submit up to 3 poems at a time. Accepts previously published poems (author must own rights only) and simultaneous submissions. Cover letter required. Time between acceptance and publication is 3 months to 1 year. Poems are circulated to an editorial board. "Our editorial board decides on all publications." Seldom comments on rejected poems. Charges criticism fees "depending on negotiations." Publishes theme issues. Guidelines and upcoming themes available for SASE. Responds within 3 weeks. Pay is negotiable. Acquires one-time rights. Staff reviews books or chapbooks of poetry or other magazines. Send books for review consideration.

Book/Chapbook Needs & How to Submit: Indian Heritage Publishing publishes chapbooks of Native American themes and/or Native American poets. Format of chapbooks varies. Query first, with a few sample poems and cover letter with brief bio and publication credits. Responds to queries within 3 weeks, varies for mss. Pays 33-50% royalties. Offers subsidy arrangements that vary by negotiations, number of poems, etc. For sample chapbooks, write to the above address.

Also Offers: Sponsors a contest for their anthology, "if approved by our editorial board. Submissions are on an individual basis—always provide a SASE."

Advice: "Any poet interested in Native American themes or any Native American poet expressing poems of any theme is invited to submit to us. If you have strong feelings for Native American people, culture, religion, or ideas, express yourself through your poetry and let us help you get published."

◧ $◯◎ **INDIANA REVIEW**, Ballantine Hall 465, 1020 E. Kirkwood Ave., Bloomington IN 47405-7103. (812)855-3439. E-mail: inreview@indiana.edu. Website: www.indiana.edu/~inreview/ir.html (includes writer's guidelines, current news, sample poetry, and fiction from past and current issues). Established 1982. **Contact:** poetry editor.

● Poetry published in *Indiana Review* has been selected for inclusion in the 1996, 1997, and 2001 volumes of *The Best American Poetry.*

Magazine Needs: *Indiana Review* is a biannual of prose, poetry, and visual art. "We look for an intelligent sense of form and language, and admire poems of risk, ambition and scope. We'll consider all types of poems— free verse, traditional, experimental. Reading a sample issue is the best way to determine if *Indiana Review* is a potential home for your work. Any subject matter is acceptable if it is written well." Has published poetry by Philip Levine, Sherman Alexie, Campbell McGrath, Charles Simic, Mark Strand, and Alberto Rios. The magazine uses about 40-60 pgs. of poetry in each issue (6×9, flat-spined, 160 pages, color matte cover, professional printing). Receives about 5,000 submissions/year, accepts up to 60. The magazine has 500 subscriptions. Sample: $8.

How to Submit: Submit 4-6 poems at a time, do not send more than 10 pages of poetry per submission. No electronic submissions. Pays $5/page ($10 minimum/poem), plus 2 copies and remainder of year's subscription. Acquires first North American serial rights only. "We try to respond to manuscripts in 2-3 months. Reading time is often slower during summer and holiday months." Brief book reviews are also featured. Send books for review consideration. Holds yearly contests. Guidelines available for SASE.

$◯◉ **INDIGENOUS FICTION**, P.O. Box 2078, Redmond WA 98073-2078. E-mail: deckr@earthlink. net (no e-mail submissions). Established 1998. **Publisher/Managing Editor:** Sherry Decker.

Magazine Needs: *Indigenous Fiction* appears 3 times/year and publishes "literary mainstream and genre fiction and poetry to provide a market for accomplished writers of 'unusual' or cross-genre fiction and poetry. We prefer poems that tell at least a story or part of a story; usually serious poems but have accepted two amusing 'spoof' type submissions. We do not want poetry that is so obscure and 'high literary' no one except the poet knows what it's about. No 'love' poems, unless they're odd or unusual." Has published poetry by Errol Miller, James S. Dorr, Margo Solod, and Holly Day. As a sample the publisher selected these lines from "The Chupacabra" by Scott Francis:

> *Water-light and/rippling up the wet tangled nighttime branches, we clothe each other in our/naked*
> *cries. Hooking scarlets from the dark, our horns become the fires of our/cries. We're gorging on blood-*
> *thick petals. It has begun to rain, each drop's/touch flaming us more and more alive. Alone, we coo,*
> *far from the/stench called men*

Indigenous Fiction is 64-84 pgs., digest-sized, digitally published and saddle-stapled with full color 30-60 lb. cover, includes drawings/watercolors/ink. Receives about 650 poems/year, accepts 9-12 poems/year. Subscription: $15. Sample: $6. Make checks payable to Sherry Decker.
How to Submit: Submit 5 poems at a time. Line length for poetry is 30 maximum. Accepts simultaneous submissions. Cover letter preferred. "Listing credits will get my attention but will not sell me your work. Do not explain your work in your cover letter. Even though we accept previously published work, we accept very little of it. Must be truly exceptional." Time between acceptance and publication is up to 6 months. Seldom comments on rejected poems. Guidelines available for SASE or by e-mail. Responds in 2 weeks. Pays $5/poem and a contributor's copy (author's choice). Acquires first North American serial rights or one-time rights for reprints. "All contributors are qualified to purchase copies at the discounted rate, as explained in contract."

THE INKWELL., % C.S. McDowell, 24031 Griffin House Lane, Katy TX 77493. Fax: (281)347-2568. Established 1999. **Contact:** C.S. McDowell.
Magazine Needs: *The Inkwell.* appears 1-2 times/year and "strives to discover and expose talent, new or old. A love of literature and a firm belief that practically nothing is stronger than the written word is my mantra. All forms and styles of poetry are accepted, from 1-100 lines. Also, prose and short fiction up to 1,000 words are included in each issue. The editor tends to stray towards well-worded, sound poetry with rhyme included, whether irregular or traditional. Free verse, haiku and all other forms are of equal importance, though. No forced rhyme. 'The leaves rustling as the dawn breaks over the horizon . . .', etc., tend to sour one's stomach. Nature and the environment are of significance to us all, but when writing on the subject try not to neuter it. In fact, save your stamp. Erotica may be stimulating, but please, all you ex-porn stars, exhibit your wares elsewhere." The journal is 15-30 pgs., digest-sized, high-quality print and saddle-stapled with cardstock or heavy weight paper cover with b&w illustration. "I receive 300-500 pieces/year of which 15-25% are accepted." Press run is 250-1,000. Sample: $1.50 (for postage).
How to Submit: Submit up to 5 pieces at a time (poetry, prose and short fiction). Line length for poetry is 1 minimum, 100 maximum. Accepts previously published poems and simultaneous submissions. Cover letter "not mandatory, but appreciated. If cover letter is included, please send a few words about oneself, life, interests (brief bio)." Include SASE for reply or return. **Reading fees:** $1/piece. Make checks payable to C.S. McDowell. Time between acceptance and publication varies. "The author should be notified of their acceptance within 4 months. Actual publication may be in up to 12 months." Always comments on rejected poems. "As a writer, I have often tired of the dreaded Form Letter Rejection. As an editor, I will always personally respond to my rejections with criticism and reason. The aforementioned reading fee covers any criticism fee there may be." Guidelines available for SASE. Responds in up to 4 months. Pays 1 copy. If response is large enough, a "Best of Each Issue" cash prize (around $10-25) may be awarded. All rights remain with the author. Byline given.
Advice: "Strong and striking poetry should be more than the goal of each poet. It should be the daily constitutional. A fine poet spills their words out on a regular basis. Remember the power of your written word; nothing in this world is of more strengh."

INKWELL MAGAZINE, Manhattanville College, Box 1379, 2900 Purchase St., Purchase NY 10577. (914)323-7239. Website: www.inkwell@manhattanville.com. Established 1995. **Editor:** Melissa Lugo.
Magazine Needs: "*Inkwell* is published biannually by Manhattanville College and publishes work by new poets and writers side by side with known poets and writers." Open to all types. Has published poetry by April Bernard, Dan Masterson, and Christian Nagle. As a sample the editor selected these lines from "The Rain-Soaked Trail" by Ace Boggess:

> *The raining season kept to the clock this year./A new father tells me he misses the sun/waiting at the*
> *nearest horizon on the outskirts of May./Thai afternoons give forests their definition,/that mythical*
> *gray text one often only reads about/in books. Such clear boundaries.*

Inkwell is 6¾ × 10, professionally printed and perfect-bound, with 4-color card cover, includes b&w art and photos. Press run is 1,000. Single copy: $10.50. Sample: $7.
How to Submit: Submit 5 poems at a time. Accepts simultaneous submissions. Accepts disk submissions, if accompanied by hard copy. Cover letter required. Name, address, phone, title, word count on cover page. SASE required for response. Reads submissions August through January. Time between acceptance and publication is up to 4 months. Poems are circulated to an editorial board. "The editor and selected readers read all manuscripts." Seldom comments on rejected poems. Guidelines available for SASE. Responds in 3 months. Pays 2 copies. Acquires first North American serial rights.
Also Offers: Sponsors annual poetry competition with $1,000 Grand Prize and 2 Honorable Mentions ($50) plus publication. Entry fee: $10 for first poem, $5 each additional. Postmark deadline in October. Send SASE for complete contest guidelines.
Advice: "*Inkwell* is dedicated to discovering new talent and to encouraging and bringing the talents of working writers and artists to a wider audience. The magazine encourages diverse voices and has an open submission policy for both art and literature."

insider report

The consolation of poetry

David Wojahn

David Wojahn may have grown up fairly conventionally in the Midwest, but his poetry is far reaching and explorative as it delves into human experience, both personal and public. Since winning the Yale Series of Younger Poets competition at 28 for his first book, *Icehouse Lights* (Yale University Press, 1982), Wojahn has published five collections of poetry through the University of Pittsburgh Press: *Glassworks* (1987), *Mystery Train* (1990), *Late Empire* (1994), *The Falling Hour* (1997), and *Spirit Cabinet* (2002). His book of essays, *Strange Good Fortune* (University of Arkansas Press) appeared in 2001. Wojahn teaches at Indiana University, where he directs the Program in Creative Writing, and in the MFA in Writing Program of Vermont College.

To a child in Minnesota during the 50s and 60s, poetry seemed "as far away as New Zealand." This changed in high school when Wojahn discovered the poetry of Ohio native James Wright. "The wonderful thing about Wright is that he wrote about the landscape I knew," says Wojahn, "like driving down Highway 55 to Rochester, Minnesota. The only thing I'd ever read that came from this landscape was Sinclair Lewis's *Main Street*, which more or less portrayed the Midwest as one of the darkest, dreariest, and most depressing places on the planet. So Wright helped me understand that poetry wasn't far away from me, but something that could be given a local habitation and a name, as Wordsworth says in the preface to *Lyrical Ballads*."

Wojahn's "local" habitation is populated by all sorts of people and events that often emerge from his eclectic reading habits. "Biography, scientific studies, history—the more you can take from all matter of sources, whether it's arcane or trash, the better it is for your poetry. You want to read with an omnivorous mind, because anything can potentially spark some connection to what you're writing about. Over the years, the things I read become more and more a part of my self-portrait."

While Wojahn's poetry engages contemporary culture, there is often a formal aspect to it, although not one that operates within a rigid set of parameters. "I try to do some things that will distort the possibilities of traditional prosody, simply because that makes it more interesting or more like speech. I like to tweak the forms a little bit. We don't necessarily profit when we're beholden merely to a sonnet's structural precepts; but I *am* interested in what a compressed poem in fourteen lines can do and what it can work against.

"Besides, most writers tend to be rather obsessive about their subject matter. There are four or five holes in our lives which each of us thinks has to be filled again and again and again. Most writers never change their basic vocabulary of subjects, but they will often radically change their approach to that subject matter. The more formal variety you have as you try to create a number of responses toward your subjects, the better and the more interesting the results can be. More and more I don't think about what I have to say in the poem as much as how to say it, and traditional prosodies provide a real opportunity for this to take place on a different sort of grid or template."

Wojahn traces his love of language back to three formative sources: rock-and-roll, the Episcopal church, and the cold war. "Listening to Top 40 radio in the mid 60s, I saw that rock-and-roll could not only convey a message but also an incredible degree of excitement for speech and utterance, the way that words could be played within musical notation and on the page. But there was also *The Book of Common Prayer* in that beautiful, exquisite Tudor and Elizabethan language that's English at its most profound and strange. Some of those passages were terrifying for a kid of five or six years. Think of the communion service and the lines 'we are so unworthy through our manifold sins and wickedness as to gather the crumbs from under Thy table.' However, the extraordinary periodic sentences I was exposed to early on gave me the sense that there was a language different from the one I spoke at home that was profound and unsettling and intensely 'other' for me."

Growing up in the shadow of a mushroom cloud was also a formative experience, not so much in a linguistic sense, as with music and liturgical language, but in a psychological sense. "I think I was nine years old during the Cuban missile crisis," Wojahn remembers. "We had 'duck and cover' drills in school and were taught that the world could end at any moment. We were told to place our heads under our desks to protect ourselves from the flash, but we all knew that wouldn't help."

"God of Journeys and Secret Tidings"

Eurydice is better off in hell.
Isn't that what Rilke says? Hermes
guides her back, unspools black gauze
to shroud her anew, and Death again is merciful,
is grave goods, unguents, clove-scented fluids,
his lips pressed deftly on nipple and thigh,
the god's long fingers, his laving hands, their slide
as they stroke and roil and spool her shroud.

And how, indeed, could such beauty be borne,
except by the shoulders of a god? Here on the dome
of hell it rains, and you are six months dead.
The answering machine tonight spins down—
February's messages, a half year unerased,
another mistake to tally. And on them is your voice.

(From *The Falling Hour*, University of Pittsburgh Press, 1997; used by permission)

Wojahn views poetry as a source of consolation. "Very few of us live lives with consoling forces in them. Tragedy is endemic to our condition, I think, and very few of us are lucky in life, or lucky in love. Many of us make so many compromises in order to arrive at some level of material comfort that we forget the value of a rich inner life, even if that richness comes largely from understanding the meaning of sorrow. Most of my poems are about conditions of grieving, of inconsolability, but I don't think I have any larger percentage of sorrow in my life than most of the other people I know, probably less. But I also grew up in a very taciturn culture in the Midwest, with a father who was severely, and clinically, depressed for most of his life; in a culture where opportunities to put your feelings into words were for the most part unavailable. The joys of poetry are for me very straightforward: poetry's an opportunity to turn an emotion into language and to try to make that language eloquent or beautiful or musical, and especially truthful.

"The consolation of poetry comes just from its making. In Auden's 'In Memory of W. B. Yeats' he writes that poetry makes nothing happen. People always remember that remark, but not the next line where Auden tells us that poetry 'survives in the valley of its making.' The valley of making is, I think, the place where all poets want to dwell. That doesn't mean it's a lush green Shangri-La, but it is a place where we are able to sing our necessary songs."

—*Michelle Moore*

INSECTS ARE PEOPLE TWO; PUFF 'N' STUFF PRODUCTIONS (Specialized), P.O. Box 146486, Chicago IL 60614-6400. Established 1989. **Publisher:** H.R. Felgenhauer.
Magazine Needs: *Insects Are People Two* is an infrequent publication focusing solely on "poems about insects doing people things and people doing insect things." Accepts poetry written by children. Has published poetry by Bruce Boston, Steve Sneyd, Paul Wieneman, and Lyn Lifshin. As a sample the editor selected these lines from an untitled poem by Steve Sneyd:

> Is time/of insect moon—/Dry chittering comes down/to us promising hour soon we/too saved

Insects Are People Two is 8½×11, with card cover, b&w art and graphics. Press run is 1,000. Sample: $6.
How to Submit: Accepts previously published poems and simultaneous submissions. Often comments on rejected poems. Publishes theme issues. Responds "immediately." Pay varies. Send books for review consideration.
Book/Chapbook Needs & How to Submit: Puff 'N' Stuff Productions publishes 1 chapbook/year. Responds to queries and mss in 10 days. Pay is negotiable.
Advice: "Hit me with your best shot. Never give up—editors have tunnel-vision. The *BEST* mags you almost *NEVER* even hear about. Don't believe reviews. Write for yourself. Prepare for failure, not success."

INTERBANG; BERTYE PRESS, INC., P.O. Box 1574, Venice CA 90294. (310)450-6372. E-mail: heather@interbang.net. Website: www.interbang.net. Established 1995. **Editor:** Heather Hoffman.
Magazine Needs: *Interbang*, published quarterly, is "Dedicated to Perfection in the Art of Writing." Wants "enticing poetry of any length on any subject. Although we do not have strict standards regarding substance, texture, or structure, your craft, in tandem with your subject matter, should elicit a strong response in the reader: love, hate, shock, sorrow, revulsion, you name it. Write your name, address, and phone number on each page of your submission." Has published poetry by Rob Lipton, John Thomas, Linda Platt Mintz, David Centorbi, and Jessica Pompei. As a sample we selected these lines from "Malted Moksha in 4C41.17" by John Marvin:

> Louie Louie please say why/you are so exciting for the FBI/Stephen King and the Kingsmen/bravissimo
> bravishiva/with the clarity of a despot/the geometry of the universe

Interbang is 30 pgs., 7½×8½, offset-printed and saddle-stapled with colored card stock cover, includes line art and photos. Receives about 500 poems/year, accepts up to 50%. Press run is 2,000 for 100 subscribers of which 10 are libraries, 20 shelf sales; 40 distributed free to other magazines, the rest distributed free at coffeehouses and bookstores in L.A. Send two stamps for a free sample copy.
How to Submit: Submit 5-15 poems at a time. Accepts previously published poems and simultaneous submissions. Accepts e-mail submissions; include text in body of message. Comments on rejected poems on request. *Interbang Writer's Guide* available by e-mail or on website. Responds in 6 months. Always sends prepublication galleys. Pays 5 copies. Reviews chapbooks of poetry and other magazines in 350-400 words, single book format. Poets may also send books for review consideration.

THE INTERFACE; BUTTERMILK ART WORKS, % GlassFull Productions, P.O. Box 57129, Philadelphia PA 19111-7129. E-mail: interface@baworks.com. Website: www.baworks.com/Interface. Established 1997. **Publisher:** Earl Weeks. **Art Director:** Willie McCoy.
Magazine Needs: *The INTERFACE* is published quarterly on the Internet. Wants "all kinds of work—romantic, political, social commentary. We want poetry that comes from your heart, that makes tears come to the eye or forces one to want to mobilize the troops. No poems of hate or discrimination." Has published poetry by Mike Emrys, Sheron Regular, Cassandra Norris, and Monique Frederick. As a sample the publisher selected his poem "Love is":

> *Love is forever until death do we part/Love is when we never send arrows through each others hearts/*
> *Love is me snuggled warmly against your breasts./Love is when you can sleep peacefully at rest.*

Receives about 20 poems/year, accepts up to 90%. Publishes 5 poems/issue.

How to Submit: Submit 7 poems at a time. Accepts previously published poems and simultaneous submissions. Accepts e-mail and disk submissions. Cover letter preferred. "We will consider accompanying illustration." Submit seasonal poems 6 months in advance. Time between acceptance and publication is 2 months. Poems are circulated to an editorial board. Occasionally publishes theme issues. Guidelines and upcoming themes available for e-mail or on website. Responds in 3 weeks. Acquires one-time rights. Reviews books and chapbooks of poetry and other magazines. Poets may send books for review consideration.

Also Offers: "We publish poetry, essays, videogame reviews, book reviews, fashion, science fiction, art, and more. We are trying to make *The INTERFACE* a meeting place for idea exchanges. We need your opinions and views, so submit them to us."

INTERIM, Dept. of English Box 5011, University of Nevada—Las Vegas, Las Vegas NV 89154. (702)895-3333. Fax: (702)895-4801. E-mail: keelanc@nevada.edu. **Editor:** Claudia Keelan.
● Member CLMP, New York. Indexed in *Index of American Periodical Verse*.

Magazine Needs: *Interim* is an annual magazine, appearing in December, that publishes poetry, short fiction, essays, and book reviews. "We seek submissions from writers who are testing the boundaries of genre." Has published poetry by Brenda Hillman, Alice Notley, Doug Powell, and Elizabeth Robinson. As a sample the editor selected this poem, "The Paragraph She gives me to Live In" by Martha Ronk:

> *"The paragraph she gives me to live in is I don't know how./Description is a phenomenon of walks as*
> *obvious as rain./All the outcroppings in a brownish moss I can't get over/The undulation of columns*
> *one after another/Through which the distance is an extension of how we think/How someone walks*
> *into the room or sits in a chair./She says again you are where you should have begun./She offers copses*
> *and seclusion./Or you don't listen to what I say how could I foresee/"bitterns crying I the lintels" or*
> *her inner being/whatever insists is what she says I have to do.*

Interim is 100 pgs., 6×9, professionally printed and perfect-bound with coated card cover. Press run is 400. Individual subscription: $12/year, $24/2 years. Single copy: $12.

How to Submit: Submit 3-5 poems at a time, SASE, and brief biographical note. No simultaneous submissions. No fax or e-mail submissions. Reads from September to April so "please do not submit anything during summer months." Responds in 3 months. Pays 2 copies. Acquires first serial rights. Poems may be reprinted elsewhere with a permission line noting publication in *Interim*.

INTERNATIONAL BLACK WRITERS; BLACK WRITER MAGAZINE (Specialized: ethnic), P.O. Box 1030, Chicago IL 60690. (312)458-5745. Established 1970. **President/CEO:** Mable Terrell.

Magazine Needs & How to Submit: *Black Writer* is a "quarterly literary magazine to showcase new writers and poets and provide educational information for writers. Open to all types of poetry." *Black Writer* is 30 pgs., magazine-sized, offset-printed, with glossy cover. Press run is 1,000 for 200 subscribers. Subscription: $19/year. Sample: $1.50. Responds in 10 days, has 1 quarter backlog. Pays 10 contributor's copies.

Book/Chapbook Needs & How to Submit: For chapbook publication (40 pgs.), submit 2 sample poems and cover letter with short bio. Accepts simultaneous submissions. Pays copies. For sample chapbook, send SASE with bookrate postage.

Also Offers: Offers awards of $100, $50, and $25 for the best poems published in the magazine and presents them to winners at annual awards banquet. International Black Writers is open to all writers.

INTERNATIONAL POETRY REVIEW (Specialized: translations), Dept. of Romance Languages, UNC-Greensboro, Greensboro NC 27412-5001. (336)334-5655. Fax: (336)334-5358. E-mail: k_mather @uncg.edu or tokyorse@aol.com. Website: www.uncg.edu/rom/ipr.htm. Established 1975. **Editor:** Kathleen Mather.

Magazine Needs: *International Poetry Review* is a biannual primarily publishing translations of contemporary poetry with corresponding originals (published on facing pages) as well as original poetry in English. Recently published work by Ana Istaru, Alexis Levitin, Coleman Barks, and Fred Chappell. *International Poetry Review* is 100 pgs., 5½×8½, professionally printed and perfect-bound with 2-3 color cover. "We accept 5% of original poetry in English and about 30% of translations submitted." Press run is 500 for 200 subscribers. Subscription: $10/$18/$25 (for one, two and three years respectively) for individuals, $15/$27/$40 for institutions. Sample: $5. Make checks payable to *International Poetry Review*.

How to Submit: Submit no more than 6 pages of poetry. Accepts simultaneous submissions; no previously published poems. Reads submissions between September 1 and April 30. Seldom comments on rejected poems. Publishes theme issues. Guidelines and upcoming themes available for SASE. Responds in up to 6 months. Pays 1 copy. All rights revert to authors and translators. Occasionally reviews books of poetry. Poets may send books for review consideration.

Advice: "We strongly encourage contributors to subscribe. We prefer poetry in English to have an international or cross-cultural theme."

⊕ ◐ **INTERPRETER'S HOUSE; BEDFORD OPEN POETRY COMPETITION**, 10 Farrell Rd., Wootton, Bedfordshire MK43 9DU United Kingdom. Established 1996. **Contact:** Merryn Williams.
Magazine Needs: *Interpreter's House* appears 3 times/year (February, June, October) and publishes short stories and poetry. Wants "good poetry (and short stories), not too long. No Christmas-card verse or incomprehensible poetry." Has published poetry by Dannie Abse, Tony Curtis, Pauline Stainer, Alan Brownjohn, Peter Redgrove, and R.S. Thomas. As a sample the editor selected these lines from "Metrics" by R.S. Thomas:

> There should be no/introit into a poem.//The listener should come/to and realize/verse has been going
> on/for some time. . . .

Interpreter's House is 74 pgs., A5 with attractive cover design. Receives about 1,000 poems/year, accepts up to 5%. Press run is 300 for 200 subscribers. Subscription: £10.00. Sample: £3 plus 44 p.
How to Submit: Submit 5 poems at a time. No previously published poems or simultaneous submissions. Cover letter preferred. Time between acceptance and publication is 2 weeks to 8 months. Often comments on rejected poems. Guidelines available for SASE or SAE and IRC. Responds "fast." Pays 1 copy.
Also Offers: Sponsors the Bedford Open Poetry Competition. Send SAE and IRC for details.

☑ ◎ **INTRO (Specialized: students)**, AWP, Tallwood House, MS 1E3, George Mason University, Fairfax VA 22030. Website: http://awpwriter.org. Established 1970. **Publications Manager:** Katherine Perry.
• See Associated Writing Programs in the Organizations section of this book.
Magazine Needs & How to Submit: Students in college writing programs belonging to AWP may submit to this consortium of magazines publishing student poetry, fiction, and creative nonfiction. Open as to the type of poetry submitted except they do not want "non-literary, haiku, etc." "In our history, we've introduced Dara Wier, Carolyn Forché, Greg Pope, Norman Dubie, and others." All work must be submitted by the writing program. Programs nominate *Intro* works in the fall. Ask the director of your writing program for more information.

◐ **INVERTED-A, INC.; INVERTED-A HORN**, 900 Monarch Way, Northport AL 35473-2663. Established 1977. **Editors:** Amnon Katz and Aya Katz.
Magazine Needs: *Inverted-A Horn* is an irregular periodical. Does not want to see anything "modern, formless, existentialist." As a sample the editor selected these lines by Delta Zahner:

> Within a boarded-up arcade/Which some dead mason's trowel laid,/The voice of law and order said:/
> "Just run. We want to shoot you dead."

Inverted-A Horn is usually 9 pages, magazine-sized, offset-printed; press run is 300.
How to Submit: Accepts simultaneous submissions. Responds to queries in 1 month, to mss in 4 months. Pays 1 copy plus a 40% discount on additional copies. Samples: SASE with postage for 2 ounces (subject to availability).
Book/Chapbook Needs & How to Submit: Inverted-A Inc. is a very small press that evolved from publishing technical manuals for other products. "Our interests center on freedom, justice, and honor." Publishes 1 chapbook/year.
Advice: "I strongly recommend that would be contributors avail themselves of this opportunity to explore what we are looking for. Most of the submissions we receive do not come close."

⊕ 🗓 ◐ **IOTA**, 67 Hady Crescent, Chesterfield, Derbyshire S41 0EB Great Britain. Phone 01246-276532. Established 1988. **Editor:** David Holliday.
Magazine Needs: *Iota* is a quarterly wanting "any style and subject; no specific limitations as to length, though, obviously, the shorter a poem is, the easier it is to get it in, which means that poems over 40 lines can still get in if they seem good enough. No concrete poetry (no facilities) or self-indulgent logorrhea." Accepts poetry written by children (but they have to take their chance with the rest). Has published poetry by James Brockway, David H.W. Grubb, Harland Ristau, Daphne Schiller, and Peter Stavropoulo. As a sample the editor selected this poem, "Advice" by Richard Cooper:

> "Whether beggar/or billionaire//the most valuable thing/you own is this moment/—use it wisely"/he
> wrote,//then made a sandwich/and watched TV

Iota is 48 pgs., professionally printed and saddle-stapled with light colored card cover. Publishes about 300 of 6,000 poems received. Their press run is 500 with 250 subscribers of which 6 are libraries. Subscription: $20 (£10). Sample: $2 (£1) "but sometimes sent free."
How to Submit: Submit 4-6 poems at a time. Prefers name and address on each poem, typed, "but provided it's legible, am happy to accept anything." Accepts simultaneous submissions, but previously published poems "only if outstanding." First response in 3 weeks (unless production of the next issue takes precedence) but final acceptance/rejection may take up to a year. Pays 2 copies. Acquires first British serial rights only. Editor usually comments on rejected poems, "but detailed comment only when time allows and the poem warrants it." Reviews books of poetry in about 200 words, single or multi-book format. Poets may send books for review consideration.
Advice: "I am after crafted verse that says something; self-indulgent word-spinning is out. All editors have their blind spots; the only advice I can offer a beginning poet is to find a sympathetic editor (and you will only do that by seeing their magazines) and not to be discouraged by initial lack of success. Keep plugging!"

$ THE IOWA REVIEW; THE TIM McGINNIS AWARD; THE IOWA AWARD, 308 EPB, University of Iowa, Iowa City IA 52242. (319)335-0462. E-mail: iowa-review@uiowa.edu. Website: www.iowa. edu/~iareview (includes excerpts, guidelines, table of contents, etc.). Established 1970. **Editor:** David Hamilton. **Contact:** poetry editor.

• Poetry published in *The Iowa Review* has also been included in the 1995, 1996, and 1997 volumes of *The Best American Poetry* and the *Pushcart Prize* anthology for 1995.

Magazine Needs: *The Iowa Review* appears 3 times/year and publishes fiction, poetry, essays, reviews, interviews, and autobiographical sketches. "We simply look for poems that at the time we read and choose, we admire. No specifications as to form, length, style, subject matter, or purpose. There are around 40 pgs. of poetry in each issue and we like to give several pages to a single poet. Though we print work from established writers, we're always delighted when we discover new talent." *The Iowa Review* is 200 pgs., professionally printed, flat-spined. Receives about 5,000 submissions/year, accepts up to 100. Press run is 2,900 with 1,000 subscribers of which about half are libraries; 1,500 distributed to stores. Subscription: $18. Sample: $6.

How to Submit: Submit 3-6 poems at a time. No e-mail submissions. Cover letter (with title of work and genre) and SASE required. Reads submissions "from Labor Day to St. Patrick's Day or until we fill our next volume year's issues." Time between acceptance and publication is "around a year. Sometimes people hit at the right time and come out in a few months." Occasionally comments on rejected poems or offers suggestions on accepted poems. Responds in up to 4 months. Pays $1/line, 2-3 copies and a 1-year subscription. Acquires first North American serial rights, non-exclusive anthology rights, and non-exclusive electronic rights.

Also Offers: Sponsors the Tim McGinnis Award. "The award, in the amount of $500, is given irregularly to authors of work with a light or humorous touch. We have no separate category of submissions to be considered alone for this award. Instead, any essay, story, or poem we publish which is charged with a distinctly comic vision will automatically come under consideration for the McGinnis Award." Also offers Iowa Award for the single work judged best of the year. Outside judge, any genre.

N ISLES OF MIST REVIEW; ISLES OF MIST PRESS, 425 N. Barbara St., Azusa CA 91702. (661)969-2668. Established 1999. **Editor:** Jessica Lee.

Magazine Needs: *Isles of Mist Review* appears quarterly. Wants "all types of poetry." As a sample the editor selected the following lines:

> Stars burn, then fall, from the sky./Hopeless realm of night./Falling, falling to the realm of green,/Into our fading sight . . .

Isles of Mist Review is 24 pgs., digest-sized, side-stapled, card stock cover, includes ads. Publishes 24 poems/issue. Press run is 100. Single copy: $7; subscription: $160. Sample: $7. Make checks payable to *Isles of Mist Review*.

How to Submit: Submit 3 poems at a time. Accepts previously published poems and simultaneous submissions. Accepts e-mail and disk submissions. Cover letter is preferred. "Please enclose a SASE." Reads submissions September 1 through June 30. Time between acceptance and publication is 6 weeks. Seldom comments on rejections. Occasionally publishes theme issues. Upcoming themes and guidelines available for SASE. Responds in 6 weeks. Always sends prepublication galleys. Pays 1 contributor's copy. Acquires first North American serial rights. Reviews books and chapbooks of poetry and other magazines. Poets may send books for review consideration to the editor.

Book/Chapbook Needs & How to Submit: Isles of Mist Press publishes novels, poetry, and short stories. "A special series of chapbooks is intended as a resource for our subscribers." Publishes 2 paperback and 8 chapbooks/year. Books/chapbooks are usually 20-30 pgs., 5×8, comb, side-stapled, or book binding, paperback cover with art/graphics. "We welcome both samples and complete manuscripts." Responds to queries in 6 weeks. Pays 1 author's copy (out of a press run of 100). Order sample books/chapbooks by sending $21.

Also Offers: "We give the Isles of Mist Award each year for high achievement in literature."

$ ITALICA PRESS (Specialized: bilingual/foreign language, translations), 595 Main St., #605, New York NY 10044-0047. (212)935-4230. Fax: (212)838-7812. E-mail: inquiries@italicapress.com. Website: www.italicapress.com. Established 1985. **Publishers:** Eileen Gardiner and Ronald G. Musto.

Book/Chapbook Needs: Italica is a small press publisher of English translations of Italian works in Smyth-sewn paperbacks, averaging 175 pgs. Has published *Guido Cavalcanti, The Complete Poems*, a dual-language (English/Italian) book with English translation and introduction by Marc Cirigliano, and *Women Poets of the Italian Renaissance*, a dual-language anthology, edited by Laura Anna Stortoni, translated by Laura Anna Stortoni and Mary Prentice Lillie.

How to Submit: Query with 10 sample translations of medieval and Renaissance Italian poets. Include cover letter, bio, and list of publications. Accepts simultaneous submissions, but translation should not be "totally"

MARKETS THAT WERE listed in the 2001 edition of *Poet's Market* but do not appear this year are listed in the General Index with a notation explaining why they were omitted.

previously published. No e-mail or fax submissions. Responds to queries in 3 weeks, to mss in 3 months. Always sends prepublication galleys. Pays 7-15% royalties plus 10 author's copies. Acquires English language rights. Sometimes comments on rejected poems.

N ☺ IVY: A QUEER POETS JOURNAL (Specialized: gay/lesbian), (formerly *Backspace*), 25 Riverside Ave., Gloucester MA 01930-2552. E-mail: IVY_ZINE@gay.com or IVYgpj@aol.com. **Publisher:** Kim Smith.
Magazine Needs: *Ivy*, published 3 times/year, is a collection of queer poetry, provides a forum for gay/lesbian poets to share their work with their peers." Prefers gay and lesbian themes. *Ivy* is digest-sized, b&w/color, and saddle-stapled. Single copy: $8; subscription: $27/4 issues. Sample: $3. Make checks payable to Kim Smith.
How to Submit: Submit up to 10 poems no longer than 30 lines, double-spaced. Accepts simultaneous submissions; no previously published poems. Accepts e-mail (in attached file) and disk submissions. Disk submissions must be on 3.5 floppy of Zip disk in QuarkXpress or MSWord; must also be accompanied by hard copy. Include SASE if you want submission returned. Cover letter with brief bio (no more than 30 words) required. Guidelines available for SASE. Responds immediately. Pays 1 contributor's copy.

N ◑ JAHBONE PRESS, 1201 Larrabee St., #207, Los Angeles CA 90069. (714)997-6609. Website: www.chapman.edu/comm/english/jahbone/index.html. Established 1991. **Publisher:** Martin Nakell.
Book/Chapbook Needs & How to Submit: Jahbone Press publishes experimental fiction and poetry. Wants to see innovative poetry, not traditional poetry. Recently published poetry by Pascuale Verdicchio, Leland Hickman, and William Crandall. Publishes a variable number of titles/year. All are perfect-bound paperbacks. Books usually have a variable number of pgs., offset-printed, perfect-bound with graphics. Query first, with a few sample poems and cover letter with brief bio and publication credits. Accepts simultaneous submissions. No e-mail or disk submissions. Responds to queries and mss in 2 months. Pays 20 author's copies (out of a press run of 1,000). Order sample books "through Small Press Distributors."

$ ☺ JAPANOPHILE (Specialized: form, ethnic), P.O. Box 7977, Ann Arbor MI 48107. (734)930-1553. E-mail: japanophile@aol.com. Website: www.japanophile.com (includes guidelines, sample material, information on the magazine and brief blurbs on the editors). Established 1974. **Editor:** Susan Aitken. **Assistant Editors:** Madeleine Vala, Jason Bredle.
Magazine Needs: *Japanophile* is a literary biannual, appearing in summer and winter, about Japanese culture (not just in Japan). Issues include articles, photos, art, a short story, and poetry. Wants haiku or other Japanese forms ("they need not be about Japanese culture") or any form if the subject is about Japan, Japanese culture, or American-Japanese relations. (Note: Karate and ikebana in the US are examples of Japanese culture.) Has published poetry by Renee Leopold, Nancy Corson Carter, Jean Jorgensen, Mimi Walter Hinman, and reprints of Basho. As a sample the editor selected this haiku (poet unidentified):
> *first snowstorm/our old cat rediscovers/the warm airduct*
There are 10-15 pgs. of poetry in each issue (digest sized, about 58 pgs., saddle-stapled). Press run is 800 with 200 subscriptions of which 30 are libraries. Receives about 500 submissions/year, accepts about 70, has a 2-month backlog. Sample: $7.
How to Submit: Summer is the best time to submit. Accepts e-mail and fax submissions. Cover letter required; include brief bio and credits if any. Guidelines and upcoming themes are available for SASE or by e-mail. Responds in 2 months. Pays $3 for haiku and up to $15 for longer poems. Poets may send books for review consideration.
Book/Chapbook Needs & How to Submit: Also publishes books under the Japanophile imprint, but so far only one has been of poetry. Query with samples and cover letter (about 1 pg.) giving publishing credits, bio.

N ◯ ◑ JEOPARDY MAGAZINE, 132 College Hall, Bellingham WA 98225. (360)650-3118. E-mail: jeopardy@cc.wwu.edu. Website: http://jeopardy.wwu.edu (includes current issue, contests, guidelines, all info about magazine). Established 1965. **Editor-in-Chief:** Carter Hasegawa. **Poetry Editor:** David McIvor.
Magazine Needs: *Jeopardy Magazine* appears annually. Wants originality, command of vocabulary, interesting perspectives, creativity. Recently published poetry by Galway Kinnell, James Bertolino, Knute Skinner, and Omar S. Castañeda. *Jeopardy Magazine* is 80-150 pgs., digest-sized, press-printed, book binding, color, hard stock cover, with photo, drawings, paintings, prints. Receives about 100 poems/year, accepts about 15-20%. Press run is 1,500 for 20 subscribers of which 20 are libraries; distributed free to students and community. Sample: $5. Make checks payable to *Jeopardy*.
How to Submit: Submit 6 poems at a time. Line length for poetry is 10 pgs. maximum. Accepts simultaneous submissions; no previously published poems. Accepts disk submissions; no e-mail submissions. Cover letter is required. Include SASE. Reads submissions January 1-May 15. Time between acceptance and publication is 3 months. Poems are circulated to an editorial board. "Assistant editors read, the head editors make decision." Never comments on rejected poems. Occasionally publishes theme issues. Upcoming themes and guidelines are available for SASE. Responds in 3 months. Pays 2 contributor's copies. Acquires one-time rights.

☑ ◯ ◑ ☺ JEWEL AMONG JEWELS ADOPTION NETWORK, INC.; JEWEL AMONG JEWELS ADOPTION NEWS (Specialized: adoption), P.O. Box 502065, Indianapolis IN 46256. (317)849-

5651. Fax: (317)915-8636. E-mail: mail@adoptionjewels.org. Website: www.adoptionjewels.org (includes history of organization, past issues of newsletters, writer's guidelines, services offered). Established 1994. **Editor:** Sherrie Eldridge.

Magazine Needs: *Jewel Among Jewels* is published "to celebrate the sovereignty of God through adoption, to educate about the realities of relinquishment, and to help each person touched by adoption to embrace God's opinion of them—a jewel among jewels." Wants "adoption-related poetry, showing the perspectives of adoptees, birth parents, and adoptive parents. We also look for a biblical perspective. No work unrelated to adoption." *Jewel Among Jewels* is a newsletter with 2-color cover, includes art/graphics. Receives about 25 poems/year, accepts about 10%. Press run is 2,000 for 1,600; distributed free to anyone who requests. Subscription: $15 suggested donation. Make checks payable to Jajani.

How to Submit: Line length for poetry is 10 minimum, 15 maximum. Accepts only e-mail and disk submissions. Cover letter preferred. Reads submissions quarterly—January, April, June, September. Poems are circulated to an editorial board. "Poems go to our advisory board of adoption professionals prior to publication." Guidelines available on website. Responds in 1 month. Acquires first or one-time rights.

☑ ♻ ⊘ ◎ JEWISH CURRENTS (Specialized: themes, religious; ethnic/nationality), 22 E. 17th St., Suite 601, New York NY 10003-1919. (212)924-5740. Fax: (212)414-2227. Established 1946.

Magazine Needs: *Jewish Currents* is a magazine appearing 11 times/year that publishes articles, reviews, fiction, and poetry pertaining to Jewish subjects or presenting a Jewish point of view on an issue of interest, including translations from the Yiddish and Hebrew (original texts should be submitted with translations). Accepts poetry written by children. *Jewish Currents* is 36 pgs., 8½×11, offset, saddle-stapled. Press run is 2,500 for 2,100 subscribers of which about 10% are libraries. Subscription: $30/year. Sample: $3.

How to Submit: Submit 1 poem at a time, typed, double-spaced, with SASE. Include brief bio. No previously published poems or simultaneous submissions. Accepts fax submissions. Cover letter required. Publishes theme issues. Upcoming themes include November: Jewish Book Month; December: Hanuka; February: Black History Month; March: Jewish Music Season, Purim, International Women's Day; April: Holocaust Resistance, Passover; May: Israel; July/August: Soviet Jewish History. Deadlines for themes are 6 months in advance. Time between acceptance and publication is 2 years. Seldom comments on rejected poems. Responds in up to 1 year. Always sends prepublication galleys. Pays 6 copies plus 1-year subscription. Reviews books of poetry.

$ ◎ JEWISH WOMEN'S LITERARY ANNUAL; JEWISH WOMEN'S RESOURCE CENTER (Specialized: ethnic, women), 820 Second Ave., New York NY 10017. (212)751-9223. Fax: (212)935-3523. Established 1994. **Editor:** Dr. Henny Wenkart.

Magazine Needs: *Jewish Women's Literary Annual* appears annually in April and publishes poetry and fiction by Jewish women. Wants "poems by Jewish women on any topic, but of the highest literary quality." Has published poetry by Alicia Ostriker, Savina Teubal, Grace Herman, Enid Dame, Marge Piercy, and Lesléa Newman. As a sample the editor selected these lines from "If It Comes" by Helen Papell:

> The glacier melting upstream/insists its right to tumble live rock/and drown them somewhere.//I ran
> from someone whose needs/were the same. Now/I wait upon this beach.

Jewish Women's Literary Annual is 160 pgs., 6×9, perfect-bound with a laminated card cover, b&w art and photos inside. Receives about 500 poems/year, accepts about 15%. Press run is 1,500 for 480 subscribers. Subscription: $18/3 issues. Sample: $7.50.

How to Submit: No previously published poems. No fax submissions. Poems are circulated to an editorial board. Often comments on rejected poems. Responds in up to 5 months. Pays 3 copies plus a small honorarium. Rights remain with the poet.

Book/Chapbook Needs & How to Submit: The Jewish Women's Resource Center holds a monthly workshop, sponsors occasional readings, and also publishes a few books of poetry. "We select only 1 or 2 manuscripts/year out of about 20 submitted. But although authors then receive editing help and publicity, they bear the cost of production. Members of the workshop we conduct and poets published in our annual receive first attention."

Advice: "It would be helpful, but not essential, if poets would send for a sample copy of our annual before submitting."

⚑ ◯ ⊘ JONES AV.; OEL PRESS, 88 Dagmar Ave., Toronto, Ontario M4M 1W1 Canada. (416)461-8739. E-mail: oel@interlog.com. Website: www.interbg.com/~oel. Established 1994. **Editor/Publisher:** Paul Schwartz.

Magazine Needs: *Jones Av.* is published quarterly and contains "poems from the lyric to the ash can; starting poets and award winners." Wants poems "up to 30 lines mostly, concise in thought and image. Prose poems sometimes. Rhymed poetry is very difficult to do well these days, it better be good." Has published poetry by Stan Rogal, Edward Mycue, rob mclennan, and Peter Bakowski. As a sample the editor selected this poem, "the red apple" by Claudia K. Grinnell:

> the red apple/sliced in/two redeems/spilling flesh/surrenders/to fingertips/inviting deep/ascension
> when/halves meet

Jones Av. is 24 pgs., 5½×8½, photocopied and saddle-stapled with card cover, uses b&w graphics. Receives about 300 poems/year, accepts 30-40%. Press run is 100 for 40 subscribers. Subscription: $8. Sample: $2. Make checks payable to Paul Schwartz

How to Submit: Submit 5-8 poems at a time. No previously published poems or simultaneous submissions. Cover letter required. Accepts e-mail and disk submissions. Include e-mail submissions in body of message. Time between acceptance and publication is up to 12 months. Often comments on rejected poems. Publishes theme issues occasionally. "Remember, US stamps cannot be used in Canada." Responds in 3 months. Pays 1 copy. Acquires first rights. Staff reviews books and chapbooks of poetry and other magazines in 50-75 words, multi-book format. Poets may send books for review consideration.

$ ☑ THE JOURNAL, Dept. of English, Ohio State University, 164 W. 17th Ave., Columbus OH 43210. (614)292-4076. Fax: (614)292-7816. E-mail: thejournal05@postbox.acs.ohio-state.edu. website www.cohums.ohio-state.edu/english/journals/the_journal/. Established 1972. **Co-Editors:** Kathy Fagan and Michelle Herman.
Magazine Needs: *The Journal* appears twice yearly with reviews, essays, quality fiction, and poetry. "We're open to all forms; we tend to favor work that gives evidence of a mature and sophisticated sense of the language." Has published poetry by Brigit Kelly, Lucia Perillo, Timothy Liu, and Heather McHugh. *The Journal* is 6×9, professionally printed on heavy stock, 128-144 pgs., of which about 60 in each issue are devoted to poetry. Receives about 4,000 submissions/year, accepts about 200, and have a 3- to 6-month backlog. Press run is 1,900. Subscription: $12. Sample: $7.
How to Submit: No submissions via fax. On occasion editor comments on rejected poems. Pays 2 copies and an honorarium of $25-50 when funds are available. Acquires all rights. Returns rights on publication. Reviews books of poetry.
Advice: "However else poets train or educate themselves, they must do what they can to know our language. Too much of the writing we see indicates poets do not in many cases develop a feel for the possibilities of language, and do not pay attention to craft. Poets should not be in a rush to publish—until they are ready."

◎ JOURNAL OF AFRICAN TRAVEL-WRITING (Specialized), P.O. Box 346, Chapel Hill NC 27514. Website: www.unc.edu/~ottotwo (includes guidelines, poetry, reviews, articles, and interviews). Established 1996. **Contact:** poetry editor.
Magazine Needs: *Journal of African Travel-Writing*, published annually, "presents and explores past and contemporary accounts of African travel." Wants "poetry touching on any aspect of African travel. Translations are also welcome." Published poets include José Craveirinha, Theresa Sengova, Charles Hood, and Sondra Meek. As a sample the editor selected the poem "Traveling" by James R. Lee:

> Thought I caught a comet's tail/The end of a poem/with tom tom beat/Langston Hughes thought about/ In one of his dreamy moments/It flashed through the skies/Of North America/Like searching phrases/ Speaking of ancient rivers/Lifted me to the Rift Valley

Journal of African Travel-Writing is 96 pgs., 7×10, professionally printed, perfect-bound, coated stock cover with cover and illustrative art, ads. Press run is 600. Subscription: $10. Sample: $6.
How to Submit: Submit up to 6 poems at a time. Include SASE. Accepts simultaneous submissions; no previously published poems. Cover letter preferred. Time between acceptance and publication is up to 1 year. "The poetry editor usually makes these selections." Sometimes comments on rejected poems. Guidelines available for SASE or on website. Publishes theme issues. Responds in up to 6 weeks. Always sends prepublication galleys. Pays 5 copies. Acquires first international publication rights. Reviews books, chapbooks or magazines of poetry. Poets may send books for review consideration.

⊕ ◖ ◔ ◎ JOURNAL OF CONTEMPORARY ANGLO-SCANDINAVIAN POETRY; ORIGINAL PLUS PRESS (Specialized: translations), 11 Heatherton Park, Bradford on Tone, Taunton, Somerset TA4 1EU England. Phone: 01823 461725. E-mail: smithsssj@aol.com. Website: http://members.aol.com/smithsssj/index.html. Established 1994. **Contact:** Sam Smith.
Magazine Needs: *Journal of Contemporary Anglo-Scandinavian Poetry*, published biannually, features English poetry or English translations of Scandinavian poems and interviews with Scandinavian poets. Wants "new poetry howsoever it comes, translations from Scandinavian and original English language poems." Does not want "staid, generalized, all form no content." Accepts poetry written by children. Has published poetry by Richard Wonnacott, Tomas Tranströmer, Staffan Söderblom, Olav H. Hauge, and Alexis Lykiard. As a sample the editor selected these lines from "We Too Are Laymen, Said the Waves" by Werner Aspenström, translated by Robin Fulton:

> Two nights in a row setting out from Stavanger/I made my way on foot over the Atlantic/between icebergs and oil-rigs/to the accompaniment/of excited conversations with the waves/who comforted me saying:/"We too are laymen."

Journal of Contemporary Anglo-Scandinavian Poetry is 44 pgs., A4, offset printed, stapled with CS1 cover stock. Receives about 1,000 poems/year, accepts approximately 5%. Press run is 100-150 for 70 subscribers of which 12 are libraries. Single copy: £6. For three issues: £7. Sample: £2 or £3 (sterling). Make checks payable to Sam Smith.
How to Submit: Submit up to 6 poems. Accepts previously published poems and simultaneous submissions. Accepts e-mail submissions but only from outside UK. Cover letter preferred. "Please send hard copy submissions with 2 IRCs." Time between acceptance and publication is 8 months. Often comments on rejected poems. Guidelines available for SASE (or SAE and IRC). Responds in 1 month. Always sends prepublication galleys. Pays 1 contributor's copy.

Also Offers: In 1997, original plus began publishing collections of poetry. Has published books by Don Ammons, Idris Caffrey, and RG Bishop. Send SASE (or SAE and IRC) for details.

JOURNAL OF NEW JERSEY POETS (Specialized: regional), English Dept., County College of Morris, 214 Center Grove Rd., Randolph NJ 07869-2086. (973)328-5471. Fax: (973)328-5425. E-mail: szulauf@ ccm.edu. Website: www.garden.net/users/swaa/JrnlNJPoets.html (includes cover picture of latest issue, names of editors, and links to the editors). Established 1976. **Editor:** Sander Zulauf.

Magazine Needs: This biannual periodical uses poetry from current or former residents of New Jersey. Wants "serious work that is regional in origin but universal in scope." Read the magazine before submitting. Has published poetry by Amiri Baraka, X.J. Kennedy, Brigit Pegeen Kelly, Gerald Stern, Renée and Ted Weiss, and Rachel Hadas. As a sample the editor selected these lines from "How I Learned to Kiss" by Tina Kelley:

> Perhaps each time I took a dare I got imperceptibly better—/the rowboat on the reservoir, the bell
> tower over Old Campus,/the night spent stowed away on top of the Empire State/Building,/abandoned
> fort at Corinth, breakdown lane of I-95,/bathroom on the train to Portland,/dressing room in the
> sporting goods store.

Journal of New Jersey Poets is digest-sized, offset-printed, with an average of 64 pgs. Press run is 900. Subscription: $10/2 issues, $16/4 issues; institutions: $12/2 issues, $20/4 issues; students/senior citizens: $10/4 issues. Sample: $5.

How to Submit: Send up to 3 poems; SASE with sufficient postage for return of mss required. Accepts e-mail and fax submissions. Electronic submissions will not be returned nor acknowledged. Responds in up to 1 year. Time between acceptance and publication is within 1 year. Pays 5 copies and 1-year subscription. Acquires first North American serial rights. Only using solicited reviews. Send books for review consideration.

JOURNAL OF THE AMERICAN MEDICAL ASSOCIATION (JAMA) (Specialized: health concerns, themes), 515 N. State, Chicago IL 60610. Fax: (312)464-5824. E-mail: charlene_breedlove @ama-assn.org. Website: www.jama.org. Established 1883. **Associate Editor:** Charlene Breedlove.

Magazine Needs: *JAMA*, a weekly journal, has a poetry and medicine column and publishes poetry "in some way related to a medical experience, whether from the point-of-view of a health care worker or patient, or simply an observer. No unskilled poetry." Has published poetry by Aimée Grunberger, Floyd Skloot, and Walt McDonald. As a sample the editor selected these lines from "In Remission" by Floyd Skloot:

> This is a spring he never thought to see./Lean dusky Alaskan geese nibbling grass/seed in his field,
> early daffodils, three/fawns moving across his lawn in the last/of a afternoon light, everything he had/
> let go with small ceremonies on dark/September nights has suddenly come back.

JAMA is magazine-sized, flat-spined, with glossy paper cover, has 360,000 subscribers of which 369 are libraries. Accepts about 7% of 750 poems received/year. Subscription: $66. Sample free. "No SASE needed."

How to Submit: Accepts simultaneous submissions, if identified; no previously published poems. "I always appreciate inclusion of a brief cover letter with, at minimum, the author's name and address clearly printed. Mention of other publications and special biographical notes are always of interest." Accepts fax submissions (include in body of message with postal address). "Poems sent via fax will be responded to by postal service." Accepts e-mail submissions; include in body of message. Publishes theme issues. Theme issues include AIDS, violence/human rights, tobacco, medical education, access to care, and end-of-life care. "However, we would rather that poems relate obliquely to the theme." A list of upcoming themes is available on website. Pays 1 contributor's copy, more by request. "We ask for a signed copyright release, but publication elsewhere is always granted free of charge."

JUBILAT, Dept. of English, Bartlett Hall, University of Massachusetts, Amherst MA 01003-0515. (413)577-1064. E-mail: jubilat@english.umass.edu. Website: www. jubilat.org (includes excerpts from current and past issues, guidelines, subscription information). Established 2000. **Managing Editor:** Lisa Olstein.

Magazine Needs: *Jubilat* appears biannually as "a new international poetry journal that bases itself on the notion that, to poetry, everything is relevant. To this end we strive to publish issues with an arresting mix of poetry, prose, art, and interviews." Wants "submissions of poetry, as well as essays and other forms of writing on poetry, poetics, or especially subjects that have nothing to do with 'poetry' but capture a quality of poetic thought. We publish work by new and established writers and strive to publish quality work regardless of school, region, or reputation." Recently published poetry by Caroline Knox, Nathaniel Mackey, Pierre Martory, Mô ng-Lan, Dean Young, and Anne Carson. *Jubilat* is 150 pgs., digest-sized, offset-printed, perfect-bound, 4-color glossy cover, with fine art features. Receives about 2,000 submissions/year, accepts about 3%. Publishes about 20-30 poems/issue. Press run is 2,000 for 1,000 subscribers of which 100 are libraries, 1,000 shelf sales. Single copy: $8; subscription: $14/1 year, $26/2 years, $38/3 years. Sample: $8. Make checks payable to Univeristy of Massachusetts.

How to Submit: Submit 3-5 poems at a time. Accepts simultaneous submissions; no previously published poems. No fax, e-mail, or disk submissions. Cover letter is preferred. "Please look at an issue or our website to get a sense to what we're up to." Reads submissions year round. Time between acceptance and publication varies. Poems are circulated to an editorial board. "*Jubilat* is collectively edited. All submissions are reviewed by at least one, often four editors." Seldom comments on rejected poems. Guidelines available for SASE and on website. Responds in up to 4 months. Always sends prepublication galleys. Acquires first North American serial rights; rights revert to author.

JUNCTION PRESS, P.O. Box 40537, San Diego CA 92164. Established 1991. **Publisher:** Mark Weiss.
Book/Chapbook Needs: Junction Press aims to publish "overlooked non-mainstream poetry." The press publishes 2 paperback books of poetry/year. Wants "modern or postmodern formally innovative work, any form or length. No academic, Iowa school, or formal poetry." Has published poetry by Armand Schwerner, Susie Mee, Richard Elman, José Kozer, and Mervyn Taylor. Books are typically 72-96 pgs., 5½×8½, offset-printed and perfect-bound with coated covers with graphics.
How to Submit: Query first with 10-15 pgs. of poetry and a cover letter (bio unnecessary). Accepts previously published poems; no simultaneous submissions. Often comments on rejected poems. Replies to queries in 6 months, to mss (if invited) "immediately." Pays 100 copies (out of a press run of 1,000).
Advice: "While I don't dismiss the possibility of finding a second Rimbaud, please note that all of my authors have been in their 50s and have written and published for many years."

K.T. PUBLICATIONS; THE THIRD HALF; KITE BOOKS; KITE MODERN POETS; KITE YOUNG WRITERS, 16 Fane Close, Stamford, Lincolnshire PE9 1HG England. Established 1989. **Editor:** Kevin Troop.
Magazine Needs: *The Third Half* is a literary magazine published irregularly. It contains "free-flowing and free-thinking material on most subjects." Accepts poetry written by children. "Open to all ideas and suggestions. No badly written or obscene scribbling." Recently published Hannah Welfare, Michael Newman, Jack Rickand, Helen Heslop, and Margaret Pelling. As a sample we selected this poem, "Without Words," by Isabel Cortan:

> a savage sound,/sharp crack of a man's hand/across a woman's chin//a ritual sound,/her weeping in
> the dark/burying her love

The Third Half is over 100 pgs., A5, neatly printed and perfect-bound with glossy card cover, includes line drawings and occasionally ads. Receives about 3,000 poems/year, accepts about 20%. Press run is 100-500. Single copy: £5.50 in UK. Sample: £10 overseas. Make checks payable to K.T. Publications.
How to Submit: Submit 6 poems at a time. No previously published poems. Cover letter preferred. Time between acceptance and publication "depends on the work and circumstances." Seldom comments on rejected poems. Occasionally publishes theme issues. Responds in 2 weeks. Always sends prepublication galleys. Pays 1-6 contributor's copies. "Copyright belongs to the poets/authors throughout."
Book/Chapbook Needs & How to Submit: Under K.T. Publications and Kite Books, they publish 6 paperbacks and 6 chapbooks/year of poetry, short stories, and books for children—"at as high a standard as humanly possible." Books are usually 50-60 pgs., A5, perfect-bound with glossy cover, and art ("always looking for more.") Query first, with up to 6 sample poems and a cover letter with brief bio and publication credits. "Also include suitable SAE—so that I do not end up paying return postage every time."
Also Offers: Offers a "reading and friendly help service to writers. Costs are reasonable." Write for details. *The Third Half* showcases 2 poets per issue. "Each poet has 24 pages with illustrations."
Advice: "Be patient—and never give up writing."

KAIMANA: LITERARY ARTS HAWAII; HAWAII LITERARY ARTS COUNCIL (Specialized: regional), P.O. Box 11213, Honolulu HI 96828. Established 1974. **Editor:** Tony Quagliano.
- Poets in *Kaimana* have received the Pushcart Prize, the Hawaii Award for Literature, the Stefan Baciu Award, Cades Award, and the John Unterecker Award.

Magazine Needs: *Kaimana*, an annual, is the magazine of the Hawaii Literary Arts Council. Poems with "some Pacific reference are preferred—Asia, Polynesia, Hawaii—but not exclusively." Has published poetry by Howard Nemerov, John Yau, Reuel Denney, Haunani-Kay Trask, Anne Waldman, Joe Balaz, and Susan Schultz. *Kaimana* is 64-76 pgs., 7½×10, saddle-stapled, with high-quality printing. Press run is 1,000 for 600 subscribers of which 200 are libraries. Subscription: $15, includes membership in HLAC. Sample: $10.
How to Submit: Cover letter with submissions preferred. Sometimes comments on rejected poems. Responds with "reasonable dispatch." Pays 2 contributor's copies.
Advice: "Hawaii gets a lot of 'travelling regionalists,' visiting writers with inevitably superficial observations. We also get superb visiting observers who are careful craftsmen anywhere. *Kaimana* is interested in the latter, to complement our own best Hawaii writers."

KALEIDOSCOPE: EXPLORING THE EXPERIENCE OF DISABILITY THROUGH LITERATURE AND FINE ARTS (Specialized: disability themes), 701 S. Main St., Akron OH 44311-1019. (330)762-9755. Fax: (330)762-0912. E-mail: mshiplett@udsakron.org. Website: www.udsakron.org (includes guidelines and themes as well as information about the United Disability Services). Established 1979. **Senior Editor:** Gail Willmott. **Editor-in-Chief:** Dr. Darshan C. Perusek.
Magazine Needs: *Kaleidoscope* is based at United Disability Services, a nonprofit agency. Poetry should deal with the experience of disability but not limited to that when the writer has a disability. "*Kaleidoscope* is interested

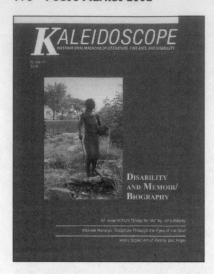

The focal point of this cover photograph is "Spirit Mother" by Native-American sculptor Michael A. Naranjo. Blinded and injured in Vietnam, he sculpts with the thumb, index finger, and middle finger of his left hand. Naranjo was the featured artist of this "Disability and Memoir/Biography" theme issue. In deciding which of Naranjo's pieces to include, *Kaleidoscope*'s editor chose "the opportunity to show this sculpture in the natural Southwestern environment of the artist's garden."

in high-quality poetry with vivid, believable images, and evocative language. Works should not use stereotyping, patronizing, or offending language about disability." Has published poetry by Sandra J. Kindow, Leah Maines, and Sheryl L. Nelms. As a sample the editors selected these lines from "Quiet Night" by Sheryl L. Nelms:

> I see shadows/of hackberry trees/curled spinach leaves/and winter/onions/leaning Sioux-like/ear/to
> the ground.

Kaleidoscope is 64 pgs., 8½ × 11, professionally printed and saddle-stapled with 4-color semigloss card cover, b&w art inside. Press run is 1,500, including libraries, social service agencies, health-care professionals, universities, and individual subscribers. Single copy: $6; subscription: $10 individual, $15 agency. Sample: $6.

How to Submit: Submit up to 5 poems at a time. Send photocopies with SASE for return of work. Accepts previously published poems and simultaneous submissions, "as long as we are notified in both instances." Accepts fax and e-mail submissions. Cover letter required. All submissions must be accompanied by an autobiographical sketch. Deadlines: March and August 1. Publishes theme issues. A list of upcoming themes is available for SASE, by e-mail, or on website. Themes for 2002 include "International Fiction/Art," "Disability: Mythology and Folklore," and "Disability and the Road Less Traveled." Responds in 3 weeks; acceptance or rejection may take 6 months. Pays $10-25 plus 2 copies. Rights return to author upon publication. Staff reviews books of poetry. Send books for review consideration to Gail Willmott, senior editor.

THE KALEIDOSCOPE REVIEW, P. O. Box 16242, Pittsburgh PA 15242-0242. Established 2000. **Editor:** Rebecca Chembars.

Magazine Needs: *The Kaleidoscope Review* appears bimonthly as a forum for fresh, creative poetry and artwork. "We tend to prefer shorter poetry. Two pages are dedicated to haiku. One (the last) page is dedicated to witty and/or humorous submissions. Writing must be effective and interesting. No preferred style, form, or school." Does not want graphic violence or pornography. As a sample the editor selected these lines from "Olé":

> ravens swoop in greeting/as you pass through faceless crowds/papier mâché hearts, pierced/cry rose
> petals at your crossing/I fall through, blindly/mad fiesta in my mind

The Kaleidoscope Review is 20 pgs., digest-sized, laser-printed, saddle-stapled, card stock cover, with art/graphics from selected submissions (2-5). Receives about 600 poems/year, accepts about 30%. Publishes about 30 poems/issue. Press run is 100 for 20 subscribers; 70 are distributed free to "friends and local business for distribution to the public." Single copy: $2; subscription: $12. Sample: $2 plus SASE. Make checks payable to *The Kaleidoscope Review*.

How To Submit: Submit 3 poems at a time, 5 if all haiku or very short poems. Line length is 35 maximum. Accepts previously published poems and simultaneous submissions. No fax, e-mail, or disk submissions. Cover letter is preferred. "Name and address on each sheet. Include SASE. Short cover letter preferred." Submit seasonal poems 3 months in advance. Time between acceptance and publication is 2-4 months. Often comments on rejected poems. "Submissions not returned to author unless SASE included." Occasionally publishes theme issues. A list of upcoming themes is available for SASE. Guidelines are available in magazine or for SASE. Responds in up to 6 weeks. Pays 1 contributor's copy; 2 subscriber/contributor's copies. Acquires one-time rights.

Advice: "Life *is* poetry in motion. Refocus!"

KALLIOPE, A JOURNAL OF WOMEN'S LITERATURE & ART (Specialized: women, translations, themes); SUE SANIEL ELKIND POETRY CONTEST, 3939 Roosevelt Blvd., Jacksonville

FL 32205. (904)381-3511. Website: www.fccj.org/kalliope (includes writer's guidelines, names of editors, poetry contest guidelines, back issues list, table of contents of recent issues, "Lollipops, Lizards and Literature," special events, poetry). Established 1978. **Editor:** Mary Sue Koeppel.

• A poem by Denise Levertov, originally published in *Kalliope*, was selected for *Best American Poetry 1999.*

Magazine Needs: *Kalliope* is a literary/visual arts journal published by Florida Community College at Jacksonville; the emphasis is on women writers and artists. "We like the idea of poetry as a sort of artesian well—there's one meaning that's clear on the surface and another deeper meaning that comes welling up from underneath. We'd like to see more poetry from Black, Hispanic and Native American women. Nothing sexist, racist, conventionally sentimental. We will have one special theme issue each year. Write for specific guidelines." Poets published include Denise Levertov, Marge Piercy, Martha M. Vertreace, Karen Subach, Maxine Kumin, and Tess Gallagher. As a sample the editor selected the following lines by Melanie Richards:

> With dried orange rind,/fragrant sage, and a blue//branch of coral, I seal/this package full of artifacts//
> in case the wild horses/all vanish from the earth,//or the red throat of the hummingbird/lies to us about
> summer;

Kalliope calls itself "a journal of women's literature and art" and publishes fiction, interviews, drama, and visual art in addition to poetry. Appearing 2 times/year, *Kalliope* is 7¼×8¼, flat-spined, handsomely printed on white stock, glossy card cover and b&w photographs of works of art. Average number of pages is 120. Press run is 1,600 for 400-500 subscribers of which 100 are libraries, 800 shelf sales. Subscription: $14.95/year or $24.95/2 years. Sample: $7.

How to Submit: Submit poems in batches of 3-5 with brief bio note, phone number, and address. No previously published poems. No fax or e-mail submissions. Reads submissions September through April only. SASE required. Because all submissions are read by several members of the editing staff, response time is usually up to 4 months. Publication will be within 6 months after acceptance. Criticism is provided "when time permits and the author has requested it." Guidelines and upcoming themes available on website or for SASE. Usually pays $10 or subscription. Acquires first publication rights. Reviews books of poetry, "but we prefer groups of books in one review." Poets may send books for review consideration.

Also Offers: Sponsors the Sue Saniel Elkind Poetry Contest. 1st Prize: $1,000; runners up published in *Kalliope.* Deadline: November 1. Details available for SASE.

Advice: "*Kalliope* is a carefully stitched patchwork of how women feel, what they experience, and what they have come to know and understand about their lives . . . a collection of visions from or about women all over the world. Send for a sample copy, to see what appeals to us, or better yet, subscribe!"

KARAMU, Dept. of English, Eastern Illinois University, Charleston IL 61920. Established 1966. **Editor:** Olga Abella.

• *Karamu* has received grants from the Illinois Arts Council and has won recognition and money awards in the IAC Literary Awards competition.

Magazine Needs: *Karamu* is an annual, usually published by May, whose "goal is to provide a forum for the best contemporary poetry and fiction that comes our way. We especially like to print the works of new writers. We like to see poetry that shows a good sense of what's being done with poetry currently. We like poetry that builds around real experiences, real images, and real characters and that avoids abstraction, overt philosophizing, and fuzzy pontifications. In terms of form, we prefer well-structured free verse, poetry with an inner, sub-surface structure as opposed to, let's say, the surface structure of rhymed quatrains. We have definite preferences in terms of style and form, but no such preferences in terms of length or subject matter. Purpose, however, is another thing. We don't have much interest in the openly didactic poem. If the poet wants to preach against or for some political or religious viewpoint, the preaching shouldn't be so strident that it overwhelms the poem. The poem should first be a poem." Has published poetry by Allison Joseph, Katharine Howd Machan, and Joanne Mokosh Riley. As a sample the editor selected these lines from "Climbing the Eiffel Tower at Night" by Barbara Crooker:

> flood-lit, so the traceries of girder and beam/seem even more insubstantial, a conjurer's vision,/an
> airy web spun out of light. It's a pyramid of X's,/row on row of kisses curving up to the sky,/meeting
> at the vanishing point, where all things come/together.

The format is 120 pgs., 5×8, matte cover, handsomely printed (narrow margins), attractive b&w art. Receives submissions from about 500 poets each year, accepts 40-50 poems. Sometimes about a year—between acceptance and publication. Press run is 350 for 300 subscribers of which 15 are libraries. Sample: $7.50.

How to Submit: Poems—in batches of no more than 5—may be submitted to Olga Abella. "We don't much care for simultaneous submissions. We read September 1 through March 1 only, for fastest decision submit January through March. Poets should not bother to query. We critique a few of the better poems. We want the poet to consider our comments and then submit new work." Publishes occasional theme issues. Upcoming themes available for SASE. Pays 1 copy. Acquires first serial rights.

Advice: "Follow the standard advice: Know your market. Read contemporary poetry and the magazines you want to be published in. Be patient."

✓ ◯ ◐ ◎ **KARAWANE: OR, THE TEMPORARY DEATH OF THE BRUITIST (Specialized: open mic/spoken word performers)**, 402 S. Cedar Lake Rd., Minneapolis MN 55405. E-mail: karawane@prodigy.net. Website: www.karawane.org (includes magazine samples, featured poets, online submissions, and open mic information). Established 1997 as *Voices From the Well*. **Editor/Publisher:** Laura Winton.
Magazine Needs: *Karawane* appears 2 times/year and "features poets, playwrights, fiction, and nonfiction writers who perform their work in public. We want innovative, thoughtful, well-crafted poetry. Poetry that needs to be poetry, rather than short stories and essays with line breaks. We are spoken word, but more in the manner of Cabaret Voltaire than a poetry slam. No poems that tell stories; no doggerel. I don't mind formal poetry, but do it well." Has published poetry by Terrence J. Folz, Dave Okar, and Richard Kostelanetz. As a sample the editor selected these lines from "Blue Highways" by William Sovern:

> Jimmy the guitar man made noise/the French surrealists made noise/the grand buddha poet will make noise/the mennonite woman walking alone/in her garden wants to make noise/i will perform a quiet/ beat rhapsody.

Karawane is 16-28 pgs., 8½×11, printed on newsprint, some inside art, ads. Receives about 300 poems/year, accepts 10-20%. Press run is 1,000 for 10 subscribers, 30 shelf sales; the remainder distributed free to festivals, open mics, inquiries, reviewers. Single copy: $3; subscription: $7/4 issues. Sample: $2, "donations of more appreciated." Make checks payable to Laura Winton. "To be considered poets *must* read at an open mic in their community. I prefer people be an ongoing part of their spoken word scene."
How to Submit: Submit 3-6 poems at a time. Accepts previously published poems and simultaneous submissions. Accepts e-mail submissions. Cover letter preferred; "Please indicate that you perform your work publicly and tell me a little about what you do, where you perform, etc. I prefer that to knowing who has published you before. SASEs essential! I *encourage* simultaneous submissions and previously published poems if you retained subsequent rights. E-mail gets a faster response from me—try any format as long as it's PC compatible." Time between acceptance and publication is up to 6 months. Seldom comments on rejected poems. Responds in 6 months. Pays in contributor's copies. Acquires one-time rights. Reviews books and chapbooks of poetry and other magazines in 500 words.
Advice: "Make your own scene! Don't wait for someone else to 'find' you. You can be a 'working poet,' with a little ingenuity and ambition. Poets should use every avenue available—lit mags, readings, self-publishing, cable access, leaving pamphlets on the bus, etc., to make themselves visible."

◐ **KATYDID BOOKS**, 1 Balsa Rd., Santa Fe NM 87505. Established 1973. **Editors/Publishers:** Karen Hargreaves-Fitzsimmons and Thomas Fitzsimmons.
Book/Chapbook Needs & How to Submit: Katydid Books publishes 3 paperbacks and 3 hardbacks/year. "We publish two series of poetry: Asian Poetry in Translation (distributed by University of Hawaii Press) and American Poets." Currently not accepting submissions.

◐ ◯ ◎ **KELSEY REVIEW (Specialized: regional)**, Mercer County Community College, P.O. Box B, Trenton NJ 08690. (609)586-4800, ext. 3326. Fax: (609)586-2318. E-mail: kelsey.review@mccc.edu. Website: www.mccc.edu (includes address, deadlines encouragement, and announced publication). Established 1988. **Editor-in-Chief:** Robin Schore.
Magazine Needs: *Kelsey Review* is an annual published in September by Mercer County Community College. It serves as "an outlet for literary talent of people living and working in Mercer County, New Jersey only." Has no specifications as to form, length, subject matter or style, but do not want to see poetry about "kittens and puppies." Accepts poetry written by children. Has published poetry by Valerie Egar, Betty Lies, Lois Harrod, Vida Chu, and Helen Gorenstein. As a sample the editor selected this poem "The Whistler" by Nancy Scott:

> A young man came to rent a room,/told me he had no job, no money./How do you live? I asked./I barter, he replied. I bet/you'd like a widescreen TV./I shook my head./Perhaps a new refrigerator?/I'd like the rent in cash./A year's supply of frozen meat?/I'm a vegetarian./He rapped his knuckles on the door,/I'll be back, he said,/and bounded down the front steps,/whistling.

Kelsey Review is about 80 glossy pgs., 7×11, with paper cover and line drawings; no ads. Receives about 60 submissions/year, accepts 6-10. Press run is 2,000. All distributed free to contributors, area libraries, bookstores, and schools.
How to Submit: Submit up to 6 poems at a time, typed. No previously published poems or simultaneous submissions. No fax or e-mail submissions. Deadline: May 1. Always comments on rejected poems. Information available for e-mail. Responds in June of each year. Pays 5 copies. All rights revert to authors.

✓ ⚲ $◐ **THE KENYON REVIEW; THE WRITERS WORKSHOP**, Kenyon College, Gambier OH 43022. (740)427-5208. Fax: (740)427-5417. E-mail: kenyonreview@kenyon.edu. Website: www.KenyonReview.org (includes submission policy, guidelines, excerpts from recent issues, interviews, "weekly feature," and soon an index to *Kenyon Review* back issues). Established 1939. **Editor:** David Lynn.
● Poetry published in *The Kenyon Review* was also selected for inclusion in the 1996, 1997, and 1998 volumes of *The Best American Poetry* and they have received, for the second consecutive year, the *Pushcart Prize* in each of the three considered genres: poetry, fiction, and nonfiction. *Kenyon Review* was the only literary magazine to win in all above categories in 1999.

Magazine Needs: *Kenyon Review* is a triquarterly review containing poetry, fiction, essays, criticism, reviews and memoirs. It features all styles and forms, lengths and subject matters. But this market is more closed than others because of the volume of submissions typically received during each reading cycle. Issues contain work by such poets as Cathy Song, John Ashbery, Mary Jo Ban, Robert Bly, Laura Kasischke, and Khaled Mattawa. The elegantly printed, flat-spined, 7×10, 180-page review has a press run of approximately 5,000, including individual subscribers institutions, and newsstand sales. Receives about 3,000 submissions/year, accepts 50 pgs. of poetry in each issue, have a 1-year backlog. The editor urges poets to read a few copies before submitting to find out what they are publishing. Sample: $9 includes postage.

How to Submit: Unsolicited submissions are typically read from September 1 through March 31. Writers may contact by phone, fax or e-mail, but may submit mss by mail only. Responds in 3 months. Pays $15/page for poetry, $10/page for prose. Acquires first North American serial rights. Reviews books of poetry in 2,500-7,000 words, single or multi-book format. "Reviews are primarily solicited—potential reviewers should inquire first."

Also Offers: Also sponsors The Writers Workshop, an annual 9-day event. 2001 dates: June 23 through July 1. Location: the campus of Kenyon College. Average attendance is 12 per class. Open to writers of fiction, nonfiction and poetry. Conference is designed to provide intensive conversation, exercises and detailed readings of participants' work. Past speakers have included Erin Belieu, Allison Joseph, P.F. Kluge, Wendy MacLeod, Pamela Painter, Nancy Zafris, David Baker, and Reginald McKnight. Other special features include a limited-edition anthology produced by workshop writers and *The Kenyon Review* that includes the best writing of the session. College and non-degree graduate credit is offered. Cost for summer 2001 conference is $1,450, including meals, a room and tuition. Application available for SASE. Early application is encouraged as the workshops are limited.

THE KERF (Specialized: animals, nature/ecology), College of the Redwoods, 883 W. Washington Blvd., Crescent City CA 95531. Established 1995. **Editor:** Ken Letko.

Magazine Needs: *The Kerf*, annually published in May, features "poetry that speaks to the environment and humanity." Wants "poetry that exhibits an environmental consciousness." Also accepts poetry written by children. Has published poetry by Ruth Daigon, Meg Files, James Grabill, and George Keithley. As a sample the editor selected these lines from "The Stones" by Janine Canan:

> Along the beach, stones/exposed by the retreating tide/greet me like friends from long ago./And I bend
> to gather eggs/mounds, ovals, crescents/smoothed by life in the tumbling sea.

The Kerf is 40 pgs., 8½×5½, printed via Docutech, saddle-stapled with CS2 cover stock. Receives about 2,000 poems/year, accepts 1-3%. Press run is 400, 150 shelf sales; 100 distributed free to contributors and writing centers. Sample: $5. Make checks payable to College of the Redwoods.

How to Submit: Submit up to 5 poems (up to 7 pgs.) at a time. No previously published poems or simultaneous submissions. Reads submissions January 15 through March 31 only. Time between acceptance and publication is 3 months. Poems are circulated to an editorial board. "Our editors debate (argue for or against) the inclusion of each manuscript." Seldom comments on rejected poems. Guidelines available for SASE. Responds in 2 months. Sometimes sends prepublication galleys. Pays 1 contributor's copy. Acquires first North American serial rights.

KIMERA: A JOURNAL OF FINE WRITING, 1316 Hollis, Spokane WA 99201. E-mail: kimera@js. spokane.wa.us. Website: www.js.spokane.wa.us/kimera/. Established 1996. **Publisher:** Jan Strever.

Magazine Needs: *Kimera* is a biannual online journal (appears yearly in hard copy) and "attempts to address John Locke's challenge—'where is the head with no chimeras.'" Wants poetry that "attempts to 'capture the soul in motion.' No flabby poems." Has published poetry by Gayle Elen Harvey, Janet McCann, and C.E. Chaffin. Accepts about 10% of poems/year. Press run is 300 for 200 subscribers. Single copy: $7; subscription: $14. Sample: $7.

How to Submit: Submit 3-6 poems at a time. Accepts simultaneous submissions; no previously published poems. Accepts e-mail submissions in ASCII text. Cover letter required. Poems are circulated to an editorial board. Seldom comments on rejected poems. Guidelines available on website. Responds in 3 months. Pays 1 copy. Acquires first rights.

KINGS ESTATE PRESS, 870 Kings Estate Rd., St. Augustine FL 32086-5033. (800)249-7485. E-mail: kep@aug.com. Established 1993. **Publisher:** Ruth Moon Kempher.

Book/Chapbook Needs & How to Submit: "Publishes the best contemporary poetry available; all books are illustrated." Publishes about 3 paperbacks/year. "Currently overstocked, not accepting submissions until after the year 2002."

THE KIT-CAT REVIEW; GAVIN FLETCHER MEMORIAL PRIZE FOR POETRY, 244 Halstead Ave., Harrison NY 10528-3611. (914)835-4833. Established 1998. **Editor:** Claudia Fletcher.

Magazine Needs: *The Kit-Cat Review* appears quarterly and is "named after the 18th century Kit-Cat Club whose members included Addison, Steele, Congreve, Vanbrugh, Garth, etc. Purpose: to promote/discover excellence and originality." Wants quality work—traditional, modern, experimental. Has published poetry by Romola Robb Allrud, Harriet Zinnes, Louis Phillips, Chayym Zeldis, and Romania's Nobel Prize nominee Marin Sorescu. As a sample the editor selected these lines from "Poet's Day Off" by Mary Kennan Herbert:

> *sleep till the rooster/has left for work/read the morning paper very slowly/sip coffee in a desultory*
> *way/imagine ostrich plumes languidly/fanning a breeze just for me*

The Kit-Cat Review is 75 pgs., 5½×8½, laser printed/photocopied, saddle-stapled with colored card cover, includes b&w illustrations. Receives about 1,000 poems/year. Press run is 500 for 200 subscribers. Subscription: $25. Sample: $7. Make checks payable to Claudia Fletcher.

How to Submit: Submit any number of poems at a time. Accepts previously published poems and simultaneous submissions. "Cover letter should contain relevant bio." Time between acceptance and publication is 2 months. Responds within 2 months. Pays up to $100 a poem and 2 copies. Acquires first or one-time rights.

Also Offers: Sponsors the annual Gavin Fletcher Memorial Prize for Poetry of $1,000.

KNUCKLE MERCHANT: THE JOURNAL OF NAKED LITERARY AGGRESSION, P.O. Box 583377, Minneapolis MN 55458-3377. (612)209-6689. E-mail: revjones@thincoyote.com. Website: www.lostpro phetpress.com. Established 2000. **Editor:** Christopher Jones.

Magazine Needs: *Knuckle Merchant: The Journal of Naked Literary Aggression* "is a bimonthly knife in the ribs of the Man." Published by Lost Prophet Press (see separate listing in this section). "We want the voice of this country (and this world) the way it should be: awake, rebellious, and vibrant. Tell us what makes you angry, joyous, frenzied, and alive; we'll put it all together and Reauchambeau Big Brother on your behalf 'cause, damn, we just don't like that guy.' " *Knuckle Merchant* is 28-32 pgs. 5½×8½, docutech-printed, type of binding: stapled, b&w cardstock cover, with b&w photos and art, and ads. Accepts about 5% of submissions. Press run is 200. Single copy: $5; subscription: $15. Make checks payable to *Knuckle Merchant*.

How to Submit: Submit 5 poems at a time. Accepts previously published poems and simultaneous submissions. Accepts fax and e-mail submissions. "Have some manners, send a cover letter." Time between acceptance and publication is 2 months. Often comments on rejected poems. Guidelines are available for SASE. Pays 1-2 contributor's copies. Acquires first rights or one-time rights. Poets may send books for review consideration to Christopher Jones.

KOJA; KOJA PRESS (Specialized: form/style), P.O. Box 140083,, Brooklyn NY 11214. Established 1996. **Editor:** Michael Magazinnik.

Magazine Needs: *Koja* is published annually and "interested in experimental poetry but also publishes experimental prose and b&w artwork." Wants "visual/concrete poetry, avant-garde poetry and experimental poetry. No religious or classical work." Accepts poetry written by children. Has published poetry by Eileen Myles, David Burlyuk, K.K. Kuzminsky, I. Weiss, Richard Kostelanetz, and Bruce Andrews. *Koja* is 64 pgs., 8½×11, various printing and binding methods, glossy color cover. Receives about 300 poems/year, accepts about 10%. Press run is 300 for 30 subscribers of which 5 are libraries, 200 shelf sales; 50 distributed free to contributors/reviewers. Subscription: $14. Sample: $7. Make checks payable to Michael Magazinnik.

How to Submit: Submit up to 10 poems at a time. No previously published poems or simultaneous submissions. "All unsolicited submissions must be accompanied by money order/check in the amount of $7 for a sample copy of the latest issue." Cover letter preferred. Time between acceptance and publication is up to 8 months. Seldom comments on rejected poems. Responds in up to 2 years. Pays 1 copy. Acquires first North American serial rights.

KONFLUENCE; KONFLUENCE PRESS, Bath House, Bath Rd., Nailsworth, Stroud, Gloucestershire GL6 0JB United Kingdom. Phone: (01453)835896. Fax: (01453)835587. E-mail: floherus@aol.com. Established 1998. **Editor:** Mark Floyer.

Magazine Needs: *Konfluence* is "an annual platform for poetry—mainly from the west country, United Kingdom, but accept anything from across the United Kingdom and the globe if it is suitable." "Open to a wide variety of poetry. It must have a content/form equation which is successfully true unto itself. No stream of consciousness ranting! We want to see some craft." Has published poetry by Mary Mamer, B.Z. Niditch, and Richard Alan Bunch. As a sample the editor selected these lines from his poem "Circle Line":

> *Slumped across his seat (a Madame/Tussaud's escapee!) he circles/Marble Arch, Baker street,/round*
> *and round and round he must/re-cycle flesh to wax, devolve-/dissolve at last to powdered dust.*

Konfluence is 50 pgs., magazine-sized, printed and staple bound with cardboard cover. Accepts about 10% of poems received. Press run is 200, 50% shelf sales; 50% distributed free to contributors. Single copy: $6. Make checks payable to Konfluence Press.

How to Submit: Submit 6 poems at a time. Line length for poetry is 10 minimum, 80 maximum. Accepts previously published poems and simultaneous submissions. Accepts fax and e-mail submissions. Cover letter preferred. Time between acceptance and publication is 10 months. Often comments on rejected poems. Responds in 1 month. Pays 1 copy.

Advice: "Do send your material in! This is an 'open' publishing venture. No rules—just quality content at the editor's whim/judgement."

KONOCTI BOOKS, 23311 County Rd. 88, Winters CA 95694. (530)662-3364. E-mail: nrpeattie@earthlin k.net. Established 1973. **Editor/Publisher:** Noel Peattie. Publishes poetry by invitation only.

✓ ▣ ◯ ◧ **KOTA PRESS; KOTA PRESS POETRY JOURNAL**. (206)297-1012. Fax: (413)647-8706. E-mail: editor@kotapress.com. Website: www.kotapress.com. Established 1999. **Editor:** Kara L.C. Jones.

Magazine Needs: *Kota Press Poetry Journal* is a quarterly online e-zine "seeking to publish new as well as seasoned poets. We seek to publish the best poetry that comes to us and then to support the poet in whatever ways she may need. While form is sometimes important, we are more interested in content. We want to know what you have to say. We are interested in the honesty and conviction of your poems. Give us accessibility over form any day. Seeing tankas, for instance, in 5-7-5-7-7 form can be interesting and accessible, but do not send us words that you have stuffed into a form just to say you could write in form." Has published poetry by Claudia Mauro, Nancy Talley, Carla Griswold, Tim Hulley, and Dana Gerringer. As a sample the editor selected these lines by Claudia Mauro from "Reading the River":

> You must know the/value of story and carry a library in each clear eye/the fine art of butch is to take
> your seat at the fire/and unfold your own story—then toss it in, to rise/as heat and light.

How to Submit: Submit 4 poems at a time. Accepts previously published poems; no simultaneous submissions. Accepts e-mail submissions *only*. Cover letter required. "Previously-published poems must include credit to prior publication. We accept e-mail submissions only; include text in body of message. Please include bio info in e-mail message. Be sure to give us contact info so we can get back to you." Reads submissions December 1 through January 30 for March issue; March 1 through April 30 for June issue; June 1 through July 30 for September issue; September 1 through October 30 for December issue. Time between acceptance and publication is 1-2 months. Publishes theme issues. Upcoming themes and guidelines available on website. Responds in 2 months. Acquires one-time electronic rights.

Also Offers: "We offer two contests per year that result in print books, so please see Journal section of site for guidelines. Because we are an Internet magazine, we are able to provide writers with resources and support through links, articles and services—as well as producing a high-quality poetry journal. Please see our website at www.kotapress.com to find out more about us and about what we offer. We look forward to hearing from you and reading your poetry."

Advice: "If you want to be a published writer you must submit your work again and again and again to anywhere and everywhere. For every 100 rejections, you will quite possibly get 1 or 2 acceptances, but you won't get rejected or accepted if you don't submit in the first place!"

🌐 ◧ ◎ **KRAX (Specialized: humor)**, 63 Dixon Lane, Leeds, Yorkshire LS12 4RR England. Established 1971. **Poetry Editor:** Andy Robson.

Magazine Needs: *Krax* appears twice yearly, and publishes contemporary poetry from Britain and America. Wants poetry which is "light-hearted and witty; original ideas. Undesired: haiku, religious, or topical politics." 2,000 words maximum. All forms and styles considered. Has published poetry by Bill Broady, Toby Litt, Maura Gage, and Dee Light. As a sample the editor selected these lines from "Waiting" by David Lang:

> A waiter is the life for me/Not serving cakes or cups of tea/Or waiting on a gent who dines/On meals
> with expensive wines/At portering I earn my pay/Waiting for the trains all day

Krax is 6×8, 64 pgs. of which 30 are poetry, saddle-stapled, offset-printed with b&w cartoons and graphics. Receives up to 1,000 submissions/year, accepts about 6%, has a 2- to 3-year backlog. Single copy: £3.50 ($7); subscription: £10 ($20). Sample: $1 (75p).

How to Submit: "Submit maximum of six pieces. Writer's name on same sheet as poem. Sorry, we cannot accept material on disk. SASE or SAE with IRC encouraged but not vital." No previously published poems or simultaneous submissions. Brief cover letter preferred. Responds in 2 months. Pays 1 copy. Reviews books of poetry (brief, individual comments; no outside reviews). Send books for review consideration.

Advice: "All editors have differing tastes so don't be upset by early rejection but please ensure you always send an address for response, whatever it may turn out to be."

◯ ◧ **KUMQUAT MERINGUE; PENUMBRA PRESS**, P.O. Box 736, Pine Island MN 55963. (507)367-4430. E-mail: moodyriver@aol.com. Website: www.geostar.com/kumquatcastle ("includes guidelines, poetry samples and all information about *Kumquat Meringue*, and our other projects."). Established 1990. **Editor:** Christian Nelson.

Magazine Needs: *Kumquat Meringue* appears on an irregular basis, using "mostly shorter poetry about the small details of life, especially the quirky side of love and sex. We want those things other magazines find just too quirky. Not interested in rhyming, meaning of life or high-flown poetry." The magazine is "dedicated to the memory of Richard Brautigan." Has published works by Gina Bergamino, T. Kilgore Splake, Antler, Monica Kershner, Lynne Douglass, and Ianthe Brautigan. As a sample the editor selected these lines from "Leaping Lizards" by Emile Luria:

> After we made love . . . Kate said,/"You're so weird, really,/Even weirder than I thought."/And I
> thought, could she taste the salt,/Feel the sea lapping on my back?/I went to sleep wondering/About
> dinosaurs and lungfish/And the deepest reaches of the sea

Kumquat Meringue is 40-48 pgs., digest-sized, "professionally designed with professional typography and nicely printed." Press run is 600 for 250 subscribers. Subscription: $10/3 issues. Sample: $5.

How to Submit: "We like cover letters but prefer to read things about who you are, rather than your long list of publishing credits. Accepts previously published and simultaneous submissions are, but please let us know."

Often comments on submissions. No fax or e-mail submissions. "Please don't forget your SASE or you'll never hear back from us. E-mail address is for 'hello, praise, complaints, threats, and questions' only." Guidelines available for SASE and on website. Usually responds in 3 months. Pays 1 copy. Acquires one-time rights.

Advice: "Read *Kumquat Meringue* and anything by Richard Brautigan to get a feel for what we want, but don't copy Richard Brautigan, and don't copy those who have copied him. We just want that same feel. We also have a definite weakness for poems written 'to' or 'for' Richard Brautigan. Reviewers have called our publication iconoclastic, post-hip, post-beat, post-antipostmodern; and our poetry, carefully crafted imagery. When you get discouraged, write some more. Don't give up. Eventually your poems will find a home. We're very open to unpublished writers, and a high percentage of our writers had never been published anywhere before they submitted here."

✓ ✿ ☁ ◯ ◑ ◎ **KWIL KIDS PUBLISHING; THE KWIL CAFÉ NEWSLETTER; THE KWIL CLUB (Specialized: children/teen/young adult)**, Box 29556, Maple Ridge, British Columbia V2X 2V0 Canada. Phone/fax: (604)465-9101. E-mail: kwil@telus.net. Website: www.members.home.com/kwilkids/ (includes guidelines, contact information, and inspirational quotations). Established 1996. **Publisher:** Kwil.

Magazine Needs: *Kwil Kids* is a quarterly newsletter "publishing stories/poems to encourage and celebrate writers in the Kwil Club." Wants poetry that is "gentle; with compassionate truth and beauty; peace; humor; for children, by children, about children. No profane, hurtful, violent, political, or satirical work. Has published poetry by Darlene Slevin (adult), Gord Brandt (adult), Wendy Matthews (adult), Torrey Janzen (age 10), Carol McNaughton (age 6), and Ben Stoltz (age 11). As a sample they selected this poem by Kwil:

> I know that I'd sigh and grimace/When you'd fight about your play/But let peace spread from the
> playground/Throughout the world one day.

Kwil Kids is 8 pgs., includes b&w graphics. Receives about 400 poems/year, accepts about 80%. Publish 8 poems/issue. Press run is 200 for 150 subscribers. Subscription: $25 (cost includes membership to the Kwil Club). Sample: SASE (or SAE and IRC) and $2. Make checks payable to Kwil Kids Publishing.

How to Submit: Submit 5 poems at a time. Include SASE and parent's signature. Cover letter preferred. Accepts fax and e-mail submissions; include in body of message, no attachments. Submit seasonal poems 3 months in advance. Time between acceptance and publication is up to 6 months. Always comments on rejected poems. "Kwil always provides encouragement and personalized response with SASE (or SAE and IRC)." Publishes theme issues occasionally. Guidelines available for SASE or on website. Responds in April, August, and December. Pays 1 copy. Acquires one-time rights.

Also Offers: "Offers 5¢ royalty (rounded to nearest dollar) on poems turned into cards for 'The Kwil Collection' sold at a local cafe, at the 'Kwil Kids Publishing Centre', and by mail order." Also sponsors The Kwil Club—a club for readers, writers, and artists of all ages. Membership features include 4 quarterly issues of the Kwil Kids newsletter, 4 quarterly issues of "Letters from the Kwil Cafe" newsletter; newsletter, newspaper, and greeting card publishing opportunities; a free subscription to Kwil's e-mail poetry list; reading, writing, and publishing tips and encouragement galore. Membership fee: $25.

Advice: "Kwil's motto: Keep your pencil moving (and your keyboard tapping!) Just be who you are, and do what you do. Then all of life's treasures will come to you."

◖ **LA JOLLA POET'S PRESS; NATIONAL POETRY BOOK SERIES; SAN DIEGO POET'S PRESS; AMERICAN BOOK SERIES**, P.O. Box 8638, La Jolla CA 92038. **Editor/Publisher:** Kathleen Iddings.

Book Needs & How to Submit: La Jolla Poet's Press and San Diego Poet's Press are nonprofit presses that publish only poets who "have published widely. No beginners here." Has published 36 individual poet's books and 5 poetry anthologies featuring poetry by Allen Ginsberg, Carolyn Kizer, Galway Kinnell, Tess Gallagher, Robert Pinsky, and Carolyn Forche. As a sample the editor included these lines from "Hester's Grammer" in *Curved Space* by Susan Terris:

> He laid his boots beside my slippers and they lay there./(Past.)/He has laid his body next to mine and
> it has lain there./(Perfect.)//Lay, lies/laid, lay/laid, lain./All quite grammatically correct and, still, it
> is not/the lay or laid that bothers him but the lies.//He may love to lie with me, yet to lie about me is
> for him/a tense not coped with in any text of standard usage./(Imperfect.)

Most books are approximately 100 pgs., 5½×8½, perfect-bound, with laminated covers. Sample: $10.

Ⓝ ◑ ◎ **LACTUCA (Specialized: translations)**, 159 Jewett Ave., Jersey City NJ 07304-2003. Phone/fax: (201)451-5411. E-mail: lactuca@mindspring.com. Website: www.mindspring.com/~lactuca. Established 1986. **Editor/Publisher:** Mike Selender.

Magazine Needs: *Lactuca* appears up to once/year. "Our bias is toward work with a strong sense of place, a strong sense of experience, a quiet dignity, and an honest emotional depth. Dark and disturbing writings are preferred over safer material. No haiku, poems about writing poems, poems using the poem as an image, light poems, or self-indulgent poems. Readability is crucial. We publish poetry that readily transposes between the spoken word and printed page. First English language translations are welcome provided that the translator has obtained the approval of the author." Has published poetry by Sherman Alexie, Joe Cardillo, Christy Beatty, and Kathleen ten Haken. *Lactuca* will resume publication with a new format: 200 pgs., perfect-bound. Sample back issues: $4. Make checks payable to Stone Buzzard Press.

How to Submit: "*Lactuca* is currently dormant. Query to find out if we're accepting new submissions. Unsolicited manuscripts will not be responded to promptly." Queries accepted via e-mail. Submit 4-5 poems at a time. No previously published material or simultaneous submissions. "We comment on rejected poems when we can. However the volume of mail we receive limits this." Always sends prepublication galleys. Pays 1-2 copies. Acquires first rights. Reviews books of poetry. Poets may send books for review consideration.

Advice: "The purpose of *Lactuca* is to be a small literary magazine publishing high-quality poetry, fiction, and b&w drawings. Much of our circulation goes to contributors' copies and exchange copies with other literary magazines. *Lactuca* is not for poets expecting large circulation. Poets appearing here will find themselves in the company of other good writers."

THE LAIRE, INC., P.O. Box 5524, Ft. Oglethorpe GA 30742. Fax: (706)858-1071. Established 1995. **Editor:** Kim Abston.

Magazine Needs: *the LAIRE* is a quarterly "newsletter for poets and poetry lovers, dedicated to bringing to our readers quality poetry, and related subject matter which is both creatively and/or socially aware. Open to all forms of poetry, provided it is well executed, both creatively and technically. Poetry may be of any length or subject, but we tend to prefer poems that are 40 lines or less and socially and/or politically aware." As a sample the editor selected these lines from a poem by Gregory Fiorini:

> In that line of neglect stand revolutionaries/portable to their cause/of wings sans feathers/among
> debris/and all other ways akimbo

the LAIRE is 8 pgs., 8½×11, photocopied, corner-stapled with line drawings and clip art. Receives about 1,500 poems/year, accepts 9%. Press run is 1,000 for 300-400 subscribers of which 50 are libraries, 400 shelf sales; 100 distributed free to schools, prisons, etc. Subscription: $10. Sample: $2.

How to Submit: Submit up to 5 poems at a time. No previously published poems or simultaneous submissions. Accepts disk submissions. "Author's name, address, and telephone number must appear on each page. One poem per page. We accept 1.44meg IBM formatted floppy disk submissions, provided name, address, and phone are on label. Nothing returned without SASE." Cover letter preferred. Time between acceptance and publication is up to 6 months. Poems are circulated to an editorial board. "Poems are reviewed by the editorial board with the editor having final approval." Seldom comments on rejected poems. Publishes theme issues occasionally. Guidelines available for SASE. Responds in 2 months. Pays 1 copy. Reviews books and chapbooks of poetry and other magazines in 150-200 words, single or multi-book format. Poets may send books for review consideration.

Also Offers: Sponsors poetry contests. Details available for SASE. Also accepts article submissions on any subject related to poetry, including critiques, biographies, book reviews, and F.Y.I. pieces.

LAKE SHORE PUBLISHING; SOUNDINGS (Specialized: anthology), 373 Ramsay Rd., Deerfield IL 60015. Phone/fax: (847)945-4324. Established 1983. **Poetry Editor:** Carol Spelius.

Magazine Needs: *Soundings* is an effort "to put out decent, economical volumes of poetry." **Reading fee:** $1/ page. Wants poetry which is "understandable and moving, imaginative with a unique view, in any form. Make me laugh or cry or think. I'm not so keen on gutter language or political dogma—but I try to keep an open mind. No limitations in length." Accepts poetry written by children. Has published poetry by Bob Mills, Gertrude Rubin, and June Shipley. The editor selected these sample lines from "It Used To Be So Easy" by Constance Vogel:

> The night before your wedding/you looked across the table/at almost-in-laws waiting for their meal/
> and wondered if, in time,/you'd be their main course.

The first 253-page anthology, including over 100 poets, is a paperback, at $7.95 (add $1 p&h), which was published (in 1985) in an edition of 2,000. It is flat-spined, photocopied from typescript, with glossy, colored card cover with art.

How to Submit: Submit 5 poems at a time, with $1/page **reading fee**, and a cover letter telling about your other publications, biographical background, personal or aesthetic philosophy, poetic goals and principles. Accepts simultaneous submissions. Any form or length. "Reads submissions anytime, but best in fall." Upcoming themes available for SASE. Responds in 1 year. Pays 1 copy and half-price for additional copies. "All rights return to poet after first printing."

Book/Chapbook Needs & How to Submit: The editor will read chapbooks, or full-length collections, with the possibility of sharing costs if Lake Shore Publishing likes the book (**$1/page reading fee**). "I split the cost if I like the book." Sample copy of anthology or random choice of full-length collections to interested poets: $5.

LANDFALL: NEW ZEALAND ARTS AND LETTERS (Specialized: regional), University of Otago Press, P.O. Box 56, Dunedin, New Zealand. Phone: 0064 3 479 8807. Fax: 0064 3 479 8385. E-mail: university.press@stonebow.otago.ac.nz. Established 1947. Originally published by Caxton Press, then by Oxford University Press, now published by University of Otago Press. **Editor:** Justin Paton.

Magazine Needs: *Landfall* appears twice/year (in May and November). "Apart from occasional commissioned features on aspects of international literature, *Landfall* focuses primarily on New Zealand literature and arts. It publishes new fiction, poetry, commentary, and interviews with New Zealand artists and writers, and reviews of New Zealand books." Single issue: NZ $21.95; subscription: NZ $39.95 for 2 issues for New Zealand subscribers, A $30 for Australian subscribers, US $30 for other overseas subscribers.

How to Submit: Submissions must be typed and include SASE. "Once accepted, contributions should if possible also be submitted on disk." No fax or e-mail submissions. Publishes theme issues. Guidelines and upcoming themes available for SASE. Pays (for poetry) NZ $15/printed page and 1 copy. New Zealand poets should write for further information.

LATERAL MOVES; AURAL IMAGES, 5 Hamilton St., Astley Bridge, Bolton BL1 6RJ United Kingdom. Phone: (01204)596369. *Lateral Moves* established 1994. Aural Images established 1993. **General Editors:** Alan White and Susan White. **Poetry Editor:** Nick Britton.

Magazine Needs: *Lateral Moves* appears 6 times/year and includes poetry, stories, criticism, reviews, humor, interviews, etc. Wants "dangerous, challenging, subversive, transgressive poetry. No new romantic, doggerel, sappy stuff, or work about seasons." Has published poetry by Dave Ward, Gerald England, Sam Smith, and Stephen Blyth. *Lateral Moves* is 48-52 pgs., magazine-sized, photocopied and stapled with card cover, includes art/graphics. Receives over 500-1,000 poems/year, accepts 10-15%. Press run is 150 for 75 subscribers. Six issue subscription is £18.00/US $30; sample copies are £3.85/$6.50.

How to Submit: Submit 6 poems maximum at a time. Line length for poetry is around 80 maximum. Accepts previously published poems; no simultaneous submissions. Cover letter optional. "All submissions should be typed, where possible, and should be clearly accompanied by your name and address. If you have no access to a typewriter, please write as legibly as possible." Reads submissions "4 times per year at 3 monthly internals." Time between acceptance and publication is up to 1 year. Seldom comments on rejected poems. Occasionally publishes theme issues. Guidelines available for SASE. Responds in 3 months. Pays 1 copy. Acquires one-time rights. Reviews books and chapbooks of poetry and other magazines in 1,500 words, single book format. Poets may send books for review consideration.

Book/Chapbook Needs & How to Submit: Aural Images publishes 0-1 paperbacks and 0-2 chapbooks per year. However, they are not currently accepting ms submissions. Also publishes occasional anthologies. Send SAE and IRC for details.

Advice: "We echo the standard advice given by all small magazines—consider buying at least one copy of the mag itself or (dare we say it) a subscription before submitting. We get a lot of material from different sources and standards are high, although new writers are also warmly encouraged. Buying a magazine or two means that you get a feel for the kinds of things we like, and that we can carry on publishing cool new literature on a nonprofitmaking basis."

LAURELS; WEST VIRGINIA POETRY SOCIETY (Specialized: membership), Rt. 2, Box 13, Ripley WV 25271. E-mail: mbush814@aol.com. Established 1996. **Editor:** Jim Bush.

Magazine Needs: *Laurels* is the quarterly journal of the West Virginia Poetry Society containing 95% poetry/5% art. Only considers work from WVPS members. Wants traditional forms and good free verse. "If it's over 100 lines it must be very, very good. No porn, foul language, shape poems; no 'broken prose.' " Also accepts poetry written by children, if members. Has published poetry by Jane Stuart, Watha Lambert, and Thomas Downing. *Laurels* is 50 pgs., digest-sized, mimeographed and saddle-stapled with paper cover, some pen-and-ink art, no ads. Receives about 2,000 poems/year, accepts about 50%. Press run is 250 for 150 subscribers. Membership: $12. Sample: $4. Make checks payable to the West Virginia Poetry Society for a subscription, to Jim Bush for a sample.

How to Submit: Requires contributors be members. For membership in WVPS, send $12 to Linda Poe, Rt. 1, Box 25, Gay WV 25244. Submit 4-5 poems at a time. Accepts previously published poems and simultaneous submissions. Accepts e-mail submissions (submit in body of message). Cover letter preferred including brief bio. Time between acceptance and publication is up to 1 year. Always comments on rejected poems. Publishes theme issues March 15, May 15, August 15, and November 15. Guidelines available for SASE. Responds "next day, usually." Sometimes sends prepublication galleys. Pays 1 copy. Acquires one-time rights. Staff briefly reviews 3-4 books/year if author is a member. Send books for review consideration.

Also Offers: Sponsors a 35-category annual contest for members. Entry fee: no fee to current WVPS members or K-12 students, $1/poem for nonmembers, maximum of $12 for 12 or more categories. Guidelines available for SASE.

Advice: "Our purpose is to encourage and aid amateur poets who believe that words can be used to communicate meaning and to create beauty."

LAZY FROG PRESS; LAZY FROG PRESS CHAPBOOK COMPETITION, P.O. Box 41253, Lafayette LA 70504-1253. E-mail: bullpen@lazyfrogpress.com. Website: www.lazyfrogpress.com (includes mission statement, guidelines, contact and ordering information). Established 2000. **Contact:** Nate Pritts.

Book/Chapbook Needs & How to Submit: "The nature of the Lazy Frog Press aesthetic is to publish and distribute bold work from new and established talents that says something about the author and his/her understanding of the form he/she is working in. Lazy Frog Press recognizes that first and foremost writing is to communicate, not to sit on a shelf and gather dust. Lazy Frog sees the best writing actively engaging the reader, forcing them to take notice of both their own place in the world and why we read. The poems and stories that most interest us are those that show an active and critical engagement with the things of this world." Publishes 2 chapbooks/year, one chosen through competition, one solicited. "We work with poets on all design elements." Pays 20 author's copies (out of a press run of 150). Order sample chapbooks by sending $6 to Lazy Frog Press.

Also Offers: The Lazy Frog Chapbook Competition awards publication and 20 copies to a poetry manuscript in even numbered years (fiction in odd). Poems can be previously in magazines, anthologies, online, etc., but the ms as a whole must be previously unpublished. "Enclose an acknowledgements page if you want but please DO include a cover letter with your contact information, the title of the manuscript, and a list of the titles of the poems in the proper sequence. Also, tell us something about yourself—some brief talk about your poetry or your life: whatever." Submit 2 copies of poetry ms of 16-28 pgs., along with the $5 entry fee and a SASE for notification. Winner will be announced in June 2002. The 2002 competition for poetry opens January 1, 2002 and closes May 1.

Advice: "As Lazy Frog Press takes its first tentative steps into the mo' money, mo' ego world of high stakes publishing, we are looking for writers and readers both, those who challenge forms and those who like to be challenged. Lazy Frog Press wants to be the stiff breeze blowing back your hair, whether you are cruising in a T-top convertible or scaling Mt. Kilimanjaro."

N $ @ THE LEADING EDGE (Specialized; science fiction/fantasy), 3146 JKHB, Provo UT 84602. E-mail: tle@byu.edu (correspondence only, no submissions). Website: http://tle.clubs.byu.edu. **Editor-in-Chief:** Brandon Sanderson.

Magazine Needs: *The Leading Edge* is a magazine appearing 2 times/year. Wants "high quality poetry reflecting both literary value and popular appeal and dealing with science fiction and fantasy. We accept traditional science fiction and fantasy poetry, but we like innovative stuff. No graphic sex, violence, or profanity." Has published poetry by Michael Collings, Tracy Ray, Susan Spilecki, and Bob Cook. As a sample the editor selected this poem, "The Spectra of Galaxies (A Zen Joke)" by Alyce Wilson:

> A man with a telescope/reduces the universe/to one red-shifted line/on a piece of graph paper.//Folds it in his pocket, forgets it.//On laundry day, he cleans/galaxies out of the lint filter./And at last, he understands.

The Leading Edge is 120 pgs., 6×9, using art. Accepts about 15 out of 150 poems received/year. Press run is 400, going to 100 subscribers (10 of them libraries) and 300 shelf sales. Single copy: $3.95; subscription: $11.85. Sample: $4.50.

How to Submit: Submit 1 or more poems with name and address at the top of each page. No simultaneous submissions or previously published poems. Cover sheet with name, address, phone number, length of poem, title, and type of poem preferred. Guidelines available for SASE. Responds in 4 months. Always sends prepublication galleys. Pays $10 for the first 1-4 typeset pages, $4.50 for each additional page; plus 2 contributor's copies. Acquires first North American serial rights.

Advice: "Poetry is given equal standing with fiction and is not treated as filler, but as art."

LEAPINGS LITERARY MAGAZINE; LEAPINGS PRESS, 2455 Pinercrest Dr., Santa Rosa CA 95403. Fax: (707)568-7531. E-mail: 72144.3133@compuserve.com. Website: http://home.inreach.com/editserv/. Established 1998. **Editor:** S.A. Warner.

Magazine Needs: *Leapings* is a semiannual literary magazine that publishes essays, book reviews, b&w artwork, literary and genre fiction, and poetry. "Open to any form, but prefer shorter verse. No rhymed for rhyming sake; no pornography." Accepts poetry written by children. Has published poetry by Kit Knight, Kenneth Pobo, Anselm Brocki, John Grey, Leslie Woolf Hedley, and John Taylor. As a sample we selected these lines from "Her love in a widened margin" by G.E. Coggshall:

> She rises at five a.m. unrebuked/for her nightgown's raveled hem. Each day/wrinkles like skin. The corners of her/wallpaper curl away from the plaster.//Her hindsight is clouded from cataracts,/yet she believes in all her layered-up/experience, her brick-and-mortar regrets.

Leapings is 35-50 pgs., digest-sized, laserjet printed and saddle-stapled with cardstock cover, uses b&w graphics. Receives about 1,000 poems/year, accepts about 10%. Press run is 200 for 25 subscribers of which 5 are libraries, about 50 shelf sales. Single copy: $6; subscription: $10/year. Sample: $5. Make checks payable to S.A. Warner.

How to Submit: Submit up to 6 poems at a time. No previously published poems or simultaneous submissions. Accepts e-mail (poetry, only in body of message) and fax submissions. Cover letter preferred. "Poetry manuscripts may be submitted single-spaced and e-mailed." SASE with sufficient postage required for return of ms sent via regular mail. Time between acceptance and publication is 6 months. Often comments on rejected poems. Guidelines available for SASE, by e-mail, or on website. Responds in 2 months. Pays 2 copies. Acquires first rights. Reviews books and chapbooks of poetry and other magazines in 300 words, single book format. Poets may send books for review consideration.

THE LEDGE, 78-44 80th St., Glendale NY 11385. Established 1988. **Editor-in-Chief/Publisher:** Timothy Monaghan. **Co-Editor:** George Held.

Magazine Needs: "We publish the best poems we receive. We seek poems with purpose, poems we can empathize with, powerful poems. Excellence is the ultimate criterion." Contributors include Sherman Alexie, Kurt Brown, Tony Gloeggler, Sherry Fairchok, Hal Sirowitz, and Brooke Wiese. As a sample the editor-in-chief selected these lines from "Crossed Lines" by Elton Glaser:

> *If you were at hand, and the night warm,/And all the crossed lines clear,/Would we undo Newton and confuse the physical,//Proving that two bodies can enclose/The same space at the same time,/As in that hybrid gift, that tourist curio//Where the Midwest finds itself/Suddenly at sea: a sand dollar/Set in the smooth belly of a buckeye burl.*

The Ledge is 128 pgs., digest-sized, typeset and perfect-bound with b&w glossy cover. Accepts 3% of poetry submissions. Press run is 1,000, including 600 subscribers. Single copy: $7; subscription: $13/2 issues, $24/4 issues or $32/6 issues.

How to Submit: Submit 3-5 poems at a time. Include SASE. Accepts simultaneous submissions; no previously published work. Reads submissions September through May only. Responds in 3 months. Pays 1 contributor's copy. Acquires one-time rights.

Also Offers: *The Ledge* sponsors an annual poetry chapbook contest, as well as an annual poetry contest. Details available for SASE.

Advice: "I believe the best poems appeal to the widest audience and consider *The Ledge* a truly democratic publication in that regard."

☑ ◯ LIBRA PUBLISHERS, INC., 3089C Clairemont Dr., PMB 383, San Diego CA 92117. Phone/fax: (858)571-1414. **Poetry Editor:** William Kroll.

Book/Chapbook Needs: Publishes two professional journals, *Adolescence* and *Family Therapy*, plus books, primarily in the behaviorial sciences but also some general nonfiction, fiction, and poetry. "At first we published books of poetry on a standard royalty basis, paying 10% of the retail price to the authors. Although at times we were successful in selling enough copies to at least break even, we found that we could no longer afford to publish poetry on this basis. Now, unless we fall madly in love with a particular collection, we offer professional services to assist the author in self-publishing." Has published books of poetry by Martin Rosner, William Blackwell, John Travers Moore, and C. Margaret Hall.

How to Submit: Prefers complete ms but accepts query with 6 sample poems, publishing credits, and bio. Responds to query in 2 days, to submissions in up to 3 weeks. Mss should be double-spaced. Sometimes sends prepublication galleys. Send 9 × 12 SASE for catalog. Sample books may be purchased on a returnable basis.

◖ THE LICKING RIVER REVIEW, Dept. of Literature and Language, Northern Kentucky University, Highland Heights KY 41099. E-mail: lrr@nku.edu. Established 1991. **Faculty Advisor:** Andrew Miller. Mail submissions to poetry editor.

Magazine Needs: *The Licking River Review,* is an annual designed "to showcase the best writing by Northern Kentucky University students alongside work by new or established writers from the region or elsewhere." No specifications regarding form, subject matter, or style of poetry. "No long poems (maximum 75 lines)." Has published poetry by Michael Cadnum, Mary Winters, and James Doyle. *The Licking River Review* is 96 pgs., 7 × 10, offset-printed on recycled paper and perfect-bound with a 16-page artwork inset (all art solicited). Accepts 5% of the poetry received. Press run is 1,500. Sample: $5.

How to Submit: Submit up to 5 poems at a time. No previously published poems, no multiple or simultaneous submissions. Reads submissions September through November only. Publishes in June or July. Poems are circulated to an editorial board. Responds in up to 6 months. Pays in copies. Rights revert to author. Requests acknowledgment if poem is later reprinted.

◉ LIFTOUTS MAGAZINE; PRELUDIUM PUBLISHERS, Dept. PM, 1414 S. Third St., Suite 102, Minneapolis MN 55454-1172. Fax: (612)305-0655. E-mail: barcass@mr.net. Established 1971. **Poetry Editor:** Barry Casselman. *Liftouts* appears irregularly as a "publisher of experimental literary work and work of new writers in translation from other languages." Currently not accepting unsolicited material.

◖ LIGHT, Box 7500, Chicago IL 60680. Established 1992. **Editor:** John Mella.

Magazine Needs: *Light* is a quarterly of "light and occasional verse, satire, wordplay, puzzles, cartoons, and line art." Does not want "greeting card verse, cloying or sentimental verse." *Light* is 64 pgs., perfect-bound, including art and graphics. Single copy: $5; subscription: $18. Sample: $4 with an additional $2 for first-class postage.

How to Submit: Submit 1 poem on a page with name, address, poem title and page number on each page. No previously published poems or simultaneous submissions. Seldom comments on rejected poems. Guidelines available for #10 SASE. Responds in 3 months or less. Always sends prepublication galleys. Pays 2 copies to domestic contributors, 1 copy to foreign contributors. Poets may send books for review consideration.

◎ LILITH MAGAZINE (Specialized: women, ethnic), 250 W. 57th St., Suite 2432, New York NY 10107. (212)757-0818. Fax: (212)757-5705. E-mail: lilithmag@aol.com. Website: www.lilithmag.com (includes material from recent issues, guidelines, a brief history and mission statement, "talent bank", etc.). Established 1976. **Editor-in-Chief:** Susan Weidman Schneider. **Poetry Editor:** Marge Piercy.

Magazine Needs: *Lilith* "is an independent magazine with a Jewish feminist perspective" which uses poetry by Jewish women "about the Jewish woman's experience. Generally we use short rather than long poems. Run four poems/year. Do not want to see poetry on other subjects." Has published poetry by Irena Klepfisz, Lyn Lifshin, Marcia Falk, and Adrienne Rich. *Lilith Magazine* is 48 pgs., magazine-sized, glossy. "We use colors. Covers are very attractive and professional-looking (one has won an award). Generous amount of art. It appears 4 times/year, circulation about 10,000, about 6,000 subscriptions." Subscription: $18 for 4 issues. Sample: $6.
How to Submit: Send up to 3 poems at a time; advise if simultaneous submission. Editor "sometimes" comments on rejected poems. Guidelines available for SASE or on website.
Advice: "(1) Read a copy of the publication before you submit your work. (2) Please be patient; it takes up to 6 months for a reply. (3) Short cover letters only. Copy should be neatly typed and proofread for typos and spelling errors."

LILLIPUT REVIEW (Specialized: form), 282 Main St., Pittsburgh PA 15201-2807. Website: http://donw714.tripod.com/lillieindex.html. Established 1989. **Editor:** Don Wentworth.
Magazine Needs: *Lilliput* is a tiny (4½ × 3.6 or 3½ × 4¼), 12- to 16-page magazine, appearing irregularly and using poems in any style or form no longer than 10 lines. Has published *What is Born* by Jen Besemer and *Footprints and Fingerprints* by Gary Hotham and poetry by Cid Corman, Linda Zeizer, Albert Huffstickler, and Miriam Sagan. As a sample the editor selected this poem, "Buried" by David Rosenthal:
> Buried in a pile/of camellia petals:/camellia petals.
Lilliput Review is laser-printed on colored paper and stapled. Press run is 250. Sample: $1 or SASE. Make checks payable to Don Wentworth.
How to Submit: Submit up to 3 poems at a time. Currently, every fourth issue is a broadside featuring the work of one particular poet. Guidelines available for SASE. Responds within 3 months. Pays 2 copies/poem. Acquires first rights. Editor comments on submissions "occasionally—always try to establish human contact."
Book/Chapbook Needs & How to Submit: Started the Modest Proposal Chapbook Series in 1994, publishing 1 chapbook/year, 18-24 pgs. in length. Chapbook submissions are by invitation only. Query with standard SASE. Sample chapbook: $3. Chapbook publications include *The Kingdom of Loose Board & Rusted Nail* by Christien Gholson.
Advice: "A note above my desk reads 'Clarity & resonance, not necessarily in that order.' The perfect poem for *Lilliput Review* is simple in style and language and elusive/allusive in meaning and philosophy. *Lilliput Review* is open to all short poems in approach and theme, including any of the short Eastern forms, traditional or otherwise."

LIMESTONE CIRCLE, P.O. Box 453, Ashburn VA 20146-0453. E-mail: rcnjcf@earthlink.net. Established 1998. **Editor:** Renee Carter Hall.
Magazine Needs: *Limestone Circle* now appears twice annually; published in spring (early May) and fall (early November). "We publish artistic, accessible poetry. Free verse is preferred." As a sample the editor selected these lines from "Cover" by Kelley Jean White:
> I lift a log and shock the thigmotactic world:/sow bugs scurry and roll, worms gleam/naked, vulnerable in the sun, a slug cowers/as my hand recoils, his thick body brown as/polished wood.
Limestone Circle is approximately 40 pgs., 8½ × 5½, digitally copied and saddle-stapled with matte cardstock cover, includes b&w artwork and photos. Each issue features 25-30 poems. Press run is 100 for 40 subscribers. Single copy: $4; subscription: $8/1 year (2 issues), $12/2 years (4 issues). Sample: $2. Make checks payable to Renee Carter Hall.
How to Submit: Submit 365 poems at a time, typed with name and address on each page, but "poets may submit work no more than twice in each calendar month." No previously published poems or simultaneous submissions. Accepts e-mail submissions "provided they are in the body of the message, not as attached files." Cover letter with bio preferred. Time between acceptance and publication is up to 4 months. Sometimes comments on rejected poems. Full guidelines available for SASE or by e-mail. Responds within 2 months for postal submissions; usually within 1 week for e-mail submissions. Pays 1 copy; additional copies available at a discount. Acquires first rights.
Also Offers: Also accepts submissions of b&w artwork and photos; guidelines available for SASE or by e-mail.
Advice: "I give respectful consideration to all submissions. That said, please remember that editors are human beings. This implies two things: first, that we like to be treated in a friendly, polite, and professional manner, and second, that any editor's decision is just one person's opinion. Keep sending out your best work and eventually someone will publish it."

LIMITED EDITIONS PRESS; ART: MAG, P.O. Box 70896, Las Vegas NV 89170. (702)734-8121. E-mail: magman@iopener.net. Established 1982. **Editor:** Peter Magliocco.
Magazine Needs: *ART:MAG* has "become, due to economic and other factors, more limited to a select audience of poets as well as readers. We seek to expel the superficiality of our factitious culture, in all its drive-thru, junk-food-brain, commercial-ridden extravagance—and stylize a magazine of hard-line aesthetics, where truth and beauty meet on a vector not shallowly drawn. Conforming to this outlook is an operational policy of seeking poetry from solicited poets primarily, though unsolicited submissions will be read, considered and perhaps used infrequently. Sought from the chosen is a creative use of poetic styles, systems and emotional morphologies other

than banally constricting." Has published poetry by Jonathan Hayes, Norman J. Olson, Vincent Suarez, Shane Jones, Lorraine Tolliver, and Jane Stuart. As a sample the editor selected these lines from "A Holding On" by Henry Tokarski:

> Life a summoning up of life,/In the constant face of death./The comfort of a crowd around an accident,/
> A blanket at midnight./Dawn, the return of October.

ART: MAG, appearing in 1-2 large issues of 100 copies/year, is limited to a few poets. Subscription: $10. Sample: $3 or more. Make checks payable to Peter Magliocco.

How to Submit: Submit 5 poems at a time with SASE. "Submissions should be neat and use consistent style format (except experimental work). Cover letters are optional." Accepts simultaneous submissions; no previously published poems. No fax or e-mail submissions. Sometimes comments on rejected poems. Publishes theme issues. Guidelines and upcoming themes are available for SASE. Responds within 3 months. Pays 1 contributor's copy. Acquires first rights. Staff occasionally reviews books of poetry. Send books for review consideration.

Book/Chapbook Needs & How to Submit: "A recently published chapbook for '00-01 is: *News from the Border* by Joyce Metzger. For any other press chapbook possibilities, query the editor before submitting any manuscript."

Advice: "The mag is seeking a futuristic aestheticism where the barriers of fact and fiction meet, where inner- and outer-space converge in the realm of poetic consciousness in order to create a more productively viable relationship to the coming 'cyberology' of the 21st century."

☑ ⤵ $ ⌨ ◎ THE LINK & VISITOR (Specialized: nationality, religious, women), % BWOQ, 414-195 The West Mall, Etobicoke, Ontario M9C 5K1 Canada. (416)651-7192. Fax: (416)651-0438. E-mail: linkvis@idirect.com. Established 1878.

Magazine Needs: *The Link & Visitor* provides monthly "encouragement, insight, inspiration for Canadian Christian women; Baptist, mission and egalitarian slant. Poetry must relate to reader's experience; must be grounded in a biblical Christian faith; contemporary in style and language; upbeat but not naive. We do not want to see anything that has already been better said in the Bible or traditional hymns." *The Link & Visitor* is 16 pgs., magazine-sized, offset-printed with self cover. Receives about 20 poems/year, accepts about 30%. "We have a few poets we use regularly because their work fits our mix." Press run is 4,500. Subscription: $14 (Canadian), $16 (US). Sample: $1.50 (Canadian).

How to Submit: Submit up to 5 poems at a time. Line length for poetry is 8 minimum, 30 maximum. Accepts previously published poems and simultaneous submissions. Accepts e-mail submissions. Cover letter required. Include SASE with Canadian stamps. Time between acceptance and publication is up to 2 years. Seldom comments on rejected poems. Occasionally publishes theme issues. Guidelines and upcoming themes are available for SASE. Pays $10-25 (Canadian). Acquires one-time rights.

Advice: "Canadian writers only, please."

☑ ⊕ ◑ LINKS, Bude Haven, 18 Frankfield Rise, Tunbridge Wells TN2 5LF United Kingdom. E-mail: linksmag.supanet.com. Established 1992. **Editor:** Bill Headdon.

Magazine Needs: *Links* is published biannually in April and October and contains good quality poetry and reviews. Wants "contemporary, strong poetry; must relate to the 'real' world; up to 80 lines. No chopped-up prose; no mock Shelley." Has published poetry by Gross, Bartlett, and Shuttle. As a sample the editor selected these lines from "Masterpiece" by Barbara Daniels:

> I am a transparent woman,/My lover looks through me,/into a collaged landscape,/where any man can
> see/tamed hills and perfect pastures,/ego ego running free.

Links is up to 32 pgs., A5, photocopied and saddle-stapled with card cover. Receives about 2,000 poems/year, accepts 7%. Press run is 200 for 150 subscribers of which 5 are libraries, 30 shelf sales. Subscription: £4/year (overseas £6), £7.50/2 years (overseas £10). Sample (with guidelines): £2 (£3 outside UK).

How to Submit: Submit 5-6 poems at a time. No previously published poems or simultaneous submissions. No fax or e-mail submissions. Cover letter preferred. "No long bios or list of previous publications." Time between acceptance and publication is up to 6 months. Seldom comments on rejected poems. Guidelines available for SASE or by e-mail. Responds in 2 weeks. Pays 1 copy. Acquires first rights. Reviews books and chapbooks of poetry and other magazines in 200 to 400 words, single or multi-book format. Poets may send books for review consideration.

☑ $ ◑ LINTEL, 24 Blake Lane, Middletown NY 10940. (845)344-1690. Established 1977. **Poetry Editor:** Walter James Miller.

Book/Chapbook Needs: "We publish poetry and innovative fiction of types ignored by commercial presses. We consider any poetry except conventional, traditional, cliché, greeting card types, i.e., we consider any artistic poetry." We have published poetry by Sue Saniel Elkind, Samuel Exler, Adrienne Wolfert, Edmund Pennant, and Nathan Teitel. "Typical of our work" is Teitel's book, *In Time of Tide*, 64 pgs., digest-sized, professionally printed in bold type, flat-spined, hard cover stamped in gold, jacket with art and author's photo on back.

How to Submit: Query with 5 sample poems. Reads submissions January and August only. "We reply to the query within a month, to the ms (if invited) in 2 months. We consider simultaneous submissions if so marked and if the writer agrees to notify us of acceptance elsewhere." Ms should be typed. Always sends prepublication galleys. Pays royalties after all costs are met and 100 copies. Acquires all rights. Offers usual subsidiary rights: 50%/50%. To see samples, send SASE for catalog and ask for "trial rate" (50%).

Advice: "Form follows function! We accept any excellent poem whose form—be it sonnet or free verse—suits the content and the theme. We like our poets to have a good publishing record in literary magazines, before they begin to think of a book."

✓ ⏱ ◎ **THE LISTENING EYE**, Kent State Geauga Campus, 14111 Claridon-Troy Rd., Burton OH 44021. (440)286-3840. E-mail: graceb@geocities.com. Website: www.geocities.com/Athens/3716. Established 1970 for student work, 1990 as national publication. **Editor:** Grace Butcher. **Assistant Editors:** Jim Wohlken and Joanne Speidel.

Magazine Needs: *The Listening Eye* is an annual publication, appearing in late summer/early fall, of poetry, short fiction, creative nonfiction, and art that welcomes both new and established poets and writers. Wants "high literary quality poetry. Prefer shorter poems (less than two pages) but will consider longer if space allows. Any subject, any style. No trite images or predictable rhyme." Accepts poetry written by children if high literary quality. Has published poetry by Alberta Turner, Virgil Suarez, Walter McDonald, and Simon Perchik. As a sample the editor selected these lines from "71" by Simon Perchik:

> You didn't hear. Or remember. But that snow/we once believed had no memory/has returned, frantic
> now, each flake/as if the sun was still in flames/will circle down, closer and closer . . .

The Listening Eye is 52-60 pgs., 5½×8½, professionally printed and saddle-stapled with card stock cover with b&w art. Receives about 200 poems/year, accepts about 5%. Press run is 300. Single copy: $4. Sample: $4. Make checks payable to Kent State University.

How to Submit: Submit up to 4 poems at a time, typed, single-spaced, 1 poem/page, name, and address in upper left-hand corner of each page, with SASE for return of work. Previously published poems occasionally accepted; no simultaneous submissions. Cover letter required. No e-mail submissions. Reads submissions January 1 through April 15 only. Time between acceptance and publication is up to 6 months. Poems are circulated to the editor and 2 assistant editors who read and evaluate work separately, then meet for final decisions. Occasionally comments on rejected poems. Guidelines available for SASE, by e-mail, or on website. Responds in 3 months. Pays 2 copies. Acquires first or one-time rights. Also awards $30 to the best sports poem in each issue.

Advice: "I look for tight lines that don't sound like prose, unexpected images or juxtapositions; the unusual use of language, noticeable relationships of sounds; a twist in viewpoint, an ordinary idea in extraordinary language, an amazing and complex idea simply stated, play on words and with words, an obvious love of language. Poets need to read the 'Big 3'—cummings, Thomas, Hopkins—to see the limits to which language can be taken. Then read the 'Big 2'—Dickinson to see how simultaneously tight, terse, and universal a poem can be, and Whitman to see how sprawling, cosmic, and personal. Then read everything you can find that's being published in literary magazines today and see how your work compares to all of the above."

☑ ◎ **LITERAL LATTÉ; LITERAL LATTÉ POETRY AWARDS**, 61 E. Eighth St., Suite 240, New York NY 10003. (212)260-5532. E-mail: litlatte@aol.com. Website: www.literal-latte.com (includes excerpts, guidelines, information on events and contests). Established 1994. **Editor:** Jenine Gordon Bockman. **Contact:** Lisa Erdman.

• Amy Holman's poem "Man Script" was just reissued in Best American Poetry.

Magazine Needs: *Literal Latté* is a bimonthly tabloid of "pure prose, poetry, and art," distributed free in coffeehouses and bookstores in New York City, and by subscription. "Open to all styles of poetry—quality is the determining factor." Has published poetry by Allen Ginsberg, Carol Muske, Amy Holman, and John Updike. As a sample we selected these lines from "What The Screech Owl Knows" by John Sokol, 1st Place winner of the annual *Literal Latté* Poetry Awards:

> That, here, in the woods/of western Pennsylvania,/life burgeons by the hour/while death rides a pig;/
> that larvae open like popcorn/and everything living/feasts on last year's detritus; . . .

Literal Latté is 24-28 pgs., 11×17, neatly printed on newsprint and unbound with b&w art, graphics and ads. Receives about 3,000 poems/year, accepts 1%. Press run is 25,000 for distribution in over 200 bookstores and coffeehouses in New York City and nationwide. Subscription: $11. Sample: $3.

How to Submit: Accepts simultaneous submissions; no previously published poems. Accepts e-mail submissions. "No attachments." Cover letter with bio and SASE required. Time between acceptance and publication is 6 months. Often comments on rejected poems. Guidelines available for SASE, by e-mail, or on website. Responds in 3 months. Pays 10 copies and 3 subscriptions (2 gift subscriptions in author's name). All rights return to author upon publication.

Also Offers: Also sponsors the *Literal Latté* Poetry Awards, an annual contest for previously unpublished work. Offers $1,500 in awards and publication. They have added a "Food Verse" award; 1st Prize $500. Entry fee: $10 for 6 poems (or buy a subscription and the entry fee for 6 poems is included). A past contest was judged by Carol Muske. Current details available for SASE, by e-mail, or on website.

☑ $ ◻ ◎ **LITERALLY HORSES (Specialized: horses, cowboy lifestyle)**, Equestrienne Ltd., 208 Cherry Hill St., Kalamazoo MI 49006. (616)345-5915. E-mail: literallyhorses@aol.com. Established 1999. **Editor:** Laurie A. Cerny.

Magazine Needs: *Literally Horses* is "a quarterly venue for creative poetry/fiction and essays that have a horse/western lifestyle theme. Any style is acceptable. Nothing sexually explicit; nothing offensive; no curse words or racial overtones." Has published poetry by John R. Tucker, Nancy Chase, Sharon Selby Merritt, Thomas Michael McDade, and Tena Bastian. As a sample the editor selected these lines from Tena Bastian:

> For in the horse's eyes, she saw a reflection of her own fear/She looked into the horse's soul/And understood what brought her here/God had brought the two together/The only way he could/This horse was not a renegade/Simply misunderstood.

Literally Horses is about 20 pgs., 5½×8½, desktop-published and saddle-stapled with b&w paper cover, includes simple drawings, classified ads. Receives about 50 poems/year, accepts about 75%. Press run is 1,000. Single copy: $2.25; subscription: $7.95. Sample (including guidelines): $2.75. Make checks payable to Equestrienne Ltd.

How to Submit: Submit 1-3 poems at a time. Line length for poetry is 5 minimum, 30 maximum. Accepts previously published poems and simultaneous submissions. No fax or e-mail submissions. Cover letter required. "Cover letters with bio and release/permission to use poems. Include SASE for return of poems and acceptance." Time between acceptance and publication is 3 months. Often comments on rejected poems. Responds in 3 months. Pays $3/poem and 5 copies. Acquires one-time rights. Reviews books and chapbooks of poetry in 150 words. Poets may send books for review consideration.

Also Offers: "Annual poetry contest. Submit up to 3 poems (under 50 lines each), bio, SASE, and $9.95 entry fee (the fee includes a one-year subscription). First place: $75. Two honorable mention awards. Deadline: July 15 of every year. Winning entries are published in winter issue."

Advice: "Know the topic of horses . . . terminology, etc. Don't try to fake it."

○ ◎ **LITERARY FOCUS POETRY PUBLICATIONS; ANTHOLOGY OF CONTEMPORARY POETRY; INTERNATIONAL POETRY CONTESTS: FALL CONCOURS, SPRING CONCOURS, SUMMER CONCOURS (Specialized: anthology)**, P.O. Box 36242, Houston TX 77236-6242. Phone/fax: (281)568-8780. E-mail: dprince1@swbell.net. Website: www.literaryfocus.com. Established 1988. **Editor-in-Chief:** Adrian A. Davieson.

Magazine Needs: Purchase of anthology may be required of poets accepted for publication. Literary Focus publishes anthologies compiled in contests, 3 times/year, with prizes of $200, $100, and $50, plus "Distinguished Mention" and "Honorable Mention." "Contemporary poetry with no restriction on themes. 20-line limit. No abusive, anti-social poetry." As a sample we selected these lines from the editor's own poem "My Deep Fears":

> Out came the fears of yester-years/Eroding my very being. As I looked/The stream of tears cascaded my/Cheeks, reminding me the journey/Was not over.//Only yesterday I thought of my arrival/At shore, but now I know it was just a/Mirage, that to be thus is nothing but/To be safely thus!

The digest-sized anthologies are either flat-spined or saddle-stapled, 70 pgs., typeset.

How to Submit: Submit maximum submission 15 poems, minimum three poems. Accepts previously published poems and simultaneous submissions. Accepts e-mail submissions. "In order to evaluate serious entries, a $5 entry fee is required for the first three poems. Poems are evaluated on an individual basis by a panel of five editors chaired by editor-in-chief. Poets are notified of acceptance two weeks after deadlines." Guidelines available for SASE or on website. Pays up to 5 copies. Reviews books of poetry.

◔ **THE LITERARY REVIEW: AN INTERNATIONAL JOURNAL OF CONTEMPORARY WRITING**, Fairleigh Dickinson University, 285 Madison Ave., Madison NJ 07940. (973)443-8564. Fax: (973)443-8364. E-mail: tlr@fdu.edu. Website: www.webdelsol.com/tlr/. Established 1957. **Editor-in-Chief:** Walter Cummins. **Contact:** William Zander.

Magazine Needs: *The Literary Review*, a quarterly, seeks "work by new and established poets which reflects a sensitivity to literary standards and the poetic form." No specifications as to form, length, style, subject matter, or purpose. Has published poetry by Thomas Halloran, Joanna Goodman and Dale M. Kushner. The magazine is 128 pgs., 6×9, professionally printed and flat-spined with glossy color cover, using 20-50 pgs. of poetry in each issue. Press run is 2,500 with 900 subscriptions of which one-third are overseas. Receives about 1,200 submissions/year, accepts 100-150, have a 8- to 16-month backlog. Sample: $5 domestic, $6 outside US, request a "general issue."

How to Submit: Submit up to 5 typed poems at a time. Accepts simultaneous submissions. No fax or e-mail submissions. Do not submit during the summer months of June, July and August. At times the editor comments on rejected poems. Publishes theme issues. Responds in 3 months. Always sends prepublication galleys. Pays 2 copies. Acquires first rights. Reviews books of poetry in 500 words, single book format. Poets may send books for review consideration.

Advice: "Read a general issue of the magazine carefully before submitting."

◔ ◎ **LITERATURE AND BELIEF (Specialized: religious)**, 3076-E Jesse Knight Humanities Building, Brigham Young University, Provo UT 84602. (801)378-3073. Fax: (801)378-8724. E-mail: richard~cracroft@em ail.byu.edu. Established 1981. **Editors:** Richard H. Cracroft and John J. Murphy. **Poetry Editor:** Lance Larsen.

Magazine Needs: *Literature and Belief* is the "biannual journal of the Center for the Study of Christian Values in Literature." It uses "carefully crafted, affirmation poetry in the Judeo-Christian tradition." Has published poetry by Ted Hughes, Donnel Hunter, Leslie Norris, Susan Elizabeth Howe, and Lance Larsen. As a sample the editor selected these lines from "Cycle" by Cyd Adams:

> The air bears the heaviness/of creation's spawning,/for Christ has borne the dogwood/to scale the last escarpment/so a risen sun can silver/the cobalt sky.

Literature and Belief is handsomely printed and flat-spined. Single copy: $5, $7 outside US; subscription: $10, $14 outside US.

How to Submit: Submit 3-4 poems at a time. No previously published poems. Responds within 6 weeks. Pays 5 copies and 10 "offprints."

Also Offers: The center also publishes religious monographs, such as *Toward the Solitary Star*, selected poems by Östen Sjöstrand. "Values in Literature" monograph series invites queries for scholarly studies of authors (C.S. Lewis, W. Cather, Leslie Norris) or works which combine fine literature and religious values and faith in God. Currently in progress: "Willa Cather and Religion" and "The York Cycle of Morality Plays"; in print: Bruce L. Edwards, *C.S. Lewis: A Rhetoric of Reaching*; *Willa Cather: Family, Community, History*.

LITHUANIAN PAPERS (Specialized: nationality), P.O. Box 777, Sandy Bay, Tasmania 7006 Australia. phone (+3)62252505. E-mail: A.Taskunas@utas.edu.au. Established 1987. **Editor:** Al Taskunas.

Magazine Needs: *Lithuanian Papers* is "an annual English-language journal aimed at fostering research into all aspects of Lithuania and its people." Wants "high-standard poetry dealing with Lithuanian topics or any topics by Lithuanian poets (in English)." Nothing unethical or offensive. Has published poetry by Bruce Dawe, J. Reilly, J. Degutytė/transl. G. Slavenas, and Julius Keleras/Vyt Bakaitis. As a sample the editor selected these lines:

> It's then that the map of dreams/soaked through and through, caves in/like a child's balloon filled with water.

Lithuanian Papers is 80 pgs., 5½×8½, offset-printed and saddle-stitched with light card cover, includes b&w photos and art, ads. Receives about 25 poems/year, accepts about 10%. Press run is 2,000 for 1,500 subscribers of which 100 are libraries, 100 shelf sales; 400 distributed free to members, students, etc. Sample: $8 (US) if available. Make checks payable to Lithuanian Studies Society (LSS).

How to Submit: Submit 2-3 poems at a time. "If translation, the originals are also required." Line length for poetry is 4 minimum, 20 maximum. No previously published poems or simultaneous submissions. Accepts e-mail (include text in body of message) and disk submissions. "Must be Mac-compatible." Cover letter required. "The cover letter must contain a concise c.v. and be accompanied by 2 letters of recommendation." Reads submissions December 1 through June 30 only. Time between acceptance and publication is up to 6 months. Poems are circulated to an editorial board. "Short list read by at least 2 referees—more if in disagreement." Pays 2 copies "or more by special arrangement." Acquires all rights. Rights returned by negotiation.

Advice: "The Chinese say that even the longest journey starts with a single step. We are open to that step—or any advanced strides along the way."

LITRAG, P.O. Box 21066, Seattle WA 98111. E-mail: litrag@hotmail.com. Website: www.litrag.com (features selections from back issues and current issue, guidelines, editors, art and information on current issues, availability and upcoming events). Established 1997. **Editor:** Derrick Hachey. **Co-Editor:** AJ Rathbun.

Magazine Needs: *LitRag* appears 3 times/year. "We strive to publish high-quality poetry, fiction and art from established and up-and-coming writers and visual artists. We look for poetry that is strong in both image and intelligence, and we admit to no thematic bias. We do not want poetry from writers who do not actually read books of contemporary poetry." Accepts poetry written by children. Has published poetry by Ed Skoog, Liz Wahler, Richard Jackson, and Mark Halliday. As a sample the editor selected this poem, "What Dying Might Be Like For You," by Kathleen McCarthy:

> Now, a man rumbles through the house asking, Where's/my oboe?, as he tosses pillows aside that land/with the soft thud of a bird/confused into a window. But this can't be/right. Where's the transcendence/in chaos?

LitRag is 40 pgs., magazine-sized, laser printed and staple bound, gloss cover, includes photos, ink drawings and illustrations. Receives about 4,000 poems/year, accepts 1%. Press run is 500 for 150 subscribers, 125 shelf sales; 150 distributed free to random people. Subscription: $12/4 issues. Sample: $3.

How to Submit: Submit 3 poems at a time. Accepts simultaneous submissions; no previously published poems. Accepts e-mail with attachments and disk submissions. Cover letter preferred. "We require a SASE." Time between acceptance and publication is 3 months. Poems are circulated to an editorial board. "One original reader who makes the initial decision to submit it to the editorial board, which makes the final decision." Seldom comments on rejected poems. Guidelines available for SASE, by e-mail, or on website. Responds in 6 weeks. Sometimes sends prepublication galleys. Pays "commemorative gift" and 4 copies. Acquires first North American serial rights. Reviews books and chapbooks of poetry and other magazines in 300 words, single book format. Poets may send books for review consideration.

Also Offers: "We host release parties for each issue."

LITTLE BROWN POETRY, P.O. Box 4533, Portsmouth NH 03802. Fax: (240)282-6418. E-mail: editor@littlebrownpoetry.com. Website: www.littlebrownpoetry.com (includes writer's guidelines, submissions page, submissions e-mail address, about the editor, subscription info). Established 1998. **Editor:** Sam Siegel.

Magazine Needs: *Little Brown Poetry* is an online quarterly poetry journal with printed anthologies. Wants "good quality emotional poetry, any style, any form." Has published poetry by Ric Masten, David Sutherland, Jarrett Keene, Yu-Cheung Cheng, Tom Perry, and O. Harrison. As a sample the editor selected these lines by Agnes Makar:

> on december barren trees/you, man of suits and cigars/disturb the peacocks/from their far off nests,/
> on some transparent glow/they fluff tails/paint eyes and lips all for the/hate of tomorrow/the
> consistency/day in and day out/you hear them cry/among the ruins of empty cages/vacant eyes/not
> belonging,/peacock woman,/a wasteland of youth.

Little Brown Poetry is over 48 pgs., journal-sized, perfect-bound with original cover art. Receives about 1,500 poems/year, accepts about 25%. Press run is 1,000 for 250 subscribers. Single copy: $5; subscription: $24/2 years. Sample: $3.

How to Submit: Submit at least 3 poems at a time. Accepts previously published poems and simultaneous submissions. Accepts fax, e-mail, and disk submissions. Cover letter preferred. Often comments on rejected poems. Publishes theme issues. Guidelines and upcoming themes available by e-mail or on website. Responds in 1 month. Pays 4 copies. Acquires one-time rights.

LONE STARS MAGAZINE; "SONGBOOK" POETRY CONTEST, 4219 Flinthill, San Antonio TX 78230. Established 1992. **Editor/Publisher:** Milo Rosebud.

Magazine Needs: *Lone Stars*, published 3 times/year, features "contemporary poetry." Wants poetry that holds a continuous line of thought. No profanity. Has published poetry by Sheila Roark, Tom Hendrix, and Patricia Rourke. As a sample the editor selected these lines from "Let Life Decide" by Terry Lee:

> A midnight rainbow, a tear never cried, words spoken in silence: a light that does not shine.

Lone Stars is 25 pgs., 8½×11, photocopied, with some hand-written poems, saddle-stapled, bound with tape, includes clip art. Press run is 200 for 100 subscribers of which 3 are libraries. Single copy: $5; subscription: $15. Sample: $4.50.

How to Submit: Submit 3-5 poems at a time with "the form typed the way you want it in print." **Charges reading fee of $1 per poem.** Accepts previously published poems and simultaneous submissions. Cover letter preferred. Time between acceptance and publication is 2 months. Publishes theme issues. Guidelines and upcoming themes available for SASE. Responds within 3 months. Acquires one-time rights.

Also Offers: Sponsors annual "Songbook" (song-lyric poems) Poetry Contest. Details available for SASE.

LONE WILLOW PRESS, P.O. Box 31647, Omaha NE 68131-0647. (402)551-0343. E-mail: lonewillowpress@aol.com. Established 1993. **Editor:** Fredrick Zydek.

Book/Chapbook Needs: Publishes 2-3 chapbooks/year. "We publish chapbooks on single themes and are open to all themes. The only requirement is excellence. However, we do not want to see doggerel or greeting card verse." Has published *Cave Poems* by Marjorie Power, *Things Like This Happen All the Time* by Eric Hoffman, *Monsters We Give Our Children* by Carolyn Riehle, and *From the Dead Before* by Clif Mason. Books are 36 pgs., digest-sized, neatly printed on gray paper and saddle-stapled with a light, gray card stock cover.

How to Submit: Query first with 5 sample poems and cover letter with brief bio and publication credits. Accepts previously published poems; no simultaneous submissions. Accepts e-mail submissions but no fax submissions. Time between acceptance and publication is 6 months. Seldom comments on rejected poems. Guidelines available for SASE. Responds to queries in 1 month, to mss (if invited) in up to 3 months. Pays 25 author's copies. "We also pay a small royalty if the book goes into a second printing." For a sample chapbook, send $7.95 in check or money order.

Advice: "If you don't know the work of Roethke, DeFrees, and Hugo, don't bother sending work our way. We work with no more than two poets at a time."

LONG ISLAND QUARTERLY (Specialized: regional), P.O. Box 114, Northport NY 11768. E-mail: Liquarterly@aol.com. Website: www.poetrybay.com. Established 1990. **Editor/Publisher:** George Wallace.

Magazine Needs: *Long Island Quarterly* uses poetry (mostly lyric free verse) by people on or from Long Island. "Surprise us with fresh language. No conventional imagery, self-indulgent confessionalism, compulsive article-droppers." Has published poetry by Edmund Pennant and David Ignatow. As a sample the editor selected this poem, "The Willow," by William Heyen:

> Crazy Horse counted the leaves of willows along the river./He realized one leaf for each buffalo,/&
> the leaves just now appearing in the Moon of Tender Grass/were calves being born. If he could keep
> the trees/from the whites, the herds would seed themselves./He watched the buffalo leaves for long, &
> long,/how their colors wavered dark & light in the running wind./If he could keep his rootedness within
> this dream,/he could shade his people to the end of time.

Long Island Quarterly is 28 pgs., digest-sized, professionally printed on quality stock and saddle-stapled with matte card cover. Press run is 250 for 150 subscribers of which 15 are libraries, 50-75 shelf sales. Subscription: $15. Sample: $4.

How to Submit: Submit 3 poems at a time. Name and address on each page. Cover letter including connection to Long Island region required. Submissions without SASE are not returned. Responds in 3 months. Sometimes sends prepublication galleys. Pays 1 copy.

Book/Chapbook Needs & How to Submit: Wants serious contemporary poetry of merit. Publishes up to 5 chapbooks per year. Chapbooks are usually 24-32 pgs. Reviews books and chapbooks of poetry. Send books for review consideration. Terms vary.

Advice: "(1) Go beyond yourself; (2) Don't be afraid to fictionalize; (3) Don't write your autobiography—if you are worth it, maybe someone else will."

☑ ◎ **LONG SHOT**, P.O. Box 6238, Hoboken NJ 07030. E-mail: dshot@mindspring.com Website: www.longshot.org. Established 1982. **Editors:** Dan Shot, Nancy Mercado, Andy Clausen, and Lynne Breitfeller.

Magazine Needs: Published biannually, *Long Shot* is, they say, "writing from the real world." Has published poetry by Wanda Coleman, Gregory Corso, Jayne Cortez, Diane di Prima, Amiri Baraka, Reg E. Gaines, and Pedro Pietri. *Long Shot* is 192 pgs., professionally printed and flat-spined with glossy card cover using b&w photos, drawings and cartoons. Press run is 2,000. Subscription: $24/2 years (4 issues). Sample: $8.

How to Submit: Accepts simultaneous submissions; no previously published poems. No e-mail submissions. Responds in 2 months. Pays 2 copies.

Also Offers: Has published *The Original Buckwheat* by Reg E. Gaines; *Sermons from the Smell of a Carcass Condemned to Begging* by Tony Medina; *Night When Moon Follows* by Cheryl Boyce Taylor; and *It Concerns the Madness* by Nancy Mercado; *I Have No Clue* by Jack Wiler.

Advice: "Unlike other publishers, we receive too many requests for writer's guidelines. Just send the poems."

☑ ◯ ◎ **LONZIE'S FRIED CHICKEN™ LITERARY MAGAZINE; SOUTHERN ESCARPMENT CO. (Specialized: regional)**, P.O. Box 189, Lynn NC 28750. E-mail: lonziesfriedchic@teleplex.net. Website: www.lonziesfriedchicken.com (includes guidelines, contributors, list of bookstores, and order form). Established 1998. **Editor:** E.H. Goree.

Magazine Needs: *Lonzie's Fried Chicken™* is "a journal of accessible southern fiction and poetry—an opportunity for writers and poets to show their stuff and satisfy readers. Our focus is well-written short fiction, self-contained novel excerpts, and poetry with a feel for the South. We welcome the best contemporary, mainstream, and historical work by published and unpublished poets and writers." Recently published poetry by Reid Bush, Gwen Hart, Wayne Hogan, Eileen Murphy, Marc Swan, and Nicole Sarrocco. *Lonzie's Fried Chicken* is about 100 pgs., digest-sized, offset-printed, perfect-bound, with light card cover containing b&w photo, ads. Receives over 500 poems/year, accepts about 10%. Press run is 1,000 for about 200 subscribers, 500 shelf sales; 100 distributed free to newspapers, reviewers, and contributors. Single copy: $8.95; subscription: $14.95/year, $26.95/2 years. Sample (including guidelines): $8.95.

How to Submit: Submit up to 5 poems at a time. Accepts simultaneous submissions; no previously published poems. No fax, e-mail, or disk submissions. Cover letter preferred. Reads submissions year round. Time between acceptance and publication is up to 5 months. Poems are circulated to an editorial board. Seldom comments on rejected poems. Send SASE or postcard for return or reply. Responds in 3 months or less. Pays 3 copies. Acquires first rights and one-time anthology rights.

Advice: "We look for humor and subtlety and always reject the quaint, as well as essays, gore, violence, hate, erotica, and science fiction."

☑ ◎ **LOS**, 150 N. Catalina St., No. 2, Los Angeles CA 90004. E-mail: lospoesy@earthlink.net. Website: http://home.earthlink.net/~lospoesy. Established 1991. **Contact:** the Editors.

Magazine Needs: *Los*, published 4 times/year, features poetry. Also accepts poetry written by children. Has published poetry by Ahmed Balfouni, David Chorlton, Thomas Feeny, Gregory Jerozal, Peter Layton, and Ed Orr. As a sample the editors selected these lines from "effusive reflection" by Christopher Mulrooney:

> the great Art Fairs and Poetry Journals/manifest a vase/curvy and full of tinselly kernals/that give us pause

Los is 5×8½ and saddle-stapled. Press run is 100 for 25 subscribers; 15 distributed free to local bookstores. Sample: $2. Make checks payable to Heather J. Lowe.

How to Submit: Submit any number of poems at a time. Accepts previously published poems and simultaneous submissions. Accepts e-mail submissions "in body of message or attachment, if necessary." Time between acceptance and publication is up to 6 months. Responds in 2 weeks. Pays 1 contributor's copy.

☑ ◐ ◎ **LOUISIANA LITERATURE; LOUISIANA LITERATURE PRIZE FOR POETRY (Specialized: regional)**, SLU-792, Southeastern Louisiana University, Hammond LA 70402. (504)549-5022. E-mail: lalit@selu.edu. Website: www.selu.edu/orgs/lalit (includes guidelines, special announcements, journal contents, and notes from the editor). **Editor:** Jack Bedell.

Magazine Needs: *Louisiana Literature* appears twice/year. "Receives mss year round although we work through submissions more slowly in summer. We consider creative work from anyone though we strive to showcase our state's talent. We appreciate poetry that shows firm control and craft, is sophisticated yet accessible to a broad readership. We don't use highly experimental work." Has published poetry by Claire Bateman, Elton Glaser, Gray Jacobik, Vivian Shipley, D.C. Berry, and Judy Longley. As a sample the editor selected these lines from "Notre Dame" by Alison T. Gray:

> Today Grandmama is as wide as Paris/and engulfs the city like smoke./She is looking for you, sister./ You think for a moment it's raining.//but it's a trick of the dead: how/in certain light smoke can seem water. . . .

Louisiana Literature is 150 pgs., 6¾ × 9¾, flat-spined, handsomely printed on heavy matte stock with matte card cover. Single copies: $8 for individuals; subscription: $12 for individuals, $12.50 for institutions.

How to Submit: Submit up to 5 poems at a time. Send cover letter, including bio to use in the event of acceptance. No simultaneous submissions. Enclose SASE "and specify whether work is to be returned or discarded." No fax or e-mail submissions. Publishes theme issues. Guidelines and upcoming themes available for SASE or on website. Sometimes sends prepublication galleys. Pays 2 copies. Send books for review consideration; include cover letter.

Also Offers: The Louisiana Literature Prize for Poetry offers a $400 award. Guidelines available for SASE. Website includes submission guidelines, special announcements, journal contents and notes from editor.

Advice: "It's important to us that the poets we publish be in control of their creations. Too much of what we see seems arbitrary."

✓ ◑ ◎ **THE LOUISIANA REVIEW (Specialized: regional)**, % Division of Liberal Arts, Louisiana State University at Eunice, P.O. Box 1129, Eunice LA 70535. (337)550-1328. E-mail: mgage@lsue.edu. Website: www.lsue.edu/LA-Review/ (includes table of contents, sample poems, cover of the second issue, and submission information). Established 1999. **Editors:** Dr. Maura Gage.

Magazine Needs: *The Louisiana Review* appears annually in August or September. "We wish to offer Louisiana residents a place to showcase their most beautiful, poignant pieces. Others may submit Louisiana-related poetry, stories, interviews with Louisiana writers, and art. We want to publish the highest-quality poetry, fiction, and drama. For poetry we like imagery, metaphor, and evidence of craft, but we do not wish to have sing-song rhymes, abstract, religious or overly sentimental work." Will publish poetry by Gary Snyder, Antler, David Cope, and Catfish McDavis. As a sample the editor selected these lines from "The Way We Used to Believe" by Sandra Meek:

> if death is a shell to split open, I want to hear/the rocking inside.

The Louisiana Review is 100-125 pgs. "depending on number of excellent poems received," magazine-sized, professionally printed and perfect-bound with glossy cover, includes 15 photographs/artwork. Receives about 200-500 poems/year, accepts 40-50 poems. Press run is 300-600. Single copy: $8. Sample copy: $5.

How to Submit: Submit 5-10 poems at a time. Accepts previously published poems. No fax submissions, accepts e-mail submissions if attached in an MS Word file. Cover letter preferred. "Send typed poems with SASE, include name, and address on each poem. If including a cover letter, please tell us your association with Louisiana: live there, frequent visitor, used to live there." Reads submissions October 1 through March 31 only. Time between acceptance and publication is up to 10 months. Poems are circulated to an editorial board. "Our board 'votes' yes or no, may request revision of a 'close' submission; it is done democratically." Sometimes comments on rejected poems. Responds in up to 5 months. Sends prepublication galleys. Pays 2 copies "depending on the size of the print run. Poets retain the rights to their works."

Advice: "Be true to yourself as a writer."

◙ **LOUISIANA STATE UNIVERSITY PRESS**, P.O. Box 25053, Baton Rouge LA 70894-5053. (225)388-6294. Fax: (225)388-6461. Established 1935. **Poetry Editor:** L.E. Phillabaum. A highly respected publisher of collections by poets such as Lisel Mueller, Margaret Gibson, Fred Chappell, Marilyn Nelson, and Henry Taylor. Currently not accepting poetry submissions; "fully committed through 2003."

◙ **LOW-TECH PRESS**, 30-73 47th St., Long Island City NY 11103. Established 1981. **Editor:** Ron Kolm. Has recently published *Bad Luck* by Mike Topp and *Goodbye Beautiful Mother* Tsaurah Litzky. "We only publish solicited mss."

◐ ◙ **LSR**, P.O. Box 440195, Miami FL 33144. Established 1990. **Editor/Publisher:** Nilda Cepero.

Magazine Needs: "Appearing 2 times per year, *LSR* publishes poetry, book reviews, interviews, and line artwork. Style, subject matter, and content of poetry open; we prefer contemporary with meaning and message.

TO RECEIVE REGULAR TIPS AND UPDATES about writing and Writer's Digest publications via e-mail, send an e-mail with SUBSCRIBE NEWSLETTER in the body of the message to newsletter-request@writersdigest.com, or sign up online at www.writersdigest.com.

No surrealism, no porn, or religious poetry. Reprints are accepted." Has published poetry by Catfish McDaris, Mike Catalano, Janine Pommey-Vega, Margarita Engle, and Evangeline Blanco. As a sample the editor selected these lines by Duane Locke:

> Death is dressed/like an old-fashioned clown/in caps and bells./Death wears silk upturned shoes./The out-of-date costume/leaves death unrecognized . . .

LSR is 20 pgs., 8½ × 11, offset-printed and saddle-stapled with a 60 lb. cover, includes line work, with very few ads. Receives about 300 poems/year, accepts about 30%. Publish 40-50 poems/issue. Press run is 3,000 for more than 100 subscribers of which 20 are libraries; the rest distributed free to selected bookstores in the US, Europe and Latin America. Single copy: $4; subscription: $8. Sample: $5, including postage.

How to Submit: Submit 4 poems at a time. Line length for poetry is 5 minimum, 45 maximum. Accepts previously published poems; no simultaneous submissions. Accepts disk submissions. Cover letter required. "We only accept disk submissions with print-out. Include SASE and bio." Reads submissions February 1 through October 31 only. Time between acceptance and publication is 1 year. Poems are circulated to an editorial board. "Three rounds by different editors. Editor/Publisher acts on recommendations." Guidelines available for SASE. Responds in 9 months. Pays 2 contributor's copies. Acquires one-time rights. Reviews books. "We will not write reviews; however, will consider those written by others to 750 words."

Advice: "Read as many current poetry magazines as you can."

✔ ▣ ◎ **LUCID MOON**, 67 Norma Rd., Hampton NJ 08827. Established 1997. E-mail: ralphy@lucidmoonpoctry.com. Website: www.lucidmoonpoetry.com. **Editor:** Ralph Haselmann Jr.

• "Ralph Haselmann Jr. was named Editor of the Year by *Cedar Hill Review* and called the hardest working editor in the small press."

Magazine Needs: "The *Lucid Moon* magazine is on indefinite hiatus but the website is thriving." The website, updated monthly, wants "underground Beat poetry and heartfelt romantic poetry. New poems each month as well as new essays, reviews, and short stories." Has published poetry by Antler, Ana Christy, Kevin M. Hibshman, Herschel Silverman, Allen Ginsberg, Gerald Locklin, Tony Moffeit, and Charles Plymell. As a sample the editor selected these lines from his poem "Lucid Moon":

> Traveling across America in all its terrible beauty, hitchhiking through history/the miles of highways and open roads a typewriter ribbon of future stories we could tell . . .

How to Submit: Submit up to 6 poems at a time. Accepts previously published poems and simultaneous submissions. Accepts snail mail, e-mail, and disk submissions. "Put name and address under each poem. Send Beat underground poems or enchanted love/nature/moon themed poems for Moon Beams section." Cover letter with 3- to 6-sentence bio and SASE required. Time between acceptance and posting on website is 3 months. "I choose poems that are moving and honest, bold and majestic." Responds same day. Rights revert to author upon posting. Poets may send poetry chapbooks, CDs, and broadsides for possible review.

Advice: "Read other poets and back issues of *Lucid Moon* to get a feel for the style wanted. Send poems you are proud of. Check out my *Lucid Moon* website and sign my guestbook!"

◖ **THE LUCID STONE**, P.O. Box 940, Scottsdale AZ 85252-0940. Established 1994. **Managing Editor:** Pauline Mounsey.

Magazine Needs: *The Lucid Stone* is a quarterly publishing "quality poetry and a small amount of quality artwork. We focus on poetry with complimentary artwork." Wants "unpublished quality poetry of any style and length. We are interested in poetry in the full poetic range, including formal, traditional and experimental poems." Nothing trite or didactic. Has published poetry by Barbara F. Lefcowitz, Jeanne Resnick, William Pitt Root, and Virgil Suarez. As a sample the editor selected these lines from "Watercolour in a Dry Country" by David Chorlton:

> . . . The view/is bordered by the deckle edges/I lay on a table/where I think like a tree/And see what the wood peckes sees. The paint//has its own life: released from the tube/it skirts a cloud, glows/ beneath a raven, rises and sets

The Lucid Stone is 56-72 pgs., 7 × 8½, offset-printed and saddle-stapled with 80 lb. Tahoe dull cover with one halftone of artwork, 5-7 b&w pieces of artwork and photography, no ads. Receives about 5,000 poems/year, accepts less than 200. Press run is 250-300 for 125 subscribers. Subscription: $16/4 issues. Sample: $6.

How to Submit: Submit 3-5 poems at a time. No previously published poems or simultaneous submissions. Cover letter preferred including "short personal biographical sketch other than the usual vita. No manuscripts or art will be returned nor queries answered unless accompanied by an SASE with adequate postage." Time between acceptance and publication is up to 6 months. Poems are circulated to an editorial board. "We have a staff of readers who individually review a group of approximately 50 poems at a time." Seldom comments on rejected poems. Guidelines available for SASE. Responds in 4 months. Pays 1 copy. Acquires first rights.

Advice: "We look for fresh language and use of images."

✔ $ ◎ **LUCIDITY; BEAR HOUSE PUBLISHING**, 14745 Memorial Dr., #10, Houston TX 77079-5200. (713)995-8159. E-mail: tedbadger@poetic.com. Established 1985. **Editor:** Ted O. Badger.

Magazine Needs: *Lucidity* is a biannual journal of poetry. **Submission fee required**—$1/poem for "juried" selection by a panel of judges or $2/poem to compete for cash awards of $15, $10, and $5. Other winners paid in both cash and in copies. Also publishes 10 pgs. of Succint Verse—poems of 12 lines or less—in most issues.

"We expect them to be pithy and significant and there is no reading/entry fee if sent along with Cash Award or Juried poems. Just think of all poetic forms that are 12 lines or less: the cinquain, limerick, etheree, haiku, senryu, lune, etc., not to mention quatrain, triolet and couplets." In addition, the editor invites a few guest contributors to submit to each issue. Contributors are encouraged to subscribe or buy a copy of the magazine. The magazine is called *Lucidity* because, the editor says, "I have felt that too many publications of verse lean to obscurity." "Open as to form, 36-line limit due to format. No restriction on subject matter except that something definitive be given to the reader. We look for poetry that is life-related and has clarity and substance." Purpose: "We dedicate our journal to publishing those poets who express their thoughts, feelings and impressions about the human scene with clarity and substance. We are open to poetry dealing with the good, bad and ugly . . . if done with finesse and style." He does not want "religious, nature or vulgar poems." Published poets include Barbara Vail, Tom Padgett, John Gorman, Penny Perry, and Katherine Zauner. As a sample the editor selected these lines by Dorothy Trautfield:

> Love like fire in grate/snuffed—turns to ash then dies as/heart and hearth grow cold.

The magazine is 72 pgs., digest-sized, photocopied from typescript and saddle-stapled with matte card cover. Publishes about 60 poems in each issue. Press run is 350 for 220 subscribers. Subscription: $6. Sample (including guidelines): $3.

How to Submit: Submit 3-5 poems at a time. Accepts simultaneous submissions. No e-mail submissions. Time between acceptance and publication is 4 months. Guidelines available for SASE or by e-mail. Responds in 4 months. Pays 1 copy plus "cash." Acquires one-time rights.

Book/Chapbook Needs & How to Submit: Bear House Press is a self-publishing arrangement by which poets can pay to have booklets published in the same format as *Lucidity,* prices beginning at 100 copies of 32 pgs. for $304. Publishes 10 chapbooks/year.

Also Offers: Sponsors the Lucidity Poets' Ozark Retreat, a 3-day retreat held during the month of April.

Advice: "Small press journals offer the best opportunity to most poets for publication."

☑ ◑ **LULLWATER REVIEW; LULLWATER PRIZE FOR POETRY**, Emory University, P.O. Box 22036, Atlanta GA 30322. (404)727-6184. Established 1990. **Editors-in-Chief:** Hilary Clark and Margarite Nathe. **Fiction Editor:** Brianne Gorod. **Poetry Editor:** Karen Edelblum.

Magazine Needs: "Appearing 2 times/year, the *Lullwater Review* is Emory University's nationally distributed literary magazine publishing poetry, short fiction and artwork." Seeks poetry of any genre with strong imagery, original voice, on any subject. No profanity or pornographic material. Has published poetry by Lyn Lifshin, Virgil Suarez, and Ha Jin. *Lullwater Review* is 104-120 pgs., magazine-sized, full color cover, includes b&w pictures. Press run is 2,500. Subscription: $10. Sample: $5.

How to Submit: Submit 5 poems at a time. Accepts simultaneous submissions; no previously published poems. Cover letter preferred. "We must have a SASE with which to reply. Poems may not be returned." Reads submissions September 1 through May 15 only. Time between acceptance and publication is up to 6 months. Poems are circulated to an editorial board. "A poetry editor selects approximately 16 poems per week to be reviewed by editors, who then discuss and decide on the poem's status." Seldom comments on rejected poems. Guidelines available for SASE. Responds in 5 months maximum. Pays 3 contributor's copies. Acquires first North American serial rights.

Also Offers: Sponsors the annual Lullwater Prize for Poetry. Award is $500 and publication. Deadline: March 15. Guidelines available for SASE. Entry fee: $8.

Advice: "Keep writing, find your voice, don't get frustrated. Please be patient with us regarding response time. We are an academic institution."

☑ $◯ ◑ **LUMMOX PRESS; LUMMOX JOURNAL; LITTLE RED BOOK SERIES; LUMMOX SOCIETY OF WRITERS**, P.O. Box 5301, San Pedro CA 90733-5301. E-mail: lumoxraindog@earthlink.net. Website: http://Raindog.tripod.com/lmx01/. Established 1994 (press), 1996 (journal). **Editor/Publisher:** R.D. Armstrong.

Magazine Needs: *Lummox Journal* appears monthly and "explores the creative process through interviews, articles, and commentary." Wants "genuine and authentic poetry—socially conscious, heartfelt, honest, insightful, experimental. No angst-ridden confessional poetry; no pretentious, pompous, racist and/or sexist work." Has published poetry by Gerald Locklin, Todd Moore, Lyn Lifshin, normal, and Scott Wannberg. As a sample we selected these lines from "The False Rhapsody of Art" by Gerald Locklin:

> oppen, edward field, bukowski—/they all sought to avoid it/while keeping their ears cocked,/their voices clear and clean,/for the new music/of the truth/of the never old emotions.

Lummox Journal is up to 24 pgs., digest-sized, photocopied and saddle-stitched with 60 lb. paper cover, includes art and ads. Receives about 600 poems/year, accepts about 10%. Press run is 200 for 150 subscribers, 50 shelf sales. Subscription: $20/12 issues. Sample: $2. Make checks payable to *Lummox Journal.*

How to Submit: Submit 3 poems at a time. Accepts previously published poems and simultaneous submissions. Accepts e-mail (include in body) and disk (PC Win 98) submissions. Cover letter with bio preferred. Time between acceptance and publication is up to 6 months. Seldom comments on rejected poems. Criticism fees: $10 to critique, $25 to advise, $50 to tutor. Guidelines available for SASE or by e-mail. Responds in 2 weeks. Pays 1 copy. Acquires one-time rights. Reviews books chapbooks, CDs of poetry/music, and other magazines. Poets may send books for review consideration.

Book/Chapbook Needs & How to Submit: Lummox Press publishes avant-garde and concrete poetry under the imprint Little Red Book. "The LRB series attempts to honor the poem as well as the poet." Publishes 12 to 15 books per year. Books are usually 50-56 pgs., digest-sized, photocopied/offset-printed, saddle-stitched/perfect-bound. Query first with a few sample poems and cover letter with brief bio. **Reading fee:** $5/submission ("or join LSW"). Responds to queries in up to 3 weeks; to mss in up to 2 months. Pays royalties of 10% (after second printing) plus 10% of press run. Offers subsidy arrangements (under the imprint of Plug Nickel Press) for the cost of printing and distribution plus ISBN #, $1.25 to $2.25 per book. Send check for $6 to Lummox for sample package or $2 for *Lummox Journal*.
Also Offers: "Lummox Society of Writers (LSW) includes a biannual newsletter listing submission guidelines and addresses for magazines and presses that the editor recommends, unlimited submissions to *Lummox Journal* for one year. Future newsletters will offer helpful tips on submitting, presentation, and updates." Annual dues are $5.

LUNA BISONTE PRODS; LOST AND FOUND TIMES (Specialized: style), 137 Leland Ave., Columbus OH 43214-7505. Established 1967. **Poetry Editor:** John M. Bennett.
Magazine Needs: John M. Bennett is a publisher (and practitioner) of experimental and avant-garde writing, sometimes sexually explicit, and art in a bewildering array of formats including the magazine, *Lost and Found Times*, postcard series, posters, chapbooks, pamphlets, labels, and audiocassette tapes. You can get a sampling of Luna Bisonte Prods for $10. Numerous reviewers have commented on the bizarre *Lost and Found Times*, "reminiscent of several West Coast dada magazines"; "This exciting magazine is recommended only for the most daring souls"; "truly demented"; "Insults . . . the past 3,000 years of literature"; "revolution where it counts, in the dangerous depths of the imagination," etc. Bennett wants to see "unusual poetry, naive poetry, surrealism, experimental, visual poetry, collaborations—no poetry workshop or academic pabulum." He has published poetry by J. Berry, J. Leftwich, S.S. Nash, Peter Ganick, I. Argüelles, and A. Ackerman. As a sample the editor selected these lines from "Far Aloft (I Traced Hostile Footprints)" by León Piñón:

> *Of course, for the order of the daz was in/chains, pintle chains,/chains you'd use in rough weather in*
> dune/roaming, *under metal clouds, and* face-spray/*upon one's hands and lips like* thumbed/blank pages.

The digest-sized, 60-page magazine, photoreduced typescript and wild graphics, matte card cover with graphics. Press run is 350 with 75 subscribers of which 30 are libraries. Subscription: $25 for 5 numbers. Sample: $6.
How to Submit: Submit anytime—preferably camera-ready (but this is not required). Responds in 2 days. Pays 1 contributor's copy. All rights revert to authors upon publication. Staff reviews books of poetry. Send books for review consideration.
Book/Chapbook Needs & How to Submit: Luna Bisonte also will consider book submissions: query with samples and cover letter (but "keep it brief"). Chapbook publishing usually depends on grants or other subsidies and is usually by solicitation. Will also consider subsidy arrangements on negotiable terms.
Advice: "I would like to see more experimental and avant-garde material in Spanish and Portuguese, or in mixtures of languages."

LUNA NEGRA, Box 26, Office of Campus Life/Student Activities or English Dept., Kent State University, Kent OH 44242. E-mail: luna-negra@listserv.kent.edu. Website: www.studentmedia.kent.edu/lunanegra (includes back issues, samples, and guidelines). **Advisor:** Kathe Davis.
Magazine Needs: *Luna Negra* is a student-run, biannual literary and art magazine of the KSU main campus appearing in May and December, open to all forms of poetry and prose. Accepts poetry written by children. *Luna Negra* is 36-42 pgs., 7½×7½, with art and photography throughout. Receives 800 poems/year, accepts 40 or 50/year. Press run is 2,000, most distributed to KSU students. Sample: $3. **Submission fee:** $2.
How to Submit: Submit up to 3 poems at a time with a reading fee of $2/poem. "Must request sample if in the published book." Line length for poetry is 100 maximum. Also accepts prose up to 1,000 words. Accepts simultaneous submissions. Accepts e-mail submissions in attached file. Reads submissions September 1 through March 30 only. Responds in 3 months. "All rights revert to author immediately after publication."

LUNGFULL! MAGAZINE, 126 E. Fourth St., #2, New York NY 10003. E-mail: lungfull@interport.net. Website: www.interport.net/~lungfull. Established 1994. **Editor/Publisher:** Brendan Lorber.
• *LUNGFULL!* was the recipient of a multi-year grant from the New York State Council for the Arts.
Magazine Needs: *LUNGFULL!*, published biannually, prints "the rough draft of each poem, in addition to the final so that the reader can see the creative process from start to finish." Wants "any style as long as its urgent, immediate, playful, probing, showing great thought while remaining vivid and grounded. Poems should be as interesting as conversation." Does not want "empty poetic abstractions." Has published poetry by Alice Notley, Allen Ginsberg, Lorenzo Thomas, Tracie Morris, Hal Sirowitz, Sparrow, Eileen Myles, and Bill Berkson. As a sample the editor selected this poem, "Jung and Restless: A Waitress Dreaming on Ernest Borgnines Birthday," by Julie Reid:

> *Your hair is combed differently than you ever wore it and a man in gray and/green with his hands up*
> *inside the working of a clock flirts lightly with the woman/beside him who's applying pink lotion from*
> *a travel size bottle to her hands./The woman ahead of you lifts her hair off her neck so you can read*
> *her tattoo . . ./She says 'To the maximum 36 . . . emotions, add umbrellas, bent and broken . . ./Add*
> *anticipation and dread, which . . . are both forms of dread . . .*

LUNGFULL! is 200 pgs., 8½×7, offset-printed, perfect-bound, desktop-published, glossy 2 color cover with lots of illustrations and photos and a few small press ads. Receives about 1,000 poems/year, accepts 5%. Press run is 1,000 for 150 subscribers, 750 shelf sales; 100 distributed free to contributors. Single copy: $7.95; subscription: $31.80/4 issues, $15.90/2 issues. Sample: $9.50. Make checks payable to Brendan Lorber.

How to Submit: "We recommend you get a copy before submitting." Submit up to 6 poems at a time. Accepts previously published poems and simultaneous submissions (with notification). "However, other material will be considered first and stands a much greater chance of publication." Accepts e-mail submissions. "We prefer hard copy by USPS—but e-submissions can be made in the body of the e-mail itself or in a file saved as text." Cover letter preferred. Time between acceptance and publication is up to 8 months. "The editor looks at each piece for its own merit and for how well it'll fit into the specific issue being planned based on other accepted work." Guidelines available by e-mail. Responds in 6 months. Pays 2 copies.

Also Offers: "Each copy of *LUNGFULL! Magazine* now contains a short poem, usually from a series of six, printed on a sticker—they can be removed from the magazine and placed on any flat surface to make it a little less flat. Innovatively designed and printed in black & white, previous stickers have had work by Sparrow, Mike Topp, Julie Reid, Donna Cartelli, Joe Maynard, and Jeremy Sharpe, among others."

Advice: "Don't just read books, mark them up, write between the lines, make your own cover, transcribe the pages you love and burn the originals, get paper cuts kissing it, massage its spine, use only the words from the book you're reading in your speech, or none of them."

✓ ◎ **THE LUTHERAN DIGEST (Specialized: humor, nature/rural/ecology, religious, inspirational)**, P.O. Box 4250, Hopkins MN 55343. (952)933-2820. Fax: (952)933-5708. E-mail: tldi@lutherandigest.com. Website: www.lutherandigest.com (include writers' guidelines and select samples from current issue). Established 1953. **Editor:** David Tank.

Magazine Needs: *The Lutheran Digest* appears quarterly "to entertain and encourage believers and to subtly persuade non-believers to embrace the Christian faith. We publish short poems (24 lines or less) that will fit in a single column of the magazine. Most are inspirational, but that doesn't necessarily mean religious. No avant-garde poetry or work longer than 25 lines." Has published poetry by Kathleen A. Cain, William Beyer, Margaret Peterson, Florence Berg, and Erma Boetkher. As a sample we selected these lines from "Easter Has Arrived" by Kathleen A. Cain:

> Sun rays streak across the rugged/mountains in the east,/Sweet warblings of the finch, wren and/
> cardinal break through the morning peace./All of God's creation arrayed in its/spring beauty begins
> to unfold,/The desert is a bright splash of purple verbena and/daisies of orange and gold.

The Lutheran Digest is 64 pgs., digest-sized, offset-printed and saddle-stitched with 4-color paper cover, includes b&w photos and illustrations, local ads to cover cost of distribution. Receives about 200 poems/year, accepts 20%. Press run is 110,000; 105,000 distributed free to Lutheran churches. Subscription: $14/year, $22/2 years. Sample: $3.50.

How to Submit: Submit 3 poems at a time. Line length for poetry is 30 maximum. Accepts previously published poems and simultaneous submissions. Cover letter preferred. "Include SASE if return is desired." Time between acceptance and publication is up to 9 months. Poems are circulated to an editorial board. "Selected by editor and reviewed by publication panel." Guidelines available for SASE or on website. Responds in 3 months. Pays credit and 1 copy. Acquires one-time rights.

Advice: "Poems should be short and appeal to senior citizens. We also look for poems that can be sung to traditional Lutheran hymns."

$ ◻ ◙ **LYNX EYE; SCRIBBLEFEST LITERARY GROUP**, 1880 Hill Dr., Los Angeles CA 90041-1244. (323)550-8522. Fax: (323)550-8243. E-mail: pamccully@aol.com. Established 1994. **Contact:** Pam McCully.

Magazine Needs: *Lynx Eye* is the quarterly publication of the ScribbleFest Literary Group, an organization dedicated to the development and promotion of the literary arts. *Lynx Eye* is "dedicated to showcasing visionary writers and artists, particularly new voices." Each issue contains a special feature called Presenting, in which an unpublished writer of prose or poetry makes his/her print debut. No specifications regarding form, subject matter, or style of poetry. Has published poetry by Bruce Curley, Dani Montgomery, Michael Neal Morris, and Whitman McGowan. As a sample the editors selected these lines from "To Aliza . . ." by Mel C. Thompson:

> The first man is every man/who was every woman's lover/since Brahman split in two/and became you
> and I.

Lynx Eye is about 120 pgs., 5½×8½, perfect-bound with b&w artwork. Receives about 2,000 poetry submissions/year and have space for about 75. Press run is 500 for 250 subscribers, 200 shelf sales. Subscription: $25/year. Sample: $7.95. Make checks payable to ScribbleFest Literary Group.

How to Submit: Submissions must be typed and include phone number, address, and an SASE. Accepts simultaneous submissions; no previously published poems. No fax or e-mail submissions. Name, address, and phone number on each piece. Guidelines available for SASE. Responds in up to 3 months. Pays $10/piece and 3 copies. Acquires first North American serial rights.

⟦N⟧ ⊘ THE LYRIC, 65 VT. SR 15, Jericho VT 05465. Phone/fax: (802)899-3993. Established 1921 ("the oldest magazine in North America in continuous publication devoted to the publication of traditional poetry"). **Editor:** Jean Mellichamp Milliken.

Magazine Needs: *The Lyric* uses about 55 poems each quarterly issue. "We use rhymed verse in traditional forms, for the most part, with an occasional piece of blank or free verse. Forty lines or so is usually our limit. Our themes are varied, ranging from religious ecstasy to humor to raw grief, but we feel no compulsion to shock, embitter or confound our readers. We also avoid poems about contemporary political or social problems—grief but not grievances, as Frost put it. Frost is helpful in other ways: If yours is more than a lover's quarrel with life, we're not your best market. And most of our poems are accessible on first or second reading. Frost again: Don't hide too far away." Has published poetry by Rhina P. Espaillat, Maureen Cannon, Ruth Parks, Henry George Fisher, R.L. Cook, and R.H. Morrison. As a sample the editor selected these lines by Jean Harris (poem untitled):

> The Warrior stands with bow forever raised/In battle, yet inexorably mute;/Never will it go singing in
> the dark/At some impending foe, but he is praised/for having every warrior attribute/Rather than that
> his arrow hit the mark.

The Lyric is 32 pgs., digest-sized, professionally printed with varied typography, matte card cover. Press run is 800 for 600 subscribers of which 40 are libraries. Receives about 3,000 submissions/year, accepts 5%. Subscription: $12 US, $14 Canada and other countries (in US funds only). Sample: $3.

How to Submit: Submit up to 5 poems at a time. Accepts simultaneous submissions; no previously published poems or translations. "Cover letters often helpful, but not required." Guidelines available for SASE. Responds in 3 months (average). Pays 1 copy, and all contributors are eligible for quarterly and annual prizes totaling $750. "Subscription will not affect publication in any way."

Advice: "Our raison d'être has been the encouragement of form, music, rhyme, and accessibility in poetry. As we witness the growing dissatisfaction with the modernist movement that ignores these things, we are proud to have provided an alternative for 75 years that helps keep the roots of poetry alive."

☑ ◎ M.I.P. COMPANY (Specialized: foreign language, erotica), P.O. Box 27484, Minneapolis MN 55427. (763)544-5915. Fax: (952)544-6077. E-mail: mp@mipco.com. Website: www.mipco.com. Established in 1984. **Contact:** Michael Peltsman.

Book/Chapbook Needs & How to Submit: M.I.P. Company publishes 3 paperbacks/year. Publishes only Russian erotic poetry and prose written in Russian. Has published poetry collections by Mikhail Armalinsky and Aleksey Shelvakh. Accepts simultaneous submissions; no previously published poems. Responds to queries in 1 month. Seldom comments on rejected poems.

☑ ⊘ THE MACGUFFIN; NATIONAL POET HUNT, Schoolcraft College, 18600 Haggerty Rd., Livonia MI 48152-2696. (734)462-4400, ext. 5292. Fax: (734)462-4679. E-mail: alindenb@schoolcrft.cc.mi.us. Website: www.macguffin.org (includes guidelines, samples from upcoming issues, special issues, and information on competitions). Established 1983. **Editor:** Arthur Lindenberg.

Magazine Needs: "*The MacGuffin* is a literary magazine which appears three times each year, in April, June, and November. We publish the best poetry, fiction, nonfiction and artwork we find. We have no thematic or stylistic biases. We look for well crafted poetry. Long poems should not exceed 300 lines. Avoid pornography, trite and sloppy poetry. We do not publish haiku, concrete, or light verse." Has published poetry by Linda Nemec Foster, Jim Daniels, and Susan Terris. *The MacGuffin* is 160 pgs., digest-sized, professionally printed on heavy buff stock, with matte card cover, flat-spined, with b&w illustrations and photos. Press run is 600 for 400 subscribers and the rest are local newsstand sales, contributor copies and distribution to college offices. Single copy: $7; subscription: $18. Sample: $6.

How to Submit: "The editorial staff is grateful to consider unsolicited manuscripts and graphics." Submit up to 5 poems at a time of no more than 300 lines; poems should be typewritten. "We discourage simultaneous submissions." Accepts fax but no e-mail submissions. Prefers submissions to be sent through the mail. Publishes theme issues. Guidelines and upcoming themes available for SASE, by e-mail, by fax, and on website. Responds in 3 months; publication backlog is 6 months. Pays 2 copies, "occasional money or prizes."

Also Offers: Also sponsors the National Poet Hunt, established in 1996, offering annual awards of $500 1st Prize, $250 2nd Prize, $100 3rd Prize, 3 honorable mentions and publication. Submissions may be entered in other contests. Submit 5 typed poems on any subject in any form. Put name and address on separate 3 × 5 index card only. Guidelines and upcoming themes available for SASE, by e-mail, by fax, and on website. Entry fee: $15/5 poems. Deadline: May 31. Judge for 2000 contest was Gary Gildner. Winners will be announced August 8, and in *Poets and Writers* in the fall.

Advice: "We will always comment on 'near misses.' Writing is a search, and it is a journey. Don't become sidetracked. Don't become discouraged. Keep looking. Keep traveling. Keep writing."

⊘ MAD POETS REVIEW; MAD POETS REVIEW POETRY COMPETITION; MAD POETS SO-CIETY, P.O. Box 1248, Media PA 19063-8248. Established 1987. **Editor:** Eileen M. D'Angelo. **Associate Editor:** Camelia Nocella.

Magazine Needs: *Mad Poets Review* is published annually in October/November. "Our primary purpose is to promote thought-provoking, moving poetry, and encourage beginning poets. We don't care if you have a 'name' or a publishing history, if your poetry is well-crafted." "Anxious for work with 'joie de vivre' that startles and inspires." No restrictions on subject, form, or style. "We are not interested in porn or obscenities used for the sake of shock value." Has published poetry by Henry Braun, Leonard Gontarek, Elaine Tetranova, Shulamith Caine, Daniel Moore, and Aaren Y. Perry. As a sample we selected these lines from "A Spoon of Sleep" by Lisa Barnett:

> We know the tenderness of spoons/the clean curve from bowl to stem,/as lying together at night/we curve into each other's dreams.

Mad Poets Review is about 80 pgs., digest-sized, attractively printed and perfect-bound with textured card cover. Receives about 500-700 poems/year, accepts 50-60. Press run is 250. Single copy: $10. Sample: $11.50. Make checks payable to either Mad Poets Society or *Mad Poets Review*.

How to Submit: Submit 6 poems at a time. "Poems without an SASE with adequate postage will not be returned or acknowledged." Accepts previously published poems and simultaneous submissions. Cover letter not necessary, but "include 3-4 sentences about yourself suitable for our Bio Notes section. Mark envelope 'contest' or 'magazine.' " Reads submissions January 1 through June 1 only. Time between acceptance and publication is 8 months. Often comments on rejected poems. Responds in 3 months. Pays 1 contributor's copy. Acquires one-time rights.

Also Offers: Sponsors the annual *Mad Poets Review* Poetry Competition. "All themes and styles of poetry are welcome, no line limit, previously unpublished work only." Complete contest guidelines available for SASE. Winners published in *Mad Poets Review*. Cash prizes awarded—amount depends on number of entries. "The Mad Poets Society is an active organization in Pennsylvania. We run several poetry series; have monthly meetings for members for critique and club business; coordinate a children's contest through Del. Co. School system; run an annual poetry festival the first Sunday in October; sponsor Mad Poets Bonfires for local poets and musicians; publish an annual literary calendar and newsletters that offer the most comprehensive listing available anywhere in the tri-state area. We send quarterly newsletters to members, as well as PA Poetry Society news covering state and national events." Membership fee: $20.

Advice: "It is advised that if someone is going to submit they see what kind of poetry we publish. We sometimes receive poetry that is totally inappropriate of our mag and it is obvious the poet does not know *Mad Poets Review*."

MAD RIVER PRESS, State Road, Richmond MA 01254. (413)698-3184. Established 1986. **Editor:** Barry Sternlieb. Mad River publishes 1 broadside and 2 chapbooks/year, "all types of poetry, no bias," but none unsolicited.

THE MADISON REVIEW; PHYLLIS SMART YOUNG PRIZE IN POETRY, Dept. of English, 7123 Helen C. White Hall, University of Wisconsin, 600 N. Park St., Madison WI 53706. (608)263-0566. E-mail: madreview@mail.student.org.wisc.edu (inquiries only). Website: http://mendota.english.wisc.edu/~Mad Rev (includes contact information, submission guidelines, contest guidelines, past issues, sample work from current issue, and a brief history of the magazine). Established 1978. **Contact:** poetry editor.

Magazine Needs: *The Madison Review*, published in August and February, wants poems that are "smart and tight, that fulfill their own propositions. Spare us: religious or patriotic dogma and light verse." Has published work by Lise Goett, David Citino, Anne Caston, Lisa Steinman, and Richard Tillinghast. Selects 15-20 poems from a pool of 750. Sample: $3.

How to Submit: Submit up to 6 poems at a time. No simultaneous submissions. Usually responds in 9 months. Pays 2 contributor's copies.

Also Offers: The Phyllis Smart Young Prize in Poetry is for $500 and publication in *The Madison Review*, for "the best group of three unpublished poems submitted by a single author, any form." Send SASE for rules before submitting for prize or see announcement for guidelines in *AWP* or *Poets & Writers* magazines. Submissions must arrive during September—winner announced December 15. Competition receives about 300 entries/year.

Advice: "Contributors: Know your market! Read before, during, and after writing. Treat your poems *better* than job applications!"

MAELSTROM, P.O. Box 7, Tranquility NJ 07879. E-mail: lmaelstrom@aol.com. Website: www.geocities.com/~readmaelstrom (includes past publications, guidelines, editors' bios, and samples of some regular features). Established 1997. **Editor:** Christine L. Reed. **Art Editor:** Jennifer Fennell.

Magazine Needs: *Maelstrom*, a quarterly, "tries to be a volatile storm of talents throwing together art, poetry, short fiction, comedy and tragedy." Wants any kind of poetry, "humor appreciated. No pornography." Has published poetry by Grace Cavalieri, Mekeel McBride, Daniela Gioseffi, and B.Z. Niditch. As a sample the editor selected this poem, "Hemingway" by John Nettles:

> Life. Too short to live/Forever in Pamplona./I'd eat my gun too.

Maelstrom is 40-50 pgs., 7 × 8½, saddle-stapled with color cover, includes b&w art. Receives about 600 poems/year, accepts about 20%. Press run is 500 for 100 subscribers. Single copy: $5; subscription: $20. Sample: $4.

How to Submit: Submit up to 4 poems at a time. Accepts previously published poems and simultaneous submissions. Accepts e-mail submissions "in the body of the e-mail message. Please do not send attached files." Cover letter preferred. Include name and address on every page. Send sufficient SASE for return of work. "There is no reading fee, however, submissions accompanied by a $1 donation will be answered immediately, all others will be answered in the order they are received." Time between acceptance and publication is up to 3 months.

Seldom comments on rejected poems. Guidelines available by e-mail or on website. Responds in up to 3 months. Pays 1 contributor's copy. Acquires first North American serial or one-time rights. Staff reviews chapbooks of poetry and other magazines. Send books for review consideration. "Materials cannot be returned."

Also Offers: Also publishes a year anthology, *Poetography*. "Send $1 and SASE for more info."

$ ◑ ◎ THE MAGAZINE OF SPECULATIVE POETRY (Specialized: horror, science fiction), P.O. Box 564, Beloit WI 53512. Established 1984. **Editor:** Roger Dutcher.

Magazine Needs: *The Magazine of Speculative Poetry* is an irregularly published magazine that features "the best new speculative poetry. We are especially interested in narrative form, but interested in variety of styles, open to any form, length (within reason). We're looking for the best of the new poetry utilizing the ideas, imagery, and approaches developed by speculative fiction and will welcome experimental techniques as well as the fresh employment of traditional forms." Has published poetry by Terry A. Garey, Bruce Boston, and Steve Rasnic-Tem. As a sample Roger Dutcher selected these lines from "Braids of Glass" by Michael Bishop:

> *We step onto a plain of braided glass,/which rattles on its topographic loom/Like a million shattered vials of valium/Spilling everywhere the stench of emptiness.*

The Magazine of Speculative Poetry is 24-28 pgs., digest-sized, offset-printed, saddle-stapled with matte card cover. Accepts less than 5% of some 500 poems received/year. Press run is 100-200, for nearly 100 subscribers. Subscription: $19/4. Sample: $5.

How to Submit: Submit 3-5 poems at a time, double-spaced. No previously published poems or simultaneous submissions. "We like cover letters but they aren't necessary. We like to see where you heard of us; the names of the poems submitted; a statement if the poetry ms is disposable; a big enough SASE; and if you've been published, some recent places." Editor comments on rejected poems "on occasion." Guidelines available for SASE. Responds in 2 months. Pays 3¢/word, minimum $5, maximum $25, plus copy. Acquires first North American serial rights. Reviews books of speculative poetry. Query on unsolicited reviews. Send speculative poetry books for review consideration.

⊕ ○ ◑ MAGMA POETRY MAGAZINE, 43 Keslake Rd., London NW6 6DH United Kingdom. E-mail: magmapoems@aol.com. Website: www.champignon.net/Magma (includes contact details, information about *Magma* and its policies and method of operating, as well as some examples of submissions for recent issues). Established 1994. **Editorial Secretary:** David Boll.

Magazine Needs: *Magma* appears 3 times/year and contains "modern poetry, reviews and interviews with poets." Wants poetry that is "modern in idiom and shortish (two pages maximum). Nothing sentimental or old fashioned." Has published poetry by Thom Gunn, Diane di Prima, and Selima Hill. *Magma* is 72 pgs., 8½ × 6, photocopied and stapled, includes b&w illustrations. Receives about 1,500 poems/year, accepts 4-5%. Press run is about 500. Subscription: £9.50 for 3. Sample: £3.50 and U.K. postage. "For foreign postage, add Europe: 2p; Far East/Pacific Rim: £1; rest of world, including USA: 80p. Make checks payable to Stukeley Press. For subscriptions contact Helen Nicholson, distribution secretary, 82 St. James's Dr., London SW17 7RR.

How to Submit: Submit up to 6 poems at a time. Accepts simultaneous submissions. Accepts e-mail submissions (ASCII only, no attachments). Cover letter preferred. Reads submissions September through November and February through July only. Time between acceptance and publication is maximum 3 months. Poems are circulated to an editorial board. "Each issue has an editor who submits his/her selections to a board for final approval. Editor's selection very rarely changed." Occasionally publishes theme issues. Responds in 4 months. Always sends prepublication galleys. Pays 1 contributor's copy.

Also Offers: "We hold a public reading in London three times/year, to coincide with each new issue, and poets in the issue are invited to read."

[N] ⊕ ○ ◑ MAGPIE'S NEST, 176 Stoney Lane, Sparkhill, Birmingham B12 8AN United Kingdom. Established 1979. **Contact:** Mr. Bal Saini.

Magazine Needs: The *Magpie's Nest* appears quarterly and publishes "cutting-edge, modern poetry and fiction which deals with the human condition. No love poetry or self-obsessed work." As a sample the editor selected this poem (poet unidentified):

> *There is something adhesive/about the first parent singular/Loose/images stick to her/where she lives in the shadow/of the absent father*

Receives about 200 poems/year, accepts about 25%. Press run is 200 for 150 subscribers, 50 shelf sales. Single copy: $2.50; subscription: $12.50. Sample: $3.

How to Submit: Submit 4 poems at a time. Line length for poetry is 10 minimum, 40 maximum. Accepts previously published poems and simultaneous submissions. Cover letter preferred. "Keep copies of poems submitted as poems which are not used are binned." Reads submissions September 1 through June 30 only. Time between acceptance and publication is 3 months. Seldom comments on rejected poems. Occasionally publishes theme issues. Responds in 3 months. Pays 1 contributor's copy. Reviews books of poetry and other magazines in 200 words, single book format. Poets may send books for review consideration.

Also Offers: "For a fee, I am willing to act as literary agent for American poets by submitting their poems to British magazines. This will save American poets postage as well as the hassle of finding out which British magazines are suitable for their poems. Please send SASE (or SAE and IRC) for further details."

Advice: "It's recommended that a sample copy be read before submission."

◐ ◿ ◎ **MAIL CALL JOURNAL (Specialized: American Civil War); DISTANT FRONTIER PRESS**, P.O. Box 5031, Dept. P1, South Hackensack NJ 07606. E-mail: mcj@historyonline.net. Website: www.historyonline.net. Established 1990. **Managing Editor:** Anna Pansini.

Magazine Needs: *Mail Call Journal* is published 6 times/year with the purpose of "keeping the spirit of the Civil War soldier alive." Accepts poetry written by children. Wants poetry with unique Civil War themes in first or third person. As a sample the editor selected these lines from "Colors" by Jim Boring:

> *"Now," he said/And the boys fell down/Down fell the blue and the gray/Down fell the stars/From the*
> *noble stripes/Down from the proud blue bars.*

Mail Call Journal is 8 pgs., 8½×11, offset-printed on colored paper and corner stapled. Receives about 100 poems/year, accepts about 10. Subscription: $24.95/year. Sample: $5.

How to Submit: "We prefer contributors order a writer's packet for $5 which includes submission guidelines and a sample copy before submitting, but it is not required." Accepts previously published poems and simultaneous submissions. Accepts e-mail submissions. Submit in body of message. Cover letter optional. "If poet is a descendant of a Civil War soldier or a member of any Civil War organizations, please provide details for publication." Time between acceptance and publication is up to 1 year. Often comments on rejected poems. Guidelines available for SASE or by e-mail. Responds in up to 1 year. Pays 2 contributor's copies.

Book/Chapbook Needs & How to Submit: Distant Frontier Press publishes book excerpts, narratives, diary entries, poems, and editorial think pieces. Details available for SASE.

Also Offers: Sponsors an annual history poetry competition, established in 1997. Awards 3 prizes of "publication on website plus percentage of proceeds." Submissions may be entered in other contests. Two categories—American Civil War and general history. Indicate whether the poem is fictional or non-fictional. Entry fee: $5/category (3 poems). Deadline: September 15.

Advice: "Don't make a Civil War movie into a poem. Write with feeling from your heart."

◑ **MAIN STREET RAG**, (formerly *Main Street Rag Poetry Journal*), P.O. Box 25331, Charlotte NC 28229-5331. (704)535-1918. E-mail: mainstrag@mindspring.com. Website: www.MainStreetRag.com. Established 1996. **Publisher/Editor:** M. Scott Douglass.

Magazine Needs: *Main Street Rag*, is a quarterly that publishes "poetry, short fiction, essays, interviews, reviews, photos, art, cartoons, (political, satirical), and poetry collections... We like publishing good material from people who are interested in more than notching another publishing credit, people who support small independent publishers like ourselves." *Main Street Rag* "will consider almost anything but prefer writing with an edge—either gritty or bitingly humorous." Has recently published poetry by Robert Cooperman, Charles Bukowski, Dana Gioia, Colette Inez, Lyn Lifshin, and A.D. Winans. As a sample the editor selected these lines from "February" by Diana Pinckney:

> *Crow shadows cross at dusk,//windows blink, shutters, drapes/close on grays and browns, questions/*
> *not yet answered, decisions/germinating, the clean slate//tarnished under a pewter moon.*

Main Street Rag is approximately 80 pgs., digest-sized, perfect bound with 80 lb. laminated color cover. Receives about 2,500 poems/year, accepts approximately 250-300. Press run is 400 for 175 subscribers of which 5 are libraries. Single copy: $7; ubscription: $15. Sample: $5.

How to Submit: Submit 6 pages of poetry at a time. No previously published poems or simultaneous submissions. No e-mail submissions. Cover letter preferred with a brief bio "about the poet, not their credits." Has backlog of up to 1 year. Guidelines available for SASE. Responds within 6 weeks. Pays 1 copy and contributor's discount for the issue in which they appear. Acquires one-time rights.

Also Offers: Also offers chapbook contest. Deadline: May 31. 1st Prize: $100 and 200 copies. Entry fee: $15. Previous winners: David Chorltan, Alan Catlin.

Advice: "Small press independent exist by and for writers. Without their support (and the support of readers) we have no means or reason to publish. Sampling is always appreciated."

✓ ○ ◎ **MALAFEMMINA PRESS; LA BELLA FIGURA (Specialized: ethnic)**, 4211 Fort Hamilton Pkwy., Brooklyn NY 11219-1237. E-mail: malafemmina.press@virgilio.it. Established 1988. **Editor:** Rose Romano.

Magazine Needs: *La Bella Figura* is published quarterly and contains "poetry by Italian-Americans concerning Italian-American history, culture, and issues." Wants poetry "on the history, culture and concerns of Italian-Americans. No stereotypes." Has published poetry by Jennifer Lagier, Barbara Crooker, Grace Cavalieri, and Eileen Spinelli. *La Bella Figura* is 20 pgs., 5½×8½, offset-printed and stapled with paper cover. Receives about 100 poems/year, accepts approximately 50%. Press run is 200 for 150 subscribers of which 27 are libraries. Subscription: $8. Sample: $2. Make checks payable to Rose Sorrentino. "Must be Italian-American and proud of it."

How to Submit: Submit 3-5 poems at a time. Accepts previously published poems; no simultaneous submissions. Accepts e-mail submissions but text "*must* be included in body of message." Cover letter preferred. Time between acceptance and publication is 3 months. Seldom comments on rejected poems. Occasionally publishes theme issues. Responds in 1 month. Pays 3 contributor's copies. Acquires first or one-time rights. Reviews books and chapbooks of poetry in 200 words, single book format. Poets may send books for review consideration.

Book/Chapbook Needs & How to Submit: Malafemmina Press publishes 3 chapbooks/year of poetry "by and about Italian-Americans to promote awareness of our culture." Chapbooks are usually 20 pgs., 5½×8½, offset-printed and saddle-stapled with paper cover. Query first, with a few sample poems and a cover letter with brief bio and publication credits. Responds to queries and mss in up to 4 months. Pays 50 author's copies (out of a press run of 200) plus 50% discount. Obtain sample books or chapbooks by sending inquiry. "Malafemmina Press will be moving to Italy soon, to publish bilingual English/Italian poetry chapbooks. Write now to be put on mailing list."

MAMMOTH BOOKS; MAMMOTH PRESS INC., 7 South Juniata St., DuBois PA 15801. E-mail: guidelines@mammothbooks.com or info@mammothbooks.com. Website: www.mammoth.books.com. Established 1997. **Publisher:** Antonio Vallone.

Book/Chapbook Needs: MAMMOTH Books, an imprint of MAMMOTH Press Inc., publishes 2-4 paperbacks/year of creative nonfiction, fiction, and poetry through annual competitions. "We are open to all types of literary poetry." Has published *The House of Sages* by Philip Terman; *The Never Wife* by Cynthia Hogue; *These Happy Eyes* by Liz Rosenberg; and *Subjects for Other Conversations* by John Stigall. Books are usually 5×7 or 6×9, offset-printed and perfect-bound, covers vary (1-4 color), include art.

How to Submit: Send mss to contest. Not currently reading outside of contests. For poetry mss, submit a collection of poems or a single long poem. Translations are accepted. "Manuscripts as a whole must not have been previously published. Some or all of each manuscript may have appeared in periodicals, chapbooks, anthologies, or other venues. These must be identified. Authors are responsible for securing permissions." Accepts simultaneous submissions. No e-mail submissions. Poetry mss should be single-spaced, no more than 1 poem/page. Reads submissions September 1 through February 28/29. Entry fee: $20. Make checks payable to MAMMOTH Books. Time between acceptance and publication is 18 months. Poems are circulated to an editorial board. "Finalists will be chosen by the staff of MAMMOTH Books and an outside editorial board and/or guest editor. Manuscripts will be selected based on merit only." Seldom comments on rejected poems. Pays royalties (10% of sales) and a least 50 free copies. Other finalist manuscripts may be selected for publication and offered a standard royalty contract and publication of at least 500 trade paperback copies. Finalists will be announced within 1 year from the end of each submission period. MAMMOTH press inc. reserves the right not to award a prize if no entries are deemed suitable. Complete rules are available for SASE or by e-mail to guidelines@mammothbooks.com. Order sample books by sending for information to their mailing address or e-mail.

Advice: "Read: literary magazines, good books of poetry (both old and new) and magazines and books seemingly unconnected to poetry. Don't learn about the world by watching TV. Go out into it, too!"

MANDRAKE POETRY REVIEW; THE MANDRAKE PRESS (Specialized: translations), Box 792, Larkspur CA 94977-0792. E-mail: mandrake@polbox.com. Website: www.angelfire.com/pc/TheMandrakePress (includes magazine in its entirety). Established 1993 in New York. **Editor:** Leo Yankevich. **Editor:** David Castleman.

Magazine Needs: *Mandrake Poetry Review* appears at least twice/year. Has published poetry by Michael Daugherty, George Held, Hugh Fox, Errol Miller, Simon Perchik, and Joan Peternel. As a sample the editor selected these lines from "By A Philosopher's Tomb" by Cornel (Adam) Lengyel:

> How may one thank in fitting terms the maker/of new and taller windows for the soul?/I turn my
> transient eyes without and see/the world's great ghostly wheels of change reduce/our mortal home to
> essences eternal—/the terror and the grandeur, all within.

Mandrake Poetry Review is 76-150 pgs., A5, offset-printed and flat-spined with glossy white card cover. Accepts about 10% of the poetry received. Press run is 500 for 100 subscribers from 3 continents. Single copy: $5 (by airmail); subscription: $20/2 years. Make checks payable to David Castleman.

How to Submit: Submit up to 7 poems at a time. "Send only copies of your poems, as we do not return poems with our reply." Accepts previously published poems and simultaneous submissions. Accepts e-mail submissions. Cover letter preferred. Responds in 2 months. Pays 2 contributor's copies "sometimes more." All rights revert to author. "Poets are encouraged to send their books for review consideration to David Castleman. All editors and publishers whose books/chapbooks are selected for review will receive one copy of the issue in which the review appears. We publish 50-100 reviews yearly."

THE MANHATTAN REVIEW (Specialized: translations), 440 Riverside Dr., Apt. 38, New York NY 10027. (212)932-1854. Established 1980. **Poetry Editor:** Philip Fried.

Magazine Needs: *The Manhattan Review* "publishes American writers and foreign writers with something valuable to offer the American scene. We like to think of poetry as a powerful discipline engaged with many other fields. We want to see ambitious work. Interested in both lyric and narrative. Not interested in mawkish, sentimental poetry. We select high-quality work from a number of different countries, including the U.S." Has published poetry by Zbigniew Herbert, D. Nurkse, Baron Wormser, Penelope Shuttle, and Peter Redgrove. *The Manhattan Review* is now "an annual with ambitions to be semiannual." 64 pgs., digest-sized, professionally printed with glossy card cover, photos and graphics. Press run is 500 for 400 subscribers of which 250 are libraries. Distributed by Bernhard DeBoer, Inc. Receives about 300 submissions/year, uses few ("but I do read everything submitted carefully and with an open mind"). "I return submissions as promptly as possible." Single copy: $5; subscription: $10. Sample: $6.25 with 6×9 envelope.

How to Submit: Submit 3-5 pgs. of poems at a time. No simultaneous submissions. Cover letter with short bio and publications required. Editor sometimes comments "but don't count on it." Responds in 3 months if possible. Pays contributor's copies. Staff reviews books of poetry. Send books for review consideration.

Advice: "Don't be swayed by fads. Search for your own voice. Support other poets whose work you respect and enjoy. Be persistent. Keep aware of poetry being written in other countries."

◐ MANKATO POETRY REVIEW, English Dept., AH230, Minnesota State University, Mankato MN 56001. (507)389-5511. E-mail: roger.sheffer@mankato.msus.edu. Established 1984. **Editor:** Roger Sheffer.

Magazine Needs: *Mankato Poetry Review* is a semiannual magazine that is "open to all forms and themes, though we seldom print 'concrete poetry,' religious, or sentimental verse. We frequently publish first-time poets." Has published poetry by Edward Micus, Gary Fincke, Judith Skillman, and Walter Griffin. *Mankato Poetry Review* is 30 pgs., 5×8, typeset on 60 lb. paper, saddle-stapled with buff matte card cover printed in one color. It appears usually in May and December and has a press run of 200. Subscription: $5/year. Sample: $2.50.

How to Submit: Submit up to 6 poems at a time. Line length for poetry is 60 maximum. "Please include biographical note on separate sheet. Poems not accompanied by SASE will not be returned." However, do not submit mss in summer (May through August). No previously published poems or simultaneous submissions. Cover letter required. Guidelines available for SASE. Deadlines are April 15 (May issue) and November 15 (December issue). Responds in about 2 months; "We accept only what we can publish in next issue." Pays 2 contributor's copies.

Advice: "We're interested in looking at longer poems—up to 60 lines, with great depth of detail relating to place (landscape, townscape)."

▼ $◐ MĀNOA: A PACIFIC JOURNAL OF INTERNATIONAL WRITING, 1733 Donaghho Rd., Honolulu HI 96822. Fax: (808)956-7808. E-mail: mjournal-1@hawaii.edu. Website www.hawaii.edu/mjournal (includes writer's guidelines, names of editors, short fiction and poetry, RealAudio readings by authors, lists of back issues and future issues, subscription info, author index, and awards received). Established 1989. **Poetry Editor:** Frank Stewart.

● Poetry published in *Mānoa* has also been selected for inclusion in the 1995 and 1996 volumes of *The Best American Poetry*.

Magazine Needs: *Mānoa* appears twice/year. "We are a general interest literary magazine, open to all forms and styles. We are not for the beginning writer, no matter what style. We are not interested in Pacific exotica." Has published poetry by Arthur Sze, Linda Hogan, and John Haines. *Mānoa* is 240 pgs., 7×10, offset printed, flat-spined using art and graphics. Receives about 3,000 poems/year, accepts 2%. Press run is 2,000 for 1,000 subscribers of which 30 are libraries, 700 shelf sales. Subscription: $22/year. Sample: $10.

How to Submit: Query by mail or e-mail. Submit 3-5 poems at a time. Guidelines available for SASE. Responds in 6 weeks. Always sends prepublication galleys. Pay "competitive" plus 2 copies. Seldom comments on rejected poems. Reviews current books and chapbooks of poetry. Poets may also send books for review consideration, attn. reviews editor.

Advice: "We welcome the opportunity to read poetry from throughout the country. We are not a regional journal, but we do feature work from the Pacific and Asia, especially in our reviews and essays. We are not interested in genre or formalist writing for its own sake, or picturesque impressions of the region."

✓ ▼ ◐ MANY MOUNTAINS MOVING; MANY MOUNTAINS MOVING LITERARY AWARDS, 420 22nd St., Boulder CO 80302. (303)545-9942. E-mail: mmm@mmminc.org. Website: www.mmm inc.org (includes submission guidelines, a list of upcoming themes, exceprts, bios, and general information about the magazine). Established 1994. **Poetry Editor:** Debra Bokur.

● Poetry published in *Many Mountains Moving* has also been included in the 1996, 1997, and 1999 volumes of *The Best American Poetry*.

Magazine Needs: Published biannually, *Many Mountains Moving* is "a literary journal of diverse contemporary voices that welcomes previously published fiction, poetry, nonfiction, and art from writers and artists of all walks of life. We publish the world's top writers as well as emerging talents." Open to any style of poetry, but they do not want any "Hallmark-y" poetry. Has published poetry by Robert Bly, Allen Ginsberg, and Adrienne Rich. As a sample they selected these lines from "Bathing Susan" by Sarah Wolbach:

> *Her vertebrae are little apples softening in the heat, rocks on the river/bottom that shimmer and*
> *dissolve in the light, little tumors like the/ones within her, spreading through her lungs and glands like*
> *a flood/of mold, a village of tiny fists. Touching her body is like reading/Braille, but nothing is*
> *explained. Lifted from the water, she is wood/dripping life, she is air with light breathing through.*

Many Mountains Moving is about 300 pgs., 6×8¾, web offset and perfect-bound with four-color cover and b&w art and photos inside. Receives 4,000 poems/year, accepts .1%. Press run is 3,000 for 400 subscribers. Single copy: $9; subscription: $16/year.

How to Submit: Submit 3-10 poems at a time, typed with SASE. No e-mail submissions. Accepts simultaneous submissions; no previously published poems. Cover letter preferred. Poems are circulated to an editorial board. "Poems are first read by several readers. If considered seriously, they are passed to the poetry editor for final decision." Seldom comments on rejected poems. Occasionally publishes theme issues. Upcoming themes and guidelines are available for SASE or on website. Responds within 1 month, "if we are seriously considering a submission, we may take longer." Sends prepublication galleys upon request. Pays 3 copies, additional copies available at $3/copy. Acquires first North American serial rights and "rights to publish in a future edition of the *Best of Many Mountains Moving Anthology.*"

Also Offers: Sponsors the annual Many Mountains Moving Literary Awards which awards $200 plus publication in the categories of poetry, fiction, and essay. Entry fee: $15 (includes subscription). Details available for SASE.

Advice: "Although we have featured a number of established poets, we encourage new writers to submit. However, we recommend that poets read through at least one issue to familiarize themselves with the type of work we generally publish."

N ◯ ◐ ◎ MANZANITA QUARTERLY (Specialized: Northwest poets), P.O. Box 1234, Ashland OR 97520. E-mail: authenticj@aol.com (for queries only; accepts only hardcopy submissions). Established 1998. **Editor:** Mariah Hegarty.

Magazine Needs: *Manzanita Quarterly* is a quarterly that publishes quality, accessible poetry. Does not want porn, rhyming poems, or Hallmark-type verse. Recently published poetry by Elizabeth Biller Chapman, Paulann Petersen, Peter Pereira, and Roger Weaver. As a sample the editor selected these lines from "Itinerary" by Paulann Peterson:

> Beyond a blue city/of bees. Hives housed inside/painted boxes. This many/small squares of sky/pulled
> down to ground level,/snugged around the thick/thrum of wings.

Manzanita Quarterly is 60 pgs. digest-sized, perfect-bound, printed card stock cover with photo. Receives about 1,000 poems/year, accepts about 25%. Publishes about 40 poems/issue. Press run is 200 for 60 subscribers of which 5 are libraries, 30 shelf sales; 10 are distributed free to libraries, reviewers. Single copy: $7.50; subscription: $25. Sample: $7.50. Make checks payable to *Manzanita Quarterly*.

How to Submit: Submit 5 poems at a time. No previously published poems or simultaneous submissions. No e-mail, fax, or disk submissions. Cover letter is preferred. "Send SASE, cover letter with short, serious bio, name and address on each page." Reads submissions all year. Deadlines: February 7, May 9, August 12, November 15. Submit seasonal poems 2 months in advance. Time between acceptance and publication is 2 months. Seldom comments on rejected poems. Guidelines are available in magazine and by e-mail. Responds in 3 months from each deadline. Pays 1 contributor's copy. Acquires first North American serial rights.

Advice: "Send your best work. Edit, preferably with the help of your writing peers, before sending. Write from your heart and life, but pay attention to technique as well."

N ▣ ◐ ◎ MARGIN: EXPLORING MODERN MAGICAL REALISM (Specialized: magical realism), 9407 Capstan Dr. NE, Bainbridge Island WA 98110. E-mail: msellma@attglobal.net. Website: www.angelfire.com/wa2/margin/index.html (includes perpetual anthology exploring all forms of magical realism [literary]). Established 2000. **Contact:** Poetry Editor.

Magazine Needs: *Margin: Exploring Modern Magical Realism* appears "perpetually. The Internet's only website dedicated to the exploration of literary magical realism." Wants "accessible poetry where metamorphoses are authentic. Metaphor alone does not qualify as magical realism. No light verse, forced rhyme, or language poetry, and *no* New Age or science fiction." *Margin* is published online. Receives about 1,000 poems/year, accepts about 10%. Publishes about 3-4 poems/issue ("publishing as we find good poetry—no schedule"). Circulation is 2,000-3,000 hits/month. Single copy: free; subscription: free, automated, private. Sample: visit website.

How to Submit: Submit 6 poems at a time. Line length for poetry is 50 maximum. Accepts previously published poems and simultaneous submissions (if notified). Accepts e-mail submissions (*no* attachments); no fax or disk submissions. "Poems submitted without SASE will not be read or returned." Reads submissions September 1 through April 30; mss received after will be held over. Time between acceptance and publication is 6 months. Poems are circulated to an editorial board. "Editors live in separate cities in the US and Canada. We nominate for Pushcart." Seldom comments on rejected poems ("Only when they are good poems but not magical realism. Send reading list of top 10 favorite magical realist poets or authors, plus bio and short definition of 'magical realism.' ") Occasionally publishes theme issues. A list of upcoming themes is available on website. Guidelines are available for SASE and on website. Responds in 6 months. Sometimes sends prepublication galleys as URL form. Pays "perpetual global exposure, nominates for literary prizes." Rights acquired are negotiable. Reviews books and chapbooks of poetry in under 500 words ("but we are flexible"), single book and multi-book format. Poets may send books for review consideration to Poetry Editor ("Nothing academic!").

Also Offers: "Broad global exposure has benefited many of our published writers."

Advice: "*Understand* what magical realism is *first* before submitting. For criteria see website guidelines."

✓ ◐ THE MARLBORO REVIEW; MARLBORO PRIZE FOR POETRY, P.O. Box 243, Marlboro VT 05344. E-mail: marlboro@marlbororeview.com. Website: www.marlbororeview.com. Established 1995. **Editor:** Ellen Dudley. **Poetry Editor:** Ruth Anderson Barnett.

Magazine Needs: *The Marlboro Review*, published biannually, is a "literary magazine containing poetry, fiction, essays, reviews, and translations." Wants long poems. Does not want greeting card verse. Has published poetry by William Matthews, Jean Valentine, Bill Knott, and Chana Bloch. *The Marlboro Review* is 80-112 pgs., 6×9, offset-printed and perfect-bound with laminated colored cover and ads. Receives about 1,000 poems/year, accepts about 7%. Press run is 1,000 for 350 subscribers of which 25 are libraries, 300 shelf sales; 50-70 distributed free to writers and institutions. Single copy: $8; subscription: $16. Sample: $8.75.

How to Submit: Submit up to 5 typed, near letter quality or better poems at a time with SASE. Accepts simultaneous submissions "if we are notified"; no previously published poems. No fax or e-mail submissions. Guidelines available for SASE. Responds in up to 3 months. Sometimes sends prepublication galleys. Pays 2 copies. Acquires all rights. Returns rights on publication. Reviews books of poetry in 500-1,000 words, single book format. Poets may send books for review consideration.

Also Offers: Sponsors the Marlboro Prize for Poetry. Awards a $1,000 honorarium and publication. Submit $10 entry fee for up to 5 poems. Deadline: March 15, 2001. Include name on cover letter only, not on ms. All entrants receive the Marlboro Prize issue and are considered for publication.

MARYLAND POETRY REVIEW; MARYLAND STATE POETRY AND LITERARY SO-CIETY ANNUAL CHAPBOOK CONTEST; MARYLAND STATE POETRY AND LITERARY SOCI-ETY, P.O. Drawer H, Catonsville MD 21228. Website: www.marylandpoetry.org (includes writer's guidelines, names of editors, poetry samples, and is "a changing, interactive site"). Established 1985. **Editor:** Rosemary Klein.

Magazine Needs: *Maryland Poetry Review* "is interested in promoting the literary arts in Maryland as well as nationally and internationally. We are interested in strong, thoughtful poetry with a slight bias to free verse. All submissions are read carefully. *Maryland Poetry Review* is open to good poets who have not published extensively as well as to those who have." Accepts poetry written by children only for website publication. Has published poetry by Josephine Jacobsen, Richard Jackson, Gary Finke, and Walter McDonald. As a sample the editor selected these lines from "Domestic Rhythm: A Pantoum" by Georgia Kreiger:

> Let us sip tea together, our knees touching/Under the oak table whose legs you carved/To crouch like
> the daunting legs of lions;/You always loved the thundering themes of nature.

Maryland Poetry Review is 75 pgs., 7×11, professionally-printed in small type on quality eggshell stock, perfect-bound, glossy color cover. Current issue: $12; back issue: $8.

How to Submit: Submit up to 5 poems at a time with brief bio. No simultaneous submissions. "We read submissions only in January, April, and September but accept all year." Publishes theme issues. Upcoming themes and guidelines are available for SASE and on website. Responds in up to 6 months. Pays 1 contributor's copy. Staff reviews books of poetry. Send books for review consideration, attn. Hugh Burgess.

Also Offers: MSPLS sponsors an annual chapbook contest. Prize includes $100 and 50 copies of winning ms. Submit mss between 20-30 pgs. Entry fee: $20/ms. Contest runs from January to October. Winners notified by Christmas. Guidelines available for SASE and on website.

MARYMARK PRESS (Specialized: form/style), 45-08 Old Millstone Dr., East Windsor NJ 08520. (609)443-0646. Website: www.experimentalpoet.com (includes samples of Mark Sonnenfeld's work, experimental writing, a spoken-word element, a listing of chapbooks with a synopsis of each, and contact information). Established 1994. **Editor/Publisher:** Mark Sonnenfeld.

Book/Chapbook Needs: Marymark Press's goal is "to feature and promote experimental poets. I will most likely be publishing only broadsides and samplers; no books at this time. I want to see experimental poetry of the outer fringe. Make up words, sounds, whatever, but say something you thought never could be explained. Disregard rules if need be." No traditional, rhyming or spiritual verse; no predictable styles. Has published poetry by Alice Olds-Ellingson, R.L. Nichols, Reed Altemus, Ash Cooke, and Bruno Sourdin. As a sample the editor selected his poem, "3-7," from the broadside, *With Conceptual Mistakes By*:

> It's to me image 222/Thought it is good/appropriate chant (semi-coma)/I so suppose, smoke, dust, oil,
> mist, etc./monday with clinical fabrics/OUT-the side a ha-street free, or gone, or barely

How to Submit: Submit 3 poems at a time. Accepts previously published poems and simultaneous submissions. Cover letter preferred. "Copies should be clean, crisp and camera-ready. I do not have the means to accept electronic submissions. A SASE should accompany all submissions, and a telephone number if at all possible." Time between acceptance and publication is 2 months. Seldom comments on rejected poems. Responds to queries and mss in up to 2 months. Pays 1-20 author's copies (out of a press run of 200-300). May offer subsidy arrangements. "I am new at this. And so it all depends upon my financial situation at the time. Yes, I might ask the author to subsidize the cost. It could be worth their while. I have good connections in the small press." Order sample publications by sending a 6×9 SAE. "There is no charge for samples."

Advice: "My advice is to find your writing voice, then go with it. Never give up trying to get published. A good alternative is to self-publish, then distribute anywhere and everywhere."

☑ ⚐ $ ⊘ **THE MASSACHUSETTS REVIEW**, South College, University of Massachusetts, Amherst MA 01003. (413)545-2689. Fax: (413)577-0740. E-mail: massrev@external.umass.edu. Website: wwwmassrevie w.org. Includes guidelines, names of editors, table of contents for recent issues, and excerpts from the latest issue). Established 1959. **Poetry Editors:** Paul Jenkins, Anne Halley, and Martín Espada.

• Work published in this review has been included in the 1995 and 1997 volumes of *The Best American Poetry.*

Magazine Needs: Mostly free verse, all lengths and topics, appears here, with emphasis in recent issues on non-narrative modes. An interesting feature: Editors run poems with long-line lengths in smaller type, to fit on the page without typographical interruption (as in other journals). Has published poetry by Tony Hoagland, Marilyn Hacker, and Juan Felipe Herrera. As a sample the editor selected these lines from "What They Did" by Vern Rutsala:

> What they decided to do was so hard/we marvelled at their courage./It was like trying to tie knots/
> with two fingers inside a matchbox/the way surgeons do, practicing./Like that only much harder.

The Massachusetts Review is 308 pgs., 6×9, offset-printed on bond paper, perfect-bound with 4-color card cover and 4-color pages of art. Receives about 2,500 poems/year, accepts about 50. Press run is 1,600 for 1,100-1,200 subscribers of which 1,000 are libraries, the rest for shelf sales. Subscription: $22/year (US), $30 outside US, $30 for libraries. Sample: $8 (US), $11 outside US.

How to Submit: No simultaneous submissions or previously published poems. Read submissions October 1 through June 1 only. Guidelines available for SASE. Responds in 6 weeks. Pays minimum of $10, or 35¢/line, plus 2 copies.

⊘ **MATCHBOOK; MATCHBOOK PRESS; LCPH MEDIA SERVICES**, 242 N. Broad St., Doylestown PA 18901. E-mail: matchgirl8@aol.com. Website: www.matchbookpress.com. Established 1994. **Editor:** Debrie Stevens.

Magazine Needs: *Matchbook,* published biannually, "presents intriguing poetry and reviews to readers interested in same." Wants "most any form, length, subject, style with the following restrictions, query first on long poems or translations." Does not want "rhymed verse, traditional forms, concrete poems." Has published poetry by Simon Perchik, Cid Corman, and Robert Peters. *Matchbook* is 64 pgs., tabloid-sized, offset-printed with cover art and ads. Receives about 500 poems/year, accepts about 20%. Press run is 300 for 12 subscribers; 25 distributed free to area bookstores. Subscription: $11.95. Sample: $6.95. Make checks payable to LCPH Media Services.

How to Submit: "Copy purchase suggested but not mandatory." Submit 5-6 poems at a time typewritten, printed out, or legible copies. Accepts simultaneous submissions OK "if noted"; no previously published poems. Cover letter preferred. Time between acceptance and publication is 6 months. Seldom comments on rejected poems. Publishes theme issues, "announced in previous issues, plus on website." Guidelines available for SASE, by e-mail, or on website. Responds in 1 month. Sometimes sends prepublication galleys. Pays 2 copies. Acquires first North American serial rights. Staff reviews books, chapbooks, magazines, and zines in 200 words, single book format. Send books for review consideration.

☑ ⦿ ◎ **MATRIARCH'S WAY, JOURNAL OF FEMALE SUPREMACY; ARTEMIS CREATIONS** **(Specialized: women/feminism)**, 3395-2J Nostrand Ave., Brooklyn NY 11229. (718)648-8215. E-mail: Arte misPub@metconnect.com. Website: www.artemiscreations.com. Established 1994. **Editor:** S. Oliveira.

Magazine Needs: *Matriarch's Way* is a biannual "matriarchal feminist" publication. Wants "powerful fem" poetry. *Matriarch's Way* is 125-200 pgs., digest-sized, offset-printed and perfect-bound, includes art. Single copy: $10; domestic subscription: $20. Sample: $10. Make checks payable to Artemis Creations.

How to Submit: Accepts previously published poems and simultaneous submissions. Accepts e-mail submissions. Time between acceptance and publication is 1 week. Comments on rejected poems. Occasionally publishes theme issues. Guidelines and a list of upcoming themes available for SASE. Responds in 1 week. Sometimes sends prepublication galleys. "Book reviews needed."

Also Offers: Annual writer's contest. "Would like to see a synopsis and 3 sample chapters." Unpublished books accepted; maximum 1,500 words.

🌐 ⊘ **MATTOID**, School of Literary & Communication Studies, Deakin University, Geelong, Victoria, Australia 3217. Fax: (035)227 2484. E-mail: bje@deakin.edu.au. Established 1977. **Contact:** Dr. Brian Edwards.

Magazine Needs: *Mattoid* appears 2 or 3 times/year. "No special requirements but interesting complexity, quality, experimentation." Has published poetry by Lauris Edmond, Kevin Hart, Judith Rodriguez, Fred Wah, Robert Kroetsch, and Pamela Banting. *Mattoid* is 200 pgs., flat-spined with 2-color cover. Receives about 800 poems/year, accepts 10-15%. Press run is 650 for 400 subscribers of which 10 are libraries, 50-100 shelf sales. Sample: $18 overseas.

How to Submit: Accepts e-mail and fax submissions. Publishes theme issues. Upcoming themes available for SASE. Responds in 3 months. Pays 1 copy. Reviews books of poetry in 1,000-2,000 words, single book format.

$ ◎ MATURE YEARS (Specialized: senior citizen, religious), P.O. Box 801, 201 Eighth Ave. S., Nashville TN 37202. (615)749-6292. Fax: (615)749-6512. E-mail: mcrepsey@umpublishing.org. Established 1954. **Editor:** Marvin W. Cropsey.

Magazine Needs: *Mature Years* is a quarterly. "The magazine's purpose is to help persons understand and use the resources of Christian faith in dealing with specific opportunities and problems related to aging. Poems are usually limited to 16 lines and may, or may not, be overtly religious. Poems should not poke fun at older adults, but may take a humorous look at them. Avoid sentimentality and saccharine. If using rhymes and meter, make sure they are accurate." *Mature Years* is 112 pgs., magazine-sized, perfect-bound, with full-color glossy paper cover. Press run is 70,000. Sample: $5.

How to Submit: Line length for poetry is 16 lines of up to 50 characters maximum. Accepts fax submissions; prefers e-mail submissions. Submit seasonal and nature poems for spring during December through February; for summer, March through May; for fall, June through August; and for winter, September through November. Guidelines available for SASE. Responds in 2 months; sometimes a year's delay before publication. Pays $1/ line upon acceptance.

⊕ ◯ MAYPOLE EDITIONS, 22 Mayfair Ave., Ilford, Essex IG1 3DQ England. (0181)252-0354.

Book/Chapbook Needs: Maypole Editions publishes 3 hardbacks/year of fiction and poetry, as well as anthologies. Wants "poems broadly covering social concerns, ethnic minorities, feminist issues, romance, lyric." Does not want "politics." Has published poetry by A. Lee Firth, Samantha Willow, Brian Jeffry, Mindy Cresswell, Denise Bell, and Paul Amphlet. As a sample we selected these lines from "Demonism Forgot" by K.M. Dersley from the anthology *Fusing Tulips: 2001-2002:*

> *Why demonise mediocrities, though?/Why do them the favor?/Do you have to attack what/is already*
> *dead?/They're decent taxpayers,/they laugh at the right places/in TV sitcoms.*

How to Submit: Query first with a few sample poems approximately 30 lines long and cover letter with brief bio and publication credits. Obtain samples of books by sending £1 and an A5 SAE for a catalog.

✓ $ ◻ ◎ MEADOWBROOK PRESS (Specialized: anthologies, children, humor), 5451 Smetana Dr., Minnetonka MN 55343. Website: www.meadowbrookpress.com (includes samples, guidelines, poetry contests for kids, and educational info for kids and teachers). Established 1975. **Contact:** Zoinks editor.

Book/Chapbook Needs: Meadowbrook Press publishes one anthology a year as part of a series of funny poetry books for children. Wants humorous poems aimed at children ages 6-12. "Poems should be fun, light and refreshing. We're looking for new, hilarious, contemporary voices in children's poetry that kids can relate to." Accepts poetry written by children "only on the website—not for publication in books." Has published poetry by Shel Silverstein, Jack Prelutsky, Jeff Moss, and Bruce Lansky. Anthologies have included *Kids Pick the Funniest Poems*; *A Bad Case of the Giggles*; and *Miles of Smiles*.

How to Submit: "Send your best work." Submit 1 poem to a page, name, and address on each. Line length for poetry is 15 maximum. Include SASE with each submission. Accepts previously published poems and simultaneous submissions. Cover letter required "just to know where the poet found us." Time between acceptance and publication is 1-2 years. Poems are tested in front of grade school students before being published. Guidelines available for SASE. Pays $50-100/poem plus 1 copy.

◻ ◎ MEDICINAL PURPOSES LITERARY REVIEW; MARILYN K. PRESCOTT MEMORIAL POETRY CONTEST; POET TO POET, INC., 86-37 120th St., #2D, Richmond Hill NY 11418. (718)776-8853 or (718)847-2150. E-mail: scarptpmp@netscape.net. Established 1994. **Executive Editor:** Robert Dunn. **Associate Editor/Poetry Editor:** Leigh Harrison.

Magazine Needs: *Medicinal Purposes* appears biannually and wants "virtually any sort of quality poetry (3 poems, up to 60 lines/poem). Please, no pornography, gratuitous violence, or hate mongering." Accepts poetry written by children for the young writers' column. Has published poetry by Patric Pepper, X.J. Kennedy, Rhina P. Espaillat, Chocolate Waters, Paul Polansky, Robert Cooperman, and George Dickerson. *Medicinal Purposes* is 80 pgs., 8½×5½ (landscape format), professionally printed and perfect-bound with card stock cover with b&w illustration, b&w illustrations also inside. Receives 1,200 poems/year, accepts about 10%. Press run is 1,000 for 270 subscribers of which 6 are libraries, 30% shelf sales. Subscription: $16/year. Sample: $9. Make checks payable to Poet to Poet.

How to Submit: Submit 3 poems at a time, up to 60 lines per poem, typed with SASE. No previously published poems or simultaneous submissions. Accepts e-mail submissions (avoid attachments, paste poems in body of message). Cover letter preferred. Time between acceptance and publication is up to 16 months. Often comments on rejected poems. Guidelines available for SASE or by e-mail. Responds in 3 months. Always sends prepublication galleys. Pays 2 contributor's copies. Acquires first rights.

Also Offers: Produces a poetry/folk music public access cable show called "Poet to Poet." Also sponsors an annual poetry contest, 1st Prize $100. Submit 3 poems of 6-16 lines each with a $5 entry fee by June 15. Winners will be published in the year's end issue. Additionally they sponsor a chapbook contest. Also administers the Marilyn K. Prescott Memorial Poetry Contest. Details available for SASE.

Advice: "Poetry cannot be created out of a vacuum. Read the work of others, listen to performances, and most important—Get A Life! Do Things! If you get struck by lightning, then share the light. Only then do you stand a chance of finding your own voice."

⬤ ◨ ◎ **MEDIPHORS (Specialized: health concerns)**, P.O. Box 327, Bloomsburg PA 17815-0327. E-mail: mediphor@ptd.net. Website: www.mediphors.org (includes writer's guidelines, sample poems, essays and short stories, letters to the editor, cover and contents, editorials, art, photographs, and staff listing/editors). Established 1992. **Editor:** Eugene D. Radice, M.D.

Magazine Needs: *Mediphors* is a biannual literary journal of the health professions that publishes literary work in medicine and health, including poetry, short story, humor, essay, drawing, art/photography. Wants "fresh insights into illness and those caregivers with the burden and joy of working in the fields of medicine and health. Optimism in the face of adversity and overwhelming sorrow. The day-to-day feelings of healthcare workers in diverse settings from hospitals in cities to war zones in military hot spots." *Mediphors* is 72 pgs., 8½×11, offset-printed and saddle-stapled with color cover and b&w art, graphics, and photos throughout. Receives about 2,000 poetry submissions/year, accepts about 100. Press run is 1,200 for 300 subscribers of which 20 are libraries, 450 shelf sales. Single copy: $6.95; subscription: $15. Sample: $6.

How to Submit: Submit "2 copies of each poem that we can keep; 6 poems maximum, 30 lines each. We do not accept previously published poems or simultaneous submissions, and it is upsetting to find out that this has occurred when we accept a poem." Cover letter not required "but helpful." No e-mail submissions. Time between acceptance and publication is up to 1 year. Seldom comments on rejected poems. Guidelines available for SASE. Responds in 3 months. Pays 2 contributor's copies. "We require authors to sign a very tight contract for first North American serial rights that makes them legally responsible for plagiarism, libel, copyright infringement, etc."

Advice: "Our goal is to place in print as many new authors as possible, particularly those working within the health/medical fields (such as doctors, nurses, technologists, therapists, etc.). We encourage unsolicited manuscripts."

N $⬤ ◨ ◎ **MEGAZINE 17 PRESENTS; KINGSTON MINES MAGAZINE (Specialized: African-American; Africa, West Indian Islands, Carribean)**, Charleston IL (e-mail for current address). E-mail: megazine 17@hotmail.com. Established 2000. **Contact:** Godfrey Logan.

Magazine Needs: *Megazine 17 Presents* appears 6 times/year. Wants "to tell the true stories of life, love, everyone has a story to tell. I like to read stories. We want poetry that is provocative, honest. Want lots of pictures. Want opinions on many topics." Does not want "hate, racism, religious persecution." As a sample the editor selected these lines from his own poem ".500" which appears in his chapbook, *Remember the Titans*:

> You win some. Love. You lose some. Love.—Cupid's aim I question sometimes. You remain my one true
> love. You make me blue sometimes. Inspire poetry in my mind. Still. Movements are like poetry to my
> eye. Love.

Megazine 17 Presents is 12-20 pgs., magazine-sized, stapled, cover photos/art, with ads. Accepts about 90% of poems submitted. Publishes about 10-20 poems/issue. Press run is 2,400. "Issues come in print and online directly through subscription." Single copy: $2; subscription $10 online, $20 print. Sample: $5. Make checks payable to *Megazine 17 Presents*, % Godfrey Logan (contact by e-mail for address).

How to Submit: Submit 5-10 poems at a time. Length for poetry is 1-2 pgs. Accepts previously published poems and simultaneous submissions. No fax submissions. Cover letter with photo is preferred. "Explain inspiration behind poetry. No long explanations, please." Reads submissions all year. **Charges $10 reading fee.** ("Part of fees and subscriptions used to fund youth athletics.") Time between acceptance and publication is 3-24 weeks. "Poems are pored over exhaustively. Examined inside and out by myself and a number of poetry-loving colleagues." Never comments on rejected poems. "Subscriptions are encouraged." Occasionally publishes theme issues. Guidelines are available by e-mail. Responds in up 6 months. Pays $100 for photos used to featured authors. Reviews books and chapbooks of poetry and other magazines/journals. Poets may send books for review consideration. "We will review them to promote to others in magazine. $20 charge to review books."

Also Offers: *Kingston Mines Magazine* focuses on African American poetry, as well as poetry from Africa, West Indian Islands, and the Carribean Islands. Appears 6 times/year, runs 12-20 pgs., magazine-sized. Accepts about 90% of poems submitted. Publishes about 10-20 poems/issue. Press run is 2,400. Charges $10 reading fee; part of fees and subscriptions used to help fund youth athletics. **For both *Megazine 17 Presents* and *Kingston Mines Magazine:*** "We encourage photos. Featured authors receive $100 and an issue when their work is featured. Can win more than once. Not just cover photos but throughout magazine as well. Will accept photos of erotic yet contemplative nature primarily but will accept other photo types as well. *Kingston Mines Magazine* accepts b&w photos only."

Advice: "There are a lot more opportunities for writers now than in the past. I've seen poetry bloom in a way that warms my heart. There are a lot of us who do it for the love."

◨ **MELLEN POETRY PRESS**, P.O. Box 450, Lewiston NY 14092-0450. (716)754-2266. Fax: (716)754-4056. E-mail: mellen@wzrd.com. Website: www.mettenpress.com. Established 1973. **Poetry Editor:** Patricia Schultz.

Book/Chapbook Needs: "Mellen Poetry Press is a division of the Edwin Mellen press, a scholarly press. We do not have access to large chain bookstores for distribution, but depend on direct sales and independent bookstores." Pays 5 copies, no royalties. "We require no author subsidies. However, we encourage our authors to seek grants from Councils for the Arts and other foundations because these add to the reputation of the volume."

Wants "original integrated work—living unity of poems, preferably unpublished, encompassable in one reading." Has published poetry by Andrew Oerke and James Sutton. Books are usually 64 pgs., 6×9, softcover binding, no graphics. Price: $14.95.

How to Submit: Submit 30-60 sample poems with cover letter including bio and publications. "We do not print until we receive at least 50 prepaid orders. Successful marketing of poetry books depends on the author's active involvement. We send out free review copies to journals or newspapers when requested. An author may, but is not required to, purchase books that count toward the needed pre-publication sales."

Advice: "We seek to publish volumes unified in mood, tone, theme."

MELTING TREES REVIEW (Specialized: social issues), P.O. Box 240268, Eclectic AL 36024. E-mail: meltingtreesreview@excite.com. Established 1995 by Mike Catalano. **Editor:** Suzanne Strickland.

Magazine Needs: *Melting Trees Review*, "The Peoples' Park of Poetry," appears quarterly and "encourages the misfits, outcasts, and bizarre nonconformists to explore their wildest imaginations." Wants "free verse only. We want stuff Hallmark would put in their shredders. Please do not send us stuff you'd read in a trite greeting card. No rhyme or academic, textbook poetry." Also accepts book, music and movie reviews, essays, short plays, lyrics, and freelance writing. Encourage b&w artwork drawn in ink. Accepts poetry written by children. Has published poetry by John Grey, Daniel Green, Virgil Suarez, John Sweet, Ward Kelley, and Mike Catalano. As a sample they selected these lines from "88" by Mike Catalano:

> She was a college grad from years past/who had her fill of sexual ultimatums/from philandering
> employers. And now,/in the final semester of her Masters,/she found a kindred spirit in the arts.

Melting Trees Review is 48 pgs., digest-sized, side-stapled with full color glossy front and back cover. "Encourages b&w art drawn in ink and honors any freelance photography of people" (editor may alter photographs with permission). "Unique magazine layout." Receives about 2,000 poems/year, accepts 15%. Press run varies. Sample: $5 postpaid. Make checks or money orders payable to Suzanne Strickland. No more back issues from prior to 2000 available.

How to Submit: Submit 3-5 typed poems at a time. Accepts published poems and simultaneous submissions. Accepts e-mail submission in body of message. Comments on rejected poems by request only. Responds in 1 month. Pays 1 contributor's copy. Acquires first rights.

Advice: "Your mommy is not judging these, so please don't send a lullabye. Send something you'd write if you saw a stright-faced mayor dancing to Eminem on top of a refrigerator because he gave the town's budget contract to a thirteen year old whiz kid who thinks the world will end in three hours because he just finished watching a movie directed by Spike Lee but thinks he should have starred in it, but now thinks he should give the contract back because the mayor is getting all goo-goo eyed with his own grandmother because he has a fetish for toothless old women who like to rap. . . We are Ms. Angelou's worst nightmare. We want talent, not reputation."

$ THE MENNONITE (Specialized: religious), P.O. Box 347, Newton KS 67114-0347. (316)283-5100. Fax: (316)283-0454. E-mail: gordonh@gcmc.org. Website: www.themennonite.org. Established 1885. **Associate Editor:** Gordon Houser.

Magazine Needs: *The Mennonite* is published weekly and wants "Christian poetry—usually free verse, not too long, with multiple layers of meaning. No sing-song rhymes or poems that merely describe or try to teach a lesson." Has published poetry by Jean Janzen and Julia Kasdorf. As a sample we selected these lines from "Her garden is the last of her love" by John Grey:

> She shares the burden of/seed, its thirst for water,/for//light, the way it bursts through the blackness,
> stands tall in/the sun. Its greatest success//climb up on their own green/backbones, press their petaled
> faces/against the parlor windows

The Mennonite is 16-24 pgs., 8½×11, 2-color cover, includes art and ads. Receives about 100 poems/year, accepts about 10%. Press run is 18,500 for 18,000 subscribers. Single copy: $1.50; subscription: $36.75. Sample: $1.

How to Submit: Submit up to 4 poems at a time. Accepts previously published poems and simultaneous submissions. E-mail submissions preferred. Cover letter preferred. Time between acceptance and publication is up to 3 months. Seldom comments on rejected poems. Publishes theme issues occasionally. Guidelines and upcoming themes are available for SASE. Responds in 2 weeks. Pays $50-75 plus 2 copies. Acquires first or one-time rights.

$ MERLYN'S PEN: FICTION ESSAYS AND POEMS BY AMERICA'S TEENS, GRADES 6-12 (Specialized: students, young adults), Dept. PM, Box 910, East Greenwich RI 02818. (401)885-5175. Fax: (401)885-5222. E-mail: merlynspen@aol.com. Website: www.merlynspen.com. Established 1985. **Editor:** R. Jim Stahl.

Magazine Needs & How to Submit: Accepts poetry only from poets aged 12 to 18. *Merlyn's Pen* appears annually in November and has published poetry by Katherine Assef, Laura Hudson, and Brian Sheppard. As a sample the editor selected the poem "Twins" by Joanna Hearne:

> Marmalade cat/sleeps in the sun/on a woven mat of wool spun/dreaming of pine-amber heights//Stormy
> Siamese/opens wide/her turquoise eyes,/onto the indigo night.

Merlyn's Pen is 100 pgs., magazine-sized, professionally printed with matte finish paper, color cover. Press run is 6,000 for 4,000 subscribers of which 2,000 are libraries. Subscription: $29, plus 10% shipping. Guidelines available for SASE or on website. Responds in 9 weeks. Pays 3 contributor's copies plus $20-200/piece.

⊘ **MIAMI UNIVERSITY PRESS**, English Dept., Miami University, Oxford OH 45056. (513)529-5110. Website: www.muohio.edu/mupress/. Established 1992. **Editor:** James Reiss.
Book/Chapbook Needs & How to Submit: Publishes 2 books/year in paperback and cloth editions by poets who have already published at least one full-length book of poems. Recent titles include *Wind Somewhere, and Shade* by Kate Knapp Johnson, Spring 2001; and *The Printer's Error* by Aaron Fogel, Spring 2001; *Ariadne's Island* by Molly Bendall, Winter 2002; *Gender Studies* by Jeffrey Skinner, Winter 2002. Currently closed to unsolicited poetry.

▼ $⊘ **MICHIGAN QUARTERLY REVIEW**, Dept. PM, 3032 Rackham Bldg., University of Michigan, Ann Arbor MI 48109. (734)764-9265. E-mail: mqr@umich.edu. Website: www.umich.edu/~mqr (includes information about the current and forthcoming issues, special issues, subscription information, guidelines, and Lawrence Foundation Prize information). Established 1962. **Editor-in-Chief:** Laurence Goldstein.
• Poetry published in the *Michigan Quarterly Review* was also selected for inclusion in the 1992, 1994, 1995, and 1998 volumes of *The Best American Poetry*.
Magazine Needs: *Michigan Quarterly Review* is "an interdisciplinary, general interest academic journal that publishes mainly essays and reviews on subjects of cultural and literary interest." Uses all kinds of poetry except light verse. No specifications as to form, length, style, subject matter, or purpose. Has published poetry by Susan Hahn, Carl Phillips, Mary Oliver, and Yusef Komunyakaa. As a sample the editor selected these lines from "Spirit Cabinet" by David Wojahn:
> *House-of-Justice-One-Way-Glass: you can't see in, not to the upper floors,/where cell rows mean to*
> *prove/that here blind justice is half cured.*

Michigan Quarterly Review is 160 pgs., 6×9, flat-spined, professionally printed with glossy card cover, b&w photos and art. Receives about 1,400 submissions/year, accepts about 30, has a 1-year backlog. Press run is 2,000, with 1,200 subscribers of which half are libraries. Single copy: $5; subscription: $18. Sample: $2.50 plus 2 first-class stamps.
How to Submit: Prefers typed mss. No previously published poems or simultaneous submissions. No fax or e-mail submissions. Cover letter preferred; "it puts a human face on the manuscript. A few sentences of biography is all I want, nothing lengthy or defensive." Publishes theme issues. Theme for winter 2002 is "Jewish in America." Responds in 6 weeks. Always sends prepublication galleys. Pays $8-12/page. Acquires first rights only. Reviews books of poetry. "All reviews are commissioned."
Advice: "There is no substitute for omnivorous reading and careful study of poets past and present, as well as reading in new and old areas of knowledge. Attention to technique, especially to rhythm and patterns of imagery, is vital."

$⊘ **MICHIGAN STATE UNIVERSITY PRESS**, 1405 S Harrison Rd., 25 Manly Miles Bldg., East Lansing MI 48823-5202. (517)355-9543. Fax: (800)678-2120. E-mail: msupress@msu.edu. Website: www.msupress.msu.edu. Established 1947. **Acquisitions Editor:** Martha Bates.
Book/Chapbook Needs: Michigan State University Press publishes 4-6 paperbacks/year. "We publish poetry of literary quality, with an emphasis on poets living and writing in Michigan." Books are usually 80-125 pgs., 6×9.
How to Submit: Send 5-10 sample poems and brief cover letter. E-mail submissions are not accepted. Include SASE "large enough to hold all materials you wish returned." Responds to queries in about 2 months, to mss in 2 years. Pays royalties and author's copies.

✓ $◯ ⊘ ◎ **THE MID-AMERICA PRESS, INC.; THE MID-AMERICA POETRY REVIEW; THE MID-AMERICA PRESS WRITING AWARD COMPETITION (Specialized: regional)**, P.O. Box 575, Warrensburg MO 64093-0575. (660)747-3481. Press established 1976. **Editor:** Robert C. Jones.
Magazine Needs: *Mid-America Poetry Review* appears 3 times/year and publishes "well-crafted poetry primarily from—but not limited to—poets living in Missouri, Illinois, Arkansas, Oklahoma, Kansas, Nebraska, and Iowa. We are open to all styles and forms; what we look for is poetry by writers who know both what they are doing and why. We have a prejudice against work with content that is primarily self-indulgent or overly private." Has published poetry by Jim Barnes, Bill Bauer, Serina Allison Hearn, Dan Jaffe, Kevin Prufer, Robert Stewart, Gloria Vando, and Jeanie Wilson. As a sample the editor selected these lines from "A Gloss Upon King Lear" by Robert Lee Mahon:
> *The toughest part of dressing out a squirrel/is removing the pelt. Years earlier//he'd watched and,*
> *childlike, asked his father,/"Why do they call it* dressing?" *His father//had looked up from the knife,*
> *then down at the squirrel, stripped to its new red skin. . . //*

The Mid-America Review is 60-70 pgs., 6×9, offset-printed and perfect-bound with matte-paper cover. Receives about 700-1,000 poems/year, accepts about 20%. Press run is 1,000. Single copy: $6; subscription: $30/2 years. Sample: $6. Make checks payable to The Mid-America Press, Inc.

How to Submit: Submit 1-3 poems at a time. No previously published poems or simultaneous submissions. Cover letter useful. "Type submissions, single- or double-spaced, on 8½×11 white paper; name, address, telephone number, and e-mail address (if available) in top left or right corner. Keep copy of your manuscript—unused submissions will be recycled; send SASE for notification. One-page cover letter (if included) should list items to be considered; contain brief paragraphs of information about author and previous publications." Time between acceptance and publication is up to 9 months. Sometimes comments on rejected poems. Guidelines available for SASE. Responds within 2 months. Sends prepublication galleys. Pays $5/poem and 2 contributor's copies. Acquires first North American serial rights. Staff occasionally reviews books of poetry. Send books for review consideration.

Book/Chapbook Needs & How to Submit: The Mid-America Press, Inc. was established "to encourage writers and the appreciation of writing." Publishes 2-6 paperbacks per year with 1 book selected through The Mid-America Press Writing Award Competition. "At present—with the exception of entries for the competition—the Press is not reading unsolicited book-length poetry mss. The competition is limited to 48- to 148-page poetry mss by poets living in Missouri, Arkansas, Oklahoma, Kansas, Nebraska, Iowa, or Illinois. Mss must be unpublished in book form." Entry fee: $20. Entry guidelines and deadline date available for SASE. The winner of Writing Award 1999 was *This Country or That* by Victoria Anderson. Recent Mid-America Press, Inc. award-winning publications include *Red Silk* (1999) by Maryfrances Wagner (winner of the 2000 Thorpe Menn Award for Writing Excellence) and *Living Off the Land, A Gathering of Writing from The Warrensburg Writers Circle* (1999) edited by Robert C. Jones (First Place in The 2000 Walter William Major Work Award, from the Missouri Writers' Guild). New publications include *Outcasts, Poems* (2000), by Brian Daldorph; *Memories & Memoirs, Essays, Poems, Stories, Letters by Contemporary Missouri Authors* (2000, edited by Sharon Kinney Hanson; and *Uncurling, Poems* (2000) by Jeanie Wilson. Obtain sample books by sending $13.95 per book (For *Memories & Memoirs*, send $18.95).

■ $□ ◐ ◎ MID-AMERICAN REVIEW; JAMES WRIGHT PRIZE FOR POETRY (Specialized: translations), Dept. of English, Bowling Green State University, Bowling Green OH 43403. (419)372-2725. Website: http://bgsu.edu/midamericanreview (includes sample work, guidelines, contact infor, and contents of previous issues). Established 1981. **Editor-in-Chief:** Michael Czyzniejewski. **Poetry Editor:** Karen Craigo.
  ● Poetry published in *Mid-American Review* was included in the 1999 volume of *Best American Poetry.*

Magazine Needs: *Mid-American Review* appears twice/year. "Poetry should emanate from strong, evocative images; use fresh, interesting language; and have a consistent sense of voice. Each line must carry the poem, and an individual vision should be evident. We encourage new as well as established writers. There is no length limit." Has published poetry by Michelle Bois-Sean, Bob Hicok, Carl Phillips, and Ted Kooser. The review is 176 pgs., offset-printed and flat-spined with laminated card cover using full-color artwork. Receives over 2,000 mss/year, accepts 40-50 poems. Press run is 1,500. Single copy: $7; subscription: $12. Sample: $5.

How to Submit: Submit up to 6 poems at a time. Reads submissions year round; responds more slowly in summer months. September 1 through May 30 only. Guidelines available for SASE. Sends prepublication galleys. Pays $10/printed page when possible plus 2 copies. Rights revert to authors on publication. Reviews books of poetry.

Also Offers: Also publishes chapbooks in translation and award the James Wright Prize for Poetry. "To be considered for the prize, send $10 fee and three poems addressed to the James Wright Prize, or write for complete guidelines."

$◎ MIDSTREAM: A MONTHLY ZIONIST REVIEW (Specialized: ethnic), 633 Third Ave., 21st Floor, New York NY 10017. (212)339-6040. E-mail: info@midstream.org. Website: www.midstream.org. **Editor:** Joel Carmichael.

Magazine Needs: *Midstream* is an international journal appearing 8 times/year. Wants short poems with Jewish themes or atmosphere. Has published poetry by Yehuda Amichai, James Reiss, Abraham Sutzkever, Liz Rosenberg, and John Hollander. The magazine is 48 pgs., about 8½×11, saddle-stapled with colored card cover. Each issue includes 4 to 5 poems (which tend to be short, lyric, and freestyle expressing seminal symbolism of Jewish history and Scripture). Receives about 300 submissions/year, accepts 5-10%. Press run is 10,000. Single copy: $3; subscription: $21.

How to Submit: Submit 2 poems at a time. Does not accept e-mail submissions. Time between acceptance and publication is within 1 year. Publishes theme issues. The April 2002 issue will be devoted to the Holocaust. Responds in 6 months. Pays $25/poem and 3 contributor's copies. Acquires first rights.

☑ $□ ◐ ◐ MIDWEST POETRY REVIEW, 7443 Oak Tree Lane, Springhill FL 34607-2324. (352)688-8116. E-mail: mariasingh@cs.com. Established 1980. **Editor/Publisher:** Pariksith Singh and Maria Scuziano.

Magazine Needs: *Midwest Poetry Review* is a quarterly, with no other support than subscriptions, contest entry fees, and an occasional advertisement. Looking for "quality, accessible verse. Evocative and innovative imagery with powerful adjectives and verbs. Poetry that opens the door to the author's feelings through sensory descriptions. We are attempting to encourage the cause of poetry by purchasing the best of modern poetry. No jingly verses or limericks. Any subject is considered, if handled with skill and taste. No pornography. Nothing which arrives without SASE is read or gets reply. We are open to new poets, but they must show talent." Accepts poetry written by children. "Must be good writing." Has published poetry by Rukmini Callamchi, B.R. Culbertson, Junette Fabian, Glenna Holloway, Mikal Lofgren, and Bettie Sellers. As a sample the editor selected these lines from "Picking" by Rukmini Callamchi:

> In your yard, we are picking blackberries:/strong, blue, and full of voice./It's the thinness of this summer I remember,/its cliff,/its way of ending before the stains/wash off my dress//I do not want your mother to see this:/her hands, soft and restless/in the kitchen sink.//She is watching, waiting,/like the summer,/for something to snap, unravel/like the breaking of clouds before rain

Midwest Poetry Review is 40 pgs., professionally printed in Univers type, digest-sized, saddle-stapled with matte card cover. Subscription: $20. Sample: $5.78 (when available).

How to Submit: Submit up to 5 poems at a time, 1 poem/page. Line length for poetry is 40 maximum. No previously published poems or simultaneous submissions. No bios or credit lists. Accepts fax submissions. Guidelines are available for $1 and SASE. "We will critique up to 10 of your poems at a time." Criticism fee: $20 plus SASE. Responds in 1 month. Pays $5/poem. Acquires first rights.

Also Offers: Has varied contests in each issue, with prizes ranging from $10-250, with "unbiased, non-staff judges for all competitions." Contests have entry fees. Details available for SASE. A 20-point self-analysis survey to assist poets in analyzing their own work is offered free to new subscribers.

THE MIDWEST QUARTERLY, Pittsburg State University, Pittsburg KS 66762. (316)235-4689. Fax: (316)235-4686. E-mail: smeats@pittstate.edu (queries only, no submissions). Website: www.pittstate.edu/engl/midwest.html. Established 1959. **Poetry Editor:** Stephen Meats.

Magazine Needs: *Midwest Quarterly* "publishes articles on any subject of contemporary interest, particularly literary criticism, political science, philosophy, education, biography, and sociology, and each issue contains a section of poetry usually 15 poems in length. I am interested in well-crafted, though not necessarily traditional poems that explore the inter-relationship of the human and natural worlds in bold, surrealistic images of a writer's imaginative, mystical experience. Sixty lines or less (occasionally longer if exceptional)." Has published poetry by David Baker, Fleda Brown Jackson, Kathleen Norris, Pattiann Rogers, Jeanne Murray Walker, and Ted Kooser. *Midwest Quarterly* is 130 pgs., digest-sized, professionally printed and flat-spined with matte cover. Press run is 650 for 600 subscribers of which 500 are libraries. Receives about 4,000 poems/year, accepts about 60. "My plan is to publish all acceptances within 1 year." Subscription: $12. Sample: $3.

How to Submit: Mss should be typed with poet's name on each page, 10 poems or fewer. Accepts simultaneous submissions; no previously published poems. No fax or e-mail submissions. Occasionally publishes theme issues. Guidelines and upcoming themes available for SASE, by fax, or by e-mail. Responds in 2 months, usually sooner. "Submissions without SASE cannot be acknowledged." Pays 3 contributor's copies. Acquires first serial rights. Editor comments on rejected poems "if the poet or poems seem particularly promising." Reviews books of poetry by *Midwest Quarterly* published poets only.

Advice: "Keep writing; read as much contemporary poetry as you can lay your hands on; don't let the discouragement of rejection keep you from sending your work out to editors."

MIDWEST VILLAGES & VOICES (Specialized: regional), P.O. Box 40214, St. Paul MN 55104. (612)822-6878. Established 1979.

Book/Chapbook Needs & How to Submit: Midwest Villages & Voices is a cultural organization and small press publisher of Midwestern poetry and prose. "We encourage and support Midwestern writers and artists. However, at this time submissions are accepted by invitation only. Unsolicited submissions are not accepted."

MIDWIFERY TODAY (Specialized: childbirth), P.O. Box 2672, Eugene OR 97402-0223. (541)344-7438. Fax: (541)344-1422. E-mail: editorial@midwiferytoday.com. Website: www.midwiferytoday.com (includes writer's guidelines, articles, and products). Established 1986. **Editor-in-Chief:** Jan Tritten. **Editor:** Alice Evans.

Magazine Needs: *Midwifery Today* is a quarterly that "provides a voice for midwives and childbirth educators. We are a midwifery magazine. Subject must be birth or profession related." Does not want poetry that is "off subject or puts down the subject." *Midwifery Today* is 75 pgs., 8½×11, offset-printed, saddle-stapled, with glossy card cover with b&w photos and b&w artwork photos, and ads inside. Uses about 1 poem/issue. Press run is 5,000 for 3,000 subscribers, 1,000 shelf sales. Subscription: $50. Sample: $10.

How to Submit: No previously published poems. Accepts fax and e-mail submissions. Cover letter required. Time between acceptance and publication is 1-2 years. Seldom comments on rejected poems. Publishes theme issues. Guidelines available for SASE and on website. Upcoming themes available for SASE. Responds in 6 months. Pays 2 contributor's copies. Acquires first rights.

Advice: "With our publication *please* stay on the subject."

MILKWOOD REVIEW, 1428 Apache, Holland MI 49424. (616)395-7613. E-mail: peckham@hope.edu. Website: www.geocities.com/milkwoodreview (includes all information about *Milkwood*). Established 2000. **Editors:** Joel Peckham and Susan Atefat Peckham.

Magazine Needs: *The Milkwood Review* is constantly updated and available year round in annual issues online. "*The Milkwood Review* is an interdisciplinary journal that seeks to create a web environment in which poetry, fiction, nonfiction, speculative essays, short scholarly articles, etc., are presented in a form appropriate to the material. All creative work appears with audio samples." Will consider "any kind of poetry from narrative to lyric, from traditional to experimental—no length or line-length restrictions. Because of the journal's commitment to real-audio technology, we favor work that concentrates on poetry as a musical form of literature in which sound is as important as meaning." Does not want "work that is uncrafted or facile." Recently published poetry by Robert Vivian and Craig Challender. *The Milkwood Review* is published online with a fine art cover and art/graphics. Accepts about 10% of poems submitted. Publishes 15-30 poems/issue.

How to Submit: Submit 4-8 poems at a time. Accepts previously published poems and simultaneous submissions. Accepts e-mail and disk submissions (if Word for Windows). Cover letter is required. "Each poem printed in *Milkwood* will include an audio file. Once a poem has been accepted (not before) we will require the author to submit a recorded version of the piece." Reads submissions year-round. Submit seasonal poems anytime. Time between acceptance and publication is 6 weeks. "Poems are read by both editors and full staff. Final decisions on the publication of work in *Milkwood* rest with the founding editors." Often comments on rejections. Occasionally publishes theme issues. A list of upcoming themes is available for SASE. Guidelines are available for SASE and on website. Responds in 6 weeks. Sometimes sends prepublication galleys. No pay; publication only. Acquires first North American serial or one-time rights, reverts to poet upon publication. Reviews books, and chapbooks of poetry and other magazines, open length, in single and multibook format. Poets may send books for review consideration to the editors.

Advice: "Read poetry—but also, *listen to it*. Pay attention not only to the precise and intentional placement of words but to the momentum they create, the surge and urge of the poem."

☑ $⃠ MILLER'S POND; LOELLA CADY LAMPHIER PRIZE FOR POETRY; H&H PRESS, RR

2, Box 241, Middlebury Center PA 16935. (570)376-3361. Fax: (570)376-2674. E-mail: cjhoughtaling@usa.net. Website: http://millerspond.tripod.com (includes contests, submission guidelines, and some poetry not found in print version). Established 1987. **Editor:** C.J. Houghtaling.

Magazine Needs: *miller's pond* is an annual magazine featuring contemporary poetry, interviews, reviews and markets. "We want contemporary poetry that is fresh, accessible, energetic, vivid and flows with language and rhythm. No religious, horror, pornographic, vulgar, rhymed, preachy, lofty, trite, or overly sentimental work." Has published poetry by Colette Inez, Barbara Crocker, Elaine Preston, Hayden Carruth, Frank van Zant, and C.S. Fuqua. As a sample the editor selected these lines from "Rediforms" by Errol Miller:

> Canning household nouns and verbs/into green-glass Mason jars/we are preserving this summer for
> ourselves

miller's pond is 48 pgs., 5½×8½, offset-printed and saddle-stapled with cardstock cover. Receives about 200 poems/year, accepts 20-25 poems/issue. Press run is 200. Single copy: $5 and $3 p&h. Sample (back issue) including guidelines: $5. Make checks payable to H&H Press.

How to Submit: Submit 3-5 poems at a time. Line length for poetry is 40 maximum. Accepts previously published poems and simultaneous submissions. Accepts disk submissions but no fax or e-mail. Cover letter preferred. "No returns without SASE." Reads submissions October 1 through December 1 only. Time between acceptance and publication is up to 1 year. Seldom comments on rejected poems. Guidelines available for SASE or on website. Responds in up to 11 months; "although we try to respond sooner, we are not always able to." Sometimes sends prepublication galleys. Pays $2/poem and 1 copy for work that appears in hard copy version. Acquires one-time rights. Reviews books of poetry in up to 500 words, single book format.

Also Offers: H&H Press sponsors the Loella Lamphier Prize for Poetry. Awards $100 for 1st Place, $50 for 2nd Place and $25 3rd Place. Guidelines available on website. Send SASE.

Book/Chapbook Needs & How to Submit: "H&H Press is a micro-publisher of poetry chapbooks and how-to-write books, with plans to expand into nonfiction and specialty books." Publishes 1 paperback and 1 chapbook per year. Books are usually 24-36 pgs., 8½×5¼, offset-printed and saddle-stapled with cardstock cover, includes some art. "By invitation only; query first for publication schedule and needs. My requirements are simple—the poem/poetry must speak to me on more than one level and stay with me for more than just those few brief moments I'm reading it." Responds in 4 months. Pays royalties of 7% minimum, 12% maximum and 25 author's copies (out of a press run of 200). Books are available for sale via website, phone, or fax.

Advice: "Believe in yourself. Perseverance is a writer's best 'tool.' Study the contemporary masters: Billy Collins, Maxine Kumin, Colette Inez, Hayden Carruth. Please check our website before submitting."

◫ ⃠ ◎ JOHN MILTON MAGAZINE; DISCOVERY MAGAZINE (Specialized: children/teen, re-

ligious, visual impairment), John Milton Society for the Blind, 475 Riverside Dr., Room 455, New York NY 10115. (212)870-3335. Fax: (212)870-3229. E-mail: order@jmsblind.org. Website: www.jmsblind.org (includes writer's guidelines, publications brochure, history of society, staff names, board of directors' names). Established 1928. **Executive Director:** Darcy Quigley.

Magazine Needs: *John Milton Magazine* is "a quarterly digest of more than 50 Christian periodicals, produced in large print (20 point) and sent free to visually impaired adults." The executive director says *John Milton Magazine* is 24 pgs., tabloid-sized, contains clip art. Receives about 30 poems/year, accepts about 5%. Press run is 5,188 for 3,776 subscribers. Subscription is free.

Magazine Needs: *Discovery* is "a quarterly Braille magazine for blind youth (ages 8-18). Articles selected and reprinted from over 20 Christian and secular periodicals for youth." Accepts poetry written by children. The executive director says *Discovery* is 44 Braille pgs. Receives about 30 poems/year, accepts 15%. Press run is 2,041 for 1,878 subscribers. Subscription is free (only available in Braille).

How to Submit: For both publications, they want "Christian themes and holidays (not exclusive), seasonal poems, subjects of interest and encouragement to blind and visually impaired persons." Submit up to 5 poems at a time. Line length for poetry is 5 minimum, 30 maximum. Accepts previously published poems and simultaneous submissions. Accepts e-mail (include in body of message) and disk submissions. Cover letter preferred. "Please enclose a SASE with regular mail submissions." Time between acceptance and publication is up to 1 year. Seldom comments on rejected poems. Publishes theme issues. Guidelines available for SASE. Responds in 3 months. *John Milton Magazine* pays 1-3 copies. *Discovery* pays 1 Braille copy. Acquires one-time or reprint rights.

Advice: "Review list of magazines we typically reprint from (available with writer's guidelines). The bulk of our material is reprinted from other periodicals."

✓ ◯ ◑ **MIND PURGE**, 6001 Skillman St., Apt. #163, Dallas TX 75231. E-mail: jivan@anet-dfw.com or bordo@yahoo.com. Established 1994. **Editor:** Jason Hensel.

Magazine Needs: *Mind Purge* is a biannual literary and art magazine appearing in April and October that publishes poetry, short fiction, one-act plays, short screenplays, essays, book reviews, and art. Wants poetry that is "well-crafted, insightful, imagistic. No specifications as to form, length, subject matter, or style. However no greeting card verse, hackneyed themes or poetry that says nothing or goes nowhere." Has published poetry by Lyn Lifshin, Danny Daniels, Wayne Hogan, B.Z. Niditch, and Ryan G. Van Cleave. As a sample the editors selected these lines from "The Last Days Of" by Holly Day:

> Harvest. Cultivation. The words fall alien and pleasing/from our lips, songs of summers past/of a
> people long since dead. Practice. The round gearshift cupped/smooth in your confused palm. The wide
> flat pedals creak/with rust beneath your sandaled feet. Someday/the machines will work again./
> Someday, it will rain.

Mind Purge is 36-52 pgs., 7 × 8½, neatly printed and saddle-stapled with matte card stock cover with b&w photo and b&w photos inside. Receives about 100 poems/year, accepts 10%. Press run is 100 for 10 subscribers. Subscription: $10. Sample: $4. Make checks payable to Jason Hensel.

How to Submit: Submit up to 5 poems or 10 pages at a time, name and address on each page. No previously published poems or simultaneous submissions. Accepts e-mail submissions, no attachments, include in body of message. Cover letter preferred. Seldom comments on rejected poems. Responds within 3 months. Pays 1 contributor's copy. Reviews books of poetry in 200 words, single book format. Poets may send books for review consideration.

Advice: "Don't give up, just keep submitting. And read, not only poetry, but everything you can get your hands on."

✓ ◑ **THE MINNESOTA REVIEW: A JOURNAL OF COMMITTED WRITING**, English Dept., University of Missouri-Columbia, 110 Tate Hall, Columbia MO 65211. Fax: (573)882-5785. E-mail: WilliamsJeff@missouri.edu. Established 1960. **Editor:** Jeffrey Williams.

Magazine Needs: *The Minnesota Review* is a biannual literary magazine wanting "poetry which explores some aspect of social or political issues and/or the nature of relationships. No nature poems, and no lyric poetry without the above focus." *The Minnesota Review* is about 200 pgs., digest-sized, flat-spined, with b&w glossy card cover and art. Press run is 1,500 for 800 subscribers. Subscription: $20 to individuals, $36 to institutions. Sample: $10.

How to Submit: Address submissions to "Poetry Editor" (not to a specific editor). No fax or e-mail submissions. Cover letter including "brief intro with address" preferred. SASE with sufficient postage required for return of mss. Publishes theme issues. Upcoming themes available for SASE. Responds in up to 4 months. Pays 2 contributor's copies. Acquires all rights. Returns rights upon request. Reviews books of poetry in single or multi-book format.

✓ ◑ ◯ ◎ **MINORITY LITERARY EXPO (Specialized: membership, minorities)**, 317 Third Ave. SW, Apt. 2E, Birmingham AL 35211. (205)297-9816. E-mail: kervin066@aol.com. Established 1990. **Editor/Publisher:** Kervin Fondren.

Magazine Needs & How to Submit: *Minority Literary Expo* is an annual literary professional publication featuring minority poets, novices and professionals. "Organization membership open to all minority poets nationally. I want poems from minority poets that are holistic and wholesome, less than 24 lines each, no vulgar or hate poetry accepted, any style, any form, any subject matter. Poetry that expresses holistic views and philosophies is very acceptable. Literary value is emphasized. Selected poets receive financial awards, certificates, honorable mentions, critiques and special poetic honors." No fee is charged for inclusion. Accepts poetry written by children ages 12 and up. As a sample the editor selected his poem "It's Lonely at the Top":

> No Man Can/Reach the Top of the Mountain/With Hate, Greed and Despair.//Because in Reaching the
> Top/He Soon Will Find Out that/he is the only one There.

Single copy: $21. Guidelines and upcoming themes available for SASE or by e-mail. Pays 1 contributor's copy. Accepts e-mail submissions, include in body of message with e-mail address for reply. "Send edited copy, no more than one page via e-mail."

Also Offers: Also sponsors an annual poetry chapbook contest and an annual "Analyze the Poem" contest. Details available for SASE.

Advice: "We seek novices and unpublished poets to breathe the new life every poetry organization needs."

☑ $◯◐ **THE MISSING FEZ; THE RED FELT AWARD**, P.O. Box 57310, Tucson AZ 85711. E-mail: missing1fez@hotmail.com. Website: www.missingfez.com (includes guidelines, sample work, contest information, and a list of book and chapbook publications). Established 1999. **Poetry Editor:** Alan Brich.

Magazine Needs: *The Missing Fez* is "a quarterly forum for the abnormal in literature. We want poems that embody some form of strangeness or oddity in either style, content, or language. Give us something different. No poems that rhyme or are about pets, or would meet parental approval." Has published poetry by Matthew Scrivner, Elise Mandernack, Ruby Jetts, Jefferson Carver, and Ian Gill. As a sample the editor selected these lines from "Mail to a Blind Man" by Michael Blackwell:

> I sit on a lamppost./Invisible tears rain down/around me and shatter like/a million broken mandalas/
> on the pavement.

The Missing Fez is 36 pgs., 7 × 8½, photocopied on laser quality paper and saddle-stapled with glossy card cover, includes b&w photos and illustrations. Receives about 150 poems/year, accepts 15%. Publish 3-5 poems/issue. Press run is 1,000 for 800 subscribers, 600 shelf sales; 100 distributed free to sponsored reading series. Single copy: $3; subscription: $10. Sample: $3. Make checks payable to Red Felt Publishing.

How to Submit: Submit 3-5 poems at a time with **$3 reading fee**. Accepts previously published poems and simultaneous submissions. No fax or e-mail submissions. Cover letter preferred. "We do require $3 reading fee and SASE since we comment on all submissions and pay on acceptance." Time between acceptance and publication is 3-6 months. Always comments on rejected poems. Occasionally publishes theme issues. Guidelines and a list of upcoming themes available for SASE or on website. Responds in 6 weeks. Pays $15 for 2-3 poems plus 2 copies. Acquires one-time rights.

Also Offers: Sponsors the annual Red Felt Award. 1st Prize winner receives $250. Complete guidelines available for SASE or on website.

Advice: "Don't write safe poetry—if you do, don't send it to us."

◐ **MISSISSIPPI REVIEW**, University of Southern Mississippi, Box 5144, Hattiesburg MS 39406-5144. (601)266-4321. Fax: (601)266-5757. E-mail: fb@netdoor.com. Website: www.sushi.st.usm.edu\mrw. **Editor:** Frederick Barthelme. **Managing Editor:** Rie Fortenberry.

Magazine Needs & How to Submit: Literary publication for those interested in contemporary literature. Poems differ in style, length and form, but all have craft in common (along with intriguing content). Sample: $8. Query first, via mail, e-mail, or their website. Does not read manuscripts in summer. Pays 3 contributor's copies. Sponsors contests. Guidelines available for SASE.

◐ **MM REVIEW; MUTANT MULE; FINISHING LINE PRESS; NEW WOMEN'S VOICES CHAP-BOOK SERIES**, P.O. Box 1016, Cincinnati OH 45201-1016. E-mail: finishingl@aol.com. Established 1998. **Editor:** C.J. Morrison.

Magazine Needs: *MM Review* is a biannual literary arts magazine publishing mostly poetry, but also short stories, short drama, essays and, sometimes, reviews. "We hope to discover new talent." Wants "quality verse. We are open to any style or form, but prefer free verse." Has published poetry by Errol Miller, Dennis Saleh, Denise Brennan Watson, Mark McCloskey, Rane Arroyo, and Alexandra Grilikhes. As a sample the editor selected these lines from "Feeling Fireworks" by Leah Maines:

> Fireflowers bloom/in the warm summer air/your hand/unaware/brushes my breast

MM Review is 40 pgs., digest-sized, laser-printed and saddle-stapled with glossy cover, includes b&w photos. Receives about 1,000 poems/year, accepts 4%. Press run is 500 for 300 subscribers. Single copy: $6; subscription: $10. Sample: $5. Make checks payable to Finishing Line Press.

How to Submit: Submit up to 3 poems at a time. Include SASE. Accepts simultaneous submissions; no previously published poems. Brief cover letter with 50- to 75-word bio required, include past publication credits. Time between acceptance and publication is 6 months. Poems are circulated to an editorial board. Often comments on rejected poems. Occasionally publishes theme issues. Guidelines available for SASE. Responds in 4 months. Sometimes sends prepublication galleys. Pays 1 contributor's copy. Acquires all rights. Returns rights upon publication. Staff reviews books and chapbooks of poetry in 200 words, multi-book format. Send books for review consideration to Finishing Line Press.

Book/Chapbook Needs & How to Submit: Finishing Line Press seeks to "discover new talent" and through their New Women's Voices Series publishes 2 chapbooks/year by women who have not previously published a book or chapbook of poetry. Has published *Looking to the East with Western Eyes* by Leah Maines; *Like the Air* by Joyce Sidman; *Startling Art* by Dorothy Sutton; *The Undertow of Hunger* by Denise Brennan Watson. Chapbooks are usually 25-30 pgs., digest-sized, laser-printed and saddle-stapled with card cover with textured matte wrapper, includes b&w photos. Submit ms of 16-24 pgs. with cover letter, bio, acknowledgements and **$10 reading fee.** Responds to queries in 3-4 weeks, to mss in 3-4 months. Pays 50 author's copies (out of a press run of 300). "Sales profits, if any, go to publish the next new poet." Obtain sample chapbooks by sending $5.

Also Offers: Sponsors New Women's Voices chapbook competition. Entry fee: $12. Deadline: December 31.

Advice: "We are very open to new talent. If the poetry is great, we will consider it for a chapbook."

◐ ◐ **MÖBIUS**, P.O. Box 7544, Talleyville DE 19803-0544. E-mail: mobiusmag@aol.com. Established 1982. **Editor:** Jean Hull Herman.

Magazine Needs: *Möbius* is published twice/year, at Memorial Day and Thanksgiving. Looks for "the informed mind responding to the challenges of reality and the expression of the imagination in poetry that demonstrates intelligence and wit. Poets should say significant, passionate things about the larger world outside themselves, using all the resources of the English language. Preference is given to poetry that pleases the ear as well as the intellect and soul; strong preference is given to work that is fine, structured, layered, as opposed to untitled, unpunctuated jottings. General topics include usage of language and the forms of poetry; the great philosophical questions; romance; relationships; war/peace; science and technology; everyday life; and humor (the editor has a weakness for humorous lines). The magazine claims no rights to poems. Delaware's only poetry magazine, Möbius has published poetry not only from 50 states but also from all seven continents." Has published poetry by Scott Sweeney, Lenore A. Reiss, Robert Feinstein, ejean lanyon, Gerald Zipper, and Ann Taylor. As a sample the editor selected these lines from "The Epmail Blues" by Peter Miller:

> *From five thousand miles across ocean and prairie/with a press of the* Send *button/you intimate your centrifugal self.*

Möbius is 60-70 pgs., magazine-sized, professionally printed and perfect-bound. Subscription: $16/year. Sample: $10.

How to Submit: Submit up to 4 poems at a time, typed with name and address on each poem, 1 submission/issue. Simultaneous submissions accepted. No electronic submissions. Submissions read year-round. Responds in 3 months. Comments on rejected poems. Pays 1 contributor's copy. Guidelines available for SASE.

🏆 $🗂 ◎ **MODERN HAIKU; FOUR HIGH SCHOOL SENIOR SCHOLARSHIPS (Specialized: form, students)**, P.O. Box 1752, Madison WI 53701-1752. (608)233-2738. Established 1969. **Poetry Editor:** Robert Spiess.

- In 2000, the editor received a Masaoka Shiki International Haiku Prize in Japan for his "Outstanding Literary Endeavor and Achievement."

Magazine Needs: *Modern Haiku* appears 3 times/year in February, June, and October and "is the foremost international journal of English language haiku and criticism. We are devoted to publishing only the very best haiku being written and also publish articles on haiku and have the most complete review section of haiku books. Issues average 124 pages." Wants "contemporary haiku in English (including translations into English) that incorporate the traditional aesthetics of the haiku genre, but which may be innovative as to subject matter, mode of approach or angle of perception, and form of expression. Haiku, senryu, and haibun only. No tanka or other forms." Accepts poetry written by children. Has published haiku by Cor van den Heuvel, George Swede, and Carol Purington. As a sample the editor included this haiku by Sandra Fuhringer:

> *plum blossoms falling/the gardener softly singing/in my father's tongue.*

The digest-sized magazine appears 3 times/year, printed on heavy quality stock with cover illustrations especially painted for each issue by the staff artist. Receives about 12,000-14,000 submissions/year, accepts about 800. There are over 260 poems in each issue. Press run is 775. Subscription: $20. Sample: $6.65.

How to Submit: Submit on "any size sheets, any number of haiku on a sheet; but name and address on each sheet." Include SASE. No previously published haiku or simultaneous submissions. Guidelines available for SASE. Responds in 2 weeks. Pays $1/haiku (but no contributor's copy). Acquires first North American serial rights. Staff reviews books of haiku in 350-1,000 words, single book format. Send books for review consideration.

Also Offers: Offers 4 annual scholarships for the best haiku by high school seniors. Scholarships range from $200-500 (total $1,400). Deadline is mid-March. Rules available for SASE. Also offers $200 Best of Issue Awards.

Advice: "Haiku achieve their effect of felt-depth, insight and intuition through juxtaposition of perceived entities, not through intellective comment or abstract words."

🌐 $◑ ◎ **MODERN POETRY IN TRANSLATION (Specialized: translations)**, King's College London, Strand, London WC2 R2LS United Kingdom. (0)207842-2360. Fax: (0)207848-2415. Website: www.kcl.ac.uk/mpt/ (includes contents of all issues from *Modern Poetry in Translation* (1992) onwards plus subscription forms). Established 1965 (original series), 1992 (new series). **Advisory and Managing Editor:** Professor Norma Rinsler. **Editor:** Daniel Weissbort.

Magazine Needs: *Modern Poetry in Translation*, published biannually, features "translations of poems from any language into English, and essays on translation (practice rather than theory). Our aim is to further international cultural understanding and exchange and to awaken interest in poetry." Wants "only translations from any language into English—'modern' refers to translation (which should be unpublished), not to original." Does not

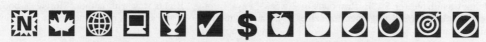

FOR EXPLANATIONS OF THESE SYMBOLS,
SEE THE INSIDE FRONT AND BACK COVERS OF THIS BOOK.

want "self-translation by those not familiar with English; work by poets or translators who are not not familiar with a range of works in the original language rarely succeeds (unless they work with original authors)." *Modern Poetry in Translation* averages 240 pgs., 5⅝ × 8½, offset-printed, perfect-bound with illustrated 2-color cover on scanchip board, matte laminated. Accept approximately 50% of the poems they receive. Press run is 500 for 350 subscribers of which 50% are libraries, 50 shelf sales. Single copy: £10 (UK/EU); £12 (foreign). Subscriptions (2 issues): £20 (UK/EU); £24 (foreign), inc. surface mail (airmail extra). Sample: £7.50. Make checks payable to King's College London (*Modern Poetry in Translation*).
How to Submit: Submit 5-6 poems at a time "unless very long, in which case 1 or 2". Disk submissions (in Word) preferred. Originals should accompany translation. No previously published poems or simultaneous submissions. Cover letter required. No fax submissions. Time between acceptance and publication is up to 9 months. The editor and managing/advisory editor discuss submissions and consult individual members of advisory board if expertise required. Often comments on rejected poems. Publishes theme issues. Upcoming themes is available for SASE (or SAE with IRC). Responds "as soon as possible—within weeks." Sometimes sends prepublication galleys. Pays £12/poem or £15/page plus 1 copy to translator, 1 for original author. "Copyright on selection as printed—general rights remain with contributors." Features reviews of poetry books often commissioned from experts in the field. Poets may send books for review consideration (translations only).

MOJO RISIN'; JOSH SAMUELS BIANNUAL POETRY COMPETITION, P.O. Box 268451, Chicago IL 60626-8451. Established 1995. **Editor:** Ms. Josh Samuels.
Magazine Needs: *mojo risin',* published quarterly, features "poetry, prose, short stories, articles, and black & white artwork in each issue." Wants "any form or style." Does not want "incest, racism, blatant sex, or anything written for shock value." Has published poetry by David Michael McNamara, Alan Catlin, Lon Schneider, and Ho Thi Kim Tuyén. As a sample we selected these lines from "Miles, Dizzy, Monk & The Duendes of Work" by Virgil Suarez:

> besides, even when the art fails us, which it won't,/there's still solace in the weight of the rock,/the
> swiftness of the stick, of the idea that without us, /the power loses, becomes powerless.

mojo risin' is 36 pgs., 8½ × 11, photocopied, saddle-stapled with colored cardstock cover and b&w artwork. Receives about 500 poems/year, accepts 30%. Press run is 300 for 200 subscribers. Subscription: $20/year; $30/ 2 years. Sample: $7.
How to Submit: Subscription not required for acceptance. Submit 3-5 poems (2 pages maximum) at a time. No previously published poems or simultaneous submissions. Cover letter preferred. Time between acceptance and publication is up to 3 months. The editor is solely responsible for all aspects of editing and publishing. Guidelines available for SASE. Responds within 10 days. Manuscripts not returned. Acquires first North American serial rights.
Also Offers: Sponsors the Josh Samuels Biannual Poetry Competition. 1st Place: $100; 2nd Place: $75; 3rd Place $50. Entry fee: $10/5 poems maximum. Any form, style or subject. No previously published poems or simultaneous submissions. Mss not returned. Deadlines: May 31 and November 30. Submissions read March through May and September through November only. Winners published and paid in February and August. Guidelines available for SASE.

MONAS HIEROGLYPHICA, 58 Seymour Rd., Hadleigh, Benfleet, Essex SS7 2HL United Kingdom. E-mail: monas_hieroglyphica@postmaster.co.uk. Website: www.geocities.com/SoHo/Museum/9668 (includes guidelines and links to other sites). Established 1994. **Contact:** Mr. Jamie Spracklen.
Magazine Needs: *Monas Hieroglyphica* appears quarterly and "supports the Gothic music movement, but aims to provide an eclectic mix of material." No racist or sexist work. Accepts poetry written by children. Has published poetry by Sean Russell Friend and Steve Sneyd. As a sample Mr. Spracklen selected this poem, "The Passing of Life & Death," by S.R. Friend:

> Come, join the game of death;/My sweet black butterfly:/There is only cloud where/The fire should be,
> sun where/We should love the moon.

Monas Hieroglyphica is 30 pgs., magazine-sized, photocopied and bound with paper cover, includes art/graphics and ads. Receives about 100 poems/year, accepts 25%. Press run is 500 for 400 subscribers. Single copy: $4; subscription: $15. Sample: $3. Make checks payable to Jamie Spracklen.
How to Submit: Submit 3 poems at a time. Line length for poetry is 60 maximum. Accepts simultaneous submissions; no previously published poems. Accepts e-mail submission, include in body of text. Cover letter required. "Poems must be typed on size A4 paper and in English." Time between acceptance and publication is 3 months. Seldom comments on rejected poems. Occasionally publishes theme issues. Upcoming themes and guidelines available for SASE. Responds in 2 weeks. Pays 1 copy. "Rights stay with author." Reviews books and chapbooks of poetry and other magazines in 20 words, multi-book format. Poets may send books for review consideration.

MOTHER EARTH INTERNATIONAL JOURNAL; NATIONAL POETRY ASSOCIATION; POETRY FILM FESTIVAL, % National Poetry Association, Box 886, Bolinas CA 94924. (415)862-8865. Fax: (415)552-9271. E-mail: gamuse@aol.com. Website: www.nationalpoetry.org. *Mother Earth International Journal* established 1991, National Poetry Association in 1976. **Editor/Publisher:** Herman Berlandt.

Magazine Needs: *"Mother Earth International* is the only on-going anthology of contemporary poetry in English translation from all regions of the world. *Mother Earth International Journal* provides a forum to poets to comment in poetic form on political, economic, and ecological issues." Wants "bold and compassionate poetry that has universal relevance with an emphasis on the world's current political and ecological crisis. No self-indulgent or prosaic stuff that lacks imagination." Has published poetry by Lawrence Ferlinghetti (USA), Tanure Ojaide (Nigeria), Marianne Larsen (Denmark), Ping Hsin (China), Simon Ortiz (USA), and Takashi Arima (Japan). As a sample the editor selected these lines from "Oath" by Gabriella Sica (Italy):

> *Let us exchange tonight/the sweet gifts of intimacy/that are a pledge of eternity.///Slowly, blessedly let*
> *us fulfill/the sacred oath of pleasure/between the glorious folds of the body./At dawn we shall part.*

Mother Earth International Journal is 60 pgs., tabloid-sized, offset-printed, includes graphics and photographs. Receives about 4,000 poems/year, accepts 15%. Press run is 2,000 for 1,200 subscribers of which 280 are libraries. Subscription: $12/year. Sample: $3.75. Make checks payable to Uniting the World Through Poetry. "We encourage the purchase of a copy or a year's subscription."

How to Submit: Submit 4 poems at a time. Accepts previously published poems and simultaneous submissions. No fax or e-mail submissions. Cover letter preferred. Time between acceptance and publication is 4 months. Occasionally publishes theme issues. Guidelines and upcoming themes available for SASE. Responds in 3 months. Sometimes sends prepublication galleys. Pays 2 copies. All rights revert to the author. Staff reviews books of poetry in 600 words, single book format. Send books for review consideration to H. Berlandt, Box 886, Bolinas CA 94924.

Also Offers: Sponsors a $50 prize to the best of "Your Two Best Lines," a benefit collage poem which will list all entries as a collective poem. As an entry fee, "a $5 check should be enclosed with submission."

Advice: *"Mother Earth International* is an ongoing anthology of world contemporary poetry. For subscribers we reduced the subscription from $18 to $12/year. While all future issues will include an American section, we hope that all who send in entries will subscribe to *Mother Earth International Journal* to get a truly world perspective of universal concerns."

MOUNT OLIVE COLLEGE PRESS; MOUNT OLIVE REVIEW; LEE WITTE POETRY CONTEST, 634 Henderson St., Mount Olive NC 28365. (919)658-2502. Established 1987 (*Mount Olive Review*), 1990 (Mount Olive College Press). **Editor:** Dr. Pepper Worthington.

Magazine Needs: *Mount Olive Review*, features "literary criticism, poetry, short stories, essays, and book reviews." Wants "modern poetry." *Mount Olive Review* is 7½ × 10. Receives about 2,000 poems/year, accepts 8%. Press run is 1,000. Single copy: $25. Make checks payable to Mount Olive College Press.

How to Submit: Submit 6 poems at a time. No previously published poems or simultaneous submissions. Cover letter preferred. Time between acceptance and publication varies. Poems are circulated to an editorial board. Seldom comments on rejected poems. Publishes theme issues. A list of upcoming themes and guidelines available for SASE. Responds in 3 months. Sometimes sends prepublication galleys. Acquires first rights. Reviews books and chapbooks of poetry and other magazines. Poets may send books for review consideration.

Book/Chapbook Needs & How to Submit: Mount Olive Press publishes 2 books/year and sponsors the Lee Witte Poetry Contest. Write to above address for guidelines. Books are usually 5½ × 8. Submit 12 sample poems. Responds to queries and mss in 3 months. Obtain sample books by writing to the above address.

MOVING PARTS PRESS (Specialized: bilingual/foreign language, regional), 10699 Empire Grade, Santa Cruz CA 95060-9474. (831)427-2271. Fax: (831)458-2810. E-mail: frice@movingpartspress.com. Website: www.movingpartspress.com (includes a full history and description of Moving Parts Press). Established 1977. **Poetry Editor:** Felicia Rice. Does not accept unsolicited mss. Published *Codex Espangliensis: from Columbus to the Border Patrol* (1998) with performance texts by Buillermo Gómez-Peña and collage imagery by Enrique Chagoya.

MUDLARK: AN ELECTRONIC JOURNAL OF POETRY & POETICS, Dept. of English, University of North Florida, Jacksonville FL 32224-2645. (904)620-2273. Fax: (904)620-3940. E-mail: mudlark@unf.edu. Website: www.unf.edu/mudlark. Established 1995. **Editor:** William Slaughter.

Magazine Needs: *Mudlark* appears "irregularly but frequently. *Mudlark* has averaged, from 1995-1999, three issues and six posters per year. *Mudlark* publishes in three formats: 'issues' of *Mudlark* are the electronic equivalent of print chapbooks; 'posters' are the electronic equivalent of print broadsides; and 'flash' poems are poems that have news is them, poems that feel like current events. The poem is the thing at *Mudlark* . . . and the essay about it. As our full name suggests, we will consider accomplished work that locates itself anywhere on the spectrum of contemporary practice. We want poems, of course, but we want essays, too, that make us read poems (and write them?) differently somehow. Although we are not innocent, we do imagine ourselves capable of surprise. The work of hobbyists is not for *Mudlark*." Has published poetry by Sheila E. Murphy, Andrew Schelling, Frances Driscoll, Van K. Brock, Robert Sward, and John Kinsella. As a sample the editor selected these lines from "Rising for You" by Michael Rothenberg:

> *I would grope over stones, sunsets, coats in the street/to reach you in the wreck of leaves, icy yards//*
> *through old obedience/press my shoulders to the load, bone, sunrise//Loving you would be tough,*
> *naked, eye to eye*

"Issues" feature 15-99 poems; "posters" feature 1-7. *Mudlark* is archived and permanently on view at www.unf.edu.

How to Submit: Submit any number of poems at a time. No simultaneous submissions. Accepts e-mail and disk submissions. "Previously published poems: Inasmuch as 'issues' of *Mudlark* are the electronic equivalent of print chapbooks, some of the individual poems in them might, or might not, have been previously published; if they have been, that previous publication must be acknowledged. Only poems that have not been previously published will be considered for *Mudlark* 'posters,' the electronic equivalent of print broadsides, or for *Mudlark* 'flash poems.' " Cover letter optional. Time between acceptance and publication is up to 3 months. Seldom comments on rejected poems. Guidelines available for SASE, by e-mail, or on website. Responds in 1 month. Always sends prepublication galleys, "in the form of inviting the author to proof the work on a private website that *Mudlark* maintains for that purpose." Does not pay. However, "one of the things we can do at *Mudlark* to 'pay' our authors for their work is point to it here and there. We can tell our readers how to find it, how to subscribe to it, and how to buy it . . . if it is for sale. Toward that end, we maintain A-Notes (on the authors) we publish. We call attention to their work." Acquires one-time rights.

Advice: "*Mudlark* has been reviewed well and often. At this early point in its history, *Mudlark* has established itself, arguably, as one of the few serious rivals in the first generation of the electronic medium, to print versions of its kind. Look at *Mudlark*, visit the website (www.unf.edu/mudlark). spend some time there. Then make your decision: to submit or not to submit."

■ ▢ ⊘ **MUSE'S KISS WEBZINE**, P.O. Box 703, Attn: L.S. Bush, Lenoir NC 28645. Fax: (603)761-7162. E-mail: museskiss@aol.com or museskiss@yahoo.com. Website: http://members.aol.com/museskiss (includes online issues, advertising information, other writing links, guidelines, and book and magazine reviews). Established 1998. **Editor:** Alex Reeves. **Publisher:** L.S. Bush.

Magazine Needs: "*Muse's Kiss* is a free quarterly webzine. It contains experimental and traditional poetry and short stories. We will consider general fiction, science fiction, historical fiction, and mystery for short stories and anything except erotica for poetry. Prefers free verse. Please do not send nonfiction, religious, romance, gay/lesbian, children's stories, or anything explicit." Accepts poetry written by children 12 and older. Has published poetry by L.B. Sedlacek, James C. Speegle, Julie Callinicos, and Jon Mathewson. As a sample the editor selected these lines from "L.A." by James C. Speegle:

> Give your guilt to the/Endless freeway that drives/Straight into the heart/Hell with an overhanging/
> Brown coughing sky that will/Blend drugs and rain in/Another time but for now/The drive is to go
> insane

Receives about 400 poems/year, accepts about 25%. Sample: $2 (by mail, online version free). Make checks payable to L.S. Bush.

How to Submit: Submit 5 poems at a time via e-mail. Line length for poetry is 8 minimum, 50 maximum. No previously published poems. Cover letter with brief bio preferred. No fax submissions. "Poems must be typed in body of e-mail—no attachments. If you prefer, you may submit offline by sending your poems and a cover letter. If you submit offline, there is a reading fee of $1 for up to 10 poems." Time between acceptance and publication is 3 months. Guidelines available on website. Responds in 3 months. Acquires one-time rights. Payment is publication; small honorarium when possible. Staff reviews chapbooks of poetry in 100 words, multi-book format. Send books for review consideration to L.S. Bush.

Also Offers: Sister offline publication: *Pop Poets* (members.aol.com/poppoets), see website for more information.

Advice: "There are plenty of exciting webzines and e-zines out there offering original work—don't get trapped by paper!"

N̄ ⊚ **THE MUSING PLACE (Specialized: poets with a history of mental illness)**, 2700 N. Lakeview, Chicago IL 60614. (773)281-3800, ext. 2465. Fax: (773)281-8790. Established 1986. **Editor:** Shannon Ford.

Magazine Needs: *The Musing Place* is an annual magazine "written and published by people with a history of mental illness. All kinds and forms of poetry are welcome." *The Musing Place* is 32 pgs., 8½×11, typeset, and stapled with art also produced by people with a history of mental illness. Receives about 300 poems/year, accepts about 40. Press run is 1,000. Single copy: $3.

How to Submit: Accepts simultaneous submissions; no previously published poems. Accepts fax submissions. Cover letter required. "Poets must prove and explain their history of mental illness." Time between acceptance and publication is up to 1 year. "The board reviews submissions and chooses those that fit into each issue." Seldom comments on rejected poems. Responds within 6 months. Pays 1 copy (additional copies at a discount).

⊕ ♥ **MUUNA TAKEENA**, Hepokuja 6B26, FIN-01200 Vantaa Finland. E-mail: lahtinen.palonen@megabaud.fi. Established 1987. **Editor:** Timo Palonen.

Magazine Needs: Appearing 2 times/year, *Muuna Takeena* publishes "reviews of underground books, zines, music, and videos. Poetry is used only to fill excess space. In every issue, I publish one or two poems that are near my hand." Does not want to see experimental poems. As a sample we selected these lines from "From Armitage to Ovid" by Rob Morrow:

From Armitage to Ovid,/It's all been done before,/To go to the house/Of the one you love/And sleep at her front door.//From palace to the poorhouse,/Sometimes against the law,/From the super rich/To the common rag,/Classless while we snore.//From lunatic to lover,/For those we cannot keep,/We think about you/And dream about you/When we are lost in sleep.

Muuna Takeena is about 30 pgs., magazine-sized, photocopied and stapled, cover includes photo/drawing, also includes photos/drawings inside, some paid ads. Receives about 50 poems/year, accepts 2%. Press run is 400 for 40 subscribers. Sample: $3. "No checks."

How to Submit: Submit 3 poems at a time. Accepts simultaneous submissions; no previously published poems. Accepts e-mail submissions. Cover letter required. Time between acceptance and publication is 6 months. Pays 1 contributor's copy. Staff reviews books and chapbooks of poetry and other magazines in up to 100 words, single book format. Send books for review consideration.

Advice: "I read, if I like, it could be printed. If I do not like, I send forward to other zine makers."

$ ▢ ◎ MYSTERY TIME (Specialized: mystery, humor); RHYME TIME (Specialized: subscribers), P.O. Box 2907, Decatur IL 62524. *Mystery Time* and *Rhyme Time* established 1983. **Poetry Editor and Vice President:** Linda Hutton.

Magazine Needs & How to Submit: *Mystery Time* is a semiannual containing 3-4 pages of humorous poems about mysteries and mystery writers in each issue. As a sample the editor selected the poem "Agatha Christie, Queen of Mystery" by Katie Chamberlin:

When I think of Agatha Christie,/I can feel my eyes grow misty./Thinking of all she did write/Can keep me up past ten at night.

Mystery Time is 44 pgs., digest-sized, stapled with heavy stock cover. Receives up to 15 submissions/year, accepts 4-6. Press run is 100. Sample: $4. Submit 3 poems at a time, up to 16 lines, "typed in proper format with SASE." Accepts previously published poems. No fax or e-mail submissions. Does not read mss in December. Guidelines available for #10 SASE. Pays $5 on acceptance.

Magazine Needs & How to Submit: *Rhyme Time* is a quarterly newsletter publishing only the work of subscribers. No length limit or style restriction. Subscription: $24. Sample: $4. Cash prize of $10 awarded to the best poem in each issue. No fax or e-mail submissions.

Also Offers: Sponsors an annual poetry contest that awards a $25 cash prize for the best poem in any style or length. Submit typed poem with SASE. No entry fee; one entry/person. Deadline: November 1. (See separate listing for the Helen Vaughn Johnson Memorial Haiku Award in the Contests & Awards section.)

Advice: "Always send for guidelines before submitting."

Ⓝ ◑ ◎ THE MYTHIC CIRCLE; THE MYTHOPOEIC SOCIETY (Specialized: fantasy), P.O. Box 31266, Omaha NE 68131-0266. E-mail: mythiccircle@hotmail.com. Website: home.earthlink.net/mythsoc/mythc ir.html. **Editor:** Gwenyth Hood.

Magazine Needs: *The Mythic Circle* is a "writer's workshop in print," with an annual issue. "*The Mythic Circle* is intended for serious writers of the mythopoeic tradition (that of C.S. Lewis, J.R.R. Tolkien, and Charles Williams)." Has published poems by Angelee Anderson, Joe Christopher and Kelly Searsmith. Receives 100 poetry submissions/year, accepts about 10%. Subscription: $8 US, $10 Canada/Mexico/Latin America, $12 Europe/Asia. Sample: $6.50.

How to Submit: No previously published poems or simultaneous submissions. Accepts e-mail submissions. Time between acceptance and publication is 6-12 months. Always comments on rejected poems. Guidelines available for SASE. Responds in up to 8 months. Pays 1 contributor's copy for 3 poems.

Advice: "Think of myth in the everyday as well as the traditional sense. Subscribers are heavily favored, since they provide the critical review which our authors need in their letters of comment. Avoid archaic use of English. Poetry requires the current language but ideas as old as humankind. Put rhyme and meter in consistent patterns or break them for a reason. Read the poem aloud: is it pleasing? Subtlety and understatement are a poet's most powerful tools. Shock has lost its shock."

◲ ◐ NANNY FANNY; FELICITY PRESS, 2524 Stockbridge Dr. #15, Indianapolis IN 46268-2670. E-mail: nightpoet@prodigy.net. Established 1998. **Editor:** Lou Hertz.

Magazine Needs: *Nanny Fanny* appears 3 times/year and "publishes accessible, high quality poetry. Some artwork wanted (b&w line art)." Wants "external, extroverted observations and character studies. Most poems published are free verse. Formal poetry discouraged. Prefer 30 lines or less. No internalized, self-pitying poetry. Nothing under 8 lines or over 30 unless exceptional. No pornography, extremes of violence or language. No political or overly religious poems." Accepts poetry written by children. Has published poetry by B.Z. Niditch, Diana Kwiatkowski, Rubin Lamar Thomas, and John Grey. As a sample the editor selected these lines from "Mr. America" by Ted Kluck:

He has his dentures out and/is working/on a slice of pie/jaw flapping up and down like/whites/on a clothesline

Nanny Fanny is 32 pgs., 5½×8½, laser-printed and side-stapled with colored 67 lb. cover, includes cover art and some b&w line drawings inside. Receives about 800 poems/year, accepts about 10%. Press run is 100 for 25 subscribers, 2 of which are libraries; 40 distributed free to contributors, etc. Subscription: $9/3 issues. Sample: $3.50. Make checks payable to Lou Hertz. "Query first about reviews."

How to Submit: Submit 3-8 poems at a time, 1 poem/page with name and address on each. Accepts previously published poems; no simultaneous submissions. No e-mail submissions. Accepts disk submissions. Cover letter with brief bio preferred. Time between acceptance and publication is up to 6 months. Sometimes comments on rejected poems. Guidelines available for SASE or by e-mail. Responds in up to 2 months. Sends prepublication galleys on request. Pays 1 contributor's copy. Acquires one-time rights.

Book/Chapbook Needs: Felicity Press is not currently open for submissions.

Advice: "I want good quality poetry that the average person will be able to understand and enjoy. Let's use poetic imagery to draw them in, not scare them away."

⊠ ⬚ ◯ ◑ ◎ THE NARROW ROAD: A HAIBUN JOURNAL (Specialized: forms, haibun); DREAMIMAGES PRESS, 38 Long Ave. #2, Cheektowaga NY 14225-2808. Fax: (716)891-8759. E-mail: kujira@buffalo.com. Established 2000. **Editor/Publisher:** Alan Mietlowski.

Magazine Needs: *The Narrow Road: a haibun journal* appears quarterly, publishing English-language haibun from around the world. "All forms and styles of haibun encouraged." Does not want anything not written in haibun style. Accepts poetry written by children. Recently published poetry by Doranna Durgin, Ken Jones, David Cobb, Gerald England, and Jerry Kilbride. *The Narrow Road* is about 32 pgs., digest-sized, computer-printed, card stock cover, with sumi-e/haiga art and ads for Japanese poetry books/magazines. Receives about 100 poems/year, accepts about 75%. Publishes about 15-20 poems/issue. Single copy: $5; subscription: $18/year. Sample: $5. Make checks payable to Alan Mietlowski.

How to Submit: Line length for poetry is open. Accepts previously published poems and simultaneous submissions. Accepts e-mail and disk submissions; no fax submissions. Cover letter is preferred. "Disk submissions in *.txt format; SASE required; electronic submissions okay." Reads submissions all year. Time between acceptance and publication is up to 1 year. "Editor reads and accepts/rejects all poems." Often comments on rejected poems. Guidelines are available for SASE or by e-mail. Responds in 1 month. Pays 1 contributor's copy. Acquires one-time rights. Reviews books and chapbooks of poetry and other magazines/journals, open length. Poets may send books for review consideration to Alan Mietlowski (may be reviewed online rather than in magazine).

Book/Chapbook Needs & How to Submit: DreamImages Press plans to publish 1-2 chapbooks/year. Chapbooks will be 32 pgs., computer-designed, card stock cover. Query first, with a few sample poems and a cover letter with brief bio and publication credits. Responds to queries in 1 month; to mss in 1 month. Pays royalties of 15-25%.

Advice: "Haibun is a style not well known in the West. Please seek out haibun online or in anthologies (such as the excellent Red Moon anthologies) before submitting work for consideration."

◉ NASSAU REVIEW, English Dept., Nassau Community College, Garden City NY 11530-6793. (516)572-7792. Established 1964. **Contact:** editorial board.

Magazine Needs: *Nassau Review* is an annual "creative and research vehicle for Nassau College faculty and the faculty of other colleges." Wants "serious, intellectual poetry of any form or style. No light verse or satiric verse." Submissions from adults only. "No college students; graduate students acceptable. Want only poems of high quality." Has published poetry by Patti Tana, Dick Allen, Louis Phillips, David Heyen, Simon Perchik, and Mario Susko. *Nassau Review* is about 190 pgs., digest-sized, flat-spined. Receives over 1,500 poems/year, accepts about 20-25. Press run is 1,200 for about 1,200 subscribers of which 200 are libraries. Sample free.

How to Submit: Submit only 3 poems per yearly issue. No previously published poems or simultaneous submissions. Reads submissions November 1 through March 1 only. Responds in up to 6 months. Pays contributor's copies.

Also Offers: Sponsors a yearly contest with $200 poetry award. Deadline: March 31.

Advice: "Each year we are more and more overwhelmed by the number of poems submitted, but most are of an amateur quality."

$ ◉ THE NATION; "DISCOVERY"/THE NATION POETRY CONTEST, 72 Fifth Ave., New York NY 10011. Established 1865. **Poetry Editor:** Grace Schulman.

Magazine Needs & How to Submit: *The Nation*'s only requirement for poetry is "excellence," which can be inferred from the list of poets they have published: Marianne Moore, Robert Lowell, W.S. Merwin, Maxine Kumin, Donald Justice, James Merrill, Richard Howard, May Swenson, Amy Clampitt, Edward Hirsch and Charles Simic. Pays $1/line, not to exceed 35 lines, plus 1 copy.

Also Offers: The magazine co-sponsors the Lenore Marshall Prize for Poetry which is an annual award of $10,000 for an outstanding book of poems published in the US in each year. For details, write to the Academy of American Poets, 584 Broadway, #1208, New York NY 10012. Also co-sponsors the "Discovery"/*The Nation* Poetry Contest ($300 each plus a reading at The Poetry Center, 1395 Lexington Ave., New York NY 10128. Deadline: mid-February. Guidelines available for SASE, on www.92ndsty.org, or by calling (212) 415-5759.

☑ $ ◑ ◎ NATIONAL ENQUIRER (Specialized: humor), Lantana FL 33464. E-mail: kmartin@nati onalenquirer.com. **Filler Editor:** Kathy Martin.

Magazine Needs: *National Enquirer* is a weekly tabloid which uses short poems, most of them humorous and traditional rhyming verse. "We want poetry with a message or reflection on the human condition or everyday life. Avoid sending obscure or 'arty' poetry or poetry for art's sake. Also looking for philosophical and inspirational material. Submit seasonal/holiday material at least three months in advance. No poetry over eight lines will be accepted."

How to Submit: Submit up to 5 poems at a time. Accepts e-mail submissions; include poetry in body of message. Requires cover letter from first-time submitters; include name, address, social security, and phone numbers. "Do not send SASE; filler material will not be returned." Pays $25 after publication; original material only. Acquires first rights.

NATIONAL FORUM: THE PHI KAPPA PHI JOURNAL, 129 Quad Center, Mell St., Auburn University, Auburn AL 36849-5306. (334)844-5200. E-mail: kaetzjp@mail.auburn.edu. Website: www.auburn.edu/natfo rum.html. Established 1915. **Editor:** James P. Kaetz. **Contact:** poetry editors.

Magazine Needs: *National Forum* is the quarterly publication of Phi Kappa Phi using quality poetry. *National Forum* is 48 pgs., magazine-sized, professionally printed, saddle-stapled, with full-color paper cover and interior. Receives about 300 poems/year, accepts about 20. Press run is 115,000 for 113,000 subscribers of which 300 are libraries. Subscription: $25.

How to Submit: Submit 3-5 short (one page) poems at a time, including a biographical sketch with recent publications. Accepts e-mail submissions. Reads submissions approximately every 3 months. Responds in about 4 months. Pays 10 contributor's copies.

NATIVE TONGUE; NATIVE TONGUE PRESS (Specialized: ethnic), P.O. Box 822, Eufaula AL 36072-0822. (334)616-7722. E-mail: ntp59@hotmail.com. Established 1998. **Submissions Editor:** Anthony Canada.

Magazine Needs: *Native Tongue* is published quarterly "to keep the voices and history of the black poet historic, and expand an audience for new black poets." Wants poetry "on or about the African-American experience. Open to all forms, subject matter, styles or purpose. Interested in poems which emphasize but are not limited to cultural issues, the exploration of self-esteem, and personal empowerment, and the exploration of the direction of African-American people. No submissions that do not deal with the African-American experience." As a sample the editor selected these lines from his poem "society's child":

> late nite lust on rooftops/society's child conceived/bewildered, beleagured/black bastard/preteen
> mother's screams/social service slaves/sing the welfare blues

National Tongue is 7-10 pgs., 8½ × 11 sheets, 3-column format, stapled. Receives about 150 poems/year, accepts about 85%. Press run is 200 for 55 subscribers, 45 shelf sales; 100 distributed free to the public, colleges, poetry groups. Subscription: $9. Sample: $2. Make checks payable to Anthony G. Canada.

How to Submit: Submit up to 5 poems at a time. Accepts previously published poems and simultaneous submissions. Accepts e-mail submissions; include text in body of message. Cover letter required. "In cover letter include basic poet information—name, address, occupation, experience, previous publishings, books, etc." SASE required for return of submitted poems. Time between acceptance and publication is 3 months. Poems are circulated to an editorial board. "Submissions reviewed by board; published pieces selected by committee." Often comments on rejected poems. Responds in 3 months. Pays 10 contributor's copies. Acquires one-time rights. Reviews books and chapbooks of poetry in 200 words, single book format. Poets may send books for review consideration.

Advice: "The aim and goal of this newsletter is to open up to a wider audience the poetic voices of our many talented brothers and sisters. The African-American community has always had a historic and rich poetic legacy. We at *Native Tongue* wish to continue and expand upon this great tradition of African-American poets. So brothers and sisters take pen to paper, and continue to make our history historic. Let your voices by heard!"

NAZARENE INTERNATIONAL HEADQUARTERS; STANDARD; LISTEN; (Specialized: religious, children), 6401 The Paseo, Kansas City MO 64131. (816)333-7000.

Magazine Needs & How to Submit: Each of the magazines published by the Nazarenes has a separate editor, focus, and audience. *Standard*, press run 177,000, is a weekly inspirational "story paper" with Christian leisure reading for adults. Free samples and guidelines available for SASE. Uses 2 poems each week. Submit maximum of 5 poems, no more than 50 lines each. Pays 25¢ a line. For *Listen* and *Holiness Today*, write individually for guidelines and samples.

THE NEBRASKA REVIEW; THE NEBRASKA REVIEW AWARDS, Creative Writing Program, FA, University of Nebraska, Omaha NE 68182-0324. (402)554-3159. Fax: (402)554-3436. Established 1973. **Fiction and Managing Editor:** James Reed. **Poetry Editor:** Susan Aizenberg.

Magazine Needs: *The Nebraska Review* is a semiannual literary magazine publishing fiction and poetry with occasional essays. Wants "lyric poetry from 10-200 lines, preference being for under 100 lines. Subject matter is unimportant, as long as it has some. Poets should have mastered form, meaning poems should have form, not simply 'demonstrate' it." Doesn't want to see "concrete, inspirational, didactic, or merely political poetry." Has published poetry by Angela Ball, Virgil Suarez, James Reiss, and Katharine Whitcomb. As a sample the editors selected these lines from "Crickets" by Pamela Stewart:

> *In every small place the eye, toe, or caught breath turns,/crickets are singing. From that shin/just above the ground they fling an edge of sound/straight through what's left of wilderness./It swings out across the trees and yards,/up to the warm sills of September.*

The Nebraska Review is 60 pgs., 6 × 9, nicely printed and flat-spined with glossy card cover. It is a publication of the Writer's Workshop at the University of Nebraska. Press run is 500 for 380 subscribers of which 85 are libraries. Single copy: $8; subscription: $15/year. Sample: $4.50.

How to Submit: Submit 4-6 poems at a time. "Clean typed copy strongly preferred." No fax submissions. Reads open submissions January 1 through April 30 only. Responds in 4 months. Time between acceptance and publication is up to 12 months. Pays 2 contributor's copies and 1-year subscription. Acquires first North American serial rights.

Also Offers: Submissions for The Nebraska Review Awards are read from September 1 through November 30 only. The Nebraska Review Awards of $500 each in poetry, creative nonfiction, and fiction are published in the spring issue. Entry fee: $15, includes discounted subscription. You can enter as many times as desired. Deadline: November 30.

Advice: "Your first allegiance is to the poem. Publishing will come in time, but it will always be less than you feel you deserve. Therefore, don't look to publication as a reward for writing well; it has no relationship."

✔ ◎ **NEDGE**, P.O. Box 2321, Providence RI 02906. Website: www.durationpress.com/nedge. Established 1994. **Co-Editor**: Henry Gould.

Magazine Needs: *Nedge* is published by the Poetry Mission, a nonprofit arts organization. Includes poetry, fiction, reviews, and essays. Wants work that "exhibits originality, talent, sincerity, skill, and inspiration." Circulation is 300. Subscription: $12/2 issues. Sample: $6. Back issues available.

How to Submit: No simultaneous submissions. SASE required. Responds in 2 months. Pays 1 contributor's copy.

◎ **THE NEOVICTORIAN/COCHLEA**, P.O. Box 55164, Madison WI 53705. E-mail: eacam@execpc.com. Established 1995. **Editor:** Esther Cameron.

Magazine Needs: *The Neovictorian/Cochlea* appears biannually and "seeks to promote a poetry of introspection, dialogue, and social concern." Wants "poetry of beauty and integrity with emotional and intellectual depth, commitment to subject matter as well as language, and the courage to ignore fashion. Welcome: well-crafted formal verse, social comment (including satire), love poems, philosophical/religious poems, poems reflecting dialogue with other writers (in particular: responses to the work of Paul Celan)." Has published poetry by Ida Fasel, Carolyn Stoloff, Joseph Salemi, Deborah Warren, and Leonard Cirino. As a sample the editor selected the poem "Astronomers" by Richard Moore:

> *Seeking the origin, man hopes/through ever larger telescopes/to probe a universe more vast/each year and deeper in its past./As they discover, so do I,/still watching with the naked eye.*

The Neovictorian/Cochlea is 28-32 pgs., 8 × 11, photocopied and saddle-stapled with cardstock cover, occasional graphics, no ads. "In the near future, the magazine will be supplemented by an electronic forum. E-mail the editor for details." Press run is 250 for 50 subscribers. Single copy: $6; subscription: $10.

How to Submit: Submit 3-5 poems at a time. Accepts simultaneous submissions and "on rare occasions a previously published poem." Accepts e-mail submissions included in body of message; no attachments. Cover letter "not necessary. Poets whose work is accepted will be asked for titles of books available, to be published in the magazine." Time between acceptance and publication is up to 12 months. Often comments on rejected poems. Does not offer guidelines because "the tradition is the only 'guideline.' We do encourage contributors to write for a sample." Responds in up to 4 months. Pays 2 contributor's copies. Acquires first rights. *The Neovictorian/Cochlea* publishes the addresses of poets who would welcome correspondence.

Advice: "Like all our social functioning, poetry today suffers from a loss of community, which translates into a lack of real intimacy with the reader. Poets can work against this trend by remaining in touch with the poetry of past generations and by forming relationships in which poetry can be employed as the language of friendship. Publication should be an afterthought."

◖ ◎ **NERVE COWBOY; LIQUID PAPER PRESS**, P.O. Box 4973, Austin TX 78765. Website: www.onr. com/user/jwhagins/nervecowboy.html. Established 1995. **Co-Editors:** Joseph Shields and Jerry Hagins.

Magazine Needs: *Nerve Cowboy* is a biannual literary journal featuring contemporary poetry, short fiction and b&w drawings. "Open to all forms, styles and subject matter preferring writing that speaks directly, and minimizes literary devices. We want to see poetry of experience and passion which can find that raw nerve and ride it." Has published poetry by Gerald Locklin, Maggie Jaffe, Fred Voss, Albert Huffstickler, and Joan Jobe Smith. As a sample the editors selected these lines from "If the Truth be Known: Little Known Facts About Superheroes," by Thomas C. Smith:

> *And Wonder Woman, well, she really is a wonder./Even with six kids and a string of alcoholic husbands,/ she is still pretending nothing is wrong.*

Nerve Cowboy is 64 pgs., 7 × 8½, attractively printed and saddle-stapled with matte card cover with b&w cover art. Currently accepts 5-10% of the submissions received. Press run is 250 for 85 subscribers. Subscription: $14/ 4 issues. Sample: $4.

How to Submit: Submit 3-7 poems at a time, name on each page. Accepts previously published poems with notification; no simultaneous submissions. Informal cover letter with bio credits preferred. Seldom comments on rejected poems. Guidelines available for SASE. Responds in 2 months. Pays 1 copy. Acquires first or one-time rights.

Book/Chapbook Needs & How to Submit: Liquid Paper Press publishes 3-4 chapbooks/year but will not be accepting unsolicited chapbook mss in the foreseeable future. Only chapbook contest winners and solicited mss will be published in the next couple of years. For information on *Nerve Cowboy*'s annual chapbook contest, please send a SASE. Deadline is January 15 of each year. Entry fee: $10. Cash prizes and publication for 1st and 2nd place finishers. Chapbooks are 24-40 pgs., 5½×8½, photocopied with some b&w artwork. Recent winners include Ralph Dranow, Christopher Jones, and Belinda Subraman. Publications include *Sunday Ritual* by Ralph Dranow; *Grappling* by Susanne R. Bowers; *The Back East Poems* by Gerald Locklin; and *Butchers and Brain Surgeons* by Fred Voss. Send SASE for a complete list of available titles.

$ NEW ENGLAND REVIEW, Middlebury College, Middlebury VT 05753. (802)443-5075. Fax: (802)443-2088. E-mail: nereview@middlebury.edu. Website: www.middlebury.edu/~nereview/ (includes guidelines, editorial staff, sample poetry from current and recent issues, ordering information, and secure online ordering). Established 1978. **Editor:** Stephen Donadio.
• Work published in this review is frequently included in volumes of *The Best American Poetry*.
Magazine Needs: *New England Review* is a prestigious, nationally distributed literary quarterly, 180 pgs., 7×10, flat-spined, elegant make-up and printing on heavy stock, glossy cover with art. Receives 3,000-4,000 poetry submissions/year, accepts about 70-80 poems/year; has a 3-6 month backlog between time of acceptance and publication. The editors urge poets to read a few copies of the magazine before submitting work. Has published poetry by Agha Shahid Ali, Carol Frost, Brigit Pegeen Kelly, Carl Phillips, and Elizabeth Spires. Subscription: $23. Sample: $7.
How to Submit: Submit up to 6 poems at a time. Address submissions to Poetry Editor. No previously published poems. "Brief cover letters are useful. All submissions by mail. Accepts questions by e-mail." Reads submissions September 1 through May 31 only. Response time is 12 weeks. Always sends prepublication galleys. Pays $10/page, $20 minimum, plus 2 contributor's copies. Also features essay-reviews. Send books for review consideration.

NEW ISSUES PRESS; NEW ISSUES PRESS POETRY SERIES; NEW ISSUES PRESS FIRST BOOK POETRY PRIZE; THE GREEN ROSE PRIZE IN POETRY FOR ESTABLISHED POETS, Dept. of English, Western Michigan University, Kalamazoo MI 49008-5092. (616)387-8185. Fax: (616)387-2562. E-mail: herbert.scott@wmich.edu. Website: www.wmich.edu/newissues. Established 1996. **Editor:** Herbert Scott.
Book/Chapbook Needs: New Issues Press First Book Prize publishes 3-6 first books of poetry per year, one through its annual New Issues Poetry Prize. Additional mss will be selected from those submitted to the competition for publication in the series. "A national judge selects the prize winner and recommends other manuscripts. The editors decide on the other books considering the judge's recommendation, but are not bound by it." Past judges include Chase Twichell, Philip Levine, C.D Wright, C.K. Williams, and Marianne Boruch. Books are published on acid free paper in editions of 1,500.
How to Submit: Open to "poets writing in English who have not previously published a full-length collection of poems in an edition of 500 or more copies." Submit 48- to 72-page ms with 1-paragraph bio, publication credits (if any), and $15 entry fee. No e-mail or fax submissions. Reads submissions June 1 through November 30 only. Complete guidelines available for SASE. Winner will be notified the following April. Winner receives $1,000 plus publication of manuscript. "We offer 33⅓% discounts on our books to competition entrants."
Also Offers: New Issues Press also sponsors the Green Rose Prize in Poetry. Award is $1,000 and publication for a book of poems by an established poet who has published one or more full-length collections of poetry. Entry fee: $20/ms. Mss accepted May 1 through September 30. Winner announced in January. *Perfect Disappearance* by Martha Rhodes won the 1999 competition and *When the Moon Knows You're Wandering* by Ruth Ellen Kocher won the 2000 competition. Other Green Rose poets include Michael Burkard, Maurice Kilwein Guevara, Mary Ann Samyn, Jim Daniels. Guidelines available for SASE or on website.
Advice: "Our belief is that there are more good poets writing than ever before. Our mission is to give some of the best of these a forum. Also, our books have been reviewed in *Publishers Weekly*, *Booklist*, and the *Library Journal* as well as being featured in the *Washington Post Book World* and the *New York Times Book Review* during 2000. New Issues books are advertised in *Poetry*, *Poets & Writers*, *APR*, *American Poet*, *The Bloomsbury Review*, etc. We are publishing 12 books of poems during the year 2001. New Issues Press is profiled in the May/June 2000 issue of *Poets & Writers*."

$ NEW LETTERS; NEW LETTERS LITERARY AWARD, University of Missouri-Kansas City, Kansas City MO 64110. (816)235-1168. Fax: (816)235-2611. Website: www.umkc.edu/newletters. Established 1934 as *University Review*, became *New Letters* in 1971. **Managing Editor:** Robert Stewart. **Editor:** James McKinley.
• Work published in *New Letters* appeared in the 2000 volume of *The Best American Poetry*.

Magazine Needs: *New Letters* "is dedicated to publishing the best short fiction, best contemporary poetry, literary articles, photography, and artwork by both established writers and new talents." Wants "contemporary writing of all types—free verse poetry preferred, short works are more likely to be accepted than very long ones." Has published poetry by Joyce Carol Oates, Amiri Baraka, Nancy Willard, Margaret Randall, Gary Gildner, and Trish Reeves. *New Letters* is 6×9, flat-spined, professionally printed quarterly, glossy 2-color cover with art, uses about 40-45 (of 120) pgs. of poetry in each issue. Press run is 2,500 with 1,800 subscriptions of which about 40% are libraries. Receives about 7,000 submissions/year, accepts less than 1%, has a 6-month backlog. Poems appear in a variety of styles exhibiting a high degree of craft and universality of theme (rare in many journals). Subscription: $17. Sample: $5.50.

How to Submit: Send no more than 6 poems at a time. No previously published poems or simultaneous submissions. Short cover letter preferred. "We strongly prefer original typescripts and we don't read between May 15 and October 15. No query needed." Responds in up to 10 weeks. Pays a small fee plus 2 copies. Occasionally James McKinley comments on rejected poems.

Also Offers: The New Letters Literary Award is given annually for a group of 3-6 poems. Entry guidelines available for SASE. Deadline: May 15. Also publishes occasional anthologies, selected and edited by McKinley.

☑ 🍎 🔘 **THE NEW MIRAGE QUARTERLY; GOOD SAMARITAN PRESS; THE MIRAGE PRIZE; THE MIRAGE GROUP**, P.O. Box 803282, Santa Clarita CA 91380-3282. (661)799-0694. E-mail: adorxyz@aol .com. Established 1996. **Editor:** Jovita Ador Lee. **Publisher:** Jerome Vallens Brooke.

Magazine Needs: *The New Mirage Quarterly* contains poetry and reviews. Wants all types of poetry. Accepts poetry written by children. Has published poetry by Linda Herring, Sharon Siekaniec, Devorie Franzwa, and Amy Jo Huffman. As a sample the editor selected this poem, "Mirage" (poet unidentified):

> Layers of false illusion lie,/Veils of lies that bind and tie./Choice returns; hope shall remain/Love
> returns, and love shall remain.

The New Mirage Quarterly is 12 pgs., 5½×8½, photocopied and saddle-stapled with bond paper cover, includes clip art and ads. Receives about 100 poems/year, accepts about 50%. Press run is 100 for 40 subscribers, 10 shelf sales; 20 distributed free to general public. Subscription: $36. Sample: $7. Make checks payable to Good Samaritan Press. "Writers are encouraged to subscribe to *The New Mirage Quarterly*."

How to Submit: Submit up to 3 poems at a time. Accepts previously published poems and simultaneous submissions. Cover letter preferred. Reads submissions September 1 through June 30 only. Time between acceptance and publication is 6 weeks. Poems are circulated to an editorial board. "Reviewed by board and editors." Seldom comments on rejected poems. Guidelines available for SASE. Responds in 6 weeks. Pays 1 contributor's copy. Acquires all rights. Returns rights upon publication. Reviews books and chapbooks of poetry and other magazines in 200-300 words, single book format. Send books for review consideration to Jovita Ador Lee.

Book/Chapbook Needs & How to Submit: Good Samaritan Press publishes chapbooks of verse in several series including the New Mirage Series and the Bright Dawn Series. Publishes 10 chapbooks per year. Chapbooks are usually 50-120 pgs., 5×8, saddle-stapled with glossy cardstock cover. "Writers may send samples or complete manuscripts. The New Mirage Series is intended as a resource for subscribers. The Bright Dawn Series is designed to give members of the Mirage Group a resource for their work." Responds to queries in 6 weeks. Pays 1 author's copy (out of a press run of 100). Order sample chapbooks (packet of 3) by sending $7. Good Samaritan Press also publishes an annual poetry anthology which is 50-100 pgs., 5½×8½, photocopied and perfect-bound, hard cover with art prints.

Also Offers: The Mirage Group offers the annual Mirage Prize for poets of special merit. Members of the Mirage Group may nominate poets for consideration. The Mirage Group offers many services to its members including mentoring. "Members may choose to work with a more experienced writer to improve their work." Membership dues (including subscription to *The New Mirage Quarterly*): $26. Also offers the New Laureate Series for Laureate Members of the Mirage Group. The series publishes chapbooks and requires mss of 5 to 40 poems. The Group also provides press support. Members may also participate in our Speakers Bureau. Additionally, the Mirage Group publishes *Bright Dawn Review*, a journal for young and new poets and *Royal Avalon Review*, poetry that has a fantasy theme, such as poems set in the Middle ages.

☑ 📷 ⊘ **NEW NATIVE PRESS (Specialized: translations)**, P.O. Box 661, Cullowhee NC 28723. (828)293-9237. E-mail: newnativepress@hotmail.com. Established 1979. **Publisher:** Thomas Rain Crowe.

Book/Chapbook Needs: New Native Press has "selectively narrowed its range of contemporary 20th century literature to become an exclusive publisher of writers in marginalized and endangered languages. All books published are bilingual translations from original languages into English." Publishes on average 2 paperbacks/ year. Recently published *Kenneth Patchen: Rebel Poet in America* by Larry Smith and Gaelic, Welsh, Breton, Cornish, and Manx poets in an all-Celtic language anthology of contemporary poets from Scotland, Ireland, Wales, Brittany, Cornwall, and Isle of Man entitled *Writing The Wind: A Celtic Resurgence (The New Celtic Poetry)*. Books are sold by distributors in four foreign countries and in the US by library vendors and Small Press Distribution. Books are typically 80 pgs., offset-printed and perfect-bound with glossy 120 lb. stock with professionally-designed color cover.

How to Submit: Not currently accepting submissions. For specialized translations only—authors should query first with 10 sample poems and cover letter with bio and publication credits. Accepts previously published poems and simultaneous submissions. Time between acceptance and publication is up to 12 months. Always comments on rejected poems. Responds in 2 weeks. Pays copies, "amount varies with author and title."

Advice: "We are still looking for work indicative of rare talent—unique and original voices using language experimentally and symbolically, if not subversively."

■ ⬚ ◯ ◉ **NEW ORLEANS POETRY FORUM; GRIS-GRIS PRESS; DESIRE STREET**, 257 Bonnabel Blvd., Metairie LA 70005-3738. Poetry forum established 1971, press and magazine established 1994. **President:** Andrea S. Gereighty. **Editor:** Jonathan Laws.

Magazine Needs: *Desire Street* is the quarterly electronic magazine of the New Orleans Poetry Forum. "The Forum, a non-profit entity, has as its chief purpose the development of poets and contemporary poetry in the New Orleans area. To this end, it conducts a weekly workshop in which original poems are presented and critiqued according to an established protocol which assures a non-judgmental and non-argumentative atmosphere. A second aim of the New Orleans Poetry Forum is to foster awareness and support for poetry in the New Orleans area through readings, publicity, and community activities. Promotion is emphasized in order to increase acceptance and support for contemporary poetry." Wants "modern poetry on any topic—1 page only. No rhyming verse; no porn, obscenity, or child molestation themes." Accepts poetry written by children. Has published poetry by Jonathan Laws, Andrea Gereighty, Yusef Komunyakaa, Beverly Matherne, and Yevgeny Yevtushenko. As a sample we selected these lines from "Bottled Mosaic" by Rebecca Morris:

> Swirls of turbulent blue/Depression spread across the canvas/Words travel around the edges/Never touching empty spaces//Shadows/Created by a single harsh stroke/Splashes of red/And anger enter the picture.//The color of whisky fills gaps/Blends the whole to a blur

Desire Street is 8-10 pgs., desktop-published, downloaded photocopied and distributed, uses clip art. Receives about 550 poems/year, accepts 10%. Press run is 200 hard copies for 200 subscribers. Single copy: $3; subscription: $12/year. Sample (including guidelines): $5. Make checks payable to New Orleans Poetry Forum.

How to Submit: Submit 2 poems at a time, 10 poem limit/year. Line length for poetry is one 8½×11 page only. Accepts previously published poems; no simultaneous submissions. Accepts disk submissions, in ASCII or MS Dos text. Cover letter required. Membership in the New Orleans Poetry Forum is required before submitting work. Annual fee: $25, includes 4 issues of *Desire Street*, 52 3-hour workshops and 1 year's free critique of up to 10 poems. Time between acceptance and publication is up to 1 year. Poems are circulated to an editorial board. "First, poems are read by Andrea Gereighty. Then, poems are read by a board of five poets." Comments on rejected poems. Occasionally publishes theme issues. Responds in 1 year. Pays 10 copies. Acquires one-time rights.

Also Offers: The Forum conducts weekly workshops on Wednesday nights at the Broadmoor Library. Also conducts workshops at schools and in prisons. Details available for SASE.

◉ **NEW ORLEANS POETRY JOURNAL PRESS**, 2131 General Pershing St., New Orleans LA 70115. (504)891-3458. Established 1956. **Publisher/Editor:** Maxine Cassin. **Co-Editor:** Charles de Gravelles.

Book/Chapbook Needs: "We prefer to publish relatively new and/or little-known poets of unusual promise or those inexplicably neglected." Does not want to see "cliché or doggerel, anything incomprehensible or too derivative, or workshop exercises. First-rate lyric poetry preferred (not necessarily in traditional forms)." Has published books by Vassar Miller, Everette Maddox, Charles Black, Malaika Favorite, Raeburn Miller, Martha McFerren, Ralph Adamo, and Charles de Gravelles.

How to Submit: *Query first.* Does not accept unsolicited submissions for chapbooks, which are flat-spined paperbacks. Unsolicited mss will not be returned. "Please enclose a reading fee of $10 for editorial comment on up to three poems total maximum line limit of one hundred lines, if sample work is submitted with query." Responds to queries in up to 3 months, mss in the same time period, if solicited. Simultaneous submissions will possibly be accepted. Sometimes sends prepublication galleys. Pays contributor's copies, usually 50-100. The press does not subsidy publish at present and does not offer grants or awards.

Advice: "1) Read as much as possible! 2) Write only when you must, and 3) Don't rush into print! No poetry should be sent without querying first! Publishers are concerned about expenses unnecessarily incurred in mailing manuscripts. *Telephoning is not encouraged.*"

☑ ◉ **NEW ORLEANS REVIEW**, Box 195, Loyola University, New Orleans LA 70118. (504)865-2295. Fax: (504)865-2294. Website: www.loyno.edu/~noreview (includes guidelines, current issue, back issues, links, subscription information, cover art, etc.). Established 1968. **Editor:** Christopher Chambers. **Poetry Editor:** Sophia Stone.

Magazine Needs: *New Orleans Review* publishes "poetry of all types, fiction, and essays." Has published poetry by Jack Gilbert, Rodney Jones, Besmilr Brigham, Mark Halliday, and Moira Crone. *New Orleans Review* is 120-200 pgs., perfect-bound, elegantly printed with glossy card cover. Press run is 1,700. Sample: $5.

How to Submit: Submit 3-6 poems at a time. No previously published work. Brief cover letter preferred. Does not accept e-mail submissions. Guidelines available on website. Responds in 3 months. Pays 3 copies. Acquires first North American serial rights.

NEW ORPHIC REVIEW; NEW ORPHIC PUBLISHERS, 706 Mill St., Nelson, British Columbia V1L 4S5 Canada. (250)354-0494. Fax: (250)352-0743. Established New Orphic Publishers (1995), New Orphic Review (1998). **Editor-in-Chief:** Ernest Hekkanen.

Magazine Needs: "Appearing 2 times/year, *New Orphic Review* is run by an opinionated visionary who is beholden to no one, least of all government agencies like the Canada Council or institutions of higher learning. He feels Canadian literature is stagnant, lacks daring, and is terribly incestuous." *New Orphic Review* publishes poetry, novel excerpts, mainstream and experimental short stories, and articles on a wide range of subjects. Each issue also contains a *Featured Poet* section. "*New Orphic Review* publishes authors from around the world as long as the pieces are written in English and are accompanied by an SASE with proper Canadian postage and/ or US dollars to offset the cost of postage." Prefers "tight, well-wrought poetry over leggy, prosaic poetry. No 'fuck you' poetry; no rambling pseudo Beat poetry." Has published poetry by Catherine Owen, Steven Michael Berzensky (aka Mick Burrs), Robert Wayne Stedingh, John Pass, and Susan McCaslin. *New Orphic Review* is 120-140 pgs., magazine-sized, laser printed and perfect-bound with color cover, includes art/graphics and ads. Receives about 400 poems/year, accepts about 10%. Press run is 500 for 250 subscribers of which 20 are libraries. Subscription: $25 (individual), $30 (institution). Sample: $15.

How to Submit: Submit 6 poems at a time. Line length for poetry is 5 minimum, 30 maximum. Accepts simultaneous submissions; no previously published poems. Cover letter preferred. "Make sure a SASE (or SAE and IRC) is included." Time between acceptance and publication is up to 8 months. Poems are circulated to an editorial board. The managing editor and associate editor refer work to the editor-in-chief. Seldom comments on rejected poems. Occasionally publishes theme issues. In the spring, *New Orphic Review* will publish a Swiss issue. Guidelines available for SASE (or SAE and IRC). Responds in 2 months. Pays 1 contributor's copy. Acquires first North American serial rights.

Also Offers: New Orphic Publishers publishes 4 paperbacks/year. However, all material is solicited.

$ THE NEW RENAISSANCE (Specialized: translations, bilingual/foreign language), 26 Heath Rd. #11, Arlington MA 02474-3645. E-mail: wmichaud@gwi.net. Established 1968. **Editor-in-Chief:** Louise T. Reynolds. **Poetry Editor:** Frank Finale.

Magazine Needs: *the new renaissance* is "intended for the 'renaissance' person—the generalist, not the specialist. Publishes the best new writing and translations and offers a forum for articles on political, sociological topics; features established as well as emerging visual artists and writers, highlights reviews of small press, and offers essays on a variety of topics from visual arts and literature to science. Open to a variety of styles, including traditional." Has published poetry by Maria Mazziotti Gullan, Jay Griswold, Marvin Solomon, and Phillip Murray. As a sample the poetry editor selected these lines from "In the Country of Higher Knowledge" by Alberto Blanco (translated by Kathleen Snodgrass from the Spanish):

> *A stone that sings the praises of its weight/a rose that at dawn weeps its own dew/a cock illuminated by an inner sun/and a human being reconciled with itself/in the country of a higher knowledge/there's a lake full of transparent mermaids/there's a boat glittering at midnight . . .*

The New Renaissance is 144-186 pgs., 6×9, flat-spined, professionally printed on heavy stock, glossy, color cover, using 24-40 pgs. of poetry in each issue. Receives about 670 poetry submissions/year, accepts 26-39; has about a 1½- to 2-year backlog. Usual press run is 1,500 for 710 subscribers of which 132 are libraries. Subscriptions: $26.50/3 issues US, $28.50 Canada, $30.50 all others. All checks in US $. "A 3-issue subscription covers 18-22 months."

How to Submit: "Until January 1, 2001, we are accepting only bilingual translations." Submit 3-6 poems at a time, "unless a long poem—then one." Accepts simultaneous submissions, if notified; no previously published poems "unless magazine's circulation was under 250." Always include SASE or SAE and IRC. No e-mail submissions. "All poetry submissions are tied to our Awards Program for poetry published in a three-issue volume; judged by independent judges. Entry fee: $15 for nonsubscribers, $10 for subscribers, for which they receive the following: two back issues or a recent issue or an extension of their subscription. Submissions without entry fee are *returned unread*." Guidelines available for SASE. Responds in 5 months. Pays $21-36, more for the occasional longer poem, plus 1 copy/poem. Acquires all rights. Returns rights provided *The New Renaissance* retains rights for any *The New Renaissance* collection. Reviews books of poetry. The Awards Program gives 3 awards of $250, $125, and $60, with 3 Honorable Mentions of $25 each.

Advice: "Read, read, read, and not just poetry but literature in general. Stay aware of what is happening in the world as well as what's happening nationally. Be familiar with the best poets of the 20th century, including, at least, the major poets from abroad. Always read those magazines, especially the literary ones, that you want to submit to, so that you know what they've been publishing, what their philosophy is, and what their guidelines are. Remember that good writing is often rewriting and don't be satisfied with your first or second draft. Try to be your own best editor and don't overwrite a poem."

A NEW SONG; NEW SONG PRESS; NEW SONG CHAPBOOK COMPETITION (Specialized: spirituality), P.O. Box 629, W.B.B., Dayton OH 45409-0629. E-mail: nsongpress@aol.com. Website: www.New SongPress.com (includes guidelines, samples, links, and subscription information). Established 1995. **Editor/ Publisher:** Susan Jelus.

Magazine Needs: *A New Song* is published 2 times/year, in January and June, and "exhibits contemporary American poetry that speaks to endeavors of faith and enriches the spiritual lives of its readers. Includes poetry that takes a fresh approach and uses contemporary, natural language." Wants "free verse that addresses spiritual life through a wide-range of topics and vivid imagery. No rhyming, sing-song, old-fashioned 'religious' poetry." Has published poetry by Claude Wilkinson, Janet McCann, Herbert W. Martin and John Grey. As a sample the editor selected these lines from "Blue" by Joanna M. Weston:

> *A hole i the sky/where heaven shines through//And blue. And blue./Blue the colour/of my true love's eyes,//blue the place/where my heart/is folded,/curled into safety,/seeing only the inside/of all that is:/ the wholly blue/of a prairie sky.*

A New Song is 40-50 pgs., 5½ × 8½, usually Docutech or offset-printed, saddle-stitched, cardstock cover, photo or artwork on cover. Receives about 600 poems/year, accepts about 20%. Press run is 300 for 150 subscribers, 100 shelf sales; 50-75 distributed free to reviewers, bookstores, editors, professors, pastors. Single copy: $6.95; subscription: $12.95. Sample back issue: $5. Make checks payable to New Song Press.

How to Submit: Submit 3-5 poems at a time with short bio and SASE. Accepts simultaneous submissions; no previously published poems. Accepts e-mail submissions if included in body of message, "up to 3 poems only and must have a mailing address and bio." Send SASE with regular mail submissions. Time between acceptance and publication is up to 18 months. Poems are circulated to an editorial board. Often comments on rejected poems. Occasionally publishes theme issues. Guidelines available for SASE or on website. Responds in 3 months. Pays 1 copy. Acquires first North American serial rights. Sometimes reviews books of poetry in 750-1,000 words, single book format. Poets may send books for review consideration.

Book/Chapbook Needs & How to Submit: New Song Press's goals are "to help develop a genre of contemporary spiritual poetry." Publishes 1-2 chapbooks per year. Has published *Remembered into Life* by Maureen Tolman Flannery. Chapbooks are usually 20-40 pgs., 5½ × 8½, usually Docutech printed, sometimes offset printed color cover, saddle-stapled, cardstock cover, include art/graphics. Query first, with a few sample poems and a cover letter with brief bio and publication credits. Responds to queries in 3 months; to mss in 6 months. Payment varies.

Also Offers: Sponsors annual chapbook contest. Prize: $150 plus copies. Deadline: July 1st. Two runners-up also recognized. Entry fee for chapbook contest entries: $15, which includes a one-year subscription to *A New Song*.

N (icons) NEW WELSH REVIEW (Specialized: Ethnic), Chapter Arts Centre, Market Rd., Cardiff CF5 1QE Wales, United Kingdom. Phone: (44)(0)2920-665529. E-mail: nwr@welshnet.co.uk. Established 1988. **Editor:** Robin Reeves.

Magazine Needs: *New Welsh Review* is a literary quarterly publishing articles, short stories, and poems. *New Welsh Review* is an average of 104 pgs., glossy paper in three colors, laminated cover, using photographs, graphics, and ads. Press run is 1,000. Subscription: £20 (£22 overseas surface mail via cheque, Visa, or MasterCard). Sample: £7.50.

How to Submit: Submit poems double-spaced. No simultaneous submissions or previously published poems. Responds in 3 months. Publication within 7 months. Reviews books of poetry.

(icons) $ THE NEW WRITER; THE NEW WRITER PROSE AND POETRY PRIZES, P.O. Box 60, Cranbrook TN17 2ZR England. Phone: 01580 212626. Fax: 01580 212041. Website: www.thenewwriter.com. E-mail: admin@thenewwriter.com. Established 1996. **Poetry Editor:** Abi Hughes-Edwards.

Magazine Needs: Published 10 times/year, "*The New Writer* is the magazine you've been hoping to find. It's *different* and it's aimed at writers with a serious intent, who want to develop their writing to meet the high expectations of today's editors. The team at *The New Writer* are committed to working with their readers to increase the chances of publication. That's why masses of useful information and plenty of feedback is provided. More than that, we let you know about the current state of the market with the best in contemporary fiction and cutting-edge poetry backed up by searching articles and in-depth features in every issue. We are interested in short fiction, 2,000 words max.; subscribers' only; short and long unpublished poems, provided they are original and undeniably brilliant; articles that demonstrate a grasp of contemporary writing and current editorial/publishing policies; news of writers' circles, new publications, competitions, courses, workshops, etc." No "problems with length/form but anything over two pages (150 lines) needs to be brilliant. Cutting edge shouldn't mean inaccessible. No recent disasters—they date. No my baby/doggie poems; no God poems that sound like hymns, dum-dum rhymes, or comic rhymes (best left at the pub)." *New Writer* is 48 pgs., A4, professionally printed and saddle-stapled with paper cover, includes clipart and b&w photos. Press run is 1,500 for 1,350 subscribers; 50 distributed free to publishers, agents. Single copy: £3.50; subscription: £45.50 in US. Sample: £4.25.

How to Submit: Submit up to 6 poems at a time. Accepts previously published poems. Accepts e-mail submissions if included in body of message. Time between acceptance and publication is up to 6 months. Often comments on rejected poems. Offers criticism service: £12/6 poems. Guidelines available for SASE (or SAE with IRC) or on website. Pays £3 voucher plus 1 copy. Acquires first British serial rights. Reviews books and chapbooks of poetry and other magazines. Poets may send books for review consideration.

Also Offers: Sponsors the New Writer Prose & Poetry Prizes. An annual prize, "open to all poets writing in the English language, who are invited to submit an original, previously unpublished poem or collection of six to ten poems. Up to 25 prizes will be presented as well as publication for the prize-winning poets in an anthology plus the chance for a further 10 shortlisted poets to see their work published in *The New Writer* during the year." Write for contest rules.

$ ◻ ◪ ◎ NEW WRITER'S MAGAZINE (Specialized: humor, writing), P.O. Box 5976, Sarasota FL 34277-5976. (941)953-7903. E-mail: newriters@aol.com. Website: www.newriters.com. Established 1986. **Editor:** George J. Haborak.

Magazine Needs: *New Writer's Magazine* is a bimonthly magazine "for aspiring writers, and professional ones as well, to exchange ideas and working experiences." Open to free verse, light verse and traditional, 8-20 lines, reflecting upon the writing lifestyle. "Humorous slant on writing life especially welcomed." Does not want poems about "love, personal problems, abstract ideas or fantasy." *New Writer's Magazine* is 28 pgs., 8½×11, offset printed, saddle-stapled, with glossy paper cover, b&w photos and ads. Receives about 300 poems/year, accepts 10%. Press run is 5,000. Subscription: $15/year, $25/2 years. Sample: $3.

How to Submit: Submit up to 3 poems at a time. No previously published poems or simultaneous submissions. No e-mail submissions. Time between acceptance and publication is up to 1 year. Guidelines available for SASE or by e-mail. Responds in 2 months. Pays $5/poem. Acquires first North American serial rights. Each issue of this magazine also includes an interview with a recognized author, articles on writing and the writing life, tips, and markets.

◐ NEW YORK QUARTERLY, P.O. Box 693, Old Chelsea Station, New York NY 10113. Established 1969. **Poetry Editor:** William Packard.

Magazine Needs: *New York Quarterly* appears 3 times/year. Seeks to publish "a cross-section of the best of contemporary American poetry" and, indeed, have a record of publishing many of the best and most diverse of poets, including W.D. Snodgrass, Gregory Corso, James Dickey, and Judson Jerome. *New York Quarterly* appears in a 6×9, flat-spined format, thick, elegantly printed, glossy color cover. Subscription: $15.

How to Submit: Submit 3-5 poems at a time with your name and address; include SASE. Accepts simultaneous submissions with notification. Responds within 2 weeks. Pays contributor's copies.

☑ ☟ $ ◓ THE NEW YORKER, 4 Times Square, New York NY 10036. Website: www.Newyorker.com. Established 1925. **Contact:** poetry editor.

● Poems appearing in *The New Yorker* have also been selected for inclusion in the 1996, 1997, 1998, and 2000 volumes of *The Best American Poetry.*

Magazine Needs: *The New Yorker*, press run 800,000, uses poetry of the highest quality (including translations). Sample: $3 (available on newsstands).

How to Submit: Mss are not read during the summer. Responds in up to 3 months. Pays top rates.

◓ NEW ZOO POETRY REVIEW; SUNKEN MEADOWS PRESS, P.O. Box 36760, Richmond VA 23235. Website: http://members.aol.com/newzoopoet. Established 1997. **Editor:** Angela Vogel.

Magazine Needs: *New Zoo Poetry Review* is published annually in September/October and "tends to publish free verse in well-crafted lyric and narrative forms. Our goal is to publish established poets alongside lesser-known poets of great promise. *New Zoo Poetry Review* wants serious, intellectual poetry of any form, length or style. Rhyming poetry only if exceptional. No light verse, song lyrics or greeting card copy. If you are not reading the best of contemporary poetry, then *New Zoo Poetry Review* is not for you." Has published poetry by Heather McHugh, Diane Glancy, D.C. Berry, and Martha Collins. As a sample the editor selected these lines from "Cityscape with pink rose" by Richard Bear:

> As he turns away, he sees in his mind's/eye, himself turning back to buy for her/one of her own roses, or bloom of her choice./Idiotic! Blooms she has, and no doubt/must throw away many; wouldn't she/ be sick, by now, of flowers?/Trading, as she does, in these symbols/of the happiness of others, what would be/happiness to her, here, today?

New Zoo Poetry Review is 36 pgs., digest-sized, photocopied and saddle-stapled with glossy card cover with b&w photography. Receives about 2,000 poems/year, accepts approximately 5%. Press run is 200. Subscription: $7 for 2 consecutive issues. Sample: $4.

How to Submit: Submit 3-5 poems at a time. Accepts simultaneous submissions; no previously published poems. Cover letter with brief bio required. Seldom comments on rejected poems. Responds in 2 months. Pays 1 contributor's copy. Acquires first North American serial rights. "Poets are discouraged from submitting more than once in a 12-month period. Please do not write to us for these submission guidelines."

Advice: "It's not enough to report something that happened to you. A great poem involves the reader in its experience. It surprises us with fresh language."

◻ ◎ NEWSLETTER INAGO (Specialized: free-verse), P.O. Box 26244, Tucson AZ 85726-6244. Established 1979. **Poetry Editor:** Del Reitz.

Magazine Needs: *Newsletter Inago* is a monthly newsletter-format poetry journal. "Free verse and short narrative poetry preferred. Rhymed poetry must be truly exceptional (nonforced) for consideration. Due to format,

---

FOR AN EXPLANATION of symbols used in this book, see the Key to Symbols on the front and back inside covers.

'epic' and monothematic poetry will not be considered. Cause specific, political, or religious poetry stands little chance of consideration. A wide range of short poetry, showing the poet's preferably eclectic perspective is best for *Newsletter Inago*. No haiku, please." Has published poetry by Debi Grace Eimer, Justin Barrett, Maureen Weldon, Jody Primoff, Vera Schwarz, and Mark J. Isham. As a sample the editor selected these lines from "Drawing Near" by Patricia G. Rourke:

> The lake is churning with conversation/night leaving her heart full of stories,/spitting out words, in sprays of laughter/wind riding its back, inspiring/unusual phrases and punctuations.

Newsletter Inago is 4-5 pgs., corner-stapled. Press run is approximately 200 for subscriptions. No price is given for the newsletter, but the editor suggests a donation of $3.50 an issue or $17.50 annually ($3.50 and $21 Canada, £8 and £21 UK). Make checks payable to Del Reitz. Copyright is retained by authors.

How to Submit: Submit 10-15 poems at a time. "Poetry should be submitted in the format in which the poet wants it to appear, and cover letters are always a good idea." Accepts simultaneous submissions and previously published poems. Sometimes comments on rejected poems. Guidelines available for SASE. Responds ASAP (usually within 2 weeks). Pays in contributor copies.

NIMROD: INTERNATIONAL JOURNAL OF POETRY AND PROSE; RUTH G. HARD-MAN AWARD; PABLO NERUDA PRIZE FOR POETRY, University of Tulsa, 600 S. College, Tulsa OK 74104-3189. (918)631-3080. Fax: (918)631-3033. E-mail: nimrod@utulsa.edu. Website: www.utulsa.edu/nimrod/ (includes guidelines, names of editors, contest rules, subscription information, and poetry samples). Established 1956. **Editor-in-Chief:** Francine Ringold. **Poetry Editor:** Manly Johnson.

● Poetry published in *Nimrod* has been included in *The Best American Poetry 1995*.

Magazine Needs: *Nimrod* "is an active 'little magazine,' part of the movement in American letters which has been essential to the development of modern literature. *Nimrod* publishes 2 issues/year, an awards issue in the fall featuring the prize winners of their national competition and a thematic issue each spring." Wants "vigorous writing that is neither wholly of the academy nor the streets, typed mss." Has published poetry by Ellen Bass, Kimberly, Jude Nutter, Sarah Flygare, Jennifer Ward, Ruth Schwartz, and Luci Getsi. *Nimrod* is 160 pgs., 6×9, flat-spined, full-color glossy cover, professionally printed on coated stock with b&w photos and art, uses 50-90 pgs. of poetry in each issue. Poems in non-award issues range from formal to freestyle with several translations. Receives about 2,000 submissions/year, accepts 1%; has a 3- to 6-month backlog. Press run is 3,500 of which 200 are public and university libraries. Subscription: $17.50/year inside USA; $19 outside. Sample: $10. Specific back issues available.

How to Submit: Submit 5-10 poems at a time. No fax or e-mail submissions. Publishes theme issues. Guidelines and upcoming themes available for SASE, by e-mail, or on website. Responds in up to 12 weeks. Pays 2 contributor's copies plus reduced cost on additional copies. "Poets should be aware that during the months that the Ruth Hardman Awards Competition is being conducted, reporting time on non-contest manuscripts will be longer."

Also Offers: Send business-sized SASE for rules for the Ruth G. Hardman Award: Pablo Neruda Prize for Poetry ($2,000 and $1,000 prizes). Entries accepted January 1 through April 30 each year. The $20 entry fee includes 2 issues. Also sponsors the Nimrod/Hardman Awards Workshop, a 1-day workshop held annually in October. Cost is approximately $30. Send SASE for brochure and registration form.

NINETY-SIX PRESS (Specialized: regional), Furman University, Greenville SC 29613. (864)294-3156. Fax: (864)294-2224. E-mail: bill.rogers@furman.edu. Website: www.furman.edu/~wrogers/96Press/home.htm (includes information about the press, publishers, and poets; a catalogue of available titles). Established 1991. **Editors:** William Rogers and Gilbert Allen.

Book/Chapbook Needs & How to Submit: Publishes 1-2 paperback books of poetry/year. "The name of the press is derived from the old name for the area around Greenville, South Carolina—the Ninety-Six District. The name suggests our interest in the writers, readers, and culture of the region." Books are usually 45-70 pgs., 6×9, professionally printed and perfect-bound with coated stock cover. For a sample, send $10. "We currently accept submissions by invitation only. At some point in the future, however, we hope to be able to encourage submissions by widely published poets who live in South Carolina."

NO EXIT, P.O. Box 454, South Bend IN 46624-0454. Fax: (801)650-3743. E-mail: no_exit@usa.net. Established 1994. **Editor:** Mike Amato.

Magazine Needs: *No Exit* is a quarterly forum "for the experimental as well as traditional excellence." Wants "poetry that takes chances in form or content. Form, length, subject matter and style are open. No poetry that's unsure of why it was written. Particularly interested in long (not long-winded) poems." Has published poetry by David Lawrence, Gregory Fiorim, and Ron Offen. *No Exit* is 32 pgs., saddle-stapled, digest-sized, card cover with art. Accepts 10-15% of the submissions received. Press run is less than 500. Subscription: $12. Sample: $4.

How to Submit: Submit up to 5 poems ("send more if compelled, but I will stop reading after the fifth"). "No handwritten work, misspellings, colored paper, multiple type faces, typos, long-winded cover letters and lists of publication credits." Accepts simultaneous submissions; no previously published poems. No e-mail submissions. Time between acceptance and publication can vary from 1 month to 1 year. Sometimes comments on rejected poems, "if the poem strikes me as worth saving. No themes. But spring issues are devoted to a single poet. Interested writers should submit 24 pgs. of work. Don't bother unless of highest caliber. There are no other guidelines for single-author issues." Guidelines available for SASE or by e-mail. Responds in up to 3 months. Pays 1 contributor's copy plus 4-issue subscription. Acquires first North American serial rights plus right to reprint once in an anthology. Reviews books of poetry. "Also looking for articles, critical in nature, on poetry/poets." Poets may send books for review consideration.

Advice: "Presentation means something; namely, that you care about what you do. Don't take criticism, when offered, personally. I'll work with you if I see something solid to focus on."

N ○ ✍ ◎ NOCTURNAL LYRIC, JOURNAL OF THE BIZARRE (Specialized: horror), P.O. Box 542, Astoria OR 97103. E-mail: nocturnallyric@melodymail.com. Website: www.angelfire.com/ca/nocturnallyric (includes upcoming authors, poetry, special deals on back issues, and news about the upcoming issue). Established 1987. **Editor:** Susan Moon.

Magazine Needs: *Nocturnal Lyric* is a quarterly journal "featuring bizarre fiction and poetry, primarily by new writers." Wants "poems dealing with the bizarre: fantasy, death, morbidity, horror, gore, etc. Any length. No 'boring poetry.' " Has published poetry by Stephanie Loy and Elisha Pierce. *Nocturnal Lyric* is 40 pgs., digest-sized, photocopied, saddle-stapled, with trade ads and staff artwork. Receives about 200 poems/year, accepts about 35%. Press run is 400 for 40 subscribers. Subscription: $10. Sample: $3, $2 for back issues; $4 for non-US addresses. Make checks payable to Susan Moon.

How to Submit: Submit up to 4 poems at a time. Accepts previously published poems and simultaneous submissions. No e-mail submissions. Seldom comments on rejected poems. Responds in up to 6 months. Pays 50¢ "discount on subscription" coupons. Acquires one-time rights.

Advice: "Please send us something really wild and intense!"

◐ NOMAD'S CHOIR, % Meander, 30-15 Hobart St. F4H, Woodside NY 11377. Established 1989. **Editor:** Joshua Meander.

Magazine Needs: *Nomad's Choir* is a quarterly. "Subjects wanted: love poems, protest poems, mystical poems, nature poems, poems of humanity, poems with solutions to world problems and inner conflict. 9-30 lines, poems with hope. Simple words, careful phrasing. Free verse, rhymed poems, sonnets, half-page parables, myths and legends, song lyrics. No curse words in poems, little or no name-dropping, no naming of consumer products, no two-page poems, no humor, no bias writing, no poems untitled." Has published poetry by Steven J. Stein, Madeline Artenberg, Wayne Wilkinson, and Jill Dimaggio. *Nomad's Choir* is 10 pgs., 8½ × 11, typeset and saddle-stapled with 3 poems/page. Receives about 150 poems/year, accepts 50. Press run is 400; all distributed free. Subscription: $5. Sample: $1.25. Make checks payable to Joshua Meander.

How to Submit: Responds in 2 months. Pays 1 contributor's copy. Publishes theme issues. Guidelines and upcoming themes available for SASE.

Advice: "Stick to your guns; however, keep in mind that an editor may be able to correct a minor flaw in your poem. Accept only minor adjustments. Go to many open poetry readings. Respect the masters. Read and listen to other poets on the current scene. Make pen pals. Start your own poetry journal. Do it all out of pure love."

✓ ♈ $◐ NORTH AMERICAN REVIEW, JAMES HEARST POETRY PRIZE, University of Northern Iowa, Cedar Falls IA 50614-0516. (319)273-6455. Fax: (319)273-4326. E-mail: nar@uni.edu. Website: http://webdelsol.com/NorthAmReview/NAR (includes masthead, history, competition guidelines, archive of selected work, and subscription forms). Established 1815. **Editor:** Vince Gotera.

 ● Work published in the *North American Review* has been included in the recent volumes of *The Best American Poetry.*

Magazine Needs: *North American Review* is a slick magazine-sized bimonthly of general interest, 48 pgs. average, saddle-stapled, professionally printed with glossy full-color paper cover, publishing poetry of the highest quality. Has published poetry by Yusef Komunyakaa, Virgil Suarez, Nance Van Winckel, and Dana Wier. Receives about 5,000 poems/year, accepts 40-50. Press run is 2,500 for 1,500 subscribers of which 1,000 are libraries. Writer's subscription: $18. Sample: $5.

How to Submit: Include SASE. No simultaneous submissions or previously published poems. No fax or e-mail submissions. Time between acceptance and publication is up to 1 year. Guidelines available for SASE. Responds in 3 months. Always sends prepublication galleys. Pays $1/line ($20 minimum) and 2 contributor's copies. Acquires first North American serial rights only. Rights revert after publication.

Also Offers: North American Review sponsors the annual James Hearst Poetry Prize. First prize $1000. Postmark deadline is October 31. Rules are available for SASE, by e-mail, by fax, or on website.

♈ $◎ NORTH CAROLINA LITERARY REVIEW (Specialized: regional), English Dept., East Carolina University, Greenville NC 27858-4353. (252)328-1537. Fax: (252)328-4889. E-mail: bauerm@mail.ecu.edu. Established 1992. **Editor:** Margaret Bauer.

 ● *North Carolina Literary Review* was awarded for best journal design in 1999 by the CELJ.

Magazine Needs: *North Carolina Literary Review* is an annual publication appearing in October that "contains articles and other works about North Carolina topics or by North Carolina authors." Wants "poetry by writers currently living in North Carolina, those who have lived in North Carolina or those using North Carolina for subject matter." Has published poetry by Betty Adcock, James Applewhite, and A.R. Ammons. *North Carolina*

Literary Review is 200 pgs. and magazine-sized. Receives about 40-50 submissions/year, accepts about 20%. Press run is 1,000 for 500 subscribers of which 150 are libraries, 200 shelf sales; 50 distributed free to contributors. Subscription: $20/2 years, $36/4 years. Sample: $10-15.
How to Submit: Submit 3-5 poems at a time. No e-mail submissions. Cover letter required. "Submit 2 copies and include SASE or e-mail address for response." Reads submissions August 1 through April 30 only. Time between acceptance and publication is up to 1 year. Often comments on rejected poems. Guidelines available for SASE, by e-mail, or on website. Responds in 2 months. Sometimes sends prepublication galleys. Pays $25-50 plus 1-2 copies. Acquires first or one-time rights. Reviews books of poetry in 2,000 words, multi-book format. Poets from North Carolina may send books for review consideration.

⬤ **NORTH DAKOTA QUARTERLY**, Box 7209, University of North Dakota, Grand Forks ND 58202-7209. Established 1910. **Poetry Editor:** Jay Meek.
Magazine Needs: *North Dakota Quarterly* is published by the University of North Dakota and includes material in the arts and humanities—essays, fiction, interviews, poems, and visual art. "We want to see poetry that reflects an understanding not only of the difficulties of the craft, but of the vitality and tact that each poem calls into play." Has published poetry by Edward Kleinschmidt, Alane Rollings, and Robert Wrigley. *North Dakota Quarterly* is 6×9, about 200 pgs., perfect-bound, professionally designed and often printed with full-color artwork on a white card cover. Publishes almost every kind of poem—avant-garde to traditional. Typically the work of about 5 poets is included in each issue. Press run is 850 for 650 subscribers. Subscription: $25/year. Sample: $8.
How to Submit: Submit 5 poems at a time, typed. No previously published poems or simultaneous submissions. No fax or e-mail submissions. Time between acceptance and publication varies. Responds in up to 6 weeks. Always sends prepublication galleys. Pays 1 contributor's copy. Acquires first serial rights.
Advice: "We look to publish the best fiction, poetry, and essays that in our estimation we can. Our tastes and interests are best reflected in what we have been recently publishing, and we suggest that you look at some current numbers."

♈ ⬤ **NORTHEAST; JUNIPER PRESS; JUNIPER BOOKS; THE WILLIAM N. JUDSON SERIES OF CONTEMPORARY AMERICAN POETRY; CHICKADEE; INLAND SEA SERIES; GIFTS OF THE PRESS**, 1310 Shorewood Dr., La Crosse WI 54601 (207)778-3454. Website: www.ddgbooks.com. Established 1962. **Contact:** editors.
   ● "Poets we have published won the Pulitzer Prize, the Posner Poetry Prize, and the Midwest Book Award."
Magazine Needs & How to Submit: *Northeast* is an annual little magazine appearing in January. Has published fiction poetry by Lisel Muller, Alan Bronghton, and Bruce Cutler. *Northeast* is digest-sized and saddle-stapled. Subscription: $33/year ($38 for institutions), "which brings you one issue of the magazine and the Juniper Books, Chickadees, the William N. Judson Series of Contemporary American Poetry Books and some gifts of the press, a total of about 3-5 items." (See our website or send SASE for catalog to order individual items; orders can be placed by calling the Order Dept. at (207)778-3454.) Sample: $3. No submissions by fax or e-mail. Responds in up to 4 months. Pays 2 copies.
Book/Chapbook Needs & How to Submit: Juniper Press does not accept unsolicited book/chapbook mss.
Advice: "Please read us before sending mss. It will aid in your selection of materials to send. If you don't like what we do, please don't submit."

✅ ⬤ **NORTHEAST ARTS MAGAZINE**, P.O. Box 4363, Portland ME 04101. Established 1990. **Publisher/Editor:** Mr. Leigh Donaldson.
Magazine Needs: *Northeast Arts Magazine* is a biannual using poetry, short fiction, essays, reviews, art, and photography that is "honest, clear, with a love of expression through simple language, under 30 lines. We maintain a special interest in work that reflects cultural diversity in New England and throughout the world." Has published poetry by Steve Lutrell, Eliot Richman, Elizabeth R. Curry, Bob Begieburg, and Alisa Aran. *Northeast Arts Magazine* is 32 or more pgs., digest-sized, professionally printed with 1-color coated card cover. Accepts 10-20% of submissions. Press run is 500-1,000 for 150 subscribers of which half are libraries, 50 to arts organizations. An updated arts information section and feature articles are included. Subscription: $10. Sample: $4.50.
How to Submit: Reads submissions September 1 through February 28 only. "A short bio is helpful." Guidelines available for SASE. Responds in 3 months. Pays 2 copies. Acquires first North American serial rights.

◖ ◯ ◕ **NORTHERN STARS MAGAZINE**, N17285 Co. Rd. 400, Powers MI 49874. website members.a ol.com/WriterNet/NorthStar.html (includes brief guidelines, poetry, and books available through North Star Publishing). Established 1997. **Editor:** Beverly Kleikamp.
Magazine Needs: *Northern Stars* is published bimonthly and "welcomes submissions of fiction, nonfiction and poetry on any subject or style. The main requirement is good clean family reading material. Nothing you can't read to your child or your mother. No smut or filth." Accepts poetry written by children. Has published poetry by Terri Warden, Julie Sanders, Najwa Salam Brax, and Gary Elam. As a sample the editor selected these lines from "Flights of Fancy" by Gary S. Elam:

> *A raven looks mysterious/With feathers black as night/An eagle perching on a cliff/Is such an awesome sight.*

Northern Stars Magazine is 32 pgs., 8½×11, photocopied and saddle-stapled with cardstock cover, may include b&w line drawings and photographs. "Send SASE for subscription information." Sample: $4. Make checks payable to Beverly Kleikamp or *Northern Stars Magazine*.

How to Submit: Submit up to 5 poems at a time, no more than 25 lines each. Accepts previously published poems and simultaneous submissions. Cover letter preferred. "Manuscripts must be typed—please do not submit handwritten material." Often comments on rejected poems. Occasionally publishes theme issues. Pays either tearsheets or copy of *Northern Stars Magazine*—except in contests where winner receives half of all entry fees—minimum $10. No fee for regular subscribers. All rights return to authors on publication.

Also Offers: Sponsors monthly alternating issues contest for poetry and fiction/nonfiction (i.e., poetry contest in March-April issue, fiction/nonfiction in May-June). Entry fee: $2.50/poem for non-subscribers, $1/poem for subscribers. Deadline: 25th of month preceding publication. Guidelines available for SASE. Publishes an annual chapbook of contest winners and honorable mentions. "I do publish a limited number of chapbooks for others now for an 'affordable' price to the writer." 100 copies or less available; sample available $5. Also has a "Somewhere In Michigan" regular column featuring people/places/events, etc., tied in with Michigan. Also includes adventures which have happened in Michigan.

[N] $ [C] THE NORTHWEST FLORIDA REVIEW; OKALOOSA ISLAND PRESS; RICHARD EB-ERHARD AWARD IN POETRY, P.O. Box 8122, Okaloosa Island, Ft. Walton Beach FL 32548. **Poetry Editor:** Lola Haskins.

Magazine Needs: *The Northwest Florida Review* appears biannually in May and December. "A magazine of high-quality literature. We are looking for serious poetry, translations, short fiction up to 5,000 words, reviews, art and articles of literary interest." Wants the best contemporary poetry. Open to all styles and subject matter. "We want to see strong images." Does not want greeting card verse, inspirational verse, or rhymed poetry unless handled with artistic excellence. As a sample the editor selected the following lines from "Neighbors" by Susan Stewart from her book *Yellow Stars and Ice*:

> . . . they climb, their sheets knotted/Around their waists, their clotheslines scarring the clouds, the
> suicides/And the maniacs, the painters and the bats,/Perch on the third story windows and slowly/Let
> go of the earth. A jet comes ripping/Across the ceiling, and the sky writing says,/"Jump, yes, jump"

The Northwest Florida Review is 96 pgs., digest-sized, press-printed, perfect-bound, glossy cover with art/graphics. Press run is 1,000. Single copy: $5; subscription: $9/year. Sample: $5. Make checks payable to *The Northwest Florida Review.*

How to Submit: Submit 3-6 poems at a time. Accepts simultaneous submissions; no previously published poems. No fax, e-mail, or disk submissions. Cover letter is preferred. "Include SASE. Single space for poetry, double space for fiction and nonfiction." Reads submissions year round. Poems are circulated to an editorial board. Never comments on rejected poems. Responds in months. Pays contributor's copies and $5/poem or $20/short story. Acquires first North American serial rights. Reviews books of poetry in 750 words, single book and multi-book format.

Books/Chapbooks & How to Submit: Okaloosa Island Press plans to publish 1 paperback title beginning in 2002 "by a poet who has published at least one book." Book will be at least 45-64 pgs., press-printed, perfect-bound, glossy cover with art/graphics. Query first, with a few sample poems and a cover letter "but not until March 2002." Responds to queries and mss in 3 months. Pays royalties of 10-15% and 10 author's copies (out of a press run of 500).

Also Offers: The Richard Eberhart Award in Poetry. 1st Prize: $300; 2nd Prize: $50. $5 entry fee. Guidelines available for SASE.

Advice: "Read *Paris Review, Georgia Review, Poetry*, and other top 20 magazines to see what kind of poetry we want."

[C] NORTHWEST REVIEW, 369 PLC, University of Oregon, Eugene OR 97403. (503)346-3957. Established 1957. **Poetry Editor:** John Witte.

Magazine Needs: "Seeking excellence in whatever form we can find it" and use "all types" of poetry. Has published poetry by Alan Dugan, Olga Broumas, and Richard Eberhart. *Northwest Review*, a 6×9, flat-spined magazine, appears 3 times/year and uses 25-40 pgs. of poetry in each issue. Receives about 3,500 submissions/year, accepts about 4%; has up to a 4-month backlog. Press run is 1,300 for 1,200 subscribers of which half are libraries. Sample: $4.

How to Submit: Submit 6-8 poems clearly reproduced. No simultaneous submissions. Guidelines available for SASE. Responds within 10 weeks. Pays 3 copies.

Advice: "Persist."

$ [] [C] NORTHWOODS PRESS, THE POET'S PRESS; NORTHWOODS JOURNAL, A MAGA-ZINE FOR WRITERS; C.A.L. (CONSERVATORY OF AMERICAN LETTERS), P.O. Box 298, Thomaston ME 04861-0298. (207)354-0998. Fax: (207)354-8953. E-mail: cal@americanletters.org. Website: www.americanletters.org. Northwoods Press established 1972, *Northwoods Journal* 1993. **Editor:** Robert Olmsted.

Magazine Needs & How to Submit: *Northwoods Journal* is a quarterly literary magazine that publishes fiction, reviews, nonfiction, and poetry. "The journal is interested in all poets who feel they have something to say and who work to say it well. We have no interest in closet poets, or credit seekers. All poets seeking an audience, working to improve their craft, and determined to 'get it right' are welcome here. Accepts poetry written by children. Please request submission guidelines before submitting." *Northwoods Journal* is about 40 pgs., digest-sized with full color cover. Subscription: $12.50/year. Sample: $5.50. **Reading fee:** $1/poem for nonmembers of C.A.L., 50¢/poem for members. One free read per year when joining or renewing membership in C.A.L. "Submission must accompany membership order." Guidelines are available for #10 SASE or on website; "see guidelines before submitting anything." Deadlines are the 1st of March, June, September, and December for seasonal publication. Responds within 2 weeks after deadline, sometimes sooner. Pays $4/page, average, on acceptance.

Book Needs & How to Submit: "For book-length poetry manuscripts, submit to Northwoods Press. Our program is designed for the excellent *working poet* who has a following which is likely to create sales of $3,000 or more. Without at least that much of a following and at least that level of sales, no book can be published. Send SASE for our 15 pt. poetry program. Please do not submit manuscripts until you have read our guidelines." Has published *Hog Killers and Other Poems* by Vernon Schmid and *Knotted Stems* by Sylvia Relation. Northwoods Press will pay a minimum of $250 advance on contracting a book. Editors "rarely" comments on rejected poems, but they offer commentary for a fee, though they "strongly recommend *against* it."

Advice: "Poetry must be non-trite, non-didactic. It must never bounce. Rhyme, if used at all, should be subtle. One phrase should tune the ear in preparation for the next. They should flow and create an emotional response."

NORTHWORDS, The Stable, Long Rd., Avoch, Ross-Shire Scotland IV9 8QR United Kingdom. E-mail. editor@northwords.co.uk. Website: www.northwords.co.uk (includes samples from past issues and contact information). Established 1991. **Editor:** Angus Dunn.

Magazine Needs: Published 3 times/year, *Northwords* is "a literary journal focusing on material relevant to the North of Scotland, the geographical North generally, fiction (short) and poetry." Does not want "vague New Age poetry; philosophical poetry without physical referents. No trite sentiments in rhyme or otherwise." Has published poetry by Gael Turnbull, Sheena Blackhall, Tom Pow, and Raymond Friel. As a sample the editor selected these lines from "The Fourth Figure in the Furnace" by Ian McDonough:

> I have made some careful calculations/based upon Nebuchadnezzar's estimation/of the mean heat of
> the furnace/and the boiling temperature of blood.//The results are conclusive in as much/as no human
> spirit is likely to survive/more than a lifetime under such conditions.

Northwords is 64 pgs., B5, perfect-bound, illustrations often used. Receives about 500 poems/year, accepts 10%. Press run is 500 for 200 subscribers of which 10 are libraries, 250 shelf sales. Subscription: £12. Sample: £4 pounds sterling (international money order preferred if overseas).

How to Submit: Submit 4-6 poems at a time. No previously published poems or simultaneous submissions. No fax or e-mail submissions. Cover letter required. Reads submissions the first week of each month only. Time between acceptance and publication is 4 months. Poems are circulated to an editorial board. "All submissions are read by the editorial board, who advise acceptance or rejection. Final decision rests with the editor." Seldom comments on rejected poems. Responds in 2 months. Pays 1 copy and a small fee. Acquires first rights. Reviews books and chapbooks of poetry in 500-1,200 words, single and multi-book format. Poets may send books for review consideration to Robert Davidson at the above address.

NOSTALGIA: A SENTIMENTAL STATE OF MIND (Specialized: nostalgia), P.O. Box 2224, Orangeburg SC 29116. E-mail: CNOSTAlgia@aol.com. Website: www.nospub.com. Established 1986. **Poetry Editor:** Connie Lakey Martin.

Magazine Needs: *Nostalgia* appears spring and fall using "content at whim of poet, style open, prefer modern prose, but short poems, never longer than one page, no profanity, no ballads." *Nostalgia* is 24 pgs., digest-sized, offset typescript, saddle-stapled, with matte card cover. Press run is 1,000. Subscription: $8. Sample: $5.

How to Submit: No e-mail submissions. Include SASE and put name and address on each poem. Guidelines available for SASE. All rights revert to author upon publication.

Advice: "I offer criticism to most rejected poems, but I suggest sampling before submitting."

NOTRE DAME REVIEW, Dept. of English, University of Notre Dame, 356 O'Shaughnessy Hall, Notre Dame IN 46556-5639. (219)631-6952. Fax: (219)631-4268. E-mail: english.ndreview.1@nd.edu. Website: www.nd.edu/~ndr/review.htm (includes writer's guidelines, names of editors, poetry, and interviews). Established 1994. **Poetry Editor:** John Matthias.

Magazine Needs: *Notre Dame Review* is "a biannual eclectic magazine of the best poetry and fiction." Open to all types of poetry. Has published poetry by Ken Smith, Robert Creeley, and Denise Levertov. As a sample the editor selected these lines from "The Watchman at Mycenae" by Seamus Heaney:

> Some people wept, and not for sorrow-joy/That the king had armed and upped and sailed for Troy,/
> But inside me life struck sound in a gong/That killing-fest, the life-warm and world wrong/It brought
> to pass still argued and endured

Notre Dame Review is 170 pgs., magazine-sized, perfect-bound with 4-color glossy cover, includes art/graphics and ads. Receives about 400 poems/year, accepts 10%. Press run is 2,000 for 500 subscribers of which 150 are libraries, 1,000 shelf sales; 350 distributed free to contributors, assistants, etc. Single copy: $8; subscription: $15/year. Sample: $6. "Read magazine before submitting."

How to Submit: Submit 3-5 poems at a time. Accepts simultaneous submissions; no previously published poems. Cover letter required. Reads submissions September through April only. Time between acceptance and publication is 3 months. Seldom comments on rejected poems. Publishes theme issues. Guidelines and upcoming themes available on website. Responds in 3 months. Always sends prepublication galleys. Pays 2 copies. Acquires first rights. Staff reviews books of poetry in 500 words, single and multi-book format. Poets may send books for review consideration.

Also Offers: Sponsors the Ernest Sandeen Prize for Poetry, a book contest open to poets with at least one other book publication. Send SASE for details.

☑ ◐ ◎ **NOVA EXPRESS (Specialized: science fiction/fantasy, horror)**, P.O. Box 27231, Austin TX 78755. E-mail: lawrenceperson@jump.net. Website: www.novaexpress.org. Established 1987. **Editor:** Lawrence Person.

• *Nova Express* was nominated for the Hugo Award.

Magazine Needs: *Nova Express* appears "irregularly (at least once/year) with coverage of cutting edge science fiction, fantasy and horror literature, with an emphasis on post-cyperpunk and slipstream. We feature interviews, reviews, fiction, poetry, and serious (but nonacademic) critical articles on important issues and authors throughout the entire science fiction/fantasy/horror/slipstream field." Wants "poetry relating to literature of the fantastic in some way." Has published poetry by Alison Wimsatt and Mark McLaughlin. As a sample we selected these lines from "The Weatherworn Banshee Declares Her Undying Love For Some Accountant She Met At A Party" by Mark McLaughlin:

> The others threw dip and salsa at me/until you, my darling, told them to stop./These hands, callused
> and scarred/from climbing rocks and tearing apart/wild dogs, long to hold you—and these lips,/puffy
> from sucking cracked rib-bones,/burn to slather you with love.

Nova Express is 48 pgs., 8½×11, stapled, desktop-published with b&w graphics and line art. Receives about 40-50 poems/year, accepts 1-2. Press run is 800 for 200 subscribers, 250 shelf sales; 200-300 distributed free to science fiction industry professionals. Subscription: $12. Sample: $5.

How to Submit: Submit up to 5 poems at a time. No previously published poems or simultaneous submissions. Cover letter preferred. E-mail submissions (in body of message) preferred. Time between acceptance and publication is 3 months. Often comment on rejected poems. Publishes theme issues. Guidelines available for SASE or by e-mail. Responds in 3 months. "Response will be slow until the slush pile is cleaned out." Sometimes sends prepublication galleys. Pays 2 copies plus 4-issue subscription. Acquires one-time rights.

Advice: "We are not interested in any poetry outside the science fiction/fantasy/horror genre. *Nova Express* is read widely and well regarded by genre professionals."

☑ $ ◻ ◎ **NOW & THEN (Specialized: regional, themes)**, ETSU, P.O. Box 70556, Johnson City TN 37614-0556. (423)439-5348. Fax: (423)439-6340. E-mail: woodsidj@etsu.edu. Website: http://cass.etsu.edu/n&t/N&T.htm (includes writer's guidelines, upcoming themes, and contact information for submission). Established 1984. **Editor-in-Chief:** Jane Woodside. **Poetry Editor:** Linda Parsons Marion.

Magazine Needs: *Now & Then* is a regional magazine that covers Appalachian issues and culture. It contains fiction, poetry, articles, interviews, essays, memoirs, reviews, photos, and drawings. Wants poetry related to the region. "Each issue focuses on one aspect of life in the Appalachian region (anywhere hilly from Northern Mississippi on up to Southern New York). Previous theme issues have featured architecture, Appalachian lives, transportation, poetry, food, and religion. We want genuine, well-crafted voices, not sentimentalized stereotypes." Has published poetry by Fred Chappell, Maggie Anderson, Robert Morgan, and Lynn Powell. *Now & Then* appears 3 times/year and is 42 pgs., magazine-sized, saddle-stapled, professionally printed, with matte card cover. Press run is 1,250-1,500 for 900 members of the Center for Appalachian Studies and Services, of which 100 are libraries. Accepts 6-10 poems an issue. Center membership is $20; the magazine is one of the membership benefits. Sample: $7.50 postage.

How to Submit: Will consider simultaneous submissions; they occasionally use previously published poems. Submit up to 5 poems, with SASE and cover letter including "a few lines about yourself for a contributor's note and whether the work has been published or accepted elsewhere." Put name, address and phone number on every poem. Accepts fax submissions. No e-mail submissions. Deadlines: March 1, July 1 and November 1. Publishes theme issues. Upcoming themes include "Appalachian Writing Re-visited" (Deadline March 1) and "Appalachia's Natural Resources" (July 1). Guidelines and upcoming themes available for SASE or on website. Editor prefers fax or e-mail to phone calls. Responds within 6 months. Sends prepublication galleys. Pays $10/poem plus 2 copies. Acquires all rights. Reviews books of poetry in 750 words. Send poetry directly to poetry editor Linda Parsons Marion, 2909 Fountain Park Blvd., Knoxville TN 37917. E-mail for correspondence lpmarion@utk.edu. Poets may send books for review consideration to Marianne Worthington, book review editor, Communication and Theatre Arts Dept., Cumberland College, 600 College Station Dr., Williamsburg KY 40769. E-mail: mworthin@cc.cumber.edn.

Also Offers: Sponsors a biennial poetry competition. Guidelines can be found at www.cass.etsu.edu/n&t/contest.htm.

N ⊟ ⊘ **NOWCULTURE.COM; NOWCULTURE.COM ANNUAL POETRY AWARD**, Eisenhower Plaza II, 354 Eisenhower Pkwy., Suite 2800, Livingston NJ 07039. E-mail: martyc@nowculture.com. Website: www.nowculture.com (includes interviews, poems, fiction, book and magazine giveaways). Established 2000. **Vice President of Artistic Development:** Ernie Hilbert.

Magazine Needs: *nowCulture.com* appears online monthly. "Our philosophy is unlike that of any other major website in existence today. The company strictly limits the number of artists appearing on its site at one time to between 15 and 25 and, thus, avoids the overcrowding of artists typical on most existing websites. Limiting the number of artists appearing on the site in this manner enables *nowCulture.com* to design each exhibit around the work of that artist, rather than forcing the company to fit the work of every artist into a single preordained format."

How to Submit: "In order to ensure that only the highest-quality artists appear on the site, *nowCulture.com* relies upon a distinguished panel of advisors, with expertise spanning the entire spectrum of fine and performing arts. This distinguished panel of advisors works closely with the company's core management team to set the standards that artists must meet to appear on the site." Reviews books of poetry and other magazines/journals in 500-1,000 words. Poets may send books for review consideration to Ernie Hilbert, 34-54 30th St., Astoria NY 11106.

Also Offers: Annual poetry award of $1,000 for a poem or group of poems up to 10 pgs. Guidelines available for SASE. "Contest finalists and winner receive monthly features."

◑ ◎ **O!!ZONE (Specialized: visual poetry, photography, collage)**, 1266 Fountain View, Houston TX 77057-2204. (713)784-2802. Fax: (713)789-5119. E-mail: HarryBurrus@juno.com. Established 1993. **Editor/ Publisher:** Harry Burrus.

Magazine Needs: *O!!Zone* is "an international literary-art zine featuring visual poetry, travel pieces, interviews, haiku, manifestos, and art. We are particularly intrigued by poets who also do photography (or draw or paint). We also do broadsides, publish small, modest saddle-stitched collections, and will consider book-length collections (on a collaborative basis) *as time and dinero permits.*" Wants visual poetry and collage. "I am interested in discovery and self-transcendence." No academic, traditional, or rhyming poetry. Has published poetry by Dmitry Babenko, Patricia Salas, Anthony Zoutra, Sasha Surikov, Willi Melnikov, Laura Ryder, and Joel Lipman. The editor did not offer sample lines of poetry because he says, "*O!!Zone* needs to be seen." *O!!Zone* is 80-100 pgs., 8½×11, desktop-published, loaded with graphics. "Write for a catalog listing our titles. Our *O!!Zone 97, International Visual Poetry* ($25) and *O!!Zone 98* ($25) and *O!!Zone 99-00* ($25) are three anthologies that cover what's going on in international visual poetry."

How to Submit: Submit 3-6 poems at a time. No previously published poems or simultaneous submissions. No fax submissions. "Submissions of visual poetry via snail mail; textual poems may come by e-mail." Inquire before submitting via e-mail. Cover letter preferred. Has a large backlog, "but always open to surprises." Seldom comments on rejected poems. Guidelines available for SASE. Responds "soon." Pays 1-2 contributor's copies.

▢ ◯ ◎ **THE OAK (Specialized: college age and up); THE ACORN (Specialized: children); THE GRAY SQUIRREL (Specialized: senior citizens); THE SHEPHERD (Specialized: inspirational)**, 1530 Seventh St., Rock Island IL 61201. (309)788-3980. **Poetry Editor:** Betty Mowery.

Magazine Needs & How to Submit: *The Oak*, established in 1990, is a "publication for writers with poetry and fiction." Wants poetry of "no more than 35 lines and fiction of no more than 500 words. No restrictions as to types and style, but no pornography. Also takes fantasy and soft horror." *The Oak* appears quarterly. Established 1991, *The Gray Squirrel* is now included in *The Oak* and takes poetry of no more than 35 lines fiction up to 500 words from poets 60 years of age and up. Uses more than half of about 100 poems received each year. Include a SASE or mss will not be returned. Press run is 250, with 10 going to libraries. Subscription: $10. Sample: $3. Make all checks payable to *The Oak*. Submit 5 poems at a time. Accepts simultaneous submissions and previously published poems. Responds in 1 week. "*The Oak* does not pay in dollars or copies but you need not purchase to be published." Acquires first or second rights. *The Oak* holds several contests. Guidelines available for SASE.

Magazine Needs & How to Submit: *The Acorn*, established in 1988, is a "newsletter for young authors and teachers or anyone else interested in our young authors. Takes mss from kids K-12th grades. Poetry no more than 35 lines. It also takes fiction of no more than 500 words." *The Acorn* appears 4 times/year and "we take well over half of submitted mss." Press run is 100, with 6 going to libraries. Subscription: $10. Sample: $3. Make all checks payable to *The Oak*. Submit 5 poems at a time. Accepts simultaneous submissions and previously published poems. Responds in 1 week. "*The Acorn* does not pay in dollars or copies but you need not purchase to be published." Acquires first or second rights. Young authors, submitting to *The Acorn*, should put either age or grade on manuscripts. *The Shepherd*, established in 1996, is a quarterly publishing inspirational poetry from all ages. Poems may be up to 35 lines and fiction up to 500 words. "We want something with a message but not preachy." Subscription: $10. Sample: $3. Include SASE with all submissions.

Also Offers: Sponsors numerous contests. Guidelines available for SASE.

Advice: "Beginning poets should submit again as quickly as possible if rejected. Study the market: don't submit blind. Always include a SASE or rejected manuscripts will not be returned. Please make checks for *all* publications payable to *The Oak*."

$ ◯ **OASIS**, P.O. Box 626, Largo FL 33779-0626. (727)449-2186. E-mail: oasislit@aol.com. Website: www.l itline.org. Established 1992. **Editor:** Neal Storrs.

Magazine Needs: *Oasis* is a quarterly forum for high quality literary prose and poetry written almost exclusively by freelancers. Usually contains 6 prose pieces and the work of 4-5 poets. Wants "to see poetry of stylistic beauty. Prefer free verse with a distinct, subtle music. No superficial sentimentality, old-fashioned rhymes or rhythms." Has published poetry by Carolyn Stoloff, Fredrick Zydek, and Kim Bridgford. As a sample the editor selected these lines from "The Lightning Speech of Birds" by Corrine DeWinter:

> But now I must comply, twisting away from the clawed/lovers, shrinking from the familiar habits/of all three wives who have built cities and spires/under my skin/from the expectant crucifixions on the shoulder of the roads,/from the blessed damned on Venus' blushing sands.

Oasis is about 75 pgs., 7×10, attractively printed on heavy book paper, perfect-bound with medium-weight card cover, no art. Receives about 2,000 poems/year, accepts 1%. Press run is 300 for 90 subscribers of which 5 are libraries. Subscription: $20/year. Sample: $7.50.

How to Submit: Submit any number of poems. Accepts simultaneous submissions; rarely accepts previously published poems. Accepts e-mail submissions (include in body of message). Cover letter preferred. Time between acceptance and publication is usually 4 months. Seldom comments on rejected poems. Guidelines available for SASE. Responds "the same or following day more than 99% of the time." Sometimes sends prepublication galleys. Pays $5/poem and 1 contributor's copy. Acquires first or one-time rights.

☑ **$** ◎ **OBLATES (Specialized: religious, spirituality/inspirational)**, Missionary Association of Mary Immaculate, 9480 N. De Mazenod Dr., Belleville IL 62223-1160. (618)398-4848. Fax: (618)398-8788. Website: www.snows.org. **Editor:** Christine Portell. **Manuscript Editor:** Mary Mohrman.

Magazine Needs: *Oblates* is a bimonthly magazine circulating free to 500,000 benefactors. "We use well-written, perceptive traditional verse, average 12 lines. Avoid heavy allusions. We prefer a reverent, inspirational tone, but not overly 'sectarian and scriptural' in content." Has published poetry by Jean Conder Soule, Carlton J. Duncan, and Jeanette M. Land. *Oblates* is 24 pgs., digest-sized, saddle-stapled, using color inside and on the cover. Sample and guidelines for SAE and 2 first-class stamps.

How to Submit: Submit up to 2 poems at a time. Considers simultaneous submissions. Time between acceptance and publication "is usually within 1 to 2 years." Editor comments "occasionally, but always when ms 'just missed or when a writer shows promise.' " Responds within 6 weeks. Pays $50 plus 3 contributor's copies. Acquires first North American serial rights.

Advice: "We are a small publication very open to mss from authors—beginners and professionals. We do, however, demand professional quality work. Poets need to study our publication, and to send no more than one or two poems at a time. Content must be relevant to our older audience to inspire and motivate in a positive manner."

☑ **$** ◓ ◎ **OCEAN VIEW BOOKS (Specialized: form/style, science fiction)**, P.O. Box 9249, Denver CO 80209. Established 1981. **Editor:** Lee Ballentine.

Book/Chapbook Needs: Ocean View Books publishes "books of poetry by poets influenced by surrealism and science fiction." Publishes 2 paperbacks and 2 hardbacks/year. No "confessional/predictable, self-referential poems." Has published poetry by Anselm Hollo, Janet Hamill, and Tom Disch. Books are usually 100 pgs., $5\frac{1}{2} \times 8\frac{1}{2}$ or 6×9, offset-printed and perfect-bound with 4-color card cover, includes art. "Our books are distinctive in style and format. Interested poets should order a sample book for $5 (in the US) for an idea of our focus before submitting."

How to Submit: Submit a book project query including 5 poems. Accepts previously published poems and simultaneous submissions. Cover letter preferred. Time between acceptance and publication is up to 3 years. "If our editors recommend publication, we may circulate manuscripts to distinguished outside readers for an additional opinion. The volume of submissions is such that we can respond to queries only if we are interested in the project. If we're interested we will contact you within 4 months." Pays $100 honorarium and a number of author's copies (out of a press run of 500). "Terms vary per project."

Advice: "In 15 years, we have published about 40 books—most consisted of previously published poems from good journals. A poet's 'career' must be well-established before undertaking a book."

$ ▢ ◎ **OF UNICORNS AND SPACE STATIONS (Specialized: science fiction/fantasy)**, P.O. Box 200, Bountiful UT 84011-0200. E-mail: gene@genedavis.com. Website: www.genedavis.com/magazine (includes samples from magazine and guidelines). Established 1994. **Editor:** Gene Davis.

Magazine Needs: *Of Unicorns and Space Stations*, published biannually, features science fiction/fantasy literature. "Material written in traditional fixed forms are given preference. Poetry of only a scientific slant or that only uses science fiction/fantasy imagery will be considered." Accepts poetry written by children. *Of Unicorns and Space Stations* is 60 pgs., digest-sized, digital press, saddle-stapled with "spot color" illustrated card cover. Receives about 200 poems/year, accepts 2%. Press run is 100 for 100 subscribers; 2-3 distributed free to convention organizers and critics. Subscription: $16/4 issues. Sample: $4. Make checks payable to Gene Davis.

How to Submit: Submit 3 poems, with name and address on each page. "Manuscripts should be paper-clipped, never stapled." Accepts previously published poems; no simultaneous submissions. E-mail submissions are only accepted from subscribers. Cover letter preferred. "If sending fixed form poetry, mention what form you used in your cover letter. Editors pulling 16-hour shifts don't always spot poem types at 1 a.m." Time between acceptance and publication is up to 9 months. Poems are circulated to an editorial board of 2 editors. "Both have veto power over every piece." Seldom comments on rejected poems. Guidelines available for SASE or on website. Responds in 3 months. Pays 1 contributor's copy and "$5 flat rate for poetry." Acquires one-time rights, both electronic and hardcopy.

OFFERINGS, P.O. Box 1667, Lebanon MO 65536-1667. Established 1994. **Editor:** Velvet Fackeldey.

Magazine Needs: *Offerings* is a poetry quarterly. "We accept traditional and free verse from established and new poets, as well as students. Prefer poems of less than 30 lines. No erotica." Accepts poetry written by children; they may submit up to 4 poems a year. Has published poetry by Charles Portolano Diane Webster, and Gerald Zipper. As a sample we selected these lines from "All Things Away" by Nick R. Zemaiduk:

> We scrubbed the room and made the bed/as if some day he may return./Kept a fire fueled, instead/of wood, with memories, to burn/away the sharper edge of pain/the mind's eye holds against all hope/of fates to which our small complaints/are no more than a way to cope.

Offerings is 50-60 pgs., digest-sized, neatly printed and saddle-stapled with paper cover. Receives about 500 poems/year, accepts about 25%. Press run is 100 for 75 subscribers, 25 shelf sales. Single copy: $5; subscription: $16. Sample: $3.

How to Submit: Submit typed poems with name and address on each page. Students should also include grade level. SASE required. No simultaneous submissions. Seldom comments on rejected poems. Guidelines available for SASE. Responds in up 1 month. All rights revert to author after publication.

Advice: "We are unable to offer payment at this time (not even copies) but hope to be able to do so in the future. We welcome beginning poets."

OFFERTA SPECIALE; BERTOLA CARLA PRESS, Corso De Nicola 20, 10-128 Torino Italy. Established 1988. **Director/Editor:** Bertola Carla. **Co-Director:** Vitacchio Alberto.

Magazine Needs: *Offerta Speciale* is a biannual international journal appearing in May and November. Has published poetry by Federica Manfredini (Italy), Bernard Heidsieck (France), Richard Kostelanetz, and E. Mycue (US). As a sample the editor selected these lines from "My Lower Back" by Sheila Murphy:

> My lower back likes to be liquid/Dose of sugar ringside/And the thought of frost/As sacrosanct as meerschaum

Offerta Speciale is 56 pgs., digest-sized, neatly printed and saddle-stapled with glossy card cover. Receives about 300 poems/year, accepts about 40%. Press run is 500 for 60 subscribers. Single copy: $25; subscription: $100. Make checks payable to Carla Bertola.

How to Submit: Submit 3 poems at a time. No previously published poems or simultaneous submissions. Time between acceptance and publication is 1 year. Often comments on rejected poems. Guidelines available for SASE (or SAE and IRC). Pays 1 contributor's copy.

OFFICE NUMBER ONE (Specialized: form), 1708 S. Congress Ave., Austin TX 78704. E-mail: onocdingus@aol.com. Established 1988. **Editor:** Carlos B. Dingus.

Magazine Needs: Appearing 2-4 times/year, *Office Number One* is a "humorous, satirical zine of news information and events from parallel and alternate realities." In addition to stories, they want limericks, 3-5-3 or 5-7-5 haiku, and rhymed/metered quatrains. "Poems should be short (2-12 lines) and make a point. No long rambling poetry about suffering and pathos. Poetry should be technically perfect." Accepts poetry written by children. As for a sample, the editor says, "No one poem provides a fair sample." *Office Number One* is 12 pgs., 8½×11, computer set in 10 pt. type, saddle-stapled, with graphics and ads. Uses about 40 poems/year. Press run is 2,000 for 75 subscribers, 50 shelf sales; 1,600 distributed free locally. Single copy: $1.85; subscription: $8.82/6 issues. Sample: $2.

How to Submit: Submit up to 5 pgs. of poetry at a time. Accepts previously published poems and simultaneous submissions. Accepts e-mail submissions included in body of message. "Will comment on rejected poems if comment is requested." Publishes theme issues occasionally. Guidelines and upcoming themes available for SASE or by e-mail. Responds in 2 months. Pays "23¢" and 1 copy. Acquires "one-time use, and use in any *Officer Number One* anthology."

Advice: "Say something that a person can use to change his life."

ON SPEC: MORE THAN JUST SCIENCE FICTION (Specialized: regional, science fiction/fantasy, horror), P.O. Box 4727, Edmonton, Alberta T6E 5G6 Canada. E-mail: onspec@earthling.net. Website: www.icomm.ca/onspec/ (includes writer's guidelines, names and bios of editors, past editorials, excerpts from back issues, links for writers, and announcements). Established 1989. **Poetry Editor:** Barry Hammond.

Magazine Needs: *On Spec* is a quarterly featuring Canadian science fiction writers and artists. Wants work by Canadian poets only and only science fiction/speculative poetry; 100 lines maximum. Has published poetry by Sandra Kasturi and Alice Major. As a sample the editor selected these lines from "Wild Things" by Eileen Kernaghan:

> *you can sing small songs to soothe them/make them soft and secret beds to lie in//still you will wake in winter dawns/to find them crouched upon your pillow/their sharp claws unravelling/the frayed edges of your dreams*

On Spec is 112 pgs., digest-sized, offset-printed on recycled paper and perfect-bound with color cover, b&w art and ads inside. Receives about 100 poems/year, accepts 5%. Press run is 1,750 for 800 subscribers of which 10 are libraries, 600 shelf sales. Single copy: $5.95; subscription: $19.95 (both in Canadian funds). Sample: $7. **How to Submit:** Submit up to 5 poems of up to 100 lines at a time with SASE (or SAE and IRC). No previously published poems or simultaneous submissions. No submissions by fax or e-mail. Cover letter with poem titles and 2-sentence bio required. Deadlines: February 28, May 31, August 31 and November 30. Responds in 4 months maximum. Time between acceptance and publication is 6 months. Usually comments on rejected poems. Publishes theme issues. Guidelines and a list of upcoming themes are available for SASE or on website. Pays $20/poem and 1 copy, pays on acceptance. Acquires first North American serial rights.

◎ ONCE UPON A TIME (Specialized: poetry about writing or illustrating), 553 Winston Court, St. Paul MN 55118. Fax: (651)457-6223. E-mail: audreyouat@aol.com. Website: http://members.aol.com/ouatmag (includes general subscription information, sample article snippets, description of magazine, representative artwork, sample covers, comments by subscribers, guidelines, etc., plus how to get a free 4-page brochure). Established 1990. **Editor/Publisher:** Audrey B. Baird.
Magazine Needs: Published quarterly, *Once Upon A Time* is a support magazine for children's writers and illustrators. Poetry should be 20 lines maximum—writing or illustration-related. "No poems comparing writing to giving birth to a baby. Very overdone!" As a sample the editor selected this poem, "Writer at Work" by Anita Hunter:

> *Spent the morning in my writing room/Sharpened pencils/Threw out stencils/Cleaned up some files/ And then, all smiles/Brought my latest manuscript to bloom./By adding one small comma./After lunch, for inspiration/I read some books/Thought up new "hooks"/Made out long lists/Cleared mental mists/ And with true, keen dedication/Took out the one small comma.*

Once Upon A Time is 32 pgs., magazine-sized, stapled with glossy cover, includes art/graphics and a few ads. Receives about 40 poems/year, accepts about 60%. Press run is 1,000 for 900 subscribers. Single copy: $6; subscription: $24.25. Sample: $5. Make checks payable to Audrey B. Baird.
How to Submit: Submit no more than 6 poems at a time. Accepts previously published poems and simultaneous submissions. Cover letter preferred. Accepts submissions by fax but not by e-mail. Time between acceptance and publication "can be up to 2 years. Short poems usually printed in less than 1 year." Often comments on rejected poems. Guidelines available for SASE or on website. Responds in 1 month. Pays 2 contributor's copies. Acquires one-time rights.
Advice: "Don't send your piece too quickly. Let it sit for a week or more. Then re-read it and see if you can make it better. If you're writing rhyming poetry, the rhythm has to work. Count syllables! Accents, too, have to fall in the right place! Most rhyming poetry I receive has terrible rhythm. Don't forget SASE!"

◐ OPEN SPACES, 6327 C SW Capitol Hwy., Suite 134, Portland OR 97201-1937. (503)227-5764. Fax: (503)227-3401. Website: www.open-spaces.com (includes submission guidelines, table of contents, covers, sample articles, literary essays, and overview). Established 1997. **Poetry Editor:** Susan Juve-Hu Bucharest.
Magazine Needs: "*Open Spaces* is a quarterly which gives voice to the Northwest on issues that are regional, national and international in scope. Our readership is thoughtful, intelligent, widely read and appreciative of ideas and writing of the highest quality. With that in mind, we seek thoughtful, well-researched articles and insightful fiction, reviews and poetry on a variety of subjects from a number of different viewpoints. Although we take ourselves seriously, we appreciate humor as well." *Open Spaces* is 64 pgs., magazine-sized, sheet-fed printed, cover art and graphics and original art throughout. "We have received many submissions and hope to use 3-4 per issue." Press run is 5,000-10,000. Subscription: $25/year. Sample: $10. Make checks payable to Open Spaces Publications, Inc.
How to Submit: Submit 3-5 poems at a time. Accepts previously published poems and simultaneous submissions. No fax of e-mail submissions. Cover letter required. Time between acceptance and publication is 2-3 months. Poems are circulated to an editorial board. Seldom comments on rejected poems. Guidelines available on website. Responds in 3 months. Payment varies. Reviews books and chapbooks of poetry."
Advice: "Poets we have published include Vern Rutsala, Pattiann Rogers, Lou Masson and William Jolliff. Poetry is presented with care and respect.

▢ ◎ OPEN UNIVERSITY OF AMERICA PRESS; OPEN UNIVERSITY OF AMERICA (Specialized: religious, nature, distance learning, English pedagogy), 3916 Commander Dr., Hyattsville MD 20782-1027. Phone/fax: (301)779-0220. E-mail: openuniv@aol.com. Website: www.openuniversityofamerica.c om. Established 1965. **Co-Editors:** Mary Rodgers and Dan Rodgers.
Book/Chapbook Needs: "We buy artistic work outright before copyright or publication by the author. We include these literary pieces always with the author's name in our university publications, catalogues, lists, etc." Publishes 4 paperbacks and 4 hardbacks/year. "No restrictions on poetry. Shorter is better. One page set up for 6×9 is good. A set of poems (short chapbook) should be uniform." Interested in receiving work on the topics of "Catholic faith and culture; morality; nature; open learning and English pedagogy (teaching English) K-Ph.D.

Pre-published or pre-copyrighted or book-length poems are beyond our capability." Accepts poetry written by children (negotiations only with parent, however). Has published poetry by Castina Kennedy, John Tormento, Emebeat Bekele, and Raphael Flores. As a sample the editors selected this poem, "Reality," by Rosalee Dansan in *Catholic Teacher Poems, 1945-1995*:

> *Yesterday/I had dreams of tomorrow./Somewhere in tomorrowland,/Life with you./But dreams shatter/ Like glass;/Like mine did when halfway to my mouth,/Before I could taste the sweetness of the wine./ Today/I do not dream./I have no guarantee of tomorrow/For today I have only today.*

Books are usually 100-200 pgs., 6×9, computer/laser printed, perfect-bound (some sewn in library binding), soft cover, includes art.

How to Submit: Submit up to 10 poems at a time. No previously published poems or simultaneous submissions. Cover letter preferred. "We buy poems and small sets of poems outright (price negotiable), so we need pre-copyrighted, pre-published literary work. No whole books. When we publish compilations, we always list the name of the artist/author. Literary work is accepted on its own merit and its usefulness in perpetuity to the Press and to Open University of America. Make sure you want to put your poem for final and irrevocable sale."
Reading fee: $1/poem. Time between acceptance and publication is up to 2 years. Poems are circulated to an editorial board. "Two editors plus one consultant select work to be purchased for publication. Note that we purchase all rights for publication, total rights." Seldom comments on rejected poems. Responds to queries and mss in up to 3 weeks. Order sample books by sending $10 or order off the web.
Advice: "Today electronic publishing, overseas sales, and other mass selling mechanisms are running rough-shod over the rights of writers. We buy your verbal art at a fair, negotiated price before copyright and publication. We use your poem/poems always with your name attached to enhance our literary productions. We keep it in perpetuity in our Literary Trust. This is an effective way to get publicity for your name and your work, as well as to earn income."

☑ ◯ ◑ OPENED EYES POETRY & PROSE MAGAZINE; KENYA BLUE POETRY AWARD CONTEST; OPENED EYES SHORT STORY COMPETITION; EVA HASKELL PROSE AWARD, P.O. Box 21708, Brooklyn NY 11202-1708. (798)284-0569. E-mail: kenyablue@juno.com or kenyablue@excite.com. Website: www.kenyablue.com. Established 1998. **Editor-in-Chief:** Kenya Blue.
Magazine Needs: Appearing 3 times/year, *Opened Eyes* is a "venue for seniors, known poets, novice poets, and minority poets; offering a supportive environment and challenging environment." Wants "free verse, traditional forms; prose—all styles; all subject matter; short, poetic stories. No hate or sexually explicit/graphic poetry." Accepts poetry written by children. Has published poetry by Lynette Grant, Jay Chollick, Evie Ivy, Sol Rubin, Jihad Qasim, and Tom Oleszczuk. As a sample the editor selected these lines from Carol D. Meeks:

> *Among my flowers/these butterflies flaunt and flash/their stained-glass wings*

Opened Eyes is 8½×11, photocopied and either strip-bound or comb-bound with cardstock cover, includes art/graphics and ads. Receives about 100 poems/year, accepts about 95%. Publish 15 poems/issue. Press run is 100 for 45 subscribers of which 5 are libraries, 24 shelf sales; 4 distributed free to Poet's House. Subscription: $18/year. Sample: $7. Make checks payable to K. Blue.
How to Submit: Submit 1-3 poems at a time with **$3 reading fee if nonsubscriber.** Line length for poetry is 30 maximum. Accepts previously published poems and simultaneous submissions. Accepts e-mail submissions; include in body of message. "Type name, address, and e-mail in upper left hand corner. Submit typed poem in desired format for magazine and editor will try to accommodate." Time between acceptance and publication is up to 2 months. "Poems are circulated to editor and poetry consultant." Occasionally publishes theme issues. Guidelines and upcoming themes available for SASE. Responds in 3 weeks. Sometimes sends prepublication galleys. Acquires one-time rights.
Also Offers: "We sponsor one contest per issue, i.e., Kenya Blue Poetry Award (open to subscribers only) contest, Opened Eyes Short Story Competition, and Eva Haskell Prose Award. One winner per contest paid in copies of magazine and featured write-up. Opened Eyes Award, Kenya Blue Award, and haiku contest topics change yearly.
Advice: "Challenge yourself and take a first step in being creative via literature and via poetry."

🌐 $◯ ORBIS: AN INTERNATIONAL QUARTERLY OF POETRY AND PROSE, 27 Valley View, Primrose, Jarrow, Tyne-and-Wear NE32 5QT United Kingdom. Phone: 44 0191-489-7055. Fax: 44 0191-430-1297. E-mail: mikeshields@compuserve.com. Established 1968. **Editor:** Mike Shields.
Magazine Needs: *Orbis*, appearing quarterly, considers "all poetry so long as it's genuine in feeling and well executed of its type." Has published poetry by Sir John Betjeman, Ray Bradbury, Seamus Heaney, and Naomi Mitchison, as well as US poets Levertov, Piercy, Bell, Geddes, Wilbur, Kumin, and many others, "but are just as likely to publish absolute unknowns." *Orbis* is 64 pgs. minimum, 6×8½, flat-spined, professionally printed with glossy card cover. Receives "thousands" of submissions/year, accepts "less than 2%." Press run is 1,000 for 600 subscribers of which 50 are libraries. Single copy: £3.95 ($6); subscription: £15 ($28). Sample: $2 (or £1).
How to Submit: "Note: ORBIS may be closing down or changing editor in the next year. Please query before submitting." Submit 1 poem/sheet, typed on 1 side only. Does not need bio. No fax or e-mail submissions.

Enclose IRCs for reply, not US postage. Responds in 2 months. Pays $10 or more/acceptance plus 1 free copy. Each issue carries £50 in prizes paid on basis of reader votes. Editor comments on rejected poems "occasionally—if we think we can help. *Orbis* is completely independent and receives no grant-aid from anywhere."

$☑ ORCHISES PRESS, P.O. Box 20602, Alexandria VA 22320-1602. E-mail: lathbury@gmu.edu. Website: http://mason.gmu.edu/~rlathbur (includes submission guidelines, sample poems, book covers, and online catalog). Established 1983. **Poetry Editor:** Roger Lathbury.
Book/Chapbook Needs: Orchises is a small press publisher of literary and general material in flat-spined paperbacks and in hardcover. "Although we will consider mss submitted, we prefer to seek out the work of poets who interest us." Regarding poetry, Orchises has "no restrictions, really; but it must be technically proficient and deeply felt. I find it increasingly unlikely that I would publish a ms unless a fair proportion of its contents has appeared previously in respected literary journals." Has published *Chokecherries* by Peter Klappert and *Full Nova* by Caley O'Dwyer. Publishes about 4 flat-spined paperbacks of poetry a year, averaging 96 pgs., and some casebound books. Most paperbacks are $12.95. Hardbacks are $20-21.95 each.
How to Submit: Submit 5-6 poems at a time. No e-mail submissions. Poems must be typed. When submitting, "tell where poems have previously been published." Brief cover letter preferred. Guidelines available on website. Responds in 1 month. Pays 36% of money earned once Orchises recoups its initial costs and has a "generous free copy policy."

☑ ◑ THE OREGON REVIEW; BACCHAE PRESS; SCOW BAY BOOKS; BACCHAE PRESS POETRY CHAPBOOK CONTEST, No. 10 Sixth St., Suite 215, Astoria OR 97103. E-mail: brown@pacifier.com. Established 1992. **Publisher/Editor:** Dr. Robert Brown.
Magazine Needs: *The Oregon Review* is "a semiannual literary journal. We publish mostly established poets and especially encourage writers from Oregon and the Pacific Northwest." Wants "short lyric poetry that takes risks. Especially like literary/intellectual poetry. A little tired of yesterday's confessions." Does not want "overly sentimental, didactic, racist, sexist, homophobic, blah, blah, blah. . . ." Recently published poetry by Julia Wendell, Bart Baxter, and Hal Sirowitz. *The Oregon Review* is 60-90 pgs. digest-sized, offset-printed, perfect-bound, paper cover, with art/graphics and ads. Receives about 1,000 poems/year, accepts about 5%. Publishes about 30 poems/issue. Press run is 300 for 50 subscribers of which 20 are libraries, 200 shelf sales; 40 are distributed free to contributors. Single copy $5. Make checks payable to *The Oregon Review*.
How to Submit: Submit 3-5 poems at a time. Accepts simultaneous submissions; no previously published poems. No fax, e-mail, disk submissions. Cover letter is preferred. Include SASE. Time between acceptance and publication is 3-6 months. Seldom comments on rejected poems. Guidelines are available for SASE. Responds in 1 month. Always sends prepublication galleys. Pays 1 contributor's copy. Acquires one-time rights. Reviews books and chapbooks of poetry in 300-500 words, single book format. Poets may send books for review consideration to Dr. Robert Brown.
Book/Chapbook Needs: Under the imprints Bacchae Press and Scow Bay Books, publishes poets who are in transition from smaller to larger publishers. Publishes 2 paperbacks and 4 chapbooks/year. Wants "high quality, literary poetry by poets who read and reflect. No greeting card verse." As a sample the editor selected these lines from "In Transit" which appears in *Sending Messages Over Inconceivable Distances* by Karen Braucher:

> *Forgive me, my new daughter, if I'm clutching you/a little hard. The third airport today, loud voices,*
> *hot air,/we stand in a long, slow line for Japanese Customs, your delicate/two-month-old Chinese face*
> *contorts into a scream, a fetus/being carried through some strange birth canal. No one knows/how far*
> *we've come, how far we've left to go . . .*

Books are usually 60-90 pgs., offset-printed, perfect-bound, heavy card stock cover, with art/graphics. Chapbooks are usually 28 pgs., offset-printed, saddle-stapled, heavy card stock cover.
How to Submit: Query first with 5 sample poems and cover letter with brief bio and publication credits. Accepts previously published poems and simultaneous submissions. No fax or e-mail submissions. Time between acceptance and publication is 6-12 months. Poems are circulated to an editorial board. Seldom comments on rejected poems. Responds to queries in 1 month; to mss in 2 months. Pays 25 author's copies (out of a press run of 300-500). Order sample books/chapbooks by sending $5 to Bacchae Press.
Also Offers: Sponsors the annual Bacchae Press Poetry Chapbook Competition. Winner receives 25 copies of the chapbook, scheduled to be published in August. Submit 16-24 typed ms pages, no more than 1 poem/pg. "With your submission, include a brief bio, acknowledgements, and a SASE for return of your manuscript and/or contest results." Entry fee: $9, includes copy of the winning chapbook. Deadlines: April 15. Winners will be announced in June.

ALWAYS include a self-addressed, stamped envelope (SASE) when sending a ms or query to a publisher within your own country. When sending material to other countries, include a self-addressed envelope and International Reply Coupons (IRCs), available at many post offices.

OSIRIS, AN INTERNATIONAL POETRY JOURNAL/UNE REVUE INTERNATIONALE (Specialized: translations, bilingual), P.O. Box 297, Deerfield MA 01342-0297. Established 1972. **Poetry Editor:** Andrea Moorhead.

Magazine Needs: *Osiris* is a semiannual that publishes contemporary poetry in English, French, and Italian without translation and in other languages with translation, including Polish, Danish, and German. Wants poetry which is "lyrical, non-narrative, multi-temporal, post-modern, well-crafted. Also looking for translations from non-IndoEuropean languages." Has published poetry by Robert Marteau (France), D.G. Jones (Canada), Vassilis Amanatidis (Greece), Flavio Ermini (Italy), and Ingrid Swanberg (US) As a sample the editor selected these lines from "Abstract As Air" by D.G. Jones:

> the whorl of intricate grass/in the grass, almost nothing, an/abstraction from song.

Osiris is 40 pgs., 6×9, saddle-stapled with graphics and photos. There are 15-20 pgs. of poetry in English in each issue of this publication. Print run is 500 with 50 subscription copies sent to college and university libraries, including foreign libraries. Receives 200-300 submissions/year, accepts about 12. Single copy: $6; subscription: $12. Sample: $3.

How to Submit: Submit 4-6 poems at a time. "Poems should be sent regular mail." Include short bio and SASE with submission. "Translators should include a letter of permission from the poet or publisher as well as copies of the original text." Responds in 1 month. Sometimes sends prepublication galleys. Pays 5 contributor's copies.

Advice: "It is always best to look at a sample copy of a journal before submitting work, and when you do submit work, do it often and do not get discouraged. Try to read poetry and support other writers."

OSRIC PUBLISHING; DISCO GOTHIC ENTERPRISES; THE WHITE CROW, P.O. Box 4501, Ann Arbor MI 48106-4501. E-mail: chris@osric.com. Website: http://osric.com and http://wcrow.com (includes guidelines, contact information, reviews, and samples). Established 1993. **Editor:** Christopher™ Herdt. **Assistant Editor:** Mrrranda L. Tarrow.

Magazine Needs: *The White Crow* is a quarterly "literate, not literary journal. It contains poetry and fiction that is meaningful and that will appeal to an educated, but not necessarily high-brow audience. Something that even an electrical engineer might enjoy." Wants "nothing bigger than a breadbox. No one-pagers that use the word black more than four times and no 'throbbing, beefy torpedo' poems." Has published poetry by Eileen Bell, Stephen Chapman, Jas Isle, and Lyn Lifshin. *The White Crow* is 32 pgs., 5½×8½, sometimes photocopied, sometimes offset-printed, saddle-stapled with black only cover, includes art and graphics. Receives about 1,000 poems/year, accepts 10%. Press run is 400 for 50 subscribers, 200 shelf sales; 50 distributed free to reviewers and associates. Single copy: $2; subscription: $6. Sample (including guidelines): $2. Make checks payable to Osric Publishing.

How to Submit: Submit 5 poems at a time. Accepts previously published poems and simultaneous submissions. No e-mail or disk submissions. Cover letter preferred. Time between acceptance and publication is about 1 month. Poems are circulated to an editorial board. "The editors all get together and drink heavily, eat some food, and rate and berate the submissions." Always comments on rejected poems. Guidelines are available for SASE or on website. Responds in about 6 months. Pays 1 contributor's copy. Acquires first rights. Staff reviews books and chapbooks of poetry and other magazines in 100 words, single book format. Send books for review consideration to Christopher™ Herdt.

Book/Chapbook Needs & How to Submit: Osric Publishing seeks "poetry and short fiction for the literate, not literary." Publishes 1 paperback and 1 chapbook/year. Books are usually 32 pgs., 8½×5½, photocopied or offset-printed and saddle-stapled with cardstock cover, uses art/graphics. Query first, with a few sample poems and a cover letter with brief bio and publication credits. Responds to queries and mss in 6 months. Pays 5 author's copies (out of a press run of 200). Order sample books by sending $2 to Osric Publishing.

Also Offers: Disco Gothic Enterprises sponsors infrequent contests.

Advice: "No poems about poetry, no poems about writing poetry, no stories about writing stories."

OTHER VOICES, Garneau P.O. Box 52059, 8210-109 St., Edmonton, Alberta T6G 2T5 Canada. Established 1988. **Contact:** poetry editors.

Magazine Needs: *Other Voices* appears 2 times/year in the Spring and Fall. "We are devoted to the publication of quality literary writing—poetry, fiction, nonfiction; also reviews and artwork. We encourage submissions by new and established writers. Our only desire for poetry is that it is good! We encourage submissions by women and members of minorities, but we will consider everyone's. We never publish popular/sentimental greeting-card-type poetry or anything sexist, racist, or homophobic." Has published poetry by Bert Almon, Heidi Greco, Robin S. Chapman, Zoë Landale, and Erina Harris. As a sample the editor selected these lines from "One Breast" by Chris Smart:

> The word cancer slips/into their house/opens lace curtains, leaves/a trail of mud. A presence/breathes
> at the window/murmurs at the door.//A breast blooms/in the garden.//Once flowers bloomed/on the
> window sills/and the scent flooded/the house.

Other Voices is 100-120 pgs., 21½×14cm, professionally printed and perfect-bound with color cover, includes art and ads. Receives about 800 poems/year, accepts 4%. Press run is 500 for 330 subscribers of which 7 are libraries, 60 shelf sales. Subscription: $18/year in Canada, $23 US, $28 overseas. Sample: $10.

How to Submit: Submit 2-6 poems at a time. Include SAE with IRC. "Please limit your submissions to a maximum of 6 pages of poetry and send only 1 submission every 6 months." No previously published poems or simultaneous submissions. Cover letter preferred. "Please include short bio. Phone numbers, fax numbers, and e-mail addresses are helpful." Spring submission deadline: March 15; fall deadline is September 15. "We are currently discussing moving our deadlines up to September 1 and March 1. Poets may want to submit by those dates to be on the safe side." Time between acceptance and publication is 1 month. Poems are circulated to an editorial board. "Poems are read and assessed independently by five poetry editors. After the deadline, we gather and 'haggle' over which poems to accept." Seldom comments on rejected poems. Publishes theme issues. Guidelines and upcoming themes are available for SASE (or SAE with IRC) or on website. Responds in up to 6 months. Pays small honorarium plus subscription. Acquires first North American serial rights. Reviews books of poetry in 1,000 words, single or double book format. Poets may send books for review consideration to Editorial Collective.

Also Offers: "We typically hold one contest per year, but the time, fees, and theme vary. Check our website for details."

Advice: "Please take note of our September and March deadlines. If you just miss a deadline, it could take up to six months for a reply."

$ OUR FAMILY (Specialized: religious, social issues, spirituality/inspirational, themes, family/marriage/parenting), Box 249, Battleford, Saskatchewan S0M 0E0 Canada. (306)937-7771. Fax: (306)937-7644. E-mail: editor@ourfamilymagazine.com. Website: www.ourfamilymagazine.com. Established 1949. **Editor:** Marie-Louise Ternier-Gommers.

Magazine Needs: *Our Family* is a monthly religious magazine for Roman Catholic families in Canada. "Any form of poetry is acceptable. In content we look for simplicity and vividness of imagery. The subject matter should center on the human struggle to live out one's relationship with the God of the Bible in the context of our modern world. We do not want to see science fiction poetry, metaphysical speculation poetry, or anything that demeans or belittles the spirit of human beings or degrades the image of God in him/her as it is described in the Bible." Has published poetry by Nadene Murphy and Arthur Stilwell. *Our Family* is 40 pgs., magazine-sized, glossy color paper cover, using drawings, cartoons, two-color ink. Publishes about 5% of all poetry received. Press run is 10,000 of which 48 are libraries. Single copy: $2; subscription: $17.95 Canada, $23.95 US. Sample: $3.

How to Submit: Will consider poems of 4-30 lines. Accepts simultaneous submissions. Accepts e-mail and fax submissions. "Please include submission in the body of the e-mail. No attachments!" Guidelines and a list of upcoming themes are available on website or by SASE, SAE with IRC, or SAE with personal check for $1.25 (as American postage cannot be used in Canada). Responds within 2 months after receipt. Pays 75¢/line.

Advice: "The essence of poetry is imagery. The form is less important. Really good poets use both effectively."

OUR JOURNEY (Specialized: recovery issues), 202 SE 188th Ave. Apt. 9, Portland OR 97233. E-mail: lynnie78@juno.com. Website: www.geocities.com/our_recovery_journey (includes writer's guidelines, upcoming issue topics, contest guidelines, non-profit information, and links to other recovery-based pages). Established 1994. **Editor:** Wendy Apgar.

 • *Our Journey* is interested in receiving poetry about hope and healing which are topics included in every issue.

Magazine Needs: Published by Our Journey, Inc., a 501(c)(3) tax deductable, nonprofit corporation, *Our Journey* is a quarterly newsletter featuring "poetry, articles, original art, and occasional book reviews by those involved or interested in the recovery process." Wants "recovery-based poetry; all inclusive, not limited to recovery of only one (e.g., addictions, incest, pain, abuse, anger, healing, etc.); will consider any length. Each issue has specific topics. No poetry which is not easily understood or which is inappropriately sexually graphic (query editor if unsure about specific poem or essay)." Accepts poetry written by children. Has published poetry by Marge Rogers, Karen Kallis, Ruth Gratlan, Sheila Roark, and Heidi Sands. As a sample the editor selected this untitled poem by Pam Clarke:

> Nobody wanted to know/what was going on in my head/To see the woman inside/Crying out for help/
> Memories haunting endlessly/Begging to be set free

Our Journey is 14-18 pgs., neatly printed on bond paper and corner stapled, no cover, contains clip art. Receives about 250-300 poems/year, accepts about 70%. Press run is 225 for 70 subscribers. Single copy: $3; subscription: $11.95/year, $14 Canada, $17 overseas. Sample: $1 with SASE.

How to Submit: Submit any number of poems; 1/page, typed with name and address in upper left corner. "Only mss with #10 SASE will be acknowledged or returned." Accepts previously published poems and simultaneous submissions. Accepts e-mail submissions (include in body of message). "Material may also be submitted via e-mail. Two poems per each e-mail, but may send as many e-mail submissions as desire (i.e., 3 e-mails total 6 poems). If accepted for publication a hard copy must then be submitted via US mail with the completed release form which will be e-mailed upon acceptance." Cover letter preferred. Time between acceptance and publication is within 1 year. If asked, will offer feedback. Publishes theme issues. Upcoming themes: March 2001: Inner Child and Parenting, Faith in Recovery; June 2001: Addictions, Guilt, Shame; September 2001: Abuse, Grief, Loneliness; December 2001: Masks, Safety and Support, Depression. Responds in 6 weeks. Pays 1 contributor's copy. Acquires one-time rights. Poets may send books for review consideration, if published.

Also Offers: Sponsors 2-4 annual contests for subscribers. Awards: 1st Prize-$20, 2nd Prize-$10, 3rd Prize-$5. Entry fee: $2/poem. Send #10 SASE for details.

⬜ ◎ **OUTER DARKNESS: WHERE NIGHTMARES ROAM UNLEASHED (Specialized: horror, mystery, science fiction, dark fantasy)**, 1312 N. Delaware Place, Tulsa OK 74110. Established 1994. **Editor:** Dennis J. Kirk.
Magazine Needs: *Outer Darkness* is a quarterly magazine featuring short stories, poetry, and art in the genres of horror, dark fantasy, and science fiction. Wants "all styles of poetry, though traditional rhyming verse is preferred. Send verse that is dark and melancholy in nature. Nothing experimental—very little of this type of verse is published in *Outer Darkness*." Has published poetry by John Grey, Steve Vertlieb, John Maclay, and Corrine De Winter. *Outer Darkness* is 40-60 pgs., 8½×5½, photocopied, saddle-stapled, glossy cover, includes cover art, cartoons and illustrations and runs ads for other publications. Receives about 200 poems/year, accepts 20%. Press run is 200, 25% to subscribers, 25% to contributors, 25% sample copy sales, 25% to advertisers, free copies, etc. Single copy: $3.95; subscription: $11.95.
How to Submit: Submit up to 3 poems at a time, no longer than 60 lines each. Accepts simultaneous submissions; no previously published poems. Cover letter preferred. "Poets are encouraged to include cover letters with their submissions, with biographical information, personal interests, past publishing credits, etc. I strongly prefer hardcopy submissions rather than disks." Always comments on rejected poems. Guidelines available for SASE. Responds in up to 6 weeks. Sends prepublication galleys, when requested. Pays 2 copies. Acquires one-time rights.
Advice: "I've noticed that interest in traditional metered verse is increasing. This is the type of poetry I feature most frequently in *Outer Darkness*. Take time and care in writing verse. Maintain a consistent mood and tone; get the most you can out of each line, each word. This obviously takes more time; but, in the end, it will pay off."

⬛ ⬜ ◪ ◎ **THE OUTER RIM (Specialized: science fiction/fantasy, horror)**, (formerly Jupiter's Freedom), P.O. Box 110217, Palm Bay FL 32911-0217. Fax: (419)844-8388. E-mail: contact@theouterrim.org. Website: www.theouterrim.org. Established 1998. **Editor:** Christine Smalldone.
Magazine Needs: *The Outer Rim* is a quarterly online journal featuring fiction, poetry, art, and articles. Looking for "works which span the regions of science fiction—from speculative fiction to horror, fantasy, and works of the surreal. I want poetry with edge, style and innovative thinking; with the ability to paint a visual landscape and go in new directions. Nothing sweet and sappy. I don't mind happy endings, just do them in an interesting way." Has published poetry by Rick Sears, Joanne Tolson, and Margaret Christmas. As a sample we selected these lines from "Eating Their Own Faces" by Rick Sears:
> they will be slain./their own laughing eyes,/driving them further/into insanity./they will be cast as dung/
> among themselves. . ./feeding madly/upon their own/worthless flesh.

Subscription: "$20/year for 3-4 CD-roms of our magazine." Sample: "$5 for a single issue or $10 for a double issue."
How to Submit: Submit 1-3 poems at a time. Accepts e-mail (as attached file) and disk submissions; format files as .txt, .doc. Cover letter preferred. Time between acceptance and publication is up to 2 months. Often comments on rejected poems. Guidelines and specifications on electronic or disk submissions are available for SASE or by e-mail. Responds in 3 weeks. Pays 1 copy on CD-rom."
Advice: "We are a SCIFI, FANTASY, & HORROR zine. I am tired of getting romance stories and poetry or stuff that is really light on the genres and subjects we cover. Don't even try to send this stuff in to us for I will just throw it away. We are ready for new and interesting works that can take us for a ride and change how we think and feel about the world in which we live. Try to evoke an emotion, any emotion, show us who you are and the voice that is your words. Freaks, weirdos, and bizarre writers unite and send in the goods. We get a lot of submissions and do not have the time and energy to spellcheck every single thing we accept. So check and double check your spelling and grammar before you send because how you send it and we accept it is how we print it."

⬜ ◪ ◎ **OUTRIDER PRESS (Specialized: women/feminism, animals, love/romance/erotica, nature/rural/ecology, gay/lesbian/bisexual, anthology, humor)**, 937 Patricia Lane, Crete IL 60417-1362. (708)672-6630. Fax: (708)672-5820. E-mail: outriderpr@aol.com. Website: www.outriderpress.com (includes publication titles, prices, ordering information, general guidelines/themes, address for complete guidelines, Tallgrass Writers Guild information, and membership). Established 1988. **Senior Editor:** Whitney Scott. **President:** Phyllis Nelson.
Book/Chapbook Needs: Outrider publishes 1-3 novels/anthologies/chapbooks annually. Wants "poetry dealing with the terrain of the human heart and plotting inner journeys; growth and grace under pressure. No bag ladies, loves-that-never-were, please." Has published poetry by Pamela Miller, David T. Lloyd, James Wheldon, Margo Tamez, and Cynthia Gallaher. As a sample we selected these lines from "Geese in Coming Rain" by Lyn Lifshin, from the anthology *Feathers, Fins & Fur*:
> only a few blood/leaves on the maple./Grass nibbled closer//to the house. The/geese move in waves/
> toward pewter, a/clot on the edge./Sky colorless on/the skin of water.

Feathers, Fins & Fur is 256 pgs., digest-sized, attractively printed and perfect-bound with glossy card cover, $15.95.

How to Submit: Submit 3-4 poems at a time with SASE. Include name, address, phone/fax number, and e-mail address on every poem. Accepts simultaneous submissions, if specified. Cover letter preferred. Responds to queries in 3 months, to mss in 6 months. Pays 1 copy.

Also Offers: Outrider publishes a themed anthology annually in August, with cash prizes for best poetry and short fiction. Submit up to 4 poems, no longer than 1 page in length (single spacing OK). **Reading fee:** $16, $12 for Tallgrass Writers Guild members. Guidelines available for SASE. Deadline: February 25, 2002. Published in August 2002. Our 2002 theme: FOOD. The press is affiliated with the Tallgrass Writers Guild, an international organization open to all who support equality of voices in writing. Annual membership fee: $30. Information available for SASE or on website.

Advice: "We look for visceral truths expressed without compromise, coyness, or cliché. Go for the center of the experience. Pull no punches."

OWEN WISTER REVIEW, Box 3625, University of Wyoming, Laramie WY 82071. (307)766-3819 or (307)766-6109. Fax: (307)766-4027. E-mail: owr@uwyo.edu. Website: www.uwyo.edu/owr (includes guidelines, samples, purchasing information, etc.). Established 1978. **Contact:** Editor.

Magazine Needs: *Owen Wister Review* is the annual literary and art magazine (appearing in February) of the University of Wyoming. Has published poetry by Robert Roripaugh, Walt McDonald, Michael McIrvin, and Alan Britt. *Owen Wister Review* is 100-120 pgs., 6×9, professionally printed and perfect-bound with art on the cover and inside and spoken word CD. Receives more than 500 submissions/year, accepts 4-6%. Press run is 500. Single copy: $8.95; subscription: $15 for 2 years/2 issues. Sample: $5. Back issues: $5 each.

How to Submit: Submit up to 5 poems. No previously published poems; simultaneous submissions discouraged. Cover letter required. May query or submit by fax (must include mailing address). Submission deadline December 1. Send spoken word submissions on cassette tape or CD. Poems are circulated to an editorial board. Guidelines available for SASE or on website. Responds in 3 months. Pays 1 copy and 10% discount on additional copies. Acquires first rights.

OXFORD MAGAZINE, 261 Bachelor Hall, Miami University, Oxford OH 45056. (513)529-1954. E-mail: oxmag@geocities.com. Website: www.geocities.com/Soho/gallery/44100. Established 1984. **Editor:** Deborah Kennedy.

 • Work published in *Oxford Magazine* has been included in the *Pushcart Prize* anthology.

Magazine Needs: *Oxford Magazine* appears annually, in the spring. "We are open in terms of form, content, and subject matter. We have eclectic tastes, ranging from New Formalism to Language poetry to Nuyorican poetry." Has published poetry by Eve Shelnutt, Denise Duhamel, and Walter McDonald. *Oxford Magazine* is 220 pgs., 6×9, professionally printed and flat-spined. Press run is 1,000. Sample: $7.

How to Submit: Submit 3-5 poems at a time. Accepts simultaneous submissions; no previously published poems. No e-mail submissions. Cover letter preferred. Reads submissions September 1 through January 31. Pays copies only. Acquires first North American serial rights.

OXYGEN, 537 Jones St., PMB 999, San Francisco CA 94102. (415)776-9681. E-mail: Oxygen@slip.net (no e-mail submissions!). Established 1991. **Editor:** Richard Hack.

Magazine Needs: *Oxygen* is published 1-2 times/year. "We are open to many forms in many categories (e.g., surrealist, expressionist, narrative, devotional, et al.). We do not like poetry that smacks too much of workshop blandness and compromise, nor do we generally like academic poetry, uninformed cafe poetry, and some others. But we are not averse to hermetic poetry, allusive poetry, or simple, clear verse. Deeper delving and passion are hoped for." Has published poetry by Victor Martinez, Sergei Yesenin, Ronald Sauer, Steve Arntson, and Maura O'Connor. *Oxygen* is 100-130 pgs., 5½×8½, offset-printed and perfect-bound with laminated solid color cover, includes drawings and photos. Receives about 4,500 poems/year, accepts 1%. Publishes 50 poems/issue. Press run is 500. "We sell about 300-350 in stores and on newsstands in the Bay Area and nationally through DeBoer." Subscription: $18/4 issues. Sample: $5.

How to Submit: Submit up to 10 poems at a time. Accepts previously published poems ("as long as previous venue and its circulation are made known") and simultaneous submissions. No e-mail submissions. Always send SASE for response. Time between acceptance and publication is up to 6 months. Guidelines available for SASE. Responds in 2 months or less. Always sends prepublication galleys. Pays 2 contributor's copies. Acquires one-time rights, "plus right to use in future anthologies (spelled out in acceptance letter)." Occasionally reviews books and chapbooks of poetry and other magazines. Poets may send books for review consideration.

OYSTER BOY REVIEW; OFF THE CUFF BOOKS, P.O. Box 83, Chapel Hill NC 27514. E-mail: editors@oysterboyreview.com. Website: wwwoysterboyreview.com (includes complete issues, contacts, and submission guidelines). Established 1993. **Poetry Editor:** Jeffery Beam.

Magazine Needs: *Oyster Boy Review* appears 4 times/year. "We're interested in the underrated, the ignored, the misunderstood, and the varietal. We'll make some mistakes. 'All styles are good except the boring kind'—

Voltaire." Accepts poetry written by children; "We're about to publish a three year-old." Has published poetry by Jonathan Williams, Cid Corman, Lyn Lifshin, and Paul Dilsaver. As a sample the editor selected these lines from "Night" by Thomas Meyer:

> When it flowers/night fills/with a cruelty/I have done you/whose fruit is sweet

Oyster Boy Review is 60 pgs., 6½×11, Docutech printed and stapled with paper cover, includes photography and ads. Receives about 1,500 poems/year, accepts 2%. Press run is 200 for 30 subscribers, 100 shelf sales; 30 distributed free to editors, authors. Subscription: $12.

How to Submit: Submit up to 5 poems at a time. No previously published poems or simultaneous submissions. Accepts e-mail submissions if poems are included in body of message. Cover letter preferred. Postal submissions require SASE. Do not submit mss in late December. "Upon acceptance, authors asked to provide electronic version of work and a biographical statement." Time between acceptance and publication is 6 months. Seldom comments on rejected poems. Guidelines are available by e-mail and on website. Responds in 3 months. Pays 2 copies. Reviews books and chapbooks of poetry in 250-500 words (1st books only), in single or multi-book format. Poets may send books for review consideration.

Book/Chapbook Needs: *Off the Cuff is not open to submissions or solicitations.* Off the Cuff Books publishes "longer works and special projects of authors published in *Oyster Boy Review.*"

Advice: "*Oyster Boy Review* responds to freshness—to the unschooled enthusiasm that leads to fresh idioms and subjects—without kowtowing to any camps, mainstream or not."

P.D.Q. (POETRY DEPTH QUARTERLY), 5836 North Haven Dr., North Highlands CA 95660. (916)331-3512. E-mail: poetdpth@aol.com Website: www.angelfire.com/biz/PoetsGuild/guide.html. Established 1995. **Publisher:** G. Elton Warrick. **Editor:** Joyce Odam.

● "*P.D.Q.* editor submits nominations for the Pushcart Prize."

Magazine Needs: *P.D.Q.* wants "original poetry that clearly demonstrates an understanding of craft. All styles accepted." Does not want "poetry which is overtly religious, erotic, inflammatory, or demeans the human spirit." Has published poetry by Jane Blue, Taylor Graham, Simon Perchik, Carol Hamilton, B.Z. Niditch, and Danyen Powell. *P.D.Q.* is 35-60 pgs., digest-sized, coated and saddle-stapled with a glossy color cover and original art. Receives 1,800-2,000 poems/year, accepts about 10%. Press run is 200 of which 5 subscribers are libraries. Single: $5; subscription: $18.50 (add $10/year for foreign subscriptions). Make checks payable to G. Elton Warrick.

How to Submit: Submit 3-5 poems of any length, "typewritten and presented exactly as you would like them to appear," maximum 52 characters/line (including spaces), with name and address on every page. All submissions should include SASE (or SAE with IRC) and cover letter with short 3-10 line bio and publication credits. "Manuscripts without SASE or sufficient postage will not be read or returned." No simultaneous submissions; accepts previously published poems "occasionally" with publication credits. Accepts e-mail submissions. Guidelines available for SASE or on website. Responds in 3 months. Pays 1 contributor's copy.

PACIFIC COAST JOURNAL; FRENCH BREAD AWARDS; FRENCH BREAD PUBLICATIONS, P.O. Box 56, Carlsbad CA 92018. E-mail: paccoastj@frenchbreadpublications.com. Website: www.frenchbreadpublications.com/pcj (includes guidelines, poetry, and contest information). Established 1992. **Editor:** Stillson Graham.

Magazine Needs: *Pacific Coast Journal* is a quarterly "unprofessional literary magazine that prints first-time authors, emerging authors, established authors, and authors who are so visible that everyone's sick of them." Wants "offbeat poetry, visual poetry, poetry that is aware of itself. We don't rule out rhyming poetry, but rarely do we accept it." Has published poetry by Nils Clausen, Joan Payne Kincaid, and Hugh Fox. As a sample the editor selected these lines by Greg Russell:

> poetry is variety, often intense,/frequently emotional, or deeply/personal. this poem isn't any of/those/
> things.

Pacific Coast Journal is 56 pgs., 5½×8½, photocopied and saddle-stapled with a card stock cover and b&w photos and artwork. Receives 400-500 poems/year, accepts about 5-10%. Press run is 200 for 100 subscribers. Single copy: $3; subscription: $12. Sample: $2.50.

How to Submit: Submit up to 6 poems or 12 pages at a time. Accepts simultaneous submissions; no previously published poems. No e-mail submissions. Cover letter preferred. Time between acceptance and publication is up to 18 months. Seldom comments on rejected poems. Guidelines available for SASE or by e-mail. Responds in 4 months. Pays 1 contributor's copy. Acquires one-time rights. Reviews novels, short story collections, and chapbooks of poetry in 1,500 words, single format. Poets may send books for review consideration.

Book/Chapbook Needs & How to Submit: French Bread Publications also occasionally publishes chapbooks of poetry, short story collections and short novellas. Books are similar to the journal in format. Has published *Literary Junkies* by Errol Miller. Query first with 5-8 sample poems, a cover letter and a list of credits for all the poems in the ms. Responds to queries in 2 months, to mss (if invited) in 4 months. Pays royalties and 10% of press run.

Also Offers: Also sponsors the French Bread Awards for short fiction/poetry. Entry fee: $6 for a group of up to 4 poems (no longer than 8 pgs. total). 1st Prize: $50. 2nd Prize: $25. Deadline: August 1. Details available for SASE.

Advice: "Most poetry looks like any other poetry. We want experiments in what poetry is."

PALANQUIN; PALANQUIN POETRY SERIES, Dept. of English, University of South Carolina-Aiken, 171 University Pkwy., Aiken SC 29801. E-mail: phebed@aiken.sc.edu. Established 1988. **Editor:** Phebe Davidson.

Book/Chapbook Needs: The press sponsors annual fall and spring chapbooks contests and publishes occasional longer books of poetry. Does not want "sentimental, religious, consciously academic" poetry. Has published poetry by Robert Parham and Dana Wildsmith. As a sample the editor selected these lines by Laura Lee Washburn:

> the clouds come down from the sky./They climb monkey-fashion on slick strings./They come leaving
> bruises/against the pale spots of where they have been.

How to Submit: Contest deadlines are May 15 and October 15 annually. Submissions should include 20-25 pages of poetry plus bio and acknowledgements. Include SASE for reply. Responds in 3 months. The $10 entry fee includes a copy of the winning chapbook. Make checks payable to Palanquin Press. The winning ms is published by Palanquin Press and the poet receives $100 and 50 copies of the chapbook. Samples are $5.

PALO ALTO REVIEW (Specialized: themes), 1400 W. Villaret Blvd., San Antonio TX 78224. (210)921-5443 or 921-5017. Fax: (210)921-5008. E-mail: EMSHULL@aol.com. Established 1992. **Editors:** Ellen Shull and Bob Richmond.

Magazine Needs: *Palo Alto Review* is a biannual publication of Palo Alto college. "We invite writing that investigates the full range of education in its myriad forms. Ideas are what we are after. *Palo Alto Review* is interested in connecting the college and the community. We would hope that those who attempt these connections will choose startling topics and find interesting angles from which to study the length and breadth of ideas and learning, a lifelong pursuit." Includes articles, essays, memoirs, interviews, book reviews, fiction, and poetry. Wants "poetry which has something to say, literary quality poems, with strong images, up to 50 lines. No inspirational verse, haiku or doggerel." Has published poetry by Walt McDonald, Diane Glancy, Virgil Suárez, and Wendy Bishop. *Palo Alto Review* is 60 pgs., 8½×11, professionally printed on recycled paper and saddle-stapled with enamel card cover with art; b&w photos, art and graphics inside. Publishes about 8 poems in each issue (16 poems/year). Press run is 700 for 400 subscribers of which 10 are libraries, 200 shelf sales. Subscription: $10. Sample: $5.

How to Submit: Submit 3-5 poems at a time. Accepts simultaneous submissions; no previously published poems. Poems are read by an advisory board and recommended to editors, who sometimes suggest revisions. Always comments on rejected poems. "Although we frequently announce a theme, the entire issue will not necessarily be dedicated to the theme." Guidelines and a list of upcoming themes available for SASE. Responds in 3 months. Pays 2 contributor's copies. Acquires first North American serial rights. "Please note poems as first published in *Palo Alto Review* in subsequent printings."

Advice: "There are no requirements for submission, though we recommend the reading (purchase) of a sample copy."

PAPER WASP: A JOURNAL OF HAIKU (Specialized: form/style); SOCIAL ALTERNATIVES (Specialized: social issues); POST PRESSED, The Graduate School of Education, The University of Queensland, Queensland 4072 Australia. E-mail: jwk@powerup.com.au. Website: http://users.bigpond.net.au/ReportWright/PaperWasp/PaperWasp.html (includes information about *Paper Wasp*, submissions, contents, and sample selections). *Paper Wasp* established 1972, *Social Alternatives* established 1971. **Editor:** Jacqui Murray. **Editor:** John Knight.

Magazine Needs: "*Paper Wasp* quarterly publishes haiku, senryu, renga, and tanka in a range of fresh tones and voices. We acknowledge a range of forms and styles from one-liners to the conventional 5-7-5 form, and variations such as development or neglect of seasonal words for regional contexts." Wants haiku, senryu, tanka, renga, linked verse, and haibun. Has published poetry by Janice Bostok, Carla Sari, Cornelis Vleeskens, Ross Clark, Tony Beyer, and Bernard Gadd. As a sample the editor selected these lines by Alan J. Summers:

> late september rain/cutting through the lane/and the mist.

Paper Wasp is 16 pgs., digest-sized, desktop-published and saddle-stapled, cardboard cover, includes art/graphics. Receives about 2,000 submissions/year, accepts 15%. Publishes about 50 haiku/issue. Press run is 200 for 67 subscribers of which 12 are libraries. Single copy: $AUD6 within Australia, $US8 elsewhere. Subscription: $AUD20 within Australia, $US26 elsewhere. Make checks payable to *Paper Wasp*. "Due to very high bank charges on overseas cheques, we prefer cash or IRCs for single copies. Copies of relevant pages only are sent to published contributors who are not subscribers or who do not pay for the relevant copy."

Magazine Needs: "*Social Alternatives* is a quarterly multidisciplinary journal which seeks to analyse, critique, and review contemporary social, cultural, and economic developments and their implications at local, national, and global levels." Has published poetry by MTC Cronin, Jules Leigh Koch, ouyang yu, John O'Connor, Gina Mercer, and Michael Sariban. As a sample the editor selected these lines from "Awaiting the Barbarians (after Cavafy)" by Ron Pretty:

> It was the golden age: they were there, sure./The barbarians, but on the borders,/the northern marches,
> walled out, or so/we were told, and kept in check. The city/prospered and its merchants. the constant
> flow/of captives kept the mines and circuses in action

Social Alternatives is 76 pgs., magazine-sized, desktop-published, saddle-stapled with cardboard cover, includes art/graphics, ads. Receives about approximately 1,200 submissions, accepts about 15%. Publishes about 30 poems/issue. Press run is about 800 for 587 subscribers of which 112 are libraries. Single copy: $8. Subscription: $30, plus $40 for overseas airmail.

How to Submit: Submit up to 12 poems at a time for *Paper Wasp*, up to 6 poems (36 lines maximum) for *Social Alternatives*. No previously published poems or simultaneous submissions. Accepts e-mail and disk submissions (IBM format with Word files, plus hard copy). Cover letter required. "If mailed within Australia, send SASE, otherwise SAE plus IRCs. Unless requested with SASE, copy is not returned." Time between acceptance and publication is up to 6 months. Poems are circulated to an editorial board. "Read by two editors." Sometimes comments on rejected poems. Responds within 6 months. *Paper Wasp* does not pay except one copy for poets publishing with them for the first time. *Social Alternatives* pays 1 contributor's copy. Copyright remains with authors.

PARADOXISM; XIQUAN PUBLISHING HOUSE; THE PARADOXIST MOVEMENT ASSOCI-ATION (Specialized: form), University of New Mexico, Gallup NM 87301. E-mail: smarand@unm.edu. Established 1990. **Editor:** Florentin Smarandache.

Magazine Needs: *Paradoxism*, (formerly *The Paradoxist Literary Movement Journal*), is an annual journal of "avant-garde poetry, experiments, poems without verses, literature beyond the words, anti-language, non-literature and its literature, as well as the sense of the non-sense; revolutionary forms of poetry. Paradoxism is based on excessive use of antitheses, antinomies, contradictions, paradoxes in creation. It was made up in the 1980s by the editor as an anti-communist protest." Wants "avant-garde poetry, one to two pages, any subject, any style (lyrical experiments). No classical, fixed forms." Has published poetry by Paul Georgelin, Titu Popescu, Ion Rotaru, Michèle de LaPlante, and Claude LeRoy. *Paradoxism* is 52 pgs., digest-sized, offset-printed, soft cover. Press run is 500. "It is distributed to its collaborators, U.S. and Canadian university libraries, and the Library of Congress as well as European, Chinese, Indian, and Japanese libraries."

How to Submit: No previously published poems or simultaneous submissions. Do not submit mss in the summer. "We do not return published or unpublished poems or notify the author of date of publication." Responds in up to 6 months. Pays 1 contributor's copy.

Book/Chapbook Needs & How to Submit: Xiquan Publishing House also publishes 2 paperbacks and 1-2 chapbooks/year, including translations. The poems must be unpublished and must meet the requirements of the Paradoxist Movement Association. Responds to queries in 2 months, to mss in up to 6 months. Pays 50 author's copies. Inquire about sample books.

Advice: "We mostly receive traditional or modern verse, but not avant-garde (very different from any previously published verse). We want anti-literature and its literature, style of the non-style, poems without poems, non-words and non-sentence poems, very upset free verse, intelligible unintelligible language, impersonal texts personalized, transformation of the abnormal to the normal. Make literature from everything; make literature from nothing!"

PARNASSUS LITERARY JOURNAL, P.O. Box 1384, Forest Park GA 30298-1384. (404)366-3177. Established 1975. **Editor:** Denver Stull.

Magazine Needs: "Our sole purpose is to promote poetry and to offer an outlet where poets may be heard. We welcome well-constructed poetry, but ask that you keep it uplifting, and free of language that might be offensive to one of our readers. We are open to all poets and all forms of poetry, including Oriental, 24-line limit, maximum 3 poems." Accepts poetry written by children. Has published poetry by Louis Cantoni, Diana Kwiatowski Rubin, Jessica Goodfellow, Ruth Schuler, Gloria Procsal, and Eugene Botelho. As a sample the editor selected these lines by Michael Skau:

> Squads of poplars break/the stripling wind of autumn/afternoon red winged black/birds guard the harvest/fields evening vibrates/with twilight shadows

Parnassus Literary Journal, published 3 times/year, is 84 pgs., photocopied from typescript, saddled-stapled, colored card cover, with an occasional drawing. Receives about 1,500 submissions/year, accepts 350. Currently have about a 1-year backlog. Press run is 300 for 200 subscribers of which 5 are libraries. Circulation includes Japan, England, Greece, India, Korea, Germany, and Netherlands. Single copy: $6 US and Canada, $9.50 overseas; subscription: $18 US and Canada, $25 overseas. Sample: $5. Offers 20% discount to schools, libraries and for orders of 5 copies or more. Make checks or money orders payable to Denver Stull.

How to Submit: Submit up to 3 poems, up to 24 lines each, with #10 SASE. Include name and address on each page of ms. "I am dismayed at the haphazard manner in which work is often submitted. I have a number of poems in my file containing no name and/or address. Simply placing your name and address on your envelope is not enough." Accepts previously published poems; no simultaneous submissions. Cover letter including something about the writer preferred. "Definitely" comments on rejected poems. "We do not respond to submissions or queries not accompanied by SASE." Guidelines available for SASE. Responds within 1 week. "We regret that the ever-rising costs of publishing forces us to ask that contributors either subscribe to the magazine, or purchase a copy of the issue in which their work appears." All rights remain with the author. Readers vote on best of each issue. Staff reviews books of poetry by subscribers only.

Also Offers: Conducts a contest periodically.

Advice: "Write about what you know. Study what you have written. Does it make sense? A poem should not leave the reader wondering what you are trying to say. Improve your writings by studying the work of others. Be professional."

$ ∅ PARNASSUS: POETRY IN REVIEW; POETRY IN REVIEW FOUNDATION, 205 W. 89th St., #8F, New York NY 10024-1835. (212)362-3492. Fax: (212)875-0148. Established 1972. **Poetry Editor:** Herbert Leibowitz.
Magazine Needs: *Parnassus* provides "comprehensive and in-depth coverage of new books of poetry, including translations from foreign poetry. We publish poems and translations on occasion, but we solicit all poetry. Poets invited to submit are given all the space they wish; the only stipulation is that the style be non-academic." Has published work by Alice Fulton, Eavan Boland, Ross Feld, Debora Greger, William Logan, Tess Gallagher, Seamus Heaney, and Rodney Jones. Subscriptions are $22/year, $46/year for libraries; has 1,100 subscribers, of which 550 are libraries.
How to Submit: Not open to unsolicited poetry. However, unsolicited essays are considered. In fact, this is an exceptionally rich market for thoughtful, insightful, technical essay-reviews of contemporary collections. Strongly recommended that writers study the magazine before submitting. Multiple submissions disliked. Cover letter required. Upcoming themes is available for SASE. Responds to essay submissions within 10 weeks (response takes longer during the summer). Pays $25-250 plus 2 gift subscriptions—contributors can also take one themselves. Editor comments on rejected poems—from 1 paragraph to 2 pages. Send for a sample copy (prices of individual issues can vary) to get a feel for the critical acumen needed to place here.
Advice: "Contributors are urged to subscribe to at least one literary magazine. There is a pervasive ignorance of the cost of putting out a magazine and no sense of responsibility for supporting one."

∅ PARTING GIFTS; MARCH STREET PRESS; FATAL EMBRACE, 3413 Wilshire, Greensboro NC 27408. E-mail: rbixby@aol.com. Website: http://members.aol.com/marchst/ (features links guidelines, sample issues, book catalog, and news). Established 1987. **Editor:** Robert Bixby.
Magazine Needs: "I want to see everything. I'm a big fan of Jim Harrison, C.K. Williams, Amy Hempel, and Janet Kauffman." He has published poetry by Eric Torgersen, Lyn Lifshin, Elizabeth Kerlikowske, and Russell Thorburn. *Parting Gifts* is 72 pgs., digest-sized, photocopied, with colored matte card cover, appearing twice/year. Press run is 200. Subscription: $12. Sample: $6.
How to Submit: Submit in groups of 3-10 with SASE. Accepts simultaneous submissions; no previously published poems. "I like a cover letter because it makes the transaction more human. Best time to submit mss is early in the year." Guidelines available for SASE or on website. Responds in 2 weeks. Sometimes sends prepublication galleys. Pays 1 copy.
Book/Chapbook Needs & How to Submit: March Street Press publishes chapbooks. **Reading fee:** $10.

▼ $ ∅ ◎ PARTISAN REVIEW (Specialized: translations, themes), Dept. PM, 236 Bay State Rd., Boston MA 02215. (617)353-4260. Fax: (617)353-7444. E-mail: partisan@bu.edu. Website: www.partisanreview.org. Established 1934. **Editor:** Edith Kurzweil. **Editor-in-Chief:** William Phillips. **Poetry Editor:** Don Share.
   • Work published in *Partisan Review* has been selected for inclusion in *The Best American Poetry* (volumes 1995 and 1998).
Magazine Needs: *Partisan Review* is a distinguished quarterly literary journal using poetry of high quality. "Our poetry section is very small and highly selective. We are open to fresh, quality translations but submissions must include poem in original language as well as translation. We occasionally have special poetry sections on specified themes." Has published poetry by Charles Wright, Glyn Maxwell, Debora Greger, and Wislawa Szymborska. *Partisan Review* is 160 pgs., 6×9, flat-spined. Press run is 8,200 for 6,000 subscriptions and shelf sales. Sample: $7.50.
How to Submit: Submit up to 6 poems at a time. No simultaneous submissions. No fax or e-mail submissions. Responds in 2 months. Pays $50 and 50% discount on copies.

∅ PASSAGES NORTH; ELINOR BENEDICT PRIZE, English Dept., 1401 Presque Isle Ave., Northern Michigan University, Marquette MI 49855. (906)227-2715. Established 1979. **Editor-in-Chief:** Kate Myers Hanson
Magazine Needs: *Passages North* is an annual magazine containing short fiction, poetry, creative nonfiction, essays, and interviews. "The magazine publishes quality work by established and emerging writers." Has published poetry by Jim Daniels, Jack Driscoll, Vivian Shipley, and Michael Delp. *Passages North* is 250 pgs. Circulation is at 1,000 "and growing." Subscription: $13/year, $26/2 years. Current issue: $7; back issue: $3.
How to Submit: Prefers groups of 3-6 poems, typed single-spaced. Accepts simultaneous submissions. "Poems over 100 lines seldom published." Time between acceptance and publication is 6 months. Reads submissions September through May only. Responds in 2 months. Pays 1 contributor's copy.
Also Offers: Sponsors the Elinor Benedict Prize in poetry and the Waasmode Fiction Contest. "We have published fiction by W.P. Kinsella, Bonnie Jo Campbell, and Lisa Stolley." Details available for SASE.

∅ PATERSON LITERARY REVIEW; ALLEN GINSBERG POETRY AWARDS; THE PATERSON POETRY PRIZE; THE PATERSON PRIZE FOR BOOKS FOR YOUNG PEOPLE; PASSAIC

COUNTY COMMUNITY COLLEGE POETRY CENTER LIBRARY, Poetry Center, Passaic County Community College, Cultural Affairs Dept., 1 College Blvd., Paterson NJ 07505-1179. (973)684-6555. E-mail: mgellan@pccc.cc.nj.us. Website: www.pccc.cc.nj.us/poetry. Established 1979. **Editor and Director:** Maria Mazziotti Gillan.

Magazine Needs & How to Submit: A wide range of activities pertaining to poetry are conducted by the Passaic County Community College Poetry Center, including the annual *Paterson Literary Review* (formerly *Footwork: The Paterson Literary Review*) using poetry of "high quality" under 100 lines; "clear, direct, powerful work." Has published poetry by David Ray, Diane Wakoski, Sonia Sanchez, Laura Boss, and Marge Piercy. *Paterson Literary Review* is 240 pgs., magazine-sized, saddle-stapled, professionally printed with glossy card 2-color cover, using b&w art and photos. Press run is 1,000 for 100 subscribers of which 50 are libraries. Sample: $10. Send up to 5 poems at a time. Accepts simultaneous submissions. Reads submissions September through January only. Responds in 1 year. Pays 1 contributor's copy. Acquires first rights.

Also Offers: The Poetry Center of the college conducts the Allen Ginsberg Poetry Awards Competition each year. Entry fee: $13. Prizes of $1,000, $200, and $100. Deadline: April 1. Rules available for SASE. Also publishes a *New Jersey Poetry Resources* book, the *Passaic County Community College Poetry Contest Anthology*, and the *New Jersey Poetry Calendar*. The Paterson Poetry Prize of $1,000 is awarded each year (split between poet and publisher) to a book of poems published in the previous year. Also sponsors the Paterson Prize for Books for Young People. Awards $500 to one book in each category (Pre-K-Grade 3, Grades 4-6, Grades 7-12). Books must be published in the previous year and be submitted by the publisher. Publishers should write with SASE for application form to be submitted by February 1 (for Poetry Prize) and March 15 (for Books for Young People Prize). Passaic County Community College Poetry Center Library has an extensive collection of contemporary poetry and seeks small press contributions to help keep it abreast. The Distinguished Poetry Series offers readings by poets of international, national, and regional reputation. Poetryworks/USA is a series of programs produced for UA Columbia-Cablevision.

○ ◎ **PATH PRESS, INC. (Specialized: ethnic)**, P.O. Box 2925, Chicago IL 60690. (847)424-1620. Fax: (847)424-1623. E-mail: pathpressinc@aol.com. Established 1969. **President:** Bennett J. Johnson.

Book/Chapbook Needs & How to Submit: Path Press is a small publisher of books and poetry primarily "by, for, and about African-American and Third World people." The press is open to all types of poetic forms; emphasis is on high quality. Submissions should be typewritten in ms format. Writers should send sample poems, credits, and bio. The books are "hardback and quality paperbacks."

☑ ◐ ♥ **PAVEMENT SAW; PAVEMENT SAW PRESS; PAVEMENT SAW PRESS CHAPBOOK AWARD; TRANSCONTINENTAL POETRY AWARD**, P.O. Box 6291, Columbus OH 43206-0291. E-mail: editor@pavementsaw.org. Website: www.pavementsaw.org (includes all information, contest rules, and a full catalog). Established 1992. **Editor:** David Baratier.

Magazine Needs: *Pavement Saw*, which appears annually in September, wants "letters and short fiction, and poetry on any subject, especially work. Length: one or two pages. No poems that tell, no work by a deceased writer and no translations." Dedicates 10-15 pgs of each issue to a featured writer. Has published poetry by Will Alexander, Sandra Kohler, Naton Leslie, Jendi Reiter, Beth Anderson, Sean Killian, and Tracy Philpot. *Pavement Saw* is 64 pgs., 6×9, perfect-bound. Receives about 14,500 poems/year, accepts less than 1%. Press run is 500 for about 250 subscribers, about 250 shelf sales. Single copy: $5; subscription: $10. Make checks payable to Pavement Saw Press.

How to Submit: Submit 5 poems at a time. "No fancy typefaces." Accepts simultaneous submissions, "as long as poet has not published a book with a press run of 1,000 or more"; no previously published poems. No e-mail submissions. Cover letter required. Seldom comments on rejected poems. Guidelines available for SASE. Responds in 6 months. Sometimes sends prepublication galleys. Pays 2 copies. Acquires first rights.

Book/Chapbook Needs & How to Submit: The press also publishes books of poetry. "Most are by authors who have been published in the journal." Published "seven titles in 2000 and nine titles in 2001, eight are full-length books ranging from 72 to 612 pages."

Also Offers: Sponsors the Transcontinental Poetry Award. "Each year, Pavement Saw Press will seek to publish at least one book of poetry and/or prose poems from manuscripts received during this competition. Competition is open to anyone who has not previously published a volume of poetry or prose. Writers who have had volumes of poetry and/or prose under 40 pgs. printed or printed in limited editions of no more than 500 copies are eligible. Submissions are accepted during June and July only." Entry fee: $15. Awards publication, $1,000 and a percentage of the press run. Include stamped postcard and SASE for ms receipt acknowledgement and results notification. Guidelines available for SASE. Also sponsors the Pavement Saw Press Chapbook Award. Submit up to 32 pgs. of poetry with a cover letter. Entry fee: $7. Awards publication, $500 and 10% of print run. "Each entrant will receive a chapbook provided a 9×12 SAE with 5 first-class stamps is supplied." Deadline: December 20. Guidelines available for SASE.

☑ ▣ ⊕ ○ ◎ **PEACE & FREEDOM; EASTERN RAINBOW; PEACE & FREEDOM PRESS (Specialized: subscribers)**, 17 Farrow Rd., Whaplode Drove, Spalding, Lincs PE12 0TS England. E-mail: peaceandfreedom@lineone.net. Website: http://website.lineone.net/~peaceandfreedom. Established 1985. **Editor:** Paul Rance.

Magazine Needs: *Peace & Freedom* is a magazine appearing 2 times/year. "We are looking for poems up to 32 lines particularly from U.S. poets who are new to writing, especially women. The poetry we publish is pro-animal rights, anti-war, environmental; poems reflecting love; erotic, but not obscene poetry; humorous verse and spiritual, humanitarian poetry. With or without rhyme/metre." Has published poetry by Dorothy Bell-Hall, Doreen King, Bernard Shough, Mona Miller, and Andrew Savage. As a sample the editor selected these lines from "No Qualms" by Daphne Richards:

> We humans want our freedom,/and the right to choose our way,/along life's many pathways/as we tread
> them every day.//And yet we ban our animals/from all that we hold dear./We rob them of their dignity,/
> and keep them bound by fear.

Peace & Freedom has a b&w glossy cover, normally 20 A4 pages. Sample: US $4; UK £1.75. "Sample copies can only be purchased from the above address, and various mail-order distributors too numerous to mention. Advisable to buy a sample copy first. Banks charge the equivalent of $5 to cash foreign cheques in the U.K., so please only send bills, preferably by registered post." Subscription: US $16, UK £7.50/4 issues.

How to Submit: No simultaneous submissions or previously published poems. No fax or e-mail submissions. Poets are requested to send in bios. Reads submissions all through the year. Publishes theme issues. A list of upcoming themes is available for SAE with IRC or on website. Responds to submissions normally under a month, with IRC/SAE. "Work without correct postage will not be responded to or returned until proper postage is sent." Pays 1 copy. Reviews books of poetry.

Also Offers: Also publishes anthologies. Details on upcoming anthologies and guidelines are available for SAE with IRC. "*Peace & Freedom* now holds regular contests as does one of our other publications, *Eastern Rainbow*, which is a magazine concerning 20th century popular culture using poetry up to 32 lines. Subscription: US, $16, UK, £7.50/4 issues. Further details of competitions and publications for SAE and IRC."

Advice: "Too many writers have lost the personal touch and editors generally appreciate this. It can make a difference when selecting work of equal merit."

◗ PEARL; PEARL POETRY PRIZE; PEARL EDITIONS, 3030 E. Second St., Long Beach CA 90803-5163. (562)434-4523 or (714)968-7530. E-mail: mjohn5150@aol.com. Website: www.pearlmag.com (includes sample issues, guidelines for submission and contests, subscription information, about the editors, book catalog, and links). Established 1974. **Poetry Editors:** Joan Jobe Smith, Marilyn Johnson, and Barbara Hauk.

Magazine Needs: *Pearl* is a literary magazine appearing 2 times/year. "We are interested in accessible, humanistic poetry that communicates and is related to real life. Humor and wit are welcome, along with the ironic and serious. No taboos stylistically or subject-wise. We don't want to see sentimental, obscure, predictable, abstract, or cliché-ridden poetry. Our purpose is to provide a forum for lively, readable poetry, the direct, outspoken type, variously known as 'neo-pop' or 'stand-up,' that reflects a wide variety of contemporary voices, viewpoints and experiences—that speaks to real people about real life in direct, living language, profane, or sublime. Our Fall/

This portrayal of Marilyn Monroe, Joan Crawford, and Barbara Stanwyck was drawn by Marilyn Johnson for *Pearl*'s 25th anniversary issue. For years, Johnson and her co-editors, Joan Jobe Smith and Barbara Hauk, were amused by the idea of sharing their first names with Monroe, Crawford, and Stanwyk. "We dare not even imagine them co-editing a poetry journal together and all the champagne, gold lame, and fur that would have flown."

Winter issue is devoted exclusively to poetry, with a 12-15 page section featuring the work of a single poet."
Has published poetry by Fred Voss, Allison Joseph, Frank X. Gaspar, Denise Duhamel, Ed Ochester, and Nin
Andrews. As a sample they selected these lines from "Wasted" by Jim Daniels:

> *This morning when I left her place, we kissed/each other's bad breath and it was all we could do/not
> to flinch. A bird squeaks its brittle song./The day ahead clearly and plainy wasted.*

Pearl is 96-121 pgs., digest-sized, perfect-bound, offset-printed, with glossy cover. Press run is 700 for 150
subscribers of which 7 are libraries. Subscription: $18/year includes a copy of the winning book of the Pearl
Poetry Prize. Sample: $7.

How to Submit: Submit 3-5 poems at a time. No previously published poems. "Simultaneous submissions
must be acknowledged as such." Prefer poems no longer than 40 lines, each line no more than 10-12 words to
accommodate page size and format. "Handwritten submissions and unreadable printouts are not acceptable."
No e-mail submissions. "Cover letters appreciated." Reads submissions September through May only. Time
between acceptance and publication is up to 1 year. Guidelines available for SASE or on website. Responds in
2 months. Sometimes sends prepublication galleys. Pays 1 contributor's copy. Acquires first serial rights. Each
issue contains the work of 80-100 different poets and a special 10- to 15-page section that showcases the work
of a single poet.

Book/Chapbook Needs: Pearl Editions "only publishes the winner of the Pearl Poetry Prize. All other books
and chapbooks are *by invitation only.*"

Also Offers: "We sponsor the Pearl Poetry Prize, an annual book-length contest, judged by one of our more
well-known contributors. Winner receives publication, $1,000 and 25 copies. Entries accepted May 1 to July 15.
There is a $20 entry fee, which includes a copy of the winning book." Complete rules and guidelines are available
for SASE or on website. Recent books include *Fluid in Darkness, Frozen in Light* by Robert Perchan, *Shelter*
by Lisa Giatt, *Transforming Matter* by Donna Hilbert, *One on One* by Tony Gloeggler, *Oyl* by Denise Duhamel
and Maureen Seaton, and *Man Climbs Out of Manhole* by David Hernandez.

Advice: "Advice for beginning poets? Just write from your own experience, using images that are as concrete
and sensory as possible. Keep these images fresh and objective. Always listen to the music."

⬤ **PECAN GROVE PRESS**, Box AL 1 Camino Santa Maria, San Antonio TX 78228-8608. (210)436-3441.
Fax: (210)436-3782. E-mail: palmer@netxpress.com. Website: http://library.stmarytx.edu/pgpress/index.html (in
cludes submission information, chapbook contest information, individual author pages with samples of work).
Established 1988. **Editor:** H. Palmer Hall. **Co-Editor:** Karen Narvarte.

Book/Chapbook Needs: Pecan Grove Press is "interested in fine poetry collections that adhere. A collection
should be like an art exhibit—the book is the art space, the pieces work together." Publishes 4-6 paperbacks and
2-3 chapbooks/year. Wants "poetry with something to say and that says it in fresh, original language. Will rarely
publish books of more than 110 pages." Does not want "poetry that lets emotion run over control. We too often
see sentiment take precedence over language." Has published *Glass* by Jenny Browne, *The Hemingway Poems*,
by Ron McFarland, *Say Hello* by Ryan G. Van Cleave, and *The Yin of It* by Jan Epton Seale. As a sample the
editor selected these lines from "This Natural History" by Gwyn McVay:

> *Three door feed in a line at the edge of the wood/And red sky, the spike-buck lifts his head, his weight/
> Suspended on three sinews from the hanging earth,/The does mythical, rounding to white, one/Held
> breath, the space between two trees/And for that reason mostly people can't return/The buck's slight
> black look when he swivels/his head to take in observers, shagbark oak*

Books or chapbooks are usually 50-96 pgs., offset, perfect-bound, one-color plus b&w graphic design or photo-
graphic cover on index stock.

How to Submit: Submit complete ms. Accepts previously published poems and simultaneous submissions. No
fax or e-mail submissions. Cover letter required, with some indication of a poet's publication history and some
ideas or suggestions for marketing the book. Time between acceptance and publication is up to 12 months. "We
do circulate for outside opinion when we know the poet who has submitted a manuscript. We read closely and
make decisions as quickly as possible." Seldom comments on rejected poems. "We do expect our poets to have
a publication history in the little magazines with some acknowledgments." Responds to queries and mss in 3
months. After the book has paid for itself, authors receive 50% of subsequent sales and 10 author's copies (out
of a press run of 500). "We have no subsidy arrangements, but if author has subvention funds, we do welcome
them. Obtain sample books by checking BIP and making purchase. We will send chapbook at random for a fee
of $5; book for $10."

Advice: "We welcome submissions but feel too many inexperienced poets want to rush into book publication
before they are quite ready. Many should try the little magazine route first instead of attempting to begin a new
career with book publication."

◨ ◻ ◎ **THE PEGASUS REVIEW (Specialized: themes)**, P.O. Box 88, Henderson MD 21640-0088.
(410)482-6736. Established 1980. **Editor:** Art Bounds.

Magazine Needs: "*The Pegasus Review* is a bimonthly, in a calligraphic format and each issue is based on a
specific theme. Since themes might be changed it is suggested to inquire as to current themes. With a magazine
in this format, strictly adhere to guidelines—brevity is the key. Poetry—not more than 24 lines (the shorter the
better); fiction (short short—about 2½ pages would be ideal); essays and cartoons. All material must pertain to

indicated themes only. Poetry may be in any style (rhyming, free verse, haiku)." Accepts poetry written by teenagers. Has published poetry by Jane Stewart, Michael Keshigian, Emma Blanch, Terry Thomas, and Carrie Jackson Karegannes. As a sample the editor selected this haiku by Robert H. Deluty:

> retired teacher . . ./eight thousand diplomas/and a gold watch

Press run is 120 for 100 subscribers, of which 2 are libraries. Subscription: $12. Sample: $2.50.

How to Submit: Submit 3-5 poems with name and address on each page. Accepts previously published poems, if there is no conflict or violation of rights agreement and simultaneous submissions, but author must notify proper parties once specific material is accepted. Brief cover letter with specifics as they relate to one's writing background welcome. Themes are January/February: Age/Youth; March/April: Gardens/Flowers; May/June: Mothers/Fathers; July/August: Friends/Enemies; September/October: Civilization/War; and November/December: Courage/Fear. Responds within a month, often with a personal response. Pays 2 copies.

Also Offers: Offers occasional book awards throughout the year.

Advice: "Keep abreast with what is going on by using *Poet's Market* and *Writer's Market*. Continue to read what was read that is still being read today and what is being written today. Constantly strive to improve your craft either with classes, seminars, or writers' groups. Above all, persevere. For most writers success does not come immediately."

$ 🗍 ◎ ⬚ **PELICAN PUBLISHING COMPANY (Specialized: children, regional)**, Box 3110, Gretna LA 70054-3110. Website: www.pelicanpub.com (includes writer's guidelines, catalog, and company history). Established 1926. **Editor-in-Chief:** Nina Kooij.

Book/Chapbook Needs: Pelican is a "moderate-sized publisher of cookbooks, travel guides, regional books, and inspirational/motivational books," which accepts poetry for "hardcover children's books only, preferably with a regional focus. However, our needs for this are very limited; we do twelve juvenile titles per year, and most of these are prose, not poetry." Accepts poetry written by children. Has published *Christmas All Over*, by Robert Bernardini. As a sample the editor selected these lines from *An Irish Hallowe'en* by Sarah Kirwan Blazek:

> Long ages ago/On an isle all green,/We started a feast/now called Hallowe'en

Books are 32-page, large-format (magazine-sized) with illustrations. Two of their popular series are prose books about Gaston the Green-Nosed Alligator by James Rice and Clovis Crawfish by Mary Alice Fontenot. Has a variety of books based on "The Night Before Christmas" adapted to regional settings such as Cajun, prairie, and Texas. Typically Pelican books sell for $14.95. Write for catalog to buy samples.

How to Submit: *Currently not accepting unsolicited mss.* Query first with 2 sample poems and cover letter including "work and writing backgrounds and promotional connections." No previously published poems or simultaneous submissions. Responds to queries in 1 month, to mss (if invited) in 3 months. Always sends prepublication galleys. Pays royalties. Acquires all rights. Returns rights upon termination of contract.

Advice: "We try to avoid rhyme altogether, especially predictable rhyme. Monotonous rhythm can also be a problem."

◉ **PEMBROKE MAGAZINE**, UNCP, Box 1510, Pembroke NC 28372-1510. (910)521-6358. Fax: (910)521-6688. Established 1969 by Norman Macleod. **Editor:** Shelby Stephenson. **Managing Editor:** Fran Oxendine.

Magazine Needs: *Pembroke* is a heavy (460 pgs., 6×9), flat-spined, quality literary annual which has published poetry by Fred Chappell, Stephen Sandy, A.R. Ammons, Barbara Guest, and Betty Adcock. Press run is 500 for 125 subscribers of which 100 are libraries. Sample: $8.

How to Submit: Sometimes comments on rejected poems. Responds within 3 months. Pays copies.

Advice: Stephenson advises, "Publication will come if you write. Writing is all."

🗍 ◯ ⬚ **PENMANSHIP: A CREATIVE ARTS CALENDAR**, P.O. Box 24833, Winston-Salem NC 27114. E-mail: penmanshipcac@yahoo.com. Website: www.geocites.com/penmanshipcalendar/masterpage.html (includes WPAP newsletter, excerpts from calendar, and guidelines). Established 1998. **Editor:** Tameka Norris. **Assistant Editor:** Sheredia Norris.

Magazine Needs: "I would like to see poetry, short stories, photography, drawings, quotes, any original work of art that one can think of. Looking for all types of work—but clean work!" *Penmanship* is a 12 plus-page calendar, bound, in b&w. Single copy: $10.95.

How to Submit: Submit 3-6 poems at a time. Length for poetry is 2 pages maximum. Accepts previously published poems and simultaneous submissions but needs to know previous and current publishers of submitted work. No fax or e-mail submission. Include cover letter, 25-50 word bio, SASE, and a check or money order for reading fee. **Reading fee: $5.** Often comments on rejected poems. Guidelines available for SASE or on website. Acquires first or one-time rights or second serial reprint rights. Reviews books and chapbooks of poetry. Poets may send books for review consideration.

OPENNESS TO SUBMISSIONS: ◯ beginners; ◉ beginners and experienced; ◕ mostly experienced, few beginners; ◎ specialized; ⬚ closed to unsolicited mss.

Also Offers: "Winner of poetry contest receives $25 award. Winner of the short story contest receives $35 award. Winner of photo/artist contest receives $35 award. One of the three winners will go on to be chosen as the final winner featured in *Penmanship*'s broadside and receive an additional $25 award."

🄐 **PENNSYLVANIA ENGLISH**, Penn State DuBois, DuBois PA 15801-3199. (814)375-4814. E-mail: ajv2 @psu.edu. Established 1988 (first issue in March, 1989). **Editor:** Antonio Vallone.
Magazine Needs: *Pennsylvania English*, appearing annually in winter, is "a journal sponsored by the Pennsylvania College English Association." Wants poetry of "any length, any style." Has published poetry by Liz Rosenberg, Walt MacDonald, Amy Pence, Jennifer Richter, and Jeff Schiff. *Pennsylvania English* is up to 180 pgs., 5½×8½, perfect-bound with a full color cover. Press run is 300. Subscription: $10/year.
How to Submit: Submit 3 or more typed poems at a time. Include SASE. Considers simultaneous submissions but not previously published poems. Guidelines available for SASE. Responds in 4 months. Pays 3 copies.

✔ ♈ 🄐 🄬 **PENNY DREADFUL: TALES & POEMS OF FANTASTIC TERROR (Specialized: horror)**, P.O. Box 719, Radio City Station, Hell's Kitchen NY 10101-0719. E-mail: MMPendragon@aol.com. Website: http://hometown.aol.com/mmppennydreadful/index.html (includes links, guidelines and subscription information). Established 1996. **Editor/Publisher:** Michael Pendragon.
   • "Works appearing in *Penny Dreadful* have received Honorable Mention in *The Year's Best Fantasy and Horror*." *Penny Dreadful* nominates best tales and poems for Pushcart Prizes.
Magazine Needs: *Penny Dreadful* is a triannual publication (Autumn, Winter, Midsummer) of goth-romantic poetry and prose. Publishes poetry, short stories, essays, letters, listings, reviews, and b&w artwork "which celebrate the darker aspects of Man, the World, and their Creator. We're looking for literary horror in the tradition of Poe, M.R. James, Shelley, M.P. Shiel, and LeFanu—dark, disquieting tales and verses designed to challenge the readers' perception of human nature, morality, and man's place within the Darkness. Stories and poems should be set prior to 1910 and/or possess a timeless quality. Avoid references to 20th century personages/events, graphic sex, strong language, excessive gore and shock elements." Has published poetry by Nancy Bennett, Michael R. Burch, Lee Clark, Louise Webster, K.S. Hardy, and Kevin H. Roberts. As a sample the editor selected these lines from "Destiny" by Tamara B Latham:
> Sand which fills the hourglass/Scattered densely thru the sky/Blown by some eternal wind/Into some
> mere mortal's eye
Penny Dreadful is about 170 pgs., 6×9, desktop-published, perfect-bound with b&w line art. Includes market listings "for, and reviews of, kindred magazines." Press run is 250 copies. Subscription: $12/year (3 issues). Sample: $5. Make checks payable to Michael Pendragon.
How to Submit: Submit 3-5 poems with name and address on opening of each page, and name, title, and page number appearing on all following pages. Poems should not exceed 3 pages; rhymed, metered verse preferred. Accepts previously published poems and simultaneous submissions. Accepts e-mail submissions; include in body of message with a copy attached. Include cover letter and SASE. Reads submissions all year. Time between acceptance and publication is up to 1 year. Poems reviewed and chosen by editor. Often comments on rejected poems. Guidelines available for SASE or on website. Responds in up to 3 months. Always sends prepublication galleys. Pays 1 contributor's copy. Acquires one-time rights.

🄐 🄬 **THE PENWOOD REVIEW (Specialized: spirituality)**, P.O. Box 862, Los Alamitos CA 90720-0862. E-mail: bcame39696@aol.com. Website: http://members.aol.com/bcame39696/penwood.htm. Established 1997. **Editor:** Lori M. Cameron.
Magazine Needs: *The Penwood Review*, published biannually, "seeks to explore the mystery and meaning of the spiritual and sacred aspects of our existence and our relationship to God." Wants "disciplined, high-quality, well-crafted poetry on any subject. Prefer poems be less than two pages. Rhyming poetry must be written in traditional forms (sonnets, tercets, villanelles, sestinas, etc.)" Does not want "light verse, doggerel, or greeting card-style poetry. Also, nothing racist, sexist, pornographic, or blasphemous." Has published poetry by Kathleen Spivack, Nina Tassi, Rachel Srubas, and Gary Guinn. As a sample the editor selected these lines from "Mount Kenya" by Michael McManus:
> Village elders told me,/if you love something immense/and beyond your reach, if your faith/is never
> diminished by famine or flood/one night the stars will turn/into white talons, and lift me to your
> summit./I believe them.
The Penwood Review has about 40 pgs, 8½×11, saddle-stapled with heavy card cover. Press run is 50-100. Single copy: $6; subscription: $12.
How to Submit: Submit 3-5 poems, 1/page with the author's full name, address and phone number in the upper right hand corner. No previously published poems or simultaneous submissions. Accepts e-mail submissions in body of message. Cover letter preferred. Time between acceptance and publication is up to 12 months. "Submissions are circulated among an editorial staff for evaluations." Seldom comments on rejected poems. Responds in 2 months. Offers subscription discount of $10 to published authors and one additional free copy in which author's work appears. Acquires one-time rights.

$ 🗋 🔾 🄐 **THE PEOPLE'S PRESS**, 4810 Norwood Ave., Baltimore MD 21207-6839. Phone/fax: (410)448-0254. Press established 1997, firm established 1989. **Contact:** submissions editor.

Book/Chapbook Needs: "The goal of the types of material we publish is simply to move people to think and perhaps act to make the world better than when we inherited it." Wants "meaningful poetry that is mindful of human rights/dignity." Has published *Tokarski Meets Acevedo* by Henry T. Tokarski and Judith Acevedo; *The Patient Presents* Kelley Jean White, MD; and *60 Pieces of My Heart* by Jennifer Closs. Accepts poetry written by children; parental consent is mandatory for publication. As a sample they selected these lines from "Miracle Enough" by Kelley Jean White, MD:

> Your hand were swollen, folder together on the Easter dress. (A pair of ducks take off low to the ground, wings long, fast, blurred.)/I cry again for your still small feet pointed in the never walked on shoes. (A robin lands on the buttress, another hops by searching the grass.)/You are silent; your remembered laugh is the only sound in the sanctuary. (I cannot see the mockingbird hidden in the highest branches of the tree.)

Books are usually 50 pgs., 5½×8, photocopied, perfect-bound and saddle-stapled with soft cover, includes art/graphics.

How to Submit: Query first with 1-5 sample poems and a cover letter with brief bio and publication credits. Accepts previously published poems and simultaneous submissions. SASE required for return of work and/or response. Time between acceptance and publication is 6-12 months. Seldom comments on rejected poems. Publishes theme issues. Guidelines available for SASE. Responds to queries in 2-6 weeks; to mss in 1-3 months. Pays royalties of 5-20% and 50 author's copies (out of a press run of 500). Order sample books by sending $8.

Also Offers: The People's Press sponsors an annual Poetry Month Contest in April. Entries accepted April 1-15. "Prizes and/or publication possibilities vary from contest to contest." Details available for SASE.

✔️ 🅾️ **PEREGRINE: THE JOURNAL OF AMHERST WRITERS & ARTISTS PRESS; THE PEREGRINE PRIZE; AMHERST WRITERS & ARTISTS**, P.O. Box 1076, Amherst MA 01004-1076. Phone/fax: (413)253-7764. E-mail: awapress@aol.com. Website: www.amherstwriters.com (includes guidelines, masthead, contest winners, and announcements). Established 1984. **Managing Editor:** Nancy Rose.

Magazine Needs: *Peregrine*, published annually in October, features poetry and fiction. Open to all styles, forms and subjects except greeting card verse. Has published poetry by Clifford Browder, G.E. Coggshall, Frank Johnson, Penelope Scambly Schott, and Virgil Suarez. As a sample the editor selected these lines from "That Summer" by Anne Carroll Fowler:

> That summer you were dying I took/a lover, took him the way you'd take/the last sticky bun on a plate, sweet/and good and then the knot/in the gut all day. . .

Peregrine is 104 pgs., digest-sized, professionally printed, perfect-bound with glossy cover. Each issue includes at least one poem in translation and reviews. Press run is 1,000. Single copy: $12; subscription: $25/3 issues; $35/5 issues; $250/lifetime. Sample: $10. Make checks payable to AWA Press.

How to Submit: Submit 3-5 poems, no more than 70 lines (and spaces) each. Accepts simultaneous submissions; no previously published work. Include cover letter with bio, 40 word maximum. No e-mail submissions. "No! No! No!" "Each ms is read by several readers. Final decisions are made by the poetry editor." Guidelines available for #10 SASE or on website. Reads submissions October through April only. Postmark deadline: April 1. Pays 2 copies. Acquires first rights.

Also Offers: The Peregrine Prize, an annual fiction and/or poetry contest. 1st Prize: $500, publication in *Peregrine*, and copies. Entry fee: $10. Submit 1-3 poems, limited to 70 lines (and spaces) per poem. *"Very specific contest guidelines!"* Guidelines available for #10 SASE or on website. After the winners of the Peregrine Prize have been chosen by an outside judge, the editorial staff will select one entry from Western Massachusetts to receive the "Best of the Nest" Award. The AWA Chapbook Series is *closed* to unsolicited submissions.

Ⓝ ⭕ 🅾️ 🎦 **PERMAFROST: A LITERARY JOURNAL; MIDNIGHT SUN POETRY CHAPBOOK CONTEST (Specialized: regional)**, ‰ English Dept., P.O. Box 755720, University of Alaska Fairbanks, Fairbanks AK 99775. Fax: (907)474-5247. Website: www.uaf.edu/english/index.html (includes guidelines, contest guidelines, published writers and electronic copy of the journal). Established 1977. **Contact:** poetry editor.

Magazine Needs: An annual published in August, *Permafrost* contains poems, short stories, creative nonfiction and b&w drawings, photographs and prints. "We survive on both new and established writers, and hope and expect to see your best work. We publish any style of poetry provided it is conceived, written, and revised with care. While we encourage submissions about Alaska and by Alaskans, we also encourage and welcome poems about anywhere and from anywhere. We have published work by E. Ethelbert Miller, W. Loran Smith, Peter Orlovsky, Jim Wayne Miller, Allen Ginsberg, Jean Genet, and Andy Warhol." *Permafrost* is about 200 pgs., digest-sized, professionally printed, flat-spined, with b&w graphics and photos. Subscription: $7. Sample: $5.

How to Submit: Submit 3-6 poems, typed, single or double-spaced, and formatted as they should appear. Considers simultaneous submissions. Accepts fax submissions. Deadline: March 15. Does not accept submissions between March 15 and September 1. Editors comment only on mss that have made the final round. Guidelines available for SASE, on website, or by e-mail. Responds in 3 months. Pays 2 copies; reduced contributor rate on additional copies.

Also Offers: *Permafrost* also sponsors the Midnight Sun Poetry Chapbook Contest, as well as an annual fiction contest and a nonfiction contest. Guidelines available for SASE or on website. Contest entry fees: $10, includes a subscription to the journal. Deadline: March 15.

⊘ ◎ **PERSPECTIVES (Specialized: religious)**, Dept. of English, Hope College, Holland MI 49422-9000. Established 1986. **Co-Editors:** Roy Anker, Leanne Van Dyk, and Dave Timmer. **Poetry Editor:** Francis Fike (send poetry submissions to Francis Fike at Dept. of English, Hope College, Holland MI 49422-9000).
Magazine Needs: *Perspectives* appears 10 times/year. The journal's purpose is "to express the Reformed faith theologically; to engage issues that Reformed Christians meet in personal, ecclesiastical, and societal life, and thus to contribute to the mission of the church of Jesus Christ." Wants "both traditional and free verse of high quality, whether explicitly 'religious' or not. Prefer traditional form. Publish one or two poems every other issue, alternating with a Poetry Page on great traditional poems from the past. No sentimental, trite, or inspirational verse, please." Has published poetry by R.L. Barth, David Middleton, and Paul Willis. As a sample the editor selected these lines from "Matthew 16:4" by Ellen Stephen, O.S.R.:

> The real will not be spited. Wisdom knows/whatever is, is God's reality./The particular and signal
> briar grows/from bud into the symbolic rose./Venture past sign into the mystery.

Perspectives is 24 pgs., 8½×11, web offset and saddle-stapled, with paper cover containing b&w illustration. Receives about 50 poems/year, accepts 6-10. Press run is 3,300 for 3,000 subscribers of which 200 are libraries. Subscription: $24.95. Sample: $3.50.
How to Submit: No previously published poems or simultaneous submissions. No e-mail submissions. Cover letter preferred. Include SASE. Time between acceptance and publication is 12 months or less. Occasionally comments on rejected poems. Responds in up to 3 months. Pays 5 contributor's copies. Acquires first rights.

☑ ⊘ ◎ **PERUGIA PRESS (Specialized: women)**, P.O. Box 108, Shutesbury MA 01072. E-mail: perugia@mindspring.com. Established 1997. **Director:** Susan Kan.
Book/Chapbook Needs: "Perugia Press publishes one collection of poetry each year, by a woman at the beginning of her publishing career. The poems that catch our attention use simple language and recognizable imagery to express complex issues, events and emotions. Our books appeal to people who have been reading poetry for decades, as well as those who might be picking up a book of poetry for the first time. Slight preference for narrative poetry." Has published poetry by Catherine Anderson, Gail Thomas, Almitra David, and Janet E. Aalfs. As a sample the director selected these lines from "Ascent" by Almitra David in *Impulse to Fly*:

> Witnesses saw the children plummet,/but she watched them fly, saw each one/soar and ride the wind,/
> then tucked her baby under her wings/and took off.

Books are usually 88 pgs., 6×9, offset-printed and perfect-bound with 2-color card cover with photo or illustration.
How to Submit: Query first with 10 sample poems and cover letter with brief bio and publication credits. Accepts previously published poems and simultaneous submissions. No fax or e-mail submissions. Cover letter preferred. Annual deadline is December 1. Time between acceptance and publication is 9 months. Seldom comments on rejected poems. Responds to queries in 1 month; to mss in 6 weeks. Pay is negotiable. Order sample books by sending $12.

☑ ⊘ **PHOEBE; GREG GRUMMER POETRY AWARD**, MSN 206, George Mason University, 4400 University Dr., Fairfax VA 22030. (703)993-2915. E-mail: phoebe@gmu.edu. Website: www.gmu.edu/pubs/phoebe (includes guidelines for contest and submission). Established 1970. **Editor:** Aviva Englander Cristy. **Poetry Editor:** Rebecca Dunham.
Magazine Needs: *Phoebe* is a literary biannual "looking for imagery that will make your thumbs sweat when you touch it." Has published poetry by C.D. Wright, Russell Edson, Yusef Komunyakaa, Rosemarie Waldrop, and Leslie Scalapino. As a sample the editor selected these lines from "Why I Cannot Write At Home" by Jeffrey Schwarz:

> Does the moon yank a black comb/through the sun?/No, Mother does that.// . . .//Then where's the
> moon all morning?///Knocking and knocking on the outhouse door.

Press run is 3,000, with 35-40 pgs. of poetry in each issue. *Phoebe* receives 4,000 submissions/year. Single copy: $6; subscription: $12/year.
How to Submit: Submit up to 5 poems at a time; submission should be accompanied by SASE and a short bio. No simultaneous submissions. Does not accept e-mail submissions. Guidelines are available for SASE or on website. Responds in 3 months. Pays 2 copies or one year subscription.
Also Offers: Sponsors the Greg Grummer Poetry Award. Awards $1,000 and publication for winner, publication for finalists and a copy of awards issue to all entrants. Submit up to 4 poems, any subject, any form, with name on cover page only. No previously published submissions. Entry fee: $10/entry. Deadline: December 15. Contest receives 400-500 submissions. Back copy of awards issue: $6. Guidelines available for SASE or on website.

⊘ ◎ **PHOEBE: JOURNAL OF FEMINIST SCHOLARSHIP THEORY AND AESTHETICS (Specialized: women/feminism)**, Women's Studies Dept., Suny-College at Oneonta, Oneonta NY 13820-4015. (607)436-2014. Fax: (607)436-2656. E-mail: omarakk@oneonta.edu. Established 1989. **Poetry Editor:** Marilyn Wesley. **Editor:** Kathleen O'Mara.
Magazine Needs: *Phoebe* is published semiannually. Wants "mostly poetry reflecting women's experiences; prefer 3 pages or less." Has published poetry by Barbara Crooker, Graham Duncan, and Patty Tana. As a sample we selected these lines from "Rosh Hodesh, In the Room of Mirrors" by Lyn Lifshin:

eyes over crystal/that a great aunt/might have polished/reflected in a/hall mirror,/candles float/like the moon,/a reflection of a/reflection.

Phoebe is 120 pgs., 7×9, offset-printed on coated paper and perfect-bound with glossy card cover, includes b&w art/photos and "publishing swap" ads. Receives about 500 poems/year, accepts 8%. Press run is 500 for 120 subscribers of which 52 are libraries. Single copy: $7.50; subscription: $15/year or $25/year institutional. Sample: $5.

How to Submit: No previously published poems. Accepts fax submissions. Cover letter preferred. Reads submissions October through January and May through July only. Time between acceptance and publication is 3 months. Seldom comments on rejected poems. Publishes theme issues occasionally. Guidelines available for SASE. Responds in up to 14 weeks. Sometimes sends prepublication galleys. Pays 1 contributor's copy. Staff reviews books and chapbooks of poetry in 500-1,000 words, single book format. Send books for review consideration.

☑ ◐ ◎ **PIANO PRESS; "THE ART OF MUSIC" ANNUAL WRITING CONTEST (Specialized: music-related topics)**, P.O. Box 85, Del Mar CA 92014-0085. (858)481-5650. Fax: (858)755-1104. E-mail: pianopress@aol.com. Website: www.pianopress.com (includes description of company, lists current and upcoming publications, and information on annual writing contest). Established 1999. **Owner:** Elizabeth C. Axford, M.A.

Book/Chapbook Needs: "Piano Press publishes poems on music-related topics to promote the art of music." Publishes 50-100 chapbooks per year. "We are looking for poetry on music-related topics only. Poems can be of any length and in any style. We do not want song lyrics." As a sample the editor selected these lines:

> *Friends close to home bring to mind/The times tuned to a cello or a flute/When I trace the fine vines/*
> *And glare at the candle with the brass root/Lighting the lazy throws.*

Chapbooks are usually 80 pgs., 5×7, photocopied and saddle-stapled with 110 lb. paper cover, includes some art/graphics.

How to Submit: Query first, with a few sample poems and cover letter with brief bio and publication credits. Accepts previously published poems and simultaneous submissions. Accepts e-mail submissions. SASE required for reply. Reads submissions September 1 through June 30 only. Submit seasonal poems 6-10 months in advance. Time between acceptance and publication is up to 18 months. Poems are circulated to an editorial board. "All submissions are reviewed by several previously published poets." Often comments on rejected poems. Responds to queries in 1 month; to mss in 3 months. Pays 5 author's copies (out of a press run of 500). Order sample chapbooks online or by sending SASE for order form.

Also Offers: Sponsors an annual writing contest for poetry, short stories, and essays on music. Open to ages 4 and up. Entry fee: $20.

☑ ▣ $◐ **PIF MAGAZINE; PIF PRIZE FOR POETRY**. (360)459-7289. Fax: (360)459-4496. E-mail: poetry@pifmagazine.com. Website: www.pifmagazine.com. Established 1995. **Poetry Editor:** Anne Doolittle. **Managing Editor:** Jen Bergmark. **Senior Editor:** Camilla Renshaw.

● "*Yahoo Internet Life* recently praised *Pif Magazine* as 'The Next Wave. With writers-only classifieds and regular fiction and poetry features, Pif targets hungry scribes eager for the chance to submit original work.' David Lehman, in the prelude to *The Best American Poetry* mentioned *Pif* as one of the 'hot new' online literary magazines."

Magazine Needs: *Pif Magazine* appears monthly and is "your home on the Internet for the best poetry, fiction, interviews, and commentary available. We are fast becoming 'the' litmus test for new authors on the Net." Open to any form or style. "We want to see poetry that is innovative and takes chances. We're plotting the course for American poetry, not following someone else's example. No stale, staid work that lacks courage or creativity." Publishes an annual print version in March. Has published poetry by Liam Rector and David Lehman. *Pif* is 30-36 electronic pgs. Receives about 2400 poems/year, accepts 3%.

How to Submit: Submit no more than 3-5 poems at a time. No previously published poems or simultaneous submissions. "Please submit all poems via our online submission form at www.pifmagazine.com/email.shtml. This will ensure that we receive your submission in the proper format." Cover letter with short bio preferred. "Tell us a little about the writing of the poem—as well as a brief bio." Time between acceptance and publication is 1 month. Does not comment on rejected poems. Guidelines available by e-mail to rules@pifmagazine.com or on website. Responds in 2 months. Sometimes sends prepublication galleys. Pays $5-50/poem. Acquires first rights. Reviews books and chapbooks of poetry and other magazines in 250-1,000 words, single book format. Query Michael Burgin at michael@pifmagazine.com .

Also Offers: Sponsors the Pif Prize for Poetry, an annual award for the best poem. Also awards Honorable mention prizes. Submit 3 poems/entry, no more than 100 lines each. Poems must be unpublished but may be on any subject or in any form. For details visit website. "*Pif* is home to Pilot-Search.com, the Net's premier literary search engine. Find the exact poem, interview, or book review you've been looking for. Pilot-Search—the Starting Point for Literary Web Searches."

$◐ ◎ **PIG IRON; KENNETH PATCHEN COMPETITION (Specialized: themes)**, P.O. Box 237, Youngstown OH 44501. (330)747-6932. Fax: (330)747-0599. Established 1975. **Poetry Editor:** Jim Villani.

Magazine Needs: *Pig Iron* is a literary annual devoted to special themes. Wants poetry "up to 300 lines; free verse and experimental; write for current themes." Does not want to see "traditional" poetry. Has published poetry by Frank Polite, Larry Smith, Howard McCord, Andrena Zawinski, Juan Kincaid, and Coco Gordon. As a sample the editors selected these lines from "Cat Call" by Andrenna Zawinski:

> *Curled in the corner of your couch,/like your amber eyed calico cat,/I dove when the earth quaked,*
> *fell/into the expanse of space stretched/between your arms. You caught me,/held me there,/hair on end,*
> *claws out, screeching./You held me to to your breast, your heart/beat my own rhythm; and I,/star struck*
> *and bewitched,/I purred in your ear.*

Pig Iron is 128 pgs., magazine-sized, flat-spined, typeset on good stock with glossy card cover using b&w graphics and art, no ads. Press run is 1,000 for 200 subscribers of which 50 are libraries. Single copy: $12.95. Subscription: $12.95/year. Sample: $5. (Include $1.75 postage.)

How to Submit: Include SASE with submission. Accepts fax submissions. Responds in 3 months. Time between acceptance and publication is 12-18 months. Publishes theme issues. Next theme issue: "Religion in Modernity." Deadline: September 2000. Guidelines and upcoming themes available for SASE. Pays $5/poem plus 2 copies (additional copies at 50% retail). Acquires one-time rights.

Also Offers: Sponsors the annual Kenneth Patchen Competition. Details available for SASE.

Advice: "Reading the work of others positions one to be creative and organized in his/her own work."

PIKEVILLE REVIEW, Humanities Dept., Pikeville College, Pikeville KY 41501. (606)432-9612. Fax: (606)432-9328. E-mail: eward@pc.edu. Website: www.pc.edu (includes names of editors, guidelines, and most recent editions). Established 1987. **Editor:** Elgin M. Ward.

Magazine Needs: "There's no editorial bias though we recognize and appreciate style and control in each piece. No emotional gushing." *Pikeville Review* appears annually in July, accepting about 10% of poetry received. *Pikeville Review* is 94 pgs., digest-sized, professionally printed and perfect-bound with glossy card cover with b&w illustration. Press run is 500. Sample: $4.

How to Submit: No simultaneous submissions or previously published poems. Editor sometimes comments on rejected poems. Guidelines available for SASE or on website. Pays 5 contributor's copies.

PINCHGUT PRESS, 6 Oaks Ave., Cremorne, Sydney, NSW 2090 Australia. Phone: (02)9908-2402. Established 1948. Publishes Australian poetry but is not currently accepting poetry submissions.

$ PINE ISLAND JOURNAL OF NEW ENGLAND POETRY (Specialized: regional), P.O. Box 317, West Springfield MA 01090-0317. Established 1998. **Editor:** Linda Porter.

Magazine Needs: *Pine Island* appears 2 times/year "to encourage and support New England poets and the continued expression of New England themes." Wants poems of "up to thirty lines, haiku and other forms welcome, especially interested in New England subjects or themes. No horror, no erotica." Has published poetry by Larry Kimmel, Roy P. Fairfield, and Carol Purington. As a sample the editor selected this poem, "Trinity," by Linda Porter.

> *a trinity of apples/grace the handturned bowl/in the parlor.//just in case the pastor should call/or God*
> *himself stop by*

Pine Island is 50 pgs., digest-sized, desktop-published and saddle-stapled, cardstock cover with art. Press run is 200 for 80 subscribers. Subscription: $10. Sample: $5. Make checks payable to Pine Island Journal.

How to Submit: "Writers must be currently residenced in New England." Submit 5 poems at a time. Line length for poetry is 30 maximum. No previously published poems or simultaneous submissions. Cover letter preferred. "Include SASE, prefer first time submissions to include cover letter with brief bio." Time between acceptance and publication is 6 months. Seldom comments on rejected poems. Responds in 1 month. Pays $1/poem and 1 contributor's copy. Acquires first rights.

PINK CADILLAC: THE MAGAZINE OF CREATIVE THOUGHT, 2822 Beale Ave., Altoona PA 16601-1708. E-mail: ikey95@aol.com or poet29@wrta.com. Website: http://hometown.aol.com/ikey95/myhomepage/business.html. Established 1996. **Editor:** Alice Balest.

Magazine Needs: *Pink Cadillac* is a quarterly forum for new and established writers. Wants any style, up to 50 lines. "No vulgar, pornographic or overly sentimental, sappy drivel." Has published poetry by Tom Hendrix, Patricia G. Rourke, Elizabeth Fuller, Ace Boggess, Ann A. Boger, and Bess Kemp. As a sample the editor selected these lines from "Notions" by Bess Kemp:

> *Plowingfields of/reverie/deep age-furrows/appeared/in neat even rows/uninvited*

Pink Cadillac is 20 pgs., 8½×11, includes line art and reading/writing related ads. Subscription: $10. Sample: $2.50.

How to Submit: Submit 4-8 typed poems at a time. "Nothing handwritten." Line length for poetry is 3 minimum, 50 maximum. Accepts previously published poems and simultaneous submissions. Accepts e-mail submissions. Cover letter preferred. Time between acceptance and publication is 4 months. Guidelines available for SASE or by e-mail. Responds in 4 months. Pays 1 copy. Acquires one-time rights. Reviews books and chapbooks of poetry and other magazines. Poets may send books for review consideration.

☑ ⊘ **PINYON**, Dept. of Languages, Literature & Communications, Mesa State College, 1100 North Ave., Grand Junction CO 81051. (970)248-1123. Established 1995. **Managing Editor:** Michele Gonzales. **Editor:** Randy Phillis.

Magazine Needs: *Pinyon* appears annually and publishes "the best available contemporary American poetry and b&w artwork." "No restrictions other than excellence. We appreciate a strong voice. No inspirational, light verse or sing-song poetry." Has published poetry by Mark Cox, Barry Spacks, Wendy Bishop, and Anne Ohman Youngs. As a sample the editor selected these lines from "The Approved Poem" by John McKernan:

> The Approved Poem sits in an oak rocker on the/front porch of a sharecropper's cabin in Logan North/ Dakota arranging the words alphabetically in a/scrapbook.

Pinyon is about 120 pgs., magazine-sized, offset-printed and perfect-bound, cover varies, includes 8-10 pgs. of b&w art/graphics, fiction, and poetry. Receives about 4,000 poems/year, accepts 2%. Press run is 300 for 150 subscribers of which 5 are libraries, 50 shelf sales; 100 distributed free to contributors, friends, etc. Subscription: $8/year. Sample: $4.50. Make checks payable to *Pinyon*, MSC.

How to Submit: Submit 3-5 poems at a time. No previously published poems or simultaneous submissions. Cover letter preferred. "Name, address and phone number on each page. SASE required." Time between acceptance and publication is 3-12 months. Poems are circulated to an editorial board. "Three groups of assistant editors, led by an associate editor, make recommendations to the editor." Seldom comments on rejected poems. Guidelines available for SASE. Responds in up to 3 months, "slower in summer." Pays 1 contributor's copy/ printed page. Acquires one-time rights.

Also Offers: "Each issue contains a 'Featured Poet.' We generally publish 8-15 pages of this one poet's work."

Advice: "Send us your best work!"

○ ◎ **THE PIPE SMOKER'S EPHEMERIS (Specialized: pipes and pipe smoking)**, 20-37 120th St., College Point NY 11356-2128. Established 1964. **Editor/Publisher:** Tom Dunn.

Magazine Needs: "The *Ephemeris* is a limited edition, irregular quarterly for pipe smokers and anyone else who is interested in its varied contents. Publication costs are absorbed by the editor/publisher, assisted by any contributions—financial or otherwise—that readers might wish to make." Wants poetry with themes related to pipes and pipe smoking. Issues range from 76-96 pgs., and are 8½×11, offset from photoreduced typed copy, saddle-stitched, with colored paper covers and illustrations. Has also published collections covering the first and second 15 years of the *Ephemeris*.

How to Submit: Cover letter required with submissions; include any credits. Pays 1-2 contributor's copies. Staff reviews books of poetry. Send books for review consideration.

☑ **PIVOT**, 505 Court St., 4N, Brooklyn NY 11231. (718)243-1055. E-mail: authur505@earthlink.com.net. Website: www.n2hos.com/acm. Established 1951. **Publisher:** Arthur Mortensen.

Magazine Needs: *Pivot* is a poetry annual appearing in September that wants "formal lyrics and narrative; not interested in confessional free verse." Has published poetry by Richard Moore, Anne Lane Sheldon, Kelly Cherry, Dick Allen, and Frederick Turner. *Pivot* is a handsome, 6×9, flat-spined, professionally printed magazine with glossy card cover. Press run is 1,200. Single copy: $10. Sample: $5.

How to Submit: Submit 3-7 poems at a time. Accepts e-mail submissions; include text in body of message. Brief cover letter preferred. Reads submissions December 1 through February 15 for June issue and June 1 through August 15 for December issue.

⊘ **PLAINSONGS**, Dept. of English, Hastings College, Hastings NE 68902-0269. (402)463-2402 or 461-7352. Established 1980. **Editor:** Dwight C. Marsh.

Magazine Needs: *Plainsongs* is a poetry magazine that "accepts manuscripts from anyone, considering poems on any subject in any style but free verse predominates. Plains region poems encouraged." Has published award poems by Michael Haskell, Jim Huffman, Heather Hutcheson, Michael L. Johnson, Deborah Phelps, and Laura Read. As a sample the editor selected these lines from "As Long As" by Brian Minturn:

> As long as night explores the empty/swimming pool, and I sleep/inside the arc of your arms, let storms/ blown from the past go flat./Your bed inhales enough air for two.

Plainsongs is 40 pgs., digest-sized, set on laser, printed on thin paper and saddle-stapled with one-color matte card cover with generic black logo. "Published by the English department of Hastings College, the magazine is partially financed by subscriptions. Although editors respond to as many submissions with personal attention as they have time for, the editor offers specific observations to all contributors who also subscribe." The name suggests not only its location on the Great Plains, but its preference for the living language, whether in free or formal verse. *Plainsongs* is committed to poems only, to make space without visual graphics, bio, or critical positions. Subscription: $10/3 issues. Sample: $3.

How to Submit: Submit up to 6 poems at a time with name and address on each page. Deadlines are August 15 for fall issue; November 15 for winter; March 15 for spring. Notification is mailed 5-6 weeks after deadlines. Pays 2 contributor's copies and 1-year subscription, with 3 award poems in each issue receiving $25. "A short essay in appreciation accompanies each award poem." Acquires first rights.

◖ ⊘ **THE PLASTIC TOWER**, P.O. Box 702, Bowie MD 20718. Established 1989. **Editors:** Carol Dyer and Roger Kyle-Keith.

Magazine Needs: *The Plastic Tower* is a quarterly using "everything from iambic pentameter to silly limericks, modern free verse, haiku, rhymed couplets—we like it all! Only restriction is length—under 40 lines preferred. So send us poems that are cool or wild, funny or tragic—but especially those closest to your soul." Accepts poetry written by children. Has published poetry by "more than 400 different poets." *The Plastic Tower* is 38-54 pgs., digest-sized, saddle-stapled; "variety of typefaces and b&w graphics on cheap photocopy paper. Line drawings also welcome." Press run is 200. Subscription: $8/year. Copy of current issue: $2.50. "We'll send a back issue free for a large (at least 6×9) SAE with 2 first-class stamps attached."

How to Submit: Submit up to 10 poems at a time. Accepts previously published poems and simultaneous submissions. Often comment on submissions. Guidelines available for SASE. Responds in 6 months. Pays 1 contributor's copy. Poets may send books for review consideration.

Advice: "*The Plastic Tower* is an unpretentious little rag dedicated to enjoying verse and making poetry accessible to the general public as well as fellow poets. We don't claim to be the best, but we try to be the nicest and most personal. Over the past several years, we've noticed a tremendous upswing in submissions. More people than ever are writing poetry and submitting it for publication, and that makes it tougher for individual writers to get published. But plenty of opportunities still exist (there are thousands of little and literary magazines in the U.S. alone), and the most effective tool for any writer right now is not talent or education, but persistence. So keep at it!"

🌐 🖥 ◑ ◎ THE PLAZA (Specialized: bilingual), U-Kan, Inc., Yoyogi 2-32-1, Shibuya-ku, Tokyo 151-0053, Japan. Phone: 81-3-3379-3881. Fax: 81-3-3379 3882. E-mail: plaza@u-kan.co.jp. Website: http://u-kan.co.jp. Established 1985. **Contact:** editor.

Magazine Needs: *The Plaza* is a quarterly, currently published only online (http://u-kan.co.jp), which "represents a borderless forum for contemporary writers and artists" and includes poetry, fiction, and essays published simultaneously in English and Japanese. Wants "highly artistic poetry dealing with being human and interculturally related. Nothing stressing political, national, religious, or racial differences. *The Plaza* is edited with a global view of mankind." Has published poetry by Al Beck, Antler, Charles Helzer, Richard Alan Bunch, Morgan Gibson, and Bun'ichirou Chino. As a sample the editors selected these lines from "To Instruct and Delight" by Charles Helzer:

> It is a music of crows,/the burden their croaking,/choreography a bone,/dancing on my skylight,/shaken, picked at, flung,/claws shuffling on glass.

The Plaza is 50 full color pgs. Available free to all readers on the Internet. Receives about 2,500 poems/year, accepts 8%. Proofs of accepted poems are sent to the authors 1 month before online publication.

How to Submit: Accepts simultaneous submissions; no previously published poems. Accepts e-mail and fax submissions. "No attachments. Cover letter required. Please include telephone and fax numbers or e-mail address with submissions. As *The Plaza* is a bilingual publication in English and Japanese, it is sometimes necessary, for translation purposes, to contact authors. Japanese translations are prepared by the editorial staff." Seldom comments on rejected poems. Responds within 2 months. Reviews books of poetry, usually in less than 500 words. Poets may send books for review consideration.

Advice: "*The Plaza* focuses not on human beings but humans being human in the borderless world."

$ ◑ PLEIADES; PLEIADES/LENA-MILES WEVER TODD POETRY SERIES; PLEIADES PRESS, Dept. of English and Philosophy, Central Missouri State University, Warrensburg MO 64093. (660)543-8106. E-mail: kdp8106@cmsu2.cmsu.edu. Website: www.cmsu.edu/englphil.pleiades.edu (includes new poems and stories, guidelines, masthead, contributors' notes, and contents for current issues). Established as *Spring Flight* in 1939, reestablished in its present format in 1990. **Editors:** R.M. Kinder and Kevin Prufer.

Magazine Needs: *Pleiades* is a semiannual journal which publishes poetry, fiction, literary criticism, belles lettres (occasionally), and reviews. It is open to all writers. Wants "avant-garde, free verse and traditional poetry, and some quality light verse. Nothing pretentious, didactic, or overly sentimental." Has published poetry by Campbell McGrath, Brenda Hillman, Kevin Young, Rafael Campo, and Carl Phillips. As a sample the editor selected these lines from "How tailors are made" by Graham Foust:

> Cipher the rate at which things are put/Together. You will discover a love for light//Sleepers who dream they are the only ones/With hands. I'll get lost on the way to your mouth.//If I could have anything I wanted, I would have/Less than I do now. Maybe your blood on a textbook,//Or your breath like some ancient hinge.

Pleiades is 160 pgs., 5½×8½, perfect-bound with a heavy coated cover and color cover art. Receives about 3,000 poems/year, accepts 1-3%. Press run is 2,500-3,000, about 200 distributed free to educational institutions and libraries across the country, several hundred shelf sales. Single copy: $6; subscription: $12. Sample: $5. Make checks payable to Pleiades Press.

How to Submit: Submit 3-5 poems at a time. Accepts simultaneous submissions with notification; no previously published poems. Cover letter with brief bio preferred. Time between acceptance and publication can be up to 1 year. Each poem published must be accepted by 2 readers and approved by the poetry editor. Seldom comments on rejected poems. Guidelines available for SASE or on website. Responds in up to 3 months. Payment varies. Acquires first and second serial rights and requests rights for *Wordbeat*, a TV/radio show featuring work published in *Pleiades*.

Also Offers: Sponsors the Pleiades/Lena-Miles Wever Todd Poetry Series. "We will select one book of poems in open competition and publish it in our Pleiades Press Series. Louisiana State University Press will distribute the collection." Entry fee: $15. Postmark deadline: March 31, 2001. Complete guidelines available for SASE.

☑ ☒ $☒ **PLOUGHSHARES**, Emerson College, 120 Boyleston St., Boston MA 02116. (617)824-8753. Established 1971.
  • Work published in *Ploughshares* appears in the 1995, 1996, 1997, and 1998 volumes of *The Best American Poetry.*

Magazine Needs: *Ploughshares* is "a journal of new writing guest-edited by prominent poets and writers to reflect different and contrasting points of view." Editors have included Carolyn Forché, Gerald Stern, Rita Dove, Chase Twichell, and Marilyn Hacker. Has published poetry by Donald Hall, Li-Young Lee, Robert Pinsky, Brenda Hillman, and Thylias Moss. The triquarterly is 250 pgs., 5½×8½. Press run is 6,000. Receives about 2,500 poetry submissions/year. Subscription: $22 domestic; $28 foreign. Sample: $9.95 current issue, $8.50 sample back issue.

How to Submit: "We suggest you read a few issues before submitting." Simultaneous submissions acceptable. Do not submit mss from April 1 to July 31. Responds in up to 5 months. Always sends prepublication galleys. Pays $50 minimum per poem, $25/printed page per poem, plus 2 copies and a subscription.

◆ $○ ◐ **THE PLOWMAN**, Box 414, Whitby, Ontario L1N 5S4 Canada. (905)668-7803. Established 1988. **Editor:** Tony Scavetta.

Magazine Needs: *The Plowman* appears semiannually using "didactic, eclectic poetry; all forms. We will also take most religious poetry except satanic and evil. We are interested in work that deals with the important issues in our society. Social and environment issues are of great importance." Has published *Rough Edge* by Don Hogan, *Once Upon a Lifetime* Volume I by Rita F. Lynch, and *Comes the New Dawn* by Scott Hallam. *The Plowman* is 20 pgs., 8½×11 (17×11 sheet folded), photocopied, unbound, contains clip art and market listings. Accepts 70% of the poetry received. Press run is 15,000 for 1,200 subscribers of which 500 are libraries. Single copy: $5; subscription: $10. Sample free.

How to Submit: Accepts previously published poems and simultaneous submissions. Cover letter required. No SASE necessary. Always comments on rejected poems. Guidelines available free. Responds in 1 week. Always sends prepublication galleys. Pays 1 copy. Reviews books of poetry.

Book/Chapbook Needs & How to Submit: Also publishes 125 chapbooks/year. Responds to queries and mss in 1 month. **Reading fee:** $25/book. Pays 20% royalties. Has published *Sense the Need* by Ken Harvey; *Just To Hear Me Yell* by Robin Merrill; *Inspiration* by Geri Ahearn; and *Jamie's Garden* by D.N. Simmers.

Also Offers: Offers monthly poetry contests. Entry fee: $2/poem. 1st Prize: 50% of the proceeds; 2nd: 25%; 3rd: 10%. The top poems are published. "Balance of the poems will be used for anthologies."

◐ **POCAHONTAS PRESS, INC.; MANUSCRIPT MEMORIES**, P.O. Drawer F, Blacksburg VA 24063-1020. (800)446-0467. Fax: (540)961-2847. E-mail: mchollim@vt.edu. Established 1984. **President:** Mary C. Holliman. Not considering new mss at this time. Accepts queries via e-mail. Has published *Arts Alive 2000: An Anthology of New River Valley Writers and Poets* and *Night and Light and the Half-Light* by Henry George Fischer.

◐ **POEM; HUNTSVILLE LITERARY ASSOCIATION**, English Dept., University of Alabama at Huntsville, Huntsville AL 35899. Established 1967. **Poetry Editor:** Nancy Frey Dillard.

Magazine Needs: *Poem*, appears twice/year, consisting entirely of poetry. "We are open to traditional as well as non-traditional forms, but we favor work with the expected compression and intensity of good lyric poetry and a high degree of verbal and dramatic tension. We equally welcome submissions from established poets as well as from less-known and beginning poets." Has published poetry by Robert Cooperman, Andrew Dillon, and Scott Travis Hutchison. *Poem* is a flat-spined, 4⅜×7¼, 90-page journal that contains more than 60 poems (mostly lyric free verse under 50 lines) generally featured 1 to a page on good stock paper with a clean design and a classy matte cover. Press run is 400 (all subscriptions, including libraries). Sample: $5.

How to Submit: "We do not accept translations, previously published works, or simultaneous submissions. Best to submit December through March and June through September. We prefer to see a sample of three to five poems at a submission, with SASE. We generally respond within a month. We are a nonprofit organization and can pay only in copy to contributors." Pays 2 contributor's copies. Acquires first serial rights.

○ ◐ **POEM DU JOUR**, P.O. Box 416, Somers MT 59932. Established 1999. **Editor:** Asta Bowen.

Magazine Needs: *Poem du Jour* is a "weekly one-page broadside circulated in the retail environment." Wants "accessible but not simplistic poetry; seasonal work encouraged; humorous, current events, slam favorites; topical work (rural, mountain, outdoors, environmental, Northwest). No erotica, forced rhyme, or poems of excessive length." As a sample the editor selected these lines from "Dandelions" by Lacie Jo Twiest:

> she called them flowers but I knew that they weren't/and I watched as she rubbed yellow on her cheeks
> and her lips/her entire face was the color of the sun and she beamed/and I watched her carefully craft
> the wreath that she placed atop her head/she was a princess though I knew she was too old to pretend . . .

Press run is 20-50. Sample: $2. Make checks payable to Asta Bowen—PDJ.

How to Submit: Submit up to 5 poems at a time. Line length for poetry is 50 maximum. Accepts previously published poems and simultaneous submissions. Cover letter preferred. "Prefer poems typed with name, address and phone on each page." Time between acceptance and publication varies. Seldom comments on rejected poems. Guidelines available for SASE. Responds in 2 months. Sometimes sends prepublication galleys. Pays 1 contributor's copy. Acquires one-time rights.
Advice: "New/young writers encouraged."

POEMS & PLAYS; THE TENNESSEE CHAPBOOK PRIZE, English Dept., Middle Tennessee State University, Murfreesboro TN 37132. (615)898-2712. Established 1993. **Editor:** Gaylord Brewer.
Magazine Needs: *Poems & Plays* is an annual "eclectic publication for poems and short plays," published in April. No restrictions on style or content of poetry. Has published poetry by Stephen Dobyns, Philip Levine, Vivian Shipley, Charles Bukowski, and Ron Koertge. *Poems & Plays* is 88 pgs., 6×9, professionally printed and perfect-bound with coated color card cover and art. "We receive 1,500 poems per issue, typically publish 30-35." Press run is 800. Subscription: $10/2 issues. Sample: $6.
How to Submit: No previously published poems or simultaneous submissions (except for chapbook submissions). Reads submissions October 1 through January 15 only. "Work is circulated among advisory editors for comments and preferences. All accepted material is published in the following issue." Usually comments on rejected poems. Responds in 2 months. Pays 1 contributor's copy. Acquires first publication rights only.
Also Offers: "We accept chapbook manuscripts (of poems or short plays) of 20-24 pages for The Tennessee Chapbook Prize. Any combination of poems or plays, or a single play, is eligible. The winning chapbook is printed as an interior chapbook in *Poems & Plays* and the author receives 50 copies of the issue. SASE and $10 (for reading fee and one copy of the issue) required. Dates for contest entry are the same as for the magazine (October 1 through January 15). Past winners include Maureen Micus Crisick, David Kirby, Angela Kelly, and Rob Griffith. The chapbook competition annually receives over 100 manuscripts from the U.S. and around the world."

N **POESY MAGAZINE**, 106 Campbell St., #5, Santa Cruz CA 95060. (831)460-1048. E-mail: poesymag@hotmail.com. Website: www.geocities.com/bmorrise2/ (includes the online version of the latest issues). Established 1994. **Editor/Publisher:** Brian Morrisey.
Magazine Needs: *POESY Magazine* appears quarterly. "*POESY* is an anthology of American poetry. *POESY*'s main concentration is Boston, MA and Santa Cruz, CA, two thriving homesteads for poets, beats, and artists of nature. Our goal is to unite the two scenes, updating poets on what's happening across the country. We like to see poems that express atmosphere and observational impacts of both Santa Cruz and Boston. Acceptence is based on creativity, composition, and relation to the goals of *POESY*. Please do not send poetry with excessive profanity. We would like to endorse creativity beyond the likes of everyday babble." Recently published poetry by A.D. Winans, Lyn Lifshin, Alan Catlin, Matt Welter, Hugh Fox, and Ed Galing. As a sample the editor selected these lines from "John Ashberry" by Normal:

> You photographed/my mind/with trees and ideas/fresh as the masque/of new dancers/forgetting your
> elementary tease

POESY is 16 pgs., 7½×10, newsprint, glued/folded, with computer generated and quarter-page ads. Receives about 1,000 poems/year, accepts about 10%. Publishes about 35 poems/issue. Press run is 1,000, most distributed free to local venues. Single copy: $1; subscription: $10/year. Sample: $2. Make checks payable to Brian Morrisey.
How to Submit: Submit 5-7 poems at a time. Line length for poetry is 32 maximum. No previously published poems or simultaneous submissions. Accepts e-mail and disk submissions; no fax submissions. Cover letter preferred. "Snail mail submissions are preferred with a SASE." Reads submissions year round. Time between acceptance and publication is 3 weeks. "Poems are accepted by the Boston editor and the publisher based on how well the poem stimulates our format." Often comments on rejected poems. Guidelines are available in magazine, for SASE, and by e-mail. Responds in 3 weeks. Sometimes sends prepublication galleys. Pays 3 contributor's copies. Acquires one-time rights. Reviews books and chapbooks of poetry and other magazines/journals in 1,000 words, single book format. Poets may send books for review consideration to *POESY*, % Brian Morrisey.
Advice: "Branch away from typical notions of love and romance. Become one with your surroundings and discover a true sense of natural perspective."

N $ **A POET BORN PRESS**, P.O. Box 24238, Knoxville TN 37933. E-mail: wm.tell.us@apoetborn.com. Website: www.apoetborn.com. Established 1998. **Contact:** Laura Skye.
Book/Chapbook Needs: A Poet Born Press publishes 6-8 paperbacks per year. Wants any style or form of poetry, 45 lines or less, including spaces. "Poems should be descriptive of the 20th Century, its people and its issues." No profanity. Has published poetry by Robin Moore, Dwhisperer, and Skye. As a sample the editor selected these lines from "One Public Servant" by J. Elsie Madding:

> What was it like—/Going to work each morning,/Calmly ordering the affairs of state,/Striving for
> wisdom amidst national crises,/Seeking to achieve honorable compromise/Among arguing, bipartitie
> factions

Books are usually 50-150 pgs., 5½×8½, perfect-bound with 80 lb. cover stock, 1 color or full bleed color covers, includes some photographs, some drawings.

How to Submit: Query first with 1-2 sample poems and cover letter with brief bio and publication credits. Line length for poetry is 45 maximum including spaces. Accepts previously published poems and simultaneous submissions. Accepts e-mail and disk submissions. "All poetry must be accompanied by author's name and address, as well as by e-mail address and URL if applicable. Also, author must specify what submission is for: contest, certain publications or call for poems, etc." Time between acceptance and publication is up to 6 months. Poems are circulated to an editorial board. "The editorial staff reviews all submissions for publication and makes their recommendations to the Senior Editor who makes the final selections." Often comments on rejected poems. "We charge for criticism only on manuscript-length work. Price varies depending on length of manuscript. E-mail for complete details." Responds to queries in 2 months. Pays 5-35% royalties "depending on individual contract." 50% of books are author-subsidy published each year. "We have four different subsidy programs. Program is dependent upon work, audience, sales track, and author/press choice. Contracts are specifically tailored to individual authors and their work. No loyalties are paid for poems accepted for anthologies."
Also Offers: Sponsors three contests per year. 1st Place: $100 plus a brass plaque of poem; 2nd Place: brass plaque of poem; 3rd Place: A Poet Born coffee mug. "All winners receive web publication within 6 weeks of contest and print publication within one year." Entry fee: $5/poem. Website includes complete contest guidelines and submission form, Call for Poems section and permission form, Winners Circle and archive of previous winning poems, Poetry Night listings, poetry news and events, resource links and Teacher's Corner. "Teacher's Corner features lessons in poetry provided by published poets, authors, professors, editors and more. Recent appearances in the Teacher's Corner include: Robert Pinsky; Robin Moore, author of the *French Connection* and *The Green Berets*; Eugene McCarthy, statesman and published poet; and Michael Bugeja, author of *The Art and Craft of Poetry*."

◐ ◒ POET LORE, The Writer's Center, 4508 Walsh St., Bethesda MD 20815. (301)654-8664. Fax: (301)654-8667. E-mail: postmaster@writer.org. Website: www.writer.org (includes magazine and contest guidelines, table of contents, subscription info, current issue, and back-issue archives). Established 1889. **Managing Editor:** Jo-Ann Billings. **Executive Editors:** Rick Cannon and Liz Poliner.
Magazine Needs: *Poet Lore* is a quarterly dedicated "to the best in American and world poetry and objective and timely reviews and commentary. We look for fresh uses of traditional form and devices, but any kind of excellence is welcome. The editors encourage narrative poetry and original translations of works by contemporary world poets." Has published poetry by William Matthews, Denise Duhamel, Susan Terris, R.T. Smith, and Cornelius Eady. *Poet Lore* is 6×9, 80 pgs., perfect-bound, professionally printed with glossy card cover. Circulation includes 600 subscriptions of which 200 are libraries. Receives about 3,000 poems/year, accepts 125. Single copy: $5.50; subscription: $18. Sample: $4.50.
How to Submit: Submit typed poems, author's name and address on each page, SASE required. No simultaneous submissions. Responds in 3 months. Pays 2 contributor's copies. Reviews books of poetry. Poets may send books for review consideration.

⊕ ◐ ◒ ◎ POETCRIT (Specialized: membership), Maranda, H.P. 176 102 India. Phone: 01894-31407. Established 1988. **Editor:** Dr. D.C. Chambial.
Magazine Needs: *Poetcrit* appears each January and July "to promote poetry and international understanding through poetry. Purely critical articles on various genres of literature are also published." Wants poems of every kind. Has published poetry by Ruth Wilder Schuller (US), Danae G. Papastratau (Greece), Shiv K. Kumar (India), Joy B. Cripps (Australia), and O.P. Bhatnagar (India). As a sample the editor selected these lines from "An Existential Question" by Manas Bakashi:

> For some days/I have lived/weaving thoughts around/All that's intractable/But poised for/An apocalypse.

Poetcrit is 100 pgs., magazine-sized, offset-printed with simple paper cover, includes ads. Receives about 1,000 poems/year, accepts 20%. Press run is 1,000 for 500 subscribers of which 100 are libraries, 200 shelf sales; 400 distributed free to new members. Single copy: $9; subscription: $15. Sample: $10. Make checks payable to Dr. D.C. Chambial. Membership required for consideration.
How to Submit: Submit 3 poems at a time. Line length for poetry is 25 maximum. Accepts simultaneous submissions; no previously published poems. Cover letter required. Reads submissions September 1 through 20 and March 1 through 20. Poems are circulated to an editorial board. "All poems reviewed by various editors and selected for publication." Occasionally publishes theme issues. Guidelines and upcoming themes are available for SASE or SAE with IRC. Responds in about 1 month. Pays 1 contributor's copy. Acquires one-time rights. Reviews books and chapbooks of poetry and other magazines in 1,000 words, single book format.
Advice: "Beginners should meditate well on their themes before writing."

⊕ ◐ POETIC HOURS, 43 Willow Rd., Carlton, Nolts NG4 3BH England. E-mail: erran@arrowgroup.frees erve,co.uk. Established 1993. Website: www.poetichours.homestead.com (includes magazine's history and charity work, submission guidelines, contacts, news of forthcoming issues, and *'Poetic Hours Online'*). **Editor:** Nicholas Clark.
Magazine Needs: *Poetic Hours*, published biannually, "is published solely to encourage and publish new poets, i.e., as a forum where good but little known poets can appear in print and to raise money for Third World charities. The magazine features articles and poetry by subscribers and others." Wants "any subject, rhyme preferred but

not essential; suitable for wide ranging readership, 30 lines maximum." Does not want "gothic, horror, extremist, political, self-interested." As a sample the editor selected these lines from his poem "School Report: Human Race":

> *Does the western world now stand for judgement/Before a clock?/There's a thought!/Whole nations*
> *check two thousand years of progress/Waiting for teachers Millennium Report*

Poetic Hours is 36 pgs., A4, printed, saddle-stapled and illustrated throughout with Victorian woodcuts. Receives about 500 poems/year, accepts about 40%. Press run is 400 of which 12 are for libraries, 300 shelf sales. Subscription: £5, overseas payments in sterling or US dollars ($20). For a subscription send bankers checks or cash. Sample: £3. Make checks payable to Erran Publishing.

How to Submit: "Poets are encouraged to subscribe or buy a single copy, though not required." Submit up to 5 nonreturnable poems at a time. Accepts previously published poems; no simultaneous submissions. Accepts e-mail submissions in attachments; accepts disk submissions. Cover letter required. Time between acceptance and publication is 3 months. "Poems are read by editors and if found suitable, are used." Always comments on rejected poems. Publishes theme issues. Upcoming themes listed in magazine. Responds "immediately, whenever possible." Acquires one-time rights. Staff reviews books or chapbooks of poetry. Send books for review consideration.

Also Offers: "Poetic Hours Online" features original content. "New Poets or beginners who are willing to subscribe to hard copy should submit up to 5 poems."

Advice: "We welcome newcomers and invite those just starting out to have the courage to submit work. The art of poetry has moved from the hands of book publishers down the ladder to the new magazines. This is where all the best poetry is found." *Poetic Hours* is non-profit-making and all proceeds go to various national charities, particularly Oxfam and Amnesty International. A page of *Poetic Hours* is set aside each issue for reporting how money is spent.

✔ ▢ ◯ **POETIC LICENSE POETRY MAGAZINE**, P.O. Box 311, Kewanee IL 61443-0311. E-mail: poeticlicense99@hotmail.com. Website: www.skybusiness.com/poetic license (includes guidelines, upcoming themes, current issue, samples from past issues and links to other sites). Established 1996. **Editor:** Denise Felt. **Children's Editor:** Nadine Shelton.

Magazine Needs: *Poetic License Poetry Magazine* is a monthly publication with "the purpose of giving new and experienced poets a chance to be published. It includes articles and contests that challenge poets to grow in their craft. We want the best free verse and rhymed poetry by adults and children. No profane, vulgar, pornographic, or sloppy work accepted." Has published poetry by Linda Creech, Terri Warden, William Middleton, and Robert Hentz. As a sample the editor selected these lines from "Inspiration" by Kimber Stonehouse:

> *I open the new book,/smelling the fresh print,/excitement like lightning flashing.*

Poetic License Poetry Magazine is 50 pgs., 8½×11, magazine-bound with full color cover, includes graphic art and ads. Receives over 2,000 poems/year, accepts about 95%. Press run is 80/issue. Subscription: $49/year, $94/2 years. Sample: $5.50. Make checks payable to *Poetic License*.

How to Submit: Submit up to 5 poems at a time. Accepts previously published poems and simultaneous submissions. Accepts e-mail submissions in body of message. Cover letter preferred. "Send double-spaced typed poems with name and address in upper right hand corner. Age required if poet is 18 or younger." Time between acceptance and publication is 1 month. "I judge poems on a 25-point system. Adult submissions with 12 points or less are rejected. Children's submissions with 10 points or less are rejected." Seldom comments on rejected poems. Publishes theme issues. Responds in 2 weeks. Acquires one-time rights. Guidelines and upcoming themes available for SASE, by e-mail, or on website.

Also Offers: Sponsors a quarterly contest anthology on a different theme each February, May, August, and November. Anthology chapbooks available at the end of each contest. Send SASE for contest rules. "Magazine and contest anthology winners throughout the year are published in an annual poetry volume called *150 Best Poems*. These are some of the best poems to be found by contemporary poets." Past volumes available.

Advice: "The most important thing poets should concern themselves with is excellence. Whether a poem is rewritten twice or twenty times, it shouldn't matter. The goal is to bring the poem to life. Then it's fit for publication. There is more talent in literate people of all ages than the poets of past centuries could have dreamed. Our goal is to encourage that talent to grow and flourish through exposure to the public."

Ⓝ ▣ $ ◖ ◯ ⊘ **THE POETIC LINK (Specialized: anthology, membership)**, 4066 Green Park Dr., Mt Joy PA 17552. (717)653-9916. E-mail: webmaster@thepoeticlink.com. Website: http://ThePoeticLink.com (includes a real time interactive poetry database; submissions post immediately and receive critiques throughout the entire month). Established 1999. **Owner:** Christopher T. Moore.

USE THE GENERAL INDEX, located at the back of this book, to find the page number of a specific publisher. Also, publishers that were listed in last year's edition but not included in this edition are listed in the General Index with a notation explaining why they were omitted.

insider report

An online editor looks at poetry on the Web

In a recent conversation between poets David Lehman and Robert Creeley, Lehman asked Creeley what he thought of the Internet. "He replied without hesitation," Lehman says. "He sees it as a hugely significant development, a potentially revolutionary method and means of distribution."

Robin Travis-Murphree

The Internet *has* proven to be a significant development, the "Brave New World" where poetry flourishes and poets are discovered. Digital publications appear in growing numbers, and hard copy publications promote their journals through websites, most including samples of their content.

However, the Internet also presents some challenges for both poets and editors.

It's true that the Web has created opportunities for poets of all skill levels to share their work in new forums. It's also true, though, that the Internet allows any person with the ability to develop a website or write e-mail to become a self-appointed editor.

When surfing the Net and deciding where to submit work, a poet should study the quality of the site's content. Are the pieces the editor selects good poetry? Are there interesting, informative articles, book reviews, features, and interviews? Is the publication affiliated with a writers' organization? Or is it some fly-by-night e-mail newsletter put together by someone whose credentials are as obscure as his or her identity? Are the editors published writers themselves? Keep these things in mind to make sure your work appears in a respected e-zine.

There are many wonderful online poetry publications. Some of my favorites are *The Cortland Review* (www.cortlandreview.com); *Pif Magazine* (www.pifmagazine.com); *Poetry Daily* (www.poems.com); *The Atlantic Monthly's Poetry Pages* (www.theatlantic.com/poetry/poetry.htm); *The Contemporary Poetry Review* (www.cprw.com); *Big Bridge* (www.bigbridge.org); and, of course, *Poetic Voices Magazine* (of which I'm executive editor—http://poeticvoices.com/).

In addition to e-zines, there are several websites full of information and resources that poets need. Two of these are the Academy of American Poets (www.poets.org) and Poetry Society of America (www.poetrysociety.org).

Poets should be cautious of sites which promise publication and require contributors to pay fees for books and other items. While online publications rarely have the funds to pay poets for publishing their works, they never *charge* contributors to do so. Just as there are predators in the book publishing world, they also inhabit cyberland.

The Web has created a mixed bag of delights and frustrations for online editors as well. On the one hand, accessibility has enabled editors to find poets they wouldn't have discovered otherwise. The lack of "space" restrictions and the low cost of publishing on the Net have given online editors the ability to publish more poetry than they could in hardcopy editions.

Distribution is easier and there are no mailing costs; once editors publish their journals online, they simply e-mail their subscribers to announce the latest edition's release.

There's also the audio/video dimension of the new multimedia. Digital publications can include audio or video clips of poets reading their work, something print publications have never been able to do.

On the other hand, digital editors face some of the same problems as print editors, only with fresh twists unique to electronic submissions.

Because of the ease of e-mail, editors are flooded with submissions. What's more, poets seem to believe that ready access to these once unreachable icons gives them the right to "Instant Message" or e-mail editors to find out if they've read their poems.

Several times while working online, I've received Instant Messages asking me to look at a poet's work. Because I like to help aspiring poets, I asked them to e-mail the poems for later review since I was busy at the time. A few moments later the poets were sending another Instant Message to say the poems had been sent, had I read them yet, and what did I think of them?

Another frustration digital editors share with print editors is dealing with poets who don't read the publication and/or disregard the importance of submission guidelines. Many editors, both digital and print, do not accept e-mail submissions. However, editors provide e-mail addresses for correspondence, inquiries, and requests. Poets take advantage of that address to submit their work electronically.

Because of the risk of viruses, software compatibility, and other concerns, many editors don't accept e-mail submissions as attached files (poems should be "pasted" into the body of the message). Yet poets continue to send their work as attachments (and some of these attached files contain everything the poet has ever written; two years ago, one poet sent me a file containing over 500 poems).

Here's an example of a more recent problem. I received two e-mails from poets who wanted their work read. First of all, I don't read submissions; my poetry editor, Ursula T. Gibson, does. This automatically let me know the poets hadn't read our guidelines. What's more, those messages read:

"*My poems are listed at [web address]. You may consider them for submission to your magazine.*" and "*I have collected my poems and ideas in the following websites: [list of seven websites]. Please have a look at them and let me know if you are interested in publishing them.*"

What these aspiring poets (and many others) do not understand is this: Editors, whether digital or print, do not have the time to go surfing for a poet's work. We already receive mountains of submissions each month.

Poets need to follow proper submission protocol, whether sending work to print or digital publications. Read the publication to see what type of work the editors are looking for. Review the submission guidelines. Poets who send work to the wrong editor, attach files to e-mail submissions, refer to website addresses where their work is posted, or submit work incompatible with the publication tell the editor they don't really care about that publication—or even their own work.

Poets also should remember that business on the Internet requires them to maintain their professionalism. They need to follow submission guidelines meticulously. After all, they no longer compete for an editor's attention from a small pool of contributors, but from a global community.

I asked a few editors and poets for their thoughts on the Internet. In closing, I'd like to share some of their responses:

"The Internet can continue the democratization of poetry. Then again, it's that very democratization that can muddle things. How do you wade through the sheer ocean of stuff and find what works for you and how your stuff can work for others? My students often encounter that disappointment, and it surprises them, and me . . ." Kevin Stein, author of *Private Poets, Worldly Acts: Public and Private History in Contemporary American Poetry* (essays) and three collections of poetry, including his most recent, *Chance Ransom.*

"I'm also very positive about the possibilities for start-up literary zines. Lots of wonderful writers will get launched in this 21st century equivalent of the mimeographed small mag started in someone's garage fifty years ago. Literary history is being made now, and it's exciting." Molly Peacock, author of several books of poetry; her guide, *How to Read a Poem and Start a Poetry Circle*; and her autobiography, *Paradise, Piece by Piece.*

"I think the Internet can save poetry in a big way. *Big Bridge* is a new community that expands with input from a changing creative environment that has a global ecology of mind . . . we are working with dynamics of a new medium that is language- and image-based and allows for relatively inexpensive access. Editing can be an art form, and the canvas of the Internet is enormous and gratifying." Michael Rothenberg, editor of *Big Bridge.*

—*Robin Travis-Murphree*

Magazine Needs: *The Poetic Link* is a website devoted to poetry posted to be shared and critiqued. "Each month every poetry submission is ranked. The best-ranked poem by each poet is placed on the 'winners list' and then published in our quarterly anthology. The top poems receive cash prizes." Wants all styles and formats, any subject matter, focus, or purpose." Does not want "poetry you have NOT given an honest effort at writing." Recently published poetry by Charles L. East, Wayne R. Leach, CJ Heck, Gene Dixon, Regina M. Heller, and Kelly Denise Evans. As a sample we selected these lines from "Summer Meditation" by Judy P. King:

> I reflect on the secret of summer/Amidst a drift of honeybees/Drunk on wine from flowers,//While a
> whisper from the wind reminds me/That everything is temporary/And must be loved to last./

How to Submit: Submit any number of poems of any length at $3/poem. Accepts previously published poems and simultaneous submissions. No e-mail submissions or disk submissions. "Submissions are ONLY accepted online at our website. The $3 submission fee is used to pay out the prizes each month. The critiques and advice you will get back on your poetry are well worth the small fee." Use the "submission link" on the main web page. Reads submissions constantly. All poetry is critiqued and scored on various points by website members (no charge for critiquing others' poetry). Guidelines available on website. Responds in 5 weeks or less. Always sends prepublication galleys. Pays in monthly prizes for both poetry and critiques. Acquires first rights.

Also Offers: *The Poetic Link Anthology*, a hardbound 8½×11 quarterly in which "each poet can have one poem per month." Single copy: $30 plus $5 shipping. Make checks payable to *The Poetic Link.*

Advice: "If you are a new or unpublished poet, this is a great place to start. You will learn a great deal here with us. If you are an experienced poet, you will teach a great deal and may earn some nice cash."

◯ POETIC SPACE: POETRY & FICTION, P.O. Box 11157, Eugene OR 97440. Fax: (541)683-1271. E-mail: poeticspac@aol.com. Established 1983. **Editor:** Don Hildenbrand.

Magazine Needs: *Poetic Space*, published annually in the fall, is a nonprofit literary magazine with emphasis on contemporary poetry, fiction, reviews (including film and drama), interviews, market news, and translations. Accepts poetry and fiction that is "well-crafted and takes risks. We like poetry with guts. Would like to see some poetry on social and political issues. We would also like to see gay/lesbian poetry and poetry on women's issues. Erotic and experimental OK." Prefers poems under 1,000 words. Has published poetry by Simon Perchik, Paul Weinman, Sherman Alexie, Albert Huffstickler, and Lyn Lifshin. *Poetic Space* is 30 pgs., magazine-sized, saddle-stapled, offset from typescript and sometimes photoreduced. Receives about 200-300 poems/year, accepts about 25%. Press run is 800 for 50 subscribers of which 12 are libraries. Single copy: $4; subscription: $7/2 issues, $13/4 issues. Send SASE for list of available back issues ($4).

How to Submit: Ms should be typed, double-spaced, clean, name/address on each page. "Submissions without SASE will not be considered." Accepts simultaneous submissions and previously published poems. Editor provides some critical comments. Guidelines available for SASE. Responds in up to 4 months. Pays 1 contributor's copy, but more can be ordered by sending SASE and postage. Reviews books of poetry in 500-1,000 words. Poets may send books for review consideration.

Book/Chapbook Needs & How to Submit: Also publishes one chapbook each spring. First chapbook was *Truth Rides to Work and Good Girls*, poetry by Crawdad Nelson and fiction by Louise A. Blum ($5 plus $1.50 p&h).

Advice: "We like poetry that takes risks—original writing that gives us a new, different perspective."

POETIC VOICES MAGAZINE, (See listing for Alden Enterprises in this section.)

■ $◨ **POETRY; THE MODERN POETRY ASSOCIATION; BESS HOKIN PRIZE; LEVINSON PRIZE; EUNICE TIETJENS MEMORIAL PRIZE; FREDERICK BOCK PRIZE; GEORGE KENT PRIZE; UNION LEAGUE PRIZE; J. HOWARD AND BARBARA M.J. WOOD PRIZE; RUTH LILLY POETRY PRIZE; RUTH LILLY POETRY FELLOWSHIP; JOHN FREDERICK NIMS PRIZE**, 60 W. Walton St., Chicago IL 60610-3380. E-mail: poetry@poetrymagazine.org. Website: www.poetrymagazine.org (includes contents of recent issues, featured poets, guidelines, subscription information, announcement of awards, etc.). Established 1912. **Editor:** Joseph Parisi.

● Work published in *Poetry* is frequently selected for inclusion in volumes of *The Best American Poetry*.

Magazine Needs: *Poetry* "is the oldest and most distinguished monthly magazine devoted entirely to verse. Established in Chicago in 1912, it immediately became the international showcase that it has remained ever since, publishing in its earliest years—and often for the first time—such giants as Ezra Pound, Robert Frost, T.S. Eliot, Marianne Moore, and Wallace Stevens. *Poetry* has continued to print the major voices of our time and to discover new talent, establishing an unprecedented record. There is virtually no important contemporary poet in our language who has not at a crucial stage in his career depended on *Poetry* to find a public for him: John Ashbery, Dylan Thomas, Edna St. Vincent Millay, James Merrill, Anne Sexton, Sylvia Plath, James Dickey, Thom Gunn, David Wagoner—only a partial list to suggest how *Poetry* has represented, without affiliation with any movements or schools, what Stephen Spender has described as 'the best, and simply the best' poetry being written." As a sample the editor selected the opening lines of "The Love Song of J. Alfred Prufrock" by T.S. Eliot, which first appeared in *Poetry* in 1915:

> *Let us go then, you and I,/When the evening is spread out against the sky/Like a patient etherized upon*
> *a table;/Let us go, through certain half-deserted streets . . .*

Poetry is an elegantly printed, flat-spined, 5½×9 magazine. Receives over 90,000 submissions/year, accepts about 300-350; has a backlog up to 9 months. Press run is 12,000 for 8,000 subscribers of which 33% are libraries. Single copy: $3.50; subscription: $30, $33 for institutions. Sample: $5.

How to Submit: Submit up to 4 poems at a time with SASE. No e-mail submissions. Guidelines available for SASE. Responds in 4 months—longer for mss submitted during the summer. Pays $2 a line. Acquires all rights. Returns rights "upon written request." Reviews books of poetry in multi-book formats of varying lengths. Poets may send books to Stephen Young, senior editor, for review consideration.

Also Offers: Eight prizes (named in heading) ranging from $200 to $3,000 are awarded annually to poets whose work has appeared in the magazine that year. Only verse already published in *Poetry* is eligible for consideration and no formal application is necessary. *Poetry* also sponsors the Ruth Lilly Poetry Prize, an annual award of $75,000, and the Ruth Lilly Poetry Fellowship, two annual awards of $15,000 to undergraduate or graduate students to support their further studies in poetry/creative writing.

◨ **POETRY & PROSE ANNUAL**, P.O. Box 541, Manzanita OR 97130. E-mail: poetry@poetryproseannual. com. Website: www.poetryproseannual.com (includes guidelines, names of editors, poetry from previous editions, and photographs). Established 1996. **Editor:** Sandra Claire Fousheé.

Magazine Needs: *Poetry & Prose Annual* is the anthology of the Gold Pen Award winners. Appearing in May, it "publishes work that focuses on the nature of consciousness and enlightens the human spirit. A general selection of poetry, fiction, nonfiction and photography. We are looking for excellence and undiscovered talent in poems of emotional and intellectual substance. Poems should be original with rhythmic and lyric strength. Innovation and fresh imagery encouraged. Metrical ingenuity recognized. Open to all forms." Has published poetry by Anita Endrezze, Mary Crow, Nancy McCleery, Renate Wood, Mark Christopher Eades, Donna K. Wright, and Carlos Reyes. As a sample the editor selected these lines from "Lucky Star" by Tom Crawford:

> *Isn't it a wonder/the way we sail out everyday/under nothing more than our lucky star./Big waves./*
> *Little waves./The shriek of birds./We go where a round world takes us.*

Poetry & Prose Annual is approximately 72 pgs., 7×8½, offset-printed and perfect-bound with glossy card cover, cover photograph, contains line art and photos inside. Press run is about 1,000. Subscription: $15.

How to Submit: A $20 entry fee is required (includes subscription and $5 reader's fee, and entry into the Gold Pen Award). "Any work submitted without submission fee or SASE will not be returned or read." Submit no more than 200 lines of poetry at a time, typed, with line count, name, address and phone number on first page. Include SASE and brief bio. Accepts previously published poems "if author holds copyright"and simultaneous submissions. Accepts e-mail submissions. "Submit text from any platform as an attached file." Cover letter preferred with short bio. Guidelines available for SASE. Responds after deadline. Sometimes sends prepublication galleys. Pays 2 contributor's copies. Acquires one-time and reprints rights. Work may also appear in the *Poetry & Prose Annual* website.

Also Offers: "Several new writers will also be chosen from the general selection to be featured in *American Portfolio*—a special selection within the journal showcasing work of several authors in a portfolio." The online journal contains original content not found in the print edition. "From poetry submissions we may use some original material on the website which may/may not be published in the Annual. Poetry needs are the same as for the journal. Writers can indicate if they wish to be considered for the website. Contact the editor.

☑ 🍎 ◯ ◐ ◎ **THE POETRY EXPLOSION NEWSLETTER (THE PEN) (Specialized: ethnic, love, subscription, nature)**, P.O. Box 4725, Pittsburgh PA 15206-0725. (412)886-1114. E-mail: aford@hillhouse.org. Established 1984. **Editor:** Arthur C. Ford.

Magazine Needs: *The Pen* is a "quarterly newsletter dedicated to the preservation of poetry." Arthur Ford wants "poetry—40 lines maximum, no minimum. All forms and subject matter with the use of good imagery, symbolism and honesty. Rhyme and non-rhyme. No vulgarity." Accepts poetry written by children; "if under 18 years old, parent or guardian should submit!" Recently published poetry by Lisa Cave, Margaret A. Brennan, and Iva Fedorka. *The Pen* is 12-16 pgs., saddle-stapled, mimeographed on both sides. Receives about 300 poems/year, accepts 80. Press run is 850 for 400 subscribers of which 5 are libraries. Subscription: $20. Send $4 for sample copy and more information. Make checks payable to Arthur C. Ford.

How to Submit: Submit up to 5 poems, maximum 40 lines, at a time with $1 **reading fee**. Also include large SASE if you want work returned. Accepts simultaneous submissions and previously published poems. No e-mail submissions. Sometimes publishes theme issues. "We announce future dates when decided. July issue is usually full of romantic poetry." Guidelines and upcoming themes available for SASE. Editor comments on rejected poems "sometimes, but not obligated." Pays 1 contributor's copy. Poetry critiques available for 15¢ a word. Poets may send books for review consideration.

Also Offers: Website includes writer's guidelines. Use code word poetry.

Advice: "Even though free verse is more popular today, we try to stay versatile."

☑ 🍎 ◯ ◐ ◎ **POETRY FORUM; THE JOURNAL (Specialized: subscription, mystery, science fiction/fantasy, social issues); HEALTHY BODY-HEALTHY MINDS (Specialized: health concerns)**, 5713 Larchmont Dr., Erie PA 16509. (814)866-2543 (also fax: 8-10 a.m. or 5-8 p.m.). E-mail: 75562.670@compuserve.com Website: www.thepoetryforum.com (includes guidelines, sample poems and stories, general information, and more). **Editor:** Gunvor Skogsholm.

Magazine Needs: *Poetry Forum* appears 3 times/year. "We are open to any style and form. We believe new forms ought to develop from intuition. Length up to 50 lines accepted. Would like to encourage long themes. No porn or blasphemy, but open to all religious persuasions." Accepts poetry written by children ages 10 and under. Has published poetry by Marshall Myers, Dana Thu, Joseph Veranneau, Ray Greenblatt, Jan Haight, and Mark Young. As a sample the editor selected these lines from his poem "Tear":

> Because the tear down the cheek of a son is the reward of a lifetime of concern, the tear down the
> cheek of a brother was what I came for

Poetry Forum is 7×8½, 38 pgs., saddle-stapled with card cover, photocopied from photoreduced typescript. Sample: $3.

How to Submit: Accepts simultaneous submissions and previously published poems. Accepts electronic submissions and by fax and e-mail (include in body). Editor comments on poems "if asked, but respects the poetic freedom of the artist." Publishes theme issues. Sometimes sends prepublication galleys. Gives awards of $25, $15, $10, and 3 honorable mentions for the best poems in each issue. Acquires one-time rights. Reviews books of poetry in 250 words maximum. Poets may send books for review consideration.

Magazine Needs & How to Submit: *The Journal*, which appears twice/year, accepts experimental poetry of any length from subscribers only. Sample: $3. *Healthy Body-Healthy Minds* is a biannual publication concerned with health issues. Accepts essays, poetry, articles, and short-shorts on health, fitness, mind, and soul. Details available for SASE.

Also Offers: Offers a poetry chapbook contest. Handling fee: $12. Prize is publication and 20 copies. Send SASE for information.

Advice: "I believe today's poets should experiment more and not feel stuck in the forms that were in vogue 300 years ago. I would like to see more experimentalism—new forms will prove that poetry is alive and well in the mind and spirit of the people."

🅽 🌐 ◯ ◐ **POETRY GREECE, A CYCLOPS PRODUCTION**, Mitropolitou Athanasiou 10, Triti Parodos, Garitsa Corfu 49100 Greece. Phone/fax: +30(0)661 47990. E-mail: poetrygreece@hotmail.com. Website: http://users.otenet.gr/~wendyhol/poetry_greece/ (includes poetry, contents, illustrations, reviews, submission and subscription guides, competition details, and details of writing courses). Established 1999. **Director/Editor:** Wendy Holborow.

Magazine Needs: *Poetry Greece* appears 3 times/year. Its purpose is "to publish good poetry in English or translated into English—to make known contemporary Greek poets to an international readership. To discuss and debate poetry and translation." Wants good, well-structured poetry with interesting themes. Does not want religious and not keen on forced rhyme. Poems do not necessarily have to be about Greece. Recently published poetry by Roger McGough, Imtiaz Dharker, Kiki Dimoula, Odysseus Elytis, and Sappho. As a sample the editor selected these lines by Adrianne Kalfopolou:

> She sits through hours/measuring cloth, her fingers/along the old lines/finding where the finer lace
> had shredded—/the white so sheer/it is the color of nightdresses.

Poetry Greece is 52 pgs., magazine-sized, perfect-bound with glossy cover, includes a guest illustrator for each issue, also ads. Receives about 300 poems/year, accepts about 20%. Publishes about 40-50 poems/issue. Press run is 500 for 200 subscribers of which 50 are libraries, 250 shelf sales; 12 distributed free to Press for reviews. Single copy: $11; subscription: $33. Sample: $6. Make checks payable to Wendy Holborow.

How to Submit: Submit no more than 6 poems at a time. Accepts previously published poems and simultaneous submissions. Accepts e-mail and disk submissions. "If e-mailing, send one single attachment. Always include SAEs and International Reply Coupons or we can't reply." Reads submissions anytime. Time between acceptance and publication is up to 6 months. "Three to four editors all read the work and decisions are reached by majority." Seldom comments on rejected poems. Regularly publishes theme issues. Upcoming themes available for SASE. Guidelines available for SASE, by e-mail, or on website. Responds in up to 6 months. Sometimes sends prepublication galleys. Pays 1 contributor's copy. Acquires one-time rights. Reviews books and chapbooks of poetry and other magazines/journals in 1,000 words. Poets may send books for review consideration to Wendy Holborow.

Also Offers: "We hold an annual open poetry competition—up to 40 lines—any theme in English. Also, the annual 'Keeley and Sherrard Translation Award for Poetry' (from Greek to English) with many cash prizes."

☑ $□ ◑ ◎ **POETRY HARBOR; NORTH COAST REVIEW (Specialized: regional)**, P.O. Box 103, Duluth MN 55801-0103. (218)279-3865. Website: www.poharb.toofarnorth.com (includes current and complete info on Poetry Harbor). Established 1989. **Director:** Patrick McKinnon.

Magazine Needs: Poetry Harbor is a "nonprofit, tax-exempt organization dedicated to fostering literary creativity through public readings, publications, radio and television broadcasts, and other artistic and educational means." Its main publication, *North Coast Review*, is a regional magazine appearing 2 times/year with poetry and prose poems by and about Upper Midwest people, including those from Minnesota, Wisconsin, North Dakota, and the upper peninsula of Michigan. "No form/style/content specifications, though we are inclined toward narrative, imagist poetry. We do not want to see anything from outside our region, not because it isn't good, but because we can't publish it due to geographics." Has published poetry by Ellie Schoenfeld, Katri Sipila, and Nancy Fitzgerald. *North Coast Review* is 56 pgs., 7 × 8½, offset and saddle-stapled, paper cover with various b&w art, ads at back. Receives about 500 submissions/year, accepts 100-150. Press run is 1,000 for 300 subscribers of which 20 are libraries, 300 shelf sales. Subscription: $19.95/4 issues. Sample: $4.95.

How to Submit: Submit 3-5 pgs. of poetry, typed single-spaced, with name and address on each page. Accepts previously published poems and simultaneous submissions, if noted. Cover letter with brief bio ("writer's credits") required. "We read three times a year, but our deadlines change from time to time. Write to us for current deadlines for our various projects." Guidelines available for SASE. Responds in up to 5 months. Pays $10 plus 2-4 contributor's copies. Acquires one-time rights.

Book/Chapbook Needs & How to Submit: Poetry Harbor also publishes 1 perfect-bound paperback of poetry and 4-8 chapbooks each biennium. "Chapbooks are selected by our editorial board from the pool of poets we have published in *North Coast Review* or have worked with in our other projects. We suggest you send a submission to *North Coast Review* first. We almost always print chapbooks and anthologies by poets we've previously published or hired for readings." Anthologies include *Poets Who Haven't Moved to St. Paul* and *Days of Obsidian, Days of Grace*, selected poetry and prose by four Native American writers. Complete publications list available upon request.

Also Offers: Poetry Harbor also sponsors a monthly reading series ("poets are paid to perform"), a weekly TV program (4 different cable networks regionally), various radio programming, and other special events.

Advice: "Poetry Harbor is extremely committed to cultivating a literary community and an appreciation for our region's literature within the Upper Midwest. Poetry Harbor projects are in place to create paying, well-attended venues for our region's fine poets. Poets are now OK to people up here, and literature is thriving. The general public is proving to us that they *do* like poetry if you give them some that is both readable and rooted in the lives of the community."

□ ◑ ◎ **POETRY INTERNATIONAL (specialized: translations)**, Dept. of English, San Diego State University, San Diego CA 92182-8140. (619)594-1523. Fax: (619)594-4998. E-mail: fmoramar@mail.sdsu.edu. Website: www-rohan.sdsu.edu:80/dept/press/poetry.html (includes subscription information and samples from each issue). Established 1996. **Editor:** Fred Moramarco.

Magazine Needs: *Poetry International*, published annually in October, is "an eclectic poetry magazine intended to reflect a wide range of poetry being written today." Wants "a wide range of styles and subject matter. We're particularly interested in translations." Does not want "cliché-ridden, derivative, obscure poetry." Has published poetry by Adrienne Rich, Robert Bly, Hayden Carruth, Kim Addonizio, Maxine Kumin, and Gary Soto. As a sample the editor selected these lines from "My Life In Over" by Al Zolynas:

> my life, I mean that life/defined by narrow boundaries/narrow concerns, by survival/and whining and
> looking over/my shoulder, that life/of the bag of skin and bones/with the little fascist ego bitching/all

*day long/That little Mussolini is dead—or/if not dead—at least stripped of his shiny/black uniform,
insignia cut/off pockets and collars,/epaulettes popped off shoulders./Not yet fully naked/but on the
way, down/to T-shirts, shorts, and socks.*

Poetry International is 200 pgs, perfect bound, with coated card stock cover. Press run is 1,000. Single copy:
$12; subscription: $24/2 years.

How to Submit: Submit up to 5 poems at a time. Accepts simultaneous submissions "but prefer not to"; no
previously published poems. No fax or e-mail submissions. Reads submissions September 1 through December
30 only. Time between acceptance and publication is 8 months. Poems are circulated to an editorial board. Seldom
comments on rejected poems. Responds in 3 months. Pays 2 contributor's copies. Acquires all rights. Returns
rights "50/50," meaning they split with the author any payment for reprinting the poem elsewhere. "We review
anthologies regularly."

Advice: "We're interested in new work by poets who are devoted to their art. We want poems that matter—that
make a difference in people's lives. We're especially seeking good translations and prose by poets about poetry."

☑ ⊕ $ ⊘ **POETRY IRELAND REVIEW; POETRY IRELAND**, Bermingham Tower, Dublin Castle,
Dublin 2, Ireland. Phone: 353.1.6714632. Fax: 353.1.6714634. E-mail: poetry@iol.ie. Established 1979. **General
Manager:** Joseph Woods.

Magazine Needs: *Poetry Ireland Review*, the magazine of Ireland's national poetry organization, "provides an
outlet for Irish poets; submissions from abroad also considered. No specific style or subject matter is prescribed.
We strongly dislike sexism and racism." Has published poetry by Seamus Heaney, Michael Longley, Denise
Levertov, Medbh McGuckian, and Charles Wright. Occasionally publishes special issues. *Poetry Ireland Review*
is 6×8 and appears quarterly. Press run is 1,200 for 800 subscriptions. Receives up to 10,000 submissions/year,
accepts about 10%; has a 2-month backlog. Prints 60 pgs. of poetry in each issue. Single copy: IR£5.99; subscription: IR£24 Ireland and UK; IR£32 overseas (surface). Sample: $10.

How to Submit: Submit up to 6 poems at a time. Include SASE (or SAE with IRC). "Submissions not
accompained by SAEs will not be returned." No previously published poems or simultaneous submissions.
Accepts e-mail submissions; attach file to e-mail. Time between acceptance and publication is up to 3 months.
Seldom comments on rejected poems. Send SASE (or SAE with IRCs) for guidelines. Responds in 2 months.
Pays IR£10/poem or 1-year subscription. Reviews books of poetry in 500-1,000 words.

Also Offers: *Poetry Ireland Review* is published by Poetry Ireland, an organization established to "promote
poets and poetry throughout Ireland." Poetry Ireland offers readings, an information service, library and administrative center, and a bimonthly newsletter giving news, details of readings, competitions, etc. for IR£6/year. Also
sponsors an annual poetry competition. Details available for SASE (or SAE with IRCs).

Advice: "Keep submitting: Good work will get through."

⊕ ⊘ **POETRY KANTO**, Kanto Gakuin University, Kamariya-cho 3-22-1, Kanazawa-Ku, Yokohama 236-
8502, Japan. Established 1984. **Editor:** William I. Elliott.

Magazine Needs: *Poetry Kanto* appears annually in August and is published by the Kanto Poetry Center. The
magazine publishes well-crafted original poems in English and in Japanese. Wants "anything except pornography,
English haiku and tanka, and tends to publish poems under 30 lines." Has published work by A.D. Hope, Peter
Robinson, Naomi Shihab Nye, Nuala Ni Dhomhnaill, and Christopher Middleton. The magazine is 60 pgs.,
digest-sized, nicely printed (the English poems occupy the first half of the issue, the Japanese poems the second),
saddle-stapled, matte card cover. Press run is 700, of which 400 are distributed free to schools, poets and presses;
it is also distributed at poetry seminars. The magazine is unpriced. For sample, send SAE with IRCs.

How to Submit: Interested poets should query from October through December with SAE and IRCs before
submitting. No previously published poems or simultaneous submissions. Often comments on rejected poems.
Responds to mss in 2 weeks. Pays 3 contributor's copies.

Advice: "Read a lot. Get feedback from poets and/or workshops. Be neat, clean, legible, and polite in submissions. SAE with IRCs absolutely necessary when requesting sample copy."

⊕ ◖ ◎ **POETRY LIFE (Specialized: subscription)**, 1 Blue Ball Corner, Water Lane, Winchester,
Hampshire SO23 0ER England. E-mail: adrian.abishop@virgin.net. Website: http://freespace.virgin.net/poetry.l
ife/. Established 1994. **Editor:** Adrian Bishop.

Magazine Needs: *Poetry Life*, published 3 times/year, describes itself as "Britain's sharpest poetry magazine
with serious articles about the poetry scene." Wants "poets who have passion, wit, style, revelation, and loads
of imagination." Does not want "poems on pets." Has published articles on James Fenton, Carol Ann Duffy,
Les Murray, Benjamin Zephaniah, and Simon Armitage. *Poetry Life* is printed on A4 paper. Accepts about 1%
of submissions received. Press run is 1,500. Single copy: £3, £5 overseas.

How to Submit: Accepts previously published poems and simultaneous submissions. Cover letter required.
"In common with most poetry magazines we now only accept recordings of the poets work on CD. Please do
not send manuscripts. If we like what we hear then we will ask for a manuscript." Time between acceptance and
publication is 6 months. Poems are circulated to an editorial board. Guidelines available for SAE with IRCs.
Responds in 6 months. Reviews books or other magazines. Poets may send books for review consideration.

Also Offers: Sponsors open poetry competitions. Send SAE with IRCs for guidelines.

N ☐ ⊘ **POETRY MOTEL; POETRY MOTEL WALLPAPER BROADSIDE SERIES**, P.O. Box 103, Duluth MN 55801-0103. Established 1984. **Editors:** Patrick McKinnon, Bud Backen, and Natalie Thompson.
Magazine Needs: *Poetry Motel* appears "every 260 days." Poetry magazine with some fiction and memoire. Wants poetry of "any style, any length." Recently published poetry by Adrian C. Louis, Ron Androla, Todd Moore, Ellie Schoenfeld, and Serena Fusek. *Poetry Motel* is 52 pgs. digest-sized, offset-printed, stapled, wallpaper cover, with collages. Receives about 1,000 poems/year, accepts about 5% Publishes about 50 poems/issue. Press run is 1,000 for 400 subscribers of which 10 are libraries. Single copy: $8.95; subscription: $26/3 issues, $99/ forever. Make checks payable to *Poetry Motel.*
How to Submit: Submit 3-6 pgs. at a time. Accepts previously published poems and simultaneous submissions. No fax, e-mail, or disk submissions. "Include SASE or brief bio." Reads submissions all year. Time between acceptance and publication varies. Never comments on rejected poems. Guidelines are available in magazine and for SASE. Responds in "1 week to never." Pays 1-5 contributor's copies. Acquires no rights. Reviews books and chapbooks of poetry and other magazines/journals in varied lengths. Poets may send books for review consideration to N. Thompson.
Advice: "All work submitted is considered for both the magazine and the broadside series."

Y ⊘ **POETRY NORTHWEST**, University of Washington, P.O. Box 354330, Seattle WA 98195. (206)685-4750. Established 1959. **Editor:** David Wagoner.
  • Poetry published here has also been included in *The Best American Poetry 1996.*
Magazine Needs: *Poetry Northwest* is a quarterly featuring all styles and forms. For instance, lyric and narrative free verse has been included alongside a sonnet sequence, minimalist sonnets and stanza patterns—all accessible and lively. *Poetry Northwest* is 48 pgs., 5½×8½, professionally printed with color card cover. Receives 10,000 poems/year, accepts approximately 160, has a 3-month backlog. Press run is 1,500. Subscription: $15. Sample: $4.
How to Submit: Occasionally comments on rejected poems. Responds in 1 month maximum. Pays 2 contributor's copies. Awards prizes of $500, $200, and $200 yearly, judged by the editors.

✓ ☐ ☐ ◎ **POETRY OF THE PEOPLE (Specialized: bilingual/foreign language, humor, love, nature, fantasy)**, 3341 SE 19th Ave., Gainesville FL 32641. (352)375-0244. E-mail: poetryforaquarter@yahoo. com. Website: www.angelfire.com/fl/poetryofthepeople (includes guidelines, poetry, and a list of back issues. Also includes original content, please contact editor). Established 1986. **Poetry Editor:** Paul Cohen.
Magazine Needs: *Poetry of the People* is a leaflet that appears several times/year. "We take all forms of poetry but we like humorous poetry, love poetry, nature poetry, and fantasy. No racist or highly ethnocentric poetry will be accepted. I do not like poetry that lacks images or is too personal or contains rhyme to the point that the poem has been destroyed. All submitted poetry will be considered for posting on website which will be updated every month." Also accepts poetry written in French and Spanish. Accepts poetry written by children. Has published poetry by Max Lizard, Prof. Jerry Reminick, Ian Ayers, and Noelle Kocot. As a sample the editor selected these lines from "Lunar" by David Vetterlein:
> *"I stumbled blindly/in coated forests/bound by howling wolves/I stagger/wandering endless/in that lunar maze/called emotion.*
Poetry of the People is 32 pgs., 5½×8 to 5½×4⅜, stapled, sometimes on colored paper. Issues are usually theme oriented. Samples: $4 for 11 pamphlets.
How to Submit: Submit up to 10 poems at a time. Include SASE. Accepts e-mail submissions. Cover letter with biographical information required with submissions. "I feel autobiographical information is important in understanding the poetry." Poems returned within 6 months. Editor comments on rejected poems "often." Pays 10 contributor's copies for poetry published in leaflet. Acquires first rights.
Advice: "Nature makes people happy."

⊕ ✓ $⊘ POETRY REVIEW; NATIONAL POETRY COMPETITION; THE POETRY SOCI-ETY, 22 Betterton St., London WC2H 9BU United Kingdom. Phone: (0044)171 420 9880. Fax: (0044)171 240 4818. E-mail: poetryreview@poetrysoc.com. Website: www.poetrysoc.com. Established 1909. **Editor:** Peter Forbes.
Magazine Needs: *Poetry Review*, published quarterly, strives "to be the leading showcase of UK poetry and to represent poetry written in English and in translation." Wants "poems with metaphoric resonance." Does not want "inconsequential disconnected jottings." Has published poetry by John Ashbery, Miroslav Holub, Sharon Olds, and Paul Muldoon. As a sample the editor selected these lines from "Whang Editorial Policy" by Mark Halliday:
> *Do not assume that to say "Barcelona" or "heart of night"/or "blue souffle" will open every door at Whang./We look for poems that embrace God because God has failed/and not the other way around.*
> *Send only such poems/ as you would choose in lieu of a cigarette before/execution by firing squad. . .*
Poetry Review is 96 pgs., 6½×9, paperback, with b&w cartoons and photos. Receives about 30-50,000 poems/ year, accepts 0.3-0.4%. Press run is 4,200 for 3,300 subscribers of which 400 are libraries, 400 shelf sales; 100 distributed free to contributors and press. Single copy: £5.95; subscription: $56. Sample: $13.
How to Submit: Submit 4 poems at a time. No previously published poems or simultaneous submissions. No fax or e-mail submissions. Time between acceptance and publication is 6 months. Poems are selected by the

editor. Seldom comments on rejected poems. Publishes theme issues. Responds in up to 3 months. Sometimes sends prepublication galleys. Pays £40 plus 1 copy. Acquires UK first publication rights. Staff reviews chapbooks of poetry or other magazines in single or multi-book format.

Also Offers: Sponsors the annual National Poetry Competition run by the Poetry Society. 1st Prize: £5,000; 2nd Prize: £1,000; 3rd Prize: £500. Entry fee: £5 for first poem, £3/poem thereafter. Deadline: October 31. Guidelines available for SASE (or SAE and IRC). "The Poetry Society promotes poetry, assists poets and campaigns for poets wherever possible." Offers "Poetry Prescription" reading service: £40 for 100 lines.

POETRY SALZBURG; THE POET'S VOICE; UNIVERSITY OF SALZBURG PRESS, Institut für Anglistik und Americanistik, Universität Salzburg, Akademiestrasse 24, A-5020 Salzburg Austria. Phone: 0049662 8044 4422. Fax: 0049 662 80 44 613. Established 1971. **Editors:** Dr. Wolfgang Görtschacher and James Hogg.

Magazine Needs: *The Poet's Voice* appears twice/year and contains "articles on poetry, mainly contemporary, and 60 percent poetry. Also includes prose and translations. We tend to publish selections by authors who have not been taken up by the big poetry publishers. Nothing of poor quality." Has published poetry by Peter Russell, Desmond O'Grady, James Kirkup, Robert Rehder, Raymond Federman, Rachel Hades, Alice Notley and Rupert Loydell. As a sample we selected "Afterwards" by Ian Robinson:

> After the phone call, she put his photograph/face down in the drawer. Then she cooked lunch./That
> night, when the television went dead,/she stared at the glistening, empty screen/and could not remember
> his face. The cat got up,/stretched and walked to the door. There was wind outside./'I must be getting
> old,' she thought/but made no move to go to bed.

The Poet's Voice is about 140 pgs., A5, professionally printed and perfect-bound with illustrated card cover, sometimes includes art. Receives about 2,000 poems/year, accepts 10%. Press run is 400 for 150 subscribers of which 30% are libraries. Single copy: about $11; subscription: $20 (cash only for those sending US funds). Make checks payable to James Hogg. "No requirements, but it's a good idea to subscribe to *Poet's Voice*."

How to Submit: No previously published poems or simultaneous submissions. Accepts fax submissions. Time between acceptance and publication is 6 months. Seldom comments on rejected poems. Occasionally publishes theme issues. Responds in 2 months. Payment varies. Acquires first rights. Reviews books and chapbooks of poetry and other magazines. Poets may send books for review consideration.

Book/Chapbook Needs & How to Submit: Poetry Salzburg publishes "collections of at least 100 pages by mainly poets not taken up by big publishers." Publishes 2-30 paperbacks/year. Books are usually 100-700 pgs., A5, professionally printed and perfect-bound with card cover, includes art. Query first, with a few sample poems and a cover letter with brief bio and publication credits. Suggests authors publish in *The Poet's Voice* first. Responds to queries in 2 weeks; to mss in about 1 month. Pays 40 author's copies (out of a press run of 300-400).

POETRY TODAY ONLINE; RING OF WORDS WEBRING, P.O. Box 8255, Jacksonville AR 72078. E-mail: editor@poetrytodayonline.com. Website: www.poetrytodayonline.com (includes how-to section by Don J. Carlson, motivations, Poet Interview by Jim Garman, and a column by E. Clark). Established 1997. **Editor:** Margaret Perkins.

Magazine Needs: "*Poetry Today Online* has served Internet poets since 1997. Its Internet traffic is approximately 15,000 hits per month during the school year and 10,000 per month during school breaks. *Poetry Today Online* owns the Ring of Words Webring with over 5,000 membership." *Poetry Today Online* encourages all forms and styles. No "adult, erotic, or X-rated material due to the fact we are used in educational facilities. No profanity."

How to Submit: Submit 1 poem at a time. Accepts previously published poems and simultaneous submissions. Accepts e-mail submissions; no disk submissions. "Submissions are accepted through Internet only." Time between acceptance and publication is 3 months. Seldom comments on rejected poems.

Also Offers: Additional features of *Poetry Today Online* include "a public forum, a listing of Internet poetry contests, how-to articles and more."

POETRYBAY, P.O. Box 114, Northport NY 11768. (631)427-1950. Fax: (631)367-0038. E-mail: poetrybay@aol.com Website: www.poetrybay.com. Established 2000. **Editor:** George Wallace.

Magazine Needs: *Poetrybay* appears quarterly and "seeks to add to the body of great contemporary American poetry by presenting the work of established and emerging writers. Also, we consider essays and reviews" Recently published poetry by Robert Bly, Yevgeny Yevtushenko, Marvin Bell, Diane Wakoski, Cornelius Eady, and William Heyen. *Poetrybay* is an online publication. Publishes about 24 poems/issue.

How to Submit: Submit 5 poems at a time. Accepts simultaneous submissions; no previously published poems. Accepts e-mail submissions; no disk submissions. "We prefer e-mail with text in body. No attachments." Time between acceptance and publication is 2 months. Seldom comments on rejected poems. Occasionally publishes theme issues. Guidelines available by fax, e-mail, or on website. Sometimes sends prepublication galleys. Acquires first time electronic rights. Reviews books and chapbooks of poetry and other magazines/journals. Poets may send books/chapbooks for review consideration.

☑ ◯ ◢ ◎ **POETS AT WORK (Specialized: subscription)**, P.O. Box 232, Lyndora PA 16045. Established 1985. **Editor/Publisher:** Jessee Poet.

Magazine Needs: All contributors are expected to subscribe. "Every poet who writes within the dictates of good taste and within my 20-line limit will be published in each issue. I accept all forms and themes of poetry, including seasonal and holiday, but no porn, no profanity, horror, bilingual/foreign language, translations, feminism." He has published poetry by Dr. Karen Springer, William Middleton, Ann Gasser, Warren Jones and Ralph Hammond. As a sample he selected his poem "An Old Romance":

> I almost loved you . . . did you know?/Sometimes you still disturb my dreams./A summer romance long
> ago/I almost loved you . . . did you know?/We danced to music soft and low/Just yesterday . . . or so
> it seems/I almost loved you . . . did you know?/Sometimes you still disturb my dreams.

Poets at Work, a bimonthly, is generally 36-40 pgs., magazine-sized, saddle-stapled, photocopied from typescript with colored paper cover. Subscription: $22. Sample: $3.75.

How to Submit: If a subscriber, submit 5-10 poems at a time. Line length for poetry is 20 maximum. Accepts simultaneous submissions and previously published poems. Guidelines available for SASE. Responds within 2 weeks. Pays nothing, not even a copy. "Because I publish hundreds of poets, I cannot afford to pay or give free issues. Every subscriber, of course, gets an issue."

Also Offers: Subscribers also have many opportunities to regain their subscription money in the numerous contests offered in each issue. Send SASE for flyer for separate monthly and special contests.

Advice: "These days even the best poets tell me that it is difficult to get published. I am here for the novice as well as the experienced poet. I consider *Poets at Work* to be a hotbed for poets where each one can stretch and grow at his or her own pace. Each of us learns from the other, and we do not criticize one another. The door for poets is always open, so please stop by; we probably will like each other immediately."

[N] ◻ ◻ ◢ **THE POET'S CUT**, P.O. Box 937, Rio Linda CA 95673. E-mail: admin@Welkinworks.com. Website: www.poetscut.com (includes poetry, forum, guidelines, name of editor, featured poet, news, links). Established 1998. **Editor:** Leslie Laurence.

Magazine Needs: *The Poet's Cut* appears monthly publishing quality, original poetry on the World Wide Web. "I am looking for poems that reflect the voice and vision of the poet, not something that reflects a current literary trend or tries to second guess what publishers want. Any form, style, or subject. Prefer works of 25 words or less. I never thought I would have to say this, but I do not want to see any hate poems or racial slurs." Accepts poetry written by children. Recently published poetry by Janet I. Buck, Taylor Graham, Duane Locke, Kevin Grossman, and Kenneth Clark. As a sample the editor selected these lines from "Acorn Issues" by Janet I. Buck:

> You had an admirable gift/for turning little acorn issues/into big fat carved pumpkins./Orange rot of
> seedless faith/stretched well beyond October nights.

The Poet's Cut is 20 pgs., published online only. Receives about 240 poems/year, accepts about 35%. Publishes about 7 poems/issue.

How to Submit: Submit up to 4 poems at a time. Line length for poetry is open. Accepts previously published poems and simultaneous submissions. Accepts e-mail submissions; no fax or disk submissions. "Submissions are accepted only as text in the body of the e-mail." Reads submissions year round. Submit seasonal poems 1 month in advance. Time between acceptance and publication is 3 months. Seldom comments on rejected poems. Occasionally publishes theme issues. A list of upcoming themes and guidelines are available on website. Responds in 1 month. No payment. Acquires one-time rights.

Advice: "Read your poems aloud. You will be amazed how the weak parts stand out. Find an honest audience for your poems. Listen to what they tell you. Read the work of others. You have to know where poetry has been if you are to be a part of where it is going."

◻ ♀ ◯ **THE POET'S HAVEN**, P.O. Box 1501, Massillon OH 44648. E-mail: VertigoXX@PoetsHaven.com. Website: www.PoetsHaven.com. Established 1997. **Publisher/Editor:** Vertigo Xi'an Xavier.

● *Poet's Haven* has received numerous small website awards including the Nocturnal Society "All-Nighter" Awards.

Magazine Needs: *Poet's Haven Digest* magazine and *The Poet's Haven* site feature poetry, artwork, stories, book reviews, essays, editorial, quotes, and much more. Wants "work that is passionate, emotional, powerful, personal, and intimate with either the author. Subjects can be fun, sad, light, deep, about love, pain, nature, insanity, or social commentary. No material that is obscene, excessively vulgar, pornographic, racist, or religious." Accepts poetry written by children (over 12 preferred). Has published poetry by Elizabeth Hendricks, Jen Pezzo, Elisha Porat, Alex Luppa, and Todd-Michael Phillips. As a sample the editor selected a poem by Kim Davis (title not given):

> Two lifetimes split, beyond the tare,/a world above, a world below,/a crescent moon of pixie dust,/you
> know not what you know./insanity-turmoil-chaos/that is existence. . . do you yet live?/nay and aye,
> different yet one./it's over, and yet, its just begun.

Poet's Haven Digest is published in an anthology format, 32-96 pgs., saddle-stapled and includes a color cover with some interior line-art and ads. The website features an unlimited number of pages, with new work added sporadically. Work published on the website will be left on the site permanently. Receives about 4,500 poems/year, accepts about 75%. Sample: $3-8 postage paid.

How to Submit: Accepts previously published poems and simultaneous submissions. Accepts e-mail and disk submissions. "Electronic submissions (e-mail, website, diskette) are highly preferred. Cover letter preferred. Time between acceptance and publication is 2 weeks to 1 year. Seldom comments on rejected poems. Responds when published by e-mail or SASE only. Pays 1 contributor's copy. Acquires rights to publish on the website and/or in the magazine. Author retains rights to have poems published elsewhere."

Also Offers: "What started our as a small e-zine has expanded into an on- and off-line community of writers and artists, growing into not only the magazine, but also an audio CD project. If a submitter wishes, his/her e-mail address will be included with any of their poems published so that readers can contact them."

POETS ON THE LINE, P.O. Box 020292, Brooklyn NY 11202-0007. E-mail: llerner@mindspring.com. Website: www.echonyc.com/~poets. Established 1995. **Editor:** Linda Lerner. Currently not accepting unsolicited work.

POETS' PODIUM, 2-3265 Front Rd., E. Hawksbury, Ontario K6A 2R2 Canada. E-mail: kennyel@hotmail.com. Established 1993. **Associate Editors:** Ken Elliott, Catherine Heaney Barrowcliffe, Robert Piquette.

Magazine Needs: *Poets' Podium* is a quarterly newsletter published "to promote the reading and writing of the poetic form, especially among those being published for the first time." Poetry specifications are open. However, does not want poetry that is gothic, erotic/sexual, gory, bloody, or that depicts violence. Publish 25 poems/issue. Subscription: $10 (US). Sample: $3 (US). "Priority is given to valued subscribers. Nevertheless, when there is room in an issue we will publish nonsubscribers."

How to Submit: Submit 3 poems at a time. Line length for poetry is 4 minimum, 25 maximum. Accepts previously published poems and simultaneous submissions. Cover letter required. Include SASE (or SAE and IRC), name, address, and telephone number; e-mail address if applicable. Time between acceptance and publication varies. Guidelines available for SASE (or SAE with IRC), by fax, or by e-mail. Pays 3 copies. All rights remain with the author.

Advice: "Poetry is a wonderful literary form. Try your hand at it. Send us the fruit of your labours."

POLYGON (Specialized: bilingual/foreign language), 22 George Square, Edinburgh EH8 9LF Scotland. Phone: (0131)650 8436. Fax: (0131)662 0053. E-mail: polygon.press@eup.ed.ac.uk. Website: www.eup.ed.ac.uk/polygon/html. Established 1969. **Contact:** poetry editor.

Book/Chapbook Needs: Polygon publishes new poets, first-time collections, young voices, and Gaelic/English translations. Publishes 3 paperbacks and 1 anthology/year. Has published poetry by Ian Hamilton Finlay, Liz Lochhead, Aonghas MacNeacail, Raymond Friel, David Kinloch, and Donny O'Rourke. Books are usually 88 pgs., 194×128mm, paperback. Anthologies are 35 pgs., 216×138mm, paperback. Polygon is currently not accepting unsolicited manuscripts.

POLYPHONIES (Specialized: translations), 8, rue des Imbergères, 92330 Sceaux, France. Established 1985. **Editor:** Pascal Culerrier. **Editorial Committee:** Pascal Boulanger, Laurence Breysse, François Comba, Emmanuelle Dagnaud, Jean-Yves Masson, and Alexis Pelletier.

Magazine Needs: *Polyphonies* appears twice/year. "Every case is a special one. We want to discover the new important voices of the world to open French literature to the major international productions. For example, we published Brodsky in French when he was not known in our country and had not yet won the Nobel Prize. No vocal poetry, no typographic effects." Has published poetry by Mario Luzi (Italy), Jeremy Reed (Great Britain), Octavio Paz (Mexico), and Claude Michel Cluny (France). It is about 110 pgs., 6½×9½, flat-spined, with glossy card cover, printed completely in French. Press run is 850 for 300 subscribers.

How to Submit: Uses translations of previously published poems. Pays 2 copies.

Advice: "Our review is still at the beginning. We are in touch with many French editors. Our purpose is to publish together, side-by-side, poets of today and of yesterday."

PORCUPINE LITERARY ARTS MAGAZINE, P.O. Box 259, Cedarsburg WI 53012. E-mail: ppine259@aol.com. Website: members.aol.com/ppine259 (features writer's guidelines, cover art, table of contents, and sample poetry). Established 1996. **Managing Editor:** W.A. Reed.

Magazine Needs: *Porcupine*, published biannually, contains featured artists, poetry, short fiction, and visual art work. "There are no restrictions as to theme or style. Poetry should be accessible and highly selective. If a submission is not timely for one issue, it will be considered for another." Has published poetry by Virgil Suarez, John Greg, Judith Ford, Peter Tomassi, and Joan Payne Kincaid. As a sample, we selected these lines from "The Scent of Lightning" by Judith Ford:

> *Certain Flowers, my mother says, bother her/Carnations, mums, some of the lilies./Funeral Flowers,*
> *she calls them. She prefers/lilacs, peonies or lumberyards littered/with Fresh-cut timber and hills of*
> *sawdust,/her old unwashed dog. . .*

Porcupine is 100-150 pgs., 8½×5, offset, perfect-bound with full-color glossy cover and b&w photos and art (occasionally use color inside, depending on artwork). Receives about 300 poems/year, accepts 10%. Press run is 1,500 for 500 subscribers of which 50 are libraries, 500 shelf sales; 100 distributed free. Single copy: $8.95; subscription: $15.95. Sample: $5.

How to Submit: Submit up to 3 poems, 1/page with name and address on each. Include SASE. "The outside of the envelope should state: 'Poetry.' " No previously published poems or simultaneous submissions. Accepts e-mail submissions include in body of message. Time between acceptance and publication is 6 months. "Poems are selected by editors and then submitted to managing editor for final approval." Seldom comments on rejected poems. Guidelines available for SASE or website. Responds in 3 months. Pays 1 contributor's copy. Acquires one-time rights.

✅ 🌾 📀 **PORTLAND REVIEW**, Box 347, Portland State University, Portland OR 97207-0347. (503)725-4533. Fax: (503)725-5860. E-mail: review@vanguard.vg.pdx.edu. Website: www.portlandreview.org ("our website is a general introduction to our magazine with samples of our poetry, fiction, and art."). Established 1954. **Editor:** Haley Hach.
• 1999 Oregon Book Award recipient for poetry, fiction, drama.
Magazine Needs & How to Submit: *Portland Review* is a literary quarterly published by Portland State University. "Experimental poetry welcomed." The quarterly is about 128 pgs. Accepts about 30 of 1000 poems received each year. "Press run is 1000 for subscribers, libraries, and bookstores throughout Oregon and Washington." Sample: $6. Accepts simultaneous submissions. Accepts e-mail submissions in body. Guidelines available for SASE. Pays 1 contributor's copy.

📀 📀 **THE POST-APOLLO PRESS (Specialized: form/style, women)**, 35 Marie St., Sausalito CA 94965. (415)332-1458. Fax: (415)332-8045. E-mail: tpapress@dnai.com. Website: www.dnai.com/~tpapress. Established 1982. **Publisher:** Simone Fattal.
Book/Chapbook Needs & How to Submit: The Post-Apollo Press publishes "quality paperbacks by experimental poets/writers, mostly women, many first English translations." Publishes 2-3 paperbacks/year. "Please note we are *not* accepting manuscripts at this time due to full publishing schedule."

✅ 🍎 ⬤ 📀 📀 **POTLUCK CHILDREN'S LITERARY MAGAZINE (Specialized: children/teen)**, P.O. Box 546, Deerfield IL 60015-0546. (847)948-1139. Fax: (847)317-9492. E-mail: nappic@aol.com. Website: http://potluckmagazine.com (includes general information, "testimonials," guidelines, where to find and how to order *Potluck*, special events, and message board). Established 1997. **Editor:** Susan Napoli Picchietti.
Magazine Needs: *Potluck* is published quarterly "to provide a forum which encourages young writers to share their voice and to learn their craft. Open to all styles, forms, and subjects—we just want well crafted works that speak to the reader. No works so abstract they only have meaning to the writer. Violent, profane, or sexually explicit works will not be accepted." *Potluck* is 34 pgs., 5½ × 8½, photocopied and saddle-stapled with 60 lb. paper cover, includes original artwork on covers. Receives about 350 poems/year, accepts about 90%. Publish 10-15 poems/issue. Press run is 400 + for 150 subscribers of which 5 are libraries, 300 shelf sales; back issues distributed free to hospitals/inner city schools. Single copy: $5.50; subscription: $18. Sample (including guidelines): $4.25.
How to Submit: Submit up to 3 poems at a time. Line length for poetry is 30 maximum. No previously published poems or simultaneous submissions. Accepts e-mail submissions in body of message. Cover letter preferred. "All works must include a SASE for reply." Submit seasonal poems 3 months in advance. Time between acceptance and publication is 4-6 weeks. Poems are circulated to an editorial board. "We each review each poem—make remarks on page then discuss our view of each—the best works make the issue." Always comments on rejected poems. Guidelines available for SASE, by fax, by e-mail, or on website. Responds 6 weeks after deadline. Pays 1 contributor's copy. Acquires first rights. Reviews chapbooks of poetry.
Advice: "Be present—now—write what you see, hear, taste, smell, observe and what you feel/experience. Be honest, clear, and choose your words with great care. Enjoy."

⬤ 📀 📀 **POTOMAC REVIEW (Specialized: regional)**, P.O. Box 354, Port Tobacco MD 20677. Website: www.meral.com/potomac (includes samplings of each issue, contents, guidelines, background on magazine). Established 1994. **Editor:** Eli Flam.
Magazine Needs: *Potomac Review*, "with a strong environmental bent and focus on nature," is published quarterly and "explores the topography and human terrain of the Mid-Atlantic region and beyond for a growing readership." Wants "poetry with a vivid, individual quality that has vision to go with competence, that strives to get at 'the concealed side' of life." Does not want "arch, banal, mannered, surface, flat, self-serving poetry." Accepts poetry written by children through high school for Young Talent Pages. Has published poetry by Lucille Clifton, Roland Flint, and Hilary Thane. As a sample the editor selected these lines from "The River at Dawn: Winter" by Fred Boltz:

> *Here in the depths/of this lost forest,/swallows have/gathered against/a flickering light/to wait for the first/wind to rise above/the trees . . .*

THE SUBJECT INDEX, located at the back of this book, can help you select markets for your work. It lists those publishers whose poetry interests are specialized 📀 .

Potomac Review is 128 pgs., 5½ × 8½, offset-printed, perfect-bound, with medium card cover, b&w graphic art, photos and ads. Receives about 1,000 poems/year, accepts 5%. Press run is 2,000 for 1,000 subscribers plus about 400 shelf sales. Subscription: $18/year (MD residents add 5%), $30/2 years. Sample: $5.

How to Submit: Submit up to 3 poems, 5 pages at a time with SASE. Accepts simultaneous submissions; no previously published poems. Cover letter preferred with brief bio and SASE. Time between acceptance and publication is up to 1 year. Poems are read "in house," then sent to poetry editor for comments and dialogue. Usually comments on rejected poems. Publishes theme issues. Guidelines and upcoming themes available for SASE or on website. Themes for fall 2001, winter 2001-2002, spring 2002, and summer 2002 are Beyond Museum Walls—First Americans Take Hold, Punch & Judies, Water, Water Everywhere?, Twining Trails, respectively. Responds in 3 months. Pays 1 contributor's copy and offers discount on additional copies. Acquires first North American serial rights. Reviews books of poetry; write first for review consideration.

Also Offers: Sponsors annual poetry contest, open January through March. 1st Prize: $300; winner's poem and some runners-up are published in fall. To enter, send $18 (provides 1-year subscription), up to 3 poems, any subject, any form. Deadline: March 31, 2002. Competition receives about 170 entries. Guidelines available for SASE or on fall/winter website.

POTPOURRI; DAVID RAY POETRY AWARD, P.O. Box 8278, Prairie Village KS 66208. (913)642-1503. Fax: (913)642-3128. E-mail: Potpourpub@aol.com. Website: www.Potpourri.org (includes general information, history, submission guidelines, sample material from back issues, and subscription information). Established 1989. **Poetry Editor:** Terry Hoyland. **Haiku Editor:** Jeri Ragan.

Magazine Needs: *Potpourri* is a quarterly magazine "publishing works of writers, including new and unpublished writers. We want strongly voiced original poems in either free verse or traditional. Traditional work must represent the best of the craft. No religious, confessional, racial, political, erotic, abusive, or sexual preference materials. No concrete/visual poetry (because of format)." Has published poetry by Lyn Lifshin, David Ray, Richard Moore, Pattiann Rogers, Sharon Kouros, and Carol Hamilton. As a sample the editor selected these lines from "Igneous Intrusion" by Elizabeth Cleary:

> Rage rose in her like magma/cooling around her feet in pools/that kept her trapped at home/Alone,/
> two children to feed,/One,/Not even sleeping,/through the night.

Potpourri is 76 pgs., 8½ × 11, professionally printed, saddle-stapled with 2-color art on glossy cover, drawings, photos and ads inside. Press run is 1,500 for 850 subscribers. Subscription: $16. Sample: $5 include 9 × 12 envelope; $7.20 overseas.

How to Submit: Submit up to 3 poems at a time, one to a page, length to 75 lines (approximately 30 preferred). Address haiku and related forms to Jeri Ragan. No e-mail submissions. Guidelines available for SASE or on website. Responds in up to 10 weeks at most. Pays 1 contributor's copy. Acquires first North American serial rights.

Also Offers: The David Ray Poetry Award ($100 or more, depending upon grant monies) is given annually for best of volume. Another annual award is sponsored by the Council on National Literatures and offers $100 and publication in *Potpourri* for selected poem or short story; alternating years (2002 fiction). Official guidelines available for SASE. Deadline: September 1, 2002. Website includes back issues, biographies, submission guidelines, sample writings and literary links.

Advice: "Keep your new poems around long enough to become friends with them before parting. Let them ripen, and, above all, learn to be your own best editor. Read them aloud, boldly, to see how they ripple the air and echo what you mean to say. Themes of unrequited love, children, grandchildren, and favorite pets find little chance here."

$ POTTERSFIELD PORTFOLIO; POTTERSFIELD PORTFOLIO SHORT POEM COMPETITION, P.O. Box 40, Station A, Sydney, Nova Scotia B1P 6G9 Canada. Website: www.pportfolio.com. Established 1979. **Contact:** poetry editor.

Magazine Needs: Appearing 3 times/year, *Pottersfield Portfolio* is a "literary magazine publishing fiction, poetry, essays and reviews by authors from all around the world. No restrictions on subject matter or style. However, we will likely not use religious, inspirational, or children's poetry. No doggerel or song lyrics. And please, no stuff that splashes symbols and images all over the page." Has published poetry by David Zieroth, Don Domanski, Jean McNeil, and Alden Nowlan. As a sample the editor selected these lines from "The Coves" by Steve McOrmond:

> You ask the wind/hard questions. Try to see/where the horizon lies, blue seam/between ocean and air,/
> between us/and the end of history.

Pottersfield is 60 pgs., 8 × 11, professionally printed and perfect-bound with b&w cover, includes photos and ads. Receives about 1,000 poems/year, accepts 5%. Press run is 1,000 for 250 subscribers of which 25 are libraries, 750 shelf sales. Single copy: $7; subscription: $26. Sample: $6. "Subscribers from outside Canada please remit in U.S. dollars."

How to Submit: Submit 6 poems at a time. Accepts simultaneous submissions; no previously published poems. Include SAE with IRCs. Cover letter strongly preferred. "Submissions should be on white paper of standard dimensions (8½ × 11). Only one poem per page." Time between acceptance and publication is 3 months. Guidelines available for SASE (or SAE with IRC). "Note: U.S. stamps are no good in Canada." Responds in 3 months. Pays $5/printed page to a maximum of $25 plus 1 contributor's copy. Acquires first Canadian serial rights.

Also Offers: Sponsors the *Pottersfield Portfolio* Short Poem Competition. Deadline: April 1 each year. Entry fee: $20 for 3 poems, which must be no more than 20 lines in length. Fee includes subscription. Write for details or consult website.

Advice: "Only submit your work in a form you would want to read yourself. Subscribe to some literary journals. Read lots of poetry."

💐 ✅ $○ ◐ ◎ THE PRAIRIE JOURNAL; PRAIRIE JOURNAL PRESS (Specialized: regional, themes), P.O. Box 61203, Brentwood Post Office, 217-3630 Brentwood Rd. NW, Calgary, Alberta T2L 2K6 Canada. E-mail: prairiejournal@iname.com. Website: www.geocities.com/prairiejournal (includes submission guidelines and poems of the month). Established 1983. **Editor:** A. Burke.

Magazine Needs: For *The Prairie Journal*, the editor wants to see poetry of "any length, free verse, contemporary themes (feminist, nature, urban, non-political), aesthetic value, a poet's poetry." Does not want to see "most rhymed verse, sentimentality, egotistical ravings. No cowboys or sage brush." Has published poetry by Mick Burrs, Lorna Crozier, Mary Melfi, Art Cuelho, and John Hicks. *Prairie Journal* is 40-60 pgs., 7 × 8½, offset, saddle-stapled with card cover, b&w drawings and ads, appearing twice/year. Receives about 500 poems/year, accepts 4%. Press run is 600 for 200 subscribers of which 50% are libraries, the rest are distributed on the newsstand. Subscription: $8 for individuals, $15 for libraries. Sample: $8 ("Use postal money order").

How to Submit: No simultaneous submissions or previously published poems. Does not accept e-mail submissions. Guidelines available for postage (but "no U.S. stamps, please"—get IRCs from the Post Office) or on website. "We will not be reading submissions until such time as an issue is in preparation (twice yearly), so be patient and we will acknowledge, accept for publication, or return work at that time." Sometimes sends prepublication galleys. Pays $10-50 plus 1 copy. Acquires first North American serial rights. Reviews books of poetry "but must be assigned by editor. Query first."

Book/Chapbook Needs & How to Submit: For chapbook publication, Canadian poets only (preferably from the region) should query with 5 samples, bio, publications. Responds to queries in 2 months, to mss in 6 months. Payment in modest honoraria. Has published *Voices From Earth*, selected poems by Ronald Kurt and Mark McCawley, and *In the Presence of Grace*, by McCandless Callaghan. "We also publish anthologies on themes when material is available."

Advice: "Read recent poets! Experiment with line length, images, metaphors. Innovate."

✅ 💐 ◐ PRAIRIE SCHOONER; STROUSSE PRIZE; LARRY LEVIS PRIZE; SLOTE PRIZE; FAULKNER AWARD; HUGH J. LUKE AWARD; STANLEY AWARD; READERS' CHOICE AWARDS, 201 Andrews, University of Nebraska, Lincoln NE 68588-0334. (402)472-0911. Fax: (402)472-9771. E-mail: eflanagan2@unl.edu. Website: www.unl.edu/schooner/psmain.htm (features writer's guidelines, names of editors, subscription info, history, table of contents, and excerpts from current issue). Established 1927. **Editor:** Hilda Raz.

● Poetry published in *Prairie Schooner* has also been selected for inclusion in *The Best American Poetry 1996* and the *Pushcart Prize* anthology.

Magazine Needs: *Prairie Schooner* is "one of the oldest literary quarterlies in continuous publication; publishes poetry, fiction, personal essays, interviews, and reviews." Wants "poems that fulfill the expectations they set up." No specifications as to form, length, style, subject matter, or purpose. Has published poetry by Alicia Ostriker, Marilyn Hacker, Radu Hotinceneasru, Mark Rudman, and David Ignatow. As a sample the editor selected these lines from "How to Get in the Best Magazines" by Eleanor Wilner:

> it is time to write/the acceptable poem—/ice and glass, with its splinter/of bone, its pit/of an olive,/the
> dregs/of the cup of abundance,/useless spill of gold/from the thresher, the dust/of it filling the sunlight,
> the chum/broadcast on the black waters/and the fish/—the beautiful, ravenous fish—/refusing to rise.

Prairie Schooner is 200 pgs., 6 × 9, flat-spined and uses 70-80 pgs. of poetry in each issue. Receives about 4,800 mss (of all types)/year, uses 300 pgs. of poetry. Press run is 3,100. Single copy: $9; subscription: $26. Sample: $6.

How to Submit: Submit 5-7 poems at a time. No simultaneous submissions. No fax or e-mail submissions. "Clear copy appreciated." Considers mss from September through May only. Publishes theme issues. Guidelines available for SASE. Responds in 4 months; "sooner if possible." Always sends prepublication galleys. Pays 3 contributor's copies. Acquires all rights. Returns rights upon request without fee. Reviews books of poetry. Poets may send books for review consideration. Editor Hilda Raz also promotes poets whose work has appeared in her pages by listing their continued accomplishments in a special section (even when their work does not concurrently appear in the magazine).

Also Offers: The $500 Strousse Prize is awarded to the best poetry published in the magazine each year. The Slote Prize for beginning writers ($500), Hugh J. Luke Award ($250), the Edward Stanley Award for Poetry ($1000) and six other *Prairie Schooner* prizes are also awarded, as well as the Faulkner Award for Excellence in Writing ($1,000) and the Larry Levis Prize for Poetry ($1,000). Also, each year 5-10 Readers' Choice Awards ($250 each) are given for poetry, fiction, and nonfiction. Editors serve as judges. All contests are open only to those writers whose work was published in the magazine the previous year.

PRAKALPANA LITERATURE; KOBISENA (Specialized: bilingual, form), P-40 Nandana Park, Kolkata 700034, West Bengal, India. Phone: (91)(033)403-0347. E-mail: prakalpana@rediffmail.com or uchandan@epatra.com. *Kobisena* established 1972; *Prakalpana Literature* press 1974; magazine 1977. **Editor:** Vattacharja Chandan.

Magazine Needs: "We are small magazines which publish only Prakalpana (a mixed form of prose and poetry), Sarbangin (whole) poetry, experimental b&w art and photographs, essays on Prakalpana movement and Sarbangin poetry movement, letters, literary news and very few books on Prakalpana and Sarbangin literature. Purpose and form: for advancement of poetry in the super-space age, the poetry must be really experimental and avant-garde using mathematical signs and symbols and visualizing the pictures inherent in the alphabet (within typography) with sonorous effect accessible to people. That is Sarbangin poetry. Length: within 30 lines (up to 4 poems). Prakalpana is a mixed form of prose, poetry, essay, novel, story, play with visual effect and it is not at all short story as it is often misunderstood. Better send six IRCs to read *Prakalpana Literature* first and then submit. Length: within 16 pages (up to 2 prakalpanas) at a time. Subject matter: society, nature, cosmos, humanity, love, peace, etc. Style: own. We do not want to see traditional, conventional, academic, religious, mainstream, and poetry of prevailing norms and forms." Has published poetry by Dilip Gupta, Sheila E. Murphy, and Jesse Glass. *Prakalpana Literature*, an annual, is 120 pgs., 7×4½, saddle-stapled, printed on thin stock, matte card cover. *Kobisena*, which also appears once/year, is 16 pgs., digest-sized, newsletter format, no cover. Both use both English and Bengali. Receive about 400 poems/year, accept approximately 10%. Press run is 1,000 for each, and each has about 450 subscribers of which 50 are libraries. Samples: 20 rupees for *Prakalpana*, 4 rupees for *Kobisena*. Overseas: 6 IRCs and 3 IRCs respectively or exchange of avant-garde magazines.

How to Submit: Submit 4 poems at a time. Cover letter with short bio and small photo/sketch of poet/writer/artist required; camera-ready copy (4×6½) preferred. Time between acceptance and publication is within a year. After being published in the magazines, poets may be included in future anthologies with translations into Bengali/English if and when necessary. "Joining with us is welcome but not a pre-condition." Editor comments on rejected poems "if wanted." Guidelines available for SAE with IRC. Pays 1 copy. Reviews books of poetry, fiction and art, "but preferably experimental books." Poets, writers, and artists may also send books for review consideration.

Advice: "We believe that only through poetry, fiction and art, the deepest feelings of humanity as well as nature and the cosmos can be best expressed and conveyed to the peoples of the ages to come. And only poetry can fill up the gap in the peaceless hearts of dispirited peoples, resulted from the retreat of god and religion with the advancement of hi-tech. So, in an attempt, since the inception of Prakalpana Movement in 1969, to reach that goal in the avant-garde and experimental way we stand for Sarbangin poetry. And to poets and all concerned with poetry we wave the white handkerchief saying (in the words of Vattacharja Chandan), 'We want them who want us.' "

PREMIERE GENERATION INK, P.O. Box 2056, Madison WI 53701-2056. E-mail: poetry@premieregeneration.com. Website: www.premieregeneration.com (includes guidelines, photography, video and spoken word, previews of upcoming journal, etc.). Established 1998. **Contact:** poetry editor.

Magazine Needs: *Premiere Generation Ink* appears twice yearly and publishes "high quality, honest poetry in a magazine/journal format and also in a multimedia format via website. We are also looking for art, photos, live recordings of poetry (audio or video) to be put on the Web. We also want experimental video poetry which can be mailed by VHS cassette. We would like to see poetry that is less concerned with being poetry than it is with being honest and true. We welcome any length, format, style or subject matter. We do not want to see pretentious and contrived poetry." Has published poetry by Yogesh Chawla, Sophia Ali, John Ejaife II, Liz Rosenberg, and Virgil Suarez. As a sample the editors selected the poem "Love Ditty" by John Ejaife II:

> Sometimes poems come to you/Other times you have to prod them out/The other day I tried to write
> you a poem./But I ended up making an ashtray instead

Premiere Generation Ink is 30-40 pgs., 8½×11, photocopied in color and saddle-stapled, cover is color or b&w "depending on issue," includes art/graphics. Single copy: $5; subscription: $16. Sample: $5.

How to Submit: Submit 5 poems at a time. Accepts previously published poems and simultaneous submissions. Accepts e-mail submissions (either in body or as attachment). Website features online submission as well. Cover letter preferred. Cover letters need not be formal, we prefer casual and personal. Time between acceptance and publication is 4 months. Poems are circulated to an editorial board. "Three editors review all submissions and a collective decision is reached." Often comments on rejected poems. Guidelines available for SASE, by e-mail, or on website. Responds in 6 weeks. Pays 5 contributor's copies. Acquires first or reprint rights.

Also Offers: "We would like to publish books in cooperation with an author. *Premiere Generation Ink* will chiefly be a means for writers to distribute their art to a larger audience via the Web and the poetry journal. The sales proceeds will go to cover the costs associated with production. Any net profit will be divided equally between the author and the publisher. The main goal of this company is not profit, but rather to distribute quality art to a larger audience. We expect to work closely with the author on the format and layout of the book, and we hope eventually they will become just as much a part of the company as the founders." Order sample books by inquiring via regular mail, e-mail, or website. "Prior to submitting for chapbook publication, a sample copy must be purchased."

☑ $ ◎ THE PRESBYTERIAN RECORD (Specialized: inspirational, religious), 50 Wynford Dr., North York, Ontario M3C 1J7 Canada. (416)441-1111. Fax: (416)441-2825. E-mail: tdickey@presbyterian.ca. Established 1876.

Magazine Needs: *The Presbyterian Record* is "the national magazine that serves the membership of The Presbyterian Church in Canada (and many who are not Canadian Presbyterians). We seek to stimulate, inform, inspire, to provide an 'apologetic' and a critique of our church and the world (not necessarily in that order!)." Wants poetry which is "inspirational, Christian, thoughtful, even satiric but not maudlin. No 'sympathy card' type verse à la Edgar Guest or Francis Gay. It would take a very exceptional poem of epic length for us to use it. Shorter poems, 10-30 lines, preferred. Blank verse OK (if it's not just rearranged prose). 'Found' poems. Subject matter should have some Christian import (however subtle)." Has published poetry by Margaret Avison, Andrew Foster, Fredrick Zydek, Kevin Hadduck, T.M. Dickey, and Charles Cooper. *The Presbyterian Record* appears 11 times/year. Press run is 55,000. Subscription: $15.

How to Submit: Submit 3-6 poems at a time; seasonal work 6 weeks before month of publication. Accepts simultaneous submissions; rarely accepts previously published poems. Poems should be typed, double-spaced. Accepts fax and e-mail submissions "but will not necessarily reply to unsolicited faxes or e-mails." Pays $30-50/poem. Acquires one-time rights. Staff reviews books of poetry. Send books for review consideration.

🌐 ◎ PRESENCE (Specialized: form), 12 Grovehall Ave., Leeds LS11 7EX United Kingdom. E-mail: martin.lucas@talk21.com. Website: http://members.netscapeonline.co.uk/haikupresence (includes samples of haiku, tanka, haibun, renga, articles, subscriptions, and submission information). Established 1995. **Contact:** Mr. Martin Lucas.

Magazine Needs: *Presence*, published 2-3 times/year, features haiku, senryu, renga, tanka, etc. Wants "haiku or haiku-related/haiku-influenced work. Maximum length: 16 lines (including title and spaces)." Does not want "anything longer than 16 lines (except renga)." Has published poetry by Ken Jones, Matt Morden, Patricia Prime, and Alison Williams. As a sample the editor selected this haiku by Martin Lucas:

> a night of stars/the footpath/sparkles with frost

Presence is 44-60 pgs., A5, photocopied, perfect-bound, with brushdrawn art on card cover and illustrations. Receives about 2,000 poems/year, accepts about 10%. Press run is 170 for 100 subscribers of which 5 are libraries, 10 shelf sales. Subscription: £10 ($20 US) for 4 issues surface mail. £3 ($6 US) per single issue air mail. Sample: £3 ($6 US). Please pay in US bills (no checks).

How to Submit: Submit 4-12 poems at a time. "Please ensure that separate poems can be identified, and not mistaken for a sequence." No previously published poems or simultaneous submissions. Accepts e-mail submissions in body of message. Cover letter preferred. Time between acceptance and publication is 4 months. Comments on rejected poems if requested. Guidelines available for SASE (or SAE with IRC) or on website. Responds within 1 month. Pays 1 contributor's copy. Copyright remains with authors. Staff reviews books or chapbooks of poetry or other magazines in 10-500 words, single format. Poets may send books for review consideration.

Advice: "The more you read the better you'll write. Those who subscribe to read make better poets than those who are motivated solely by seeing their own name in print."

◎ THE PRESS OF THE THIRD MIND (Specialized: form), 1301 North Dearborn #1007, Chicago IL 60610. Phone/fax: (312)337-3122. Established 1985. **Poetry Editor:** Bradley Bongwater.

Book/Chapbook Needs: Press of the Third Mind is a small press publisher of artist books, poetry, and fiction. "We are especially interested in found poems, Dada, surrealism, written table-scraps left on the floors of lunatic asylums by incurable psychotics, etc." Has published poetry by Anthony Stark, Jorn Barger, Michael Kaspar, and Eric Forsburg. As a sample the editor selected this excerpt from the prose-poem "Needle Porn at the Mütter Museum" (poet unnamed):

> "Screw the fetal alcohol syndrome bubble gum cards; rotogravure needle porn gives my athiest brain cells a Christian burial! . . . . Separated by a gulf of two inches according to my ruler, and two light years according to the tape measure of my undoing, they wait to be bridged by a Mason and Dixon of hell.

Press run is 1,000 with books often going into a second or third printing. Sample for $1.43 postage.

How to Submit: For book publication submit up to 20 sample poems. "No anthologized mss where every poem has already appeared somewhere else." Accepts simultaneous submissions, if noted. "Cover letter is good, but we don't need to know everything you published since you were age nine in single-spaced detail." Upcoming themes available for SASE. "Authors are paid as the publication transcends the break-even benchmark." The press has released an 80-page anthology entitled *Empty Calories* and published a deconstructivist novel about the repetition compulsion called *The Squeaky Fromme Gets the Grease*.

N ◎ PRESSTHEEDGE, 1015 E. Yager Lane #62, Austin TX 78753. E-mail: mogreen@flash.net. Established 1996. **Contact:** Morrie W. Greene.

Magazine Needs: "*presstheEDGE*, a literary magazine, is a journal-sized annual anthology published in summer consisting of approximately 100 pages of quality poetry, short stories, and art. The only factor affecting acceptance or rejection is quality work. Do not hesitate to submit. Our goal is to provide opportunities for writers so the fine art of writing will flourish as well as provide a quality magazine. We want to see poetry that reaches in deep and grabs the reader. Poetry that is fresh, real contemporary and hits the senses with well-crafted use of metaphor, symbolism, etc. It must be meaningful. Any form or style acceptable. No porn, nothing trite. Traditionalists should submit elsewhere."

How to Submit: Submit up to 10 poems at a time. Accepts previously published poems ("please specify") and simultaneous submissions ("notify please"). Cover letter preferred. "Format: single spaced, name and address on bottom of each page. E-mail submissions preferred, but snail mail is OK. Include brief bio in cover letter. No handwritten submissions." **Reading fee: $2/poem.** Make check payable to M.W. Greene. Time between acceptance and publication is approximately 1 year. Occasionally comments on rejected poems. "Send SASE for notification within 4-6 weeks. If accepted, your realtime address will be required to send author's release form, etc. Hard copy (paper copy) of poems or short stories will not be returned (no need to waste anybody's postage). Author retains all rights, but if the piece is republished, author will credit *presstheEDGE* as the original publisher whenever and wherever else the work may be placed."

Also Offers: Sponsors $50 Editors Choice Award for contributors.

PRIMAVERA (Specialized: women), P.O. Box #37-7547, Chicago IL 60637. (773)324-5920. Established 1975. **Co-Editor:** Ruth Young.

Magazine Needs: *Primavera* is "an irregularly published but approximately annual magazine of poetry and fiction reflecting the experiences of women. We look for strong, original voice and imagery, generally prefer free verse, fairly short length, related, even tangentially, to women's experience." Has published poetry by Dixie Seuss and Caroline D. Goodwin. As a sample the editors selected these lines by Laurie Lemon:

> The fall is true this year;/I wear its cold sweater./It's the dying color/that attracts us, a season/raked
> and burned.

The elegantly printed publication, flat-spined, generously illustrated with photos and graphics, uses 25-30 pgs. of poetry in each issue. Receives over 1,000 submissions of poetry/year, accepts about 25. Press run is 1,000. Single copy: $10. Sample: $5.

How to Submit: Submit up to 6 poems anytime, no queries. No simultaneous submissions. Editors comment on rejected poems "when requested or inspired." Guidelines available for SASE. Responds in up to 3 months. Pays 2 contributor's copies. Acquires first-time rights.

PRINCETON UNIVERSITY PRESS; LOCKERT LIBRARY OF POETRY IN TRANSLATION (Specialized: translations, bilingual), 41 William St., Princeton NJ 08540. (609)258-4916. Fax: (609)258-6305. Website: http://pup.princeton.edu. **Assistant Editor:** Fred Appel.

Book Needs: "In the Lockert Library series, we publish simultaneous cloth and paperback (flat-spine) editions for each poet. Clothbound editions are on acid-free paper, and binding materials are chosen for strength and durability. Each book is given individual design treatment rather than stamped into a series mold. We have published a wide range of poets from other cultures, including well-known writers such as Hölderlin and Cavafy, and those who have not yet had their due in English translation, such as Göran Sonnevi. Manuscripts are judged with several criteria in mind: the ability of the translation to stand on its own as poetry in English; fidelity to the tone and spirit of the original, rather than literal accuracy; and the importance of the translated poet to the literature of his or her time and country."

How to Submit: Accepts simultaneous submissions if informed. Accepts fax submissions. Cover letter required. Send mss only during respective reading periods stated in guidelines. "Manuscripts returned only with SASE." Comments on finalists only. Send SASE for guidelines to submit. Responds in 3 months.

PRISM INTERNATIONAL, Creative Writing Program, University of British Columbia, Vancouver, British Columbia V6T 1Z1 Canada. (604)822-2514. Fax: (604)822-3616. E-mail: prism@interchange.ubc. ca. Website: www.arts.ubc.ca/prism (includes writer's guidelines, names of editors, samples from past issues and "virtually everything you'd want to know." Website also publishes a quarter of the poetry appearing in the print issue). Established 1959. **Editors:** Chris Labonté and Andrea MacPherson. **Executive Editor:** Belinda Bruce.

● *Prism International* is known in literary circles as one of the top journals in Canada.

Magazine Needs: "*Prism* is an international quarterly that publishes poetry, drama, short fiction, imaginative nonfiction and translation into English in all genres. We have no thematic or stylistic allegiances: Excellence is our main criterion for acceptance of mss. We want fresh, distinctive poetry that shows an awareness of traditions old and new. We read everything." Has published poetry by Di Brandt, Esta Spalding, Karen Connelly, Derk Wynand, and a translation by Seamus Heaney. As a sample the editors selected these lines from "The Bends" by Aurian Haller:

> its body lost all signs of passage:/jolted out of its riverskin,/furious at the barbless hook,/red bags of
> reeking oil

Prism is 96 pgs., 6×9, elegantly printed, flat-spined with original color artwork on a glossy card cover. Circulation is for 1,100 subscribers of which 200 are libraries. Receives 1,000 submissions/year, accepts about 80; has a 3 to 4 month backlog. Subscription: $18, $27/2 years. Sample: $5.

How to Submit: Submit up to 6 poems at a time, any print so long as it's typed. Include SASE (or SAE with IRCs). No previously published poems or simultaneous submissions. Accepts fax submissions. Cover letter with brief introduction and previous publications required. "Translations must be accompanied by a copy of the original." Guidelines available for SASE (or SAE with IRCs) or on website. Responds in up to 6 months. Pays $40/printed page plus subscription; plus an additional $10/printed page to selected authors for publication on the World Wide Web. Editors sometimes comment on rejected poems. Acquires first North American serial rights. **Advice:** "While we don't automatically discount any kind of poetry, we prefer to publish work that challenges the writer as much as it does the reader. We are particularly looking for poetry in translation."

☑ ◯ **THE PROSE POEM: AN INTERNATIONAL JOURNAL**, English Dept. Providence College, Providence RI 02918. (401)865-2217. Website: http://webdelsol.com/TPP. **Editor:** Peter Johnson. **Assistant Editor:** Brian Johnson.
Magazine Needs: *The Prose Poem* is published annually in September. "Please don't send verse poems. Although we don't want to say that we can define 'prose poetry,' we do expect our contributors to at least know the difference between verse and prose poetry, so that they don't waste their time and postage." Has published poetry by Charles Simic, Russell Edson, and Robert Bly.
How to Submit: Submit 3-5 poems at a time with SASE. No simultaneous submissions. Cover letter with 2-sentence bio required. Reads submissions December through March only. "Won't be accepting until December 2001." Time between acceptance and publication is 4-6 months. Subscription: $8/year, $12/2 years. Make checks payable to Providence College. Responds in 3 months. "If we publish an anthology we reserve the right to reprint your published poem in it; we also reserve the right to publish it on our web page."

☑ ◯ **PROSODIA**, New College of California, 766 Valencia St., San Francisco CA 94110. E-mail: prosodia @ncgate.newcollege.edu Established 1990. **Faculty Advisor:** George Mattingly.
Magazine Needs: "*Prosodia* is the annual publication of the graduate Poetics Department at the New College of California. Wants experimental, imaginative, adventurous, and stimulating poetry. No religious or sentimental work." Has published poetry by Andrei Codrescu, Barbara Guest, Tom Clark, Gloria Frym, Anselm Hollo, and Pat Nolan. As a sample they selected these lines from "There are a thousand doors to let out life" by Adam Cornford:

> 1. Already in the womb in one, the placenta's aperture/like a telescope's tiny eyepiece, just opposite/
> the still locked, only door into this life

Prosodia is 160 pgs., magazine-sized, offset-printed and perfect-bound with soft cover, includes sometimes art. Receives about 300 poems/year, accepts about 15%. Press run is 500 for 100 subscribers. Sample: $10. Make checks payable to GMD.
How to Submit: Accepts simultaneous submissions; no previously published poems. Accepts disk and e-mail submissions (attach file to e-mail; "please also send hardcopy for proofing"). Cover letter required. Submission deadline is October 1; publication in May. Poems are circulated to an editorial board. "Editorial staff changes with each issue." Occasionally publishes theme issues. Responds by mid-February. Pays 2 contributor's copies.

☑ $ ◯ **PROVINCETOWN ARTS; PROVINCETOWN ARTS PRESS**, 650 Commercial St., Provincetown MA 02657-1725. (508)487-3167. Fax: (508)487-4791. E-mail: cbusa@mediaone.net. Established 1985. **Editor:** Christopher Busa.
Magazine Needs: An elegant annual using quality poetry. "*Provincetown Arts* focuses broadly on the artists and writers who inhabit or visit the tip of Cape Cod and seeks to stimulate creative activity and enhance public awareness of the cultural life of the nation's oldest continuous art colony. Drawing upon a century-long tradition rich in visual art, literature, and theater, *Provincetown Arts* publishes material with a view towards demonstrating that the artists' colony, functioning outside the urban centers, is a utopian dream with an ongoing vitality." Has published poetry by Bruce Smith, Franz Wright, Sandra McPherson, and Cyrus Cassells. *Provincetown Arts* is about 170 pgs., 8¾ × 11⅞, perfect-bound with full-color glossy cover. Press run is 10,000 for 500 subscribers of which 20 are libraries, 6,000 shelf sales. Sample: $10.
How to Submit: Submit up to 3 typed poems at a time. All queries and submissions should be via regular mail. Reads submissions October through February. Guidelines available for SASE. Responds in 3 months. Usually sends prepublication galleys. Pays $25-100/poem plus 2 contributor's copies. Acquires first rights. Reviews books of poetry in 500-3,000 words, single or multi-book format. Poets may send books for review consideration.
Book/Chapbook Needs & How to Submit: The Provincetown Arts Press has published 8 volumes of poetry. The Provincetown Poets Series includes *At the Gate* by Martha Rhodes, *Euphorbia* by Anne-Marie Levine, a finalist in the 1995 Paterson Poetry Prize, and *1990* by Michael Klein, co-winner of the 1993 Lambda Literary Award.

◯ ◯ **THE PUCKERBRUSH PRESS; THE PUCKERBRUSH REVIEW**, 76 Main St., Orono ME 04473-1430. (207)866-4868 or 581-3832 Press established 1971. *Review* established 1978. **Poetry Editor:** Constance Hunting.
Magazine Needs & How to Submit: *The Puckerbrush Review* is a literary, twice-a-year magazine. Looks for freshness and simplicity, but does not want to see "confessional, religious, sentimental, dull, feminist, incompetent, derivative" poetry. As a sample the editor selected these lines from "Breughel's Two Monkeys" by Beth Thomas:

> O bestial side, starry-and strong-eyed,/set like twin pupils, balled on hanch,/clamped at thigh,
> glowering over Antwerp

insider report

Exploring a personal landscape

Cynthia Huntington's approach to writing—and to life—is one of reciprocity. It's a recognition of *relationship* in all things (creative, emotional, human, or geographic) and the need to give something back, to feel equal to what one has been given. Huntington is the author of two collections of poetry, *The Fish Wife* (University of Hawaii Press, 1986) and *We Have Gone to the Beach* (Alice James Books, 1996), as well as a memoir, *The Salt House: A Summer on the Dunes of Cape Cod* (University Press of New England, 1999).

A prominent feature in her work is her sense of connection with landscape, which she sees as very much related to personal relationships and self-discovery. Although Huntington grew up in Western Pennsylvania (northern Appalachia), the landscape she feels closest to is Cape Cod, specifically about eight square miles around Provincetown, Rhode Island, home to the Fine Arts Work Center, from which Huntington received a grant.

Cynthia Huntington

© 1999 Brad Fowler

"That's hallowed ground to me," says Huntington, "the streets, the trails, and the beaches. I have a natural affinity for this landscape, but it's also a place where I stood on this corner and had a conversation, or sat in that bar and cried because my manuscript got rejected, or walked on this path with my husband before we were married. So there's an investment in that landscape—and I mean in terms of the human landscape and the natural landscape. I've fed it and it's fed me back, so in my imagination we're so entwined."

Huntington has mixed feelings about the human and natural landscapes of her childhood. "My imaginative life on the page seems to start at about age 26. There are a lot of really rich things in my childhood but it was also very painful. I feel like I've spent the first fifty years of my life making a self away from that world. The next move is for the frail and hardy adult self now to go back and look at all that. For a long time I couldn't because I was having to create myself with other materials. It amazes and impresses me that some people make themselves out of these painful situations, that they're able to write about them and stay in contact with them."

Huntington has made herself out of her own painful situations, one of which was being diagnosed with Multiple Sclerosis. "We had moved to California, I started teaching, my son was born, my book came out, and then I got sick." However, she was unable write about the disease for a long while. "I just didn't see any imaginative way of describing it. Then recently, I tried to find what interested me about it and to describe that rather than just describing it clinically. In a poem called 'A Picture of My Brain,' all these little ghost things show up on the MRI, and it's about how something invisible that comes and goes and can't be tracked can change your life so much.

"The biggest challenge with MS has been the way if effects my energy," Huntington continues. "Anything with the central nervous system really affects your overall physical and mental energy, so it had a very detrimental effect on my writing for a long time simply because writing takes a lot of mental energy. But I've become more comfortable with it since my mid-40s. I have a much greater understanding now that everybody has *something*. I don't feel so singled out."

"Balch Hill"

The birds were talking about me, passing ideas
back and forth along the branches.
They said I had been sick too long,
that I walked among the trees like a tall stranger,
and that where I put my foot was not certain.
They said there was a lightness of uncertainty, and a sliding,
as if my weight would not fall evenly on the earth,
that my head never moved to the left or to the right,
my chin held down, not looking up—oh that one,
I heard them finally agree: she has been sick too long.

The birds were talking to hear themselves agree on anything,
to make a convention out of the rowdiness of June.
Their notes unbirdlike intrusions,
to recall that they alone were birds.
I went on. I was not tired. I could walk forever,
if forever lived in that town, but the path ended
on a steep hillside where apple trees grew wild
and I could see four mountains, and the clock tower
rising above the college library, then the highway and the river,
and Vermont in the distance like another country.

The birds were talking to put me in the ground,
to sing me down from their sky. They said that
a broken thing must be ended. My feet bruised the fallen
apples under the leaves, and overhead the treetops
were circling in air. But when I raised my head to answer them,
the wind blew in among the trees, and the flock scattered,
disappearing, becoming nothing, just specks on the sky,
distant, like ash blown up from a fire. I stood and sniffed
the spice of the apples, rotting under last year's leaves,
their heavy fragrance sweet, like the sweetest taste of ruin.

(first published in *Third Coast*, 1996; reprinted by permission of the author)

Huntington's next book of poems, *The River of Doubt*, was written through a time of great personal crisis when her illness collided with problems in her marriage. "It seemed like my sense of inadequacy in every way was being shown to me. There's a sense of physical inadequacy when you have a disease; not that you're being judged, but you can't do what you want to do or be what you want to be. And there's certainly a sense of failing and being failed in a marital crisis, so those had to be very inward poems. I ask in one poem, 'if everything is taken away, do you still have a self?' And there's a very tenuous 'yes,' but it's not necessarily a self you're immediately going to recognize."

Huntington's process of writing includes recording things without judgment. "I really put down a lot of crazy stuff, but it's usually propelled by something I don't understand or anticipate. Something gets me going. I think that's the greatest mystery for every writer: We know how we work once we have something on the page to work with, but where it originally comes from is so wonderful. Something in you contacts some deeper layer that brings together a lot of things you could never rationally bring together. The closest thing I can relate it to is a sense of smell. There's some energy there and you're going after it with words and images.

"The group of poems I was writing this summer started with this carcass of a 30-foot shark that was washed up on this beach we were going to every day—a very familiar poetic image about how the mighty are fallen and how the flies are eating him, but I knew there was something in that image that was speaking to me beyond what I originally could see. I was drawn in just a slightly different way than before into the feel of the images of that particular beach, about the things that were eating each other and feeding each other, that sense of scale and the flatness of the beach, how large you feel in terms of height compared to all the little things.

"But even to explain it isn't the point. It's suddenly the sense that you are drawn toward an intuition of something that language is going to show you the way through and into."

As a teacher of creative writing at Dartmouth College and Vermont College, Huntington believes the most important thing for a writer is to respect his or her own creative process. "If your imagination insists it will only speak to you between the hours of three and four a.m. and you have to be in the laundry room, I'd go. I'd show up. Maybe it would become less perverse if you're nicer to it.

"It's like the relationship between landscape and person, the relationship between the poet and the poem. You get all these poems in the notebook; but unless you're ready to sit with them and rear them like children, to invest in them, to be willing to be right and wrong, to be in a relationship with them and give your intelligence and spirit over to them, then it's a wasted gift. I don't worry where they come from, but I do have a great religious concern about being equal to the task because we're so lucky that we're able to do this."

—*Michelle Moore*

For the review, submit 5 poems at a time. Pays 2 copies.
Book/Chapbook Needs & How to Submit: The Puckerbrush Press is a small press publisher of flat-spined paperbacks of literary quality. Has published *Settling* by Patricia Ranzoni and *A Voice*, translation of Celan by Irask Nagel. For book publication, query with 10 samples. Prefers no simultaneous submissions. Offers criticism for a fee: $100 is usual. Pays 10% royalties plus 10 copies.

PUDDING HOUSE PUBLICATIONS; PUDDING MAGAZINE: THE INTERNATIONAL JOURNAL OF APPLIED POETRY; PUDDING HOUSE CHAPBOOK COMPETITIONS; PUDDING HOUSE BED & BREAKFAST FOR WRITERS; PUDDING HOUSE WRITERS INNOVATION CENTER (Specialized: political, social issues, popular culture), 60 N. Main St., Johnstown OH 43031. (740)967-6060. E-mail: pudding@johnstown.net. Website: www.puddinghouse.com. Established 1979. **Editor:** Jennifer Bosveld.
Magazine Needs: Pudding House Publications provides "a sociological looking glass through poems that speak to the pop culture, struggle in a consumer and guardian society and more—through 'felt experience.' Speaks for the difficulties and the solutions. Additionally a forum for poems and articles by people who take poetry arts into the schools and the human services." Publishes *Pudding* every several months, also chapbooks, anthologies, broadsides. "Wants what hasn't been said before. Speak the unspeakable. Don't want preachments or sentimentality. Don't want obvious traditional forms without fresh approach. Long poems OK as long as they aren't windy. Interested in receiving poetry on popular culture, rich brief narratives, i.e. 'virtual journalism.' (sample sheet $1

plus SASE)." Has published poetry by Knute Skinner, David Chorlton, Mary Winters, and Robert Collins. Uses up to 60 pgs. of poetry in each issue—5½ × 8½, 70 pgs., offset-composed on Microsoft Word PC. Press run is 2,000 for 1,400 subscribers of which 40 are libraries. Subscription: $18.95/3 issues. Sample: $7.95.

How to Submit: Submit 3-10 poems at a time with SASE. "Submissions without SASEs will be discarded." No postcards. No simultaneous submissions. Previously published submissions respected but include credits. Likes cover letters and "cultivates great relationships with writers." Sometimes publishes theme issues. Guidelines available for SASE. Responds on same day (unless traveling). Pays 1 copy; to featured poet $10 and 4 copies. Returns rights "with *Pudding* permitted to reprint." Staff reviews books of poetry. Send books for review consideration. "See our website for vast calls for poems for magazine, chapbooks, and anthologies; for poetry and word games, and essays and workshop announcements."

Book/Chapbook Needs & How to Submit: Has recently published *Dancing with the Switchman* by Conrad Squires, *When I Had it Made* by Will Nixon, and *Subject Apprehended* by Hans Ostrom. Chapbooks considered outside of competitions, no query. **Reading fee:** $10. Send complete ms and cover letter with publication credits and bio. Editor sometimes comments, will critique on request for $4/page of poetry or $75 an hour in person.

Also Offers: Pudding House is the publisher of the nationwide project POETS' GREATEST HITS—an invitational. They have over 250 chapbooks and books in print. Pudding House offers 2 annual chapbook competitions— each requires a $10 reading fee with entry. Deadlines: June 30 and September 30. The competitions award $100, publication, and 20 free copies. Pudding House Bed & Breakfast for Writers offers "pretty, comfortable, clean rooms with desk and all the free paper you can use" as well as free breakfast in large comfortable home ½ block from conveniences. Location of the Pudding House Writers Innovation Center and Library on Applied Poetry. Bed & Breakfast is $85 single or double/night, discounts to writers. Reservations recommended far in advance. Details available for SASE. "Our website is one of the greatest poetry websites in the country—calls, workshops, publication list/history, online essays, games, guest pages, calendars, poem of the month, poet of the week, much more." The website also links to the site for The Unitarian Universalist Poets Cooperative, a national organization. Membership: $10/year.

Advice: "Editors have pet peeves. I won't respond to postcards or on them. I require SASEs. I don't like cover letters that state the obvious, poems with trite concepts, or meaning dictated by rhyme. Thoroughly review our website; it will give you a good idea about our publication history and editorial tastes."

PUERTO DEL SOL, Box 3E, New Mexico State University, Las Cruces NM 88003-0001. E-mail: kwest@nmsu.edu. Established 1972 (in present format). **Poetry Editor:** Kathleene West. **Editor-in-Chief:** Kevin McIlvoy.

Magazine Needs: "We publish a literary magazine twice per year. Interested in poems, fiction, essays, photos, originals, and translations, usually from the Spanish. Also (generally solicited) reviews and dialogues between writers. We want top quality poetry, any style, from anywhere. We are sympathetic to Southwestern writers, but this is not a theme magazine. Excellent poetry of any kind, any form." Has published poetry by Judith Sornberger, Ana Castillo, Marilyn Hacker, Virgil Suarez, and Lois-Ann Yamanaka. As a sample the editor selected these lines from "And Seeing It" by Valerie Martínez:

> Orange, orange. And the hand arching up/to hold it. The woman's hand, the arching./Up. And the
> star exploding, seeing it/where it wasn't, a telescope on the night sky./The thermonuclear flash. The
> explosion.

Puerto del Sol is 6 × 9, flat-spined, professionally printed, matte card cover with art. Press run is 1,250 for 300 subscribers of which 25-30 are libraries. Devotes 40-50 pgs. to poetry in each 150-page issue. Uses about 50 of the 800 submissions (about 6,000 poems) received each year to fill up the 90 pgs. of poetry the 2 issues encompass. Subscription: $10/2 issues. Sample: $7.

How to Submit: Submit 3-6 poems at a time, 1 poem to a page. Accepts simultaneous submissions. Cover letter welcome. Reads mss September 1 to March 1 only. Offers editorial comments on most mss. Responds in 6 months. Sometimes sends prepublication galleys. Pays 2 contributor's copies.

Advice: "We're looking for poems that are risk-taking and honest."

PULSAR POETRY MAGAZINE; LIGDEN PUBLISHERS, 34 Lineacre, Grange Park, Swindon, Wiltshire SN5 6DA United Kingdom. Phone: (01793)875941. E-mail: david.pike@virgin.net. Website: www.btint ernet.com/~pulsarpoetry. Established 1992. **Editor:** David Pike. **Editorial Assistant:** Jill Meredith.

Magazine Needs: *Pulsar*, published quarterly, "encourages the writing of poetry from all walks of life. Contains poems, reviews and editorial comments." Wants "hard-hitting, thought-provoking work; interesting and stimulating poetry." Does not want "racist material. Not keen on religious poetry." Has published poetry by Merryn Williams, Joy Martin, Li Min Hua, Virgil Suarez, and Wincey Willis. As a sample the editor selected these lines from "The Watcher" by Lewis Hosegood:

> Somewhere in this tall terraced house, somewhere,/somewhere lives a boy/who surely cannot see me,/
> nor speak my name aloud, yet senses/my interest in origins./He will never go away though I wait here
> and wait. . . .

Pulsar is 36 pgs., A5, professionally printed, saddle-stapled, glossy 2-color cover with photos and ads. Press run is 300 for 100 subscribers of which 40 are libraries; several distributed free to newspapers, etc. Subscription: $30 (£12 UK). Sample: $7. Make checks payable to Ligden Publishers.

How to Submit: Submit 3 poems at a time "preferably typed." No previously published poems or simultaneous submissions. Send no more than 2 poems via e-mail; file attachments will not be read. Cover letter preferred; include SAE with IRCs. "Poems can be published in next edition if it is what we are looking for. The editor and assistant read all poems." Time between acceptance and publication is about 1 month. Seldom comments on rejected poems. Guidelines available for SASE (or SAE with IRC). Responds within 3 weeks. Pays 1 contributor's copy. Acquires first rights. Staff reviews poetry books and poetry audio tapes (mainstream); word count varies. Send books for review consideration.

Advice: "Give explanatory notes if poems are open to interpretation. Be patient and enjoy what you are doing. Check grammar, spelling, etc. (should be obvious). Note: we are a non-profit making society."

✓ 🌐 $ ◯ ◐ **QUADRANT MAGAZINE**, P.O. Box 82, Balmain, 2041 NSW, Australia. Phone: (02)9818-1155. Fax: (02)9818-1422. E-mail: quadrantmonthly@ozemail.com.au. Established 1956. **Editor:** P.P. McGuinnes. **Literary Editor:** Les Murray.

Magazine Needs: *Quadrant*, published 10 times/year, is a "magazine of literature and ideas; about 10% of pages devoted to poetry." Has published poetry by Bruce Dawe, Geoff Page, and Kathleen Stewart. *Quadrant* is 88 pgs., 7⅞×10¾, professionally printed on newsprint, saddle-stapled, CS2 cover stock with some art and ads. Receives several thousand poems/year, accepts about 5%. Press run is 8,000 for 3,000 subscribers of which 500 are libraries, 2,500 shelf sales; 130 distributed free. Subscription: $59.40 (in Australia). Sample: $6.50 plus $1.40 postage (in Australia).

How to Submit: No previously published poems or simultaneous submissions. Cover letter preferred. Time between acceptance and publication is 6 months. "Assessment made by literary editor." Seldom comments on rejected poems. Guidelines available for SASE (or SAE with IRCs). Pays $40/poem plus 1 contributor's copy. Acquires first Australian serial rights. Reviews books of poetry.

🌐 $ ⬚ ◯ ◐ **QUANTUM LEAP; Q.Q. PRESS**, York House, 15 Argyle Terrace, Rothesay, Isle of Bute PA20 0BD Scotland, United Kingdom. Established 1997. **Editor:** Alan Carter.

Magazine Needs: *Quantum Leap* is a quarterly poetry magazine. Wants "all kinds of poetry—free verse, rhyming, whatever—as long as it's well written and preferably well punctuated, too. We rarely use haiku." Also accepts poetry written by children. Has published poetry by Pamela Constantine, Ray Stebbing, Leigh Eduardo, Sam Smith, Sky Higgins, Norman Bissett, and Gordon Scapens. As a sample we selected these lines from "Topography of Mind" by Sky Higgins:

> A map like none other, encompassing me: from the hard, distant stones of stars/to the blood-pulse in
> my eyes, and all/the time I ever savoured, stretched or lost,/where sand deserts the hourglass, is freed/
> into landscape whorls. . .

Quantum Leap is 40 pgs., digest-sized, desktop-published and saddle-stapled with card cover, includes clip art and ads for other magazines. Receives about 2,000 poems/year, accepts about 10%. Press run is 200 for 180 subscribers. Single copy: $9; subscription: $32. Sample: $8. Make checks payable to Alan Carter. "All things being equal in terms of a poem's quality, I will sometimes favor that of a subscriber (or someone who has at least bought an issue) over a nonsubscriber, as it is they who keep us solvent."

How to Submit: Submit 6 poems at a time. Line length for poetry is 36 ("normally"). Accepts previously published poems (indicate magazine and date of first publication) and simultaneous submissions. Cover letter required. "Within the UK, send a SASE, outside it, send IRCs to the value of what has been submitted." Time between acceptance and publication is usually 3 months "but can be longer now, due to magazine's increasing popularity." Sometimes comments on rejected poems. Guidelines available for SASE (or SAE and IRC). Responds in 3 weeks. Pays £2 sterling. Acquires first or second British serial rights.

Book/Chapbook Needs: Under the imprint "Collections," Q.Q. Press offers subsidy arrangements "to provide a cheap alternative to the 'vanity presses'—poetry only." Charges £120 sterling for 50 32-page books (A4), US $250 plus postage. Please write for details. Order sample books by sending $12 (postage included). Make checks payable to Alan Carter.

Also Offers: Sponsors open poetry competitions and competitions for subscribers only. Send SAE and IRC for details.

Advice: "Submit well-thought-out, well-presented poetry, preferably well punctuated, too. If rhyming poetry, make it flow and don't strain to rhyme. I don't bite, and I appreciate a short cover letter, but not a long, long list of where you've been published before!"

◐ ◎ **QUARTER AFTER EIGHT; PROSE WRITING CONTEST (Specialized: form/style)**, Ellis Hall, Ohio University, Athens OH 45701. (740)593-2827. Fax: (740)593-2818. E-mail: quarteraftereight@excite. com. Website: www.geocities.com/quarteraftereight. Established 1993. **Editors-in-Chief:** Christina Veladota and Thom Conroy.

Magazine Needs: *Quarter After Eight* is "an annual journal of prose and commentary devoted to the exploration of prose in all its permutations. We are interested in reading fiction, sudden fiction, prose poetry, creative and critical non-fiction, interviews, reviews, letters, memoirs, translations, and drama. We do not publish traditional (lineated) poetry, but we do welcome work that provocatively explores—even challenges—the prose/poetry distinction. Our primary criteria in evaluating submissions are freshness of approach and an address to the prose form." Has published poetry by Colette Inez, Richard Kostelanetz, Christine Boyka Kluge, Alanna Bondar, and Sandra Alcosser. As a sample the editors selected these lines from "Whining Prairie" by Maureen Seaton:

> *I don't want to die in this wild onion smelly belly mire of the midwest stinking marsh this drenchy swaly swamp but I might and who would note the fragrant corruption of my poor elan this moorish bog this poachy few who come from sea with salt and myrrh to burn my rotting flesh?*

Quarter After Eight is 310 pgs., 6×9, professionally printed and perfect-bound with glossy card cover, includes b&w photos and ads. Receives about 1,000 poems/year, accepts 3%. Press run is 800 for 200 subscribers of which 50 are libraries, 300 shelf sales. Sample: $10.

How to Submit: Submit 4-6 poems at a time. Accepts simultaneous submissions; no previously published poems. Accepts disk submissions with hard copy. "Include publishing history. We encourage readers/submitters to obtain a copy of the magazine." Reads submissions September 15 through March 15 only. Poems are circulated to an editorial board. "Editorial board makes final decisions; a pool of readers handles first reads and commentary/input on editorial decisions." Often comments on rejected poems. Guidelines available for SASE or on website. Responds in up to 3 months. Pays 2 contributor's copies. Acquires first North American serial rights. Reviews books of poetry in 800-1,200 words, single or multi-book format. Send books for review consideration to Patrick Madden, Book Review Editor.

Also Offers: Sponsors an annual Prose Writing Contest with $300 cash award. Reading fee: $10. Winner is published in subsequent issue. Maximum length 10,000 words—can be a sequence of poems Guidelines available for SASE or on website.

Advice: *"Quarter After Eight* is a somewhat specialized niche. Check out the magazine and explore the boundaries of genre."

QUARTERLY WEST, 200 S. Central Campus Dr., Room 317, University of Utah, Salt Lake City UT 84112-9109. (801)581-3938. Website: www.utah.edu/quarterly/ (includes guidelines, staff, examples of recently published poems, graphic of cover, and a list of contributors). Established 1976. **Editor:** Margot Schilpp and Lynn Kilpatrick. **Poetry Editor:** David Hawkins.

- Poetry published in *Quarterly West* has appeared in *The Best American Poetry* 1997 and 2000 and has won the Pushcart Prize several times.

Magazine Needs: *Quarterly West* is a semiannual literary magazine that seeks "original and accomplished literary verse—free or formal. No greeting card or sentimental poetry." Also publishes translations. Has published poetry by Robert Pinsky, Eavan Boland, Albert Goldbarth, William Matthews, Agha Shahid Ali, and Heather McHugh. *Quarterly West* is 220 pgs., 6×9, offset-printed with 4-color cover art. Receives 1,500 submissions/year, accepts less than 1%. Press run is 1,900 for 500 subscribers of which 300-400 are libraries. Subscription: $12/year, $21/2 years. Sample: $7.50.

How to Submit: Submit 3-5 poems at a time; if translations, include original. Accepts simultaneous submissions, with notification; no previously published poems. Seldom comments on rejected poems. Guidelines available for SASE or on website. Responds in up to 6 months. Pays $15-100 plus 2 contributor's copies. Acquires all rights. Returns rights with acknowledgement and right to reprint. Reviews books of poetry in 1,000-3,000 words.

QUEEN OF ALL HEARTS (Specialized: religious), 26 S. Saxon Ave., Bay Shore NY 11706. (631)665-0726. Fax: (631)665-4349. E-mail: pretre@worldnet.att.net. Established 1950. **Poetry Editor:** Joseph Tusiani.

Magazine Needs: *Queen of All Hearts* is a magazine-sized bimonthly that uses poetry "dealing with Mary, the Mother of Jesus—inspirational poetry. Not too long." Has published poetry by Fernando Sembiante and Alberta Schumacher. *Queen of All Hearts* is professionally printed, 48 pgs., heavy stock, various colors of ink and paper, liberal use of graphics and photos, has approximately 2,5000 subscriptions at $22/year. Single copy: $3.50. Sample: $4. Receives 40-50 submissions/year, accepts 1-2/issue.

How to Submit: Submit double-spaced mss. Accepts fax submissions but not e-mail submissions. Responds within 1 month. Pays 6 contributor's copies (sometimes more) and complimentary subscription. Editor sometimes comments on rejected poems.

Advice: "Try and try again! Inspiration is not automatic!"

ELLERY QUEEN'S MYSTERY MAGAZINE (Specialized: mystery), 475 Park Ave. S, 11th Floor, New York NY 10016. Established 1941. **Contact:** Janet Hutchings.

Magazine Needs: *Ellery Queen's Mystery Magazine*, appearing 11 times/year, uses primarily short stories of mystery, crime, or suspense. As a sample we selected these lines from "Mean Clara" by Katherine H. Brooks:

> *Employed as a bagger, intent upon packing/the food in a way the ice cream would run,/She distributed eggs so the shells would be cracking,/then scrambled the contents, and thought it was fun/. . ./The person responsible wasn't detected./They called him a hero—delighted and flip—/And suggested, as Clara was duly collected,/that he who had bagged her deserved a nice tip.*

Ellery Queen's Mystery Magazine is 144 pgs., 5¼×8⁵⁄₁₆, professionally printed on newsprint, flat-spined with glossy paper cover. Subscription: $33.97. Sample: $2.95 (available on newsstands).

How to Submit: Accepts simultaneous submissions; no previously published poems. Include SASE with submissions. Responds in 3 months. Pays $5-50 plus 3 contributor's copies.

$ ☑ ⓘ **QUEEN'S QUARTERLY: A CANADIAN REVIEW (Specialized: regional),** Queen's University, Kingston, Ontario K7L 3N6 Canada. (613)533-2667. Fax: (613)533-6822. E-mail: qquarter@post.que ensu.ca. Website: www.info.queensu.ca/quarterly. Established 1893. **Editor:** Boris Castel.
Magazine Needs: *Queen's Quarterly* is "a general interest intellectual review featuring articles on science, politics, humanities, arts and letters, extensive book reviews, some poetry and fiction. We are especially interested in poetry by Canadian writers. Shorter poems preferred." Has published poetry by Evelyn Lau, Sue Nevill, and Raymond Souster. Each issue contains about 12 pgs. of poetry, 6×9, 224 pgs. Press run is 3,500. Receives about 400 submissions of poetry/year, accepts 40. Subscription: $20 Canadian, $25 US for US and foreign subscribers. Sample: $6.50 US.
How to Submit: Submit up to 6 poems at a time. No simultaneous submissions. Accepts e-mail submissions. Responds in 1 month. Pays usually $50 (Canadian)/poem, "but it varies," plus 2 copies.

☑ ☀ ◯ **THE RABBIT HOLE PRESS**, 2 Huntingwood Crescent, Brampton, Ontario L6S 1S6 Canada. E-mail: rabbitholepress@hotmail.com. Established 1999. **Publisher:** Alice.
Magazine Needs: "*Rabbit Hole* is a small, quarterly literary journal that publishes poetry, short fiction, short shorts, essays, original art, and photography. We are eclectic, imaginative, edgy, insightful, sensual, provocative, rebellious in nature: 'how deep is the rabbit hole.' " Specifications for poetry are open: "We want original, quality, well-crafted work which shows the poet has his/her own voice. Poetry should be accessible, provocative, poignant, vital, honest. Feel it, mean it, be it, craft it and then share it. If it's quality, professional work and it touches me, I'll publish it. No doggerel or 'Hallmark' verse. No ranting, whining, or gushing. Nothing illegal or offensive. (You should know what is illegal. I'll decide what is offensive.) Erotica is okay but no porn." Has published poetry by Alex Morgan and Kevin Hoag. As a sample they selected these lines from "New Year's Day" by Alex Morgan:

> All the promises/I made at midnight/slip my grasp and float/downstream on the backs of mallards.//I
> wish that I could follow,/escape that hollow confection/like the honking geese/etching secret messages
> to the sun/on the icing-sugar sky.

The Rabbit Hole Press is 35-50 pgs., 5½×8½, desktop-published and saddle-stapled with card cover, includes original art and photography. Receives about 500 poems/year, accepts 20%. Publishes 10 poems/issue. Press run is 300. Subscription: $20 (US). Sample: $5 (US). Make checks payable to A. Cobham. "All payment in U.S. dollars unless you are Canadian."
How to Submit: Submit 5 poems at a time. Line length for poetry is 100 maximum. Accepts simultaneous submissions; no previously published poems. Accepts e-mail submissions. Cover letter preferred. "SASE required for all submissions and correspondence. IRC requested if outside Canada. International contributors and subscribers welcomed." Time between acceptance and publication is 4 months. Seldom comments on rejected poems. Guidelines available for SASE (or SAE with IRC). Responds in 1 month. Pays 1 contributor's copy. Acquires one-time rights.
Advice: "Read, read and write, write. Join a group of kindred spirits for constructive criticism and encouragement. Believe in yourself and never give up. Subscribe to small presses and buy books of poetry; support your craft."

☑ ❤ ◎ **THE RAINTOWN REVIEW (Specialized: form/style)**, P.O. Box 370, Pittsboro IN 46167. E-mail: hmpeditor@hotmail.com. Website: www.hstanbrough.com/ (includes detailed guidelines, reviews of Harvey Stanbrough's poetry collections, samples of his poetry, and rates for his freelance editorial services). Established 1996. **Editor:** Harvey Stanbrough.
Magazine Needs: *The Raintown Review* is published irregularly and contains only poetry. Wants well-crafted poems—metered, syllabic, or free-verse. Has published poetry by Andrea B. Geffner, Mary Gribble, Robert Michael O'Hearn, and Ted Simmons. As a sample the editor selected these lines from "Suicide Note" by William Baer:

> The night that she committed suicide/her brother in New Jersey played the horses,/drinking with his
> buddies all night long;/her friend at Yale thumbed through a recent novel/looking in vain for meaning
> and for love;/her mother was asleep in New Rochelle;/her father, dead, was knocking on his box,/
> hoping to distract his little girl.

The Raintown Review is about 60 pgs., chapbook-sized, desktop-published and saddle-stapled with card cover. Receives about 900 poems/year, accepts 10-15%. Press run is about 200 with most going to subscribers and contributors. Subscription: $24/year. Sample: $7.
How to Submit: Submit up to 6 poems at a time. Accepts previously published poems and simultaneous submissions. No e-mail submissions. Cover letter preferred. "We prefer contributors write for guidelines before submitting work." Often comments on rejected poems. Guidelines available for SASE or on website. Responds in 1 month. Pays at least 1 contributor's copy. Acquires first or one-time rights.

THE GEOGRAPHICAL INDEX, located at the back of this book, can help you discover the publishers in your region.

Also Offers: *The Raintown Review* Poetry Awards with $1,500 prize; guidelines available on website.
Advice: "To help regain the poetry audience, study your craft and write accessible, aesthetic poetry."

☑ ◯ ◐ ◎ **RALPH'S REVIEW; RC'S STAMP HOT LINE (Specialized: horror, nature/rural/ecology, psychic/occult, science fiction/fantasy)**, 129A Wellington Ave., Albany NY 12203. E-mail: rcpub @juno.com. Established 1988. **Editor:** R. Cornell.
Magazine Needs: *Ralph's Review*, published quarterly, contains "mostly new writers, short stories and poems." Wants "horror/fantasy, environmental. No more than 30 lines." Does not want "rape, racial, political poems." Has published "Moods of Madness" by R. Cornell and poetry by Joanne Tolson, Joseph Danoski, Jim Sullivan, and Brendan J. MacDonald. *Ralph's Review* is 20-35 pgs., 8½ × 11, photocopied, sometimes with soft cover, with art, cartoons and graphics. Receives about 80-100 poems/year, accepts 40%. Press run is 75-100 for 35 subscribers of which 3 are libraries; 30-40 distributed free to bookstores, toy stores, antique, and coffee shops. Single copy: $2; subscription: $15. Make checks payable to R. Cornell.
How to Submit: Submit up to 5 poems, with a $3 reading fee and SASE. Accepts previously published poems and simultaneous submissions. No e-mail submissions. Cover letter required. Time between acceptance and publication is 2-4 months. Seldom comments on rejected poems. Publishes theme issues. Guidelines and upcoming themes available for SASE or by e-mail. Responds in 3 weeks. Pays 1 copy. Acquires all rights. Returns rights 1 year after acceptance. Reviews books in up to 5,000 words in single-book format. Poets may send books for review consideration.
Advice: "Books are selling like crazy; keep writing, check out current trends, submit to as many publications as you can afford."

◎ ◐ **RARACH PRESS (Specialized: bilingual/foreign language, ethnic/nationality)**, 1005 Oakland Dr., Kalamazoo MI 49008. (616)388-5631. Established 1981. **Owner:** Ladislav Hanka. Not open to unsolicited mss.

☑ $ ◯ ◐ **RATTAPALLAX; RATTAPALLAX PRESS**, 532 La Guardia Place, Suite 353, New York NY 10012. (212)560-7459. E-mail: devineni@rattapallax.com. Website: www.rattapallax.com (includes information about the journal, submission guidelines, bios, upcoming readings, names of editors, sample poems, chat room, and links). Established 1998. **Editor-in-Chief:** Martin Mitchell.
Magazine Needs: "A biannual journal of contemporary literature, *Rattapallax* is Wallace Steven's word for the sound of thunder." Wants "extraordinary work in poetry and short fiction—words that are well-crafted and sing, words that recapture the music of the language, words that bump into each other in extraordinary ways and leave the reader touched and haunted by the experience. We do not want ordinary words about ordinary things." Has published poetry by Anthony Hecht, Kate Light, Karen Swenson, Mark Nickels, Bill Kushner, Michael T. Young, and James Rayan. As a sample the editors selected these lines from "This kindled by *Guade Virgo Salutata*, a motet by John Dunstable, c. 1400" by Mark Nickels:

> *Slow-spreading English music, as though/we watched a pale drawing-off of the night/from delicate*
> *fields, and heard a haunt/of griffins in a fog close by the house./How one of the griffins, without fire,*
> *has wrought,/by a concentration of time, a face in gnarled elmwood. . . .*

Rattapallax is 128 pgs., magazine-sized, offset-printed and perfect-bound, with 12 pt. C1S cover, includes photos, drawings, and CD with poets. Receives about 5,000 poems/year, accepts 2%. Press run is 2,000 for 100 subscribers of which 50 are libraries, 1,200 shelf sales; 200 distributed free to contributors, reviews and promos. Single copy: $7.95; subscription: $14/1 year. Sample (including guidelines): $7.95. Make checks payable to Rattapallax.
How to Submit: Submit 3-5 poems at a time. Accepts simultaneous submissions; no previously published poems. Accepts e-mail submissions from outside of the US and Canada. "SASE is required and e-mailed submissions should be sent as simple text." Cover letter preferred. Reads submissions all year; issue deadlines are June 1 and December 1. Time between acceptance and publication is 6 months. Poems are circulated to an editorial board. "The editor-in-chief, senior editor and associate editor review all the submissions then decide on which to accept every week. Near publication time, all accepted work is narrowed and unused work is kept for the next issue." Often comments on rejected poems. Guidelines available by e-mail on on website. Responds in 2 months. Pays 2 contributor's copies. Always sends prepublication galleys. Acquires first rights.
Book/Chapbook Needs & How to Submit: Rattapallax Press publishes "contemporary poets and writers with unique powerful voices." Publishes 5 paperbacks and 3 chapbooks/year. Books are usually 64 pgs., 6 × 9, offset-printed and perfect-bound with 12 pt. C1S cover, include drawings and photos. Query first with a few sample poems and cover letter with brief bio and publication credits and SASE. Requires authors to first be published in *Rattapallax*. Responds to queries in 1 month; to mss in 2 months. Pays royalties of 10-25%. Order sample books by sending SASE and $7.

◑ ◐ **RATTLE**, 13440 Ventura Blvd. #200, Sherman Oaks CA 91423. (818)788-3232 or (818)788-2831. Fax: (818)788-2831. E-mail: stellasuel@aol.com. Website: www.rattle.com (includes all back issues, subscription information, and shopping cart). Established 1994. **Editor:** Alan Fox. **Poetry Editor:** Stellasue Lee. Address submissions to Stellasue Lee.
Magazine Needs: *RATTLE* is a biannual poetry publication which also includes interviews with poets, essays, and reviews. Wants "high quality poetry of any form, three pages maximum. Nothing unintelligible." Accepts

some poetry written by children ages 10 to 18. Has published poetry by Billy Collins, Anne Waldman, James Ragan, Philip Levine, Yusef Komunyakaa, and Simon Ortiz. As a sample the editor selected these lines from "Thinking of Li Po" by Glenn McKee:

> Island flowers blossom/unpicked by human hands./Small boats at sunset cast giant/shadows on calm waters./Adolescent Herring Gulls play the/wind's latest composition./Love searches for companionship in/a crowd of strangers./I remain stranded in time/with only words for wine.

RATTLE is 196 pgs., 6×9, neatly printed and perfect-bound with 4-color coated card cover. Receives about 8,000 submissions/year, accepts 250. Press run is 4,000. Subscription: $28/2 years. Sample: $8. Make checks payable to *RATTLE*.

How to Submit: Submit up to 5 poems at a time with name, address, and phone number on each page in upper right hand corner. Include SASE. No previously published work or simultaneous submissions. Accepts e-mail ("cut and paste into text file") and fax submissions. Cover letter and e-mail address, if possible, is required as well as a bio. Reads submissions all year. Seldom comments on rejected poems unless asked by the author. Responds in up to 2 months. Pays 2 contributor's copies. Rights revert to authors upon publication. Welcomes essays up to 2,000 words on the writing process and book reviews on poetry up to 250 words. Send books for review consideration.

RAW DOG PRESS; POST POEMS, 151 S. West St., Doylestown PA 18901-4134. (215)345-6838. Website: www.freeyellow.com/members/rawdog (includes basic Raw Dog Press information, general poets' Q and A, and general writer's guidelines). Established 1977. **Poetry Editor:** R. Gerry Fabian.

Magazine Needs: "Publishes Post Poems annual—a postcard series. We want short poetry (three to seven lines) on any subject. The positive poem or the poem of understated humor always has an inside track. No taboos, however. All styles considered. Anything with rhyme had better be immortal." Has published poetry by Don Ryan, John Grey, Wes Patterson, and the editor, R. Gerry Fabian, who selected his poem, "Kiowa," as a sample:

> I placed my tired head/where the just new moon/emits your presence

How to Submit: Submit 3-5 poems at a time. Send SASE for catalog to buy samples. Always comments on rejected poems. Guidelines available on website. Pays contributor's copies. Acquires all rights. Returns rights on mention of first publication. Sometimes reviews books of poetry.

Book/Chapbook Needs & How to Submit: Raw Dog Press welcomes new poets and detests second-rate poems from 'name' poets. We exist because we are dumb like a fox, but even a fox takes care of its own."

Also Offers: Offers criticism for a fee; "if someone is desperate to publish and is willing to pay, we will use our vast knowledge to help steer the ms in the right direction. We will advise against it, but as P.T. Barnum said. . . ."

Advice: "I get poems that do not fit my needs. At least one quarter of all poets waste their postage because they do not read the requirements."

RB'S POETS' VIEWPOINT, 2043 S. Coleman, Shepherd MI 48883. Established 1989. **Editor:** Robert Bennett.

Magazine Needs: *RB's Poets' Viewpoint* published bimonthly, features poetry and cartoons. Wants "general and religious poetry, sonnets, and sijo with a 21-line limit." Does not want "vulgar language." Has published poetry by Marion Ford Park, Ruth Ditmer Ream, Ruth Halbrooks, and Delphine Ledoux. As a sample the editor selected these lines from "Star Fantasy" by Mary Strand:

> On the hill where Will-O-Wisps camp/I danced to the chirpings of crickets/by the glow of the lightning-bug's lamp./When the stars in their celestial thickets/beckoned me with come-hither winks/I climbed a dangling moonbeam/& skipped on heavenly rinks.

RB's Poets' Viewpoint is 34 pgs., digest-sized, photocopied, saddle-stapled with drawings and cartoons. Receives about 400 poems/year, accepts about 90%. Press run is 60. Subscription: $8. Sample: $2. Make checks payable to Robert Bennett.

How to Submit: Submit 3 poems typed single space. **Reading fee:** $1.50/poem. Accepts previously published poems and simultaneous submissions. Reads submissions February, April, June, August, October, and December only. Time between acceptance and publication is 1 month. "Poems are selected by one editor." Often comments on rejected poems. Guidelines available for SASE. Responds in 1 month. Pays 1 contributor's copy. Acquires one-time rights.

Also Offers: Sponsors contests for general poetry, religious poetry, sonnets, and sijo with 1st Prizes of $20, $6, and $5, respectively, plus publication in *RB's Poets' Viewpoint*. There is a $1.50 per poem entry fee, except the sijo category, which has a 50¢ per poem fee. Guidelines available for SASE.

RE:AL—THE JOURNAL OF LIBERAL ARTS, Dept. PM, Box 13007, Stephen F. Austin State University, Nacogdoches TX 75962. (409)468-2059. Fax: (409)468-2190. E-mail: f_real@titan.sfasu.edu. Website: www.libweb.sfasu.edu/real/default.htm (includes the entire journal). Established 1968. **Editor:** W. Dale Hearell.

Magazine Needs: *RE:AL* is a "Liberal Arts Forum" using short fiction, reviews, criticism, and poetry; contains editorial notes and personalized "Contributors' Notes"; printed in the fall and spring. Aims "to use from 90 to 110 pages of poetry per issue, typeset in editor's office. *RE:AL* welcomes all styles and forms that display craft, insight, and accessibility." Accepts poetry written by children. Receives between 60-100 poems/week. "We need

a better balance between open and generic forms. We're also interested in critical writings on poems or writing poetry and translations with a bilingual format (permissions from original author)." It is handsomely printed, "reserved format," perfect-bound with line drawings and photos. Circulation approximately 400, "more than half of which are major college libraries." Subscriptions also in Great Britain, Ireland, Italy, Holland, the Phillipines, Puerto Rico, Brazil, Croatia, and Canada. Subscription: $40 for institutions, $30 individual. Sample: $15.
How to Submit: Submit original and copy. "Editors prefer a statement that ms is not being simultaneously submitted; however, this fact is taken for granted when we receive a ms." Writer's guidelines available for SASE. They acknowledge receipt of submissions and strive for a 1-month decision. Submissions during summer semesters may take longer. Pays 2 contributor's copies. Reviews are assigned, but queries about doing reviews are welcome.

[N] [□] [⊘] RED BOOTH REVIEW; RED BOOTH CHAPBOOKS, Owen House, JHU, 3400 N. Charles St., Baltimore MD 21218. (410)516-7545. E-mail: rbr@wtp62.com. Website: http://wtp62.com/rbr.htm (includes archive, current issue, guidelines). Established 1998. **Contact:** W. T. Pfefferle.
Magazine Needs: *Red Booth Review* appears 3 times/year online, 1 time/year in print. Publishes "best poetry we see, moving poems about driving, meagre love, compact and focused." Recently published poetry by John Hicks, David McNaron, and Roy Schwartzman. The editor selected these lines by Beau Boudreaux:

> *a woman approaches/who I'd shared a booth, a pitcher/in college, her touch was like an ice/cube*
> *sliding the length of your sleeve./This woman called me angel./I could not introduce her/for the life of*
> *me.*

Red Booth Review is 64 pgs., digest-sized, digitally-printed, perfect-bound, slick cover, with some art/graphics. Receives about 700 poems/year, accepts about 5%. Publishes about 10 poems/issue online, about 40 in print. Press run is 250 for 30 subscribers; 220 are distributed free to writers and editors. Single copy: $11. Sample: $6. Make checks payable to W.T. Pfefferle.
How to Submit: Submit 5 poems at a time. Accepts simultaneous submissions; no previously published poems. Accepts e-mail submissions; no fax or disk submissions. Cover letter is preferred. Reads submissions all year. Time between acceptance and publication is 1 week. Usually one editor and one guest editor select poems. Often comments on rejected poems. Guidelines are available on website. Responds in 1 week. Pays 1 contributor's copy. Acquires first North American serial rights, rights revert to author upon publication.
Book/Chapbook Needs & How to Submit: Red Booth Chapbooks prefers moving and compact poetry. Publishes 1-2 chapbooks/year. Chapbooks are chosen through annual contest. Deadline: August 1. Chapbooks are usually 30 pgs., digitally-printed, saddle-stapled, slick cover, with art/graphics. Submit less than 30 pgs. of poetry with $10 entry fee. Responds to queries in 1 month; to mss in 4 months. Pays winner $100 plus 30 copies of the finished chapbook. Order sample books/chapbooks by sending $6 to W. T. Pfefferle.

[N] [🌐] [⊘] THE RED CANDLE PRESS; CANDELABRUM POETRY MAGAZINE, 9 Milner Rd., Wisbech, Cambs PE13 2LR England. E-mail: rcp@poetry7.fsnet.co.uk. Website: www.members.tripod.com/redcandlepress (includes information about the press and its publications, a profiles link, and a mini-anthology of poems). Established 1970. **Editor:** M.L. McCarthy, M.A.
Magazine Needs: Red Candle Press was "established to encourage poets working in traditional-type verse, metrical unrhymed or metrical rhymed. We're more interested in poems than poets: that is, we're interested in what sort of poems an author produces, not in his or her personality." Publishes the magazine, *Candelabrum*, twice yearly (April and October). Wants "good-quality metrical verse, with rhymed verse specially wanted. Elegantly cadenced free verse is acceptable. Accepts 5-7-5 haiku. No weak stuff (moons and Junes, loves and doves, etc.) No chopped-up prose pretending to be free verse. Any length up to about 40 lines for *Candelabrum*, any subject, including eroticism (but not porn)—satire, love poems, nature lyrics, philosophical—any subject, but nothing racist or sexist." Has published poetry by Amanda Rochford, M.L. McCarthy, Eric Martin, Michael Axtell, Esther Cameron, and John Lord. We selected these lines from "Roman Temple" by Janet Farady:

> *Abandoned by its god, bereft of worshippers,/The ruined temple rises on the valley's rim;/Sparrows*
> *lark among its flaking capitals and/Henbane sprigs the roofless sanctuary walls./Now, the light of*
> *evening on its crumbling face,/It sits serene, like some old man outside his door . . .*

Candelabrum is digest-sized, staple-spined, small type, exemplifies their intent to "pack in as much as possible, wasting no space, and try to keep a neat appearance with the minimum expense." Uses about 40 pgs. (some 70 poems) in each issue. Receives about 2,000 submissions/year, of which 10% is accepted, sometimes holds over poems for the next year. Press run is 900 for 700 subscribers of which 22 are libraries. Sample: $5 in bills only; checks not accepted.
How to Submit: "Submit anytime. Enclose one IRC for reply only; three IRCs if you wish manuscript returned. If you'd prefer a reply by e-mail, without return of unwanted manuscript, please enclose one British first-class stamp, IRC, or U.S. dollar bill to pay for the call. Each poem on a separate sheet please, neat typescripts or neat legible manuscripts. Please no dark, oily photostats, no colored ink (only black or blue). Author's name and address on each sheet, please." No simultaneous submissions. No e-mail submissions. Responds in about 2 months. Pays 1 contributor's copy.
Advice: "Traditional-type poetry is much more popular here in Britain, and we think also in the United States, now than it was in 1970, when we established *Candelabrum*. We always welcome new poets, especially traditionalists, and we like to hear from the U.S.A. as well as from here at home. General tip: Study the various outlets

at the library, or buy a copy of *Candelabrum*, or borrow a copy from a subscriber, before you go to the expense of submitting your work. The Red Candle Press regrets that, because of bank charges, it is unable to accept dollar cheques. However, it is always happy to accept U.S. dollar bills."

RED CEDAR REVIEW, 17C Morrill Hall, Dept. of English, Michigan State University, East Lansing MI 48824. E-mail: rcreview@msu.edu. Website: www.msu.edu/~rcreview (includes guidelines, subscription information, order forms for sample copies, and biographical information about our staff). Established 1963. **General Editor:** Douglas Dowland. **Contact:** Meg McClure.
Magazine Needs: *Red Cedar Review* is a literary biannual which uses poetry—"any subject, form, length; the only requirement is originality and vision." Encourages work from both students and professionals. Has published poetry by Margaret Atwood, Diane Wakoski, Jim Harrison, and Stuart Dybek. *Red Cedar Review* is 120 pgs., digest-sized. Receives about 500 submissions/year, accepts 20. Press run is 400 for 200 subscribers of which 100 are libraries. Single copy: $6; subscription: $12. Sample: $4.
How to Submit: Submit up to 5 poems at a time with SASE. No previously published poems. Simultaneous submissions are discouraged. No e-mail submissions. Responds in up to 4 months. Pays 2 copies. Sometimes comments on rejected poems. Publishes theme issues. Guidelines and upcoming themes available for SASE or on website.

RED CROW; REDBUD HILL PRESS (Specialized: political, social issues, Appalachian and Beat poetry), 265 Glencoe Ave., Decatur IL 62522. E-mail: RedCrowPoetry@aol.com. Website: www.redc rowguidelines.cjb.net (includes complete submission guidelines and information on contests). Established 1998. **Editor:** Scott Goebel.
Magazine Needs: *Red Crow* is a biannual poetry journal publishing a Beat issue in autumn and an Appalachian issue in spring (as part of the Jack Kerouac Poetry Prize and the Bob Snyder Poetry Awards). All styles and forms. Has published poetry by Larry Fontenot, Richard Hague, Joe Enzweiler, and Nelson Pilsner. *Red Crow* is digest-sized, laser printed, perfect-bound or saddle-stapled, with color card cover. Receives about 500 poems/year, accepts 20%. Publishes over 40 poems/issue. Press run is 300 for 35 subscribers of which 8 are libraries, 100 shelf sales; 30 distributed free to reviewers and schools. Single copy: $8; subscription: $15. Sample: $5. Make checks payable to Red Crow.
How to Submit: Submit 5 poems at a time. Accepts simultaneous submissions; no previously published poems. No fax or e-mail submissions. Cover letter required. "Cover letter should be separate from manuscript. Cover letter contains name, address, e-mail, brief bio, and a list of titles." Reads submissions for Beat issue through June 1st; for Appalachian issue through March 1st. Time between acceptance and publication is 3-4 months. Poems are circulated to an editorial board "then final decisions made by the managing editor." Seldom comments on rejected poems. Guidelines available for SASE. Responds in 10 weeks. Sometimes sends prepublication galleys. Pays 2 contributor's copies. Acquires first North American serial rights.
Book/Chapbook Needs & How to Submit: "Redbud Hill Press publishes the best modern Appalachian and Beat poetry written today. We believe poetry serves as a record of the times." Publishes chapbooks by query and by invitation. Pays 25 author's copies (out of a press run of 100).
Also Offers: Also sponsors the Jack Kerouac Poetry Prize and the Bob Snyder Poetry Awards. (See separate listings in the Contest & Awards section).
Advice: "Edit, cut, edit, cut. . . ."

RED DANCEFLOOR PRESS; RED DANCEFLOOR, P.O. Box 4974, Lancaster CA 93539-4974. Fax: (805)946-8082. E-mail: dubpoet@as.net. Website: www.web.as.net/~dubpoet. Established 1989. **Editor:** David Goldschlag.
Magazine Needs & How to Submit: The press publishes the magazine, *Red Dancefloor*. However, the magazine has suspended publication until further notice.
Book Needs: Red Dancefloor Press also publishes full-length books and poetry audiotapes. No restrictions on form, length, or subject matter. Has published poetry by Sean T. Dougherty, Gerry Lafemina, Laurel Ann Bogen, Marc. C. Jacksina, Gary P. Walton, and Michael Stephans. As a sample the editor selected these lines from "Ladybugs" in *Estrogen Power* by Nancy Ryan Keeling:

> Allergic to "pink,"/she camouflages/her exquisite figure/in layers of baggy clothes./She is content to
> live the/sexual life of a porcupine/testing and cataloging/feelings and emotions/because she knows/
> nobody is ever pure twice.

The editor suggests sampling a book, chapbook, or tape prior to submission. Send 5½×8½ SASE with first-class stamp for catalog. Sample: $10.
How to Submit: "We openly accept submissions for books and tapes, but *please* query first with ten samples and a cover letter explaining which area of our press you are interested in. Listing credits in a cover letter is fine, but don't go crazy." Accepts e-mail and fax submission. "E-mail submissions may be embedded in the message itself or attached as ASCII, MS Word, or Wordperfect files." Queries and submissions via e-mail "strongly encouraged." Payment negotiable.

☑ ☒ $☑ **RED DEER PRESS**, Room 813, MacKimmie Library Tower, 2500 University Dr. NW, Calgary, Alberta T2N 1N4 Canada. (403)220-4334. Fax: (403)210-8191. E-mail: Khanson@ucalgary.ca. Established 1975. **Poetry Editor:** Nicole Marcotic.
Book/Chapbook Needs & How to Submit: Red Deer Press publishes 1 poetry paperback per year under the imprint Writing West. Has published poetry by Susan Holbrook, Monty Reid, Stephen Scobie, Ian Samuels, and Nicole Marcotic. Books are usually 80-100 pgs. Submit 8-10 poems at a time. Accepts simultaneous submissions. Cover letter required. "Must include SASE. Canadian poets only." Time between acceptance and publication is 6 months. Responds to queries in 6 months. Pays royalties.

☑ **RED DRAGON PRESS**, P.O. Box 19425, Alexandria VA 22320-0425. Website: www.reddragonpress.com (includes statement of purpose, guidelines for submissions, book list, order information, sample poems, book descriptions, and author biographical information). Established 1993. **Editor/Publisher:** Laura Qa.
Book/Chapbook Needs: Red Dragon Press publishes 3-4 chapbooks/year. Wants "innovative, progressive, and experimental poetry and prose using literary symbolism, and aspiring to the creation of meaningful new ideas, forms, and methods. We are proponents of works that represent the nature of man as androgynous, as in the fusing of male and female symbolism, and we support works that deal with psychological and parapsychological topics." Has published *Spectator Turns Witness* by George Karos and *The Crown of Affinity* by Laura Qa. As a sample the editor selected these lines from "Visitarte" by James Kerns:

> Tonight the world is awake in the moon's embrace./I have turned everywhere but cannot outrun/the black shadow spreading from my feet./I like the brief side late light offers,/but I am unsure of what lies outside the beams/in the shade of things that have already been.

Chapbooks are usually 64 pgs., 8½×5⅜, offset-printed, perfect-bound on trade paper with 1-10 illustrations.
How to Submit: Submit up to 5 poems at a time with SASE. Accepts previously published poems and simultaneous submissions. Cover letter preferred with brief bio. **Reading fee:** $5 for poetry and short fiction, $10 for novels; check or money order payable to Red Dragon Press. Time between acceptance and publication is 8 months. Poems are circulated to an editorial board. "Poems are selected for consideration by the publisher, then circulated to senior editor and/or poets previously published for comment. Poems are returned to the publisher for further action; i.e., rejection or acceptance for publication in an anthology or book by a single author. Frequently submission of additional works is required before final offer is made, especially in the process for a book by a single author." Often comments on rejected poems. Charges criticism fee of $10 per page on request. Responds to queries in 10 weeks, to mss in 1 year. For sample books, purchase at book stores or mail order direct from Red Dragon Press at the above address.

☑ $☑ **RED HEN PRESS; RED HEN POETRY CONTEST**, P.O. Box 3537, Granada Hills CA 91394. Fax: (818)831-6659. E-mail: editors@redhen.org. Website: www.redhen.org. Established 1993. **Publisher:** Mark E. Cull. **Editor:** Kate Gale.
Book/Chapbook Needs: Red Hen Press wants "good literary fiction and poetry" and publishes 10 paperbacks, one selected through a competition. "Translations are fine. No rhyming poetry." Has published poetry by Dr. Benjamin Saltman, Dr. Angela Ball, Ricardo Means Ybarra, and Marlene Pearson. Books are usually 64-96 pgs., 5×7 or 6×9, professionally printed and perfect-bound with trade paper cover. Includes paintings and photos.
How to Submit: Submit 5 poems at a time. Accepts previously published poems and simultaneous submissions. Accepts e-mail submissions. Cover letter preferred. Time between acceptance and publication is 1 year. Poems are circulated to an editorial board. "One main poetry editor plus three to four contributing editors review the work." Seldom comments on rejected poems. Responds to queries in 1 month. Pays 10% royalties and 50 author's copies. To obtain sample books "write to our address for a catalog."
Also Offers: Sponsors the Benjamin Saltman Poetry Contest for a full-length collection (46-68 pgs.). Deadline is October 31.
Advice: "Be willing to help promote your own book and be helpful to the press. Writers need to help small presses survive."

☑ ⊕ ☉ ○ ☑ **RED HERRING**, MidNAG, East View, Stakeford, Choppington, Northumberland NE62 5TR England. Phone: 01670 844240. Fax: 01670 844298. E-mail: n.baumfield@warrbeck.gov.uk. **Contact:** Nicholas Baumfield.
Magazine Needs: *Red Herring* appears 2-3 times/year and "welcomes new original poetry of all kinds." Accepts poetry written by children. Has published poetry by W.N. Herbert, Sean O'Brien, and Matthew Sweeney. As a sample they selected these lines from "Sometimes" by Tom Kelly:

> He's making his point,/stabbing his fingers/at the air, his kids, I presume,/stand near the mother,/as he seethes/intoning his hate, his troubles/to those he loves/sometimes.

Red Herring is 1 A3 sheet folded. Receives about 350 poems/year, accepts 15%. Press run is 3,000. "Most available free in Northumberland libraries." Single copy: £1. Make checks payable to MidNAG.
How to Submit: Accepts simultaneous submissions; no previously published poems. Accepts fax and e-mail submissions. "Copies preferred, as submissions cannot be returned." Time between acceptance and publication is 4 months. Poems are circulated to an editorial board. Seldom comments on rejected poems. Responds in 4 months. Pays 5 contributor's copies.

$⬚ ⬚ ⬚ ◎ **RED MOON PRESS; THE RED MOON ANTHOLOGY; AMERICAN HAIBUN & HAIGA (Specialized: form/style)**, P.O. Box 2461, Winchester VA 22604-1661. (540)722-2156. Fax: (708)810-8992. E-mail: redmoon@shentel.net. Established 1994, *American Haibun & Haiga* established 1999. **Editor/Publisher:** Jim Kacian.

Magazine Needs: *American Haibun & Haiga*, published annually in January, is the first western journal dedicated to these forms. *American Haibun & Haiga* is 128 pages, digest-sized, offset-printed on quality paper with heavy stock four-color cover. Receives several hundred submissions per year, accepts approximately 10%. Accepts poetry written by children. Expected print run is 1,000 for subscribers and commercial distribution. Subscription: $15 plus $3 shipping and handling. A brief sample of the form will be available for SASE.

How to Submit: Submit up to 3 haibun or haiga at a time with SASE. No previously published work or simultaneous submissions. Accepts fax and e-mail submissions (include in body of message). Submissions will be read by at least two editors. Time between acceptance and publication varies according to time of submission. Pays $1/page. Acquires first North American serial rights. "Only haibun and haiga will be considered. If the submitter is unfamiliar with the form, consult *Journey to the Interior*, edited by Bruce Ross, or previous issues of *American Haibun & Haiga*, for samples and some discussion."

Book/Chapbook Needs: Red Moon Press "is the largest and most prestigious publisher of English-language haiku and related work in the world." Publishes *The Red Moon Anthology,* an annual volume, the finest English-language haiku and related work published anywhere in the world in the previous 12 months. *The Red Moon Anthology* is 160 pgs., digest-sized, offset-printed, perfect-bound, glossy 4-color heavy-stock cover. Inclusion is by nomination of the editorial board only. The press also publishes 6-8 volumes per year, usually 3-5 individual collections of English-language haiku, as well as 1-3 books of essays or criticism of haiku. As a sample the editor selected the following haiku from *The Tree as It Is* by Bernard Lionel Einbond:

> *frog pond—/a leaf falls in/without a sound*

Under other imprints the press also publishes chapbooks of various sizes and formats.

How to Submit: Query with book theme and information, and 30-40 poems, or draft of first chapter. Responds to queries in 2 weeks, to mss (if invited) in 2-3 months. "Each contract separately negotiated."

Advice: "Haiku is a burgeoning and truly international form. It is nothing like what your fourth-grade teacher taught you years ago, and so it is best if you familiarize yourself with what is happening in the form (and its close relatives) today before submitting. We strive to give all the work we publish plenty of space in which to resonate, and to provide a forum where the best of today's practitioners can be published with dignity and prestige. All our books have either won awards or are awaiting notification."

⬚ ⬚ **RED OWL MAGAZINE**, 35 Hampshire Rd., Portsmouth NH 03801-4815. (603)431-2691. E-mail: RedOwlMag@aol.com. Established 1995. **Editor:** Edward O. Knowlton.

Magazine Needs: *Red Owl* is a biannual magazine of poetry and b&w art published in the spring and fall. "Ideally, poetry here might stress a harmony between nature and industry; add a pinch of humor for spice. Nothing introspective or downtrodden. Sometimes long poems are OK, yet poems which are 10 to 20 lines seem to fit best." Also open to poems on the subjects of animals, gay/lesbian issues, horror, psychic/occult, science fiction/fantasy, and women/feminism. Has published poetry by John Binns, John Grey, Albert Huffstickler, Nancy McGovern, and Dawn Zapletal. As a sample the editor selected these lines from "Night Eye" by Nancy McGovern:

> *colors shifting to mute tones/as though the skull of earth/held a candle within whose/wax draws sun-fire to/illuminate the center/and glow in the moon.*

Red Owl is about 70 pgs., 8½×11, neatly photocopied in a variety of type styles and spiral-bound with a heavy stock cover and b&w art inside. "Out of a few hundred poems received, roughly one third are considered." Single copy: $10; subscription: $20. Sample (including brief guidelines): $10 includes shipping and handling. Make checks payable to Edward O. Knowlton.

How to Submit: Submit 4 poems at a time. No previously published poems or simultaneous submissions. Accepts e-mail submissions. Cover letter preferred. "Relay cover letter and each poem separately. I mostly use the 'Net to answer questions; this isn't the best home for 'noetics' or 'noetry.' I'd prefer to receive the submissions I get via the U.S.P.S. since I feel it's more formal—and I'm not in that big of a hurry, nor do I feel that this world has reached a conclusion. . . ." Seldom comments on rejected poems. Responds in up to 3 months. Pays 1 contributor's copy.

Advice: "Try and be bright; hold your head up. Yes, there are hard times in the land of plenty, yet we might try to overshadow them. . . ."

⬚ ⬚ ⬚ **RED RIVER REVIEW**, E-mail: Editor@RedRiverReview.com. Website: www.RedRiverReview.com. Established 1999. **Editor:** Bob McCranie.

Magazine Needs: "Published quarterly, *Red River Review* is a fully electronic literary journal. Our purpose is to publish quality poetry using the latest technology. *Red River* is a journal for poets who have studied the craft of writing and for readers who enjoy being stirred by language." Wants "poetry which speaks to the human experience in a unique and accessible way. No rhyming poetry or poetry that is annoyingly obscure." Has published poetry by Marin Sorescu, Padi Harman, Barbara F. Lefcowitz, Deborah DeNicola, Ed Madden, and Jeanne P. Donovan. As a sample the editor selected this poem, "This Day" by Meghan Ehrlich:

> *This is a day to wear./Grackles whistle and click in the leaves,/damp plaid flannel shirts salute, flap from balconies,/fragrant green horse-apples molder underfoot./I lay out my laundry, too, like an offering,/like a sponge. I will keep this sun in my closet/and wear it often.*

Receives about 750 poems/year, accepts about 25%.

How to Submit: Submit 4-6 poems at a time. No previously published poems or simultaneous submissions. Cover letter preferred. Electronic submissions only. Time between acceptance and publication is 3 months. Often comments on rejected poems. Guidelines available on website. Responds in 3 months. Sometimes sends prepublication galleys. Acquires first rights and anthology rights, "if we want to do a *Red River Review Anthology*." For address and query information e-mail Editor@RedRiverReview.com.

Advice: "Write about who you are and who we are in the world. Read other writers as much as possible."

◯ ◉ **RED ROCK REVIEW; RED ROCK POETRY AWARD**, English Dept. J2A, Community College of Southern Nevada, 3200 E. Cheyenne Ave., North Las Vegas NV 89030. (702)651-4094. E-mail: rich_logsdon@ ccsn.nevada.edu. Website: www.ccsn.nevada.edu/academics/departments/english/redrockreview/default.html (includes editorial staff, samples from current issue, guidelines, and contest information). Established 1994. **Editor-in-Chief:** Dr. Rich Logsdon. **Associate Editor:** Todd Moffett.

Magazine Needs: *Red Rock Review* appears biannually and publishes "the best poetry available." Also publishes fiction, creative nonfiction, and book reviews. Has published poetry by Dorianne Laux, Kim Addonizio, Ellen Bass, Cynthis Hogue, and Dianne di Prima. As a sample the editors selected these lines (poet unidentified):

> *Oil paint, I've read/never completely dries./The breasts of Venus droop./Mona Lisa finally drops the smile./Glass, I've heard, is a liquid./Windows silently slide at night,/a slow motion sink, always/toward the floor, Christ ascending*

Red Rock Review is about 130 pgs., magazine-sized, professionally printed and perfect-bound with 10 pt. cornwall, C1S cover. Accepts about 15% of poems received/year. Press run is 1,000. Sample: $5.50.

How to Submit: Submit 2-3 poems at a time, "mailed flat, not folded, into a letter sized envelope." Line length for poetry is 80 maximum. Accepts simultaneous submissions; no previously published poems. Accepts e-mail (in body of message) and disk submissions. Cover letter with SASE required. Do not submit mss June 1 through August 31. Time between acceptance and publication is 3 months. Poems are circulated to an editorial board. "Poems go to poetry editor, who then distributes them to three readers." Seldom comments on rejected poems. Guidelines available for SASE or on website. Responds in 2 months. Pays 2 contributor's copies. Acquires first North American serial rights. Reviews books and chapbooks of poetry in 500-1,000 words, multi-book format. Poets may send books for review consideration.

Also Offers: Sponsors the annual Red Rock Poetry Award. Winner receives $500 plus publication in the *Red Rock Review*. Submit up to 3 poems of not more than 20 lines each, typed on 8½×11 white paper. Reading fee: $6/entry (3 poems). Deadline: October 31. Complete rules available for SASE.

☑ ◉ **RED WHEELBARROW**, (formerly *Bottomfish*), De Anza College, 21250 Stevens Creek Blvd., Cupertino CA 95014. (408)864-8600. E-mail: rns2107@mercury.fhda.edu. Website: www.deanza.fhda.edu/bottomfish. Established 1976. **Editor:** Randolph Splitter.

Magazine Needs: This college-produced magazine appears annually in May or June. *Red Wheelbarrow* has published poetry by Steve Fellner, Nola Perez, Virgil Suarez, and Walter Griffin. As a sample the editor selected these lines from "After Watching George Romero's *The Night of the Living Dead*" by Steve Fellner:

> *Only now (as I approach sixty) do I appreciate/the zombies' slow shuffle, their refusal to hurry/someone else's death. Human flesh should be considered/a delicacy. Something to be savored. Like créme brulée/ and Mel Torme albums.*

Bottomfish is 100 pgs., 6×9, well-printed on heavy stock with b&w graphics, perfect-bound. Press run is 500. Single copy: $5.

How to Submit: Submit 3-5 poems at a time. "Before submitting, writers are strongly urged to purchase a sample copy." Accepts e-mail submissions. Best submission times: September through December. Annual deadline: December 31. Responds in up to 6 months, depending on backlog. Include SASE for reply. "We cannot return manuscripts." Pays 2 contributor's copies.

Ｎ $ ◉ ◎ **THE REJECTED QUARTERLY (Specialized: rejected literature); BLACK PLANKTON PRESS**, P.O. Box 1351, Cobb CA 95426. (707)928-5511. E-mail: bplankton@juno.com. Website: www.geocities.com/area51/aurora/9291/index.html. Press established 1983, magazine established 1998. **Editor:** Daniel Weiss. **Associate Editor:** Jeff Ludecke.

Magazine Needs: *The Rejected Quarterly* is published "to provide an outlet for literature that doesn't fit anywhere else"; poetry submitted should have been rejected at least five time by other magazines. Wants "original, unassuming, out-of-state poetry." Has published poetry by Michael Stegner, James Rossignol, and Brent Duffin. As a sample the editor selected these lines from "To the Erstwhile Contributor" by Ken Waldman:

> *Dear Poetry, he writes,/forgetting Editor, and signs/A new Poet, Billy Rochester. Typical/of the submission, which, full/of typos, does charm enough/to almost win me, I respond:*

The Rejected Quarterly is 40-48 pgs., magazine-sized, saddle-stapled, with glossy 80 lb. coated cover, ads. Receives about 150 poems/year, accepts about 5%. Press run is 125 for 50 subscribers, 25 shelf sales; 20 distributed free to editors, book companies, etc. Sample: $6. Make checks payable to Black Plankton Press.

How to Submit: Submit up to 3 poems at a time. No previously published poems or simultaneous submissions. Cover letter preferred. "We prefer five rejection slips to accompany poems." Time between acceptance and publication is 3 weeks to 6 months. "Poems are circulated to both editors." Often comments on rejected poems. Guidelines available for SASE. Responds in up to 6 months. Pays $5 and/or 1 contributor's copy. Acquires first rights.

Advice: "We like things that are different—but not for the sake of being different."

✓ ▣ ⬭ ⊘ RENAISSANCE ONLINE MAGAZINE, P.O. Box 3246, Pawtucket RI 02861. E-mail: submit@renaissancemag.com. Website: www.renaissancemag.com (contains entire magazine as well as archives, guidelines, and contact information). Established 1996. **Editor:** Kevin Ridolfi. E-mail submissions only.

Magazine Needs: "Updated monthly, *Renaissance Online* strives to bring diversity and thought-provoking writing to an audience that usually settles for so much less. Poetry should reveal a strong emotion and be able to elicit a response from the reader. No nursery rhymes or profane works." Accepts poetry written by teenagers "but still must meet the same standard as adults." Has published poetry by Kevin Larimer, Josh May, and Gary Meadows. As a sample the editor selected these lines from "Dasein" by David Hunter Sutherland:

> What can't be held send/into sleep, into turn by gentle turn/if ring worn age, covetable grace/beauty,
> sadness and you spread/over this air-woven awning of clouds/to defy life's strange author

Receives about 60 poems/year, accepts about 50%.

How to Submit: Submit 3 poems at a time. Does not accept previously published poems or simultaneous submissions. Prefers e-mail submissions (include text in body of message). "We prefer e-mail submissions, include in body of message. Cover letter preferred. *Renaissance Online Magazine* is only published online and likes to see potential writers read previous works before submitting." Time between acceptance and publication is 3 months. Poems are circulated to an editorial board. "Poems are read by the editor, when difficult acceptance decisions need to be reached, the editorial staff is asked for comments." Often comments on rejected poems. Occasionally publishes theme issues. Guidelines available for SASE or on website. Responds in 2 months. Acquires all online publishing rights. Reviews books of poetry.

Also Offers: Website includes the entire magazine, including content, archives, guidelines and contact information.

✓ ⊕ $ ◎ RENDITIONS: A CHINESE-ENGLISH TRANSLATION MAGAZINE (Specialized: translations), Research Center for Translation, CUHK, Shatin, NT, Hong Kong. Phone: 852-2609-7399. Fax: 852-2603-5110. E-mail: renditions@cuhk.edu.hk. Website: www.renditions.org (includes information on *Renditions* magazine and the Research Centre for Translation, ordering information for paperback books and forthcoming issues of *Renditions*, links to related sites, authors' and translators' indexes, contact information, and sample translations). **Editor:** Dr. Eva Hung.

Magazine Needs: *Renditions* appears twice/year. "Contents exclusively translations from Chinese, ancient and modern." Also publishes a paperback series of Chinese literature in English translation. Has published translations of the poetry of Yang Lien, Gu Cheng, Shu Ting, Mang Ke, and Bei Dao. *Renditions* is about 150 pgs., magazine-sized, elegantly printed, perfect-bound, all poetry with side-by-side Chinese and English texts, using some b&w and color drawings and photos, with glossy 4-color card cover. Annual subscription: $25/1 year; $42/2 years: $58/3 years. Single copy: $17.

How to Submit: Accepts e-mail and fax submissions. "Chinese originals should be sent by regular mail because of formatting problems. Include 2 copies each of the English translation and the Chinese text to facilitate referencing." Publishes theme issues. Responds in 2 months. Pays "honorarium" plus 2 contributor's copies. Use British spelling. "Will consider" book mss. Query with sample translations. Submissions should be accompanied by Chinese originals. Books pay 10% royalties plus 10 copies. Mss usually not returned. Editor sometimes comments on rejected poems.

⊘ RE:VERSE! A JOURNAL IN POETRY; RE:PRINT! PUBLISHING COMPANY, P.O. Box 8518, Erie PA 16505. E-mail: reverse@email.com. Website: www.geocities.com/reversepoetry (contains an overview of the contents, sample work from recent artists, guidelines, and a "writer's workshop" section as a poet's resource). Established 1999. **Editor:** Eric Grignol.

Magazine Needs: "*Re:Verse!* is a yearly anthology of contemporary literary poetry from American artists. We are committed to putting moving written experiences in the hands of the reading public. As the world moves into a new century, we call for a time when the American people enjoyed poetry and felt a part of the experience. We are looking for literary poetry—taut writing, which is free from affectation. Open to all forms and styles of poems; steer clear of excessively long poems. Some themes we are interested in are healing and renewal, the extraordinary in the everyday, struggles with dichotomous situations, serious explorations of social issues—but do not limit yourself to this list! No pornographic, demeaning, or vulgar poems." As a sample the editor selected "Construction Accident" by Larry Shug:

> He'd been workin'/demolition sites/since Jericho;/thought he knew/all about/tumblin' walls./But you
> know/them demo sites,/so noisy sometimes/you can't hear/a trumpet blow/

Re:Verse! is 90 pgs., 5½×8½, offset-printed and perfect-bound with 2-color cardstock cover, includes line illustrations and some photos. Receives about 8,000 poems/year, accepts about 10%. Publishes 65-70 poems/issue. Press run varies according to demand. Single copy: $9.99. Sample: $6. Make checks payable to Re:Print! Publishing.
How to Submit: Submit 5 poems at a time. Accepts previously published poems and simultaneous submissions, "but both must be noted as such on cover letter." Cover letter preferred. "Must include SASE or no reply will be made. Please state whether you would like your manuscript returned. If they are unable to be used, we prefer to recycle them and simply send a letter of reply back. Name and address atop each page, please. Has a "revolving door approach to submissions. We review them constantly up to the point when this year's issue is full. After that point, all subsequent submissions are considered for next year's volume. So your best chance of getting in is by submitting early." Time between acceptance and publication is 10 months. Seldom comments on rejected poems. Occasionally publishes theme issues. Guidelines and upcoming themes available for SASE or on website. Responds in 5 months. Always sends prepublication galleys. Pays 1 contributor's copy. Acquires one-time rights.
Also Offers: "We are working on a companion volume to *Re:Verse!* which is intended to act as a workshop, or textbook so to speak, for poets looking to strengthen their craft by analysis of contemporary poetic works, poetry history, writing exercises and editors' comments. Contact us for details on this."
Advice: "Read constantly, explore your piece of the world, observe intently, write every day, revise your work unceasingly!"

REVISTA/REVIEW INTERAMERICANA (Specialized: ethnic, regional), Inter-American University of Puerto Rico, Box 5100, San Germán, Puerto Rico 00683. Phone: (787)264-1912, ext. 7229 or 7230. Fax: (787)892-6350. E-mail: reinter@sg.inter.edu. **Editor:** Anibal José Aponte.
Magazine Needs: The *Revista/Review* is a bilingual scholarly journal oriented to Puerto Rican, Caribbean and Hispanic American and inter-American subjects, poetry, short stories, and reviews. Press run is 400.
How to Submit: Submit at least 5 poems, but no more than 7, in Spanish or English, blank verse, free verse, experimental, traditional, or avant-garde, typed exactly as you want them to appear in publication. Name should not appear on the poems, only the cover letter. No simultaneous submissions. Accepts fax submissions. Cover letter with brief personal data required. Publishes theme issues. Guidelines and upcoming themes available for SASE. Pays 2 copies.

RHINO, P.O. Box 554, Winnetka IL 60093. Website: www.rhinopoetry.org (includes writer's guidelines, ordering info, table of contents and excerpts from current issue, literary challenges and a schedule of Chicago-area workshops, events and literary links). Established 1976. **Editors:** Deborah Rosen, Alice George, Kathleen Kirk, and Helen Degen Cohen.
• "*Rhino* recently won two Illinois Literary Awards."
Magazine Needs: *Rhino* "is an annual poetry journal, appearing in March, which also includes short-shorts and occasional essays on poetry. Translations welcome. The editors delight in work which reflects the author's passion, originality and artistic conviction. We also welcome experiments with poetic form, sophisticated wit, and a love affair with language. Prefer poems, appearing in March, under 100 lines." Has published poetry by Maureen Seaton, James Armstrong, Susan Terris, Barry Silesky, Richard Jones, and Rustin Larson. *Rhino* is a 96-page journal, digest-sized, card cover with art, on high-quality paper. Receives 1,500 submissions/year, accepts 60-80. Press run is 1,500. Sample: $7.
How to Submit: Submit 3-5 poems with SASE. Accepts simultaneous submissions with notification; no previously published submissions. Submissions are accepted April 1 through October 1. Guidelines available for SASE or on website. Responds in 3 months. Pays 2 contributor's copies. Acquires first rights only.

THE RIALTO, P.O. Box 309, Alysham, Norwich, Norfolk NR11 6LN England. Website: www.therialto.co.uk. Established 1984. **Editor:** Michael Mackmin.
Magazine Needs: *The Rialto* appears 3 times/year and "seeks to publish the best new poems by established and beginning poets. *The Rialto* seeks excellence and originality." Has published poetry by Les Murray, Selima Hill, Penelope Shuttle, George Szirtes, Philip Gross, and Ruth Padel. *The Rialto* is 56 pgs., A4 with full color cover, occasionally includes art/graphics. Receives about 12,000 poems/year, accepts about 1%. Publishes 50 poems/issue. Press run is 1,500 for 1,000 subscribers of which 50 are libraries. Subscription: £16. Sample: £6. Make checks payable to *The Rialto*. "Checks in sterling only please."
How to Submit: Submit 6 poems at a time. Accepts simultaneous submissions; no previously published poems. Cover letter preferred. "SASE or SAEs with IRCs essential. U.S. readers please note that U.S. postage stamps are invalid in U.K." Time between acceptance and publication is 3 months. Seldom comments on rejected poems. Responds in 3 months. "A large number of poems arrive every week, so please note that you will have to wait at least 10 weeks for yours to be read." Pays £20/poem. Poet retains rights.
Advice: "It is a good idea to read the magazine before submitting to check if you write our kind of poem."

RIO: A JOURNAL OF THE ARTS, P.O. Box 165, Port Jefferson NY 11777. E-mail: rioarts@angelfire.com. Website: www.engl.uic.edu/rio/rio.html and www.rioarts.com. Established 1997. **Editors:** Cynthia Davidson and Gail Lukasik.

Magazine Needs: *Rio* is a biannual online journal containing "poetry, short fiction, creative nonfiction, scannable artwork/photography, and book reviews. Query for anything else." Wants poetry of any length or form. "Experiments encouraged with voice, image, or language. No greeting card verse or sentimentality; no purely therapeutic rants against mom, dad, boss, or gender." Has published poetry by Michael Anania, Liviu Ioan Stoiciu, Eleni Fourtourni, Michael Waters, Terry Wright, Ralph Mills, Jr., David Shevin, and Briar Wood. As a sample the editors selected these lines from "XI. The Sun Has Wings" by Roberta Gould:

> *Each worm in the cabbage/is joyous/Each saw-toothed form/smiles freely/Even the question mark shimmers/flexed to new functions*

Accepts about 20% of poems received/year. Back issues are available on the website.
How to Submit: Submit 5-8 poems at a time. Accepts previously published poems and simultaneous submissions "as long as you inform us of publication elsewhere." Accepts e-mail and disk submissions. "For electronic submissions, use text (ASCII) or Macintosh attachments, or e-mail submissions in body of e-mail message." Cover letter preferred. "Unaccepted entries without the SASE will be discarded." Time between acceptance and publication is 6 months. Sometimes comments on rejected poems. Guidelines available website. Responds in up to 6 months. Acquires all rights. Rights revert to authors immediately upon publication. Reviews books and chapbooks of poetry in 500-1,200 words, single book format. Send books for review consideration.
Advice: "We're looking for writers who do not fall into an easy category or niche."

RIO GRANDE REVIEW, 105 East Union, El Paso TX 79968-0622. **Contact:** poetry editor.
Magazine Needs: *Rio Grande Review*, a annual student publication from the University of Texas at El Paso, contains poetry; flash, short, and nonfiction; short drama; photography and line art. *Rio Grande Review* is 168 pgs., 6×9, professionally printed and perfect-bound with card cover with line art, line art inside. Subscription: $8/year, $15/2 years.
How to Submit: Include bio information with submission. "Submissions are recycled regardless of acceptance or rejection." SASE for reply only. Guidelines available for SASE. Pays copies. "Permission to reprint material remains the decision of the author. However, *Rio Grande Review* does request it be given mention."

RISING, 80 Cazenove Rd., Stoke Newington, London N16 6AA England. Phone: 0956 992974. E-mail: timmywells@hotmail.com. Website: www.saltpetre.com. Established 1995. **Editor:** Tim Wells.
Magazine Needs: *Rising* is a "quarterly-ish journal of poetry." Wants "short, pithy work, preferably nonrhyming; epigrams; analogies. No animals, fluffy, lazy, rhyming, anything that has 'like a . . .' in it." Has published poetry by Salena Saliva, Francesca Beard, Cheryl B, Sean O'Brien, Gerald Locklin, and Tim Turnbull. As a sample we selected these lines from "Go Tell It to the Spartans" by Ivan Penaluna:

> *It was once said by a lady friend/that I have the kind of smile that would foreshadow a nearby mailbox exploding/whereas the lads at the Post Office just said;//You're an anarchist aren't you?*

Rising is 28 pgs., A5, photocopied and saddle-stapled, colored card cover, includes b&w graphics. Receives about 250 poems/year, accepts 30%. Press run is 500 for 30 subscribers, 100 shelf sales. Sample: £1.
How to Submit: Submit 5 poems at a time. Line length for poetry is 60 maximum. Accepts previously published poems and simultaneous submissions. Accepts e-mail submissions. Cover letter required. Time between acceptance and publication is 6 months. Poems are circulated to an editorial board. "If I like it, it's in. If I'm not sure, I consult others who work on *Rising*." Seldom comments on rejected poems. Occasionally publishes theme issues. Responds in 1 month. Pays 1 contributor's copy.
Advice: "Give 'em hell."

RIVELIN GRAPHEME PRESS, Merlin House, Church St., Hungerford, Berkshire RG17OJG England. Established 1984. **Poetry Editor:** Snowdon Barnett, D.F.A.
Book/Chapbook Needs & How to Submit: Rivelin Grapheme Press publishes only poetry. Query first with biographical information, previous publications, and a photo, if possible. If invited, send book-length manuscript, typed, double-spaced, photocopy OK. Payment is 20 copies of first printing up to 2,000, then 5% royalties on subsequent printings.

RIVER CITY, English Dept., University of Memphis, Memphis TN 38152. (901)678-4591. Fax: (901)678-2226. E-mail: rivercity@memphis.edu. Website: www.people.memphis.edu/~rivercity (includes submission guidelines, samples from previous issue, and staff and contact info). Established 1980. **Editor:** Dr. Thomas Russell. **Web Contact:** Mark Yakich.
Magazine Needs: *River City* appears biannually and publishes fiction, poetry, interviews, and essays. Has published poetry by Marvin Bell, Maxine Kumin, Jane Hirshfield, Mary Leader, Deborah Tall, and Pamela Ditchoff. *River City* is 160 pgs., 7×10, perfect-bound, professionally printed with 4-color glossy cover. Publishes 40-50 pgs. of poetry/issue. Subscription: $12. Sample: $7. Press run is 2,000.
How to Submit: Submit no more than 5 poems at a time. Include SASE. Does not read mss June through August. Publishes theme issues. Guidelines and upcoming themes available for SASE, e-mail, and on website. Responds in up to 3 months. Pays 2 contributor's copies (and cash when grant funds available).

◪ $◨ **RIVER STYX MAGAZINE; BIG RIVER ASSOCIATION**, 634 N. Grand Ave., 12th Floor, St. Louis MO 63103. Website: www.riverstyx.org (includes writer's guidelines, masthead, samples from current and recent issues, "ask the editor" section, and calendar of upcoming themes and events). Established 1975. **Editor:** Richard Newman. **Managing Editor:** Carrie Robb.

• Poetry published in *River Styx* has been selected for inclusion in past volumes of *The Best American Poetry* and *Pushcart Prize* anthologies.

Magazine Needs: *River Styx*, published 3 times/year, is "an international, multicultural journal publishing both award-winning and previously undiscovered writers. We feature poetry, short fiction, essays, interviews, fine art and photography." Wants "excellent poetry—original, energetic, musical and accessible. Please don't send us chopped prose or opaque poetry that isn't about anything." Has published work by Louis Simpson, Molly Peacock, David Kirby, Marilyn Hacker, Timothy Liu, and Lucia Perillo. As a sample the editor selected these lines from "The Dismal Science" by Donald Finkel:

> He could pick up an epic this morning/from the take-away rack at the local supermarket./All over the
> city young men are scribbling, scribbling,/and old women, and schoolchildren, and several
> chimpanzees.//The young man persists in his kitchen, parboiling a dithyramb/while the sows go
> farrowing on in Iowa./Welcome to the eleventh plague: plenty.

River Styx is 100 pgs., 6×9, professionally printed on coated stock, perfect-bound with color cover and b&w art, photographs, and ads. Receives about 8,000 poems/year, accepts 60-75. Press run is 2,500 for 1,000 subscribers of which 80 are libraries. Sample: $7.

How to Submit: Submit 3-5 poems at a time, "legible copies with name and address on each page." Time between acceptance and publication is within 1 year. Reads submissions May 1 through November 30 only. Publishes theme issues. Guidelines available for SASE or on website. Editor sometimes comments on rejected poems. Responds in up to 5 months. Pays 2 contributor's copies plus 1-year subscription plus $15/page if funds available. Acquires one-time rights.

Also Offers: Sponsors annual poetry contest. Past judges include Marilyn Hacker, Philip Levine, Mark Doty, Naomi Shihab Nye, Billy Collins, and Molly Peacock. Deadline: May 31. Guidelines available for SASE.

◨ **RIVERSTONE, A PRESS FOR POETRY; RIVERSTONE POETRY CHAPBOOK AWARD**, 7571 E. Visao Dr., Scottsdale AZ 85262. Established 1992. **Contact:** Editor.

Book/Chapbook Needs: Riverstone publishes 1 perfect-bound chapbook/year through an annual contest. Has published chapbooks by Jefferson Carter, Marcia Hurlow, Margo Stever, Cathleen Calbert, Gary Myers, and Anita Barrows. As a sample the editor selected these lines by Martha Modena Vertreace:

> With vertical loops/the Ferris wheel weds Navy Pier to clouds/as if the resurrection were not enough/
> to tether poor humans to shifting Earth./So whose permission/do I need to know your holy body?

That's from "Creating Space with Light" in *Dragon Lady: Tsukimi*, which won the 1999 Riverstone Poetry Chapbook Award. The year 2000 winner was G. Timothy Gordon's *Everything Speaking Chinese*. It is 44 pgs., digest-sized, attractively printed on 80 lb. paper and perfect-bound with spruce green endleaves and a stippled beige card stock cover.

How to Submit: To be considered for the contest, submit $8 entry fee and chapbook ms of 24-36 pgs., "including poems in their proposed arrangement, title page, contents, and acknowledgments. All styles welcome." Accepts previously published poems, multiple entries, and simultaneous submissions. Include 6×9 SASE or larger for notification and copy of last year's chapbook. No further guidelines. Contest deadline: June 30 postmark. Winner receives publication, 50 author's copies, and a cash prize of $100. Sample: $5.

◪ ◨ ◎ **RIVERWIND (Specialized: Regional)**, 312 Oakley Hall, Hocking College, Nelsonville OH 45764. (740)753-3591, ext. 2363. Established 1976. **Contact:** Demi Naffzigger, J.A. Fuller.

Magazine Needs: *Riverwind* is a literary annual publishing quality work by new and established writers mainly from Ohio, West Virginia, and Kentucky. Very open to various forms. Biased toward image poems and "voice" poems. No "genre poems (i.e., erotic, juvenile, etc.)." Recently published poetry by Paul Nelson, Roy Bentley, P.K. Harmon, Amy Newman, Betsy Brown. As a sample the editors selected these lines from "Mantle Dying" by Roy Bentley:

> If I needed a hero, you'd be him/a second liver in the bloated gut,/fielding questions about the new
> cancer./Everyone's going where you are/and still they marvel because it's you./

Riverwind is 112-130 pgs., 7×7, offset-printed, perfect-bound, photo offset-printed cover, with art/graphics. Receives about 300 poems/year, accepts about 25%. Publishes about 65 poems/issue. Press run is 400 for 300 subscribers of which 75 are libraries, 225 shelf sales; 80 are distributed free to contributors. Single copy $7.50; subscription: $7.50. Sample: $3. Make checks payable to *Riverwind*.

How to Submit: Submit 6 poems at a time. Accepts previously published poems; no simultaneous submissions. Accepts e-mail submissions; no fax or disk submissions. Cover letter is preferred. Reads submissions October 1-May 30. Time between acceptance and publication varies. Poems circulated to an editorial board. "One editor chooses what she's interested in publishing. The two editors meet to make final decision." Seldom comments on rejected poems. Occasionally publishes theme issues. Guidelines are available in magazine and for SASE. Responds in up to 3 months. Pays 2 contributor's copies. Acquires first rights. Poets may send books for review consideration to Demi Naffziger.

Advice: "Writers may want to purchase a sample copy before sending work."

ROANOKE REVIEW, English Dept., Roanoke College, Salem VA 24153. Established 1968. **Poetry Editor:** Robert R. Walter.

Magazine Needs: *Roanoke Review* is a semiannual literary review which uses poetry that is "conventional; we have not used much experimental or highly abstract poetry." Has published poetry by Peter Thomas, Norman Russell, and Mary Balazs. *Roanoke Review* is 52 pgs., 6×9, professionally printed with matte card cover with decorative typography. Uses 25-30 pgs. of poetry in each issue. Press run is 250-300 for 150 subscribers of which 50 are libraries. Receives 400-500 submissions of poetry/year, accepts 40-60; has a 3- to 6-month backlog. Subscription: $9. Sample: $3.

How to Submit: Submit original typed mss, no photocopies. Responds in 3 months. No pay.

Advice: "There is a lot of careless or sloppy writing going on. We suggest careful proofreading and study of punctuation rules."

ROCKET PRESS, P.O. Box 672, Water Mill NY 11976. E-mail: rocketpress@hotmail.com. Website: www.BouncePass.com. Established 1993. **Editor:** Darren Johnson.

Magazine Needs: *Rocket Press* features "styles and forms definitely for the 21st century." Wants "experimental and eccentric poetry that's tight and streamlined. No rhyme. Don't use the words 'poem,' 'love,' or 'ode.' " Has published poetry by Ben Ohmart, Albert Huffstickler, and Cheryl Townsend. As a sample the editor selected these lines from "The Bovine Photograph" by Brandon Freels:

> At the art museum/we both stood in front of the/bovine photograph.//"It's sexy," Kris said./"I think it's just a sexy photo!"//"Look at those thighs!"/Someone in the background/mumbled.//"You know,"/I said. "It is kind of sexy."

Rocket Press is a newspaper tabloid, 20 pgs., professionally printed. Receives about 1,000 poems/year, accepts 1-2%. Press run is 2,000 for 200 subscribers of which 2 are libraries, 400 shelf sales. Sample: $1.50.

How to Submit: Submit 3 poems at a time. Accepts simultaneous submissions; no previously published poems. Accepts e-mail submissions. Time between acceptance and publication is up to 1 year. Often comments on rejected poems. "Subscribers get fuller critiques." Responds in less than 3 months. Pays 1 contributor's copy. Acquires one-time rights. Editor includes his own blurb reviews "of anything cool."

Advice: "In our sixth year of publication, we've just about seen it all—please change that. Let's break all the rules in the new millennium."

THE ROCKFORD REVIEW; ROCKFORD WRITERS' GUILD, 7721 Venus St., Loves Park IL 61111. E-mail: haikupup@aol.com. Website: www.welcome.to/rwg. Established 1971. **Editor:** Cindy Guentherman.

Magazine Needs: *The Rockford Review* is a publication of the Rockford Writers' Guild which appears 3 times/year, publishing their poetry and prose, that of other writers throughout the country and contributors from other countries. *The Rockford Review* seeks experimental or traditional poetry of up to 50 lines. "We look for the magical power of the words themselves, a playfulness with language in the creation of images and fresh insights on old themes, whether it be poetry, satire, or fiction." Has published poetry by John Grey, Richard Luftig, and Laura Wilson. *The Rockford Review* is about 50 pgs., digest-sized, professionally printed and saddle-stapled with card cover with b&w illustration. Press run is 350. Single copy: $6; subscription: $20 (3 issues plus the Guild's monthly newsletter, *Write Away*).

How to Submit: Submit up to 3 poems at a time with SASE. Accepts simultaneous submissions; no previously published poems. No electronic submissions. "Include a cover letter with your name, address, phone number, e-mail address (if available), a three-line bio, and an affirmation that the submission is unpublished in print or electronically." Responds in 2 months. Pays 1 contributor's copy and "you will receive an invitation to be a guest of honor at a Contributors' Reading & Reception in the spring." Acquires first North American serial rights.

Also Offers: Offers Editor's Choice Prizes of $25 for prose, $25 for poetry each issue. Also sponsors a Spring Stanzas Contest and a Fall Short Story Contest with cash prizes and publication in *The Rockford Review.* Accepts work by children for both contests. The Rockford Writers' Guild is a nonprofit, tax-exempt corporation established "to encourage, develop and nurture writers and good writing of all kinds and to promote the art of writing in the Rockford area." Offers lectures by Midwest authors, editors, and publishers, conduct several workshops and publish a monthly newsletter. Membership: $30/year. Further information available for written request or on website.

$ ROCKY MOUNTAIN RIDER MAGAZINE (Specialized: animals, regional), P.O. Box 1011, Hamilton MT 59840-1011. (406)363-4085. Fax: (406)363-1056. Website: www.rockymountainrider.com. Established 1993. **Editor:** Natalie Riehl.

THE CHAPBOOK INDEX, located at the back of this book, lists those publishers who consider chapbook mss. A chapbook, a small volume of work (usually under 50 pages), is often a good middle step between magazine and book publication.

Magazine Needs: *Rocky Mountain Rider Magazine* is a regional, monthly, all-breed horse magazine. Wants "cowboy poetry; western or horse-themed poetry. Please keep length to no more than 5 verses." *Rocky Mountain Rider Magazine* is 64 pgs., 8½×11, web offset on newsprint and stapled. Publish 1 poem/issue.

How to Submit: Submit 1-10 poems at a time. Accepts previously published poems and simultaneous submissions. Cover letter preferred. Seldom comments on rejected poems. Occasionally publishes theme issues. Guidelines and upcoming themes available for SASE. "We'll send a free copy if requested in a letter asking for writer's guidelines." Pays $10/poem. Acquires one-time rights. Reviews books of poetry. Send books for review consideration.

ROMANTIC OUTSIDER, 44 Spa Croft Rd., Ossett, West Yorkshire WF5 0HE United Kingdom. Phone: (01924)275814. E-mail: susandarlington@ukonline.co.uk. Established 1997. **Editor:** Susan Darlington.

Magazine Needs: "*Romantic Outsider* appears 2-3 times/year and provides exposure to new writers (and musicians); celebrates the social outsider." Wants "anything with passion. No overly sentimental or bigoted work." Has published poetry by Giovanni Malito, Jacqueline Disler, and Ian Sawicki. As a sample we selected these lines from "Tomorrow" by Giovanni Malito:

> . . . by morning/the moon/will have gone//and its tides/will have stolen/my footprints

Romantic Outsider is about 40 pgs., A5, photocopied and stapled with colored paper cover and occasional illustrations. Receives about 100 poems/year, accepts about 30%. Press run is about 100. Sample: $4 US, (£1 in UK). Make checks (sterling only) payable to Susan Darlington.

How to Submit: Submit 5 poems maximum at a time. Accepts previously published poems and simultaneous submissions. Accepts disk submissions (Word format) and e-mail submissions (attachments preferred). "Reply not guaranteed unless SAE/IRC included." Time between acceptance and publication is up to 5 months. Often comments on rejected poems. Responds in 1 month. Pays 1 contributor's copy. Reviews books and chapbooks of poetry in 250 words, single book format. Poets may send books for review consideration.

Advice: "More submissions from women especially welcome."

ROMANTICS QUARTERLY; A.C. SWINBURNE POETRY PRIZE; ROMANTICS POETRY GROUP (Specialized: form/style, love/romance/erotica, inspirational), 4921 SW 59th Ave., Suite #5, Portland OR 97221. Fax: (503)296-7991. E-mail: knracs@aol.com. Website: http://hometown.aol.com/romantics quarter/index.html and www.thehypertexts.com/RQ.htm. Established 2000. **Editor:** Kevin. **Assistant Editors:** Celeste and Michael.

Magazine Needs: "Our goal is to resurrect the voice of the Victorian Romantic poet and renew popular interest in traditional, rhyming, musical verse. We have no restrictions; we want to see all varieties of quality poetry. However, we are partial to traditional rhyming verse in the style of the Victorian Romantics. We do not want to see limericks, greeting card verse, political poetry, splatter—gore, children's poetry or poems containing cliché, harsh language, or graphic violence." Has published poetry by Kevin N. Roberts, Michael Burch, Michael Pendragon, Harvey Stanbrough, and Annie Finch. As a sample the editor selected these lines from "Ophelia" by Kevin Roberts:

> Her fierce and frantic fingers wound/and wept for every word he said,/And tore glad grasses from the
> ground/And wove a garland for her head,/The blowing of her hair unbound,/Her guilded skirts that
> billowed 'round,/composed an eerie rustling sound/like choirs of wretched restless dead.

Romantics Quarterly is 40 pgs., 5½×8½, desktop-published and saddle-stapled, includes b&w line art, considers ads from gothic and poetry-related companies/publications. Receives about 400 poems/year, accepts about 50%. Publish about 50 poems/issue. Press run is 500 of which 50 are libraries, 100 shelf sales; 50 distributed free to reviewers and colleagues of university. Subscription: $20. Sample: $5 (when available). Make checks payable to K. Roberts. (Cash and money orders preferred, $25 fee for returned checks.) "No requirements for contributors, but we encourage contributors to subscribe and keep in touch or become members of the Romantics Poetry Group."

How to Submit: Submit 1-10 poems at a time with reading fee. Accepts previously published poems and simultaneous submissions. Accepts e-mail submissions included in body of e-mail or attached in MS Word. Cover letter preferred. "We prefer poems to be typed with name and address of poet on each page. Include SASE for reply. Enclose reading fee in cash, check, or money order made out to K. Roberts." **Reading fee:** $2/poem, $3/essay or story. Time between acceptance and publication is up to 1 year. Poems are circulated to an editorial board. "The poetry editor reads all submissions and passes selected works on to 2-3 members of the editorial board (made up of graduate students). Editorial board makes the final decisions." Often comments on rejected poems. "If a poet wants professional criticism from graduate students/professors, please include letter stating the type of guidance you require. Include $10 per piece for thorough critique and suggestions." Upcoming themes and guidelines available for SASE, on website, or by e-mail. Responds in 1 month. Sometimes sends prepublication galleys. Pays 2 contributor's copies per piece accepted. Acquires one-time rights. Reviews books and chapbooks of poetry and other magazines in 35 words, multi-book format. Poets may send books for review consideration.

Also Offers: Sponsors the annual A.C. Swinburne Poetry Prize. Submit 1 poem and $10 entry fee. Winner will receive $100, publication of poem and 5 free copies of zine. Contest rules available for SASE.

Advice: "If you really want to impress us, study the works of Romantic poets like A.C. Swinburne, E.A. Poe, S.T. Coleridge, Lord Byron, and Shelley, and take your lead from them both in terms of music and subject matter. Make us feel it was written in the 1800s."

☑ 🐿 $ ▢ ◎ **RONSDALE PRESS (Specialized: anthology, nature/rural/ecology, social issues, regional)**, 3350 W. 21st Ave., Vancouver, British Columbia V6S 1G7 Canada. (604)738-4688. Fax: (604)731-4598. Website: www.ronsdalepress.com (includes catalogs, list of upcoming events, and writer's guidelines). Established 1988. **Director:** Ronald B. Hatch.
Book Needs: Publishes 3 flat-spined paperbacks of poetry/year—by Canadian poets only—classical to experimental. "Ronsdale looks for poetry manuscripts which show that the writer reads and is familiar with the work of some of the major contemporary poets. It is also essential that you have published some poems in literary magazines. We have never published a book of poetry when the author has not already published a goodly number in magazines." Has published *Taking the Breath Away* by Harold Rhenisch, *Two Shores/Deux rives* by Thuong Vuong-Riddick, *Cobalt 3* by Kevin Roberts, *Ghost Children* by Lillia Boraks-Vemetz, *Vintage 2000* by the League of Canadian Poets, and *Cleaving* by Florence Treadwell. As a sample we selected these lines from "Flirt" in the *Green Man* by John Donlan:

> People are such flirts. Their animal spirits/rise and quit their dreary doppelgängers/as easily as you'd leave a chair./I've given up even trying to figure that out:/these tracks were laid for a lot of trains to run on—/maybe escape is in our nature.

How to Submit: Query first, with sample poems and cover letter with brief bio and publication credits. Accepts previously published poems and simultaneous submissions. Often comments on rejected poems. Responds to queries in 2 weeks, to mss in 2 months. Pays 10% royalties and 10 author's copies. Write for catalog to purchase sample books.
Advice: "Ronsdale looks for poetry with echoes from previous poets. To our mind, the contemporary poet must be well-read."

∅ **ROSE ALLEY PRESS**, 4203 Brooklyn Ave. NE #103A, Seattle WA 98105. (206)633-2725. E-mail: rosealleypress@juno.com. Established 1995. **Publisher/Editor:** David D. Horowitz. "We presently do not read unsolicited manuscripts."

🌐 ○ **ROSE TINTED WINDOWS; CARAVAN OF LOVE**, 3 Belleville Rd., London SW11 6QS England, United Kingdom. Phone: (0171)223 1014. Established 1998. **Contact:** Miss Arabella Millett.
Magazine Needs: "*Rose Tinted Windows* is a very irregular, but almost annual publication. Mainly a music fanzine, but I do include some poetry and some political articles. No specifications but original poetry is always good. No clichéd poetry." Has published poetry by Steve Sneyd, Jon Summers, Colin Cross, and Jim Dewitt. As a sample the editor selected this poem "Irrational Minds" by Chris Clayton:

> They send human beings to war./You can copulate at sixteen./Yet the word "cunt",/Is considered obscene and dirty./How strange and irrational humans are./They make little sense.

Rose Tinted Windows is 28 pgs., A5, photocopied and saddle-stapled with paper cover. Receives about 70 poems/year, accepts about 43%. Press run is 70. Sample: £1.
How to Submit: Submit 3-6 poems at a time. Accepts previously published poems and simultaneous submissions. Cover letter preferred. Include SASE or SAE and IRC. Seldom comments on rejected poems. Response time "depends—I try to reply ASAP." Poet retains rights. Staff reviews books and chapbooks of poetry and other magazines in 40 words. Send books for review consideration.
Also Offers: "*Caravan of Love* is a pen-friend/advertising zine, but we occasionally include a few poems."

🅽 ○ ∅ **ROSEWATER PUBLICATIONS; THROUGH SPIDER'S EYES**, 223 Chapel St., Leicester MA 01524-1115. (508)728-6564. E-mail: RoseWaterBooks@aol.com. Established 1997. **Editor:** April M. Ardito.
Magazine Needs: *Through Spider's Eyes* appears several times/year. It's "a short zine highlighting the best of what RoseWater Publications receives. The best art is about art or has a strong message. We prefer coffeehouse and slam style poems, work that is just as powerful spoken as written. Multi-layered work always appreciated. Prefer modern and experimental work. Rhymed poetry must be exceptional; biased against 'God is great' and 'See the pretty trees and flowers' poetry." Recently published poetry by D.R. Middleton, Gwen Ellen Rider, Ed Fuqua, Jay Walker, Craig Nelson, and April M. Ardito. As a sample the editor selected these lines from "Absolutes" by Paul William Gagnon which appears in his chapbook, *The Darkness is Habitable*:

> On the way home, we talk religion. You believe in demons, hell and/original sin./You tell me Buddhists and Wiccans worship Satan./I indulge you for the sake of conversation./Outside your window, I see your devil looking in./He's big and solid as an anvil . . .

Through Spider's Eyes is 8-12 pgs., magazine-sized, photocopied b&w, corner-stapled, plain white paper cover, accepts original artwork. Receives and accepts varied number of poems/year. Publishes about 10-40 poems/issue. Press run is 50. Single copy: $1.95; subscription: $4.75/5 issues. Sample: $2.50. Make checks payable to April M. Ardito.
How to Submit: Submit up to 5 poems at a time. Line length for poetry is 3 minimum, 250 maximum. Accepts previously published poems; no simultaneous submissions. Accepts e-mail submissions; no fax of disk submissions. Cover letter is preferred. Likes "disposable manuscripts; casual, personal cover letter; SASE re-

quired; e-mail submissions in body or as attached .doc file." Reads submissions year round. Does not publish seasonal poems. **Charges $1/pg. reading fee.** Accepts personal checks, money orders, or PayPal for all reading fees and subscriptioins. Time between acceptance and publication is up to 1 year. "Editor always attempts to read all submissions personally, but has a few people who help out when submissions get overwhelming." Seldom comments on rejected poems. "Prefer that poets submit a full chapbook-length manuscript. Otherwise, there is $1 reading fee per page." Responds in up to 2 months. Pays 3 contributor's copies. Acquires one-time rights and reprint rights (possible inclusion in an anthology at a later date). Reviews books and chapbooks of poetry and other magazines/journals in less than 1 pg., single book format. Poets may send books for review consideration to April M. Ardito.

Book/Chapbook Needs & How to Submit: RoseWater Publications "wants to create an aesthically pleasing product for poets who spend as much time on the stage as with the page." Hopes to publish full-length anthologies in the future. Publishes 5-10 chapbooks/year. Chapbooks are usually 20-64 pgs., photocopied b&w, stapled, colored paper, cardstock, or business stock cover with original cover design. "Please send full manuscript (16-60 pages) with a $10 reading fee. We do not wish to see queries. We would prefer to see a poet's full vision." Responds to mss in up to 2 months. Pays 25-50 author's copies (out of a press run of 50-100). **Approximately 20% of titles are author-subsidy published.** "Poet pays for layout and editing fees. RoseWater Publications would like to discontinue subsidy publishing in the next 1-2 years." Order sample books/chapbooks by sending $6.50 to April M. Ardito.

Also Offers: Also publishes poetry for vending machines. Send full ms (up to 120 lines), titled. Press run of 40, author receives 20 copies. Format is $11 \times 18\frac{1}{2}$ sheet folded in eighths. **$1 reading fee.**

Advice: "Spend a lot of time reading and re-reading, writing and re-writing. Always try to keep one finger on the pulse of contemporary poetry, as much to know what isn't working as what is. Stay true to yourself and your vision. Use your words to lure others into your experiences."

ROWAN BOOKS (Specialized: regional), #410, 10113-104 St., Edmonton, Alberta T5J 1A1 Canada. (780)421-1544. Fax: (780)421-1588. E-mail: jonrach@msn.com. Website: www.rowan-books.com. Established 1992. **Publisher:** H. Marshall.

Book/Chapbook Needs: Rowan Books aims "to publish emerging Western Canadian poets, previously unpublished in book form." Publishes 2 paperbacks per year. Wants "well-written (i.e., we look for artistic quality); feminist; regional (Alberta, Western Canadian); links with the experience of a particular group (e.g., women, lesbian/gay, ethnic minorities, youth, etc.). No pornography, racist, or homophobic work." Has published poetry by Mary T. McDonald, Alice Major, Jannie Edwards, Shirley A. Serviss, Anna Mioduchowska, and Lori Miseck. Books are usually 64 pgs., $5\frac{1}{2} \times 8\frac{1}{2}$, offset-printed and perfect-bound with soft 4-color laminate cover, uses photo or art for cover.

How to Submit: Query first, with a few sample poems and cover letter with brief bio and publication credits. "Prefers poets be previously published in some recognized Canadian journals. Prefer typewritten, but will accept and read legible handwritten manuscripts. Submit samples by mail; accepted manuscripts may be sent electronically upon acceptance." Time between acceptance and publication is up to 6 months. Poems are circulated to an editorial committee. Responds to queries in 1 month; to mss in 3 months. Pays royalties of 8% minimum, 11% maximum and 5 author's copies (out of a press run of 500). Order sample books by sending $15 (Canadian)/book, include shipping.

Also Offers: "We occasionally publish anthologies; watch for calls for submissions."

RUAH; POWER OF POETRY (Specialized: spirituality), Dominican School of Philosophy/Theology, 2401 Ridge Rd., Berkeley CA 94709. E-mail: cjrenz@usa.net. Established 1990. **General Editor:** C.J. Renz, O.P. **Editor:** Gregory Thielen.

Magazine Needs: *Ruah*, an annual journal published in May, "provides a 'non-combative forum' for poets who have had few or no opportunities to publish their work. Theme: spiritual poetry. The journal has three sections: general poems, featured poet, and chapbook contest winners." Wants "poetry which is of a 'spiritual nature,' i.e., describes an experience of the transcendent. No religious affiliation preferences; no style/format limitations. No 'satanic verse'; no individual poems longer than four typed pages." Has published poetry by Benjamin Alire Saens, Jean Valentine, Alberto Rios, and Naomi Shihab Nye. *Ruah* is 60-80 pgs., $5\frac{1}{2} \times 8\frac{1}{2}$, photocopied and saddle-stapled or perfect-bound, glossy card stock cover, b&w photo, includes occasional b&w sketches of original artwork. Receives about 250 poems/year, accepts 10-20%. Press run is 250 for about 100 subscribers of which 7 are libraries, 10 shelf sales; 50 distributed free to authors, reviewers and inquiries. Subscription: $10. Sample: $5 plus $1.50 postage/handling. Make checks payable to Power of Poetry/DSPT.

How to Submit: Submit 3-5 poems at a time. Accepts simultaneous submissions; no previously published poems. Accepts e-mail submissions in MS Word 97 file attachments; Chapbooks, however, cannot be submitted by e-mail. "Do not mail submissions to publisher's address. Contact general editor via e-mail for current address or send written inquiries to Dominican School." Reads submissions December through March only. Time between acceptance and publication is up to 6 months. Poems are circulated to an editorial board. "Poems reviewed by writers and/or scholars in field of creative writing/literature." Guidelines available for SASE. Responds in up to 6 months. Pays 1 copy/poem. Acquires first rights.

Book/Chapbook Needs & How to Submit: Power of Poetry publishes 1 chapbook of spiritual poetry through their annual competition. Chapbooks are usually 24 pgs., and are included as part of *Ruah*. "Poets should e-mail editor for contest guidelines and submission address or write to Dominican School." Entry fee: $10. Deadline: December 15. Responds to queries in up to 6 weeks; to mss in up to 6 months. Winner receives publication in a volume of *Ruah* and 25 author's copies (out of a press run of 250).

Advice: "*Ruah* is a gathering place in which new poets can come to let their voice be heard alongside of and in the context of 'more established' poets. The journal hopes to provide some breakthrough experiences of the Divine at work in our world."

N 🔘 RUNES, A REVIEW OF POETRY, Arctos Press, P.O. Box 401, Sausalito CA 94966-0401. (415)331-2503. Fax: (415)331-3092. E-mail: RunesRev@aol.com. Website: http://runes.cc (includes guidelines, names of editors, poetry, interviews). Established 2000. **Editors:** C.B. Follett and Susan Terris. Member: SPAN, BAIPA.

Magazine Needs: *RUNES, A Review Of Poetry* appears annually. "Our taste is eclectic, but we are looking for excellence in craft." Wants "poems that have passion, originality, and conviction. We are looking for narrative and lyric poetry that is well-crafted and has something surprising to say. No greeting card verse." Recently published poetry by Jane Hirshfield, David St. John, Richard Wilbur, Ronald Wallace, Ruth Daigon, and Martha Rhodes. *RUNES* is 96 pgs., digest-sized, professionally-printed, flat-spined, glossy card cover, with art/graphics. Receives about 1,000 poems/year, accepts 50-60. Press run is 500. Single copy: $10; subscription: $10. Sample: $10. Make checks payable to Arctos Press.

How to Submit: Submit 3-5 poems at a time. Prefers poems under 100 lines. Accepts simultaneous submissions if notified; no previously published poems. No e-mail or disk submissions. SASE required. Reads submissions April 1-May 31. Time between acceptance and publication is 6 months. Seldom comments on rejections. Publishes theme issues regularly. "Theme for 2002 is 'Mystery.'" Guidelines available for SASE or on website. Responds in 4 months. Sometimes sends prepublication galleys. Pays 1 contributor's copy. Acquires first North American serial rights. Reviews books of poetry. Poets may send books for review consideration to *RUNES*.

Also Offers: "Our first competition will be in 2002. The theme will be the same as the theme for the 2002 issue: 'Mystery'. Three poems plus a one-year subscription for $10; but, for publication, it is *not* necessary to enter competition. All submitted poems will be read." Make checks payable to Arctos Press. (See separate listing for Arctos Press in this section.)

Advice: "No one can write in a vacuum. If you want to write good poetry, you must read good poetry—classic as well as modern work."

$ 🔲 ◎ RURAL HERITAGE (Specialized: rural, humor, agriculture), 281 Dean Ridge Lane, Gainesboro TN 38562-5039. (931)268-0655. E-mail: editor@ruralheritage.com. Website: www.ruralheritage.com. Established 1976. **Editor:** Gail Damerow.

Magazine Needs: *Rural Heritage* uses poetry related to the modern use of draft animals. "We are interested in action-oriented rather than image-oriented verse that offers insight into human nature and/or working with livestock, especially draft animals. Traditional meter and rhyme only. Poems must have touch of humor or other twist. Please, no comparisons between country and city life and no religious, political, or issues-oriented material." As a sample we selected these lines from "Down to Earth" by John M. Floyd:

> . . . *Well, that may be, but what I see/Ahead for my old mule and me/Is taking pains to use our brains/*
> *To plan the beans before it rains.*

Rural Heritage is magazine-sized, bimonthly, using b&w photos, graphics and ads, 4-6 poems/issue. Press run is 4,600. Subscription: $24. Sample: $7.

How to Submit: Submit up to 3 poems at a time, one/page. Prefers short poems (12 lines or less). "Previously published poems are OK if we are told where and when. Simultaneous submissions must be withdrawn before we publish. We welcome submissions via e-mail in body of message—one verse per message please. Don't forget your snail mail address so we'll know where to send the check if your verse is accepted." Time between acceptance and publication is 6 months. "We often group poems by theme, for example plowing, threshing and so forth according to season. Verse may also be coupled with an article of similar theme such as plowing, mule teams, etc." Guidelines available for SASE or on website. Responds ASAP. Pays on publication, $5 and up (depending on length), and 2 copies. Acquires first English language rights.

Advice: "We receive too much modern poetry (free verse), not enough traditional (true meter & rhyme), not enough humor. We get too much image poetry (we prefer action) and most poems are too long—we prefer 12 lines or less."

N $ 🔲 🔘 JAMES RUSSELL PUBLISHING, 780 Diogenes Dr., Reno NV 89512. E-mail: scrnplay@po wernet. Website: www.powernet.net/~scrnplay. Established 2000. **Publisher:** James Russell.

Book/Chapbook Needs & How to Submit: James Russell Publishing is "a new publishing firm." Wants "religious, inspirational, daily devotional books. No obscene or offensive material." Books are usually 150 pgs., produced or through color cover, with art/graphics. Query first, with 2 sample poems and a cover letter with brief bio and publication credits. "No previously published material from books or magazines. We are looking for new material." Accepts simultaneous and e-mail submissions; no disk submissions. Responds to queries in 3 weeks; to mss in 1 month. Pays royalties of 10-15%. "We have bestselling books. We use Ingram and Baker & Taylor book distributors."

Advice: "Have your poems professionally edited before submitting. Enter contests to see how your poems rank. Don't quit. Keep the faith."

N ◯ ⊕ S.W.A.G., THE MAGAZINE OF SWANSEA'S WRITERS AND ARTISTS; S.W.A.G. NEWSLETTER, Dan-y-Bryn, 74 CWM Level Rd., Brynhyfryd, Swansea SA5 9DY Wales, United Kingdom. Established 1992. **Chairman/Editor:** Peter Thabit Jones.

Magazine Needs: *S.W.A.G.* appears biannually and publishes poetry, prose, articles, and illustrations. "Our purpose is to publish good literature." Wants "first-class poetry—up to 40 lines, any style." Has published poetry by Adrian Mitchell, Alan Llwyd, Mike Jenkins, and Dafydd Rowlands. As a sample the editor selected these lines from his poem "Castle Gardens, Swansea":

> In the park, Christmas Eve,/A woman shares her lunch/With a throbbing puddle/Of pigeons at her feet.

S.W.A.G. is 48 pgs., A4, professionally printed on coated paper and saddle-stapled with glossy paper cover, photos and illustrations. Accepts 12-20 poems/issue. Press run is 500 for 120 subscribers of which 50 are libraries. Subscription: £5. Sample (including guidelines): £2.50 plus postage.

How to Submit: "Interested poets should obtain sample beforehand (to see what we offer)." Submit 6 poems, typed. No previously published poems or simultaneous submissions. Cover letter required. Time between acceptance and publication is 4-6 months. Poems are circulated to an editorial board. "Editor chooses/discusses choices with board." Guidelines available for SASE (or SAE with IRCs). Responds ASAP. Pays 2 contributor's copies plus a copy of S.W.A.G.'s newsletter. Staff reviews books or poetry (half page to full). Send books for review consideration.

Also Offers: The Swansea Writers and Artists Group (S.W.A.G.) also publishes a newsletter containing information on the group's events. Send SASE for details on the organization. "We also publish Welsh language poetry."

$ ◐ ◎ SACHEM PRESS (Specialized: translations, bilingual), P.O. Box 9, Old Chatham NY 12136-0009. Established 1980. **Editor:** Louis Hammer.

Book/Chapbook Needs: Sachem, a small press publisher of poetry and fiction, both hardcover and flat-spined paperbacks. Wants to see "strong, compelling, even visionary work, English-language or translations." He has published poetry by Cesar Vallejo, Yannis Ritsos, 24 leading poets of Spain (in an anthology), Miltos Sahtouris and himself. The paperbacks average 120 pgs. and the anthology of Spanish poetry contains 340 pgs. Each poem is printed in both Spanish and English, and there are biographical notes about the authors. The small books cost $6.95 and $9.95 and the anthology $24.

How to Submit: No new submissions, only statements of projects, until January 2001. Submit mss January through April only. Royalties are 10% maximum, after expenses are recovered, plus 50 author's copies. Rights are negotiable. Book catalog is free "when available," and poets can purchase books from Sachem "by writing to us, 33⅓% discount."

N ◯ ◯ ◎ SAHARA (Specialized: regional/Central New England), P.O. Box 20705, Worcester MA 01602. (508)798-5672. E-mail: SaharaJournal@aol.com. Established 2000. **Managing Editor:** Lydia Mancevice.

Magazine Needs: *Sahara* appears biannually. "We are dedicated to the poetry of our region, Central New England." Wants "unaffected, clear writing in any style. Poems may exist, but they should mean something, too. No pointless obscenities." Accepts poetry written by children. Recently published poetry by Susan Roney-O'Brien, Patricia Fargnoli, Robert Cording, Christopher Merrill, Trevor Code, and Michael Milligan. *Sahara* is 90 pgs., digest-sized, offset-printed, perfect-bound, b&w printed card cover with graphics. Receives about 600 poems/year, accepts about 10%. Publishes about 30-40 poems/issues. Press run is 300 for 70 subscribers of which 5 are libraries, 100-150 shelf sales. Single copy: $10; subscription: $18. Sample: $11.50. Make checks payable to Elizabethan Press.

How to Submit: Submit 5 poems at a time. No previously published poems or simultaneous submissions. No fax, e-mail, or disk submissions. Cover letter is required. "Please state the titles of the poems and include a bio." Reads submissions continually. Submit seasonal poems 6 months in advance. Time between acceptance and publication is 6 months. "Material is circulated among several editors and must find at least one strong advocate to be considered." Seldom comments on rejected poems. "Subscribers are preferred." Responds in up to 2 months. Sometimes sends prepublication galleys. Pays 1 contributor's copy. Acquires one-time rights. Reviews books and chapbooks of poetry in 300-600 words. Poets may send books for review consideration to *Sahara*.

Advice: "As always, be yourself but not autocentric. Confessional poetry is *out* unless you actually have something to confess."

$ ◎ ST. ANTHONY MESSENGER (Specialized: religious), 1615 Republic St., Cincinnati OH 45210-1298. Website: www.americancatholic.org. **Poetry Editor:** Susan Hines-Brigger.

Magazine Needs: *St. Anthony Messenger* is a monthly 56-page magazine, press run 340,000, for Catholic families, mostly with children in grade school, high school, or college. Some issues feature a poetry page that uses poems appropriate for their readership. Poetry submissions are always welcome despite limited need. As a sample here is "A Valentine for Darby" by Jean M. Syed:

> Why do I love you, my potbellied love?/Not for your pregnant form or shiny pate./Were these on tender
> those decades ago,/would I have been so indiscriminate/as to let you win my heart? No princess/from
> passion ever took a frog to mate.

How to Submit: "Submit seasonal poetry (Christmas/Easter/nature poems) several months in advance. Submit a few poems at a time; do not send us your entire collection of poetry. We seek to publish accessible poetry of high quality." Guidelines available for standard SASE, free sample for 9×12 SASE. Pays $2/line on acceptance. Acquires first worldwide serial rights. *St. Anthony Messenger* poetry occasionally receives awards from the Catholic Press Association Annual Competition.

$ ▢ ◎ ST. JOSEPH MESSENGER AND ADVOCATE OF THE BLIND (Specialized: religious), 537 Pavonia Ave., P.O. Box 288, Jersey City NJ 07303. Established 1898. **Poetry Editor:** Sister Mary Kuiken, C.S.J.P.

Magazine Needs: *St. Joseph Messenger* is semiannual, (16 pgs., 8×11). Wants "brief but thought-filled poetry; do not want lengthy and issue-filled." Most of the poets they have used are previously unpublished. Receives 400-500 submissions/year, accepts about 50. There are about 2 pgs. of poetry in each issue. Press run 15,000. Subscription: $5.

How to Submit: Sometimes comments on rejected poems. Publishes theme issues. Guidelines, a free sample, and upcoming themes available for SASE. Responds within 1 month. Pays $10-25/poem and 2 copies.

☑ ▢ SANSKRIT, UNC Charlotte, Cone University Center, Charlotte NC 28223. (704)687-2326. Fax: (704)687-3394. E-mail: sanskrit@email.uncc.edu. Website www.uncc.edu/life/sanskrit (features online format) or www.uncc.edu/life/smp/smp_sanskrit.html (includes guidelines and information about student media). Established 1965. **Editor-in-Chief:** Jennifer Bonacci. **Editor:** Jason Hughes.

Magazine Needs: *Sanskrit* is a literary annual appearing in April that uses poetry. "No restrictions as to form or genre, but we do look for maturity and sincerity in submissions. Nothing trite or sentimental." Has published poetry by Kimberleigh Luke-Stallings. As a sample the editor selected these lines from "The World Will Always Be With Us" by Kristina Wright:

> The blues, the scent of lilacs on the tongue, tiny cherries/softly push from my mouth like the first buds
> still straining,//Though once I walked stupid-faced: shambling through dairy/products, putrid flowers,
> the confusion of menus, guns, women/skinny as switches on scratch and sniff pages, children with/
> tremulous liquid hearts like firing glass vases, . . .

Seeks "to encourage and promote beginning and established artists and writers." *Sanskrit* is 60-65 pgs., 9×12, flat-spined, printed on quality matte paper with heavy matte card cover. Press run is 3,500 for about 100 subscribers of which 2 are libraries. Sample: $10.

How to Submit: Submit up to 15 poems at a time. Accepts simultaneous submissions. Accepts fax and e-mail submissions (include in body of message). Cover letter with 30-70 word bio required. Submission deadline is the first Friday in November. Editor comments on submissions "infrequently." Responds in 2 months. Pays 1 contributor's copy.

$ ▢ SARABANDE BOOKS, INC.; THE KATHRYN A. MORTON PRIZE IN POETRY, 2234 Dundee Rd., Suite 200, Louisville KY 40205. (502)458-4028. Fax: (502)458-4065. E-mail: sarabandeb@aol.com. Website: www.SarabandeBooks.org (includes guidelines and application form for contest, interviews with authors, ordering information, and general information on press). Established 1994. **Editor-in-Chief:** Sarah Gorham.

Book/Chapbook Needs: Sarabande Books publishes books of poetry and short fiction. Wants "poetry of superior artistic quality. Otherwise no restraints or specifications." Has published poetry by Michael Burkard, Belle Waring, Baron Wormser, and Afaa Michael Weaver.

How to Submit: Query with 10 sample poems during the month of September only. No fax or e-mail submissions. SASE must always be enclosed. Accepts previously published poems if acknowledged as such and simultaneous submissions "if notified immediately of acceptance elsewhere." Seldom comments on rejected poems. Responds to queries in 3 months, to mss (if invited) in 6 months. Guidelines available for SASE. Pays 10% royalties and author's copies.

Also Offers: The Kathryn A. Morton Prize in Poetry is awarded to a book-length ms (at least 48 pgs.) submitted between January 1 and February 15. $20 handling fee and entry form required. Guidelines available in November for SASE or on website. Winner receives a $2,000 cash award, publication, and a standard royalty contract. All finalists are considered for publication. "At least half of our list is drawn from contest submissions." Entry fee: $20. Reads entries January 1 through February 15 only. Competition receives 1,200 entries. Most recent contest winner was Cate Marvin for "World's Tallest Disaster." Judge was Robert Pinsky.

◎ SATURDAY PRESS, INC., Box 43548, Upper Montclair NJ 07043. (973)256-5053. Fax: (973)256-4987. E-mail: saturdaypr@aol.com. Established 1975. **Editor:** S. Ladov. "We do not plan to read manuscripts in the foreseeable future."

$ ◎ SCAVENGER'S NEWSLETTER; KILLER FROG CONTEST (Specialized: science fiction/ fantasy, horror, mystery, writing), 833 Main, Osage City KS 66523-1241. (785)528-3538. E-mail: foxscav1 @jc.net. Website: www.jlgiftsshop.com/scav/index.html (features guidelines, information about *Scavenger's Newsletter*, Killer Frog Contest information, and other projects). **Editor:** Janet Fox.

Magazine Needs: *Scavenger's Newsletter* is a booklet packed with news about science fiction and horror publications. Prefers science fiction/fantasy, horror, and mystery poetry and will read anything that is offbeat or bizarre. Writing-oriented poetry is occasionally accepted but "poems on writing must present fresh ideas and viewpoints. Poetry is used as filler so it must be ten lines or under. I like poems with sharp images and careful craftsmanship." Has published poetry by Ann K. Schwader, Deborah P. Kolodji, and Joey Froehlich. As a sample the editor selected this poem, "Spider Fingers" by Deborah P. Kolodji:

> *Creeping keyboard clicks/spin clandestine data links/weaving web horror*

Scavenger's Newsletter is 22-28 pgs., printed at a quick printing shop for 800 subscribers. Subscription: $22/year; $11/6 months. Send 1st class. Sample (including guidelines): $2.50.

How to Submit: Submit 3-6 poems at a time. Accepts previously published poems, submissions by e-mail (no attachments) and simultaneous submissions (if informed)—reprints if credit is given. Guidelines available for SASE, by e-mail, or on website. At last report was "accepting about 1 out of 20 poems submitted. I am currently reading selectively. I have made the notice 'reading selectively due to backlog' a permanent part of the guidelines, since I do usually have quite a bit of material on hand yet do not want to close to the exceptional piece." Responds in 1 month or less. Pays $2 on acceptance plus one contributor's copy. E-mail submissions may choose cash or subscription. Acquires one-time rights. Staff reviews science fiction/fantasy/horror and mystery chapbooks, books and magazines only. Send materials for review to either: Jim Lee, 801 - 26th St., Windber PA 15963 or Steve Sawicki, 186 Woodruff Ave., Watertown CT 06795.

Also Offers: "I hold an annual 'Killer Frog Contest' for horror so bad or outrageous it becomes funny. There is a category for horror poetry. Has been opening April 1, closing July 1 of each year. Prizes are $50 each in four categories: poetry, art, short stories and short short stories." The last contest had no entry fee but entrants wanting the anthology pay $4.50. Winners list available for SASE.

☑ $ ◎ **SCIENCE OF MIND (Specialized: spirituality/inspirational)**, 3251 W. Sixth St., P.O. Box 75127, Los Angeles CA 90020-5096. (213)388-2181. Fax: (213)388-1926. E-mail: edit@scienceofmind.com. Website: www.scienceofmind.com. Established 1927. **Editor-in-Chief:** Kenneth Lind. **Assistant Editor:** Jim Shea. Send all poetry mss to edit@scienceofmind.com.

Magazine Needs: *Science of Mind*, published monthly, "is a correlation of laws of science, opinions of philosophy, and revelations of religion applied to the needs and aspirations of humankind. A practical teaching, it helps thousands of people experience health, happiness, peace, and love." Wants "poems inspirational and spiritual in theme and characterized by an appreciation of *Science of Mind* principles. Average length is 8-12 lines. Maximum length is 25-30 lines." Does not want "religious poetry, stuff about Christ and redemption." *Science of Mind* is 112 pgs., digest-sized, web offset-printed, perfect-bound with 4-color cover and color ads. Receives about 200 poems/year, accepts 6-8. Press run is 78,000 for 55,000 subscribers, 15,000 shelf sales. Single copy: $2.95; subscription: $24.95. Sample: $5.

How to Submit: Submit maximum of 3 poems at a time. Accepts simultaneous submissions; no previously published poems. No fax submissions. Cover letter preferred. "Only accepts will be contacted. Allow 3 months. Manuscript will not be returned." Time between acceptance and publication is 1 year ("each issue has a theme, so we may keep a poem until the right theme comes along"). Poems are read by the editorial associate, and if approved, sent to the editor for final decision. Publishes theme issues. Responds "not soon at all—most are rejected right away, but acceptances may take months." Pays $25 and 10 contributor's copies. Acquires first North American serial rights.

☑ ◎ ◎ **SCORE MAGAZINE; SCORE CHAPBOOKS AND BOOKLETS (Specialized: form)**, 1111 E. Fifth, Moscow ID 83843. (509)332-1120. E-mail: orion@pullman.com. **Poetry Editors:** Crag Hill and Spencer Selby.

Magazine Needs: Score Chapbooks and Booklets is a small press publisher of visual poetry in the annual magazine *Score*, booklets, postcards, and broadsides. Wants "poetry which melds language and the visual arts such as concrete poetry; experimental use of language, words, and letters—forms. The appearance of the poem should have as much to say as the text. Poems on any subject; conceptual poetry; poems which use experimental, non-traditional methods to communicate their meanings." Doesn't want "traditional verse of any kind—be it free verse or rhymed." Has published poetry by Karl Kempton, John Vieira, Bruce Andrews, Larry Eigner, and Pete Spence. They say that it is impossible to quote a sample because "some of our poems consist of only a single word—or in some cases no recognizable words." *Score* is 48-72 pgs., magazine-sized, offset-printed, saddle-stapled, using b&w graphics, 2-color matte card cover. Press run is 200 for 25 subscribers, of which 6 are libraries, about 50-60 shelf sales. Sample: $10.

How to Submit: We strongly advise looking at a sample copy before submitting if you are not familiar with visual poetry. Accepts previously published poems "if noted"; no simultaneous submissions. Guidelines available for SASE. Pays 2 contributor's copies. Open to unsolicited reviews. Poets may send books for review consideration.

Book/Chapbook Needs & How to Submit: For chapbook consideration send entire ms. No simultaneous submissions. Almost always comments on rejected poems. Pays 25% of the press run. Subsidy publishing available "if author requests it."

♣ ◎ **SCRIVENER**, Poetry Dept., McGill University, 853 Sherbrooke St. W., Montreal, Quebec H3A 2T6 Canada. (514)398-6588. E-mail: scrivenermag@hotmail.com. Established 1980. **Contact:** Sophie Boyer or Sergio Jimenez Barrante.

Magazine Needs: *Scrivener* is an annual review of contemporary literature and art published in April by students at McGill University. With a circulation throughout North America, *Scrivener* publishes the best of new Canadian and American poetry, short fiction, criticism, essays, reviews, and interviews. "*Scrivener* is committed to publishing the work of new and unpublished writers." Recently published poetry by Nicola Little, Shane Neilson, Giovanni Malito, and Sharon Desmarais. *Scrivener* is perfect-bound, 8½×7, 120 pgs., with 25 pages of b&w photography printed on coated paper. Text and graphics are printed in b&w duotone cover. Subscription: $9 Canadian in Canada, $11 Canadian in US and $13 Canadian anywhere else. Prices include postage.

How to Submit: January 15 deadline for submissions; contributors encouraged to submit in early fall. Send 5-10 poems, one poem/page; be sure that each poem is identified separately, with titles, numbers, etc. Accepts e-mail submissions (attachments or within text of message). Submissions require SASE for return. Comments or questions regarding back issues or submissions may be sent to scrivenermag@hotmail.com. *Scrivener* only operates fully between September and April. Responds in 6 months. Pays 1 copy (multiple copies available upon request).

☑ $ ▨ ◯ **SCROLL PUBLICATIONS INC.; SCROLL ORIGINAL ARTIST MAGAZINE**, (formerly Scroll Publications), P.O. Box 562, Swink CO 81077. (917)384-8220. E-mail: scrollpubl@ria.net. Website: www.scrollpublications.com. Established 1990. **Editor:** Cherylann Gray.

Magazine Needs: *Scroll Original Artist Magazine* contains "humor, comics, slogans, music, short stories, fiction/nonfiction, artwork, recipes, and poetry. We are strictly devoted to preserving the works and dreams of the original artist." Wants poetry of any form or style, on any subject; length, no more than 30 lines. Nothing profane or vulgar. Accepts poetry written by children. Has published poetry by Dr. Robert Spector and Natalia Radula. As a sample the editor selected these lines from "Grandmothers" by Eve Mackintosh:

> Grandmothers are rocks thrown into deep wells/Each brick fitted painstakingly to form/Solid
> foundations for dream castles created/by her children and offspring.

Scroll is 75-80 pgs., 8½×11½, soft paperback, includes art, ads. Receives about 500 poems/year, accepts about 65%. Press run is 150. Single copy: $6; subscription: $20. Sample: $4. Make checks payable to Cherylann Gray.

How to Submit: Submit up to 5 poems at a time. **Reading fee:** $4/5 poems. Accepts previously published poems and simultaneous submissions. Cover letter preferred. Time between acceptance and publication is up to 3 months. Poems are circulated to an editorial board. Often comments on rejected poems. Occasionally publishes theme issues. Guidelines and upcoming themes available for a large SASE. Responds in 1 month. Pays 1 contributor's copy. Acquires first or one-time rights. Reviews chapbooks of poetry. Poets may send books for review consideration.

Book/Chapbook Needs & How to Submit: Scroll Publications publishes 3 chapbooks and 3 anthologies/year. Query first, with 3-4 sample poems and a cover letter with brief bio and publication credits. Responds to queries in 2 months; to mss in 3 months. Pays 40-50% royalties and 25 author's copies (out of a press run of 300).

Also Offers: Sponsors biannual contest. Awards prizes of $250, $100, and $50 plus publication. Submit up to 7 poems, 30 lines maximum, with large SASE. Arrangements for co-publishing and subsidy publishing available.

Advice: "We want poetry that's strong in nature, life and real experiences, thoughts and dreams."

"*Seam* 13 was a summer issue and the shells reminded us of seasides and holidays," says editor Maggie Freeman. She also took the photograph that was reworked graphically in Photoshop by James Freeman (presently working towards an MA at Aberdeen University in Scotland). The cover's design is also by James Freeman.

⊕ ◐ **SEAM**, P.O. Box 3684, Danbury, Chelmsford CM3 4GP, United Kingdom. Established 1994. **Editors:** Maggie Freeman and Frank Dullaghan.

Magazine Needs: *Seam* appears twice/year (in January and July) to publish "good contemporary poetry." Wants "high quality poems that engage the reader in any length." Has published poetry by Annemarie Austin, Sheenagh Pugh, Virgil Suarez, and Michael Gregg Michael. *Seam* is 64 pgs., A5, folded with b&w cover photo. Receives about 2,000 poems/year, accepts about 5%. Press run is 300. Subscription: £6/year, £10 overseas. Sample: £3, £5 overseas.

How to Submit: Submit 5-6 poems at a time; each poem on 1 sheet of paper (A4 size). No poems previously published in UK or simultaneous submissions. Sometimes comments on rejected poems. Pays 1 contributor's copy.

✔ ⊕ ⊘ **SECOND AEON PUBLICATIONS**, 19 Southminster Rd., Roath, Cardiff CF23 5AT Wales. Phone/fax: 01222-493093. E-mail: peter@peterfinch.co.uk. Website: www.peterfinch.co.uk. Established 1966. **Poetry Editor:** Peter Finch. Does not accept unsolicited mss.

◖ ◖ ⊘ **SEEDHOUSE**, P.O. Box 883009, Steamboat Springs CO 80477. Phone/fax: (970)879-6978. E-mail: seedhouse98@yahoo.com. Website: www.seedhousemag.org (includes writer's guidelines, editor's names, upcoming themes, contest guidelines, subscription information, and titles and authors by issue). Established 1998. **Editor-in-Chief:** Barbara Block.

Magazine Needs: *Seedhouse* is "a bimonthly literary magazine for modern writers and poets. Accepts poetry, essays, short stories, nonfiction, b&w artwork, and photography." Wants "any good poetry. No juvenile work." Accepts poetry written by children ages 15 and over. Has published poetry by Michael White, Colorado Award Winner, and Mary Crow, Poet Laureate of Colorado. As a sample the editor selected these lines from "Cliff Dwellers" by Ron Chappell:

> still they roam the hidden reaches/ . . . archaic margins of my mind/and they call me, seek to know
> me/from an age beyond some border/where the eons gather stardust/from a people lost in time.

Seedhouse is 16 pgs., magazine-sized, saddle-stapled, includes b&w art/graphics. Press run is 1,000 for 500 subscribers. Single copy: $2.75; subscription: $15. Sample: $3.50. Make checks payable to *Seedhouse Magazine*.

How to Submit: Submit 3 poems at a time. Line length for poetry is 80 maximum. Accepts simultaneous submissions; no previously published poems. Accepts e-mail and disk submissions in Word Perfect or MS Word. Cover letter preferred. "We prefer typed submissions, double-spaced, in an easy to read font. Include name, address, phone, and three-sentence bio." Often comments on rejected poems. Occasionally publishes theme issues. Guidelines and upcoming themes available for SASE or on website. Responds in 3 months. Pays 2 contributor's copies. Acquires one-time rights.

Also Offers: Sponsors an annual summer writing contest for short stories and poetry. 1st Place winners: $50 plus 1-year subscription; 2nd Place winners: $30; 3rd Place: $20.

Advice: "Proofread your work carefully. Be sure to retain original."

⊠ ▱ ○ **SEEDS POETRY MAGAZINE; HIDDEN BROOK PRESS; SEEDS POETRY CONTEST**, 412-701 King St. W., Toronto, Ontario M5V 2W7 Canada. E-mail: writers@hiddenbrookpress.com. Website: www.hiddenbrookpress.com. Established 1994. **Publisher/Editor:** Richard M. Grove.

Magazine Needs: *SEEDS* is an online publication dedicated to being an accessible venue for writers, no matter what their status is in the publishing world. "It doesn't matter whether you've ever been published or not. We publish well-crafted poetry from around the world, so send us any style of poetry you love to write. Send us your newly written or previously published work but be sure it is your absolute top shelf, best stuff. Don't save it for the bottom drawer or the future. We do not appreciate obscure, self-indulgent word games. We are not very interested in reading rhymed verse though we do on occasion publish such poetry if it suits us personally. We are not at all interested in reading about one-night stands, love-lorn angst, or the teen heart throb. Save this for your bottom drawer. Religious dogma and spiritually sappy work are usually not our cup of tea but we have published some interesting references to God, the universe, and spiritual epiphanies. Our goal is to publish well-written, memorable work whether it is humorous, traumatic, nature poems, cityscapes, or just the insight or outlook about life. Push your poetry to the edge but not too far over the edge for us. Oh, and keep the four letter words to a minimum. We have published very few of them."

How to Submit: Submit "any number of poems by e-mail or ASCII-text file on disk with hard copy." Line length for poetry is 3-200 maximum. Accepts previously published poems and simultaneous submissions. "Work, if accepted, is filed to fit with future themes, styles and formats of other works. Authors will be notified as to whether or not the editor is interested in keeping work on file." Guidelines available on website. Responds "as soon as possible."

Also Offers: Sponsors the *SEEDS* Poetry Contest, awards $100, $50, and $25 plus publication. Entry fee: $12 for 6 poems. "Send as many sets of 3 by the same author as you like on white paper, single spaced, font size 12 pt. (no fancy fonts) with your name, mailing address, phone, and e-mail address on the back of each sheet. Please no cover letter, bio, comments, or pleadings. After you have mailed your hard copy with your submission fee, then and only then, e-mail your submission in the body of the e-mail." Deadline: May 1 and October 1. Also sponsors *No Love Lost* and *The Open Window* poetry anthology contests. For *No Love Lost*, submit poems of love, hate, lust, desire, passion, jealousy and ambivalence, brotherly, sisterly, parental love, and love of country, city. Deadline: January 1. For *The Open Window*, send any style, theme, and length. Deadline: June 1. For *No Love Lost* and *The Open Window* contests, send 5 poems, previously unpublished, of any styles, any length. Submission fee: $15/£7 includes purchase of book. Authors retain copyright. 1st, 2nd, 3rd Prizes plus 10 honorable mentions will be chosen plus up to 300 poems published. Send your submissions with a SASE or SAE with IRCs to Hidden Brook Press. Electronic and hard copy submissions required. All non-Canadian destinations pay in US dollars or British sterling if from Great Britain. For overseas submissions add $1 US or £1.

Advice: "The paper-based *SEEDS* and the website *SEEDS* are two different poetry publications containing a different selection of poems and published at different times of the year."

SEEMS, P.O. Box 359, Lakeland College, Sheboygan WI 53082-0359. (920)565-1276 or (920)565-3871. Fax: (920)565-1206. E-mail: kelder@excel.net. Website: www.lakeland.edu/faculty/~elder/seemsweb.htm (currently consists of a home page with basic information, including images of the covers of two issues). Established 1971. **Editor:** Karl Elder.

Magazine Needs: *Seems* is published irregularly (35 issues in 30 years). This is a handsomely printed, nearly square (7×8¼) magazine, saddle-stapled, generous with white space on heavy paper. Two of the issues are considered chapbooks, and the editor, suggests sampling *Seems #14, What Is The Future Of Poetry?* for $5, consisting of essays by 22 contemporary poets, and "If you don't like it, return it and we'll return your $5." *Explain That You Live: Mark Strand with Karl Elder* (#29) is available for $3. There are usually about 20 pgs. of poetry/issue. Has published poetry by Kim Bridgford, William Greenway, William Heyen, Mary MacGowan, and Terry Savoie. The editor said it was "impossible" to select 6 illustrative lines, but for an example of his own recent work see *The Best American Poetry 2000* or *The 2001 Pushcart Prize* anthology. Print run is 350 for 200 subscribers of which 20 are libraries. Single copy: $4; subscription: $16/4 issues.

How to Submit: There is a 1- to 2-year backlog. "People may call or fax with virtually any question, understanding that the editor may have no answer." No simultaneous submissions. No fax or e-mail submissions. Responds in up to 3 months. Pays 1 copy. Acquires first North American serial rights. Returns rights upon publication.

Advice: "We'd like to consider more prose poems."

SEMIQUASI PRESS; RED DOT (Specialized: form/style), 803A N. Congress St., Jackson MS 39202. (601)969-9324. E-mail: autopolar@hotmail.com. Established 1989. **Publisher/Editor:** A. di Michele. **Editor (chapbooks):** Yum Cax.

● Semiquasi Press has been featured in Boise State University's SZ2 (Some Zines Two) exhibition (1996) and in the annual Poets House Poetry Publication Showcase.

Magazine Needs: *Red Dot*, published in association with La College de Phénomenographie, is an annual "barrage of disjointed, articulated poems and poetic discourse." Wants "experimental work—meaning: concrete, cut-up, automatic, post-syntactic, collaborative, phenomenological, chance; poetry that combines or fuses the style/direction of, say, *Popol Vuh* with haiku . . . epic instances." Does not want "witty, sentimental work, or rhyming poems (unless unintentional)." Has published poetry by Joel Dailey and Jake Berry. As a sample the editor selected these lines from "Untitled" by Frank O'Royler:

> *Apropos, reverse vulnerable, a gem/abrigate could even structure an ear of worry/to be helium of ol'*
> *you soulmates. Her's is/quorum diabetes, (to menthol)*

Red Dot is 20-60 pgs., 8½×7, offset- or letterpress-printed, saddle-stapled or hand-bound with cardstock cover, includes collage art. Receives about 500 poems/year, accepts about 10%. Press run is 200-400 for 100 subscribers of which 10 are libraries, 100 shelf sales; 50 distributed free (traded) to like publishers.

How to Submit: Submit 5-10 poems at a time. Accepts previously published poems and simultaneous submission. Accepts e-mail submissions included in body of message. Cover letter preferred. Reads submissions February 14 through November 2 only. Sometimes comments on rejected poems. Responds "sometimes." Sometimes sends prepublication galleys. Pays 1 contributor's copy.

Book/Chapbook Needs & How to Submit: Semiquasi Press is interested in "post-experimental, post-colonial, post-primal, and post-leftist work" and publishes 3-6 chapbooks/year under the imprint Semiquasi Editions. Chapbooks are usually 8-24 pgs., size varies, offset- or letterpress-printed or photocopied, saddle-stapled or hand-bound with cardstock cover. Query first with 5-10 sample poems and cover letter with brief bio and publication credits. Responds to queries "sometimes." Pays up to 25 author's copies (out of a press run of 200).

SENECA REVIEW, Hobart and William Smith Colleges, Geneva NY 14456-3397. (315)781-3392. Fax: (315)781-3348. Website: www.hws.edu/~senecareview/ (includes guidelines, excerpts from current issue, profile of editors, available back issues, subscription info, info for advertisers and book stores). Established 1970. **Editor:** Deborah Tall. **Associate Editor:** John D'Agata.

● Poetry published in *Seneca Review* has also been included in the 1997 and 2000 volumes of *The Best American Poetry* and in *The 1998 Pushcart Prize* anthology.

Magazine Needs: *Seneca Review* is a biannual. Wants "serious poetry of any form, including translations. No light verse. Also essays on contemporary poetry and lyrical nonfiction." Has published poetry by Seamus Heaney, Rita Dove, Denise Levertov, Stephen Dunn, and Hayden Carruth. *Seneca Review* is 100 pgs., 6×9, professionally printed on quality stock and perfect-bound with matte card cover. You'll find plenty of free verse here—some accessible and some leaning toward experimental—with the emphasis on voice, image, and diction. All in all, poems and translations complement each other and create a distinct editorial mood each issue. Receives 3,000-4,000 poems/year, accepts about 100. Press run is 1,000 for 500 subscribers of which half are libraries, about 250 shelf sales. Subscription: $11/year, $20/2 years, $28/3 years. Sample: $5.

How to Submit: Submit 3-5 poems at a time. No simultaneous submissions or previously published poems. Reads submissions September 1 through May 1 only. Responds in up to 3 months. Pays 2 contributor's copies and a 2-year subscription.

SENSATIONS MAGAZINE, 2 Radio Ave., A5, Secaucus NJ 07094. Website: www.sensationsmag.com. Established 1987. **Publisher/Executive Editor:** David Messineo.

• *Sensations Magazine* won first place in the American Literary Magazine Awards in 1994 and 1996.

Magazine Needs and How to Submit: "Please check our website, www.sensationsmag.com, for submission requirements."

Advice: "If you would like to be treated with personal courtesy and decency instead of as 'one among thousands' for a change, it's definitely worth your time to give us a try. Purchase of a back issue, as always, is recommended; rates and availability will be included with all inquiries we receive. Good luck!"

SERPENT & EAGLE PRESS, 10 Main St., Laurens NY 13796. (607)432-2990. Established 1981. **Poetry Editor:** Jo Mish. Currently not accepting poetry submissions.

THE SEWANEE REVIEW, University of the South, Sewanee TN 37383-1000. (931)598-1246. E-mail: rjones@sewanee.edu. Website: www.sewanee.edu/sreview/home.html (includes submission guidelines, subscription costs, selections from the magazine, and links to useful references, publishers, etc.). Established 1892, thus being our nation's oldest continuously published literary quarterly. **Editor:** George Core.

Magazine Needs: Fiction, criticism, and poetry are invariably of the highest establishment standards. Many of our major poets appear here from time to time. *Sewanee Review* has published poetry by Robert Bly, Neal Bowers, Catharine S. Brosman, Robert Cording, Debora Greger, John Haines, and David Middleton. Each issue is a hefty paperback of nearly 200 pgs., conservatively bound in matte paper, always of the same typography. Open to all styles and forms, the issues we reviewed featured formal sequences, metered verse, structured free verse, sonnets, and lyric and narrative forms—all accessible and intelligent. Press run is 3,200. Sample: $7.25.

How to Submit: Submit up to 6 poems at a time. Line length for poetry is 40 maximum. No simultaneous submissions. No electronic submissions. "Unsolicited works should not be submitted between June 1 and August 31. A response to any submission received during that period will be greatly delayed." Responds in 6 weeks. Pays 60¢/line, plus 2 copies (and reduced price for additional copies). Also includes brief, standard, and essay-reviews.

Also Offers: Presents the Aiken Taylor Award for Modern American Poetry to established poets. Poets *cannot* apply for this prize.

Advice: "Please keep in mind that for each poem published in *Sewanee Review*, approximately 250 poems are considered."

SHADES OF DECEMBER, P.O. Box 244, Selden NY 11784. E-mail: fiction@shadesofdecember.com or poetry@shadesofdecember.com. Website: www.shadesofdecember.com (includes guidelines, subscription/ordering information, upcoming themes, and sample pieces). Established 1998. **Poetry Editor:** Alexander C.P. Danner. **Fiction Editor:** Brandy L. Donner.

Magazine Needs: Published quarterly, *Shades of December* "provides a forum that is open to all forms of writing (poetry, prose, drama, etc.). Topics and tones range from the academic to the whimsical. We are open to any genre and style. No trite greeting-card verse." Has published poetry by Joe Lucia, William Doreski, Virgil Suarez, and Claudia Grinnell. *Shades of December* is 84 pgs., digest-sized, neatly printed and perfect-bound with colored cardstock cover, uses b&w graphics. Single copy: $7; subscription: $18. Sample: $7. Make checks payable to Alexander C.P. Danner.

How to Submit: Submit 2-6 poems at a time. Accepts simultaneous submissions; no previously published poems. Accepts e-mail submissions in an attached file. Cover letter preferred. "Cover letter should include brief 50-word bio listing previous publications/noteworthy facts. Include SASE. All electronic submissions should be in an IBM-recognizable format (any version MS Word, Corel Word Perfect)." Time between acceptance and publication is 1-4 months. Seldom comments on rejected poems. Occasionally publishes theme issues . Guidelines and upcoming themes available for SASE or on website. Responds in 6 weeks. Sometimes sends prepublication galleys. Pays 2 contributor's copies. Acquires one-time rights.

SHATTERED WIG REVIEW, 425 E. 31st, Baltimore MD 21218. (410)243-6888. Website: www.normals.com/~normals/. Established 1988. **Contact:** Sonny Bodkin.

Magazine Needs: *Shattered Wig Review* is a semiannual using "everything in particular. Prefer sleaking nurse stories, absurdist trickles, and blasts of Rimbaud. Exploring the thin line between reality and societal hallucination." Has published poetry by Gary Blankenburg, Cynthia Hendershot, and Dan Raphael. As a sample the editor selected these lines from "Answering" by John M. Bennett:

Seems like falling over chair, rings I skull-clapped/that stoney wall he dandruffs in, dithering before's/
slump in the socket, an (eye slucked back in)/what I doubled seeing, like "crawling over air, sinks/I"
dreaming my lid-blink closed . . . (so the far down/dull flat seems, like's phoney) all night looking

Shattered Wig Review is approximately 70 pgs., 8½ × 8½, photocopied, side-stapled with card stock covers with original artwork, art and graphics also inside. Receives about 10 submissions a week, accepts about 20%. Press run is 300 for 100 subscribers of which 10 are libraries, 100 shelf sales. Subscription: $9 (2 issues). Sample: $4.
How to Submit: Accepts previously published poems and simultaneous submissions. Seldom comments on rejected poems. Responds within 1 month. Pays 1 copy. Acquires one-time rights. Occasionally reviews books of poetry in 100 words. Poets may send books for review consideration. There are no requirements for contributors except "that the contributor include us in their nightly prayers."

SHEMOM (Specialized: motherhood), 2486 Montgomery Ave., Cardiff CA 92007. E-mail: peggyfrench@home.com. Established 1997. **Editor:** Peggy French.
Magazine Needs: "Appearing 2-4 times/year, *Shemom* celebrates motherhood and the joys and struggles that present themselves in that journey. It includes poetry, essays, book and CD reviews, recipes, art, and children's poetry. Open to any style, prefer free verse. We celebrate motherhood and related issues. Haiku and native writing also enjoyed. Love to hear from children." As a sample the editor selected these lines from her poem "Ode to Motherhood":

Motherhood/that often/thankless job/yet one filled/with some of life's/greatest rewards/in the early
years/there are diapers/sleepless nights/unread books but/priceless/infant smiles.

Shemom is a 10-20-page zine. Receives about 20 poems/year, accepts 100%. Press run is 50 for 30 subscribers. Single copy: $3; subscription: $12/4 issues. Sample: $3.50. Make checks payable to Peggy French.
How to Submit: Submit 3 poems at a time. Accepts previously published poems and simultaneous submissions included in body of message. Accepts e-mail submissions included in body of message. "Prefer e-mail submission, but not required if material is to be returned, please include a SASE." Time between acceptance and publication is 3 months. Responds in 1 month. Pays 1 copy. Acquires one-time rights.

SHENANDOAH; THE JAMES BOATWRIGHT III PRIZE FOR POETRY, Troubadour Theater, 2nd Floor, Washington and Lee University, Lexington VA 24450-0303. (540)463-8765. E-mail: lleech@wlu. edu. Website: www.wlu.edu/~shenando (includes guidelines, samples, editors, and subscription form). Established 1950. **Editor:** R.T. Smith.
● Poetry published in *Shenandoah* has been included in the 1999 and 2000 volumes of *The Best American Poetry.*
Magazine Needs: Published at Washington and Lee University, *Shenandoah* is a quarterly literary magazine. Has published poetry by Mary Oliver, Ted Kooser, W.S. Merwin, and Marilyn Hacker. As a sample the editor selected "Penumbra" by Betty Adcock:

And something as cold as winter's breath/tightens in her, as later the asthma's vise/will tighten—hands
on the throat, the truth.

The magazine is 160 pgs., 6 × 9, perfect-bound, professionally printed with full-color cover. Generally, it is open to all styles and forms. Press run is 1,900. Subscription: $22/year; $35/2 years; $45/3 years. Sample: $5.
How to Submit: All submissions should be typed on one side of the paper only. Your name and address must be clearly written on the upper right corner of the ms. Does not accept e-mail submissions. Include SASE. Reads submissions September 1 through May 30 only. Responds in 3 months. Pays $2.50/line, 1-year subscription, and 1 contributor's copy. Acquires first publication rights. Staff reviews books of poetry in 7-10 pages, multi-book format. Send books for review consideration. Most reviews are solicited.
Also Offers: Sponsors the James Boatwright III Prize For Poetry. A $1,000 prize awarded annually to the author of the best poem published in *Shenandoah* during a volume year.

SHIRIM, A JEWISH POETRY JOURNAL (Specialized: ethnic), 4611 Vesper Ave., Sherman Oaks CA 91403. (310)476-2861. Established 1982. **Editor:** Marc Dworkin.
Magazine Needs: *Shirim* appears biannually and publishes "poetry that reflects Jewish living without limiting to specific symbols, images or contents." Has published poetry by Robert Mezcy, Karl Shapiro, and Grace Schulmon. *Shirim* is 40 pgs., 4 × 5, desktop-published and saddle-stapled with card stock cover. Press run is 200. Subscription: $7. Sample: $4.
How to Submit: Submit 4 poems at a time. No previously published poems or simultaneous submissions. Cover letter preferred. Seldom comments on rejected poems. Publishes theme issues regularly. Responds in 3 months. Acquires first rights.

SENDING TO A COUNTRY other than your own? Be sure to send International Reply Coupons (IRCs) instead of stamps for replies or return of your manuscript.

◐ ◎ **SIERRA NEVADA COLLEGE REVIEW**, P.O. Box 4269, Incline Village NV 89450. Established 1990. **Editor:** June Sylvester Saraceno.

Magazine Needs: *Sierra Nevada College Review* is an annual literary magazine published in May, featuring poetry and short fiction by new writers. "We want image-oriented poems with a distinct, genuine voice. Although we don't tend to publish 'light verse,' we do appreciate, and often publish, poems that make us laugh. We try to steer clear of sentimental, clichéd, or obscure poetry. No limit on length, style, etc." Has published poetry by Carol Frith, Simon Perchik, Taylor Graham, and Maximilian Werner. As a sample the editor selected these lines from "The Small Town in the Heart" by Brendan McCormack:

> *Closing in/on a red bead/on the red line of a white map/and a cloud goes by on the radio./Out of the last curve into the straightaway/the wind leans in behind you./There is a familiar comfort in the flow./ The smell of wet leaves and cedar/gets in through a crack in the window.*

Sierra Nevada College Review is about 75 pgs., with cover art only. "We receive approximately 500 poems/ year and accept approximately 50." Press run is 500. Subscription: $5/year. Sample: $2.50.

How to Submit: Submit 5 poems at a time. Accepts simultaneous submissions; no previously published poems. Include brief bio. Reads submissions September 1 through April 1 only. Sometimes comments on rejected poems. Responds in about 3 months. Pays 2 contributor's copies.

Advice: "We're looking for poetry that shows subtlety and skill."

$ ◐ ◎ **THE SILVER WEB: A MAGAZINE OF THE SURREAL** (Specialized: science fiction, horror), P.O. Box 38190, Tallahassee FL 32315. Fax: (850)385-4063. E-mail: annk19@mail.idt.net. Established 1989. **Editor:** Ann Kennedy.

Magazine Needs: *The Silver Web* is a semiannual publication featuring fiction, poetry, art, and thought-provoking articles. Wants "works ranging from speculative fiction to dark tales and all weirdness in between; specifically works of the surreal. We are looking for well-written work that is unusual and original. No genre clichés, that is, no vampires, werewolves, zombies, witches, fairies, elves, dragons, etc. Also no fantasy, sword, and sorcery. Poems must use standard poetic conventions whether free verse or rhyming." Has published poetry by Glenna Holloway, Simon Perchik, Tippi N. Blevins, and Jacie Ragan. As a sample we selected these lines from "Empty House" by Fabian Peake:

> *You walk the pavement/of my street in your/scuffed black shoes,/dragging behind you/(on lengths of string/tied to your belt),/a hundred paintbrushes/dancing like drumsticks . . .*

The Silver Web is 90 pgs., 8½ × 11, offset printed, perfect-bound with full-color cover and b&w photos, art and ads. Receives 10-20 poems a week, accepts 10-20/year. Press run is 2,000 for more than 300 subscribers. Subscription: $12. Sample: $7.20, $7.95 Canada and overseas.

How to Submit: Submit up to 5 poems at a time. Accepts previously published poems, but note previous credit and simultaneous submissions. E-mail for queries and information only. "Cover letters are enjoyed but not essential. Provide an SASE with proper postage to ensure a response." Reads submissions January 1 through August 31 only. "You may receive a form rejection, but I will do my best to give personal comments as time allows." Guidelines available for SASE or by e-mail. Responds in 2 months. Always sends prepublication galleys. Pays $10-50, 2 contributor's copies, and discount on additional copies. Acquires first or one-time rights.

✓ ◐ ◎ **SILVER WINGS/MAYFLOWER PULPIT** (Specialized: religious, spirituality/inspirational); **POETRY ON WINGS, INC.**, P.O. Box 1000, Pearblossom CA 93553-1000. (661)264-3726. E-mail: jacksonwx@iopener.net. Established 1983. Published by Poetry on Wings, Inc. **Poetry Editor:** Jackson Wilcox.

Magazine Needs: "As a committed Christian service we produce and publish *Silver Wings/Mayflower Pulpit*, a bimonthly poetry magazine. We want poems with a Christian perspective, reflecting a vital personal faith and a love for God and man. Will consider poems from 3-20 lines. Short poems are preferred. Poems over 20 lines will not even be read by the editor. Quite open in regard to meter and rhyme." Accepts poetry written by children. Has published poetry by Patricia G. Rourke, June Gilchrist, and Dr. J.W. McMillan. As a sample we selected these lines from "Into the Flame" by Michael Cross:

> *Tossed at last into the flame,/We sputter, hiss, but do not die./Transformed, we steam towards heaven . . ./ Home.*

Silver Wings/Mayflower Pulpit is 16 pgs., digest-sized, offset with cartoon-like art. Each issue contains a short inspirational article or sermon plus 15-20 poems. Receives about 1,500 submissions/year, accepts about 260. Press run is 300 with 250 subscribers, 50 shelf sales. Subscription: $10. Sample: $2.

How to Submit: Submit typed ms, double-spaced. Include SASE. Accepts simultaneous submissions; no previously published poems. Time between acceptance and publication can be up to 2 years. Guidelines and upcoming themes are available for SASE. Responds in 3 weeks, providing SASE is supplied. Pays 1 contributor's copy. "We occasionally offer an award to a poem we consider outstanding and most closely in the spirit of what *Silver Wings* seeks to accomplish." Acquires first rights.

Also Offers: Sponsors an annual contest. For theme and details send SASE.

Advice: "We are interested in poetry that has a spiritual content and may be easily understood by people of humble status and simple lifestyle."

☑ $⊘ **SILVERFISH REVIEW PRESS; GERALD CABLE BOOK AWARD**, (formerly Silverfish Review), P.O. Box 3541, Eugene OR 97403. (541)344-5060. E-mail: sfrpress@aol.com. Website: www.qhome.com/silverfish. Established 1979. **Editor:** Rodger Moody.

Book/Chapbook Needs & How to Submit: Silverfish Review Press sponsors the Gerald Cable Poetry Contest. A $1,000 cash award and publication is awarded annually to the best book-length ms or original poetry by an author who has not yet published a full-length collection. No restrictions on the kind of poetry or subject matter; translations not acceptable. A $20 entry fee must accompany the ms; make checks payable to Silverfish Review Press. Guidelines available for SASE.

☑ ⛱ ◖ ◗ **SIMPLYWORDS**, 605 Collins Ave., Centerville GA 31028. (912)953-9482 (between 10 a.m. and 5 p.m. only). E-mail: simplywords@hotmail.com. Website: http://welcome.to/simplywords and http://mypage.goplay.com/simplywords. Established 1991. **Editor:** Ruth Niehaus.

Magazine Needs: *SimplyWords* is a quarterly magazine open to all types, forms, and subjects. "No foul language or overtly sexual works." Accepts poetry written by children; "there are no reading fees for children." Has published poetry by Jan Bavet, Helen McIntosh Gordon, Sarah Jensen, and James Cannon. *SimplyWords* is 20-30 pgs., magazine-sized, deskjet printed and spiral-bound, photo on cover, uses clip art. Receives about 500 poems/year, accepts about 90%. Press run is 60-100 depending on subscriptions and single issue orders in house." Subscription: $18.50/year. Sample: $5.

How to Submit: Send SASE for guidelines before submitting and write 'guidelines' in big block letters on left hand corner of envelope. No e-mail submissions. Line length for poetry is 28 maximum. "Name, address, phone number, e-mail, and line count must be on each page submitted." SASE required. **Reading fee:** $1/poem. Time between acceptance and publication "depends on what issue your work was accepted for."

Also Offers: Sponsors a poetry contest with small cash prize. Winning poem is showcased on cover. Now offers quarterly contest. Prizes are 1 Place: $15, 2nd Place: $10, and 3rd Place: $5. Also uses 10-12 short stories/year. Publishes chapbooks; send SASE for details.

Advice: "It is very important that you send for guidelines before you submit to any publication. They all have rules and expect you to be professional enough to respect that. So learn the ropes—read, study, research your craft. If you want to be taken seriously prove that you are by learning your chosen craft."

◎ **SINISTER WISDOM (Specialized: lesbian, feminist)**, P.O. Box 3252, Berkeley CA 94703. E-mail: sinister@sirius.com. Webiste: www.sinisterwisdom.org. Established 1976. **Editor:** Alexis Alexander. **Poetry Editor:** Joan Aunsfire.

Magazine Needs: *Sinister Wisdom* is a multicultural lesbian journal. "We want poetry that reflects the diversity of lesbian experience—lesbians of color, Third World, Jewish, old, young, working class, poor, disabled, fat, etc.—from a lesbian perspective. No heterosexual themes. We will not print anything that is oppressive or demeaning to women, or which perpetuates negative stereotypes." The journal has published work by Gloria Anzaldúa and Betsy Warland. The quarterly magazine is 128-144 pgs., digest-sized, flat-spined, with photos and b&w graphics. Press run is 3,500 for 1,000 subscribers of which 100 are libraries; newsstand sales and bookstores are 1,500. Single copy: $6; subscription: $20 US, $25 foreign. Sample: $7.50.

How to Submit: No simultaneous submissions. Time between acceptance and publication is 6 months to 1 year. Publishes theme issues. Upcoming themes available for SASE. Responds in up to 9 months. Pays 2 contributor's copies. Reviews books of poetry in 500-1,500 words, single or multi-book format.

Advice: "Send anything *other* than love poetry and want work by lesbians only."

🌐 ◯ **SKALD**, 2 Greenfield Terrace, Menai Bridge, Anglesey LL59 5AY Wales, United Kingdom. Phone: 1248-716343. Established 1994. **Contact:** Ms. Zoë Skoulding.

Magazine Needs: *Skald* appears approximately 3 times/year and contains "poetry and prose in Welsh or English. We focus on writers in Wales though submissions from elsewhere are welcome." Wants "interesting and varied poetry in Welsh and English. Nothing didactic, sentimental, or nostalgic." As a sample the editor selected these lines from "Life Story" by Malcolm Bradley:

> Unexplored eccentric swelling/fills my lunar skull./An atrocity of emptiness/leaves each glib cell/to
> the slow abstract/click of extinction.

Skald is 30-40 pgs., A5, professionally printed and saddle-stapled with textured card cover, contains b&w artwork. Receives about 300 poems/year, accepts about 25%. Press run is 300 for 20 subscribers, 250 shelf sales; 20 distributed free to other magazines, art boards. Single copy: £3; subscription: £8/year (payments in sterling only).

How to Submit: Submit 2 poems at a time. No previously published poems or simultaneous submissions. Cover letter preferred. Time between acceptance and publication is 4 months. Often comments on rejected poems. Responds in 1 month. Pays 1 contributor's copy.

◗ **SKIDROW PENTHOUSE**, 44 Four Corners Rd., Blairstown NJ 07825. (908)362-6808 or (212)286-2600. Established 1998. **Editor:** Rob Cook. **Editor:** Stephanie Dickinson.

Magazine Needs: *Skidrow Penthouse* is published "to give emerging and idiosyncratic writers a new forum in which to publish their work. We are looking for deeply felt authentic voices, whether surreal, confessional, New York School, formal, or free verse. Work should be well crafted: attention to line-break and diction. We want poets who sound like themselves, not workshop professionals. We don't want gutless posturing, technical precision with

insider report

A formal take on human relationships

Sex, in all its complex emotional and physical permutations, is one of the trickiest subjects for a poet to tackle. The villanelle, a traditional poetic form involving a pattern of repeated lines and rhyme schemes, is one of the most difficult forms for a poet to master. And a feminist point of view, the female perspective that runs counter to centuries of conventional male ideas about poetic subjects, can be a challenge as well.

Beth Gylys

Photo by Michael Cipperman

Needless to say, feminist villanelles about sex don't appear easy to write. Beth Gylys is a poet, though, who writes such poems—and makes writing them seem as easy as having a conversation with a good friend.

With the publication in 1999 of her first book, *Bodies that Hum*, Gylys rapidly has gained recognition as an up-and-coming poet on the national scene. The book, a formal *tour-de-force*, won the Gerald Cable Book Award from Silverfish Review Press. The aspect of the book that has attracted the most critical notice and praise has been its numerous, edgy, frequently hilarious villanelles about various aspects of human relationships, including love and, yes, sex.

"The villanelle can be very serious or funny," Gylys says. "It's easier to be funny. Dylan Thomas created a masterpiece, 'Do Not Go Gentle into that Good Night.' It's hard to write a poem with that kind of impact."

In a villanelle, the concluding lines of each stanza, which rhyme, repeat according to a predetermined pattern. Poets can vary the lines somewhat for syntactical reasons, word play, or the desire for variety, to achieve certain effects. In the case of Thomas' famous poem ("Do not go gentle into that good night,/Rage, rage against the dying of the light") the repetition achieves a kind of grandeur.

By contrast, the repeating lines of Gylys's poem "Personal" meld the snap of rhyme and meter with the language of personal ads: "I want a man whose body makes mine hum./Don't call me if you're rigid, mean or dumb." The tone is humorous, parodying—one seldom sees such personal ads so succinctly phrased—and longing.

Gylys began writing villanelles as a challenge to herself. Her first attempt "was bad. I wanted to learn how to do them." She eventually found that the comic possibilities of the form were especially appropriate to her most frequent subject, human relationships. "I don't know if I was all that conscious of it," she says. "The humor emerges from the form. The rhyme accentuates it."

Gylys doesn't write exclusively in villanelles. *Bodies that Hum* features poems in other forms, such as sestinas, and a significant number in free verse. "People have talked about me as a New Formalist," she says, referring to a group of contemporary poets devoted to promoting traditional styles of verse. "I don't really think of myself that way. Form can be helpful, but I think I've written about similar subject matter in free verse."

"Personal"

I want a man whose body makes mine hum,
who when he looks my way the sky goes hazy.
Don't call me if you're boring, crude or dumb.

Discussions about sports teams turn me numb,
and men who can't stop talking drive me crazy.
I want a man whose body makes mine hum,

who sweetly cries my name out as we come,
a sensual man, whose touch makes me feel dizzy.
Don't call me if you're angry, cheap or dumb.

I like full lips, bare skin, long winter nights, some
good red wine. I like to spend a lazy
morning with a man who makes me hum.

I like to wade in fountains just for fun,
to decorate my hairband with a daisy,
skinny-dipping, hopscotch, playing dumb.

I love good jazz, dancing till I'm numb,
deep snow, strong wind, a girl dressed up in paisley.
I want a man whose body makes mine hum.
Don't call me if you're rigid, mean or dumb.

(from *Bodies that Hum*, 1999, Silverfish Review Press; reprinted by permission)

Gylys makes her living as a university professor. After earning a Ph.D. in English from the University of Cincinnati in 1997, she taught for three years at Mercyhurst College in Pennsylvania and now teaches in one of the country's leading writing programs, Georgia State University.

As a teacher, Gylys tries to be supportive of her students' work, to give them ample space to try out various approaches to writing poetry. "I'm not a dictator. I really encourage students to talk a lot. I think they like that," she says. "I try to take them where they are."

She urges beginning writers to read poetry as well as write it. "Many of them have never read poetry," she says, but it's essential for developing writers to get exposure to the great writing of the past. With graduate students, by contrast, she focuses more on creating "a space for writers to do their own thing."

Not content with the success of *Bodies that Hum*, Gylys is now hard at work on her second collection of poems, which is "definitely going to address relationships." It will be some time before the collection fully takes shape. *Bodies that Hum* was drawn from several years of work, and Gylys circulated it to more than fifty publishers and writing competitions before it was finally accepted.

Though she continues to work on new material, she does appreciate the positive feedback she's gotten on *Bodies that Hum*. "I'm really happy with how it turned out."

—Kevin Walzer

no subject matter, explicit sex and violence without craft, or abstract intellectualizing. We are not impressed by previous awards and publications." Has published poetry by Andrew Demcak, Antler, Simon Perchik, Rodger Moody, Denise Dumars, and Nancy Gannon. As a sample we selected these lines from "Nocturne for the Nocturnal" by Karl Tierney:

> *the redundancies of your male side—hostile indifference—/Are doomed to glorious basking in street*
> *light, no other./But you need not be beautiful, only self-sustaining.*

Skidrow Penthouse is 166 pgs., 5½ × 8½, professionally printed and perfect-bound with 2-color cover, includes original art and photographs as well as contest announcements, magazine advertisements. Receives about 500 poems/year, accepts 3%. Publish 35-40 poems/issue. Press run is 300 for 50 subscribers; 10% distributed free to journals for review consideration. Single copy: $10; subscription: $20. Make checks payable to Rob Cook or Stephanie Dickinson.

How to Submit: Submit 3-5 poems at a time. Accepts previously published poems and simultaneous submissions. "Include a legal sized SASE; also name and address on every page of your submission. No handwritten submissions will be considered." Time between acceptance and publication is 1 year. Seldom comments on rejected poems. Responds in 2 months. Pays 1 contributor's copy. Acquires one-time rights. Reviews books and chapbooks of poetry and other magazines in 1,500 words, single book format. Poets may send books for review consideration.

Also Offers: "We're trying to showcase a poet in each issue by publishing up to 60 page collections within the magazine." Send SASE for details about chapbook competitions.

◻ ◯ ◑ ◎ **SKIPPING STONES: A MULTICULTURAL CHILDREN'S MAGAZINE; ANNUAL YOUTH HONOR AWARDS (Specialized: bilingual, children/teen, ethnic/nationality, nature/ecology, social issues)**, P.O. Box 3939, Eugene OR 97403. (541)342-4956. E-mail: skipping@efn.org. Website: www.efn.org/~skipping (includes guidelines, sample poetry, and details on the Youth Honor Awards). Established 1988. **Editor:** Arun Toké.

Magazine Needs: *Skipping Stones* is a "nonprofit magazine published bimonthly during the school year (5 issues) that encourages cooperation, creativity and celebration of cultural and ecological richness." Wants poetry by youth under 19; 30 lines maximum on "nature, multicultural and social issues, family, freedom . . . uplifting." No work by adults. As a sample we selected these lines from "Dry Reflections" by Amanda Marusich, age 16 from Eugene, OR:

> *velvet green/carpets the wet dirt heavy with rain and a deep, rocky scent/clear, clean water/gushes*
> *over the riverbed with thunderous cascades/showers of mist/it is a vibrant/tangled/living web.*

Skipping Stones is 8½ × 11, saddle stapled, printed on recycled paper. Receives about 500-1,000 poems/year, accepts 10%. Press run is 3,000 for 1,700 subscribers. Subscription: $25. Sample: $5.

How to Submit: Submit up to 3 poems at a time. Accepts simultaneous submissions; no previously published poems. Accepts e-mail submissions included in body of message. Cover letter preferred. "Include your cultural background, experiences and what was the inspiration behind your creation." Time between acceptance and publication is up to 9 months. Poems are circulated to a 3-member editorial board. "Generally a piece is chosen for publication when all the editorial staff feel good about it." Seldom comments on rejected poems. Publishes theme issues. Guidelines and upcoming themes available for SASE. Responds in up to 4 months. Pays 1 contributor's copy, offers 25% discount for more. Acquires all rights. Returns rights after publication, but "we keep reprint rights."

Also Offers: Sponsors Annual Youth Honor Awards for 7-17 year olds. Theme for Annual Youth Honor Awards is "Multicultural and Nature Awareness." Deadline: June 20. Entry fee: $3 which includes free issue featuring winners. Details available for SASE.

☑ ◻ ◯ ◑ ◎ **SKYLARK (Specialized: themes)**, Purdue University Calumet, 2200 169th St., Hammond IN 46323. (219)989-2273. Fax: (219)989-2165. Established 1972. **Editor-in-Chief:** Pamela Hunter. **Poetry Editor:** Cathy Michniewicz.

Magazine Needs: *Skylark* is "a fine arts annual, one section (about 25 pages) of which is devoted to a special theme." *Skylark* publishes short stories, poetry, short essays, translations, illustrations, and photographs. Looking for "fresh voices, original images, concise presentation and honesty; poems up to 30 lines. No horror, nothing extremely religious, no pornography." Also interested in receiving more prose poems and more well-crafted surrealistic poems. Accepts poetry written by children, ages 5-18. Has published poetry by Sandra Fowler, Mick Kennedy, Charles Tinkham, Henry White, and Fredrick Zydek. As a sample the editor selected these lines from "Boys and Men" by Sandra Goldsmith:

> *Splayed across cold bushes,/little Perry cried/into spindly branches,/an unyielding autumn ground/the*
> *sole comfort for his pain.*

Published in December, *Skylark* is 100 pgs., magazine-sized, professionally printed, perfect-bound, with four-color cover and numerous color illustrations inside the magazine. Publishes 80 poems/issue. Press run is 900-1,000 for 50 subscribers of which 12 are libraries. Single copy: $8. Sample (back issues): $6.

How to Submit: Submit up to 6 poems at a time. "Cover letter encouraged. No previously published poems or simultaneous submissions. Inquire (with SASE) as to annual theme for special section." Accepts fax submissions followed by SASE within 2 weeks. The theme for 2002 is "Holidays, including Halloween." Guidelines and themes available for SASE. Mss are read between November 1 and April 30. Responds in 3 months. Pays 1 copy/published poem. Acquires first rights. Editor may encourage rejected but promising writers.

Advice: "Send poems with greater coordination of form and content, sharper, more original imagery and a carefully-edited text."

SLANT: A JOURNAL OF POETRY, Box 5063, University of Central Arkansas, 201 Donaghey Ave., Conway AR 72035-5000. (501)450-5107. Website: www.uca.edu/divisions/academic/english/Slant/HOMP AGE.html (includes guidelines, editor/board of readers, table of contents from 2001 volume, and index 1987-1996). Established 1987. **Editor:** James Fowler.

Magazine Needs: *Slant* is an annual using *only* poetry. Uses "traditional and 'modern' poetry, even experimental, moderate length, any subject on approval of Board of Readers; purpose is to publish a journal of fine poetry from all regions of the United States and beyond. No haiku, no translations." Accepts poetry written by children ("although we're not a children's journal.") Has published poetry by Alberto Ríos and Lois Marie Harrod. As a sample the editor selected these lines from "The French Language Tapes" by Richard Broderick:

> By the end of tape 4-B I'm ready to kill them:/Madame Durand and Monsieur Lelong/trying to decide
> where and at what time/to have lunch; Janine, the young woman/who will not fail to pass along M.
> Durand's/good wishes to her parents . . .

Slant is 125 pgs., professionally printed on quality stock, flat-spined, with matte card cover. Receives about 1,500 poems/year, accepts 70-80. Press run is 200 for 70-100 subscribers. Sample: $10.

How to Submit: Submit up to 5 poems of moderate length with SASE between September and mid-November. "Put name, address (including e-mail if available) and phone on the top of each page." No simultaneous submissions or previously published poems. Editor comments on rejected poems "on occasion." Allow 3-4 months from November 15 deadline for response. Pays 1 contributor's copy.

Advice: "I would like to see more formal and narrative verse."

SLAPERING HOL PRESS, 300 Riverside Dr., Sleepy Hollow NY 10591-1414. (914)332-5953. Fax: (914)332-4825. E-mail: info@writerscenter.org. Website: www.writerscenter.org (includes listing/brief description of publications, ordering info, contest guidelines). Established 1990. **Contact:** Stephanie Strickland and Margo Stever.

Book/Chapbook Needs: "Slapering Hol Press is the small press imprint of the Hudson Valley Writers' Center, created in 1990 to provide publishing opportunities for emerging poets who have not yet published a book or chapbook, and to produce anthologies of a thematic nature. Chapbooks are selected for publication on the basis of an annual competition judged by a nationally known poet." Recently published poetry by Andrew Krivak, Rachel Loden, Ellen Goldsmith, Lynn McGee, Paul-Victor Winters, and Pearl Karrer. As a sample the editors selected these lines from "The Osprey" by Andrew Krivak from his chapbook *Islands*:

> When the ebb falls slack and the bay has stopped/the wind to appease the mud and stiletto reeds/
> basking in the stench of dead low tide,//the yearly visitors use their oars and ride/the current in as it
> turns. I hear them talk/of food, the smell; the flies out there are cruel.

Slapering Hol Press publishes 1 chapbook/year. Chapbooks are usually 28-32 pgs., offset-printed, stapled or hand sewn, 80 lb. cover weight cover.

How to Submit: For submission guidelines, see separate listing for Slapering Hol Press Chapbook competition in the Contests & Awards section. Order sample chapbooks by sending $9.50 postage paid to Hudson Valley Writers' Center. (See separate listing for Hudson Valley Writers' Center in the Organizations section.)

SLATE & STYLE (Specialized: blind writers), Dept. PM, 2704 Beach Dr., Merrick NY 11566. (516)868-8718. Fax: (516)868-9076. E-mail: LoriStay@aol.com. **Editor:** Loraine Stayer.

Magazine Needs: *Slate & Style* is a quarterly for blind writers available on cassette, in large print, Braille and e-mail, "including articles of interest to blind writers, resources for blind writers. Membership/subscription is $10 per year, all formats. Division of the National Federation of the Blind." Poems may be "5-36 lines. Prefer contributors to be blind writers, or at least writers by profession or inclination, but prefer poems not about blindness. No obscenities. Will consider all forms of poetry including haiku. Interested in new talent." Has published poetry by Stephanie Pieck, Louise Hope Bristow, Janet Wolff, and Ken Volonte. As a sample the editor selected these lines from Meditation at a Water Pump" by David Plumlee:

> The villagers have gone elsewhere/Their water pails to fill,/And cold darkness settles over the sleepy
> town./The village square, alone, deserted, stands—/All except for that water pump—/That dusty, rusty,
> old water pump—/and the little old lady/Leaning on the handle—/Living alone in her memories.

The print version of *Slate & Style* is 28-32 pgs., magazine-sized, stapled, with a fiction and poetry section. Press run is 200 for 160 subscribers of which 4-5 are libraries. Subscription: $10/year. Sample: $2.50.

How to Submit: Submit 3 poems once or twice/year. No simultaneous submissions or previously published poems.Accepts fax and e-mail submissions; for e-mail, include text in body of message. Cover letter preferred. "On occasion we receive poems in Braille. I prefer print, since Braille slows me down. Typed is best." Do not submit mss in July. Editor comments on rejected poems "if requested." Guidelines available for SASE. Responds in "two weeks if I like it." Pays 1 contributor's copy. Reviews books of poetry. Poets may send books for review consideration.

Also Offers: Offers an annual poetry contest. Entry fee: $5/poem. Deadline: May 1. Write for details. Also holds a contest for blind children; write for details.

Advice: "Poetry is one of the toughest ways to express oneself, yet ought to be the easiest to read. Anything that looks simple is the result of much work."

✔ ◐ **SLIDE**, 309 Lullwater Dr., Wilmington NC 28403. Phone/fax: (910)395-4564. E-mail: Editors@Slidem ag.com. Website: www.slidemag.com. Established 1999. **Editors:** Aimee Lind and Jesse Waters. **Associate Editor:** Meggen Lyon.

Magazine Needs: *Slide*, appearing in October, is published "to bring forward good art to our subscribers in a fashion that ensures a wide range of provocative original voices in each issue. *Slide* is looking for poems that illuminate something about ourselves, or how we live; art which keeps us buoyant in the mass culture. No erudite, cryptic, self-loathing, or otherwise insular poetry." Has published poetry by Zarina Mullan Plath, Thomas David Lisk, Doug Martin, and Clyde Edgerton. As a sample the editor selected these lines from "A Few Notes on Leaving Someone to Die with Small Pox" by Doug Martin:

> Sooner or later, I had to leave./A chain-link fence of stars in the sky/disappearing in snow that fell/ like an enema bag from heaven/Fighting small pox, you the girl/that vomited about the room/stared out the window/at the old road grader.

Slide is 75 pgs., 6×9, perfect-bound with 80 lb. preset color cover. Press run is 3,000, Subscription: $11/year. Sample: $5.

How to Submit: Submit 3-5 poems at a time. Accepts simultaneous submissions; no previously published poems. Accepts e-mail and disk submissions but no fax submissions. "Disk and e-mail submissions must be in RTF, Word, or Word Perfect format. Please include SASE with proper postage or IRC coupons." Cover letter preferred. Reads submissions September 1 through May 31 only. Time between acceptance and publication is 1 year. Poems are circulated to an editorial board. Seldom comments on rejected poems. Publishes theme issues occasionally. Guidelines and upcoming themes available for SASE, by e-mail, or on website. Responds in 4 months. Pays 5 contributor's copies. Acquires all rights. Returns rights upon publication. Reviews books of poetry in 500 words, single book format.

Also Offers: "*Slide* occasionally publishes chapbooks, novels, novellas, plays, juried art shows, etc. in installment series. Artists should be aware of their eligibility to submit large pieces in confidence."

Advice: "Don't listen to anyone, send what is closest to your heart and mind."

◑ ◎ **SLIPSTREAM (Specialized: themes)**, Box 2071, New Market Station, Niagara Falls NY 14301-0071. (716)282-2616 (after 5PM, EST). E-mail: editors@slipstreampress.org. Website: www.slipstreampress.org (includes guidelines, announcements, samples of poetry, annual poetry chapbook winner, chapbook competition guidelines, audio/video information, back issues, and order form). Established 1980. **Poetry Editors:** Dan Sicoli, Robert Borgatti, and Livio Farallo.

Magazine Needs: *Slipstream* is a "small press literary mag published in the spring and is about 90% poetry and 10% fiction/prose, with some artwork. Likes new work with contemporary urban flavor. Writing must have a cutting edge to get our attention. We like to keep an open forum, any length, subject, style. Best to see a sample to get a feel. Like city stuff as opposed to country. Like poetry that springs from the gut, screams from dark alleys, inspired by experience." No "pastoral, religious, traditional, rhyming" poetry. Has published poetry by M. Scott Douglass, Johnny Cordova, Douglas Goetsch, Gerald Locklin, Alison Miller, Jim Daniels, James Snodgrass, and Chrys Darkwater. As a sample the editors selected these lines from "Song about a Girl" by Rachel Kuble:

> She was a population in exile once/& she came marching in long lines/over the green hills & the green hills shook/like falling cities under her feet.

Slipstream appears 1-2 times/year in a 7×8½ format, 80-100 pgs., professionally printed, perfect-bound, using b&w photos and graphics. It contains mostly free verse, some stanza patterns. Receives over 2,500 submissions of poetry/year, accepts less than 10%. Press run is 500 for 400 subscribers of which 10 are libraries. Subscription: $15/2 issues and 2 chapbooks. Sample: $6.

How to Submit: No e-mail submissions. Editor sometimes comments on rejected poems. Publishes theme issues. Guidelines and upcoming themes available for SASE. "Reading for a general issue through 2000." Responds in up to 2 months, "if SASE included." Pays 1-2 copies.

Also Offers: Annual chapbook contest has December 1 deadline. Reading fee: $10. Submit up to 40 pgs. of poetry, any style, previously published work OK with acknowledgments. Winner receives $1,000 and 50 copies. All entrants receive copy of winning chapbook and an issue of the magazine. Past winners have included Sherman Alexie, Katharine Harer, Robert Cooperman, Leslie Anne Mcilroy, Serena Fusek, Rene Christopher, Gerald Locklin, Alison Pelegrin, and most recently Laurie Mazzaferro for "Breaking the Captive's Fetters."

Advice: "Do not waste time submitting your work 'blindly.' Sample issues from the small press first to determine which ones would be most receptive to your work."

N ◐ **SLOPE**, E-mail: ethan@slope.org. Website: www.slope.org. Established 1999. **Editor:** Ethan Paquin.

Magazine Needs: *Slope* "is a bimonthly, online journal of poetry featuring work that is challenging, dynamic, and innovative. The main credo of *Slope* is that vital voices, from both new and established poets alike, must reach a wider audience via the electronic medium." Wants "no particular style. Interested in poetry being written in English around the world, as well as translations." Recently published poetry by Franz Wright, Heather McHugh, Dara Wier, James Tate, Charles Bernstein, Forrest Gander, and Lee Upton. Submit 3-6 poems at a time. No previously published poems; or simultaneous submissions. Accepts e-mail submissions or disk submissions. "Submit poems via e-mail to the address at the website." Reads submissions year round. Time between acceptance and publication is 3-6 months. Seldom comments on rejections.

How to Submit: Guidelines available by e-mail or on website. Responds in 3 months. Acquires one-time rights. Reviews books and chapbooks of poetry in 400 words, single book format. Poets may send books for review consideration; "query first."

N ◯ SLUGFEST, LTD., P.O. Box 1238, Simpsonville SC 29681. Established 1991. **Contact:** M.T. Nowak.
Book/Chapbook Needs: Wants "any type of poetry, less than 3 pages or 300 lines. No pornographic or bad work." Has published poetry by Conti, Semenovich, Nowak, and Arnold.
How to Submit: Submit 3-5 poems at a time. Accepts previously published poems and simultaneous submissions. Time between acceptance and publication is 6 months. Poems are circulated to an editorial board. Responds in 1 month. Always comments on rejected poems. Pays 1 copy. More details available for SASE.

■ ⊙ A SMALL GARLIC PRESS (ASGP); AGNIESZKA'S DOWRY (AgD), 5445 Sheridan #3003, Chicago IL 60640. E-mail: asgp@enteract.com or marek@enteract.com or ketzle@aa.net. Website: www.enteract .com/~asgp/. Established 1995. **Co-Editors:** Marek Lugowski, katrina grace craig.
Magazine Needs: *Agnieszka's Dowry (AgD)* is "a magazine published both in print and as a permanent Internet installation of poems and graphics, letters to Agnieszka, and a navigation in an interesting space, all conducive to fast and comfortable reading. No restrictions on form or type. We use contextual and juxtapositional tie-ins with other material in making choices, so visiting the online *AgD* is assumed to be part of any submission." Single copy: usually $3. Make checks payable to A Small Garlic Press.
How to Submit: Submit 5-10 poems at a time. "Please inform us of the status of publishing rights." E-mail submissions only, plain text ("unless poet doesn't have the means to e-mail us—then we will accept submissions by regular mail"). Sometimes comments on rejected poems. Guidelines available on website. Responds online usually in 2 months. Pays 1 contributor's copy. Acquires one-time rights where applicable.
Book/Chapbook Needs & How to Submit: A Small Garlic Press (ASGP) publishes 2-7 chapbooks of poetry/ year. Query with a full online ms, ASCII (plain text) only.
Also Offers: "See our webpage for policies and submission guidelines. The press catalog and page of links to other markets and resources for poetry and a Broadsides section are maintained online at our website. Chat and other features are expected soon."

⊘ SMALL POND MAGAZINE OF LITERATURE, P.O. Box 664, Stratford CT 06615. (203)378-4066. Established 1964. **Editor:** Napoleon St. Cyr.
Magazine Needs: *Small Pond Magazine of Literature* is a literary triquarterly that features poetry . . . "and anything else the editor feels is interesting, original, important." Poetry can be "any style, form, topic, except haiku, so long as it is deemed good, but limit of about 100 lines." Napoleon St. Cyr wants "nothing about cats, pets, flowers, butterflies, etc. Generally nothing under eight lines." *Small Pond* is 40 pgs., digest-sized, offset from typescript on off-white paper, with colored matte cover, saddle-stapled, artwork both on cover and inside. Press run is 300, of which about a third go to libraries. Subscription: $10/3 issues. Sample (including guidelines): $3 for a random selection, $4 current. "Random back issue for $1; same quality, famous editor's comments."
How to Submit: Doesn't want 60 pages of anything; "dozen pages of poems max." Name and address on each page. No previously published poems or simultaneous submissions. Brief cover letter preferred. Time between acceptance and publication is within up to 15 months. Responds in up to 30 days. Pays 2 copies. Acquires all rights. Returns rights with written request including stated use. "One-time use per request." All styles and forms are welcome here. The editor usually responds quickly, often with comments to guide poets whose work interests him.

✓ ⊘ SMARTISH PACE; ERSKINE J. POETRY PRIZE, P.O. Box 22161, Baltimore MD 21203. Website: wwwsmartishpace.com (includes interviews, samples, guidelines, links, contact information, poetry submission link, advertising rates, contest information, and more). Established 1999. **Editor:** Stephen Reichert.
Magazine Needs: *Smartish Pace*, published in spring and fall, contains poetry, translations, essays on poetry, reviews, and interviews. "*Smartish Pace* is an independent poetry journal and is not affiliated with any institution." No restrictions on style or content of poetry. Has published poetry by Mary Gillialand, David Kirby, Susan Wood, Stephen Cushman, Cleopatra Mathis, and David Wagoner. As a sample the editor selected "Metamorphosis" by Pulitzer Prize winner Henry Taylor:

> The bar in the attic closet/sags with jackets and trousers/from lives I barely remember.//My breath still
> short from the stairway,/I stack them up for the goodwill box./The dark air thickens with promise.

Smartish Pace is about 80 pgs., 6×9, professionally printed and perfect-bound with color, heavy stock cover, original artwork appears on the cover of each issue. Receives about 3,000 poems/year, accepts 3%. Publish 50-60 poems/issue. Press run is 500 for 300 subscribers. Subscription: $12. Sample: $6.

How to Submit: Submit no more than 6 poems at a time. Accepts simultaneous submissions; no previously published poems. "Please provide prompt notice when poems have been accepted elsewhere. Cover letter with bio and SASE is required. Electronic submissions are encouraged and can be made at the website." Accepts e-mail submissions. Submission deadlines: June 1 for fall issue, December 1 for spring issue. Submit seasonal poems 6 months in advance. Time between acceptance and publication is up to 1 year. Poems are circulated to an editorial board. "All poems are initially screened by editor Stephen Reichert and senior editor Daniel J. Todd. Promising poems are then considered by a four member editorial board." Guidelines available for SASE or on website. Responds in up to 8 months. Pays 1 copy. Acquires first rights. Encourages unsolicited reviews. Poets and publishers encouraged to send review copies. All books received will also be listed in the books received sections of each issue and at the website along with ordering information and a link to the publisher's website.
Also Offers: "*Smartish Pace* also hosts the prestigious annual Erskin J. Poetry Prize. Submit 3 poems with $5 entry fee in either check or money order made payable to *Smartish Pace*. Additional poems may be submitted for $1 per poem. No more than 7 poems may be submitted (7 poems = $5 + $4 = $9). Winners receive cash prizes and publication. See website for complete information."

⊕ **$**○✎ **SMITHS KNOLL**, 49 Church Rd., Little Glemham, Woodbridge, Suffolk IP13 0BJ England. Established 1991. **Co-Editors:** Roy Blackman and Michael Laskey.
Magazine Needs: *Smiths Knoll* is a magazine appearing 3 times/year. Looks for poetry with honesty, depth of feeling, lucidity, and craft. As a sample the editors selected these lines from "Cut Lip" by John Lynch:

> The way she held out her hand/As if to say Daddy, what's this?//I hushed her, wiped her tears,/It's only
> blood I said//Later, on the motorway,/streams of tail-lights pouring red.

Smiths Knoll is 60 pgs., A5, offset-litho, perfect-bound, with 2-color card cover. Receives up to 10,000 poems/year, "accepts about one in sixty." Press run is 500 for 350 subscribers. Single copy: £4.50; subscription: £12/3 issues (outside UK).
How to Submit: Submit up to 5 poems at a time to the co-editors. "We would consider poems previously published in magazines outside the U.K." No simultaneous submissions. Poems only. Doesn't commission work. "Cover letters should be brief: name, address, date, number of poems sent (or titles). We don't want life histories or complete publishing successes or what the poems are about. We do want sufficient IRCs for return of work. Constructive criticism of rejected poems where possible." Tries to respond within 1 month (outside UK). Pays £5 plus 1 copy/poem.

N ⊕ ✎ **SMOKE; SPIKE**, First Floor, Liver House, 96 Bold St., Liverpool L1 4HY England. Phone: (0151)709-3688. Established 1974. **Editor:** Dave Ward.
Magazine Needs: *Smoke* is a biannual publication of poetry and graphics. Wants "short, contemporary poetry, expressing new ideas through new forms." Has published poetry by Carol Ann Duffy, Roger McGough, Jackie Kay, and Henry Normal. *Smoke* is 24 pgs., A5, offset-litho printed and stapled with paper cover, includes art. Receives about 3,000 poems/year, accepts about 40 poems. Press run is 750 for 350 subscribers of which 18 are libraries, 100 shelf sales; 100 distributed free to contributors/other mags. Subscription: $5 (cash). Sample: $1. Make checks payable to Windows Project (cash preferred/exchanges rate on cheques not viable).
How to Submit: Submit 6 poems at a time. Accepts previously published poems and simultaneous submissions. Cover letter preferred. Time between acceptance and publication is 6 months. Seldom comments on rejected poems. Responds in 2 weeks. Pays 1 copy.
Book/Chapbook Needs & How to Submit: Spike publishes "challenging and 'non-literary' work—mainly Merseyside." Publishes 2 paperbacks and 3 chapbooks/year. Books are usually 64 pgs., A5, offset-litho printed and perfect-bound with laminated board cover, cover art only. Query first, with a few sample poems and a cover letter with brief bio and publication credits. Responds to queries and mss in 2 months. Pays 160 author's copies (out of a press run of 1,000).

⊕ ✎ ◎ **SNAPSHOTS; SNAPSHOT PRESS; TANGLED HAIR; SNAPSHOT PRESS COLLECTION COMPETITION; THE HAIKU CALENDAR COMPETITION (Specialized: form/style)**, P.O. Box 35, Sefton Park, Liverpool L17 3EG United Kingdom. E-mail: jb@snapshotpress.freeserve.co.uk. Website: www.mccoy.co.uk/snapshots (includes information on publications, reviews, sample poems, competition rates and entry forms, and submission and subscription guidelines). Established 1998. **Editor:** John Barlow.
Magazine Needs: Snapshot Press publishes two journals, *Snapshots* and *Tangled Hair*. *Snapshots* is published 3-4 times/year and *Tangled Hair* 2-3 times/year. Whereas *Tangled Hair* is the first journal published in the UK to be devoted exclusively to tanka. Both journals contain brief contributor biographies, a "Books Received and Recommended" section, and an award for the best poem in each issue as voted by readers. Poems are printed one to a page for maximum effect. It also contains brief biographies on its contributors, and there is an award for the best poem in each issue, as voted for by subscribers." *Snapshots* has published poetry by Tom Clausen, Janice Bostok, Garry Gay, and Christopher Herold. *Tangled Hair* has published poetry by Sanford Goldstein, Laura Maffei, Jane Reichhold, and Cherie Hunter Day. As a sample of work published in *Snapshots*, the editor selected this haiku by David Steele:

> long weekend alone/the click of buttons/in the wash cycle.

As a sample of work published in *Tangled Hair*, the editor selected this tanka by Phillip Rowland:

> wondering how much/she hides from me—/no telling/the first touch of dusk/this dark winter's day

Snapshots is 64-80 pgs., 4×6, professionally printed and perfect-bound with glossy card cover featuring a full-color photograph. *Tangled Hair*'s format is similar except it is 4×4. *Snapshots* receives about 4,000 poems/year (2,000 for *Tangled Hair*), accept 5% for each. Press run for both journals is 250-300. Subscription: $24. Sample of each publication: $12. Make checks payable to Snapshot Press. (US banknotes accepted.)

How to Submit: For *Snapshots*, submit up to 20 haiku/senryu; for *Tangled Hair*, submit up to 12 tanka at a time. No previously published poems or simultaneous submissions. Accepts e-mail submissions. Cover letter required. Submissions must be accompanied by a SAE and 2 IRCs. Time between acceptance and publication is up to 6 months. Sometimes comments on submissions. Guidelines available for SAE and IRC or by e-mail. Responds in 1 month. Always sends prepublication galleys. No payment. Acquires first rights.

Book/Chapbook Needs & How to Submit: Snapshot Press publishes 2-4 paperbacks and 4-8 chapbooks per year. Chapbooks are 32-40 pgs., 4×6, professionally printed, saddle-stitched with full-color glossy card covers. Order sample books by sending $10, or SAE and IRC for further details/order forms. One paperback and up to 4 chapbooks are selected biennially through the Snapshot Press Collection Competition. "No unsolicited manuscripts other than entries to Snapshot Press Collection Competition. All other material for anthologies and collections is solicited." Send SAE and IRC for catalog.

Also Offers: Sponsors two competitions: the Snapshot Press Collection Competition, for unpublished collections of haiku, senryu and tanka, held biennially. 1st Prize: $250 and publication of collection as a perfect-bound book; four runners-up: publication of collection as a full-color chapbook. The Haiku Calendar Competition is held annually (closing date July 31). Prize money: $600. Send SAE and IRC for rules/entry forms.

$ SNOWAPPLE PRESS, P.O. Box 66024, Heritage Postal Outlet, Edmonton, Alberta T6J 6T4 Canada. Established 1991. **Editor:** Vanna Tessier.

Book/Chapbook Needs: Snowapple Press is an "independent publisher dedicated to writers who wish to contribute to literature." Publishes 4-5 paperbacks/year. Wants "contemporary, expansive, experimental and literary poetry." Has published poetry by Gilberto Finzi, Peter Prest, Vanna Tessier, Bob Stallworthy, I.B. Iskov, and Paolo Valesio. Books are usually 120-160 pgs., offset-printed with #10 colored card cover with "art/graphics suitable to theme."

How to Submit: Submit 5 poems at a time, 14-70 lines each. Accepts previously published poems and simultaneous submissions. Cover letter preferred. Reads submissions September through March 31 only. Time between acceptance and publication is up to 18 months. Poems are circulated to an editorial board. Responds in 1 month. Pays 10% royalty, $100 honorarium, and 25 author's copies (out of a press run of 500).

Also Offers: Sponsors an occasional anthology contest. Send SASE (or SAE and IRC) with all correspondence. "Queries welcome for 10th anniversary 2001 Celebration Anthology to be available spring 2002."

$ SNOWY EGRET (Specialized: nature), P.O. Box 9, Bowling Green IN 47833. Established 1922 by Humphrey A. Olsen. **Contact:** editors.

Magazine Needs: Wants poetry that is "nature-oriented: poetry that celebrates the abundance and beauty of nature or explores the interconnections between nature and the human psyche." As a sample they selected the middle and final lines of "Night Song" by Conrad Hilberry:

> *All creatures/sleep,/except the fish./. . . all night long,/barracuda weave and angle/through the weeds,/
> bluefins rise, flash/in the broken moonlight,/and dive again./Sharks graze old wrecks,/and marlins/
> slice the dark.*

Snowy Egret appears twice/year in a 60-page, magazine-sized format, offset, saddle-stapled, with original graphics. Receives about 500 poems/year, accepts about 30. Press run is 800 for 500 subscribers of which 50 are libraries. Sample: $8; subscription: $12/year, $20/2 years.

How to Submit: Writer's guidelines available for #10 SASE. Responds in 1 month. Always sends prepublication galleys. Pays $4/poem or $4/page plus 2 copies. Acquires first North American and one-time reprint rights.

SO TO SPEAK: A FEMINIST JOURNAL OF LANGUAGE AND ART (Specialized: women/feminism), George Mason University, 4400 University Dr., MS 2D6, Fairfax VA 22030-4444. (703)993-3625. E-mail: sts@gmu.edu. Established 1991. **Poetry Editor:** Susan Gardner Dillon.

Magazine Needs: *So to Speak* is published 2 times/year. "We publish high-quality work about women's lives—fiction, nonfiction (including book reviews and interviews), b&w photography and artwork along with poetry. We look for poetry that deals with women's lives, but also lives up to a high standard of language, form and meaning. We are most interested in experimental, high-quality work. There are no formal specifications. We like work that takes risks successfully. No unfinished/unpolished work." Has published poetry by Marcella Durand, Jean Donnelly, Heather Fuller, Carolyn Forché, Allison Joseph, Jenn McCreary, and Elizabeth Treadwell. As a sample they selected these lines from "Sister Cell" by Allison Cobb:

> *close/vanish appear/kin knees sis/my toes is/divided half whole/live split to/cry sister/the pull*

So To Speak is 128 pgs., digest-sized, photo-offset printed and perfect-bound, with glossy cover, includes b&w photos and art, ads. Receives about 300 poems/year, accepts 10%. Press run is 1,300 for 40 subscribers, 50 shelf sales; 500 distributed free to students/submitters. Subscription: $11. Sample: $5.

How to Submit: Submit 3-5 poems at a time. Accepts simultaneous submissions; no previously published poems. Accepts disk submissions. Cover letter preferred. "Please submit poems as you wish to see them in print. We do have an e-mail address but do not accept e-mail submissions. Be sure to include a cover letter with contact info, publications credits, and awards received." Reads submissions August 15 through October 15 and December 31 through March 15 . Time between acceptance and publication is 6-8 months. Seldom comments on rejected poems. Occasionally publishes theme issues. Guidelines and upcoming themes available for SASE. Responds in 3 months if submissions are received during reading period. Pays 2 copies. Acquires one-time rights. Reviews books and chapbooks of poetry and other magazines in 750 words, single book format. Poets may send books for review consideration.

Also Offers: *So to Speak* runs an annual poetry contest. "Our 2000 judge was Judy Grahn."

Advice: "We are looking for poetry that, through interesting use of language, locates experiences of women."

SO YOUNG!; ANTI-AGING PRESS, INC., P.O. Box 141489, Coral Gables FL 33114. (305)662-3928. Fax: (305)661-4123. E-mail: julia2@gate.net. Established 1992 press, 1996 newsletter. **Editor:** Julia Busch.

Magazine Needs: *So Young!* is a bimonthly newsletter publishing "anti-aging/holistic health/humorous/philosophical topics geared to a youthful body, attitude, and spirit." Wants "short, upbeat, fresh, positive poetry. The newsletter is dedicated to a youthful body, face, mind and spirit. Work can be humorous, philosophical fillers. No off color, suggestive poems or anything relative to first night, or unrequited love affairs." *So Young!* is 12 pgs., 8½×11 (11×17 sheets folded), unbound. Receives several hundred poems/year, accepts 6-12. Press run is 700 for 500 subscribers. Subscription: $35. Sample: $6.

How to Submit: Submit up to 10 poems at a time. Accepts previously published poems and simultaneous submissions. Cover letter preferred. Time between acceptance and publication "depends on poem subject matter—usually 6-8 months." Guidelines available for SASE. Responds in 2 months. Pays 10 copies. Acquires one-time rights.

THE SOCIETY OF AMERICAN POETS (SOAP); IN HIS STEPS PUBLISHING COMPANY; THE POET'S PEN; PRESIDENT'S AWARD FOR SUPERIOR CHOICE (Specialized: religious), P.O. Box 3563, Macon GA 31205-3563. (478)788-1848. Fax: (478)788-0925. E-mail: DrRev@msn.com. Established 1984. **Editor:** Dr. Charles E. Cravey.

Magazine Needs: *The Poet's Pen* is a literary quarterly of poetry and short stories. "Open to all styles of poetry and prose—both religious and secular. No gross or 'X-rated' poetry without taste or character." Accepts poetry written by children. Has published poetry by Allen Walker, Najwa Salam Brax, Henry Goldman, and Elizabeth Hammill. As a sample the editor selected these lines from "Praise Song" by Norma Woodbridge:

> *The mountains rise in harmony, as they press against the sky./The jet blue lake, serene and still, the forests sing nearby.//The snows send anthems in the air, they greet a new day's morn;/And deer run wild in freedom's path, the trilliums are born.//How great the wonder of our God, His majesty to sing;/ The praises to His wondrous love, the gifts of joy to bring!*

The Poet's Pen uses poetry primarily by members and subscribers, but outside submissions are also welcomed. Sample copy: $15. Membership: $25/year.

How to Submit: Submit 3 poems at a time, include name and address on each page. "Submissions or inquiries will not be responded to without a #10 business-sized SASE. We do stress originality and have each new poet and/or subscriber sign a waiver form verifying originality." Accepts simultaneous submissions and previously published poems, if permission from previous publisher is included. Publishes seasonal/theme issues. Upcoming themes and guidelines available for SASE or by e-mail. Sometimes sends prepublication galleys. Editor "most certainly" comments on rejected poems.

Book/Chapbook Needs & How to Submit: In His Steps publishes religious and other books. Also publishes music for the commercial record market. Query for book publication.

Also Offers: Sponsors several contests each quarter which total $100-250 in cash awards. Editor's Choice Awards each quarter. President's Award for Superior Choice has a prize of $50; deadline is November 1. Also publishes a quarterly anthology that has poetry competitions in several categories with prizes of $25-100.

Advice: "We're looking for poets who wish to unite in fellowship with our growing family of poets nationwide. We currently have over 850 poets and are one of the nation's largest societies, yet small enough and family operated to give each of our poets individual attention and pointers."

SOLO FLYER; SPARE CHANGE PRESS, 3470 Wales NW, Suite A-6130, Massillon OH 44646. Established 1979. **Editor:** David B. McCoy.

Magazine Needs: *Solo Flyer* appears 3-5 times/year. It features the work of a single poet in each issue. Wants "poems with a common theme." Does not want poems "that lack punctuation and capitalization." *Solo Flyer* is 4 pgs., folded and photocopied. Receives about 100 poems/year, accepts about 2%. Publishes about 3 poems/issue. Press run is 100. Sample copy free for SASE.

How to Submit: Submit 5 poems at a time. Accepts previously published poems and simultaneous submissions. "Must include SASE." Reads submissions year-round. Time between acceptance and publication is 3 months. Seldom comments on rejected poems. Responds in 4 months. Always sends prepublication galleys. Pays 25 contributor's copies. Acquires one-time rights.

SOUL FOUNTAIN, 90-21 Springfield Blvd., Queens Village NY 11428. Phone/fax: (718)479-2594. E-mail: davault@aol.com. Website: www.TheVault.org (includes guidelines). Established 1997. **Editor:** Tone Bellizzi.

Magazine Needs: *Soul Fountain* appears 4 times/year and publishes poetry, art, photography, short fiction, and essays. "Open to all. Our motto is 'Fear no Art.' We publish all quality submitted work, and specialize in emerging voices. We are particularly interested in visionary, challenging and consciousness-expanding material. We are especially seeking poetry from North and South Dakota, Utah, Vermont, Alaska, Nevada, and Kansas for our 50 states issue. We're hungry for artwork, particularly small black on white drawings." Accepts poetry written by children, teens only. Has published poetry by Robert Dunn, Thomas Catterson, Jay Chollick, and Paula Curci. *Soul Fountain* is 28 pgs., 8½×11, offset-printed and saddle-stapled. Subscription: $10. Sample: $3.50. Make checks payable to Hope for the Children Foundation.
How to Submit: Submit 2-3 "camera-ready" poems at a time. One page in length for each piece maximum. No cover letters necessary. Accepts previously published poems and simultaneous submissions. Accepts e-mail submissions (include in body of message); when e-mailing a submission, it is necessary to include your mailing address. Time between acceptance and publication is 1 year. Theme issues for 2002 are as follows: March, Women's Voices; September, Dangerous Visions; January, Channeling the 21st Century; June All-USA. An updated list of themes is available for SASE. Pays 1 copy. "For each issue there is a release/party/performance, 'Poetry & Poultry in Motion,' attended by all poets, writers, artists, etc., appearing in the issue."
Also Offers: *Soul Fountain* is published by The Vault, "a not-for-profit arts project of the Hope for the Children Foundation; a growing, supportive community committed to empowering young and emerging artists of all disciplines at all levels to develop and share their talents through performance, collaboration, and networking."

SOUNDINGS EAST, Salem State College, Salem MA 01970. (978)542-6494. Established 1978. **Advisory Editor:** J.D. Scrimgeour.
Magazine Needs: "*Soundings East* is published twice a year by Salem State College. We accept short fiction, creative nonfiction, short reviews, and contemporary poetry. We publish both established and previously unpublished writers and artists. All forms of poetry welcome." Recently published poetry by Allison Joseph, Martín Espada, and Virgil Suarez. *Soundings East* is 64 pgs., digest-sized, flat-spined, b&w drawings and photos, glossy card cover with b&w photo. Receives about 500 submissions/year, accepts about 40-50. Press run is 2,000 for 120 subscribers of which 35 are libraries. Subscription: $10/year. Sample: $5.
How to Submit: Submit 5 poems at a time. Accepts simultaneous submissions with notification. Be prompt when notifying *Soundings East* that work was accepted elsewhere. Reads submissions September 1 through April 20 only. Fall deadline: November 20; spring: April 20. Responds within 4 months. Pays 2 copies. Rights revert to author upon publication.

SOUNDS OF A GREY METAL DAY; CREATIVE EXPRESSIONS PROJECT (Specialized: prisoners), % Jacqueline Helfgott, Dept. of Criminal Justice, Seattle University, 900 Broadway, Seattle WA 98122. (206)296-5477. Fax: (206)296-5997. E-mail: jhelfgot@seattleu.edu. Established 1993. **Outside Program Coordinator/Associate Professor of Criminal Justice:** Jacqueline Helfgott. **Inside Coordinator:** Patrick Bolt.
Magazine Needs: *Sounds of a Grey Metal Day* appears annually in November/December and publishes writing and art by prisoners and volunteers participating in the Creative Expressions Project. Welcomes "poetry by prisoners about anything or poetry about prisons/imprisonment." Accepts poetry written by children of incarcerated parents or relatives. *Sounds of a Grey Metal Day* is 75-85 pgs., magazine-sized, printed in "prison print shop" and saddle-stapled, textureed card stock cover, includes b&w drawings. Press run is 500. Single copy: $5. Make checks payable to Jackie Helfgott, money orders to CIPC.
How to Submit: Submit up to 3 poems at a time. No previously published poems or simultaneous submissions. Accepts fax and e-mail submissions. Accepts disk submissions. Cover letter preferred. Time between acceptance and publication varies. Poems are circulated to an editorial board. "Poems are circulated among committee of prisoners, volunteers, coordinators and selected by vote based on available space for outside submissions." Responds in 2 months. Pays 2 copies.

THE SOUNDS OF POETRY; THE LATINO POETS' ASSOCIATION (Specialized: bilingual/foreign language, ethnic/nationality), 2076 Vinewood, Detroit MI 48216-5506. (313)843-2352. E-mail: jacqueraesan@aol.com (queries only). Website: http://hometown.aol.com/jacqueraesan/myhomepage/business.html (includes information on regarding the magazine and the Latino Poets' Association). Established 1983. **Publisher/Editor:** Jacqueline Rae Sanchez.
Magazine Needs: *The Sounds of Poetry* is published 3 times/year to "promote throughout the world an awareness (through poetry) that we are quite diverse, yet the same. We all love, hurt, laugh, and suffer. We are open to all types of poetry with substance, grit, feeling; prefer one column and/or shorter poetry. Always in need of fillers. Do not want to see fluff, insincere gibberish, foul language, nor porn, although light erotica is acceptable." Accepts poetry written by children ages 14 and over. Has published poetry by s.t. kilgore splake, Liberty R.V. Daniels, Jessica Sanchez, John Payne Kincaid, and Nancy L. Dahl. As a sample the editor selected these lines from "In Search of Home" by Tumika Patrice Cain:

> When I was hungry/You fed me with your words/Spooning me knowledge and widsom for breakfast/
> Whetting my carnal appetite in the twilight/Easing those yearnings/With whispered dialogue/Until my
> belly swelled with fullness

The publisher says *Sounds of Poetry* is 24-32 pgs., digest-sized, saddle-stapled. "We use approximately 50-98 poems per issue representing at least 18 different states plus three or more other countries as well." Press run is 200. Subscription: $10. Sample: $5.

How to Submit: Submit 5 poems at a time. Accepts previously published poems ("only if credit is listed on poem sheet submitted"); prefer no simultaneous submissions. No e-mail submissions; e-mail queries only. Cover letter with titles of poems and bio preferred. "Type poems on an 8½×11 sheet of white paper, one poem per page unless submitting brief fillers (four titled fillers per sheet is OK), handwritten poems will be returned. Name, address, and phone number should appear on each sheet submitted." Reads submissions January through October only. Time between acceptance and publication can be from several months to a couple years. Seldom comments on rejected poems. Publishes theme issues. Theme for 2002 is childhood memories. Guidelines available for SASE. Responds in up to 6 months. Pays 1 copy to contributor, 2 to subscriber. Poets may send books for review consideration; "mark 'Review Copy' and enclose cover letter. We do not review excerpts of books/chapbooks."

Also Offers: "The Latino Poets' Association is a multicultural, multilingual, non-profit association whose 'purpose is to promote within the community and throughout the USA an appreciation and education of the writing/recitals of poetry by Latinos and those people who support the work of Latinos.' A person does not have to be Latino in order to join the L.P.A. Some L.P.A. poets write and recite only in Spanish, others write/recite in English, Spanish, and French." Yearly membership: $25. Members have the opportunity to read at scheduled events. The L.P.A. meets at the Bowen Branch Library-DPL, 3648 W. Vernor, Detroit MI, (313)297-9381. Send SASE for a schedule of L.P.A. events.

Advice: "Write poetry using the knowledge you have, research and expand, add your own feelings, emotions then take that same poetry to your ultimate heights. Write and rewrite until you are comfortable with your work. Attend poetry readings, listen closely to other poets as they read their material. Participate in open-mike readings, get feedback from other poets but ultimately use your own gut instincts."

N ▣ ◎ **SOUR GRAPES: ONLINE VINE FOR REJECTED WRITERS AND OTHER TOR-MENTED SOULS (Specialized)**, 26 Sheridan St., Woburn MA 01801-3542. E-mail: sandyberns@netscape.net. Website: members.NBCi.com/Sandyberns/sourgrapes.htm. Hardcopy established 1995, discontinued 1998, website established 1997. **Editor/Publisher:** Sandy Bernstein.

Needs: *Sour Grapes* website, published "haphazardly," is "dedicated to the discouraged, disgruntled, disillusioned, and dejected writers of the universe." Wants "insightful verse that is thought-provoking, creates an image or stirs a feeling. Poems don't have to be gripe-related, but should be of normal length—no epics, please. Almost any form style or subject is acceptable." Doesn't want " 'Experimental Poems' such as lines printed horizontally and vertically. If it looks like a crossword puzzle—don't send it here. No 'Gratuitous Profanity,' show us poetic language—not street talk."

How to Submit: Submit no more than 5 poems at one time. If submitting all haiku or very short poems, the limit is 5. Prefer e-mail submissions ("text in the body of the e-mail is preferred"). Please include cover letter with short bio and credits. Regular mail submissions should include SASE for return of mss. Often comments on rejected poems. Response time "may vary but will not be unreasonable." Guidelines available on the website. "Payment, none. We're too cheap. Our site is free and open to everyone."

Advice: "Only submissions that follow our guidelines will be considered."

🌐 ◗ **SOUTH–A POETRY MAGAZINE FOR THE SOUTHERN COUNTIES; WANDA PUBLI-CATIONS**, 75 High St., Wimborne, Dorset BH21 1HS England. Phone: (01202)889669. Fax: (01202)881061. E-mail: wanda@wanda.demon.co.uk. Established 1972.

Magazine Needs: *South* is published biannually "to give voice to poets writing in the South of England. As the magazine passes through the hands of several editorial groups, our policy is open." Accepts poetry written by children. Has published poetry by Ian Caws, Stella Davis, Finola Holiday, Elsa Corbluth, and Brian Hinton. *South* is 68 pgs., 6×9, litho-printed and saddle-stapled with gloss laminated, duotone cover, includes photographs. Receives about 1,000 poems/year, accepts about 10%. Press run is 400 for 200 subscribers of which 15 are libraries, 170 shelf sales; 15 distributed free to other magazines and reviewers. Single copy: £3.50; subscription: £6/2 issues, £11/4 issues. Make checks payable to Wanda Publications.

How to Submit: Submit 6 poems at a time. Accepts previously published poems; no simultaneous submissions. Accepts e-mail and disk submissions; include e-mail submissions in attached file. Cover letter preferred. Time between acceptance and publication is 5 months. Poems are circulated to an editorial board. "Each issue is selected by a different editorial group." Responds in 5 months. Pays 1 copy. Staff reviews books of poetry and other magazines in 400 words, multi-book format. Send books for review consideration.

THE OPENNESS TO SUBMISSIONS INDEX at the back of this book lists all publishers in this section by how open they are to submissions.

N **回** **🗂** **$🗆** THE SOUTH BOSTON LITERARY GAZETTE, P.O. Box 443, South Boston MA 02127. (617)426-0791. E-mail: johnshea@msn.com. Website: www.thesouthbostonliterarygazette.com (includes poetry and prose excerpts, guidelines, names of editors, prize descriptions, artwork). Established 1999. **Editor:** John Shea.

Magazine Needs: *The South Boston Literary Gazette* appears quarterly, dedicated to promoting quality work by both new and established writers. Very open to diversity in style, content, age groups. Does not want "acid ramblings; no extreme pornography (although foul language is considered); amateurish, grammatically disordered writing." Accepts poetry written by children. Recently published poetry by Leonard Peltier, W.D. Ehrhardt, Michael Brown, Lyn Lifshin, David Connolly, and Harris Gardner. As a sample the editor selected these lines from "What Better Way to Begin" by W.D. Ehrhardt:

> *You can just keep your rocket's red glare./And as for the bombs bursting in air,/with all that noise and fire and smoke/there has to be plenty of jagged steel/looking for someone to hit.*

The South Boston Literary Gazette is 70 pgs., magazine-sized, computer copied on 70 lb. higloss paper, perfect-bound, 80 lb. 4-color higloss cover. Also published in online format. Receives about 400 poems/year, accepts about 25%. Publishes about 25 poems/issue. Press run is 500 for 100 subscribers, 100 shelf sales; 50 are distributed free to contributors and donors. Single copy: $5; subscription: $20/year (4 issues). Sample: $6. Make checks payable to *The South Boston Literary Gazette*.

How to Submit: *The South Boston Literary Gazette* Submit up to 4 poems at a time. Maximum length for poetry is 3,000 words. Accepts previously published poems and simultaneous submissions. Accepts e-mail and disk submissions; no fax submissions. Cover letter is preferred. "Put name on each page, all pages numbered." Reads submissions at all times. Submit seasonal poems 1 month in advance. **Reading Fee: $2.** Time between acceptance and publication is 1-3 months. Poems are circulated to an editorial board, "four editors; independent reviews using a 1-3 grading system; roundtable discussions follow." Often comments on rejected poems. Guidelines are available in magazine, for SASE, by e-mail, or on website. Responds in up to 3 months. Sometimes sends prepublication galleys. Pays 1 contributor's copy. "Author and *Gazette* share rights."

Also Offers: Each issue awards at least two $50 prizes for poetry and prose.

Advice: "Interesting poetry can be blunt or devious, shocking or thoughtful; but greeting card sugar won't cut it. If you have 34 cents, a name, and a thought, send it."

◯ SOUTH CAROLINA REVIEW, English Dept., 801 Strode Tower, Clemson University, Box 340523, Clemson SC 29634-0523. (864)656-3151 or 656-5399. Fax: (864)656-1345. Established 1968. **Editor:** Wayne Chapman.

Magazine Needs: *South Carolina Review* is a biannual literary magazine "recognized by the *New York Quarterly* as one of the top 20 of this type." Will consider "any kind of poetry as long as it's good. No stale metaphors, uncertain rhythms, or lack of line integrity. Interested in seeing more traditional forms. Format should be according to new MLA Stylesheet." Has published poetry by Pattiann Rogers, J.W. Rivers, and Claire Bateman. *South Carolina Review* is 200 pgs., 6×9, professionally printed, flat-spined and uses about 8-10 pgs. of poetry in each issue. Reviews of recent issues back up editorial claims that all styles and forms are welcome; moreover, poems were accessible and well-executed. Press run is 600, for 400 subscribers of which 250 are libraries. Receives about 1,000 submissions of poetry/year, accepts about 10; has a 2-year backlog. Sample: $10.

How to Submit: Submit 3-10 poems at a time in an "8×10 manila envelope so poems aren't creased." No previously published poems or simultaneous submissions. "Editor prefers a chatty, personal cover letter plus a list of publishing credits." Do not submit during June, July, August, or December. Publishes theme issues. Responds in 3 months. Pays copies. Staff reviews books of poetry.

◐ **◎** THE SOUTHERN CALIFORNIA ANTHOLOGY (Specialized: anthology); ANN STANFORD POETRY PRIZES, c/o Master of Professional Writing Program, WPH 404, University of Southern California, Los Angeles CA 90089-4034. (213)740-3252. Established 1983.

Magazine Needs: *The Southern California Anthology* is an "annual literary review of serious contemporary poetry and fiction. Very open to all subject matters except pornography. Any form, style OK." Has published poetry by Robert Bly, Donald Hall, Allen Ginsberg, Lisel Mueller, James Ragan, and Amiri Baraka. *The Southern California Anthology* is 144 pgs., digest-sized, perfect-bound, with a semi-glossy color cover featuring one art piece. A fine selection of poems distinguish this journal, and it has an excellent reputation, well-deserved. The downside, if it has one, concerns limited space for newcomers. Press run is 1,500, 50% going to subscribers of which 50% are libraries, 30% are for shelf sales. Sample: $5.95.

How to Submit: Submit 3-5 poems between September 1 and January 1 only. No simultaneous submissions or previously published poems. All decisions made by mid-February. Guidelines available for SASE. Responds in 4 months. Pays 2 contributor's copies. Acquires all rights.

Also Offers: The Ann Stanford Poetry Prizes ($1,000, $200, and $100) have an April 15 deadline, $10 fee (5 poem limit), for unpublished poems. Include cover sheet with name, address, and titles as well as SASE for contest results. All entries are considered for publication, and all entrants receive a copy of *The Southern California Anthology*.

⬤ SOUTHERN HUMANITIES REVIEW; THEODORE CHRISTIAN HOEPFNER AWARD, 9088 Haley Center, Auburn University, Auburn AL 36849-5202. E-mail: shrengl@auburn.edu. Website: www.auburn.edu/english/shr/home.htm. Established 1967. **Co-Editors:** Dan Latimer and Virginia M. Kouidis.
Magazine Needs: *Southern Humanities Review* is a literary quarterly "interested in poems of any length, subject, genre. Space is limited, and brief poems are more likely to be accepted. Translations welcome, but also send written permission from the copyright holder." Has published poetry by Eamon Grennan, Donald Hall, Brendan Galvin, Susan Ludvigson, Andrew Hudgins, Bin Ramke, and Fred Chappell. *Southern Humanities Review* is 100 pgs., 6×9, press run 700. Subscription: $15/year. Sample: $5.
How to Submit: "Send 3-5 poems in a business-sized envelope. Include SASE. Avoid sending faint computer printout." No previously published poems or simultaneous submissions. No e-mail submissions. Responds in 2 months, possibly longer in summer. Always sends prepublication galleys. Pays 2 copies. Copyright reverts to author upon publication. Reviews books of poetry in approximately 750-1,000 words. Send books for review consideration.
Also Offers: Sponsors the Theodore Christian Hoepfner Award, a $50 award for the best poem published in a given volume of *Southern Humanities Review*.
Advice: "For beginners we'd recommend study and wide reading in English and classical literature, and, of course, American literature—the old works, not just the new. We also recommend study of or exposure to a foreign language and a foreign culture. Poets need the reactions of others to their work: criticism, suggestions, discussion. A good creative writing teacher would be desirable here, and perhaps some course work too. And then submission of work, attendance at workshops. And again, the reading: history, biography, verse, essays—all of it. We want to see poems that have gone beyond the language of slippage and easy attitudes."

✔ ⬤ SOUTHERN POETRY REVIEW; GUY OWEN POETRY PRIZE, English Dept., Central Piedmont Community College, Charlotte NC 28235. (704)330-6275. Fax: (704)330-6455. Established 1958. **Editor:** Ken McLaurin.
Magazine Needs: *Southern Poetry Review* a semiannual literary magazine "with emphasis on effective poetry. There are no restrictions on form, style or content of poetry; length subject to limitations of space." Has published work by R.T. Smith, Colette Inez, Dabney Stuart, Peter Cooley, and Susan Ludvigson. *Southern Poetry Review* is 80 pgs., 6×9, handsomely printed on buff stock, flat-spined with textured, one-color matte card cover. Press run is 1,000. Subscription: $10/year. Sample: $3.
How to Submit: Queries answered with SASE. Submit up to 3-5 poems at a time. Does not accept fax submissions. Reads submissions September 1 through May 31 only. Pays 1 contributor's copy. Acquires first-time rights. Staff reviews books of poetry. Send books for review consideration.
Also Offers: Also sponsors the annual Guy Owen Poetry Prize of $500. Entry fee is an $10 subscription; submission must be postmarked in April. Submit 3-5 poems with SASE.
Advice: "This is the type of literary magazine to settle back with in a chair and read, particularly during dry creative spells, to inspire one's muse. It is recommended as a market for that reason. It's a tough sell, though. Work is read closely and the magazine reports in a timely manner."

✔ ⬆ $⬤ THE SOUTHERN REVIEW, 43 Allen Hall, Louisiana State University, Baton Rouge LA 70803-5005. (225)578-5108. Fax: (225)578-5098. E-mail: bmacon@lsu.edu. Website: www.lsu.edu/guests/www tsm (includes guidelines, subscription information, current table of contents, relevant addresses, names, etc.). Established 1935 (original series), 1965 (new series). **Poetry Editors:** James Olney and Dave Smith.
● Work published in this review has been frequently included in *The Best American Poetry* and appeared in *The Beacon's Best of 1999*.
Magazine Needs: *The Southern Review* "is a literary quarterly that publishes fiction, poetry, critical essays, and book reviews, with emphasis on contemporary literature in the U.S. and abroad, and with special interest in southern culture and history. Selections are made with careful attention to craftsmanship and technique and to the seriousness of the subject matter. We are interested in any variety of poetry that is well crafted, though we cannot normally accommodate excessively long poems (say 10 pgs. and over)." Has published poetry by Norman Dubie, Margaret Gibson, Seamus Heaney, Yusef Komunyakaa, Susan Ludvigson, and Robert Penn Warren. The beautifully printed quarterly is massive: 6¾×10, 240 pgs., flat-spined, matte card cover. Receives about 6,000 submissions of poetry/year. All styles and forms seem welcome, although accessible lyric and narrative free verse appear most often in recent issues. Press run is 3,100 for 2,100 subscribers of which 70% are libraries. Subscription: $25. Sample: $8.
How to Submit: "We do not require a cover letter but we prefer one giving information about the author and previous publications." Prefers submissions of up to 4 pgs. No fax or e-mail submissions. Guidelines available for SASE or on website. Responds in 2 months. Pays $20/printed page plus 2 contributor's copies. Acquires first North American serial rights. Staff reviews books of poetry in 3,000 words, multi-book format. Send books for review consideration.

⬤ SOU'WESTER, Box 1438, Southern Illinois University, Edwardsville IL 62026. (618)650-3190. Established 1960. **Managing Editor:** Fred W. Robbins. **Associate Editor:** Nancy Avdoian.
Magazine Needs: *Sou'wester* appears twice/year. "We lean toward poetry with strong imagery, successful association of images, and skillful use of figurative language." Has published poetry by R.T. Smith, Susan

Swartwout, and William Jolliff. There are 30-40 pgs. of poetry in each 6×9, 100-page issue. *Sou'wester* is professionally printed, flat-spined, with textured matte card cover, press run is 300 for 500 subscribers of which 50 are libraries. Receives 3,000 poems (from 600 poets) each year, accepts 36-40, has a 6-month backlog. Subscription: $10/2 issues. Sample: $5.

How to Submit: Accepts simultaneous submissions. Does not read May 1 through September 1. Rejections usually within 4 months. Pays 2 copies. Acquires all rights. Returns rights. Editor comments on rejected poems "usually, in the case of those that we almost accept."

Advice: "Read poetry past and present. Have something to say and say it in your own voice. Poetry is a very personal thing for many editors. When all else fails, we may rely on gut reactions, so take whatever hints you're given to improve your poetry, and keep submitting."

THE SOW'S EAR POETRY REVIEW, 19535 Pleasant View Dr., Abingdon VA 24211-6827. (540)628-2651. E-mail: richman@preferred.com. Established 1988. **Editor:** James Owen. **Managing Editor:** Larry Richman.

Magazine Needs: *The Sow's Ear* is a quarterly. "We are open to many forms and styles, and have no limitations on length. We try to be interesting visually, and we use graphics to complement the poems. Though we publish some work from our local community of poets, we are interested in poems from all over. We publish a few by previously unpublished poets." Has recently published poetry by Charles Atkinson, Rhina P. Espaillat, Richard Hague, James T. McGowan, Dannye Romine Powell, and Jendi Reiter. As a sample, the editor selected these lines from "Geese in the Graveyard" by Judson Evans:

> They are calling us to the embarrassment/of prayer, to the aching adhesions/of unknown tongues.
> When they see their own/likenesses in marble slune, they bluster/without recognition, then sensing/the
> defenseless of words, raid/each niche for its eatable flowers.

The Sow's Ear Poetry Review is 32 pgs., 8½×11, saddle-stapled, with matte card cover, professionally printed. Receives about 2,000 poems/year, accepts about 100. Press run is 600 for 500 subscribers of which 15 are libraries, 20-40 shelf sales. Subscription: $10. Sample: $5.

How to Submit: Submit up to 5 poems at a time with SASE. Accepts simultaneous submissions if you tell them promptly when work is accepted elsewhere; no previously published poems. Enclose brief bio. No e-mail submissions. Guidelines available for SASE or by e-mail. Responds in up to 6 months. Pays 2 copies. Acquires first publication rights. Most prose (reviews, interviews, features) is commissioned.

Also Offers: Offers an annual contest for unpublished poems, with fee of $2/poem, prizes of $1,000, $250, and $100, and publication for 15-20 finalists. For contest, submit poems in September/October, with name and address on a separate sheet. Submissions of 5 poems/$10 receive a subscription. Include SASE for notification. 1998 Judge: Maggie Anderson. Also sponsors a chapbook contest in March/April with $10 fee, $1,000 1st Prize, publication, 25 copies and distribution to subscribers; 2nd Prize $200 and 3rd Prize $100. Send SASE or e-mail for chapbook contest guidelines.

Advice: "Four criteria help us to judge the quality of submissions: Does the poem make the strange familiar or the familiar strange or both? Is the form of the poem vital to its meaning? Do the sounds of the poem make sense in relation to the theme? Does the little story of the poem open a window on the Big Story of the human situation?"

$ SPACE AND TIME (Specialized: science fiction/fantasy, horror), 138 W. 70th St. (4B), New York NY 10023-4468. Established 1966. **Poetry Editor:** Linda Addison.

Magazine Needs: *Space and Time* is a biannual that publishes "primarily science fiction/fantasy/horror; some related poetry and articles. We do not want to see anything that doesn't fit science fiction/fantasy/weird genres." Has published poetry by Lyn Lifshin, Susan Spilecki, Mark Kreighbaum, and Cynthia Tedesco. As a sample we selected these lines from "Dark Waiting" by Catherine Mintz:

> An unceasing rain/lamp light gold in the gutters./I refold bat wings.

The issue of *Space and Time* we received was about 100 pgs., 5½×8½, perfect-bound. However, the magazine will be reformatted to 48 pgs., 8½×11, web press printed on 50 lb. stock and saddle-stapled with glossy card cover and interior b&w illustrations. Receives about 500 poems/year, accepts 5%. Press run is 2,000 for 200 subscribers of which 10 are libraries, 1,200 shelf sales. Single copy: $5; subscription: $10. Sample: $6.25.

How to Submit: Submit up to 4 poems at a time. No previously published poems or simultaneous submissions. Time between acceptance and publication is up to 9 months. Often comments on rejected poems. Poets may send SASE for guidelines "but they won't see more than what's here." Responds in up to 6 weeks, "longer if recommended." Pays 1¢/word ($5 minimum) plus 2 copies. Acquires first North American serial rights.

SPILLWAY, P.O. Box 7887, Huntington Beach CA 92615-7887. (714)968-0905. Established 1991. **Editors:** Mifanwy Kaiser and J.D. Lloyd.

Magazine Needs: *Spillway* is a biannual journal, published in March and September, "celebrating writing's diversity and power to affect our lives. Open to all voices, schools, and tendencies. We usually do not use writing which tells instead of shows, or writing which contains general, abstract lines not anchored in images. We publish poetry, translations, reviews, essays and b&w photography." Has published poetry by John Balaban, Sam Hamill,

Robin Chapman, Richard Jones, and Susan Terris. *Spillway* is about 176 pgs., digest-sized, attractively printed, perfect-bound, with 2-color or 4-color card cover. Press run is 2,000. Single copy: $9; subscription: $16/2 issues, $28/4 issues. Sample (including guidelines): $10. Make checks payable to *Spillway*.

How to Submit: Submit 3-6 poems at a time, 10 pages total. Accepts previously published work ("say when and where") and simultaneous submissions ("say where also submitted"). Cover letter including brief bio and SASE required. "No cute bios." Responds in up to 6 months. Pays 1 copy. Acquires one-time rights. Reviews books of poetry in 500-2,500 words maximum. Poets may send books for review consideration.

Advice: "We have no problem with simultaneous or previously published submissions. Poems are murky creatures—they shift and change in time and context. It's exciting to pick up a volume, read a poem in the context of all the other pieces, and then find the same poem in another time and place. And, we don't think a poet should have to wait until death to see work in more than one volume. What joy to find out that more than one editor values one's work. Our responsibility as editors, collectively, is to promote the work of poets as much as possible—how can we do this if we say to a writer you may only have a piece published in one volume and only one time?"

⊕ ◯ ◒ **SPIN; POETRY ORBITAL WORKSHOPS,** % Postal Agency, Ngakawau, Buller, New Zealand. Phone: 03 7828608. Established 1986. **Contact:** Leicester Kyle.

Magazine Needs: *SPIN* appears 3 times/year (March, July, November) and publishes poetry. "We have no hard and fast rules but appreciate poetry that excels in its form and content. No stereotyped, imitative, or boring work." Has published poetry by George Gott, Catherine Maur, John O'Connor, and Joanna Weston. As a sample the editor selected these lines from "Like Florida" by David Gregory:

> No new ways of telling time,/winking heart monitor digitals,/cruel and precise./Autumn is made
> apocryphal,/she extends herself south,/ahead of the shadows.

SPIN is 72 pgs., A5, photocopied and saddle-stapled with light card cover. Receives about 600 poems/year, accepts about 25%. Press run is 160 for 130 subscribers of which 6 are libraries. Single copy: NZ 6.50; subscription: NZ 20. Sample: NZ 5.

How to Submit: "We expect contributors to subscribe/purchase. We are unable to supply contributors copies." Submit approximately 6 poems at a time. No previously published poems or simultaneous submissions. Cover letter preferred. "All submissions returned at each publication." Time between acceptance and publication is 1 month. Sometimes comments on rejected poems. Publishes theme issues. Responds within 3 months. Reviews books of poetry in 1-page (or more), or in multi 3-4 line notices. Poets may send books for review consideration.

Also Offers: Subscription covers (optional) membership in poetry orbital workshops. "Each workshop or 'orbit' comprises four or five poets who by post submit poems to each other for reading and comment." Send SASE (or SAE and IRC) for details.

◪ **SPINDRIFT,** Shoreline Community College, 16101 Greenwood Ave. N., Seattle WA 98133. (206)546-5864. Established 1962. **Faculty Advisor:** varies each year, currently Carol Orlock.

Magazine Needs: *Spindrift* is open to all varieties of poetry except greeting card style. Has published poetry by Lyn Lifshin, Mary Lou Sanelli, James Bertolino, Edward Harkness, and Richard West. *Spindrift*, an annual, is 125 pgs., handsomely printed in an 8" square, flat-spined. Press run is 500. Single copy: $6.50. Sample: $5.

How to Submit: "Submit two copies of each poem, six lines maximum. The author's name should not appear on the submitted work. Include SASE and cover letter with 2-3 lines of biographical information including name, address, phone number, e-mail address, and a list of all materials sent. We accept submissions postmarked by February 1; editorial responses are mailed by March 15." Guidelines available for SASE. Pays 2 copies. All rights revert to author upon publication.

Advice: "Read what the major contemporary poets are writing. Read what local poets are writing. Be distinctive, love the language, avoid sentiment."

◪ ◓ **SPINNING JENNY,** Black Dress Press, P.O. Box 213, New York NY 10014. Website: www.blackdress press.com (includes guidelines, address/contact information, subscription, links, author bios, etc.). Established 1994. First issue Fall 1995. **Editor:** C.E. Harrison.

Magazine Needs: *Spinning Jenny* appears once/year. Has published poetry by Denise Duhamel, Matthew Lippman, Michael Loncar, Sarah Messer, and a play by Jeff Hoffman. As a sample the editor selected these lines from "Infidelity" by Michael Morse:

> The stranger takes off his shirt,/and in your own good mind it's the kiss.//When you lean forward and
> close the eyes,/the stars and their just torments/wheel off to the somewhere-else.

Spinning Jenny is 96 pgs., 5¼×9¼, perfect-bound with heavy card cover. "We accept less than 5% of unsolicited submissions." Press run is 1,000. Single copy: $8; subscription: $15/2 issues. Sample: $8.

How to Submit: No previously published poems; simultaneous submissions not encouraged. Accepts e-mail submissions (include in body of message). Seldom comments on rejected poems. Guidelines available for SASE or on website. Responds within 2 months. Pays contributor copies. Authors retain rights.

◪ **THE SPIRIT THAT MOVES US; THE SPIRIT THAT MOVES US PRESS,** P.O. Box 720820-PM, Jackson Heights, Queens NY 11372-0820. (718)426-8788. Established 1974. **Poetry Editor:** Morty Sklar.

Magazine Needs & How to Submit: *"The Spirit That Moves Us* will be continuing its *Editor's Choice* series and publishing regular issues only occasionally. *Editor's Choice* consists of selections from other literary magazines and small presses, where we choose from nominations by the editors of those magazines and presses." Has published poetry by Steve Kowit, Naomi Shibab Nye, Wendell Berry and Dorothy Allison. As a sample the editor selected these lines from "Everybody Says Hello" by Bob Jacob:

> Sometimes when the trees out back/Talk to one another/And the sky rumbles just before rain,/I'll stand at the window and listen./Sometimes, everybody says hello.

That poem appeared in *The Day Seamus Heaney Kissed My Cheek in Dublin* by Bob Jacob, which they offer as a sample for $8 plus $1 postage (regularly $12 plus $1.50 postage) or their *15th Anniversary Collection* for $6 and free shipping. Publishes theme issues. Upcoming themes and time frames are available for SASE.

Advice: "Write what you would like to write, in a style (or styles) which is/are best for your own expression. Don't worry about acceptance, though you may be concerned about it. Don't just send work which you think editors would like to see, though take that into consideration. Think of the relationship between poem, poet, and editor as personal. You may send good poems to editors who simply do not like them, whereas other editors might."

■ □ ◎ SPISH (Specialized: fish stories, poetry related to fishing), % Progressive, 5785 Yucca Lane North, Minneapolis MN 55446. E-mail: spishmagazine@aol.com. Website: www.spish.com (includes poetry and stories, art and photography, submission guidelines, about the editors, past issues, and links). Established 1999. **Contact:** editors.

Magazine Needs: *Spish* is an electronic magazine featuring fish stories, poetry, art, and photography. Appears "as we find time to produce it. We publish alternative, edgy, humorous poetry and short prose with a tie to fishing; along the lines of Brautigan, Bukowski, or Jim Harrison. We aren't likely to publish rhyming or greeting card verse. If we have to read it twice to 'get it,' it probably won't make it." Has published poetry by Charlie Bukowski, Bill Meissner, and Michael Hall. As a sample the editor selected this poem, "The Ice Fisherman" by Michael Hall:

> They sit on stools/like cats/staring into a mouse hole./Thinking perhaps,/about the unpaid loan/or the unfaithful wife,/praying/that there's something/down there/that will get them through/another winter.

How to Submit: Submit 3-5 poems at a time. Accepts previously published poems and simultaneous submissions. E-mail submissions preferred (in body of message with "Submissions" in subject line.) Include brief bio (less than 3 sentences). Time between acceptance and publication is up to 4 months. Poems are circulated to an editorial board. Often comments on rejected poems. Guidelines are available on website. Responds in 1 month. Acquires one-time rights and anthology rights.

Advice: "Spend more time focusing on the story rather than the language. Write something that will be fun to read!"

☑ ⊕ □ SPLIZZ, 4 St. Marys Rise, Burry Port, Carms SA16 OSH Wales. E-mail: a_jmorgan@yahoo.co.uk. Website: www.stmarys4.freeserve.co.uk (includes general information about *Splizz* as well as a sample issue). Established 1993. **Editor:** Amanda Morgan.

Magazine Needs: *Splizz*, published quarterly, features poetry, prose, reviews of contemporary music and background to poets. Wants "any kind of poetry. We have no restrictions regarding style, length, subjects." However, they do not want "anything racist or homophobic." Has published poetry by writers from throughout the world. *Splizz* is 40-44 pgs., A5, saddle-stapled with art and ads. Receives about 200-300 poems/year, accepts about 90%. Press run is 150 for 35 subscribers. Single copy: £1.30, 5 IRCs elsewhere; subscription: £5 UK, £10 elsewhere. Sample: £1.30 UK, 5 IRCs elsewhere. Make checks payable to Amanda Morgan (British checks only).

How to Submit: Submit 5 poems, typed submissions preferred. Include SAE with IRCs. Accepts previously published poems and simultaneous submissions. Accepts e-mail submissions in attached file. Cover letter required with short bio. Time between acceptance and publication is 4 months. Often comments on rejected poems. Charges criticism fee: "Just enclose SAE/IRC for response, and allow one to two months for delivery." Guidelines available for SASE (or SAE and IRC). Responds in 2 months. Sometimes sends prepublication galleys. Reviews books or chapbooks of poetry or other magazines in 50-300 words. Poets may send books for review consideration. E-mail for further enquiries.

Advice: "Beginners seeking to have their work published, send your work to *Splizz*, as we specialize in giving new poets a chance."

⒩ ⊕ ◖ SPOKES, 319a Hills Rd., Cambridge, Cambs CB22QT United Kingdom. Phone: (44)1223-243657. Established 1982. **Contact:** Alistair and Gina Wisker.

Magazine Needs: *Spokes*, published biannually, contains "general poetry—international and national." They have published poetry by Les Murray and Peter Porter. The editor says *Spokes* is 50 pgs. with graphics. They receive about 1,000 poems a year, accept approximately 10%. Press run is 400 for 200 subscribers of which 20 are libraries; 20 distributed free. Subscription: £4.50. Sample: £3.

How to Submit: Although not required, the editor prefers contributors to purchase a copy. Submit up to 5 poems at a time. Accepts previously published poems; no simultaneous submissions. Cover letter preferred. Time between acceptance and publication is 3 months. Poems are circulated to an editorial board of 2. Seldom comments on rejections. Guidelines available for SASE (or SAE and IRC). Staff reviews books or chapbooks of poetry or other magazines. Poets may send books for review consideration.

Advice: The editor says, "We prefer shorter poems. International submissions are encouraged."

🔵 **THE SPOON RIVER POETRY REVIEW; EDITORS' PRIZE CONTEST**, 4240/English Dept., Illinois State University, Normal IL 61790-4240. Website: www.litline.org/spoon (includes guidelines, cover art, contest guidelines, subscription information, and poems). Established 1976. **Editor:** Lucia Getsi.

Magazine Needs: *Spoon River Poetry Review* is a "poetry magazine that features newer and well-known poets from around the country and world." Also features 1 Illinois poet/issue at length for the magazine's Illinois Poet Series. "We want interesting and compelling poetry that operates beyond the ho-hum, so-what level, in any form or style about anything; language that is fresh, energetic, committed, filled with a strong voice that grabs the reader in the first line and never lets go." Also uses translations of poetry. Has published poetry by Stuart Dybek, George Kalamaras, Leslie Andrienne Miller, Allison Joseph, Sheryl St. Germain, and Rachel Levine. *Spoon River Poetry Review* appears biannually, 128 pgs., digest-sized, laser set with card cover using photos, ads. Receives about 3,000 poems a month, accepts 1%. Press run is 1,500 for 700 subscribers, of which 100 are libraries and shelf sales. Subscription: $15. Sample (including guidelines): $10.

How to Submit: "No simultaneous submissions unless we are notified immediately if a submission is accepted elsewhere. Include name and address on every poem." Do not submit mss May 1 through September 1. Editor comments on rejected poems "many times, if a poet is promising." Responds in 2 months. Pays a year's subscription. Acquires first North American serial rights. Reviews books of poetry. Send books for review consideration.

Also Offers: Sponsors the Editor's Prize Contest for previously unpublished work. One poem will be awarded $1,000 and published in the fall issue of *Spoon River Poetry Review*, and two runners-up will receive $100 each and publication in the fall issue. Entries must be previously unpublished. Entry fee: $16, including 1-year subscription. Deadline: April 15. Write for details. Recent winners were Kathleen Lynch and Aleida Rodríguez.

N 🔵 **SPORT LITERATE**, P.O. Box 577166, Chicago IL 60657-7166. Website: www.sportliterate.org. Established 1995. **Editor:** William Meiners. **Poetry Editor:** Frank Van Zant.

Magazine Needs: *Sport Literate*, published biannually, "covers leisure/sport life outside the daily grind of making a living. Stay out of your sentimental backyard where you had that eternal game of catch with dad. But don't avoid the image if it burns like a house fire. Be richly literary, but don't avoid fun. Avoid heady stuff that says nothing which matters. Send quality." Recently published poetry by Bob Harrison, Marilyn Kallet, and Ron McFarland. As a sample the editor selected these lines from "Baseball: A Short History" by Robert L. Harrison:

> *The dark ages came and went,/with no night games played,/and little was known about/the bunt or hit and run/as the monks sold fine wine.*

Sport Literate is digest-sized with glossy cover. Receives about 500 poems/year, accepts 2%. Publishes about 3-4 poems/issue. Press run is 1,500. Single copy: $7.75; subscription: $20/4 issues. Make checks payable to *Sport Literate*.

How to Submit: Submit 3 poems at a time. Accepts simultaneous submissions; no previously published poems. No e-mail or disk submissions. Reads submissions year round. Submit seasonal poems 4 months in advance. Time between acceptance and publication is up to 6 months. Often comments on rejected poems. Occasionally publishes theme issues. Guidelines available for SASE, by e-mail, or on website. Responds in 5 weeks. Always sends prepublication galleys. Pays 2 contributor's copies. Acquires first North American serial rights.

◎ **SPRING: THE JOURNAL OF THE E.E. CUMMINGS SOCIETY (Specialized: membership/subscription)**, 33-54 164th St., Flushing NY 11358-1442. (718)353-3631 or (718)461-9022. Fax: (718)353-4778. **Editor:** Norman Friedman.

Magazine Needs: *Spring* is an annual publication, usually appearing in fall, designed "to maintain and broaden the audience for cummings and to explore various facets of his life and art." Wants poems in the spirit of Cummings, primarily poems of one page or less. Nothing "amateurish." Has published poetry by John Tagliabue, Ruth Whitman, M.L. Rosenthal, William Jay Smith, and Theodore Weiss. *Spring* is about 180 pgs., 5½ × 8½, offset and perfect-bound with light card stock cover. Press run is 700 for 200 subscribers of which 15 are libraries, 450 shelf sales. Subscription or sample: $17.50.

How to Submit: No previously published poems or simultaneous submissions. Accepts fax submissions. Cover letter required. Reads submissions January through March only. Seldom comments on rejected poems. Responds in 6 months. Pays 1 copy.

Advice: "Contributors are encouraged to subscribe."

🔲 ◎ **SPRING TIDES (Specialized: children)**, Savannah Country Day School, 824 Stillwood Dr., Savannah GA 31419-2643. (912)925-8800. Fax: (912)920-7800. E-mail: Houston@savcds.org. Website: www.savcds.org. Established 1989. **Contact:** Connie Houston.

Magazine Needs: *Spring Tides* is an annual literary magazine by children 5-12 years of age. "Children from ages five through twelve may submit material. Please limit stories to 1,200 words and poems to 20 lines. All material must be original and created by the person submitting it. A statement signed by the child's parent or teacher attesting to the originality must accompany all work." *Spring Tides* is 28 pgs., digest-sized, attractively printed and saddle-stapled with glossy card cover, includes b&w and 4-color art. Press run is 500; given to students at Savannah Country Day School and sold to others. Single copy: $5.

How to Submit: Accepts simultaneous submissions. SASE required. "Poems with or without illustrations may be submitted." Reads submissions January through August only. Poems are circulated to an editorial board. Always comments on rejected poems. Guidelines available for SASE. Responds in 4 months. Pays 1 copy.

☑ $ Ⓩ ◎ **SPS STUDIOS, INC., PUBLISHERS OF BLUE MOUNTAIN ARTS®** (Specialized: greeting cards), Dept. PM, P.O. Box 1007, Boulder CO 80306-1007. Fax: (303)447-0939. E-mail: editorial@spsstudios.com. Established 1971. **Contact:** editorial staff.

Book/Chapbook Needs: SPS Studios publishes greeting cards, calendars, prints, and mugs. Looking for poems, prose, and lyrics ("usually nonrhyming") appropriate for publication on greeting cards and in poetry anthologies. "Poems should reflect a message, feeling, or sentiment that one person would want to share with another. We'd like to receive creative, original submissions about love relationships, family members, friendships, philosophies, and any other aspect of life. Poems and writings for specific holidays (Christmas, Valentine's Day, etc.) and special occasions, such as graduation, anniversary, and get well are also considered. Only a small portion of the material we receive is selected each year and the review process can be lengthy, but be assured every manuscript is given serious consideration."

How to Submit: Submissions must be typewritten, 1 poem/page or sent via e-mail. Enclose SASE if you want your work returned. Simultaneous submissions "discouraged but OK with notification." Submit seasonal material at least 4 months in advance. Guidelines available for SASE or by e-mail. Responds in up to 6 months. Pays $200/poem all rights for each of the first 2 submissions chosen for publication (after which payment scale escalates), for the worldwide, exclusive right, $25/poem for one-time use in an anthology.

Advice: "We strongly suggest that you familiarize yourself with our products before submitting material, although we caution you not to study them too hard. We do not need more poems that sound like something we've already published. Overall, we're looking for poetry that expresses real emotions and feelings."

☑ ◖ Ⓩ **SPUNK**, Box 55336, Hayward CA 94545. (415)974-8980. Established 1996. **Editor:** Violet Jones.

Magazine Needs: Appearing 2 times/year, *Spunk: The Journal of Unrealized Potential* contains "writings and artwork of every nature. We are an outlet for spontaneous expressions only. Save the self-satisfied, over-crafted stuff for *The New Yorker*, please." Accepts poetry written by children. *Spunk* is 30-50 pgs. though "its size varies; silkscreened and photocopied, hand bound, no ads." Receives about 800-1,000 poems/year, accepts 10%. Press run is 500; all distributed free to anyone who really, really wants them. Sample: $1. No checks.

How to Submit: Submit any number of poems at a time. No previously published poems or simultaneous submissions. Cover letter preferred. "Just make us happy we opened the envelope—how you do this is up to you." Time between acceptance and publication is up to 1 year. Poems are circulated to an editorial board. "Our extremely small staff gets together now and then, we drink large amounts of coffee/tea and work through the 'in' pile until we have a zine." Often comments on rejected poems. Occasionally publishes theme issues. Guidelines and upcoming themes available for SASE. Responds in up to 1 year. Pays 1 contributor's copy. Acquires first North American serial rights. Staff occasionally reviews books and chapbooks of poetry and other magazines in 100-500 words, single book format. Send books for review consideration. "Our review section has expanded, we run reviews every issue now."

☑ ⊕ $ ◻ Ⓩ ◎ **STAND MAGAZINE; NORTHERN HOUSE; STAND MAGAZINE BIEN-NIAL POETRY COMPETITION** (Specialized: translations), School of English, University of Leeds, Leeds LS2 9JT England. Phone: +44 (0)113 233 4794. Fax: +44 (0)113 233 4791. E-mail: stand@english.novell.leeds.ac.uk. Website: saturn.vcu.edu/~dlatane/stand.html (includes the history of the magazine, current competition winners, and entry forms to download, subscription details, contents lists and cover images, information about the editors and poetry links). **Contact:** Mr. Michael Hulse and John Kinsella. **US editor:** David Latané. Department of English, VCU, Richmond VA 23284-2005. E-mail: dlatane@vcu.edu.

Magazine Needs: *Stand*, established by Jon Silkin in 1952, is a highly esteemed literary quarterly. *Stand* seeks more subscriptions from US readers and also hopes that the magazine will be seriously treated as an alternative platform to American literary journals. The New Series edited by Michael Hulse and John Winsella has published poems by such poets as Michael Hamburger, Wole Soyinka, Penelope Shuttle, Peter Porter, Ruth Padel, and Christopher Hope. *Library Journal* calls *Stand* "one of England's best, liveliest, and truly imaginative little magazines." Among better-known American poets whose work has appeared here are John Ashbery, Mary Jo Bang, Brian Henry, and Michael Mott. Poet Donald Hall says of it, "among essential magazines, there is Jon Silkin's *Stand*, politically left, with reviews, poems, and much translation from continental literature." Its current format is 9²/₁₀×6 (portrait), flat-spined, 128 pgs., professionally printed on smooth stock with matte color cover and uses ads. Press run is 4,500 for 2,800 subscribers of which 600 are libraries. Subscription: $49.50. Sample: $13.

How to Submit: No fax or e-mail submissions. Cover letter required with submissions, "assuring us that work is not also being offered elsewhere." Publishes theme issues. Always sends prepublication galleys. Pays £25/

poem (unless under 6 lines) and 1 copy (⅓ off additional copies). Acquires first world serial rights for 3 months after publication. If work(s) appear elsewhere *Stand*/Northern House must be credited. Reviews books of poetry in 3,000-4,000 words, multi-book format. Poets may send books for review consideration.

Also Offers: Sponsors the *Stand* Magazine Biennial Poetry Competition during even-numbered years. 1st Prize: £1,500. Send SASE (or SAE and IRC) for rules.

N ⊕ ◐ STAPLE, Padley Rise, Nether Padley, Grindleford, Hope Valley, Derbys S32 2HE United Kingdom. Phone: 01433-631949. Established 1982. **Co-Editor:** Ann Atkinson and Elizabeth Barrett.

Magazine Needs: This literary magazine appears 3 times/year including supplements. "Nothing barred: Evidence of craft, but both traditional and modernist accepted." Has published poetry by Richard Epstein, Ulf Goebel, William Oxley, D.A. Prince, and Christine McNeill. As a sample they selected these lines from "Haunting" by Janet Loverseed:

> When I'm dead, please do try on all my clothes/And ransack all my cupboards. Seek my life./Don't be
> the squeamish type, the sort who loathes/To look in secret drawers or use a knife/To prise the locks
> that guard dark hidden things.

Staple is professionally printed, flat-spined, 90 pgs., with card cover. Receives 10,000 poems/year, accepts about 2%. Press run is 800 for 350 subscribers. Subscription: £14 (surface), £17.50 (air). Sample: £3.

How to Submit: Submit 6 poems at a time. No simultaneous submissions or previously published poems. Cover letter preferred. Editors sometimes comment on rejected poems. Submission deadlines are end of March, July, and November. Responds in up to 3 months. Sometimes sends prepublication galleys. Pays overseas writers complimentary copies.

Also Offers: Send SASE (or SAE with IRC) for *Staple First Editions* collections (sample: £8). Published collections include *Two Plus Two* by Ruth Sharman, et al. Also produces (to order) poetry postcards of poetry published in the magazine.

Advice: "In general, we don't go for haiku, performance pieces, concrete poetry, 'found' items."

N ◯ ◐ STATE STREET REVIEW, FCCJ North, 4501 Capper Rd., Jacksonville FL 32218. (904)766-6697. Fax: (904)766-6654. E-mail: hdenson@fccj.cc.fl.us. Website: www.fccj.org/wf/. Established 1990. **Poetry and Fiction Editor:** Howard Denson, Brian Hale, Sohrab Fracis, and Michele Boyette.

Magazine Needs: A biannual that "sometimes has to settle for being an annual," *State Street Review* strives "to publish the best prose and poetry that we can get our hands on." Wants "good, sharp poems. Generally no longer than 30 lines. No restrictions other than quality." Doesn't want "stuff that's been done before." Has published poetry by Peter Meinke, Enid Shomer, Scott Ward, and Jane Ellen Glasser. As a sample the editor selected these lines from "Piet Mondrian" by Louis Phillips:

> Mondrian. Piet/Did not sculpt the Piet/Instead he settled on subjects less theatrical,/But slightly more
> geometrical.

State Street Review is 70-90 pgs., 5 × 8, offset-printed, true binding with b&w photos and line art. Receives about 300-500 poems/year, accepts 40-60. Press run is 300-500 for 20 subscribers, 200-400 shelf sales, with 100 distributed free to libraries. Single copy: $5. Sample: $3.

How to Submit: Submit 5 poems at a time. Accepts simultaneous sumbissions; no previously published poems. "It won't hurt our feelings if a piece has been accepted elsewhere while we scraped together the money for our next issue." No fax or e-mail submissions. Cover letter preferred with information for contributors' page. "For longer poems, we appreciate diskettes in WordPerfect, ASCII, or RTF format." Time between acceptance and publication is up to 6 months. Poems are circulated to an editorial board. Always comments on rejected poems. Guidelines available for SASE or by e-mail. Responds in 6 months. Always sends prepublication galleys. Pays 2 copies. Acquires first North American serial rights. May review books or chapbooks of poetry in the future. Poets may send books for review consideration.

☑ ▣ ◯ STELLALUNA-POETRY CIRCLE, (formerly part of *Endemoniada*). E-mail: stella_22@quepas a.com or Lucifera999@yahoo.com. Website: www.angelfire.com/pa3/stellaluna. **Contact:** Olga and 'Lucifera' Elena León. Bilingual-Spanish and English.

Needs: StellaLuna-Poetry Circle is a site dedicated to sharing poetry of all kinds. "Specifically we enjoy occult, vampiric, romantic, radical, traditional, passionate, dreamy, demonik, angelik, wiccan, pagan. We invite anyone who writes their own poetry to add their creation to our poetic temples. We prefer poems that are short and appeal to a mature audience. We also have an area to discuss poetry, and we have an area to add links to other poetic sites. We are very open to submissions. This is a ying yang experiment. Try it out." As a sample the editors selected these lines by Stan (Incarnedine):

> Leaves may fall and wings may struggle/Though nature damns restraint,/In their spheres, their destined
> bubbles,/Every beast will see its way.

How to Submit: "Once you enter the site you may post your poem in the area called 'Temple of Poetry.' You can post it yourself; it's very easy. The Spanish version and the English version are not translations of each other, they are different so if you speak both languages, visit both. One or two poems at a time please. There are no payments. You may link your personal poetry website to our site to help boost your visits." E-mail submissions are also accepted; include text in body of message.

THE WALLACE STEVENS JOURNAL (Specialized: Wallace Stevens), Liberal Arts, Clarkson University, Box 5750, Potsdam NY 13699-5750. (315)268-3967. Fax: (315)268-3983. E-mail: duemer@clarkson. edu. Established 1977. **Poetry Editor:** Prof. Joseph Duemer.

Magazine Needs: *The Wallace Stevens Journal* appears biannually using "poems about or in the spirit of Wallace Stevens or having some relation to his work. No bad parodies of Stevens' anthology pieces." Has published poetry by David Athey, Jacqueline Marcus, Charles Wright, X.J. Kennedy, A.M. Juster, and Robert Creeley. As a sample the editor selected these lines from "A Holograph Draft" by Richard Epstein:

> Dear Sir:/I have received your letter of/the 26th. The offer it contains,/that in exchange for ~~mermaids~~
> a warranty deed/to 1464 we drop our claim/for 16,000 ~~blackbirds~~ dollars, will not do./Our client has
> decided to obtain/~~a pair of scarlet boots~~ a writ of execution to be served/at his discretion. I remain,
> most truly,/~~the Rajah of Molucca~~ blithely yours/your obedient servant, Wallace Stevens

The Wallace Stevens Journal is 80-120 pgs., 6×9, typeset, flat-spined, with cover art on glossy stock. Receives 200-300 poems/year, accepts 15-20. Press run is 900 for 600 subscribers of which 200 are libraries. Subscription: $25, includes membership in the Wallace Stevens Society. Sample: $6.

How to Submit: Submit 3-5 poems at a time. "We like to receive clean, readable copy. We generally do not publish previously published material, though we have made a few exceptions to this rule. No fax or e-mail submissions, though requests for information are fine." Responds in up to 10 weeks. Always sends prepublication galleys. Pays 2 copies. Acquires all rights. Returns rights with permission and acknowledgment. Staff reviews books of poetry. Send books for review consideration "only if there is some clear connection to Stevens." *The Wallace Stevens Journal* is published by the Wallace Stevens Society.

Advice: "Brief cover letters are fine, even encouraged. Please don't submit to *Wallace Stevens Journal* if you have not read Stevens. We like parodies, but they must add a new angle of perception. Most of the poems we publish are not parodies but meditations on themes related to Wallace Stevens and those poets he has influenced. Those wishing to contribute might wish especially to examine the Fall 1996 issue which has a large and rich selection of poetry."

STONE SOUP, THE MAGAZINE BY YOUNG WRITERS AND ARTISTS; THE CHILDREN'S ART FOUNDATION (Specialized: children), P.O. Box 83, Santa Cruz CA 95063. (831)426-5557. Fax: (831)426-1161. E-mail: editor@stonesoup.com. Website: www.stonesoup.com (features writer's guidelines, sample issue, philosophy, and related materials featuring children's writing and art). Established 1973. **Editor:** Ms. Gerry Mandel.

• *Stone Soup* has received both Parents' Choice and Edpress Golden Lamp Honor Awards.

Magazine Needs: *Stone Soup* publishes writing and art by children through age 13; wants free verse poetry but no rhyming poetry, haiku, or cinquain. *Stone Soup*, published 6 times/year, is a handsome 7×10 magazine, professionally printed on heavy stock with 10-12 full-color art reproductions inside and a full-color illustration on the coated cover, saddle-stapled. A membership in the Children's Art Foundation at $33/year includes a subscription to the magazine. Receives 5,000 poetry submissions/year, accepts about 12. There are 2-4 pgs. of poetry in each issue. Press run is 20,000 for 14,000 subscribers, 5,000 to bookstores, 1,000 other. Sample: $5.

How to Submit: Submissions can be any number of pages, any format. Include name, age, home address and phone number. Must send SASE for response. No simultaneous submissions. No e-mail submissions. Criticism will be given when requested. Guidelines available for SASE, by e-mail, or on website. Responds in 1 month. Pays $25, a certificate, and 2 copies plus discounts. Acquires all rights. Returns rights upon request. Open to reviews by children. Children through age 13 may also send books for review consideration.

STORY LINE PRESS; NICHOLAS ROERICH POETRY PRIZE, Three Oaks Farm, P.O. Box 1240, Ashland OR 97520-0055. (541)512-8792. Fax: (541)512-8793. E-mail: mail@storylinepress.com. Website: www.storylinepress.com (includes catalog, contest guidelines, online orders, sample books, and e-mail links). Story Line Press. Established 1985. **Executive Director:** Robert McDowell.

• Books published by Story Line Press have recently received such prestigious awards as the Lenore Marshall Prize, the Whiting Award, and the Harold Morton Landon Prize.

Book/Chapbook Needs: Story Line Press publishes each year the winner of the Nicholas Roerich Poetry Prize ($1,000 plus publication and a paid reading at the Roerich Museum in New York; a runner-up receives a full Story Line Press Scholarship to the Wesleyan Writers Conference in Middletown, CT [see listing in Conferences and Workshops section]; $20 entry and handling fee). The press also publishes books about poetry and has published collections by such poets as Alfred Corn, Annie Finch, Donald Justice, Mark Jarman, and David Mason.

How to Submit: Deadline for Nicholas Roerich Poetry Prize competition is October 31st. Complete guidelines available for SASE.

Also Offers: Story Line Press annually publishes 10-15 books of poetry, literary criticism, memoir, fiction, and books in translation. Query first.

THE STORYTELLER, 2441 Washington Rd., Maynard AR 72444. (870)647-2137. Website: www.ang elfire.com/ar/coolwriters (includes guidelines, contact info, and sample poetry). Established 1996. **Editor:** Regina Williams.

Magazine Needs: *The Storyteller*, a quarterly magazine, "is geared to, but not limited to new writers and poets." Wants "any form up to 40 lines, any matter, any style, but must have a meaning. Do not throw words together and call it a poem. Nothing in way of explicit sex, violence, horror or explicit language. I would like it to be understood that I have young readers, ages 9-18." Accepts poetry written by children of all ages. As a sample the editor selected this poem by Bryan Byrd:

> *This is the land of my memories:/Where forgotten river towns leak slowly into the Mississippi;/ Crumbling and ivy covered,/They jealously watch the trains and barges go by.*

Storyteller is 64 pgs., 8½×11, desktop-published with slick cover, original pen & ink drawings on cover, ads. Receives about 300 poems/year, accepts about 40%. Press run is 600 for over 500 subscribers. Subscription: $20; $24 Canada & foreign; $8 Canada & foreign. Sample: $6 (if available).

How to Submit: Submit 2 poems at a time, typed and double-spaced. Accepts previously published poems and simultaneous submissions, "but must state where and when poetry first appeared." Cover letter preferred. Reading fee: $1/poem. Time between acceptance and publication is 9 months. Poems are circulated to an editorial board. "Poems are read and discussed by staff." Often comments on rejected poems. Offers criticism service for $5/poem. Occasionally publishes theme issues. Upcoming themes and guidelines available for SASE. Responds in up to 5 weeks. Acquires first or one-time rights. Reviews books and chapbooks of poetry by subscribers only. Poets may send books for review consideration to associate editor Ruthan Riney.

Also Offers: Sponsors a quarterly contest. "Readers vote on their favorite poems. Winners receive copy of magazine and certificate suitable for framing."

Advice: "I want to read what comes from your heart, whether good or bad. This is probably the easiest place to get your work in print—if it is well written. Thrown together words will not find a place in *The Storyteller*."

✅ 🅞 **STOVEPIPE, A JOURNAL OF LITTLE LITERARY VALUE; SWEET LADY MOON PRESS; SOCIETY OF UNDERGROUND POETS**, P.O. Box 1076, Georgetown KY 40324. E-mail: troyteegarden@ worldradio.org. Website: www.wrvg-fm.org/poets.html (includes links to past guests, summary of show contents, and further information). Established 1995. **Editor:** Troy Teegarden.

Magazine Needs: *STOVEPIPE* is a quarterly journal of poetry, short fiction, and b&w art. "Open to most anything, but we suggest you order a copy of *STOVEPIPE* first. We extremely dislike forced rhyme poetry, cheesy Hallmark-esque lines, and religious rants." Has published poetry by Robin Merrill, Mark Wisniewski, Richard Taylor. As a sample we selected these lines from "Impenetrable" by Sherrie Bennett:

> *She wants me to be soft, like velvet/able to bend around the edges/But I'm hard like nails,/I go straight into the matter/Holding on to what I know is solid*

STOVEPIPE is 24-60 pgs., 5½×8½, offset-printed and saddle-stapled with card stock cover, includes b&w art and photos. Accepts about 10% of poems received. Press run is 250 for 75 subscribers of which 5 are libraries, 100 shelf sales. Subscription: $10, "includes free chapbook." Sample: $2 US; $2.50 Can/Mex; $3.50 world. Make checks payable to Troy Teegarden.

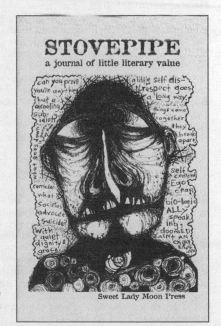

This issue of *Stovepipe* features literary and artistic work by J. Todd Dockery (Kentucky writer/artist/musician/performer/interviewer). The pen and ink drawing was considered most representative of the works included in the journal.

How to Submit: Submit 3-5 poems at a time. Accepts simultaneous submissions. Must be informed of simultaneous submissions. "Please include an informal cover letter and short bio with all submissions." Time between acceptance and publication is up to 3 months. Often comments on rejected poems. Responds in 1 month. Pays 1 year subscription.

Book/Chapbook Needs & How to Submit: Sweet Lady Moon Press publishes 2-4 chapbooks/year—"if we like it, we publish it." Chapbooks are usually 60 pgs., 5½ × 8½, offset-printed and saddle-stapled with heavy card stock cover, includes b&w art and photos. "We usually solicit the poets we'd like to publish, but are open to a sample of five poems and cover letter with bio." Responds to queries in 1 month. Payment varies. Obtain sample chapbooks by writing for free catalog (include SASE).

Also Offers: Sponsors The Society of Underground Poets (SoUP), a weekly one-hour radio show broadcast on WRVG from Georgetown, KY and broadcast in Real Audio on the web. More info at www.wrvg-fm.org/poets.html. "We are interested in poetry along with music, spoken word performances, taped recordings of poets and writers reading their works, and lots of other stuff. We regularly interview national award-winning poets along with writers and editors from the smallest of presses. We also receive large amounts of books from established publishers and review them on the show right beside the latest issue of your zine or chapbook. Send us your best stuff and we'll get it on the air." More information is available for SASE.

Advice: "Send us your best stuff. We enjoy reading poetry and short prose all year round."

$ ☑ **THE STRAIN**, 11702 Webercrest, Houston TX 77048. **Poetry Editor:** Norm Stewart Jr.

Magazine Needs: *The Strain* is a monthly magazine using "experimental or traditional poetry of very high quality." Does not include sample lines of poetry here as they "prefer not to limit style of submissions."

How to Submit: Accepts simultaneous submissions and previously published poems. Guidelines issue: $5 and 8 first-class stamps. Pays "no less than $5. We would prefer you submit before obtaining the guidelines issue which mostly explains upcoming collections and collaborations." Send books for review consideration.

N ☑ **STRAY DOG; PRILLY & TRU PUBLICATIONS, INC.**, P.O. Box 713, Amawalk NY 10501. E-mail: straydog@bestweb.net. Website: www.prillyandtru.com (includes guidelines, rights aquired, name of editor/publisher, subscription rates, e-mail address, submissions address). Established 2000. **Editor/Publisher:** j.v. morrissey.

Magazine Needs: *Stray Dog* appears annually in June and seeks "to publish the best, most powerful work we can find," including contemporary poetry, short-shorts, and art. "We print high-quality poetry, short-shorts and b&w art in any form or style. We're looking for work that is evocative and incisive, work that will leave skid marks on the reader's emotional highway. Prior publication credits admired but not required." Does not want to see anything "preachy, whiny, obscure, pornographic, gratuitously violent, or trite." Recently published poetry by Virgil Suarez, Stephanie Dickinson, Derek Kannemeyer, Catfish McDaris, Mary Boyes, and Will Nixon. *Stray Dog* is 60-80 pgs., 6¾ × 8⅛, Docutech printed, saddle stapled, 4 color glossy card cover with b&w art. Receives about 500 poems/year, accepts 5%. Publishes about 20-25 poems/issue. Press run is 300. Single copy: $8; subscription: $8/year, $15/2 years. Sample: $8. Make checks payable to Stray Dog.

How to Submit: Submit 3-5 poems at a time. Line length for poetry is 2 pgs. maximum. Accepts simultaneous submissions; no previously published poems. No e-mail or disk submissions. Cover letter is preferred. "All submissions and correspondence must be accompanied by SASE for response and return of work; name/address/phone number on each page. No handwritten work. Include 2-3 line bio." Reads submissions year round. Time between acceptance and publication is within 1 year. "Publisher/editor makes initial selections. These are passed on to assistant editors for comments and recommendations. Final selections made by publisher/editor." Sometimes comments on rejected poems. Guidelines available for SASE. Responds in up to 5 months. Pays 2 contributor's copies. Acquires first North American serial rights.

Book/Chapbook Needs & How to Submit: Prilly & Tru Publications, Inc. is "not publishing books or chapbooks at this time, but plans to in the future."

Advice: "Surprise me! Blow me away! We receive too many works that are technically flawless, but lack emotional impact. Think 'indie' film, not network TV."

N 🌐 ☑ **STRIDE PUBLICATIONS**, 11 Sylvan Rd., Exeter, Devon EX4 6EW England. E-mail: editor@stridebooks.co.uk. Website: www.stridebooks.co.uk or stridemagazine.co.uk. Established 1982. **Managing Editor:** R.M. Loydell.

Book/Chapbook Needs: Stride Publications publishes poetry, poetry sequences, prose, and experimental novels, and an occasional arts magazine. Wants to see any poetry that is "new, inventive, nothing self-oriented, emotional, no narrative or fantasy, rhyming doggerel, light verse, or the merely-confessional." Has published work by Peter Redgrove, William Everson, Sheila E. Murphy, Peter Finch, and Charles Wright. Stride Publications publishes paperbacks 60-100 pgs. of poetry, plus a few novels and anthologies.

How to Submit: Unsolicited submissions for book publication are accepted. "All submissions must be typewritten/word-processed and have an SAE included" with IRCs. Authors should obtain submission guidelines first via e-mail or by sending SASE with return postage or IRCs. Cover letter required with bio, summary, and review quotes. Queries will be answered in 6 weeks and mss reported on in 3 months or more. Pays 30 author's copies. Magazine reviews books and tapes of poetry in 100-200 words, multi-book format. Send books etc. for review consideration.

◯ ◔ ◉ **STRUGGLE: A MAGAZINE OF PROLETARIAN REVOLUTIONARY LITERATURE** (Specialized: political, ethnic/nationality, gay/lesbian/bisexual, socialism, workers' social issues, women/feminism, anti-racism), P.O. Box 13261, Detroit MI 48213-0261. (313)273-9039. E-mail: timhall11 @yahoo.com. Established 1985. **Editor:** Tim Hall.

Magazine Needs: *Struggle* is a "literary quarterly, content: the struggle of the working people and all oppressed against the rich. Issues such as: racism, poverty, women's rights, aggressive wars, workers' struggle for jobs and job security, the overall struggle for a non-exploitative society, a genuine socialism." The poetry and songs printed are "generally short, any style, subject matter must criticize or fight—explicitly or implicitly—against the rule of the billionaires. We welcome experimentation devoted to furthering such content. We are open to both subtlety and direct statement." Has published poetry by Cynthia Hatten, Peter Dolack, Vincent Johnson, and Luis Cuauhtémoc Berriozábal. As a sample the editor selected these lines by Timothy Carter:

   My vote/rode the weight of a penny/in a thousand plate dinner.

Struggle is 36 pgs., digest-sized, photocopied with occasional photos of artwork, short stories, and short plays as well as poetry and songs. Subscription: $10 for 4 issues. Sample: $2.50. Make checks payable to "Tim Hall— Special Account."

How to Submit: Submit up to 8 poems at a time. Accepts e-mail submissions in body of message (no attachments). Accepted work usually appears in the next or following issue. Editor tries to provide criticism "with every submission." Tries to respond in 4 months. Pays 2 copies. "If you are unwilling to have your poetry published on our website, please in form us."

Also Offers: "Coming soon: website at STRUGGLEMAGAZINE.com"

Advice: "Show passion and fire. Humor also welcome. Prefer powerful, colloquial language over academic timidity. Look to Neruda, Lorca, Brecht, Bly, Whitman, Braithwaite, Pietri, Tupac Shakur, Aimé Césaire. Experimental, traditional forms both welcome. Especially favor: works reflecting rebellion by the working people against the rich; works against racism, sexism, militarism, imperialism; works critical of our exploitative culture; works showing a desire for—or fantasy of—a non-exploitative society; works attacking the Republican New Stone Age and the Democrats' surrender to it."

$ ◉ **STUDENT LEADERSHIP JOURNAL (Specialized: students, religious),** Dept. PM, P.O. Box 7895, Madison WI 53707-7895. (608)274-4823, ext. 425 or 413. Website: www.ivcf.org/slj. **Editor:** Jeff Yourison.

Magazine Needs: *Student Leadership* appears 3 times/year and is a "magazine for Christian student leaders on secular campuses. We want poetry with solid Biblical imagery, not preachy or trite. We get too many prayerpoems. Also, we accept little rhymed poetry; it must be very, very good." *Student Leadership* is 32 pgs., magazine-sized, full color, with no advertising, 70% editorial, 30% graphics/art. Press run is 10,000 going to college students in the US and Canada. Subscription: $12. Sample: $4.

How to Submit: Accepts previously published poems; no simultaneous submissions. "Would-be contributors should read us to be familiar with what we publish." Best time to submit mss is March through July ("We set our year's editorial plan"). Editor "occasionally" comments on rejected poems. Guidelines available for SASE. Responds in 3 months. Time between acceptance and publication is 1-24 months. Pays $25-50/poem plus 2 copies. Acquires first or reprint rights.

Advice: "Try to express feelings through images and metaphor. Religious poetry should not be overly didactic, and it should never moralize!"

Ⓝ ◻ ◯ ◉ **STUDENTSWRITE.COM (Specialized: teen/young adult),** P.O. Box 90046, San Antonio TX 78209. E-mail: editor@StudentsWrite.com. Website: www.StudentsWrite.com. Established 1994. **Editor:** Susan Curne.

Magazine Needs: *StudentsWrite.com*, published 9 times/year, is an "online publication publishing information on the art and business of writing for young writers, as well as poetry and short stories by young people ages 12-19." Wants "positive poetry, upbeat, no more than 30 lines—rhymed or unrhymed." Does not want "depressing poetry, boring poetry, unoriginal poetry, 'roses-are-red-violets-are-blue' poetry." Receives about 100 poems/year, accepts about 25%.

How to Submit: Contributors must be 12-19 years old. Submit 3-5 poems at a time. No previously published poems or simultaneous submissions. Cover letter preferred with author's age and bio. Accepts submissions on disk in .doc or .txt formats. Time between acceptance and publication is 8 months. Always comments on rejected poems. Guidelines available for SASE or by e-mail. Responds in 1 month. Sometimes sends prepublication galleys. Acquires first rights.

Advice: "We look for good writing. But we also look for potential in our submitters, and even if their work is returned, we work with them to improve. We're more than willing to help."

THE BOOK PUBLISHERS INDEX, located at the back of this book, lists those publishers who consider full-length book collections.

☑ ⊕ ☑ ◎ **STUDIO, A JOURNAL OF CHRISTIANS WRITING (Specialized: religious, spiritu-ality)**, 727 Peel St., Albury, New South Wales 2640 Australia. Phone/fax: 61 2 6021 1135. E-mail: pgrover@bigpond.com. Established 1980. **Publisher:** Paul Grover.

Magazine Needs: *Studio* is a quarterly journal publishing "poetry and prose of literary merit, offering a venue for previously published, new and aspiring writers, and seeking to create a sense of community among Christians writing." The journal also publishes occasional articles as well as news and reviews of writing, writers, and events of interest to members. In poetry, the editors want "shorter pieces but with no specification as to form or length (necessarily less than 200 lines), subject matter, style, or purpose. People who send material should be comfortable being published under this banner: *Studio, A Journal of Christians Writing*." Has published poetry by John Foulcher and other Australian poets. *Studio* is 36 pgs., digest-sized, professionally printed on high-quality recycled paper, saddle-stapled, matte card cover, with graphics and line drawings. Press run is 300, all subscriptions. Subscription: $48 (Aud) for overseas members. Sample available (airmail to US) for $8 (Aud).

How to Submit: Submissions must be typed and double-spaced on one side of A4 white paper. Accepts simultaneous submissions. Name and address must appear on the reverse side of each page submitted. Cover letter required; include brief details of previous publishing history, if any. SASE (or SAE with IRC) required. Response time is 2 months and time to publication is 9 months. Pays 1 contributor's copy. Acquires first Australian rights. Reviews books of poetry in 250 words, single format. Poets may send books for review consideration.

Also Offers: The magazine conducts a biannual poetry and short story contest.

Advice: "The trend in Australia is for imagist poetry and poetry exploring the land and the self. Reading the magazine gives the best indication of style and standard, so send a few dollars for a sample copy before sending your poetry. Keep writing, and we look forward to hearing from you."

☐ ☑ **STUDIO ONE**, Haehn Campus Center, College of St. Benedict, St. Joseph MN 56374. E-mail: studio1 @csbsju.edu. Established 1976. Editor changes yearly.

Magazine Needs: *Studio One* an annual literary and visual arts magazine appearing in May is designed as a forum for local, regional, and national poets/writers. No specifications regarding form, subject matter or style of poetry submitted. However, poetry no more than 2 pgs. stands a better chance of publication. Accepts poetry written by children. Has published poetry by Bill Meissner, Eva Hooker, and Larry Schug. As a sample the editor selected these lines from "Jewels for Waking" by Tiffaney Dawn Dressen:

> Do not touch me/when I sleep/my bones are breaking/into sapphires frozen/deep arctic blue

Studio One is 50-80 pgs., soft cover, typeset. Includes 1-3 short stories, 22-30 poems and 10-13 visual art representations. Receives 600-800 submissions/year. No subscriptions, but a sample copy can be obtained by sending a self-addressed stamped manilla envelope and $6 for p&h. Make checks payable to *Studio One*.

How to Submit: Accepts previously published poems and simultaneous submissions. Accepts e-mail submissions included in body of message; clearly show page breaks and indentations. Deadline: February 1 for spring publication. Seldom comments on rejected poems. Pays 1 contributor's copy. Send stamped, addressed postcard for confirmation of submissions received and SASE for results only.

⬚N⬚ ☑ **THE STYLES; META CARPAL PUBLISHING (M.C.P.)**, P.O. Box 7171, Madison WI 53707. E-mail: thestylesorg@yahoo.com. Website: www.thestyles.org (includes mission statement, contributors, subscription information, submissions guidelines). Established 20000. **Poetry Editor:** Amara Dante Verona.

Magazine Needs: *The Styles* appears biannually. Publishes "ambitious original and creative ideas and standards of what writing should be. *The Styles* encourages new ideas about how writing should be written, read, evaluated, and what it should accomplish. Experimental work." Looking for "highly experimental poetry. Most of the poetry we publish is prose poetry." Does not want "anything sentimental." Recently published poetry by Jennie Trivanovich, Sarah Lindsay, Laura Mullen, Scott Bently, Mark Terrill, and Brian Johnson. *The Styles* is over 100 pgs., 8 × 8, offset-printed, perfect-bound, soft point-spot laminated color cover. Accepts about 2% of poems submitted. Publishes 12-20 poems/issue. Press run is 1,000. Single copy: $8; subscription: $10/year (2 issues). Sample: $5. Make checks payable to *The Styles*.

How to Submit: Submit 3 or more poems at a time. Line length for poetry is open. Accepts simultaneous submissions; no previously published poems. No fax, e-mail, or disk submissions. Cover letter is preferred. "Always send a SASE. Cover letters and bios are appreciated, but not required." Reads submissions all year. Time between acceptance and publication is 1-9 months. Often comments on rejected poems. Guidelines are available in magazine, for SASE, or on website. Responds in 1 month. Sometimes sends prepublication galleys. Pays $3 and 2 contributor's copies. Acquires first North American serial rights. Poets may send books for review consideration. "We will make 'comments,' quotes, and advanced comments for books, chapbooks, and other magazines. We don't have a section in our publication for reviews."

Advice: "We publish very little poetry in each issue. We are looking for poets who are using language in new ways. Read our publication. Our readers enjoy work that is accessible and yet still challenging."

☑ ⬚ ☑ **SUB-TERRAIN; ANVIL PRESS; LAST POEMS POETRY CONTEST**, P.O. Box 3008, MPO, Vancouver, British Columbia V63 3X5 Canada. (604)876-8710. Fax: (604)899-2667. E-mail: subter@portal.ca. Website: www.anvilpress.com. Established 1988. **Contact:** poetry editor.

Magazine Needs: Anvil Press is an "alternate small press publishing *sub-TERRAIN*—a socially conscious literary quarterly whose aim is to produce a reading source that will stand in contrast to the trite and pandered—

as well as broadsheets, chapbooks and the occasional monograph." Wants "work that has a point-of-view; work that has some passion behind it and is exploring issues that are of pressing importance (particularly that with an urban slant); work that challenges conventional notions of what poetry is or should be; work with a social conscience. No bland, flowery, uninventive poetry that says nothing in style or content." As a sample the editor selected these lines from "Eidetic" by Quentin Tarantino:

> *In fluid and electrics the alligator brain holds it all/rigid, refined and encyclopedic, the chemical well/*
> *contains a green bathing suit, improbable sex acts,/inclusive results from the elector of nineteen eighty-*
> *six/a bowl of stinging Thai soup and the origin of scars/all held static and wet in the ancient clock,*
> *the first mind.*

Sub-TERRAIN is 40 pgs., 7½ × 10½, offset-printed, with a press run of 3,000. Subscription: $15. Sample: $5.

How to Submit: Submit 4-6 poems at a time. Accepts simultaneous submissions; no previously published poems. No fax or e-mail submissions. Responds in up to 6 months. Pays money only for solicited work; for other work, 3-issue subscription. Acquires one-time rights for magazine. "If chapbook contract, we retain right to publish subsequent printings unless we let a title lapse out-of-print for more than one year." Staff occasionally reviews small press poetry chapbooks.

Book/Chapbook Needs & How to Submit: For chapbook or book publication submit 4 sample poems and bio, no simultaneous submissions. No fax or e-mail submissions. "Only those manuscripts accompanied by a self-addressed stamped envelope (SASE) will be considered. But I must stress that we are a co-op, depending on support from an interested audience. New titles will be undertaken with caution. We are not subsidized at this point and do not want to give authors false hopes—but if something is important and should be in print, we will do our best. Response time can, at times, be lengthy; if you want to be assured that your manuscript has been received, include a self-addressed stamped postcard for notification." Editor provides brief comment and more extensive comments for fees.

Also Offers: Sponsors Last Poems Poetry Contest for "poetry that encapsulates North American experience at the close of the 20th Century." Submit up to 4 poems. Entry fee: $15. Deadline: January 31. Winner announced March 1. Prize: $250, plus publication in Spring issue. Entrants receive a 4-issue subscription. More information is available for SASE (or SAE and IRC).

Advice: "It is important that writers intending to submit work have an idea of what work we publish. Read a sample copy before submitting."

SULPHUR RIVER LITERARY REVIEW, P.O. Box 19228, Austin TX 78760-9228. (512)292-9456. Established 1978, reestablished 1987. **Editor/Publisher:** James Michael Robbins.

Magazine Needs: *Sulphur River* is a semiannual of poetry, prose and artwork. "No restrictions except quality." Does not want poetry that is "trite or religious or verse that does not incite thought." Has published poetry by Hugh Fox, B.Z. Niditch, Alexandra Grilikher, Lyn Lifshin, Catherine Stepler, and Sophia M. Starner. *Sulphur River* is digest-sized, perfect-bound, with glossy cover. Receives about 2,000 poems/year, accepts 4%. Press run is 400 for 200 subscribers, 100 shelf sales. Subscription: $12. Sample: $7.

How to Submit: No previously published poems or simultaneous submissions. Often comments on rejected poems, although a dramatic increase in submissions has made this increasingly difficult. Responds in 1 month. Always sends prepublication galleys. Pays 2 contributor's copies.

Also Offers: "*Sulphur River* also publishes full-length volumes of poetry; latest book: *Plenum* by Ben Norwood."

Advice: "Poetry is, for me, the essential art, the ultimate art, and there can be no compromise of quality if the poem is to be successful."

SUMMER STREAM PRESS, P.O. Box 6056, Santa Barbara CA 93160-6056. (805)962-6540. E-mail: geehossiffer@aol.com. Established 1978. **Poetry Editor:** David D. Frost.

Book/Chapbook Needs: Publishes a series of books (Box Cars) in hardcover and softcover, each presenting 6 poets, averaging 70 text pgs. for each poet. "The mix of poets represents many parts of the country and many approaches to poetry. The poets previously selected have been published, but that is no requirement. We welcome traditional poets in the mix and thus offer them a chance for publication in this world of free-versers. The six poets share a 15% royalty. We require rights for our editions worldwide and share 50-50 with authors for translation rights and for republication of our editions by another publisher. Otherwise all rights remain with the authors." Accepts poetry written by children. Has published poetry by Virginia E. Smith, Sandra Russell, Jennifer MacPherson, Nancy Berg, Lois Shapley Bassen, and Nancy J. Wallace.

How to Submit: To be considered for future volumes in this series, query with about 12 sample poems, no cover letter. No e-mail submissions. Responds to query in 6 months, to submission (if invited) in 1 year. Accepts previously published poetry and simultaneous submissions. Editor usually comments on rejected poems. Always sends prepublication galleys. Pays 6 contributor's copies plus royalties.

Advice: "We welcome both traditional poetry and free verse. However, we find we must reject almost all the traditional poetry received simply because the poets exhibit little or no knowledge of the structure and rules of traditional forms. Much of it is rhymed free verse."

A SUMMER'S READING, 409 Lakeview Dr., Sherman IL 62684. (217)496-3012. E-mail: t_morrissey @hotmail.com. Established 1996. **Contact:** Ted Morrissey.

Magazine Needs: *A Summer's Reading*, published annually in June, strives "to provide one more well edited, attractive outlet for new and emerging writers, poets and artists. Willing to look at all kinds of poetry, prefer free verse or blank verse with clear images and ideas." Does not want "sappy 'greeting card' stuff." Has published poetry by Robert Cooperman, Alice Marie Tarnowski, and Dianalee Velie. As a sample the editor selected these lines from "I Went Searching for the Past" by Patty Dickson Pieczka:

> Ghosts carrying bottles/stumbled away like revelers/staggering through wisps of dawn./Old jokes slept
> beneath fallen leaves/as birds picked at remnants of hardened laughter,/winging them off to build nests.

A Summer's Reading is approximately 80 pgs., offset-printed, with color cover, b&w artwork. Press run is 200 for 50 subscribers. Subscription: $6. Sample: $4.

How to Submit: Submit up to 10 poems with name, address, phone, and line count on each. Accepts simultaneous submissions if so noted. Cover letter preferred with brief bio and publishing history. Time between acceptance and publication is 3-12 months. Sometimes comments on rejected poems. Guidelines available for SASE. Responds in 3 months. Always sends prepublication galleys. Pays 2 copies. Acquires one-time rights plus request for acknowledgement if reprinted. May include staff-written reviews of poetry books in the future. Poets may send books for review consideration.

Advice: "Don't hesitate to submit—we will be respectful and fair to your work. We strive to publish newcomers with emerging and established artists. We would like to see more translations (include original text)."

$ ◻ THE SUN, 107 N. Roberson St., Chapel Hill NC 27516. Website: www.thesunmagazine.org. Established 1974. **Editor:** Sy Safransky.

Magazine Needs: *The Sun* is "noted for honest, personal work that's not too obscure or academic. We avoid traditional, rhyming poetry, as well as limericks, haiku, and religious poetry. We're open to almost anything else: free verse, prose poems, short and long poems." Has published poetry by William Snyder Jr., Alison Luterman, Donna Steiner, David Budbill, Susan Terris, and Michael Chitwood. As a sample the editor selected these lines from "Dog on the Floor in the Pet-Food Aisle" by Ruth L. Schwartz:

> We watch our loves through airplane windows,/small and dim and scarred,/and even so, life noses up,/
> rolling before us/like a black dog,/its brown eyes steady as the sun,/its belly in the air, asking for touch.

The Sun is 48 pgs., magazine-sized, printed on 50 lb. offset, saddle-stapled, with b&w photos and graphics. Circulation is 50,000 for 48,000 subscriptions of which 500 are libraries. Receives 3,000 submissions of poetry/year, accepts about 36; has a 1- to 3-month backlog. Subscription: $34. Sample: $5.

How to Submit: Submit up to 6 poems at a time. Poems should be typed and accompanied by a cover letter. Accepts previously published poems, but simultaneous submissions are discouraged. Guidelines available for SASE. Responds within 3 months. Pays $50-200 on publication plus copies and subscription. Acquires first serial or one-time rights.

N ◯ ◕ SUN POETIC TIMES, 10362 Sahara Dr. #2203, San Antonio TX 78216. (210)530-9849. E-mail: sunpoets@hotmail.com. Established 1994. **Editor:** Rod C. Stryker.

Magazine Needs: *Sun Poetic Times, a literary & artistic magazine*, appears quarterly to "publish all types of literary and visual art from all walks of life. We take all types. Our only specification is length—1 page in length if typed, 2 pages if handwritten (legibly)." Has published poetry by Naomi Shihab Nye, Chris Crabtree, Trinidad Sanchez, Jr., and Garland Lee Thompson, Jr. As a sample the editors selected these lines from "Measurements" by Tom Cox:

> We talk among ourselves in mysterious tongues/telling each other lies with stiff lips/in the place where
> the mountain meets the moon/amplified guitars screaming in the night/bonfires illuminating the paths
> converging on what we have/called sacred ground

Sun Poetic Times is 24-28 pgs., magazine-sized, attractively printed and saddle-stapled with glossy card stock cover, uses b&w line drawings/halftones. Receives about 200 poems/year, accepts about 30%. Press run is 300, 200 shelf sales. Subscription: $6 for 2 issues, $12/1 year (4 issues). Sample: $3 and SASE. Make checks payable to Sun Poetic Times.

How to Submit: Submit 3-5 poems at a time. Accepts simultaneous submissions; no previously published poems. Accepts e-mail submissions included in body of message (no attached files). Cover letter preferred. "In cover letters, we like to hear about your publishing credits, reasons you've taken up the pen and general BS like that (biographical info)." Time between acceptance and publication is up to 8 months. Seldom comments on rejected poems. Occasionally publishes theme issues. Guidelines and upcoming themes available for SASE. E-mail queries welcome. Responds in up to 4 months. Pays 1 contributor's copy. Rights revert back to author upon publication.

◕ SUNSTONE, 343 N. 300 W., Salt Lake City UT 84103-1215. (801)355-5926. Established 1974. **Poetry Editor:** Dixie Partridge.

Magazine Needs: Appearing 6-8 times/year, *Sunstone* publishes "scholarly articles of interest to an open, Mormon audience; personal essays; fiction; and poetry." Wants "both lyric and narrative poetry that engages the reader with fresh, strong images, skillful use of language, and a strong sense of voice and/or place. No didactic poetry, sing-song rhymes, or in-process work." Has published poetry by Susan Howe, Anita Tanner, Robert Parham, Ryan G. Van Cleave, Robert Rees, and Virgil Suarez. As a sample the editor selected these lines from "Sonora" by Georganne O'Connor:

. . . the wind's hot breath steals the air from your chest/and every bead of sweat from your skin./From the canyon floor, I see hills/robbed of rain, studded with giant saguaro,/the sentinels. They have seen us coming./In the accordian folds of their flesh,/elf owl rests, insulated from heat. . . .

Sunstone is 96 pgs., 8½×11, professionally printed and saddle-stapled with a semi-glossy paper cover. Receives over 500 poems/year, accepts 40-50. Press run is 10,000 for 8,000 subscribers of which 300 are libraries, 700 shelf sales. Subscription: $36/6 issues. Sample: $5.95.

How to Submit: Submit up to 5 poems with name and address on each poem. "We rarely use poems over 40 lines." No previously published poems or simultaneous submissions. Time between acceptance and publication is 18 months or less. Seldom comments on rejected poems. Guidelines available for SASE. Responds in 3 months. Pays 3 contributor's copies. Acquires first North American serial rights. Poets may send books for review consideration. "Address to *book review editor—poetry,* not to poetry editor."

Advice: "Poems should not sound like a rewording of something heard before. Be original; pay attention to language, sharp imagery. Contents should deepen as the poem progresses. We've published poems rooted strongly in place, narratives seeing life from another time or culture, poems on religious belief or doubt—a wide range of subject matter."

SUPERIOR POETRY NEWS (Specialized: translations, regional, humor); JOSS (Specialized: multi-cultural, philosophical); SUPERIOR POETRY PRESS, P.O. Box 424, Superior MT 59872. Established 1995. **Editors:** Ed and Guna Chaberek.

Magazine Needs: *Superior Poetry News* appears 4 times/year and "publishes the best and most interesting of new poets, as well as established poets, we can find. Also, we encourage lively translation into English from any language." Wants "general, rural, Western, or humorous poetry; translations; 40 lines or under. Nothing graphically sexual; containing profanity." Accepts poetry written by children, but it has to be very good or unusual for the age level. Has published poetry by makyo, Roberts Mūks, Simon Perchik, Arthur Winfield Knight, and Kit Knight. As a sample the editor selected these lines from "Amrita" by Roberts Mūks, translated from Latvian:

Birds and other flying things die quietly/making no noise about life/and death, no last words/leaving no trace

Superior Poetry News is 12-24 pgs., 8½×5, photocopied and saddle-stapled, "relevant artwork accepted, ads open to subscribers (1 free per issue)." Receives about 2,000 poems/year, accepts 10%. Press run is 75 for 50 subscribers; 3-5 distributed free to libraries. Single copy: $2; subscription: $5.50. Sample: $2.

How to Submit: Submit 3-5 poems at a time. Accepts previously published poems and simultaneous submissions (if stated). Cover letter with short bio preferred. Time between acceptance and publication is 3 months. Seldom comments on rejected poems, "but will if requested." Guidelines available for SASE. Responds in 1 week. Pays 1 copy. Acquires first rights. Staff reviews books and chapbooks of poetry and other magazines in 50-100 words, single book format. Send books for review consideration with return postage (overseas contributors please include two IRCs).

Magazine Needs & How to Submit: Superior Poetry Press also publishes *JOSS: A journal for the 21st century.* Published annually, *JOSS* features "material which serves to project and uplift the human spirit for the great adventure of the next one hundred years. Writers and poets in mainstream religious, philosophical, scientific, and social disciplines are encouraged to submit." Subscription: $2/year. Sample: $2. Submit poems of up to 40 lines in length; articles 400 words maximum. Pays 1 contributor's copy.

SUZERAIN ENTERPRISES; LOVE'S CHANCE MAGAZINE; FIGHTING CHANCE MAGAZINE (Specialized: romance, horror, mystery, science fiction), P.O. Box 60336, Worcester MA 01606. Established 1994. **Editor/Publisher:** Milton Kerr.

Magazine Needs: *Love's Chance Magazine* and *Fighting Chance Magazine* are each published 3 times/year to "give unpublished writers a chance to be published and to be paid for their efforts." *Love's Chance* deals with romance; *Fighting Chance* deals with dark fiction, horror, and science fiction. "No porn, ageism, sexism, racism, children in sexual situations." Has published poetry by Gary McGhee, David A. Ross, David Hurd, Ellaraine Lockie, and Matar. As a sample the editor selected these lines from "Floater" by Matar:

Sincerely longing/for the street's soul,/but smart enough to hover above it./Levitating/as the heat shimmers up.

Both magazines are 15-30 pgs., 8½×11, photocopied and side-stapled, computer-designed paper cover. Both receive about 500 poems/year, accept about 10%. Press runs are 100 for 70-80 subscribers. Subscription: $12/year for each. Samples: $4 each. Make checks payable to Suzerain Enterprises.

How to Submit: For both magazines, submit 3 poems at a time. Line length for poetry is 20 maximum. Accepts previously published poems and simultaneous submissions. Cover letter preferred. "Proofread for spelling errors, neatness; must be typewritten in standard manuscript form. No handwritten manuscripts." Time between acceptance and publication is 3 months. Often comments on rejected poems. Guidelines available for SASE. Responds in 6 weeks. Acquires first or one-time rights.

Advice: "Proofread and edit carefully. Read and write, then read and write some more. Keep submitting and don't give up."

SWEET ANNIE & SWEET PEA REVIEW, 7750 Highway F-24 W, Baxter IA 50028. (515)792-3578. Fax: (515)792-1310. E-mail: anniespl@netins.net. Established 1995. **Editor/Publisher:** Beverly A. Clark.

Magazine Needs: *Sweet Annie & Sweet Pea Review*, published quarterly, features short stories and poetry. Wants "poems of outdoors, plants, land, heritage, women, relationships, olden times—simpler times." Does not want "obscene, violent, explicit sexual material, obscure, long-winded materials, no overly religious materials." Has published poetry by Anne Carol Betterton, Mary Ann Wehler, Susan Clayton-Goldner, Celeste Bowman, Dick Reynolds, and Brenda Serotte. As a sample the editor selected these lines from "Brooding the Heartlands" by M.L. Liebler:

> There were those days/Lonesome out on/The Dakota Plains. Lonesome/In my prairie rose daydreams—/
> memories brooding across the heartland.

Sweet Annie & Sweet Pea Review is 30 pgs., 5¼ × 8½, offset-printed, saddle-stapled, bond paper with onion skin page before title page, medium card cover, and cover art. Receives about 200 poems/year, accepts 25-33%. Press run is 50 for 75 subscribers; 25-35 distributed free to contributors. Subscription: $24. Sample: $7. Make checks payable to Sweet Annie Press.

How to Submit: Submit 6-12 poems at a time. "Effective 2001, **reading fee** $5/author submitting. Strongly recommend ordering a sample issue prior to submitting and preference is given to poets and writers following this procedure and submitting in accordance with the layout used consistently by this Press." Accepts simultaneous submissions; no previously published poems. No e-mail submissions. Cover letter preferred with personal comments about yourself and phone number. Time between acceptance and publication is 9 months. Often comments on rejected poems. Publishes theme issues. "We select for theme first, select for content second; narrow selections through editors." Themes for 2002 are Eclectic Woman, Eclectic Man, and Celebrating Gaia. Upcoming themes and guidelines available for SASE. Responds in 6 months or sooner. Pays 1 contributor's copy. Acquires all rights. Returns rights with acknowledgment in future publications. Will review chapbooks of poetry or other magazines of short length, reviews 500 words or less. Poets may send books for review consideration.

SYCAMORE REVIEW, Dept. of English, Purdue University, West Lafayette IN 47907. (765)494-3783. Fax: (765)494-3780. E-mail: sycamore@expert.cc.purdue.edu. Website: www.sla.purdue.edu/academic/engl/sycamore/ (includes current issue information, writer's guidelines, online versions of out-of-print editions, back issue information, and subscription information). Established 1988 (first issue May, 1989). **Editor-in-Chief:** Numsiri C. Kunakemakorn. Poetry Editor changes each year; submit to Poetry Editor.

Magazine Needs: "We accept personal essays, short fiction, drama, translations, and quality poetry in any form. We aim to publish many diverse styles of poetry from formalist to prose poems, narrative, and lyric." Has published poetry by Lucia Perillo, Theresa Pappas, Virgil Suarez, Dale Hushner, Christine Sneed, John O'Connor, and Kevin Prufer. *Sycamore Review* is semiannual in a digest-sized format, 160 pgs., flat-spined, professionally printed, with matte, color cover. Press run is 1,000 for 500 subscribers of which 50 are libraries. Subscription: $12; $14 outside US. Sample: $7. Make checks payable to Purdue University (Indiana residents add 5% sales tax.)

How to Submit: Submit 3-6 poems at a time. Name and address on each page. Accepts simultaneous submissions, if notified immediately of acceptance elsewhere; no previously published poems except translations. No submissions accepted via fax or e-mail. Cover letters not required but invited; include phone number, short bio and previous publications, if any. "We read September 1 through March 31 only." Guidelines available for SASE. Responds in 4 months. Pays 2 copies. Acquires first North American rights. After publication, all rights revert to author. Staff reviews books of poetry. Send books to editor-in-chief for review consideration.

Advice: "Poets who do not include SASE do not receive a response."

SYMBIOTIC OATMEAL; SYMBIOTIC PRESS, SYMBIOSIS PRESS, SLAP-DASH-UGLY CHAPBOOK SERIES, P.O. Box 14938, Philadelphia PA 19149. Established 1997. **Editor:** Ms. Juan Xu.

Magazine Needs: *Symbiotic Oatmeal* is published 2 times/year and contains poetry, art, and fun." Wants poetry of "any style under three pages, would like to see more work from Asian Americans. No poor taste, poorly written work." Has published poetry by Giovanni Malito, Yen Li, John Sweet, and Michael Hafer. As a sample the editor selected these lines from "Zodiac" by Joseph Farley:

> There is a morning out there,/beyond the horizon,/waiting for prayers/to call it out of darkness/and
> light the world

Symbiotic Oatmeal is about 6 pgs., magazine-sized, photocopied and side-stapled. Receives about 50 poems/year, accepts about 25%. Press run is 100. Single copy: $3 cash or 6 first-class stamps.

How to Submit: Submit 5 poems at a time. Accepts previously published poems and simultaneous submissions. Accepts disk submissions. "Disk submissions must be on a diskette formatted in DOS and in WordPerfect format." Cover letter required. Time between acceptance and publication is up to 5 months. Seldom comments on rejected poems. Offers criticism service. "I have a M.A. in English. If someone wants me to read a book manuscript, proof, and give feedback I will need compensation of $25 or more, depending on length." Responds in 3 months. Pays 1 contributor's copy.

Book/Chapbook Needs & How to Submit: Symbiotic Press/Symbiosis Press publishes chapbooks. Query before submitting. **Reading fee:** $10 per ms. Make checks payable to Juan Xu.

☑ $ ◐ **SYNAESTHESIA PRESS; SYNAESTHESIA PRESS CHAPBOOK SERIES**, P.O. Box 1763, Tempe AZ 85280-1763. (602)280-9092. E-mail: synaepress@aol.com. Website: www.chapbooks.org. Established 1995. **Editor:** Jim Camp.

Book/Chapbook Needs: Synaesthesia Press wants to publish "work seldom seen elsewhere." Under the Synaesthesia Press Chapbook Series, they publish 4 chapbooks/year. "No real specifications to form/style; I want to read fresh poetry that stimulates the reader." He does not want to see "the same garbage most little mags publish." Has published poetry by Jack Micheline, Tszurah Litzky, Roxie Powell, and Steve Fisher. Chapbooks are usually 16 pgs., digest-sized, offset/hand press printed, sewn-wrap binding, 80 lb. cardstock cover.

How to Submit: Query first with *one* sample poem. Accepts previously published poems and simultaneous submissions. Cover letter preferred. Time between acceptance and publication is 6 months. Responds to queries in 1 month. Pays honorarium of $200 and 6 author's copies (out of a press run of about 250). Order sample chapbooks by sending $15.

Advice: "Don't quit—submit!"

☑ ◯ ◉ **SYNCOPATED CITY**, P.O. Box 2494, Providence RI 02906. E-mail: samuelgray@bigfoot.com. Established 1995. **Editor:** Liti Kitiyakara. **Poetry Editors:** Margaret Balch-Gonzalez, Jerry Fogel, and Milton Mannix.

Magazine Needs: *Syncopated City*, published quarterly, strives "to provide an outlet for the expression of creativity." Wants "poetry of any subject and style; generally 50 lines or less, but will consider longer poems if truly outstanding." Does not want greeting card verse or untitled work. Has published poetry by John Grey, Hugh Fox, Lorette Thiessen, and Ryan G. Van Cleave. As a sample the editor selected these lines from "Maybe Birds Would Carry It Away" by Christopher Woods:

> *But she won't open the locket./She can't./Maybe it's been too long./The hair might dissolve in the air./*
> *Maybe birds would carry it away.*

Syncopated City is 60 pgs., 5½×8½, photocopied, saddle-stapled with cardstock cover, original b&w artwork and ads. Receives about about 800 poems/year, accepts about 20%. Press run is 150-200, mostly shelf sales, about 10% subscriptions including the Rockefeller Library at Brown University; 20-25 distributed free to reviewers and contributors. Subscription: $15. Sample: $4. Make checks payable to Gerald Fogel.

How to Submit: Submit up to 3 poems at a time, preferably under 50 lines, with full name on every page. Accepts previously published poems and simultaneous submissions "if notified and poet retains rights." Accepts e-mail submissions ("attach file"). Cover letter preferred. Time between acceptance and publication is 6-12 months. Often comments on rejected poems. Guidelines available for SASE. Responds in up to 6 months. Pays 1 copy, additional copies half price. Acquires one-time rights.

Advice: "Quality is important, but it is equally important to make us think, make us feel. Don't feel it's necessary to conform—originality is important. We lean toward poetry that is more art than craft. Don't be afraid to be original, evoke thoughts and feelings."

🌐 ◉ **TAK TAK TAK**, BCM Tak, London WC1N 3XX England. Established 1986. **Editors:** Andrew and Tim Brown. *Tak Tak Tak* appears occasionally in print and on cassettes. "However, we are currently not accepting submissions."

☑ 🌐 $ ◯ ◉ **TAKAHE**, P.O. Box 13335, Christchurch 8001 New Zealand. (03)359-8133. Established 1990. **Poetry Editor:** Victoria Broome.

Magazine Needs: "*Takahe* appears three to four times/year, and publishes short stories and poetry by both established and emerging writers. The publisher is the Takahe Collective Trust, a nonprofit organization formed to help new writers and get them into print. While insisting on correct British spelling (or recognized spellings in foreign languages), smart quotes, and at least internally consistent punctuation, we, nonetheless, try to allow some latitude in presentation. Any use of foreign languages must be accompanied by an English translation." No style, subject, or form restrictions. Length: "A poem can take up to two pages, but we have published longer." Has published poetry by John O'Connor, John Allison, Patricia Prime, Jennifer Compton, David Eggleton, Mark Pirie, and James Norcliff. *Takahe* is 60 pgs., A4. Receives about 250 poems/year, accepts about 30%. Press run is 340 for 250 subscribers of which 30 are libraries, 40 shelf sales. Single copy: $NZ6; subscription: $NZ24 within New Zealand, $NZ32 elsewhere.

How to Submit: Accepts previously published poems; no simultaneous submissions. Accepts IBM compatible disk submissions. Cover letter required. Time between acceptance and publication is 4 months. Often comments on rejected poems. Guidelines available for SASE. Responds in 4 months. "Payment varies but currently NZ$30 total for any and all inclusions in an issue plus 2 copies." Acquires first or one-time rights.

🔁 ◯ ◎ **TALE SPINNERS; MIDNIGHT STAR PUBLICATIONS (Specialized: rural/pastoral)**, R.R. #1, Ponoka, Alberta T4J 1R1 Canada. (403)783-2521. Established 1996. **Editor/Publisher:** Nellie Gritchen Scott.

Magazine Needs: *Tale Spinners* is a quarterly " 'little literary magazine with a country flavour,' for writers who love country and all it stands for." Wants poetry, fiction, anecdotes, personal experiences, etc. pertaining to country life. Children's poetry welcome." No scatological, prurient or sexually explicit or political content." She has published poetry by Norma West Lindner, Don Winter, Harold T. Little, Daniel Green, Larsen Bowker, and Kurt Metzler. As a sample the editor selected these lines from "Quest For Happiness" by Melvin Sandberg:

> *I've combed this globe from pole to pole/by trail and boulevard,/But found what I was looking for/*
> *Right in my own back yard.*

Tale Spinner is 48 pgs., 5½×8, photocopied and saddle-stapled with light cardstock cover, uses clip art or freehand graphics. Receives about 100 poems/year, accepts about 80%. Press run is 75 for 50 subscribers. Subscription: $18. Sample: $4.

How to Submit: Submit up to 6 poems at a time. Accepts previously published poems. Cover letter ensures a reply. Foreign submissions should include a SAE and IRC. "Short poems preferred, but will use narrative poems on occasion." Time between acceptance and publication is 3 months. Often comments on rejected poems. Responds in 2 weeks. Pays 1 copy.

Book/Chapbook Needs & How to Submit: "Due to health reasons, Midnight Star Publications is not accepting chapbook manuscripts at present. Tale Spinners will continue."

TALKING RIVER REVIEW, Lewis-Clark State College, 500 Eighth Ave., Lewiston ID 83501. Established 1994. **Contact:** Poetry Editor.

Magazine Needs: *Talking River Review*, published biannually, considers itself a "high-quality literary magazine." Wants "any length, any style, any subject. We print one long poem each issue (up to 15 pages). Send your best work." Does not want "sexist, racist, or simple-minded poetry." Has published poetry by Stephen Dunn, Robert Wrigley, and Dorianne Laux. As a sample the editor selected these lines from "Poverty" by Pattiann Rogers:

> *The lament wasn't in the stiff/whips of willow or the ice-captures/on pondweed and underwater tubers,/*
> *as we expected. No moan rose/from the frost-blackened spikelets/of bluejoint or twisted cattail.*

Talking River Review is 150 pgs., perfect-bound with color cover and some color art. Receives about 3,000 poems/year, accepts less than 5%. Press run is 600 for 350 subscribers of which 50 are libraries, 100 shelf sales; 150 distributed free to students/contributors. Single copy: $6; subscription: $14. Sample: $5.

How to Submit: Submit up to 5 poems at a time. Accepts simultaneous submissions. Cover letter preferred. Reads submissions September 1 through March 1 only. Time between acceptance and publication is 4 months. "Faculty advisor picks poems for board to consider; majority rules." Often comments on rejected poems. Guidelines available for SASE. Responds in up to 3 months. Sometimes sends prepublication galleys. Pays 1-year subscription and 2 contributor's copies. Acquires first rights.

TAMEME (Specialized: bilingual, regional), 199 First St., #335, Los Altos CA 94022. Website: www.tameme.org (includes overview, content, contributors notes, purchase information, and guidelines.) Established 1999. **Contact:** Poetry Editor.

• *Tameme* was awarded a grant from the foundation for US—Mexico Culture.

Magazine Needs: "*Tameme* is an annual literary magazine dedicated to publishing new writing from North America in side-by-side English-Spanish format. *Tameme*'s goals are to play an instrumental role in introducing important new writing from Canada and the United States to Mexico, and vice versa, and to provide a forum for the art of literary translation. By 'new writing' we mean the best work of serious literary value that has been written recently. By 'writing from North America' we mean writing by citizens or residents of Mexico, the United States, and Canada." *Tameme* is open in regard to poetry. They say, "surprise us." Has published poetry by Alberto Blanco, Jaime Sabines, T. Lopez Mills, Marianne Toussaint, and W.D. Snodgrass. *Tameme* is 225 pgs., 5½×8½. Receives about 200 poems/year, accepts 1%. Press run is 2,000. Subscription: $14.95. Sample: $14.95. Make checks payable to Tameme, Inc.

How to Submit: Accepts previously published poems and simultaneous submissions. Cover letter preferred. Include SASE for reply. "If the work you submit has been published elsewhere, be sure to indicate where and when and who holds the copyright. If the work has not been previously published, *Tameme* reserves the right to publish it twice, once in the magazine and again in any future anthology of work that has appeared in *Tameme*. If the work has not been translated, it will be translated by an experienced literary translator chosen by *Tameme*'s editors. Time between acceptance and publication is 4 months. Poems are circulated to an editorial board. Seldom comments on rejected poems. Guidelines available for SASE (or SAE and IRC) or on website. Responds in 4 months. Always sends prepublication galleys. Pays 2 contributor's copies. Acquires first North American serial rights or one-time rights.

Advice: "Submissions via e-mail are not wanted. Poems cannot be read properly online. Do your work justice— send it snail mail with SASE."

TAMPA REVIEW, Dept. PM, University of Tampa, 401 W. Kennedy Blvd., Tampa FL 33606-1490. Website: http://tampareview.utampa.edu. Established 1964 as *UT Poetry Review*, became *Tampa Review* in 1988. **Editor:** Richard Mathews. **Poetry Editor:** Donald Morrill. Send poems to Poetry Editor, *Tampa Review*, Box 19F, The University of Tampa, Tampa FL 33606-1409.

Magazine Needs: *Tampa Review* is an elegant semiannual of fiction, nonfiction, poetry, and art (not limited to US authors) wanting "original and well-crafted poetry written with intelligence and spirit. We do accept translations, but no greeting card or inspirational verse." Has published poetry by Richard Chess, Naomi Shihab Nye, Jim Daniels, and Stephen Dunn. As a sample the editors selected these lines from "91st Birthday" by Peter Meinke:

> *her brown eyes must have lit every room/she entered showing there's a brief time bright/for everyone:*
> *a flushed spell when our blood comes/together the music all trumpets and drums . . .*

Tampa Review is 72-96 pgs., 7½×10½ flat-spined, with acid free text paper and hard cover with color dust jacket. Receives about 2,000 poems/year, accepts 50-60. Press run is 1,000 for 175 subscribers of which 20 are libraries. Sample: $7.

How to Submit: Submit 3-6 poems at a time, typed, single-spaced. No previously published poems or simultaneous submissions. Unsolicited mss are read between September and December only. Guidelines available for SASE. Responds by mid-February. Sometimes sends prepublication galleys. Pays $10/printed page plus 1 contributor's copy and 40% discount on additional copies. Acquires first North American serial rights.

◖ ◗ **TAPROOT LITERARY REVIEW; TAPROOT WRITER'S WORKSHOP ANNUAL WRITING CONTEST**, P.O. Box 204, Ambridge PA 15003. (724)266-8476. E-mail: taproot10@aol.com. Established 1986. **Editor:** Tikvah Feinstein.

Magazine Needs: *Taproot* is an annual publication, open to beginners. "We publish some of the best poets in the U.S. *Taproot* is a very respected anthology with increasing distribution. We enjoy all types and styles of poetry from emerging writers to established writers to those who have become valuable and old friends who share their new works with us." Writers published include Hilary Koski, Lila Julius, Tammy Pegher, Charles Cingolani, B.Z. Niditch, and James Doyle. As a sample the editor selected these lines from "Autumn Croquis" by Elizabeth Howkins:

> *against the sky, reaching upwards/like arms, toward something distant/our eyes, still clouded by summer/cannot see—a world disrobing*

Taproot Literary Review is approximately 95 pgs., offset printed on white stock with one-color glossy cover, art and no ads. Circulation is 500, sold at bookstores, barnesandnoble.com, amazon.com. readings and through the mail. Single copy: $6.95; subscriptions $7.50. Sample: $5.

How to Submit: Submit up to 5 poems, "no longer than 30 lines each." Nothing previously published or pending publication will be accepted. Accepts e-mail submissions (no attached files); "we would rather have a printed copy.'We would rather have a hard copy. Also, we cannot answer without a SASE." Cover letter with general information required. Submissions accepted between September 1 and December 31 only. Guidelines available for SASE. Sometimes sends prepublication galleys. Pays 2 contributor's copies. Open to receiving books for review consideration. Send query first.

Also Offers: Sponsors the annual Taproot Writer's Workshop Annual Writing Contest. 1st Prize: $25 and publication in *Taproot Literary Review*; 2nd Prize: publication; and 3rd Prize: publication. Submit 5 poems of literary quality, any form and subject except porn. Entry fee: $10/5 poems (no longer than 35 lines each), provides copy of review. Deadline: December 31. Winners announced the following March.

Advice: "We publish the best poetry we can in a variety of styles and subjects, so long as it's literary quality and speaks to us. We love poetry that stuns, surprises, amuses, and disarms."

◖ **TAR RIVER POETRY**, English Dept., East Carolina University, Greenville NC 27858-4353. Website: www.ecu.edu/journals (includes guidelines, masthead, sample poetry, and subscription information). Established 1960. **Editor:** Peter Makuck. **Associate Editor:** Luke Whisnant.

Magazine Needs: "We are not interested in sentimental, flat-statement poetry. What we would like to see is skillful use of figurative language." *Tar River* is an "all-poetry" magazine that accepts dozens of poems in each issue, providing the talented beginner and experienced writer with an excellent forum that features all styles and forms of verse. Has published poetry by Samuel Hazo, Carolyn Elkins, R.S. Gwynn, Philip Dacey, Elizabeth Dodd, and Michael Mott. As a sample the editors selected these lines from "Garage Sale Mirror" by Richard Foerster:

> *Where the silver backing's peeled away,/absence blooms upon its surface./Apale impetigo now stipples the face//of the settled room, or take a step and an algae/film seems to have floated from the depth/of a shadowed steam-fed pond . . .*

Tar River appears twice yearly and is 60 pgs., digest-sized, professionally printed on salmon stock, some decorative line drawings, matte card cover with photo. Receives 6,000-8,000 submissions/year, accepts 150-200. Press run is 900 for 500 subscribers of which 125 are libraries. Subscription: $10. Sample: $5.50.

How to Submit: Submit 3-6 poems at a time. "We do not consider previously published poems or simultaneous submissions. Double or single-spaced OK. Name and address on each page. We do not consider mss during summer months." Reads submissions September 1 through April 15 only. Editors will comment "if slight revision will do the trick." Guidelines available for SASE or on website. Responds in 6 weeks. Pays 2 contributor's copies. Acquires first rights. Reviews books of poetry in 4,000 words maximum, single or multi-book format. Poets may send books for review consideration.

Advice: "Read, read, read. Saul Bellow says the writer is primarily a reader moved to emulation. Read the poetry column in *Writer's Digest*. Read the books recommended therein. Do your homework."

☑ ✿ ◖ ◗ ◎ **"TEAK" ROUNDUP (Specialized: subscribers); THE WAY PUBLISHING & CONSULTING, INC.**, P.O. Box 1477, Vernon, British Columbia V1T 6N7 Canada. (250)260-7768. Fax: (250)542-3661. E-mail: vzaitseff@hotmail.com. **Editors:** Valerie Zaitseff and Helen Burmatoff.

Magazine Needs: *"Teak" Roundup* is an international quarterly open to the work of subscribers only. Publishes work from authors and poets across North America and beyond. Accepts poetry written by children. As a sample the editors selected these lines from "A Joyous Moment" by Martin Goorhigian:

> Let the rivers flow/Through verdant lands/Where flocks browse/Carelessly beneath/The endless sun/
> And flowers bloom for eternity.

"Teak" Roundup is 52 pgs., A5, offset-printed, saddle-stapled, medium card cover with clip art, photos, and ads. Subscription: $17 Canadian, $13 US, $24 overseas. Sample: $5 Canadian, $3 US, $8 overseas. **How to Submit:** Accepts work from subscribers only. Submit 3-5 poems at a time. Line length for poetry is 40 maximum, but "good work makes room for exceptions." Accepts fax and e-mail submissions included in body of message. SASE (or SAE with IRC) required for response. Deadlines are Spring issue: January 15; Summer issue: April 15; Fall issue: July 15; Winter issue: October 15. Publishes theme issues. Guidelines and upcoming themes available for SASE. No payment. "It is our goal to become a paying market when circulation makes it feasible." Responds in 1 week.

TEARS IN THE FENCE, 38 Hodview, Stourpaine, Nr. Blandford Forum, Dorset DT11 8TN England. Phone: 0044 1258-456803. Fax: 0044 1258-454026. E-mail: westrow@cooperw.fsnet.co.uk. Established 1984. **General Editor:** David Caddy.
Magazine Needs: *Tears in the Fence* is a "small press magazine of poetry, fiction, interviews, articles, reviews and graphics. We are open to a wide variety of poetic styles. Work that is unusual, perceptive, risk-taking as well as imagistic, lived, and visionary will be close to our purpose. However, we like to publish a variety of work." Has published poetry by Joan Jobe Smith, Kim Taplin, Jay Ramsay, Andrea Moorhead, John Welch, and Linda Healey. As a sample the editors selected these lines by Pansy Maurer-Alvarez from "I must grieve I speak":

> I must grieve I speak/the romance of people the last music/a simple matter of lovers, everything to do/
> with concentration/all one breath the perspective and the voice

Tears in the Fence appears 3 times/year, is 112 pgs., A5, docutech printed on 110 gms. paper and perfect-bound with matte card cover and b&w art and graphics. It has a press run of 700, of which 412 go to subscribers. Subscription: $20/4 issues. Sample: $7.
How to Submit: Submit 6 typed poems with IRCs. Does not accept fax or e-mail submissions. Cover letter with brief bio required. Publishes theme issues. Upcoming themes available for SASE. Responds in 3 months. Time between acceptance and publication is 10 months "but can be much less." Pays 1 contributor's copy. Reviews books of poetry in 2,000-3,000 words, single or multi-book format. Send books for review consideration.
Also Offers: The magazine is informally connected with the East Street Poets literary promotions, workshops and events, including the annual Wessex Poetry Festival and the annual East Street Poets International Open Poetry Competition. Also publishes books. Books published include *Hanging Windchimes In A Vacuum*, by Gregory Warren Wilson, *Heart Thread* by Joan Jobe Smith, and *The Hong Kong/Macao Trip* by Gerald Locklin.
Advice: "I think it helps to subscribe to several magazines in order to study the market and develop an understanding of what type of poetry is published. Use the review sections and send off to magazines that are new to you."

TEBOT BACH, P.O. Box 7887, Huntington Beach CA 92615-7887. (714)968-0905. **Editors/Publishers:** Mifanwy Kaiser
Book/Chapbook Needs & How to Submit: Tebot Bach (Welsh for "little teapot") publishes books of poetry. Titles include *48 Questions* by Richard Jones, *The Way In* by Robin Chapman, and *Written in Rain: New and Selected Poems 1985-2000* by M.L. Liebler. Query first with sample poems and cover letter with brief bio and publication credits. Include SASE. Responds to queries and mss, if invited, in 1 month. Time between acceptance and publication is up to 2 years. Write to order sample books.

TEEN VOICES (Specialized: teen, women), P.O. Box 120-027, Boston MA 02112-0027. E-mail: womenexp@teenvoices.com. Website: www.teenvoices.com (includes creative writing, horoscopes, bulletin boards, activision tips, information about the print magazine, and other topics of interest for our writers and readers). Established 1988; first published 1990. **Contact:** Submission Director.
Magazine Needs: *Teen Voices*, published quarterly, is a magazine written by, for, and about teenage girls. Regular features are family, cultural harmony, surviving sexual assault, teen motherhood, and all other topics of interest to our writers and readers. Accepts poetry written by young women ages 13-19. As a sample the editor selected these lines from "Seraph" by Rachel D.:

> Not long ago in a kingdom by the sea/winged seraphs of heaven protected me/the winds would blow
> their vow/to guide me for eternity

Teen Voices is 72 pgs., with glossy cover, art and photos. "We accept 10% of the poems we receive, but can't afford to publish all of them timely." Press run is 25,000. Single copy: $3; subscription: $20. Sample: $5. Make checks payable to *Teen Voices*.
How to Submit: Submit any number of poems with name, age and address on each. Accepts simultaneous submissions; no previously published poems. Accepts fax submissions and e-mail submissions included in body of message. Cover letter preferred. "Confirmation of receipt of submission sent in 6-8 weeks." Poems are circulated to a teen editorial board. Pays 5 contributor's copies. Open to unsolicited reviews.

TEMPORARY VANDALISM RECORDINGS; THE SILT READER, P.O. Box 6184, Orange CA 92863-6184. E-mail: tvrec@yahoo.com. Website: www.csulb.edu/~rroden. Established 1991 (Temporary Vandalism Recordings), 1999 (*The Silt Reader*). **Editors:** Robert Roden and Barton M. Saunders.

Magazine Needs: *The Silt Reader*, is published biannually. "Form, length, style and subject matter can vary. It's difficult to say what will appeal to our eclectic tastes." Does not want "strictly rants, overly didactic poetry." Has published poetry by M. Jaime-Becerra, Daniel McGinn, Jerry Gordon, Margaret Garcia, and S.A. Griffin. As a sample the editor selected these lines from "The Woman Next Door" by Duane Locke:

> Under her dark hair,/a white bowl/of ashes from burnt poppies.//She is afraid/she'll hear her clothes
> drop/and become apples.//She is afraid/her hands will turn into magpies/and have shadows.//She is
> afraid her mirror might vanish./She only bares her breasts to mirrors.

The Silt Reader is 32 pgs., 4¼ × 5½, saddle-stapled, photocopied with colored card cover and some ads. Accepts less than 15% of poems received. Press run is 500. Sample: $2. Make checks payable to Robert Roden.

How to Submit: Submit 5 neatly typed poems at a time. Accepts previously published poems and simultaneous submissions. Does not accept e-mail submissions. Cover letter preferred. Time between acceptance and publication is 3 months. "Two editors' votes required for inclusion." Seldom comments on rejected poems. Responds in up to 6 months. Pays 2 contributor's copies. Acquires one-time rights.

Book/Chapbook Needs & How to Submit: Temporary Vandalism Recordings strives "to make the world safe for poetry (just kidding)." Publishes 3 chapbooks/year. Chapbooks are usually 40 pgs., photocopied, saddle-stapled, press run of 100 intially, with reprint option if needed. Submit 10 sample poems, with SASE for response. "Publication in some magazines is important, but extensive publishing is not required." Responds in 3 months. Pays 50% royalty (after costs recouped) and 5 author's copies (out of a press run of 100). For sample chapbooks send $5 to the above address.

10TH MUSE, 33 Hartington Rd., Southampton, Hants SO14 0EW England. Established 1990. **Editor:** Andrew Jordan.

Magazine Needs: *10th Muse* "includes poetry and reviews, as well as short prose (usually no more than 2,000 words) and graphics. I prefer poetry with a strong 'lyric' aspect. I enjoy experimental work that corresponds with aspects of the English pastoral tradition. I have a particular interest in the cultural construction of landscape." Has published poetry by Peter Riley, Andrew Duncan, Dr. Charles Mintern, Ian Robinson, John Welch, and Jeremy Hooker. As a sample the editor selected these lines from *City Walking (1)* by Jeremy Hooker:

> The brown Thames/laps against timbers.//A fragment of Roman wharf/is bound against a pillar,/ancient
> water-worn wood/against carved stone.

10th Muse is 48-72 pgs., A5, photocopied, saddle-stapled, with card cover, no ads. Press run is 200. "U.S. subscribers—send $8 in bills for single copy (including postage)."

How to Submit: Submit up to 6 poems. Include SASE (or SAE with IRCs). Often comments on rejected poems. Responds in 3 months. Pays 1 contributor's copy. Staff reviews books of poetry. Send books for review consideration.

Advice: "Poets should read a copy of the magazine first."

TERRA INCOGNITA, A BILINGUAL LITERARY REVIEW; TERRA INCOGNITA—EN-CUENTRO CULTURAL BILINGÜE, P.O. Box 150585, Brooklyn NY 11215-0585. (718)492-3508. E-mail: terraincognita@worldonline.es. Website: http://inicia.es/de/ti (includes guidelines, excerpts from current issue, names of editors, new content when possible, etc.). Established 1998 (first issue publised in summer 2000). **US Poetry Editor:** Alexandra van de Kamp. **Spanish Poetry Editor:** Luciano Priego. **Member:** CLMP.

Magazine Needs: *Terra Incognita, A Bilingual Literary Review* appears biannually. Goal "is to print the best work we can find from established and emerging writers in English and Spanish on both sides of the Atlantic and to act as a cultural bridge between the various Spanish and English-speaking communities. We are open to all forms and subject matter except for that of pornography and material with racist/sexist themes. We're looking for work with guts and intelligence that shows a love of the craft. We do not want to see poetry that asks only so much of itself. We want poetry that rises out of a true, sure urgency, out of a need to be written." Recently published poetry by Billy Collins, Virgil Suarez, Laurie Blauner, J'Laine Robnolt, Donna Stonecipher, and José Hierro. As a sample the editor selected these lines from "Under the Mermaid's Moon" by Laurie Blauner:

> You should see aquatic life: the twist and shouts of color,/the knots of light, the vague features of the
> drowned waving/good-bye. In our own backyard we find desire,/not the kind that endless explorers
> spread over continents,/not the gold distortion of treasure winking conspiratorially,/but the way life
> repeats itself, the retelling/of the amorous red rose.

Terra Incognita is 90 pgs., magazine-sized, printed, perfectly-bound, card stock cover, with b&w photos, sketches, and selective ads for mainly independent presses and companies. Accepts about 3% of poems submitted. Publishes about 25-30 poems/issue. Press run is 1,000. Single copy $7.50; subscription: $14/year or $25/2 years. Sample: $6 plus $2 postage. Make checks payable to Alexandra van de Kamp.

How to Submit: Submit 5 poems at a time. Line length for poetry is 100 maximum. Accepts simutaneous submissions with notification; no previously published poems. No fax, e-mail, or disk submissions. Cover letter is preferred. Note: **Submissions in Spanish should be sent to Apartado 14.401, 28080, Madrid, Spain with 2-3 IRCs.** Reads submissions all year. Time between acceptance and publication is 2-10 months. "The final decision on poetry submissions lies with the poetry editor, but other editors are consulted as well." Sometimes comments on rejected poems. Guidelines are available in magazine, for SASE, by e-mail, or on website. Responds in up to 2 months. Sometimes sends prepublication galleys. Pays 2 contributor's copies. Acquires first North American serial rights. Reviews books and chapbooks of poetry in 1,000 words, single book format. Poets may send books for review consideration to Alexandra van de Kamp.

Also Offers: *Terra Incognita* is part of a larger cultural association that does bilingual readings and encourages cultural exchanges.

Advice: "We look for poetry that is not merely good or capable, but which is actually exciting and thrilling to read—something that bubbles up from deeper, more complex sources. Poetry that is not only confident but comes from a conviction of its need to be written. Beginners, ask yourself why your poem or piece *needs* to be in the world."

TEXAS TECH UNIVERSITY PRESS (Specialized: series), P.O. Box 41037, Lubbock TX 79409-1037. (806)742-2982. Fax: (806)742-2979. E-mail: ttup@ttu.edu. Website: www.ttup.ttu.edu. Established 1971. **Editor:** Judith Keeling. Does not read unsolicited manuscripts.

THALIA: STUDIES IN LITERARY HUMOR (Specialized: subscribers, humor), Dept. of English, University of Ottawa, Ottawa, Ontario K1N 6N5 Canada. (613)230-9505. Fax: (613)565-5786. E-mail: jtaverni@aixl.uottawa.ca. **Editor:** Dr. J. Tavernier-Courbin.

Magazine Needs: *Thalia* appears twice/year using "humor (literary, mostly). Poems submitted must actually be literary parodies." *Thalia* is 7 × 8½, flat-spined, "with illustrated cover." Press run is 500 for 475 subscribers. Subscription: $25 (US funds) for individuals, $27 (US funds) for libraries. Sample: $8 up to volume 11, $15 and $20 for volume 12-15 respectively (double issues).

How to Submit: Contributors must subscribe. Accepts simultaneous submissions but *Thalia* must have copyright. Will authorize reprints. Publishes occasional theme issues. Query for guidelines and upcoming themes. "Accepts queries via phone, fax, or e-mail. Accepts fax submissions. However, submissions must be in hard copy." Editor comments on submissions. Responds in 4 months. Reviews books of poetry. "Send queries to the editor concerning specific books."

THEMA (Specialized: themes), Thema Literary Society, P.O. Box 8747, Metairie LA 70011-8747. E-mail: thema@home.com. Website: www.litline.org/THEMA (includes general information, guidelines and upcoming themes, a list of past issues, and sample writing from past issues). Established 1988. **Editor:** Virginia Howard. **Poetry Editor:** Gail Howard. Address poetry submissions to Gail Howard.

Magazine Needs: *Thema* is a triannual literary magazine using poetry related to specific themes. "Each issue is based on an unusual premise. Please, please send SASE for guidelines before submitting poetry to find out the upcoming themes. Upcoming themes (and submission deadlines) include: 'The Power Within (November 1, 2001); 'Paper Tigers' (March 1, 2002); 'Lost in Translation' (July 1, 2002). No scatologic language, alternate life-style, explicit love poetry." Accepts poetry written by children, but quality counts. Poems will be judged with all others submitted. Has published poetry by John Grey, Lynn Veach Sadler, Max Money, and L.G. Mason. As a sample the editor selected these lines from "Visitor" by Carol Kanter:

This *Thema* cover shows the birthplace of the issue's theme, "On the Road to the Villa." After reworking her photograph in Corel to add "richness" to the two-toned photograph, editor Virginia Howard admits, "Adding the text was the easy part."

A young September day./Crisp./The cameo moon/pins half its wispy face/on the cloudless sapphire sky.
Thema is 200 pgs., digest-sized, professionally printed, with matte card cover. Receives about 400 poems/year, accepts about 8%. Press run is 500 for 270 subscribers of which 30 are libraries. Subscription: $16. Sample: $8.
How to Submit: Submit up to 3 poems at a time with SASE. All submissions should be typewritten and on standard 8½ × 11 paper. Submissions are accepted all year, but evaluated after specified deadlines. Guidelines and upcoming themes available for SASE, on website, or by e-mail. Editor comments on submissions. Pays $10/poem plus 1 contributor's copy. Acquires one-time rights.

N: ⬤ THIN AIR MAGAZINE: A JOURNAL OF THE LITERARY ARTS, Graduate Creative Writing Association of Northern Arizona University, P.O. Box 23549, Flagstaff AZ 86002. (520)523-6743. Fax: (520)523-7074. Website: www.nau.edu/~english/thinair/. Established 1995. **Poetry Editor:** Mandi Merrifield. **Editor-in-Chief:** A. Vaughn Wagner.
Magazine Needs: *Thin Air* is a biannual literary magazine of poetry, fiction, nonfiction, and essays. "The aesthetic we use in selecting work for our magazine is a simple one: Does it catch our eyes and our minds? Is it something we want not only to read, but to re-read? If this describes your writing then we would love to see a submission." Has published poetry by Vivian Shipley, Nancy Johnson, and Charles H. Webb. As a sample we selected these lines from "Tarantula Dreams" by James Jay:

> *"You see I'm in low orbit. Sometimes it's longer,/then I must be in high orbit." From the rim/I reply*
> *"ah, hah, ah" when Dostoesvky/would have said "what . . . what . . . what" or Kerouac/"who . . .*
> *skoo di dee skoo di dee doo . . . who,"/So low from orbit the man says to wait, so I do/from down here*
> *on a rutted road of brown that meanders/over the rim and into the space of the high desert/below.*

Thin Air is 50 pgs., 5½ × 8½, attractively printed and permabound with coated color cover, includes art. Receives about 300 poems/year, accepts 10%. Press run is 300-500 for 70 subscribers of which 5 are libraries, 225-425 shelf sales. Single copy: $4.95; subscription: $9. Sample: $4.
How to Submit: Submit up to 10 poems at a time. Accepts simultaneous submissions with notification; no previously published poems. Cover letter preferred. Reads submissions August through May only, but accepts submissions all year. Time between acceptance and publication is 2 months. Seldom comments on rejected poems. Guidelines available for SASE. Responds in 1 month. Pays 2 contributor's copies. Acquires all rights and extends republishing rights to the author subject to acknowledgement of original publication in *Thin Air*. Reviews books and chapbooks of poetry and other magazines in 700-1,200 words, single book format. Poets may send books for review consideration.
Also Offers: Sponsors annual contest for fiction/creative nonfiction and one poetry. Deadline: January 31. Rules available for SASE.

☑ ⬤ THIN COYOTE; LOST PROPHET PRESS, P.O. Box 583377, Minneapolis MN 55458-3377. (612)209-6689. E-mail: revjone@thincoyote.com. Website: www.thincoyote.com. Established 1992. **Publisher/Editor:** Christopher Jones.
Magazine Needs: *Thin Coyote* is a quarterly magazine "churning up whirlwinds of creative endeavor by the planet's scofflaws, mule skinners, seers, witchdoctors, maniacs, alchemists, and giant-slayers. Get in touch with your inner shapeshifter and transcribe his howls, growls, and wails. No singsong rhyming crap; no greeting card devotional stuff or I'll come over to your house and put a terrible hurtin' on you." Has published poetry by Jonis Agee, John Millett, Pat McKinnon, and Paul Weinman. As a sample the editor selected these lines from "Beelzebub the Geometer" by Joseph Carrella:

> *God works not in angles/but in folds. Fat girls/curled in concupiscence/sing hosannas. Damn, damn/*
> *the Angel of the straitedge.*

Thin Coyote is 40-60 pgs., 8½ × 11, docutech printed and perfect-bound with b&w cardstock cover, includes b&w photos and ads. Receives about 3,000 poems/year, accepts 2-5%. Press run is 300 for 30 subscribers of which 20 are libraries, 270 shelf sales. Single copy: $6; subscription: $18. Sample: $6. Make checks payable to Christopher Jones/*Thin Coyote*.
How to Submit: Submit 5 poems at a time. Accepts previously published poems and simultaneous submissions. Accepts e-mail submissions. Cover letter preferred. Time between acceptance and publication is 4 months. Often comments on rejected poems. Guidelines available for SASE. Responds in 1 month. Pays 1 contributor's copy. Acquires first or one-time rights. Reviews books and chapbooks of poetry and other magazines. Poets may send books for review consideration to Christopher Jones.
Book/Chapbook Needs & How to Submit: Lost Prophet Press publishes "primarily poetry, some short stories." Publishes 2-3 chapbooks/year. Chapbooks are usually 30-40 pgs., 5½ × 8, offset-printed and saddle-stapled with cardstock cover, includes art. Query first, with a few sample poems and a cover letter with brief bio and publication credits. Responds to queries in 1 month; to mss in 2 weeks. Pays advance or 25% of run.

MARKETS THAT WERE listed in the 2001 edition of *Poet's Market* but do not appear this year are listed in the General Index with a notation explaining why they were omitted.

Also Offers: Annual chapbook competition; submit $24 pages of poetry or shor fiction and a $13 reading fee before August 31 (annual deadline). First prize is $100, publication, and up to 50 author's copies. "Lost Prophet Press is now also publishing a new magazine, *Knuckle Merchant: the Journal of Naked Literary Aggression.*"

THORNY LOCUST, P.O. Box 32631, Kansas City MO 64171-5631. established 1993. E-mail: kofler@tot o.net. **Editor:** Silvia Kofler. **Associate Editor:** Celeste Kuechler.
Magazine Needs: *Thorny Locust*, published quarterly, is a "literary magazine that wants to be thought-provoking, witty, and well-written." Wants "poetry with some 'bite' e.g., satire, epigrams, black humor and bleeding-heart cynicism." Does not want "polemics, gratuitous grotesques, sombre surrealism, weeping melancholy, or hate-mongering." Has published poetry by B.Z. Niditch, Phyllis Becker, Simon Perchik, and Philip Miller. As a sample the editor selected these lines from "Writings" by Brian Daldorph:
> writing's/easy just/paper and/blade/to cut the vein/do it/bleed . . .

Thorny Locust is 28-32 pgs., $7 \times 8\frac{1}{2}$, desktop-published, saddle-stapled with medium cover stock, drawings and b&w photos. Receives about 350-400 poems/year, accepts about 35%. Press run is 150-200 for 30 subscribers of which 6 are libraries; 60 distributed free to contributors and small presses. Single copy: $4; subscription: $15. Sample: $3. Make checks payable to Silvia Kofler.
How to Submit: Submit 3 poems at a time. "If you do not include a SASE with sufficient postage, your submission will be pitched!" Accepts simultaneous submissions; no previously published poems. Cover letter preferred. "Poetry and fiction must be typed, laser-printed or in a clear dot-matrix." Time between acceptance and publication is 2 months. Seldom comments on rejected poems. Guidelines available for SASE. Responds in 3 months. Pays 1 contributor's copy. Acquires one-time rights.
Advice: "Never perceive a rejection as a personal rebuke, keep on trying. Take advice."

THOUGHTS FOR ALL SEASONS: THE MAGAZINE OF EPIGRAMS (Specialized: form, humor, themes), % editor Prof. Em. Michel Paul Richard, 478 NE 56th St., Miami FL 33137-2621. Established 1976.
Magazine Needs: *Thoughts for All Seasons* "is an irregular serial: designed to preserve the epigram as a literary form; satirical. All issues are commemorative." Rhyming poetry and nonsense verse with good imagery will be considered although most modern epigrams are prose. As a sample the editor selected this poem by Rex E. Moser:
> If Shakespeare had two IBMs/And I a humble quill/Would I produce artistic gems/And he this awful
> swill?

Thoughts for All Seasons is 80 pgs., offset from typescript and saddle-stapled with full-page illustrations, card cover. Accepts about 20% of material submitted. Press run is 500-1,000. There are several library subscriptions but most distribution is through direct mail or local bookstores and newsstand sales. Single copy: $6 (includes postage and handling).
How to Submit: Submit at least 1 full page of poems at a time, with SASE. Accepts simultaneous submissions, but not previously published epigrams "unless a thought is appended which alters it." Editor comments on rejected poems. Publishes theme issues. Theme for Volume 6 is "Time Travel." Guidelines available for SASE. Responds in 1 month. Pays 1 contributor's copy.

THREE CANDLES, E-mail: editor@threecandles.org. Website: www.threecandles.org (includes an extensive links and resource section). Established 1999. **Editor:** Steve Mueske.
Magazine Needs: *Three Candles* appears weekly ("post updates when qualified poetry is available, generally once or twice a week"). "Though I am not particular about publishing specific forms of poetry, I prefer to be surprised by the content of the poems themselves. I believe that poetry should have some substance and touch, at least tangentially, on human experience." Does not want poems that are "overtly religious, sexist, racist, or unartful." Recently published poetry by Jim Moore, Deborah Keenan, Peter Kane Dufault, Jim Brock, and Jacqueline Marcus. As a sample the editor selected these lines from "Question From the Floor" by Peter Kane Dufault:
> Could you call it Dead Motion—/that of the atoms, planets,/stars, galaxies—seeing/it can no more
> cease/than dead men can collect/old bones and resume being

Three Candles is a "high-quality online journal, professionally designed and maintained." Receives about 1,000 poems/year. Publishes "approximately 4-6 poets/month, about 10 poems. Many poems I publish are solicited directly from poets." Receives over 3,000 hits/month "and growing."
How to Submit: Submit 3-5 poems at a time. Accepts simultaneous submissions, if noted; no previously published poems. Accepts *only* e-mail submissions; no disk submissions. Send poems "as the body of the text or, if special formatting is used, as attachments in Word or rich text format. In the body of the e-mail, I want a short bio, a list of previous publications, and a brief note about what writing poetry means to you as an artist." Accepts submissions year round. Time between acceptance and publication is "nominal, usually less than 2 weeks." Sometimes comments on rejected poems. "Reading the journal is important to get an idea of the level of craft expected." Guidelines available on website. Responds within 2 months. Does not send prepublication galleys but "allows author to make any necessary changes before a formal announcement is e-mailed to the mailing list." No payment "at this time." Acquires first rights. Copyright reverts to author after publication.

Advice: "The online poetry community is vital and thriving. Take some time and get to know the journals that you are submitting to. Don't send work that is like what is published. Send work that is as good but different in a way that is uniquely your own."

☑ ⚘ ◯ **3 CUP MORNING; SOMETIMES I SLEEP WITH THE MOON ... ELECTRONIC PUB-LICATION,** 1372 Grantley Rd., Chesterville, Ontario K0C 1H0 Canada. Fax: (613)448-1478. E-mail: cards@canada.com. Website: http://3cupmorning.8k.com. Established 1999. **Editor:** H. Moodie. **Webzine Editor:** Gen O'Neil.

Magazine Needs: Published bimonthly, *3 cup morning* is "a platform for the beginning and novice poet to showcase their work. We firmly believe that seeing your work in print is the single greatest encouragement needed to continue. Every poet should have the opportunity to see their work in print—at least once anyway." Accepts all types of poetry, haiku, traditional, experimental, free form, etc. No graphic violence, hate, profanity, or graphic sex. Has published poetry by Robert Hogg, Valerie Poynter, J. Kevin Wolfe, Mary-Ann Hazen, and Ruth Witter. As a sample the editor selected these lines from "Immortality" by Ruth Ritter:

> On wisps of rare, invisible silk/Soul eludes in mystery whispers./No face but a lonesome breath.//She slips through mortal fingers/Occupied with dust.

3 cup morning is 20 pgs., 5½×8½, photocopied and saddle-stapled with illustrated card cover, includes art/graphics. Publish about 15 poems/issue. Press run is about 200 copies. Subscription: $30. Sample: $5. Make checks or money order payable to Gen O'Neil.

How to Submit: Submit 5 poems at a time. Line length for poetry is 3 minimum, 40 maximum. Accepts previously published poems and simultaneous submissions. Prefers e-mail submissions but accepts "anything that is neatly typed or printed." Electronic submissions can be sent in html or plain text. "All work must be neatly typed on white paper with your name and address on every page. SAE with an IRC must be included if you want to have work returned or a review of your work sent to you. Would prefer to have an e-mail address to send critique to." Submit seasonal poems well in advance. Time between acceptance and publication is 4 months. Poems are circulated to an editorial board. Guidelines available on website. "We guarantee that at least one poem from each submission will be printed in our publication. If you would like to be published on the web, please say so in your cover letter."

Advice: "We look for poetry that is visible. Poetry you can see and touch and feel."

☑ ⬭ ◔ **360 DEGREES,** 1229 Reece Rd., Charlotte NC 28209. Established 1993. **Managing Editor:** Karen Kinnison.

Magazine Needs: *360 Degrees* is a biannual review, containing literature and artwork. "We are dedicated to keeping the art of poetic expression alive." "No real limits" on poetry, "only the limits of the submitter's imagination." However, they do not want to see "greeting card verse, simplified emotions, or religious verse." Accepts poetry written by children. Has published poetry by Rochelle Holt, Anselm Brocki, Aaron Petrovich, and Christopher Brisson. As a sample the editor selected these lines from "Where Heroes Gather" by David Demarest.

> "It is the encounter of a lifetime,/the endless struggle, like Sisyphus and his rock,/where the sun confronts the moon's sad and silent side/and rises again the better for it,/free, perhaps, yet forever locked within dark gates."

360 Degrees is 40 pgs., digest-sized, neatly printed and saddle-stapled. Receives about 1,000 poems/year, accepts about 80. Press run is 500 for 100 subscribers and one library. Subscription: $17. Sample: $3.

How to Submit: Submit 3-6 poems at a time. Include SASE. Accepts simultaneous submissions; no previously published poems. "Just let us know if a particular piece you have submitted to us has been accepted elsewhere." Cover letter preferred. Seldom comments on rejected poems. Guidelines available for SASE. Responds within 3 months. Pays 1 contributor's copy.

Advice: "We are a small, but excellent review. Most of the poems we accept not only show mastery of words, but present interesting ideas. The mastery of language is something we expect from freelancers, but the content of the idea being expressed is the selling point."

☑ ⬭ $◔ **THE THREEPENNY REVIEW,** P.O. Box 9131, Berkeley CA 94709. (510)849-4545. Website: www.threepennyreview.com (includes sample work, advertising and submission guidelines, internet order forms for single issues, and subscription information). Established 1980. **Poetry Editor:** Wendy Lesser.

● Work published in this review has also been included in *The Best American Poetry*.

Magazine Needs: *Threepenny Review* "is a quarterly review of literature, performing and visual arts, and social articles aimed at the intelligent, well-read, but not necessarily academic reader. Nationwide circulation. Want: formal, narrative, short poems (and others). Prefer under 100 lines. No bias against formal poetry, in fact a slight bias in favor of it." Has published poetry by Thom Gunn, Frank Bidart, Seamus Heaney, Czeslaw Milosz, and Louise Glück. Features about 10 poems in each 36-page tabloid issue. Receives about 4,500 submissions of poetry/year, accepts about 12. Press run is 10,000 for 8,000 subscribers of which 150 are libraries. Subscription: $20. Sample: $10.

How to Submit: Submit up to 5 poems at a time. Do not submit mss June through August. Guidelines available for SASE or on website. Responds in up to 2 months. Pays $100/poem plus year's subscription. Acquires first serial rights. "Send for review guidelines (SASE required)."

☑ ◯ **THE THRESHOLD; CROSSOVER PRESS**, P.O. Box 101362, Pittsburgh PA 15237. (412)364-9009. Fax: (412)364-3273. E-mail: threshmag@aol.com. Website: www.thresholdmagazine.com (includes guidelines, editor's name, excerpts from poetry, and short story collections). Established 1996. **Editor:** Don H. Laird. **Poetry Editor:** Halley White.
Magazine Needs: *The Threshold* is a quarterly magazine. "The types of works we tend to find most interesting are epic or adventure poetry, fantasy and gothic verse, or mythological narrative poetry." *The Threshold* is 48 pgs., magazine-sized, attractively printed and saddle-stitched with glossy color cover, includes b&w illustrations. Receives about 200 poems/year, accepts about 5%. Publishes about 2 poems/issue. Press run is 600 for 100 subscribers, 500 shelf sales. Sample copy: $5.95; subscription: $19.95. Make checks payable to Crossover Press.
How to Submit: Submit up to 2 poems at a time. Accepts simultaneous submissions; no previously published poems. No fax or e-mail submissions. "Poets should provide a brief biography." Time between acceptance and publication is 6 months. Occasionally publishes theme issues. Guidelines available for SASE. Responds in up to 8 months. Pays 1 contributor's copy. Acquires one-time rights.
Advice: "Good writers are a dime a dozen. Good story tellers are priceless!"

Ⓝ ⊕ ◪ **THUMBSCREW**, P.O. Box 657, Oxford OX2 6PH United Kingdom. E-mail: tim.kendall@bristol. ac.uk. Website: www.bristol.ac.uk/thumbscrew (includes an archive section for past and present issues). Established 1994. **Editor:** Tim Kendall.
Magazine Needs: "Appearing 3 times/year, *Thumbscrew* is an international poetry magazine featuring poetry and criticism from well-known and new writers." Has published poetry by Paul Muldoon, Anne Stevenson, Michael Longley, and Seamus Heaney. *Thumbscrew* is 100 pgs., magazine-sized, perfect-bound with laminated board cover. Receives about 6,000 poems/year, accepts 1%. Press run is 600 for 400 subscribers of which 50 are libraries, 200 shelf sales. Subscription: $27.50. Sample: $9.50.
How to Submit: Submit 2-5 poems at a time. No previously published poems or simultaneous submissions. E-mail submissions are not accepted. Cover letter preferred. "Send clear typed copies, with each page including name and address of author." Time between acceptance and publication is 3 months. Seldom comments on rejected poems. Occasionally publishes theme issues. Responds in 3 months. Pays 1-2 contributor's copies. Acquires all rights. Copyright returned to author after publication. Reviews books and chapbooks of poetry in 1,000 words, single book format. Poets may send books for review consideration.

☑ ▣ ◯ **THUNDER RAIN PUBLISHING, CORP.; L'INTRIGUE WEB MAGAZINE; THUNDER RAIN WRITER AWARD**, P.O. Box 1000, Livingston LA 70754. (225)686-2002. Fax: (225)686-2285. E-mail: rhi@thunder-rain.com. Website: www.thunder-rain.com or www.intrigue.org. Established 1996. **Managing Editor:** Katherine Christoffel. **Associate Editors:** Phyllis Jean Green and Elizabeth Hebron.
Magazine Needs: *L'Intrigue* is published 3 times a year on the Internet. Accepts quality work by beginning and established poets. Accepts submissions of poetry, fiction, nonfiction, feature stories, and reviews on all literary material. Welcomes information on literary events. Has published *Mixing Cement* by Peter Tomassi. As a sample the editors selected these lines from "Housewife" in *Mixing Cement* by Peter Tomassi:

> She managed to ignore all summer/That strange crackling in the fireplace/The skulk of handymen storming her nave/The porch door locked and shut/It was time to kindle the fire/To flirt with the screen/ A whisper one more time/Her kiss of breeze/To be her last

Receives about 250 poems/year, accepts approximately 35%.
How to Submit: Accepts simultaneous submissions if notified. Short bio requested. E-mail submissions preferred. Acquires first North American serial rights. Copyright remains with author.
Also Offers: Sponsors the annual Thunder Rain Writer Award of $100 for all genre published in *L'Intrigue*. Winner notified in January of following year. "Voice in the Mind" by Sara Claytor was the 2000 Thunder Rain Award-winning poem. Also has an ongoing project, *The Louisiana Poetry Book*, for which poetry about Louisiana is accepted. Pays $5 a poem. Publication date has not been set.

◪ **TIGHTROPE; SWAMP PRESS**, 15 Warwick Rd., Northfield MA 01360. Established 1977. **Editor:** Ed Rayher.
Magazine Needs: *Tightrope*, appearing annually, is a "limited edition letterpress magazine of fine poetry and original art." Has published poetry by Robert Bensen and Gian Lombardo. The format of *Tightrope* varies though it is usually 60 pgs. and letterpress-printed. Receives about 1,000 poems/year, accepts 2%. Publishes 60 poems/ issue. Press run is 300 for 50 subscribers of which 20 are libraries and 150 are shelf sales. Subscription: $10/2 issues. Sample: $6.
How to Submit: Submit 6 poems at a time. No simultaneous submissions or previously published poems. Time between acceptance and publication is 1 year. Seldom comments on rejected poems. SASE required. Responds in 3 months. Pays 2 contributor's copies. Acquires one-time rights.
Book/Chapbook Needs & How to Submit: *Not presently accepting unsolicited submissions for chapbook publication.* Swamp Press is a small press publisher of poetry and graphic art in limited edition, letterpress chapbooks. Swamp Press has published books by Edward Kaplan, editor Ed Rayher, Alexis Rotella (miniature, 3×3, containing 6 haiku), Sandra Dutton (a 4 foot long poem), Frannie Lindsay (a 10×13 format containing 3 poems), Andrew Glaze, Tom Haxo, Carole Stone, and Steven Ruhl. Publishes 1-6 titles a year in either hardback

or paperback. Books are usually 60 pgs., letterpress-printed, hand-sewn/Smyth-sewn with a wrap cover/cloth-bound cover and art. Responds to queries and mss in 6 months. Pays 5-10% of press run. Catalog available for SASE.

$ ⊘ TIMBERLINE PRESS, 6281 Red Bud, Fulton MO 65251. (573)642-5035. Established 1975. **Poetry Editor:** Clarence Wolfshohl.
Book/Chapbook Needs: "We do limited letterpress editions with the goal of blending strong poetry with well-crafted and designed printing. We lean toward natural history or strongly imagistic nature poetry but will look at any good work. Also, good humorous poetry." Has published *The White Rose* by Wally Swist; *The Lighthouse Keeper* by Larry D. Thomas; and *Wildcat Road* by William Hart. Sample copies may be obtained by sending $5, requesting sample copy, and noting you saw the listing in *Poet's Market*. Responds in under 1 month. Pays "50-50 split with author after Timberline Press has recovered its expenses."
How to Submit: Query before submitting full ms.

■ ○ ◎ TIMBOOKTU (Specialized: ethnic/nationality), P.O. Box 933, Mobile AL 36601-0933. E-mail: editor@timbooktu.com. Website: www.timbooktu.com. Established 1996. **Editor:** Memphis Vaughan, Jr.
Magazine Needs: *TimBookTu* is a monthly online journal. Wants "positive, creative, and thought-provoking poetry that speaks to the diverse African-American culture and the African diaspora." Has published poetry by Zamoundie Allie, Jamal Sharif, John Riddick, Rodney Coates, Michael Rodriguez, and Richard "Rip" Parks. Receives about 1,500 poems/year, accepts about 75%.
How to Submit: Submit 3 poems at a time. Accepts previously published poems and simultaneous submissions. Accepts e-mail and disk submissions; no fax submissions. Cover letter preferred. Time between acceptance and publication is 2 months. Always comments on rejected poems. Guidelines are available for SASE. Responds in 1 month. Poets may send books for review consideration.

✿ ○ ◎ TIME FOR RHYME (Specialized: form/style), P.O. Box 1055, Battleford, Saskatchewan S0M 0E0 Canada. (306)445-5172. Established 1995. **Editor:** Richard W. Unger.
Magazine Needs: *Time for Rhyme*, published quarterly, aims to "promote traditional rhyming poetry. Other than short editorial, contents page, review page, PoeMarkets (other markets taking rhyme), this magazine is all rhyming poetry." Wants "any rhyming poetry in any form up to about 32 lines on nearly any subject." Does not want poetry that is "obscene (4-letter words), pornographic, profane, racist, or sexist. No e.e. cummings' style either." Has published poetry by Elizabeth Symon, Sharron R. McMillan, Anthony Chalk, and J. Alvin Speers. *Time for Rhyme* is 32 pgs., 4 × 5½, photocopied, hand-bound with thread, hand press printed cover, with clip art, handmade rubber stamps, letterpress art and ads. Receives several hundred poems/year, accepts about 10%. Subscription: $12. Sample: $3.25.
How to Submit: "Preference given to subscribers, however, no requirements." Accepts previously published poems ("But must ensure poet retained rights on it. Prefer unpublished"). No simultaneous submissions. Cover letter preferred and if first submission here give brief list of publications poet has been published in. No poems published yet? Send some general information." Often comments on rejected poems. Guidelines available for SASE (or SAE with IRC). "Americans submitting can save money by sending SAE and $1 U.S. bill (cheaper than IRC). Please no SASE with U.S. stamps." Responds ASAP. Pays 1 copy. Acquires first North American serial rights—will consider second serial rights. Staff reviews books/magazines containing mostly or all rhyming poetry. Reviews vary in length but up to about 100 words. Send books for review consideration.
Advice: "Though non-rhyming poetry can be excellent, *Time for Rhyme* was created to be a platform for poets who prefer rhyme and as a source for those who prefer to read it. Old-fashioned values popular here too. Might be best to read a back issue before submitting."

✓ ⊘ ◎ TIME OF SINGING, A MAGAZINE OF CHRISTIAN POETRY (Specialized: religious, themes), P.O. Box 149, Conneaut Lake PA 16316. E-mail: timesing@toolcity.net. Website: http://timeofsinging. bizland.com (includes themes, guidelines, sample poems, and subscription information). Established 1958-1965, revived 1980. **Editor:** Lora H. Zill.
Magazine Needs: *Time of Singing* appears 4 times/year. "We tend to be traditional. We like poems that are aware of grammar. Collections of uneven lines, series of phrases, preachy statements, unstructured 'prayers,' and trite sing-song rhymes usually get returned. We look for poems that 'show' rather than 'tell.' The viewpoint is unblushingly Christian—but in its widest and most inclusive meaning. Moreover, it is believed that the vital message of Christian poems, as well as inspiring the general reader, will give pastors, teachers, and devotional leaders rich current sources of inspiring material to aid them in their ministries. Would like to see more forms. Has published poetry by Tony Cosier, John Grey, Luci Shaw, Bob Hostetler, Evelyn Minshull, Frances P. Reid, and Charles Waugaman. As a sample the editor selected these lines from "Stone Pillars" by Elizabeth Howard:

> Manoah brought his broken/body home. We grieved/two wheat straws leaning/into each other for
> succor,/but one pale day, joy/crept onto the hearth,/legs as spindly/as a grasshopper nymph's/on a
> frosty morning.

Time of Singing is 40 pgs., digest-sized, offset from typescript with decorative line drawings scattered throughout. The bonus issues are not theme based. Receives over 800 submissions/year, accepts about 175. Press run is 300 for 150 subscribers. Single copy: $6; subscription: $15 US, $18 Canada, $27 overseas. Sample: $4.

How to Submit: Submit up to 5 poems at a time, single-spaced. "We prefer poems under 40 lines, but will publish up to 60 lines if exceptional." Accepts simultaneous submissions and previously published poems. Accepts e-mail submissions, include in body of message. Time between acceptance and publication is up to 1 year. Editor comments with suggestions for improvement if close to publication. Publishes theme issues "quite often." Guidelines and upcoming themes are available for SASE, by e-mail, and on website. Responds in 2 months. Pays 1 contributor's copy.

Also Offers: Sponsors several theme contests for specific issues. Guidelines and upcoming themes available for SASE.

TO' TO' POS: AN ANNUAL ANTHOLOGY OF POETRY FOR THE INTERNATIONALLY MINDED (Specialized: themes), (formerly *To Topio*), 712 NW 13th St., Corvallis OR 97330. (541)753-9955. E-mail: weaverroger@hotmail.com. Established 1996. **Founder:** Roger Weaver. **Contact:** Editor.

Magazine Needs: *To' To' Pos* is published annually (Summer/Fall). "The landscape, site or locality that *To' To' Pos* refers to is global, so we welcome quality poetry from all over the world and in any language, so long as it is accompanied by an English translation approved by the author and so indicated with the author's legible signature." Has published *From Roots to Branches* edited by Chris Pine. As a sample the editors selected these lines from "The Free Song" by Gerard Bocholier, translated by J. Krause:

> *Becoming simple obsesses us,/Writing smooth like water,/Speaking peony or sparrow,/Finding one's rhyme under light.*

To' To' Pos is 50-100 pgs., digest-sized, perfect-bound with card cover. Subscription: $6.

How to Submit: Submit up to 6 poems or pages with name and address on each page. Accepts simultaneous submissions; no previously published poems. Cover letter preferred. Reads submissions September 1 through April 15 only. Poems are circulated to an editorial board with two editors agreeing on the acceptances. Seldom comments on rejected poems. Publishes theme issues. Guidelines and upcoming themes available for SASE. Pays 1 copy. Acquires one-time rights.

Also Offers: "Poetry Enterprises provides copyrighted but free materials for poets and artists, students and teachers. Send a SASE and request for information on traditional poetry, free verse, or prose poetry."

TORRE DE PAPEL (Specialized: ethnic/nationality), 111 Phillips Hall, Iowa City IA 52242-1409. (319)335-0487. E-mail: torredepapel@uiowa.edu. Website: www.uiowa.edu/~spanport. Established 1991. **Editor:** Eduardo Gúizar Alvarez.

Magazine Needs: Appearing 3 times/year, *Torre de Papel* is a "journal devoted to the publication of critical and creative works related to Hispanic and Luso-Brazilian art, literature, and cultural production. We are looking for poetry written in Spanish, Portuguese, or languages of these cultures; translations of authors writing in these languages; or poems in English representative of some aspect of Hispanic or Luso-Brazilian culture." Does not want to see "poetry for children; no religious or esoterical work." As a sample the editor selected these lines from David William Foster and Daniel Altamiranda's translation of "Cadáveres" by Néstor Perlongher:

> *Along the tracks of a train that never stops/In the wave of a sinking ship/In a small wave, vanishing/ On the wharves the steps the trampolines the piers/There are Corpses*

Torre de Papel is 110 pgs., 8¾ × 11½. Press run is 200 for 50 subscribers of which 19 are libraries. Single copy: $7; subscription: $21. Sample: $10.

How to Submit: Submit up to 5 poems at a time. No previously published poems or simultaneous submissions. Accepts e-mail submissions, include as attached file. Cover letter with brief bio required. Include e-mail address. Submit 3 copies of each poem and a Macintosh or IBM diskette of the work. Reads submissions September through April only. Poems are circulated to an editorial board for review. "We send creative work to three readers of our advisory board for comments. However, since we publish articles and stories as well, space for poetry can be limited." Responds in 6 months. Pays 1 contributor's copy.

$ TOUCH (Specialized: religious, young teens, themes), P.O. Box 7259, Grand Rapids MI 49510. (616)241-5616. Established 1970. **Managing Editor:** Sara Lynne Hilton.

Magazine Needs: *Touch* is a 24-page edition "written for girls 9-14 to show them how God is at work in their lives and in the world around them. *Touch* is theme-oriented. We like our poetry to fit the theme of each issue. We send out a theme update biannually to all our listed freelancers. We prefer short poems with a Christian emphasis that can show girls how God works in their lives." Has published poetry by Janet Shafer Boyanton and Iris Alderson. As a sample the editor selected this poem, "Thanks for Funny Things," by Lois Walfrid Johnson:

> *Thank You for funny things,/for the bubbling feeling of/giggles that fill my insides,/push up,/and spill over/in a shout of joy!/Thank You, Lord./Thank You!*

Touch is published 9 times/year, magazine-sized. *Keeping In-Touch* newsletter is published in the summer. Receives 150-200 submissions of poetry/year, accepts 1 poem/issue; has a 6-month backlog. Circulation is 15,500 subscribers. Subscription: $12.50 US, $15 Canada, $20 foreign. Sample and guidelines: $1 with 8 × 10 SASE.

How to Submit: Poems must not be longer than 20 lines—prefer much shorter. Accepts simultaneous submissions. Query with SASE for theme update. Responds in 2 months. Pays $10-15 and contributor's copies.

✓ ◉ **TOUCHSTONE LITERARY JOURNAL (Specialized: bilingual/foreign language, form/ style, translations); PANTHER CREEK PRESS**, P.O. Box 8308, Spring TX 77387-8308. E-mail: guidamj@fl ex.net or panthercreek3@hotmail.com. Website: www.panthercreekpress.com (includes guidelines, names of editors, display of current titles, and ordering information). Established 1975. **Poetry Editor:** William Laufer. **Managing Editor:** Guida Jackson. (Mail for book projects should be sent to Panther Creek Press, P.O. Box 130233, Panther Creek Station, Spring TX 77393-0233, attn: Guida Jackson.)
Magazine Needs: *Touchstone Literary Journal* is an annual appearing in December that publishes "experimental or well-crafted traditional form, including sonnets, and translations. No light verse or doggerel." Has published poetry by Walter Griffin, Walter McDonald, Paul Ramsey, Omar Pound, and Christopher Woods. *Touchstone* is 100 pgs., digest-sized, flat-spined, professionally printed in small, dark type with glossy card cover. Subscription: $7.50.
How to Submit: Submit 5 poems at a time. "Cover letter telling something about the poet piques our interest and makes the submission seem less like a mass mailing." Sometimes sends prepublication galleys. Pays 2 contributor's copies. Reviews books of poetry. Poets may send books for review consideration to Review Editor.
Book/Chapbook Needs & How to Submit: Panther Creek Press also publishes an occasional chapbook. Send SASE for chapbook submission guidelines. Recent titles include *Leopards, Oracles, and Long Horns: Three West African Epic Cycles* by chichi layor, *Watching the Worlds Go By, Selected Poems* by Omar Pound; and *Under a Riverbed Sky* by Christopher Woods. "Query first, with SASE. Absolutely no mail is answered without SASE or e-mail address."

🅽 ✓ ◉ **TOWER POETRY SOCIETY; TOWER**, % McMaster University, 1200 Main St. W., Box 1021, Hamilton, Ontario L8S 1C0 Canada. (905)648-4878. Established 1951. **Editor-in-Chief:** Joanna Lawson.
Magazine Needs: "The Tower Poetry Society was started by a few members of McMaster University faculty to promote interest in poetry. We publish *Tower* twice/year. We want rhymed or free verse, traditional or modern, but not prose chopped into short lines, maximum 40 lines in length, any subject, any comprehensible style." Has published poetry by Bill Moore and Helen Fitzgerald Dougher. As a sample the editor selected these lines by Joanna Lawson:

> A poem is/a slide under a microscope/one thin slice/of then,/or now,/or what might be,/magnified for
> meaning

Tower is 40 pgs., digest-sized. Press run is 250 for 60 subscribers of which 8 are libraries. Receives about 400 poems/year, accepts about 70. Subscription: $8; $9.50 abroad. Sample: $3.
How to Submit: Submit up to 4 poems at a time. Reads submissions during February or August. Responds in 2 months. Pays 1 contributor's copy.
Advice: "Read a lot of poetry before you try to write it."

✓ ◉ **TRANSCENDENT VISIONS (Specialized: psychiatric survivors, ex-mental patients)**, 251 S. Olds Blvd. 84-E, Fairless Hills PA 19030-3426. (215)547-7159. Established 1992. **Editor:** David Kime.
Magazine Needs: *Transcendent Visions* appears 1-2 times/year "to provide a creative outlet for psychiatric survivors/ex-mental patients." Wants "experimental, confessional poems; strong poems dealing with issues we face. Any length or subject matter is OK but shorter poems are more likely to be published. No rhyming poetry." Has published poetry by Alan Catlin, John Greg, and Mike Lazarchuk. As a sample the editor selected these lines from "It (Fear)" by Gloria del Vecchio:

> What has happened to the rat?/Is it on some remote street with its/mouth and anus ruining space?/
> Suddenly, out of the chimney/the rat leaps into the room and/climbs up the paintings of large women.

Transcendent Visions is 24 pgs., 8½×11, photocopied and corner-stapled with paper cover, b&w line drawings. Receives about 100 poems/year, accepts 20%. Press run is 200 for 50 subscribers. Subscription: $6. Sample: $2. Make checks payable to David Kime.
How to Submit: Submit 5 poems at a time. Accepts previously published poems and simultaneous submissions. Cover letter preferred. "Please tell me something unique about you, but I do not care about all the places you have been published." Time between acceptance and publication is 3 months. Responds in 3 weeks. Pays 1 contributor's copy of issue in which poet was published. Acquires first or one-time rights. Staff reviews books and chapbooks of poetry and other magazines in 20 words. Send books for review consideration.
Also Offers: "I also publish a political zine called *Crazed Nation*, featuring essays concerning mental illness."

✓ ◉ ◉ **TRESTLE CREEK REVIEW (Specialized: regional)**, English Dept., LHA-2, North Idaho College, 1000 W. Garden Ave., Coeur d'Alene ID 83814-2199. (208)769-5915. Fax: (208)769-3431. E-mail: gala_muench@nic.edu. Established 1982-83. **Editor:** Gala Muench et al.
Magazine Needs: *Trestle Creek Review* is a "2-year college creative writing program production. Purposes: (1) expand the range of publishing/editing experience for our small band of writers; (2) expose them to editing experience; (3) create another outlet for serious, beginning writers. We're fairly eclectic but prefer poetry on the Northwest region, particularly the innermountain West (Idaho, Montana, etc.). We favor poetry strong on image and sound, and country vs. city; spare us the romantic, rhymed clichés. We can't publish much if it's long (more

than two pgs.).'' Features both free and formal verse by relative newcomers. Has published poetry by Sean Brendan-Brown, E.G. Burrows, Ron McFarland, and Mary Winters. As a sample the editor selected these lines from "under my skin" by Rande Mack:

> there are targets taking shape in the brains/of the yellowstone wolves—there are edges/over which they'll never know they've stumbled

Trestle Creek Review is a 57-page annual, digest-sized, professionally printed on heavy buff stock, perfect-bound, matte cover with art. Press run is 500 for 6 subscribers of which 4 are libraries. Receives 100 submissions/year, accepts about 30. Sample: $5.

How to Submit: Submit before March 1 (for May publication), no more than 5 pgs. No previously published poems or simultaneous submissions. Accepts fax and e-mail submissions (in attached file). Responds by May 30. Pays 2 contributor's copies.

Advice: "Be neat; be precise; don't romanticize or cry in your beer; strike the surprising, universal note. Know the names of things."

✓ 🏵 ◐ **TRIQUARTERLY MAGAZINE; TRIQUARTERLY BOOKS/NORTHWESTERN UNI- VERSITY PRESS**, 2020 Ridge Ave., Evanston IL 60208-4302. (847)491-3490. Fax: (847)467-2096. Website: www.triquarterly.nwu.edu. **Editor:** Susan Hahn.

● Work appearing in *TriQuarterly* has been included in *The Best American Poetry* and the *Pushcart Prize* anthologies.

Magazine Needs: *TriQuarterly* magazine "accepts a wide range of verse forms and styles of verse (long poems, sequences, etc.) with the emphasis solely on excellence, and some issues are published as books on specific themes." Has published poetry by Tom Sleigh, Carl Phillips, Edward Hirsch, Campbell McGrath, Susan Stewart, and Theodore Weiss. *TriQuarterly*'s three issues per year are 250 pgs., 6×9, professionally printed and flat-spined with b&w photography, graphics, glossy card cover. Each issue has about 40 or more pgs. of poetry. Receives about 3,000 poems/year, accepts 60; 1 year backlog. Press run is 5,000 for 2,000 subscribers of which 35% are libraries. Single copy: $11.95; subscription: $24. Sample: $5.

How to Submit: No simultaneous submissions. No fax or e-mail submissions. Reads submissions October 1 through March 31 only. Sometimes works with poets, inviting rewrites of interesting work. Responds in 3 months. Always sends prepublication galleys. Pays 2 contributor's copies, additional copies available at a 40% discount. Acquires first North American serial rights. "We suggest prospective contributors examine sample copy before submitting." Reviews books of poetry "at times."

Book Needs & How to Submit: TriQuarterly Books (an imprint of Northwestern University Press) publishes 8-10 books/year of fiction and poetry. Has published poetry by William Meredith, Pimone Triplett, and Muriel Rukeyser. Query with up to 10 sample pages of poetry with SASE, "but we cannot consider unsolicited manuscripts without a prior query." Send SASE for additional information.

$ ◑ ◎ **TRUE ROMANCE (Specialized: women); STERLING MACFADDEN**, 233 Park Ave. S., New York NY 10003. **Editor:** Pat Vitucci.

Magazine Needs: *True Romance* is a monthly magazine publishing "subjects of interest to women—family, careers, romance, tragedy, personal crises." Wants "poems that express a unique point of view. Poems that address topics. No Hallmark greeting cards." *True Romance* is 108 pgs., magazine-sized.

How to Submit: Submit 3 poems at a time. Line length for poetry is 8 minimum, 24 maximum. No previously published poems or simultaneous submissions. Send SASE for guidelines before submitting. Responds in 3 months. Pays $10-40. Acquires all rights.

◐ ◎ **TSUNAMI, INC.; THE TEMPLE (Specialized: foreign language)**, P.O. Box 100, Walla Walla WA 99362-0033. (509)529-0813. E-mail: tsunami@innw.net. Website: www.tsunami-inc.net (includes guidelines, names of editors, sample poems, and covers of books). Established 1995. **Editor:** Charles Potts.

Magazine Needs: *The Temple,* is a quarterly poetry magazine containing poems in Chinese, Spanish, and English; also news, reviews and events. Wants "signature poems exhibiting artistic control, intellectual rigor, emotional commitment, and a command of subject matter. No rhymes, haiku; formalist, overly clever, or academic work." Has published poetry by Teri Zipf, John Oliver Simon, Jim Bodeen, and Sharon Doubiago. As a sample the editor selected these lines from "The Wheel" by Stephen Thomas:

> My daddy made me reinvent the wheel . . ./on the lathe which I'd invented more than once/and would again. The spoke wire/trembled like a martyr,/as I drew it out from the/extruder in the hissing workshop air.

The Temple is 80 pgs., 7×10, web press printed on newsprint and saddle-stapled, includes ads for books and other magazines. Receives about 5,000 poems/year, accepts about 1%. Press run is 5,000 for 300 subscribers of which 10 are libraries; 600 distributed free to poets at festivals. Subscription: $20. Sample: $5. Make checks payable to Tsunami, Inc. "Familiarity is critical, poets must buy and read a sample first or be a subscriber."

How to Submit: Submit 3-5 poems at a time. Accepts previously published poems; no simultaneous submissions. Accepts e-mail submissions. Cover letter preferred. "Send poems in 9×12 envelopes." Send Chinese mss to Denis Mair, 9200 Glendon Way, Rosemead CA 91770. Time between acceptance and publication is 3 months.

Seldom comments on rejected poems. Guidelines available for SASE or on website. Responds in 2 months. Pays 10 contributor's copies. Acquires first North American serial or one-time rights. Reviews books and chapbooks of poetry and other magazines in single or multi-book format. Poets may send books for review consideration.

Book/Chapbook Needs: Tsunami Inc. publishes 3 paperbacks/year. Books are published by invitation only.

Advice: "Beginners send one to three poems, large envelope, SASE for reply. Know the contents of the magazine to date: we publish original poetry in Spanish and Chinese with English translations."

TUCUMCARI LITERARY REVIEW (Specialized: cowboy, form/style, humor, regional, social issues, memories, nostalgia), 3108 W. Bellevue Ave., Los Angeles CA 90026. Established 1988. **Editor:** Troxey Kemper.

Magazine Needs: *Tucumcari* appears every other month. "Prefer rhyming and established forms, including sonnet, rondeau, triolet, kyrielle, villanelle, terza rima, limerick, sestina, pantoum and others, 2-100 lines, but the primary goal is to publish good work. No talking animals. No haiku. No disjointed, fragmentary, rambling words or phrases typed in odd-shaped staggered lines trying to look like poetry. The quest here is for poetry that will be just as welcome many years later as it is now." Has published poetry by Bobby S. Rivera, Helen McIntosh Gordon, Mary Gribble, Richard Moore, Virgil Suarez, and Ruth Daniels. As a sample the editor selected this limerick by William J. Middleton:

> A motto that's presently shared/By all the Boy Scouts was declared/when a tenderfoot tyke/Fixed the horn on his bike/An proudly announced, "Beep repaired."

Tucumcari Literary Review is 48 pgs., digest-sized, saddle-stapled, photocopied from typescript, with card cover. Press run is 150-200. Subscription: $12, $20 for overseas. Sample: $2, $4 for overseas.

How to Submit: Submit up to 4 poems at a time. Accepts simultaneous submissions and previously published poems. Sometimes comments on rejected poems. Guidelines available for SASE. Responds within 1 month. Pays 1 contributor's copy. Acquires one-time rights.

Advice: "Writing is welcomed from amateurs, in-betweens and professors/scholars. Oddly, some of the work by amateurs is more honest, earnest, and heart-felt. The main measure of acceptability is: Is it interesting? Is it good? What counts is what it says not whether the work is handwritten on lined notebook paper or presented on expensive computer-generated equipment/paper which often is very difficult to read. *Tucumcari Literary Review* often is overstocked with material, but if something arrives that I like, I will make room for it. I publish two or three extra or bonus issues a year (free to subscribers) trying to use up the backlog. It is gratifying to me to see the number of college and university professors who submit their work here, and a few 'famous' writers have sent their work."

TURKEY PRESS, 6746 Sueno Rd., Isla Vista CA 93117-4904. Established 1974. **Poetry Editors:** Harry Reese and Sandra Reese. "We do not encourage solicitations of any kind to the press. We seek out and develop projects on our own."

TURNSTONE PRESS LIMITED (Specialized: regional), 607-100 Arthur St., Winnipeg, Manitoba R3B 1H3 Canada. (204)947-1555. Fax: (204)942-1555. E-mail: editor@turnstonepress.mb.ca. Website: www.TurnstonePress.com (includes writer's guidelines, list of books, and samples of writing). Established 1976. **Contact:** Acquisitions Editor-Poetry.

• Books published by Turnstone Press have won numerous awards, including the McNally Robinson Book of the Year Award, the Canadian Author's Association Literary Award for Poetry and the Lampert Memorial Awards.

Book/Chapbook Needs: "Turnstone Press publishes Canadian authors with special priority to prairie interests/themes." Publishes 2 paperbacks/year. Has published poetry by Di Brandt, Catherine Hunter, Patrick Friesen, and Dennis Cooley. Books are usually 5½ × 8½, offset-printed and perfect-bound with quality paperback cover.

How to Submit: Query first with 10 sample poems and cover letter with brief bio and publication credits. Accepts previously published poems and simultaneous submissions. Cover letter preferred. "Please enclose SASE (or SAE with IRC) and if you want the submission back, make sure your envelope and postage cover it." Time between acceptance and publication is 1 year. Poems are circulated to an editorial board. "The submissions that are approved by our readers go to the editorial board for discussion." Receives more than 1,200 unsolicited mss/year, about 10% are passed to the editorial board. Responds to queries in 3 months; to mss in 4 months. Pays royalties of 10% plus advance of $200 and 10 author's copies.

Advice: "Competition is extremely fierce in poetry. Most work published is by poets working on their craft for many years."

24.7; RE-PRESST, 30 Forest St., Providence RI 02906. Established 1994. **Poetry Editor:** David Church. Currently not accepting submissions.

TWILIGHT ENDING, 21 Ludlow Dr., Milford CT 06460-6822. (203)877-3473. Established 1995. **Editor/Publisher:** Emma J. Blanch.

Magazine Needs: *Twilight Ending* appears 3 times/year publishing "poetry and short fiction of the highest caliber, in English, with universal appeal." Has featured the work of poets from the US, Canada, Europe, Middle East, Japan, and New Zealand. Wants "poems with originality in thought and in style, reflecting the latest trend in writing, moving from the usual set-up to a vertical approach. We prefer unrhymed poetry, however we accept rhymed verse if rhymes are perfect. We look for the unusual approach in content and style with clarity. No haiku. No poems forming a design. No foul words. No translations. No bio. No porn." *Twilight Ending* is 5½×8½, "elegantly printed on white linen paper with one poem with title per page (12-30 lines)." Receives about 1,500 poems/year, accepts 10%. Press run is 120 for 50 subscribers of which 25 are libraries. Sample: $6 US, $6.50 Canada, $7 Europe, $8 Middle East, Japan, and New Zealand. Make checks payable to Emma J. Blanch.

How to Submit: Submit only 3-4 poems at a time, typed, single spaced. No previously published poems or simultaneous submissions nor poems submitted to contests while in consideration for *Twilight Ending*. Include white stamped business envelop for reply (overseas contributors should include 2 IRCs). No fax or e-mail submissions. "When accepted, poems and fiction will not be returned so keep copies." Submission deadlines: mid-December for Winter issue, mid-April for Spring/Summer issue, mid-September for Fall issue. No backlog, "all poems are destroyed after publication." Often comments on rejected poems. Guidelines available for SASE. Responds in 1 week. Pays nothing—not even a copy. Acquires first rights.

Advice: "If editing is needed, suggestions will be made for the writer to rework and resubmit a corrected version. The author always decides; remember that you deal with experts."

☑ Ⓞ **TWO RIVERS REVIEW; ANDERIE POETRY PRESS**, P.O. Box 158, Clinton NY 13323. E-mail: tworiversreview@juno.com (guidelines/inquiries only). Website: http://members.tripod.lycos.com/tworr/trr.html. Established 1998. **Editor:** Philip Memmer.

Magazine Needs: *Two Rivers Review* appears biannually and "seeks to print the best of contemporary poetry. All styles of work are welcome, so long as submitted poems display excellence." Has published poetry by Billy Collins, Gary Young, Lee Upton, Baron Wormser, and Olga Broumas. *Two Rivers Review* is 44-52 pgs., digest-sized, professionally printed on cream-colored paper, with card cover. Subscription: $12. Sample: $6. "Poets wishing to submit work may obtain a sample copy for the reduced price of $4."

How to Submit: Submit no more than 4 poems at a time with cover letter (optional) and SASE (required). Simultaneous submissions are considered with notification. No electronic submissions. Guidelines available for SASE, by e-mail, or on website. Responds to most submissions within 1 month. Acquires first rights.

Also Offers: Sponsors the annual *Two Rivers Review* Poetry Prize. In 2001, the *Two Rivers Review* chapbook series will also be introduced, with books chosen through a competition. Guidelines available for SASE or on website.

☑ $ Ⓞ **U.S. CATHOLIC; CLARETIAN PUBLICATIONS**, 205 W. Monroe St., Chicago IL 60606. (312)236-7782. E-mail: aboodm@claretianpubs.org. Website: www.uscatholic.org. Established 1935. **Literary Editor:** Maureen Abood.

Magazine Needs: "Published monthly, *U.S. Catholic* engages a broad range of issues as they affect the everyday lives of Catholics." Has no specifications for poetry, but does not necessarily want poems religious in nature. No light verse. Has published poetry by Naomi Shihab Nye. *U.S. Catholic* is 51 pgs., magazine-sized, printed in 4-color and stapled, includes art/graphics. Receives about 1,000 poems/year, accepts about 12 poems. Publishes 1 poem/issue. Press run is 50,000. Subscription: $22.

How to Submit: Submit 3 poems at a time. Line length for poetry is 50 maximum. Accepts simultaneous submissions; no previously published poems. Accepts e-mail submissions (include in body of message); no fax submissions. Cover letter preferred. Always include SASE. Time between acceptance and publication is 3 months. Poems are circulated to an editorial board. Seldom comments on rejected poems. Guidelines available for SASE. Responds in 3 months. Pays $75 and 5 contributor's copies. Acquires first North American serial rights.

☑ Ⓞ ◎ **THE U.S. LATINO REVIEW (Specialized: ethnic, ecology, political, social issues); HISPANIC DIALOGUE PRESS**, P.O. Box 150009, Kew Gardens NY 11415. E-mail: andrescastro@aol.com or editor@uslatinoreview.org. Website: www.uslatinoreview.org (includes writer's guidelines, mission statement, poetry, interview, etc.). Established 1999. **Managing Editor:** Andres Castro.

Magazine Needs: "*U.S. Latino Review* is a biannual literary review for Latinos, our friends, and critics. It is indeed a labor of love dedicated to promoting the best we as a community of creative artists have to offer. We expect truth, excellence and passion from ourselves and contributors. We include poetry, short short story, essay, sketch art and other forms considered if queried. Submissions of all content and form are considered, but writers and artists should understand that we heavily favor work that focuses concretely on the urgent social, political, economic and ecological issues of our time. We stress that *U.S. Latino Review* is not exclusionary—we are won over easily by care, craft and conscience. Hate to say, but if you are going to be egocentric you better send a masterpiece." Has published poetry by Alma Luz Villianueva, L.S. Asekoff, Jack Agüeros, Cornelius Eady, Virgil Suarez, Kimiko Hahn, and Tony Medina. As a sample we selected these lines from "Always Things Pressing Flat" by Lorraine Lopez:

> damp palms mash my brother's/cowlick to his scalp. I remember/always her pushing things down/so
> that they would stay. You,/girls, she would say if we rose/to storm, shouldn't be angry.//never lose your
> temper. Never shout/nor punch. Don't shove, don't bite./never rattle windows, slam doors. You/girls,
> you have your outlet, your release.

U.S. Latino Review is 64 pgs., 5½×8½, printed on 100% recycled 24 lb. stock and flat-spined with semi-gloss card cover, includes black ink sketch art/prints. Receives about 500 poems/year, accepts 3-5%. Press run is 500 for 50 subscribers, 300 shelf sales. Single copy: $6 US; subscription: $12 US; $22 US/2 years. Make checks payable to *The U.S. Latino Review*.

How to Submit: Submit 3-5 poems at a time. Accepts previously published poems and simultaneous submissions. Accepts e-mail submissions in body of message (no attachments). Cover letter preferred. "SASE must accompany submissions. A short bio is requested but not necessary for contributors page." Time between acceptance and publication is up to 6 months. Poems are circulated to an editorial board. "Editor does early screening and poems forwarded to editorial board of at least three others for final selection." Often comments on rejected poems. Guidelines available for SASE. Responds in 3 months. Sends prepublication galleys if requested. Acquires first rights.

Advice: "Please, send your best."

☑ ◑ **U.S. 1 WORKSHEETS; U.S. 1 POETS' COOPERATIVE**, P.O. Box 127, Kingston NJ 08528-0127. Established 1973. **Contact:** Poetry Editors. **Managing Editor:** Winifred Hughes.

Magazine Needs: *U.S. 1 Worksheets* is a literary annual, double issue December or January, circulation 400, which uses high-quality poetry and fiction. "We use a rotating board of editors; it's wisest to query when we're next reading before submitting. A self-addressed, stamped postcard will get our next reading period dates (usually in the spring)." Has published poetry by Alicia Ostriker, James Richardson, Frederick Tibbetts, Lois Marie Harrod, James Haba, Charlotte Mandel, and David Keller. *U.S. 1 Worksheets* is 72 pgs., 5½×8½, saddle-stapled, with color cover art. "We read a lot but take very few. Prefer complex, well-written work." Subscription: $7, $12/2 years.

How to Submit: Submit 5 poems at a time. Include name, address, and phone number in upper right-hand corner. No simultaneous submissions; rarely accepts previously published poems. Requests for sample copies, subscriptions, queries, back issues, and all mss should be addressed to the editor (address at beginning of listing). Pays 1 contributor's copy.

☑ ⊕ ◯ ◑ **UNDERSTANDING MAGAZINE; DIONYSIA PRESS LTD.**, 20 A Montgomery St., Edinburgh, Lothion EH7 5JS Great Britain. Phone/fax: (0131)4770754. E-mail: denise.smith@cablenet.co.uk. Established 1989. **Contact:** Denise Smith.

Magazine Needs: *Understanding Magazine*, published 1-2 times/year, features "poetry, short stories, parts of plays, reviews and articles." Wants "original poetry." Has published poetry by Susanna Roxman, D. Zervanou, and Ron Butlin. As a sample we selected these lines from "Private Axis" by Thom Nairn:

> The circles grow relentlessly,/His passage, inscrutably centrifugal/On this terminal cycle to silence.

Understanding is A5 and perfect-bound. Receives 2,000 poems/year. Press run is 1,000 for 500 subscribers. Single copy: £4.50; subscription: £9. Sample: £3. Make checks payable to Dionysia Press.

How to Submit: Submit 5 poems at a time. Accepts simultaneous submissions; no previously published poems. Accepts e-mail and fax submissions. Time between acceptance and publication is 6-10 months. Poems are circulated to an editorial board. Often comments on rejected poems. Responds in 6 months or more. Always sends prepublication galleys. Pays 1 contributor's copy. Acquires all rights. Returns rights after publication. Staff reviews books or chapbooks of poetry or other magazines. Send books for review consideration.

Book/Chapbook Needs & How to Submit: Dionysia Press Ltd., publishes 14 paperbacks and chapbooks of poetry/year. "Sometimes we select from submissions or competitions." Has published *Let Me Sing My Song* by Paul Hullah; *Poems* by Klitos Kyrou, translated by Thom Nairn and D. Zervnaou; *Sailing the Sands* by James Andrew; and *The Feeble Lies of Orestes Chalkiopoulos* by Andreas Mitsou. Books are usually A5, perfect-bound, hard cover with art. Query first, with a few sample poems and cover letter with brief bio and publication credits. Responds to queries in 2-6 months. Pays author's copies. "We usually get arts council grants or poets get grants for themselves." For sample books or chapbooks, write to the above address.

Also Offers: Sponsors poetry competitions with cash prizes. Guidelines available for SASE.

⬛ $ **UNIVERSITY OF ALBERTA PRESS**, Ring House 2, Edmonton, Alberta T6G 2E1 Canada. (780)492-3662. Fax: (780)492-0719. E-mail: u.a.p@ualberta.ca. Website: www.ualberta.ca/~uap (includes contact information and description of publishing program). Established 1969. **Managing Editor:** Leslie Vermeer.

Book/Chapbook Needs: "The University of Alberta Press is a scholarly press, generally publishing nonfiction plus some literary titles." Publishes 1-2 paperback poetry titles per year. Looking for "mature, thoughtful work—nothing too avant-garde. No juvenile or 'Hallmark verse.'" Has published poetry by E.D. Blodgett, Alice Major, Bert Almon, Fred Wah, Monty Reid, and Nigel Darbasie.

How to Submit: Query first, with 10-12 sample poems and cover letter with brief bio and publication credits. "Do not send complete manuscript on first approach." Accepts previously published poems and simultaneous submissions. Accepts e-mail and disk submissions. Time between acceptance and publication is 6-10 months. Poems are circulated to an editorial board. "The process is: acquiring editor to editorial group meeting to two external reviewers to press committee to acceptance." Seldom comments on rejected poems. Responds to queries in 2 months. Pays royalties of 10% of net plus 10 author's copies. See website to order sample books.

◐ **UNIVERSITY OF GEORGIA PRESS; CONTEMPORARY POETRY SERIES**, 330 Research Dr., Suite B100, University of Georgia, Athens GA 30602-4901. (706)369-6135. Fax: (706)369-6131. E-mail: mnunne ll@ugapress.uga.edu. Website: www.uga.edu/ugapress (includes competition guidelines). Press established 1938, series established 1980. **Series Editor:** Bin Ramke. **Poetry Competition Coordinator:** Margaret Nunnelley.
Book/Chapbook Needs: Through its annual competition, the press publishes 4 collections of poetry/year, 2 of which are by poets who have not had a book published, in paperback editions. Has published poetry by Marjorie Welish, Arthur Vogelsang, C.D. Wright, Martha Ronk, and Paul Hoover.
How to Submit: "Writers should query first for guidelines and submission periods. Please enclose SASE." There are no restrictions on the type of poetry submitted, but "familiarity with our previously published books in the series may be helpful." No fax or e-mail submissions. $15 submission fee required. Make checks payable to University of Georgia Press. Manuscripts are *not* returned after the judging is completed.

✓ ◐ **UNIVERSITY OF IOWA PRESS; THE IOWA POETRY PRIZES**, 119 West Park Rd., 100 Kuhl House, Iowa City IA 52242-1000. Fax: (319)335-2055. E-mail: rhonda-wetjen@uiowa.edu. Website www.uiowa. edu/~uipress (includes "all our books, some with samples").
Book/Chapbook Needs: The University of Iowa Press offers annually the Iowa Poetry Prizes for book-length mss (50-150 pgs.) by new or established poets. Winners will be published by the Press under a standard royalty contract. Winning entry for 2000 was *The Penultimate Suitor* by Mary Leader. (This competition is the only way in which this press accepts poetry.)
How to Submit: Mss are received annually in April only. All writers of English are eligible. Poems from previously published books may be included only in mss of selected or collected poems, submissions of which are encouraged. Accepts simultaneous submissions if press is immediately notified if the book is accepted by another publisher. $15 entry fee is charged; stamped, self-addressed packaging is required or mss will not be returned. Include name on the title page only. Single copy: $13.95 plus postage.
Advice: "These awards have been initiated to encourage all poets, whether new or established, to submit their very best work."

N ◐ **UNIVERSITY OF TEXAS PRESS**, P.O. Box 7819, Austin TX 78713-7819. Website: www.utexas. edu/utpress. Established 1950. Not accepting unsolicited manuscripts.

✓ ◐ **UNIVERSITY OF WISCONSIN PRESS; BRITTINGHAM PRIZE IN POETRY; FELIX POL-LAK PRIZE IN POETRY**, 2537 Daniels St., Madison WI 53718-6772. Website: www.wisc.edu/wisconsinpress/ index.html. Brittingham Prize inaugurated in 1985. **Poetry Editor:** Ronald Wallace.
Book/Chapbook Needs: The University of Wisconsin Press publishes primarily scholarly works, but they offer the annual Brittingham Prize and the Felix Pollak Prize, both $1,000 plus publication. These prizes are the only way in which this press publishes poetry. Send SASE for rules. Qualified readers will screen all mss. Winners will be selected by "a distinguished poet who will remain anonymous until the winners are announced in mid-February." Past judges include Henry Taylor, Carolyn Kizer, Philip Levine, Rita Dove, Donald Hall, Alicia Ostriker, Mark Poty, and Robert Bly. Winners include Stefanie Marlis, Tony Hoagland, Stephanie Strickland, Lisa Lewis, Derick Burleson, and Greg Rappleye.
How to Submit: For both prizes, submit between September 1 and October 1, unbound ms volume of 50-80 pgs., with name, address, and telephone number on title page. No translations. Poems must be previously unpublished in book form. Poems published in journals, chapbooks, and anthologies may be included but must be acknowledged. There is a non-refundable $20 entry fee which must accompany the ms. (Checks to University of Wisconsin Press.) Mss will not be returned. Enclose SASE for contest results.
Advice: "Each submission is considered for both prizes (one entry fee only)."

N ○ ◐ **THE UNKNOWN WRITER**, P.O. Box 698, Ramsey NJ 07446. E-mail: unknown_writer_2000@ yahoo.com. Website: http://munno.net/unknownwriter/ (includes guidelines, staff info, samples of works from each issue, previous tables of contents). Established 1995. **Co-Editors:** Amy Munno and Jamie McNeely.
Magazine Needs: "We are a quarterly print magazine that publishes poetry and fiction by up-and-coming writers with limited publishing credits. We publish some art on covers and inner pages. We are the place for quality writers who need a start. We print original, insightful poems by up-and-coming writers. Send us strong, rich poetry with attention to imagery, emotion and detail. We enjoy the traditional and structured forms like sonnet and haiku as much as experimental and modern free verse. Any subject matter is acceptable as long as the poem makes a direct connection with the reader. Keep the work fresh, intelligent and mindful." Does not want forced rhyme, limericks or vulgar work. No profane or sexually explicit material and no graphic violence. *The Unknown Writer* is usually 40-60 pgs., digest-sized, saddle-stapled, cardstock cover and b&w line art and photos (at times). Publishes up to 6 poems/issue.
How to Submit: Submit 3-5 poems at a time. Line length for poetry is 2 minimum, 100 maximum. Accepts simultaneous submissions; no previously published poems. Accepts e-mail and disk submissions. Cover letter is preferred. "Through postal mail, include a SASE, full address and e-mail address. Through e-mail, attach poems as a file or include them in the message body. With e-mail submissions, please introduce yourself in a short note; don't just send poems. Tell us if the submission is simultaneous." Reads submissions all year. Submit seasonal poems 4 months in advance. Time between acceptance and publication is 3 months. Poems are circulated to an

editorial board. "Two of four editors must accept poem. Poem may be read by some or all of editorial board members." Occasionally publishes theme issues. Guidelines available by e-mail or on website. Responds in 3 months. Pays 3 contributors copies. Acquires first worldwide rights.

Advice: "This is not the magazine for the established poet. We want to discover new, talented writers who need their first break or have a handful of previous acceptances. Remember to keep writing regularly, even when you're turning out drivel. Writing is a practice and a craft. If we reject your first submission but tell you to submit again, we mean it. Keep trying."

✓ ▣ ○ **UNLIKELY STORIES: A COLLECTION OF LITERARY ART**, P.O. Box 2085, Marietta GA 30061. (770)422-9731. E-mail: unlikely@flash.net. Website: http://go.to/unlikely. Established 1998. **Editor:** Jonathan Penton.

Magazine Needs: "*Unlikely Stories* is a monthly online publication containing poetry, fiction and nonfiction which falls under my own highly subjective definition of 'literary art.' I especially like work that has trouble finding publication due to adult, offensive or weird content." Wants "any subject matter, including those normally considered taboo. I like informal poetry, but am open to formal poetry that demonstrates an understanding of good meter. No emotionless poetry, lies. 'I'll love you forever' is a lie; spare me." Has published poetry by Scott Holstad, Wendy Carlisle, Laurel Ann Boyer, and Elisha Porat. As a sample the editor selected these lines from an untitled poem by Shari Nettles:

> *even the little white flowers/in the yard/trembled when they heard you scream.*

Receives about 500 poems/year, accepts about 30%.

How to Submit: Submit 3 or more poems at a time. Accepts previously published poems and simultaneous submissions. Accepts e-mail and disk submissions. Cover letter preferred. "*Unlikely Stories* is designed to promote acquaintanceship between readers and authors therefore, only multiple submissions will be accepted. I greatly prefer to see a bio; there is no maximum length." Time between acceptance and publication is 1 month. Often comments on rejected poems, if requested. Guidelines available for SASE, by e-mail, or on website. Responds in up to 6 weeks. Acquires one-time rights.

Also Offers: "If a contributor asks me a question, or for editorial or business advise, I'll answer. I have edited full manuscripts for a fee."

Advice: "Write from the heart, if you must, but write from that part of you which is unique."

◪ ◉ **UNMUZZLED OX**, 43B Clark Lane, Staten Island NY 10304 or Box 550, Kingston, Ontario K7L 4W5 Canada. (212)226-7170. Established 1971. **Poetry Editor:** Michael Andre.

Magazine Needs & How to Submit: *Unmuzzled Ox* is a tabloid literary biannual. Each edition is built around a theme or specific project. "The chances of an unsolicited poem being accepted are slight since I always have specific ideas in mind." Has published poetry by Allen Ginsberg, Robert Creeley, and Denise Levertov. As a sample the editor selected these lines from "CL" by Daniel Berrigan:

> *Let's be grandiose, it's a game/Let's climb a balcony/Let's issue a manifesto//Why, we're turning things on their head/we're making history/we're—//Harmless.*

Only unpublished work will be considered, but works may be in French as well as English." Subscription: $20.

◉ **UNO MAS MAGAZINE**, P.O. Box 1832, Silver Spring MD 20915. E-mail: unomasmag@aol.com. Website: www.unomas.com/ (includes fiction, poetry samples, reviews, interviews, photography, and articles). Established 1990. **Contact:** poetry editor.

Magazine Needs: *UNo Mas*, published quarterly, features "general culture, music, fiction, essays, photography, art." Wants "general poetry of short to medium length." Has published poetry by Sparrow. As a sample the editor selected these lines from "Krishna Harry and His Voice" by Kristine Durden:

> *pulling me across a river bed/baptism of sound/floating on ripples/riding each dip and wave/like dream flying*

UNo Mas is 50 pgs., 8½×11, offset-printed with a glossy 2-color cover. Receives about 100-150 poems/year, accepts 20-25%. Press run is 3,000 for 40 subscribers and which 1 is a library, most are shelf sales; 100 distributed free to advertisers. Single copy: $2.50; subscription: $9. Sample: $3. Make checks payable to Jim Saah.

How to Submit: Submit up to 5 poems with name on each page. Accepts previously published poems and simultaneous submissions. Accepts fax and e-mail submissions. Cover letter preferred with SASE. Time between acceptance and publication is 6 months. Poems are circulated to an editorial board, "if we like it, we publish it." Seldom comments on rejected poems. Guidelines available for SASE. Responds in up to 6 weeks. Sometimes sends prepublication galleys. Pays 3 contributor's copies. Acquires one-time rights. Staff reviews books or chapbooks of poetry. Send books for review consideration.

N: ⬜ ◎ **UPRISING; THE JEREMIAH REEVES POETRY PRIZE FOR JUSTICE (Specialized: social issues, ethnic/nationality),** 241 Noble Ave., Montgomery AL 36104. (334)265-7613. E-mail: Geri34825 @aol.com. Established 1997. **Editor:** Geri Moss.

Magazine Needs: *Uprising* is a quarterly poetry journal especially interested in political poems and work on Native Americans. Wants "free verse, well written work, very little if any rhyme. I want fire, thought, and feeling; make the reader feel what you feel. Poems should be 32 lines or under, more if poem is exceptional. No religious, haiku, or pornography." Has published poetry by David Store, John Gray, Gerald Zipper, and Nihda Cepero. As a sample the editor selected these lines from "On the Corner" by Jeffrey Forrest Grice:

> Pool rooms, churches/even love/is down on the corner/supplying your every need/when the cries of
> poverty shattered your dreams/go look on the corner

Uprising is 15-20 pgs., 8½ × 11, desktop-published and glued into paper cover. Receives about 300 poems/year, accepts about 25%. Press run is 150. Subscription: $20/year. Sample: $5. Make checks payable to Geri Moss.

How to Submit: Submit 3 poems at a time. Accepts simultaneous submissions; no previously published poems. Accepts e-mail submissions, "no more than 30 lines." Time between acceptance and publication is 3 months. Seldom comments on rejected poems. Occasionally publishes theme issues. Guidelines and upcoming themes available for SASE or by e-mail. Responds in 6-12 months. Pays 1 contributor's copy. Acquires first rights. Send books for review consideration.

Also Offers: Sponsors the Jeremiah Reeves Poetry Prize for Justice. 1st Prize: $500, publication in contest issue and free copy; 2nd Prize: $150; 3rd Prize: $75; 4th Prize: $25. Poems can be up to 2 pgs. long. Entry fee: $5/3 poems. Proceeds from contest will go to support the E.J.I. & the Southern Poverty Law Center of Alabama to help fight injustice. Contest announced March each year. Deadline: January 15, but submissions accepted all year.

Advice: "Poets write what you feel, don't be afraid to submit your work with the best out there. Read. Join a book swapping club and remember editors are poets who were not great poets."

⬜ ⬜ ◎ **UPSOUTH (Specialized: regional, religious),** 323 Bellevue Ave., Bowling Green KY 42101-5001. (502)843-8018. E-mail: galen@ky.net. Website: www.expage.com/upsouth (includes current info about the newsletter, editor's biographical information, and editor's favorite links). Established 1993. **Editor:** Galen Smith.

Magazine Needs: "*Upsouth* is a quarterly international newsletter for Southern and Catholic writers. We ask for tasteful poems, columns, essays, etc. No works of non-Christian views will be accepted. But the works do not necessarily have to be religious or spiritual to be accepted. Our intention is to be a creative outlet for spiritual or inspirational works, but *Upsouth* also has an interest in Southern culture and its literary figures and their writings, too. We do accept works from writers and poets from other regions of the U.S. and other parts of the world. We also accept works from non-Catholic writers and writers with other religious beliefs." Has published poetry by Rory Morse, Joyce Bradshaw, and Leah Maines. As a sample the editor selected these lines from "Dear Heavenly Father" by Raymond Flory:

> This day,/in this place/hold me once again./May I feel the touch

Upsouth is 12-16 pgs., 8½ × 11, photocopied and corner-stapled, includes clip art. Receives about 100 poems/year, accepts about 10%. Press run is 100 for 50 subscribers of which 10 are libraries, 10 shelf sales. Subscription: $8. Sample: $2. "We are more likely to publish your poem if you subscribe."

How to Submit: Submit 3 poems at a time. Line length for poetry is 21 maximum. Include SASE. Accepts previously published poems and simultaneous submissions. No e-mail submissions. Cover letter preferred. Seldom comments on rejected poems. Occasionally publishes theme issues (related to the seasons). Guidelines available for SASE. Responds in up to 2 months. Pays 1 contributor's copy. Author retains all rights. Reviews books and chapbooks of poetry and other magazines in 250 words. Poets may send books for review consideration.

Advice: "We like for you to subscribe to *Upsouth*. We consider you as a friend and write you personal and encouraging letters. Our motto is 'your writing can change the world!' "

⬜ **URBAN SPAGHETTI: LITERARY ARTS JOURNAL,** P.O. Box 5186, Mansfield OH 44901-5186. (419)524-8527. E-mail: editor@urban-spaghetti.com. Website: www.urban-spaghetti.com (includes guidelines, editors, list of previously published writers, sample poetry, and links). Established 1998. **Contact:** Cheryl Dodds.

Magazine Needs: "*Urban Spaghetti* is a biannual literary arts journal located in mid-Ohio featuring poetry, short stories and artwork from around the world. Our focus extends a hand to new poets who share a sense of social responsibility in their writing, and offer a fresh presentation and language which challenges us." Wants "quality verse. All styles are accepted, but please send your best. Rhymed verse has its place. However, that place is not *Urban Spaghetti*." Has published poetry by Sascha Feinstein, Ann Filemyr, Duane Locke, B.Z. Niditch, Marge Piercy, and Andrea Potos. As a sample we selected these lines from "Slogans" by Philip Avery:

> He's folding into madness/The way his mother used to be/Asking questions of his feet/Does the ocean
> rush ashore/Or push the land away/Does the sky turn black/When there's nothing left to see/And what
> time is dinner served/When there's nothing left to eat

Urban Spaghetti is 90-200 pgs., digest-sized, offset litho printed and perfect-bound with slick 90 lb. paper cover, includes b&w photos and drawings. Receives about 1,200 poems/year, accepts about 10%. Press run is 500. Single copy: $10; subscription: $17.

How to Submit: Line length for poetry is 100 maximum. Accepts simultaneous submissions (with notification). No e-mail submissions. Cover letter and bio preferred. "All poetry submitted to *Urban Spaghetti* will be considered for publication and must be accompanied by SASE. Non-accepted submissions will be returned if proper postage and envelope are provided." *Urban Spaghetti* accepts submissions throughout the year. Seldom comments on rejected poems. Occasionally publishes theme issues . Guidelines available for SASE or on website. Responds in up to 6 months. Pays 2 contributor's copies. Copyright reverts to author upon publication.

N **$** **⊘** **◎** **THE URBANITE; URBAN LEGEND PRESS (Specialized: horror, fantasy, themes)**, P.O. Box 4737, Davenport IA 52808-4737. Website: http://theurbanite.tripod.com/. Established 1991. **Editor:** Mark McLaughlin.

Magazine Needs: *The Urbanite* appears 3 times/year "to promote literate, character-oriented, and entertaining fiction and poetry in the genre of surrealism." Wants contemporary fantasy/surrealism (maximum 2 pages/poem). No "slice-of-life, sentimental, gore, porn, Western, haiku, or rambling rants against society." Has published poetry by John Benson, Tina Reigel, Marni Scofidio Griffin, and Wayne Edwards. As a sample the editor selected these lines from "Tree" by Pamela Briggs:

> Another cold spring/Is that a train a siren a wolf howling/or just a chainsaw cutting into something
> living/because it doesn't fit everyone's idea/of what a tree should be?

The Urbanite is 64-92 pgs., 8½×11, saddle-stapled or perfect-bound with 2-color glossy cover. Receives 500 poems/year, accepts less than 10%. Press run is 500-1,000. Subscription: $13.50/3 issues. Sample: $5. Make checks payable to Urban Legend Press.

How to Submit: Submit up to 3 poems at a time. No simultaneous submissions. "Query first regarding previously published work." Cover letter required. Sends checklist reply form, but sometimes comments on rejected poems. Publishes theme issues. Guidelines and upcoming themes are available for SASE. Responds within 1 month, sometimes longer. Pays $10/poem and 2 contributor's copies. Acquires first North American serial rights and nonexclusive rights for public readings. ("We hold readings of the magazine at libraries, literary conventions and other venues.") Rights revert to the writer after publication.

Book/Chapbook Needs & How to Submit: In addition to the magazine, Urban Legend Press publishes 1 or more chapbooks/year. Interested poets should "submit to the magazine first, to establish a relationship with our readers." More poetry chapbooks are planned for the future.

✓ **⊕** **⊘** **◎** **URTHONA MAGAZINE (Specialized: religious, Buddhism)**, 3 Coral Park, Henley Rd., Cambridge CB1 3EA United Kingdom. Phone: 01223 472417. Fax: 01223 566568. E-mail: urthona.mag@virgin. net. Website: www.urthona.com. Established 1992. **Contact:** poetry editor.

Magazine Needs: *Urthona*, published biannually, explores the arts and western culture from a Buddhist perspective. Wants "poetry rousing the imagination." Does not want "undigested autobiography, political, or New-Agey poems." Has published poetry by Peter Abbs, Robert Bly, and Peter Redgrove. As a sample the editor selected these lines from "The Shower" by Ananda:

> And somewhere there is gold,/and a song almost getting started/in the street we're leaving by://
> something like tenderness, how/the spring light races and dies/over the washed squares

Urthona is 60 pgs., A4, offset-printed, saddle-stapled with 4-color glossy cover, b&w photos, art and ads inside. Receives about 300 poems/year, accepts about 40. Press run is 900 for 50 subscribers of which 4 are libraries, 500 shelf sales; 50 distributed free to Buddhist groups. Subscription: £8.50 (surface), £11.50 (airmail)/2 issues; £15 (surface), £22 (airmail)/4 issues. Sample (including guidelines): £3.50.

How to Submit: Submit 6 poems at a time. No previously published poems or simultaneous submissions. Accepts fax but not e-mail submissions. Cover letter preferred. Time between acceptance and publication is 8 months. Poems are circulated to an editorial board and read and selected by poetry editor. Other editors have right of veto. Responds in 2 months. Pays 1 contributor's copy. Acquires one-time rights. Reviews books or chapbooks of poetry or other magazines in 600 words. Poets may send books for review consideration.

♥ **UTAH STATE UNIVERSITY PRESS; MAY SWENSON POETRY AWARD**, Logan UT 84322-7800. (801)797-1362. Fax: (801)797-0313. E-mail: mspooner@press.usu.edu. Website: www.usu.edu/usupress (includes current book information, submission guidelines, May Swenson Poetry Award guidelines, and purchasing information). Established 1972. **Poetry Editor:** Michael Spooner. Publishes poetry only through the May Swenson Poetry Award competition annually. Has published *May Out West* by May Swenson; *Plato's Breath* by Randall Freisinger; *The Hammered Dulcimer* by Lisa Williams; *Necessary Light* by Patricia Fargnoli; *All That Divides Us* by Elinor Benedict. See website for details.

N **◎** **VALEE PUBLICATIONS (Specialized: women from all backgrounds)**, P.O. Box 1092, Wilkes-Barre PA 18703. Established 2000. **Publisher:** Hilda L. McMullins.

Book/Chapbook Needs: Valee Publications wants "to publish writers who are very talented, but have not been 'discovered.'" Wants to see poetry of "any form, length, style, but no pornography or anything in bad taste." Does not want "poetry that can't be deciphered." As a sample the editor selected these lines from her own poem "Angry Eyes":

> Teacher never taught me black was beautiful/mother never told me female was beautiful/me—tall and
> big boned/a female beauty from lands unknown//I have been betrayed.

Publishes 1 chapbook/year. Books are usually 30-75 pgs., stapled, glossy cover with artwork on cover. Sample: $10.

How to Submit: Send complete ms with cover letter. Accepts simultaneous submissions. No queries necessary, just submit complete ms. Manuscript will not be returned unless SASE enclosed. Reads submissions February through April. Responds in 2 months. Pays 50 author's copies (out of a press run of 100). "Hope to give honorarium in the future."

Advice: "I seek writers who aren't in it for the money, but as an expression to share with others. Write with your heart, send out your work, have faith in God—you are a writer even if you never get published. Treasure your gift."

N ✉ $ ◑ VALLUM MAGAZINE, P.O. Box 48003, 5678 du Parc, Montreal, Quebec H2V 4S8 Canada. E-mail: vallummag@hotmail.com. Website: www.vallummag.com. Established 2000. **Contact:** Joshua Auerbach, Helen Zisimatos.

Magazine Needs: *Vallum Magazine* appears biannually. "We are looking for poetry that's fresh and edgy, something that reflects contemporary experience and is also well-crafted. Open to all styles. We publish new and established poets." Recently published poetry by jwcurry, David Solway, Robert Allen, Ronnie R. Brown, Blaine Marchand. *Vallum Magazine* is 60 pgs., $7 \times 8\frac{1}{2}$, digitally-printed, perfect-bound, color images on coated stock cover, with art/graphics. Publishes about 45 poems/issue. Press run is 500. Single copy: $7; subscription: $12. Make checks payable to *Vallum Magazine*.

How to Submit: Submit 4-7 poems at a time. No previously published poems or simultaneous submissions. No fax, e-mail, or disk submissions. Cover letter is preferred. Include SASE. Time between acceptance and publication is several months. Sometimes comments on rejected poems. Guidelines are available in magazine. Responds in 3 months. Pays a "small honorarium" and 2 contributor's copies. Acquires first North American serial rights. Reviews books and chapbooks of poetry in 250-500 words. Poets may send books for review consideration to *Vallum Magazine*.

Advice: "Hone your craft, read widely, be original."

N ▣ ◑ VALPARAISO POETRY REVIEW, Dept of English, Valparaiso University, Valparaiso IN 46383-6493. (219)464-5278. Fax: (219)464-5511. E-mail: vpr@valpo.edu. Website: www.valpo.edu/english/vpr/. Established 1999. **Editor:** Edward Byrne.

Magazine Needs: *Valparaiso Poetry Review: Contemporary Poetry and Poetics* is "a biannual online poetry journal accepting submissions of unpublished or previously published poetry, book reviews, author interviews, and essays on poetry or poetics that have not yet appeared online and for which the rights belong to the author. Query for anything else." Wants poetry of any length or style, free verse or traditional forms. Recently published poetry by Charles Wright, Jonathan Holden, Reginald Gibbons, Janet McCann, Laurence Lieberman, Beth Simon, and Margot Schilpp. As a sample the editor selected these lines from "Leaving the Scene" by Walt McDonald:

> Sleet clicking in the trees, and finches flicking/maize and millet from the feeder. This late in spring,/
> and still the thin smoke whips from chimneys/a mile away. We rock and watch the dawn,/a ten-watt
> bulb beyond the clouds. Is all/this sideshow spring a barker's promise of warmth?

Valparaiso Poetry Review is published online only. Receives about 500 poems/year, accepts about 7%. Publishes about 17 poems/issue.

How to Submit: Submit 3-5 poems at a time. Accepts previously published poems ("original publication must be identified to ensure proper credit") and simultaneous submissions. Accepts e-mail submissions (but prefers postal mail); no fax or disk submissions. Cover letter is preferred. Include SASE. For e-mail submissions, include text in body of message rather than as an attachment. Submit no more than 5 poems at a time. Reads submissions year round. Time between acceptance and publication is 6-12 months. Seldom comments on rejected poems. Guidelines are available on website. Responds in up to 6 weeks. Acquires one-time rights. "All rights remain with author." Reviews books of poetry in single book and multi-book format. Poets may send books for review consideration to Edward Byrne, editor.

N ♥ VAN WEST & COMPANY, PUBLISHERS, 5341 Ballard Ave. NW, Seattle WA 98107. (206)297-0469. Fax: (206)784-6759. E-mail: info@vanwestco.com. Website: www.vanwestco.com. (includes catalog, news and events, retailer information, online ordering information, editorial guidelines, contact information). Established 1999. **Contact:** Jennifer Van West, publisher.

Book/Chapbook Needs: Van West & Company, Publishers wants "poetry manuscripts for a general audience of the highest literary quality. We look for writers who have published extensively in literary magazines and journals or who have published previous collections of poetry. All styles considered. We do not publish poetry for children/adolescents or religious poetry." Recently published poetry by Molly Tenenbaum and Melinda Mueller. As a sample the editor selected these lines from "Neither Now" by Molly Tenenbaum:

> All summer I lived in the bees' house,/but by then it wasn't I,/it was what the bees flowed by,/what
> they danced/some distance from. What they didn't notice,/coming and going.

Van West & Company publishes 2 paperbacks/year. Books are usually 96 pgs., offset-printed, perfect-bound.

How to Submit: "*Queries only:* 7-10 pgs. of poetry, brief cover letter, résumé with list of publications. Must have published in literary journals. Responds to queries and mss in 1 month. Pays royalties of 7% minimum plus 10 author's copies out of a press run of 1,000. Order sample books by sending $16 to Van West & Co.

▣ ◎ **VEGETARIAN JOURNAL; THE VEGETARIAN RESOURCE GROUP (Specialized: children/teens, vegetarianism)**, P.O. Box 1463, Baltimore MD 21203. Website: www.vrg.org. Established 1982.
Magazine Needs: The Vegetarian Resource Group is a publisher of nonfiction. *Vegetarian Journal* is a bimonthly, 36 pgs., 8½×11, saddle-stapled and professionally printed with glossy card cover. Press run is 20,000. Sample: $3.
How to Submit: "Please no submissions of poetry from adults; 18 and under only."
Also Offers: The Vegetarian Resource Group offers an annual contest for ages 18 and under, $50 savings bond in 3 age categories for the best contribution on any aspect of vegetarianism. "Most entries are essay, but we would accept poetry with enthusiasm." Postmark deadline: May 1. Details available for SASE.

N: ⊕ ◐ **VERANDAH**, c/o Faculty of Arts, Deakin University, 221 Burwood Hwy., Bwwood, Victoria, Australia 3125. Phone: 61.3.9251.7134. Fax: 61.3.9244.6755. E-mail: verandah@deakin.edu.an. Website: www.deakin.edu.au/~ctgeorge/verandah (includes guidelines, subscription info, samples from each issue, photos, links, events, and news). Established 1986.
Magazine Needs: *Verandah* appears annually in October and is "a high-quality literary journal edited by professional writing students. It aims to give voice to new and innovative writers and artists." Has published poetry by Christos Tsiolka, Dorothy Porter, Seamus Heaney, Les Murray, Ed Burger, and Joh Muk Muk Burke. As a sample the editor selected the poem "Perspective" by Jane Williams:
> I do not care to know/Your lover as you know her/But I would care/To crawl inside her/And there inside her/Be known to you.

Verandah is 100 pgs., flat-spined with full-color glossy card cover, professionally printed on glossy stock. Sample: A$11.50.
How to Submit: Annual deadline: May 31. Accepts e-mail submissions in attached file (pdf, word.doc format, or rtf). Pays 1 contributor's copy plus cash as funds allow. Acquires first Australian publishing rights.

✅ ⏳ ◑ **VERSE**, Dept. of English, University of Georgia, Athens GA 30602. Website: www.versemag.com (includes information on recent and forthcoming issues, criticism, ordering information, and sample poems). Established 1984. **Editors:** Brian Henry and Andrew Zawacki.
● Poetry published in *Verse* also appeared in *The Best American Poetry*.
Magazine Needs: *Verse* appears 3 times/year and is "an international poetry journal which also publishes interviews with poets, essays on poetry, and book reviews." Wants "no specific kind; we look for high-quality, innovative poetry. Our focus is not only on American poetry, but on all poetry written in English, as well as translations." Has published poetry by Heather McHugh, John Ashbery, James Tate, Karen Volkman, Matthew Rohrer, and Eleni Sikelianos. *Verse* is 128-256 pgs., digest-sized, professionally printed and perfect-bound with card cover. Receives about 5,000 poems/year, accepts 1%. Press run is 1,000 for 600 subscribers of which 200 are libraries, 200 shelf sales. Subscription: $18 for individuals, $33 for institutions. Current issue $8. Sample: $6.
How to Submit: Submit up to 5 poems at a time. Accepts simultaneous submissions; no previously published poems. Cover letter required. Time between acceptance and publication is up to 18 months. Responds in 6 months. Often comments on rejected poems. "The magazine often publishes special features—recent features include younger American poets, Mexican poetry, Scottish poetry, Latino poets, prose poetry, women Irish poets, and Australian poetry—but does not publish 'theme' issues." Always sends prepublication galleys. Pays 2 contributor's copies plus a one-year subscription. Poets may send books for review consideration.

N: ◐ **VIA DOLOROSA PRESS; ERASED, SIGH, SIGH. (Specialized: themes—"dark" poetry and death)**, 701 E. Schaaf Rd., Cleveland OH 44131-1227. E-mail: hyacinthe@disinfo.net. Website: www.angelfire.com/oh2/dolorosa (includes VDP background/history and current catalog). Established 1994. **Editor:** Ms. Hyacinthe L. Raven.
Magazine Needs: *Erased, Sigh, Sigh* appears biannually. Literary journal "showcasing free verse poetry/fiction with a dark tinge. Our theme is death/suicide." Prefers "free verse poetry that is very introspective and dark. We do not publish light-hearted works. No traditional or concrete poetry. Vampire poems will be thrown away." Recently published poetry by John Sweet, William Kopecky, Laura Haynes, and Emma Hooper. As a sample the editor selected these lines from "that the baby will be born" by Joh Sweet from his chapbook, *Seasons of Rust*:
> and anything left/unsaid after the/sky bleeds away/is left unsaid for/obvious reasons

Erased, Sigh, Sigh is 28-40 pgs. (depends on amount of submissions), digest-sized, Xerox-printed, saddle-stapled/hand-bound, parchment paper cover and pages, with pen & ink drawings, print-ready ads accepted. Receives 200 poems/year, accepts about 25%. Publishes about 25 poems/issue. Press run is 300-1,000 of which 75% are shelf sales; 25% are distributed free to "other journals for review and also to charity organizations (teen crisis centers, especially)." Single copy: $3; does not offer subscriptions. Sample copy: $4 postage paid. Make checks payable to Hyacinthe L. Raven.
How to Submit: Submit any number of poems at a time. Line length for poetry is open. Accepts previously published poems and simultaneous submissions. No fax, e-mail, or disk submissions. Cover letter is preferred. "SASE's are always appreciated." Reads submissions any time. Submit seasonal poems 6 months in advance. Time between acceptance and publication is up to 7 months. "Poems are chosen by the editor. Writers will receive an acceptance/rejection letter usually within a month of receipt. We print when our target journal size is

reached, usually twice a year, so publication may be a month to seven or eight months from acceptance." Often comments on rejected poems. Publishes theme issues on "death, poets, and suicide. We publish dark poetry on these themes in every issue." Guidelines are available for SASE. "Send for submission guidelines! We are strict about our theme and style. We also recommend reading a couple issue prior to considering us." Responds in 1 month. Pays 1 contributor's copy. Acquires one-time rights.

Book/Chapbook Needs & How to Submit: Via Dolorosa Press publishes "poetry, fiction, and nonfiction with an existential/humanist feel. Darker works preferred." Publishes 2-10 chapbooks/year. Chapbooks are usually 10-50 pgs., Xerox- or offset-printed, saddle-stapled or hand-bound, card stock, parchment, or other cover, with pen & ink drawings. "We ask that poets request our submission guidelines first. Then, if they think their work is fitting, we prefer to read the entire manuscript to make our decision." Responds to queries in 1 month; to mss in 2 months. Pays royalties of 25% plus 10% of press run. "See submission guidelines—our payment terms are listed in there." Send for free catalog.

Advice: "If you are repeatedly rejected because editors label your work as 'too depressing,' try us before you give up! We want work that makes us cry and that makes us think."

VIGIL; VIGIL PUBLICATIONS, 12 Priory Mead, Bruton, Somerset BA10 ODZ England. Established 1979. **Poetry Editor:** John Howard Greaves.

Magazine Needs: *Vigil* appears 2 times/year. Wants "poetry with a high level of emotional force or intensity of observation. Poems should normally be no longer than 40 lines. Color, imagery and appeal to the senses should be important features. No whining self-indulgent, neurotic soul-baring poetry. Form may be traditional or experimental." Has published poetry by Michael Newman, Claudette Bass, David Flynn, Sheila Murphy, and Karen Rosenberg. As a sample the editor selected these lines from Colin Mackay:

> Your night, Svetlana,/was a song of pine and water/and the sigh of gently stirring bracken/as the valley
> slid off to sleep in the owl light. . .

Vigil is 40 pgs., digest-sized, saddle-stapled, professionally printed with colored matte card cover. Receives about 400 poems/year, accepts about 60. Press run is 250 for 85 subscribers of which 6 are libraries. Subscription: £8. Sample: £3.

How to Submit: Submit up to 6 poems at a time in typed form. No previously published poems. Guidelines available for SASE (or SAE and IRC). Sometimes sends prepublication galleys. Pays 1 contributor's copy. Sometimes comments on rejected poems.

Book/Chapbook Needs & How to Submit: Query regarding book publication by Vigil Publications. Offers "appraisal" for £10 for a sample of a maximum of 6 poems.

VIRGINIA ADVERSARIA, P.O. Box 2349, Poquoson VA 23662. Established 2000. **Poetry Editor:** Nancy Powell.

Magazine Needs: *Virginia Adversaria* appears quarterly "to further the literary arts." Wants high-quality poetry without restriction to form, style, or subject matter. Does not want greeting card-type verse. Recently published poetry by Serena Fusek, Virginia O'Keefe, Nancy Powell, Robert Young, Doris Gwaltney, and Adrienne Morton. As a sample we selected these lines from "My Daddy's Shoes" by Doris Gwaltney:

> He had walked so many miles/over field clods and barnyard droppings.//You would find them resting
> on the back steps/while he napped on the daybed in the kitchen./Or waiting on the porch at night/
> while he read the farm journals.

Virginia Adversaria is 64 pgs., 7×10, digitally printed, perfect-bound, full color, 100 lb. white gloss cover, with b&w artwork/illustrations and ¼ page to full-page ads. Receives about 400 poems/year, accepts about 5%. Publishes about 6 poems/issue. Press run is 1,000 for 250 subscribers of which 5 are libraries, 700 shelf sales. Single copy: $4.50; subscription: $15. Sample: $4.95. Make checks payable to Empire Publishing.

How to Submit: Submit 3-6 poems at a time. Accepts previously published poems and simultaneous submissions. Accepts e-mail submissions, no fax submissions. Cover letter is preferred. "Always inlcude SASE." Reads submissions all year. Submit seasonal poems 5 months in advance. "Poetry editor reads all poems, selects posssible acceptances, then three editors decide which will be published." Often comments on rejected poems. Guidelines are available for SASE. Responds in up to 6 weeks. Pays 1¢/word and 1 contributor's copy. Acquires one-time rights.

Advice: "Read as much as possible the current poets being published today. Continue to study and work at the craft."

THE VIRGINIA QUARTERLY REVIEW; EMILY CLARK BALCH PRIZE, 1 West Range, P.O. Box 400223, Charlottesville VA 22904-4223. (804)924-3124. Fax: (804)924-1397. Established 1925.

Magazine Needs: *The Virginia Quarterly Review* uses about 15 pgs. of poetry in each issue, no length or subject restrictions. Issues have largely included lyric and narrative free verse, most of which features a strong message or powerful voice. *The Virginia Quarterly Review* is 220 pgs., digest-sized, flat-spined. Press run is 4,000.

How to Submit: Submit up to 5 poems and include SASE. "You will *not* be notified otherwise." No simultaneous submissions. Responds in 3 months or longer "due to the large number of poems we receive." Submission details available for SASE; do not request by fax. Pays $1/line.

Also Offers: Also sponsors the Emily Clark Balch Prize, an annual prize of $500 given to the best poem published in the review during the year.

$ ◎ VISTA PUBLISHING, INC. (Specialized: nurses), 422 Morris Ave., Suite 1, Long Branch NJ 07740. (732)229-6500. Fax: (732)229-9647. E-mail: info@vistapubl.com. Website: www.vistapubl.com (includes contact information and a list of all current titles with prices and ordering information). Established 1991. **Contact:** Carolyn S. Zagury.
Book/Chapbook Needs: Provides "a forum for the creative and artistic side of our nursing colleagues." Publishes 10 paperback/year. Wants "poetry written by nurses, relating to nursing or healthcare." Has published *Broken Butterflies* by Jodi Lalone and *Drifting Among the Whales* by Carol Battaglia. Books are usually 100 pgs., 6×9, trade paper, perfect-bound with illustrations if appropriate and 4-color cover.
How to Submit: Submit complete typed ms. "We are interested only in poetry collections with an average of 100 poems." Accepts simultaneous submissions; no previously published poems. No fax or e-mail submissions. Cover letter preferred. Has backlog to Fall 2000. Time between acceptance and publication is 2 years. Often comments on rejected poems. Responds in 3 months. Pays "percentage of profits."

[N] ○ ◑ VOCE PIENA, 1011½ W. Micheltorena, Santa Barbara CA 93101. (805)962-7068. E-mail: dslaght @aol.com. Established 2000. **Contact:** Deborah Slaght, editor.
Magazine Needs: *Voce Piena* appears annually in October. Publishes experimental poetry. *Voce Piena* is magazine-sized, desktop-published, white glossy 90 lb. paper cover, with abstract art. Receives varied number of poems/year. Publishes about 35-50 poems/issue. Single copy: $10; subscription: $10. Make checks payable to *Voce Piena.*
How to Submit: Submit 3-5 poems at a time. Length for poetry is 4 lines minimum, 3 pgs. maximum. Accepts previously published poems; no simultaneous submissions. Accepts e-mail and disk submissions; no fax submissions. Cover letter is required. "If there are graphics in poem, include an explanation of how the graphics should be reproduced." Reads submissions June-August. Time between acceptance and publication is up to 4 months. Never comments on rejected poems. Responds in 1 week. Pays 1 contributor's copy. Acquires first North American serial rights.
Advice: "Do not send any submissions using profanity. All experimental poetry, including experimental lyricism are read and considered thoughtfully."

[N] ⊕ ○ ◎ VOICES ISRAEL (Specialized: anthology); REUBEN ROSE POETRY COMPETITION; MONTHLY POET'S VOICE (Specialized: members), P.O. Box 661, Metar Israel 85025. Phone: 972-7-6519118. Fax: 972-7-6519119. E-mail: aschatz@bgumail.bgu.ac.il. Website: members.tripod.com/~Voices Israel. Established 1972. **Editor-in-Chief:** Amiel Schotz; with an editorial board of 7.
Magazine Needs: "*Voices Israel* is an annual anthology of poetry in English coming from all over the world. You have to buy a copy to see your work in print. Submit all kinds of poetry (up to 4 poems), each no longer than 40 lines, in seven copies." Has published poetry by Yehuda Amichai, Hsi Muren, Alexander Volovick, Péter Kántor, and Ada Aharoni. As a sample the editor selected these lines from "Milk" by Orit Perlman:

> I want to marry a goat man/with jitter in his socks and drums in his hip/with saffron in his curls and
> sun/and blue blue wind in his eye/and crime on his teeth when he smiles.

Voices Israel is approximately 121 pgs , 6½×9⅜, offset from laser output on ordinary paper, flat-spined with varying cover. Press run is 350. Subscription: $15. Sample back copy: $10. Contributor's copy: $15 airmail. "All money matters—including $35 annual membership—must be handled by the treasurer. Mel Millman, 15 Shachar St., Jerusalem, Israel 96263."
How to Submit: Accepts previously published poems, "but please include details and assurance that copyright problems do not exist." No simultaneous submissions. Accepts e-mail submissions with attachment. Cover letter with brief biographical details required with submissions. Deadline: end of November; responds as per receipt.
Also Offers: Sponsors the annual Reuben Rose Poetry Competition. Send poems of up to 40 lines each, plus $5/poem to P.O. Box 236, Kiriat Ata, Israel. Poet's name and address should be on a separate sheet with titles of poems. *The Monthly Poet's Voice*, a broadside edited by Ezra Ben-Meir, is sent only to members of the Voices Group of Poets in English.
Advice: "We would like to see more humorous but well constructed poetry. We like to be surprised."

✓ ⊕ $ ○ ◑ ◎ VOICEWORKS MAGAZINE (Specialized: children/teen/young adult), 156 George St., 1st Floor, Melbourne, Victoria, Fitzroy 3065 Australia. Phone: (03)9416-3305. Fax: (03)9419-3365. E-mail: vworks@vicnet.net.au. Website: www.expressmedia.org.au. Established 1985. **Editor:** Ms. Aizura Hankin.
Magazine Needs: *Voiceworks* appears 4 times/year to publish "young," "new," "emerging" writers under 25 years of age. "We have no specifications for poetry. Only the poets must be under 25 years of age. No racist, stolen, or libelous work." *Voiceworks* is 80 pgs., 8½×11, perfect-bound, includes art/graphics and ads. Receives about 400 poems/year, accepts 14%. Publish 14 poems/issue. Press run is 1,000. Single copy: $5; subscription: $25/year. Sample: $3. Make checks payable to Express Media/*Voiceworks Magazine.*
How to Submit: Submit no more than 8 poems at a time. Accept simultaneous submissions; no previously published poems. Accepts e-mail and disk submissions. Cover letter required. "We need a short bio and SASE (or SAE and IRC). If giving a disk or submitting by e-mail save the file as a Rich Text format." Reads submissions January 4 through 11, April 4 through 11, July 4 through 11, and October 4 through 11 only. Time between acceptance and publication is 2 months. Poems are circulated to an editorial board. "We all read the submissions, make comments and decide what to publish." Often comments on rejected poems. Publishes theme issues.

Guidelines and upcoming themes are available for SASE (or SAE with IRCs), by fax, or by e-mail. Responds in 2 months. Pays $50. Poets retain rights. Staff reviews books and chapbooks of poetry and other magazines. Send books for review consideration.

☑ ▣ ◖ **VOIDING THE VOID**, % E.E. Lippincott, 8 Henderson Place, New York NY 10028. (718)784-6593. E-mail: eelipp@aol.com. Website: www.vvoid.com (includes writer's guidelines, correspondence information, e-mail access to editor, all back issues as well as the main display of the current issue of the hard copy). Established 1997. **Editor-in-Chief:** E. E. Lippincott.

Magazine Needs: *Voiding The Void* is "a monthly existential-esque reader." Their poetry needs are "very open, if author feels the work is in keeping with *Voiding The Void*'s themes of 'tangibility' and amusement value." Has published poetry by Bryon Howell, Sue Batterton, and Paul D. McGlynn. As a sample the editor selected these lines by Charles O'Hay:

> It is better to do one thing catastrophically/than to do a hundred acceptably./Disaster/done well/can
> set the experts chattering for decades

Voiding The Void appears both on hard copy (b&w, 8-page tabloid format) and on the web. Receives about 1,000 poetry submissions/year, accepts about 50%. First press run is about 150 for about 100 subscribers. Single copy: 1 first-class stamp; subscription: $3.96/year. Make checks payable to E.E. Lippincott.

How to Submit: Submit up to 5 poems at a time. Accepts simultaneous submissions. Accepts e-mail and disk submissions. Cover letter preferred. Time between acceptance and publication is 3 months. Always comments on rejected poems. Occasionally publishes theme issues . Guidelines available for SASE. Responds in 2 months. Pays 5 copies. Acquires one-time rights. Reviews books of poetry. Poets may send books for review consideration.

Ⓝ ◖ ◖ **VOODOO SOULS QUARTERLY**, P.O. Box 4117, Lawrence KS 66046. E-mail: sayers@hometc .com. Established 2000. **Editor:** Meredith Sayers.

Magazine Needs: *Voodoo Souls Quarterly* is "a place where quality writing—poetry, essays, and short fiction—can find a home, regardless of the fame of its author. I've no real inclination toward a particular school of poetry. To be accepted, it will need to be precise, meaningful, and possess a sense of its own power. Innovation and clarity are appreciated." Does not want "inspirational, gratuitously violent, watered-down, imitations, or just plain poorly-written." Accepts poetry written by children. Recently published poetry by Alan Britt, Anne Gatschet, Stephen Meats, and Paul B. Roth. As a sample the editor selected these lines from "Loretta" by Anne Gatschet:

> each final dispersion where silence regains you/will wake me with night cries for nipples,/i'll call up
> your name again tiny Loretta/and the hollow compartment will shift/to the fluttering sound of your r.

Voodoo Souls Quarterly is 20-40 pgs., digest-sized, high-quality photocopied, saddle-stapled, cardstock cover with b&w art/graphics. Receives about 100 poems/year, accepts about 50%. Publishes about 5-10 poems/issue. Press run is 50 for 10 subscribers of which 1 is a library, 30 shelf sales; 10 are distributed free to contributors. Single copy: $4; subscription: $12. Sample: $4. Make checks payable to Meredith Sayers.

How to submit: Submit 3-5 poems at a time. No previously published poems or simultaneous submissions. No fax, e-mail, or disk submissions. Cover letter is preferred. "Include SASE and bio. Please tell a bit about yourself—not just your publications!" Reads submissions year round. Submit seasonal poems 6 months in advance. Time between acceptance and publication is 3-6 months. Often comments on rejected poems. Guidelines are available in magazine, for SASE, and by e-mail. Responds in 2 months. Always sends prepublication galleys. Pays 1 contributor's copy. Acquires one-time rights. Reviews books and chapbooks of poetry in single book format. Poets may send books for review consideration to Meredith Sayers.

Book/Chapbook Needs & How to Submit: "I would encourage poets to submit book/chapbook mss for consideration, as that will be my next venture. Please include SASE for return, if desired."

Advice: "Put your ego on the line and send what you love. Don't bother checking popular literary mags to see if you're following the current trend. Set your own!"

☑ ▣ 🍎 ◎ **VQONLINE (Specialized: volcanoes)**, 8009 18th Lane SE, Lacey WA 98503. (360)455-4607. E-mail: jmtanaka@webtv.net. Website: http://community.webtv.net/JMTanaka/VQ. Established 1992. **Editor:** Janet Tanaka.

Magazine Needs: *VQOnline* is an "interest" publication for professional and amateur volcanologists and volcano buffs. Wants "any kind of poetry as long as it is about volcanoes and/or the people who work on them." Does not want "over-emotive, flowery stuff or anything not directly pertaining to volcanoes." Accepts poetry written by children. Has published poetry by Dane Picard and C. Martinez. As a sample the editor selected these lines from "Farewell Observatory" by C. Scarpinati, translated from Italian by Claude Grandpey:

> A coat of fire shrouded your shoulders/and your sides, as tho' you were cold./Your masks, walls of
> iron/didn't collapse.

Free on the Internet, no subscription costs.

How to Submit: Submit any number of poems. Accepts previously published poems with permission of the original copyright holder and simultaneous submissions. Accepts disk and e-mail submissions (in body of message). Time between acceptance and publication is 6 months. Always comments on rejected poems. "I try not to outright reject, preferring to ask for a rewrite." Guidelines available for SASE. Responds in 1 month. Pays 3 copies. "Contributors may copyright in the usual fashion. But there is as yet no mechanism on the Internet to keep users honest. We also need written permission to publish on the Internet." Reviews books or chapbooks of poetry or other magazines by guest reviewers. Poets may send books for review consideration if they are about volcanoes.

N ☻ WAKE UP HEAVY (WUH); WAKE UP HEAVY PRESS, P.O. Box 4668, Fresno CA 93744-4668. E-mail: wuheavy@yahoo.com. Established 1998. **Editor/Publisher:** Mark Begley.

Magazine Needs: *Wake Up Heavy* appears 1-2 times/year. "Our magazine issues contain work from 5-7 established writers and the occasional local author. Most work is new, but we have reprinted viable work. There are no specifications as to style, form, etc., but *Wake Up Heavy* is partial to writers associated with the Black Sparrow Press." Does not want beginning/amateur, pornographic, overtly political or racist poetry. Recently published poetry by Laura Chester, Wanda Coleman, Fielding Dawson, Edward Field, Sherril Jaffe, and Diane Wakoski. "In lieu of a sample poem, I would suggest reading a book by any of the writers *Wake Up Heavy* has published for an idea of what we're looking for." *Wake Up Heavy* is 20-28 pgs., digest-sized, copied/offset-printed, saddle-stapled, linen cover stock, with line drawings, photos. Receives about 100 poems/year, accepts about 90%. Publishes about 30 poems/issue. Press run is 150 for 50 subscribers, 25 shelf sales; 75 are distributed free to authors and patrons. Single copy: ranges from $5-8; inquire for subscription rates. Sample: $8 postpaid. Make checks payable to Mark Begley.

How to Submit: Submit 5-20 poems at a time. Accepts previously published poems; no simultaneous submissions. Accepts e-mail submissions; no fax or disk submissions. Cover letter is required. Submit seasonal poems 4 months in advance. Time between acceptance and publication is 4-5 months. "I choose *everything* myself, based simply on my own likes and dislikes. Again, most work is taken because I contact writers I am already a fan of." Often comments on rejected poems. "Only submit work if you are an established writer, or inquire via e-mail for more information." A list of upcoming themes and guidelines are available for SASE and by e-mail. Responds in 2 weeks. Always sends prepublication galleys. Pays 5-6 contributor's copies. Acquires one-time rights. Poets may send books for review consideration to Mark Begley.

Book/Chapbook Needs & How to Submit: "Chapbooks and broadsides by single authors are becoming our main focus. They can be single poems, groups of poems, stories, memoirs, or chapters from novels." Wake Up Heavy Press publishes 2-3 chapbooks/year. Chapbooks are usually copied/offset-printed, glued or saddle-stapled, heavy card/cover stock, with drawings, photos. "Books and chapbooks are *strictly* solicited. Please do not send mss for chaps." Responds to solicited submissions in 2 months. Pays author's copies, 50% of a press run of 130-200. Order sample chapbooks by sending $10 to Mark Begley.

Also Offers: "Besides magazine issues and chapbooks, *Wake Up Heavy* publishes broadsides by individual authors. Each publication includes signed limited edition copies for sale."

$ ☐ ◎ THE WAR CRY (Specialized: religious), 615 Slaters Lane, P.O. Box 269, Alexandria VA 22313. (703)684-5500. Fax: (703)684-5539. E-mail: warcry@usn.salvationarmy.org. Website: http://publications.salvationarmyusa.org (features writer's guidelines, interviews, and forums). Established 1880. **Editor-in-Chief:** Lt. Colonel Marlene Chase.

Magazine Needs: *The War Cry*, appearing biweekly, publishes "reports, commentary, and testimonies that proclaim the gospel of Jesus Christ and His power to change lives today." Wants "Christian poetry, any style, 16 lines maximum." As a sample the editor selected these lines from "Merciful Heavens!" by Ruth Glover:

> Today my skies are clear;/The night is gone,/And all my midnight sighs/And foolish fears/Have faded
> with the dawn;

The War Cry is 24 pgs., with photos and graphics. Press run is 300,000. Sample available for SASE.

How to Submit: Submit up to 6 poems at a time. Accepts previously published poems and simultaneous submissions. Accepts fax and e-mail submissions, for e-mail include as attached file (Word or WordPerfect) or in body of message. Cover letter preferred. Time between acceptance and publication varies. "Poems are screened by an editor who acts as a 'first reader,' then good ones are passed on to the editor-in-chief." Seldom comments on rejected poems. Publishes theme issues. Guidelines and upcoming themes available for SASE. Responds in up to 1 month. Pays $10-65 and 1 complimentary copy. Acquires one-time and reprint rights.

☐ WARTHOG PRESS, 29 South Valley Rd., West Orange NJ 07052. (973)731-9269. Established 1979. **Poetry Editor:** Patricia Fillingham.

Book/Chapbook Needs: Warthog Press publishes books of poetry "that are understandable, poetic." Has published *From the Other Side of Death* by Joe Lackey; *Wishing for the Worst* by Linda Portnay; and *Hanging On* by Joe Benevento.

How to Submit: Query with 5 samples, cover letter, and SASE. "A lot of the submissions I get seem to be for a magazine. I don't publish anything but books." Accepts simultaneous submissions. Ms should be "readable." Comments on rejected poems, "if asked for. People really don't want criticism." Pays copies, but "I would like to get my costs back."

Advice: "The best way to sell poetry still seems to be from poet to listener."

N⊕◻◎ WASAFIRI (Specialized: ethnic/nationality), Dept. of English, Queen Mary and Westfield College, University of London, Mile End Rd., London E1 4NS United Kingdom. Phone: +44 020 7882 3120. Fax: +44 020 7882 3357. E-mail: wasafiri@qmw.ac.uk. Website: www.english.qmw.ac.uk/wasafiri. Established 1984. **Editor:** Susheila Nasta. **Managing Editor:** Richard Dyer.

Magazine Needs: *Wasafiri*, published biannually, "promotes new writing and debate on African, Asian, Caribbean and associated literatures." Wants "African, Asian, Caribbean, diaspora, post-colonial, innovative, high-quality poetry." Has published poetry by Vikram Seth, Fred D'Aguiar, Marlene Nourbese Philip and Kamau Brathwaite. *Wasafiri* is 80 pgs., A4, professionally printed on coated stock, perfect-bound, with full color glossy cover, graphics, photos and ads. Receives about 350 poems/year, accepts about 30%. Press run is 1,500 for 1,000 subscribers of which 450 are libraries, 300 shelf sales; 50 distributed free to arts council literature panel and education board. Single copy: $14; subscription: £18 individuals; £30 institutions/overseas. Sample: £5, £6 overseas.

How to Submit: Submit 3 poems at a time. No simultaneous submissions. Cover letter required. Accepts disk submissions (Word or WordPerfect). Time between acceptance and publication is 6-12 months. Poems are circulated to an editorial board. "Poems are considered by the editor and managing editor. Where guest editors are involved, poetry is considered by them also. Associate editors with expertise are asked to participate also." Often comments on rejected poems. Publishes theme issues. Guidelines and upcoming themes available for SASE, by e-mail, or on website. Themes for future issues include "Travel Writing" and "African Literature." Responds in up to 1 year. Sometimes sends prepublication galleys. Pays 1 copy. Acquires all rights. Returns rights with editor's permission. Reviews books or chapbooks of poetry or other magazines. Poets may send books for review consideration.

♣ $◻ WASCANA REVIEW, Dept. of English, University of Regina, Regina, Saskatchewan S4S 0A2 Canada. (306)585-4302. Fax: (306)585-4827. E-mail: Kathleen.Wall@uregina.ca. Website: www.uregina.ca./English/wrhome/htm (includes a description of magazine, a list of contributing writers, a description of special issues, and submission guidelines). Established 1966. **Editor:** Kathleen Wall.

Magazine Needs: *Wascana Review* appears twice/year publishing contemporary poetry and short fiction along with critical articles on modern and post-modern literature. "We look for high-quality literary poetry of all forms. No haiku or doggerel. No long poems. No concrete poetry." Has published poetry by Beth Goobie, Robert Cooperman, Lea Littlewolfe, and Susanna Roxman. *Wascana Review* is a trade-sized paperback, 75-100 pgs., no art/graphics, no ads. Receives about 200-300 submissions/year, accepts under 10%. Press run is 400 for 192 subscribers of which 134 are libraries, 100 shelf sales. Subscription: $10/year, $12 outside Canada. Sample: $5.

How to Submit: No previously published poems or simultaneous submissions. Cover letter required. SASE (or SAE and IRCs) necessary for return of mss. "Poems are read by at least two individuals who make comments and/or recommendations. Poetry editor chooses poems based on these comments. Poets may request information via e-mail. But no faxed or e-mailed submissions, please." Guidelines and upcoming themes are available for SASE or on website. Often comments on rejected poems. Publishes theme issues. Responds within 6 months. Pays $10/page plus contributor's copy and 1-year subscription. Acquires first North American serial rights. Reviews books of poetry in both single and multi-book format.

Advice: "*Wascana Review* will be featuring special issues from time to time. Poets should watch for news of these in upcoming editions."

◻ WASHINGTON SQUARE, A JOURNAL OF THE ARTS, 19 University Place, Third Floor, New York University Graduate Creative Writing Program, New York NY 10003. Established 1994 as *Washington Square* (originally established in 1979 as *Ark/Angel*).

Magazine Needs: Published semiannually, *Washington Square* is "a non-profit literary journal publishing fiction, poetry and essays by new and established writers. It's edited and produced by the students of the NYU Creative Writing Program." Wants "all poetry of serious literary intent." Has published poetry by Marilyn Chin, Paul Muldoon, W.S. Merwin, Sharon Olds, and Philip Levine. *Washington Square* is 128 pgs. Press run is 1,000. Subscription: $12. Sample: $6.

How to Submit: Submit up to 6 poems at a time. Accepts simultaneous submissions if noted. Time between acceptance and publication is up to 6 months. Poems are circulated to an editorial board. "The poetry editors and editorial staff read all submissions, discuss and decide which poems to include in the journal." Sometimes comments on rejected poems. Guidelines available for SASE or on website. Responds in up to 6 weeks. Acquires first North American serial rights. Sometimes reviews books and chapbooks of poetry and other magazines in 300 words. Poets may send books for review consideration.

◻ WATER MARK PRESS, 138 Duane St., New York NY 10013. Established 1978. **Editor:** Coco Gordon. Currently does not accept any unsolicited poetry.
  ● Note: Please do not confuse Water Mark Press with the imprint Watermark Press, used by other businesses.

◻◎ WATERWAYS: POETRY IN THE MAINSTREAM (Specialized: themes); TEN PENNY PLAYERS (Specialized: children/teen/young adult); BARD PRESS, 393 St. Paul's Ave., Staten Island NY

10304-2127. (718)442-7429. E-mail: water@tenpennyplayers.org. Website: www.tenpennyplayers.org (contains "material from our publication, programs, curriculum"). Established 1977. **Poetry Editors:** Barbara Fisher and Richard Spiegel.

Magazine Needs: Ten Penny Players "publishes poetry by adult poets in a magazine [*Waterways*] that is published 11 times/year. We do theme issues and are trying to increase an audience for poetry and the printed and performed word. The project produces performance readings in public spaces and is in residence year round at the New York public library with workshops and readings. We publish the magazine *Waterways*, anthologies, and chapbooks. We are not fond of haiku or rhyming poetry; never use material of an explicit sexual nature. We are open to reading material from people we have never published, writing in traditional and experimental poetry forms. While we do 'themes,' sometimes an idea for a future magazine is inspired by a submission so we try to remain open to poets' inspirations. Poets should be guided however by the fact that we are children's and animal rights advocates and are a NYC press." Has published poetry by Ida Fasel, Albert Huffstickler, Jay Hewitt Mann, and Will Inman. *Waterways* is 40 pgs., 4¼×7, photocopied from various type styles, saddle-stapled, using b&w drawings, matte card cover. Uses 60% of poems submitted. Press run is 150 for 58 subscribers of which 12 are libraries. Subscription: $20. Sample: $2.60.

How to Submit: Submit less than 10 poems for first submission. Accepts simultaneous submissions. Accepts e-mail submissions. Guidelines for approaching themes are available for SASE. "Since we've taken the time to be very specific in our response, writers should take seriously our comments and not waste their emotional energy and our time sending material that isn't within our area of interest. Sending for our theme sheet and for a sample issue and then objectively thinking about the writer's own work is practical and wise. Manuscripts that arrive without a return envelope are not sent back." Editors sometimes comment on rejected poems. Responds in less than a month. Pays 1 copy. Acquires one-time publication rights.

Book/Chapbook Needs & How to Submit: Chapbooks published by Ten Penny Players are "by children and young adults only—*not by submission*; they come through our workshops in the library and schools. Adult poets are published through our Bard Press imprint, *by invitation only*. Books evolve from the relationship we develop with writers we publish in *Waterways* and whom we would like to give more exposure."

Advice: "We suggest that poets attend book fairs. It's a fast way to find out what we are publishing. Without meaning to sound 'precious' or unfriendly, the writer should understand that small press publishers doing limited editions and all production work inhouse are working from their personal artistic vision and know exactly what notes will harmonize, effectively counterpoint and meld. Many excellent poems are sent back to the writers by *Waterways* because they don't relate to what we are trying to create in a given month."

[N] ◯ ◎ **WAVELENGTH: A MAGAZINE OF POETRY**, 1753 Fisher Ridge Rd., Horse Cave KY 42749-9706. E-mail: David.Rogers@wku.edu. Established 1999. **Editor/Publisher:** David P. Rogers.

Magazine Needs: *Wavelength: A Magazine of Poetry* appears 3 times/year. "We want poems approximately 30 lines or less that use lively images, intriguing metaphor, and original language. Rhyme is almost always a liability. All subjects and styles considered as long as the poem is thought-provoking or uses language in an innovative way. Prose poems are fine." Does not want "rhymed, very religious—anything that sacrifices creativity for convention or poems over 30 lines." Recently published poetry by Francis Blessington, Ann Taylor, Albert Haley, and Virgil Suarez. As a sample the editor selected these lines from "How to make love to a poem" by Kelly Donaldson:

> Let each syllable be tensed and quivering/with near ecstasy/at the touch of your tongue. Then/the poem
> will unhook it stanzas/and part its longest lines for you.

Wavelength is 35 pgs., digest-sized, laser-printed, perfect-bound with heavy cardstock cover and cover illustration. Receives about 450 poems/year, accepts 15-20%. Publishes about 30 poems/issue. Press run is 150 for 25 subscribers, 20-25 shelf sales; 100 distributed free to the public. Single copy: $5; subscription: $15. Sample: $5. Make checks payable to Dr. David P. Rogers.

How to Submit: Submit 1-10 poems at a time. Line length for poetry is 30 maximum. No previously published poems or simultaneous submissions. No e-mail or disk submissions. Cover letter is preferred. "SASE required. Brief bio preferred. Poet's name and address must appear on every page. Poets who want poems returned should include sufficient postage." Reads submissions May 1 through September 1 and November 1 through April 1 only. Submit seasonal poems 3 months in advance. Time between acceptance and publication is 4 months. Poems are circulated to an editorial board. "We look for the most original, interesting poems; vote and publish the winners. We like to publish new and young poets." Seldom comments on rejected poems. Responds in 3 weeks. Pays 1 copy. Acquires one-time rights. Reviews books and chapbooks of poetry in 100-150 words, single book format. Poets may send books/chapbooks for review consideration to David P. Rogers.

Advice: "If a poet sends 10 poems, we usually see at least one worthy of publication. Read and write as much as possible. Be original. If a poem still seems good a year after you wrote it, publish it."

◯ ◎ **WAY STATION MAGAZINE**, 1319 S. Logan-MLK, Lansing MI 48910-1340. Established 1989. **Managing Editor:** Randy Glumm. **Guest Editor:** Robin Lynch.

Magazine Needs: *Way Station*, published occasionally, strives "to provide access and encourage beginning writers, while courting the established." Wants "emerging cultures, world view, humanity direction, relationships—try all. No rhyme unless truly terrific." Does not want "religious or openly militant gay or lesbian poetry. Use common sense and discretion." Has published poetry by Charles Bukowski, Diane Wakoski, Stuart Dybek,

Ethridge Knight, and Terri Jewell. *Way Station* is 7×8½, offset-printed, saddle-stapled with heavy card cover, b&w art, photos and ads. Receives about 300 poems/year, accepts 20-30%. Press run is 1,000 for 35 subscribers of which 2 are libraries, 200 shelf sales; 500 distributed free to potential advertisers, readers, libraries and universities. Subscription: $18. Sample: $6.

How to Submit: Submit 5 poems with name and address on each page and $5 processing fee (returned if work is rejected). Accepts previously published poems and simultaneous submissions. Cover letter preferred. Time between acceptance and publication is 2 months, sometimes longer. "If not struck immediately, I then put it aside and re-read later 3-4 times. I might also circulate if through a panel of volunteer readers." Often comments on rejected poems. Guidelines available for SASE. Responds in 2 months. Pays 2 contributor's copies. Acquires one-time or first North American serial rights. Reviews books or chapbooks of poetry or other magazines "if I have time." Poets may send books for review consideration.

Advice: "It's best to check out your own work. Get advice from coaches, instructors prior to submitting. Also get sample copies of magazines you intend to submit to—this can only help you."

N ◯ ◑ WAYNE LITERARY REVIEW, % Dept. of English, Wayne State University, Detroit MI 48202. Established 1960. **Editor:** Richard Brixton.

Magazine Needs: *Wayne Literary Review* appears biannually. "Our philosophy is to encourage a diversity of writing styles. Send your favorites. If you like them, others probably will, too." Does not want "lack of craft, gratuitous sex and violence." As a sample the editor selected these lines from "The Picture in the Shoebox" by Ray McNiece:

> *I remember just where I put it, only it's gone now./Nothing there but pinches of wood-rot spaced/across the floor, a wad of newspaper packing,/a bit of spider chaff on the one, square window,/and a blue bottle fly bouncing against the pane.*

Wayne Literary Review is 75 pgs., digest-sized. Receives about 1,000 poems/year, accepts about 5%. Publishes about 25 poems/issue. Press run is 500 which are distributed free to the public.

How to Submit: Submit 3 poems at a time. No previously published poems or simultaneous submissions. No fax, e-mail, or disk submissions. Cover letter is preferred. "Send SASE with proper postage." Reads submissions anytime. Submit seasonal poems 6 months in advance. Time between acceptance and publication is 6 months. Poems are circulated to an editorial board. Seldom comments on rejected poems. Guidelines are available for SASE. Responds in 3 months. Pays 2 contributor's copies. Acquires first North American serial rights.

☑ ♉ $◑ WēBER STUDIES—VOICES AND VIEWPOINTS OF THE CONTEMPORARY WEST, 1214 University Circle, Weber State University, Ogden UT 84408-1214. (801)626-6473. Website: http://weberstudies.weber.edu (contains on electronic version of the magazine). Established 1983. **Editor:** Sherwin W. Howard.

● Poetry published here has appeared in *The Best American Poetry*.

Magazine Needs: *Wēber Studies* appears 4 times/year and publishes fiction, poetry, criticism, personal essays, nonfiction, and interviews. It is an interdisciplinary journal interested in relevant works covering a wide range of topics. Wants "three or four poems; we publish multiple poems from a poet." Does not want "poems that are flippant, prurient, sing-song, or preachy." Has published poetry by Mark Strand, Janet Sylvester, Ingrid Wendt, and Katharine Coles. As a sample the editor selected these lines from "Rhapsody for the Good Night" by David Lee:

> *nightbird/and the hum of pickup tires/on hardscrabble/I listen//behind the mockingbird behind the wind/behind the sound a taproot makes/working its way down to water/past that I can hear them/they can hear me too/if they want to*

Wēber Studies is 120 pgs., 7½×10, offset-printed on acid-free paper, perfect-bound, with 2-3 color cover, occasional color plates and exchange ads (with other journals). Receives about 150-200 poems/year, accepts 30-40. Press run is 1,200 for 1,000 subscribers of which 90 are libraries. Subscription: $20, $20 institutions. Sample: $7-8.

How to Submit: Submit 3-4 poems, 2 copies of each (one without name). Accepts simultaneous submissions; no previously published poems. Cover letter preferred. Time between acceptance and publication is 15 months. Poems are selected by an anonymous (blind) evaluation. Seldom comments on rejected poems. Publishes theme issues. Upcoming themes and guidelines available for SASE. Responds in up to 6 months. Always sends prepublication galleys. Pays $10-15/page; depending on fluctuating grant monies. Acquires all rights. Copyright reverts to author after first printing.

Also Offers: Cash award given every three years for poems published in *Wēber Studies*. Only poetry published in *Wēber Studies* during 3-year interval considered.

Advice: "This journal is referred by established poets—beginners not encouraged."

☑ $◎ WELCOME HOME; MOTHERS AT HOME, INC. (Specialized: mothers, parenting, families, children), 9493-C Silver King Court, Fairfax VA 22031. E-mail: mah@mah.org. Website: www.mah.org (includes writer's guidelines and samples). Established 1984. **Manuscript Coordinator:** Diane Bognar.

Magazine Needs: *Welcome Home* is a monthly publication of "support and encouragement for at-home mothers." Wants "poetry about the experience of parenting. Nothing long or obscure." *Welcome Home* is 32 pgs., digest-sized, professionally printed and saddle-stapled with paper cover, includes original art and photos. Receives about 240 poems/year, accepts about 8%. Press run is 16,000 for 14,000 subscribers of which 200 are libraries. Subscription: $18. Sample: $2. Make checks payable to *Welcome Home*.

How to Submit: Accepts previously published poems and simultaneous submissions. Accepts disk submissions. "We prefer paper mailed to the office." Cover letter preferred. Time between acceptance and publication is 6 months or more. Poems are circulated to an editorial board. Seldom comments on rejected poems. Guidelines available on website. Responds in 1 month. Pays $10 and 5 copies. Acquires one-time rights.

WELLSPRING: A JOURNAL OF CHRISTIAN POETRY (Specialized: religious, spirituality/inspirational). E-mail: wellspring@poetrypages.com. Website: www.angelfire.com/wa2/wellspring (includes complete guidelines, author biographies, the editor's statement of faith, ABC's of salvation, and other items of interest). Established 1999. **Editor:** Deborah Beachboard.

Magazine Needs: "*Wellspring* is an online journal featuring quality Christian poetry by various authors. Poems are published on an ongoing basis. I am looking for quality Christian poetry that touches every aspect of Christian living—from the worship of God to the activities of daily life. No pornography, no senseless violence, nothing New Age." Has published poetry by Joyce Freeman-Clark, Nancy Spiegelberg, H. Arlequin, Robert K. Meyer II, and Jean Calkins. As a sample the editor selected these lines from "A Farmer's Prayer" by Jane F. Hutto:

> *Perhaps I'll go today, dear Lord,/A tramping 'cross some fresh-tilled soil,/Then sit beside a tree-lined*
> *stream/To contemplate Your graciousness,/And dream . . .*

Accepts about 60% of poems received/year.

How to Submit: Submit 5 poems at a time. Accepts previously published poems and simultaneous submissions. Accepts e-mail submissions included in body of message. "Currently I am accepting submissions by e-mail only. When submitting, indicate it is for *Wellspring*. Include e-mail address and name with each poem submitted." Cover letter preferred. Submit seasonal poems 1 month in advance. Time between acceptance and publication is 2 weeks. Seldom comments on rejected poems. Guidelines available on website. Responds in 2 weeks. Sometimes sends prepublication galleys. Acquires one-time rights.

Advice: "Heartfelt poetry is wonderful, but quality poetry will show an understanding of the craft of poetry. Learn how to incorporate poetic device into your poetry even when writing free verse!"

WEST ANGLIA PUBLICATIONS, P.O. Box 2683, La Jolla CA 92038. **Editor:** Helynn Hoffa. **Publisher:** Wilma Lusk.

Book Needs: West Anglia Publications wants only the best poetry and short stories and publishes 1 paperback/year. Wants "contemporary poems, well wrought by poets whose work has already been accepted in various fine poetry publications." Has published poetry by Gary Morgan, Robert Wintringer and John Theobald. As a sample the editor selected this poem from *Sticks, Friction & Fire, Selected and New Poems, 2001* by Kathleen Iddings:

> *We stutter to the rimless surface./No smell of parsley or almond,/no slit of starlight/nor sheen of*
> *whispering stream.//A stereo fugue/shrieks like a dying dream./Wardens of the wind swing from a*
> *gibbet./locked in a cross-grained knot.*

Books are usually 75-100 pgs., 5½×8½, perfect-bound. Sample book: $10 plus $1.50 postage and handling.

How to Submit: Query with 6 poems, cover letter, professional bio, and SASE.

WEST BRANCH, Bucknell Hall, Bucknell University, Lewisburg PA 17837. E-mail: westbranch @bucknell.edu. Website: www.departments.bucknell.edu/stadler_center/westbranch. Established 1977. **Editor:** Paula Closson Buck. **Managing Editor:** Andrew Ciotola.

Magazine Needs: *West Branch* is a literary biannual "publishing high-quality poetry, fiction, essays, reviews. We're open to both conventional and experimental forms, both free verse and metered poetry." Has published poetry by Denise Duhamel, Beth Ann Fennelly, Victoria Redel, Wyn Cooper, Linda Allardt, and Charles Harper Webb. *West Branch* is 120 pgs., digest-sized, press run 1,000. Subscription: $10/year, $16/2 years. Sample: $3.

How to Submit: Submit 3-6 poems. Simultaneous submissions accepted; "ASAP notification of publication elsewhere." No e-mail submissions. Reads September through May only. Responds within one month. Pays 3 copies and $10/page, $20 minimum and $100 maximum (payment always subject to grant funding). Acquires first rights. Rights revert to author on publication.

Advice: *West Branch* "publishes 3% of submissions—always send your best work."

✔ ⬇ $ ◐ ◎ **WEST COAST LINE (Specialized: ethnic/nationality, gay/lesbian/bisexual, love/romance/erotica, nature/rural/ecology, regional, social issues, women/feminism)**, 2027 EAA, Simon Fraser University, Burnaby, British Columbia V5A 1S6 Canada. (604)291-4287. Fax: (604)291-4622. E-mail: wcl@sfu.ca. Website: www.sfu.ca/west-coast-line. Established 1990. **Editor:** Miriam Nichols. **Managing Editor:** Roger Farr.

Magazine Needs: *West Coast Line* is published 3 times/year and "favors work by both new and established Canadian writers, but it observes no borders in encouraging original creativity. Our focus is on contemporary poetry, short fiction, criticism, and reviews of books." Has published poetry by Bruce Andrews, Dodie Bellamy, Clint Burnham, Lisa Robertson, Aaron Vidaver, and Rita Wong. As a sample we selected these lines by Charles Bernstein:

> Sometimes/you burn a book because/it is cold/and you need the fire/to keep warm/and/sometimes/you
> read a/book for the same reason./This is not a theory of reading/this is about staying alive

The magazine is 144 pgs., 6×9, handsomely printed on glossy paper and flat-spined. Receives 500-600 poems/year, accepts about 20. Approximately 40 pages of poetry/issue. Press run is 800 for 500 subscribers of which 350 are libraries, 150 shelf sales. Single copy: $10; subscription: $25.

How to Submit: Submit poetry ". . . in extended forms; excerpts from works in progress; experimental and innovative poems; to 400 lines." No previously published poetry or simultaneous submissions. No e-mail submissions. Time between acceptance and publication is up to 8 months. Publishes theme issues. Guidelines available for SASE or by e-mail. Responds in 4 months. Pays $8 (Canadian)/printed page plus a 1-year subscription and 2 copies. Mss returned only if accompanied by sufficient Canadian postage or IRC.

Advice: "We have a special concern for contemporary writers who are experimenting with, or expanding the boundaries of, conventional forms of poetry, fiction, and criticism. That is, poetry should be formally innovative. We recommend that potential contributors send a letter of inquiry before submitting a manuscript."

🌐 $ ◐ **WESTERLY; PATRICIA HACKETT PRIZE**, Centre for Studies in Australian Literature, University of Western Australia, Nedlands 6907, Australia. Phone: (08)9380-2101. Fax: (08) 9380-1030. E-mail: westerly@uniwa.uwa.edu.au. Website: www.arts.uwa.edu.au/westerly (currently being updated). Established 1956. **Editors:** Dennis Haskell and Delys Bird. **Poetry Editor:** Marcella Polain.

Magazine Needs: *Westerly* is a literary and cultural annual, appearing in November, which publishes quality short fiction, poetry, literary critical, socio-historical articles, and book reviews with special attention given to Australia and the Indian Ocean region. "We don't dictate to writers on rhyme, style, experimentation, or anything else. We are willing to publish short or long poems. We do assume a reasonably well-read, intelligent audience. Past issues of *Westerly* provide the best guides. Not consciously an academic magazine." *Westerly* is 200 pgs., 5½×8½, "electronically printed," with some photos and graphics. Press run is 1,200. Subscription: $16 (US) airmail, $16 by e-mail.

How to Submit: Submit up to 6 poems at a time. Accepts fax and e-mail submissions in an attached file, Word 6; if submission is short, include in body of e-mail. "Please do not send simultaneous submissions. Covering letters should be brief and nonconfessional." Time between acceptance and publication is 3 months. Occasionally publishes theme issues. Responds in 3 months. Pays minimum of $30 plus 1 contributor's copy. Acquires first publication rights; requests acknowledgment on reprints. Reviews books of poetry. Poets may send books to Reviews Editor for review consideration.

Also Offers: The Patricia Hackett Prize (value approx. $500) is awarded in March for the best contribution published in *Westerly* during the previous calendar year.

Advice: "Be sensible. Write what matters for you but think about the reader. Don't spell out the meanings of the poems and the attitudes to be taken to the subject matter—i.e., trust the reader. Don't be swayed by literary fashion. Read the magazine if possible before sending submissions."

✔ ◯ ◎ **WESTERN ARCHIPELAGO REVIEW; WESTERN ARCHIPELAGO PRESS (Specialized: ethnic/nationality, regional)**, P.O. Box 803282, Santa Clarita CA 91380. (213)383-3447. E-mail: adorxyz@aol.com. Established 1999. **Editor:** Jovita Ador Lee.

Magazine Needs: *Western Archipelago Review* "publishes verse with a focus on the civilizations of Asia and the Pacific. All types of verse considered." As a sample the editor selected these lines (poet unidentified):

> Angel of Death, the High Priestess dances,/Turning in her silk;/Servant of the temple, covered in black
> robes,/Black cloth of Bali.

Western Archipelago Review is 12 pgs., 5½×8½, with glossy cover. Press run is 100. Subscription: $36. Sample: $7. Make checks payable to GoodSAMARitan Press

How to Submit: Submit 3 poems at a time. Accepts previously published poems and simultaneous submissions. Accepts e-mail and disk submissions. Cover letter with SASE required. Reads submissions September to June. Time between acceptance and publication is 6 weeks. Poems are circulated to an editorial board. Guidelines available for SASE. Responds in 6 weeks. Reviews books and chapbooks of poetry and other magazines in 100 words. Poets may send books for review consideration.

Book/Chapbook Needs & How to Submit: *Western Archipelago Review* publishes chapbooks and other monographs in the Western Archipelago series. The series is a resource for subscribers.

◑ WESTVIEW: A JOURNAL OF WESTERN OKLAHOMA, 100 Campus Dr., SWOSU, Weatherford OK 73096. (580)774-3168. Established 1981. **Editor:** Fred Alsberg.

Magazine Needs: *Westview* is a semiannual publication that is "particularly interested in writers from the Southwest; however, we are open to work of quality by poets from elsewhere. We publish free verse, prose poems and formal poetry." Has published poetry by Miller Williams, Walter McDonald, Robert Cooperman, Alicia Ostriker, and James Whitehead. *Westview* is 64 pgs., magazine-sized, perfect-bound, with glossy card cover in full-color. Receives about 500 poems/year, accepts 7%. Press run is 700 for 300 subscribers of which about 25 are libraries. Subscription: $10/2 years. Sample: $5.

How to Submit: Submit 5 poems at a time. Cover letter including biographical data for contributor's note requested with submissions. "Poems on 3.5 computer disk are welcome so long as they are accompanied by the hard copy and the SASE has the appropriate postage." Editor comments on submissions "when close." Mss are circulated to an editorial board; "we usually respond within two to three months." Pays 1 copy.

⊕ ◑ WEYFARERS; GUILDFORD POETS PRESS, 1 Mountside, Guildford, Surrey GU2 5JD United Kingdom (for submissions), 9, White Rose Lane, Woking, GU22 7JA United Kingdom (for subscriptions). Phone: (01483)504566. Established 1972. **Administrative Editor:** Martin Jones.

Magazine Needs: "We publish *Weyfarers* magazine three times/year. All our editors are themselves poets and give their spare time free to help other poets." Wants "all types of poetry, serious and humorous, free verse and rhymed/metered, but mostly 'mainstream' modern. Excellence is the main consideration. Any subject publishable, from religious to satire. Not more than 45 lines." Has published poetry by Kenneth Pobo, Richard Ball (US), Michael Henry, and Susan Skinner. As a sample the editors selected these lines from "The Lonely Places" by R.L. Cook:

> . . . *Set in the rim of the globe, spots on the atlas,/Stern, hard & desolate,/Far from the bedlam towns,*
> *these lonely places,/Have waited & will wait,//Till they are left, one day, to the cold-eyed seabirds,/*
> *Gannet, guillemot, gull,/And the last croft, crumbling covered by the bracken,/And the wild sheep's*
> *skull* . . .

The digest-sized, saddle-stapled format of *Weyfarers* contains about 31 pgs. of poetry (of a total of 36 pgs.). Receives about 1,200-1,500 poems/year, accepts 125. Press run is "about 300," including about 200 subscribers of which 5 are libraries. Sample (current issue): $6 in cash US or £2.50 UK.

How to Submit: Submit up to 6 poems, one poem/sheet. No previously published poems or simultaneous submissions. Closing dates for submissions are end of January, May, and September. Usually comments briefly on rejected poems. Pays 1 contributor's copy.

Advice: "Always read a magazine before submitting. And read plenty of modern poetry."

◑ WHISKEY ISLAND MAGAZINE, English Dept., Cleveland State University, Cleveland OH 44115. (216)687-2056. Fax: (216)687-6943. E-mail: whiskeyisland@popmail.csuohio.edu. Website: www.csuohio.edu/whiskey_island ("provides writer's guidelines, contest information, a history of the publication, and will, in the future, include poetry and fiction."). Established 1968. Student editors change yearly. **Contact:** poetry editor.

Magazine Needs: *Whiskey Island* appears biannually in January and July and publishes poetry, fiction, and nonfiction. Wants "advanced writing. We want a range of poetry from standard to experimental and concrete poetry. Thought provoking." Has published poetry by Vivian Shipley, Kathleene West, Claudia Rankine, Patricia Smith, and Dennis Saleh. As a sample the editor selected these lines from "Pigeon Bones & A Pair of Pants" by Ben Gulyas:

> *he is . . . in his dreams/a man, mad with the deep blue of wooden corners/under a high eclipse where*
> *moon & sun/make dark luminous love/he is a man mad with something that breaks him open/and*
> *makes him sing—*

Whiskey Island Magazine is 86-120 pgs., 6×9, professionally printed and perfect-bound with glossy stock cover and b&w art. Receives 1,000-1,500 poetry mss/year, accepts 6%. Press run is 1,200 for 200 subscribers of which 20 are libraries, about 200 shelf sales. Subscription: $12, $20 overseas. Sample: $6. Make checks payable to *Whiskey Island Magazine*.

How to Submit: Submit up to 10 pgs. of poetry at a time. Include SASE for reply/ms return. Include name, address, e-mail, fax, and phone number on each page. No previously published poems or simultaneous submissions. Include cover letter with brief bio. Accepts fax and e-mail submissions for mss outside of US; send as Rich Text format (.RTF) or ASCII files. Reads submissions September through April only. "Poets may fax inquiries and work that runs a few pages (longer submissions should be mailed). They may e-mail requests for submission and contest information." Poems are circulated to an editorial committee. Guidelines available for SASE or on website. Responds within 4 months. Pays 2 contributor's copies, and 1 year subscription.

Also Offers: Sponsors an annual poetry contest. 1st Prize: $300; 2nd Prize: $200; 3rd Prize: $100. Entry fee: $10. Entries accepted October 1 through January 31. Query regarding contest for 2000.

Advice: "Include SASEs and your name, address, and phone for reply. List contents of submission in a cover letter."

◑ WHITE EAGLE COFFEE STORE PRESS; FRESH GROUND, P.O. Box 383, Fox River Grove IL 60021-0383. E-mail: wecspress@aol.com. Website: http://members.aol.com/wecspress. Established 1992.

Magazine Needs & How to Submit: *Fresh Ground* is an annual anthology, appearing in November, that features "some of the best work of emerging poets. We're looking for edgy, crafted poetry. Poems for this annual are accepted during May and June only."

Book/Chapbook Needs: White Eagle is a small press publishing 5-6 chapbooks/year. "Alternate chapbooks are published by invitation and by competition. Author published by invitation becomes judge for next competition." "Open to any kind of poetry. No censorship at this press. Literary values are the only standard. Generally not interested in sentimental or didactic writing." Has published poetry by Timothy Russell, Connie Donovan, Scott Lumbard, Linda Lee Harper, Scott Beal, and Jill Peláez Baumgaertner. As a sample the editors included these lines from "Volunteer" in *The Wide View* by Linda Lee Harper:

> Her Head-Start students love her bosom plush as a divan./They celebrate and grieve there, noodle/
> their faces deeper, deeper, dangerous comfort./But she holds their fears close as if to absorb them/into
> her girth like calories from so much pasta,/each little rigatoni head, a child's dread allayed.

Sample: $5.95.

How to Submit: Submit complete chapbook ms (20-24 pgs.) with a brief bio, 125-word statement that introduces your writing and $10 reading fee. Accepts previously published poems and simultaneous submissions, with notice. No e-mail submissions. Competition deadlines: March 30 for spring contest; September 30 for fall contest. Guidelines available for SASE or on website. "Each competition is judged by either the author of the most recent chapbook published by invitation or by previous competition winners." Seldom comments on rejected poems. Responds 3 months after deadline. All entrants will receive a copy of the winning chapbook. Winner receives $200 and 25 copies.

Advice: "Poetry is about a passion for language. That's what we're about. We'd like to provide an opportunity for poets of any age who are fairly early in their careers to publish something substantial. We're excited by the enthusiasm shown for this press and by the extraordinary quality of the writing we've received."

WHITE HERON; WHITE HERON PRESS, P.O. Box 15259, San Luis Obispo CA 93406-5259. Established 1997. **Editor:** Kevin Hull.

Magazine Needs: *White Heron* is a biannual magazine. "We are interested in lyric poetry, vivid imagery, open form, natural landscape, philosophical themes but not at the expense of honesty and passion; model examples: Wendell Berry, Gabriela Mistral, and Issa." Has published poetry by Penny Harter, Bill Witherup, Joseph Duemer and Michael Hannon. As a sample the editor selected the poem "Creature" by Dark Cloud:

> Tired, so tired, it feels later than it probably is,/the wild world hushed as though obedient to poetry/
> or a god who wishes to be free of form and worshippers,/free, even, of consciousness, this dubious
> sense of self./The owl stares into its sorcery . . ./something tender and fierce disguised as a bird

White Heron Review is 30 pgs., 8½×5½, professionally printed and saddle-stapled with card stock cover, sometimes includes art. Single copy: $6; subscription: $10. Sample (including guidelines): $4.

How to Submit: Submit 4 poems at a time. Accepts previously published poems "by request only" and simultaneous submissions. Cover letter preferred. "Poets should send one copy of each poem and a cover letter that provides a brief bio." Time between acceptance and publication is up to 6 weeks. Seldom comments on rejected poems. Responds "within a week or two." Pays 1 contributor's copy.

Book/Chapbook Needs & How to Submit: White Heron Press also considers chapbook publication. "Only interested in poetry, but he will consider prose pieces as well. Each manuscript considered on its own merits, regardless of name recognition. Basic production costs variable. Query or send manuscript and I'll respond."

Advice: "Do the work. Get used to solitude and rejection."

WHITE PELICAN REVIEW, P.O. Box 7833, Lakeland FL 33813. Established 1999. **Editor:** Nancy J. Wiegel.

Magazine Needs: *White Pelican Review* is a biannual literary journal dedicated to publishing poetry of the highest quality. Wants "expertly-crafted, imaginatively-powerful poems rich in insight, music, and wit. No pornography." Has published poetry by Fred Chappell, Aleida Rodríguez, and Peter Meinke. As a sample the editor selected these lines from "Leaving Rabies" by Thérése Halscheid:

> and his fur was matted/over his body/curved, in a way/of a stone,/wet curved stone/the kind you think/
> skims five times across water/before sinking,

White Pelican Review is about 48 pgs., digest-sized, photocopied from typescript and saddle-stapled with matte cardstock cover. Receives about 3,000 poems/year, accepts 3%. Press run is 250 for 80 subscribers of which 25 are libraries. Subscription: $8, sample: $4.

How to Submit: Submit 3-5 poems at a time. No previously published poems or simultaneous submissions. Cover letter and SASE required. "Please include name, address, and telephone number on each page. No handwritten poems." Time between acceptance and publication is 3 months. Poems are circulated to an editorial board which reviews all submissions. Seldom comments on rejected poems. Guidelines available for SASE. Responds in 6 months. Pays 1 contributor's copy. Acquires one-time rights.

WHITE PINE PRESS; THE WHITE PINE PRESS POETRY PRIZE, P.O. Box 236, Buffalo NY 14201. E-mail: wpine@whitepine.org. Website: www.whitepine.org (includes writer's guidelines, poetry contest guidelines, list of current, and backlist titles). Established 1973. **Editor:** Dennis Maloney. **Managing Director:** Elaine LaMattina.

Book/Chapbook Needs & How to Submit: White Pine Press publishes poetry, fiction, literature in translation, essays—perfect-bound paperbacks. "*At present we are accepting unsolicited mss only for our annual competition, The White Pine Poetry Prize.* This competition awards $1,000 plus publication to a book-length collection of poems by a US author. Entry fee: $20. Deadline: December 31. Send SASE for details." No e-mail submissions. Has published *In the Pines* by David St. John, *Trouble in History* by David Kellor (winner of the Poetry Prize), *The Cartographer's Tongue* by Susan Rick, *The Way Back* by Wyn Cooper. Send for free catalog.

WHITE PLUME PRESS, 2442 NW Market St., PMB 370, Seattle WA 98107-4177. (206)768-9594. E-mail: bd072@scn.org. Established 1989. **Publisher:** Gene Nelson.
Book/Chapbook Needs: White Plume looks for poetry that "says something, or at least entertains, in an easy to read understandable manner." Publishes 1-2 paperbacks/year. "Open to anything, except personal drivel that has not been critiqued." Has published poetry by Kyle Kimberlin. Books are usually very simple, 64 pgs., 6×9, perfect-bound.
How to Submit: Submit up to 10 sample poems with a list of publication credits and bio. "Include a cover letter stating why this poetry is important and what the poet plans to do to help market it." Accepts previously published poems and simultaneous submissions. Accepts disk submissions. Has a 1-2 year backlog. "All poetry is reviewed by a select group of poets." Seldom comments on rejected poems. Responds to queries in 1 month. Pay is "open to negotiation."
Advice: The publisher says, "Get yourself involved with a group—listen to the group—be open to suggestions and changes. Help critique others' works."

WHITE WALL REVIEW, 63 Gould St., Toronto, Ontario M5B 1E9 Canada. Established 1976. Editors change every year.
Magazine Needs: *White Wall Review* is an annual, appearing in May, "focused on publishing clearly expressed, innovative poetry. No style is unacceptable." Has published poetry by Vernon Mooers and David Sidjak. As a sample the editors selected these lines from "The Journal of Robert Delaunay" by John Allison:

> *1912; The poet gives the Orphic Word. And/the veil is torn asunder, an open Mystery/now before us:*
> *Light. All is Light.//Paris, City of Light. Roof-line and gable are/luminous intersections of thought;*
> *my mind/a mordant, holding the image.*

White Wall Review is about 90-144 pgs., digest-sized, professionally printed and perfect-bound with glossy card cover, using b&w photos and illustrations. Press run is 250. Subscription: $9 in Canada, $9.50 in US and elsewhere. Sample: $5.
How to Submit: Submit up to 5 poems at a time. A critique composed of 5 editors' comments is available for $5. "Please do not submit between January and August of a given year." Cover letter required; include short bio. Responds "as soon as we can (usually in April or May)." Pays 1 contributor's copy. "Poets should send what they consider their best work, not everything they've got."

TAHANA WHITECROW FOUNDATION; CIRCLE OF REFLECTIONS (Specialized: animals, ethnic, nature, spirituality/inspirational), 2350 Wallace Rd. NW, Salem OR 97304. (503)585-0564. E-mail: tahana@open.org. Website: www.open.org/tahana (includes veterans page, alcohol/drug, mental health alert). Established 1987. **Executive Director:** Melanie Smith.
● **Note: Poets are advised that at press time, this market was completely closed to submissions of any kind.**
Magazine Needs & How to Submit: The Whitecrow Foundation conducts one spring/summer poetry contest on Native American themes in poems up to 30 lines in length. Deadline for submissions: May 31. No haiku, Seiku, erotic or porno poems. Fees are $2.75 for a single poem, $10 for 4. Winners, honorable mentions and selected other entries are published in a periodic anthology, *Circle of Reflections.* Winners receive free copies and are encouraged to purchase others for $4.95 plus $1 handling in order to "help ensure the continuity of our contests." Guidelines available by e-mail. Reviews books of poetry for $10 reading fee (average 32 pages).
Advice: "We seek unpublished Native American writers. Poetic expressions of full-bloods, mixed bloods, and empathetic non-Indians need to be heard. Future goals include chapbooks and native theme art. Advice to new writers: Keep writing, honing and sharpening your material; don't give up—keep submitting."

THE W!DOW OF THE ORCH!D (Specialized: dark, decadent, surreal), 3472 Laurel St., New Orleans LA 70115. E-mail: widow_orchid@yahoo.com. Website: http://widow-orchid.iwarp.com (includes guidelines, links, upcoming themes, and subscription information). Established 1994. **Poetry Editor:** Mr. Cimon Krow. **Co-Editor:** Emella Loran.
Magazine Needs: *W!dow* appears quarterly and publishes work with "no happy endings . . . without a price. I want to see dark poetry—any length or style or form is absolutely welcome—but the poetry must be of a dark and macabre nature. Surreal is a plus." Does not want "pretty, happy, mushy poetry. There are places for that sort of behavior." Has published poetry by Gary Jurechka, Cinsearae Santiago, Craig Sernotti, Wayne Wilkinson, Timothy Hodor and John Grey. As a sample the editor selected this excerpt from *winter's ghosts* by eroquela aruever ami:

> *people have no faces/there are no leaves to rustle/no meaning to life//i do not see them in their reality//*
> *i am a shade outside their existence/a shadow/angel/and watcher of them*

W!dow is about 50 pgs., full-sized, photocopied and comb-bound with colored card cover, b&w illustrations with occasional clip art if available, ads. Receives about 40 poems/year, accepts about 60%. Press run is 100 for 70 subscribers, 30 shelf sales. Subscription: $20/4 issues. Sample: $6 for recent issue. Make checks payable to Raquel Wright.

How to Submit: "Please invest in a copy if you're not sure about us. Then decide if we're the right zine for you." Must be 18 years or older to submit. "The maximum on submissions goes as follows: 10 pages at 3-5 lines; 6 at 1-2 page length, 1 at 6 page length or more." Include SASE. Accepts previously published poems; simultaneous submissions OK. E-mail submissions OK. Cover letter preferred including bio. "Please do not explain the 'darkness' of your work in the letter. Let your work speak for itself. Also please include a bio with your cover letter that is more than just a list of publications." Always comments on rejected poems. Publishes theme issues. Upcoming themes and guidelines available for SASE, on website, or by e-mail. Responds in 1 month or less. Pays 1 contributor's copy. Acquires first North American serial or one-time rights. Reviews chapbooks, magazines, art, or music (including books on tape). Poets may send books for review consideration.

Advice: "The best way to find if a market is best is to get guidelines or an issue. This way you can tell whether your work will work for the publication."

THE WILLIAM AND MARY REVIEW, Campus Center, College of William and Mary, P.O. Box 8795, Williamsburg VA 23187-8795. (757)221-3290. Established 1962. **Poetry Editors:** Philip Clark and Jen Scaife.

Magazine Needs: *The William and Mary Review* is a 120-page annual, appearing in April, "dedicated to publishing new work by established poets as well as work by new and vital voices." Has published poetry by Cornelius Eady, Amy Clampitt, Robert Hershon, Agha Shahid Ali, Henry Hort, and Virgil Suarez. *The William and Mary Review* is about 120 pgs., 6×9, professionally printed on coated paper and perfect-bound with 4-color card cover, includes 4-color artwork and photos. Receives about 5,000 poems/year, accepts 15-20. Press run is 3,500. Has 250 library subscriptions, about 500 shelf sales. Sample: $5.50.

How to Submit: Submit 1 poem/page, batches of up to 6 poems addressed to Poetry Editors. Cover letter required; include address, phone number, past publishing history, and brief bio note. Reads submissions September 15 through February 15 only. Responds in approximately 4 months. Pays 5 contributor's copies.

WILLOW REVIEW; COLLEGE OF LAKE COUNTY READING SERIES, College of Lake County, 19351 W. Washington St., Grayslake IL 60030-1198. (847)223-6601, ext. 2956. Fax: (847)548-3383. Established 1969. **Editor:** Paulette Roeske.

Magazine Needs: "We are interested in poetry and fiction of high quality with no preferences as to form, style or subject." Has published poetry by Lisel Mueller, Lucien Stryk, David Ray, Louis Rodriguez, John Dickson, and Garrett Hongo and interviews with Gregory Orr, Diane Ackerman, and Li-Young Lee. As a sample the editor selected this poem, "Daddy Long Legs" by Elaine Fowler Palencia:

> *His mind trapped forever/In a dream of shadows/My son hunts bugs./All the day long/Along the house*
> *foundations/Mewling gently/He pulls up grass/Lets daylight under bricks/To watch the bugs scurry./*
> *One day while I'm sunning/He opens his palm to me/And smiles./There sit five grey buttons/Pulsing*
> *with surprise/At the loss of their legs//How like a god he is,/My thoughtless child.*

The editor selected this particular sample because "Palencia's powerful poem represents the simultaneous simplicity of language and complexity of idea I admire, along with a relentless credibility." *Willow Review* is an 88- to 96-page, flat-spined annual, 6×9, professionally printed with a 4-color cover featuring work by an Illinois artist. Editors are open to all styles, free verse to form, as long as each poem stands on its own as art and communicates ideas. Press run is 1,000, with distribution to bookstores nationwide. Subscription: $15 for 3 issues, $25 for 5 issues. Sample back issue: $4.

How to Submit: Submit up to 5 poems or short fiction/creative nonfiction up to 4,000 words. "We read year round but response is slower in the summer months." Sometimes sends prepublication galleys. Pays 2 contributor's copies. Acquires first North American serial rights. Prizes totaling $400 are awarded to the best poetry and short fiction/creative nonfiction in each issue.

Also Offers: The reading series, 4-7 readings/academic year, has included Angela Jackson, Thomas Lux, Charles Simic, Isabel Allende, Donald Justice, Gloria Naylor, David Mura, Galway Kinnell, Lisel Mueller, Amiri Baraka, Stephen Dobyns, Heather McHugh, Linda Pastan, Tobias Wolff, William Stafford, and others. One reading is for contributors to *Willow Review*. Readings are usually held on Thursday evenings, for audiences of about 150 students and faculty of the College of Lake County and other area colleges and residents of local communities. They are widely publicized in Chicago and suburban newspapers.

WIND MAGAZINE; WIND PUBLICATIONS; JOY BALE BOONE CHAPBOOK AWARD; THE QUENTIN R. HOWARD POETRY PRIZE, P.O. Box 24548, Lexington KY 40524. (859)277-6849. E-mail: wind@wind.org. Website: http://wind.wind.org (includes examples of the magazine and its history, submission guidelines for the magazine and contests, literary links, and essential advice to beginning writers about avoiding literary scams and selecting worthwhile literary venues). Established 1971. **Editor:** Chris Green.

Magazine Needs: *Wind Magazine* appears 3 times/year. "Using poetry, fiction, and nonfiction, *Wind* operates on the metaphor of neighborly conversation between writers about the differing worlds they live in. Founded in 1971 in rural Kentucky, *Wind* looks to bring the vision and skill of writers from all concerns and walks of life into dialogue." *Wind*'s goal is "to publish a wide scope of literary work from diverse communities. Hence, we believe that each piece must be evaluated on its own terms based on its context. As not all poets and communities in America are like ourselves, and context does not travel with a poem, if you need to explain the rhetoric of your piece, please do!" Recently published poetry by Michelle Boisseau, George Eklund, James Baker Hall, Marcia Hurlow, and Richard Taylor. As a sample the editor selected these lines from "The Unspoken Appeal of Autumn" by Devin Brown:

> *This barn must be eighty,/no a hundred, maybe./Along the gleaming interstate,/its beams and posts lean/half off their timbered foundation—/dry, creaking trusses . . .*

Wind is 100 pgs., digest-sized, perfect-bound, with photo portraits. Receives about 3,000 poems/year, accepts about 1%. Publishes 15 poems/issue. Press run is 400 for 200 subscribers of which 75 are libraries, 100 shelf sales. Single copy: $6; subscription: $15/year or $25/2 years. Sample: $4.50. Make checks payable to *Wind*.
How to Submit: Submit up to 5 poems at a time. Accepts simultaneous submissions; no previously published poems. No e-mail or disk submissions. Cover letter is preferred. Include "a brief letter of introduction letting us know a little bit about your place in life and the world." Reads submissions year round. Time between acceptance and publication is 1-2 months. "Three staff readers review each manuscript. Editor makes final selection." Comments on rejections "when near misses." Guidelines available for SASE. Responds in 4 months. Pays 1 contributor's copy and discount on extras. Acquires first North American serial rights. Reviews books of poetry and other magazines in 250-500 words, single books format. Poets may send books for review consideration to Chris Green, *Wind Magazine*.
Also Offers: Joy Bale Boone Poetry Award, $500, deadline: March 1st; The Quentin R. Howard Chapbook Prize, published as summer issue of magazine; $100 and 25 copies, deadline: October 31st. Guidelines available for SASE. Each issue of *Wind* also features a portrait of a community of writers. "We highlight literary communities in the greater Ohio Valley—anywhere from Indianapolis to Knoxville, from the Mississippi to the Appalachians. Write '*Wind*: Literary Community Portraits' for guidelines."
Advice: "Be honest and relentless. There are hundreds of different poetries being written in America. As a way of selecting the appropriate place to submit work, find the community to which your voice and vision belong. Want to read every poem in whatever journal you submit to, then read them and join the conversation."

WINDSOR REVIEW, English Dept., University of Windsor, Windsor, Ontario N9B 3P4 Canada. (519)253-3000, ext. 2290. Fax: (519)971-3676. E-mail: uwrevu@uwindsor.ca. Established 1965. **Poetry Editor:** Dr. John Ditsky.
Magazine Needs: *Windsor Review* appears twice/year and features poetry, short fiction, and art. "Open to all poetry but no epics." Has published poetry by Rosemary Sullivan, Wendell Berry, Walter Griffin, and Eva Tihanyi. *Windsor Review* is professionally printed, 100 pgs., digest-sized. Receives about 500 poems/year, accepts about 15%. Press run is 400. Subscription: $19.95 (+7% GST) individuals, $29.95 (+7% GST) institutions (Canadian); $19.95 individuals, $29.95 institutions (US). Sample: $7.
How to Submit: Submit 5-10 poems at a time, typed. No simultaneous submissions. Accepts poetry submissions by fax; by e-mail, accepts queries and submissions in an attached file. Responds in 6 weeks. Pays 1 contributor's copy.

$ WINDSTORM CREATIVE, (formerly Pride Imprints), 7419 Ebbert Dr. SE, Port Orchard WA 98367. Website. www.windstormcreative.com (includes writer's guidelines, complete catalog, and individual book pages). Established 1989. **Senior Editor:** Ms. Cris Newport.
Book/Chapbook Needs: Windstorm Creative Ltd. publishes "thoughtful, quality work; must have some depth." Publishes 12 paperbacks/year. Wants "a minimum of 100 publishable, quality poems; book length. Previously published poets only: chapbooks, major magazines and journals or book-length work. No sexually explicit material. You must be familiar with our published poetry before you submit work." Has published poetry by Jack Rickard, Vacirca Vaughn, and Rudy Kikel.
How to Submit: "Visit our website first. Read at least two of our poetry volumes. In initial query, comment on how your work fits into what we do and indicate which volumes you have read. SASE must be included." If invited, send entire mss, 100 poems minimum. Accepts previously published poems and simultaneous submissions. No e-mail queries. Cover letter preferred. "A bio with publishing history, a page about the collection's focus, theme, etc., will help in the selection process." Guidelines available on website. Time between acceptance and publication is 2 years. Poems are circulated to an editorial board. "Senior editor reviews all work initially. If appropriate for our press, work given to board for review." Seldom comments on rejected poems. Responds to queries and to mss in 3 months. Pays 10-15% royalties.

WINGS MAGAZINE, INC., E-mail: tomjones1965@juno.com. Website: www.nywcafe.com/wings/. Established 1991. **Publisher/Poetry Editor:** Thomas Jones.
Magazine Needs: *Wings* is an exclusively online publication. "We want to publish the work of poets who are not as widely known as those published in larger journals but who nevertheless produce exceptional, professional material. We also publish personal essays, fiction, and plays." Wants "poetry with depth of feeling. No jingly, rhyming poetry. Rhyming poetry must show the poet knows how to use rhyme in an original way. Poetry on any theme, 80 lines or less, any style." As a sample the editor has selected these lines from "The Southern Ocean" by Robert James Berry:

> *The wind blusters big waves/Glacial spring is coming//If you listen to the ocean's measured voice/In*
> *the wide pale eyes of Wakatipu//Sky father and earth mother/are making footsteps on the sea*

Receives about 500 poems/year. "No requirements, but we encourage poets to check out our website and get an idea of the kind of material we publish."

How to Submit: Submit up to 5 poems at a time. Accepts previously published poems but no simultaneous submissions. "We take submissions through e-mail only. Send e-mail to the above juno address. Copy and paste the poem and bio into the e-mail message. The bio should be five lines or less." Always responds to submissions. Responds in 2 months. Staff reviews books and chapbooks of poetry in single book format. Send inquiries to pamwings@juno.com.

Also Offers: "Our needs are eclectic. Content can be on any topic as long as the poet shows mastery of subject matter and craft, as well as penetration into depths." Also, published a Best of Wings CD-ROM.

Advice: "We don't want doggerel. We want sincere, well-crafted work. Poetry has been reduced to second class status by commercial publishing, and we want to restore it to the status of fiction (novels) or plays."

✔ ◐ ◎ **WINSLOW PRESS (Specialized: children/teen/young adult)**, 115 E. 23rd St., 10th Floor, New York NY 10010. (212)254-2025. Fax: (212)254-2410. E-mail: winslow@winslowpress.com. Website: www. winslowpress.com (includes Winslow's virtual library of books, plus games, links, activities, and teachers' guides). Established 1997. **Assistant Editor:** Sarah Nielsen.

Book/Chapbook Needs & How to Submit: Winslow Press publishes children's books and young adult novels. "Winslow Press is a new company, and while we are open to publishing poetry, we haven't published any as of yet. Please keep in mind, we are a children's book publisher, thus no adult material will be considered." Guidelines available for SASE.

✔ ◐ ◎ **WISCONSIN ACADEMY REVIEW (Specialized: regional)**, 1922 University Ave., Madison WI 53705. (608)263-1692. Fax: (608)265-3039. E-mail: joanfischer@facstaff.wisc.edu. Website: www.wiscconsi nacademy.org. Established 1954. **Editor:** Joan Fischer.

Magazine Needs: *Wisconsin Academy Review, The Magazine of Wisconsin Thought and Culture*, "publishes articles on intellectual and cultural life of Wisconsin and provides a forum for Wisconsin (or Wisconsin background) artists and authors. Publishes original poetry." Wants "good poetry of any kind; traditional meters acceptable if content is fresh. We rarely accept poems over 65 lines." Has published poetry by Credo Enriquez, Jean Feraca, Felix Pollak, Ron Wallace, Sara Rath, and Lorine Niedecker. *Wisconsin Academy Review* is a quarterly of 56 pages, magazine-sized, professionally printed on glossy stock, glossy card color cover. Press run is 3,000 for members, bookstores, and libraries around the state. Uses 6 pgs. of poetry/issue. Has a 6- to 12-month backlog. Sample: $5.

How to Submit: Submit 5 pages maximum, double-spaced, with SASE. Must include Wisconsin connection if not Wisconsin return address. Poems not returned. Responds in 4 months. Pays 3 contributor's copies. Staff reviews books of poetry with Wisconsin connection only. Send related books for review consideration.

Advice: "We will consider traditional or experimental poetry but not light verse or sentimental rhymes."

◯ ◪ **WISCONSIN REVIEW; WISCONSIN REVIEW PRESS**, 800 Algoma Blvd., University of Wisconsin-Oshkosh, Oshkosh WI 54901. (920)424-2267. Established 1966. **Contact:** Poetry Editor.

Magazine Needs: *Wisconsin Review* is published 3 times/year. "The poetry we publish is mostly free verse with strong images and fresh approaches. We want new turns of phrase." Has published poetry by Lyn Lifshin, Karla Huston, Cathryn Cofell, Shoshauna Shy, and Troy Schoultz. As a sample the editor selected these lines from "Paint on Canvas" by G. Bryan Anderson:

> *I whisper American dreams of the Mississippi,/bronzed shoulders, jump from Wisconsin bridges,/*
> *leeches licking toes, paddle-fish slapping tummies,/we swallow emerald water and our underwear dyes*
> *green//You whisper Russian dreams of the Mediterranean,/bleached hair, jump from Grecian cliffs,*
> *eels/wrapping thighs, urchins stabbing hearts, we/swallow cobalt water until our eyes turn blue.*

Wisconsin Review is 80-100 pgs., 6×9, elegantly printed on quality white stock, glossy card cover with color art, b&w art inside. Receives about 1,500 poetry submissions/year, accepts about 75; 40-50 pgs. of poetry in each issue. Press run is 1,600 for 40 subscribers of which 20 are libraries. Single copy: $4; subscription: $10.

How to Submit: Submit mss September 15 through May 15. Offices checked bimonthly during summer. Submit up to 4 poems at a time, one poem/page, single-spaced with name and address of writer on each page. Accepts simultaneous submissions, but previously unsubmitted works preferable. Cover letter required; include brief bio. Mss are not read during the summer months. Guidelines available for SASE. Responds in up to 9 months. Pays 2 contributor's copies.

N ◎ **WOLFSONG PUBLICATIONS (Specialized: regional)**, 3123 S. Kennedy Dr., Sturtevant WI 53177. E-mail: wolfsong@wi.net. Established 1974. **Editor/Publisher:** Gary C. Busha.

Book/Chapbook Needs: Wolfsong is "a small press with a well known, respected reputation for publishing talented, serious poets." Publishes 1-3 chapbooks/year. Open to all types of poetry, but have a bias toward nature/fishing. Publishes only Wisconsin/Midwest Writers. Has published poetry by Chris Halla, Dave Etter, Russell King, Michael Koehler, Robert Schuler, and Doug Flaherty. As a sample the editor selected these lines from "April 10" in *Grace: A Book of Days* by Robert Schuler:

> *Crocuses blossom/lavendar out of snow and mud/Canada geese honking/circling the house/in the soft*
> *evening rain.*

Chapbooks are usually 30-36 pgs., 5½×8½, offset-printed or photocopied, saddle-stapled with line art on cover. Sample: $3.50. $5 list; $12 signed.

How to Submit: Query first. "Serious poets should send SASE for guidelines. Poets should have 5-10 publishing credits in respectable magazines and journals." No previously published poems or simultaneous submissions. Accepts only queries by fax and e-mail. Seldom comments on rejected poems. Responds to queries in up to 2 weeks. Pays 5 author's copies (out of a press run of 200-300).

Advice: "You need to develop a critical eye and apply that eye to your own work. You need to know the elements of good writing and understand why something that is good stands the test of time, while the 95% of everything else is—thankfully—soon forgotten."

✔ ◎ **WOODLEY MEMORIAL PRESS (Specialized: regional)**, English Dept., Washburn University, Topeka KS 66621. (785)234-1032. E-mail: zzlaws@washburn.edu. Website: www.washburn.edu/reference/woodley-press (features descriptions of books, board members' short bios, and writers' guidelines). Established 1980. **Editor:** Robert Lawson.

Book/Chapbook Needs: Woodley Memorial Press publishes 1-2 flat-spined paperbacks/year, about half being collections of poets from Kansas or with Kansas connections, "terms individually arranged with author on acceptance of ms." Has published *Looking for the Pale Eagle* by Stephen Meats, *Killing Seasons* by Christopher Cokinos, and *Gathering Reunion* by David Tangeman. As a sample the editor selected these lines from "Noah's Teenage Daughters" in *Lot's Wife* by Caryn Mirriam-Goldberg:

> *I hate this life./They wanted to take a boy for me/but he got more interested in my best friend,/so now*
> *they're both drowned/. . . //I think of throwing myself overboard/I think of throwing some rabbit over/*
> *or one of the mice.*

Samples may be individually ordered from the press for $5.

How to Submit: Guidelines available on website. Accepts e-mail queries. Responds to queries in 2 weeks, to mss in 2 months. Time between acceptance and publication is 1 year.

◑ ◎ **WORCESTER REVIEW; WORCESTER COUNTY POETRY ASSOCIATION, INC. (Specialized: regional)**, 6 Chatham St., Worcester MA 01609. (508)797-4770. Website: www.geocities.com/Paris/LeftBank/6433. Established 1973. **Managing Editor:** Rodger Martin.

Magazine Needs: *Worcester Review* appears annually "with emphasis on poetry. New England writers are encouraged to submit, though work by other poets is used also." Wants "work that is crafted, intuitively honest and empathetic, not work that shows the poet little respects his work or his readers." Has published poetry by May Swenson, Robert Pinsky, and Walter McDonald. *Worcester Review* is 160 pgs., 6×9, flat-spined, professionally printed in dark type on quality stock with glossy card cover. Press run is 1,000 for 300 subscribers of which 50 are libraries, 300 shelf sales. Subscription: $20 (includes membership in WCPA). Sample: $5.

How to Submit: Submit up to 5 poems at a time. "I recommend three or less for most favorable readings." Accepts simultaneous submissions "if indicated." Previously published poems "only on special occasions." Editor comments on rejected poems "if ms warrants a response." Publishes theme issues. Guidelines and upcoming themes available for SASE. Responds in up to 9 months. Pays 2 copies. Acquires first rights.

Also Offers: Has an annual contest for poets who live, work, or in some way (past/present) have a Worcester County connection or are a WCPA member.

Advice: "Read some. Listen a lot."

▢ ◎ **WORD DANCE (Specialized: children/teen)**, P.O. Box 10804, Wilmington DE 19850. (302)894-1950. Fax: (302)894-1957. E-mail: playful@worddance.com. Website: www.worddance.com (includes samples of writing and art, subscription information, submission guidelines, word games, and links for kids). Established 1989. **Director:** Stuart Ungar.

Magazine Needs: "Published quarterly, *Word Dance* magazine encourages the love of reading and writing in a nonthreatening, playful environment. It was created to give young people a quality vehicle for creative expression, a place where their voices can be heard. It includes short stories, poems and artwork by kids in kindergarten through Grade 8." *Word Dance* features haiku, but accepts all forms of poetry. As a sample we selected this haiku by Ernie Blais:

> *In the early dawn/The insects were gathering/Food for their new born.*

Word Dance is 32 pgs., 6×9, professionally printed and saddle-stapled, two-color card cover, includes two-color drawings. Subscription: $18/year US, $23 Canada, $28 other countries.

How to Submit: Accepts poetry for four of their six sections. Field Trip accepts poems and stories about family and school trips; World Word accepts poems and short stories about the environment, war and peace, endangered species, etc.; for Haiku Corner send your Haiku poetry; Grab Bag accepts poems and short stories about any topic. "*Word Dance* receives many submissions for the Grab Bag section of the magazine, so competition is greater in this category. We recommend that students contribute to the other sections of the magazine to increase their chances of getting published." No previously published poems or simultaneous submissions. "Our submission form must be included with each submission." Submission form available in magazine, on website, by

telephone, or by written request. Submission deadlines: February 25, May 25, August 25, November 25. Time between acceptance and publication is up to 9 months. Poems are circulated to an editorial board. Guidelines available for SASE or on website. Copies are available at cost.
Advice: "A subscription is suggested to see examples of work. We are a nonprofit organization. Parents and teachers are encouraged to help their child/student revise and edit work."

N $ ☑ WORD PRESS; WORD PRESS POETRY PRIZE, P.O. Box 541106, Cincinnati OH 45254-1106. (513)474-3761. Fax: (513)474-9034. E-mail: connect@wordtechweb.com. Website: www.wordtechweb. com (includes guidelines). Established 2000. **Editor:** Kevin Walzer.
Book/Chapbook Needs & How to Submit: Word Press "is a new, independent literary press devoted to publishing and distributing the best new poetry through an annual competition and other channels." Pays $1,000 and 25 author's copies (out of a press run of 300-500. Publishes one paperback/year chosen through the Word Press Poetry Prize. Books are 48-96 pgs. offset-printed, perfect-bound, paper/laminated cover, with photos. "Submit at least 48 pgs. of poetry. Individual poems may be previously published, but manuscript may not." Open to both new and published poets. Guidelines available on website. Competition receives 100-200 entries/year. Judges are the Word Press staff. Winners will be announced 2 months after deadline (check website for deadline information). 2001 winner was *Rare Space* by Leslie Anne Mcilroy. Copies of previous winning books are available from Word Press for $15.
Advice: "Submit your best work."

N ▣ ◯ ☑ WORD PROCESS, E-mail: sensitive@earthlink.net. Website: www.home.earthlink.net/~sen sitive. Established 1996. **Editor:** Don Craig Campbell.
Magazine Needs: *Word Process* is a weekly online publication featuring a poet of the week, a "Web Shrine to San Gabriel Valley Poetry," and more. "Our motto is 'cool poetry . . . for your refrigerator!' " Wants "quality poetry—35 lines maximum (including line breaks)." Does not want "poetry without images." As a sample the editor selected these lines by Yvonne M. Estrada:

> *I breathe deep, drive away fast, racing/your blood to the corner, making the siren/a prayer too loud for your God to ignore.*

How to Submit: Submit 3-5 poems at a time. Accepts previously published poems and simultaneous submissions. Only accepts e-mail submissions included in body of message. "Please send brief biographical information (i.e., recent publications, reading notice, chapbook available, geographical, etc.).

☑ ☑ THE WORD WORKS; THE WASHINGTON PRIZE, P.O. Box 42164, Washington DC 20015. Fax: (703)527-9384. E-mail: editor@WORDSWORKSDC.com. Website: www.WORDWORKSDC.com. Established 1974. **Editor-in-Chief:** Hilary Tham.
Book/Chapbook Needs: Word Works "is a nonprofit literary organization publishing contemporary poetry in single author editions usually in collaboration with a visual artist. We sponsor an ongoing poetry reading series, educational programs, the Capital Collection—publishing metropolitan Washington, D.C. poets, and the Washington Prize—an award of $1,500 for a book-length manuscript by a living American poet." Previous winners include *Last Heat* by Peter Blair; *Following Fred Astaire* by Nathalie Anderson; *Tipping Point* by Fred Marchant; *Stalking the Florida Panther* by Enid Shomer; and *Toward Desire* by Linda Lee Harper. Submission open to any American writer except those connected with Word Works. Send SASE for rules. Entries accepted between February 1 and March 1. Postmark deadline is March 1. Winners are announced at the end of June. Publishes perfect-bound paperbacks and occasional anthologies and want "well-crafted poetry, open to most forms and styles (though not political themes particularly). Experimentation welcomed." As a sample the editors selected these lines from "You can count on it" in the 2000 Washington Prize winning *Gandhi's Lap* by Charlotte Gould Marren:

> *In that country-of-so-many,/where families lie on the grit of sidewalks,/a thin cloth their only roof and window,/their locked door and chimney—/in that courtyard,//they break your legs/on purpose/so you can grow up begging . . .*

"We want more than a collection of poetry. We care about the individual poems—the craft, the emotional content and the risks taken—but we want manuscripts where one poem leads to the next. We strongly recommend you read the books that have already won the Washington Prize. Buy them, if you can, or ask for your libraries to purchase them. (Not a prerequisite.)" Most books are $10.
How to Submit: "Currently we are only reading unsolicited manuscripts for the Washington Prize." Accepts simultaneous submissions, if so stated. No fax or e-mail submissions. Always sends prepublication galleys. Payment is 15% of run (usually of 1,000). Guidelines and catalog available for SASE or on website. Occasionally comments on rejected poems.
Advice: "Get community support for your work, know your audience, and support contemporary literature by buying and reading the small press."

☑ $ ◎ WORDSONG; BOYDS MILLS PRESS (Specialized: children/teen/young adult), 815 Church St., Honesdale PA 18431. (800)490-5111. Website: www.boydsmillspress.com (includes info on books, book reviews, author bios, Boyds Mills Press staff, and author tours). Established 1990. **Manuscript Coordinator:** Beth Troop. **Editor-in-Chief:** Dr. Bernice E. Cullinan.

● Wordsong's *Been to Yesterdays* received the Christopher Award and was named a Golden Kite Honor Book.

Book/Chapbook Needs: Wordsong is the imprint under which Boyds Mills Press (a *Highlights for Children* company) publishes books of poetry for children of all ages. Wants quality poetry which reflects childhood fun, moral standards, and multiculturalism. "We are not interested in poetry for adults or that which includes violence or sexuality or promotes hatred." Has published *Storm Coming!* by Audrey Baird and *Sing of the Earth and Sky* by Aileen Fisher. As a sample the editor selected this excerpt from *Storm Coming!* by Audrey Baird:

> "*Firebolt!*"*—Sparks fly/from a giant's hobnailed boots;/flinting into ebony skies./Jagged/heat/hiss-s-s-s-s-ing through space.*

How to Submit: "Wordsong prefers original work but will consider anthologies and previously published collections. We ask poets to send collections of 25-45 poems with a common theme; please send complete book manuscripts, not single poems. We buy all rights to collections and publish on an advance-and-royalty basis. Wordsong guarantees a response from editors within one month of our receiving submissions or the poet may call us toll free to inquire. Please direct submissions to Beth Troop, manuscript coordinator." No fax or e-mail submissions. Always sends prepublication galleys.

Advice: "Poetry lies at the heart of the elementary school literature and reading program. In fact, poetry lies right at the heart of children's language learning. Poetry speaks to the heart of a child. We are anxious to find poetry that deals with imagination, wonder, seeing the world in a new way, family relationships, friends, school, nature, and growing up."

✓ ◯ ◿ ◎ **THE WRITE WAY (Specialized: writing); TAKING CARE OF YOURSELF (Specialized: health concerns); ANN'S ENTERPRISES**, P.O. Box 220102, Glenwood FL 32722. E-mail: annlarberg @hotmail.com. Established 1988. **Editor:** Ann Larberg.

Magazine Needs: *The Write Way* is a quarterly using poems of up to 20 lines on the theme of writing. As a sample the editor selected "Limerick Lamentation" by Donna Bickley:

> *Composing a limerick's not easy/Although my attempts make me queasy,/I jot down a line, I stretch for a rhyme,/Reaching as far as it pleases me.*

The Write Way is an 6-page newsletter with articles on writing and ads. Single copy: $2; subscription: $6. Sample free with SASE.

How to Submit: Nonsubscribers must include $1 reading fee and SASE with submissions (up to 5 poems). Do not submit in summer. Reads submissions January 1 through June 30 only. Accepts e-mail submissions included in an attached file; 20 line limit. Publishes theme issues: winter, writing (the writing life); spring, nature; summer, travel; fall, greeting card rhymed verse. Upcoming themes available for SASE. Responds in 6 weeks. Pays 1 copy. Poets may send books for review consideration.

Also Offers: Publishes an annual holiday poetry edition. Deadline for annual holiday issue is November 15. *Taking Care of Yourself*, a 4-page newsletter of well-being, is also published quarterly and accepts 1-2 short poems/issue on the theme of health. Sample free with SASE. Pays contributor's copies.

✓ $ ◯ ◿ **THE WRITER; POET TO POET**, 21027 Crossroads Circle, P.O. Box 1612, Waukesha WI 53187-1612. (800)533-6644. Fax: (262)798-6468. E-mail: editor@writermag.com. Website: www.writermag.com. Established 1887. **Managing Editor:** Rebecca Dian Schneider.

Magazine Needs: *The Writer* is a monthly magazine about writing for writers. It features how-to and inspirational articles focusing on the writing of fiction, nonfiction, poetry, and children's and young adult literature. Also publishes a monthly aritcle, "Poet to Poet," in which poets discuss specific aspects of writing poetry and to which poets may submit previously unpublished work for possible publication and comment. Also "welcomes poetry shorts, especially humorous verse, up to 10 lines, on any aspect of writing." Single copy: $3.50 newsstand; subscription: $29 (introductory offer: 5 issues for $12).

How to Submit: For "Poet to Poet," published poets may submit an article up to 1,000 words; include poems for specific examples as well as a brief bio. Prefers e-mail submissions attached in a Word file; accepts disk submissions formatted for Mac. "Otherwise, send double-spaced printed manuscript and a SASE if you would like unaccepted manuscripts returned. Be sure to include your name, address, phone number, and e-mail address." Poetry shorts will not be returned so SASE is not required. Payment for poetry shorts is $20-35. Payment for "Poet to Poet" varies. Acquires first North American serial rights.

Advice: "It may be helpful to review recent copies of the magazine or the website to see what types of subjects are covered."

◫ $ ◯ **WRITER'S BLOCK MAGAZINE; WRITER'S BLOCK CONTEST**, P.O. Box 32, 9944-33 Ave., Edmonton, Alberta T6N 1E7 Canada. Established 1994. **Editor:** Shaun Donnelly.

Magazine Needs: *Writer's Block Magazine* appears biannually and publishes assorted fiction, nonfiction, and poetry. Wants poetry of any form, length or subject matter. *Writer's Block Magazine* is 48 pgs., digest-sized, professionally printed and saddle-stapled with 4-color card cover. Receives about 500 poems/year, accepts about 12. Press run is 10,000 for 500 subscribers, 2,000 shelf sales; 7,500 distributed free to Edmonton neighborhoods. Single copy: 3.50; subscription: $12/2 years. Sample: $5.

How to Submit: Submit 3 poems at a time. Accepts previously published poems and simultaneous submissions. Cover letter preferred. Time between acceptance and publication is 6 months. Always comments on rejected poems. Guidelines available for SASE (or SAE and IRC). Responds in 2 months. Pays $25. Acquires first North American serial rights.

Also Offers: Sponsors the biannual Writer's Block Contest for novice poets. Entry deadlines are March 1 and September 1. Awards $75 plus publication to the best poem.

☑ ◯ **WRITER'S EXCHANGE; R.S.V.P. PRESS; NEW MARKETS**, 129 Thurman Lane, Clinton TN 37716. E-mail: eboone@aol.com. Website: http://members.aol.com/writernet/wrinet.htm. Established 1983. **Editor:** Eugene Boone.

Magazine Needs: *Writer's Exchange* published quarterly, "is a small press magazine for writers and poets that covers the small press and its ever-changing array of diverse publications. Seeks articles on writing-related topics, particularly those that relate to small press writers and poets, such as how-to techniques for writing various types of poetry (from haiku to sonnets!), personal experiences about writing groups, conferences, writing courses, etc." Wants "poetry in various forms, including free verse, light verse, sonnets, tanka, haiku and other fixed-forms. Length: 3-35 lines. Topics of interest include relationships, personal experience, nature, etc. However, what the editor is most interested in is what interests the poet, the subjects he or she choses to write about, these are the poems that will convey the uniqueness of the poet. What the editor does not want to see: poems that preach or 'say' what the poet feels about problems facing our society. Take homelessness, for example. Show what the homeless person sees through his or her eyes and that will show your feelings as well and help to evoke a response, sometimes a deep, emotional reaction in the reader. I like writing that is upbeat or at least positive, enlightening or inspiring, especially humorous poetry about every day life, writing, etc. I will not consider material that is anti-religious, racist or obscene." He has published poetry by Victor Chapman, Najwa Salam Brax, Sarah Jensen, and Edd McWatters. As a sample he selected these lines by Diane L. Krueger:

> all my hopes and dreams/feel possible once more with/resurgence of dreams . . . hopes/and . . . belief
> in our tomorrows

Writer's Exchange is 36 pgs., digest-sized, saddle-stapled, with a full-color cover. Accepts about half or more of the poetry received. Press run is 250. Subscription: $12. Sample: $3.

How to Submit: Submit no more than 8 poems at a time with SASE. "I prefer typed mss, one poem per page, readable. Poets should always proofread mss before sending them out. Errors can cause rejection." Accepts previously published poetry; no simultaneous submissions. "Submissions may be made in MSWord, MSWorks RTF, text, and ASCII formats on diskette or via e-mail download: webbase1@aol.com." Cover letter appreciated; list "prior credits, if any, and other details of writing background, such as writing interests." Time between acceptance and publication is 4 months. Guidelines available for SASE, by e-mail, or on website. Responds in 1 month. Pays 1 contributor's copy. Acquires one-time rights. Staff reviews books of poetry. Send books for review consideration.

Also Offers: Offers cash awards for quarterly contests sponsored through the magazine. Send SASE for current rules. In 1995 they began publishing *New Markets*, a newsletter featuring information on small press and New Age markets. Send SASE for details. The newsletter may become a column feature in *Writer's Exchange* when a new Paying Small Press Markets column is added to the magazine. *The Best of New Markets*, a compilation of the first six issues, is available for $3.95 postpaid. *Remembrance*, formerly a paper-format journal, is now published as an electronic ezine online at http://members.aol.com/eboone/remember/htm. *Remembrance Online* features poetry about unforgettable people (living and deceased), memorable moments, special places, and perfekt pets. Send SASE for complete guidelines. Same address as *Writer's Exchange*. The editor says he comments on rejected poems, "if I feel it will benefit the poet in the long run, never anything too harsh or overly discouraging." Website features guidelines for *Writer's Exchange* and other small press publications, including paying publications and others. Website includes WriterNet http://members.aol.com/writernet/wrinet.htm (the *Writer's Exchange* website) which features columns on writing techniques by established writers and poets: Mary H. Sayler, Mickey Clark, Diane L. Krueger, Lois Green Stone. Also features writing markets for those involved in the small press. Our sister website, WebBase1, features links to Research, Reference and other material of interest to writers and others at http://members.aol.com/webbase1/index1.html.

Advice: "Support the small press publications you read and enjoy. Without your support these publications will cease to exist. The small press has given many poets their start. In essence, the small press is where poetry lives!"

N ⊕ ◎ **WRITERS FORUM; AND MAGAZINE (Specialized: form)**, 89A Petherton Rd., London N5 2QT England. Phone: 020 7226 2657. Established 1963. **Editors:** Bob Cobbing and Adrian Clarke.

Magazine Needs: Writers Forum is a small press publisher of experimental work including sound and visual poetry in cards, leaflets, chapbooks, occasional paperbacks, and a magazine. Seeks "explorations of 'the limits of poetry' including 'graphic' displays, notations for sound and performance, as well as semantic and syntactic developments, not to mention fun." Has published poetry by Bruce Andrews, Maggie O'Sullivan, Lawrence Upton, Adrian Clarke, and Karen MacCormack. *And Magazine* is published "irregularly" and uses "very little unsolicited poetry; practically none." Press run "varies."

How to Submit: Submit 6 poems at a time. "We normally don't publish previously published work." Work should generally be submitted camera-ready. Pays 2 contributor's copies, additional copies at half price.

Book/Chapbook Needs & How to Submit: Under the imprint Writers Forum they publish 12-18 books/ year averaging 28 pgs. Samples and listing: £3. For book publication, query with 6 samples, bio, publications. Pays 12 copies, additional copies at half price.

Advice: "We publish only that which surprises and excites us; poets who have a very individual voice and style."

[N] ○ ◎ WRITES OF PASSAGE (Specialized: teens/young adult), P.O. Box 1935, Livingston NJ 07039. E-mail: wopassage@aol.com. Website: www.writes.org. Established 1994. **Editor/Publisher:** Wendy Mass.

Magazine Needs: *Writes of Passage* is a biannual literary journal for teenagers across the country. Only publishes poems by teenagers (12-19). "We accept all topics and forms, but do not want poems longer than three pages." As a sample the editor selected these lines from "We Were Bandits" by Megan McConnel:

> . . . *And one of the saddest things/about being able to drive these days/is that you never really go anywhere—/like across America,/or all those places/you only pretended to go in the car/parked in the garage of your childhood.*

Writes of Passage is 100 pgs., 5½×8½, professionally printed and perfect-bound with semiglossy color cover. Receives about 2,500 poems/year, accepts 100. Press run is 3,000 for 500 subscribers of which 100 are libraries, 1,500 shelf sales. Subscription: $12. Sample: $6.

How to Submit: Submit up to 5 poems at a time. Accepts previously published poems; no simultaneous submissions. Cover letter with brief bio (2-3 lines) preferred. Three editors review poems. Seldom comments on rejected poems. Guidelines available for SASE or by e-mail. Responds in 2 months. Pays 2 contributor's copies.

Also Offers: Writes of Passage USA is a nonprofit educational organization dedicated to providing teenagers with a forum for their creative writing. In addition to publishing the literary journal, they also occasionally conduct workshops and organize readings.

Advice: "Our motto is: 'your poem may make your parents cringe, your teachers blush, but your best friend will understand it.' We also accept tips and advice on writing poetry by authors and educators."

◎ WRITING FOR OUR LIVES; RUNNING DEER PRESS (Specialized: women, feminism), 647 N. Santa Cruz Ave., The Annex, Los Gatos CA 95030-4350. Established 1991. **Editor/Publisher:** Janet McEwan.

Magazine Needs: Appearing annually, "*Writing For Our Lives* serves as a vessel for poems, short fiction, stories, letters, autobiographies, and journal excerpts from the life stories, experiences, and spiritual journeys of women." Wants poetry that is "personal, women's real life, life-saving, autobiographical, serious—but don't forget humorous, silence-breaking, many styles, many voices. Women writers only, please." Has published poetry by Sara V. Glover, Kennette Harrison, Sara Regina Mitcho, and Eileen Tabios. As a sample the editor selected these lines from "To the Great Blue Heron" by Joyce Greenberg Lott:

> *Teach me how to swallow without chewing,/To hold a fish in my gullett until its scales become wings// Show me how to puff down into a secret/So only those who know me can find me/Teach me how to open my wings and fly,/unexpected and perfect, a crone in the sky.*

Writing For Our Lives is 80-92 pgs., 5¼×8¼, printed on recycled paper and perfect-bound with matte card cover. Receives about 400 poems/year, accepts 5%. Press run is 700. Subscription: $15.50/2 issues. (CA residents add 8.25% sales tax). Back issues and overseas rates available, send SASE for info. Sample: $8, $11 overseas.

How to Submit: Submit up to 5 typed poems with name and phone number on each page. Accepts previously published poems ("sometimes") and simultaneous submissions. Include 2 SASEs; "at least one of them should be sufficient to return manuscripts if you want them returned." Closing date is August 15. Usually responds in 3 days, occasionally longer. "As we are now shaping 2-4 issues in advance, we may ask to hold certain poems for later consideration over a period of 18 to 24 months." Seldom comments on rejected poems. Guidelines available for SASE. Pays 2 contributor's copies, discount on additional copies, and discount on 2-issue subscription. Acquires first world-wide English language serial (or one-time reprint) rights.

Advice: "Our contributors and circulation are international. We welcome new writers, but cannot often comment or advise. We do not pre-announce themes. Subscribe or try a sample copy—gauge the fit of your writing with *Writing For Our Lives*—support our ability to serve women's life-sustaining writing."

◖ XAVIER REVIEW, Box 110C, Xavier University, New Orleans LA 70125. (504)483-7303. Fax: (504)485-7917. E-mail: rskinner@xula.edu. Established 1961. **Editor:** Thomas Bonner, Jr. **Managing Editor:** Robert E. Skinner.

Magazine Needs: *Xavier Review* is a biannual that publishes poetry, fiction, nonfiction, and reviews (contemporary literature) for professional writers, libraries, colleges, and universities. Wants writing dealing with African/ Americans, the South, and the Gulf/Caribbean Basin. Has published *I Am New Orleans* by Marcus Christian; *Three Poets in New Orleans* by Lee Grue; and poetry by Biljiana Obradovic and Patricia Ward. Press run is 500.

How to Submit: Submit 3-5 poems at a time with SASE. Pays 5 contributor's copies.

◖ ◎ XCP: CROSS-CULTURAL POETICS (Specialized: anthropology), ℅ College of St. Catherine-Mpls, 601 25th Ave., South Minneapolis MN 55454. Website: http://bfn.org/~xcp. Established 1997. **Editor:** Mark Nowak. Member: Council of Literary Magazines and Presses.

Magazine Needs: *Xcp: Cross-Cultural Poetics* is published biannually. About *Xcp*, *The Poetry Project Newsletter* said, "Welcome to a writer's manual on how to detonate the Master-Axis of Big Brother Narratives." Has published poetry by Amiri Baraka, Diane Glancy, Juan Felipe Herrera, and Edwin Torres. *Xcp* is 175 pgs., 6×9, perfect-bound, includes ads. Subscription: $18/2 issues individuals, $40/2 issues institutions (outside US add $4). Sample (including guidelines): $10. Make checks payable to College of St. Catherine.

How to Submit: Submit 6-8 poems at a time. No previously published poems or simultaneous submissions. Cover letter preferred. Time between acceptance and publication is 4 months. Seldom comments on rejected poems. Publishes theme issues. Responds in up to 2 months. Always sends prepublication galleys. Pays 2 copies. Acquires first rights. Reviews books of poetry in 1,500-2,000 words, single or multi-book format. Open to unsolicited reviews. Poets may send books for review consideration.

Advice: "We advise all potential contributors to read several back issues (cover to cover) before submitting work." Sample copies also available from Small Press Distribution, 1-800-869-7553.

YALE UNIVERSITY PRESS; THE YALE SERIES OF YOUNGER POETS COMPETITION, P.O. Box 209040, New Haven CT 06520-9040. (203)432-0900. E-mail: tamara.belknap@yale.edu. Website: www.yale.edu/yup/. Established 1919. **Poetry Editor** (Yale University Press): Tamara Belknap.

Book/Chapbook Needs & How to Submit: The Yale Series of Younger Poets Competition is open to poets under 40 who have not had a book previously published. Submit ms of 48-64 pgs. in February. Entry fee: $15. Guidelines and rules are available for SASE. No e-mail submissions. Poets are not disqualified by previous publication of limited editions of no more than 300 copies or previously published poems in newspapers and periodicals, which may be used in the book ms if so identified. Previous winners include Richard Kenney, Carolyn Forché, and Robert Hass.

$ YANKEE MAGAZINE; YANKEE ANNUAL POETRY CONTEST, P.O. Box 520, Dublin NH 03444-0520. (603)563-8111. Established 1935. **Poetry Editor** (since 1955): Jean Burden.

Magazine Needs: Though it has a New England emphasis, the poetry is not necessarily about New England or by New Englanders. Wants to see "high-quality contemporary poems in either free verse or traditional form. Does not have to be regional in theme. Any subject acceptable, provided it is in good taste. We look for originality in thought, imagery, insight—as well as technical control." Does not want translations or poetry that is "cliché-ridden, banal verse." Has published poetry by Maxine Kumin, Liz Rosenberg, Josephine Jacobsen, Nancy Willard, Linda Pastan, Paul Zimmer, and Hayden Carruth. As a sample the editor selected these lines from "Planting the Impatiens on St. Norbert's Day" by Joan Vayo:

> three Saturdays ago/the dogwood foamed//gone green now/I see white shells of it/in the impatiens/I
> rest around its roots

Yankee Magazine is 6×9, 144 pgs., professionally printed, saddle-stapled, using full-color and b&w ads and illustrations, with full-color glossy paper cover. Receives over 30,000 submissions/year, accepts 50-60 poems, use 4-5 poems/monthly issue. Has a national distribution of more than 700,000 subscribers. Single copy: $2.99. Subscription: $24.

How to Submit: Submit up to 6 poems at a time, up to 32 lines each, free verse or traditional. No previously published poems or simultaneous submissions. "Cover letters are interesting if they include previous publication information." Submissions without SASE "are tossed." Editor comments on rejected poems "only if poem has so many good qualities it only needs minor revisions." Responds in up to 6 weeks. Approximately 18-month backlog. Pays $50/poem. Acquires first North American magazine rights.

Also Offers: Sponsors an annual poetry contest judged by a prominent New England poet and published in the March issue, with awards of $150, $100, and $50 for the best 3 poems in the preceding year.

Advice: "Study previous issues of *Yankee* to determine the kind of poetry we want. Get involved in poetry workshops at home. Read the best contemporary poetry you can find."

YA'SOU! A CELEBRATION OF LIFE, 2025 Taraval St., Rear, San Francisco CA 94116-2268. (415)665-0294. E-mail: poetjo@mymailstation.com. Established 2000. **Editor:** Joanne M. Olivieri.

Magazine Needs: *Ya'sou! A celebration of life* appears quarterly. "Our purpose is to celebrate life. We like thought-provoking and uplifting material in any style and subject matter. We would like to see poetry essays, short stories, articles, and b&w artwork." Does not want "sexually explicit, violence. I'd like more poetry written by children." Recently published poetry by C. David Hay, Joseph Verrilli, Geri Ahearn, and Daphne Baumbach. As a sample the editor selected these lines from "Call of the Wild" by C. David Hay:

MARKET CONDITIONS are constantly changing! If you're still using this book and it is 2003 or later, buy the newest edition of *Poet's Market* at your favorite bookstore or order directly from Writer's Digest Books (800)289-0963 or www.writersdigest.com.

> *The call of the wild is a restless voice/Of wind and sky and sea/Beckons all—both great and small/*
> *With the yearning to be free.*

Ya'Sou! is 15-25 pgs., magazine-sized, photocopied, side-stapled, paper cover with color photo, with art/graphics, classified ads, recipes, book and music reviews. Receives about 200 poems/year, accepts about 75%. Publishes about 40-50 poems/issue. Press run is 40 for 20 subscribers; 10 are distributed free to coffeehouses. Single copy: $3; subscription: $10/year. Make checks payable to Joanne Olivieri.

How to Submit: Submit 3 poems at a time. Line length for poetry is open. Accepts previously published poems and simultaneous submissions. Accepts e-mail submissions; no fax or disk submissions. Cover letter is preferred. "Work submitted by regular mail should be camera-ready. SASE required." Reads submissions all year. Time between acceptance and publication varies. "All work is read and chosen by the editor." Never comments on rejected poems. "Subscribers will be published in each issue. Subscribers only also receive special editions throughout the year." Guidelines are available in magazine and by e-mail. Responds in 1 week. Pays one contributor's copy. Acquires one-time rights.

Advice: "Let your own unique voice be heard. Remember, express your heart, live your soul, and celebrate life."

YEFIEF, P.O. Box 8505, Santa Fe NM 87504-8505. (505)753-3648. Fax: (505)753-7049. E-mail: arr@image sformedia.com. Established 1993. **Editor:** Ann Racuya-Robbins.

Book/Chapbook Needs: *yefief* is a serial imprint of Images For Media that was originally designed "to construct a narrative of culture at the end of the century." Wants "innovative visionary work of all kinds and have a special interest in exploratory forms and language. There is no set publication schedule." Has published poetry by Michael Palmer, Simon Perchik, and Carla Harryman. *yefief* is 250 pgs., printed on site and perfect-bound with color coated card cover with color and b&w photos, art and graphics inside. Initial artbook press run is 500. Single copy: $24.95. Write for information on obtaining sample copies.

How to Submit: Submit 3-6 poems at a time. Accepts previously published poems and simultaneous submissions. Responds in 2 months. Pays 2-3 contributor's copies. Poets may send books for review consideration.

YEMASSEE; YEMASSEE AWARDS, Dept. of English, University of South Carolina, Columbia SC 29208. (803)777-2085. E-mail: yemassee@gwm.sc.edu. Website: www.cla.sc.edu/ENGL/index.html (includes writer's guidelines, editor's names, sponsor's names, table of contents, and cover of most recent issues). Established 1993. **Editor:** Corinna McLeod.

Magazine Needs: *Yemassee* appears semiannually and "publishes primarily fiction and poetry, but we are also interested in one-act plays, brief excerpts of novels, essays, reviews, and interviews with literary figures. Our essential consideration for acceptance is the quality of the work; we are open to a variety of subjects and writing styles." Accepts 10-25 poems/issue. "No poems of such a highly personal nature that their primary relevance is to the author; bad Ginsberg." Has published poetry by Kwame Dawes, Virgil Saurez, Phoebe Davidson, Pamela McClure, and Catherine Davidson. *Yemassee* is 60-80 pgs., $5\frac{1}{2} \times 8\frac{1}{2}$, professionally printed and saddle-stapled, quality uncoated cover stock, one-color cover graphic, no ads. Receives about 400 poems/year, accepts about 10%. Press run is 750 for 63 subscribers, 10 shelf sales; 275-300 distributed free to English department heads, creative writing chairs, agents and publishers. Subscription: $6 for students, $15 regular. Sample: $4. Make checks payable to Education Foundation/English Literary Magazine Fund.

How to Submit: Submit up to 5 poems at a time. Line length for poetry is fewer than 50, "but poems of exceptional quality are considered regardless of length." No previously published poems. No fax or e-mail submissions. Cover letter required. "Each issue's contents are determined on the basis of blind selections. Therefore we ask that all works be submitted, without the author's name or address anywhere on the typescript. Include this information along with the title(s) of the work(s) in a cover letter. For longer submissions, please include an approximate word count." Reads submissions October 1 through November 15 and March 15 through April 30. Time between acceptance and publication is 4 months. "Staff reads and votes on 'blind' submissions." Seldom comments on rejected poems. Guidelines available for SASE or on website. Responds in up to 10 weeks after submission deadline. Pays 2 contributor's copies with the option to purchase additional copies at a reduced rate. Acquires first rights.

Also Offers: Sponsors the *Yemassee* Awards when funding permits. Awards $400/issue, usually $200 each for poetry and fiction.

ZILLAH: A POETRY JOURNAL, P.O. Box 202, Port Aransas TX 78373-0202. E-mail: islundim p@yahoo.com. Established 2001. **Editor/Publisher:** Pamela M. Smith.

Magazine Needs: *Zillah* is a new publication which will appear quarterly. Is " 'not your mother's poetry.' Simply put, in the year 3999 an archaeologist's dig produces a copy of *Zillah* in situ and, reading it, the treasure hunter knows what it was like to live during the second and third millenia." Does not want pornography, gratuitous violence, evil or devil worship, or anything that lacks quality. *Zillah* is 8 pgs., $7 \times 8\frac{1}{2}$, stapled, 50 lb. cover stock, with b&w graphics. Single copy: $3; subscription: $12. Make checks payable to Pamela M. Smith.

How to Submit: Submit 5-6 poems at a time. Line length for poetry is 80 maximum. Accepts previously published poems and simultaneous submissions. Accepts disk submissions; no fax or e-mail submissions. "SASE essential, typed, double-spaced, one poem to a page." Reads submissions all year. Submit seasonal poems 6 months in advance. Time between acceptance and publication is 3 months. Never comments on rejected poems. Responds in 2 months. Pays 1 contributor's copy. Acquires first North American serial rights or second reprint rights; rights revert to author after publication.

Also Offers: The *Zillah* Poetry Contest. Winners will be published and receive 2 copies of magazine. Guidelines available for SASE.

Advice: "Everyone should write, everyone should write poetry. Take a leap of faith. Think of writing as a natural state of being. Let go from a stream of consciousness, from the heart, from depth—edit and refine later."

ZINE ZONE, 47 Retreat Place, London E9 6RH United Kingdom. Fax: (+44)20-8985-7488. E-mail: getzz@zinezone.co.uk. Website: www.zinezone.co.uk. Established 1992. **Contact:** "editorial".

Magazine Needs: *Zine Zone* appears 8 times/year and publishes "a chaotic mix of illustrative works with poetry, short stories, music reviews, etc." For their poetry wants, they say, "anything goes. Although, we mostly publish obscure unpublished poets and students." As a sample they selected these lines from "Laughing at Nothing" by Steve Andrews (Wales):

> Doing something ordinary is only an act;/There's freedom of expression in the ethers./I was talking to
> a Neanderthal face/And inspecting rooms on a personal pilgrimage,/Running like a child under smiling
> Heavens,/Laughing at nothing is too much for some it seems.

Zine Zone is 44 pgs., A4, photocopied and stapled with b&w paper cover, b&w graphics. Receives about 200 poems/year, accepts 50-70%. Press run is 500 for 120 subscribers. Single copy: £1.95 ($4 US); subscription: £18 ($32 US)/8 copies, £11 ($30 US)/4 copies. Sample: £3 ($5 US).

How to Submit: Accepts previously published poems and simultaneous submissions. Accepts fax, e-mail, and disk submissions (text format). Cover letter preferred. Time between acceptance and publication is 2 months. Reviews books and chapbooks of poetry and other magazines, single book format.

Also Offers: "Poetry nights organized in and around London (UK) where poets read their work to an audience."

$ ZOLAND BOOKS INC., 384 Huron Ave., Cambridge MA 02138. (617)864-6252. Fax: (617)661-4998. E-mail: info@zolandbooks.com. Website: www.zolandbooks.com (includes reviews, frontlist, backlist, and Amazon.com links). Established 1987. **Publisher:** Roland Pease.

Book/Chapbook Needs: Zoland is a "literary press: fiction, poetry, photography, gift books, books of literary interest." Wants "high-quality" poetry, not sentimental. Has published poetry by Kevin Young, Bill Berkson, Joel Sloman, and Ange Mlinko. Publishes 15 books/year, flat-spined, averaging 104 pgs.

How to Submit: Query first with 5-10 sample poems and cover letter with brief bio and publication credits. Include SASE. Sometimes sends prepublication galleys. Pays 5-10% royalties plus 5 author's copies. Acquires all rights.

ZUZU'S PETALS QUARTERLY ONLINE, P.O. Box 4853, Ithaca NY 14852. (607)387-6916. E-mail: info@zuzu.com. Website: www.zuzu.com. Established 1992. **Editor:** T. Dunn.

Magazine Needs: "We publish high-quality fiction, essays, poetry, and reviews on our award-winning website, which was featured in *USA Today Online*, *Entertainment Weekly*, and *Web Magazine*. Becoming an Internet publication allows us to offer thousands of helpful resources and addresses for poets, writers, editors, and researchers, as well as to greatly expand our readership. Free verse, blank verse, experimental, visually sensual poetry, etc. are especially welcome here. We're looking for a freshness of language, new ideas, and original expression. No 'June, moon, and spoon' rhymed poetry. No light verse. I'm open to considering more feminist, ethnic, alternative poetry, as well as poetry of place." Has published poetry by Ruth Daigon, Robert Sward, Laurel Bogen, W.T. Pfefferle, and Kate Gale. As a sample the editor selected these lines from "San Francisco Earthquake" by Kathryn Young:

> Padre Pablo, in the dream I could understand/how the angels of death like wild birds/can be entertained
> with kind gestures/like strangers, how white their teeth,/how warm and dark their skin

Zuzu's Petals averages 70-100 pgs., using full-color artwork, and is an electronic publication available free of charge on the Internet. "Many libraries, colleges, and coffeehouses offer access to the Internet for those without home Internet accounts." Receives about 3,000 poems/year, accepts about 10%. A copy of *Zuzu's Petals Poetry Buffet*, a sample of writing from the past 4 years is available for $5.

How to Submit: Submit up to 4 poems at a time. Accepts previously published poems and simultaneous submissions. Submissions via e-mail are welcome, as well as submissions in ASCII (DOS IBM) format on 3½″ disks. Include e-mail submissions in the body of the message. "Cover letters are not necessary. The work should speak for itself." Seldom comments on rejected poems. Guidelines available for SASE, by e-mail, or on website. Responds in up to 2 months. Acquires one-time electronic rights. Staff reviews books of poetry in approximately 200 words. Send books, galleys, or proofs for review consideration.

Advice: "Read as much poetry as you can. Support the literary arts: Go to poetry readings, read chapbooks and collections of verse. Eat poetry for breakfast, cultivate a love of language, then write!"

Contests & Awards

This section contains a wide array of poetry competitions and literary awards. These range from state poetry society contests with a number of modest monetary prizes to prestigious honors bestowed by private foundations, elite publishers, and renowned university programs. Because there is such a variety of skill levels and degrees of competitiveness, it's important to read these listings carefully and note the requirements of each. *Never* enter a contest without consulting the guidelines and following directions to the letter (including manuscript formatting, number of lines or pages of poetry accepted, amount of entry fee, entry forms needed, and other details).

WHERE TO ENTER?

While it's perfectly okay to "think big" and aim high, being realistic may actually improve your chances of winning a prize for your poetry. Many of the listings in the Contests & Awards section begin with symbols that reflect their level of difficulty:

Contests ideal for beginners and unpublished poets are coded with the (☐) symbol. That's not to say these contests won't be highly competitive—there may be a very large number of entries. However, you may find that the work entered is more on a level with your own, increasing your chances of being "in the running" for a prize. Don't assume that these contests reward low quality, though. If you submit less than your best work, you're wasting your time and money (in postage and entry fees).

Contests for poets with more experience are coded with the (◨) symbol. Beginner/unpublished poets are usually still welcome to enter, but it's understood that the competition is keener here. Your work may be judged against that of widely published, prize-winning poets, so consider carefully whether you're ready for this level of competition. (Of course, nothing ventured, nothing gained—but those entry fees *do* add up!)

Contests for accomplished poets are coded with the (◪) symbol. Note that these may have stricter entry requirements, higher entry fees, and other conditions that signal that these programs are not intended to be "wide open" to all poets.

Specialized contests are coded with the (◎) symbol. These may include regional contests; awards for poetry written in a certain form or in the style of a certain poet; contests for women, gay/lesbian, ethnic, or age-specific poets (for instance, children or older adults); contests for translated poetry only; and many others.

There are also symbols which give additional information about contests. The (N) symbol indicates that the contest is new to this edition; the (✔) symbol signals a change in the contact information for that listing. The (♥) symbol identifies a Canadian contest or award and the (🌐) symbol an international listing. Sometimes Canadian and international contests require that entrants live in certain countries, so pay extra close attention when you see these symbols.

ADDITIONAL CONTESTS & AWARDS

Often magazines and presses prefer to include their contests within their listings in the Publishers of Poetry section. Therefore we provide a supplement at the end of this section as a cross reference to these opportunities. For full details about a contest in this list, locate that market in the General Index and turn to the appropriate page number.

WHAT ABOUT ENTRY FEES?

You'll find that most contests charge entry fees, and these are usually quite legitimate. The funds are used to cover expenses such as paying the judges, putting up prize monies, printing prize editions of magazines and journals, and promoting the contest through mailings and ads. If you're concerned about a poetry contest or other publishing opportunity, see Are You Being Taken? on page 14 for advice on some of the more questionable practices in the poetry world.

OTHER RESOURCES

Be sure to widen your search for contests beyond those listed in *Poet's Market*. Many Internet writer's sites have late-breaking announcements about competitions old and new (see Websites of Interest on page 468). Often these sites offer free electronic newsletter subscriptions, so sign up! Information will come right to you via your e-mail inbox.

Publications such as *Poets & Writers*, *The Writer*, and *Writer's Digest* regularly include listings for upcoming contests, as well as deadlines for artist's grants at the state and national level. (See Publications of Interest on page 462 for contact information; also, State & Provincial Grants on page 418.) Associated Writing Programs (AWP) is a valuable resource, including its publication, *Writer's Chronicle*. (See Organizations, page 444.) State poetry societies are listed throughout this book; they offer many contests as well as helpful information for poets (and mutual support). To find a specific group, search the General Index for listings under your state's name or look under "society"; also consult the Geographical Index on page 502.

Finally, don't overlook your local connections. City and community newspapers, radio and TV announcements, bookstore newsletters and bulletin boards, and your public library can be terrific resources for competition news, especially regional contests.

☘ ✓ $ ☺ ◎ **THE ACORN-RUKEYSER CHAPBOOK CONTEST; THE SANDBURG-LIVESAY ANTHOLOGY CONTEST; THE HERB BARRETT AWARD**, 237 Prospect St. S., Hamilton, Ontario L8M 2Z6 Canada. (905)312-1779. E-mail: meklerdeahl.com. Website: www.meklerdeahl.com. **Managing Partner:** James Deahl. Offers three contests: The Acorn-Rukeyser Chapbook Contest awards $100 (US), publication, and 50 copies; runner-up receives $100 (US). Submissions may be entered in other contests. Submit a poetry ms of up to 30 pgs., poems must be within the People's Poetry tradition, as exemplified by the work of Milton Acorn and Muriel Rukeyser. Guidelines available for SASE. Entry fee: $10 (US). All entrants receive a copy of the winning chapbook. Postmark deadline: September 30. Winner will be notified in the spring. Also sponsors the Sandburg-Livesay Anthology Contest awards 1st Prize: $250 (US) and publication; 2nd Prize: $150 (US) and anthology publication; 3rd Prize: $100 and anthology publication; and anthology publication for other prizes. Submit up to 10 poems of up to 70 lines each; poems must be within the People's Poetry tradition, as exemplified by the work of Carl Sandburg and Dorothy Livesay. Entry fee: $12 (US). All entrants receive a copy of the anthology ($14 value). Postmark deadline: October 31. Winners will be notified in the spring. The Herb Barrett Award for short poetry in the haiku tradition awards publication and 1st Prize: $200 (US); 2nd Prize: $150 (US); 3rd Prize: $100 (US); and anthology publication for other prizes. Winning poems will be published in an anthology. All entrants will receive 1 copy of the anthology. "What is most important is that each haiku be a concise image of life." Entry fee: $10 (US). "Up to 10 poems may be submitted per entry." Postmark deadline: November 30. Winners will be notified the following summer. Guidelines for any of the 3 competitions are available for SASE or on website. Entry fees payable by check or bank money order to Mekler & Deahl, Publishers.

✓ $ ☺ **AKRON POETRY PRIZE**, The University of Akron Press, 374B Bierce Library, Akron OH 44325-1703. (330)972-5342. Fax: (330)972-5132. E-mail: uapress@uakron.edu. Website: www.uakron.edu/uapress/(includes a list of publications, ordering information, and guidelines for poetry contest). **Award Director:** Elton Glaser. Offers annual award of $1,000 plus publication. Submissions must be unpublished and may be entered in other contests (with notification of acceptance elsewhere). Submit 60-100 pages maximum, typed, preferably double-spaced, with SASE for results. Mss will not be returned. Do not send mss bound or enclosed in covers. Guidelines available for SASE or by fax or e-mail. Accepts inquiries by fax and e-mail. Entry fee: $25. Deadline: entries are accepted May 15 through June 30 only. Competition receives 450-500 entries. Most recent contest winners were John Minczeski, Dennis Hinrichsen, Beckian Fritz Goldberg, and Jeanne E. Clark. Judge for the 2001 prize was Billy Collins. Winner will be announced in September. Copies of previous winning books are available from UAP or through your local bookstore. The University of Akron Press "is committed to publishing poetry that, as Robert Frost said, 'begins in delight and ends in wisdom.' Books accepted must exhibit three essential qualities: mastery of language, maturity of feeling, and complexity of thought."

☑ ◎ ◎ **AMERICAN ANTIQUARIAN SOCIETY VISITING FELLOWSHIPS FOR CREATIVE AND PERFORMING ARTISTS AND WRITERS (Specialized: American history and culture)**, Artists and Writers Fellowship, American Antiquarian Society, 185 Salisbury St., Worcester MA 01609-1634. (508)363-1131. Fax: (508)754-9069. E-mail: jmoran@mwa.org. Website: www.americanantiquarian.org/artistfellowship.htm. Established 1994. **Award Director:** James David Moran. Offers at least 3 fellowships for 4-week residencies at the Society. Awards a stipend of $1,200 plus an allowance for travel expenses. Fellowships provide recipients "with the opportunity for a period of uninterrupted research, reading, and collegial discussion at the Society in Worcester, Massachusetts." Library is devoted to pre-20th century materials. Entry form and guidelines available for SASE; additional information available on website. Accepts inquiries by fax and e-mail. Deadline October 5. 2001 winners included poet Geoffrey Brock (winner profiles for 1995-2001 available on website). Winners will be announced in December. "Established in 1812. As the country's first national historical organization, the American Antiquarian Society is both a learned society and a major independent research library. The AAS library today houses the largest and most accessible collection of books, pamphlets, broadsides, newspapers, periodicals, sheet music and graphic arts material produced through 1876 in what is now the United States, as well as manuscripts and a substantial collection of secondary works, bibliographies, and other reference works related to all aspects of American history and culture before the twentieth century." Potential candidates should "learn about the collections in the library; consult *Under Its Generous Dome, A Guide to the Collections and Programs of the American Antiquarian Society.*"

◖ **ARKANSAS POETRY DAY CONTEST; POETS' ROUNDTABLE OF ARKANSAS**, 605 Higdon, Apt. 109, Hot Springs AR 71913. (501)321-4226. E-mail: vernalee@lpt.net. **Contact:** Verna Lee Hinegardner. Over 25 categories, many open to all poets. Brochure available in June; deadline in September; awards given in October. Guidelines available for SASE.

$◖ **ART COOP FELLOWSHIP IN POETRY**, % Charli Valdez, 725 Ashland, Houston TX 77007. E-mail: art_coop@yahoo.com. Website: www.geocities.com/~cottonwood. Established 1996. **Director:** Charli Valdez. Offers annual fellowship in poetry. Open to poets everywhere. Awards cash prize (not less than $250) and publication. Pays winners from other countries by cashier's check. Include cover sheet, bio, and list of publications. Guidelines and information available for SASE, by e-mail, or on website. Entry fee(s): $5 for first poem, $2 each thereafter. Does not accept entry fees in foreign currencies. "For flat $10 fee and SASE, feedback on poems provided." Deadline: May 31. Competition received 20 entries last year.

☑ $◪ **"ART IN THE AIR" POETRY CONTEST**, Inventing the Invisible/"Art in the Air" Radio Show, 3128 Walton Blvd., PMB 186, Rochester Hills MI 48309. Fax: (248)693-7344. E-mail: lagapvp@aol.com. Website: www.wpon.com (includes guidelines). Established 1991. **Award Director:** Margo LaGattuta. Offers biannual award of 1st Prize: $100; 2nd Prize: $50; and 4 Honorable Mentions. Pays winners from other countries by check. ("All winners read poems on the radio.") Submissions may be entered in other contests. Submit 3 poems maximum in any form, typed, single-spaced, limit 2 pages per poem. Guidelines available for SASE or on website. Accepts inquiries by fax or e-mail. Entry fee: $5 for up to 3 poems. Accepts entry fees in foreign currencies. Deadlines: October 30 and April 30. Competition receives over 600 entries/year. Past contest winners were Simone Muench, Marilyn Krysl, Julie Moulds, Elizabeth Rosner, Bill Rudolph, Jenny Brown, and Wyatt Townley. Judges were Mary Jo Firth Gillett and Margo LaGattuta. Winners will be announced 2 months after deadline. Copies of previous winning poems or books may be obtained by sending an SASE to the Inventing the Invisible address. " 'Art in the Air' is an interview radio show on WPON, 1460 AM, in Bloomfield Hills, MI, hosted by Margo LaGattuta. The theme is creativity and the creative process, especially featuring writers both local and national. Send only your best work—well crafted and creative. Judges look for excellence in content and execution."

$◎ **ARTIST TRUST; ARTIST TRUST GAP GRANTS; ARTIST TRUST FELLOWSHIPS (Specialized: regional)**, 1402 Third Ave., Suite 404, Seattle WA 98101. (206)467-8734. Fax: (206)467-9633. E-mail: info@artisttrust.org. Website: www.artisttrust.org (includes applications and other grant/publication opportunities). **Program Director:** Heather Dwyer. Artist Trust is a nonprofit arts organization that provides grants to artists (including poets) who are residents of the state. Accepts inquiries by fax and e-mail. Competition receives 1,000 entries/year. Contest winners include Donna Miscolta, Thomas Gribble, and Bruce Beasley. Also publishes, three times a year, a journal of news about arts opportunities and cultural issues.

☑ $◖ ◪ **THE BACKWATERS PRIZE**, The Backwaters Press, 3502 N. 52nd St., Omaha NE 68104-3506. (402)451-4052. E-mail: gkosm62735@aol.com. Website: www.thebackwaterspress.homestead.com. Established 1998. **Award Director:** Greg Kosmicki. Offers annual prize of $1,000 plus publication, promotion, and distribution. "Submissions may be entered in other contests and this should be noted in cover letter. Backwaters Press must be notified if manuscripts are accepted for publication at other presses." Submit up to 80 pgs. on any subject, any form. "Poems must be written in English. No collaborative work accepted. Parts of the manuscript may be previously published in magazines or chapbooks, but entire manuscript may not have been previously published." Manuscript should be typed (or word processed) in standard poetry format—single spaced, one poem per page, one side only. Guidelines only available for SASE. Entry fee: $20. Does not accept entry fees in foreign currencies. Send postal money order or personal check in US dollars. Deadline: postmarked by June 1 of each year. Competition receives 200-250 entries/year. Most recent contest winner was David Staudt (2000). Judge was Ted Koozer. Winner will be announced in *Poets & Writer's* "Recent Winners." Copies of previous winning books may be obtained by writing to the press. "The Backwaters Press is a nonprofit press dedicated to publishing the best new literature we can find. Send your best work."

[N] $□ ☑ BALCONES POETRY PRIZE, Austin Community College, 1212 Rio Grande, Austin TX 78701. (512)223-3236. E-mail: dbarnett@austin.cc.tx.us. Established 1995. **Contest Director:** Dorothy Barnett. Offers annual prize of $1,000 for a book of poetry, in English, published during the award year. Submissions must be previously published in the year of the award and may be entered in other contests. Winning poet is expected to come to Austin to read from ms. Submit 42-page ms on any subject or in any form. Guidelines and information available for SASE and by e-mail. Entry fee: $20. Deadline: April 1st, 2001. Competition receives approximately 80 entries. Most recent contest winner was Dana Levin. Judges were John Herndon, Dave Oliphant, and Peggy Kelley. Winner will be announced in late June or early July. "The Austin Community College is a 2-year college of 26,000 students in urban Central Texas."

☑ ◎ BAY AREA BOOK REVIEWERS ASSOCIATION AWARDS (BABRA); FRED CODY AWARD (Specialized: regional), 1450 Fourth St., #4, Berkeley CA 94710. (510)525-5476. Fax: (510)525-6752. Established 1981. **Contact:** Joyce Jenkins. Offers annual awards which recognize "the best of Northern California (from Fresno north) fiction, poetry, nonfiction, and children's literature." Submissions must be previously published. Submit 3 copies of each book entered. The authors of the submitted books must live in Northern California. Guidelines available for SASE. Deadline: December 1. BABRA also sponsors the Fred Cody Award for lifetime achievement given to a Northern California writer who also serves the community. Also gives, on an irregular basis, awards for outstanding work in translation and publishing. The Cody Award winner for 1998 was Maxine Hong Kingston. **Note:** *The Fred Cody Award does not accept applications.*

⊕ ◎ BBC WILDLIFE MAGAZINE POET OF THE YEAR AWARDS (Specialized: nature), *BBC Wildlife Magazine*, Broadcasting House, Whiteladies Rd., Bristol BS8 2LR United Kingdom. Phone: +44(0)117 973 8402. Fax: +44(0)117 946 7075. E-mail: wildlife.magazine@bbc.co.uk. Established in 1994. **Award Director:** Nina Epton. Offers annual prize of £500, publication in *BBC Wildlife Magazine* plus the poem is read on BBC radio 4's "Poetry, Please" program. Runners-up receive cash prizes plus publication in *BBC Wildlife Magazine*. Pays winners from other countries by international money order. Submissions must be unpublished. Submit 1 poem on the natural world in any form, 50 lines maximum. Send SASE (or SAE and IRC) for guidelines only. Accepts inquiries by fax or e-mail. "No entry fees, but entry form appears in magazine, so you have to buy magazine to enter." Deadline varies from year to year. Competition receives 1,500-2,000 entries/year. Most recent award winner was Geri Rosenzweig (2000). Judges were Simon Rae (poet), Philip Gross (poet), Sara Davies (producer of "Poetry, Please"), Frank Delaney (presenter of "Poetry, Please"), Helen Dunmore (poet and novelist), Libby Houston (poet and conservationist), and Rosamund Kidman Cox (editor of *BBC Wildlife Magazine*). Winner announced in *BBC Wildlife Magazine*. "Contact us for information before sending a poem in."

⊕ $□ BECH PUBLICATIONS WRITING COMPETITION, BECH Publications (Ballarat East Community House), P.O. Box 2038, Ballarat Mail Centre, Ballarat, Victoria 3354 Australia. Phone/fax: (03)53314107. E-mail: bech@netconnect.com.au. Website: www.yarranet.net.au/cedric/balleast/hom.htm. Established 1998. **Coordinator:** Janelle Johnson. Offers annual prizes (Australian dollars) in 3 categories. Poetry: open to 60 lines—$150, $80. Short Story: open to 2,000 words—$150, $80. Prose: theme to 750 words—$100, $80. Submissions must be unpublished. Submit any number of poems. Entry form and guidelines available for SASE (or SAE and IRC). Entry fee: $4 (AUS)/entry. Does not accept entry fees in foreign currencies. Send International Bank Exchange rate or 3 IRCs plus 1 additional IRC for results. Competition receives 900 entries/year. Judges have included David Farnsworth, Ruth Strachan, and Vicky Lowe. Winners will be announced by mail and on the Internet. "Ballarat East Community House sponsors the BECH Publications Writing Competitions and has done so since 1998. It is a provider of Adult Community Education and vocational training and education with the State of Victoria Australia. Judges are hand-picked professional writers or dedicated wordsmiths with judging experience. The competition is open to all. We encourage everyone to 'have a go.' "

$☑ GEORGE BENNETT FELLOWSHIP, Phillips Exeter Academy, 20 Main St., Exeter NH 03833-2460. Website: www.exeter.edu (includes information about Phillips Exeter Academy and the Fellowship with application materials). Established 1968. **Selection Committee Coordinator:** Charles Pratt. Provides a $6,000 fellowship plus room and board to a writer with a ms in progress. The Fellow's only official duties are to be in residence while the academy is in session and to be available to students interested in writing. The committee favors writers who have not yet published a book-length work with a major publisher. Application materials available for SASE or on website. Deadline: December 1. Competition receives 125 entries. Recent award winners were Ilya Kaminsky (1999-2000) and Laura Moriarty (2001).

$ ◎ BEST OF OHIO WRITERS WRITING CONTEST (Specialized: regional); OHIO WRITER MAGAZINE, P.O. Box 91801, Cleveland OH 44101. Offers annual contest for poetry, fiction, creative nonfiction, and "Writers on Writing" (any genre). 1st Prize: $150, 2nd Prize: $50, plus publication for first-place winner of each category in a special edition of *Ohio Writer*. Submit up to 3 typed poems, no more than 2 pages each unpublished mss only. Open only to Ohio residents. "Entries will be judged anonymously, so please do not put name or other identification on manuscript. Attach a 3×5 card with name, address, city, state, zip, and day and evening phone number. Manuscripts will not be returned." Entry form and guidelines available for SASE. Entry fee: $10/first entry in each category (includes subscription to *Ohio Writer*); $2 for each additional entry (limit 3 per category). Deadline: July 31. Competition receives 300 entries/year. Most recent winners were Philip Brady, Rita Grabowski, and Cheryl McPeek. Judges have included Larry Smith, editor of Bottom Dog Press; Richard Hague, author of *Milltown Natural*; Ron Antonucci, editor of *Ohio Writer*; Sheila Schwartz, author of *Imagine a Great White Light*. Winners will be announced in the November/December issue of *Ohio Writer*. (See listing for *Ohio Writer* in Publications of Interest.)

$ ◙ BLUESTEM PRESS AWARD, Emporia State University, English Dept., Box 4019, Emporia KS 66801-5087. (316)341-5216. Fax: (316)341-5547. Website: www.emporia.edu/bluestem/index.htm (includes guidelines, announcements, previous winners, and booklist). Established in 1989. **Editor/Contest Coordinator:** Philip Heldrich. Offers annual award of $1,000 and publication for an original book-length collection of poems. Submissions must be unpublished and may be entered in other contests (with notification). Submit a typed ms of at least 48 pages on any subject in any form with a #10 SASE for notification. Guidelines and information available for SASE and by e-mail. Entry fee: $18. Deadline: March 1. Competition receives 500-700 entries/year. Recent award winner was Katharine Whitcomb. Judge was Lucia Perillo. Winner will be announced in May. Copies of previous winning poems or books may be obtained by contacting the Bluestem Press at the above number. Enter early to avoid missing the deadline. Also, looking at the different winners from past years would help. Manuscripts will *not* be accepted after the deadline and will not be returned.

✓ ⊕ $ ◎ THE BOARDMAN TASKER AWARD (Specialized: mountain literature), The Boardman Tasker Charitable Trust, 40 Wingate Rd., London W6 OUR United Kingdom. Phone: 0208 743 4845. E-mail: pippa@pippasouthward.demon.co.uk. Established in 1983. **Contact:** Pippa Southward. Offers prize of £2,000 to "the author or authors of the best literary work, whether fiction, nonfiction, drama, or poetry, the central theme of which is concerned with the mountain environment. Entries for consideration may have been written by authors of any nationality but the work must be published or distributed in the United Kingdom between November 1, 2001 and October 31, 2002. (If not published in the U.K., please indicate name of distributor.) The work must be written or have been translated into the English language." Submit ms in book format. "In a collection of essays or articles by a single author, the inclusion of some material previously published but now in book form for the first time will be acceptable." *Submissions accepted from the publisher only.* Four copies of entry must be submitted with application. Accepts inquiries by e-mail; does not accept inquiries by fax. Deadline: August 1, 2002. Competition receives about 25 entries. Most recent winner was *The Wildest Dream*, by Peter and Leni Gillman, published by Headline.

⬛ $ ◎ BP NICHOL CHAPBOOK AWARD (Specialized: regional), 316 Dupont St., Toronto, Ontario M5R 1V9 Canada. (416)964-7919. Fax: (416)964-6941. Established 1985. Offers $1,000 (Canadian) prize for the best poetry chapbook (10-48 pgs.) in English published in Canada in the preceding year. Submit 3 copies (not returnable) and a brief curriculum vitae of the author. Accepts inquiries by fax. Deadline: March 31. Competition receives between 40-60 entries on average.

Ⓝ ⊕ $ ◙ THE BRIDPORT PRIZE; INTERNATIONAL CREATIVE WRITING COMPETITION, Bridport Arts Centre, South St., Bridport, Dorset DT6 3NR United Kingdom. Phone: (01308) 427183. E-mail: arts@bridport.co.uk. Website: www.bridportprize.org.uk (includes entry forms, rules, info about competition, anthology order forms). Established 1980. **Contact:** Competition Secretary. Offers annual award for an original poem of not more than 42 lines and an original story of not more than 5,000 words. 1st Prize: £3,000, 2nd Prize: £1,500, and 3rd Prize: £500 in each category plus small supplementary prize. Prize-winning entries also published in anthology. Submissions must be previously unpublished. Open as to subject or form. Entry fee: £5 sterling/entry. Accepts foreign entry fees by VISA, Mastercard. Deadline: June 30 of each year. Competition receives approximately 8,000 entries. Most recent contest winners are Victotia Worsley and Linda Rogers. Judges for 2001 contest were Kate Atkinson and Maura Dooley. Winners will be announced at the end of September. Copies of the previous winning anthologies may be obtained by sending £11 sterling to Competition Secretary at the above address (VISA and Mastercard also accepted).

Ⓝ ⬛ $ ◎ ◙ CANADIAN AUTHORS ASSOCIATION AWARDS FOR ADULT LITERATURE (Specialized: regional); CANADIAN AUTHORS ASSOCIATION; AIR CANADA AWARD, Box 419, Campbellford, Ontario K0L 1L0 Canada. (705)653-0323. Fax: (705)653-0593. E-mail: canauth@redden.on.ca. Website: www.CanAuthors.org. **Administrator:** Alec McEachern. The CAA Awards for Adult Literature offers $2,500 and a silver medal in each of 5 categories (fiction, poetry, short stories, Canadian history, Canadian biography) to Canadian writers, for a book published during the year. Entry fee: $20/title. Deadline: December

15; except for works published after December 1, in which case the postmark deadline is January 15.Competition receives 300 entries/year. Most recent award winners were Helen Humphreys (poetry) and Alistair MacLeod (fiction). The CAA Air Canada Award is an annual prize of two tickets to any Air Canada destination, awarded to a Canadian author under 30 who shows the most promise in the field of literary creation (any field or form). **Nominations are made before March 31 by CAA branches, or other writers' organizations, agents or publishers.** All awards are given at the CAA banquet in June.

☑ ⊕ $◖ **CATALPA WRITER'S PRIZE**, (formerly Irish Famine Commemorative Literary Prize), Australian-Irish Heritage Association, P.O. Box 1583, Subiaco, West Australia 6904 Australia. Phone: 08 9381 8306. Fax: 08 9382 1283. E-mail: aiha@ireland.com. Website: www.multiline.com.au/~aiha (includes rules, prize-winning poems, and description of contest). Established 1997. **Award Director:** Joe O'Sullivan. Offers annual awards in 3 categories: short fiction, essay, poetry. Winner in each category will receive AUS $250. Best entry overall will receive additional AUS $500. Pays winners from other countries with bankdraft. Submissions must be unpublished. Submit unlimited number of poems on the theme "Separation" in any form—100 lines maximum. Guidelines available for SASE (or SAE and IRC) or on website. Accepts inquiries by fax and e-mail. Entry fee: AUS $10/entry, will be donated to Community Aid Abroad/OXFAM to relieve world hunger. Accepts entry fees in foreign currencies. Deadline: January 17, 2002. Competition receives 150-200 entries/year. Most recent winner was Libby Hart (Australia). Judge was Joyce Parkes. Copies of previous winning poems are published on the Internet. "AIHA conserves and publishes our Irish heritage. Contest commemorates famine in a practical way by donating entry fees in their entirety to OXFAM for relief of world hunger. Enter and help a good cause."

Ⓝ $◎ **CAVE CANEM POETRY PRIZE (Specialized: ethnic/African American); CAVE CANEM FOUNDATION, INC.**, 39 Jane St. GB, New York NY 10014. (804)979-8825. Fax: (804)977-8106. E-mail: cavecanempoets@aol.com. Website: http://cavecanempoets.org. Award established 1999; organization 1996. **Award Director:** Carolyn Micklem, Cave Canem director. Offers "a first book award dedicated to presenting the work of African American poets who have not been published by a professional press. The winner will receive $500 cash, publication, and 50 copies of the book." U.S. poets only. "Send two copies of manuscript of 50-75 pgs. The author's name should not appear on the manuscript. Two title pages should be attached to each copy. The first must include the poet's name, address, telephone and the title of the manuscript; the second should list the title only. Number the pages. Manuscripts will not be returned, but a SASE postcard can be included for notice of manuscript receipt. Simultaneous submissions should be noted. If the manuscript is accepted for publication elsewhere during the judging, immediate notification is requested." Guidelines available for SASE, by fax, by e-mail, or on website. There is no entry fee. Deadline: May 15 of each year. Send ms to Cave Canem, P.O. Box 4286, Charlottesville, VA 22905-4286. Receives 78 entries/year (so far). Most recent award winners are Major Jackson (2000) and Natasha Trethewey (1999). Judges were Al Young (2000) and Rita Dove (1999). Winners will be announced by press release in October of year of contest. Copies of previous winning books are available from "any book seller, because the publishers are Graywolf Press ('99), University of Georgia ('00), and University of Pittsburgh ('01). Cave Canem sponsors a week-long workshop/retreat each summer and regional workshops in New York City and Minnesota. It sponsors readings in Philadelphia, Virginia Festival of the Book, and New York City each year and in other venues as opportunities arise." Recommends "since this is a highly competitive contest, you should be at a stage in your development where some of your poems have already been published in literary journals." (See the Insider Report on Cave Canem on pg. 425 of the Conferences & Workshops section.)

☑ $◑ **THE CENTER FOR BOOK ARTS' ANNUAL POETRY CHAPBOOK COMPETITION**, 28 W. 27th St., 3rd Floor, New York NY 10001. (212)481-0295. E-mail: info@centerforbookarts.org. Website: www.centerforbookarts.org/ (includes guidelines, application form, center information and history, class schedule, events). Established in 1995. **Award Director:** Sharon Dolin. Offers $500 cash prize, a $500 reading honorarium, and publication of winning manuscript in a limited edition letterpress-printed and handbound chapbook. Pays winners from other countries in US dollars. Submissions may be entered in other contests. Submit no more than 500 lines or 24 pgs. on any subject, in any form. Mss must be typed on one side of 8½ × 11 paper. Guidelines available for SASE and on website. Entry fee: $15/ms. Postmark deadline: December 1. Competition receives 500-1,000 entries/year. Most recent contest winner was Terri Witek. Judges were Sharon Dolin and Rachel Hadas. Winner will be contacted mid-April by telephone. Each contestant receives a letter announcing the winner. Copies of previous winning books may be ordered by sending $25. Reading fee is credited toward the purchase of the winning chapbook. "Center for Book Arts is a non-profit organization dedicated to the traditional crafts of bookmaking and contemporary interpretations of the book as an art object. Through the Center's Education, Exhibition and Workspace Programs we ensure that the ancient craft of the book remains a viable and vital part of our civilization."

$◻ CNW/FFWA FLORIDA STATE WRITING COMPETITION, Florida Freelance Writers Association, P.O. Box A, North Stratford NH 03590-0167. (603)922-8338. E-mail: contest@writers-editors.com. Website: www.writers-editors.com (includes announcement of winners, list of previous winners, tips for poetry). Established 1978. **Award Director:** Dana K. Cassell. Offers annual awards for nonfiction, fiction, children's literature, and poetry. Awards for each category are: 1st Place: $100 plus certificate, 2nd Place: $75 plus certificate, 3rd Place: $50 plus certificate, plus Honorable Mention certificates. Submissions must be unpublished. Submit any number of poems on any subject in traditional forms, free verse, or children's. Entry form and guidelines available for SASE or on website. Accepts inquiries by e-mail. Entry fee: $3/poem (members), $5/poem (nonmembers). Deadline: March 15. Competition receives 350-400 entries/year. Competition is judged by writers, librarians, and teachers. Winners will be announced on May 31 by mail and on website.

$◎ COLORADO BOOK AWARDS (Specialized: regional), Colorado Center for the Book, 2123 Downing, Denver CO 80205. (303)839-8320. Fax: (303)839-8319. E-mail: ccftb@compuserve.com. Website: www.aclin.org/~ccftb. **Executive Director:** Christiane Citron. Offers annual award of $350 plus promotion for books published in the year prior to the award. Submissions may be entered in other contests. Submit 6 copies of each book entered. Open to residents of Colorado. Entry form and guidelines available for SASE, by e-mail, or on website. Entry fee: $40. Deadline: December 15. Competition receives 120 entries/year. Most recent award winner was Robert Cooperman. Winner will be announced at an annual ceremony/dinner. "We are a nonprofit organization affiliated with the Library of Congress Center for the Book. We promote the love of books, reading, and literacy. We annually sponsor the Rocky Mountain Book Festival which attracts tens of thousands of people. It's free and includes hundreds of authors from throughout the country. We are located in the home of Thomas Hornsby Ferril, Colorado's late former poet laureate. This historic landmark home is used as a literary center and a tribute to Ferril's life and work."

$◎ COUNCIL FOR WISCONSIN WRITERS, INC. (Specialized: regional), Box 55322, Madison WI 53705. Offers annual awards of $500 or more for a book of poetry by a Wisconsin resident, published within the awards year (preceding the January 13 deadline). Competition receives 250 entries/year. Entry form and entry fee ($10 for members of the Council, $25 for others) required.

$◻◎ CREATIVE WRITING FELLOWSHIPS IN POETRY (Specialized: regional), Arizona Commission on the Arts, 417 W. Roosevelt St., Phoenix AZ 85003. (602)255-5882. Fax: (602)256-0282. E-mail: general@ArizonaArts.org. Website: http://az.arts.asu.edu/artscomm (includes competition deadlines). **Literature Director:** Jill Bernstein. Offers biennial prizes of $5,000-7,500. Poetry fellowships awarded in odd-numbered years. Submissions can be previously published or unpublished and can be entered in other contests. Submit 10 pgs. maximum on any subject. Open to Arizona residents over 18 years old. To request an application form, contact the Literature Director at (602)229-8226 or via e-mail. Entry deadline: September of the year prior to the award.

N̄ $◻ DANA AWARD IN POETRY, 7207 Townsend Forest Ct., Browns Summit NC 27214. (336)656-7009. E-mail: danaawards@pipeline.com (for emergency questions only). Website: http://danaawards@pipeline.com (includes submission information and guidelines, all competitions, information on winners, judges, and the philosophy behind the awards). Established 1996. **Award Chair:** Mary Elizabeth Parker. Offers annual award of $1,000 for the best group of 5 poems. Pays winners from other countries by check in US dollars. Submissions must be unpublished; may be entered in other contests. Submit 5 poems on any subject, in any form; no light verse. Include SASE for winners list. No mss will be returned. Include a separate cover sheet with name, address, phone, e-mail address, and titles of poems. Guidelines available for SASE, by e-mail, or on website. "We will not send guidelines via e-mail." Entry fee: $10/5 poems. Does not accept entry fees in foreign currencies,; accepts "bank draft or traveller's check in U.S. dollars only, drawn on U.S. banks. No personal checks written on foreign banks." Postmark deadline: October 31. Competition receives 200-400 poetry entries. Winner will be announced in early spring.

☑ $◻ DANCING POETRY CONTEST, Artists Embassy International, 704 Brigham Ave., Santa Rosa CA 95404-5245. Phone/fax: (707)528-0912 (for fax, call first after 5 p.m.). E-mail: jhcheung@aol.com. Website: www.DANCINGPOETRY.com (includes description of the Dancing Poetry Festival where winners are read and performed; also description of Artist Embassy International). Established 1993. **Contest Chair:** Judy Cheung. Annual contest offers three Grand Prizes of $100, five 1st Prizes of $50, 10 2nd Prizes of $25, 20 3rd Prizes of $10. The 3 Grand Prize-winning poems will be danced, choreographed, costumed, premiered, and videotaped at the annual Dancing Poetry Festival at Palace of Legion of Honor, San Francisco. Natica Angilly's Poetic Dance Theater Company will perform the 3 Grand Prize-winning poems. Pays winners from other countries in international money orders with US value at the time of the transaction. Submissions must be unpublished or poet must own rights. Submit 2 copies of any number of poems, 40 lines maximum (each), with name, address, phone on one copy only. Foreign language poems must include English translations. Include SASE for winners list. Entry form available for SASE. No inquiries by fax or e-mail. Entry fee: $5/poem or $10/3 poems. Does not accept entry fees in foreign currencies; send international money order in US dollars. Deadline: May 15. Competition receives about 500-800 entries. Most recent contest winners include Claire J. Baker, Richard Brostoff, and Barbara Crooker. Judges for upcoming contest will be members of Artists Embassy International. Artist Embassy International has been a nonprofit educational arts organization since 1951, "Furthering intercultural understanding and peace through the universal language of the arts."

☑ $ ☑ THE DOROTHY DANIELS ANNUAL HONORARY WRITING AWARD, The National League of American Pen Women, Inc.—Simi Valley Branch, P.O. Box 1485, Simi Valley CA 93062. E-mail: cdoering@gte.net. Established 1980. **Award Director:** Carol Doering. Offers annual award of 1st Prize: $100 in each category: poetry, fiction, nonfiction. Pays winners from other countries by check in US currency. Submissions must be unpublished. Submit any number of poems, 50 lines maximum each, on any subject, free verse or traditional. Manuscript must not include name and address. Include cover letter with name, address, phone, title, category of each entry, and line count for each poem. Poem must be titled and typed on 8½×11 white paper, single- or double-spaced, one poem per page. Guidelines and winners list available for SASE. Entry fee: $3/poem. Does not accept entry fees in foreign currencies; send "checks which consider the exchange rate, or U.S. cash money." Deadline: July 30. Competition receives 1,500 entries/year. Recent award winner was Sandra Becker. Winners will be announced by mail on or before November 1. The National League of American Pen Women, a nonprofit organization headquartered in Washington, DC, was established in 1897 and has a membership of more than 7,000 professional writers, artists, and composers. The Simi Valley Branch, of which noted novelists Dorothy Daniels and Elizabeth Forsythe Hailey are Honorary Members, was established in 1977. "Request rules and follow them carefully—always include SASE."

☑ ⊕ $ ☐ ☑ ◎ DAVID THOMAS CHARITABLE TRUST OPEN POETRY AWARD (Specialized: themes), (formerly DTCT Open Poetry Award), David Thomas Charitable Trust, P.O. Box 6055, Nairn 1V12 5YB Scotland. Phone: (01667) 453351. Fax: (01667) 452365. Established 1990. **Award Director:** David St. John Thomas. Offers annual £1,000 prize split into 4 categories plus £250 for "Winner of Winners." Cash prize paid by sterling cheque/draft only. Submissions must be unpublished. Submit any number of poems any form; subject changes each year. Entry form only available for SASE (or SAE and IRC); accepts inquiries by fax. Entry fee: £2.50 in sterling, IRCs to the value. Does not accept entry fees in foreign currencies. Deadline: January 15. Competition receives over 1,000 entries/year. Most recent award winner was Pam Gidney Groney. Judges are Alison Chesholm and Denis Corti. Winners will be announced mid-March.

⊕ $ ☐ DUNCTON COTTAGE SHORT STORY AND POETRY COMPETITION, Duncton Cottage Bird and Animal Sanctuary, 12 Hylton Terrace, Rookhope, Weardale, County Durham DL13 2BB United Kingdom. Phone: +44(0)1388 517005. Fax: +44(0)1388 517041. E-mail: farplace@hotmail.com. Established 1999. Offers annual cash prizes as a percentage of entry fees. Poems can be any subject and in any style. Please include SASE or SAE with IRC. Entry form and guidelines available for SASE. Accepts inquiries by fax and e-mail. Entry fee: £5 for up to 2 poems, £1.50 each additional poem. Entry fees must be in UK sterling. Make checks payable to Duncton Cottage Bird & Animal Sanctuary. Competition receives 150 entries or more/year. Most recent contest winners were Fiona Thakeray (Brazil, fiction), E.G. Williams (U.K., poetry). "For blind or partially sighted entrants, we will accept entries on cassette or on Word-compatible disk."

⊕ $ ☑ T.S. ELIOT PRIZE, The Poetry Book Society, Book House, 45 East Hill, London SW18 2Q2 United Kingdom. Phone: (020)8874 6361. Fax: (020)8877 1615. E-mail: info@poetrybooks.co.uk. Website: www.poetrybooks.co.uk. Established 1993. **Award director** Clare Brown. Offers annual award for the best poetry collection published in the UK/Republic of Ireland each year. Prize: £10,000 (donated by Mrs. Valerie Eliot) and "winning book is bound in Moroccan leather." Pays winners from other countries via publisher. Submissions must be previously published. **Book/ms must be submitted by publisher** and have been published (or scheduled to be published) the year of the contest. Entry form and guidelines available for SASE. Accepts inquiries by fax and e-mail. Deadline: early August. Competition receives 100 entries/year. Most recent contest winner was Hugo Williams. Winners will be announced in January.

$ ☑ T.S. ELIOT PRIZE FOR POETRY; TRUMAN STATE UNIVERSITY PRESS, 100 E. Normal, Kirksville MO 63501-4221. (660)785-7199. Fax: (660)785-4480. E-mail: tsup@truman.edu. Website: www2.truman.edu/tsup/ (includes T.S. Eliot Prize guidelines, past winners and judges, also books and order form). Established in 1984. **Director:** Paula Presley. Offers annual award of $2,000, publication, and 10 copies first prize. All entrants will receive a copy of the winning book. Submit 60-100 pages, include 2 title pages, 1 with name, address, phone and ms title; the other with only the title. Individual poems may have been previously published in periodicals or anthologies, but the collection must not have been published as a book. Include SASE if you wish acknowledgement of receipt of your ms. Mss will not be returned. Guidelines available for SASE. Accepts inquiries by fax and e-mail. Entry fee: $25. Deadline: October 31. Competition receives 500 entries/year. Most recent contest winners were Harvey L. Hix, 2000; David Keplinger, 1999; Rhina Espaillat, 1998. Truman State University Press also publishes critical books about poetry or poets, as well as hardcover and paperback originals and reprints.

$ ☑ THE WILLIAM FAULKNER CREATIVE WRITING COMPETITION/POETRY CATEGORY; THE DOUBLE DEALER REDUX, The Pirate's Alley Faulkner Society, Inc., 632 Pirate's Alley, New Orleans LA 70116. (504)586-1612. Fax: (504)522-9725. E-mail: faulkhouse@aol.com. Website: www.wordsandmusic.o rg (includes competition guidelines, entry form, information about annual Writers' Conference, and Words & Music). Established 1992. **Award Director:** Rosemary James. Offers annual publication in *The Double Dealer Redux*, cash prize of $750, gold medal, and trip to New Orleans from any continental US city. "Foreign nationals are eligible but the society pays transportation to awards ceremony from US cities only. Winners must be present at annual meeting to receive award." Submissions must be unpublished. Submit 1 poem on any subject in any English language form. Entry form and guidelines available for SASE and on website. Accepts inquiries by fax and e-mail. Entry fee: $25/entry. Deadline: April 1. Competition receives 1,000 (for 5 categories) entries/year. Most recent contest winner was Vivian Shipley (2000). Judge was James Nolan. Winners will be announced on the society's website by September 1. "Competition is keen. Send your best work."

☑ $ ☑ ◎ FLORIDA INDIVIDUAL ARTIST FELLOWSHIPS (Specialized: regional), Florida Division of Cultural Affairs, Dept. of State, The Capitol, Tallahassee FL 32399-0250. (850)487-2980. Website: www.dos.state.fl.us/dca (includes general information about the Florida Department of State, Division of Cultural Affairs, and application guidelines). **Arts Administrator:** Valerie Ohlsson. Annually offers an undetermined number of fellowships in the amount of $5,000 each. "The Individual Artist Fellowship Program is designed to recognize practicing professional creative artists residing in Florida through monetary fellowship awards. The program provides support for artists of exceptional talent and demonstrated ability to improve their artistic skills and enhance their careers. Fellowships may be awarded in the following discipline categories: dance, folk arts, interdisciplinary, literature, media arts, music, theatre, and visual arts and crafts." Submissions can be previously published or unpublished. Submit 3-5 representative poems, single- or double-spaced. "Reproductions of published work may not be submitted in published format. Open to Florida residents of at least 18 years of age who are not enrolled in undergraduate or graduate programs. Eight copies of the work sample must be included with 8 copies of the application form. Write for entry form and guidelines." Deadline: 2002 not yet determined. Competitions receive 500 entries. Most recent winners were Nancy Reisman, Martin Simpson, Max Ruback, Rhonda Nelson, Geoffrey Brock, Elizabeth Stuckey-French, and Vicki Hunt. Also publishes the *Dept. of State, Division of Cultural Affairs Informational Memo*, a newsletter of "information of concern to writers at state, regional, national and international levels."

ℕ $ ○ ☑ THE ROBERT FROST FOUNDATION ANNUAL POETRY AWARD, The Robert Frost Foundation, Heritage Place, 439 S. Union St., Lawrence MA 01843. Phone/fax: (978)725-8828. E-mail: mejanelro@aol.com. Website: www.frostfoundation.org. Established 1997. **Award Director:** Mary Ellen Janeiro. Offers annual award of $1,000. Pays winners from other countries in dollars (US). Submissions may be entered in other contests. Submit up to 3 poems of not more than 3 pages written in the spirit of Robert Frost. Guidelines available for SASE and on website. Entry fee: $10/poem. Does not accept entry fees in foreign currencies. Deadline: September 1st of each year. Competition receives over 200 entries/year. 2000 award winner was Len Krisak. Winners will be announced at the annual Frost Festival and by SASE following the Festival (late October).

☑ $ ○ ☑ GLIMMER TRAIN'S APRIL POETRY OPEN, Glimmer Train Press, 710 SW Madison St., #504, Portland OR 97205-2900. (503)221-0836. Fax: (503)221-0837. E-mail: info@glimmertrain.com. Website: www.glimmertrain.com (includes poetry presentation, top 25 winners of past contests, glimpses into issues of *Glimmer Train Stories* and *Writers Ask*). Established 1998. **Co-Editor:** Linda Swanson-Davies. Offers annual prizes. 1st Prize: $500, publication in *Glimmer Train Stories*, and 20 copies of that issue; 2nd Prize: $250; 3rd Prize: $100. Pays winners from other countries by check in US dollars. Submissions must be unpublished and may be entered in other contests. Submit up to 3 poems with no subject or form restrictions. "Name, address, and phone number need to appear on all submitted poems." Entry fee: $10 for up to 3 poems (sent together). Does not accept entry fees in foreign currencies. Will accept Visa or Mastercard. Postmark deadline: April 30. Competition receives several hundred entries/year. Most recent contest winners were Ron Egatz and Karen Kovacik. Judged by the editors of Glimmer Train Press. Winners will be contacted by September 1. Glimmer Train Press publishes the quarterly *Glimmer Train Stories*, circulation 13,000.

☑ $ ○ ☑ GLIMMER TRAIN'S OCTOBER POETRY OPEN, Glimmer Train Press, 710 SW Madison St., #504, Portland OR 97205-2900. (503)221-0836. Fax: (503)221-0837. E-mail: info@glimmertrain.com. Website: www.glimmertrain.com (includes poetry presentation, top 25 winners of past contests, glimpses into issues of *Glimmer Train Stories* and *Writers Ask*). Established 1998. **Co-Editor:** Linda Swanson-Davies. Offers annual prizes. 1st Prize: $500, publication in *Glimmer Train Stories* and 20 copies of that issue; 2nd Prize: $250; 3rd Prize: $100. Pays winners from other countries by check in US dollars. Submissions must be unpublished and may be entered in other contests. Submit up to 3 poems with no subject or form restrictions. "Name, address and phone number need to appear on all submitted poems." Entry fee: $10 for up to 3 poems (sent together). Does not accept entry fees in foreign currencies. Will accept Visa or MasterCard. Postmark deadline: October 31. Competition receives "several hundred" entries/year. Most recent contest winners were Ron Egatz and Karen Kovacik. Judged by the editors of Glimmer Train Press. Winners will be contacted by March 1. Glimmer Train Press publishes the quarterly *Glimmer Train Stories*, circulation 13,000.

$☑ GRANDMOTHER EARTH NATIONAL AWARD, Grandmother Earth Creations, P.O. Box 241986, Memphis TN 38124. (901)682-6936. Fax: (901)682-8274. E-mail: grmearth@gateway.net. Website: www.grand motherearth.com. Established 1994. **Award Director:** Frances Cowden. Offers annual award of $1,250 with varying distributions each year. $1,250 minimum in awards for poetry and prose; $200 first, etc., plus publication in anthology; non-winning finalists considered for anthology if permission is given. Send published or unpublished work. Submissions may be entered in other contests. Submit at least 3 poems, any subject, in any form. Include SASE for winners list. Send 2 copies with name and address on one copy and on a 3×5 card. Guidelines available for SASE or on website. Entry fee: $10/3 works, $2 each additional work. Entry fee includes a copy of the anthology. Deadline: July 15. Most recent award winners were Marilyn Kemph and others. Judges were Stephen Malin, University of Memphis, and others. Winner will be announced on October 1 at the Mid-South Poetry Festival in Memphis. Copies of previous winning poems or books may be obtained by writing the above address.

$☑ THE GREAT BLUE BEACON POETRY CONTEST; THE GREAT BLUE BEACON, 1425 Patriot Dr., Melbourne FL 32940. (321)253-5869. E-mail: ajircc@juno.com. Established in 1997. **Award Director:** A.J. Byers. Offers prizes approximately 3 times/year, as announced, of 1st: $25; 2nd: $15; 3rd: $10. "Winning poem to be published in *The Great Blue Beacon* (amounts will be increased if sufficient entries are received.)" *The Great Blue Beacon* is a quarterly newsletter for all writers. Sample copy: $1 and 55¢ stamp (or IRC). Subscription: $10/year, students $8; outside the US $14. Submissions must be unpublished and may be entered in other contests. Submit up to 3 poems maximum on any subject in any form. "Submit two typed copies of each entry no more than 24 lines/poem. On one copy, place your name, address, and telephone number on the upper left-hand corner of the first page. No name or address on the second copy." Guidelines available for SASE. Accepts inquiries by e-mail. Entry fees: $3/poem ($2 for subscribers to *The Great Blue Beacon*). Does not accept entry fees in foreign currencies; US dollars only. Competition receives 200-300 entries/year. Most recent contest winner was JANUS (2000). Winners will be announced approximately 2 months after deadline date. "Contestants must send SASE or e-mail address with entry to receive notification of results. Submit your best work."

☑ $☑ GREAT LAKES COLLEGES ASSOCIATION NEW WRITERS AWARD, GLCA, English Department, Denison University, Granville OH 43023. (740)587-5740. Fax: (740)587-5680. Website: www.glca. org/new.writers.tour/index.shtml (includes contact information, GLCA mission statement, tour dates, and more). **Director:** Linda Krumholz. Offers annual award to "the best first book of poetry and the best first book of fiction among those **submitted by publishers**. The winning authors tour several of the Great Lakes Colleges reading, lecturing, visiting classes, doing workshops, and publicizing their books. Each writer receives an honorarium of at least $300 from each college visited, as well as travel expenses, hotel accommodations, and hospitality. Usually, one winner (fiction) tours in the fall, and the other winner (poetry) tours in the spring, following the competition." Submissions must be previously published. Submit 4 copies of galleys or the printed book plus a statement stating author's agreement to commit to the college tour. Guidelines available for SASE. Accepts inquiries by fax. Deadline: February 28. Competition receives about 50 entries for poetry, 35 for fiction/year. Most recent award winners were *Zombi, You My Love* (fiction) by William Orem (published by La Quesla Press) and *In the Surgical Theatre* by Dana Levin (published by *American Poetry Review*).

$☑ GUGGENHEIM FELLOWSHIPS, John Simon Guggenheim Memorial Foundation, 90 Park Ave., New York NY 10016. (212)687-4470. Fax: (212)697-3248. E-mail: fellowships@gf.org. Website: www.gf.org. Guggenheims are awarded each year to individuals who have already demonstrated exceptional capacity for productive scholarship or exceptional creative ability in the arts. The amounts of the grants vary. The average grant in 2000 was $34,800. Most recent award winners for poetry were David Baker, Rigoberto Gonzalez, Linda Gregerson, Brooks Haxton, Tony Hoagland, Eric Pankey, and Bruce Smith (2000). In 2000, there were 182 winners awarded fellowships in the US out of 2,927 applications. Accepts inquiries by fax and e-mail. Application deadline: October 1.

☑ $☑ HACKNEY LITERARY AWARDS, Birmingham-Southern College, Box 549003, Birmingham AL 35254. (205)226-4921. Fax: (205)226-3072. E-mail: dcwilson@bsc.edu. Website: www.bsc.edu. Sponsored by the Cecil Hackney family since 1969, offers $10,000 in prizes for novels, poetry and short stories as part of the annual Birmingham-Southern Writing Today Conference. (See separate listing for the Writing Today Conference in the Conferences & Workshops section.) Prizes for poetry awarded at both the state and national levels. Submissions must be previously unpublished. Submit no more than 50 lines of poetry (may submit more than one poem, but total lines of all poems together must not exceed 50 lines). Guidelines available for SASE. Entry fee: $10/50-line entry. Postmark deadline (poems and short stories): December 30. Most recent award winners were Dwight Eddins, Denise Wadsworth Trimm, and Lauren Terry (state); Gloria Evangelista, Anthony Russell White, and Diane DiRoberto (national). Writer's Conference winners are announced and prizes awarded. Hackney Award winners will be announced at the *Writing Today* Conference in March.

$ ⊙ ◎ J.C. AND RUTH HALLS; THE DIANE MIDDLEBROOK; AND ANASTASIA C. HOFF-MANN FELLOWSHIPS IN POETRY (Specialized: MFA or equivalent degree in creative writing), Wisconsin Institute for Creative Writing, English Dept., 600 North Park St., Madison WI 53706. Website: http://polyglot.lss.wisc.edu/english. Established 1986. **Director:** Jesse Lee Kercheval. Offers annual fellowships will pay $23,000 for one academic year. Applicants will teach one creative writing class per semester at U. of Wisconsin and give a public reading at the end of their stay. Submissions may be entered in other contests. Submit 10 poems maximum on any subject in any form. *Applicants must have an MFA or equivalent degree in creative writing.* Applicants cannot have published a book (chapbooks will not disqualify an applicant). Guidelines available for SASE. Deadline: last day of February. Competitions receive 200 entries/year. Judges are faculty of creative writing program. Results will be sent to applicants by May 1. Winners announced in *Poets & Writers* and *AWP Chronicle*. "The fellowships are administered by the Program in Creative Writing at the University of Wisconsin-Madison. Funding is provided by the Jay C. and Ruth Halls Writing Fund and the Carl Djerassi and Diane Middlebrook Fund through the University of Wisconsin Foundation."

✓ $ ◯ THE HODDER FELLOWSHIP, The Council of the Humanities, Joseph Henry House, Princeton University, Princeton NJ 08544. (609)258-4717. E-mail: humcounc@princeton.edu. Website: www.princeton.edu/~humcounc. Awarded to a humanist in the early stages of a career. The recipient has usually written one book and is working on a second. Preference is given to applicants outside academia. "The Fellowship is designed specifically to identify and nurture extraordinary potential rather than to honor distinguished achievement." **Candidates for the Ph.D. are not eligible.** The Hodder Fellow spends an academic year in residence at Princeton working on an independent project in the humanities. Stipend is approximately $46,500. Submit a résumé, sample of previous work (10 pgs. maximum, not returnable), a project proposal of 2 to 3 pgs., and SASE. Guidelines available on website. Announcement of the Hodder Fellow is made in February by the President of Princeton University. Postmark deadline: November 1.

✓ $ ◯ HENRY HOYNS FELLOWSHIPS, Creative Writing Program, 219 Bryan Hall, P.O. Box 400121, University of Virginia, Charlottesville VA 22904-4121. (804)924-6675. Fax: (804)924-1478. E-mail: lRS9E@virginia.edu. Website: www.engl.virginia.edu/cwp (includes general information, applications, and faculty biographies). **Program Administrator:** Lisa Russ Spaar. Fellowships in poetry and fiction of varying amounts for candidates for the M.F.A. in creative writing. Sample poems/prose required with application. Accepts inquiries by fax and e-mail. Deadline: January 1. Competition receives 300-400 entries.

N $ ◯ INTRO PRIZE IN POETRY; LEVIS POETRY PRIZE; FOUR WAY BOOKS; FRIENDS OF WRITERS, INC., P.O. Box 535, Village Station, New York NY 10014. (212)619-1105. Fax: (212)406-1352. E-mail: four-way-editors@yahoo.com. Website: www.fourwaybooks.com (includes announcement of winners). **Award Director:** Karen Clarke. Offers 2 biennial contests with prizes including book publication, honorarium (approximately $1,500 but amount will vary year to year), and a reading at 1 or more participating series, including the Barrow Street Reading Series, The CCS Reading Series, Grolier Poetry Book Shop Inc., Cody's, and Chapters Literary Bookstore. Contests are open only to US residents. The Intro Prize is open to poets who have not yet published a book. The Levis Prize is open to any US poet. "For both prizes, submit one manuscript, 48-100 pages suggested. More than one manuscript may be submitted but each one must be entered separately. Your name should appear on the entry form and the title page of the manuscript and nowhere else. Include SASE if you would like notification of the winner." Entry form and guidelines available for SASE and on website. Entry fee: $20. Postmark deadline: Intro, March 31, 2002; Levis, March 31, 2003. Receives about 1,000 entries/year. Most recent contest winners were Noelle Kocot (Levis, 1999) and Gwen Ebert (Intro, 2000). Judges were Lynn Emanuel (Intro, 2000) and Susan Mitchell (Levis, 2001). Winners will be announced Labor Day in the same year as the entry date. "Winners announced by mail and on our website." Copies of previous winning books are available through Four Way Books or local bookstores. "Four Way Books is the publishing arm of Friends of Writers, Inc., a Vermont-based not-for-profit organization dedicated to encouraging, supporting, and promoting the craft of writing and identifying and publishing writers at decisive stages in their careers."

✓ $ ◎ JAPANESE LITERARY TRANSLATION PRIZE (Specialized: translation of Japanese classical or modern literature into English), Donald Keene Center of Japanese Culture, Columbia Univer-

---

ALWAYS include a self-addressed, stamped envelope (SASE) when sending a ms or query to a publisher within your own country. When sending material to other countries, include a self-addressed envelope and International Reply Coupons (IRCs), available at many post offices.

sity, 507 Kent Hall, New York NY 10027. (212)854-5036. Fax: (212)854-4019. E-mail: donald-keene-center@col umbia.edu. Website: www.columbia.edu/cu/ealac/dkc (includes mission and history, calendar of events, scholarly activities, translation prizes, and corporate sponsors). Established 1981. Offers annual $2,500 prize for translation of a work of Japanese classical literature into English and a $2,500 prize for translation of a work of Japanese modern literature into English. Pays winners from other countries in US dollars. "Special attention is given to new or unpublished translators, and citizens of all nationalities are eligible." Submissions may be entered in other contests. Submit 7 copies of book-length ms or published book. Entry form and guidelines available for SASE. Accepts inquiries by fax and e-mail. Deadline: February 15. Competition receives 20-25 entries/year. Most recent award winners were Meredith McKinney (modern Japanese literature) and Roger K. Thomas (classical Japanese literature). Judges were Donald Keene, Hortense Calisher, Howard Hibbett, Bonnie Crown, and Robert Gottlieb.

JOHANN-HEINRICH-VOSS PRIZE FOR TRANSLATION, German Academy for Language and Literature, Alexandraweg 23, 64287 Darmstadt, Germany. Phone: (06151)40920. Fax: (06151)409299. E-mail: deutsche.akademie@t-online.de. Website: www.deutscheakademic.de. **President:** Prof. Dr. Christian Meier. Offers an annual award of DM 20,000 for outstanding lifetime achievement for translating into German, **by nomination only**.

HELEN VAUGHN JOHNSON MEMORIAL HAIKU AWARD (Specialized: forms/ haiku), Hutton Publications, P.O. Box 2907, Decatur IL 62524. Established 2001. **Award Director:** Linda Hutton. Offers annual award for traditional haiku. 1st Prize: $25 and 1 year's subscription to *Rhyme Time*, 2nd Prize: $15, 3rd Prize: $10. Pays winners from other countries by money order. Submissions may be entered in other contests. Submit unlimited number of poems of 5 lines on nature in traditional 5-7-5 haiku format; must not refer to people. Name, address, and phone number should appear in upper righthand corner of each page. Guidelines available for SASE. Entry fee: $1/haiku. Accepts entry fees in foreign currencies. Deadline: January 17 annually. "This is our first year; we expect to receive 100 entries." Judge is Linda Hutton. Winners will be announced February 20 annually. Poets may obtain copies of previous winning poems by purchasing the *Rhyme Time* winner's issue ($4). "*Rhyme Time* endeavors to encourage beginning poets. Study traditional haiku; we do not accept anything but 5-7-5." (See separate listing for *Rhyme Time* in the Publishers of Poetry section.)

BARBARA MANDIGO KELLY PEACE POETRY CONTEST, Nuclear Age Peace Foundation, PMB 121, 1187 Coast Village Rd. #1, Santa Barbara CA 93108-2794. (805)965-3443. Fax: (805)568-0466. E-mail: wagingpeace@napf.org. Website: www.wagingpeace.org. Established 1996. Offers an annual series of awards "to encourage poets to explore and illuminate positive visions of peace and the human spirit." Awards $1,000 to adult contestants, $200 to youth (13 to 18), $200 to youth (12 and under), and honorable mentions in each category. Pays winners from other countries in US currency. Submissions must be unpublished and may be entered in other contests. Submit up to 3 poems on "positive visions of peace and the human spirit" in any form. Send 2 copies; maximum of 40 lines per poem. Put name, address, phone number, and age in upper right hand corner of one copy. Guidelines available for SASE or on website. Entry fee: $5/1 poem, $10/2-3 poems. Free for youth. Does not accept entry fees in foreign currencies but will accept US money order. Postmark deadline: July 1. Competition receives over 500 entries. Recent contest winner was Nikko. Judged by a committee of poets. Winners will be announced through press release and mail notification by October. The Foundation reserves the right to publish the winning poems. "Nuclear Age Peace Foundation is a nonprofit peace and international security-related organization, focusing on the abolition of nuclear weapons, the strengthening of international law, the empowerment of youth, and the responsible and sustainable use of technology." Poets thinking about entering contest should "be creative and positive."

THE JACK KEROUAC POETRY PRIZE, Redbud Hill Press, 265 S. Glencoe Ave., Decatur IL 62522. (217)425-9144. E-mail: kerouacpoetry@aol.com. Website: www.redcrowguidelines.cjb.net. Established 2001. **Award Director:** Dennis Kurlas. Offers annual award. First Prize: $500, publication, and a featured reading at the Lowell Celebrates Kerouac Festival in October. Pays winners from other countries in US dollars. Submissions must be unpublished. Submit up to 5 poems (8 pgs. maximum). Guidelines available for SASE, by e-mail, and on website. Entry fee: $10/ms. Does not accept entry fees in foreign currencies; US dollars only. Deadline: June 1, 2002. See website for most recent award winners. Winners will be announced upon publication at the Lowell Celebrates Kerouac Festival. Send for a sample. "Redbud Hill is a publisher of *Red Crow Poetry Journal*, Appalachian and beat poetry. Also sponsors the Bob Snyder Poetry Awards." (See separate listing for *Red Crow Poetry Journal* in Publishers of Poetry section; see separate listing for The Bob Snyder Poetry Awards in this section.) "Don't worry about themes of interest to us—just send us your best work! We're *not* looking for odes to dead writers."

THE LEAGUE OF MINNESOTA POETS CONTEST, 432 Tyrol Dr., Brainerd MN 56401-2920. **Contest Chairman:** Joan Wiesner. Offers 19 different contests in a variety of categories (including student-only) and 3 prizes in each category ranging from $10-125 for poems up to 55 line limit. Entry form and guidelines available for SASE. Nonmember fees: $1/poem per category; $2/poem (limit 6) for Grand Prize category. Members fee: $3 for 18 categories; $1/poem (limit of 6) for Grand Prize category. Deadline: July 31. Nationally known judges. Competition receives over 1,200 entries total. Most recent winners include Majorie Millison and Susan Stevens Chambers (2000 Grand Prize).

☑ $⃠ ◎ **MARIN ARTS COUNCIL INDIVIDUAL ARTIST GRANTS (Specialized: regional)**, 650 Las Gallinas Ave., San Rafael CA 94903. (415)499-8350. Fax: (415)499-8537. E-mail: alison@marinarts.org. Website: www.marinarts.org (includes general info about the Marin Arts Council and the grants program, plus copies of application forms which can be downloaded). Established 1987. **Grants Coordinator:** Alison DeJung. Offers biennial grants starting at $2,000 to residents of Marin County, CA only. Submissions must have been completed within last 3 years. Submit 10 pgs. on any subject in any form. *Open to Marin County residents only*—"must have lived in Marin County for one year prior to application, be 18 or over and not in an arts degree program." Entry form and guidelines available for SASE. Accepts inquiries by fax and e-mail. Winners will be announced June of each year. "The Marin Arts Council offers grants in 13 different categories to individual artists living in Marin County. Deadlines and categories alternate each year. Call for more information." Competition receives 50-100 entries.

☑ $◎ **MATURE WOMEN'S GRANTS (Specialized: women)**, National League of American Pen Women, 1300 17th St., Washington DC 20036-1973. (978)443-2165. E-mail: nlapw1@juno.com. Website: http://members.aol.com/penwomen/pen.htm. Established 1976. **Award Director:** Mary Jane Hillery. Offers biennial (even-numbered years) award of $1,000 each for the categories of arts, letters, and music for women aged 35 and older. Must be US citizen. Submit 3 poems. Accepts previously published submissions. Include SASE for information or winners list. Open to women over the age of 35 during the calendar year of the award. "Women who enter may never have been a member of the Pen women." Include letter stating age, creative purpose, and how you learned of the grant. Guidelines available during odd-numbered years for SASE. Entry fee: $8. Deadline: October 1 of the odd-numbered year. Competition receives 200 entries in art, 400 in letters, and 10 entries in music/year. Winner will be announced March 1 of even-numbered year. (See listing for National League of American Pen Women in Organizations sections.)

⊕ $⃠ ◎ **MELBOURNE POETS UNION ANNUAL NATIONAL POETRY COMPETITION (Specialized: regional)**, (formerly Melbourne Poets Union Annual National Poetry Competition), Melbourne Poets Union, P.O. Box 266, Flinders Lane, Victoria 8009 Australia. Established 1977. **Contact:** The Secretary. Offers annual prizes to a total of $1,000. Pays winners from other countries "with a cheque in foreign currency, after negotiation with winner." Submissions must be unpublished. Submit unlimited number of poems on any subject in any form. "Open to Australian residents living in Australia or overseas." Entry form and guidelines available for SASE (or SAE and IRC). Entry fee: AUS $5/poem. Accepts entry fees in foreign currencies. Deadline: October 31. Competition receives over 500 entries/year. Winners will be announced on the last Friday of November. "The $1,000 prize money comes directly from entry money, the rest going to paying the judge and costs of running the competition."

$⃠ **MID-LIST PRESS FIRST SERIES AWARD FOR POETRY**, Mid-List Press, 4324 12th Ave. S., Minneapolis MN 55407-3218. E-mail: guide@midlist.org. Website: www.midlist.org (includes information about publishing program, describes and lists titles published, and provides links to online booksellers; guidelines and entry forms are available as are special offers on most recent First Series titles). Established 1990. **Senior Editor:** Lane Stiles. "The First Series Award for Poetry is an annual contest we sponsor for poets who have never published a book of poetry. The award includes publication and a $500 advance against royalties." Individual poems within the book ms can be previously published and can be entered in other contests. Submit at least 60 single-spaced pages. "Note: We do not return manuscripts. Other than length we have no restrictions, but poets are encouraged to read previous award winners we have published." Recent award winners include Katherine Starke, Adam Sol, and Jennifer O'Grady. Submissions are circulated to an editorial board. Guidelines are available for #10 SASE or on website; no inquiries by fax or e-mail. Entry fee: $20. Does not accept entry fees in foreign currencies. Accepts submissions October 1 through February 1. Competition receives 750 entries/year. "The First Series Award contest is highly competitive. We are looking for poets who have produced a significant body of work but have never published a book-length collection. (A chapbook is not considered a 'book' of poetry.)"

$⃠ **VASSAR MILLER PRIZE IN POETRY**, Univeristy of Missouri, English Dept., Tate 103, Columbia MO 65211. (573)882-6421. Fax: (573)882-5785. Established 1991. **Award Director:** Scott Cairns. Offers annual award of $1,000 and publication by the University of North Texas Press. Submit 50-80 pgs., include an additional title page without the name of the poet and #10 SASE for winners list. Guidelines available for SASE. Entry fee: $20. Make checks payable to UNT Press. Entries are read September 1 through November 30 only. Most recent award winner was Karen Homberg. Judge was Sheron Sontos. Winner will be announced by March 15.

☑ $◎ **MILTON CENTER POST GRADUATE FELLOWSHIP (Specialized: religious)**, (formerly Milton Center Poetry Fellowship), The Milton Center, 3100 McCormick Ave., Wichita KS 67213-2097. (316)942-4291, ext. 226. Fax: (316)942-4483. E-mail: miltonc@newmanu.edu. Established 1986. **Program Director:** Essie Sappenfield. Awards stipend of $1,225/month and residency in Wichita, KS from September-May. Two fellowships awarded/year. Offered annually to new writers of Christian commitment to complete their first book-length ms of fiction, poetry, or creative nonfiction. "The Milton Center exists to encourage work by writers who seek to animate the Christian imagination, foster intellectual integrity, and explore the human condition with honesty and compassion. Write well and have mature work habits. Don't worry about doctrinal matters, counting Christian symbols, etc. What you believe will automatically show up in you writing." Submit 10 poems on any subject or in any form. Entry form and guidelines available for SASE. Accepts inquiries by fax and e-mail. Entry fee: $15. Does not accept entry fees in foreign currencies. Send check or money order. The 2001 deadline was March 15. Competition receives 200 entries. Most recent award winners were Michelle Roop and Cindy Slates. Winner will be announced in mid-April. Notification is by letter, phone, or e-mail.

☑ $◯ ◐ MISSISSIPPI VALLEY POETRY CONTEST, sponsored by Midwest Writing Center, P.O. Box 3188, Rock Island IL 61204. (319)359-1057. **Chairman:** Max J. Molleston. Offers annual prizes of approximately $1,700 for unpublished poems in categories for students (elementary, junior, and senior high), adults, Mississippi Valley, senior citizens, jazz, religious, humorous, rhyming, haiku, ethnic, and history. Fee: $5 for up to 5 poems; 50 lines/poem limit. Fee for children: $3 for up to 5 poems. Send check or US dollars. Professional readers present winning poems to a reception at an award evening in May. Deadline: April 1. Competition receives 1,000-2,000 entries.

$◎ MONEY FOR WOMEN (Specialized: women/feminism); GERTRUDE STEIN AWARD, FANNIE LOU HAMER AWARD, Barbara Deming Memorial Fund, Inc., P.O. Box 630125, Bronx NY 10463. **Administrator:** Susan Pliner. Offers biannual small grants of up to $1,500 to feminists in the arts "whose work addresses women's concerns and/or speaks for peace and justice from a feminist perspective." Pays winners from other countries with a US check. Application form available for SASE. Applicants must be citizens of US or Canada. Application fee: $10. Does not accept entry fees in foreign currencies. Must send check drawn on US bank or cash (US). Deadlines: December 31 and June 30. Competition receives 400 entries/year. Most recent award winners were Shara McCallum, Marilyn Bogusca Pryle, and Lyrae Van Clief-Stefanon. Winners will be announced in May and October. Also offers the Gertrude Stein Award for outstanding work by a lesbian, and the "Fannie Lou Hamer Award" for work which combats racism and celebrates women of color.

$◑ JENNY McKEAN MOORE WRITER IN WASHINGTON, Dept. of English, George Washington University, Washington DC 20052. (202)994-6515. Fax: (202)994-7915. E-mail: dmca@gwu.edu. Website: www.gwu.edu/~english (includes some initial description of program, course description, readings schedule, other info). Offers fellowship for a visiting lecturer in creative writing, about $48,000 for 2 semesters. Apply by November 15 with résumé and writing sample of 25 pgs. or less. Awarded to poets and fiction writers in alternating years.

$◑ SAMUEL FRENCH MORSE POETRY PRIZE, English Dept., 406 Holmes, Northeastern University, Boston MA 02115. E-mail: grotella@lynx.neu.edu. Website: www.casdn.neu.edu/~english/morse.htm (includes contest rules). **Editor:** Prof. Guy Rotella. Offers book publication (ms 50-70 pgs.) by Northeastern University Press and an award of $1,000. Open to US poets who have published no more than 1 book of poetry. Accepts inquiries by e-mail. Entry fee: $15. Deadline of August 1 for inquiries, September 15 for single copy of ms. Manuscripts will not be returned. Competition receives approximately 400 entries/year. Most recent award winners include Michelle Boisseau, Charles Webb, Jeffrey Greene, and Jennifer Atkinoor.

$◯ NASHVILLE NEWSLETTER POETRY CONTEST, P.O. Box 60535, Nashville TN 37206-0535. Established 1977. **Editor/Publisher:** Roger Dale Miller. Offers prizes of $50, $25, and $10 plus possible publication in newsletter, and at least 50 Certificates of Merit. Pays winners from other countries with check in US funds. Submit one unpublished poem to a page, any style or subject up to 40 lines, with name and address in upper left corner. Send large #10 SASE for more information and/or extra entry forms for future contests. Entry fee: $5 for up to 3 poems. Must be sent all at once. Does not accept entry fees in foreign currencies but will accept check/money order in US funds. "All other nonwinning poems will be considered for possible publication in future issues." Competition receives over 700 entries/year. Most recent winners were Christine Haluszka and Millie Hughes. *Nashville Newsletter* appears quarterly. Sample: $3. Responds in up to 10 weeks.

$◑ NATIONAL BOOK AWARD, National Book Foundation, 260 Fifth Ave., Room 904, New York NY 10001. (212)685-0261. E-mail: natbkfdn@mindspring.com. Website: www.nationalbook.org. Offers annual grand prize of $10,000 plus 4 finalist awards of $1,000. Awards in fiction, nonfiction, poetry, and young people's literature. Submissions must be previously published and **must be entered by the publisher**. Entry form and guidelines available for SASE. Entry fee: $100/title. Deadline: July 10.

☑ ◯ NATIONAL WRITERS UNION ANNUAL NATIONAL POETRY COMPETITION, P.O. Box 2409, Aptos CA 95001. E-mail: lstaple@earthlink.net. Website: www.mbay.net/~NWU (includes information about local and national events and links for writers). Co-chairs: Stephanie Bryand and Susan Heinlein. **Contact:** Local 7 Coordinator. The 2001 competition is sponsored by Santa Cruz/Monterey Local 7 of the NWU. Entry fee: $4/poem. Prizes: $500, $300, $200, plus publication in union newsletter. Possible additional 1st place publication in *Poetry Flash*. For rules, send SASE to Local 7 Coordinator see website. Postmark deadline: December 1. Competition receives 1,000 entries/year. Judge for 2000 was Adrienne Rich.

☑ $ ▢ ▨ **NEW MILLENNIUM AWARD FOR POETRY, NEW MILLENNIUM WRITINGS**, P.O. Box 2463, Knoxville TN 37901. E-mail: donwill@aol.com. Website: www.mach2.com (includes publication of winners, table of contents, photos of contributors, contest guidelines, cover graphics, how to order past issues, subscription information and much more). **Editor:** Don Williams. Offers 2 annual awards of $1,000 each. Pays winners from other countries by money order. Submissions must be previously unpublished but may be entered in other contests. Submit up to 3 poems, 5 pages maximum. No restrictions on style or content. Include name, address, phone number, and a #10 SASE for notification. Manuscripts are not returned. Guidelines available for SASE. Accepts inquiries by e-mail. Entry fee: $15. Make checks payable to New Millennium Writings. Does not accept entry fees in foreign currencies; send money order drawn on US bank. Deadlines: June 15 and November 15. Competition receives 2,000 entries/year. "Two winners and selected finalists will be published." Most recent award winners include Ken McCullough and Sam Witt. "Contests are not the only avenues to publication. We also accept—at no cost, no entry fee—general submissions for publication, year round. These should be addressed to Editor. There are no restrictions as to style, form, or content. Submitters should enclose SASE for correspondence purposes."

▨ ▨ **THE NEW PHYSICIAN'S CREATIVE ARTS CONTEST (Specialized: premedical/medical students and medical residents)**, *The New Physician*, 1902 Association Dr., Reston VA 20191. (703)620-6600. Fax: (703)620-6445. E-mail: tnp@www.amsa.org. Website: www.amsa.org/tnp/artcontest.htm (includes guidelines, examples of past winners in poetry, short story, photography, and art). Established 1995. Offers annual award for poetry, fiction, photography, and art; $250 for first place in each category. Pays winners from other countries by check in American dollars. Must be premedical or medical student or medical resident to enter. Guidelines and entry form available on website. No entry fee. Deadline: March. Competition receives 100 entries/year. Judges for the contest in 2001 were the editorial staff of *The New Physician*. Winners will be announced in the July/August issue of *The New Physician*. Copies of previous winning poems are available on the website.

☑ ▢ **NEW YORK UNIVERSITY PRIZE FOR POETRY**, New York University Press, 70 Washington Square S., New York NY 10012. (212)998-2575. Fax: (212)995-3833. E-mail: nyupress.info@elmer5.bobst.nyu.edu. Website: www.nyupress.nyu.edu (includes guidelines and information on previous winners). Established 1990. **Contact:** Prize Coordinator. Offers annual award of a $1,000 honorarium, plus book publication. Guidelines available for SASE. No inquiries by fax or e-mail. Most recent award winner was Veronica Patterson.

☑ $ ▨ **NEWBURYPORT ART ASSOCIATION ANNUAL SPRING POETRY CONTEST**, 12 Charron Dr., Newburyport MA 01950. E-mail: cspmosk@juno.com. Website: www.newburyportart.org (includes contest information and guidelines). Established 1990. **Contest Coordinator:** Rhina P. Espaillat. Offers annual awards of 1st Prize: $200, 2nd Prize: $150, 3rd Prize: $100, plus Honorable Mentions and certificates. "All winners, including Honorable Mention poets, are invited to read their own entries at the Awards Day Reading in May." Open to anyone over 16 years old. Pays winners from other countries with NAA check. Submissions must be previously unpublished. Submit any number of poems, each no more than 3 pages in length. Must be typed, single- or double-spaced, on white 8½×11 paper; each poem must have a title. Send 2 copies of each poem— one without identification, one bearing your name, address, and telephone number. Include SASE for notification of contest results. Any number of poems accepted, but all must be mailed together in a single envelope with one check covering the total entry fee. Guidelines available for SASE, by e-mail, and on website. Entry fee: $3/poem. Does not accept entry fees in foreign currencies; send US cash, check, or money order. Make checks payable to NAA Poetry Contest (one check for all entries). Postmark deadline: mid-March. Competition received 585 entries in 2000. Winners for the 2001 contest were Robert Crawford, Bill Coyle, and Alfred Nicol and Len Krisak (co-winners, split 3rd Prize). Judges were Diana Der-Hovanessian (2000) and Dr. Bruce Bennett (2001).

⊕ ☑ $ ▨ **NSW PREMIER'S LITERARY AWARD "THE KENNETH SLESSOR PRIZE" (Specialized: regional)**, NSW Ministry for the Arts, P.O. Box A226, Sydney South NSW 1235 Australia. E-mail: ministry@arts.nsw.gov.au. Website: www.arts.nsw.gov.au. Established 1980. Offers annual award of AUS $15,000 for a book of poetry published in the previous year (i.e., for the 2000 contest, book must have been published between November 21, 2000 and November 23, 2001). Submissions *must* be previously published and may be entered in other contests. Submit 4 copies of published book. Open to Australians only. Write for entry form and guidelines. Accepts inquiries by fax and e-mail. Competition receives 80 entries/year. Most recent award winner was Jennifer Maiden (2000). Judged by a panel of 15. Winners will be announced in May. "Obtain copy of guidelines before entering."

$ ▢ ▨ ▨ **FRANK O'HARA AWARD CHAPBOOK COMPETITION; THORNGATE ROAD PRESS (Specialized: gay/lesbian/bisexual)**, Campus Box 4240, English Dept., Illinois State University, Normal IL 61790-4240. (309)438-7705. Fax: (309)438-5414. E-mail: jmelled@ilstu.edu. Website: www.litline.org/html/thorngate.html. Established 1996. **Award Director/Publisher:** Jim Elledge. Offers annual award of

$500, publication, and 25 copies. Submissions may be a combination of previously published and unpublished work and may be entered in other contests. Submit 16 pages on any topic, in any form. Another 4 pages for front matter is permitted, making the maximum total of 20 pages. Poets must be gay, lesbian, or bisexual (any race, age, background, etc.). One poem/page. Guidelines available for SASE. Accepts inquiries by fax and e-mail. Entry fee: $15/submission. Deadline: February 1. Competition receives 200-300 entries. Most recent contest winner was *Good Long Enough* by Holly Iglesias. Judge is a nationally recognized gay, lesbian, or bisexual poet. Judge remains anonymous until the winner has been announced. Winners will be announced by April 15. Copies of previous winning books may be obtained by sending $6 to the above address made out to Thorngate Road Press. "Thorngate Road publishes at least two chapbooks annually, and they are selected by one of two methods. The first is through the contest. The second, the Berdache Chapbook Series, is by invitation only. We published chapbooks by Kristy Nielsen, David Trinidad, Reginald Shepherd, Karen Lee Osborne, and Maureen Seaton in the Berdache series." Although the contest is only open to gay, lesbian, bisexual, and transgendered authors, the content of submissions does not necessarily have to be gay, lesbian, bisexual, or transgendered."

☑ $ ◎ **OHIOANA BOOK AWARDS; OHIOANA POETRY AWARD (Helen and Laura Krout Memorial); OHIOANA QUARTERLY; OHIOANA LIBRARY ASSOCIATION (Specialized: regional)**, Ohioana Library Association, 274 E. First Ave., Columbus OH 43201. (614)466-3831. Fax: (614)728-6974. E-mail: ohioana@SLOMA.state.oh.us. Website: www.oplin.lib.oh.us/ohioana. **Director:** Linda Hengst. Offers annual Ohioana Book Awards. Up to 6 awards may be given for books (including books of poetry) by authors born in Ohio or who have lived in Ohio for at least 5 years. The Ohioana Poetry Award of $1,000 (with the same residence requirements), made possible by a bequest of Helen Krout, is given yearly "to an individual whose body of published work has made, and continues to make, a significant contribution to poetry, and through whose work as a writer, teacher, administrator, or in community service, interest in poetry has been developed." Nominations to be received by December 31. Competition receives several hundred entries. Most recent award winners were Alvin Greenberg and Rita Dove. *Ohioana Quarterly* regularly reviews Ohio magazines and books by Ohio authors and is available through membership in Ohioana Library Association ($25/year).

$ ◻ **PANHANDLE PROFESSIONAL WRITERS; FRONTIERS IN WRITING ANNUAL WRITING CONTEST; FRONTIERS IN WRITING CONFERENCE**, P.O. Box 19303, Amarillo TX 79114. Website: www.users.arn.net/~ppw (includes details about summer conference and upcoming meetings, contest rules and winners, history of the organization, membership information, contact information, and useful links). **Contact:** Contest Chairman. Offers cash awards. Pays winners from other countries in US dollars. Open to all poets, 2 categories (long, short) any subject or form, 50 lines maximum. Fee $7.50/poem. Does not accept entry fees in foreign currencies; US dollars only. Other categories include short stories, book-length nonfiction, book-length fiction, and nonfiction article. Guidelines available for SASE. Deadline: postmarked on or before March 15. Competition receives 100-200 entries. Past winners include Pauline Robertson, Lynn Lewis, Marianne McNeil Logan, Jean Ravenscroft, Margaret Schultz, and Lynn Olson.

$ ◪ **PAUMANOK POETRY AWARD COMPETITION; THE VISITING WRITERS PROGRAM**, SUNY Farmingdale, Farmingdale NY 11735. E-mail: brownml@farmingdale.edu. Website: www.farmingdale.edu/CampusPages/ArtsSciences/EnglishHumanities/paward.html (includes Paumanok Poetry Award guidelines and other links to information on the Visiting Writers Program). Established 1990. **Director:** Dr. Margery Brown. Offers a prize of $1,000 plus an all-expense-paid feature reading in their 2002-2003 series (*Please note:* travel expenses within the continental US only). Also awards two runner-up prizes of $500 plus expenses for a reading in the series. Pays winners from other countries in US dollars. Submit cover letter, 1-paragraph literary bio, up to 5 poems of up to 10 pgs. (published or unpublished). Entry fee: $12. Postmark deadline: by September 15. Make checks payable to SUNY Farmingdale Visiting Writers Program (VWP). Does not accept entry fees in foreign currencies. Send money order in US dollars. Send SASE for results (to be mailed by late December). Guidelines available for SASE or on website. Accepts inquiries by e-mail. Competition receives over 600 entries. Most recent contest winners include Charles Atkinson (winner), Edward Bartok-Baralta and Virginia Chase Sutton (runners-up). Poets who have read in this series include Hayden Carruth, Allen Ginsberg, Linda Pastan, Marge Piercy, Joyce Carol Oates, Louis Simpson, and David Ignatow. The series changes each year so entries in the 2001 competition will be considered for the 2002-2003 series, and so on.

$ ◎ **PENNSYLVANIA POETRY SOCIETY ANNUAL CONTEST (Specialized: students)**, 801 Spruce St., West Reading PA 19611-1448. (610)374-5848. E-mail: aubade@juno.com. Website: www.homestead.juno.com/aubade/index.html. **Contact:** Contest Chairman. Offers annual contest with grand prize awards of $100,

---

USE THE GENERAL INDEX, located at the back of this book, to find the page number of a specific publisher. Also, publishers that were listed in last year's edition but not included in this edition are listed in the General Index with a notation explaining why they were omitted.

$50, and $25; 3 poems may be entered at $2 each for members and nonmembers alike. A total of 17 categories are open to all poets; nonmembers pay $1.50/poem; categories 2-12 and 17-21, one poem/category. Categories 13-16 are for members only. PPS members pay $2.50 total for entries in categories 2-21, inclusive. Guidelines available for SASE or on website. Deadline for PPS Annual Contest: January 15. Also sponsors the Pegasus Contest for PA Students in grades 5-12. For information send SASE to Anne Pierre Spangler, contest chairman, 1685 Christine Dr., R.D. #2, Lebanon PA 17042. **"Pegasus Contest is open only to Pennsylvania students!"** Deadline for the Pegasus Contest: March 1. Deadline for the Charles Ferguson Environmental Contest: September 15. Deadline for the Wine and Roses Contest: October 15. Deadline for the Carlisle "Kids' 'N Critters" Contest: October 15. Guidelines available for SASE. The society publishes a quarterly newsletter containing pages of poetry by members and an annual *Prize Poems* soft cover book, containing prize-winning poems. Prize-winning Pegasus poems are published in a booklet sent to schools which enter. PPS membership dues are $15/year. Make check payable to PPS, Inc. and mail to Richard R. Gasser, Treasurer, at the above address.

☑ $☐ ◎ **PENUMBRA POETRY & HAIKU COMPETITION (Specialized: form; anthology)**, Tallahassee Writers' Association, P.O. Box 15995, Tallahassee FL 32317-5995. E-mail: gtimin@unr.net. Website: http://twaonline.org (includes complete contest guidelines, postal address, information on Tallahassee Writers' Association membership, programs, and publications). Established 1987. **Editor:** Carole Clark Timin. Offers cash prizes plus publication in and one copy of a chapbook of winners and finalists. Prizes: $100, $30, and $20 for poetry; $50, $20, and $10 for haiku. Pays winners from other countries by US check. Submission must be unpublished. No simultaneous submissions. First category is poetry of up to 50 lines (shorter poetry is of equal value); second category is 3-line haiku. Poets may submit to both categories. Poems must be typed on 8½ × 11 paper; haiku on 3 × 5 cards. Send 2 copies of each entry. On the back of one copy, *only* write author's name, address, telephone, e-mail, and source of contest information. Send 1-paragraph bio with personal information and publications. Guidelines available for SASE or on website. Accepts inquiries by e-mail. Entry fee: $5/poem, $3/haiku. Does not accept entry fees in foreign currencies, send check or money order in US dollars only. Deadline: June 30. Competition receives 500-600 entries/year from US, Canada, Europe, and others. Most recent winners were Anne Meisenzahl (poetry) and Tim Russell (haiku). Past judges: Lola Haskins and Janet Holmes. Sample copy of *Penumbra* chapbook with 60 pgs. of top winners and finalists available for $7.50 from TWA Penumbra. "Includes essays by judges and contributor bios."

☑ $◎ **PEW FELLOWSHIPS IN THE ARTS (Specialized: regional)**, 230 S. Broad St., Suite 1003, Philadelphia PA 19102. (215)875-2285. Fax: (215)875-2276. Website: www.pewarts.org (includes past panelists and PEW fellows, application forms, and guidelines). Established 1991. **Award Director:** Melissa Franklin. "The Pew Fellowships in the Arts provide financial support directly to artists so they may have the opportunity to dedicate themselves wholly to the development of their artwork for up to 2 years. Up to 12 fellowships of $50,000 each (in 3 different categories) awarded each year." Must be a Pennsylvania resident of Bucks, Chester, Delaware, Montgomery, or Philadelphia county for at least two years; must be 25 or older. Matriculated students, full or part-time, are not eligible. Application and guidelines available mid-August for SASE. Accepts inquiries by phone, fax, and e mail. Deadline: December of the preceding year. Most recent judge was a panel of artists and art professionals. Winner will be announced by letter.

☑ $◙ **THE RICHARD PHILLIPS POETRY PRIZE**, The Phillips Publishing Co., 719 E. Delaware St., Siloam Springs AR 72761. Established 1993. **Award Director:** Richard Phillips, Jr. Annual award of $1,000, open to all poets. Submit 48-page ms, published or unpublished poems, any subject, any form. Guidelines available for SASE. Include $15 entry fee/ms, payable to Richard Phillips Poetry Prize. Accepts entry fees in foreign currencies. Manuscripts are not returned. Postmark deadline: January 31. "Winner will be announced and check for $1,000 presented by March 31." Publication is the following September. Competition receives approximately 100 entries. Most recent prize winners were: Clark Doane (2001), Patricia Lang (2000), Paul Davidson (1999), and Jana Klenburg (1998). "There are no anthologies to buy, no strings attached. The best manuscript will win the prize."

$◙ **POETIC LICENSE CONTEST; MKASHEF ENTERPRISES**, P.O. Box 688, Yucca Valley CA 92286-0688. E-mail: alayne@inetworld.net. Website: www.asidozines.com (includes guidelines, sample poetry, editor's biography). Established 1998. **Poetry Editor:** Alayne Gelfand. Offers a biannual poetry contest. 1st Prize: $500, 2nd Prize: $100, 3rd Prize: $40, plus publication in anthology and 1 copy. Five honorable mentions receive 1 copy; other poems of exceptional interest will also be included in the anthology. Themes and deadlines available for SASE. Submit any number of poems, any style, of up to 50 lines/poem. Include name, address, and phone on each poem. Enclose a SASE for notification of winners. "Judges prefer original, accessible, and unforced works." Entry fee: $1/poem. "We're looking for fresh word usage and surprising imagery. Each contest seeks to explode established definitions of the theme being spotlighted. Be sure to SASE for current theme and deadline."

☐ ◙ **POETIC POTPOURRI QUARTERLY CONTESTS**, P.O. Box 13, Lattimore NC 28089. **Award Director:** Dennis Norville. Offers quarterly awards of $100, $75, $50, and three Honorable Mentions. Submissions may be previously published and may be entered in other contests. Submit any number of poems on any subject in any style. "No porn! Put name and address on each page. Send SASE for guidelines." Entry fee: $3 for the first poem, $2 each additional poem. Postmark deadlines: March 31, June 30, September 30, and December 31. Include SASE with your entry for a winners' list. Winners will be announced within one month after contest deadlines.

POETRY FOREVER; MILTON ACORN PRIZE FOR POETRY; ORION PRIZE FOR POETRY; TIDEPOOL PRIZE FOR POETRY, Poetry Forever, P.O. Box 68018, Hamilton, Ontario L8M 3M7 Canada. (905)312-1779. Fax: (905)312-8285. **Administrator:** James Deahl. Poetry Forever sponsors 3 annual contests for poets everywhere—the Milton Acorn Prize, the Orion Prize, and the Tidepool Prize. Each contest awards 50% of its entry fees in 1st, 2nd, and 3rd Place prizes (amount varies, but no less than $100). The top 3 poems also receive broadsheet publication. For all 3 contests, poems may be no longer than 30 lines. "Poems should be typed or neatly printed and no longer than 30 lines. Photocopied submissions OK." Send SASE or e-mail address to receive winners' list. Entry fee: $3/poem. Make checks payable to Poetry Forever. Deadlines: May 15 (Milton Acorn), June 15 (Orion Prize), July 15 (Tidepool Prize). "The purpose of the contests is to fund the publication of full-size collections by the People's Poet, Milton Acorn (1923-1986); Ottawa poet Marty Flomen (1942-1997); and Hamilton poet Herb Barrett (1912-1995)." Recent winners include Ellen Jaffe (Orion Prize), Dorothy Stott (Milton Acorn), and Margaret Malloch Zielinski (Tidepool Prize).

THE POETRY SOCIETY OF VIRGINIA ANNUAL CONTESTS (Specialized: forms/sonnet, haiku, limerick; humor; students; themes), 11027 Becontree Lake Dr., Apt. 303, Reston VA 20190. **Contest Cordinator:** Lori C. Fraind. E-mail: PoetryInVa@aol.com. Website: www.PoetrySocietyOfVirginia.org (includes info about the PSU, history, newsletters, member publications and websites, and several round robin poems written by a group of poets who each contributed a line—see the sonnet "Grief"). Offers contests in various categories including the Bess Gresham Memorial (garden or gardeners); Brodie Herndon Memorial (the sea); Judah, Sarah, Grace, and Tom Memorial (inter-ethnic amity); Cenie H. Moon Prize (women); Karma Deane Ogden Memorial (PSV members only); and the Edgar Allan Poe Memorial. (All of the previous categories are open to any form, have limits of 32-48 lines, and some have specific subjects as noted.) The following group of contests require specific forms: the J. Franklin Dew Award (series of 3-4 haiku), Carleton Drewry Memorial (lyric or sonnet about mountains), Handy Andy Prize (limerick), Emma Gray Trigg Memorial (lyric, 64-line limit, PSV members only), Nancy Byrd Turner Memorial (sonnet). The final group of contests is open to students only: Elementary School Prize (grades 1-5, any form or subject, 24-line limit), Middle School Prize (grades 6-8, any form or subject, 24-line limit), High School Prize (grades 9-12, any form or subject, 32-line limit); Undergraduate College Prize (any form or subject, 48 line limit). All poems are open to nonmembers except those noted above. Cash prizes range from $10-100. Pays winners from other countries with IRCs or through PayPal account. Contest information available for SASE or on website (guidelines *must* be followed). Does not accept submissions by e-mail. Entry fee: Adults, $2/poem; no fee for student entries. Send **all entries** to Lori C. Fraind at the address above. Deadline for all contests is January 19 (Edgar Allan Poe's birthday). Each category averages about 80 entries/year. Winning entries will be published in a booklet unless author indicates otherwise. Also publishes the *Poetry Society of Virginia Newsletter*, which provides PSV members with information about upcoming meetings and local events. Includes some poetry by members, book reviews, and notices of publication/contest opportunities.

POETS' CLUB OF CHICAGO; HELEN SCHAIBLE SHAKESPEAREAN/PETRARCHAN SONNET CONTEST (Specialized: form, sonnet), 1212 S. Michigan Ave., Apt. 2802, Chicago IL 60605. (312)786-1959. Fax: (312)461-0217. E-mail: tomroby@mindspring.com. **Chairman:** Tom Roby. The Helen Schaible Shakespearean/Petrarchan Sonnet Contest is open to anyone **except** members of Poets' Club of Chicago. Submit only 1 entry (2 copies) of either a Shakespearean or a Petrarchan sonnet, which must be original and unpublished. Entry must be typed on $8\frac{1}{2} \times 11$ paper, double-spaced. Name and address in the upper right-hand corner on only one copy. No entry fee. Prizes of $50, $35, and $15. Postmark deadline: September 1. Competition receives 120 entries/year. Most recent contest winners were Joyce Schiver, Geneva Fulgham, and Len Krisak. Winners will be notified by October 15. Include SASE with entry to receive winners' list. The Poets' Club of Chicago meets monthly at the Harold Washington Library to critique their original poetry, which the members read at various venues in the Chicago area and publish in diverse magazines and books. Members also conduct workshops at area schools and libraries by invitation.

POETS' DINNER CONTEST (Specialized: regional), 2214 Derby St., Berkeley CA 94705-1018. (510)841-1217. **Contact:** Dorothy V. Benson. Three typed copies of original, unpublished poems in not more than 3 of the 8 categories [Humor, Love, Nature, Beginnings & Endings, Spaces & Places, People, Theme (changed annually), and Poet's Choice] are submitted anonymously without fee, and the winning poems (Grand Prize, 1st, 2nd, 3rd) are read at the banquet and honorable mentions awarded. **Contestant must be present to win.** Cash prizes awarded; Honorable Mention receives books. The event is nonprofit. Since 1927 there has been an annual awards banquet sponsored by the ad hoc Poets' Dinner Committee, usually at Spenger's Fish Grotto (a Berkeley Landmark). Contest guidelines available for SASE. Deadline: January. Competition receives about 300 entries. Recent contest winners include Danyen Powell (Grand Prize); 1st Prizes: Marcene Gandolfo, Robin Michel, Deborah Cooper, LaVerne Smith, Sandy Stark, Gayle Eleanor, John Rowe, and Charles Sullivan.

N: $□ POETS OF THE VINEYARD CONTEST; VINTAGE, 704 Brigham Ave., Santa Rosa CA 95404-5245. E-mail: jhchueng@aol.com. **Contest Chair:** Emma J. Blanch. Offers annual contest sponsored by the Sonoma County Chapter (P.O.V.) of the California Federation of Chaparral Poets with entries in 5 categories. Includes traditional forms, free verse poems that tell a story, short free verse, and a theme-category on grapes, vineyards, wine. Contest rules and deadline available for SASE from Contest Chair at 21 Ludlow Dr., Milford CT 06460. Prizes in each category are $50, $25, and $15, with a grand prize chosen from category winners ($75). Pays winners from other countries with international money order at US value at time of issue. Entry fee: nonmembers $4/poem or $10/3 poems; members $3/poem or $10/5 poems. Prize-winning poems will be published in the annual anthology, *Vintage*. Every winning poet will receive a complimentary copy of the anthology in which his/her poem appears. Most recent contest winners were Ruth Wilder Schuler, Elizabeth Howard, and Patricia Wellingham Jones.

N: □ PORTLANDIA CHAPBOOK CONTEST; THE PORTLANDIA GROUP, PMB 225, 6663 SW Beaverton-Hillsdale Hwy., Portland OR 97225. E-mail: braucher@portlandia.com. Established 1999. **Award Director:** Karen Braucher. Offers annual prize of publication of chapbook and 30 free copies. Submissions may be entered in other contests. Submit 24 pgs. of poetry with title page, table of contents, and bio. Poems may be in free verse and/or formal verse. "See guidelines for the year you are submitting." Guidelines available for SASE and by e-mail. Entry fee: $10/chapbook ms (as of 2001). Does not accept entry fees in foreign currencies; accepts check on US bank or US money order. Deadline: check annual guidelines. Competition receives approximately 200/year. Most recent contest winner was Kurt S. Olsson for *I Know Your Heart, Hieronymus Bosch* (2000). "Panel of judges is used. Most have M.F.A. or Ph.D degrees and have published." Winner will be announced in spring of each year. Copies of previous winning chapbooks are available by sending check to The Portlandia Group. "The Portlandia Group, a fine poetry press, was founded by Karen Braucher, M.F.A., to publish the best emerging poets in the hope that they will go on to publish full-length books. This is happening. We are looking for the finest poetry being written in English. Judges are published poets who have read widely in contemporary poetry. You are unlikely to win if you have not published some poems in journals."

☑ $□ PULITZER PRIZE IN LETTERS, % The Pulitzer Prize Board, 709 Journalism, Columbia University, New York NY 10027. (212)854-3841. Fax: (212)854-3342. E-mail: pulitzer@www.pulitzer.org. Website: www.pulitzer.org (includes downloadable entry form and guidelines, bios and photos of winners from 1995 to present, and an archive of past winners). **Contact:** the Pulitzer Prize Board. Offers 5 prizes of $5,000 each year, including 1 in poetry, for books published in the calendar year preceding the award. Accepts inquiries by fax and e-mail. Submit 4 copies of published books (or galley proofs if book is being published after November), photo, bio, entry form, and $50 entry fee. July 1 deadline for books published between January 1 and June 30; November 1 deadline for books published between July 1 and December 31. Competition receives 150 entries/year. Most recent award winner was C.K. Williams for *Repair* published by Farrar, Straus and Giroux.

☑ $□ QUINCY WRITERS GUILD WRITING CONTEST, P.O. Box 433, Quincy IL 62306. E-mail: chillcbr@adams.net. Website: www.quincylibrary.org/guild.htm (includes updated guidelines). Established 1990. **Contact:** Contest Coordinator. Offers annual award for original, unpublished poetry (serious poetry and light poetry), fiction, and nonfiction. Cash prizes based on dollar amount of entries. 1st, 2nd, and 3rd Prizes will be awarded in all categories. Guidelines available for SASE. Accepts inquiries by e-mail. Entry fee: $2/poem; $4/nonfiction or fiction piece. Does not accept entry fees in foreign currencies; accepts cash in US dollars as well as Western Union and American Express checks. Entries accepted from January 1 through April 1. Competition receives 110-125 entries. Recent contest winners were Maryann Westoff for "The Wedding of Jacob," Shawna Mayer for "The Ethereal Adena," and Alika Tanaka for "Wrench." The Quincy Writers Guild meets monthly and consists of Quincy-area writers working in various genres.

☑ ✂ $◎ QWF A.M. KLEIN PRIZE FOR POETRY; QUEBEC WRITERS' FEDERATION; QW-RITE (Specialized: regional, translations), (formerly QWF Literary Awards), 1200 Atwater Ave., Montreal, Quebec H3Z 1X4 Canada. (514)933-0878. Fax: (514)934-2485. E-mail: qspell@total.net. Website: www.qwf.org. **Contact:** Award Director. Offers annual awards of $2,000 each for poetry, fiction, nonfiction, and translation. Also offers a $1,000 first book award. Submissions must be previously published. Open to authors "who have lived in Quebec for at least 3 of the past 5 years." Submit 4 copies of a book at least 48 pgs. Write for entry form. Accepts inquiries by fax and e-mail. Entry fee: $10/submission. Deadline for books published between October 1 and May 15 is May 31. Deadline for books published between May 15 and September 30 is August 15 (bound proofs are acceptable; the finished book must be received by September 30). Competition receives approximately 50 entries. Recent award winners were Bruce Taylor (poetry), Elyse Gasco (fiction), Elaine K. Naves (nonfiction), and Sheila Fischman (translation). Poetry judges have included NourBese Philip, Carolyn Souai, and John Steffler. Winners will be announced in November. "QWF was formed in 1988 to honor and promote literature written in English by Quebec authors." QWF also publishes *QWRITE*, "a newsletter offering information and articles of interest to membership and the broader community."

○ **REDWOOD ACRES FAIR POETRY CONTEST**, P.O. Box 6576, Eureka CA 95502. (707)445-3037. Fax: (707)445-1583. Offers an annual contest with various categories for both juniors and seniors. Entry fee: 50¢/poem for the junior contests and $1/poem for the senior contests. Deadline: late May. Competition receives 200 entries.

✓ ◎ **ROANOKE-CHOWAN POETRY AWARD (Specialized: regional)**, North Carolina Literary and Historical Association, 4610 Mail Service Center, Raleigh NC 27699-4610. (919)733-9375. Fax: (919) 733-8807, E-mail: mhill@ncsl.dcr.state.nc.us. Website: www.lib.unc.edu/ncc/onl/litawards.html (includes list of past winners). **Awards Coordinator:** Michael Hill. Offers annual award for "an original volume of poetry published during the twelve months ending June 30 of the year for which the award is given." Open to "authors who have maintained legal or physical residence, or a combination of both, in North Carolina for the three years preceding the close of the contest period." Submit 3 copies of each entry. Deadline: July 15. Competition receives about 15 entries. Recent award winners were Margaret Rabb, Stephen Knauth, and Kathryn Stripling Byer. Winner will be announced during the annual meeting in November.

✓ ◎ ◑ **ANNA DAVIDSON ROSENBERG AWARD, FOR POEMS ON THE JEWISH EXPERI-ENCE (Specialized: ethnic)**, Judah L. Magnes Museum, 2911 Russell St., Berkeley CA 94705. E-mail: pfpr@magnesmuseum.org. Website: www.magnesmuseum.org/. Established 1987. Offers prizes of $100, $50, and $25, as well as honorable mentions, for unpublished poems (in English) on the Jewish Experience. "This award is open to all poets. You needn't be Jewish to enter."

  • There was no award given in 2001; poets should query regarding the status of the award for 2002 before submitting.

✓ $ ◎ **SAN FRANCISCO FOUNDATION; JOSEPH HENRY JACKSON AWARD; JAMES D. PHELAN AWARD (Specialized: regional, young adult)**, % Intersection for the Arts, 446 Valencia St., San Francisco CA 94103. (415)626-2787. Fax: (415)626-1636. E-mail: info@theintersection.org. Website: www.t heintersection.org (includes calendar of events at Intersection for the Arts and general guidelines for San Francisco Foundation awards). **Contact:** Awards Coordinator. Offers the Jackson Award ($2,000), established in 1955, to the author of an unpublished work-in-progress in the form of fiction (novel or short stories), nonfictional prose, or poetry. Applicants must be residents of northern California or Nevada for three consecutive years immediately prior to the deadline date of January 31 and must be between the ages of 20 and 35 as of the deadline. Offers the Phelan Award ($2,000), established in 1935, to the author of an unpublished work-in-progress in the form of fiction (novel or short stories), nonfictional prose, poetry, or drama. Applicants must be California-born (although they may now reside outside of the state), and must be between the ages of 20 and 35 as of the January 31 deadline. Mss for both awards must be accompanied by an application form. The award judge will use a name-blind process. Mss should be copied on the front and back of each page and must include a separate cover page that gives the work's title and the applicant's name and address. The applicant's name should only be listed on the cover page; do not list names or addresses on the pages of the ms. Applicants may, however, use the mss title and page numbers on the pages of the ms. Mss with inappropriate identifying information will be deemed ineligible. Three copies of the ms should be forwarded with one properly completed current year's official application form to the address listed above. Entries accepted November 15 through January 31. Competitions receive 150-180 entries. Most recent contest writers include Richard Dry, Kristen Hanlon, and Angela Morales.

✓ ⊕ ◑ **AILEEN & ALBERT SANDERS MEMORIAL TROPHY**, 33 Alledge Dr., Woodford, North-amptonshire NN14-4JQ Great Britain. Established 1995. **Award Director:** Ivan Sanders. Offers annual open poetry competition. 1st Prize: annual trophy, certificate and publication; 2nd to 10th Prize: certificate and publica-tion; best overseas poem entered receives certificate and publication; 11th to 25th Prize: publication. All entrants: free "AAS" anthology. Submissions must be unpublished and may be entered in other contests. Submit up to 5 poems maximum on any subject in any form/style. "Poems must be in English and no longer than 30 lines excluding title and lines between stanzas. Each poem should be typed on a separate A4 size page, and must not bear the author's details. Any poem bearing either the author's name or address is automatically disqualified, without refund of the entry fee. Poems may not be amended, and will not be returned. Retain copies of your work!" Entry form and guidelines available for SASE (or SAE and IRC). Entry fee: £5 (total). "All entries must be accompanied by a completed entry form (this may be photocopied), and entry fee. Each entrant is eligible to have more than 1 poem published. Cheques/postal orders/bank drafts should be crossed and made payable to Ivan Sanders. No cheques/bank drafts drawn on overseas accounts are acceptable due to high U.K. bank charges. Overseas entrants (only) are allowed to pay by International Postage Coupons if preferred. (Entry fee: 11 cou-pons.)" Deadline: January 31, 2002. Competition receives 750 entries/year. "The AAS committee and helpers prepare a short list of poems for the judge, who has discretion on whether or not to examine any or all of the other entries. The trophy is retained by the winner on a May to May basis, and this may not be removed from the U.K." Most recent award winner was Elizabeth Rapp. "Winner will be announced 2-3 weeks after close of competition by post to entrants providing a SAE." Anthologies are post free. Additional copies £5. Ivan Sanders says, "Read the rules. Submit in good time. Your work must be interesting/entertaining, as well as well written."

N $☐ ☑ ◎ **SARASOTA POETRY THEATRE PRESS; EDDA POETRY CHAPBOOK COM-PETITION FOR WOMEN; SARASOTA POETRY THEATRE CHAPBOOK COMPETITION; ANI-MALS IN POETRY; SPRING POETRY CHAPBOOK PRIZE (Specialized: women/feminism)**, P.O. Box 48955, Sarasota FL 34230-6955. (941)366-6468. Fax: (941)954-2208. E-mail: soulspeak1@home.com. Website: www.soulspeak.org (includes general info about Soulspeak/Sarasota Poetry Theatre, the press, competitions, and all books published, plus samples of poetry from each book). Established 1994-1998. **Award Director:** Scylla Liscombe. Offers 4 annual contests for poetry with prizes ranging from 1st Prize: $25 plus publication in an anthology to 1st Prize: $100 plus 25 published chapbooks. Honorable Mentions also awarded. Pays winners from other countries in copies. Guidelines and details about theater available for SASE or on website. Accepts queries by e-mail. Entry fees range from $4/poem to $10/ms. Postmark deadline: Animals in Poetry, April 30 (winners notified in July); Sarasota Poetry Theatre Chapbook Competition, August 31 (winners notified in November); Edda Poetry Chapbook Competition for women, February 28 (winners notified in May); Spring Poetry Chapbook Prize, October 31 (winners notified in January). Competition receives an average of 1,000 entries/year. Judges for contests are the staff of the press and ranking state poets. Winners are notified by mail. "Sarasota Poetry Theatre Press is a division of Soulspeak/Sarasota Poetry Theatre, a nonprofit organization dedicated to encouraging poetry in all its forms through the Sarasota Poetry Theatre Press, Therapeutic Soulspeak for at-risk youth and the Soulspeak Performance Center. We are looking for honest, not showy, poetry; use a good readable font. Do not send extraneous materials."

☑ $☐ ◎ **CLAUDIA ANN SEAMAN POETRY AWARD (Specialized: students)**, The Community Foundation of Dutchess County, 80 Washington St., Suite 201, Poughkeepsie NY 12601. (845)452-3077. Fax: (845)452-3083. Established 1983. Offers annual award of $500 (1st Prize). Submissions may be entered in other contests. Submit 1 or 2 poems on any subject or in any form. Open to students in grades 9-12. "Entry must contain student and school names, addresses, and phone numbers and the name of the English or writing teacher." Entry form and guidelines available for SASE. Accepts inquiries by fax. Deadline: June 1. Most recent award winner was Gemma Cooper-Novack. Judged by "a panel of judges, including Donna Seaman (Claudia's sister)." Winner announced in September each year at the Barnes & Noble in Manhattan. Copies of last year's winning poem may be obtained by contacting The Community Foundation by phone or in writing. "The Community Foundation is a nonprofit organization serving Dutchess County, NY; it administers numerous grant programs, scholarship funds, and endowment requests. This is an excellent opportunity for young, previously unpublished poets to earn recognition for their work. Since there's no fee, there is little to lose; realize, however, that a national contest will have more entries than a regional competition."

☑ $☐ ☑ ◎ **SENIOR POET LAUREATE POETRY COMPETITION (Specialized: senior citizen)**, Goodin Communications & Penny Peephole Publications, Chapbook Dept., P.O. Box 6003, Springfield MO 65801. E-mail: goldenword@aol.com. Website: http://hometown.aol.com/goldenword/index.html (includes basic facts of contest). Established 1993. **Contact:** SPL Coordinator. Offers annual award to "American poets age 50 and older. Top winner will receive $75 and the Senior Poet Laureate title. Cash awards will also be given 1st Place winners in ten poetry categories. Pays winners from other countries by money order. The top 61 winning poems will be published in *Golden Words* chapbook of poems by leading older American poets." Submit any number of poems; 32 lines or less (unless specified otherwise); 1/page. Categories are haiku, short poem (12 lines or less), nostalgic, long poem (over 32 lines), sonnet, love, inspirational, light verse, western/pioneer/tall tales poem, and Pissonnet. Entry form and guidelines available for SASE. Accepts inquiries by e-mail. Entry fee: $1/poem. Does not accept entry fees in foreign currencies; send money order. Deadline: August 1. Competition receives 1,000 entries/year. Most recent contest winner was Reese Danley-Kilgo. Winners will be announced in October. The top winning poems from the 9 categories and the new Senior Poet Laureate's poem will also be published in *Hodgepodge* literary magazine. (See listing in Publishers of Poetry).

$☐ **SKY BLUE WATERS POETRY CONTESTS; SKY BLUE WATERS POETRY SOCIETY**, 232 SE 12th Ave., Faribault MN 55021-6406. (507)332-2803. **Contact:** Marlene Meehl. sponsors monthly contests with prizes of $40, $30, $20, $10, plus 3 paid Honorable Mentions of $5 each. Pays winners from other countries by check. Accepts simultaneous submissions. Submit any number of poems on any subject. Guidelines available for SASE. Entry fee: $2 first poem, $1 each additional poem. Does not accept entry fees in foreign currencies; send check or money order. All winning poems automatically entered in the Best of the Best Contest to be judged each January. No fee required. 1st Prize: $50, 2nd Prize: $30, 3rd Prize: $20. Winners will be announced by mail one month following deadline date. "The Sky Blue Waters Poetry Society is a group of Southern Minnesota poets who exist for the sheer 'love of writing.' Most members agree that writing is not just a love but a necessity. Keep writing. Keep submitting. Today's creation will be tomorrow's winner."

☑ ⊕ **SENDING TO A COUNTRY** other than your own? Be sure to send International Reply Coupons (IRCs) instead of stamps for replies or return of your manuscript.

☑ $◑ **SLAPERING HOL PRESS CHAPBOOK COMPETITION**, The Hudson Valley Writers' Center, 300 Riverside Dr., Sleepy Hollow NY 10591. (914)332-5953. Fax: (914)332-4825. E-mail: info@writerscenter.org. Website: www.writerscenter.org (includes information about the Writers' Center and the Slapering Hol Press, including titles in print and contest guidelines). Established 1990. **Coeditors:** Stephanie Strickland and Margo Stever. Offers annual award of $500 plus 10 author's copies. Pays winners from other countries with check in US currency. Submissions must be from poets who have not previously published a book or chapbook. Submit 16-20 pgs. of poems with acknowledgements, any form or style, SASE and $10 entry fee. "Manuscript should be anonymous with second title page containing name, address, and phone." Guidelines available for SASE or on website. Accepts entry fees in foreign currencies as well as US currency (check, postal order, etc.). Deadline: May 15. Competition receives 200-300 entries. Most recent contest winner was Sondra Upham, *Freight.* Copies of previous winning books may be obtained by requesting order form.

☑ $◐ ◑ **KAY SNOW WRITING AWARDS; WILLAMETTE WRITERS**, 9045 SW Barbur Blvd., Suite 5A, Portland OR 97219-4027. (503)452-1592. Fax: (503)452-0372. E-mail: wilwrite@teleport.com. Website: www.willamettewriters.com. Established 1986. **Award Director:** Elizabeth Shannon. Offers annual awards of 1st Prize: $300, 2nd Prize: $150, 3rd Prize: $50 and publication of excerpt only in December issue of *The Willamette Writer.* Pays winners from other countries by postal money order. Submissions must be unpublished. Submit 1-5 pages on any subject in any style or form, single spaced, one side of paper only. Entry form and guidelines available for SASE. Accepts inquiries by fax and e-mail. Entry fee: $10 for members of Willamette Writers; $15 for nonmembers. Does not accept entry fees in foreign currencies; only accepts a check drawn on a US bank. Deadline: May 15. Competition receives 150 entries. Most recent award winner was Elaine Lockie. Winners will be announced July 31. "Write and send in your very best poem. Read it aloud. If it still sounds like the best poem you've ever heard, send it in."

Ⓝ ◑ ◎ **THE BOB SNYDER POETRY AWARDS (Specialized: poetry written by or about Appalachian people)**, Redbud Hill Press, 265 S. Glencoe Ave., Decatur IL 62522. (217)425-9144. E-mail: RedbudHillPress@aol.com. Website: www.redcrowguidelines.cjb.net. Established 2001. **Award Director:** Jim Webb. Offers annual awards, $300 total cash prizes (plus publication). Cash awards vary. Pays winners from other countries in US dollars. Submissions must be unpublished. Submit up to 5 poems (8 pgs. maximum) of Appalachia-related poetry, all genres. Guidelines available for SASE, by e-mail, and on website. Entry fee: $8/ms. Does not accept entry fees in foreign currencies. Send US dollars. Deadline: March 1, 2002. See website for most recent award winners. Judge for the upcoming contest will be poet Richard Hague. Winners will be announced in June (by phone or mail). Send for a sample. "Redbud Hill is a publisher of contemporary Appalachian and beat poetry in *Red Crow Poetry Journal.* Also sponsors The Jack Kerouac Poetry Prize." (See separate listing for *Red Crow Poetry Journal* in Publishers of Poetry section; see separate listing for The Jack Kerouac Poetry Prize in this section.) "Don't worry about themes of interest to us—just send us your best work! Social, beautiful, profane, or political."

Ⓝ $◐ ◑ **SOUTH DAKOTA STATE POETRY SOCIETY (SDSPS) ANNUAL POETRY CONTEST; PASQUE PETALS**, South Dakota State Poetry Society, 115 W. 25th St., Sioux Falls SD 57105. (605)338-0113. Established 1975. **SDSPS Contest Chairman:** Martha Hegdahl. Offers annual awards for poetry in several categories; some are for South Dakota residents only, others are open to all poets. Grand Prize—1st Prize: $75, 2nd Prize: $50, 3rd Prize: $25; all other categories—1st Prize: $25, 2nd Prize: $15, 3rd Prize: $10 (unless otherwise specified by sponsor). Poems must be original, unpublished, and have won no more than $10 in competition. Send as many poems as desired for Grand Prize category; send only one poem/category for rest of competition. No poem may be entered in more than one category and, except where noted in guidelines, length is limited to 40 lines/poem. All poems except haiku and tanka must be titled. Send one original and one copy with the category on the upper left of both, and your name and address on the upper right of copy only. Entry form and guidelines (including list of categories and prizes) available for SASE. Entry fees: range from $2-7, depending on category and membership status; see guidelines for complete information. Deadline: mid-August. Competition receives about 490 entries/year. Most recent award winners were Maria V. Bakkum, Susan Rose, and Maureen Lavender (Grand Prize). Complete list of winners in all categories available for SASE after October 31. Judges are selected from National Federation of State Poetry Society members during their summer meeting. There were 13 individual judges from across the US for the 2000 contests, a different judge for each category. The contest chairman announces the winners during the SDSPS Fall Conference in October. Winners not present are notified by mail. Winning poems will be published in *Pasque Petals,* the SDSPS magazine—free to winners and available by request to others for a fee. (See separate listing for South Dakota State Poetry Society in the Organizations section.) "Send SASE for rules and regulations—*read thoroughly!*"

$◑ **WALLACE E. STEGNER FELLOWSHIPS**, Creative Writing Program, Stanford University, Stanford CA 94305. (650)725-1208. Fax: (650)723-3679. E-mail: gay.pierce@forsythe.stanford.edu. Website: www.stanford.edu/dept/english/cw/. **Program Administrator:** Gay Pierce. Offers 5 fellowships in poetry of $18,000 plus tuition of over $6,000 for promising writers who can benefit from 2 years instruction and criticism at the Writing Center. Previous publication not required, although it can strengthen one's application. Deadline: postmarked by the first working day after December 1. Accepts inquiries by fax and e-mail. Competition receives 1,000 entries/year. Past winners were Gabrielle Calvocoressi, Matthew Doherty, Susan Kim, Mon-Lan Anne Pham, and Brian Teare.

🌐 $🔲 **THE TABLA POETRY COMPETITION; THE TABLA BOOK OF NEW VERSE**, Dept. of English, University of Bristol, 3-5 Woodland Rd., Bristol BS8 1TB England. Fax: (0117)928 8860. E-mail: stephen.james@bristol.ac.uk. Website: www.bris.ac.uk/tabla. Established 1991. **Award Director:** Dr. Stephen James. Offers annual poetry competition. 1st Prize: £500, 2nd Prize: £200, 3 runners-up: £100 each plus publication. Cash prizes are paid in UK sterling only. Submissions must be unpublished. Submit any number of poems on any subject in any form and any length. Poems must be typed on one side only; no names on poems to be judged. Entry form and guidelines available for SASE (or SAE and IRC) or on website. Accepts inquiries by fax and e-mail. "One free entry with purchase of *The Tabla Book of New Verse* (£6 UK); all other entries: £3 UK each. Book costs £7 (Eur), £8 (rest of world) to cover postage. Only UK standing fees and payments accepted." Deadline: June 30. Competition receives about 1,200 entries/year. Most recent contest winner was Henry Shukman (2000). Judge was Anne Stevenson. Judge for upcoming contest will be George Szirtes. Winners are announced by mail and on the website by September each year. "All above prices correct in 2001; subject to revision in 2002."

$🔲 🎯 **TOWSON UNIVERSITY PRIZE FOR LITERATURE (Specialized: regional)**, Towson University, College of Liberal Arts, Towson MD 21252. (410)830-2128. Fax: (410)830-6392. **Award Director:** Dean of the College of Liberal Arts. Offers annual prize of $1,500 "for a single book or book-length manuscript of fiction, poetry, drama, or imaginative nonfiction by a young Maryland writer. The prize is granted on the basis of literary and aesthetic excellence as determined by a panel of distinguished judges appointed by the university. The first award, made in the fall of 1980, went to novelist Anne Tyler." The work must have been published within the three years prior to the year of nomination or must be scheduled for publication within the year in which nominated. Open to Maryland residents under 40 years of age. Submit 5 copies of work in bound form or in typewritten, double-spaced ms form. Entry form and guidelines available for SASE. Accepts inquiries by e-mail. Deadline: May 15. Competition receives 8-10 entries. Most recent contest winner was Jane Satterfield.

🌐 $🔲 🔲 🎯 **THE TREWITHEN POETRY PRIZE (Specialized: rural); THE TREWITHEN CHAPBOOK**, Trewithen Poetry, Chy-An-Dour, Trewithen Moor, Stithians, Truro, Cornwall TR3 7DU England. Established 1995. **Award Secretary:** D. Atkinson. Offers annual award of 1st Prize: £300, 2nd Prize: £150, 3rd Prize: £75, plus 3 runner-up prizes of £25 each and publication in *The Trewithen Chapbook*. Pays winners from other countries by "sterling cheque" or draft only. Submissions may be entered in other contests "*but* must *not* previously have won another competition." Submit any number of poems on a rural theme in any form. Entry form available for SASE. Entry fee: £3 for the first poem and £2 for each additional poem. Does not accept entry fees in foreign currencies; send "sterling cheque" or draft only. Deadline: October 31. Competition receives 1,000-1,500 entries. Recent contest winners were Glenda Beagen and Roger Elkin. Judged by a panel of 3-4 working poets who remain anonymous. Winners will be announced at the end of December by results sheet and through poetry magazines and organizations. Winning poems published biennially in March/April. Copies of *The Trewithen Chapbook* may be obtained by using order form on entry form or by writing direct to the secretary and enclosing a SAE with IRC. "We are seeking good writing with a contemporary approach, reflecting any aspect of nature or rural life in any country."

✅ $🔲 **KATE TUFTS DISCOVERY AWARD; KINGSLEY TUFTS POETRY AWARD**, Claremont Graduate University, 160 E. 10th St., Harper B7, Claremont CA 91711-6165. (909)621-8974. Fax: (909)621-8390. Website: www.cgu.edu/commun/tuftsent.html. Established 1992 (Kingsley Tufts Award) and 1993 (Kate Tufts Award). **Awards Administrator:** Betty Terrell. Kate Tufts Discovery Award offers $10,000 annually "for a first or very early work by a poet of genuine promise." Kingsley Tufts Poetry Award offers $100,000 annually to honor "an emerging poet, one who is past the very beginning, but has not yet reached the acknowledged pinnacle of his/her career." Books must be published between September 15, 2001 and September 15, 2002. Entry form and guidelines available for SASE or on website. Deadline: September 15. Kingsley Tufts Competition receives up to 500 entries/year. Most recent award winner was Alan Shapiro (2001).

🌐 $🔲 **V.B. POETRY PRIZE**, Look and Learn Productions Limited, 20, Clifton House, Club Row, London E2 7HB United Kingdom. Phone: +44(20)7390759. E-mail: looklearn@aol.com. Website: www.looklearn.com. Established 1999. **Award Director:** Nicholas Morgan. Offers annual cash awards of 1st Prize: £400, 2nd Prize: £100, 3rd Prize: £50. Pays winners from other countries by international money order. Submissions must be unpublished and in English. Submit any number of poems on any subject in no more than 40 lines (including title). "Name of poet must not appear on ms. Poems must be typed on one side only of A4 sheet, one poem/sheet; no stapled sheets. Poems will be accepted only with entry form." Entry forms may be copies and may cover multiple entries. Entry form and guidelines available for SASE (or SAE and IRC) or visit website for information. Accepts inquiries by e-mail. Entry fees: £3 sterling for each of the first two poems; subsequent entries are £1.50 each. Does not accept entry fees in foreign currencies. Send international money order. Deadline: June 30. Competition receives 200 entries/year. Most recent award winners were Olivia Weatherall, Colin Searle, and Cara Bowen and Anna Wigley (2000). Winners announced in August in writing and on website. "We are a film and video productions company (i.e., we are looking for scripts). We also run an artist's shop including artist's books and may be interested in new talent."

⊕ $ ◎ WESTERN AUSTRALIAN PREMIER'S BOOK AWARDS (Specialized: regional), Library & Information Service of W.A., Alexander Library Bldg., Perth Cultural Centre, Perth, Western Australia 6000 Australia. Phone: (61 8)9427 3330. Fax: (61 8)9427 3336. E-mail: jham@liswa.wa.gov.au. Website: www.liswa.w a.gov.au/pba.html. Established 1982. **Award Director:** Ms. Julie Ham. Offers annual poetry prize of AUS $5,000 for a published book of poetry. Winner also eligible for Premier's Prize of AUS $20,000. Submissions must be previously published. Open to poets born in Western Australia, current residents of Western Australia, or poets who have resided in Western Australia for at least 10 years at some stage. Entry form and guidelines available by mail or on website. Accepts inquiries by fax and e-mail. No entry fee. Deadline: December 31 each year. Competition receives about 10-15 entries in poetry category/year (120 overall). Past award winners were Tracy Ryan's *The Willing Eye*, John Kinsella's *The Hunt*, and Fay Zwicky's *The Gatekeeper's Wife* (1998). Judges were Dr. David Black, Andre Malan, Terri-ann White, and Jill Midolo. Winners announced in June each year (i.e., June 2001 for 2000 awards) at a presentation dinner given by the Premier of Western Australia. "The contest is organized by the Library and Information Service of Western Australia, with money provided by the Western Australian State Government to support literature."

☑ $ ◿ STAN AND TOM WICK POETRY PRIZE, Wick Poetry Program, Kent State University, P.O. Box 5190, Kent OH 44242-0001. (330)672-2067. Fax: (330)672-2567. E-mail: wickpoet@kent.edu. Website: http://dept.Kent.edu/english/wick/wickpoetry.htm (includes contest guidelines, reading series schedule). Established 1994. **Award Director:** Maggie Anderson. Offers annual award of $2,000 and publication by The Kent State University Press. Submissions must be unpublished as a whole and may be entered in other contests as long as the Wick program receives notice upon acceptance elsewhere. Submit 48-68 pages of poetry. Open to poets writing in English who have not yet published a full-length collection. Entries must include cover sheet with poet's name, address, telephone number, and title of ms. Guidelines available for SASE. Entry fee: $15. Does not accept entry fees in foreign currencies; send money order or US check. Deadline: May 1, 2002. Competition receives 700-800 entries. 2000 contest winner was Morri Creech. Judge for 2001 contest was Lynne Emanuel.

$ ◎ THE RICHARD WILBUR AWARD (Specialized: nationality), Dept. of English, University of Evansville, 1800 Lincoln Ave., Evansville IN 47722. (812)479-2963. Offers a biennial award (even-numbered years) of $1,000 and book publication to "recognize a quality book-length manuscript of poetry." Submissions must be unpublished ("although individual poems may have had previous journal publications") original poetry collections and "public domain or permission-secured translations may comprise up to one-third of the manuscript." Submit ms of 50-100 typed pages, unbound, bound, or clipped. Open to all American poets. Manuscripts should be accompanied by 2 title pages: one with collection's title, author's name, address, and phone number and one with only the title. Include SASE for contest results. Manuscripts are *not* returned. Guidelines available for SASE. Entry fees: $25/ms. Next postmark deadline: December 1, 2002. Competition receives 300-500 entries. Recent contest winner was A.E. Stallings. Judge for last contest was Mary Jo Salter. The winning ms is published and copyrighted by the University of Evansville Press.

$ ◿ OSCAR WILLIAMS & GENE DERWOOD AWARD, New York Community Trust, 2 Park Ave., New York NY 10016. An award given annually to nominees of the selection committee "to help needy or worthy artists or poets." **Selection Committee for the award does not accept submissions or nominations.** Amount varies from year to year.

☑ $ ◻ ◿ WINTER WOOD POETRY AWARD, Heather's Teddy Bear Organization, Inc., 16 Oakdale Rd., Terryville CT 06786. (860)585-1735. E-mail: StarlenHTBO@aol.com. Website: http://ctnow.com (under Communities Regional Nonprofit Groups). Established 1999. Offers annual awards of 1st Prize: $100, 2nd Prize: $50, and 3rd Prize: $25. Pays winners from other countries with a bank check. Submissions must be unpublished and may be entered in other contests. Submit any number of poems on any subject in any style/form. Line length is 20 maximum per poem. Guidelines and winners list available for SASE. Accepts inquiries by e-mail. Entry fees: $5/poem. Does not accept entry fees in foreign currencies. Make checks payable to the Heather's Teddy Bear Organization, Inc., "a nonprofit organization, 501-(c)(3)." Deadline: submissions must be postmarked no earlier than January 1 and no later than June 30. Judges are Sue Bacon, Linda Foster, Nancy Giudice, Lisa Lavoie, and Garth Pelton. Winners will be announced in July.

☑ $ ◿ ◎ WISCONSIN ARTS BOARD FELLOWSHIPS (Specialized: regional), Wisconsin Arts Board, 101 E. Wilson St., 1st Floor, Madison WI 53702. (608)264-8191. Fax: (608)267-0380. E-mail: mark.fraire @arts.state.wi.us. Website: www.arts.state.wi.us. **Awards Director:** Mark Fraire. Offers fellowships to "recognize the significant contributions of professional artists." Open to Wisconsin residents who are *not* fulltime students in the fine arts. Entry form and guidelines available—please write. Accepts inquiries by phone, fax, and e-mail. Deadline: September ("call for exact date").

$ ☑ ◎ **WORLD ORDER OF NARRATIVE AND FORMALIST POETS (Specialized: subscription, form)**, P.O. Box 580174, Station A, Flushing NY 11358-0174. Established 1980. **Contest Chairman:** Dr. Alfred Dorn. This organization sponsors contests in at least 15 categories of traditional and contemporary poetic forms, including the sonnet, blank verse, ballade, villanelle, free verse, and new forms created by Alfred Dorn. Prizes total at least $5,000 and range from $20 to $300. Only subscribers to *The Formalist* will be eligible for the competition, as explained in the complete guidelines available from the contest chairman. "We look for originality of thought, phrase and image, combined with masterful craftsmanship. Trite, trivial or technically inept work stands no chance." Postmark deadline for entries: November 14. Competition receives about 3,000 entries. Recent contest winners include Brian E. Drake, Rachel Hadas, Len Krisak, Albert Sterbak, Carolyn Raphael, and Rhina P. Espaillat. (For more information on *The Formalist*, see their listing in the Publishers of Poetry section.)

🌐 **$** ☐ ☑ **THE WRITERS BUREAU POETRY AND SHORT STORY COMPETITION**, The Writers Bureau, Sevendale House, 7 Dale St., Manchester M1 1JB England. Phone: (0161)228 2362. Fax: (0161)228 3533. E-mail: comp@writersbureau.com. Website: www.writersbureau.com. Established 1994. Offers annual prizes. First place: £1,000, 2nd: £400, 3rd: £200, 4th: £100, six 5th place prizes of £50, and publication in *Freelance Market News*. Submissions must be unpublished. "Any number of entries may be sent. There is no set theme or form. Entries must be typed, and no longer than 40 lines." Entry form available for SASE. Accepts inquiries by fax or e mail. Accepts entry fees in foreign currencies as bank drafts in US currency. Deadline: late July. Judge for last contest was Alison Chisholm. Winner(s) will be announced in September. "The Writers Bureau is a distance learning college offering correspondence courses in Journalism, Creative Writing, and Poetry."

$ ☑ **THE W.B. YEATS SOCIETY ANNUAL POETRY COMPETITION**, W.B. Yeats Society of New York, National Arts Club, 15 Gramercy Park S, New York NY 10003. (212)780-0605. Website: www.YeatsSociety .org (includes a "guestbook, where inquiries may be left; full information on our programs and links to numerous other relevant sites"). Offers $250 cash prize for 1st Place, $100 cash prize for 2nd Place, and optional honorable mentions. Open to beginner as well as established poets; winners are invited to read their winning entries at the Taste of the Yeats Summer School, held each April in New York. They are also inducted as Honorary Members of the Society, a 501 (c)(3) charitable organization established in 1994, Andrew McGowan president. Judges have included poets Eamon Grennan, L.S. Asekoff, Campbell McGrath, Billy Collins, and Paul Muldoon. Annual deadline for submissions is February 15. No entry form is required. Submit any number of unpublished poems in any style or form, up to 50 lines each, typed on letter-size paper without poet's name. Enclose reading fee ($7 for first poem, $6 per additional poem) and attach a 3×5 card to each entry containing the poem's title along with the poet's name, address, and phone/fax/e-mail. Winners are selected by March 31 and announced in April. Winning entries and judge's report are posted on the Society's website. Printed report available for SASE. Receives 200-300 entries/year. Most recent contest winners were Michele Madigan Somerville, H.R. Stoueback, and Griffin Hanshury.

(See pg. 416 for Additional Contests & Awards.)

Additional Contests & Awards

The following listings also contain information about contests and awards. See the General Index for page numbers, then read the listings and send SASEs (or SAEs and IRCs) for specific details about their offerings.

Academi
Academy of American Poets
ACM (Another Chicago Magazine)
Acorn, The
African Voices
Alabama State Poetry Society
Albatross
Alice James Books
Allegheny Review, The
Alsop Review, The
Amelia
America
American Literary Review
American Research Press
American Tolkien Society
Amethyst & Emerald Publishing
Amethyst Review, The
Anamnesis Press
Ancient Paths
Anhinga Press
Anthology of New England Writers
Antietam Review
Appalachia
Apples & Oranges International Poetry Magazine
Arizona Authors Association
Artisan
ArtWord Quarterly
Associated Writing Programs
Association of Christian Writers
Atlanta Review
Bay Area Poets Coalition
Beacon Street Review
Bear Star Press
Bellingham Review
Bell's Letters Poet
Beloit Poetry Journal, The
Bibliophilos
Bitter Oleander, The
Black Bear Publications
Black Warrior Review
Blue Collar Review
Blue Light Press
Blue Unicorn
Bordighera, Inc.
Boston Review
Bread Loaf Writers' Conference
BrickHouse Books, Inc.
British Haiku Society
Bulk Head
Burnaby Writers' Society
Burning Bush Publications
Button Magazine
Byline Magazine
California Quarterly
Canadian Poetry Association
Cape Rock, The
Caribbean Writer, The
Center Press
Chelsea
Children, Churches and Daddies
Chiron Review
Christian Science Monitor, The
Cleveland State University Poetry Center

Cló Iar-Chonnachta
Cochran's Corner
College of New Jersey Writers Conference, The
Colorado Review
Columbine State Poetry Society of Colorado
Common Threads
Comstock Review, The
Connecticut Poetry Society
Connecticut River Review
Copper Canyon Press
Correction(s)
Country Woman
Crab Orchard Review
Creative With Words Publications (C.W.W.)
Creativity Unlimited Press®
Cricket
Crucible
Cutbank
Dallas Poets Community
Davidson County Writers' Guild
Dead Metaphor Press
Defined Providence
Denver Quarterly
Disquieting Muses
Driftwood Review, The
1812
Ekphrasis
Ellipsis Magazine
Emerald Coast Review
Emotions Literary Magazine
Experimental Forest Press
Explorations
Fauquier Poetry Journal
Field
Firewater Press Inc.
First Time
Fishtrap
Five Points
Floating Bridge Press
Flyway
Formalist, The
Free Lunch
Frogmore Papers
Frogpond
Funny Paper, The
Gentle Survivalist, The
George & Mertie's Place
Georgia Poetry Review
Georgia Poetry Society
Gertrude
Gig Harbor Writers' Conference
Grain
Grasslands Review
Great Blue Beacon, The
Greensboro Review, The
GSU Review
Haiku Headlines
Harp-Strings Poetry Journal
Harpweaver, The
HEArt—Human Equity Through Art
Heaven Bone Magazine
Hippopotamus Press
Hodgepodge Short Stories & Poetry

Hubbub
Hunger Magazine
Idiom 23
Illinois State Poetry Society
Images Inscript
Indian Heritage Publishing
Inkwell Magazine
International Black Writers
Interpreter's House
Iowa Review, The
Isles of Mist Review
Kalliope
Kit-Cat Review, The
La Jolla Poet's Press
LAIRE, Inc., The
Laurels
Lazy Frog Press
Ledge, The
Life Press Christian Writers' Conference
Literal Latté
Literally Horses
Literary Focus Poetry Publications
Lone Stars Magazine
Louisiana Literature
Lucidity
Lucidity Poets' Ozark Retreat
Lullwater Review
Lyric, The
MacGuffin, The
Mad Poets Review
Madison Review, The
Mail Call Journal
Main Street Rag
Mammoth Books
Manitoba Writers' Guild Inc.
Many Mountains Moving
Marlboro Review, The
Maryland Poetry Review
Massachusetts State Poetry Society, Inc.
Medicinal Purposes Literary Review
Mid-America Press, Inc., The
Mid-American Review
Midwest Poetry Review
Miller's Pond
Minority Literary Expo
Missing Fez, The
Mississippi Poetry Society, Inc.
Mississippi Review
Mississippi Valley Writers Conference
Modern Haiku
mojo risin'
Mother Earth International Journal
Mount Olive College Press
Nassau Review
Nation, The
National Federation of State Poetry Societies, Inc.
National League of American Pen Women, Inc.
National Writers Association
Nebraska Review, The
Nerve Cowboy
Nevada Poetry Society

New Hampshire Writers' Project
New Issues Press
New Letters
New Mirage Quarterly, The
New Renaissance, The
New Song, A
New Writer, The
Nimrod
North American Review
North Carolina Writers' Network
Northern Stars Magazine
Northwest Florida Review, The
Notre Dame Review
Now & Then
nowCulture.com
Oak, The
Oakland University Writers'
    Conference
Ohio Poetry Association
Opened Eyes Poetry & Prose
    Magazine
Oregon Review, The
Oregon State Poetry Association, The
Osric Publishing
Other Voices
Our Journey
Outrider Press
Ozark Creative Writers Conference
Pacific Coast Journal
Palanquin
Parnassus Literary Journal
Passages North
Paterson Literary Review
Pavement Saw
Peace & Freedom
Pearl
Pegasus Review, The
PEN American Center
Pennwriters Annual Conference
People's Press, The
Peregrine
Permafrost
Phoebe (VA)
Piano Press
Pif Magazine
Pig Iron
Pikeville Review
Plainsongs
Pleiades
Plowman, The
Poems & Plays
Poet Born Press, A
Poetic License Poetry Magazine
Poetic Link, The
Poetry
Poetry & Prose Annual
Poetry Forum
Poetry Greece
Poetry Ireland Review

Poetry Life
Poetry Northwest
Poetry Review
Poetry Society of America
Poetry Society of Tennessee
Poetry Society of Texas, The
Poets at Work
Poets House
Potomac Review
Potpourri
Pottersfield Portfolio
Prairie Schooner
presstheEDGE
Pudding House Publications
Quantum Leap
Quarter After Eight
Raintown Review, The
RB's Poets' Viewpoint
Red Booth Review
Red Crow
Red Hen Press
River Styx Magazine
Riverstone
Rockford Review, The
Romantics Quarterly
Ruah
Runes, A Review Of Poetry
San Diego State University Writers'
    Conference
Sandhills Writers Conference, The
Santa Barbara Writers' Conference
Sarabande Books, Inc.
Scavenger's Newsletter
Scroll Publications Inc.
Seedhouse
Seeds Poetry Magazine
Shenandoah
Silver Wings/Mayflower Pulpit
Silverfish Review Press
Sinipee Writers Workshop
Skidrow Penthouse
Skipping Stones
Slate & Style
Slipstream
Smartish Pace
Snapshots
Snowapple Press
So To Speak
Society of American Poets, The
South Boston Literary Gazette, The
South Dakota State Poetry Society
Southern California Anthology, The
Southern California Writers'
    Conference
Southern Humanities Review
Southern Poetry Association
Southern Poetry Review
Southwest Writers Contest and
    Conference

Sow's Ear Poetry Review, The
Spoon River Poetry Review, The
Stand Magazine
Story Line Press
Storyteller, The
Studio
sub-TERRAIN
Taos Summer Writers' Workshop
Taproot Literary Review
Tears in the Fence
Thin Air Magazine
Thin Coyote
Thunder Rain Publishing
Time of Singing
Two Rivers Review
Understanding Magazine
University of Arizona Poetry Center
University of Georgia Press
University of Iowa Press
University of Wisconsin Press
Unterberg Poetry Center of the 92nd
    Street Y, The
Uprising
Urban Spaghetti
Urthona Magazine
Vegetarian Journal
Victoria School of Writing
Virginia Quarterly Review, The
Voices Israel
Weber Studies
West Virginia Poetry Society
    (WVPS)
Westerly
Whiskey Island Magazine
White Eagle Coffee Store Press
White Pine Press
Whitecrow Foundation, Tahana
Willow Review
Wind Magazine
Wings Magazine, Inc.
Wisconsin Fellowship of Poets
Wisconsin Regional Writers'
    Association Inc.
Worcester Review
Word Press
Word Works, The
World-Wide Writers Service, Inc.
Writer's Block Magazine
Writer's Exchange
Writers' Federation of Nova Scotia
Writers Guild of Alberta
Writers' News
Writers' Union of Canada, The
Yale University Press
Yankee Magazine
Yeats Society of New York, W.B.
Yemassee
Zillah

State & Provincial Grants

Arts councils in the United States and Canada provide assistance to artists (including poets) in the form of fellowships or grants. These grants can be substantial and confer prestige upon recipients; however, **only state or province residents are eligible**. Because deadlines and available support vary annually, query first (with a SASE).

UNITED STATES ARTS AGENCIES

Alabama State Council on the Arts, *201 Monroe St., Montgomery AL 36130-1800. (334)242-4076. E-mail: staff @arts.state.al.us. Website: www.arts.state.al.us.*

Alaska State Council on the Arts, *411 W. Fourth Ave., Suite 1-E, Anchorage AK 99501-2343. (907)269-6610 or (888)278-7424. E-mail: info@aksca.org. Website: www.aksca.org.*

Arizona Commission on the Arts, *417 W. Roosevelt, Phoenix AZ 85003. (602)255-5882. E-mail: general@ArizonaArts.org. Website: http://az.arts.asu.edu/artscomm/.*

Arkansas Arts Council, *1500 Tower Bldg., 323 Center St., Little Rock AR 72201. (501)324-9766. E-mail: info@dah.state.ar.us. Website: www.arkansasaarts.com.*

California Arts Council, *1300 I St., Suite 930, Sacramento CA 95814. (916)322-6555. E-mail: cac@cwo.com. Website: www.cac.ca.gov/.*

Colorado Council on the Arts, *750 Pennsylvania St., Denver CO 80203-3699. (303)894-2617. E-mail: coloarts@artswire.org. Website: www.coloarts.state.co.us/.*

Connecticut Commission on the Arts, *755 Main St., 1 Financial Plaza, Hartford CT 06103. (860)566-4770. Website: www.ctarts.org.*

Delaware State Arts Council, *Carvel State Office Bldg., 820 N. French St., Wilmington DE 19801. (302)577-8278. E-mail: delarts@artswire.org. Website: www.artsdel.org.*

District of Columbia Commission on the Arts & Humanities, *410 Eighth St., 5th Floor, Washington DC 20004. (202)724-5613. E-mail: dcarts@dcgov.org. Website: http://dcarts.dc.gov.*

Florida Arts Council, *Division of Cultural Affairs, Florida Dept. of State, The Capitol, Tallahassee FL 32399-0250. (850)487-2980. Website: www.dos.state.fl.us/dcal/.*

Georgia Council for the Arts, *530 Means St. NW, Suite 115, Atlanta GA 30318-5793. (404)651-7920. Website: www.state.ga.us/georgia-arts/.*

Hawaii State Foundation on Culture & Arts, *44 Merchant St., Honolulu HI 96813. (808)586-0300. E-mail: sfca@sfca.state.hi.us. Website: www.state.hi.us/sfca.*

Idaho Commission on the Arts, *P.O. Box 83720, Boise ID 83720-0008. (208)334-2119 or (800)278-3863. E-mail: bgarrett ca.state.id.us. Website: www2.state.id.us/arts.*

Illinois Arts Council, *100 W. Randolph, Suite 10-500, Chicago IL 60601. (312)814-6750. E-mail: info@arts.state.il.us. Website: www.state.il.us/agency/iac.*

Indiana Arts Commission, *402 W. Washington St., Indianapolis IN 46204-2739. (317)232-1268. E-mail: arts@state.in.us. Website: www.state.in.us/iac/.*

Iowa Arts Council, *600 E. Locust, Capitol Complex, Des Moines IA 50319-0290. (515)281-4451. Website: www.culturalaffairs.org/iac/.*

Kansas Arts Commission, *SW 700 Jackson, Suite 1004, Topeka KS 66603. (785)296-3335. Website: http://arts.state.ks.us/.*

Kentucky Arts Council, *Old Capitol Annex, 300 W. Broadway, Frankfort KY 40601-1942. (502)564-3757. E-mail: kyarts@mail.state.ky.us. Website: www.kyarts.org.*

Louisiana State Arts Council, *P.O. Box 44247, Baton Rouge LA 70804-4247. (225)342-8180. E-mail: arts@crt.state.la.us. Website: www.crt.state.la.us/arts/.*

Maine Arts Commission, *55 Capitol St., 25 State House Station, Augusta ME 04333-0025. (207)287-2724. E-mail: jan.poulin@state.me.us. Website: www.mainearts.com.*

Maryland State Arts Council, *175 West Ostend St., Suite E, Baltimore MD 21230. (410)767-6555. E-mail: tcolvin@mdbusiness.state.md.us. Website: www.msac.org/.*

Massachusetts Cultural Council, *10 St. James Ave., 3rd Floor, Boston MA 02116. (617)727-3668. E-mail: web@art.state.ma.us. Website: www.massculturalcouncil.org/.*

Michigan Council for Arts & Cultural Affairs, *525 W. Ottawa, P.O. Box 30705, Lansing MI 48909. (313)256-3735. E-mail: artsinfo@cis.state.mi.us. Website: www.commerce.state.mi.us/arts/home.htm.*

Minnesota State Arts Board, *Park Square Court, 400 Sibley St., Suite 200, St. Paul MN 55101-1928. (651)215-1600 or (800)8MN-ARTS. E-mail: msab@state.mn.us. Website: www.state.mn.us/ebranch.msab.*

Mississippi Arts Commission, *239 N. Lamar St., Suite 207, Jackson MS 39201. (601)359-6030. E-mail: vlindsay@arts.state.ms.us. Website: www.arts.state.ms.us/.*

Missouri Arts Council, *111 N. Seventh St., Suite 105, St. Louis MO 63101-2188. (314)340-6845. E-mail: moarts@mail.state.mo.us. Website: www.missouriartscouncil.org.*

Montana Arts Council, *P.O. Box 202201, Helena MT 59620-2201. (406)444-6430. E-mail: mac@state.mt.us. Website: www.art.state.mt.us.*

Nebraska Arts Council, *3838 Davenport St., Omaha NE 68131-2329. (402)595-2122. Website: www.nebraskaartscouncil.org.*

Nevada State Council on the Arts, *716 N. Curry, Suite A, Carson City NV 89701. (775)687-6680. Website: http://dmla.clan.lib.nv.us/docs/arts.*

New Hampshire State Council on the Arts, *40 N. Main St., Concord NH 03301-4974. (603)271-2789. Website: http://webster.state.nh.us/nharts.*

New Jersey State Council on the Arts, *P.O. Box 306, 225 W. State St., Trenton NJ 08625. (609)292-6130. E-mail: njsca@arts.sos.state.nj.us. Website: www.artswire.org/Artswire/njsca/.*

New Mexico Arts Division, *P.O. Box 1450, Santa Fe NM 87504-1450. (505)827-6490. Website: www.artsnet.org/nmu.*

New York State Council on the Arts, *915 Broadway, New York NY 10010. (212)387-7000. Website: www.nysca.org.*

North Carolina Arts Council, *Dept. of Cultural Resources, Raleigh NC 27699-4632. (919)733-2111. Website: www.ncarts.org/home.html.*

North Dakota Council on the Arts, *418 E. Broadway, Suite 70, Bismarck ND 58501-4086. (701)328-3954. E-mail: comserv@state.nd.us. Website: www.state.nd.us/arts/index.html.*

Ohio Arts Council, *727 E. Main St., Columbus OH 43205-1796. (614)466-2613. E-mail: wlawson@mail.oac.ohio.gov. Website: www.oac.state.oh.us/home.html.*

Oklahoma Arts Council, *P.O. Box 52001-2001, Oklahoma City OK 73152-2001. (405)521-2931. E-mail: okarts@arts.state.ok.us. Website: www.state.ok.us/~arts/.*

Oregon Arts Commission, *775 Summer St. NE, Suite 200, Salem OR 97310-1280. (503)986-0123. E-mail: oregon.artscomm@state.or.us. Website: http://art.econ.state.or.us/.*

Pennsylvania Council on the Arts, *Room 216, Finance Bldg., Harrisburg PA 17120. (717)787-6883. Website: www.artsnet.org/pca/.*

Institute of Puerto Rican Culture, *P.O. Box 9024184, San Juan PR 00902-4184. (787)725-5137.*

Rhode Island State Council on the Arts, *83 Park St., 6th Floor, Providence RI 02903. (401)222-3880. E-mail: info@risca.state.ri.us. Website: www.risca.state.ri.us/.*

South Carolina Arts Commission, *1800 Gervais St., Columbia SC 29201. (803)734-8696. Website: www.state.sc.us/arts/.*

South Dakota Arts Council, *800 Governors Dr., Pierre SD 57501-2294. (605)773-3131. E-mail: sdac@stlib.state.sd.us. Website: www.state.sd.us/state/executive/deca/sdarts/.*

Tennessee Arts Commission, *401 Charlotte Ave., Nashville TN 37243-0780. (615)741-1701. Website: www.arts.state.tn.us/index.html.*

Texas Commission on the Arts, *P.O. Box 13406, Austin TX 78711-3406. (512)463-5535. E-mail: front.desk@arts.state.tx.us. Website: www.arts.state.tx.us/.*

Utah Arts Council, *716 E. South Temple, Salt Lake City UT 84102-1177. (801)236-7555. Website: www.dced.state.ut.us/arts/index.html.*

Vermont Arts Council, *136 State St., Drawer 33, Montpelier VT 05602. (802)828-3291. E-mail: info@arts.vca.state.vt.us. Website: www.vermontartscouncil.org.*

Virgin Islands Council on the Arts, *41-42 Norre Gada, P.O. Box 103, St. Thomas VI 00804. (340)774-5984. E-mail: vicouncil@slands.vi.*

Virginia Commission for the Arts, *Lewis House, 2nd Floor, 223 Governor St., Richmond VA 23219-2010. (804)225-3132. E-mail: vacomm@artswire.org. Website: www.artswire.org/~vacomm/.*

Washington State Arts Commission, *234 E. Eighth Ave., P.O. Box 42675, Olympia WA 98504-2675. (360)753-3860. E-mail: wsac@artswire.org. Website: www.wa.gov/art/.*

West Virginia Arts Commission, *Cultural Center, 1900 Kanawha Blvd. E., Charleston WV 25305-0300. (304)558-0220. Website: www.wvculture.org/arts/.*

Wisconsin Arts Board, *101 E. Wilson St., 1st Floor, Madison WI 53702. (608)266-0190. E-mail: artsboard@arts.state.wi.us. Website: http://arts.state.wi.us.*

Wyoming Arts Council, *2320 Capitol Ave., Cheyenne WY 82002. (307)777-7742. Website: commerce.state.wy.us/cr/arts/index.htm.*

CANADIAN PROVINCES ARTS AGENCIES

Alberta Foundation for the Arts, *901 Standard Life Centre, 10405 Jasper Ave., 9th Floor, Edmonton, Alberta T5J 4R7. (780)427-6315. Website: www.affta.ab.ca/.*

British Columbia Arts Council, *P.O. Box 9819, Stn. Prov. Gov., Victoria, British Columbia V8W 9W3. (250)356-1718. Website: www.bcartscouncil.gov.bc.ca.*

The Canada Council, *350 Albert St., P.O. Box 1047, Ottawa, Ontario K1P 5V8. (613)566-4414. Website: www.canadacouncil.ca/.*

Manitoba Arts Council, *525-93 Lombard Ave., Winnipeg, Manitoba R3B 3B1. (204)945-2237. E-mail: manart1@mb.sympatico.ca. Website: www.artscouncil.mb.ca.*

New Brunswick Department of Economic Development, Tourism & Culture, *Arts Branch, P.O. Box 6000, Fredericton, New Brunswick E3B 5H1. (506)453-3984.*

Newfoundland & Labrador Arts Council, *P.O. Box 98. St. John's, Newfoundland A1C 5H5. (709)726-2212. E-mail: nlacmail@newcomm.net. Website: www.nlac.nf.ca/.*

Nova Scotia Arts Council, *P.O. Box 1559, CRO, Halifax, Nova Scotia B3J 2Y3. (902)422-1123. E-mail: nsartscouncil@ns.sympatico.ca. Website: www.novascotiaartscouncil.ns.ca.*

Ontario Arts Council, *151 Bloor St. W., 5th Floor, Toronto, Ontario M5S 1T6. (416)961-1660. E-mail: info@arts.on.ca. Website: www.arts.on.ca/.*

Prince Edward Island Council of the Arts, *115 Richmond, Charlottetown, Prince Edward Island C1A 1H7. (902)368-4410.*

Saskatchewan Arts Board, *3475 Albert St., Regina, Saskatchewan S4S 6X6. (306)787-4056. Website: www.artsboard.sk.ca.*

Yukon Arts Branch, *Box 2703, Whitehorse, Yukon Y1A 2C6. (867)667-8589. E-mail: arts@gov.yk.ca. Website: www.artsyukon.com.*

Resources
Conferences & Workshops

As poets, we keep learning day to day. Perhaps a helpful comment on a rejection slip, feedback from a writer's group, or an enlightening essay by an admired master provides that special lesson we need to improve our writing just that much more.

However, there are times when we want to immerse ourselves in learning. Or perhaps we crave a change of scenery, the creative stimulation of being around other artists, or the uninterrupted productivity of time alone to work.

That's what this section of *Poet's Market* is all about. Not only will you find a selection of writing conferences and workshops listed, but also artist colonies and retreats, poetry festivals, and even a few opportunities to go travelling with your muse. These listings give the basics: contact information, a brief description of the event, lists of past presenters, and offerings that may be of special interest to poets. If an event interests you, get in touch with the director for additional information, including up-to-date costs and housing details. (Please note that most directors had not finalized their 2002 plans when we contacted them for this edition of *Poet's Market*. However, where possible, they provided us with their 2001 dates, costs, faculty names, or themes to give you a better idea of what each event has to offer.)

Before you seriously consider a conference, workshop, or other event, determine what you hope to get out of the experience. Would a general conference with one or two poetry workshops among many other types of sessions be acceptable? Or are you looking for something exclusively focused on poetry? Do you want to hear poets speak about poetry writing, or are you looking for a more participatory experience such as a one-on-one critiquing session or a group workshop? Do you mind being one of hundreds of attendees or do you prefer a more intimate setting? Are you willing to invest in the expense of travelling to a conference, or would something local better suit your budget? Keep these questions and others in mind as you read these listings, view websites, and study conference brochures.

Some listings are coded with symbols to provide certain "information at a glance." The (N) symbol indicates a listing new to this edition; the (☑) symbol signals a change in the contact information for that listing. The (☒) symbol denotes a Canadian listing and the (🌐) symbol an international one.

Finally, this section includes an Insider Report about **Cave Canem**, the renowned African-American poetry workshop, and its founders **Toi Derricotte** and **Cornelius Eady**. See this piece on page 425 for a moving account of the workshop's creation and how much a conference/workshop experience can mean to a poet.

For additional information about workshops and conferences, see *The Guide to Writers Conferences* by ShawGuides (or log on to www.shawguides.com) and *Writer's Market* as well as *Writer's Digest*, *The Writer*, and *Poets & Writers*.

☑ **AMERICAN CHRISTIAN WRITERS CONFERENCES**, P.O. Box 110390, Nashville TN 37222. (800)21-WRITE. E-mail: regaforder@aol.com. Website: www.ecpa.org/acw. **Director:** Reg Forder. Established 1981. Annual 2-day events, 30 conferences/year held in cities including Houston, Boston, Minneapolis, Chicago, St. Louis, Detroit, Atlanta, Miami, Phoenix, and Los Angeles. Location: Usually a major hotel chain like Holiday Inn. Average attendance: 50-80.
Purpose/Features: Open to anyone. Conferences cover fiction, poetry, writing for children.

Costs/Accommodations: Cost is $99-169, participants responsible for their own meals. Accommodations include special rates at host hotel.

Additional Info: Also sponsors an annual Caribbean Christian Writers Conference Cruise each November. Brochure and registration form available for SASE.

⊞ ANTIOCH WRITERS' WORKSHOP, P.O. Box 494, Yellow Springs OH 45387. (877)914-3349. E-mail: ml_Carpenter@yahoo.com. Website: writersworkshop@yellowsprings.com (includes workshop, faculty, schedule, and housing information, registration form). **Director:** Mindy Carpenter. Established 1986. Annual 7-day event usually held in late July or early August. Location: Antioch College in the village of Yellow Springs. "The campus is quiet, shady, relaxed. The village is unusual for its size: a hotbed of artists, writers, and creative people." Average attendance: 70.

Purpose/Features: Open to everyone. "We create an intense community of writers and cover fiction, poetry, and nonfiction. Also talks by editors, agents, and others in the industry." Offerings for poets include an introductory class in writing poetry, intensive seminar, night sessions for participants to share poetry, and critiquing. 2001 conference faculty included David Lee Garrison, Julia Levine, and William Least Heat Moon.

Costs/Accommodations: 2001 conference tuition was $460 regular, $410 local/returning participants, with a $50 nonrefundable registration fee. Scholarships available (including the Judson Jerome Scholarship sponsored by *Writer's Digest* magazine). Both graduate and undergraduate credit available for an additional fee. Campus dining room meal ticket is $27.50 (for 5 meals, breakfast, lunch, or dinner); must be purchased in advance, or single meals may be purchased at the door. Banquet before keynote address (optional but recommended) costs $19. Information on overnight accommodations available and includes local hotels, camping, or lodging with a village host.

Additional Info: Individual critiques available. Submit work for critique in advance with $60 fee for poetry, fiction, nonfiction, or plays. Brochure and registration form available for SASE or on website.

⊕ ART WORKSHOPS IN GUATEMALA, 4758 Lyndale Ave. S., Minneapolis MN 55409-2304. (612)825-0747. Fax: (612)825-6637. E-mail: info@artguat.org. Website: www.artguat.org (includes complete information). **Director:** Liza Fourré. Established 1995. Ten-day creative writing courses offered by educational travel program. Location: workshops held in Antigua, the old colonial capital of Guatemala. 2002 dates to be announced. Average attendance: limit 10 students.

Purpose/Features: Offerings for poets include "Poetry/Snapshots in Words" with Roseann Lloyd and "Voice of the Soul" with Sharon Doubiago. "This workshop is designed for those desiring to write from their true voice through aesthetic exercises, self-exploration, memory retrieval, independent writing, and lively class discussions."

Costs/Accommodations: Cost is $1,725; includes "air transportation from US, tuition, lodging in a beautiful old colonial home, a hearty breakfast, ground transport, and some pretty interesting field trips." Offers the "Buddy Discount. If you've already attended one of our workshops and tell a friend who decides to take a workshop, too, you'll get $50 off the tuition of your next workshop." Lodging and classes held in private home; overflow goes to nearby hotels.

Additional Info: Call, write, e-mail, fax, or check website.

⊞ ASHLAND WRITERS CONFERENCE, 295 E. Main St., #5, Ashland OR 97520. (541)482-2783. Fax: (541)482-4923. E-mail: awcore@aol.com. Website: www.ashlandwriters.com. Director: Jonah Bornstein. Annual five-day workshop/conference. Established in 1997. Students work with a specified instructor three hours daily for five days and in individual conferences. Usually held last week of July or first week of August. Location: Southern Oregon University. Registration limited.

Purpose/Features: Designed to provide intensive writing and learning experience with workshops, writing time, panel discussions, and faculty readings. Open to all writers, beginners to advanced. Workshops cover poetry, fiction, and creative nonfiction. Speakers/panelists for past conferences have included Yusef Komunyakaa, Mark Jarman, Sharon Olds, Quincy Troupe, Olga Broumas, Sharon Doubiago, Dana Gioia, Dorianne Laux.

Costs/Accommodations: 2000 conference cost was $400. Does not include meals or lodging. Housing available at university residence halls for less than $200 for the week. Other accommodations available through the Ashland Chamber of Commerce, (541)482-3486. Ashland is home of the world class Oregon Shakespeare Festival; tickets for a specific play are available through the conference.

Additional Info: Participants send four poems (no more than six pages) or six prose pages with registration for instructors to familiarize themselves with student's work. Additional individual conferences may be available with conference staff/writers.

☑ ASPEN SUMMER WORDS WRITING RETREAT AND LITERARY FESTIVAL; ASPEN WRITERS' FOUNDATION, P.O. Drawer 7726, Aspen CO 81612. (970)925-3122 or (800)925-2526. Fax: (970)920-5700. E-mail: Aspenwrite@aol.com. Website: www.aspenwriters.org (includes general information about Aspen Writers' Foundation, including history; all programs; registration forms; information about past presenters; and links to visiting Aspen). **Executive Director:** Julie Comins. Established 1976. Three-day writing retreat, followed by three-day literary festival. Held the third week of June. Location: The Aspen Institute, Aspen Meadows campus, or other site in Aspen. Average attendance: 100-200 for the festival, 50 for the retreat.

Purpose/Features: Open to all writers. Retreat includes intensive workshops in poetry, fiction, memoir, and essay. Offerings for poets include poetry workshops, craft lectures, and readings by faculty and participants. Faculty at past conferences included Carol Muske (poetry), Ron Carlson (fiction), and Madeline Blais (memoir and essay).

Costs/Accommodations: Cost for retreat is $325; cost for the Literary Festival is $150; cost for both is $475. Transportation to and from on-site lodging and event available. Information on overnight accommodations available for registrants. Cost of accommodations was $60/person/day double occupancy or $120/person/day single occupancy.

Additional Info: "We accept poetry manuscripts in advance that will be discussed during workshop." Brochure and registration form available for SASE or on website, or request by phone, fax, or e-mail. Include mailing address with all e-mail requests.

AUSTIN WRITERS' LEAGUE SPRING AND FALL WORKSHOPS (soon to be The Writers' League of Texas); THE AUSTIN WRITERS' LEAGUE; THE AUSTIN WRITER, P.O. Box 33096, Austin TX 78764-0096. (512)499-8914. Fax: (512)499-0441. E-mail: awl@writersleague.org. Website: www.writersleague.org. **Executive Director:** Jim Bob McMillan. Established 1982. Biannual workshops "usually three- or six-hour sessions. Intensive classes last from 10-15 weeks and meet for three hours each week." Usually held weekends in March, April, May; and September, October, November. Location: Austin Writers' League Resource Center/Library. Average attendance: limited.

Purpose/Features: Open to all writers, beginners and advanced. Workshops cover fiction, poetry, writing for children, nonfiction, screenwriting, book promotion/marketing, working with agents/publishers, journal writing, special interest writing, creativity, grantwriting, copyright law, and taxes for writers. Offerings for poets include at least 2 workshops during each series. Poetry presenters have included Ralph Angel, Rosellen Brown, Reginald Gibbons, and Marion Winik. Past speakers have included Sandra Scofield, Sue Grafton, Peter Mehlman, Gregg Levoy, Lee Merrill Byrd, and several New York agents and editors. "Occasionally, presenters agree to do private consults with participants. Also, workshops may incorporate hands-on practice and critique."

Costs/Accommodations: Cost is $35-75. Members get discount.

Additional Info: Requirements for critiques are posted in workshop brochure. Brochure and registration form available for SASE or request by fax or e-mail (include mailing address). The Austin Writers' League publishes *The Austin Writer*, a monthly publication of prose and poetry selected from submissions each month. Poetry guidelines for other publications, awards and grants programs, and market listings are available through the League library.

BREAD LOAF WRITERS' CONFERENCE; BAKELESS LITERARY PUBLICATION PRIZES, Middlebury College, Middlebury VT 05753. (802)443-5286. Fax: (802)443-2087. E-mail: blwc@middlebury.edu. Website: www.middlebury.edu/~blwc. **Administrative Coordinator:** Noreen Cargill. Established 1926. Annual 11-day event usually held in mid-August. Average attendance: 230.

Purpose/Features: Conference is designed to promote dialogue among writers and provide professional critiques for students. Conference usually covers fiction, nonfiction, and poetry.

Costs/Accommodations: 2001 conference cost was $1,798, including tuition, room, and board. Fellowships and scholarships for the conference available. "Candidates for fellowships must have a book published. Candidates for scholarships must have published in major literary periodicals or newspapers. A letter of recommendation, application, and supporting materials due by March 15. Awards are announced in June for the conference in August." Taxis to and from the airport or bus station are available.

Additional Info: Individual critiques also available. Sponsors the Bakeless Literary Publication Prizes, an annual book series competition for new authors of literary works in poetry, fiction, and creative nonfiction. Details, conference brochure, and application form are available for SASE or on website. Accepts inquiries by fax and e-mail.

BRISTOL POETRY FESTIVAL, 20-22 Hepburn Rd., Bristol B52 8UD United Kingdom. Phone: (0044)117 9426976. Fax: (0044)117 9441478. E-mail: festival@poetrycan.demon.co.uk. Website: www.poetrycan.demon.co.uk (includes information about the festival, Poetry Can, projects, published poetry, links). **Festival Director:** Hester Cockcroft. Established 1996. Annual, usually held in October. Location: across the city of Bristol in a variety of venues. Average attendance: about 6,000.

Purpose/Features: Open to "everyone who is interested, from practicing poets to the general public. The festival aims to celebrate the best in local, national, and international poetry in all its manifestations, with events for everyone including performances and workshops, competitions and exhibitions, public poetry interventions, community work, cross art form, and digital projects." Offerings for poets include master classes from famous poets, workshops on poetry writing and performance, debates, and competitions.

Costs/Accommodations: Cost varies. "Discounts are available for students, elderly people, the unwaged, or the disabled."

Additional Info: Accepts inquiries by fax and e-mail. "Bristol Poetry Festival is organized and funded by Bristol's Poetry Development Agency, the Poetry Can, which is based at the same address and managed by the same personnel."

CANYONLANDS WRITERS RIVER TRIP, P.O. Box 68, Moab UT 84532. (435)259-7750. Fax: (435)259-2335. E-mail: cfinfo@canyonlandsfieldinst.org. Website: www.canyonlandsfieldinst.org. **Contact:** registrar. Established 2000. Annual usually held for five days in August on the San Juan or Colorado River. Average attendance: is a maximum of 16.

Purpose/Features: Open to all. Workshop covers instruction/critique on writing about relationships to the natural world while floating down the river observing anazazi ruins and red rock walls.

Costs/Accommodations: Cost ranges from $500-600, includes instruction, lodging, all river meals.

[N] CAPE COD WRITERS' CENTER SUMMER CONFERENCE, % Cape Cod Writers' Center, P.O. Box 186, Barnstable MA 02630. (508)375-0516. Fax: (508)362-2718. E-mail: ccwc@capecod.net. Website: www.capecod.net/writers (includes event schedules, conference/workshop information, news about members and the World Television Interview Program). **Executive Director:** Jacqueline M. Loring. Established 1963. Annual week-long event usually held the third week of August. Location: the Craigville Conference Center in a rustic setting overlooking Nantucket Sound. Average attendance: 150.

Purpose/Features: Open to everyone. Covers poetry, fiction, mystery writing, nonfiction, children's writing, screenwriting, plus one-evening Master Class.

Costs/Accommodations: Participants responsible for their own meals. "It is recommended that participants stay at the Craigville Conference Center (early registration necessary)." Other housing information available from Bed & Breakfast Cape Cod.

Additional Info: Manuscript evaluations and personal conferences also available. For ms evaluation, submit a few poems, short story, article, or one book chapter by July 1st. Cost, brochure, and registration form available for SASE or on website. Accepts inquiries by fax and e-mail. Sponsors workshops and seminars in the fall and spring.

[N] CAVE CANEM, P. O. Box 4286, Charlottesville VA 22905-4286. E-mail: cavecanempoets@aol.com. **Contact:** Carolyn Micklem, foundation director. Established 1996. Annual week-long workshop for African-American poets. 2001 dates: June 24-July 1. Location: the beautiful grounds of the Cranbrook Schools in Bloomfield Hills, MI. Average attendance: 50.

Purpose/Features: Open to all African-American poets. Participants selected based on a sample of 6-8 poems. Offerings include workshops by fellows and faculty and evening readings. Participants are assigned to groups of about 8 and remain together throughout session, with different faculty leading each workshop. 2001 faculty included Toi Derricotte, Cornelius Eady, Nikky Finney, Harryette Mullen, Sonia Sanchez, and Tim Seibles, with guest poets Elizabeth Alexander and Sekou Sundiata.

Costs/Accommodations: 2001 cost was $450. For complete information contact Cave Canem.

Additional Information: Poets should submit 6-8 poems with cover letter. 2001 postmark deadline was March 15, with accepted poets notified by April 20. Cave Canem Foundation also sponsors the Cave Canem Poetry Prize (see separate listing in Contest & Awards section). Accepts queries by regular mail and e-mail.

[N] [■] CHAUTAUQUA WRITING SEMINARS. E-mail: vandeneynden@fuse.net. Website: www.creative writing.cc (includes class overviews, courses in creative writing, discussion threads). **President:** Keith Vanden Eynden. Established 1999. "We offer online writing seminars. Students can read the lessons at their convenience. They post comments to a discussion thread, so no matter what their work schedule, they can get feedback from other writers."

Purpose/Features: "It's difficult to hold a day job and focus on your writing. Writing groups and classes are helpful, but you have to make a commitment to meet at a specific time each week. It's much easier if you can participate any time you are free." Contact by e-mail for further information.

THE COLLEGE OF NEW JERSEY WRITERS CONFERENCE, College of New Jersey, Department of English, P.O. Box 7718, Ewing NJ 08628-0718. (609)771-3254. E-mail: write@tcnj.edu. **Director:** Jean Hollander. Established 1981. Annual 1-day event usually held in April at the College of New Jersey campus. Average attendance: 800.

Purpose/Features: Open to anyone. Conference covers all genres of writing. "We usually have a special presentation on breaking into print." Offers 20 separate workshops as well as readings. Recent featured speaker was John Updike.

Costs/Accommodations: Cost for past conference was $40 for 1-day session; additional cost for workshops and evening session. Discounts available for students. Information on overnight accommodations available.

Fostering diversity in poetry

While vacationing in Italy in 1995, poet Toi Derricotte mentioned the idea of an African-American poetry workshop to fellow poet Cornelius Eady. "People have always thought about this and usually it goes no further than 'it would be a nice idea,' " Eady says. Then Eady's wife, Sarah Micklem, suggested "that we simply pay for it out of our own pockets—and that made all the difference because that meant we didn't have to go looking, waiting to see if we could get funding for this idea that's kind of strange, crazy. We didn't have to ask anybody." That simple suggestion gave the founders complete autonomy. Cave Canem became more than just "a nice idea."

Toi Derricotte and Cornelius Eady

The poetry workshop has been held annually since 1996 and serves as a haven for African-American poets to form bonds with one another. To promote relationships, the attendance is small—no more than forty or fifty poets; to achieve quality, the participants and faculty must have talent and skill to propel them to even greater levels of achievement.

History itself seems to have been awaiting Cave Canem. Virginia Woolf and Malcom X long ago endorsed a space for one's own self, one's own people, ideas that beckon from ancient times. Visiting the ruined city of Pompeii, Derricotte noticed the mosaic of a dog guarding the House of the Tragic Poet. She adopted the tiled picture as a logo, the Latin inscription Cave Canem ("Beware the Dog") as a name. "In one way," Derricotte says, "it's a spoof on literary traditions and yet it's also about our organization being a protector of the treasures of the African-American people, the memories and voices of these people."

With more than eleven books of poetry between them and many prestigious awards and fellowships, Derricotte and Eady have thoroughly navigated the world of poetry. Despite their success, they feel the need for a responsive, welcoming community where, as Derricotte says, African-American poets are "able to deal with material that brings forth the vulnerable side, to feel safe enough, that you're not going to be attacked or misunderstood. You're not going to be the only one.

"African-Americans have always had this special little slot over on the side as if we can't really do poetry like everybody else," Derricotte continues, "the sense that there's something within us that is inferior, either in spirit or intellect, that makes us incapable of doing great poetry."

To Eady, "African-Americans feel disenfranchised in writing programs because they realize they don't get that kind of 'I see who you are, I recognize you.' Even if you're perceived as a star of the program, you sometimes wonder under what conditions are you doing this? And what's the price?

"There is no price at Cave Canem. There is none of that pressure. We want to know what your story is, so tell us. Tell us what you are, tell us what you know, right? That's an important thing, that kind of recognition."

Once the initial idea of a workshop took hold, the founding of Cave Canem gathered momentum. "Toi immediately thought of a priest at a retreat center in upstate New York," Eady recalls. "She called him from Italy to explain what it was she wanted to do." The priest's response? "Yeah, sure, c'mon!"

"Once we had the idea that we could fund this and once we had a location, it was simply a matter of advertising and seeing who would show up. Which was the *scary* part!" Eady says with a laugh.

As it turned out, the Cave Canem concept of an African-American poetry workshop was very well received. Derricotte and Eady invited Michael Weaver and Elizabeth Alexander to join the faculty, and the two poets responded with enthusiasm. Then came the following summer when twenty participants arrived at the conference site. Says Eady, "Often when you get people from a lot of different points of view, a lot of aesthetics, they'll decide they cannot agree upon anything, cannot stay in the same space together. What people sort of realized toward the middle of the first week of the first year was that we had stumbled upon something very unique and precious, and we needed to protect it at all costs."

Even with the passage of time and a move from upstate New York to Cranbrook School in Michigan, that sense of community and family has only strengthened. Both Derricotte and Eady credit the workshop structure—about fifty people divided into four or five groups, with faculty rotating from group to group. "That's good," explains Derricotte, "because the group's main allegiance is to themselves and each other, not to their teacher. People really form a loyalty to the others in their group.

"One of the things that happens at Cave Canem that doesn't happen at any other place I've ever taught is people hug each other all the time," Derricotte adds. "Every time you pass somebody, you touch them, you hug them, you smile. You want to be close to these people; they're beautiful to you."

A highlight of the workshop session is the series of nightly readings, by participants as well as faculty. "That's where you get this range of voices and ages," Derricotte notes. "It's so exciting just to hear these people read in all of these diverse ways. It's so inspiring. People just leave there, you know, *high*!"

Eady agrees. "They're wonderful readers from the get-go. People feel permission to push themselves and take a chance. And people who are not necessarily comfortable reading all the time feel safe and able to do a couple really wonderful, wonderful readings of their own work."

Derricotte and Eady have noticed the effect of this choir of strong, variegated voices on audiences elsewhere. "When we had a reading at the Academy of American Poets, the director said it was one of the best he'd ever heard there," notes Derricotte. "The high quality of the work coupled with the diversity of the poets just blew people away."

Once their initial workshop is completed, Cave Canem participants may return to any two sessions during the next five years. Derricotte explains, "If we keep this small family group of 50 people and 40 people stay every year, we're not going to have many spaces. Last year we had 108 applicants for 12 spaces."

An applicant's manuscript must stand out. "A good manuscript is one that announces itself, says that writer is ready, has some experience and skill, is on to something," says Eady. "We look for some sense of uniqueness, and if we both can agree upon it, then that person gets into the workshop."

Once at Cave Canem, however, that manuscript is set aside. "Everybody has to write a poem everyday," Derricotte states firmly. "We're not coming here to decide whether the comma you put in ten years ago should be taken out now. We're really here to work and talk about poetry that's alive for you."

When asked if Cave Canem poets write from an African-American tradition, Eady points out that such an idea is faulty. "The one thing Cave Canem basically illuminates is that there is no uniform tradition. There are a lot of different elements and interesting ebbs and currents within that tradition. Some may be writing from a more spiritual vocation, some might be writing experimentally or what people consider a very narrative form, right? But it all becomes part of the African-American aesthetic because what binds them together isn't the forms but the experiences they articulate."

From the start, Cave Canem has attracted skilled teachers and guest poets, including Harryette Mullen, Lucille Clifton, Sonia Sanchez, Tim Seibles, Sekou Sundiata, and Elizabeth Alexander, as well as Derricotte and Eady. Yusef Komunyakaa, Al Young, and Nikkey Finney will join the co-founders for the 2002 session. "We ask people who are excellent poets," says Eady. "What we really go for is how we feel about their work and their teaching."

Cave Canem has experienced remarkable serendipity to this point. Location, students, faculty—everything has fallen naturally into place as if these elements were simply biding time. "There's been a need for this kind of organization," says Derricotte. "But you have to have the support to do it. It takes a lot of support to do it well. And that's why it works, because we're doing this well."

Eady believes that Cave Canem, on some level, will "enact some sort of transition in the way we conceive what literature, American literature, is supposed to be about. I mean," Eady laughs, "in a small way."

Derricotte's vision is similar. "Cave Canem is showing that kind of mind we've had to develop in order to use all of the literary traditions. We've had to take in the knowledge of all of these things. Not only that, but the double consciousness you have to develop where you're always not only doing your own thing but looking through the eyes of an outsider. This has strengthened our poetry.

"I think in the next century, African-American poets are going to be the greatest poets in our country. That's what Cave Canem is doing right now. It's blowing people away, they can't believe all of the diversity. It's making people think, 'Wow, this is a different way of thinking about poetry.' "

—*Vanessa Lyman*

Additional Info: Writers of poetry, drama, journalism, literature for the young, nonfiction, and fiction may submit ms to be critiqued in writing by workshop leaders. Poetry and short story contest sponsored as part of conference. 1st Prize: $100; 2nd Prize: $50. Judges are workshop leaders and a special panel from the English Dept. Brochure and registration form available—write or call. Accepts inquiries by e-mail.

☑ **COLORADO MOUNTAIN WRITERS' WORKSHOP,** P.O. Box 85394, Tucson AZ 85754. (520)206-9479. E-mail: mfiles@pimacc.pima.edu. Website: www.sheilabender.com (includes information on upcoming conference, photos, and evaluations of previous conference). **Director:** Meg Files. Established 1999. Annual 5-day event. 2001 dates were June 25-29. Location: Steamboat Springs, CO, on the mountaintop campus of Colorado Mountain College. Average attendance: 50.

Purpose/Features: Open to all writers, beginning and experienced. "The workshop includes sessions on writing and publishing fiction, nonfiction, and poetry, as well as manuscript workshops and individual critiques and writing exercises." Faculty includes Sheila Bender, Jack Heffron, and Meg Files. Other special features include "a beautiful high-country site, extensive and intensive hands-on activities, individual attention, and a supportive atmosphere."

Costs/Accommodations: Cost is $300; dorm rooms and meals are available on site.

Additional Info: Individual critiques are available. Submit 5 poems in advance to Meg Files.

DESERT WRITERS WORKSHOP, P.O. Box 68, Moab UT 84532. (435)259-7750. Fax: (435)259-2335. E-mail: cfinfo@canyonlandsfieldinst.org. Website: www.canyonlandsfieldinst.org. **Contact:** Registrar. Established 1985. Annual 3-day event usually held the first weekend in November. Location: a ranch in the foothills of the LaSal Mountains. Attendance: maximum of 33.

Purpose/Features: Open to all. Workshop covers 3 categories—fiction, nonfiction, and poetry—and focuses on relationship to natural world.

Costs/Accommodations: Cost ranges from $440-520, including meals, instruction, and lodging. Scholarships available.

Additional Info: Individual critiques also available. Participants will be able to mail some samples to their instructor before the workshop for critique.

✅ **EASTERN KENTUCKY UNIVERSITY CREATIVE WRITING CONFERENCE**, Case Annex 467, Richmond KY 40475-3102. (859)622-5861. E-mail: engbrown@acs.eku.edu. Website: www.english.eku.edu/conferences (includes the brochure which lists the visiting writers and their bios, schedule of events, registration information, cost, etc.). **Co-Directors:** Dorothy Sutton and Harry Brown. Established 1964. Annual 5-day event usually held Monday through Friday of the third week in June. Location: Eastern Kentucky University. Average attendance: 15.

Purpose/Features: Open to poetry and fiction. Provides lectures, workshops, and private conferences with visiting writers to "help writers increase their skills in writing poetry and fiction." A ms of 4-8 poems (8 pgs. maximum) must be submitted by May 20 and accepted before enrollment in conference is allowed. Offerings for poets include workshop discussions and individual conferences. Visiting writers have included David Citino, X. J. Kennedy, Donald Justice, Greg Orr, Maggie Anderson, and Sena Naslund.

Costs/Accommodations: Costs are $106 undergraduate and $153 graduate (in-state fees), $287 undergraduate and $418 graduate (out-of-state fees); participants responsible for their own meals, available on campus. Cost for housing in on-site facilities is $57/week single occupancy, $41/week double occupancy. "Must bring your own sheets, pillow, blanket."

Additional Info: Brochure available for SASE or request by e-mail.

[N] FESTIVAL OF POETRY; CONFERENCE ON TEACHING AND POETRY, Robert Frost Place, Franconia NH 03580. (603)823-5510. E-mail: donald.sheehan@dartmouth.edu. Executive Director: Donald Sheehan. **Director of Admissions:** David Keller. Established 1978. Annual week-long event usually held first week of August at Robert Frost's mountain farm (house and barn), made into a center for poetry and the arts. Average attendance: 50-55.

Purpose/Features: Open to poets only. Faculty has included Maxine Kumin, Jean Valentine, Galway Kinnell, Grace Paley, Molly Peacock, Martin Espada, Dana Gioia, and Ellen Bryant Voigt.

Costs/Accommodations: Cost is $585 tuition, plus a $25 reading fee. "Room and board available locally; information sent upon acceptance to program."

Additional Info: Application should be accompanied by 3 sample pages of your work. Brochures and registration forms available for SASE. Also offers the Conference on Teaching and Poetry, an annual event usually held in late June. Guest faculty for 2001 were Betsy Sholl, Afaa Michael Weaver, Gray Jacobik, and David Graham. "The conference is intended for high school and middle school classroom teachers. Daily sessions include talks on poetry and teaching, workshops on teaching poems, workshops for teachers who write poems, and teacher sharing sessions as well as talks by working teachers on poetry in the curriculum." Fee for 4½-day program: $450 (NH teachers $350), plus $372 for 3 graduate credits. To apply, send letter describing current teaching situation and your literary interests, along with $15 processing fee to Donald Sheehan, Teacher Conference, The Frost Place, Franconia NH 03580.

FISHTRAP, P.O. Box 38, Enterprise OR 97828. (541)426-3623. E-mail: rich@fishtrap.org. Website: www.fishtrap.org (includes general information; information on writers retreat; winter and summer events, and ongoing programs in schools and local communities; fellowships; and updated dates and instructors/presenters). **Director:** Rich Wandschneider. Established 1988. Holds 3 annual 3- to 4-day events. 2001 dates were Winter Fishtrap—February 23-25; Summer Workshop—July 9-12; Summer Gathering—July 13-15. Location: "Winter site is a meeting room attached to a motel at Wallowa Lake, Oregon (off season); summer site is an old Methodist church camp." Average attendance: 50 for Winter Fishtrap ("always sold out"); 8 workshops (12 people/workshop) for Summer Workshop; 90 for Summer Gathering.

Purpose/Features: Open to anyone. "Fishtrap's goal is to promote good writing and clear thinking about the West. Also to encourage and promote new writers. There are always craft workshops on fiction, poetry, nonfiction; sometimes in children's writing, playwriting, radio, etc." Offerings for poets include a poetry workshop. Themes for 2001 were "Humor" (winter) and "Legacy of Vietnam" (summer).

Costs/Accommodations: Cost for 2001 Winter Fishtrap was $225-335 including meals (higher price includes lodging); Summer Workshop was $225, Gathering was $175, meals and lodging available at $32/day at camp. Lodging also available at nearby motels.

Additional Info: Awards 5 fellowships annually. Receives 80-100 entries/year. Most recent winners were Mary Tanquay Webb, Bucky Achilles, Ann Nelson, Geronimo Tagatac, and Kamala Bremer. "Award is room and board and workshop registration for Summer Fishtrap." Brochure and registration form available for SASE or request by e-mail. Each year the selected writings of workshop students and workshop instructors are published in an anthology.

N GIG HARBOR WRITERS' CONFERENCE, P. O. Box 826, Gig Harbor WA 98335. (253)265-1904. Fax: (253)265-8532. E-mail: ghwritersconf@aol.com. Website: http://ghkp-culturalarts.org/members/ (includes dates, place, presenters, bios, contact info). **Director:** Kathleen O'Brien. Established 1996. Annual 3-day conference usually held the first weekend in May. 2001 dates: May 4, 5, 6. Location: Wesley Inn in Gig Harbor, "a new Best Western with conference capabilities." Average attendance: 100.

Purpose/Features: Open to all writers, with sessions offered in poetry, fiction, nonfiction, and children's writing. Offerings for poets include workshops. 2001 faculty included Heather McHugh, Linda Andrews, Linda Burmeister-Davies, Greg Bear, and Peter Archer.

Costs/Accommodations: 2001 cost: $125, including lunch. Discounts for early registration. Offers special arrangements for transportation to and from the conference. Information on overnight accommodations is available. Special rates available at area hotels.

Additional Information: Poetry critiques available. Contests sponsored as part of conference. Brochures and registration forms available by fax, e-mail, or on website; also sent to those on mailing list. Accepts inquiries by fax and e-mail. Affiliated with AWP and WCC.

N GREEN LAKE WRITERS CONFERENCE, Green Lake Conference Center, W2511 State Highway 23, Green Lake WI 54941-9599. (800)558-8898. Fax: (920)294-3848. E-mail: blythean@greenlake-aba.org. Website: www.greenlake-aba.org (includes conference and registration information, accommodations, grounds and building descriptions). **Vice President of Adult Programming:** Blythe Ann Cooper. Established 1946. Annual weeklong event. 2001 dates: June 30 to July 1. Location: "Attendees stay in one of our three hotels. The Inn overlooks beautiful Green Lake 30 miles southwest of Oshkosh. Large private bath, double occupancy rooms, with singles available, extra charge. Located on 1,000 acres and is the national conference center for American Baptists. Alcoholic beverages are not permitted." Average attendance: 65-80.

Purpose/Features: Open to regional and national participants. Conference covers writing for children, fiction, autobiography, inspirational/devotional, humor, and feature articles. Instructors at last year's conference were Ellen Kort (poet laureate for Wisconsin), Carol Pierskalla, Barbara Smith, Deb D. Sandro, Janet Reihecky, and Jerry Apps.

Costs/Accommodations: Cost: $95 program fee plus $485.50/person for double occupancy room with meals. Camping available. Shuttle service to and from the airport provided for an additional fee. Information on overnight accommodations available for registrants.

Additional Info: Individual critiques also available. Call for brochure and registration form. Accepts inquiries by fax and e-mail. "A past participant wrote, 'I would recommend this conference to anyone committed to writing and sharing their work in a spiritual atmosphere. What I found to be most incredible was the fact that everyone was friendly, willing to talk, and incredibly generous with their time.' "

HARVARD SUMMER WRITING PROGRAM, 51 Brattle St., Dept. S810, Cambridge MA 02138. (617)495-4024. Fax: (617)495-9176. E-mail: summer@hudce.harvard.edu. Website: www.summer.harvard.edu (includes catalog, courses, program policies, and registration materials). Annual 8-week event. 2001 dates: June 25 through August 17. Location: Harvard University. Average attendance: 700.

Purpose/Features: Open to all levels, from beginner to published author. Course offerings include creative, expository, and professional writing. Offerings for poets include beginning poetry, intermediate poetry, and graduate level poetry courses. Other special features include small classes, undergraduate and graduate credit, individual conferences, access to the Writing Center at Harvard, visiting writers, a reading series, and a literary magazine. Instructors are writers, editors, and faculty members from Harvard as well as other universities.

Costs/Accommodations: 2001 conference cost was $1,800/course (2 courses considered full-time), plus $3,050 for room and board (dormitory housing).

Additional Info: Accepts inquiries by e-mail.

✓ HAYSTACK WRITING PROGRAM, Summer Session, Portland State University, P.O. Box 1491, Portland OR 97207. (800)547-8887, ext. 4186 or (503)725-4186. Fax: (503)725-4840. E-mail: herrinm@pdx.edu. Website: www.haystack.pdx.edu. **Director:** Maggie Herrington. Established 1969. Annual summer program. One-week and weekend courses over the five-week program. Location: local school of small coastal community; some evening lectures and other activities. Average attendance: 10-15/class; 400 total.

Purpose/Features: Open to all writers. One-week workshops cover fiction, poetry, mystery, screenplay, nonfiction, and more.

Costs/Accommodations: Cost for workshops is $125-450; participants pay for their own lodging and meals. Wide range of options for accommodations. Listing provided upon registration.

Additional Info: Brochure and registration form available by mail. Accepts inquiries by fax and e-mail.

HOFSTRA UNIVERSITY SUMMER WRITERS' CONFERENCE, Hofstra University, University College for Continuing Education, Hempstead NY 11549. (516)463-5016. Fax: (516)463-4833. E-mail: Kenneth.A.Henwood@hofstra.edu. Website: www.hofstra.edu/Academics/UCCE/ (includes descriptions of workshops, faculty bios, conference information, and registrations form). **Director:** Kenneth Henwood. Established 1972. Annual 10-day event usually starts the Monday after July 4th. Location: Hofstra University. Average attendance: 60-70.

Purpose/Features: Open to all writers. Conference covers fiction, nonfiction, poetry, children's writing, stage/screenwriting and, on occasion, one other area (science fiction, mystery, etc.). Guest speakers (other than the workshop leaders) "usually come from the world of publishing." There are also "readings galore and various special presentations."

Costs/Accommodations: 2000 conference cost was $400/workshop, $625 for 2. Additional fee of $350 for air-conditioned dorm room during conference. For those seeking credit, other fees apply.

Additional Info: Individual critiques also available. "Each writer receives a half hour one-on-one with each workshop leader." Does not sponsor a contest, but "we submit exceptional work to various progams sponsored by Writers Conferences and Festivals." Write for brochure and registration form (available as of April). Accepts inquiries by fax and e-mail.

⚙ IMAGINATION, Cleveland State University, English Dept., Euclid at 24th, Cleveland OH 44115. (216)687-4522. Fax: (216)687-6943. E-mail: n.chandler@csuohio.edu. **Director (Creative Writing Program):** Neal Chandler. Established 1991. Annual 5½-day event usually held in mid-July "in Mather Mansion, located on the campus of Cleveland State University. There are several large conference rooms and a number of smaller workshop rooms." Average attendance: 90.

Purpose/Features: Open to "all writers, in any genre, who have submitted a writing sample to the director and been accepted on the basis of that writing sample. *Imagination* is a writing conference about strong, imaginative writing from minimalism to magical realism; from mainstream to science fiction; from poetry to the novel. It includes classes and workshops without genre bias or boundaries. Courses are about distinctive creative writing, period." 2000 speakers and workshop leaders included Pamela Alexander, Samuel R. Delany, Candas Jane Dorsey, Elizabeth Evans, Karen Joy Fowler, Steve Lattimore, and David Young.

Costs/Accommodations: 2001 conference cost was $525 (higher with graduate or undergraduate credit). Participants responsible for their own meals. A limited number of scholarships available. Information on overnight accommodations available for registrants. "Limited housing is available on campus through the university. Campus housing is one block from conference site. Participants are responsible for their own transportation to and from the conference." Housing in on-site facilities costs approximately $35/night.

Additional Info: Individual critiques also available. "Every participant has her/his work critiqued twice—once in a workshop, once in an individual conference with another faculty member." Submit 8-10 pgs. to Dr. Neal Chandler with $10 fee. Send a first-class stamp for brochure and registration form. Accepts inquiries by fax and e-mail. Cleveland State University's Poetry Center publishes 2-6 books of poetry/year, including the winners of its national poetry prize competition. (See separate listing in the Publishers of Poetry section.)

✓ INDIANA UNIVERSITY WRITERS' CONFERENCE, Ballantine Hall 464, Indiana University, Bloomington IN 47405. (812)855-1877. Fax: (812)855-9535. E-mail: rrubinas@indiana.edu. Website: php.indiana.edu/~iuwc/. **Director:** Romayne Rubinas. Established 1940. Annual week-long event usually held the last week in June at the university student union. Average attendance: 100.

Purpose/Features: Open to all. Conference covers fiction, creative nonfiction, and poetry. Offerings for poets include workshops and classes. 2001 speakers/panelists in poetry included Susan Mitchell, Alan Shapiro, Jean Valentine, Cindy Chinelly, and Beth Ann Fennelly.

Costs/Accommodations: Cost for last conference was $200 for conference and classes, $300 for conference, classes, and one workshop; plus $25 application fee. Information on overnight accommodations available for registrants. "Rooms available in the student union or in a dorm."

Additional Info: Individual critiques also available. Submit 10 pgs. of poetry in advance. "All manuscripts are considered for scholarships." Brochure and registration form available for SASE. Accepts inquiries by fax and e-mail.

✓ IOWA SUMMER WRITING FESTIVAL, University of Iowa, 100 Oakdale Campus, W310, Iowa City IA 52242-5000. (319)335-4160. Fax: (319)335-4039. E-mail: iswfestival@uiowa.edu. Website: www.uiowa.edu/

VISIT THE WRITER'S DIGEST WEBSITE at www.writersdigest.com for books on craft, hot new markets, daily market updates, writers' guidelines and much more.

~iswfest (includes complete catalog of courses, faculty, workshop descriptions, registration forms, schedules, etc.). **Coordinator:** Amy Margolis. Established 1987. Annual event held each summer in June and July for six weeks. Includes one-week and weekend workshops at the University of Iowa campus. Average attendance: 150/week.
Purpose/Features: Open to "all adults who have a desire to write." Conference offers courses in nearly all writing forms. In 2001, offerings for poets included 21 classes for all levels. Poetry faculty included Michael Dennis Browne, Stuart Dischell, Ben Doyle, Vince Gotera, Timothy Liu, and Liz Waldner.
Costs/Accommodations: 2001 conference cost was $175 for a weekend course and $400-425 for a one-week course. Participants are responsible for their own meals. Accommodations available at the Iowa House and the Sheraton. Housing in residence hall costs about $29/night.
Additional Info: Participants in week-long workshops will have private conference/critique with workshop leader. Send for brochure and registration form. Requests for info are accepted by phone, fax, or e-mail.

THE IWWG SUMMER CONFERENCE, The International Women's Writing Guild, P.O. Box 810, Gracie Station, New York NY 10028. (212)737-7536. Fax: (212)737-9469. E-mail: dirhahn@aol.com. Website: www.iwwg.com. **Executive Director:** Hannelore Hahn. Established 1978. Annual week-long event usually held the second Friday in August through the following Friday. Location: Skidmore College in Saratoga Springs, NY. Average attendance: over 500.
Purpose/Features: Open to all women. Seventy workshops offered. "At least four poetry workshops offered for full week."
Costs/Accommodations: Cost is $860 for conference program and room and board.
Additional Info: "Critiquing available throughout the week." Brochure and registration form available for SASE. Accepts inquiries by e-mail (include mailing address for response). The International Women's Writing Guild's bimonthly newsletter features hundreds of outlets for poets. (See separate listing for The International Women's Writing Guild in the Organizations section.)

N KALANI HONUA OCEANSIDE ECO RESORT, RR2, Box 4500, Pahoa Beach Road HI 96778-9724. (808)965-7828 or (800)800-6886. Fax: (808)965-9613. E-mail: kalani@kalani.com. Website: www.kalani.com. Established 1980. **Director:** Richard Koob.
Purpose/Features: Offers 2-week to 2-month residencies on a year-round basis for visual, literary, folk, and performing artists. "Kalani Honua is situated near Kalapana on the big island of Hawaii on 113 acres of secluded forest and dramatic coastline, 45 minutes from the city of Hilo and 5 minutes from Hawaii Volcanoes National Park. Visitors stay in 3 two-story wooden lodges and 16 private cottage units that provide comfortable accommodations." Accommodates 100 (generally about 5 artists-in-residence) at a time in private rooms with full meal service plus optional kitchen facilities and shared or private baths; private desks and access to computers, ports and reference material available. Activities include a variety of yoga, dance, drawing, fitness, and mind/body classes; also available are an olympic pool, sauna, fitness room, and nearby beach and thermal springs.
Costs/Accommodations: Residency cost ranges from $105/night to $210/night (private cottage); plus $29/day for meals. Stipends are most available in the periods of May through July and September through December. Stipends provide for 50% of lodging costs; balance is responsibility of the artist (stipends may *not* be applied toward dorm lodging or camping, or reduction in food or transportation costs).
Additional Information: Application form and guidelines available for SASE, by e-mail, or on website. When sending application, include $10 fee.

☑ KEY WEST WRITERS' WORKSHOP, 5901 College Rd., Key West FL 33040. (305)296-9081, ext. 302. Fax: (305)292-2392. E-mail: weinman_i@firn.edu. Website: www.firn.edu/fkcc/kwww.htm (includes full details of current program/workshop leaders; all application information with form; information on travel and accommodations). **Director:** Irving Weinman. Established 1996. Five annual weekend events usually held from late January to early March. Location: "the conference room of Key West's historic Old City Hall—a modernized 1890's landmark building in the heart of the old town. Subsidiary activities (introductory get-together and optional Literary Walking Tour) also held in Old Town, Key West." Average attendance: limited to 10 for poetry weekends, 12 for fiction.
Purpose/Features: Open to all. However, "not for beginners." Workshop's purpose is to "bring the best writers into an intimate workshop setting with serious writers at all but beginning stages of their writing careers. Workshops are offered in poetry and fiction." Speakers/panelists for past workshops have included John Ashbery, Carolyn Forché, Sharon Olds, and Richard Wilbur.
Costs/Accommodations: 2001 conference cost was $275/weekend. Participants responsible for their own meals. Information on overnight accommodations available.
Additional Info: Brochure and registration form available for SASE. Accepts inquiries by fax and e-mail. "Interested poets will be put on our brochure mailing list for the upcoming season."

N LIFE PRESS CHRISTIAN WRITERS' CONFERENCE; LIFE PRESS CHRISTIAN WRITERS' ASSOCIATION, P.O. Box 241986, Memphis TN 38124. (901)682-6936. Fax: (901)682-8274. E-mail: grmeath @gateway.net. Website: www.grandmotherearth.com/ (includes contest rules, information about contest and publications). **Contact:** Frances Cowden. Established 1998. Annual 1-day event usually held the first or second Saturday in August. Location: "A church fellowship hall with nearby classroom for small critique groups." Average attendance: 45.

Purpose/Features: Open to all writers. Writing poetry or prose is the focus of the conference, with a special feature each year (for example, writing for children, humor, markets, etc.). A special humor workshop was presented in 2001. Offerings for poets include critiquing of work. 2001 speakers included Patricia Smith, Dr. Malra Treece, Mike Denington, Florence Bruce, and Cherry Pryon.

Costs/Accommodations: 2001 conference cost was $20, meals and other services included. Discounts available "upon request." Special arrangements for transportation to and from conference can be made "if prearranged and person stays in nearby hotel." Special overnight accommodations can be made.

Additional Info: Individual poetry critiques available. Poets should submit a limit of 6 works/category and $10 fee. "One payment for all entries—send with entries." Contest sponsored for "poetry and prose in general, open to all writers. Other contests require attendance. Small entry fee. Money prizes do not include publication." Special Awards for poetry (open to everyone, 50-line limit) are $50, $25, $15, $10, and $5. Conference Awards for poetry (open to those who register for the conference, 30-line limit) are $25, $15, $10, and $5. "A fee of $5 entitles you to enter one entry. $2 for each additional entry. (Three poems is an entry.) Critique from the judges is available for $10 for all entries. Write the work 'critique' on the upper right corner of each copy. (Limit 6 works in each category)."

LIGONIER VALLEY WRITERS CONFERENCE; THE LOYALHANNA REVIEW, P.O. Box B, Ligonier PA 15658. (724)537-3341. Fax: (724)537-0482. Established 1986. Annual 3-day event usually held in early July. "A relaxing, educational, inspirational conference in a scenic, small town." Average attendance: 80.

Purpose/Features: Open to anyone interested in writing. Conference covers fiction, creative nonfiction, and poetry.

Costs/Accommodations: Conference cost is approximately $200. Participants responsible for their own dinner and lodging. Information on overnight accommodations available for registrants.

Additional Info: Send 9×6 SASE for brochure and registration form. "We also publish *The Loyalhanna Review*, a literary journal, which is open to participants."

THE LITERARY FESTIVAL AT ST. MARY'S, St. Mary's College of Maryland, St. Mary's City MD 20686. E-mail: msglaser@osprey.smcm.edu. Website: www.smcm.edu/academics/litfest. **Contact:** Dr. Michael S. Glaser. Semiannual event held during the last 2 weekends in May in even years (i.e., 2002, 2004). Approximately 18 guest poets and artists participate in and lead workshops, seminars, and readings. Concurrent with the festival, St. Mary's College offers 2-week intensive writing workshops in poetry and fiction and a 10-day writer's community retreat.

Purpose/Features: The poetry and fiction workshop engages the participants in structured writing experiences. Intended for anyone with a serious interest in writing. Offers 4 college credits or may be taken as non-credit courses. The retreat, designed for the serious writer, offers individual plans for writing alone or in conjunction with other participants..

Additional Info: For application or more information on these workshops or the festival, write to Michael S. Glaser at the above address. Accepts inquiries by e-mail.

[N] LUCIDITY POETS' OZARK RETREAT, 11025 Larkwood #1701, Houston TX 77096. (713)995-8159. E-mail: tedbadger@poetic.com. **Director:** Ted O. Badger. Established 1990. Annual 3-day event ("always midweek"). 2001 dates were April 24-26 (Tuesday, Wednesday, and Thursday). Location: The Best Western Inn of the Ozarks in Eureka Springs. Average attendance: 65.

Purpose/Features: Open to all poets. Retreat features lectures, workshops, and read-arounds—all poetry. "No stated theme other than giving opportunity to meet other poets from across the USA, have one's own work critiqued, and read poems to the group. If there be a theme, it would be 'The Fellowship of Poets.'" Offerings include "critiquing of poems done in small groups; lectures by distinguished poets and teachers." Speakers at past retreats were Tom Padgett, college English professor from Bolivar, MO, and Laurence Thomas, international teacher, poet, and author from Ypsilanti, MI. Other special features include an "awards banquet on closing night with several hundred dollars given as awards."

Costs/Accommodations: 2001 cost was $20; participants responsible for their own meals. Housing in on-site facilities costs $39 (couple).

Additional Info: Individual critiques also available. Submit 2 poems with a limit of 36 lines/page in advance to *Lucidity Poetry Journal* at above address. Contest sponsored as part of retreat. Submit 1 poem of 36 lines or less—any form or subject. Brochure and registration form available for SASE. Accepts inquiries by e-mail. "We are loosely affiliated with a dozen state poetry societies which offer annual competitions with cash awards, some of which are underwritten by our own *Lucidity Poetry Journal*, which offers publication and cash payments." (See separate listing for *Lucidity* in Publishers of Poetry section.) "*Lucidity* has tried since 1985 to promote and publish understandable poetry as opposed to obscure or highly esoteric verse. Nowhere else will you find a poetry conference offering three days of activity for only $20."

MANHATTANVILLE'S WRITERS' WEEK, Manhattanville College, 2900 Purchase St., Purchase NY 10577. (914)694-3425. Fax: (914)694-3488. E-mail: dowdr@mville.edu. Website: www.manhattanville.edu. **Dean—Graduate and Profession Studies:** Ruth Dowd, RSCJ. Established 1983. Annual 5-day event usually held the last week in June at the Manhattanville College campus (June 25-29, 2001). Location: "suburban surroundings 45 minutes from downtown Manhattan." Average attendance: more than 90.
Purpose/Features: Open to "published writers, would-be writers, and teachers of creative writing. The conference offers workshops in five genres: short story, creative nonfiction, poetry, screenwriting, children's/young adult literature. There is also a special workshop in The Writers' Craft for beginners." Offerings for poets include a workshop conducted by Jessica Greenbaum. "In past years we have had such distinguished poet/workshop leaders as Mark Doty, Marie Howe, Stephanie Strickland, and Honor Moore. We generally feature a lecture by a distinguished writer."
Costs/Accommodations: Conference cost is $560. Participants responsible for their own meals. Information on overnight accommodations is available. "Rooms in the residence halls are available or students may choose to stay at area hotels. Housing in on-site facilities costs $25-30/night."

☑ **MIDLAND WRITERS CONFERENCE**, Grace A. Dow Memorial Library, 1710 W. St. Andrews, Midland MI 48640. (517)837-3435. Fax: (517)837-3468. E-mail: ajarvis@midland-mi.org. Website: www.gracedowli brary.org (includes a page about the conference). **Conference Coordinator:** Ann Jarvis. Established 1979. Annual 1-day event. 2000 date was June 10. Location: Grace A. Dow Memorial Library in Midland, MI. Average attendance: 100.
Purpose/Features: Open to any writer, published or unpublished. Conference includes sessions that vary in content. Recent keynote speaker was Arthur Golden. "We always have a well-known keynoter. In the past we have had Judith Viorst, Kurt Vonnegut, David McCullough, P.J. O'Rourke, Dave Barry, and Pat Conroy." In 2000, presenters included Russell Thorburn (poetry), Pete Hautman (young adult fiction), Sue Robishaw (creativity), and Daniel King (literary agent).
Costs/Accommodations: Cost for past conference $50 until 2 weeks prior to the event ($60 after that). For students, senior citizens, and handicapped participants, cost was $40 until 2 weeks prior to the event ($50 after that). Information on overnight accommodations available.
Additional Info: Brochure and registration form available by mail. Accepts inquiries by fax and e-mail (include mailing address for response). Brochures mailed in late April.

MISSISSIPPI VALLEY WRITERS CONFERENCE, 3403 - 45th St., Moline IL 61265. (309)762-8985. E-mail: kimseuss@aol.com. **Founder/Director:** David R. Collins. Established 1973. Annual week-long event usually held the second week in June. Location: Liberal Arts College of Augustana College. Average attendance: 80.
Purpose/Features: Open to all writers, "beginners to polished professionals." Conference provides a general professional focus on many genres of writing. Offers week-long workshop in poetry. Evening programs as well as daily workshops included.
Costs/Accommodations: Cost for past conference was $25 registration, $50 one workshop, $90 two workshops, $40 each additional workshop. Conferees may stay on campus or off. Board and room accommodations available at Westerlin Hall on Augustana campus, 15 meals and 6 nights lodging approximately $200.
Additional Info: Individual critiques also available. Submit up to 10 poems. Awards presented by workshop leaders. Brochure and registration form available for SASE. Accepts inquiries by e-mail.

MOUNT HERMON CHRISTIAN WRITERS CONFERENCE, P.O. Box 413, Mount Hermon CA 95041. (831)335-4466. Fax: (831)335-9413. E-mail: dtalbott@mhcamps.org. Website: www.mounthermon.org. **Director of Specialized Programs:** David R. Talbott. Established 1970. Annual 5-day event held Friday through Tuesday over Palm Sunday weekend. 2002 dates: March 22-26. Location: Full hotel-service-style conference center in heart of California redwoods. Average attendance: 350-450.
Purpose/Features: Open to "anyone interested in the Christian writing market." Conference is very broad based. Always covers poetry, fiction, article writing, writing for children, plus an advanced track for published authors. Offerings for poets have included several workshops, sessions on the greeting card industry, and individual one-hour workshops. "We usually have 45-50 teaching faculty. Faculty is made up of publishing reps of leading Christian book and magazine publishers, plus selected freelancers." Other special features have included an advance critique service (no extra fee); residential conference, with meals taken family-style with faculty; private appointments with faculty; and an autograph party. "High spiritual impact."
Costs/Accommodations: 2001 conference cost was $850 deluxe; $705 standard; $575 economy; including 13 meals, snacks, on-site housing, and $315 tuition fee. No-housing fee: $570. $25 airport, Greyhound, or Amtrack shuttle from San Jose, CA.
Additional Info: Brochures and registration forms available for SASE. Accepts inquiries by fax and e-mail.

☑ **OAKLAND UNIVERSITY WRITERS' CONFERENCE**, College of Arts and Sciences, 221 Varner Hall, Oakland University, Rochester MI 48309-4401. (248)370-4386. Fax: (248)370-4280. E-mail: gjboddy@oak land.edu. Website: www.oakland.edu/contin-ed/writersconf/ (includes comprehensive description of conference with photos from previous conferences; downloadable PDF copy of the conference brochure). **Director:** Gloria

J. Boddy. Established 1961. Annual 1½-day event. 2001 dates: October 19-20. Location: in the university student center, in meeting rooms and large dining/meeting areas, plus adjoining classroom buildings with lecture halls. Average attendance: 400-500.
Purpose/Features: Open to beginning through professional adult writers. "No restrictions as to geographic area." Designed to "help writers develop their skills; to provide information (and contact) for getting published; to provide a current picture of publishing markets; to furnish a venue for networking. All genres of writing are covered." Offers "critiques, both one-on-one and group, on Friday. On Saturday, 36 concurrent sessions dealing with all aspects of writing in a variety of genres are available in four time slots. A well-known professional writer speaks at lunch. A panel of the major speakers answers questions in the concluding session."
Costs/Accommodations: 2001 conference cost: $48-58 for Friday critiques; $85 for Saturday conference plus $15 for lunch. "Discounts are not offered." Information on overnight accommodations available for registrants.
Additional Info: Work must be submitted, in advance, for individual critiques. Brochure and registration form available each September 1 prior to the October conference. Accepts inquiries by fax and e-mail. Also offers the Mary Kay Davis Scholarships for high school and college students to attend conference. Check website for details.

OZARK CREATIVE WRITERS CONFERENCE, 6817 Gingerbread Lane, Little Rock AR 72204-4738. (501)565-8889. Fax: (501)565-7220. E-mail: pvining@aristotle.net. **Conference Counselor:** Peggy Vining. Established 1968. Annual 3-day event held the second full weekend in October. 2001 conference: October 11-13. Location: Inn of the Ozarks in Eureka Springs, Arkansas.
Purpose/Features: Open to all writers.
Costs/Accommodations: Registration fee is $50 prior to September 1. "Eureka Springs is a resort town so register early for lodging (say you are with OCWI). Eighty rooms are blocked at the Inn of The Ozarks for the conference."
Additional Info: Various writing contests sponsored as part of conference. Sizeable monetary awards given for all types of writing. Brochure available for #10 SASE after April 1. Accepts inquiries by e-mail. "If requesting by e-mail, please include regular mailing address."

✔ **PENNWRITERS ANNUAL CONFERENCE; PENNWRITERS, INC.; PENNWRITERS ANNUAL WRITING CONTEST; IN OTHER WORDS CONTEST; PENNWRITERS POETRY CONTEST**, RR2, Box 241, Middlebury Center PA 16935. (570)376-3361(day) /2821 (evening). Fax: (570)376-2674. E-mail: cjhoughtaling@usa.net. Website: http://pennwriters.org (includes mission statement, bulletin board, events calendar and details, Board of Directors' bios, chat room, store, and membership form). **Treasurer:** C.J. Houghtaling. Established 1987. Annual 3-day event. 2001 dates were May 18-20. Location: Grantville Holiday Inn, Grantville PA (near Hershey). Average attendance: 200.
Purpose/Features: Open to all writers, novice to multi-published. Covers fiction, nonfiction, and poetry. Offers workshops/seminars, appointments with agents and editors, autograph party, contests—all multi-genre oriented. Theme for 2001 conference was "A Way With Words."
Costs/Accommodations: 2001 conference cost was $130, including some meals. Special dinner event costs $35. "Scholarship awards are presented to Pennwriter members who are winners in our annual writing contests." Transportation to and from airport/train station arranged with advance notice. Information on overnight accommodations available. Housing in on-site facilities costs $82/room double occupancy.
Additional Info: Sponsors three separate contests: 1. Annual Writing Contest for novel (first chapter), article, and short story (unpublished and published). Open to members only. Complete guidelines on website. Awards scholarships to annual Pennwriters Conference. All entries receive critiques from judges. Categories receive anywhere from 5-30 submissions each. 2. In Other Words Contest, held during annual conference, open to conference attendees only. Divisions for poetry, fiction, and nonfiction (published and unpublished). Complete rules on website. Awards prizes; judged by peers. 3. Pennwriters Poetry Contest, open to all; nonmembers pay slightly higher fee. Cash prizes of $50, $25, $10. Complete guidelines on website. Brochure and registration form available for SASE or on website. Accepts inquiries by fax and e-mail. "The Pennwriters Annual Conference is sponsored by Pennwriters, Inc., a nonprofit organization with goals to help writers get published."

✔ **PIMA WRITERS' WORKSHOP**, Pima College, 2202 W. Anklam Rd., Tucson AZ 85709. (520)206-6084. Fax: (520)206-6020. E-mail: mfiles@pimacc.pima.edu. **Director:** Meg Files. Established 1987. Annual 3-

---

TO RECEIVE REGULAR TIPS AND UPDATES about writing and Writer's Digest publications via e-mail, send an e-mail with SUBSCRIBE NEWSLETTER in the body of the message to newsletter-request@writersdigest.com, or sign up online at www.writersdigest.com.

day event. 2001 dates were May 25-27. Location: Pima College's Center for the Arts, "includes a proscenium theater, a black box theater, a recital hall, and conference rooms, as well as a courtyard with amphitheater." Average attendance: 250.

Purpose/Features: Open to all writers, beginning and experienced. "The workshop includes sessions on all genres (nonfiction, fiction, poetry, writing for children and juveniles, screenwriting) and on editing and publishing, as well as manuscript critiques and writing exercises." Past faculty has included Robert Morgan, Jack Heffron, Sharman Apt Russell, David Ray, Nancy Mairs, and others, including 2 agents. Other special features include "accessibility to writers, agents, and editors; and the workshop's atmosphere—friendly and supportive, practical and inspirational."

Costs/Accommodations: Cost is $65; participants are responsible for their own meals. Information on overnight accommodations is available.

Additional Info: Individual poetry critiques available. Submit 3 poems in advance to Meg Files. Accepts inquiries by fax and e-mail.

✔ **POETRY ALIVE! SUMMER RESIDENCY INSTITUTE FOR TEACHERS**, 20 Battery Park, Suite 505, Asheville NC 28801. (800)476-8172 or (828)232-1045. Fax: (828)232-1045. E-mail: poetry@poetryalive.com. Website: www.poetryalive.com (includes photos, descriptions, dates and prices). **Contact:** Rodney Bowling. Established 1990. Annual 6-day event. 2001 dates were June 17-23, July 15-21, July 22-28. Location: University of North Carolina at Asheville. Average attendance: 20/session.

Purpose/Features: Open to anyone. Themes or panels for conference have included "creative writing (poetry), reader response techniques, poem performance techniques and teaching." Speakers at past conferences have included Allan Wolf (performance poetry, writing) and Cheryl Bromley Jones (reader response, writing). Other special features include a trip to Connemara, the Carl Sandburg Home Place, and dinner out at the Grove Park Inn.

Costs/Accommodations: 2000 conference cost was $700, including meals and housing in on-site facilities; discounts available to local commuters "who don't pay the cost of food and lodging." Transportation to and from the event not provided. "We provide transportation from the airport."

Additional Info: Call or write for brochure and registration form. Accepts inquiries by fax and e-mail. "This workshop is designed specifically for teachers or any poet interested in working with students in the schools or as an educational consultant."

N **POETRY WEEKEND INTENSIVES**, 40 Post Ave., Hawthorne NJ 07506. (973)423-2921. Fax: (973)523-6088. E-mail: mgillan@pccc.cc.nj.us or mgillan@msn.com. Website: www.pccc.cc.nj.us. **Contact:** Maria Mazziotti Gillan. Established 1997. Usually held 4 times/year, Friday evening to Sunday in March, June, October, and December. Location: St. Marguerite's Retreat House, an English manor house at the Convent of St. John the Baptist in Mendhan, NJ. Average attendance: 24.

Purpose/Features: Open to all writers. "The purpose of this retreat is to give writers the space and time to focus totally on their own work in a serene and beautiful setting away from the pressures and distractions of daily life." 2001 theme was "Writing Your Way Home—Poetry of Memory and Place." "Writing weekend poets will find support and encouragement, stimulating activities leading to the creation of new work, workshop leaders who are actively engaged in the writing life, opportunities to read their work aloud to the group, a circle of writer friends, and networking opportunities." Poetry Weekend Intensives are lead by Maria Mazziotti Gillan and Laura Boss. Other special features include one-on-one conferences with lead poet faculty.

Costs/Accommodations: Cost for 2001 weekends was $295, including meals. Offers a $25 early bird discount. Housing in on-site facilities included in the $295 price.

Additional Info: Individual poetry critiques available. Poets should bring poems to weekend. Brochures and registration forms available for SASE and by e-mail. Accepts inquiries by fax and e-mail. Maria Mazziotti Gillan is the executive director of the Poetry Center at Passaic County Community College and edits *Paterson Literary Review*. Laura Boss is the editor of *Lips* magazine. Fifteen professional development credits are available for each weekend.

SAGE HILL WRITING FALL POETRY COLLOQUIUM, P.O. Box 1731, Saskatoon, Saskatchewan S7K 3S1 Canada. Phone/fax: (306)652-7395. E-mail: sage.hill@sk.sympatico.ca. Website: www.lights.com/sagehill (includes program information, scholarship information, tuition, course outlines, faculty profiles, application information and down-loadable application forms). **Executive Director:** Steven Ross Smith. Established 1995. Annual 21-day event. 2001 dates: November 12-December 2. Location: "The peaceful milieu of St. Peter's College, adjoining St. Peter's Abbey, in Muenster, 125 kilometers east of Saskatoon."

Purpose/Features: Open to poets, 19 years of age and older, who are working in English. The colloquium offers "an intensive three-week workshop/retreat designed to assist poets with manuscripts-in-progress. Each writer will have established a publishing record in books or periodicals and will wish to develop his/her craft and tune a manuscript. There will be ample time for writing, one-on-one critiques, and group meetings to discuss recent thinking in poetics. Eight writers will be selected. Writers in and outside Saskatchewan are eligible." Instructor for the 2001 colloquium: Erin Mouré.

Costs/Accommodations: 2001 cost: $975, including tuition, accommodations, and meals. "A university registration fee of $25 will be added if taking this course for credit." Transportation from Saskatoon can be arranged as needed. On-site accommodations included in cost.

Additional Info: Brochure and registration form available for SASE. Most recent application deadline: July 31, 2001.

SAGE HILL WRITING SUMMER EXPERIENCE, P.O. Box 1731, Saskatoon, Saskatchewan S7K 3S1 Canada. Phone/fax: (306)652-7395. E-mail: sage.hill@sk.sympatico.ca. Website: www.lights.com/sagehill (includes program information, scholarship information, tuition, application information and down-loadable application forms). **Executive Director:** Steven Ross Smith. Established in 1990. Annual 7-day and 10-day events usually held the end of July through the beginning of August. Location: St. Michael's Retreat, "a tranquil facility in the beautiful Qu'Appelle Valley just outside the town of Lumsden, 25 kilometers north of Regina." Average attendance: 54, with participants broken into small groups of 5-11.

Purpose/Features: Open to writers, 19 years of age and older, who are working in English. No geographic restrictions. The retreat/workshops are designed to "offer a special working and learning opportunity to writers at different stages of development. Top quality instruction, a low instructor-writer ratio, and the rural Saskatchewan setting offers conditions ideal for the pursuit of excellence in the arts of fiction, poetry, playwriting, and creative nonfiction." Offerings specifically available for poets include a poetry workshop and poetry colloquium. The 2001 faculty included Fred Wah, Betsy Warland, and Robert Kroetsch.

Costs/Accommodations: 2001 conference cost was $675, including instruction, accommodations, and meals. Limited local transportation to the conference is available. "Van transportation from Regina airport to Lumsden will be arranged for out-of-province travellers." On-site accommodations offer individual rooms with a writing desk and washroom.

Additional Info: Individual critiques offered as part of workshop and colloquium. Writing sample required with application. Application deadline: April 25, 2001. Brochure and registration form available for SASE.

SAN DIEGO STATE UNIVERSITY WRITERS' CONFERENCE, 5250 Campanile Dr., San Diego CA 92182-1920. (619)594-2517. Fax: (619)594-8566. E-mail: lkoch@mail.sdsu.edu. Website: www.ces.sdsu.edu (includes complete conference brochure posted in November prior to the January conference). **Director of Noncredit Community Education:** Leslie Koch. Established 1984. Annual 3-day event. 2002 dates: January 18-20. Location: Doubletree Hotel (Mission Valley), 7450 Hazard Center Dr., San Diego. Average attendance: 400.

Purpose/Features: Open to writers of fiction, nonfiction, children's books, poetry, and screenwriting. "We have participants from across North America." Offers numerous workshops in fiction, nonfiction, general interest, children's books, screenwriting, magazine writing, and poetry. Speakers at last conference included Peter Gethers (vice president and editor-at-large for Random House Inc.), Amy Scheibe (senior editor, Doubleday), Abby Zidie (assistant editor, Bantam Dell Publishing Group), and screenwriter Madeline DiMaggio. Other special features include networking lunch, editor/agent appointments and consultations, and novel writing workshops.

Costs/Accommodations: Cost is $265-355, including 1 meal; discounts are available for early registration. Transportation to and from the event provided by the Doubletree Hotel. Information on overnight accommodations available. Accommodations include special rates at the Doubletree Hotel.

Additional Info: Individual poetry critiques available. See brochure for details. Contest sponsored as part of conference. "Editors and agents give awards for favorite submissions." Brochure and registration form available for SASE or on website. Accepts inquiries by fax and e-mail.

SAN JUAN WRITERS WORKSHOP, P.O. Box 68, Moab UT 84532. (435)259-7750. Fax: (435)259-2335. E-mail: cfinfo@canyonlandsfieldinst.org. Website: www.canyonlandsfieldinst.org. **Contact:** Registrar. Annual 4-day event usually held in March. Location: based out of the Recapture Lodge in scenic Bluff, Utah. Attendance: a maximum of 24.

Purpose/Features: Open to all. Workshop focuses on small group sessions discussing a sense of place and developing writing skills, related to natural history and community life.

Costs/Accommodations: Cost is $440, includes instruction, lodging, and meals.

THE SANDHILLS WRITERS CONFERENCE, Augusta State University, Augusta GA 30904. (706)737-1500. Fax: (706)667-4770. E-mail: akellman@aug.edu. Website: www.aug.edu/langlitcom/sand_hills_conference. **Conference Director:** Anthony Kellman. Established 1975. Annual 3-day event. Facilities are handicapped accessible. Usually held the third weekend in March. 2002 dates: March 21-23. Average attendance: 100.

Purpose/Features: Open to all aspiring writers. Conference designed to "hone the creative writing skills of participants and provide networking opportunities. All areas are covered—fiction, poetry, children's literature, playwriting, screenwriting, and writing of song lyrics, also nonfiction." Offerings for poets include craft lectures, ms evaluations, and readings. 2001 conference speakers were Maxine Hong Kingston (keynote); Declan Spring, editor at New Directions; Louisiana Poet-Laureate Pinkie Gordon-Lane; and Robert Bausch. Faculty will give craft sessions and readings.

Costs/Accommodations: 2001 cost was $156, including lunches; participants responsible for dinners only. Information on overnight accommodations available.

Additional Info: Individual poetry critiques available. Submit 6 poems with a limit of 15 pages. Contest sponsored as part of conference. "All registrants who submit a manuscript for evaluation are eligible for the contest determined by the visiting authors in each respective genre." Brochure and registration form available for SASE. Accepts inquiries by fax and e-mail.

N: SANTA BARBARA WRITERS' CONFERENCE, P.O. Box 304, Carpinteria CA 93014. (805)684-2250. Fax: (805)684-7003. **Conference Director:** Barnaby Conrad. Established 1973. Annual week-long event held the last Friday in June. Location: Westmont College in Montecito. Average attendance: 350.
Purpose/Features: Open to everyone. Covers all genres of writing. Workshops in poetry offered. Past speakers have included Ray Bradbury, Phillip Levine, Sol Stein, Gore Vidal, and Willian Styron.
Costs/Accommodations: 2001 conference cost including all workshops and lectures, 2 al fresco dinners, and room and board, was $1,340 single, $1,240 double occupancy; $400 day students.
Additional Info: Individual poetry critiques available. Submit 1 ms of no more than 3,000 words in advance with SASE. Competitions with awards sponsored as part of conference. Brochure and registration form available for SASE.

✓ SEWANEE WRITERS' CONFERENCE, 310 St. Luke's Hall, 735 University Ave., Sewanee TN 37383-1000. (931)598-1141. E-mail: cpeters@sewanee.edu. Website: www.sewaneewriters.org (includes History, The Conference, Sewanee Writers' Series, Alumni, Contact Us, and Applications Admissions). **Creative Writing Programs Manager:** Cheri B. Peters. Established 1990. Annual 12-day event held the last 2 weeks in July. Location: the University of the South ("dormitories for housing, Women's Center for public events, classrooms for workshops, Sewanee Inn for dining, etc."). Attendance: about 105.
Purpose/Features: Open to poets, fiction writers, and playwrights who submit their work for review in a competitive admissions process. "Genre, rather than thematic, workshops are offered in each of the three areas." 2001 speakers/panelists included poets Debora Gregory, Robert Hass, John Hollander, and William Logan. Other speakers included editors, agents, and additional writers.
Costs/Accommodations: Conference cost is $1,205, including room and board. Each year scholarships and fellowships based on merit are available on a competitive basis. "We provide free bus transportation from the Nashville airport on the opening day of the conference and back to the airport on the closing day."
Additional Info: Individual critiques also available. "All writers admitted to the conference will have an individual session with a member of the faculty." A ms should be sent in advance after admission to the conference. Write for brochure and application forms; no SASE necessary. Accepts inquiries by e-mail.

SINIPEE WRITERS WORKSHOP, Continuing Education, Loras College, Dubuque IA 52004-0178. (319)588-7139. Fax: (319)588-7964. E-mail: lcrosset@loras.edu. **Director:** Linda Crossett. Established 1986. Annual 1-day event usually held the third or fourth Saturday in April. Location: the campus of Loras College. Average attendance: 50-100.
Purpose/Features: Open to anyone, "professional or neophyte," interested in writing. Conference covers fiction, poetry, and nonfiction.
Costs/Accommodations: Cost for the last workshop was $60 pre-registration, $65 at the door. Scholarships covering half of the cost are traditionally available to senior citizens and to full-time students, both college and high school. Cost includes handouts, coffee and donut break, lunch, snacks in afternoon, and book fair with authors in attendance available to autograph their books. Information on overnight accommodations available.
Additional Info: Annual contest for nonfiction, fiction, and poetry sponsored as part of workshop. There is a $5 reading fee for each entry (article/essay of 1,500 words, short story of 1,500 words, or poetry of 40 lines). 1st Prize in each category: $100 plus publication, 2nd Prize: $50, and 3rd Prize: $25. Competition receives 50-100 entries. Entrants in the contest may also ask for a written critique by a professional writer. The cost for critique is an additional $15/entry. Brochure and registration form available for SASE.

✓ SOCIETY OF THE MUSE OF THE SOUTHWEST (S.O.M.O.S.); CHOKECHERRIES, P.O. Box 3225, Taos NM 87571. (505)758-0081. Fax: (505)758-4802. E-mail: somos@laplaza.com. Website: http://somostaos.org (includes calendar and descriptions of special events). **Executive Director:** Dori Vinella. Established 1983. "We offer readings, special events, and workshops at different times during the year, many during the summer." Length of workshops varies. Location: various sites in Taos. Average attendance: 10-50.
Purpose/Features: Open to anyone. "We offer workshops in various genres—fiction, poetry, nature writing, etc." Past workshop speakers have included Denise Chavez, Alfred Depew, Marjorie Agosin, Judyth Hill, Robin Becker, and Robert Westbrook. Other special features include writing in nature/nature walks and beautiful surroundings in a historic writer's region.
Costs/Accommodations: Cost for workshops ranges from $30-175, excluding room and board. Information on overnight accommodations available.
Additional Info: Brochure and registration form available for SASE. Accepts inquiries by fax and e-mail. "Taos has a wonderful community of dedicated and talented writers who make SOMOS workshops rigorous, supportive, and exciting." Also publishes *Chokecherries*, an annual anthology.

☑ **SOUTHAMPTON COLLEGE WRITERS CONFERENCE**, 239 Montauk Hwy., Southampton NY 11968. (631)287-8175. Fax: (631) 287-8253. E-mail: summer@southampton.liu.edu. Website: www.southampton .liu.edu. **Summer Director:** Carla Caglioti. Established 1976. Annual 8-day to 2-week events. 2001 dates were June 29-July 6. Location: Southampton College of Long Island University "in the heart of the Hamptons, one of the most beautiful and culturally rich resorts in the country." Average attendance: 15/workshop.
Purpose/Features: Open to writers, graduate students, and upper-level undergraduate students. Conference covers poetry, fiction, short story, and nonfiction. 2001 conference theme was "On Publishing." Offerings for poets include a workshop. 2001 conference speakers were Billy Collins, Robert Phillips, Mary Karr, Matthew Klam, Roger Rosenblatt, Larry Heinemann, Kaylie Jones, Stefan Kanfer, and Robert Reeves.
Costs/Accommodations: Past cost was $610; participants responsible for own meals, discounts available. "Each additional workshop is at the reduced rate of $370." Information on overnight accommodations available. Housing in on-site facilities costs $240 to share a room with another participant, $355 for a single.
Additional Info: Brochure and registration form available for SASE or on website. Accepts inquiries by fax and e-mail.

N **SOUTHERN CALIFORNIA WRITERS' CONFERENCE*SAN DIEGO**, 4406 Park Blvd., Suite E, San Diego CA 92116. Phone/fax: (619)282-2983. E-mail: wewrite@writersconference.com. Website: www.writer sconference.com. **Executive Director:** Michael Gregory. Established 1986. Annual 4-day event. 2002 dates are February 15-18. Location: Holiday Inn Hotel and Suites in historic Old Town, San Diego. Average attendance: 300.
Purpose/Features: Open to all aspiring and accomplished writers of fiction, nonfiction, screen, and poetry. Conference offers 50 read-and-critique sessions as well as Q&A workshops.
Costs/Accommodations: 2001 conference cost was $250; participants responsible for own meals. Individual day rates available; see website for details. Information on overnight accommodations available for registrants. Accommodations include special rates at area hotels.
Additional Info: Individual poetry critiques available. Submit poetry in advance to Leroy V. Quintana at the above address. Contest sponsored as part of conference. Competition receives 50-100 entries. Brochure and registration form available for SASE and on website.

☑ **SOUTHWEST WRITERS CONTEST AND CONFERENCE**, (formerly Southwest Writers Work-shop), 8200 Mountain Rd. NE, Suite 106, Albuquerque NM 87110. (505)265-9485. Fax: (505)265-9483. E-mail: swriters@aol.com. Website: www.southwestwriters.org (includes contest rules, past winners, prize information, registration forms, membership information). **Contact:** Contest Chair. Established 1982. Annual 3- to 4-day event. 2001 dates were September 20-23. Location: Hyatt Regency, Albuquerque. Average attendance: 500.
Purpose/Features: Open to all writers. Workshop covers all genres, focus on getting published—over 20 editors, agents, and producers as presenters. "As part of the conference, SWW has an annual writing contest with a category for poetry. Contest judges are editors and agents." Recent contest winners were Joan Mitchell, Sudasi Clement, and Lori Johnson. Other special features include preconference sessions; appointments with editors, agents, producers, and publicists.
Costs/Accommodations: Cost is $180-260. Early Bird discount if registered by July 15. Information on overnight accommodations available. Accommodations include special rates at area hotels.
Additional Info: Individual critiques available through entry in annual contest. Submit poems with a limit of 50 lines in advance with $18 (member), $23 (nonmember) fee. Each must have separate entry form and fee. Contest receives 750 entries/year, 100 of which are poetry. Deadline for entries is May 1, 2002. Entry form and rules, brochure, and registration form available for SASE or on website. Accepts inquiries *only* by fax and e-mail.

N **SPLIT ROCK ARTS PROGRAM**, University of Minnesota, 360 Coffey Hall, 1420 Eckles Ave., St. Paul MN 55108-6084. (612)625-8100. Fax: (612)624-6210. E-mail: srap@mail.cce.umn.edu. Website: www.cce.umn. edu/splitrockarts/ (includes full catalog with program/workshop descriptions, instructor bios, registration and housing information and forms, scholarship information and application forms). **Program Associate:** Vivien Oja. Established 1983. Annual week-long workshop. 2002 dates: July 7-August 10. Location: "Workshops are held on the University's Duluth campus overlooking Lake Superior; some retreat-style workshops are held at the University of Minnesota's Cloquet Forestry Center, which offers the peaceful seclusion of the north woods." Average attendance: 550.
Purpose/Features: Open to "anyone over 18 years old who has an interest in the arts. Participants are lifelong learners from all walks of life—novices, professionals, passionate hobbyists, and advanced amateurs. Our program offers uninterrupted time and space for them to explore their art in an inviting, supportive community and an opportunity to work with renowned practising artists, writers, and craftspeople. Areas of concentration include poetry, stories, memoirs, novels, and personal essays." 2000 program instructors included Jonis Agee, Paulette Bates Alden, Ron Carlson, Sharon Doubiago, Bill Holm, Susan Hubbard, Kent Meyers, Lawrence Sutin, and Catherine Watson. Offerings for poets included presentations by Michael Dennis Browne, Ray Gonzalez, Kate Green, Jesse Lee Kercheval, and Pattiann Rogers.

Costs/Accommodations: 2000 cost for each workshop was $465/workshop; participants are responsible for their own meals. "Limited scholarships are available based on artistic merit and financial need." Housing in on-site facilities costs $168-258/week.

Additional Info: Write or call for free catalog or visit website (registration forms available online beginning in March of each year). Accepts inquiries by fax and e-mail.

☑ **SQUAW VALLEY COMMUNITY OF WRITERS POETRY WORKSHOP**, 10626 Banner Lava Cap, Nevada City CA 95959. (530)274-8551. E-mail: svcw@oro.net. Website: www.squawvalleywriters.org (includes "all the information contained in our brochure and more; a FAQ section which contains most information applicants will need"). **Executive Director:** Brett Hall Jones. Established 1969. Annual 7-day event. 2001 dates were July 21-28. Location: The Squaw Valley Ski Corporation's Lodge in the Sierra Nevada near Lake Tahoe. "The workshop takes place in the off-season of the ski area. Participants can find time to enjoy the Squaw Valley landscape." Average attendance: 64.

Purpose/Features: Open to talented writers of diverse ethnic backgrounds and a wide range of ages. "The Poetry Program differs in concept from other workshops in poetry. Our project's purpose is to help participants break through old habits and write something daring and difficult. Workshops are intended to provide a supportive atmosphere in which no one will be embarrassed, and at the same time to challenge the participants to go beyond what they have done before. Admissions are based on quality of the submitted manuscripts." Offerings include regular morning workshops, craft lectures, and staff readings. "Participants gather in daily workshops to discuss the work they wrote in the previous 24 hours." 2001 staff poets: Lucille Clifton, Brenda Hillman, Galway Kinnell, and Sharon Olds.

Costs/Accommodations: Past workshop cost was $595, included regular morning workshops, craft lectures, staff readings, and dinners. Scholarships available. "Requests for financial aid must accompany submission/application and will be granted on the perceived quality of manuscript submitted and financial need of applicant." Transportation to workshop available. "We will pick poets up at the Reno/Lake Tahoe Airport if arranged in advance. Also, we arrange housing for participants in local houses and condominiums. Participants can choose from a single room for $385/week or a double room for $285/week within these shared houses. We do offer inexpensive bunk bed accommodations on a first come, first served basis."

Additional Info: Individual conferences available. "Only work-in-progress will be discussed." Brochure available for SASE or by e-mail (include mailing address for response). Accepts inquiries by e-mail. Also publishes the annual *Squaw Valley Community of Writers Omnium Gatherum and Newsletter* containing "news and profiles on our past participants and staff, craft articles, and book advertising.'

☑ **STEAMBOAT SPRINGS WRITERS CONFERENCE**, P.O. Box 774284, Steamboat Springs CO 80477. (970)879-8079. E-mail: thefreibergers@cs.com. **Director:** Harriet Freiberger. Established 1981. Annual 1-day event. 2001 conference was held in mid-July. Location: a "renovated train station, the Depot is home of the Steamboat Springs Arts Council—friendly, relaxed atmosphere." Average attendance: 35-40 (registration limited).

Purpose/Features: Open to anyone. Conference is "designed for writers who have limited time. Instructors vary from year to year, offering maximum instruction during a weekend at a nominal cost." 2001 speakers included poet James Tipton and children's writer Avi.

Costs/Accommodations: 2001 cost was $35 (early registration, which is limited), including lunch. "A variety of lodgings available. Special discounts at Steamboat Resorts."

Additional Info: Brochure and registration form available for SASE. Accepts inquiries by e-mail. Affiliated with *Seedhouse*, "a new publication with rapidly expanding circulation that encourages submissions from unpublished writers. It is a 'not-for-profit' and 'no advertisement' publication." (See separate listing for *Seedhouse* in the Publishers of Poetry section.)

☑ **SUMMER WRITING PROGRAM AT THE UNIVERSITY OF VERMONT**, 322 S. Prospect St., Burlington VT 05401. (800)639-3210. Fax: (802)656-0306. E-mail: EveningUniversity@uvm.edu. Website: http://learn.uvm.edu. Established 1994. Annual event. Credit courses held during the summer. Location: University of Vermont's campus, located in Burlington and close to Lake Champlain. Average attendance: 75-100.

Purpose/Features: Open to all writers. Credit courses in fiction, poetry, nonfiction, and autobiographies. Features university faculty.

Costs/Accommodations: Summer 2001 tuition: $281/credit hour (Vermont resident); $618/credit hour (nonresident). Most courses are three-credit hours. Residency option not available.

Additional Info: Accepts inquiries by e-mail.

ALWAYS include a self-addressed, stamped envelope (SASE) when sending a ms or query to a publisher within your own country. When sending material to other countries, include a self-addressed envelope and International Reply Coupons (IRCs), available at many post offices.

☑ **SWT SUMMER CREATIVE WRITING CAMP**, Dept. of English, Southwest Texas State University, San Marcos TX 78666. (512)245-3717. Fax: (512)245-8546. E-mail: sw13@swt.edu. Website: www.English.swt.edu/Camp.html (includes "an overview of our program, application details, and links to information about SWT and San Marcos"). **Director:** Steve Wilson. Established 1989. Annual week-long event usually held the last week in June. Location: "The camp is held on the campus of the 21,000-student Southwest Texas State University, which is also home to a nationally recognized Master of Fine Arts program in creative writing. SWTSU is located in Central Texas, roughly 20 miles from Austin." Attendance: limited to 20 participants.

Purpose/Features: Open to all high school students. "Because the camp is for high school students, we ask that participants take workshops in both fiction and poetry. In addition to our standard workshops in poetry, we offer workshops in revision, and each camper takes part in one-on-one tutorials with the poetry workshop leaders. On the final day of the writing camp, campers present a public reading of their writing for friends, family, and people from the local community."

Costs/Accommodations: Cost is $250, including meals. All campers stay in SWT residence halls. Costs included in program fee.

Additional Info: Brochure and registration form available for SASE. "Our application deadline is April 15 of each year." Accepts inquiries by fax and e-mail. "Our writing camp is quite competitive, so we encourage interested poets to send their best work."

N. TAOS SUMMER WRITERS' WORKSHOP, Dept. of English, Humanities Bldg. #235, Albuquerque NM 87131-1106. (505)277-6248. Website: www.unm.edu/~taosconf (includes e-mail link, instructor profiles, workshop descriptions, price and travel information, photos). **Director:** Sharon Oard Warner. Established 1999. Annual 5-day (weeklong) and 2-day (weekend) workshops usually held the third week in July. Location: Taos, NM, at the "historic Sagebrush Inn. Beautiful views of Taos mountain. Next door sister hotel offers more modern rooms with refrigerator/microwave and computer hookups." Average attendance: 75 total; 120 places available in weeklong workshop. Class size limited to 12/class, usually smaller.

Purpose/Features: Open to everyone, beginners to experienced. Minimum age is 18. Friendly, relaxed atmosphere with supportive staff and instructors. Purpose is "to encourage writers in all areas. We offer both weekend and weeklong workshops in fiction, short story and novel, creative nonfiction, memoir, travel writing, magazine article writing, and poetry. We have offered classes in the past in historical fiction, screenplay writing, and children's writing." 2001 workshop presenters included Pam Houston, Carolyn Meyer, Laurie Kutchins, Patricia Clark Smith, Elizabeth Hadas, and Brent Spencer. At least one week-long workshop and one weekend devoted to poetry. Previous guest speakers have included John Nichols (*Milagro Beanfield War*) in 1999 and Luci Tapahonso (*Blue Horses Rush In*) in 2000. All workshop instructors give readings. Other special features include open mic sessions daily. "We offer free tours of the nearby D.H. Lawrence Ranch and a museum crawl—many famous artists lived and worked in Taos, including Georgia O'Keefe. All of our instructors have some connection to the Southwest."

Costs/Accommodations: 2001 conference cost was $200 for weekend, $475 for weeklong sessions. Participants responsible for own meals, but lunches available on site. Opening and closing dinners included in workshop cost. Offers $50 discount if one person takes both a weekend and week-long workshop. Nearest airport is Albuquerque Sunport. Shuttle bus available (a commercial service not provided by the conference) for approximately $100. Auto rental services available at the airport. Taos is about 2½ hours north of Albuquerque. Information on overnight accommodations available. Sagebrush Inn and Comfort Suites offer special rates.

Additional Info: Conference contest in both fiction and poetry. Submit five poems, not to exceed 10 pages/poetry entry. Prize (one for poetry, one for fiction) is a scholarship to the conference. ("Some years this includes travel and motel accommodations, some years it doesn't. Check website for details.") Judges: staff from the Creative Writing Dept., University of New Mexico. Brochure and registration form available by snail mail (no SASE required), by fax, or on website. Accepts inquiries by fax and e-mail. Participants encouraged to submit work to the University of New Mexico's *Blue Mesa Review* (see separate listing for *Blue Mesa Review* in the Publishers of Poetry section). "Taos is a unique experience of a lifetime. The setting and scenery are spectacular; historical and natural beauty abound. Our previous attendees say they have been inspired by the place and by the friendly, personal attention of our instructors."

🌐 ☑ **TŶ NEWYDD WRITERS' CENTRE**, Taliesin Trust, Llanystumdwy, Cricieth, Gwynedd LL52 0LW Wales, Great Britain. Phone: 0441766 523552. Fax: 0441766 523095. E-mail: tynewydd@dial.pipex.com. Website: www.tynewydd.org (includes information about courses: accommodation, tutors, travel, etc.). **Director:** Sally Baker. Established 1990. Holds 4½-day courses throughout the year, Monday evening through Saturday morning. Location: Tŷ Newydd, "a house of historical and architectural interest situated near the village of Llanystumdwy. It was the last home of Lloyd George, the former British prime minister." Average attendance: 12/course.

Purpose/Features: Open to anyone over 16 years of age. Courses are designed to "promote the writing and understanding of literature by providing creative writing courses at all levels for all ages. Courses at Tŷ Newydd provide the opportunity of working intimately and informally with two professional writers." Courses specifically for poets of all levels of experience and ability are offered throughout the year.

Costs/Accommodations: Cost for a 4½-day course is £300 (inclusive); some weekend courses available, cost is £125 (inclusive). Transportation to and from Centre available if arranged at least a week in advance. Participants

stay at Tŷ Newydd House in shared bedrooms or single bedrooms. "Vegetarians and people with special dietary needs are catered for but please let us know in advance. Course participants help themselves to breakfast and lunch and help to prepare one evening meal as part of a team. Participants should bring towels and their own writing materials. Some typewriters and word processors are available."
Additional Info: Brochure and registration form available for SASE. Accepts inquiries by fax and e-mail.

✓ **UND WRITERS CONFERENCE**, University of North Dakota, Department of English, Grand Forks ND 58202-7209. (701)777-3321. Fax: (701)777-2373. E-mail: james_mckenzie@und.nodak.edu. Website: www.und writersconference.org (includes biographies of visiting writers, complete conference schedule, archive listing past conferences). **Director/Professor:** James McKenzie. Established 1970. Annual 4- to 5-day event. 2001 dates were March 18-23. Location: The "UND student Memorial Union, with occasional events at other campus sites, especially the large Chester Fritz Auditorium or the North Dakota Museum of Art." Average attendance: 3,000-5,000. "Some individual events have as few as 20, some over 1,000."
Purpose/Features: All events are free and open to the public. "The conference is really more of a festival, though it has been called a conference since its inception, with a history of inviting writers from all genres. The conference's purpose is public education, as well as a kind of bonus curriculum at the University. It is the region's premier intellectual and cultural event." 2001 conference theme was "Worklife/Lifework." Guests included Peter Carey (fiction), Gary Fisketjon (editing, fiction), Kent Haruf (fiction), Natasha Trethewey (poetry), Joy Williams (fiction, essay), and Ofelia Zepeda (poetry). "They read, participate in panels, and otherwise make themselves available in public and academic venues." The 2002 conference theme will be "Explore!" to coincide with the upcoming Lewis and Clark Bicentennial. Other special features include open mic student/public readings every morning, informal meetings with writers, autograph sessions, dinners, and receptions.
Additional Info: Brochure available for SASE. Accepts inquiries by fax and e-mail.

✓ **UNIVERSITY OF WISCONSIN-MADISON'S SCHOOL OF THE ARTS AT RHINELANDER**, 715 Lowell Center, 610 Langdon St., Madison WI 53703-1195. Fax: (608)262-1694. E-mail: kberigan@dcs.wisc. edu. Website: www.dcs.wisc.edu/lsa. **Administrative Coordinator:** Kathy Berigan. Established 1964. Annual 5-day event. 2001 session held July 23-27. Location: local junior high school. Average attendance: 300.
Purpose/Features: Open to all levels and ages. Offerings for poets include poetry workshops and related workshops in creativity.
Costs/Accommodations: 2001 workshop cost ranged from $120-335. Information on overnight accommodations available.
Additional Info: Write for brochure and registration form.

🍁 ✓ **VICTORIA SCHOOL OF WRITING**, Box 8152, Victoria, British Columbia V8W 3R8 Canada. (250)595-3000. E-mail: vicwrite@islandnet.com. Website: www.islandnet.com/vicwrite/ (includes description of school, faculty, and workshops; registration details; comments from former students and contest winners). **Director:** Ruth Slavin. Established 1996. Annual 5-day event. 2001 dates were July 16-20. Location: "Residential school in natural, park-like setting. Easy parking, access to university, downtown." Average attendance: 100.
Purpose/Features: "A three- to ten-page manuscript is required as part of the registration process, which is open to all. The general purpose of the workshop is to give hands-on assistance with better writing, working closely with established writers/instructors. We have workshops in fiction, poetry, and nonfiction; plus three other workshops which vary." Offerings for poets include two of the intensive 5-day workshops (16 hours of instruction and one-on-one consultation). 2000 workshop leaders were Marlene Cookshaw and Don MacKay (Governor General's Award 1991 and 2001). In 2001, leaders included Sue Wheeler (poetry) and Keath Fraser and M.A.C. Farrant (fiction).
Costs/Accommodations: 2001 workshop cost was $575 Canadian; included 5 lunches and 1 dinner. Other meals and accommodations available on site. "For people who register with payment in full before May 1, the cost is $525 Canadian."
Additional Info: Contest sponsored as part of conference. Most recent contest winners were Susan Ellenton, Paul Willcocks, and Heather Walker. Competition receives approximately 200 entries. Brochure and registration form available for SASE. Accepts inquiries by e-mail.

WESLEYAN WRITERS CONFERENCE, Wesleyan University, Middletown CT 06457. (860)685-3604. Fax: (860)685-2441. E-mail: agreene@wesleyan.edu. Website: www.wesleyan.edu/writing/conferen.html (includes overview of conference, information on schedule and faculty, scholarship information, rates and registration form). **Director:** Anne Greene. Established 1956. Annual 5-day event usually held the last week in June. Location: the campus of Wesleyan University "in the hills overlooking the Connecticut River, a brief drive from the Connecticut shore. Wesleyan's outstanding library, poetry reading room, and other university facilities are open to participants." Average attendance: 100.
Purpose/Features: "Open to both experienced and new writers. The participants are an international group. The conference covers the novel, short story, fiction techniques, fiction-and-film, poetry, literary journalism, and memoir." Recent special sessions included "The Poetry of Engagement," "The Writer's Life," "Writing Memoirs," and "Publishing." Offerings for poets include manuscript consultations and daily seminars. Past faculty included Honor Moore, C.D. Wright, William Meredith, and Henry Taylor.

Costs/Accommodations: Cost in 2000, including meals, was $725 (day rate); $845 (boarding rate). "Wesleyan has scholarships for journalists, fiction writers, nonfiction writers, and poets. Request brochure for application information." Information on overnight accommodations available. "Conference participants may stay in university dormitories or off campus in local hotels."

Additional Info: Individual poetry critiques available. Registration for critiques must be made before the conference. Accepts inquiries by fax and e-mail.

WHIDBEY ISLAND WRITERS' CONFERENCES; THE WHIDBEY ISLAND WRITERS' ASSOCI-ATION, 5456 Pleasant View Lane, Freeland WA 98249. (360)331-6714. E-mail: writers@whidbey.com. Website: www.whidbey.com/writers (includes conference information: presenters, accommodations, links to Whidbey Island, registration forms, how to make the most of agent/editor/publisher meetings and conference opportunities). **Director:** Celeste Mergens. Established 1997. Annual event held the first weekend in March. 2002 dates: March 2-4. Location: "South Whidbey High School's state-of-the-art facility, except for Friday's Author Fireside Chats, which are held in private residencies within the community." Average attendance: 250.

Purpose/Features: Open to writers of every genre and skill level. Conference covers fiction, nonfiction, poetry, children's writing, and screenwriting. Offerings for poets include workshops, panels, and readings. Past speakers have included poets Pattiann Rogers, Maurya Simon, Bart Baxter, and Susan Zwinger. Other special features include "Author Fireside Chats, which are opportunities to meet and learn from the faculty in personable home settings with groups of 20 or less. Participants spend the day focusing on their chosen genre."

Costs/Accommodations: 2001 conference cost was $308, including 3 meals. Volunteer discounts available. "Rideshare board available through our website." Information on overnight accommodations available. Accommodations include special rates at "local B&B's, as well as roommate share lists and dorm-style accommodations as low as $10/night.

Additional Info: Individual poetry critiques available. Submit 8 poems with a limit of 2 poems/page by February 15. Brochure and registration form available for SASE or on website. Accepts inquiries by e-mail. Conference is sponsored by the Whidbey Island Writers' Association and is "designed to offer personable interaction and learning opportunities. We consider all presenters and participants to be part of the 'team' here. We emphasize practical application strategies for success as well as workshop opportunities. We try to invite at least one poetry publisher per year."

WINTER POETRY & PROSE GETAWAY IN CAPE MAY, 18 North Richards Ave., Ventnor NJ 08406. (609)823-5076. E-mail: wintergetaway@hotmail.com. Website: www.wintergetaway.com. **Founder/Director:** Peter E. Murphy. Established 1994. Annual 4-day event. 2002 dates: January 18-21. Location: The Grand Hotel on the Oceanfront in Historic Cape May, New Jersey. "Participants stay in comfortable rooms with an ocean view, perfect for thawing out the muse. Hotel facilities include a pool, sauna, and whirlpool, as well as a lounge and disco for late evening dancing for night people." Average attendance: 175.

Purpose/Features: Open to all writers, beginners and experienced, over the age of 18. "The poetry workshop meets for an hour or so each morning before sending you off with an assignment that will encourage and inspire you to produce exciting new work. After lunch, we gather together to read new drafts in feedback sessions led by experienced poet-teachers who help identify the poem's virtues and offer suggestions to strengthen its weaknesses. The groups are small and you receive positive attention to help your poem mature. In late afternoon, you can continue writing or schedule a personal tutorial session with one of the poets on staff." Previous staff have included Renee Ashley, Robert Carnevale, Cat Doty, Stephen Dunn, Kathleen Rockwell Lawrence, Charles Lynch, Peter Murphy, Jim Richardson, and Robbie Clipper Sethi. There are usually 10 participants in each poetry workshop and 7 in each of the prose workshops. Other special features include extra-supportive sessions for beginners.

Costs/Accommodations: 2001 conference cost was $380, including breakfast and lunch for 3 days, all sessions, as well as a double room; participants responsible for dinner only. Discounts available. "Early Bird Discount: Deduct $25 if paid in full by November 15, 2001." Single-occupancy rooms available at additional cost.

Additional Info: Individual poetry critiques available. "Each poet may have a 20-minute tutorial with one of the poets on staff." Brochure and registration form available by mail or on website. "The Winter Getaway is known for its challenging, yet supportive atmosphere that encourages imaginative risk-taking and promotes freedom and transformation in the participants' writing."

WISCONSIN REGIONAL WRITERS' ASSOCIATION INC.; WISCONSIN REGIONAL WRITER, 510 W. Sunset Ave., Appleton WI 54911-1139. (920)734-3724. Fax: (920)734-5146. E-mail: wrwa@lakefield.net. Website: www.inkwells.net/wrwa (includes conference information and a registration form; membership application; local club network; links to numerous other writer websites; link to upcoming speakers). Biannual conferences held first Saturday in May and last weekend in September. Location: various hotel-conference centers around the state. Average attendance: 100-150.

Purpose/Features: Open to all writers, "aspiring, amateur, or professional." All forms of writing/marketing presentations rotated between conferences. "The purpose is to keep writers informed and prepared to express and market their writing in a proper format." At least one session dedicated to poetry at every conference. Book fair held at the fall conference where members can sell their published works. Banquet also held at the fall conference Saturday and Sunday, where the Jade Ring writing contest winners from 6 categories receive awards. Winners of two additional writing contests also receive awards at the spring conference in May.

Costs/Accommodations: Spring conference is approximately $35-40, the 2-day fall conference approximately $40-60. Conferences also include Saturday morning buffet; fall conference offers hors d'oeuvres buffet at the Book Fair and entertainment at the Jade Ring Banquet. Meals (Saturday luncheon and dinner) are at an additional cost. Information about overnight accommodations available. "Our organization 'blocks' rooms at a reduced rate."

Additional Info: Sponsors 3 writing contests/year. Membership in the WRWA and small fee required. Brochure and registration form available for SASE. "We are affiliated with the Wisconsin Fellowship of Poets and the Council of Wisconsin Writers. We also publish a newsletter, *Wisconsin Regional Writer*, four times a year for members."

☑ **THE WRITERS' CENTER AT CHAUTAUQUA**, The Chautauque Institution, Special Studies Office, Chautauqua NY 14722. (800)836-ARTS. Website: www.chautauqua-inst.org (includes the latest news from Chautauqua). **Program Director:** Clara Silverstein. Established 1988. Annual event held 9 weeks in summer from late June to late August. Participants may attend for 1 week or more. "We are an independent, cooperative association of writers located on the grounds of Chautauqua Institution." Average attendance: 60 for readings and speeches, 12 for workshops.

Purpose/Features: Readings and speeches open to anyone; workshops open to writers. Purpose is "to make creative writing one of the serious arts in progress at Chautauqua; to provide a vacation opportunity for skilled artists and their families; and to help learning writers improve their skills and vision." Workshops available all 9 weeks. Poetry Works meets 2 hours each day. 2001 leaders included Neil Shepard, Liz Rosenberg, Margaret Gibson, Brad Comann, Kevin Pilkington, Julia Kasdorf, Elaine Terranova, Dan Masterson, and Douglas Goetsch. Prose Works offers 2 hours/day in fiction and nonfiction, writing for children, and Young Writers' Workshops. Poets welcome to explore other fields. Other special features include 2 speeches/week and 1 reading, usually by the Writers-In-Residence.

Costs/Accommodations: Cost is $100/week. Participants responsible for gate fees, housing and meals; "may bring family; sports, concerts, activities for all ages. A week's gate ticket to Chautauqua is $190/adult (less if ordered early); housing cost varies widely, but is not cheap; meals vary widely depending on accommodations— from fine restaurants to cooking in a shared kitchen." Access best by car or plane to Jamestown, NY.

Additional Info: List of workshops available by mail, phone, or on website.

☑ **WRITING TODAY**, Birmingham-Southern College, Box 549003, Birmingham AL 35254. (205)226-4921. Fax: (205)226-3072. E-mail: mross@bsc.edu. Website: www.bsc.edu/events/specialevents/writingtoday/2001.h tm. **Director of Special Events:** Martha Ross. Established 1978. Annual 2-day event. 2001 dates were March 16-17. Location: Birmingham-Southern College campus. Average attendance: 400-500.

Purpose/Features: Open to "everyone interested in writing—beginners, professionals, and students. Conference topics vary year to year depending on who is part of the faculty." 2001 speakers/panelists included Galway Kinnell, James Redfield, Barry Hannah, and Josephine Humphries.

Costs/Accommodations: 2001 conference cost was $120 before deadline ($130 after deadline), including lunches. Cost for a single day's events was $65, including luncheon. Either day's luncheon was $25. $10 cancellation fee. Information on overnight accommodations is available. Accommodations include special rates at area hotels.

Additional Info: Individual critiques available. In addition, the Hackney Literary Awards competition is sponsored as part of the conference. Open to writers nationwide, offers $5,000 ($2,500 state level, $2,500 national level) in prizes for poetry and short stories and a $5,000 award for the novel category. (See listing for the Hackney Literary Awards in the Contests and Awards section.) Conference information and brochure available for SASE or on website.

Organizations

There are many organizations of value to poets. These groups may sponsor workshops and contests, stage readings, publish anthologies and chapbooks, or spread the word about publishing opportunities. A few provide economic assistance or legal advice. The best thing that organizations offer, though, is a support system where poets can turn for a pep talk, a hard-nosed (but sympathetic) critique of a manuscript, or simply the comfort of talking and sharing with others who understand the challenges (and joys) of writing poetry.

Whether national, regional, or as local as your library or community center, each organization has something special to offer. The listings in this section reflect the membership opportunities available to poets with a variety of organizations. Note, too, that many groups provide certain services to both members and nonmembers.

Certain symbols may appear at the beginning of some listings. The (🔃) symbol indicates an organization that is new to this edition; the (✔) symbol signals a change in the contact information from the previous edition. The (⬇) symbol denotes a Canadian organization and the (🌐) symbol an international one.

Since some organizations are included in listings in the Publishers of Poetry, Contest & Awards, and Conferences & Workshops sections of this book, we've included these markets in a cross reference at the end of this section called Additional Organizations. For full information on a listing that interests you, locate it in the General Index and turn to the appropriate page number.

To find out more about groups in your area (including those that may not be listed in *Poet's Market*), contact your YMCA, community center, local colleges and universities, public library, and bookstores (and don't forget newspapers and the Internet). And if you can't find a group that suits your needs, consider starting one yourself. You might be surprised to find there are others in your locality who would welcome the encouragement, feedback, and moral support of a writer's group.

🌐 **ACADEMI–YR ACADEMI GYMREIG/THE WELSH ACADEMY; TALIESIN; NWR; A470: WHAT'S ON IN LITERARY WALES**, Mount Stuart House, 3rd Floor, Cardiff, Wales CF10 5FQ United Kingdom. Phone: 029 2047 2266. Fax: 029 2049 2930. E-mail: post@academi.org. Website: www.academi.org (includes contact details, list of writers, events, competitions). **Chief Executive:** Peter Finch. Established in 1959 to "promote literature in Wales and to assist in the maintaining of its standard." The Welsh National Literature Promotion Agency and Society of Writers is open to "the population of Wales and those outside Wales with an interest in Welsh writing." Currently has 2,000 total members. Levels of membership: associate, full, and fellow. Offerings include promotion of readings, events, conferences, exchanges, tours; employment of literature-development workers; publication of a bimonthly events magazine; publication of a literary magazine in Welsh (*Taliesin*) and another (*NWR*) in English. Sponsors conferences/workshops and contests/awards. Publishes *A470: What's On In Literary Wales*, a magazine appearing 5 times/year that contains information on Welsh literary events. Also available to nonmembers for £15 (annual subscription). Members and nationally known writers give readings that are open to the public. Sponsors open mic readings for members and the public. Membership dues: £15/year (waged) or £7.50/year (unwaged). Additional information available for SASE (or SAE and IRC) by fax, e-mail, or on website.

🔃 **$ THE ACADEMY OF AMERICAN POETS; FELLOWSHIP OF THE ACADEMY OF AMERICAN POETS; WALT WHITMAN AWARD; THE JAMES LAUGHLIN AWARD; HAROLD MORTON LANDON TRANSLATION AWARD; THE LENORE MARSHALL POETRY PRIZE; THE ATLAS FUND; THE RAIZISS/DE PALCHI TRANSLATION AWARD; THE WALLACE STEVENS AWARD; THE AMERICAN POET**, 584 Broadway, Suite 1208, New York NY 10012-3250. (212)274-0343. Fax: (212)274-9427. E-mail: academy@poets.org. Website: www.poets.org. **Executive Director:** William Wadsworth. Established 1934. Robert Penn Warren wrote in *Introduction to Fifty Years of American Poetry*, an anthology published in 1984 containing one poem from each of the 126 Chancellors, Fellows, and Award Winners of the Academy: "What does the Academy do? According to its certificate of incorporation, its purpose is 'To encourage, stimulate and foster the production of American poetry. . . .' The responsibility for its activities lies with the Board of Directors and the Board of 18 Chancellors, which has included, over the years, such figures as Louise Bogan, W.H. Auden, Witter Bynner, Randall Jarrell, Robert Lowell, Robinson Jeffers, Marianne Moore, James Merrill, Robert Fitzgerald, F.O. Matthiessen and Archibald MacLeish—certainly not members of the same poetic church." The Academy Fellowship is a $35,000 award for a distinguished American poet at mid-career. **No applications are accepted.** The Walt Whitman Award pays $5,000 plus publication of a poet's first book by Louisiana State University Press. Winner also receives a 1-month residency at the Vermont Studio Center. Mss of 50-100 pgs. must be submitted between September 15 and November 15 with a $20 entry fee. Entry form required. Send SASE. The James Laughlin Award, for a poet's second book, is also a prize of $5,000. Submissions must be made by a publisher in ms form. The Academy distributes over 9,000 copies of the Whitman Award- and Laughlin Award-winning books to its members. Poets entering either contest must be American citizens. The Harold Morton Landon Translation Award is for translation of a book-length poem, a collection of poems, or a verse-drama translated into English from any language. One award of $1,000 is given each year to a US citizen. Write for guidelines. Most recent award winner was Cola Franzen (2000). The Lenore Marshall Poetry Prize is a $10,000 award for the most outstanding book of poems published in the US in the preceding year. The contest is open to books by living American poets published in a standard edition (40 pgs. or more in length with 500 or more copies). Self-published books are not eligible. Publishers may enter as many books as they wish. Deadline: June 1. Most recent award winner was David Ferry (2000). Guidelines available for SASE. The Atlas Fund assists noncommercial publishers of poetry. Guidelines available for SASE. The Raiziss/de Palchi Translation Award is for outstanding translations of modern Italian poetry into English. A $5,000 book prize and a $20,000 fellowship are given in alternate years. Submissions for the book prize are accepted in odd-numbered years from September 1 through November 1. Submissions for the fellowship are accepted in even-numbered years from September 1 through November 1. Most recent fellow was Geoffrey Brock (1998). Most recent book prize winners were Ruth Feldman and John P. Welle (1999). The Wallace Stevens Award of $150,000 is given annually for proven mastery in the art of poetry. Most recent winner was Frank Bidart. **No applications are accepted.** *American Poet* is an informative periodical sent to those who contribute $25 or more/year. Membership: $45/year. The Academy inaugurated the first Annual National Poetry Month in April, 1996. It also sponsors a national series of poetry readings and panel discussions and offers for sale select audio tapes from its archive of poetry readings. Call or write for a catalog.

☑ **ADIRONDACK LAKES CENTER FOR THE ARTS**, P.O. Box 205, Rte. 28, Blue Mountain Lake NY 12812. (518)352-7715. Fax: (518)352-7333. E-mail: alca@telenet.net. **Program Coordinator:** Darren Miller. Established in 1967 to promote "visual and performing arts through programs and services, to serve established professional and aspiring artists and the region through educational programs and activities of general interest." An independent, private, nonprofit educational organization open to everyone. Currently has 1,300 members. Levels of membership: individual, family, and business. Offerings include workshops for adults and children, reading performances, discussions, and lectures. Offers a "comfortable, cozy performance space—coffeehouse setting with tables, candles, etc." Computers available for members and artists. Publishes a triannual newsletter/schedule that contains news, articles, photos, and a schedule of events. "All members are automatically sent the schedule and others may request a copy." Sponsors a few readings each year. "These are usually given by the instructor of our writing workshops. There is no set fee for membership, a gift of any size makes you a member." Members meet each July. Additional information is available for SASE and by fax and e-mail.

N **ALABAMA STATE POETRY SOCIETY; THE SAMPLER; THE MUSE MESSENGER**, 420 20th St. N., Suite 1600, Birmingham AL 35203-5202. (205)250-8333. Fax: (205)322-8007. E-mail: bsm@blik.com. Website: http://poetry.wecre8.com (includes information on contests, programs, meetings, and events). **Contact:** Barry S. Marks. Established in 1969 to promote poetry and help members improve, publish, and perform their work. Statewide organization open to anyone. Affiliated with the National Federation of State Poetry Societies (NFSPS). Currently has 175 total members. Offerings include contests (including annual chapbook contests), publishing and performing opportunities, and critiques by committee. Sponsors conferences/workshops. Publishes anthologies (*The Sampler* now in its 32nd year). Also publishes *The Muse Messenger*, a quarterly newsletter featuring contest and meeting information. Members and nationally known writers give readings. "We hold festivals for the public." Membership dues: $20/year. Members meet 3 times/year. Additional information is available for SASE, by e-mail or on website.

ARIZONA AUTHORS ASSOCIATION; ARIZONA LITERARY MAGAZINE; ARIZONA AUTHORS NEWSLETTER, P.O. Box 87857, Phoenix AZ 85080-7857. (623)780-0053. Fax: (623)780-0468. E-mail: vijayaschartz@az.rmci.net. Website: http://home.rmci.net/vijayaschartz/azauthors.htm (includes information about the Arizona Authors Association, membership, meetings, and book signings as well as contest forms and guidelines, member news, and links). President: Vijaya Schartz. **Contact:** Contest Coordinator. Established in 1978 to provide education and referral for writers and others in publishing. State-wide organization. Currently has 250 total members. Levels of memberships: Published, Unpublished (seeking publication), Professional (printers, agents, and publishers), and Student. Sponsors conferences, workshops, contests, awards. Sponsors annual literary contest with 4 categories: poetry, short story, essay, and unpublished and published books. Awards publication in *Arizona Literary Magazine*, radio interview, publication of novel by 1stbooks.com in e-book and print-on-demand, and $100 1st Prize in each category. Pays winners from other countries by international money order. Does not accept entry fees in foreign currencies. Poetry submissions must be unpublished and may be entered in other contests. Submit any number of poems on any subject of up to 42 lines. Entry form and guidelines available for SASE. Entry fee: $10/poem. Submission period: January 1 through July 1. Competition receives 1,000 entries/year. Most recent contest winners include Michael Murphy, Marion Ekholm, Betty Brownlow, and Constance Gelvin. Judges are Arizona authors. Winners will be announced by November 15. Publishes *Arizona Literary Magazine* and *Arizona Authors Newsletter*. Membership dues: $45. Members meet bimonthly. Additional information and guidelines available for SASE, by fax, e-mail, and on website.

✓ **ASSOCIATED WRITING PROGRAMS; WRITER'S CHRONICLE; THE AWP AWARD SERIES**, Tallwood House, MS 1E3, George Mason University, Fairfax VA 22030. (703)993-4301. Fax: (703)993-4302. E-mail: awp@gmu.edu. Website: www.awpwriter.org (includes information on AWP's core services, contest guidelines, conference information, links to other writer's organizations and creative writing programs). **Publications Manager:** Katherine Perry. Established 1967. Offers a variety of services to the writing community, including information, job placement assistance, writing contests, literary arts advocacy, and forums. Annual individual membership: $59; placement service extra. Publishes *The Writer's Chronicle* containing information about grants and awards, publishing opportunities, fellowships, and writing programs. Available for $20/6 issues. Also publishes a directory, *The AWP Official Guide to Writing Programs*, of over 250 college and university writing programs, available for $25.95 (includes shipping); and the *AWP Job List* magazine, approximately 20 pgs., that contains employment opportunity listings for writers in higher education, editing, and publishing. The AWP Award Series selects a volume of poetry (48 pg. minimum) each year ($10 entry fee for members; $20 for nonmembers) with an award of $2,000 and publication. Deadline: February 28. Submission guidelines available for business-sized SASE. Query after November. Competition receives approximately 1,400 entries. Most recent contest winners include Joanie V. Mackowski, Alexander Parsons, Brian Lennon, and Michelle Richmond. Offers placement service that helps writers find jobs in teaching, editing, and other related fields.

🌐 ✓ **ASSOCIATION OF CHRISTIAN WRITERS; CANDLE AND KEYBOARD**, 73 Lodge Hill Rd., Farnham, Surrey GU10 3RB England. Phone/fax: (01252)715746. E-mail: admin@christianwriters.org.uk. Website: www.christianwriters.org.uk. **Administrator:** Warren Crawford. Established in 1971 "to inspire, train, equip, and encourage Christian writers." National charity with regional affiliations open to "anyone who affirms and practises the Christian faith and writes for pleasure or profit." Currently has 1,000 total members. Levels of membership: New Writers (exploring), Noncommercial Writers, Intermediate (few pieces published), and Experienced Writers (regularly published). Offerings include "market news in quarterly magazine, poetry adviser for personal manuscript critiques, postal workshops with other poets, and poetry competitions." Arranges 3 training days/year and annual contests. Publishes *Candle and Keyboard*, a quarterly magazine. Membership dues: £17 sterling/year. Additional information available for SASE and by fax and e-mail.

✓ **THE AUTHORS GUILD, INC.; THE BULLETIN**, 31 E. 28th St., New York NY 10016. (212)564-5904. Fax: (212)564-8363. E-mail: staff@authorsguild.org. Website: www.authorsguild.org. **Executive Director:** Paul Aiken. Established in 1912, it "is the largest association of published writers in the United States. The Guild focuses its efforts on the legal and business concerns of published authors in the areas of publishing contract terms, copyright, taxation, and freedom of expression. The Guild provides free 75-point book and magazine contract reviews to members and makes group health insurance available to its members. The Guild also sponsors Backinprint.com, a service that allows members to republish and sell their out-of-print books. Writers must be published by a recognized book publisher or periodical of general circulation to be eligible for membership. We do not work in the area of marketing mss to publishers nor do we sponsor or participate in awards or prize selections." Also publishes *The Bulletin*, a quarterly journal for professional writers. Additional information available by mail, phone, and e-mail.

✓ **AUTHORS LEAGUE FUND**, 31 E. 28th St., 10th Floor, New York NY 10016. **Administrator:** Sarah Heller. Makes interest-free loans to published authors and professional playwrights in need of temporary help because of illness or an emergency. No grants.

✓ **THE BEATLICKS; BEATLICK NEWS**, 1016 Kipling Dr., Nashville TN 37217. (615)366-9012. Fax: (615)366-4117. E-mail: beatlick@bellsouth.net. Website: www.geocities.com/SoHo/Studios/9307/beatlick.html or beatlickontour.homestead.com/ (includes mission statement, poetry, pictures, and calendar and Beatlick products). **Editor:** Joe Speer. Established in 1988 to "promote literature and create a place where writers can share their work." International organization open to "anyone interested in literature." Currently has 200 members. "There is no official distinction between members, but there is a core group that does the work, writes reviews, organizes readings, etc." Offerings include publication of work (they have published poets from Australia, Egypt, India, and Holland), reviews of books and venues, readings for local and touring poets, and a poetry hotline. "We have also hosted an open mic reading in Nashville since 1988. We have read in bars, bookstores, churches, libraries, festivals, TV, and radio. We produce an hour show every Friday, Saturday, and Sunday on CATV, Channel 19. Poets submit audio and video tapes from all over. We interview poets about their work and where they are from." Publishes *Beatlick News*, a bimonthly networking tool designed to inform poets of local events and to bring awareness of the national scene. "We include poems, short fiction, art, photos, and articles about poets and venues." Submit short pieces, no vulgar language. "We try to elevate the creative spirit. We publish new voices plus well-established talents." Subscription: $12/year. Members meet twice a month. Additional information available for SASE and by fax and e-mail. "We promote all the arts."

BURNABY WRITERS' SOCIETY, 6584 Deer Lake Ave., Burnaby, British Columbia V5G 3T7 Canada. Website: www.bws.bc.ca (includes contest details, markets, resources). **Contact:** Eileen Kernaghan. Established 1967. Corresponding membership in the society, including a newsletter subscription, is open to anyone, anywhere. Yearly dues: $30. Sample newsletter in return for SASE with Canadian stamp. Holds monthly meetings at The Burnaby Arts Centre (located at 6450 Deer Lake Ave.), with a business meeting at 7:30 followed by a writing workshop or speaker. Members of the society stage regular public readings of their own work. Sponsors a contest for poetry open to British Columbia residents. Competition receives about 200-400 entries/year. Past contest winners include Mildred Tremblay, Frank McCormack, and Kate Braid. Additional information and contest guidelines available for SASE or on website.

THE WITTER BYNNER FOUNDATION FOR POETRY, INC., P.O. Box 10169, Santa Fe NM 87504. (505)988-3251. Fax: (505)986-8222. E-mail: bynnerfoundation@aol.com. Website: www.bynnerfoundation.org (includes information concerning the foundation's history, mission statement, grant programs, and application process). **Director:** Steven Schwartz. Awards grants, ranging from $1,000 to $15,000, exclusively to nonprofit organizations for the support of poetry-related projects in the area of: 1) support of individual poets through existing nonprofit institutions; 2) developing the poetry audience; 3) poetry translation and the process of poetry translation; and 4) uses of poetry. "May consider the support of other creative and innovative projects in poetry." Letters of intent accepted annually from September 1 through December 1; requests for application forms should be submitted to Steven Schwartz, executive director. Applications, if approved, must be returned to the Foundation postmarked by February 1. Additional information is available by fax and e-mail.

CANADIAN CONFERENCE OF THE ARTS (CCA); BLIZZART, 130 Albert St., Suite 804, Ottawa, Ontario K1P 5G4 Canada. (613)238-3561. Fax: (613)238-4849. E-mail: cca@mail.culturenet.ca. Website: www.c ulturenet.ca/cca (includes CCA activities and information). National, nongovernmental, not-for-profit arts service organization dedicated to the growth and vitality of the arts and cultural industries in Canada. The CCA represents all Canadian artists, cultural workers, and arts supporters and works with all levels of government, the corporate sector, and voluntary organizations to enhance appreciation for the role of culture in Canadian life. Each year, the CCA presents awards for contribution to the arts. Regular meetings held across the country ensure members' views on urgent and ongoing issues are heard and considered in organizing advocacy efforts and forming Board policies. Members stay informed and up-to-date through *Blizzart*, a newsletter published 4 times/year, and receive discounts on conference fees and on all other publications. Membership dues: $35 (plus GST) for Canadian individual members, $40 for US members, and $45 for international members.

CANADIAN POETRY ASSOCIATION; POEMATA; THE SHAUNT BASMAJIAN CHAP-BOOK AWARD; CPA ANNUAL POETRY CONTEST, P.O. Box 22571, St. George PO, Toronto, Ontario M5S 1V8 Canada. (905)312-1779. Fax: (905)312-8285. E-mail: writers@sympatico.ca. Website: www.mirror. org/cpa. **National Coordinator:** Wayne Ray. Established 1985 "to promote all aspects of the reading, writing, publishing, purchasing and preservation of poetry in Canada. The CPA promotes the creation of local chapters to organize readings, workshops, publishing projects, and other poetry-related events in their area." Membership is open to anyone with an interest in poetry, including publishers, schools, libraries, booksellers and other literary organizations. Publishes a bimonthly magazine, *Poemata*, featuring news articles, chapter reports, poetry by new members, book reviews, markets information, announcements and more. Sample: $3. Membership dues: $30/ year; seniors and students: $20. Membership form available for SASE and on website. Also sponsors the following contests: The Shaunt Basmajian Chapbook Award offers $100 (Canadian) and publication, plus 50 copies. Guidelines available for SASE and on website. Annual deadline: April 30. The CPA Annual Poetry Contest offers prizes of $50, $40, $30, $20, $10, $5, with up to 10 Honorable Mentions. Winning poems published in *Poemata* and on CPA website. Postmark deadline: June 30 annually. Guidelines available for SASE and on website.

COLUMBINE STATE POETRY SOCIETY OF COLORADO, P.O. Box 461131, Denver CO 80246. (303)465-0883. E-mail: copoets@aol.com. Website: http://members.aol.com/copoets. **Secretary/Treasurer:** Anita Gilbert. Established in 1978 to promote the writing and appreciation of poetry throughout Colorado. State-wide organization open to anyone interested in poetry. Currently has 90 total members. Levels of membership: Members at Large, who do not participate in the local chapters but who belong to the National Federation of State Poetry Societies and at the state level; and Members, who belong to the national, state, and local chapter in Denver, Colorado. Offerings for the Denver Chapter include weekly workshops and monthly critiques. Sponsors contests, awards for students and adults. Sponsors the Annual Poets Fest where members and nationally known writers give readings and workshops that are open to the public. Also sponsors a chapbook contest in alternate years under Riverstone Press. Membership dues: $10 state and national; $25 local, state, and national. Members meet weekly. Additional information available for SASE or by e-mail.

N CONNECTICUT POETRY SOCIETY; CT RIVER REVIEW; CPS NEWSLETTER, P.O. Box 4053, Waterbury CT 06704-0053. (203)753-7815. Fax: (203)753-1703. E-mail: wtarzia@nvctc.5commnet.edu. Website: http://pagesprodigy.net/mmwalhercpsindex.html. **Co-Presidents:** Joan Ketrys and Joan Malerba-Foran. Established in 1974 to promote interest in and regard for good poetry; to assist members regarding writing techniques, markets, critiques, etc. Affiliated with the National Federation of State Poetry Societies (NFSPS). Organization open to anyone. Currently has approximately 200 total members. Offerings include annual meetings, chapters. Sponsors contests/awards. Publishes *CT River Review*, a national poetry magazine. Also publishes *CPS Newsletter*, a quarterly that contains a variety of poetry, members, and event news. Not available to nonmembers. Members and nationally known writers give readings that are open to the public. Sponsors open mic readings for members and the public. Membership dues: $25/year. Members meet monthly. Additional information available for SASE, by e-mail, or on website.

N COUNCIL OF LITERARY MAGAZINES AND PRESSES; DIRECTORY OF LITERARY MAGAZINES, 154 Christopher St., Suite 3C, New York NY 10014-2839. (212)741-9110. Website: www.clmp.org (includes member directory, publishing resources, discussion boards, The Literary Landscape). Compiles an annual directory useful to writers: the *Directory of Literary Magazines*, which has detailed descriptions of over 600 literary magazines, including type of work published, payment to contributors, and submission requirements. The directory is $17 postage paid and may be ordered by sending a check to CLMP. Additional information available by fax and e-mail.

N DALLAS POETS COMMUNITY, P.O. Box 225435, Dallas TX 75222-5435. Website: www.dallaspoets. org (includes history, mission statement, goals, guidelines for joining, and contests). **Director:** Christopher Soden. Established 1990 to provide a "safe" workshop environment for the nurturing and refining of talent, facilitate recognition for talented poets, and organize readings and events. Regional (Dallas-Ft. Worth metroplex). Organization open to poets writing at the appropriate level. Currently has 10-15 total members. "There is a 'probationary' period before a poet is allowed to join as a permanent member." Member benefits include workshops twice a month, readings throughout the year, opportunities to teach poetry in the schools and assist with the publication of *Illya's Honey*, a poetry/short fiction magazine published 4 times/year. (See separate listing for *Illya's Honey* in the Publishers of Poetry section). Sponsors conferences/workshops and contests/awards. "We have poetry workshops twice a month and an annual poetry contest to raise money for our organization." Members and nationally known writers give readings that are open to the public. Membership dues: $50/year. Members meet every two weeks (every first and third Sunday afternoon).

✓ DAVIDSON COUNTY WRITERS' GUILD, Arts Council for Davidson County, 23 W. Second Ave., Lexington NC 27292. (336)248-2551. Fax: (336)248-2000. E-mail: fraziers@lexcominc.net. **President:** Marge Doty. Established in 1972 to "encourage creative writing; to bring together writers and those interested in writing; to share ideas and inspiration and to critique original pieces; to provide resources and programs to help develop writing talents; to provide opportunities to have writing talents recognized; and to promote writing through contests for children, youth, and adults." A county-wide organization open to any interested person 16 years of age and older. Currently has 15 active members. Membership benefits include "monthly meetings that offer opportunities to read original work, and occasional guest speakers conducting workshops—including poetry-related topics. The Guild's monthly meetings are conducted in a conference room above Frazier's Bookstore." Sponsors 3 annual writing contests—Adult, High School, and Youth. "Winning and runner-up entries are published for the High School and Youth Contests in a book entitled *Ventures in Writing*." Competition receives over 300 entries/year. Members give readings that are open to the public. Sponsors open-mic readings. Membership dues: $15/year. Members meet monthly. Additional information available for SASE, by fax, or by e-mail.

🌐 THE EASTERN SUBURBS POETRY GROUP-N.S.W., Off Oxford St. Complex, Bondi Junction, N.S.W. Australia. Phone: (02)96992129. E-mail: merlyn@easy.com.au. **Coordinator/Founder:** Merlyn Swan. Established in 1988 to provide "a platform for poets to express themselves, the publishing of group's contributions, improvement of skills through themes set by group, and occasional workshops." Open to "anyone interested in writing and/or listening to poetry." Currently has 50 core members. "Many others come in and out for the occasional meeting." Membership benefits include having audience reaction and comments; an annual Public Reading; meeting and communicating with fellow poets/writers; chance to enhance skills; meeting and tackling new ideas. Also sponsors conferences/workshops. Members give readings that are open to the public. Sponsors

MARKET CONDITIONS are constantly changing! If you're still using this book and it is 2003 or later, buy the newest edition of *Poet's Market* at your favorite bookstore or order directly from Writer's Digest Books (800)289-0963 or www.writersdigest.com.

open mic readings for members. "We have an annual festival, and poets who have attended three meetings in the year can read a couple or more poems." Membership dues: $3/attendance. "We meet every first Friday of the month at Church in the Market Place. The Waverley Library sponsors our annual festival." Additional information available for SASE (or SAE and IRC) or by e-mail.

☑ **GEORGIA POETRY SOCIETY; BYRON HERBERT REECE CONTEST; EDWARD DAVIN VICKERS CONTEST; CHARLES B. DICKSON CHAPBOOK CONTEST; MARGERY CARLSON YOUTH AWARDS; OCTAVIO PAZ SPANISH LANGUAGE POETRY WRITING CONTEST; GEORGIA POETRY SOCIETY NEWSLETTER**, P.O. Box 371123, Decatur GA 30037-1123. (404)289-9428. E-mail: lancethrower@iopener.net. Website: http://pages.prodigy.net/elcampbell (includes history of GPS, membership, contests, events, publications, resources and links, outreach programs, members' news, featured poet, and acknowledgements). **President:** Herbert W. Denmark. Established in 1979 to further the purposes of the National Federation of State Poetry Societies, Inc. (NFSPS) in securing fuller public recognition of the art of poetry; to stimulate a finer and more intelligent appreciation of poetry; and to provide opportunity for study of and incentive for practice in the writing and reading of poetry. State-wide organization open to any person who is in accord with the objectives listed above. No restrictions as to age, race, religion, color, national origin, or physical or mental abilities. Currently has 190 total members. Levels of membership: Active, fully eligible for all aspects of membership; Student, same as Active except pays lower dues, does not vote or hold office, and must be full-time enrolled student through college level; Lifetime, same as Active but pays a one-time membership fee the equivalent of approximately 15 years' dues, receives free anthologies each year, and pays no contest entry fees. Offerings include affiliation with NFSPS. At least one workshop is held annually, contests are throughout the year, some for members only and some for general submissions. Workshops deal with specific areas of poetry writing, publishing, etc. Contests include the Byron Herbert Reece Contest, Edward Davin Vickers Contest, Charles B. Dickson Chapbook Contest (members only), and many ongoing or one-time contests, with awards ranging from $250 downwards. Most recent contest winner: Patricia Posey (1st Place, the 2000 Ed Vickers Contest). Entry fees and deadlines vary. Does not accept entry fees in foreign currencies. Send US dollars or money orders. Guidelines available for SASE. Publishes *Georgia Poetry Society Newsletter*, a quarterly. Also available to nonmembers on request. Readings held annually to celebrate National Poetry Day (October) and National Poetry Month (April) in public forums such as libraries; some with specified poets reading their own poetry or works of famous poets, and some open mic readings. At each quarterly meeting (open to the public) members have an opportunity to read their own poems. Current annual membership dues: Active, $20; Family, $35; Student, $10; Lifetime, $300. Members meet quarterly. "Our bylaws require rotation in office. We sponsor an active and popular Poetry in the Schools project, conducting workshops or readings in schools throughout the state by invitation. We also sponsor the annual Margery Carlson Youth Awards contest in all Georgia schools and winning poems are submitted to the Manningham Youth Awards contest of NFSPS. Our membership ranges from 9 to 93 years of age." Also sponsors The Octavio Paz Spanish Language Poetry Writing Contest with prizes of $50, $25, $10. Entry fee: $1/poem. Deadline: June 15.

☑ **GREATER CINCINNATI WRITERS' LEAGUE**, 2735 Rosina Ave., Covington KY 41015. (859)491-2130. E-mail: karenlgeo@aol.com. **President:** Karen George. Established in 1930s "to promote and support poetry and those who write poetry in the Cincinnati area and the attainment of excellence in poetry as an art and a craft. We believe in education and discipline, as well as creative freedom, as important components in the development of our own poetry and open, constructive critique as a learning tool." Regional organization open to anyone interested in and actively writing. Currently has 35 total members. Offerings include a monthly meeting/workshop or critique. Critics are published poets, usually faculty members from local universities, who critique poems submitted by members. The group also joins in the critique. Sponsors workshops, contests (none planned for 2001-2002), awards with monetary prizes, and an anthology published every few years. Members give readings that are open to the public or sponsor open mic readings at bookstores and other locations. Membership dues: $25. Members meet monthly. Additional information available for SASE.

Ⓝ THE HUDSON VALLEY WRITERS' CENTER; CROSSCURRENTS, 300 Riverside Dr., Sleepy Hollow NY 10591-1414. (914)332-5953. Fax: (914)332-4825. E-mail: info@writerscenter.org. Website: www.writerscenter.org (includes events calendar, class schedule, publications, chapbook competition guidelines). **Executive Director:** Dare Thompson. Established 1988. "The Hudson Valley Writers' Center is a nonprofit organization devoted to furthering the literary arts and literacy in our region. Its mission is to promote the appreciation of literary excellence, to stimulate and nurture the creation of literary works in all sectors of the population, and to bring the diverse works of gifted poets and prose artists to the attention of the public." National organization open to all. Currently has 350 total members. Levels of membership: individual, family, senior, student, and donor. Offerings include public readings by established and emerging poets/writers, workshops and classes, monthly open mic nights, paid and volunteer outreach opportunities, and an annual chapbook competition. "We are housed in the former Philipse Manor Railroad Station in Sleepy Hollow, NY. The main room of the station serves as our class and performance space, with a maximum occupancy of approximately 85 people. Our building overlooks the Hudson River. Our small press imprint, Slapering Hol Press, holds an annual chapbook competition for emerging poets who have not yet published a book or chapbook. The winner receives a cash award, publication, and a reading at the Writers' Center." (See separate listing for Slapering Hol Press in Publishers of Poetry section;

see separate listing for Slapering Hol Press Chapbook Competition in the Contests & Awards section.) Also publishes *Crosscurrents*, an occasional newsletter with program information and interviews with writers. "We also send class and event flyers and brochures on a regular basis, averaging one per month." Available to nonmembers. Members and nationally known writers give readings that are open to the public. Sponsors open mic readings for members and the public. "Open mics are held on the third Friday of each month and are open to all writers, with a five minute limit for each reader." Membership dues: $35 individual, $45 family, and $15 senior/student. Additional information available for SASE, by fax, e-mail, or on website.

ILLINOIS STATE POETRY SOCIETY; ISPS NEWS, 5515 E. Lake Dr. #A, Lisle IL 60532. (630)969-8473. Website: www.illinoispoets.org (includes club information and member poetry). **President:** Dr. Mardelle Fortier. Established in 1991 "to promote and enhance poetry." Statewide, affiliated with the National Federation of State Poetry Societies (NFSPS). Organization open to adult and college student members. Currently has 35 total members. Offerings include local newsletter, NFSPS newsletter (*Strophes*), meetings and workshops, annual poetry contest, and club website. Publishes *ISPS News*, a bimonthly newsletter which contains messages and news of interest to members, contest news, member poetry, and biographies of members. Not available to nonmembers. "Club has a monthly coffeehouse reading open to members and the public." Membership dues: $15/year. Members meet bimonthly "at various libraries and other community facilities." Additional information available for SASE and on website.

INTERNATIONAL WOMEN'S WRITING GUILD; NETWORK, P.O. Box 810, Gracie Station, New York NY 10028. (212)737-7536. Fax: (212)737-9469. E-mail: dirhahn@aol.com. Website: www.iwwg.com (includes membership services, calendar of events, profiles of members, etc.). **Contact:** Hannelore Hahn. Established 1976 as "a network for the personal and professional empowerment of women through writing." The Guild publishes a bimonthly 32-page journal, *Network*, which includes members' needs, achievements, contests, and publishing information. A manuscript referral service introduces members to literary agents. Other activities and benefits are annual national and regional events, including a summer conference (see separate listing for The IWWG Summer Conference in the Conferences & Workshops section); "regional clusters" (independent regional groups); round robin manuscript exchanges; and group health insurance. Membership dues: $45/year (domestic and overseas). Additional information available by fax and e-mail.

LIVING SKIES FESTIVAL OF WORDS; THE WORD, 88 Saskatchewan St. E., Moose Jaw, Saskatchewan S6H 0V4 Canada. (306)691-0557. Fax: (306)693-2994. E-mail: word.festival@sk.sympatico.ca. Website: www3.sk.sympatico.ca/praifes (includes excerpts from the newsletter, past presenters featured, news of upcoming events, and news of Festival). **Operations Manager:** Lori Dean. "Established in 1996, the purpose/philosophy of the organization is to celebrate the imaginative uses of languages. The Festival of Words is a registered nonprofit group of over 150 volunteers who present an enjoyable and stimulating celebration of the imaginative ways we use language. We operate year round bringing special events to Saskatchewan, holding open microphone coffeehouses for youth, and culminating in an annual summer festival in July which features activities centered around creative uses of language." National organization open to writers and readers. Currently has 142 total members. Offerings include "The Festival of Words programs with readings by poets, panel discussions, and workshops. In addition, poets attending get to share ideas, get acquainted, and conduct impromptu readings. The activities sponsored are held in the Moose Jaw Library/Art Museum complex, as well as in various venues around the city." Sponsors workshops as part of the Festival of Words. "We are also associated with *FreeLance* magazine, a publication of the Saskatchewan Writers' Guild. This publication features many useful articles dealing with poetry writing and writing in general." Also publishes *The Word*, a newsletter appearing approximately 6-7 times/year that contains news of Festival events, fund-raising activities, profiles of members, reports from members. Also available to nonmembers. First issue is free. Members and nationally known writers give readings that are open to the public. Sponsors open mic readings for members and for the public. Membership dues: $5. Additional information available for SASE, by fax, e-mail, or on website.

THE LOFT LITERARY CENTER (Specialized: Regional); A VIEW FROM THE LOFT, Suite 200, Open Book, 1011 Washington Ave. S, Minneapolis MN 55414. (612)215-2575. Fax: (612)215-2576. E-mail: loft@loft.org. Website: www.loft.org. Established 1974. "The Loft was started by a group of poets looking for a place to give readings and conduct workshops and has evolved into the most comprehensive literary center in the country, offering opportunities for Minnesota writers in all genres and at all levels of development." Managed by a 35-member board of directors and staff of 15. Currently has 1,800 total members. In addition to membership dues, financial support comes from tuition for creative writing classes, fees from benefit performances, and contributions from individuals, corporations, and foundations. The Loft offers over 150 courses each year in addition to 80 workshops and panels. Its reading series presents established and emerging writers throughout Minnesota. Programs also bring in visiting writers from around the country to serve as mentors. The Loft publishes *A View from the Loft*, a monthly magazine on craft. Grants and fellowships are awarded only to writers who are residents of Minnesota.

MANITOBA WRITERS' GUILD INC.; MANITOBA WRITING AND PUBLISHING AWARDS; WINNIPEG INTERNATIONAL WRITERS FESTIVAL; WORDWRAP, 206-100 Arthur St., Winnipeg,

Manitoba R3B 1H3 Canada. (204)942-6134. Fax: (204)942-5754. E-mail: mbwriter@escape.ca. Website: www.m bwriter.mb.ca. Established in 1981 to "promote and advance the art of writing, in all its forms, throughout the province of Manitoba." Regional organization open to "any individual with an interest in the art of writing." Currently has 550 members. Levels of membership: Regular and Student/Senior/Fixed Income. Programs and services include the Manitoba Workshop Series, intensive 1-day sessions conducted by professional writers; monthly Blue Pencil Sessions held in the fall and winter; an Annual Spring Conference, a 1-day event which includes panel discussions, readings, performances, and special events; the Mentor Program, a limited number of promising writers selected to work one-on-one with experienced mentors; the Manitoba Writing and Publishing Awards which include the McNally Robinson Book of the Year Award and the John Hirsch Award for Most Promising Manitoba Writer (all awards are to "recognize and celebrate excellence in Manitoba writing and publishing"); the Writers' Resource Centre, containing information about writing, publishing, markets, as well as Canadian periodicals and books by Manitoba authors; and 2 studios offering writers comfortable, private work space. Also sponsors the Winnipeg International Writers Festival in the fall. *WordWrap*, a newsletter published 6 times/year, includes feature articles, regular columns, information on current markets and competitions, and profiles of Manitoba writers. Also publishes *The Writers' Handbook*, the Guild's "comprehensive resource manual on the business of writing." Membership dues: $50 Regular, $25 Student/Senior/Fixed Income. Additional information available for SASE.

☑ **MASSACHUSETTS STATE POETRY SOCIETY, INC.; BAY STATE ECHO; THE NATIONAL POETRY DAY CONTEST; THE GERTRUDE DOLE MEMORIAL CONTEST; POET'S CHOICE CONTEST; THE NAOMI CHERKOFSKY MEMORIAL CONTEST; OF THEE I SING! CONTEST**, 64 Harrison Ave., Lynn MA 01905. **President:** Jeanette C. Maes. Established in 1959, dedicated to the writing and appreciation of poetry and promoting the art form. State-wide organization open to anyone with an interest in poetry. Currently has 200 total members. Offerings include critique groups. Sponsors workshops, contests including The National Poetry Day Contest, with prizes of $25, $15, and $10 (or higher) for each of 30 categories. Pays winners from other countries in US currency. Entry fee: $5. Deadline: August 1. Competition receives about 2,000 entries/year. Also sponsors these contests: The Gertrude Dole Memorial Contest, with prizes of $25, $15, and $10. Entry fee: $3. Deadline: March 1. The Poet's Choice Contest, with prizes of $50, $25, and $15. Entry fee: $3/poem. Deadline: November 1. The Naomi Cherkofsky Memorial Contest, with prizes of $50, $30, and $20. Entry fee: $3/poem. Deadline: June 30. The "Of Thee I Sing!" Contest, with prizes of $50, $25, and $15. Deadline: January 15. Does not accept entry fees in foreign currencies. Guidelines available for SASE. Publishes a yearly anthology of poetry and a yearly publication of student poetry contest winners. Also publishes *Bay State Echo*, a newsletter, 5 times/year. Members or nationally known writers give readings that are open to the public. Sponsors open mic readings. Membership dues: $10/year. Members meet 5 times/year. Additional information available for SASE.

MISSISSIPPI POETRY SOCIETY, INC.; THE MAGNOLIA MUSE, 5713 Belle Fontaine, Ocean Springs MS 39564-9084. **State President:** Brenda B. Finnegan. ("This changes annually when new officers are installed.") Established in 1932 "to foster interest in the writing of poetry through a study of poetry and poetic form; to provide an opportunity for, and give recognition to, individual creative efforts relating to poetry; and to create an audience for poetry; and suggest or otherwise make known markets and contests for poetry to its members." Statewide organization, affiliated with the National Federation of State Poetry Societies (NFSPS), consisting of three branches open to "anyone who writes poetry or is interested in fostering the interests of poetry." Currently has 108 total members. Offerings include monthly meetings, annual contests, and an annual awards banquet. State also holds a 1-day Mini-Festival in the fall and an annual 2-day Spring Festival; includes noted speakers and contests. Publishes bimonthly newsletter *Magnolia Muse*, branches publish a newsletter of the same name on a monthly basis. "The state organization also publishes journals of all winning poems each year, and often of other special contests. There are occasionally 'featured poets,' and two or three of their poems are featured in an issue of *Magnolia Muse*." Members or nationally known writers give readings that are open to the public. Membership dues: $20. Members meet monthly at branches, semiannually at the state level. Additional information available for SASE.

☑ **MOUNTAIN WRITERS SERIES; MOUNTAIN WRITERS CENTER NEWSLETTER**, Mountain Writers Center, 3624 SE Milwaukee Ave., Portland OR 97202. (503)236-4854. Fax: (503)731-9735. E-mail: pdxmws@aracnet.com. Website: www.aracnet.com/~pdxmws (includes upcoming programs, workshop registrations, and information about the MWS community). **Associate Director:** Jennifer Grotz. Established in 1973, "Mountain Writers Series is an independent non-profit organization dedicated to supporting writers, audiences, and other sponsors by promoting literature and literacy through artistic and educational literary arts events in the Pacific Northwest." The Center is open to both members and nonmembers. Currently has about 100 total members. Levels of membership: Contributing ($100), Supporting ($500), Patron ($1,000), Basic ($50), Student/ Retired ($25), and Family ($75). "Poets have access to our extensive poetry library, resource center, and space as well as discounts to most events. Members receive a seasonal newsletter as well. Poets may attend 1-day workshops, weekend master classes, 5-week and 10-week courses about writing." Authors who participated in 2000-2001 season include Tony Hoagland, Robert Wrigley, Bruce Smith, Maggie Anderson, Marvin Bell, Peter Coyote, Li-Young Lee, Patricia Goedicke, Nance Van Winckel, and Michael Collier. "The Mountain Writers

Center is an 100-year-old Victorian house with plenty of comfortable gathering space, a reading room, visiting writers room, library, resource center, garden, and Mountain Writers Series offices." Sponsors conferences/workshops. Publishes the *Mountain Writers Center Newsletter*. Also available to nonmembers for $12/year. Sponsors readings that are open to the public. Nationally and internationally known writers are sponsored by the Mountain Writers Series Northwest Regional Residencies Program (reading tours) and the campus readings program (Pulitzer Prize winners, Nobel Prize winners, MacArthur Fellows, etc.). Additional information available for SASE, by fax, e-mail, or on website.

N NATIONAL COWBOY POETRY GATHERING, Western Folklife Center, 501 Railroad St., Elko NV 89801. (775)738-7508. Fax: (775)738-2900. E-mail: wfc@westernfolklife.org. Website: www.westernfolklife.org (includes information about the Western Folklife Center and its programs as well as an online gift shop). **Contact:** Gathering Manager. An 8-day gathering of cowboy poets and musicians in Elko each January. "The well-established tradition of cowboy poetry is enjoying a renaissance, and hundreds of cowboy poets participate in the Gathering each year. The Western Folklife Center distributes books and tapes of cowboy poetry and songs as well as other cowboy memorabilia, and it also sponsors a variety of other community programs throughout the year." Additional information is available by fax, e-mail, and on website.

NATIONAL FEDERATION OF STATE POETRY SOCIETIES, INC.; STEVENS MANUSCRIPT COMPETITION; ENCORE; STROPHES. Membership Chairperson: Sy Swann, 2736 Creekwood Lane, Ft. Worth TX 76123-1105. (817)292-8598 or (605)768-2127 (June and July). Fax: (817)531-6593. E-mail: JFS@fl ash.net. Website: www.nfsps.com (includes history, contact info, contests, publications). **Contest Chairs:** Irvin and Patricia Kimber, 1220 W. Koradine Dr., South Jordan UT 84095 (e-mail: irvkimber@lgcy.com). Established in 1959, "NFSPS is a nonprofit organization exclusively educational and literary. Its purpose is to recognize the importance of poetry with respect to national cultural heritage. It is dedicated solely to the furtherance of poetry on the national level and serves to unite poets in the bonds of fellowship and understanding." Any poetry group located in a state not already affiliated but interested in affiliating with NFSPS may contact the membership chairperson. Canadian groups may also apply. "In a state where no valid group exists, help may also be obtained by individuals interested in organizing a poetry group for affiliation." Most reputable state poetry societies are members of the National Federation and advertise their various poetry contests through the quarterly bulletin, *Strophes*, available for SASE and $1, edited by Vera Bakker, 784 W. 1400 North, West Bountiful UT 84087 (e-mail: veraobakker@msn.com). **Beware of organizations calling themselves state poetry societies (however named) that are not members of NFSPS,** as such labels are sometimes used by vanity schemes trying to sound respectable. Others, such as the Oregon State Poetry Association, are quite reputable, but they don't belong to NFSPS. NFSPS holds an annual meeting in a different city each year with a large awards banquet, addressed by a renowned poet and writer. Sponsors 50 national contests in various categories each year, including the NFSPS Prize of $1,500 for 1st Prize; 2nd Prize: $500; 3rd Prize: $250 with entry fees ($3 for the entire contest for members, $5 for NFSPS Award; $1/poem for nonmembers and $5 for NFSPS Award, up to 4 poems/entry). All poems winning over $15 are published in the anthology, *ENCORE*. Rules for all contests are given in a brochure available from Vera Bakker at *Strophes* or Irvin and Patricia Kimber at the address above and on website; you can also write for the address of your state poetry society. Sponsors the annual Stevens Manuscript Competition with a 1st Prize of $1,000 and publication, 2nd Prize: $500; October 1 deadline. Contact Amy Zook, 3520 St. Rt. 56, Mechanicsburg OH 43044. Scholarship information available from Madelyn Eastlund, 310 S. Adams St., Beverly Hills FL 34465 (e-mail: verdure@digitalusa.net). Additional information available by fax or e-mail.

☑ $ NATIONAL LEAGUE OF AMERICAN PEN WOMEN, INC.; THE PEN WOMAN, 1300 17th St. NW, Washington DC 20036-1973. Phone/fax: (978)443-2165. E-mail: nlapw1@juno.com. Website: http://members.aol.com/penwomen/pen.htm. **National Scholarship Chair:** Mary Jane Hillery. Established in 1897, national organization open to professional women in the creative arts. Currently has 4,500 total members. Levels of membership: "full members, those who provide proof of payment for creative work—writers, artists, composers; associate members, those in the creative arts who have not supplied proof of payment for sufficient works." Offerings include opportunities for publication and cash prizes in contests. "The National Headquarters is in Northwest Washington DC within walking distance of the White House and many DC landmarks and memorials. It is a converted mansion in which Robert Todd Lincoln and his family lived for several months. We are near DuPont Circle with bookstores, computer center." Sponsors conferences/workshops and contests/awards. "A penwoman publishes *The Pen Woman*, a quarterly magazine in which previously published poems are published for greater exposure." Members and nationally known writers give readings that are open to the public. Membership dues: $30 to NLAPW, branch dues vary. Additional information available for SASE or on website. Also sponsors a biennial $1,000 grant for which only nonmember women poets are qualified to enter; receives over 1,000 entries total. Flyer available for SASE. (See separate listing for Mature Women's Grants in the Contests & Awards section.)

☑ THE NATIONAL POETRY FOUNDATION; SAGETRIEB; PAIDEUMA, University of Maine, 5752 Neville Hall, Room 302, Orono ME 04469-5752. (207)581-3813. Fax: (207)581-3886. E-mail: sapiel@maine.e du. Website: www.ume.maine.edu/~npf/ (includes a listing of available books, order forms, and mission statement). **Contact:** Burton Hatlen. "The NPF is a nonprofit organization concerned with publishing scholarship on the work of 20th century poets, particularly Ezra Pound and those in the Imagist/Objectivist tradition. We publish *Paideuma*, a journal devoted to Ezra Pound scholarship, and *Sagetrieb*, a journal devoted to poets in the imagist/objectivist tradition, as well as books on and of poetry. NPF occasionally conducts a summer conference." Sample copies: $8.95 for *Paideuma* or *Sagetrieb*. Additional information available for SASE, by fax, or on website.

NATIONAL WRITERS ASSOCIATION; AUTHORSHIP, 3140 S. Peoria, #295, Aurora CO 80014. (303)841-0246. Fax: (303)751-8593. Website: www.nationalwriters.com. **Executive Director:** Sandy Whelchel. Established 1937. National organization with regional affiliations open to writers. Currently has 3,000 total members. Levels of membership: Published Writers and Other Writers. Hosts an annual Summer Conference where workshops, panels, etc. are available to all attendees, including poets. Also offers a yearly poetry writing contest with cash awards of $100, $50, and $25. Pays winners from other countries by US check. Entry fee: $10/poem. Accepts entry fees in foreign currencies. Deadline: October 1. Send SASE for judging sheet copies. Publishes *Authorship*, an annual magazine. Sample copy available for 9×12 envelope with $1.21 postage. Also available to nonmembers for $18. Memberships dues: Professional $85; others $65. Members meet monthly. Additional information available for SASE, by fax, or e-mail. Contest forms available on website.

NEVADA POETRY SOCIETY, P.O. Box 7014, Reno NV 89510. (775)322-3619. **President:** Sam Wood. Established in 1976 to encourage the writing and critiquing of poetry. State-wide organization. Currently has 30 total members. Levels of membership: Active and Emeritus. Offerings include membership in the National Federation of State Poetry Societies (NFSPS), including their publication, *Strophes*; monthly challenges followed by critiquing of all new poems; lessons on types of poetry. Members of the society are occasionally called upon to read to organizations or in public meetings. Membership dues: $10 (this includes membership in NFSPS). Members meet monthly. "We advise poets to enter their poems in contests before thinking about publication."

N: NEW HAMPSHIRE WRITERS' PROJECT; EX LIBRIS, P.O. Box 2693, Concord NH 03302-2693. (603)226-6649. Fax: (603)226-0035. E-mail: nhwp@ultranet.com. Website: www.nhwritersproject.org (includes updated calendar of events, articles of interest to writers, links to author's homepages, and information about NHWP). **Executive Director:** Katie Goodman. Established in 1988 "to foster the literary arts community in New Hampshire, to serve as a resource for and about New Hampshire writers, to support the development of individual writers, and to encourage an audience for literature in New Hampshire." State-wide organization open to anyone. Currently has 850 members. Offerings include workshops, seminars, and information about poetry readings held throughout northern New England. Sponsors day-long workshops and 4- to 6-week intensive courses. Also sponsors biennial awards for outstanding literary achievement. Publishes *Ex Libris*, a bimonthly newsletter for members only. Members and nationally known writers give readings that are open to the public. Also sponsors open mic readings. Membership dues: $35/year; $20/year for Seniors and students. Members meet annually. Additional information available for SASE, by fax, or e-mail.

N: NORTH CAROLINA WRITERS' NETWORK; THE WRITERS' NETWORK NEWS; NORTH CAROLINA'S LITERARY RESOURCE GUIDE; RANDALL JARRELL POETRY PRIZE, P.O. Box 954, Carrboro NC 27510. (919)967-9540. Fax: (919)929-0535. E-mail: mail@ncwriters.org. Website: www.ncwriters.org (includes complete information about NCWN and all its programs and services). **Program & Services Director:** Shannon Woolfe. Established 1985. Supports the work of writers, writers' organizations, independent bookstores, little magazines and small presses, and literary programming statewide. Membership dues: $55 annually brings members *The Writers' Network News*, a 24-page bimonthly newsletter containing organizational news, national market information, and other literary material of interest to writers; and access to the Resource Center, other writers, workshops, conferences, readings and competitions, and a critiquing service. Currently has 1,700 total members nationwide. Publishes *North Carolina's Literary Resource Guide*, an annual including information about retreats, fellowships, markets, writer's groups, conferences, agents, and literary organizations. Available for $10 members/$12 nonmembers. Annual fall conference features nationally known writers, publishers, and editors, held in a different North Carolina location each November. Sponsors competitions in short fiction, nonfiction essays, and chapbooks of poetry for North Carolinians and members. Also sponsors 3 international competitions: Randall Jarrell Poetry Prize, Thomas Wolfe Fiction Prize, and Paul Green Playwrights Prize. The Randall Jarrell Poetry Prize annually awards $1,000 and publication in *Parnassus: Poetry in Review*. Submissions must be unpublished. Entry fee: $7. Deadline: November 1. Competitions receive 600-800 entries/year. Most recent poetry contest winner was Julie Buchsbaum (1999). Winner announced in February. Guidelines available for SASE, by fax, e-mail, or on website.

FOR AN EXPLANATION of symbols used in this book, see the Key to Symbols on the front and back inside covers.

N OHIO POETRY ASSOCIATION; OHIO POETRY ASSOCIATION NEWSLETTER, 348 S. Monroe St., Tiffin OH 44883-3006. (419)443-1140. E-mail: TiffinPoetry@hotmail.com. Website: www.crosswinds. net/~theopa (includes history, officers, library, newsletter, posted poetry, contests). **President:** Henry B. Stobbs. Established in 1929 as Verse Writers' Guild of Ohio to promote the art of poetry and further the support of poets and others who support poetry. "We sponsor contests, seminars, readings, and publishing opportunities for poets of all ages and abilities throughout and beyond Ohio." Statewide membership with additional members in Japan, New Zealand, Australia, and several other states. Affiliated with the National Federation of State Poetry Societies (NFSPS). Organization open to "poets and writers of all ages and ability, as well as to nonwriting lovers of poetry in all its forms." Currently has over 300 total members. Levels of membership: Regular, Student, Associate, Honorary Life, Paid Life, and Honorary. Member benefits include regular contests, newsletter, publication in *Common Threads* for selected writers, access to NFSPS contests at reduced cost, meeting/workshop participation, assistance with writing projects, and networking. Sponsors conferences/workshops and contests/awards. "We are cosponsors of Ohio Poetry Day. Individual chapters regularly host workshops and seminars. We publish *Common Threads*, a semiannual, saddle-bound anthology of poetry." (See separate listing for *Common Threads* in the Publishers of Poetry section.) Publishes the *Ohio Poetry Association Newsletter*, a quarterly which includes general news, member accomplishments, publishing opportunities, contests, editorials, items of interest to poets and writers. First issue is complementary to nonmembers. Members and nationally known writers give readings that are open to the public. Sponsors open mic readings for members and the public. "We host or sponsor a variety of readings throughout the state. Local chapters hold open mic and members-only readings as well. Past readers include Lisa Martinovic, David Shevin, Michael Bugeja, David Citino, and Danika Dinsmore." Membership dues: $12 senior; $15 regular; $5 associate and student. Members meet quarterly at the state level; monthly at the local level. Additional information available for SASE, by e-mail, or on website.

✓ THE OREGON STATE POETRY ASSOCIATION; VERSEWEAVERS, P.O. Box 602, West Linn OR 97068. (503)655-1274. E-mail: OSPA@teleport.com. Website: www.oregonstatepoetryassoc.org (includes contest and organization information). **President:** David Hedges. Established in 1936 for "the promotion and creation of poetry." Member of the National Federation of State Poetry Societies, Inc. (NFSPS), sponsors workshops, readings, and seminars around the state and an annual contest for students (K-12). Currently has over 400 total members. Membership dues: $18, $12 (65 and older), $5 (18 and under). Publishes a quarterly *OSPA Newsletter*, annual *Verseweavers* book, and annual *Cascadia* book of Oregon student poetry. Sponsors contests twice yearly, awards prizes in October during Fall Poetry Conference and in April during Spring Poetry Conference, with total cash prizes of $700 each (no entry fee to members, $3/poem for nonmembers; out-of-state entries welcome). Pays winners from other countries by International Money Order. Does not accept entry fees in foreign currencies. Send International Money Order. Themes and categories vary; special category for New Poets. Competition receives 1,400 entries/year. Most recent contest winners include Eleanor Berry, Alan Contreras, Linda H. Elegant, Alice C. Fick, Ruth F. Harrison, and Glenna Holloway. For details send SASE to OSPA, contest chair Joan Henson, 6071 SW Prosperity Park Rd., Tualatin OR 97062, phone (503)638-7488 after June 1 and December 1 each year, or check website.

PEN AMERICAN CENTER; PEN WRITERS FUND; PEN TRANSLATION PRIZE; GRANTS AND AWARDS, 568 Broadway, New York NY 10012. (212)334-1660. Website: www.pen.org. PEN American Center "is the largest of more than 100 centers which comprise International PEN, established in London in 1921 by John Galsworthy to foster understanding among men and women of letters in all countries. Members of PEN work for freedom of expression wherever it has been endangered, and International PEN is the only worldwide organization of writers and the chief voice of the literary community." Total membership on all continents is approximately 10,000. The 2,700 members of the American Center include poets, playwrights, essayists, editors, novelists (for the original letters in the acronym PEN), as well as translators and those editors and agents who have made a substantial contribution to the literary community. Membership in American PEN includes reciprocal privileges in foreign centers for those traveling abroad. Branch offices are located in Cambridge, Chicago, Portland/Seattle, New Orleans, and San Francisco. Among PEN's various activities are public events and symposia, literary awards, assistance to writers in prison and to American writers in need (grants and loans up to $1,000 from PEN Writers Fund). Medical insurance for writers is available to members. The quarterly *PEN News* is sent to all members. The PEN Translation Prize is sponsored by the Book-of-the-Month Club, 1 prize each year of $3,000 for works published in the current calendar year. Publishes *Grants and Awards* biennially, containing guidelines, deadlines, eligibility requirements, and other information about hundreds of grants, awards, and competitions for poets and other writers: $18. Send SASE for booklet describing activities and listing publications, some of them available free.

✓ PITTSBURGH POETRY EXCHANGE, P.O. Box 4279, Pittsburgh PA 15203. (412)481-POEM. Website: http://trfn.clpgh.org/forpoems/ (includes description of organization, activities, list of upcoming events, listing of publications by members). **Contact:** Michael Wurster. Established in 1974 as a community-based organization for local poets, it functions as a service organization and information exchange, conducting ongoing workshops, readings, forums, and other special events. No dues or fees. "Any monetary contributions are voluntary, often from outside sources. We've managed not to let our reach exceed our grasp." Reading programs are primarily committed to local and area poets, with honorariums of $25-75. Sponsors a minimum of three major events each year in addition to a monthly workshop. Some of these have been reading programs in conjunction with community arts festivals, such as the October South Side Poetry Smorgasbord—a series of readings throughout the evening at different shops (galleries, bookstores). Poets from out of town may contact the Exchange for assistance in setting up readings at bookstores to help sell their books.

THE POETRY LIBRARY, Royal Festival Hall, London SE1 8XX United Kingdom. Phone: (0207)921 0943/0664. Fax: (0207)921 0939. E-mail: poetrylibrary@rfh.org.uk. Website: www.poetrylibrary.org.uk (includes information about library's collections and services, interactive "Lost Quotations Noticeboard"). **Poetry Librarian:** Mary Enright. Established in 1953 as a "free public library of modern poetry. It contains a comprehensive collection of all British poetry published since 1912 and an international collection of poetry from all over the world, either written in or translated into English. As the United Kingdom's national library for poetry, it offers loan and information service and large collections of poetry magazines, tapes, videos, records, poem posters and cards; also press cuttings and photographs of poets." National center with "open access for all visitors. Those wishing to borrow books and other materials must be residents of U.K." Offerings include "library and information service; access to all recently published poetry and to full range of national magazines; only source of international poetry, including magazines; and information on all aspects of poetry." Offers browsing facilities and quieter area for study; listening facilities for poetry on tape, video record, and CD. Adjacent to "Voice Box" venue for literature readings. Nationally known writers give readings that are open to the public. "Separate administration for readings in 'The Voice Box'—a year-round program of readings, talks, and literature events for all writing. Contact the literature section, Royal Festival Hall." Additional information available for SASE, by fax, e-mail, or on website. "Our focus is more on published poets than unpublished. No unpublished poems or manuscripts kept or accepted. Donations welcome but please write or call in advance."

POETRY SOCIETY OF AMERICA; POETRY SOCIETY OF AMERICA AWARDS; CROSSROADS: A JOURNAL OF THE POETRY SOCIETY OF AMERICA, 15 Gramercy Park, New York NY 10003. (212)254-9628. Fax: (212)673-2352. Website: www.poetrysociety.org (includes information and calendar for contests, awards, and seminars; information on journal contest winners; postcards to send; discussion groups, etc.). **Executive Director:** Elise Paschen. Established in 1910, the society is a nonprofit cultural organization in support of poetry and poets, member and nonmember, young and established. Sponsors readings, lectures, and workshops both in New York City and around the country. Peer Group Workshop is open to all members and meets on a weekly basis. Publishes *Crossroads: A Journal of the Poetry Society of America*, approximately 40 pgs., letter-sized. **Poetry Society of America does not publish poems in its journal or on website.** Contest guidelines available for SASE. The following are open to members only: Alice Fay Di Castagnola Award ($1,000); *Writer Magazine*/Emily Dickinson Award ($250); Cecil Hemley Memorial Award ($500); Lucille Medwick Memorial Award ($500); Lyric Poetry Award ($500). Nonmembers may enter as many of the following contests as they wish, no more than 1 entry for each, for a $5 fee: Louise Louis/Emily F. Bourne Student Poetry Award, $250 for students in grades 9-12; George Bogin Memorial Award, $500 for a selection of 4 to 5 poems which take a stand against oppression; Robert H. Winner Memorial Award, $2,500 for a poem written by a poet over 40, still unpublished or with one book (all have a deadline of December 21; awards are made at a ceremony and banquet in late spring). The Society also has 2 contests open to works submitted by publishers only, who must obtain an entry form. There is a $10 fee for each book entered. Book awards are: Norma Farber Award, $500 for a first book; William Carlos Williams Award, a purchase prize of $500-1,000 for a book of poetry by a permanent resident of the US published by a small, nonprofit or university press—translations not eligible. The Shelley Memorial Award of $5,000-7,500 and The Frost Medal ($2,500) are by nomination only. For necessary rules and guidelines for their various contests send a 55¢ SASE between October 1 and December 21. Additional information available by fax or on website. Rules and awards are subject to change. Membership: $40.

POETRY SOCIETY OF TENNESSEE; TENNESSEE VOICES, 18 S. Rembert St., Memphis TN 38104. (901)726-4582. E-mail: RSTRpoet@cs.com. **President:** Russell H. Strauss. Established in 1953 to "promote the creative poetry of its members, poetry in the community, improving poetry writing skills, and creative poetry among young people." Statewide "but we have some associate members out of state." Affiliated with the National Federation of State Poetry Societies (NFSPS). Organization open to anyone interested in poetry. Currently has 85 total members. "We have an adult membership and a student membership." Offerings include monthly speakers, contests, and poetry readings; an annual poetry festival; and two student poetry contests each year. Sponsors conferences/workshops. "We publish a yearly anthology of poems, *Tennessee Voices*, that has won in various festival, monthly, and special contests." Also publishes a newsletter called *Tennessee Voices* 4-6 times/year as needed; contains information on meetings and speakers, contests and winners, various activities, etc. Not available to nonmembers. "We have a monthly reading at Deliberate Literate bookstore in Memphis. Nonmembers are sometimes invited to participate also." Membership dues: $20/year for adults, $5 for students. Additional information available by e-mail. "Our meetings are held at 2 p.m. on the first Saturday of the month from September through May at Clough Hall on the campus of Rhodes College in Memphis."

THE POETRY SOCIETY OF TEXAS; POETRY SOCIETY OF TEXAS BULLETIN; A BOOK OF THE YEAR, 235 Shady Hill Lane, Double Oak TX 75077-8270. (817)430-1182. E-mail: jpaulholcomb@prodigy.net. Website: http://members.nbci.com/PoetrySocTX/pstindex.htm (includes history, purpose, officers, current activities, contact information, Poetry in Schools, membership application). **President:** J. Paul Holcomb. Established 1921. "The purpose of the society shall be to secure fuller public recognition of the art of poetry, to encourage the writing of poetry by Texans, and to kindle a finer and more intelligent appreciation of poetry, especially the work of living poets who interpret the spirit and heritage of Texas." National organization with regional affiliations. Offers " 'Active' membership to native Texans, Citizens of Texas, or former Citizens of Texas who were active members; 'Associate' membership to all who desire to affiliate." Currently has 400 total members. Levels of membership: Active Membership, Associate Membership, Sustaining Membership, Benefactors, Patrons of the Poets, and Student Membership. Offerings include annual contests with prizes in excess of $5,000 as well as monthly contests (general and humorous); eight monthly meetings; annual awards banquet; annual summer conference in a different location each year; round-robin critiquing opportunities sponsored at the state level; and Poetry in Schools with contests at state and local chapter levels. "Our monthly state meetings are held at the Preston Royal Branch of the Dallas Public Library. Our annual awards banquet is held at the Marriott Market Suites Hotel in Dallas. Our summer conference is held at a site chosen by the hosting chapter. Chapters determine their meeting sites." Publishes *A Book of the Year* which presents annual and monthly award-winning poems, coming contest descriptions, minutes of meetings, by-laws of the society, history, and information. Also publishes the *Poetry Society of Texas Bulletin*, a monthly newsletter that features statewide news documenting contest winners, state meeting information, chapter and individual information, news from the National Federation of State Poetry Societies (NFSPS), and announcements of coming activities and offerings for poets. "*A Book of the Year* is available to nonmembers for $8." Members and nationally known writers give readings. "All of our meetings are open to the public." Membership dues: $20 for Active and Associates Memberships, $10 for students. Members meet monthly. Additional information is available by e-mail or on website.

POETS & WRITERS, INC. See separate listing in the Publications of Interest section.

☑ **POETS HOUSE; DIRECTORY OF AMERICAN POETRY BOOKS; THE REED FOUNDATION LIBRARY; THE POETS HOUSE SHOWCASE; POETRY IN THE BRANCHES; NYC POETRY TEACHER OF THE YEAR**, 72 Spring St., New York NY 10012. (212)431-7920. Fax: (212)431-8131. E-mail: info@poetshouse.org. Website: www.poetshouse.org (includes Poets House news, general information about programs, comprehensive calendar of events, Directory of American Poetry Books online). **Contact:** Betsy Fagin. Established 1985, Poets House is a 40,000-volume (noncirculating) poetry library of books, tapes, and literary journals, with reading and writing space available. Comfortably furnished literary center open to the public year-round. Over 50 annual public events include 1) poetic programs of cross-cultural and interdisciplinary exchange, 2) readings in which distinguished poets discuss and share the work of other poets, 3) workshops and seminars on various topics led by visiting poets, 4) an annual $1,000 award for the designated NYC Poetry Teacher of the Year, and 5) the People's Poetry Gathering. In addition, Poets House continues its collaboration with public library systems, Poetry in The Branches, aimed at bringing poetry into NYC neighborhoods through collection building, public programs, seminars for librarians, and poetry workshops for young adults (information available upon request). Finally, in April Poets House hosts the Poets House Showcase, a comprehensive exhibit of the year's new poetry releases from commercial, university, and independent presses across the country. Related Showcase events include receptions, panel discussions, and seminars which are open to the public and of special interest to poets, publishers, booksellers, distributers, and reviewers. (**Note: Poets House is not a publisher.**) Following each Showcase, copies of new titles become part of the library collection and comprehensive listings for each of the books are added to the online version of the *Directory of American Poetry Books*, accessible on www.poetshouse.org. "Poets House depends, in part, on tax-deductible contributions of its nationwide members." Membership levels begin at $40/year, and along with other graduated benefits each new or renewing member receives free admission to all regularly scheduled programs. Additional information is available by fax or e-mail.

☑ **POETS THEATRE**, RR2, Box 241, Middlebury Center PA 16935. (570)376-3361. Fax: (570)376-2674. E-mail: cjhoughtaling@usa.net. Website: http://poetstheater.tripod.com (includes information on upcoming readings, workshops, contests). **Contact:** C.J. Houghtaling, co-director with Julie Damerell. Established 1981, sponsors monthly poetry readings and performances with limited funding from *Poets & Writers* and the Hornell Arts Council. For a mostly conservative, rural audience. A featured poet, followed by open reading. Sponsors a summer poetry festival and an annual poets picnic in September. Meets March-November at Senior Citizens Center in Hornell, NY. Additional information available by e-mail or on website.

POETS-IN-THE-SCHOOLS. Most states have PITS programs that send published poets into classrooms to teach students poetry writing. If you have published poetry widely and have a proven commitment to children, contact your state arts council, Arts-in-Education Dept., or other writing programs in your area to see whether you qualify. Here are three of the biggest: 1) Teachers & Writers Collaborative, Inc., 5 Union Square W., New York NY 10003-3306. (212)691-6590. E-mail: info@twc.org. Website: www.twc.org. Requires poets in its program have some prior teaching experience. 2) California Poets-in-the-Schools, 870 Market St., Suite 1148, San Francisco CA 94102. (415)399-1565. E-mail: info@cpits.org. Website www.cpits.org. 3) Writers & Artists in the Schools, COMPAS, 304 Landmark Center, 75 W. Fifth St., St. Paul MN 55102. (651)292-3254. E-mail: waits@compas.org. Website: www.compas.org. Includes both Minnesota-based writers and artists in their program.

SCOTTISH POETRY LIBRARY; SCHOOL OF POETS; CRITICAL SERVICE; SCOTTISH POETRY INDEX, 5 Crichton's Close, Edinburgh EH8 8DT Scotland. Phone: (0131)557-2876. Fax: (0131)557-8393. E-mail: inquiries@spl.org.uk. Website: www.spl.org.uk (includes About the Library; members; catalogue; publications; outreach works; SPL projects; events and diary; links). **Director:** Robyn Marsack. **Librarian:** Penny Duce. A reference information source and free lending library, also lends by post and has a travelling van service lending at schools, prisons, and community centres. The library has a web-based catalogue at www.slainte. org.uk allowing searches of all the library's resources, including books, magazines, and audio material, over 20,000 items of Scottish and international poetry. The School of Poets is open to anyone; "at meetings members divide into small groups in which each participant reads a poem which is then analyzed and discussed." Meetings normally take place at 7:30 p.m. on the second Tuesday of each month at the library. Also offers a Critical Service in which groups of up to 6 poems, not exceeding 200 lines in all, are given critical comment by members of the School: £15 for each critique (with SAE). Publishes the *Scottish Poetry Index*, a multi-volume indexing series, photocopied, spiral-bound, that indexes poetry and poetry-related material in selected Scottish literary magazines from 1952 to present, and an audio CD of contemporary Scottish poems, *The Jewel Box* (January 2000). Additional information available by fax or e-mail.

SMALL PUBLISHERS ASSOCIATION OF NORTH AMERICA (SPAN); SPAN CONNECTION, P.O. Box 1306, Buena Vista CO 81211. (719)395-4790. Fax: (719)395-8374. E-mail: span@spannet.org. Website: www.spannet.org. **Executive Director:** Marilyn Ross. Established 1996 to "advance the image and profits of independent publishers and authors through education and marketing opportunities." Open to "authors, small- to medium-sized publishers, and the vendors who serve them." Currently has 1,300 total members. Levels of membership: regular and associate vendor. Offerings include marketing ideas, sponsors annual conference. Publishes *SPAN Connection*, "a 24-page monthly newsletter jam-packed with informative, money-making articles." Also available to nonmembers for $8/issue. Membership dues: $95/year (Regular), $120/year (Associate Vendor). Additional information available for SASE, by fax, or on website. Accepts inquiries by fax.

SOUTH DAKOTA STATE POETRY SOCIETY; PASQUE PETALS, Box 398, Lennox SD 57039. (605)647-2447. **Membership Chair:** Verlyss V. Jacobson. Established 1926 to provide a place for members to publish their poetry. Regional organization open to anyone. Currently has 200-225 total members. Levels of membership: Regular, Patron, Foreign, Student. Sponsors conferences, workshops, and 2 annual contests, one for adults and one for students, with 12 categories. Deadlines: August 15 for adults, February 1 for students. Competition receives 300-500 entries/year for both contests. Most recent contest winner was Maria Bakkum. (See separate listing for South Dakota State Poetry Society Annual Contest in the Contests & Awards section.) Publishes the magazine *Pasque Petals* 6 times/year. Membership dues: $20 regular, $30 patron, $5 students. Members meet biannually. Additional information available for SASE.

SOUTHERN POETRY ASSOCIATION; THE POET'S VOICE; THE SPA HANDBOOK; THE POET'S VOICE POETRY CONTEST, P.O. Box 524, Pass Christian MS 39571. E-mail: southpoets@aol.com. Website: www.southernpoetry.com (includes poetry, contests, book reviews, information about our Student Writing Program, and many other interesting features). **Poetry Editor:** Mildred Klyce. Established in 1986 to provide networking, publishing, free critique service for members through Round Robin Groups, and assistance in publishing chapbooks. Sponsors a number of contests, including Voices of the South, Yarn Spinner, Poetry in Motion, and Special People. Some are for members only; while others, such as the Voices of the South Contest, are open to all. High-scoring poems are published in an anthology (which the poet is not required to purchase). Send #10 SAE with 64¢ postage for details. Annual membership fee: $12, includes *The Poet's Voice* quarterly newsletter, which contains poetry book reviews, articles on great poets of the past, current activities, input from SPA members, and contest-winning poems. Also sponsors *The Poet's Voice* Poetry Contest. Send SASE or visit website for guidelines. Also publishes *The SPA Handbook*, 46 pgs., 5½ × 8½, perfect-bound, $8.95, "This book is filled to the brim with helpful tips and many answers to questions often asked by writers. This basic reference book is a guide to important aspects of writing such as: copyright, pen names, legal rights, query letters, manuscript preparation, and much more."

UNIVERSITY OF ARIZONA POETRY CENTER, 1216 N. Cherry Ave., Tucson AZ 85721-0410. (520)626-3765. Fax: (520)621-5566. E-mail: poetry@u.arizona.edu. Website: www.coh.arizona.edu/poetry/ (includes info about programs and events, newsletter and guidelines). **Director:** Jim Paul. Established in 1960 "to maintain and cherish the spirit of poetry." Open to the public. The Center is located in 3 historic adobe houses near the main campus and contains a nationally acclaimed poetry collection that includes over 40,000 items. Programs and services include a library with a noncirculating poetry collection and space for small classes; poetry-related meetings and activities; facilities, research support, and referral information about poetry and poets for local and national communities; the Free Public Reading Series of 12-18 readings each year featuring poets, fiction writers, and writers of literary nonfiction; a guest house for residencies of visiting writers and for use by other University departments and community literary activities; a 1-month summer residency at the Center's guest house offered each year to an emerging writer selected by jury; and poetry awards, readings, and special events for undergraduate and graduate students. Publishes a biannual newsletter. Additional information available for SASE, by fax, or e-mail. "We do not have members, though one can become a 'Friend' through a contribution to our Friends of the Poetry Center account."

☑ **THE UNTERBERG POETRY CENTER OF THE 92ND STREET Y; "DISCOVERY"/THE NATION POETRY CONTEST**, 1395 Lexington Ave., New York NY 10128. (212)415-5759. Website: www.92ndsty.org (includes guidelines). Offers annual series of readings by major literary figures (weekly readings October through May), writing workshops, master classes in fiction and poetry, and lectures and literary seminars. Also co-sponsors the "Discovery"/*The Nation* Poetry Contest. Deadline: January. Competition receives approximately 2,000 entries/year. Most recent contest winners include Erin Grace Brooks, Anthony Deaton, Andrew Feld, and Sue Kwock Kim. Additional information available for SASE or on website. No queries by phone, fax, or e-mail.

☑ **VIRGINIA WRITERS CLUB; THE VIRGINIA WRITER**, P.O. Box 300, Richmond VA 23218. (804)648-0357. Fax: (804)782-2142. E-mail: charfinley@mindspring.com. **Editor/Executive Director:** Charlie Finley. Established in 1918 "to promote the art and craft of writing; to serve writers and writing in Virginia." State-wide organization with 7 local chapters open to "any and all writers." Currently has 350 total members. Offerings include networking with other poets and writers, discussions on getting published, workshops, and a newsletter, *The Virginia Writer*, published 5 times/year. Nationally known writers give readings that are open to the public. Membership dues: $25/year. Members meet 5 times/year as well as at workshops and monthly chapter meetings. Additional information available for SASE or by fax.

☒ **WEST VIRGINIA POETRY SOCIETY (WVPS); WV CROSSROADS; LAURELS**, 678 West View Ave., Morgantown WV 26505. (304)598-2672. **President:** Beverly Taylor. Established in 1950 to "encourage creative writing and an appreciation of poetry; to foster the establishment of active community chapters of WVPS." Has statewide, regional, and national membership; "not limited to WV residents." Affiliated with the National Federation of State Poetry Societies (NFSPS). Open to "all poets and lovers of poetry." Currently has 185 total members. Levels of membership: local/community chapters of WVPS; state membership automatically includes being a member of NFSPS (the National Society). Membership benefits include a quarterly newsletter (state and national); annual poetry contests; and state and national conventions "with outstanding presenters." Sponsors conferences/workshops and contests/awards. Publishes *WV Crossroads*, a quarterly newsletter which contains president's message; state, local, regional, and national news; and contest information. *WV Crossroads* editor is Betty Grugin (jbgrug@citynet.net). Members also receive *Laurels*, quarterly anthology, and the NFSPS newsletter, *Strophes*. Not available to nonmembers. Members and nationally known writers give readings that are open to the public. Sponsors open mic readings for members and the public. "Meetings and annual conventions may be attended by nonmembers. Many readings are in conjunction with special occasions such as National Poetry Month/Day." Membership dues: $12 annually. Local chapters of WVPS meet monthly and at the annual state convention. "The West Virginia Poetry Society is an important link to the arts in WV. It maintains active involvement locally, regionally, and nationally in the realm of creative writing."

☑ **WISCONSIN FELLOWSHIP OF POETS; MUSELETTER; WISCONSIN POETS' CALENDAR**, 736 W. Prospect Ave., Appleton WI 54914. E-mail: 2mutsch@vbe.com. **Vice President:** Cathryn Cofell. **President:** Peter Sherrill. Established in 1950 to secure fuller recognition of poetry as one of the important forces making for a higher civilization and to create a finer appreciation of poetry by the public at large. State-wide organization open to current and past residents of Wisconsin who write poetry acceptable to the Credentials Chairperson. Currently has 415 total members. Levels of memberships: Associate, Active, Student and Life. Sponsors biannual conferences, workshops, contests and awards. Publishes *Wisconsin Poets' Calendar*, poems of Wisconsin (resident) poets. Also publishes *Museletter*, a quarterly newsletter. Members or nationally known writers give readings that are open to the public. Sponsors open mic readings. Membership dues: Active $15, Associate $10, Student $7.50, Life $100. Members meet biannually. Additional information available for SASE to WFOP Vice President Cathryn Cofell at the above address. Also available by e-mail; no inquiries by fax.

🌐 ☑ **THE WORDSMITHS (CHRISTIAN POETRY GROUP); WORDSMITHS NEWSLETTER**, 493 Elgar Rd., Box Hill North, Victoria 3129 Australia. Phone/fax: (03) 98905885. **Leader:** Jean Sietzema-

Dickson. Established 1987 to provide a meeting place where poets could share their work for critique and encouragement. "We have met monthly (except in January) since 1987 and began publishing in 1990. Our concern, as a group, has been to encourage the development of excellence in our writing and to speak out with a distinctive voice." Currently has 37 members, mostly from the greater Melbourne area. Offerings include monthly workshops, plus "we subscribe to several magazines, have occasional guests poets and a Quiet Day once a year when we meet from 10 a.m.-4 p.m. to spend some time together in directed silence and writing." Holds occasional public readings. Through publishing arm, Poetica Christi Press, has published 4 group anthologies of the writing of the Wordsmiths and the works of 3 individual poets. Also sends out the *Wordsmiths Newsletter*, appearing "roughly" bimonthly, available to nonmembers for AUS $5/year. Membership dues: $15/year or $2/meeting. Additional information available by fax.

☑ **WORLD-WIDE WRITERS SERVICE, INC. (3WS); WRITERS INK; WRITERS INK PRESS; WRITERS UNLIMITED AGENCY, INC.**, 233 Mooney Pond Rd., P.O. Box 2344, Selden NY 11784. (631)451-0478. Fax: (631)451-0477. E-mail: axelrodthepoet@poetrydoctor.com. Website: www.poetrydoctor. com or www.worldwidewriters.com (includes editorial services; in-residence programs; college credit, State University of New York certified, and non-credit courses; publishing opportunities; and information on conferences and workshops). **Director:** Dr. David B. Axelrod. Established 1976; Writers Ink Press established 1978. "World-Wide Writers Service is a literary and speakers' booking agency. With its not-for-profit affiliate, Writers Unlimited Agency, Inc., it presents literary workshops and performances, conferences, and other literary services, and publishes through Writers Ink Press, chapbooks and small flat-spined books as well as arts editions. **We publish only by our specific invitation at this time.**" *Writers Ink* is "a sometimely newsletter of events on Long Island, now including programs of our conferences. We offer 3 conferences a year: Healing Power of Writing, Long Island Literature Conference, Florida Writing Workshop and Poetry Conference. We welcome news of other presses and poets' activities. Review books of poetry. We fund raise for nonprofit projects and are associates of Long Island Writers Festival and Jeanne Voege Poetry Awards as well as the Key West Poetry Writing January Workshops, and Writing Therapy Trainings throughout the year in various locations. Arts Editions are profit productions employing hand-made papers, bindings, etc. We have editorial services available at small fees. Also inquire if appropriate." Also sponsors a new contest. Most recent winner was George Wallace.

☑ **THE WRITER'S CENTER; WRITER'S CAROUSEL**, 4508 Walsh St., Bethesda MD 20815. (301)654-8664. E-mail: postmaster@writer.org. Website: www.writer.org (includes news and information about the Washington metropolitan literary community as well as market basket for tapes, books, membership; writers/editors registry; special "members only" page). **Founder and Artistic Director:** Allan Lefcowitz. **Executive Director:** Jane Fox. Established 1976. An outstanding resource for writers not only in Washington DC but in the wider area ranging from southern Pennsylvania to North Carolina and West Virginia. Offers 260 multi-meeting workshops each year in writing, word processing, and graphic arts. Open 7 days/week, 10 hours/day. Some 2,600 members support the center with $30 annual donations, which allows for 7 paid staff members. Includes a book gallery in which publications of small presses are displayed and sold. Publishes *Writer's Carousel*, a 24-page magazine that comes out 6 times/year. Also sponsors 80 annual performance events, which include presentations of poetry, fiction, theater, and film. Also publishes *Poet Lore*—110 years old in 1999 (see separate listing for *Poet Lore* in the Publishers of Poetry section). Additional information available by e-mail.

☑ **WRITERS' FEDERATION OF NOVA SCOTIA; ATLANTIC POETRY PRIZE; ATLANTIC WRITING COMPETITION; EASTWORD**, 1113 Marginal Rd., Halifax, Nova Scotia B3H 4P7 Canada. (902)423-8116. Fax: (902)422-0881. E-mail: talk@writers.ns.ca. Website: www.writers.ns.ca. Established in 1975 "to foster creative writing and the profession of writing in Nova Scotia; to provide advice and assistance to writers at all stages of their careers; and to encourage greater public recognition of Nova Scotian writers and their achievements." Regional organization open to anybody who writes. Currently has 600 total members. Offerings include resource library with over 1,200 titles, promotional services, workshop series, annual festivals, manuscript reading service, and contract advice. Sponsors the Atlantic Writing Competition for unpublished works by beginning writers, and the annual Atlantic Poetry Prize for the best book of poetry by an Atlantic Canadian. Publishes *Eastword*, a bimonthly newsletter containing "a plethora of information on who's doing what, markets and contests, and current writing events and issues." Additional information available for SASE, by fax, e-mail, or on website.

☑ ☑ **WRITERS GUILD OF ALBERTA; STEPHAN STEPHANSSON AWARD FOR POETRY**, 11759 Groat Rd., Edmonton, Alberta T5M 3K6 Canada. (780)422-8174. Fax: (780)422-2663. E-mail: wga@oanet .com. Website: www.writersguild.ab.ca (includes directory of writers, job and market listings, workshop/conference information). Executive Director: Norma Lock. **Program Coordinator:** Renate Donnovan. Office Administrator: Lorraine Carson. Established in 1980 "to provide a community of writers which exists to support, encourage, and promote writers and writing; to safeguard the freedom to write and read; and to advocate for the well-being of writers." Provincial organization open to emerging and professional writers. Currently has 750 total members. Offerings include workshops/conferences, bimonthly newsletter with market section, and the Stephan Stephansson Award for Poetry (Alberta residents only). Deadline: December 31. Most recent award winner was Shawna LeMay. Also publishes a bimonthly magazine that includes articles on writing, poems, and a market section. Available to nonmembers for $60 Canadian/year. Members and nationally known writers give readings that are open to the public. Sponsors open mic readings for members. Additional information available by fax, e-mail, or on website.

THE WRITERS ROOM, 10 Astor Place, 6th Floor, New York NY 10003. (212)254-6995. Fax: (212)533-6059. Website: www.writersroom.org (includes general information, books for sale by members, application form). Established in 1978 to provide a "home away from home" for any writer who needs a place to work. Open 24 hours a day, 7 days a week, offering desk space, storage, and comradery at the rate of $185/quarter. Supported by the National Endowment for the Arts, the New York State Council on the Arts, the New York City Department of Cultural Affairs, and private sector funding. Call for application or download from website.

THE WRITERS' UNION OF CANADA; THE WRITERS' UNION OF CANADA NEWSLETTER, 40 Wellington St. E, 3rd Floor, Toronto, Ontario M5E 1C7 Canada. (416)703-8982. Fax: (416)504-7656. E-mail: twuc@the-wire.com. Website: www.writersunion.ca (includes general information about publishing, members web pages, competition information). Established 1973. Dedicated to advancing the status of Canadian writers by protecting the rights of published authors, defending the freedom to write and publish, and serving its members. National organization open to poets who have had a trade book published by a commercial or university press; must be a Canadian citizen or landed immigrant. Currently has over 1,370 total members. Offerings include contact with peers, contract advice/negotiation, grievance support, and electronic communication. Sponsors conferences/workshops. Sponsors Annual General Meeting, usually held in May, where members debate and determine Union policy, elect representatives, attend workshops, socialize, and renew friendships with their colleagues from across the country. Publishes *The Writers' Union of Canada Newsletter* 9 times/year. Membership dues: $180/year. Regional reps meet with members when possible. For writers not eligible for membership, the Union offers, for a fee, publications on publishing, contracts, and more; a Manuscript Evaluation Service for any level writer; Contract Services, including a Self-Help Package, a Contract Evaluation Service, and a Contract Negotiation Service; and three annual writing competitions for developing writers. Additional information available for SASE (or SAE and IRC), by fax, e-mail, or on website.

W.B. YEATS SOCIETY OF NEW YORK, National Arts Club, 15 Gramercy Park S, New York NY 10003. Website: www.YeatsSociety.org (includes a "guestbook, where inquiries may be left; full information on our programs; links to numerous other relevant sites"). **President:** Andrew McGowan. Established in 1990 "to promote the legacy of Irish poet and Nobel laureate William Butler Yeats through an annual program of lectures, readings, poetry competition and special events." National organization open to anyone. Currently has 400 total members. Offerings include an annual poetry competition and *Poet Pass By!*, an annual "slam" of readings, songs, and music by poets, writers, entertainers. Also sponsors conferences/workshops. Members and nationally known writers give readings that are open to the public. Sponsors open mic readings for members and the public. Membership dues: $15/year. Members meet monthly, September to June. Additional information available for SASE or on website; no inquiries by fax or e-mail.

Additional Organizations

The following listings also contain information about organizations. See the General Index for page numbers.

Alden Enterprises
American Tolkien Society
Anthology of New England Writers
Arkansas Poetry Day Contest
Artist Trust
Asian Pacific American Journal
Aspen Summer Words Writing
    Retreat and Literary Festival
Austin Writers' League Spring and
    Fall Workshops
Baltimore Review, The
Bay Area Poets Coalition
Borderlands
Borderlines
Bridport Prize, The
Bristol Poetry Festival
British Haiku Society
California Quarterly
Canadian Authors Association
    Awards for Adult Literature
Cave Canem Poetry Prize
CNW/FFWA Florida State Writing
    Competition
Colorado Book Awards
Comstock Review, The
Connecticut River Review
Council for Wisconsin Writers, Inc.
Creative Writing Fellowships in
    Poetry
Daniels Annual Honorary Writing
    Award, The Dorothy
Diner
Eliot Prize, T.S.
Emerald Coast Review
Faulkner Creative Writing
    Competition/Poetry Category,
    The William

First Draft: The Journal of the
    Alabama Writers' Forum
FreeFall Magazine
Frogpond
Handshake
HQ Poetry Magazine
Intro
Intro Prize in Poetry
Jewish Women's Literary Annual
Kwil Kids Publishing
Laurels
Life Press Christian Writers'
    Conference
Lummox Press
Mad Poets Review
Maryland Poetry Review
Midwest Villages & Voices
Milton Center Post Graduate
    Fellowship
New Orleans Poetry Forum
Newburyport Art Association Annual
    Spring Poetry Contest
Northwoods Press
Ohioana Book Awards
Outrider Press
Panhandle Professional Writers
Pennsylvania Poetry Society Annual
    Contest
Pennwriters Annual Conference
Peregrine
Poem
Poetic Hours
Poetry Book Society
Poetry Flash
Poetry Harbor
Poetry Ireland Review
Poetry Kanto

Poetry Review
Poets & Writers, Inc.
Poets' Club of Chicago Helen
    Schaible Sonnet Contest
Pudding House Publications
Quincy Writers Guild Writing
    Contest
QWF A.M. Klein Prize for Poetry
Red Herring
Rockford Review, The
Romantics Quarterly
S.W.A.G.
San Francisco Foundation
Seaman Poetry Award, Claudia Ann
Sky Blue Waters Poetry Contests
Slapering Hol Press Chapbook
    Competition
Snow Writing Awards, Kay
Society of American Poets, The
Society of the Muse of the Southwest
Sounds of Poetry, The
SPIN
Terra Incognita
Tower Poetry Society
Whidbey Island Writers' Conferences
Whitecrow Foundation, Tahana
Wisconsin Regional Writers'
    Association Inc.
Worcester Review
Word Works, The
Writers' News
Writes of Passage
Yeats Society Annual Poetry
    Competition, The W.B.

Publications of Interest

This section lists publications of special interest to poets, with a focus on information about writing and publishing poetry. While there are few actual markets for your work, some of these publications do identify promising leads for your submission efforts. There is also a wealth of advice on craft, poet interviews, reviews of books and chapbooks, events calendars, and other valuable information contained in these publications. While each listing includes contact information, you may also find these publications in your library or bookstore; or you may be able to order them through your favorite online bookseller.

Certain symbols may appear at the beginning of some listings. The (**N**) symbol indicates a publication that is new to this edition; the (✓) symbol alerts you to a change in the contact information from the previous edition. The (❖) symbol denotes a Canadian publication and the (🌐) symbol an international one.

Some listings in the Publishers of Poetry, Contests & Awards, and Conferences & Workshops sections include informative publications (such as handbooks and newsletters). We've included these markets in a cross reference at the end of this section called Additional Publications of Interest. To find out more about a market cross referenced in this list, see the General Index for the appropriate page number.

🌐 **THE BBR DIRECTORY**, P.O. Box 625, Sheffield S1 3GY United Kingdom. E-mail: directory@bbr-online.com. Website: www.bbr-online.com/directory (includes "a fully searchable archive of every issue of the *BBR Directory*, plus a free Message Board facility where readers can post their publishing news for immediate viewing by other visitors to the website, network with other writers, or discuss issues relevant to small press and independent publishing.") **Editor/Publisher:** Chris Reed. Established 1996. *The BBR Directory* "is a monthly e-mail newssheet for everyone involved with or interested in the small press. Providing accurate and up-to-date information about what's happening in independent publishing all over the world, *The BBR Directory* is the ideal starting point for exploring the small press and for keeping tabs on who exactly is publishing what, and when." To subscribe, send a blank e-mail to directory-subs-on@bbr-online.com or sign up through website. Accepts inquiries by e-mail. *The BBR Directory* also has a special website of resources for writers at www.bbr-online.com/writers.

✓ **CANADIAN POETRY**, English Dept., University of Western Ontario, London, Ontario N6A 3K7 Canada. (519)661-3403 ext. 83403 or 85834. Fax: (519)661-3776. Website: www.arts.uwo.ca/canpoetry. **Editor:** Prof. D.M.R. Bentley. Founded 1977. A biannual journal of critical articles, reviews, and historical documents (such as interviews). Professionally printed, scholarly edited, flat-spined, 150 pgs. Pays contributors in copies. Subscription: $15. Sample: $7.50. **Publishes no poetry except as quotations in articles.** Also offers Canadian Poetry Press Scholarly Editions; DocuTech printed, perfect-bound, containing scholarship and criticism of Canadian poetry. Details available for SASE.

DUSTBOOKS; INTERNATIONAL DIRECTORY OF LITTLE MAGAZINES AND SMALL PRESSES; DIRECTORY OF POETRY PUBLISHERS; SMALL PRESS REVIEW; SMALL MAGAZINE REVIEW, P.O. Box 100, Paradise CA 95967. (530)877-6110. Fax: (530)877-0222. E-mail: dustbooks@de si.net. website www.dustbooks.com. Dustbooks publishes a number of books useful to writers. Send SASE for catalog. Regular publications include *The International Directory of Little Magazines & Small Presses*, published annually with almost 6,000 entries. In addition to a wide range of magazine and book publisher listings (with full editorial information), *The International Directory* offers 1,000 pages of indexes plus sources of unique subject material for readers and researchers. *Directory of Poetry Publishers* has similar information for over 2,000 poetry markets. *Small Press Review* is a bimonthly newsprint magazine carrying updates of listings in *The International Directory*, small press needs, news, announcements, and reviews—a valuable way to stay abreast of the literary marketplace. It also incorporates *Small Magazine Review*. Additional information is available by fax, e-mail, or on website.

FIRST DRAFT: THE JOURNAL OF THE ALABAMA WRITERS' FORUM; THE ALABAMA WRITERS' FORUM, Alabama State Council on the Arts, 201 Monroe St., Montgomery AL 36130-1800. (334)242-

4076 ext. 233, Fax: (334)240-3269. E-mail: awfl@arts.state.al.us. Website: www.writersforum.org (includes complete coverage of forum programs and services; back issues of the quarterly journal *First Draft* are posted in PDF format). **Editor:** Jeanie Thompson. Established 1992. Appears 4 times/year with news, features, book reviews, and interviews relating to Alabama writers. "We do not publish original poetry or fiction." *First Draft* is 32 pgs., 8½ × 11, professionally printed on coated paper and saddle-stapled with b&w photos inside and a full color cover. Lists markets for poetry, contests/awards, and workshops. Sponsored by the Alabama Writers' Forum, "the official literary arts advocacy organization for the state of Alabama and a partnership program of the Alabama State Council on the Arts." Reviews books of poetry, fiction, and nonfiction by "Alabama writers or from Alabama presses." Subscription: $25/year plus membership. Sample: $3.

🌐 **FREELANCE MARKET NEWS**, Sevendale House, 7 Dale St., Manchester M1 1JB England. phone (+ 44) 161 228 2362, Fax: (+ 44) 161 228 3533. E-mail: fmn@writersbureau.com. Website: http://writersbureau. com. **Editor:** Angela Cox. Established 1968. A monthly newsletter providing market information for writers and poets, *Freelance Market News* is 16 pgs., A4-sized. Lists markets for poetry, contests/awards, conferences/ workshops, and features how-to articles. Associated with the Writers College which offers correspondence courses in poetry. Occasionally reviews books or chapbooks of poetry. Subscription: £29. Sample: £2.50. Accepts inquiries by fax and e-mail.

THE GREAT BLUE BEACON, 1425 Patriot Dr., Melbourne FL 32940. (321)253-5869. E-mail: ajircc@juno. com. **Editor/Publisher:** Andy J. Byers. Established 1996. A quarterly newsletter for writers of all genres and skill levels. Contains writing tips, book reviews, humor, quotations, and contest/publisher information. Occasionally publishes poetry, but only through periodic contests. *The Great Blue Beacon* is 8 pgs., magazine-sized, desktop-published, and unbound. Poets may send books for review consideration. Single copy: $4; subscription: $10, $8 for students, $14 outside US. Sample: $1 plus 2 first-class stamps or IRC. Accepts inquiries by e-mail.

🌐 **HANDSHAKE; THE EIGHT HAND GANG**, 5 Cross Farm Station Rd., Padgate, Warrington, Cheshire WA2 0QG England. **Contact:** John Francis Haines. Established 1992. Published irregularly to "encourage the writing of genre poetry, to provide a source of news and information about genre poetry, to encourage the reading of poetry of all types, including genre, and to provide an outlet for a little genre poetry." *Handshake* is 1 A4-sized pg., printed on front and back. Lists markets for poetry and contests/awards. Single copy available for SAE and IRC.

N; **LAUGHING BEAR NEWSLETTER; LAUGHING BEAR PRESS**, P.O. Box 613322, Dallas TX 75261-3322. (817)858-9515. E-mail: editor@laughingbear.com. Website: www.LaughingBear.com. **Editor:** Tom Person. Established 1976. *Laughing Bear Newsletter* is a monthly publication of small press news, information, and inspiration for writers and publishers containing articles, news, and reviews. Subscription: $15/year. Sample copy available for SASE or by e-mail. *Laughing Bear Newsletter* uses short (200- to 300-word) articles on self-publishing and small press. Pays copies.

✅ 🌐 **LIGHT'S LIST**, 37 The Meadows, Berwick-Upon-Tweed, Northumberland, TD15 1NY England. Phone: (01289)306523. E-mail: photon.press@cwcom.net. **Editor:** John Light. Established 1986. *Light's List* is an annual publication "listing some 1,450 small press magazines publishing poetry, prose, market information, articles, and artwork with address and brief note of interests. All magazines publish work in English. Listings are from the United Kingdom, Europe, United States, Canada, Australia, New Zealand, South Africa, and Asia." *Light's List* is 62 pgs., A5-sized, photocopied, saddle-stapled with card cover. Single copy: $6 (air $7). Accepts inquiries by e-mail.

✅ **MINNESOTA LITERATURE**, 1387 Berkeley Ave., St. Paul MN 55105. (651)698-4770. Fax: (651)698-3059. E-mail: mnlit@aol.com. **Editor:** Diane Wilson. Established 1975. *Minnesota Literature* appears 10 times/ year (September through June), providing news and announcements for Minnesota writers. Regularly features "Minnesota literary events such as readings, lectures, workshops, conferences, and classes; news of publications written by Minnesotans or published in Minnesota; and opportunities for writers, such as grants, awards, and want-ads." *Minnesota Literature* is magazine-sized, 8 pgs. (two 11 × 17 sheets folded), unbound. Subscription: $10/10 issues. Sponsors annual reading for creative writing nominees for Minnesota Book Awards. Publishes biennial bibliography of Minnesota publishers and literary publications.

✅ **OHIO WRITER**, P.O. Box 91801, Cleveland OH 44101. (216)932-8444. E-mail: poetsleague@yahoo.com. **Editor:** Ron Antonucci. A bimonthly newsletter for Ohio writers or those connected with Ohio. *Ohio Writer* is 16-24 pgs., professionally printed on off-white stock, containing news and reviews of Ohio writing events, publications, and regional opportunities to publish. Subscription: $15/year, $20 for institutions. Also sponsors an annual contest for Ohio writers. Competition receives about 300 entries. (See separate listing for the Best of Ohio Writers Writing Contest in the Contests & Awards section). Also accepts poems on writing, the writing life, etc. Payment on publication, $5-50.

PARA PUBLISHING, Box 8206-880, Santa Barbara CA 93118-8206. (805)968-7277, orders (800)727-2782. Fax: (805)968-1379. E-mail: danpoynter@parapublishing.com. Website: www.parapublishing.com (over 500 pages of valuable book writing, publishing and promoting information. A good way to sample Para Publishing's offerings). Author/publisher Dan Poynter offers how-to books on book publishing and self-publishing. *Writing Nonfiction: Turning Thoughts Into Books* shows how to get your book out. *The Self-Publishing Manual, How to Write, Print and Sell Your Own Book* is all about book promotion. Also available are *Publishing Contracts on Disk, Book Fairs*, and 45 Special Reports on various aspects of book production, promotion, marketing, and distribution. Free book publishing information kit. Accepts inquiries by e-mail only.

PERSONAL POEMS, % Jean Hesse, 56 Arapaho Dr., Pensacola FL 32507. (850)492-9828. F. Jean Hesse started a business in 1980 writing poems for individuals for a fee (for greetings, special occasions, etc.). Others started similar businesses after she began instructing them in the process, especially through a cassette tape training program and other materials. Send SASE for free brochure or $20 plus $4.50 p&h for training manual, *How to Make Your Poems Pay*. Make checks payable to F. Jean Hesse.

N 🌐 **POETRY BOOK SOCIETY; PBS BULLETIN**, Book House, 45 East Hill, London SW18 2QZ England. Phone: +44 (0)20 8870 8403. Fax: +44 (0)20 8877 1615. E-mail: info@poetrybooks.co.uk. Website: www.poetrybooks.co.uk. Established 1953 "to promote the best newly published contemporary poetry to as wide an audience as possible." A book club with an annual subscription rate of £42, which covers 4 books of new poetry, the *PBS Bulletin*, and a premium offer (for new members). The selectors also recommend other books of special merit, which are obtainable at a discount of 25%. The Poetry Book Society is subsidized by the Arts Council of England. Please write (Attn: Clare Brown), fax, or e-mail for details.

✓ **THE POETRY CONNECTION**, 13455 SW 16 Court #F-405-PM, Pembroke Pines FL 33027. (954)431-3016. Fax: (509)351-7401. E-mail: poetryconnect@webtv.net (for news) or MagicCircle@webtv.net (for poetry). **Editor/Publisher:** Sylvia Shichman. *The Poetry Connection*, a monthly newsletter, in flyer format, provides poets, writers, and performing artists with information on how to sell their poetry/books, poetry and performing artists publications and contests, and obtain assistance in getting poetry published. Also info on "how to win cash for your talent" and mailing list rental. *The Poetry Connection* has information on "writing for greeting cards" directories, and a directory listing poetry contests with cash awards. Subscription: $20. Sample (including guidelines): $7. Make checks payable to Sylvia Schichman. Also sponsors The Magic Circle, a poetry publicity distribution network service. "Join the Magic Circle and have your bio and one poem sent directly to editors and publishers. Fifty copies for $40 or 100 copies for $70. The Magic Circle will distribute your flyers in a reciprocal exchange. For information, please enclose a large SASE and write to Sylvia Shichman."

N **POETRY FLASH; BAY AREA BOOK REVIEWERS ASSOCIATION**, 1450 Fourth St. #4, Berkeley CA 94710. (510)525-5476. Fax: (510)525-6752. E-mail: editor@poetryflash.org (NOTE: **does not respond by e-mail to poetry submissions**) or BABRA@poetryflashorg. Website: www.poetryflash.org (includes BABRA button). **Editor:** Joyce Jenkins. Established 1972. Appears 6 times/year. "*Poetry Flash*, a Poetry Review & Literary Calendar for the West, publishes reviews, interviews, essays, and information for writers. Poems, as well as announcements about submitting to other publications, appear in each issue." *Poetry Flash* focuses on poetry, but its literary calendar also includes events celebrating all forms of creative writing in areas across the nation. *Poetry Flash* is about 48 pgs., printed on newsprint. Lists markets for poetry, contests/awards, and workshops. *Poetry Flash* also sponsors a weekly poetry reading series at Cody's Books in Berkeley and sponsors the Bay Area Book Reviewers Association. (See separate listing in Contests & Awards section.) Reviews books and chapbooks of poetry. Poets may send books for review consideration. Subscription $16/year. Sample: $2. "We publish at least three poems per issue—sometimes more in a special feature." Accepts inquiries by fax.

✓ **POETS & WRITERS, INC.; A DIRECTORY OF AMERICAN POETS AND FICTION WRITERS; LITERARY AGENTS; POETS & WRITERS MAGAZINE**, 72 Spring St., New York NY 10012. (212)226-3586. Website: www.pw.org. Subscription office: *Poets & Writers Magazine*, P.O. Box 543, Mount Morris IL 61054. (815)734-1123. Poets & Writers, Inc., was founded in 1970 to foster the development of poets and fiction writers and to promote communication throughout the literary community. A nonmembership organization, it offers information, support, and exposure to writers at all stages in their careers. Publishes the bimonthly *Poets & Writers Magazine*, which delivers to its readers profiles of noted authors and publishing professionals, practical how-to articles, a comprehensive listing of grants and awards for writers, and special sections on subjects ranging from small presses to writers conferences. The Readings/Workshops Program supports public literary events through matching grants to community organizations. The Literary Horizons Program

VISIT THE WRITER'S DIGEST WEBSITE at www.writersdigest.com for books on craft, hot new markets, daily market updates, writers' guidelines and much more.

offers how-to-publish seminars, panel discussions, a lecture series, festivals, and online or audiotape seminars. The program also provides a publishing information packet free of charge and compiles the biennial *A Directory of American Poets and Fiction Writers*, which lists contact information and publication credits for more than 7,400 published U.S. authors.

⦿ BERN PORTER INTERNATIONAL, 50 Salmond St., Belfast ME 04915-6111. (207)338-4303. **Director:** Bern Porter. **Co-Editors:** Natasha Bernstein and Sheila Holtz. Established 1911. A bimonthly literary newsletter and bulletin of the Institute of Advanced Thinking, *Bern Porter International* specializes in "the bizarre, the strange, the conceptual: poetry and prose which stretches the envelope." Reviews books of poetry and publishes poetry, prose, and visual essays. Sample copy: $2 cash. Guidelines available for SASE.

PUSHCART PRESS, P.O. Box 380, Wainscott NY 11975. Publishes a number of books useful to writers including the Pushcart Prize Series, annual anthologies representing the best small press poetry, essays, and short stories, according to the judges; The Editors' Book Award Series, "to encourage the writing of distinguished books of uncertain financial value"; *The Publish-It-Yourself Handbook*; and the Literary Companion Series. Catalog available for SASE.

RAIN TAXI REVIEW OF BOOKS, P.O. Box 3840, Minneapolis MN 55403. E-mail: raintaxi@bitstream.net. Website: www.raintaxi.com (includes a selection of the contents of each issue, full table of contents for current and back issues, and information about the organization). **Editor:** Eric Lorberer. Established 1996. "*Rain Taxi Review of Books* is a quarterly publication available by subscription and free in bookstores nationwide. Our circulation is 20,000 copies. We publish reviews of books that are overlooked by mainstream media, and each issue includes several pages of poetry reviews, as well as author interviews and original essays." Devotes 20% of publication to poetry. "We review poetry books in every issue and often feature interviews with poets." *Rain Taxi* is 56 pgs., magazine-sized, web offset-printed on newsprint, saddle-stapled. Poets may send books for review consideration. Subscription: $12. Sample: $3. Accepts inquiries via e-mail. "We DO NOT publish original poetry. Please don't send poems."

SHAW GUIDES, INC., 10 W. 66 St., #30H, New York NY 10023. (212)799-6464. Fax: (212)724-9287. E-mail: info@shawguides.com. Website: www.shawguides.com (includes *Guide to Writers Conferences* with detailed descriptions of over 500 conferences and workshops worldwide). Established 1988 "to publish true stories of educational travel and creative career programs worldwide." **President:** Dorlene Kaplan. Publishes material on an ongoing basis on website. Accepts inquiries by fax and e-mail.

☑ ⦿ WORDS & PICTURES, 134 Glasgow Rd., Perth, Perthshire PH2 0LX Scotland. E-mail: elizabeth_gatland@email.msn.com. Website: www.wordpool.co.uk/scbwi (includes information regarding British region of Society of Children's Book Writers & Illustrators, including contacts and forms). Established 1996. **Editor:** Elizabeth Wein. *Words & Pictures* "is the quarterly regional newsletter for the British Isles branch of The Society of Children's Book Writers & Illustrators. It serves as a forum for the discussion of issues in the professional field of children's literature and an organ which publicizes SCBWI business and activities. Occasionally we have market listings for poetry, articles focusing on poetry, or announcements of events relating to poetry (for children)." *Words & Pictures* is 16-20 pgs., A5-sized, photocopied, folded and saddle-stapled. Also lists markets for contests/awards and conferences/workshops. Single copy: $4; subscription: $17. Make checks payable in $US to E. Gatland. Accepts inquiries by surface mail or e-mail. "Include SASE with U.K. postage or International Postal Coupon, with inquiry. Sample copies of text only available with e-mail inquiry."

☑ ⦿ WRITERS' BULLETIN, Cherrybite Publications, Linden Cottage, 45 Burton Rd., Little Neston, Cheshire CH64 4AE United Kingdom. E-mail: helicon@globalnet.co.uk. **Editor:** Shelagh Nugent. Established 1997. "Published bimonthly, *Writers' Bulletin* aims to give writers the most reliable and up-to-date information on markets for fiction, nonfiction, poetry, photographs, artwork, cartoons; information on resources, courses, and conferences; book reviews (books about writing); editors' moves, publishing news, address changes; advice and tips on writing. All markets are verified with the editor—no guesswork or second-hand information." *Writer's Bulletin* is about 28 pgs., saddle-stapled, colored paper cover. Single copy: £2.40 Europe, £3 USA sterling only, £2 UK. Will accept the equivalent in US dollars (cash). Sample issue also available for 2 International Reply Coupons. Accepts inquiries by e-mail. "Because we are adding news right up to publication day, *Writers' Bulletin* has the most up-to-date information available in print."

WRITER'S DIGEST BOOKS; WRITER'S DIGEST, 1507 Dana Ave., Cincinnati OH 45207. (800)289-0963 or (513)531-2690. Website: www.writersdigest.com. **Contact:** Jack Heffron. Writer's Digest Books publishes a remarkable array of books useful to all types of writers. In addition to *Poet's Market*, books for poets include *Writing Personal Poetry* by Sheila Bender, *You Can Write Poetry* by Jeff Mock, *The Poet's Handbook* by Judson Jerome, *Creating Poetry* by John Drury, and *The Art and Craft of Poetry* by Michael J. Bugeja. Call or write for a complete catalog. *Writer's Digest* is a monthly magazine about writing with frequent articles and market news about poetry, in addition to a monthly poetry column.

☑ ⊕ WRITERS' NEWS; DAVID THOMAS CHARITABLE TRUST, P.O. Box 168, Wellington St., Leeds LS1 1RF United Kingdom. Phone: +44(0113)2388333. Fax: +44(0113)2388330. E-mail: JanetEvans@ypn.co.uk. **Editor:** Derek Hudson. Established 1989. A monthly magazine containing news and advice for writers. Devotes up to 10% to poetry and regularly features a poetry workshop, critiques, "method and type explained," and annual and monthly competitions. *Writer's News* is 32-64 pgs., A4-sized, saddle-stapled. Lists markets for poetry, contests/awards, conferences/workshops, and readings. Associated with the David Thomas Charitable Trust (P.O. Box 6055, Nairn 1V12 54B) which sponsors poetry competitions. Occasionally reviews books and chapbooks of poetry and other magazines. Poets may send books for review consideration. Subscription: £49.90 overseas. Sample: £4.50. Accepts inquiries by fax and e-mail.

⊕ ZENE, TTA Press, 5 Martins Lane, Witcham, Ely Cambs CB6 2LB England. E-mail: ttapress@aol.com. Website: www.tta-press.freewire.co.uk (includes details of *Zene* plus other TTA Press publications, extracts, news, link, and secure credit card subscription facility). **Contact:** Team Zene. Established 1994. A bimonthly "definitive guide to the vast independent press, recognised throughout the world as the creative writer's bible when it comes to looking for markets not normally found in more staid, mainstream writers' magazines. *Zene* covers all kinds of markets for fiction, nonfiction, and poetry from all genres, from mainstream to fantasy, from science fiction to horror, from thriller to romance. Neither does *Zene* restrict its coverage to the U.K., with regular reports from across the globe: Ireland, America, Canada, Australia, New Zealand, Europe, South Africa . . . in fact, everywhere there are independent titles publishing in the English language!" *Zene* is 36 pgs., A5-sized, lithographed and saddle-stapled. Also lists contests/awards, conferences/workshops, and readings. Reviews poetry collections, anthologies, and poetry magazines. Poets may send books for review consideration. Subscription: $24 including airmail (6 issues). Accepts inquiries by e-mail.

Additional Publications of Interest

The following listings also contain information about instructive publications for poets. See the General Index for page numbers.

Websites of Interest

The resources for poetry on the Internet are growing daily, and there are far too many to list here. However, below you'll find those key sites every poet should bookmark. Content ranges from postal and copyright information to links, forums, articles, and reviews. (Although we confirmed every address at press time, connections can become outdated; if a site comes up "not found," enter the name of the site in a search engine to check for a new address.)

SEARCH ENGINES:

Best of the Web: www.bestoftheweb.com
Dogpile: www.dogpile.com
Google: www.google.com

RESOURCES:

Canadian Postal Service: www.canadapost.ca
IRS: www.irs.ustreas.gov/basic/cover.html
US Copyright Office: www.loc.gov/copyright
US Postal Service: www.usps.gov

ESPECIALLY FOR POETS:

The Academy of American Poets: www.poets.org/index.cfm
Alien Flower: www.xdrom.com/alienflower/
Electronic Poetry Center: http://epc.buffalo.edu
National Federation of State Poetry Societies (NFSPS): www.nfsps.com
Poetic Voices: http://poeticvoices.com/
Poetry Society of America: www.poetrysociety.org
Poetry Today Online: www.poetrytodayonline.com
Poets & Writers: www.pw.org
Rhyming Dictionary: www.rhymezone.com
Slam News Service: www.slamnews.com

OTHER GREAT SITES FOR WRITERS:

Associated Writing Programs: www.awpwriter.org
Literary Terms/Rhetorical Devices: www.uky.edu/AS/Classics/Harris/rhetform.htm/
The Word Wizard: http://wordwizard.com/
The Writer: www.writermag.com
Writer Beware: www.sfa.org/beware
Writer Online: www.novalearn.com/wol/
The Writer's Center: www.writer.org/
Writer's Digest: www.writersdigest.com
Writers Write™—The Write Resource™: www.writerswrite.com
Zuzu's Petals: www.zuzu.com

PUBLICATIONS ACCEPTING E-MAIL SUBMISSIONS

The following publications accept e-mail submissions. See the General Index for page numbers. For e-mail submission instructions, see the publication's listing or obtain a copy of its writer's guidelines.

Aardvark Adventurer, The
Able Muse
Acorn
Acorn, The
African Voices
Ag-Pilot International
    Magazine
Albatross
Along the Path
Alsop Review, The
American Tanka
Amethyst & Emerald
Ancient Paths
Anna's Journal
Antigonsih Review, The
Apples & Oranges
Arkansas Review
Artisan
Avalanche
Avocet
Awakening Review, The
Bathtub Gin
Bear Deluxe, The
Bell's Letters Poet
Between Whisper and Shout
    Poetry
Bible Advocate
Black Bear Review
Black Spring Review
Bookpress, The
Brother Jonathan Review
Bugle, Journal of Elk Country
Bulk Head
Bridge Burner's Publishing
Canadian Dimension
Canadian Woman Studies
Canadian Writer's Journal
Candle, The
Caribbean Writer, The
Chaff
Challenger International
Children, Churches and
    Daddies
Clay Palm Review
Climbing Art, The
Comfusion
Concho River Review

Concrete Wolf
Copious Magazine
Cortland Review
Country Folk
Creative Juices
Cyber Oasis
Dalhousie Review
Dead Fun
Devil Blossoms
Discovery Magazine
Disquieting Muses
Dovetail
Dwan
Edgar
1812
Emerald Coast Review
Emotions
Eratosphere
Ethereal Green
Exit 13
Experimental Forest Press
failbetter.com
Fairfield Review
Fat Tuesday
Feelings of the Heart
Flaming Omelet, The
Flesh and Blood
For Poetry.Com
4*9*1*Imagination
Freefall
Freexpression
Frogpond
Funny Paper, The
Futures Magazine
Gentle Reader
George & Mertie's Place
Geronimo Review
Glass Tesseract
Gotta Write Network Litmag
Guerrilla Poetry
Hadrosaur Tales
Harp-Strings Poetry Journal
Harpweaver, The
HEart
Heaven Bone Magazine
Heliotrope
Herb Network, The

Hernando Medic
Hey, Listen!
Hidden Oak
Higginsville Reader, The
Hodgepodge
Hunger Magazine
Idiom 23
Idiot, The
Illuminations
Images Inscript
Imago
Interbang
Interface, The
International Poetry Review
Isles of Mist Review
Ivy
Japanophile
Jewel Among Jewels
Jones Av.
Journal, The
Journal of Contemporary
    Anglo-Scandinavian
    Poetry
Journal of New Jersey Poets
Journal of the American
    Medical Association
    (JAMA)
Kaleidoscope
Karawane
Kimera
Knuckle Merchant
Konfluence
Kota Press Poetry Journal
Kwil Cafe Newsletter, The
La Bella Figura
Lactuca
Laurels
Leapings Literary Magazine
Left Curve
Legend, The
Limestone Circle
L'intrigue Web Magazine
Link & Visitor, The
Literal Latte
Lithuanian Papers
Litrag
Little Brown Poetry

Los
Louisiana Review, The
Lucid Moon
Lummox Journal
Luna Negra
Lungfull! Magazine
Maelstrom
Magma Poetry Magazine
Mail Call Journal
Mandrake Poetry Review
Manzanita Quarterly
Margin
Matriarch's Way
Mattoid
Mature Years
Mayfly
Medicinal Purposes Literary
    Review
Melting Trees Review
Mennonite, The
Midwifery Today
Milkwood Review
Milton Magazine, John
Mind Purge
Minority Literary Expo
Monas Hieroglyphica
Monkey Flower
Mudlark
Murderous Intent
Muse Journal
Muse's Kiss Webzine
Musicworks
Muuna Takeena
Narrow Road
National Enquirer
National Forum
Native Tongue
Neovictorian/Cochlea, The
New Song, A
New Writer, The
Nova Express
O!!Zone
Oasis
Obsessed with Pipework
Of Unicorns and Space
    Stations
Office Number One
Opened Eyes Poetry & Prose
    Magazine
Our Family
Our Journey
Outer Rim, The
Oyster Boy Review

P.D.Q.
Paper Wasp
Penny Dreadful
Penwood Review, The
Pif Magazine
Pink Cadillac
Pivot
Plaza, The
Poesy Magazine
Poet to Poet
Poetic Hours
Poetic License Poetry
    Magazine
Poetic Voices Journal
Poetic Voices Magazine
Poetry & Prose Annual
Poetry Forum
Poetry Greece
Poetry Ireland Review
Poetry of the People
Poetry Today Online
Poetrybay
Poet's Cut, The
Poet's Haven, The
Porcupine Literary Arts
    Magazine
Portland Review
Potluck Children's Literary
    Magazine
Premiere Generation Ink
Presbyterian Record, The
Presence
Presstheedge
Prosodia
Pulsar Poetry Magazine
Queen's Quarterly
Rattapallax
Rattle
Red Booth Review
Red Dancefloor
Red Dot
Red Herring
Red Moon Press
Red Owl Magazine
Red River Review
Red Rock Review
Red Wheelbarrow
Renaissance Online Magazine
Renditions: A Chinese-
    English Translation
    Magazine
Rio
Rising

Romantic Outsider
Romantics Quarterly
Ruah
Rural Heritage
Sanskrit
Scavenger's Newsletter
Seedhouse
Shades of December
Shemom
Sisterwrite
Skipping Stones
Slate & Style
Slide
Slope
Small Garlic Press, A
Smartish Pace
Snapshots
Sometimes I Sleep with the
    Moon
Soul Fountain
Sounds of a Grey Metal Day
Sour Grapes
South
South Boston Literary
    Gazette, The
Spish
Splizz
Spoofing
Stellaluna
Struggle
Studio One
Sun Poetic Times
Syncopated City
Taproot Literary Review
Teak Roundup
Teen Voices
Temple, The
Ten Penny Players
Thin Coyote
Three Candles
3 Cup Morning
TimBookTu
Time of Singing
Torre de Papel
Trestle Creek Review
U.S. Catholic
U.S. Latino Review, The
Understanding Magazine
Unknown Writer, The
Unlikely Stories
Uno Mas Magazine
Uprising
Valparaiso Poetry Review

Verandah
Voce Piena
Voices Israel
Voiceworks Magazine
Voiding the Void
VQOnline
Wake Up Heavy
War Cry, The
Waterways

We Are Writers, Too!
Wellspring
Westerly
Western Archipelago Review
Whiskey Island Magazine
White Heron
W!dow of the Orch!d, The
Windsor Review
Wings Magazine

Wisconsin Academy Review
Word Process
Write Way, The
Writer, The
Writer's Exchange
Ya'sou!
Zine Zone
Zuzu's Petals Quarterly
    Online

U.S. and Canadian Postal Codes

United States

AL	Alabama	MI	Michigan	VT	Vermont
AK	Alaska	MN	Minnesota	VI	Virgin Islands
AZ	Arizona	MS	Mississippi	VA	Virginia
AR	Arkansas	MO	Missouri	WA	Washington
CA	California	MT	Montana	WV	West Virginia
CO	Colorado	NE	Nebraska	WI	Wisconsin
CT	Connecticut	NV	Nevada	WY	Wyoming
DE	Delaware	NH	New Hampshire		
DC	District of Columbia	NJ	New Jersey	**Canada**	
FL	Florida	NM	New Mexico	AB	Alberta
GA	Georgia	NY	New York	BC	British Columbia
GU	Guam	NC	North Carolina	LB	Labrador
HI	Hawaii	ND	North Dakota	MB	Manitoba
ID	Idaho	OH	Ohio	NB	New Brunswick
IL	Illinois	OK	Oklahoma	NF	Newfoundland
IN	Indiana	OR	Oregon	NT	Northwest Territories
IA	Iowa	PA	Pennsylvania	NS	Nova Scotia
KS	Kansas	PR	Puerto Rico	ON	Ontario
KY	Kentucky	RI	Rhode Island	PEI	Prince Edward Island
LA	Louisiana	SC	South Carolina	PQ	Quebec
ME	Maine	SD	South Dakota	SK	Saskatchewan
MD	Maryland	TN	Tennessee	YT	Yukon
MA	Massachusetts	TX	Texas		
		UT	Utah		

Glossary of Listing Terms

A3, A4, A5. Metric equivalents of $11\frac{3}{4} \times 16\frac{1}{2}$, $8\frac{1}{4} \times 11\frac{3}{4}$ and $5\frac{7}{8} \times 8\frac{1}{4}$ respectively.

Anthology. A collection of selected writings by various authors.

Attachment. A computer file electronically "attached" to an e-mail message.

b&w. Black & white (photo or illustration).

Bio. A short biographical statement often requested with a submission.

Camera-ready. Poems ready for copy camera platemaking; camera-ready poems usually appear in print exactly as submitted.

Chapbook. A small book of about 24-50 pages.

Contributor's copy. Copy of book or magazine containing a poet's work, sometimes given as payment.

Cover letter. Brief introductory letter accompanying a poetry submission.

Cover stock. Heavier paper used as the cover for a publication.

Digest-sized. About $5\frac{1}{2} \times 8\frac{1}{2}$, the size of a folded sheet of conventional printer paper.

Electronic magazine. See Online magazine.

E-mail. Mail sent electronically using computer and modem or similar means.

FAQ. Frequently Asked Questions.

Font. The style/design of type used in a publication; typeface.

Galleys. First typeset version of a poem, magazine, or book/chapbook.

Honorarium. A token payment for published work.

Internet. A worldwide network of computers offering access to a variety of electronic resources.

IRC. International Reply Coupon, a publisher can exchange IRCs for postage to return a manuscript to another country.

Magazine-sized. About $8\frac{1}{2} \times 11$, the size of an unfolded sheet of conventional printer paper.

ms. Manuscript; **mss.** Manuscripts.

Multi-book review. Several books by the same author or by several authors reviewed in one piece.

Offset-printed. Printing method in which ink is transferred from an image-bearing plate to a "blanket" and then from blanket to paper.

Online magazine. Publication circulated through the Internet or e-mail.

p&h. Postage & handling.

Perfect-bound. Publication with glued, flat spine; also called "flat-spined."

Publishing credits. A poet's magazine publications and book/chapbook titles.

Query letter. Letter written to an editor to raise interest in a proposed project.

Rights. A poet's legal property interest in his/her literary work; an editor or publisher may acquire certain rights from the poet to reproduce that work.

Royalties. A percentage of the retail price paid to the author for each copy of a book sold.

Saddle-stapled. A publication folded, then stapled along that fold; also called "saddle-stitched."

SAE. Self-addressed envelope.

SASE. Self-addressed, stamped envelope.

Simultaneous submission. Submission of the same manuscript to more than one publisher at the same time.

Subsidy press. Publisher who requires the poet to pay all costs, including typesetting, production, and printing; sometimes called a "vanity publisher."

Tabloid-sized. 11×15 or larger, the size of an ordinary newspaper folded and turned sideways.

Unsolicited manuscript. A manuscript an editor did not ask specifically to receive.

Website. A specific address on the Internet that provides access to a set of documents (or "pages").

Indexes

Chapbook Publishers

A poetry chapbook is a slim volume of 24-50 pages (although chapbook lengths can vary; some are even published as inserts in magazines). Many publishers and journals solicit chapbook manuscripts through competitions. Read listings carefully, check websites where available, and request guidelines before submitting. See Who Wants to Be a Published Poet? on page 8 for further information about chapbooks and submission formats.

CHAPBOOK PUBLISHERS INDEX

Book Publishers Index

The following are magazines and publishers that consider full-length book manuscripts (over 50 pages, often much longer). See Who Wants to Be a Published Poet? on page 8 for further information about book manuscript submission.

Openness to Submissions Index

In this section all magazines, publishers, and contests/awards with primary listings in *Poet's Market* are categorized according to their openness to submissions (as indicated by the symbols that appear at the beginning of each listing). Note that some markets are listed in more than one category.

☐ OPEN TO BEGINNING POETS

◢ OPEN TO BEGINNING & EXPERIENCED POETS

◙ OPEN MOSTLY TO EXPERIENCED POETS, FEW BEGINNERS

◎ SPECIALIZED—OPEN TO POETS FROM SPECIFIC AREAS OR GROUPS OR POEMS IN SPECIFIC FORMS OR ON SPECIFIC THEMES

Geographical Index

This section offers a breakdown of US publishers and conferences/workshops arranged alphabetically by state or territory, followed by listings for Canada, Australia, France, Japan, the United Kingdom, and other countries—a real help when trying to locate publishers in your region as well as conferences and workshops convenient to your area.

ALABAMA
Publishers of Poetry
Alden Enterprises
Birmingham Poetry Review
Black Warrior Review
Catamount Press
Inverted-A, Inc.
Melting Trees Review
Minority Literary Expo
National Forum
Native Tongue
Poem
Southern Humanities Review
TimBookTu
Uprising

Conferences & Workshops
Writing Today

ALASKA
Publishers of Poetry
Alaska Quarterly Review
Explorations
Permafrost

ARIZONA
Publishers of Poetry
Allisone Press
Bilingual Review Press
Creosote
Hayden's Ferry Review
Lucid Stone, The
Missing Fez, The
Newsletter Inago
Riverstone
Synaesthesia Press
Thin Air Magazine

Conferences & Workshops
Pima Writers' Workshop

ARKANSAS
Publishers of Poetry
Arkansas Review
Lucidity
Poetry Today Online
Slant
Storyteller, The

Conferences & Workshops
Ozark Creative Writers Conference

CALIFORNIA
Publishers of Poetry
Able Muse
Acorn, The
Along the Path
Amelia
Amethyst & Emerald Publishing
Anamnesis Press
Aphasia Press
Arctos Press
Avocet
Bay Area Poets Coalition
Bear Star Press
Blue Unicorn
Broken Boulder Press
Brother Jonathan Review
Burning Bush Publications
California Quarterly
Caveat Lector
CC. Marimbo Communications
Center Press
Chase Park

Conferences & Workshops

San Diego State University Writers'
    Conference
Santa Barbara Writers' Conference
Southern California Writers'
    Conference*San Diego
Squaw Valley Community of Writers
    Poetry Workshop

COLORADO
Publishers of Poetry
Arjuna Library Press
Bible Advocate
Bombay Gin
Clark Street Review
Climbing Art, The
Cloud Ridge Press
Clubhouse Jr.
Colorado Review
Dead Metaphor Press
Denver Quarterly
Gertrude
High Plains Literary Review
Many Mountains Moving
Ocean View Books
Pinyon
Scroll Publications Inc.
Seedhouse
SPS Studios, Inc.

Conferences & Workshops
Aspen Summer Words Writing Retreat and
    Literary Festival
Colorado Mountain Writers' Workshop
Steamboat Springs Writers Conference

CONNECTICUT
Publishers of Poetry
Clay Palm Review
Connecticut Poetry Review, The
Connecticut Review
Connecticut River Review
Creative Juices
Dirigible
Fairfield Review, The
Hanover Press, Ltd.
Small Pond Magazine of Literature
Twilight Ending

Yale University Press

Conferences & Workshops
Wesleyan Writers Conference

DELAWARE
Publishers of Poetry
Möbius
Word Dance

DISTRICT OF COLUMBIA
Publishers of Poetry
Word Works, The

FLORIDA
Publishers of Poetry
Anhinga Press
Apalachee Review
Australian Gothica
Emerald Coast Review
4*9*1 Neo-Naive Imagination
Gecko
Gulf Stream Magazine
Harp-Strings Poetry Journal
Hernando Medic
Home Times
Kalliope
Kings Estate Press
LSR
Mudlark
National Enquirer
New Writer's Magazine
Northwest Florida Review, The
Oasis
Outer Rim, The
Poetry of the People
Silver Web, The
So Young!
State Street Review
Tampa Review
Thoughts for All Seasons
White Pelican Review
Write Way, The

Conferences & Workshops
Key West Writers' Workshop

GEORGIA
Publishers of Poetry
Anna's Journal
Atlanta Review
babysue
Chattahoochee Review, The
Classical Outlook, The
Five Points
Georgia Poetry Review
Georgia Review, The
GSU Review
LAIRE, Inc., the
Lullwater Review
Midwest Poetry Review
Parnassus Literary Journal
SimplyWords
Society of American Poets, The
Spring Tides
University of Georgia Press
Unlikely Stories
Verse

Conferences & Workshops
Sandhills Writers Conference, The

HAWAII
Publishers of Poetry
Hawaii Pacific Review
Kaimana
Manoa

Conferences & Workshops
Kalani Honua Oceanside Eco Resort

IDAHO
Publishers of Poetry
Arsenic Lobster
Confluence Press
Fugue
Talking River Review
Trestle Creek Review

ILLINOIS
Publishers of Poetry
ACM (Another Chicago Magazine)
Aim Magazine
Artisan
Awakenings Review, The
Baybury Review
Chaff
Children, Churches and Daddies
Crab Orchard Review
Cricket
Dream International Quarterly
Gotta Write Network Litmag
High/Coo Press
Insects Are People Two
International Black Writers
Journal of the American Medical
    Association
Karamu
Lake Shore Publishing
Light
Megazine 17 Presents
mojo risin'
Musing Place, The
Mystery Time
Oak, The
Oblates
Outrider Press
Path Press, Inc.
Poetic License Poetry Magazine
Poetry
Potluck Children's Literary Magazine
Press of the Third Mind, The
Primavera
Red Crow
Rhino
Rio
Rockford Review, The
Small Garlic Press, A
Sou'wester
Spoon River Poetry Review, The
Sport Literate
Summer's Reading, A
TriQuarterly Magazine
U.S. Catholic
White Eagle Coffee Store Press
Willow Review

Beloit Poetry Journal, The
Café Review, The
Northeast Arts Magazine
Northwoods Press
Puckerbrush Press, The

MARYLAND
Publishers of Poetry
Abbey
Alsop Review, The
Antietam Review
Baltimore Review, The
BrickHouse Books, Inc.
Cochran's Corner
Dolphin-Moon Press
Feminist Studies
Flaming Omelet Press
In the Family
Maryland Poetry Review
Open University of America Press
Pegasus Review, The
People's Press, The
Plastic Tower, The
Poet Lore
Potomac Review
Red Booth Review
Shattered Wig Review
Smartish Pace
UNo Mas Magazine
Vegetarian Journal

Conferences & Workshops
Literary Festival at St. Mary's, The

MASSACHUSETTS
Publishers of Poetry
Adastra Press
Agni
Albatross
American Dissident, The
Amherst Review, The
Appalachia
Atlantic Monthly, The
Aurorean, The
Bay Windows
Beacon Street Review
Boston Review

Button Magazine
Christian Science Monitor, The
Crooked River Press
Diner
Dreams of Decadence
Godine, Publisher, David R.
Houghton Mifflin Co.
Ibbetson St. Press
Ivy
Jubilat
Mad River Press
Massachusetts Review, The
New Renaissance, The
Osiris
Partisan Review
Peregrine
Perugia Press
Pine Island Journal of New England Poetry
Ploughshares
Provincetown Arts
RoseWater Publications
Sahara
Soundings East
Sour Grapes
South Boston Literary Gazette, The
Suzerain Enterprises
Teen Voices
Tightrope
Worcester Review
Zoland Books Inc.

Conferences & Workshops
Cape Cod Writers' Center Summer
    Conference
Harvard Summer Writing Program

MICHIGAN
Publishers of Poetry
Affable Neighbor
American Tolkien Society
Angelflesh
Bennett & Kitchel
Dead Fun
Driftwood Review, The
Ethereal Green
Expedition Press
freefall

Gravity Presses
Japanophile
Literally Horses
MacGuffin, The
Michigan Quarterly Review
Michigan State University Press
Milkwood Review
New Issues Press
Northern Stars Magazine
Osric Publishing
Passages North
Perspectives
Rarach Press
Red Cedar Review
Sounds of Poetry, The
Struggle
Touch
Way Station Magazine
Wayne Literary Review

Conferences & Workshops
Cave Canem
Midland Writers Conference
Oakland University Writers' Conference

MINNESOTA
Publishers of Poetry
ArtWord Quarterly
Bulk Head
Coffee House Press
Futures Magazine
Heeltap
Karawane
Knuckle Merchant
Kumquat Meringue
Liftouts Magazine
Lutheran Digest, The
M.I.P. Company
Mankato Poetry Review
Meadowbrook Press
Midwest Villages & Voices
Once Upon A Time
Poetry Harbor
Poetry Motel
Spish
Studio One
Thin Coyote

Xcp: Cross-Cultural Poetics

Conferences & Workshops
Split Rock Arts Program

MISSISSIPPI
Publishers of Poetry
Bell's Letters Poet
Feelings of the Heart
Mississippi Review
Semiquasi Press

MISSOURI
Publishers of Poetry
Boulevard
Cape Rock, The
Chariton Review, The
Country Folk
Debut Review
Funny Paper, The
Green Hills Literary Lantern
Helicon Nine Editions
Hodgepodge Short Stories & Poetry
Mid-America Press, Inc., The
Nazarene International Headquarters
New Letters
Offerings
Pleiades
River Styx Magazine
Thorny Locust
Timberline Press

MONTANA
Publishers of Poetry
Bugle
Cutbank
Poem du Jour
Rocky Mountain Rider Magazine
Superior Poetry News

NEBRASKA
Publishers of Poetry
Beggar's Press
Herb Network, The
Lone Willow Press
Nebraska Review, The
Plainsongs

Get America's #1 Poetry Resource Delivered to Your Door—and Save!

Completely UPDATED Each Year

100% UPDATED!

POET'S MARKET

1,800 PLACES TO PUBLISH YOUR POETRY

- 300 new publishing opportunities
- 1,000+ journals & magazines
- 500+ book publishers
- 200+ chapbook publishers
- 150+ contests
- 1,500 phone numbers
- 1,100 e-mail addresses & Web sites

From the Publishers of Writer's Market

SUBMISSION GUIDELINES, CONTACT NAMES & REPORTING TIMES

Finding the right outlets for your poetry is crucial to publishing success. With constant changes in the industry, it's not always easy to stay informed. That's why every year poets trust the newest edition of *Poet's Market* for the most up-to-date information on the people and places that will get their poetry published (more than 1,800 editors and publishers are included). This definitive resource also features insider tips from successful poets and editors that will further increase publishing opportunities.

2003 Poet's Market will be published and ready for shipment in August 2002.

Through this special offer, you can reserve your 2003 *Poet's Market* at the 2002 price—just $23.99. Order today and save!

Turn over for more books to help you write great poems and get them published!

□ **Yes!** I want the most current edition of *Poet's Market*. Please send me the *2003* edition at the 2002 price—just $23.99. (#10790·K)

| # 10790-K | $ 23.99 |

(NOTE: *2003 Poet's Market* will be shipped in August 2002.)

I also want these books listed on back:

Book	Price
# -K	$
# -K	$
# -K	$
# -K	$
Subtotal	$
Postage & Handling	$

In the U.S., please add $3.95 s&h for the first book, $1.95 for each additional book. In OH and NY add applicable sales tax. In Canada, add US$5.00 for the first book, US$3.00 for each additional book, and 7% GST. Payment in U.S. funds must accompany order.

| Total | $ |

Credit card orders call
TOLL FREE 1-800-221-5831
or visit
www.writersdigest.com/catalog

□ Payment enclosed $ _____ (or)
Charge my: □ VISA □ MC □ AmEx Exp. _____

Account # _____

Signature _____

Name _____

Address _____

City_____

State/Prov._____ ZIP/PC_____

□ Check here if you do not want your name added to our mailing list.

30-Day Money Back Guarantee on every book you buy!

ZAH01B5

Mail to: Writer's Digest Books • PO Box 9274 • Central Islip, NY 11722-9274

More Great Books to Help You Write and Publish Your Poetry!

Pencil Dancing
New ways to free your creative spirit
by Mari Messer
Learn to dance between your right and left brain as you move between creator and critic, and creativity and logic. You'll develop creative confidence and discover how to overcome writer's block as you explore these fun and effective methods to tap into your imagination.
#10733-K/$15.99/240 p/pb

NEW!
Roget's Thesaurus of Phrases
by Barbara Ann Kipfer, Ph.D.
Sure, you go to the thesaurus when you need a synonym for a word, but now you can do the same for a phrase! Need to know a different way to say "crowning achievement" or "budget deficit?" Look no further that Kipfer's indispensible reference. You'll make your writing precise and colorful, with more than 10,000 multiword entries and example lists!
#10734-K/$22.99/432 p/hc

Keeping a Journal You Love
by Sheila Bender
This mix of practical instruction from Bender and advice from respected writers—including Ron Carlson, Philip Lopate and others—is chock-full of writing prompts and inspiration to help you get more enjoyment and fulfillment from your journal. You'll learn how to write about travel, hobbies, personal thoughts, insights, emotions and theories—and how to move from personal writing to published piece.
#10750-K/$14.99/240 p/pb

The Art & Craft of Poetry
by Michael J. Bugeja
Nurture your poetry-writing skills with inspiration and insight from the masters of the past and present, including Louise Glück, Dana Gioia, Walt Whitman, and Robert Frost. From idea generation to methods of expression, you'll find everything you need to create well-crafted poetry!
#10781-K/$15.99/352 p/pb

Write Your Heart Out
by Rebecca McClanahan
Discover how to turn personal experiences, ideas and emotions into stories, essays, poems and memoirs. McClanahan will help you learn to write deeply, honestly and imaginatively about the most important people, events and emotions in your life, leading you on a path to both catharsis and self-discovery.
#10735-K/$17.99/224 p/pb

Order these helpful references today from your local bookstore, or use the handy order card on the reverse side.

Prairie Schooner

NEVADA
Publishers of Poetry
Interim
Limited Editions Press
Red Rock Review
Russell Publishing, James
Sierra Nevada College Review

NEW HAMPSHIRE
Publishers of Poetry
Brown Bottle, The
Concrete Wolf
Little Brown Poetry
Red Owl Magazine
Slope
Yankee Magazine

Conferences & Workshops
Festival of Poetry

NEW JERSEY
Publishers of Poetry
Adept Press
Between Whisper and Shout Poetry
Devil Blossoms
Edgar
Exit 13
Flesh and Blood
Higginsville Reader, The
Journal of New Jersey Poets
Kelsey Review
Lactuca
Literary Review, The
Long Shot
Lucid Moon
Maelstrom
Mail Call Journal
Marymark Press
nowCulture.com
Paterson Literary Review
Princeton University Press
St. Joseph Messenger and Advocate of the
      Blind
Saturday Press, Inc.
Sensations Magazine

Skidrow Penthouse
U.S. 1 Worksheets
Unknown Writer, The
Vista Publishing, Inc.
Warthog Press
Wings Magazine, Inc.
Writes of Passage

Conferences & Workshops
College of New Jersey Writers Conference,
      The
Poetry Weekend Intensives
Winter Poetry & Prose Getaway in Cape
      May

NEW MEXICO
Publishers of Poetry
American Research Press
Blue Mesa Review
Gentle Survivalist, The
Hadrosaur Tales
Katydid Books
Paradoxism
Puerto del Sol
RB's Poets' Viewpoint
yefief

Conferences & Workshops
Society of the Muse of the Southwest
Southwest Writers Contest and
      Conference
Taos Summer Writers' Workshop

NEW YORK
Publishers of Poetry
Aardvark Adventurer, The
Adrift
Advocate
African Voices
America
American Tanka
Amicus Journal, The
Antipodes
Art Times
Asian Pacific American Journal
Barbaric Yawp
Barrow Street

Birch Brook Press
Bitter Oleander, The
Black Diaspora Magazine
Black Spring Press
Black Thistle Press
Blind Beggar Press
Blueline
Boa Editions, Ltd.
Bookpress, The
Breakaway Books
Chelsea
Chronicles of Disorder
Commonweal
Comstock Review, The
Confrontation Magazine
Correction(s)
Cross-Cultural Communications
Edgewise Press, Inc.
1812
Epoch
failbetter.com
Fantastic Stories of the Imagination
Farrar, Straus & Giroux/Books for Young
      Readers
Fish Drum
Free Focus
Frogpond
Fullosia Press
Grand Street
Green Bean Press
Guide Magazine
Hanging Loose Press
HarperCollins Publishers
Hazmat Review
Heaven Bone Magazine
Holiday House, Inc.
Home Planet News
Hudson Review, The
Hunger Magazine
Iconoclast, The
Inkwell Magazine
Italica Press
Jewish Currents
Jewish Women's Literary Annual
Kit-Cat Review, The
Koja
Ledge, The

Lilith Magazine
Lintel
Literal Latté
Long Island Quarterly
Low-Tech Press
LUNGFULL! Magazine
Malafemmina Press
Manhattan Review, The
Matriarch's Way
Medicinal Purposes Literary Review
Mellen Poetry
Midstream
Milton Magazine, John
Narrow Road, The
Nassau Review
Nation, The
New York Quarterly
New Yorker, The
Nomad's Choir
Opened Eyes Poetry & Prose Magazine
Parnassus
Penny Dreadful
Phoebe
Pipe Smoker's Ephemeris, The
Pivot
Poetrybay
Poets on the Line
Queen of All Hearts
Queen's Mystery Magazine, Ellery
Ralph's Review
Rattapallax
Rocket Press
Sachem Press
Seneca Review
Serpent & Eagle Press
Shades of December
Slapering Hol Press
Slate & Style
Slipstream
Soul Fountain
Space and Time
Spinning Jenny
Spirit That Moves Us, The
Spring
Stevens Journal, The Wallace
Stray Dog
Terra Incognita

Conferences & Workshops
Antioch Writers' Workshop
Chautauqua Writing Seminars
Imagination

OKLAHOMA
Publishers of Poetry
Attic Magazine
Byline Magazine
Cimarron Review
Eagle's Flight
Nimrod
Outer Darkness
Westview

OREGON
Publishers of Poetry
Bear Deluxe, The
Bridges
Calyx
Eighth Mountain Press, The
Horse Latitudes Press
Hubbub
Manzanita Quarterly
Midwifery Today
Nocturnal Lyric
Northwest Review
Open Spaces
Oregon Review, The
Our Journey
Poetic Space
Poetry & Prose Annual
Portland Review
Romantics Quarterly
Silverfish Review Press
Skipping Stones
Story Line Press
To' To' Pos
Whitecrow Foundation, Tahana

Conferences & Workshops
Ashland Writers Conference
Fishtrap
Haystack Writing Program

PENNSYLVANIA
Publishers of Poetry
Acorn

Aguilar Expression, The
Allegheny Review, The
American Writing
Apropos
Axe Factory Review
Black Bear Publications
Blind Man's Rainbow, The
Brilliant Corners
Dwan
Experimental Forest Press
Fat Tuesday
5 AM
Gettysburg Review, The
HEArt—Human Equity Through Art
Herald Press
Hidden Oak
Highlights for Children
Interface, The
Kaleidoscope Review, The
Lilliput Review
Mad Poets Review
Mammoth Books
Matchbook
Mediphors
Miller's Pond
Pennsylvania English
Pink Cadillac
Poetic Link, The
Poetry Explosion Newsletter, The
Poetry Forum
Poets at Work
Raw Dog Press
Re:Verse!
Symbiotic Oatmeal
Taproot Literary Review
Threshold, The
Time of Singing
Transcendent Visions
Valee Publications
West Branch
Wordsong

Conferences & Workshops
Ligonier Valley Writers Conference
Pennwriters Annual Conference

PUERTO RICO
Publishers of Poetry
Revista/Review Interamericana

RHODE ISLAND
Publishers of Poetry
Defined Providence
Hunted News, The
Hurricane Alice
Merlyn's Pen
Nedge
Prose Poem, The
Renaissance Online Magazine
Syncopated City
24.7

SOUTH CAROLINA
Publishers of Poetry
Emrys Journal
Illuminations
Ninety-Six Press
Nostalgia
Palanquin
Slugfest, Ltd.
South Carolina Review
Yemassee

SOUTH DAKOTA
Publishers of Poetry
Beatnik Pachyderm, The

TENNESSEE
Publishers of Poetry
Aethlon
Alive Now
Firefly Magazine
Indian Heritage Publishing
Mature Years
Now & Then
Poems & Plays
Poet Born Press, A
River City
Rural Heritage
Sewanee Review, The
Writer's Exchange

Conferences & Workshops
American Christian Writers Conferences
Life Press Christian Writers' Conference
Sewanee Writers' Conference

TEXAS
Publishers of Poetry
American Literary Review
Black Tie Press
Borderlands
Chachalaca Poetry Review
Concho River Review
Descant
Didactic, The
Gulf Coast
Illya's Honey
Inkwell, The
Literary Focus Poetry Publications
Lone Stars Magazine
Mind Purge
Nerve Cowboy
Nova Express
O!!Zone
Office Number One
Palo Alto Review
Pecan Grove Press
presstheEDGE
RE:AL
Red River Review
Rio Grande Review
Strain, The
Studentswrite.com
Sulphur River Literary Review
Sun Poetic Times
Texas Tech University Press
Touchstone Literary Journal
University of Texas Press
Zillah

Conferences & Workshops
Austin Writers' League Spring and Fall
    Workshops
Lucidity Poets' Ozark Retreat
SWT Summer Creative Writing Camp

UTAH
Publishers of Poetry
Ellipsis Magazine

Rowan Books
Scrivener
Seeds Poetry Magazine
Snowapple Press
sub-TERRAIN
Tale Spinners
"Teak" Roundup
Thalia
3 Cup Morning
Time for Rhyme
Tower Poetry Society
Turnstone Press Limited
University of Alberta Press
Unmuzzled Ox
Vallum Magazine
Wascana Review
West Coast Line
White Wall Review
Windsor Review
Writer's Block Magazine

Conferences & Workshops
Sage Hill Writing Fall Poetry Colloquium
Sage Hill Writing Summer Experience
Victoria School of Writing

AUSTRALIA
Publishers of Poetry
FreeXpresSion
Ginninderra Press
Idiom 23
Imago
Lithuanian Papers
Mattoid
Paper Wasp
Pinchgut Press
Quadrant Magazine
Studio
Verandah
Voiceworks Magazine
Westerly

FRANCE
Publishers of Poetry
Doc(k)s
Handshake Editions
Polyphonies

JAPAN
Publishers of Poetry
Abiko Annual with James Joyce FW
	Studies
Plaza, The
Poetry Kanto

UNITED KINGDOM
Publishers of Poetry
Aabye
Acumen Magazine
Blackwater Press
Borderlines
Brando's Hat
British Haiku Society
Carn
Chapman
Dandelion Arts Magazine
Darengo
Dialogos
Enitharmon Press
European Judaism
Feather Books
Fire
Firewater Press Inc.
First Time
Flarestack Publishing
Frogmore Papers
Gairm
Gentle Reader
Handshake
Hilltop Press
Hippopotamus Press
HQ Poetry Magazine
Interpreter's House
Iota
Journal of Contemporary Anglo-
	Scandinavian Poetry
K.T. Publications
Konfluence
Krax
Lateral Moves
Links
Magma Poetry Magazine
Magpie's Nest
Maypole Editions
Modern Poetry in Translation

Conferences & Workshops

OTHER COUNTRIES

Publishers of Poetry

Conferences & Workshops

Subject Index

This index focuses on markets indicating a specialized area of interest, whether regional, poetic style, or specific topic (these markets show a ◎ symbol at the beginning of their listings). Subject categories are listed alphabetically, with additional subcategories indicated under the "Specialized" heading. Please note that this index only partially reflects the total markets in this book; many do not identify themselves as having specialized interests and so are not included here. Also, many specialized markets have more than one area of interest and will be found under multiple categories. Note, too, that when a market indicates a specialized subject, it does not necessarily mean that it considers *only* poetry associated with that subject. It's still best to read all listings carefully as part of a thorough marketing plan.

Animal

Bibliophilos
Bugle
Creative Juices
Kerf, The
Literally Horses
Outrider Press
Rocky Mountain Rider Magazine
Whitecrow Foundation, Tahana

Anthology

Acorn Rukeyser Chapbook Contest
Arctos Press
Asian Pacific American Journal
Bay Area Poets Coalition
Birch Brook Press
Blind Beggar Press
Catamount Press
Cross-Cultural Communications
Feather Books
Floating Bridge Press
Lake Shore Publishing
Literary Focus Poetry Publications
Meadowbrook Press
Outrider Press
Peace & Freedom
Penumbra Poetry & Haiku
    Competition
Plowman, The
Poetic Link, The
Polygon

Prairie Journal, The
Pudding House Publications
Red Moon Press
Ronsdale Press
Scroll Publications Inc.
Seeds Poetry Magazine
Southern California Anthology, The
Spirit That Moves Us, The
Voices Israel
Waterways
White Eagle Coffee Store Press

Bilingual/Foreign Language

Bibliophilos (French, German,
    Romanian)
Bilingual Review Press (Spanish)
Borderlands (multilingual)
Carn (Celtic)
Cló Iar-Chonnachta (Irish Gaelic)
Cross-Cultural Communications (African,
    Asian, Cajun, Dutch, Finnish, Israeli,
    Italian, Scandinavian, Spanish,
    Swedish, Turkish, Yiddish)
Doc(k)s (French)
Dwan (Spanish)
Écrits des Forges (French)
Experimental Forest Press
Gairm (Scottish Gaelic)
Italica Press (Italian)
M.I.P. Company (Russian)
Moving Parts Press

Children/Teen/Young Adult

Cowboy

Ethnic/Nationality

Journal of Contemporary Anglo-
Scandinavian Poetry
Lilith Magazine (Jewish)
Link & Visitor, The
Lithuanian Papers
Malafemmina Press (Italian-
American)
Megazine 17 Presents
Midstream (Jewish)
Native Tongue (African-American)
New Welsh Review
Path Press, Inc. (African-
American, Third World)
Poetry Explosion Newsletter, The
Rarach Press (Czech)
Revista/Review Interamericana (Puerto
Rican, Caribbean,
Hispanic, Latin America)
Rosenberg Award, Anna Davidson
Shirim (Jewish)
Skipping Stones (multicultural)
Sounds of Poetry, The (Spanish, French)
Struggle
TimBookTu (African-American)
Torre de Papel
U.S. Latino Review, The
Uprising (Native American)
Wasafiri (African, African
Diaspora, Caribbean, Asian)
West Coast Line (Canada)
Western Archipelago Review (Asia, Pacific)
Whitecrow Foundation, Tahana
Wilbur Award, The Richard
(American)

Form/Style
Able Muse
Acorn
Amelia (all forms)
American Tanka
American Writing (experimental)
Anthology of New England
Writers, The (free verse)
Bennett & Kitchel
Bibliophilos (structured form)
Bogg Publications
British Haiku Society

Broken Boulder Press
Catamount Press
Clark Street Review
Dirigible (avant-garde,
experimental)
Formalist, The (metrical, rhymed)
4*9*1 Neo-Naive Imagination (neo-naive
genre)
Free Focus
frisson
Frogpond (haiku, senryu, sequences, linked
poems, haibun)
Generator (experimental, language, concrete,
visual)
Haiku Headlines (haiku, senryu)
High/Coo Press (haiku)
Hippopotamus Press (modernist)
Hunger Magazine (language/image
experimentation)
Japanophile (haiku or other
Japanese forms)
Johnson Memorial Haiku Award, Helen
Vaughn
Koja (visual, concrete, avant-garde,
experimental)
Lilliput Review (10 lines or less)
Luna Bisonte Prods (experimental, avant-
garde)
Lyric, The (rhymed, traditional)
Margin
Marymark Press (experimental)
Modern Haiku
Narrow Road, The
Newsletter Inago
Ocean View Books (surrealist-
influenced)
Office Number One (limericks, haiku,
rhymed/metered
quatrains)
Paper Wasp
Paradoxism (experimental, avant-garde)
Penumbra Poetry & Haiku
Competition
Poetry Society of Virginia Annual Contests,
The
Poets' Club of Chicago Helen Schaible
International

Spirituality/Inspirational

Sports/Recreation

Students

Themes

Translations

General Index

Markets and resources that appeared in the *2001 Poet's Market* but are not included in this edition are identified by two-letter codes in parentheses explaining why these entries no longer appear.

The Codes are: **(ED)—Editorial Decision; (NR)—No (or late) Response to Requests for updated information; (NS)—Not Accepting Submissions** (which includes publishers who are overstocked as well as those who no longer publish poetry); **(OB)—Out of Business** (or, in the case of contests, cancelled); **(RR)—Removed by Request** (no reason given); and **(UF)— Uncertain Future** (which includes publishers who have suspended publication or are reorganizing their operations).

Markets that appeared in the 2001 edition of *Poet's Market*, but do not appear this year, are listed in this General Index with the following codes explaining why these entries were omitted: (ED)—Editorial Decision, (NS)—Not Accepting Submissions, (NR)—No (or late) Response to Request for Updated Information, (OB)—Out of Business, (RR)—Removed by Market's Request, (UF)—Uncertain Future.

Markets that appeared in the 2001 edition of *Poet's Market*, but do not appear this year, are listed in this General Index with the following codes explaining why these entries were omitted: (ED)—Editorial Decision, (NS)—Not Accepting Submissions, (NR)—No (or late) Response to Request for Updated Information, (OB)—Out of Business, (RR)—Removed by Market's Request, (UF)—Uncertain Future.

Markets that appeared in the 2001 edition of *Poet's Market*, but do not appear this year, are listed in this General Index with the following codes explaining why these entries were omitted: (ED)—Editorial Decision, (NS)—Not Accepting Submissions, (NR)—No (or late) Response to Request for Updated Information, (OB)—Out of Business, (RR)—Removed by Market's Request, (UF)—Uncertain Future.

Markets that appeared in the 2001 edition of *Poet's Market*, but do not appear this year, are listed in this General Index with the following codes explaining why these entries were omitted: (ED)—Editorial Decision, (NS)—Not Accepting Submissions, (NR)—No (or late) Response to Request for Updated Information, (OB)—Out of Business, (RR)—Removed by Market's Request, (UF)—Uncertain Future.

Markets that appeared in the 2001 edition of *Poet's Market*, but do not appear this year, are listed in this General Index with the following codes explaining why these entries were omitted: **(ED)**—Editorial Decision, **(NS)**—Not Accepting Submissions, **(NR)**—No (or late) Response to Request for Updated Information, **(OB)**—Out of Business, **(RR)**—Removed by Market's Request, **(UF)**—Uncertain Future.

Markets that appeared in the 2001 edition of *Poet's Market*, **but do not appear this year, are listed in this General Index with the following codes explaining why these entries were omitted: (ED)—Editorial Decision, (NS)—Not Accepting Submissions, (NR)—No (or late) Response to Request for Updated Information, (OB)—Out of Business, (RR)—Removed by Market's Request, (UF)—Uncertain Future.**

GENERAL INDEX

Markets that appeared in the 2001 edition of *Poet's Market*, but do not appear this year, are listed in this General Index with the following codes explaining why these entries were omitted: (ED)—Editorial Decision, (NS)—Not Accepting Submissions, (NR)—No (or late) Response to Request for Updated Information, (OB)—Out of Business, (RR)—Removed by Market's Request, (UF)—Uncertain Future.

Markets that appeared in the 2001 edition of *Poet's Market*, but do not appear this year, are listed in this General Index with the following codes explaining why these entries were omitted: (ED)—Editorial Decision, (NS)—Not Accepting Submissions, (NR)—No (or late) Response to Request for Updated Information, (OB)—Out of Business, (RR)—Removed by Market's Request, (UF)—Uncertain Future.

Markets that appeared in the 2001 edition of *Poet's Market*, but do not appear this year, are listed in this General Index with the following codes explaining why these entries were omitted: (ED)—Editorial Decision, (NS)—Not Accepting Submissions, (NR)—No (or late) Response to Request for Updated Information, (OB)—Out of Business, (RR)—Removed by Market's Request, (UF)—Uncertain Future.

GENERAL INDEX

NOTES